by Carl Beck
Thomas McKechnie
Paul Evan Peters

Published by the University Center for International Studies,
University of Pittsburgh,
in conjunction with
the American Political Science Association

Library of Congress Cataloging in Publication Data

Beck, Carl, 1930-
Political science thesaurus II.

First ed. published in 1975 under title: Political science thesaurus.
1. Subject headings—Political science.
I. McKechnie, Thomas, 1942- joint author.
II. Peters, Paul Evan, 1947- joint author.
III. Pittsburgh. University. University Center for International Studies. IV. Title.
Z695.1.P63B4 1979 025.3'332 79-21402
ISBN 0-916002-47-0

First edition compiled by Carl Beck
Eleanor Dym and
Thomas McKechnie

Published by the American Political Science Association
1527 New Hampshire Avenue, N.W.
Washington, D.C. 20036

Second edition
Published by the University Center for International Studies
University of Pittsburgh
in conjunction with the American Political Science Association

Oh what a tangled web we weave,
when first we practice to retrieve.

With Apologies to Sir Walter Scott

This mass of words is dedicated to the staff, particularly Cynthia Carbine, Retrieval Specialist; Gail Ricketts, Retrieval Specialist; and Jan P. Miller, Manager, and the thousands of users of the Social Sciences Information Utilization Laboratory and the United States Political Science Information System in the hopes that it will help to untangle their webs.

ACKNOWLEDGEMENTS

We would like to acknowledge the contributions of the following people, each of whom worked hard to produce a finely tuned instrument:

Felix Boni, Indexing, Candidate Term Identification
Keith Cameron, Indexing, Candidate Term Identification
Cynthia Carbine, Geographical Terminology Analysis, Retrieval Analysis, Candidate Term Identification
Linda Davoli, Production Advisor
Kristine Demko, Administrative Assistant
Robert Donaldson, Scope Note Construction, Indexing, Candidate Term Identification
William Flurry, Document Analysis
Lynne Foote, Retrieval Analysis
Kimberly Gordish, Technical Operations
James Haberman, Sales and Fulfillment
Anne Healey, Cover Design, Promotional Artwork
Marie Hutchison, Production Assistant
William Jarzabek, Indexing, Candidate Term Identification
Joanne Juzwa, Technical Operations, Sales and Fulfillment
Pamela Kelley, Technical Operations
Loretta Kuhn, Technical Operations
Cole Mazur, Technical Operations
Jan Miller, Book Design Coordination, Retrieval Analysis, Candidate Term Identification
Henrietta Moss, Administrative Assistant
Peter Nehnevajsa, Technical Operations
Thomas Pittock, Technical Operations
Gail Ricketts, Retrieval Analysis, Candidate Term Identification
Michelle Russo, Technical Operations
Jerome Smith, Technical Operations
Gertrude Whitman, Administrative Assistant

C.B.
T.M.
P.P.

CONTENTS

PREFACE TO THE SECOND EDITION

This revised and expanded second edition of the *Political Science Thesaurus* reflects our concern with mapping the ever-expanding language of the study of politics. In the first edition which we published in 1975, we concentrated on the core language of political science. We drew the preponderance of candidate terms from political science sources. We have refined our presentation of the core language of political science in this second edition, but we have concentrated on adding the language of cognate fields of interest to political scientists.

Our goals in this second edition remain the same as in the first edition: to create a terminological regulation system which will assist users in seeking the information and data that they need for their own research and teaching purposes; to assist those who operate computerized information systems in matching the interests of their clients or themselves with the information contained in that system, whether the client is concerned with scanning the literature or identifying that one piece of literature which matches his or her needs; and to assist those who write in the field of politics by presenting to them a structured list of alternative terms from which they can choose that term which best conveys their meaning.

When we published the *Political Science Thesaurus* in 1975 and initiated a Political Science Information Service, we knew that within a four or five year period we would have to publish a revised edition of the Thesaurus. We, therefore, initially built into the information service mechanisms for the collection of candidate terms, mechanisms for the evaluation of posted terms, and mechanisms for the evaluation of the structure that we presented as the language of political science. We could not have revised the first edition of the *Political Science Thesaurus* without having that formative evaluation system in place from the very beginning of this project. The way in which we built the first edition of the *Political Science Thesaurus* is discussed at length in the Preface and Forward to the first edition of the *Political Science Thesaurus* which we have produced in this volume as Appendices V and VI. In revising the *Thesaurus* we followed the same methodology. We had at our disposal, however, the experiences of the United States Political Science Information Service; *United States Political Science Documents*; the retrieval specialists of the Social Sciences Information Utilization Laboratory at the University Center for International Studies, a client-based organization which accesses over 800,000 abstracts for over 100 clients per week on the campus of the University of Pittsburgh; and the experiences of the clients of all these systems.

A. Selection of Candidate Terms.

The United States Political Science Information Service is a service which abstracts, indexes, and further categorizes every article that appears in over 150 journals relevant to political science published in the United States (See Appendix VII for a description of the design philosophy of this service). The data base of over 12,000 documentary descriptions served as the major source of candidate terms, particularly those candidate terms which would be used to refine the core language of the study of politics. To gain an understanding of how candidate terms were collected, it is useful to have an understanding of how each documentary representation in the *United States Political Science Documents* is indexed. There are three separate human operations and two computerized indexing operations performed on each abstract. The first step is the most relevant to the development of this *Thesaurus*. The first indexing is done in free form. Each abstractor lists those terms which he or she thinks are most relevant to the article without reference to the existing terminological control system. An indexer then converts these terms into "Postable" (*Thesaurus*) terms and "Other" terms. "Other" terms are marked with a + sign in order to identify them as outside the *Thesaurus* and therefore as candidate terms for revision. A third indexer reviews the entire indexing process and makes final judgements as to what goes into both machine readable and printable form. We then augment these human operations through two machine operations discussed later in this Preface. We feel through this process, applied as it has been to 12,000 abstracts, that we have identified those terms which are core political science terms relevant to revision of the *Thesaurus*.

The second source of candidate terms came from the conversations between the users of the Social Sciences Information Utilization Laboratory (SSIUL) and the retrieval specialists in that Laboratory. In the SSIUL, over 100 clients, student and faculty members at the University of Pittsburgh, initiate searches in an average week with SSIUL retrieval specialists. In the conversations that lead to the development of a search, candidate terms for this revised *Thesaurus* were recorded. As the retrieval system at the University of Pittsburgh allows full text searching to be a retrieval option, it was easy to test the usage of such candidate terms against machine readable abstracts.

A third source of terms was that drawn from a mixture of empirical data and our own knowledge of the structure of the system that we had designed. As we had constructed the first edition of the *Thesaurus*, we were aware of and kept track of gaps in the *Thesaurus*, particularly gaps in cognate fields. We deliberately set out then to identify from other sources candidate terms to fill these gaps. The cognate fields which we emphasized include: Social Psychology, Service Industries, Public Policy Analysis, The Humanities (particularly Linguistics where we were fortunate enough to have access to the candidate terms of the *Modern Language Association Thesaurus* now being constructed), Economics, Sociology, History, Anthropology, and Geography. Sources used to fill these gaps are listed in Appendix III.

A fourth source of candidate terms was created when we decided to analyze what we call the amplitude of each hierarchy. By amplitude we mean the distance between a term and its narrower term or between a term and its broader term. Such linguistic distance is something for which we had no instruments for measuring, but a careful analyst can develop a sense when the distance or amplitude is too great. One way that we identify a problem with amplitude is by the number of narrower terms associated with one term. An inordinate number of narrower terms indicates to us that the amplitude is too great and that a filter term is necessary. We therefore added terms in order to create such filters. Adding filters often led to the reconstruction of a hierarchy. Political Movements is an excellent example of this process. In the original *Thesaurus* there were 28 first level terms out of 40 which did not have any narrower terms associated with them. Only 1 second level term out of 21 had a narrower term associated with it. Obviously, this was more a listing than a hierarchy. In the revised *Thesaurus* through the use of filter terms we were able to restructure the Political Movement hierarchy so that it is hierarchical. Assisting us in defining amplitude or identifying amplitude problems were the two computer indexing operations that take place as we construct the machine readable files and the *United States Political Science Documents*. As far as we know these are unique in the field of information service design. We augment our human indexing with machine-added terms. We do this in two ways. The first way is what we have named one-way reciprocity. If there is a relationship between two terms outside of the same hierarchy and that relationship can be stated as "it is not possible to discuss term A without discussing term B," we then add that statement to a dictionary of one-way reciprocally related terms so that every time term A is used as an index term, term B is automatically added. If the reciprocity holds in both directions, then one of the terms is redundant and is deleted. As an example: It is difficult to conceive of an article in which an author discusses "Adjudicator" without discussing "Adjudication;" however, it is possible to discuss "Adjudication" without discussing "Adjudicator". We call this process machine augmented related term indexing. A second form of machine augmentation of indexing which is unique to our indexing system is the automatic inclusion of the broader term in the indexing process. Every time a term appears as an index term, the computer automatically adds the immediate broader term to the indexing array. In this way we can get a sense of the symmetry of our amplitude. By analyzing the impact of this machine augmented broader term indexing in the context of a particular document, we can sharpen our evaluation of the *Thesaurus* as a terminological regulation system.

Through these four processes we collected approximately 40,000 candidate terms to consider as additions to the original *Thesaurus*.

B. Deletion

The data base of used terms that we have constructed in building *United States Political Science Documents* over a five-year period could have served as a basis for deleting terms. Approximately 836 terms in the *Thesaurus* have not been used in a five-year period. However, we were reluctant to delete terms on the basis of non-usage alone. We deleted terms in this revision of the *Thesaurus* only on the basis of redundancy or editing. Approximately 287 terms have been deleted.

C. Hierarchical Structuring

We reduced the number of hierarchies from 43 to 38 by incorporating Bureaucracy into Institutions and Coalition Type into Agreement Type and Veto into Process and Voting Device into Politics and Weapon into Security Forces. We were concerned about regrouping hierarchies because of usage of automatic broader term indexing. In restructuring hierarchies our analysis of amplitude was of great assistance. In this revised *Thesaurus* there are no cases in which we reversed the broader to narrower term relationship.

D. Editing

In many cases we made editorial changes for the purpose of greater precision in machine searching. For example, since the term "Budget" was used more than "Budgetary," we substituted where we could without destroying the English language "Budget" for "Budgetary." "Budgetary Process" becomes "Budget Process." Whenever we did this, we created a USED FOR statement.

There are three additional elements of the *Thesaurus* that we paid particular attention to in this revised edition.

I. Related Terms

We have completely restructured the Related Terms listing for each postable term. Of invaluable help in this process was the See Also list that we created for each *Thesaurus* term and which appears for the first time in Volume 4 of *United States Political Science Documents*. We made so many changes in related terms that we did not keep track of them. We can say, however, that each term's Related Terms were evaluated at least three times in the process of creating a new Related Terms listing. We also reduced the number of such relationships because the first *Thesaurus* suffered from overkill. Finally, we assured reciprocity in related terms by the development of a computer program that allowed us to edit both deletions and additions to related terms listing.

II. Use and Used For References

We have developed for this revision of the *Thesaurus* a number of Use and Used For references. The source of these was our candidate terms listing and our editing decisions. Because of the intensive manner in which we have presented this map of political science and its cognate fields, there are not many Use and Used For references in this *Thesaurus*. We will reevaluate Use and Used For references when we do the third edition.

III. Scope Notes

Scope Notes have been constructed to provide definitions of the senses in which possibly ambiguous descriptors are used. We believe that the addition of Scope Notes will increase the utility of the *Thesaurus* to persons not well acquainted with the language of Political Science.

THE FUTURE

In four years we will publish a revised edition of this *Thesaurus*. We fully expect that instead of being the third revised edition of *Political Science Thesaurus*, it will be an integrated *Social Science Thesaurus* developed through incremental steps emphasizing the expansion of the scope of this version. We are adding to our information base service journals and book reviews that will give us the empirical basis for soliciting candidate terms for that revision.

It should be noted that as with everything else involving *United States Political Science Documents* or the United States Political Science Information System, we have created this *Thesaurus* on our own time without funding from any agency except the University of Pittsburgh. The good will and contributions of those who assisted us are cited in the Acknowledgements. We are particularly grateful to the University of Pittsburgh for nurturing the United States Political Science Information System. Without the support of the University, this project would not have come to fruition nor would it be in existence today. It has been a commitment at the highest level of the University, including the Chancellor, Wesley W. Posvar, the Provost, Rhoten A. Smith, and the Senior Vice Chancellor for Planning and Budget, Jack E. Freeman.

Carl Beck, 1979

POLITICAL SCIENCE THESAURUS (PST)
DESCRIPTION AND USE OF THE THESAURUS

PURPOSE OF A SPECIALIZED THESAURUS

In recent years, practitioners in most of the accepted academic disciplines have consciously or unconsciously realized that material of import to their field is being generated not only from within their own discipline but from other disciplines. In addition, the investigation of areas of subject interest have led to the development of interdisciplinary fields, e.g., socioeconomics, that produce material of interest to other disciplines. This proliferation of sources, and, therefore, material, is one dimension of the *information explosion*.

The approach that has, generally, been employed for handling the material available for a given discipline has been to establish a specialized information center that acquires possibly relevant materials from all germane subject areas. To facilitate the dissemination of the disciplinary-interdisciplinary acquisitions, various approaches to an *automated* system have been designed and implemented. In practice, an essential component of the various automated systems has been the design and development of a terminology control mechanism that will permit the storage and retrieval of information on a consistent basis regardless of the discipline of the source material. One of the most generally used terminology control devices has been the information storage and retrieval thesaurus.

DEVELOPMENT OF POLITICAL SCIENCE THESAURUS

Since the *Political Science (PS) Thesaurus* was created *a priori* to the development of an operating information storage and retrieval system, it was possible to take into account the terminology control needs of additional levels of the discipline. In addition to the vocabulary base for an information system, these needs included: (1) a listing of the basic terminology of the field of political science; (2) a point of reference for authors, researchers, or editors to identify useful terminology; (3) a tool to be employed by students of the discipline to determine the terms that may be used to express various concepts; (4) a standard by which practitioners in the field may organize their individual files; and, (5) a guideline that might be employed by periodical publications in the generation of subject indexes.

Levels of Political Science Terminology Control Needs.

Information system vocabulary base: Since the primary motivation for the development of the *PS Thesaurus* was to provide a terminology normalization device for a computer-based information storage and retrieval system, considerable attention was given to this terminology need in the establishment of the *Rules and Conventions* and the analysis of the candidate terms.

It is extremely important that, when the *essential features* of a document are described for storage and retrieval purposes, language is employed that is available to and understandable by the requester. When reviewing a document, an analyst may be tempted to use terms or descriptors found in the document. However, terminology used by an individual author may reflect *his*, idiosyncratic viewpoint and are *not* necessarily, the terms that would be used in information requests. As a result, the document analyst has to describe the *essential features* of a document in anticipation of the searcher's point of view.

Conversely, the terminology used by *any* individual user may reflect *his* idiosyncratic viewpoint and are *not*, necessarily, the terms that would be used to store the information. The questioner or system operator, therefore, has to describe the *essential features* of a question based upon *his* experience with the terminology employed by the analyst.

When a terminology normalization device, such as a thesaurus, is employed to bridge the gap between the language used by the analyst in describing the *essential features* of a document and the language used by the questioner or system operator in describing the *essential features* of a question, predictable relevant document retrieval is possible.

Basic terminology listing: Over a period of time, the terminology of most disciplines is altered by the addition of new concepts, the experience of the times, and the discarding of out-moded concepts. The discipline of political science is one that must be particularly responsive to these elements of terminology change. This does not imply that previous language should be abandoned, but only that the language must reflect both previous and current terminology.

In addition, in a discipline such as political science, which is closely associated in purpose, methods, and investigation with other disciplines, e.g. anthropology, economics, psychology, sociology, a contamination of the language of the discipline may occur by: (1) imprecise usage of political science terminology in describing interdisciplinary phenomenon: (2) adaptation of terminology from other disciplines to describe similar (but *not* exact) observations in political science; and (3) the attempt to separate new interpretations of political science concepts from previous interpretations by varying the terminology.

As a result of the dynamics of the terminology of political science, a device that supplies the basic language of the field and provides a mechanism that permits revision and up-dating is essential. It is anticipated that the user will find this *Thesaurus* such a device. The basic terminology of political science may be identified and reviewed through perusal of the hierarchically associated term listing (*Thesaurus of Terms*), the *Hierarchical Display*, or the *Rotated Descriptor Display*.

Author/researcher/editor terminology need: The process of selecting meaningful terminology when drafting papers, proposals, or reports or when preparing surrogates, e.g., abstracts, index entries, of papers for publication in technical publications will be assisted by this *Thesaurus*.

The desirability of expressing an idea or concept more than once in alternative terminology to increase the probability of understanding by the reader is a basic principle of technical writing. When an author is drafting a paper or when a researcher is preparing a proposal or a research report, the *Thesaurus* may be consulted to identify desirable terminology that will prevent repetition and aid comprehension.

Many technical publications have adopted the practice of requesting authors to provide abstracts and index entries for their articles. The *PS Thesaurus* will assist both the authors of the articles and the editors of the publications in selecting meaningful terms for surrogates as well as titles of the articles. The concepts discussed in the papers may be expressed in specific terms as provided in the *Thesaurus*.

Educational reference tool: The *PS Thesaurus* provides students of political science, as well as individuals from other disciplines interested in political science, with a reference tool that will aid: (1) in identifying a term for a given meaning, and (2) in determining the meaning of a term by its relationship to associated terms. Unlike a dictionary or a glossary, the major purpose of a thesaurus is not to define or express the meaning of a term, but to indicate a term for a given meaning. However, by reviewing the concepts that are associated with a term, a meaning for a term may be determined. For these purposes, students will find the *Thesaurus of Terms* useful.

Individual file organization: As the proliferation of available information has affected the political science discipline, it has also affected the individual political scientist. More material, conventional and unconventional, from more sources, discipline-oriented and interdisciplinary, is being received and retained for future use. Once the individual has decided to retain material, the problem of storing it in a manner that will permit retrieval at some future time is presented. In the past, it might have been possible to organize materials by date of arrival or by source or by some other broad classification. As long as the pile of material remained relatively small, the total search of the material that was required to identify a desired item was not time consuming. But, as the volume of material increases, the application of broad classification becomes more difficult and the time required for the total search to identify a desired item becomes greater.

The *PS Thesaurus* may be used by political scientists to organize their individual files on a subject-oriented basis. The advantages of using consistent, identifiable terminology for filing are as important for the individual as they are for the computer-based information system. By using specific subject entries to describe the material, the time required for future identification will be expedited. In addition, by noting in *his Thesaurus* when a term is employed as a subject entry, the individual will have a file listing available when storing or retrieving material.

Journal subject index terminology: In many instances, the technical journal publications are involved in developing subject indexes. The lack of author-generated index terms, the quality of the author's index entries, and the development of cumulative publications are only a few of the reasons for which journal publications will find the *Thesaurus* useful in identifying index entries for subject indexes. In addition, normalization of the terminology employed by the various publications in indexing will provide a commonality of language that will facilitate the task of the user when reviewing these indexes.

Procedures for Developing the PS Thesaurus.

In order to design and develop a thesaurus that would serve the needs of these information handling levels, two conceptual criteria were identified: (1) that the thesaurus should contain the current terminology of the field of political science, and (2) that individuals with subject expertise should perform the tasks associated with term identification, term analysis, and term relating.

It was agreed by the Scientific Information Exchange Committee (SIEC) of the American Political Science Association (APSA) that the thesaurus construction technique developed at the Knowledge Availability Systems Center (KASC) of the University of Pittsburgh would be employed in the design and development of the *PS Thesaurus*. This technique involved: (1) the establishment of *Rules and Conventions* for the *Thesaurus*; (2) the determination of sources to be employed in the identification of candidate terms; (3) the designing of an analytical taxonomy of the language of political science to be employed in preliminary term analysis; and (4) the establishing of hierarchical and collateral relationships for the analyzed terminology.

Project staff from the University Center for International Studies (UCIS) of the University of Pittsburgh and KASC drafted preliminary rules and conventions and a list of sources for candidate terms. These were reviewed by the members of SIEC. The *Rules and Conventions*, as accepted by the Committee, are reproduced in Appendix 1, and the listing of sources employed in the identification of candidate terms is provided in Appendix 2.

More than 300 political scientists individually scanned copies of the selected periodical publications and underlined each word or term which he felt was important for political science. In addition: (1) a concordance was generated from abstracts stored in two mechanized data bases and key words were identified; (2) subject indexes of books were reviewed for candidate terms; and (3) dictionaries for political science, economics, and sociology were perused for candidate terms. A total of 292,632 terms were identified from all of the sources and keyed into machine processable form. Editing of the identified terms to remove duplicates, variant forms, non-nouns, inverted word forms, and inappropriate terms resulted in a listing of 23,207 candidate terms. Since many of the terms had import in other disciplines, e.g., anthropology, economics, adequate technical knowledge of the field was necessary to determine each term's specific significance for political science.

The next phase in the construction of the *PS Thesaurus* was a preliminary analysis to obtain groupings of linguistically similar terms. A taxonomy of the language of political science was developed and graphically displayed by using the *roadmap** technique developed at KASC. The areas of the language of the field were divided into seven major headings: (1) *device*; (2) *process/method technique*; (3) *prescriptive statement*; (4) *ideology/belief*; (5) *characteristic/property*; (6) *role/position*; and (7) *institution/structure*. Each of these major headings was then subdivided into more specific categories for a total of 38 category locations. For those terms that did not fall into one of the seven major headings, a *miscellaneous* category was established. After the initial decision that a term *should be analyzed* had been made and it had been placed into one of the major headings, subsequent decisions were made by following the *roadmap* to reduce all *process/method technique* terms or all *role/position* terms, etc., into more specific locations.

From the roadmaps, the terms with their analyses were recorded in machine processable form and then sorted alphabetically into like groupings. Each grouping was then printed out and employed in the hierarchical relating phase of the *Thesaurus* construction.

Eventually, two different approaches for establishing hierarchical and collateral relationships for the terms had to be employed. The necessity for using two approaches was realized when, following the review of the *first* rough draft of the *Thesaurus*, a total redevelopment of all the hierarchies was required. The reasons for this redevelopmment are numerous and in some instances speculative. It may be that the difficulties that were experienced are the problems that have historically faced the *soft sciences* in classification and organization. Though differing in methodology, since the objectives of the two approaches were the same, it was possible to incorporate the results of one into the operations of the other.

After the explicit relationships, e.g., broader terms, narrower terms, related terms, had been established, for the second time a rough draft of the *Thesaurus* was prepared. This draft was then reviewed, revised, and typeset. A total of 5,721 main entry terms are contained in the *Thesaurus of Terms*.

In addition to the construction of the political science associated term listing contained in the *Thesaurus of Terms*, a separate geographical/political areas associated term listing was constructed. The *Geographical/Political Areas* was developed *off-line* from the construction of the main *Thesaurus of Terms* construction activity since proper nouns are not, normally, thesaural terms. However, the importance of geographical/political areas to the discipline necessitated their inclusion. The addition of these proper nouns will permit a more specific analysis of a document by subject entry as well as by geographical/political area.

ORGANIZATION AND ARRANGEMENT

The *Political Science* (*PS*)*Thesaurus* has been divided into three sections to assist the user in identifying the appropriate terminology from varying approaches. The *Thesaurus* divisions are: (1)*Thesaurus of Terms* which has two parts—(a) the associated terms of political science and (b) the geographical/political areas associated listing; (2) the *Permuted Index*; and (3) the *Hierarchical Index*. The functions of each division are explained below, and at the beginning of each division additional explanations of symbols, notations, or other arrangement features appear.

Thesaurus of Terms

As previously described, the *Thesaurus of Terms* is organized into two parts: (1) associated terms of political science, and (2) the associated listing of geographical/political areas. In both parts, the descriptors and USE references are interfiled alphabetically word-by-word. This alphabetizing technique was agreed upon in the *Rules and Conventions* in order to keep multiword terms together and to prevent their being interfiled with other terms. As a result, an array such as the following is maintained:

Behavior
Behavior Analysis
Behavioral Measurement
Behavioral Psychology
Behavioral Science

Each descriptor, in either part of the *Thesaurus of Terms*, is displayed with its hierarchical structuring and other cross references. All hierarchical structuring and cross references are reciprocal: for each broader term there is a narrower term; for each related term there is a reciprocating related term: and for each reference there is a used for reference.

In order to identify a term for a given meaning or to determine the relationships for a given term, the user of the *PS Thesaurus* should first consult the political science associated term part of the *Thesaurus of Terms*. To determine the proper term for the concept that is being contemplated, the user may consult the broader terms, narrower terms, and related terms that are displayed for a term. If the term to represent a concept that the user has in mind is not found, one or both of the indexes may be reviewed to determine another term or term form that might represent the desired concept.

The identification of the descriptors and the structuring of the hierarchical arrays included in the *Thesaurus of Terms* have been performed in accordance with the *Rules and Conventions* (Appendix 1) that were adopted by the Scientific Information Exchange Committee of the American Political Science Association (APSA). Since any use of the *Thesaurus* will be more effective and efficient with an understanding of the methodology employed in its construction, users are referred to Appendix 1 to review the procedures.

---

*"Roadmap" is the description of the term analysis and grouping technique developed at KASC and described in Dym, Eleanor D."A New Approach to the Development of a Technical Thesaurus," *Proceedings of the American Documentation Institute*, annual meeting, vol. 4. New York, American Documentation Institute, October 22-27, 1967. pp. 126-131.

Permuted Index

If the user cannot find the desired term to represent a concept of the political science in the *Thesaurus of Terms*, he should consult the *Permuted Index*. This is an alphabetical listing of every significant word comprising the terms in the associated terms of political science part of the *Thesaurus of Terms*.

The user will find this *Index* useful in: (1) providing the proper word order for multiword terms, and (2) providing listings of generic words for review. Since it is often possible to arrange the words in a multiword term in more than one order, e.g., behavior theory or theory of behavior, the *Permuted Index* will permit the user to determine the accepted word order in the *Thesaurus*. In addition, when the user only has a general concept in mind rather than a specific term, by reviewing the listings of generic terms, e.g., characteristics, specific terms may be identified and then looked up in the *Thesaurus of Terms*.

Hierarchical Index.

Those users interested in determining the position of membership of a term in an overall family of descriptors should consult the *Hierarchical Index*. Those descriptors that were considered heads of families are those that do not have broader terms in the *Thesaurus of Terms*. The user will find this *Index* useful not only in determining hierarchical arrangement for searching and indexing, but, also, in dealing with more complex term taxonomies.

EXPLANATION AND EXAMPLES

EXPLANATION		EXAMPLES
(Refer to numbers opposite; Examples drawn from actual *Thesaurus* entries.)		
1. This represents the main entry position for the descriptors. When a descriptor is in the main entry position is appears in uppercase bold face type.	1.	**ADMINISTRATION**
2. **Codes.** There are two forms of numerical codes associated with *Thesaurus* entries, one for terms in the *Thesaurus* (a.) and one for terms deleted from the *Thesaurus* (b.)		
a. *Hierarchy Line Number* (*s-xx-nnnn*). The s indicates a parent subject hierarchy (as opposed to a g for a geographical hierarchy), and the xx-nnnn indicates the parent hierarchy number and line within that hierarchy. As such, this code provides a cross reference to the hierarchy display.	2a.	**ADMINISTRATIVE THEORY** S-38-0039 1975 00043
Entry Date and Postings (*1975- 0037*). The entry date indicates when a term officially became a part of the *Thesaurus*. The postings total shows how many times a term has been used in indexing all of the first three and part of the fourth volumes of *United States Political Science Documents*.		
b. *Entry Date, Exit Date and Postings* (*1975-1979 0037*). The entry date indicates when a term officially became part of the *Thesaurus*. The exit date indicates when a term was officially deleted from the *Thesaurus*. The postings total shows how many times a term has been used in indexing for all of the first three and part of the fourth volumes of *United States Political Science Documents*.	2b.	**AD HOC COMMITTEE** 1975-1979 00002
3. **Scope Note.** Scope Notes are used to provide definitions of the senses in which possibly ambiguous descriptors are used.	3.	**ADJUDICATION** SN Conflict resolution by judicial procedure
4. **Used For (UF) Reference.** The UF reference indicates that the descriptor in the main entry position is to be used for any descriptor listed under this notation.	4.	**ACADEMIC AREAS** UF Academic Departments
5. **USE Reference.** The USE reference refers the user to the preferred descriptor of usage. The UF and USE references are reciprocations of thought. USE references are most often provided to link various expressions of an idea as found in literature with applicable descriptors as provided in the *Thesaurus*. Such references have also been provided for deleted terms whenever possible.	5.	**AFRICA SOUTH OF SAHARA** USE Central Africa East Africa South Africa West Africa
6. **Broader Term (BT).** A broader term provides the generic hierarchical relationship for the descriptor in the main entry position. In the broader class, the main entry descriptor is a lesser term.	6.	**ACADEMIC SPECIALIZATION** BT Education Characteristics
7. **Narrower Term (NT).** The narrower term provides the specific hierarchical relationship for the descriptor in the main entry position. It is the reciprocal of a broader term.	7.	**ADMINISTRATIVE BEHAVIOR** NT Bureaucratic Behavior Executive Behavior Organization Behavior

8. **Related Term (RT).** The related term notation indicates those terms that are related in concept but do not possess a hierarchical or preferential relationship.

8. **ADMINISTRATIVE ACCOUNTABILITY**
RT Administrative Discretion
Administrative Law System
Bureaucratic Capability Characteristics
Bureaucratic Socialization
Bureaucratic Structural Characteristics
Government Accountability
Legislative Accountability

9. **Rotated Descriptor Display.** The Rotated Descriptor Display (see third section of the *Thesuarus* proper) provides an index to the Political Science and Geographical Terminology sections in a format such that each descriptor phrase is listed alphabetically according to each word in the phrase, instead of simply the first word in the phrase. Thus, a descriptor phrase will appear in this index as many times as there are words in the phrase.

10. **Hierarchical Displays.** The Hierarchical Displays (see fourth section of the *Thesaurus* proper) present the political science and geographical descriptors in outline format as determined by their hierarchy membership. This enables visualization of broader/narrower and generic/specific relationships.

POLITICAL SCIENCE TERMINOLOGY

POLITICAL SCIENCE TERMINOLOGY

ABDICATION
S-31-0461 1975 00000
BT Executive Dissolution
RT Emperor
Government Instability
Government Overthrow
King
Monarchy
Regent
Resignation

ABORTION LAW
S-21-0085 1975 00024
BT Social Law
RT Abortion Policy
Birth Control Policy
Birth Rate
Family Law
Family Planning
Family Policy
Gambling Law
Gender Ideology
Health Care Rights
Illegal Abortion
Public Health Policy
Womens Rights

ABORTION POLICY
S-26-0372 1979 00000
BT Social Policy
RT Abortion Law
Birth Control Policy
Birth Rate
Family Planning
Family Policy
Health Care Rights
Public Health Policy
Womens Rights

ABSENTEE BALLOT
S-29-0157 1975 00000
BT Paper Ballot
RT Absentee Voter
Absentee Voting
Electoral Law
Voting Rights

ABSENTEE LANDLORD SYSTEM
S-37-0051 1975 00000
BT Property Ownership System
RT Collective Ownership
Foreign Ownership
Ghetto Business
Housing Code
Land Estate System
Land Ownership Pattern
Land Tenure System
Landless Peasant Class
Plantation Economy
Slavery

ABSENTEE VOTER
S-32-0294 1975 00000
BT Voter
RT Absentee Ballot
Absentee Voting
Eligible Voter
Voter Qualification

ABSENTEE VOTING
S-29-0122 1975 00000
BT Voting
RT Absentee Ballot
Absentee Voter
Electoral Law
Political Party Voting Indicator
Proxy Voting
Student Voter
Voter Qualification
Voting Behavior Analysis
Voting Rights

ABSENTEEISM
USE Employment Record

ABSOLUTE MAJORITY ELECTORAL OUTCOME
S-29-0112 1975 00002
BT Majority Electoral Outcome
RT Majoritarianism
Single Member District

ABSOLUTE MONARCH
S-36-0055 1975 00000
BT Monarch
RT Absolute Monarchy
Absolutism
Absolutist Government
Ancient Regime
Authoritarian Regime
Authoritarianism
Autocrat
Autocratic Government
Constitutional Monarch
Despot
Dictatorship
Emperor
Hereditary Ruler
Hobbesian Absolutism
Imperial Government
Kaiser
King
Machiavellian Thought
Monarchy
Renaissance State Theory
Royalist
Royalist State Theory
Statecraft Theory
Totalitarian Political System
Traditional Authority
Traditional Leadership
Tyranny

ABSOLUTE MONARCHY
S-16-0073 1975 00001
BT Monarchy
RT Absolute Monarch
Absolutism
Absolutist Government
Ancient Regime
Aristocratic Class
Authoritarian Regime
Authoritarianism
Autocrat
Autocratic Government
Constitutional Monarchy
Despot
Dictator
Dictatorship
Emperor
Hereditary Ruler
Hobbesian Analysis
Integrated Authority
Kaiser
King
Prince
Republican Monarchy
Sheik
Totalitarian Political System
Tyranny

ABSOLUTISM
S-38-0177 1975 00004
BT Ideologies
RT Absolute Monarch
Absolute Monarchy
Absolutist Government
Ancient Regime
Authoritarian Attitude
Authoritarian Personality
Authoritarian Regime
Authoritarianism
Authoritarianism Scale
Autocratic Government
Centralized Authority
Centralized Government
Closed Society
Concentrated Power
Corporatism
Despot
Despotism
Dictator
Dictatorial Regime
Dogmatism
Fascist Council
Fascist Economy
Fascist Theory
Feudal State
Hobbesian Absolutism
Hobbesian Analysis
Integrated Authority
Political Authority
Totalitarian Dictatorship
Totalitarian Leadership
Totalitarian Political System
Traditional Authority
Tsar
Tutelary Democracy
Tyranny

ABSOLUTIST GOVERNMENT
S-16-0003 1975 00003
BT Government Type
RT Absolute Monarch
Absolute Monarchy
Absolutism
Authoritarian Regime
Authoritarianism
Autocratic Government
Centralized Government
Closed Society
Communist Government
Despotism

Dictatorship
King
Military Government
One Political Party System
Political Repression
Totalitarian Dictatorship
Totalitarian Political System
Tutelary Democracy
Tyranny

ABSTRACTING
S-24-0154 1975 00000
BT Information Storage
RT Abstracting Service
Bibliographic Service
Data Storage
Documentation Service
Indexing
Information Network

ABSTRACTING SERVICE
S-18-0047 1975 00000
BT Information Service
RT Abstracting
Bibliographic Service
Citation Analysis
Documentation Service
Government Information Service
Indexing
Information Network
Information Retrieval
Legislative Information Service
Private Information Service
University Information Service

ACADEMIC
S-32-0002 1979 00000
BT Roles
RT Academic Areas
Academy Of Science
Advisor
Anthropologist
Economist
Geographer
Higher Education
Historian
Policy Scientist
Political Scientist
Professor
Psychologist
Research And Development
Teacher
University
University Education

ACADEMIC AREAS
S-01-0001 1975 00011
UF Academic Departments
NT Administrative Science
Agricultural Science
Anthropology Discipline
Archaeology
Architectural Studies
Area Studies
Behavioral Science
Biological Sciences
Business Studies
Communist Studies
Computer Science
Demographic Studies
Earth Sciences
Ecology Discipline
Economics Discipline
Education Discipline
Engineering Discipline
Environmental Studies
Ethnic Studies
Geography Discipline
Gerontology
History Discipline
Humanities Discipline
Information Science
Interdisciplinary Studies
Language Studies
Legal Studies
Library Science Studies
Linguistics
Literature Studies
Mathematics Discipline
Medical Science
Military Science
Natural Science Discipline
Peace Studies
Philosophy Discipline
Political Science Discipline
Psychology Discipline
Religious Studies
Sociology Discipline
Statistics Discipline
Strategic Studies
Urban Studies
Womens Studies
RT Academic
Academic Community
Academic Elite
Academic Freedom
Academic Specialization
Academy Of Science
Education Planner
Education Policy
Education Process
Interdisciplinary Research
Professor
Research Center
Research Institution
Theory
Traditional Education
University
University Information Service

ACADEMIC COMMUNITY
S-07-0002 1979 00000
BT Community Type
RT Academic Areas
Academy Of Science
College
Cooperative Community
Heterogeneous Community
Higher Education
Pedagogical Institute
Research Institution
University
University Education

ACADEMIC DEPARTMENTS
USE Academic Areas

ACADEMIC ELITE
S-14-0002 1975 00012
BT Elite Type
RT Academic Areas
Academic Freedom
Academic Imperialism
Academic Tenure Policy
Academy Of Science
Basic Research
Cultural Elite
Education Policy Making
Institutional Elite Identification
Intellectual Elite
Intelligentsia
Literary Elite
Meritocracy
Modernizing Elite
Scientific Elite
Social Elite
Technological Elite
Tenure Policy

ACADEMIC FREEDOM
S-15-0011 1975 00006
BT Freedom Of Inquiry
RT Academic Areas
Academic Elite
Academic Tenure Policy
Censorship Process
Education Policy Making
Freedom Of Information
Freedom Of Press
Freedom Of Speech
Scientific Freedom

ACADEMIC IMPERIALISM
S-37-0067 1975 00005
BT Imperialism System
RT Academic Elite
Cultural Imperialism
Economic Imperialism
Field Research
Political Imperialism

ACADEMIC MANAGEMENT
USE Education Planning

ACADEMIC SPECIALIZATION
S-06-0362 1979 00000
BT Education Characteristics
RT Academic Areas
Education Planning
Education Type
Higher Education Planning
Higher Education Policy
Policy Research
Professional Occupational Role
Professional Socialization
Technical Education
Traditional Education
Vocational Education

ACADEMIC TENURE POLICY
S-26-0209 1975 00003
BT Tenure Policy
RT Academic Elite
Academic Freedom
Education Agency
Education Policy
Education Policy Making
Education Politics
Field Research
Higher Education Administration
Private College
Private University

ACADEMICIAN
USE Professor

ACADEMY OF SCIENCE
S-19-0202 1975 00002
BT Higher Education Institution
RT Academic
Academic Areas

Academic Community
Academic Elite
Graduate School
Higher Education
Higher Education Planning
Pedagogical Institute
Research Institution
Science Information Policy
University

ACCESS TO CULTURE
USE Cultural Policy

ACCESS TO EDUCATION
USE Education Opportunity

ACCESS TO UNIVERSITY
USE Education Opportunity

ACCIDENT INSURANCE
S-26-0299 1979 00000
BT Insurance
RT Catastrophe Insurance
Compulsory Insurance
Disability Insurance
Fire Insurance
Life Insurance
Malpractice Insurance
Motor Vehicle Insurance
No Fault Insurance

ACCOMMODATION
S-31-0221 1975 00008
BT Conflict Resolution
RT Accommodative Social Behavior
Acculturation
Adaptive Behavior
Agreement
Appeasement
Bargaining
Conciliation
Mediation
Negotiation

ACCOMMODATIVE SOCIAL BEHAVIOR
S-05-0023 1975 00026
UF Individual Accommodation
BT Social Behavior
NT Adaptive Behavior
Conformity Behavior
Cooperative Behavior
RT Accommodation
Acculturation
Acculturation Theory
Avoidance Behavior
Consensual Norms
Consensual Politics
Consensus Theory
Habitual Behavior
Mass Behavior
Pragmatic Political Culture
Sexual Behavior
Social Adjustment

ACCOUNTANT
USE Financial Accounting

ACCREDITATION PROCESS
S-31-0002 1979 00000
BT Process
NT Education Accreditation Process
Professional Accreditation Process
RT Degree Requirement
Professional Occupational Role
Professional School
Sociology Of The Professions
Testing

ACCULTURATION
S-34-0002 1975 00024
BT Socialization
RT Accommodation
Accommodative Social Behavior
Acculturation Theory
Adaptive Behavior
Assimilation
Cultural Adaptation
Cultural Assimilation
Culture Shock
Enculturation
Ethnic Assimilation Theory
Homogeneous Culture
Learning Theory
Political Socialization
Psychology Discipline
Social Adjustment
Socialization Context
Socialization Type

ACCULTURATION THEORY
S-38-0003 1975 00006
BT Anthropological Theory
RT Accommodative Social Behavior
Acculturation
Adaptive Behavior
Anthropological Functionalism
Assimilation
Assimilation Theory
Cultural Adaptation
Cultural Assimilation
Cultural Evolutionism
Ethnographic Theory
Kinship Systematics Theory
Social Learning Theory
Socialization Theory

ACCUMULATED CAPITAL
S-06-0260 1975 00017
BT Capital
RT Assets
Capital Surplus
Classical Economic Theory
Fixed Assets
Investment Capital
Laissez Faire Theory

ACHIEVED STATUS
S-06-0787 1975 00030
BT Status Stratification Division
RT Achieved Status System
Achievement Theory
Achieving Society
Ascribed Status
Class Stratification Division
Objectively Derived Status
Prestige Hierarchy
Status Equality
Subjectively Derived Status

ACHIEVED STATUS SYSTEM
S-37-0146 1975 00014
BT Status Social System
RT Achieved Status
Achievement Theory
Achieving Society
Ascribed Status System

ACHIEVEMENT MOTIVATION
S-06-0131 1975 00062
BT Self Interest
RT Achievement Theory
Achieving Society
Economic Incentive System
Inner Directedness
Personality Development

ACHIEVEMENT THEORY
S-38-0530 1975 00034
BT Psychological Theory
RT Achieved Status
Achieved Status System
Achievement Motivation
Achieving Society
Cross Pressure Theory
Frustration Aggression Theory
Learning Theory
Meritocracy
Motivation Theory
Psychopolitical Theory
Relative Deprivation Theory

ACHIEVING SOCIETY
S-35-0002 1975 00009
SN Society in which individual attainment and ambition are highly valued.
BT Society Type
RT Achieved Status
Achieved Status System
Achievement Motivation
Achievement Theory
Affluent Society
Gesellschaft
Industrial Society
Meritocracy
Modernizing Society
Secular Society
Urban Society
Western Society

ACQUITTAL
S-31-0478 1975 00000
BT Court Action
RT Cease Desist Order
Consent Judgment
Conviction
Criminal Law System
Defendants Rights
Law System
Military Justice
Plea Bargaining
Verdict
Writ Of Mandamus

ACTIVIST
S-32-0179 1975 00010
BT Political Role
NT Demonstrator
Economic Activist
Political Activist
Rioter
Student Activist
War Protestor
RT Civil Rights Leader
Militancy
Political Activist
Political Efficacy
Politician
Protest Politics
Racial Militancy
Rioter
Student Activism
Student Activist
Student Militancy
War Protestor

AD HOC COMMITTEE
1975-1979 00002
USE Ad Hoc Congressional Committee

AD HOC CONGRESSIONAL COMMITTEE
S-19-0263 1979 00000
UF Ad Hoc Committee
BT Congressional Committee
RT Committee Staffing
Congressional Delegation
Congressional Subcommittee
Joint Congressional Committee
Joint Standing Congressional Committee
Senate House Conference Committee
Standing Congressional Committee

ADAPTATION
USE Adaptive Behavior

ADAPTIVE BEHAVIOR
S-05-0024 1975 00040
UF Adaptation
Individual Adaptation
BT Accommodative Social Behavior
RT Accommodation
Acculturation
Acculturation Theory
Assimilation
Conformity Behavior
Cooperative Behavior
Coping Behavior
Ethnic Assimilation
Functional Adaptation
Learning Feedback
Mass Behavior
Psychological Anthropology
Psychological Theory
Social Adjustment
Social Integration
Social Learning Theory
Socialization Analysis
Socialization Type
Structural Adaptation

ADJOURNMENT DEBATE
S-31-0582 1975 00000
BT Legislative Action
RT Legislative Behavior
Legislative Procedure
Legislative Voting

ADJUDICATION
S-31-0222 1975 00013
SN Conflict resolution by judicial procedure.
BT Conflict Resolution
NT International Adjudication
International Conciliation
RT Adjudicator
Agreement
Appeasement
Arbitration
Bargaining
Case Law
Conciliation
Decision Making Process
Judicial Administration
Judicial Administration Agency
Judicial Behavior
Judicial Decision Making
Judicial Procedure
Law Administration
Law System
Mediation
Military Court
Negotiation

ADJUDICATOR
S-32-0003 1975 00000
BT Roles
NT Arbitrator
Bargainer
Broker
Mediator
Moderator
Negotiator
Ombudsman
RT Adjudication
Bargaining
Decision Maker
Judicial Behavior
Judicial Decision Making

ADMINISTRATION
USE Administrative Behavior

ADMINISTRATIVE ACCOUNTABILITY
S-06-0432 1975 00029
BT Administrative Normative Characteristics
NT Executive Accountability
Ministerial Responsibility
RT Administrative Discretion
Administrative Law System
Bureaucratic Capability Characteristics
Bureaucratic Socialization
Bureaucratic Structural Characteristics
Government Accountability
Legislative Accountability

ADMINISTRATIVE ADVISOR
S-32-0012 1975 00005
BT Advisor
NT Chief Executive Advisor
RT Administrative Officer
Administrative Personnel
Administrative Staff Personnel
Economic Advisor
Education Advisor
Legal Advisor
Military Advisor
Political Advisor
Science Advisor
Technical Advisor

ADMINISTRATIVE BEHAVIOR
S-05-0002 1975 00024
UF Administration
BT Behavior
NT Bureaucratic Behavior
Executive Behavior
Organization Behavior
RT Administrative Characteristics
Administrative Leadership
Administrative Personnel
Administrative Reform
Administrative Science
Administrative Theory
Avoidance Behavior
Behavioral Science
Behavioral Theory
Bureaucratic Leadership
Bureaucratic Theory
Decision Making Theory
Government Bureaucracy
Habitual Behavior
Mass Behavior
Organization Environment
Public Administration Studies
Social Behavior

ADMINISTRATIVE CAPABILITY CHARACTERISTICS
S-06-0428 1975 00009
BT Administrative Characteristics
NT Administrative Effectiveness
Administrative Efficiency
RT Administrative Law System
Administrative Normative Characteristics
Bureaucratic Characteristics

ADMINISTRATIVE CHARACTERISTICS
S-06-0427 1975 00021
BT Management Characteristics
NT Administrative Capability Characteristics
Administrative Normative Characteristics
Bureaucratic Characteristics
RT Administrative Behavior
Administrative Planning
Association Characteristics
Bureaucratic Theory
Public Administration Studies

ADMINISTRATIVE COURT
S-19-0125 1975 00001
BT Courts
NT Administrative Tribunal
Tax Court
RT Administrative Jurisdiction
Civil Court
Colonial Court
Court Jurisdiction
Criminal Court
International Court
Jurisdiction Characteristics
Justice Administration Agency
Local Court
Military Court
Probate Court

ADMINISTRATIVE DEVELOPMENT THEORY
S-38-0022 1975 00012
BT Development Theory
RT Administrative Theory
Bureaucratic Politics
Bureaucratic Rationality
Institutionalization
Organization Behavior
Organization Change
Organization Development
Organization Formation
Organization Innovation
Organization Theory
Political Development Theory
Social Development Theory
Technological Development Theory
Urban Development Theory

ADMINISTRATIVE DISCRETION
S-06-0437 1975 00003
BT Administrative Normative Characteristics
NT Executive Discretion
Executive Prerogative

Executive Privilege
RT Administrative Accountability
Bureaucratic Capability Characteristics
Pocket Veto

ADMINISTRATIVE EFFECTIVENESS
S-06-0429 1975 00017
BT Administrative Capability Characteristics
RT Administrative Efficiency
Administrative Planning
Bureaucratic Efficiency

ADMINISTRATIVE EFFICIENCY
S-06-0430 1975 00015
BT Administrative Capability Characteristics
RT Administrative Effectiveness
Administrative Planning
Bureaucratic Efficiency

ADMINISTRATIVE JURISDICTION
S-06-0401 1975 00013
BT Jurisdiction Characteristics
RT Administrative Court
Executive Jurisdiction
Government Bureaucracy
Legal Jurisdiction
Legislative Jurisdiction
Territory Jurisdiction
Union Jurisdiction

ADMINISTRATIVE LAW
S-21-0002 1975 00006
BT Law Type
RT Administrative Policy Making
Administrative Theory
Administrative Tribunal
Civil Law
Code Enforcement
Constitutional Law
Constitutional Law System
Judicial Administration
Law Administration
Law Enforcement System
Legal Studies
Public Administration Studies

ADMINISTRATIVE LAW SYSTEM
S-37-0097 1975 00000
BT Law System
RT Administrative Accountability
Administrative Capability Characteristics
Administrative Policy Making
Administrative Tribunal
Civil Law System
Commercial Law
Common Law System
Constitutional Law System
International Law System
Legal Studies
Military Law System
Sociology Of Law

ADMINISTRATIVE LEADERSHIP
S-22-0004 1975 00023
UF Administrator
BT Leadership Authority Base
NT Bureaucratic Leadership
RT Administrative Behavior
Administrative Management
Administrative Normative Characteristics
Administrative Officer
Administrative Personnel
Administrative Theory
Bureaucratic Leadership
Bureaucratic Politics
Bureaucratic Rule
Bureaucratic Theory
Collective Leadership
Collegial Leadership
Entrepreneurship
Executive Behavior
Executive Policy
Governing Elite
National Leadership
Political Leadership
Public Policy Management
Rational Legal Leadership
Totalitarian Leadership
Traditional Leadership

ADMINISTRATIVE MANAGEMENT
S-23-0002 1975 00066
BT Management
NT Personnel Management
RT Administrative Leadership
Administrative Normative Characteristics
Administrative Science
Administrative Theory
Bureaucratic Politics
Bureaucratic Structural Characteristics
Business Management
Central Economic Management
Corporate Management
Crisis Management
Democratic Economic Planning
Development Management
Economic Management
Energy Management
Executive Behavior
Executive Budget
Executive Reorganization
Management Training Program
Monetary Management
Public Administration Studies
Public Authorities
Research Management
Worker Self Management

ADMINISTRATIVE NORMATIVE CHARACTERISTICS
S-06-0431 1975 00009
BT Administrative Characteristics
NT Administrative Accountability
Administrative Discretion
RT Administrative Capability Characteristics
Administrative Leadership
Administrative Management
Bureaucratic Goal
Bureaucratic Normative Characteristics
Institutional Socialization

ADMINISTRATIVE OFFICER
S-36-0003 1975 00006
BT Administrative Personnel
NT Bureau Chief
Dean
Department Head
Executive Director
RT Administrative Advisor
Administrative Leadership
Administrative Staff Personnel
Dean
Subnational Government Bureaucracy

ADMINISTRATIVE PERSONNEL
S-36-0002 1975 00009
BT Status
NT Administrative Officer
Administrative Staff Personnel
RT Administrative Advisor
Administrative Behavior
Administrative Leadership
Advisor
Government Official
Military Officer
Military Personnel
Political Party Official
Subnational Government Bureaucracy

ADMINISTRATIVE PLANNING
S-31-0635 1975 00009
BT Planning Process
NT Planification
RT Administrative Characteristics
Administrative Effectiveness
Administrative Efficiency
Administrative Reform
Bureaucratic Rationality
Centrally Planned Economy
Contingency Theory
Defense Planning
Development Planning
Economic Planning
Environmental Planning
Government Planner
Management Characteristics
Management Training Program
Military Planning
Model Building
National Planning Policy
Planning Commission
Planning Policy
Public Administration Studies
Public Policy Management
Public Policy Planning
Regional Planning Policy
Social Engineering
Social Planning
State Planner
Urban Planner

ADMINISTRATIVE POLICY MAKING
S-31-0675 1975 00013
BT Policy Making Process
RT Administrative Law
Administrative Law System
Administrative Politics
Administrative Reform
Administrative Theory
Bureaucratic Structural Characteristics
Executive Agreement
Executive Assistant
Executive Budget Proposal
Executive Discretion
Executive Power
Executive Prerogative
Fiscal Management
Goal Specificity
Hierarchical Model

International Agency
Management Training Program
National Policy Making
Policy Implementation
Policy Incrementalism
Public Administration Studies
Public Policy Management
Public Policy Studies

ADMINISTRATIVE POLITICS
S-29-0002 1975 00019
BT Politics
NT Bureaucratic Politics
Interagency Rivalry
RT Administrative Policy Making
Administrative Reform
Administrative Theory
Administrative Tribunal
Bureaucratic Behavior
Bureaucratic Hierarchy
Executive Agreement
Executive Diplomacy
Executive Discretion
Executive Judicial Policy
Executive Jurisdiction
Executive Policy
Executive Power
Executive Prerogative
Executive Reorganization
Executive Trial Balloon Policy
Executive Veto
Extraparliamentary Politics
Group Hierarchy
Hierarchical Authority
Hierarchical Model
Public Administration Studies

ADMINISTRATIVE RECORD
S-18-0020 1975 00001
BT Government Document
NT Census Record
Proclamation
Regulatory Agency Record
Veto Message
RT Executive Communique
Intergovernmental Document
Judicial Record
Legislative Record
Licensing Record
White Paper

ADMINISTRATIVE REFORM
S-31-0087 1979 00000
BT Reform
RT Administrative Behavior
Administrative Planning
Administrative Policy Making
Administrative Politics
Administrative Science
Administrative Theory
Education Reform
Executive Reform
Judicial Reform
Legislative Reform

ADMINISTRATIVE SCIENCE
S-01-0002 1975 00023
UF Management Science
BT Academic Areas
RT Administrative Behavior
Administrative Management
Administrative Reform
Administrative Theory
Behavioral Science
Bureaucratic Normative Characteristics
Bureaucratic Socialization
Decision Making Theory
Evolutionary Economics
Expertise
Institutional Change
Institutional Socialization
Iron Law Of Oligarchy
Labor History
Management Characteristics
Management Training Program
Organization Characteristics
Organization Environment
Organization Model
Organization Theory
Policy Incrementalism
Policy Science Studies
Political Behavior Studies
Political Science Discipline
Political Science Methodology Studies
Psychology Discipline
Public Administration Studies
Social Organization Theory
Social Psychology
Sociology Discipline
Weberian Theory

ADMINISTRATIVE STAFF PERSONNEL
S-36-0009 1975 00003
BT Administrative Personnel
NT Executive Staff Personnel
Judicial Staff Personnel
Legislative Staff Personnel
RT Administrative Advisor
Administrative Officer
Executive Assistant
Government Employee

ADMINISTRATIVE THEORY
S-38-0039 1975 00043
BT Organization Theory
RT Administrative Behavior
Administrative Development Theory
Administrative Law
Administrative Leadership
Administrative Management
Administrative Policy Making
Administrative Politics
Administrative Reform
Administrative Science
Bureaucracy
Bureaucratic Normative Characteristics
Bureaucratic Parallelism
Bureaucratic Rigidity
Bureaucratic Rule
Bureaucratic Socialization
Bureaucratic Society
Bureaucratic Theory
Executive Role Orientation
Hierarchical Integration
Hierarchical Model
Institutional Socialization
Organization Behavior
Organization Characteristics
Organization Environment
Political Theory Studies
Public Administration Studies
Weberian Analysis

ADMINISTRATIVE TRIBUNAL
S-19-0126 1975 00000
SN Bureaucratic agency invested with adjudicative powers.
BT Administrative Court
RT Administrative Law
Administrative Law System
Administrative Politics
Bureaucratic Rule
Civil Service System
Investigation Commission

ADMINISTRATOR
USE Administrative Leadership

ADMIRALTY
S-33-0050 1975 00001
BT Armed Forces
RT Admiralty Law
Army
Coast Guard
Marines
Mercenary Armed Forces
Military Management
Navy
Peoples Army
Professional Military Forces

ADMIRALTY LAW
S-21-0067 1975 00002
BT Political Law
RT Admiralty
Commercial Law
Maritime Court
Maritime Law

ADMISSION POLICY
S-26-0002 1979 00000
UF University Admission
BT Policy
RT Affirmative Action Employment Policy
Education Policy
Exclusionary Policy
Fair Employment Policy

ADOLESCENCE
S-06-0181 1975 00019
BT Age
RT Adolescent Political Socialization
Adolescent Socialization
Childhood
Infancy
Peer Group
Youth
Youth Culture
Youth Politics
Youth Voter

ADOLESCENT POLITICAL SOCIALIZATION
S-34-0019 1975 00015
BT Adolescent Socialization
RT Adolescence
Adult Political Socialization
Childhood Political Socialization
Family Political Socialization
Learning Theory
Psychology Discipline
Youth Culture
Youth Movement
Youth Politics

ADOLESCENT SOCIALIZATION
S-34-0018 1975 00018
BT Group Socialization
NT Adolescent Political Socialization
RT Adolescence
Adult Socialization
Childhood Socialization
Class Social System
Cohort Group Socialization
Family Socialization
Interest Group Socialization
Learning Theory
Peer Group Socialization
Primary Group Socialization
Psychology Discipline
Youth Culture
Youth Movement
Youth Politics

ADULT EDUCATION
S-13-0002 1979 00000
BT Education Type
RT Civic Education
Continuing Education
Education Service
Informal Education
Outreach Education
Professional Education
Service Delivery System
Technical Education

ADULT POLITICAL SOCIALIZATION
S-34-0021 1975 00006
BT Adult Socialization
RT Adolescent Political Socialization
Learning Theory
Peer Group Socialization
Primary Group Socialization

ADULT SOCIALIZATION
S-34-0020 1975 00007
BT Group Socialization
NT Adult Political Socialization
RT Adolescent Socialization
Cohort Group Socialization
Elite Socialization
Ethical Socialization
Family Socialization
Interest Group Socialization
Learning Theory
Peer Group Socialization
Primary Group Socialization

ADVANCED INDUSTRIAL SOCIETY
S-35-0021 1975 00047
BT Industrial Society
RT Advanced Technology
American Area Studies
Commodity Production
Diversified Economic System
Economic Development Level
Economic Development Stage
Economic Development Theory
Economic Modernization
Economic Process
Industrial Economic Stage
Mature Capitalism
Post Industrial Economic Stage
Post Industrial Society
Post Industrial Society Theory
Preindustrial Society
Rich Nation
Technological Development Theory
Technological Obsolescence
Technology
Technology Policy

ADVANCED TECHNOLOGY
S-06-0800 1975 00043
BT Technology
RT Advanced Industrial Society
American Area Studies
Computer Programming
Futurology
Industrial Society
Man Machine Simulation
Middle Level Technology
Modernization
Patent Law
Research And Development
Solar Energy
Technocracy
Technological Obsolescence
Technology Policy
Technology Transfer
Technology Transfer Policy
Tidal Energy

ADVERSARY PROCESS
S-31-0476 1975 00003
BT Judicial Process
RT Adversary System
Appellate Court
Court Procedure
Defender
Defense Attorney
Judicial Decision Making
Judicial Procedure
Judicial System
Law System
Litigation
Public Trial
Trial
Trial Court
Trial System

ADVERSARY SYSTEM
S-37-0089 1975 00003
BT Justice System
RT Adversary Process
Appeal Procedure
Appellate Court
Conflict Resolution
Criminal Lawyer
Grand Jury System
Judicial Process
Jury Trial
Law Enforcement System
Public Trial
Trial
Trial Court
Trial Jury
Trial Strategy
Trial System

ADVERTISING INDUSTRY
S-17-0067 1979 00000
BT Service Industry
RT Communication Industry
Magazine Industry
Marketing
Political Advertising
Publication Industry

ADVISOR
S-32-0011 1975 00002
BT Roles
NT Administrative Advisor
Economic Advisor
Education Advisor
Legal Advisor
Military Advisor
Political Advisor
Science Advisor
Technical Advisor
RT Academic
Administrative Personnel
Expert

ADVOCACY RESEARCH
S-24-0374 1979 00000
BT Research Orientation
RT Applied Research
Basic Research
Data Selection Orientation
Descriptive Research
Dialectic
Law System
Legal Studies
Qualitative Research
Theoretical Research

AEROSPACE INDUSTRY
S-17-0036 1975 00006
BT Defense Industry
RT Aircraft Industry
Arms Industry
Space Exploration Policy

AESTHETICS
S-25-0002 1975 00166
BT Philosophical Concept
RT Artisan
Artistic Elite
Arts Policy
Classical Education
Cultural History
Culture Type
Fine Arts
German Romanticism
Humanistic Education
Humanistic Research
Humanities Discipline
Metaphysics
Romanticism
Socialist Realism
Sociology Of Art
Structuralism
Theater Censorship

AFFECTIVE MEASUREMENT
S-24-0180 1975 00080
SN Specification of value and emotional dimension of attitude or belief.
BT Attitude Measurement
RT Belief Measurement
Cognitive Measurement
Intelligence Quotient
Motivation Measurement

AFFIRMATIVE ACTION EMPLOYMENT POLICY
S-26-0198 1975 00023
BT Employment Policy
RT Admission Policy
Civil Rights Litigation
Employment Opportunity
Equal Employment Policy

Equal Opportunity
Fair Employment Policy
Job Discrimination
Job Training
Opportunity Characteristics
Quota System Policy
Womens Rights

AFFLUENT SOCIETY
S-35-0003 1975 00009
BT Society Type
RT Achieving Society
Bourgeois Society
Capitalist Society
Modernizing Society
Prosperity
Secular Society
Urban Society
Western Society

AFRICAN AREA STUDIES
S-01-0025 1975 00094
BT Area Studies
NT Central African Area Studies
East African Area Studies
North African Area Studies
South African Area Studies
West African Area Studies
RT Black Culture
Black History
Comparative Literature Studies
Comparative Political Studies
Comparative Sociology
Cultural Anthropology
Cultural History
Ethnic Studies
Ethnicity
Political Science Discipline
Social Anthropology

AFRICAN CIVILIZATION
S-11-0003 1979 00000
BT Civilization
RT Ancient Civilization
Eastern Civilization
Greek Civilization
Historical Analysis
History Discipline
Homogeneous Culture
Islamic Civilization
Political Culture
Roman Civilization

AFRO ASIAN BLOC
S-02-0046 1975 00001
BT Third World Bloc
RT Arab Bloc
Asian Area Studies
Black Culture
Black Nationalism
Community Identity
Cultural Revolution
Neutral Bloc
Security Community
Western Bloc

AGE
S-06-0180 1975 00061
BT Demographic Characteristics
NT Adolescence
Childhood
Infancy
Middle Age
Old Age
Youth
RT Demographic Indicator
Demographic Profile
Gerontocracy
Population Attribute
Population Composition
Population Distribution

AGE GROUP VOTING
S-29-0129 1975 00009
BT Group Voting
RT Class Voting
Ethnic Group Voting
Geographic Voting
Gerontology
Group Theory
Protest Voting
Racial Voting
Regional Voting
Religious Voting
Rural Voting
Sex Group Voting
Student Voting
Suburban Voting
Urban Voting

AGENCIES
S-19-0002 1975 00015
BT Institutions
NT Agricultural Agency
Business Agency
Censorship Agency
Consumer Agency
Cultural Agency
Economic Agency
Education Agency
Environmental Agency
Foreign Affairs Agency
Government Agency
Information Agency
Intelligence Agency
International Agency
Judicial Administration Agency
Justice Administration Agency
Military Agency
Planning Agency
Testing Agency
Transportation Agency
Welfare Agency
RT Authorities
Characteristics
Commissions
Councils
Economic Institution
Health Care Institution
Interagency Rivalry
Political Party Institution

AGGREGATE DATA ANALYSIS
S-09-0002 1975 00023
BT Contemporary Analytic Modes
RT Aggregate Data Selection
Aggregate Data Statistics
Analysis Unit
Career Analysis
Cluster Analysis
Cross Level Analysis
Cross National Analysis
Data Archives
Data Collection Methodology
Data Retrieval
Descriptive Research
Econometrics
Economic Index
Electoral Data
Field Data
Graph Theory Analysis
Political Statistics
Social Statistics
Statistical Analysis
Statistical Data
Survey Analysis
Voting Behavior Analysis

AGGREGATE DATA SELECTION
S-24-0378 1975 00004
BT Data Selection Orientation
RT Aggregate Data Analysis
Aggregate Data Statistics
Economic Index
Electoral Data
Statistical Data

AGGREGATE DATA STATISTICS
S-18-0080 1975 00006
BT Statistical Data
RT Aggregate Data Analysis
Aggregate Data Selection
Census Record
Data Collection Methodology
Data Processing
Data Storage
Descriptive Statistics
Economic Statistics
Field Data
Frequency Table
Mass Public Opinion
Political Statistics
Public Opinion Survey
Social Statistics
Statistical Analysis
Statistical Table
Statistics Type
Survey Data
Typology

AGGREGATION PROCESS
1975-1979 00002

AGGRESSION
S-08-0002 1975 00024
BT Conflict Type
NT Cultural Aggression
Military Aggression
Psychological Aggression
RT Aggression Scale
Aggression Theory
Aggressiveness
Aggressor State
Agitation
Belligerence
Economic Conflict
Ideological Conflict
Institutional Conflict
Insurgency
Interpersonal Conflict
Political Violence
Social Conflict
Struggle
Tyranny
Violence
War
Warfare State

AGGRESSION SCALE
S-24-0222 1975 00002
BT Scale Type
RT Aggression
Aggressiveness
Aggressor State
Anomie Scale
Authoritarianism Scale
Belligerence
Dogmatism Scale
Frustration Scale
Psychological Aggression
Psychological Theory
Scale Type
Social Frustration Scale
Warfare State

AGGRESSION THEORY
S-38-0122 1975 00020
BT Conflict Theory
RT Aggression
Aggressiveness
Aggressor State
Belligerence
Motivation Theory
Power Theory
Psychopolitical Theory
Social Conflict
War
Warfare State

AGGRESSIVENESS
S-06-0103 1975 00015
BT Hostility
NT Belligerence
RT Aggression
Aggression Scale
Aggression Theory
Aggressor State
Ambition
Assertiveness
Belligerence
Extremism
Hostile Nation
Militancy
Psychological Aggression

AGGRESSOR STATE
S-16-0159 1975 00002
UF Belligerent
BT State Type
RT Aggression
Aggression Scale
Aggression Theory
Aggressiveness
Declared War
First Strike Policy
Hostile Nation
Military State
State Type
War
Warfare State

AGING
S-31-0055 1979 00000
BT Development Process
RT Middle Age

AGITATION
S-08-0007 1975 00000
BT Conflict Type
NT Economic Agitation
Political Agitation
RT Aggression
Election Campaign Propaganda
Information Policy
Propaganda Policy
Protest
Social Conflict
Struggle

AGITATION PROPAGANDA
S-08-0014 1975 00001
BT Political Agitation
RT Class Polarization
Communist Education
Economic Agitation
Ideological Conflict
Propaganda Policy
Protest
Psychological Aggression

AGITATOR
USE Political Agitator

AGRARIAN DEMOCRACY
S-16-0012 1975 00000
BT Democratic Government
RT Agrarian Economy
Agrarian Movement
Agrarian Political Party
Agrarian Socialism
Agrarianism
Bourgeois Democracy
Democratic Regime
Direct Democracy
Farmer
Farmer Union
Mass Democracy

AGRARIAN ECONOMY
S-12-0002 1975 00025
BT Economy Type
NT Farm Economy
RT Agrarian Democracy
Agrarian Socialism
Agrarian Syndicalism
Agrarianism
Barter Economy
Consumer Economy
Cottage Industry Economy
Craft Economy
Farm Subsidy
Farming
Hunting And Fishing Society
Hunting And Trapping Economy
Kibbutz
Mixed Economy
Nomadic Economy
Peasant Economy
Self Sufficient Economy
Subsistence Economy
Underdeveloped Economy

AGRARIAN MOVEMENT
S-27-0047 1975 00007
BT Sector Based Political Movement
NT Agrarian Reform Movement
RT Agrarian Democracy
Agrarian Political Party
Agrarian Socialism
Agrarianism
Chiliastic Movement
Class Based Movement
Farm Economy
Farm Production
Farmer Union
Farming
Grass Roots Movement
Maoist Movement
Peasant Class
Peasant Society
Populist Movement
Socialist Revolution

AGRARIAN PARTY
1975-1979 00001

AGRARIAN POLITICAL PARTY
S-28-0035 1979 00000
BT Sector Based Political Party Type
RT Agrarian Democracy
Agrarian Movement
Agrarian Reform Movement
Agrarian Reform Policy
Farmer Union
Peasant Class
Peasant Political Party
Peasant Society

AGRARIAN REFORM MOVEMENT
S-27-0048 1975 00003
BT Agrarian Movement
RT Agrarian Political Party
Agricultural Cooperative
Farmer Union
Green Revolution
Land Reform Policy
Populist Movement

AGRARIAN REFORM POLICY
S-26-0004 1975 00014
BT Agricultural Policy
NT Land Reform Policy
RT Agrarian Political Party
Agricultural Collectivization Policy
Agricultural Cooperative
Agricultural Subsidization Policy
Farm Economy
Farm Income
Farm Production
Farm Subsidy
Farmer Union

AGRARIAN SOCIALISM
S-38-0289 1975 00001
BT Socialist Theory
RT Agrarian Democracy
Agrarian Economy
Agrarian Movement
Agrarian Syndicalism
Agrarianism
Aprista Socialism
Christian Socialism
Democratic Socialism
Green Revolution
Kibbutz
Land Reform Policy
Maoism
Marxism
Marxist Theory
Socialist Market Economy
Socialist Revolution

AGRARIAN SYNDICALISM
S-38-0337 1975 00001
BT Syndicalism
RT Agrarian Economy
Agrarian Socialism
Agrarianism
Green Revolution
Land Reform Policy

AGRARIANISM
S-38-0178 1975 00005
BT Ideologies
RT Agrarian Democracy
Agrarian Economy
Agrarian Movement
Agrarian Socialism
Agrarian Syndicalism
Caudillism
Farm Subsidy
Farm Voter
Farmer
Farmer Union
Populism

AGREEMENT
S-31-0225 1975 00005
BT Conflict Resolution
NT Treaty Making
RT Accommodation
Adjudication
Agreement Type
Appeasement
Bargaining
Conciliation
Decision Making Process
Deescalation
Mediation
Negotiation
Peace

AGREEMENT TYPE
S-02-0001 1975 00003
NT Alliance
Coalition Type
Compact
Contract Type
Extranational Bloc
International Bloc
Political Front
State Agreement Declaration
State Agreement Form
State Agreement Type
RT Agreement
Alliance Theory
Defense Policy
Foreign Policy
International Policy
Military Policy

AGRICULTURAL ADVISORY BOARD
S-19-0004 1975 00000
BT Agricultural Agency
RT Agricultural Policy
Commerce
Consumer Advisory Board
Demand Analysis
Economic Advisory Board
Food Industry
Food Policy
Government Agricultural Enterprise
Tenant Farmer
Tenant Farming

AGRICULTURAL AGENCY
S-19-0003 1975 00004
BT Agencies
NT Agricultural Advisory Board
RT Agricultural Extension Service
Agricultural History
Agricultural Policy
Business Agency
Consumer Agency
Farming

AGRICULTURAL COLLECTIVIZATION POLICY
S-26-0006 1975 00009
BT Agricultural Policy
RT Agrarian Reform Policy
Agricultural Subsidization Policy
Farming
Forced Requisitioning
Land Nationalization
Land Ownership Pattern
Red Commune

AGRICULTURAL COOPERATIVE
S-03-0003 1975 00007
UF Farm Cooperative
BT Cooperatives
RT Agrarian Reform Movement
Agrarian Reform Policy
Cooperative Farm Economy
Credit Cooperative
Dairy Industry
Farm Production
Marketing Cooperative
Peasant Cooperative
Producer Cooperative
Village Cooperative

AGRICULTURAL DEVELOPMENT
S-31-0130 1975 00070
BT Rural Development
RT Agricultural Extension Service
Agricultural History
Agricultural Policy
Agrochemical Industry
Agronomy
Animal Husbandry
Development Policy
Economic Development Characteristics
Farm Subsidy
Food Policy
Food Scarcity
Horticulture
Hunger
Land Use Policy
Malnutrition
Resource Utilization
Starvation

AGRICULTURAL ECONOMIC STAGE
S-06-0160 1975 00007
BT Economic Development Stage
RT Agricultural Growth Rate
Feudal Economic Stage
Industrial Economic Stage
Pretakeoff Period

AGRICULTURAL EDUCATION
S-13-0049 1979 00000
BT Technical Education
RT Agricultural History
Agronomy
Animal Husbandry
Horticulture

AGRICULTURAL EXTENSION SERVICE
S-37-0138 1979 00000
BT Service Delivery System
RT Agricultural Agency
Agricultural Development
Agricultural Policy
Agricultural Subsidization Policy
Agronomy
Horticulture

AGRICULTURAL GROWTH RATE
S-06-0154 1975 00014
BT Economic Growth Rate
RT Agricultural Economic Stage
Agricultural Policy
Agricultural Production
Productivity Rate

AGRICULTURAL HISTORY
S-01-0104 1979 00000
BT Economic History
RT Agricultural Agency
Agricultural Development
Agricultural Education
Agricultural Policy
Agricultural Science
Agronomy
Animal Husbandry
Cultural History
Farming
History Of Technology
Horticulture

AGRICULTURAL OCCUPATION
S-32-0062 1975 00005
BT Occupational Role
NT Agricultural Worker
Farmer
RT Animal Husbandry
Commercial Occupation
Farm Industry
Farming
Foreign Worker
Industrial Occupation
Occupation Characteristics
Rural Community
Rural Sociology

AGRICULTURAL POLICY
S-26-0003 1975 00035
BT Policy
NT Agrarian Reform Policy
Agricultural Collectivization Policy
Agricultural Subsidization Policy
Food Policy
Forced Requisitioning
RT Agricultural Advisory Board
Agricultural Agency
Agricultural Development
Agricultural Extension Service
Agricultural Growth Rate
Agricultural History
Agricultural Price Support Policy
Agricultural Production
Agricultural Science
Agrochemical Industry
Agronomy
Consumer Policy
Farm Industry
Farm Subsidy
Farming
Forced Requisitioning
Land Reform Policy

AGRICULTURAL PRICE SUPPORT POLICY
S-26-0128 1975 00001
BT Price Support Policy
RT Agricultural Policy
Business Price Support Policy
Farm Income
Farm Subsidy

Soil Bank Policy

AGRICULTURAL PRODUCTION
S-31-0425 1975 00079
UF Farm Production
BT Production Process
NT Farm Production
RT Agricultural Growth Rate
Agricultural Policy
Agricultural Science
Agricultural Subsidization Policy
Agrochemical Industry
Agronomy
Dairy Industry
Farm Economy
Farm Industry
Food Industry
Food Policy
Horticulture
Hunger
National Production
Soil Bank Policy

AGRICULTURAL SCIENCE
S-01-0003 1975 00016
BT Academic Areas
NT Agronomy
Animal Husbandry
Horticulture
RT Agricultural History
Agricultural Policy
Agricultural Production
Agrochemical Industry
Agronomy
Biological Sciences
Dairy Industry
Earth Sciences
Ecology Discipline
Environmental Studies
Farm Industry
Farming
Geography Discipline
Labor History
Natural Science Discipline
Rural Sociology

AGRICULTURAL SECTOR
S-37-0027 1975 00014
BT Economic Sector
RT Agronomy
Commercial Sector
Farm Economy
Farm Industry
Farmer
Farmer Union
Farming
Private Sector
Public Sector

AGRICULTURAL SUBSIDIZATION POLICY
S-26-0007 1975 00004
BT Agricultural Policy
NT Soil Bank Policy
RT Agrarian Reform Policy
Agricultural Collectivization Policy
Agricultural Extension Service
Agricultural Production
Food Policy
Land Reform Policy
Land Use Policy

AGRICULTURAL WORKER
S-32-0063 1975 00013
BT Agricultural Occupation
NT Migrant Worker
RT Agricultural Working Class
Day Laborer
Farmer
Farmer Union
Farming
Migrant Worker

AGRICULTURAL WORKING CLASS
S-06-0781 1975 00010
BT Working Class
RT Agricultural Worker
Farmer
Farmer Union
Industrial Working Class
Proletariat
Unionized Working Class

AGROCHEMICAL INDUSTRY
S-17-0003 1979 00000
BT Chemical Industry
RT Agricultural Development
Agricultural Policy
Agricultural Production
Agricultural Science
Agronomy
Rubber Industry
Synthetics Industry

AGRONOMY
S-01-0004 1979 00000
UF Soil Science
BT Agricultural Science
RT Agricultural Development
Agricultural Education
Agricultural Extension Service
Agricultural History
Agricultural Policy
Agricultural Production
Agricultural Science
Agricultural Sector
Agrochemical Industry
Animal Husbandry
Climatology
Eugenics
Farming
Horticulture
Topography

AIR FARE REGULATION
1975-1979 00001
USE Air Fare Regulation Policy

AIR FARE REGULATION POLICY
S-26-0425 1979 00000
UF Air Fare Regulation
BT Airline Regulation Policy
RT Air Transportation Industry
Aircraft Industry
Airline Regulation Policy
Business Regulation Policy
Commercial Law
Regulatory Commission

AIR FORCE
S-33-0051 1979 00000
UF Air Forces
BT Armed Forces
RT Aircraft Industry
Marines
Mercenary Armed Forces
Military Aircraft

AIR FORCES
1975-1979 00060
USE Air Force

AIR PIRACY
S-10-0053 1975 00001
BT Piracy
RT Air Safety Policy
Guerrilla Activity
International Law
Pilot
Political Crime
Terrorist

AIR POLLUTION
S-31-0104 1975 00009
BT Environmental Pollution
RT Air Pollution Policy
Ecological Analysis
Ecological Model
Ecological Revolution
Ecology Discipline
Ecosystem
Environmental Control Agency
Pollution Policy

AIR POLLUTION POLICY
S-26-0225 1975 00015
BT Pollution Policy
RT Air Pollution
Environmental Agency
Environmental Control Agency
Environmental Management
Environmental Planning
Environmental Pollution
Natural Resource Management
Water Pollution Policy

AIR SAFETY POLICY
S-26-0404 1975 00002
BT Traffic Safety Policy
RT Air Piracy
Air Transportation Policy
Highway Safety Policy

AIR TRANSPORTATION INDUSTRY
S-17-0071 1975 00012
BT Transportation Industry
NT Aircraft Industry
RT Air Fare Regulation Policy
Air Transportation Policy
Mass Transportation Industry
Shipping Industry
Transportation System
Trucking Industry

AIR TRANSPORTATION POLICY
S-26-0423 1975 00010
BT Mass Transit Policy
NT Airline Regulation Policy
RT Air Safety Policy
Air Transportation Industry
Railroad Policy
Transportation System

AIRCRAFT INDUSTRY
S-17-0072 1979 00000
UF Airplane Industry
BT Air Transportation Industry
RT Aerospace Industry
Air Fare Regulation Policy
Air Force
Airline Regulation Policy
Arms Industry
Military Aircraft
Production Industry

AIRLINE REGULATION
1975-1979 00003
USE Airline Regulation Policy

AIRLINE REGULATION POLICY
S-26-0424 1979 00000
UF Airline Regulation
BT Air Transportation Policy
NT Air Fare Regulation Policy
RT Air Fare Regulation Policy
Aircraft Industry
Commercial Law
Regulatory Commission

AIRPLANE INDUSTRY
USE Aircraft Industry

ALCOHOLISM
S-06-0373 1979 00000
BT Health Characteristics
RT Disease
Drug Addiction
Epidemic
Health Clinic
Mental Health Policy
Public Health Institution

ALDERMAN
S-36-0197 1975 00002
BT Local Legislative Member
RT City Councilman
Local Legislature

ALGEBRA
1975-1979 00000

ALIEN
S-36-0016 1975 00007
BT Citizenship Status
NT Dual Citizen
Native Born Citizen
Naturalized Citizen
RT Immigrant
Repatriate
Stateless Person

ALIENATED VOTER
S-32-0295 1975 00004
BT Voter
RT Apathetic Voter
Marginal Voter
Nonvoter
Protest Voter

ALIENATION
S-06-0076 1975 00035
BT Attitude Characteristics
NT Cultural Alienation
Cynicism
Distrust
Estrangement
Normlessness
Political Alienation
Powerlessness
RT Alienation Process
Alienation Psychological Theory
Alienation Scale
Ambivalence
Anomic Process
Anomie
Anomie Scale
Apathy
Atomistic Society
Efficacy
Extremism
Hostility
Job Dissatisfaction
Marxist Alienation Theory
Militancy
Pessimism
Social Distance Theory
Submissiveness

ALIENATION PROCESS
S-31-0787 1975 00015
BT Structural Process
RT Alienation
Alienation Psychological Theory
Alienation Scale
Cleavage Process
Decay
Existential Psychologism
Fragmentation
Group Theory
Marxist Alienation Theory
Political Fragmentation
Stateless Person

ALIENATION PSYCHOLOGICAL THEORY
S-38-0531 1975 00005
BT Psychological Theory
RT Alienation
Alienation Process
Alienation Scale
Attitude Characteristics
Freudian Theory
Frustration Aggression Theory
Learning Theory
Motivation Theory
Personality Theory
Political Normlessness
Psychopolitical Theory
Relative Deprivation Theory
Social Psychiatry

ALIENATION SCALE
S-24-0223 1975 00001
BT Scale Type
NT Political Alienation Scale
RT Alienation
Alienation Process
Alienation Psychological Theory
Anomie Scale
Authoritarianism Scale
Civic Competence Scale
Cynicism Scale
Dogmatism Scale
Efficacy Scale
Frustration Scale
Legitimacy Scale
Liberalism Conservatism Scale
Optimism Pessimism Scale
Satisfaction Scale
Social Distance Scale
Social Frustration Scale
Stability Index
Support Opposition Scale

ALIGNED NATION
S-16-0115 1975 00003
BT Nation Type
RT Alliance
Alliance Process
Client Nation
Debtor Nation
Dependent Nation
Empire
Fourth World Nation
Global System
Military Treaty
Nonaligned Nation
Third World Nation

ALL PARTY COALITION
S-02-0027 1975 00000
SN Governing alliance comprised of all of the parliamentary parties.
BT Political Party Coalition
NT Grand Coalition
RT Democratic Coalition
Electoral Tactics
Governing Coalition
Intraparty Coalition
Legislative Coalition
Multiparty Coalition
Parliamentary Coalition
United Front
Voting Coalition

ALLIANCE
S-02-0002 1975 00023
BT Agreement Type
NT Economic Alliance
Electoral Alliance
Military Alliance
Multilateral Alliance
Wartime Alliance
World Alliance
RT Aligned Nation
Alliance Process
Alliance Theory
Compact
East West Detente
Extranational Bloc
Institution Building
International Bloc
Military Treaty
Political Front
State Agreement Declaration
State Agreement Form
State Agreement Type

ALLIANCE PROCESS
S-31-0014 1975 00025
BT Associational Process
RT Aligned Nation
Alliance
Alliance Theory
Coalition Process
East West Detente
Group Process

ALLIANCE THEORY
S-38-0129 1975 00017
BT Coalition Theory
RT Agreement Type
Alliance
Alliance Process
International Alliance Theory
International Power Theory
International Relations Studies
Military Treaty
Security Community Theory

ALLOCATION PROCESS
S-31-0323 1975 00043
BT Decision Making Process
RT Approval Process
Authorization Process
Distributive Justice Theory
Economic Process
Economic Resource Allocation
Fiscal Process
Implementation Process

Telephone Allocation Policy

ALTERNATIVE EDUCATION
S-13-0003 1975 00004
SN Educational methods and curriculum in contrast to their traditional counterparts.
BT Education Type
RT Apprenticeship
Continuing Education
Ideological Education
Mass Education
Progressive Education
Self Taught Education
Technical Education

ALTRUISM
S-06-0500 1975 00023
BT Personality Characteristics
RT Assertiveness
Charity
Courage
Creativity
Curiosity
Egocentrism
Empathy
Femininity
Gregariousness
Honesty
Imagination
Masculinity
Optimism
Other Directedness
Persistence
Tolerance

AMATEUR ATHLETE
S-32-0024 1979 00000
BT Athlete
RT Amateur Sports
Professional Athlete
Professional Sports
Sports

AMATEUR SPORTS
S-31-0784 1979 00000
BT Sports
RT Amateur Athlete
Athlete
Professional Athlete
Professional Sports

AMBASSADOR
S-36-0121 1975 00003
BT Embassy Official
RT Charge D'Affaires
Civil Servant
Consul General
Diplomatic Relations
Embassy Attache
Foreign Service Officer

AMBITION
S-06-0132 1975 00020
BT Self Interest
RT Aggressiveness
Opportunity Characteristics
Social Mobility
Status Mobility
Upward Mobility

AMBIVALENCE
S-06-0501 1975 00001
BT Personality Characteristics
NT Role Ambivalence
RT Alienation
Anomie
Assertiveness
Courage
Creativity
Culture Shock
Curiosity
Egocentrism
Empathy
Femininity
Honesty
Masculinity
Normlessness
Optimism
Persistence
Pessimism

AMERICAN AREA STUDIES
S-01-0031 1975 00037
BT Area Studies
NT Caribbean Area Studies
Central American Area Studies
Latin American Area Studies
North American Area Studies
RT Advanced Industrial Society
Advanced Technology
American Conservatism
American Enlightenment Thought
Americanism
Comparative Literature Studies
Comparative Political Studies
Cultural Anthropology
Cultural History
Ethnic Studies
Political Science Discipline

AMERICAN CONSERVATISM
S-38-0194 1975 00000
BT Conservatism
RT American Area Studies
Americanism
Anticommunism
Burkean Conservatism
Christian Conservatism
Liberalism Conservatism Scale
McCarthyism
Neoconservatism
Objectivist Political Thought
Reactionary Conservatism

AMERICAN ENLIGHTENMENT THOUGHT
S-38-0398 1975 00003
BT Enlightenment Thought
NT Jeffersonian Thought
Madisonian Thought
RT American Area Studies
American Political Thought
Classical Liberalism
Democratic Theory

AMERICAN INDIAN STUDIES
S-01-0083 1975 00142
UF Indian Studies
BT Ethnic Studies
RT Area Studies
Black Studies
Chicano Studies
Cultural Anthropology
Cultural History
Ethnic Studies
Ethnicity
Human Geography
Puerto Rican Studies
Reservation

AMERICAN POLITICAL THOUGHT
S-38-0387 1979 00000
BT Modern Political Thought
RT American Enlightenment Thought
Americanism
Conservatism
Conservative
Enlightenment Liberalism
Federalism
Jeffersonian Thought
Liberal Political Thought
Lockean Contractualism
Madisonian Thought
Separation Of Power

AMERICANISM
S-38-0262 1975 00003
BT Nationalism
RT American Area Studies
American Conservatism
American Political Thought
Americanization
Identity Characteristics
Isolationism
Isolationist
McCarthyism
National Characteristics
Patriotism

AMERICANIZATION
S-34-0004 1975 00008
BT Enculturation
RT Americanism
Assimilation
Ethnic Assimilation Theory
Socialization Type

AMICUS CURIAE
S-36-0094 1975 00000
SN Brief filed with a court by persons or groups who are not parties to the case but who have pertinent expertise related to the case.
BT Court Official
RT Civil Rights Litigation
Class Action Litigation
Constitutional Litigation
Right To Counsel

AMNESTY
S-31-0536 1975 00003
BT Judicial Procedure
RT Appeal Procedure
Clemency
Conscientious Objector
Desertion
Judicial Discretion
Legal Immunity
Penal Law

ANABAPTISM
S-38-0374 1975 00000
SN Sixteenth century Protestant Sect's belief in separation of church and state, social reform and baptism of believers.
BT Quietistic Thought
RT Protestant Sectarianism
Sectarian Movement

ANALYSIS FRAMEWORK
S-24-0341 1975 00108
BT Research Design
NT Analysis Unit
RT Decision Making Theory
Interaction Analysis
Normative Analysis
Paradigm
Typologizing
Value Analysis

ANALYSIS METHODOLOGY
S-24-0002 1975 00143
BT Methodology
NT Causal Analysis
Deductive Method
Education Testing
Forecasting Methodology
Hermeneutical Analysis
Inductive Method
Logical Analysis
Mathematical Analysis
Normative Analysis
Qualitative Analysis
Statistical Analysis
RT Analytic Process
Contemporary Analytic Modes
Data Collection Methodology
Data Presentation Methodology
Decision Making Theory
Group Analysis
Hermeneutical Analysis
Interaction Analysis
Measurement
Models
PERT Analysis
Reductionist Analysis
Research Design
Theoretical Framework

ANALYSIS OF PLAY
S-09-0003 1979 00000
UF Recreation
BT Contemporary Analytic Modes
RT Group Analysis
Interaction Analysis
Leisure Time Analysis
Recreation District
Social Area Analysis
Sociology Discipline
Sports
Tourist Industry

ANALYSIS OF VARIANCE
S-24-0039 1975 00021
BT Multivariate Analysis
RT Canonical Correlation Analysis
Covariance Analysis
Data Presentation Methodology
Dimensional Analysis
Discriminant Analysis
Factor Analysis
Multiple Correlation Analysis
Multiple Regression Analysis
Partial Correlation Analysis
Path Analysis
Social Statistics
Statistical Significance Test
Statistics Type

ANALYSIS UNIT
S-24-0342 1975 00002
BT Analysis Framework
NT Event
Individual
Social Classification
Territory Classification
RT Aggregate Data Analysis
Area Sampling
Research Unit
Social Indicator

ANALYTIC PROCESS
S-31-0005 1975 00009
BT Process
NT Classification Process
Evaluating
Formalization
Judging
Testing
Typologizing
RT Analysis Methodology
Change Process
Concept Explication Research
Contemporary Analytic Modes
Decision Making Process
Economic Process
Policy Making Process
Research Design
Research Orientation
Social Role Process
Statistical Analysis
Structural Model
Structural Process
System Analysis
Value Analysis

ANALYTIC SYSTEM CHARACTERISTICS
S-06-0570 1975 00002
BT System Characteristics
NT Feedback Loop
System Boundary
System Capacity
System Change
System Disequilibrium
System Function
System Inputs
System Integration
System Interdependence
System Maintenance
System Outputs
RT Economic System Characteristics
Functional Equivalent
Organization Environment
Political System Characteristics
Social System
Social System Characteristics
System Analysis

ANARCHISM
S-38-0179 1975 00011
BT Ideologies
RT Anarchist
Anarchosyndicalism
Anarchy
Authority Theory
Counter Culture Ideology
Libertarianism
Nihilism
Syndicalism

ANARCHIST
S-32-0267 1975 00001
BT System Politicist
RT Anarchism
Anarchosyndicalism
Anarchy
Nihilism

ANARCHOSYNDICALISM
S-38-0180 1975 00000
BT Ideologies
RT Anarchism
Anarchist
Anarchy
Communalism
Economic Ideology
Nihilism
Syndicalism

ANARCHY
S-04-0011 1975 00004
BT Authority Structure
RT Anarchism
Anarchist
Anarchosyndicalism
Authority Theory
Counter Culture Ideology
Decay
Decentralized Authority
Diffuse Authority
Fragmentation

ANCESTRY
S-06-0199 1975 00002
BT Origin
NT Black Ancestry
RT Class Origin
Ethnic Origin
Extended Kinship System
Geographic Origin
Kindred Family
Kinship
Population Attribute
Racial Background

ANCIEN REGIME
USE Ancient Regime

ANCIENT CIVILIZATION
S-11-0004 1979 00000
BT Civilization
RT African Civilization
Ancient Times
Byzantine Civilization
Eastern Civilization
Greek Civilization
Historical Analysis
History Discipline
Homogeneous Culture
Islamic Civilization
Political Culture
Roman Civilization

ANCIENT HISTORY
S-01-0098 1979 00000
BT History Discipline
RT Ancient Times
Aristotelian Thought
Classical Political Thought
Cultural History
Cynic Thought
Diplomatic History
Economic History
Historical Analysis
Historiography

History Of Philosophy
History Of Technology
Intellectual History
Legal History
Military History
Oral History
Platonic Political Thought
Political History
Presocratic Political Thought
Religious History
Social History
Thucydidean Political Thought

ANCIENT REGIME
S-16-0133 1975 00001
UF Ancien Regime
BT Political Regime
RT Absolute Monarch
Absolute Monarchy
Absolutism
Aristocratic Class
Authoritarian Regime
Conservative Regime
Dictatorial Regime
Feudal Government
Old Middle Class

ANCIENT TIMES
S-06-0168 1979 00000
BT Historical Periods
NT Antiquity
RT Ancient Civilization
Ancient History
Archaeology
Byzantine Civilization
Classical Period
Classical Political Thought
Dark Ages
Greek Civilization
Medieval Ages
Prehistorical Times
Roman Civilization

ANGLICANISM
S-38-0566 1975 00000
BT Protestantism
RT Calvinism
Hussite Thought
Lutheranism
Protestant Sectarianism
Religious Group
Unitarianism

ANIMAL BEHAVIOR
S-05-0006 1979 00000
BT Behavior
RT Anthropology Discipline
Behavior Modification
Behavioral Psychology
Behavioral Science
Behavioral Science Research
Behavioral Theory
Psychological Anthropology
Psychology Discipline

ANIMAL HUSBANDRY
S-01-0005 1979 00000
BT Agricultural Science
RT Agricultural Development
Agricultural Education
Agricultural History
Agricultural Occupation
Agronomy
Eugenics
Farming
Horticulture

ANIMOSITY
USE Hostility

ANNEXATION
S-31-0152 1975 00006
BT Extraterritorial Development
RT Border Conflict
Colonization
Decolonization
Expansionist War
International Law
Manifest Function
Military Aggression
Secession
Social Integration Theory

ANOMIC PROCESS
S-31-0793 1975 00006
BT Fragmentation
RT Alienation
Anomie
Anomie Scale
Crowd Behavior
Group Disintegration
Mass Society Theory
Normlessness
Political Fragmentation
Social Pathology
Social Stability

ANOMIE
S-06-0089 1975 00016
SN State of being without guiding norms or values.
BT Attitude Characteristics
RT Alienation
Ambivalence
Anomic Process
Anomie Scale
Apathy
Estrangement
Group Disintegration
Marxist Alienation Theory
Normlessness
Organization Disintegration
Political Fragmentation
Role Ambivalence
Social Fragmentation
Social Pathology

ANOMIE SCALE
S-24-0225 1975 00004
BT Scale Type
RT Aggression Scale
Alienation
Alienation Scale
Anomic Process
Anomie
Authoritarianism Scale
Civic Competence Scale
Cynicism Scale
Dogmatism Scale
Efficacy Scale
Frustration Scale
Left Right Scale
Legitimacy Scale
Liberalism Conservatism Scale
Normlessness
Optimism Pessimism Scale
Organization Disintegration
Satisfaction Scale
Social Distance Scale
Social Frustration Scale
Stability Index
Support Opposition Scale

ANTHROPOLOGICAL FUNCTIONALISM
S-38-0004 1975 00002
BT Anthropological Theory
RT Acculturation Theory
Anthropology Discipline
Cultural Anthropology
Cultural Change Process
Cultural Evolution
Cultural Evolutionism
Ethnographic Theory
Hydraulic Theory
Methodology
Myth Analysis
Polyandry
Polygyny
Psychological Anthropology
Role Theory
Structural Functional Political Theory
Structural Marxism
Structuralism

ANTHROPOLOGICAL LINGUISTIC THEORY
S-38-0005 1975 00007
BT Anthropological Theory
RT Anthropology Discipline
Communication Theory
Cultural Anthropology
Cultural Change Process
Cultural Evolution
Cultural Identity
Ethnolinguistics
Linguistic Ethical Theory
Linguistic Theory
Linguistics
Morphology
Myth Analysis
Sociolinguistics
Structural Linguistics
Structuralism

ANTHROPOLOGICAL THEORY
S-38-0002 1975 00036
BT Theory
NT Acculturation Theory
Anthropological Functionalism
Anthropological Linguistic Theory
Antievolutionist Anthropological Theory
Cultural Evolutionism
Ethnographic Theory
Geographic Determinism Theory
Hydraulic Theory
Kinship Systematics Theory
Myth Analysis
Structuralism
RT Anthropologist
Anthropology Discipline
Cultural History
Development Theory
Ethnic Studies
Ethnographic Data
Explanatory Political Theory
Field Research
Folkways
General System Theory

Kinship System
Matrilineal Family Descent Pattern
Participant Observation
Philosophical Anthropology
Political Theory
Psychological Theory
Social Theory
Structural Linguistics

ANTHROPOLOGIST
S-32-0108 1979 00000
BT Social Scientist
RT Academic
Anthropological Theory
Anthropology Discipline
Economist
Field Research
Geographer
Historian
Policy Scientist
Political Scientist
Psychologist
Social Psychologist
Social Worker

ANTHROPOLOGY DISCIPLINE
S-01-0007 1975 00039
BT Academic Areas
NT Applied Anthropology
Cultural Anthropology
Philosophical Anthropology
Physical Anthropology
Political Anthropology
Psychological Anthropology
Social Anthropology
RT Animal Behavior
Anthropological Functionalism
Anthropological Linguistic Theory
Anthropological Theory
Anthropologist
Antievolutionist Anthropological Theory
Archaeology
Area Studies
Cultural Change Process
Cultural Evolutionism
Cultural Universalism
Ecology Discipline
Ethnic Studies
Field Research
Fine Arts
Folk Literature
Folkways
Gerontology
Group Behavior
Habitual Behavior
History Discipline
Human Geography
Ideographic Science
Parent
Political Science Discipline
Political Science Methodology Studies
Social History
Social Psychology
Sociolinguistics
Sociological Analysis
Sociology Discipline
South African Area Studies
West African Area Studies

ANTIBALLISTIC MISSILE
S-33-0028 1975 00006
BT Ballistic Missile
RT Nuclear Weapon
Strategic Advantage
Strategic Arms Race

ANTICLERIC
S-32-0268 1975 00000
BT System Politicist
RT Anticlericalism
Atheism
Sectarian

ANTICLERICALISM
S-38-0181 1975 00000
BT Ideologies
RT Anticleric
French Revolutionary Thought

ANTICOLONIALISM
S-38-0182 1975 00010
BT Ideologies
RT Antiimperialism
Decolonization
Democratic Theory
Imperialism
International Court
Liberation Movement
Liberation Process

ANTICOMMUNISM
S-38-0183 1975 00018
BT Ideologies
NT McCarthyism
RT American Conservatism
Cold War
Conservatism
Containment Policy
Counterrevolution
Extremism
Fascist Council
Ideological Struggle
McCarthyism
Right Wing Activist

ANTIEVOLUTIONIST ANTHROPOLOGICAL THEORY
S-38-0006 1975 00000
BT Anthropological Theory
RT Anthropology Discipline
Cultural Evolutionism

ANTIFASCISM
S-38-0185 1975 00000
BT Ideologies
RT Antiimperialism
Communist Government
Democratic Theory
Popular Front
Socialist Theory

ANTIIMPERIALISM
S-38-0186 1975 00008
BT Ideologies
RT Anticolonialism
Antifascism
Antimilitarism
Decolonization
Democratic Theory
Leninist Imperialism Theory
Liberation Movement
Liberation Process
Nationalism
Political Rebellion
Socialist Theory

ANTIINFLATION POLICY
S-26-0093 1979 00000
BT Fiscal Policy
RT Capital Formation Policy
Capital Investment Policy
Currency Revaluation Policy

ANTIMILITARISM
S-38-0187 1975 00002
BT Ideologies
RT Antiimperialism
Democratic Theory
Pacifism

ANTIQUITY
S-06-0169 1979 00000
BT Ancient Times
RT Archaeology
Classical Period
Greek Civilization
Prehistorical Times
Roman Civilization

ANTISEMITISM
S-38-0218 1975 00034
BT Racism
RT Apartheid Theory
Black Racism
Fascist Council
Persecution
White Racism

ANTITRINITARIANISM
S-38-0375 1975 00000
BT Quietistic Thought
RT Religious Authority

ANTITRUST AGENCY
S-19-0007 1975 00001
BT Business Regulation Agency
RT Antitrust Law
Antitrust Policy
Consumer Protection Policy
Economic Bureaucracy
Economic Control Agency
Economic Council
Productivity Policy

ANTITRUST LAW
S-21-0032 1975 00009
BT Economic Law
RT Antitrust Agency
Antitrust Policy
Big Business
Cartel
Consumer Protection Law
Labor Law
Law Enforcement
Monopoly
Tax Law

ANTITRUST POLICY
S-26-0014 1975 00005
BT Business Regulation Policy
RT Antitrust Agency
Antitrust Law
Big Business
Cartel
Monopoly

ANTIWAR MOVEMENT
S-27-0041 1975 00006
BT Peace Movement
RT Pacifism
Peace Activist
Protest Politics

APARTHEID
S-26-0381 1975 00028
BT Racial Policy
RT Racial Persecution
Racism
Segregated Community
Segregation Policy
White Racism

APARTHEID THEORY
S-38-0219 1975 00002
BT Racism
RT Antisemitism
Black Racism
Institutional Racism
Integration
Intermarriage
Segregated Community
Segregation Policy
Segregationist
White Racism

APATHETIC VOTER
S-32-0296 1975 00003
BT Voter
RT Alienated Voter
Apathy
Deferential Voter
Marginal Voter
Negative Voting Abstention
Nonvoter
Positive Voting Abstention

APATHY
S-06-0090 1975 00010
BT Attitude Characteristics
NT Political Apathy
RT Alienation
Anomie
Apathetic Voter
Cynicism
Normlessness
Pessimism
Powerlessness
Submissiveness

APPEAL PROCEDURE
S-31-0537 1975 00001
BT Judicial Procedure
RT Adversary System
Amnesty
Appellate Court
Clemency
Grievance Procedure
Judicial Review
Procedural Due Process

APPEASEMENT
S-31-0227 1975 00003
BT Conflict Resolution
RT Accommodation
Adjudication
Agreement
Balance Of Power Theory
Bargaining
Coercion
Conciliation
Deescalation
Foreign Policy
International Peace Negotiation
Mediation
Negotiation

APPELLATE COURT
S-19-0136 1975 00006
BT Constitutional Court
RT Adversary Process
Adversary System
Appeal Procedure
Appellate Court Review
Appellate Jurisdiction
District Court
Grand Jury Indictment
Judicial Review
Law System
Right To Appeal
Supreme Court
Trial Court

APPELLATE COURT REVIEW
S-31-0544 1975 00007
BT Judicial Review
RT Appellate Court
Law System
Supreme Court Review

APPELLATE JURISDICTION
S-06-0405 1975 00003
SN Judicial prerogative to review a decision made by another court.
BT Court Jurisdiction
RT Appellate Court
Constitutional Jurisdiction
Law System
Law Type
Original Jurisdiction

APPLIANCE INDUSTRY
S-17-0057 1979 00000
BT Light Industry
RT Clothing Industry
Consumerism
Machinery Industry
Production Industry

APPLIED ANTHROPOLOGY
S-01-0008 1979 00000
BT Anthropology Discipline
RT Applied Research
Applied Sociology
Policy Evaluation Research
Policy Research
Policy Science Studies
Problem Solving Behavior
Public Policy Studies
Quantitative Research
Research And Development

APPLIED LINGUISTICS
S-01-0135 1979 00000
BT Linguistics
RT Applied Research
Policy Research
Quantitative Research
Research And Development
Sociolinguistics

APPLIED RESEARCH
S-24-0375 1975 00092
BT Research Orientation
RT Advocacy Research
Applied Anthropology
Applied Linguistics
Applied Sociology
Basic Research
Deductive Method
Descriptive Research
Evaluating
Experimental Research
Explanatory Research
Inductive Method
Operationalization
Policy Evaluation Research
Policy Research
Policy Science Studies
Predictive Research
Qualitative Research
Quantitative History
Quantitative Research
Research Center
Research Council
Research Evaluation
Research Laboratory
Research Management
Scientific Research
Theoretical Research

APPLIED SOCIOLOGY
S-01-0183 1979 00000
BT Sociology Discipline
RT Applied Anthropology
Applied Research
Basic Research
Comparative Sociology
Criminology
Historical Sociology
Historical Sociology Analysis
Industrial Sociology
Macrosociology
Policy Research
Political Sociology
Problem Solving Behavior
Public Policy Analysis
Public Policy Studies
Quantitative Research
Research And Development
Rural Sociology
Social Pathology
Sociobiology
Sociology Discipline
Sociology Of Knowledge

APPOINTMENT PROCESS
S-31-0729 1975 00003
BT Selection Process
NT Presidential Appointment
Reappointment
RT Delegate Selection
Endorsement
Government Formation Process
Legislative Nominating Process
National Judge
Political Party Convention
Recruitment Process
Slate Making

APPORTIONMENT
S-31-0706 1975 00001
BT Representation
NT Districting
Malapportionment
Reapportionment
RT Legislative District
Legislative Districting
Representation Theory

APPORTIONMENT REFORM
S-31-0097 1975 00002
BT Legislative Reform
RT Congressional Reform
Legislative Redistricting
Legislative Reorganization

National Planning Policy
Parliamentary Reform
Reapportionment
Territory Classification

APPRENTICESHIP
S-13-0004 1975 00001
BT Education Type
RT Alternative Education
Professional Education
Self Taught Education
Skill Acquisition
Technical Education
Vocational Education

APPROPRIATION AGENCY
S-19-0022 1975 00003
BT Fiscal Agency
RT Budget Agency
Defense Appropriation
Government Economic Management
Government Economic Planning
Legislative Appropriation
Monetary Agency
Revenue Agency
Tax Agency

APPROVAL PROCESS
S-31-0324 1975 00000
BT Decision Making Process
RT Allocation Process
Authorization Process
Confirmation Process
Gubernatorial Veto
Implementation Process
National Decision Making Process
Veto

APRISTA SOCIALISM
S-38-0290 1975 00000
SN Socialist movement originating in Peru which spread to other Latin American countries.
BT Socialist Theory
RT Agrarian Socialism
Christian Socialism
Democratic Socialism
Evolutionary Socialism
Guild Socialism
Marxism
Marxist Theory
Socialist Political Party
Syndicalism

APTITUDE
USE Skill Acquisition

APTITUDE MEASUREMENT
S-24-0177 1979 00000
BT Measurement Object
NT Intelligence Quotient
RT Attitude Measurement
Education Testing
Individual Measurement
Measurement
Measurement Evaluation
Measurement Level
Measurement Problem
Measurement Scale
Test Results

ARAB BLOC
S-02-0047 1975 00027
BT Third World Bloc
RT Afro Asian Bloc
Islamic Thought
Middle East Area Studies
Neutral Bloc
Pan Islamism
Religious Authority
Security Community

ARBITRARY ARREST
S-31-0508 1975 00001
BT Arrest
RT Arbitrary Imprisonment
Evidence Admissibility
Habeas Corpus
On View Arrest
Political Arrest
Right To Due Process
Warrant Arrest

ARBITRARY IMPRISONMENT
S-31-0493 1975 00000
BT Imprisonment
RT Arbitrary Arrest
Evidence Admissibility
Habeas Corpus
Jailing
Right To Due Process
Sentencing

ARBITRATION
S-31-0237 1975 00001
BT Mediation
NT International Arbitration
Labor Arbitration
RT Adjudication
Arbitrator
Compulsory Arbitration Policy
Industrial Union
International Arbitration
International Mediation
Labor Arbitration
Labor Mediation

ARBITRATOR
S-32-0004 1975 00000
BT Adjudicator
RT Arbitration
Bargainer
Broker
Mediator
Moderator
Negotiator
Ombudsman

ARCHAEOLOGY
S-01-0022 1975 00015
BT Academic Areas
RT Ancient Times
Anthropology Discipline
Antiquity
Classical Period
Exploration
Explorer
Geography Discipline
Natural Resource Policy
Natural Science Discipline
Prehistorical Times

ARCHITECTURAL STUDIES
S-01-0023 1979 00000
UF Building Design
BT Academic Areas
RT Business Economics
Environmental Studies
Housing Code
Housing Policy
Housing Rights
Urban Design
Urban History
Urban Policy Planning
Urban Politics
Urban Population
Urban Redevelopment
Urban Renewal

ARCHIVES
S-18-0002 1975 00004
UF Repository
BT Information Sources
NT Data Bank
National Archives
RT Documentation Service
Government Information Service
Information Network
Information Retrieval
Information Service
Legislative Information Service
Library
Library Science Studies
Machine Readable Data
Machine Readable Information
National Archives
Private Information Service
University Information Service

AREA SAMPLING
S-24-0117 1975 00001
SN Multi-stage probability sample design based on regional stratification of a geographic unit.
BT Sampling Procedure
RT Analysis Unit
Nonprobability Sampling
Political Statistics
Probability Sampling
Social Area Analysis
Social Stratification Division

AREA STUDIES
S-01-0024 1975 00003
UF Regional Studies
BT Academic Areas
NT African Area Studies
American Area Studies
Asian Area Studies
British Commonwealth Area Studies
Middle East Area Studies
Soviet And East European Area Studies
West European Area Studies
RT American Indian Studies
Anthropology Discipline
Black Studies
Chicano Studies
Comparative Analysis
Comparative Law
Comparative Political Studies
Comparative Sociology
Cultural Anthropology
Demographic Studies
Economics Discipline
Education Discipline
Ethnic Studies
Ethnography
Ethnolinguistics
Geography Discipline
Global Education
Graduate School
History Discipline

Ideographic Science
International Relations Studies
Language Studies
Literature Studies
Physical Geography
Political Economy Studies
Political Geography
Political Science Discipline
Political Sociology
Puerto Rican Studies
Social Anthropology
Sociology Discipline
Territory Classification

ARISTOCRACY
USE Aristocratic Class

ARISTOCRACY POLITICAL PARTY
S-28-0037 1979 00000
BT Class Based Political Party
RT Aristocratic Class
Class Analysis
Labor Political Party
Middle Class Political Party
Peasant Political Party
Proletarian Political Party
Working Class Political Party

ARISTOCRATIC CLASS
S-06-0762 1975 00009
UF Aristocracy
Nobility
BT Class Stratification Division
RT Absolute Monarchy
Ancient Regime
Aristocracy Political Party
Caste Society
Feudal Lord
Feudal Society
Governing Elite
Landowning Class
Nobility
Propertied Class
Ruling Class
Upper Class

ARISTOTELIAN THOUGHT
S-38-0048 1975 00011
BT Classical Political Thought
RT Ancient History
Classical Period
Classification Process
Distributive Justice Theory
Epicurean Thought
History Of Philosophy
Medieval Islamic Thought
Medieval Natural Law Theory
Platonic Political Thought
Political Man Theory
Pythagorean Thought
Remedial Justice Theory
Statecraft Theory
Stoic Thought
Teleological Model
Teleology
Thomism

ARMAMENT INDUSTRY
1975-1979 00014
USE Arms Industry

ARMED FORCES
S-33-0049 1975 00037
UF Seaman
BT Military Establishment
NT Admiralty
Air Force
Army
Coast Guard
Conscripted Armed Forces
Marines
Mercenary Armed Forces
Merchant Marine
Navy
Peoples Army
Voluntary Armed Forces
RT Arms Industry
Defense Agency
Defense System
Military Budget
Offensive Weapon System
Officer Corps
Paramilitary Forces
Professional Military Forces
Reserve Military Forces
Tactical Force
Weapon
Weapon Delivery Subsystem
Weapon Delivery System

ARMED INTERVENTION POLICY
S-26-0326 1975 00012
BT Military Policy
RT Escalation Policy
Guerrilla Activity
Guerrilla War
Militarism
Military Aggression
Reprisal Policy
Undeclared War
War Policy
World War

ARMISTICE POLICY
S-26-0051 1975 00003
BT Defense Policy
RT Arms Control Policy
Cease Fire Policy
International Conflict Resolution Theory
International Peace
Military Policy
Peace
Truce
War Declaration Policy

ARMS CONTROL AGENCY
S-19-0060 1975 00003
BT Defense Agency
RT Arms Control Agreement
East West Detente
Foreign Affairs Agency
Strategic Arms Limitation
Strategic Arms Race
Strategic Arms Reduction Policy

ARMS CONTROL AGREEMENT
S-02-0067 1975 00026
BT State Agreement Type
NT Arms Control Treaty
RT Arms Control Agency
Disarmament Agreement
Friendship Agreement
International Law
International Sanction
Nuclear Stockpiling
Strategic Arms Limitation
Strategic Arms Reduction Policy
Test Ban Agreement

ARMS CONTROL POLICY
S-26-0052 1975 00063
BT Defense Policy
NT Arms Inspection Policy
Arms Reduction Policy
Arms Verification Policy
Disarmament Policy
Nuclear Weapon Nonproliferation Policy
RT Armistice Policy
Balanced Force
Declared War
Deescalation Policy
Deterrence Policy
Disarmament
MARV
Military Policy
MIRV
Mutual Deterrence System
Nuclear Strategy
Nuclear Weapon Nonproliferation Policy
Peace
Rearmament Policy
Strategic Advantage
Strategic Arms Limitation
Strategic Arms Reduction Policy
Test Ban Agreement
Test Ban Treaty
Truce

ARMS CONTROL TREATY
S-02-0068 1975 00013
BT Arms Control Agreement
RT Disarmament Treaty
International Law
Nonaggression Treaty
Peace Treaty
Peaceful Coexistence
Strategic Arms Limitation
Strategic Arms Reduction Policy
Test Ban Treaty

ARMS INDUSTRY
S-17-0037 1979 00000
UF Armament Industry
BT Defense Industry
RT Aerospace Industry
Aircraft Industry
Armed Forces
Arms Inspection Policy
Arms Race
Arms Sales
Bomb
Military Aircraft
Military Establishment
Military Industrial Complex
Military Policy
Military Weapon
Strategic Studies

ARMS INSPECTION POLICY
S-26-0053 1975 00003
BT Arms Control Policy
RT Arms Industry
Arms Reduction Policy
Arms Verification Policy

Military Policy
Nuclear Weapon Nonproliferation Policy
Strategic Arms Limitation
Strategic Arms Race
Strategic Arms Reduction Policy
Test Ban Agreement
Test Ban Treaty

ARMS RACE
S-06-0660 1975 00050
BT International Political System Characteristics
NT Nuclear Arms Race
Nuclear Weapon Proliferation
Strategic Arms Race
RT Arms Industry
Arms Sales
Balance Of Power
Global War Policy
International Relations Studies
Military Alliance
Power Politics
Strategic Arms Reduction Policy

ARMS REDUCTION POLICY
S-26-0054 1975 00020
BT Arms Control Policy
NT Balanced Force Reduction Policy
Strategic Arms Reduction Policy
RT Arms Inspection Policy
Arms Verification Policy
Disarmament Policy
Military Policy
Nuclear Weapon Nonproliferation Policy
Peace
Strategic Arms Limitation
Strategic Arms Race

ARMS SALES
S-02-0069 1979 00000
UF Weapons Sales
BT State Agreement Type
RT Arms Industry
Arms Race
Arms Verification Policy
Commercial Agreement
Defense Industry
Government Regulation
Weapon

ARMS VERIFICATION POLICY
S-26-0057 1979 00000
BT Arms Control Policy
RT Arms Inspection Policy
Arms Reduction Policy
Arms Sales
Defensive Capability
Disarmament Policy
Inductive Method
International Relations Studies
Military Science
Strategic Studies
Threat Indicator

ARMY
S-33-0052 1975 00052
BT Armed Forces
NT Army Organization
RT Admiralty
Coast Guard
Conscripted Armed Forces
Marines
Mercenary Armed Forces
Navy
Peoples Army
Professional Military Forces
Reserve Military Forces
Soldier

ARMY ORGANIZATION
S-33-0053 1975 00007
BT Army
NT Mass Militia Army
National Guard
Regular Army
Standing Army
RT Military Agency
Military Characteristics
Military Elite
Military Management
Military Planning
Military Policy
Professional Military Forces

ARRAIGNMENT
S-31-0506 1975 00000
BT Pretrial Procedure
RT Arrest
Bail
Constable
Crime Commission
Criminal Law System
Detention
Detention Center
Ex Post Facto Protection
Indictment
Magistrate
Pretrial Release

ARREST
S-31-0507 1975 00004
BT Pretrial Procedure
NT Arbitrary Arrest
On View Arrest
Political Arrest
Warrant Arrest
RT Arraignment
Law Enforcement System
Preventive Detention

ART HISTORY
S-01-0099 1979 00000
BT History Discipline
RT Cultural History
Fine Arts
Graphic Arts
Historical Analysis
History Of Philosophy
Humanities Discipline
Intellectual History
Plastic Arts
Religious History
Visual Arts

ARTISAN
S-32-0070 1979 00000
BT Occupational Role
RT Aesthetics
Business Leader
Commercial Occupation
Marketplace
Professional Occupational Role
Small Businessman

ARTISTIC ELITE
S-14-0012 1979 00000
BT Cultural Elite
RT Aesthetics
Classical Education
Humanistic Education
Humanities Discipline
Humanities Education
Intelligentsia
Liberal Arts Education
Literary Elite

ARTS POLICY
S-26-0048 1975 00046
BT Cultural Policy
RT Aesthetics
Cultural Advisory Board
Humanities Discipline
Sociology Of Art

ASCRIBED STATUS
S-06-0788 1975 00023
BT Status Stratification Division
RT Achieved Status
Ascribed Status System
Objectively Derived Status
Prestige Hierarchy
Social Distance Theory
Status Equality
Subjectively Derived Status
Traditional Authority
Traditional Political Elite
Traditional Social Elite
Traditional Society

ASCRIBED STATUS SYSTEM
S-37-0147 1975 00011
BT Status Social System
RT Achieved Status System
Ascribed Status

ASIAN AREA STUDIES
S-01-0036 1975 00113
UF Far East Studies
BT Area Studies
NT East Asian Area Studies
South Asian Area Studies
Southeast Asian Area Studies
RT Afro Asian Bloc
Comparative Literature Studies
Comparative Political Studies
Comparative Sociology
Cultural Anthropology
Cultural History
Eastern Political Thought
Hinduism
Political Science Discipline

ASSASSINATION
S-10-0056 1975 00004
BT Political Crime
NT Tyrannicide
RT Assault
Murder
Organized Crime
Political Assassin

ASSAULT
S-10-0027 1975 00004
BT Individual Crime
RT Assassination
Child Molestation
Child Neglect
Kidnapping
Murder
Police Brutality

Rape
Robbery
Sex Crime
Street Crime
Vandalism
Violent Crime

ASSEMBLER LANGUAGE
USE Computer Programming

ASSERTIVENESS
S-06-0503 1979 00000
BT Personality Characteristics
RT Aggressiveness
Altruism
Ambivalence
Charity
Courage
Creativity
Curiosity
Egocentrism
Empathy
Femininity
Gregariousness
Honesty
Imagination
Masculinity
Optimism
Persistence

ASSETS
S-06-0261 1979 00000
BT Capital
NT Fixed Assets
RT Accumulated Capital
Capital Formation
Capital Surplus
Economic Gain
Foreign Capital
Income
Investment Capital
Investment Policy
Private Capital
Public Capital

ASSIMILATION
S-31-0797 1975 00015
BT Integration
NT Cultural Assimilation
Ethnic Assimilation
Linguistic Assimilation
Racial Assimilation
RT Acculturation
Acculturation Theory
Adaptive Behavior
Americanization
Assimilation Theory
Bilingualism
Ethnic Assimilation Theory
Ideological Polarization
Local Political Integration
Nation Building

ASSIMILATION THEORY
S-38-0582 1975 00014
BT Social Theory
RT Acculturation Theory
Assimilation
Consensus Model
Homogeneous Society
Identity Change
Role Theory
Social Action Theory
Social Integration Theory
Social Learning Theory
Socialization Theory

ASSOCIATION CHARACTERISTICS
S-06-0002 1975 00003
BT Characteristics
NT Community Characteristics
Group Characteristics
Organization Characteristics
RT Administrative Characteristics
Associations
Education Association
Education Characteristics
Group Theory
Institution Building
Kinship Group
Youth Organization

ASSOCIATION INTEREST GROUP
S-03-0014 1975 00005
SN Formally structured group which attempts to influence government policy.
BT Interest Group
RT Cultural Interest Group
Economic Interest Group
Education Association
Ethnic Community
Interest Group Theory
Latent Interest Group
Medical Association
Occupational Interest Group
Policy Interest Group
Political Interest Group
Social Group
Voluntary Association

ASSOCIATIONAL PROCESS
S-31-0013 1975 00003
BT Process
NT Alliance Process
Coalition Process
Group Process
Organization Process
RT Associations
Education Association
Institution Building
Secret Society
Social System
Youth Organization

ASSOCIATIONS
S-03-0001 1975 00001
NT Cooperatives
Groups
Organizations
Voluntary Association
Youth Organization
RT Association Characteristics
Associational Process

ASSURED DESTRUCTION POLICY
S-26-0067 1979 00000
UF Assured Destruction Strategy
BT Nuclear Strategy
RT Counterforce Theory
MARV
MIRV

ASSURED DESTRUCTION STRATEGY
1975-1979 00005
USE Assured Destruction Policy

AT LARGE REPRESENTATION
S-31-0716 1975 00001
BT Representation Type
RT District Representation
Functional Representation
Geographic Representation
Indirect Representation
Minority Group Representation
Proportional Representation
Single Member District Representation

ATHEISM
S-38-0553 1979 00000
BT Religious Thought
RT Anticleric
Religious Authority
Sectarian Movement
Secular Society

ATHENIAN DEMOCRATIC THEORY
S-38-0083 1975 00001
BT Democratic Theory
RT City State Political System
Concurrent Majority Theory
Democratic Elite Theory
Direct Democracy
Economic Theory Of Democracy
General Will Democratic Theory
Guided Democracy Theory
Jacksonian Democratic Theory
Jeffersonian Democratic Theory
Majoritarianism
Minority Rights Democratic Theory
Participatory Democratic Theory
Populist Democratic Theory
Republic Theory
Socialist Democratic Theory

ATHLETE
S-32-0023 1979 00000
BT Roles
NT Amateur Athlete
Professional Athlete
RT Amateur Sports
Professional Sports
Sports

ATLANTIC COMMUNITY
S-02-0042 1975 00030
BT Extranational Bloc
RT International Bloc
Latin American Bloc
Political Front
Security Community
Third World Bloc
Trade Bloc
Treaty Making
West European Area Studies
Western Bloc

ATOMISTIC FAMILY
S-20-0007 1975 00000
BT Family Type
RT Atomistic Model
Atomistic Society
Cultural History
Family Court
Mass Society
Mass Society Theory
Monogamy
Nuclear Family
Social Change
Social Role Process

Social Stress
Stem Family

ATOMISTIC MODEL
S-24-0289 1975 00000
BT Social Science Model
RT Atomistic Family
Atomistic Society
Diffusion Model
Mass Society
Rational Model

ATOMISTIC SOCIETY
S-35-0024 1975 00002
BT Mass Society
RT Alienation
Atomistic Family
Atomistic Model
Heterogeneous Society
Mass Society Theory
Normlessness
Nuclear Family
Possessive Individualism

ATTENTIVE PUBLIC
S-14-0020 1975 00013
BT Opinion Elite
RT Decision Making Elite
Foreign Policy Elite
Governing Elite
Intellectual Elite
Local Elite
Opinion Socialization
Political Activist
Political Attitude
Potential Elite

ATTITUDE CHANGE THEORY
S-38-0532 1975 00122
BT Psychological Theory
NT Cognitive Dissonance Theory
RT Attitude Characteristics
Attitude Cluster
Cognitive Dissonance Theory
Freudian Theory
Identity Theory
Learning Theory
Methodology
Motivation Theory
Opinion Change
Political Attitude
Psychopolitical Theory
Relative Deprivation Theory

ATTITUDE CHARACTERISTICS
S-06-0075 1975 00310
BT Characteristics
NT Alienation
Anomie
Apathy
Attitude Cluster
Authoritarian Attitude
Deference
Dogmatism
Efficacy
Extremism
Hostility
Inner Directedness
Intolerance
Militancy
Military Mind
Other Directedness
Political Attitude
Political Awareness
Prejudice
Racial Attitude
Satisfaction
Self Interest
Submissiveness
Tolerance
Trust
RT Alienation Psychological Theory
Attitude Change Theory
Attitude Measurement
Black Racism
Cognitive Theory
Group Attitude
Identity Characteristics
Individual
Individual Attitude
Motivation Theory
National Political Culture
Personality Characteristics

ATTITUDE CLUSTER
S-06-0092 1975 00043
BT Attitude Characteristics
NT Perception
RT Attitude Change Theory
Attitude Measurement
Authoritarianism Scale
Identity Characteristics
National Character
National Political Culture
Opinion Change
Opinion Coalition
Political Attitude

ATTITUDE MEASUREMENT
S-24-0179 1975 00094
BT Measurement Object
NT Affective Measurement
Belief Measurement
Cognitive Measurement
Motivation Measurement
RT Aptitude Measurement
Attitude Characteristics
Attitude Cluster
Authoritarian Attitude
Behavioral Measurement
Change Measurement
Decision Maker Perception
Group Measurement
Individual Measurement
Intelligence Quotient
Interviewer Effect
Opinion Change
Opinion Coalition
Perception Measurement
Structured Interview

ATTORNEY GENERAL
S-36-0103 1975 00000
BT Prosecuting Attorney
NT District Attorney
Military Prosecutor
RT Crime Commission
Criminal Law System
Criminal Lawyer
Defender
Judicial Discretion
Solicitor

ATTRIBUTION THEORY
S-38-0534 1979 00000
BT Psychological Theory
RT Cognitive Theory
Identity Theory
Learning Theory
Motivation Theory
Personality Theory
Psychopolitical Theory
Stereotyping

AUGUSTINIAN ANALYSIS
S-38-0365 1975 00001
BT Medieval Political Thought
RT Catholicism
Lutheranism
Neoplatonic Political Thought
Platonic Political Thought
Religious Authority
Religious Bureaucracy
Religious Law
Roman Catholicism

AUSTRALIAN BALLOT
S-29-0151 1975 00000
SN Election ballot which is marked privately.
BT Ballot
RT Long Ballot
Machine Ballot
Office Block Ballot
Political Party Column Ballot
Political Party List Ballot
Secret Ballot
Short Ballot

AUTARCHIC ECONOMY
S-12-0042 1975 00004
SN Self-sufficient economic system.
BT Self Sufficient Economy
RT Autarchic Government
Balanced Economy
Centrally Planned Economy
Collective Farm Economy
Dual Economy
Fascist Economy
Planned Economy
Protective Tariff
Socialist Economy

AUTARCHIC GOVERNMENT
S-16-0004 1975 00002
BT Government Type
RT Autarchic Economy
Planned Economy
Political Development Theory

AUTARCHY
USE Autocratic Government

AUTHORITARIAN ATTITUDE
S-06-0095 1975 00005
BT Attitude Characteristics
RT Absolutism
Attitude Measurement
Authoritarian Personality
Authoritarianism Scale
Dogmatism
Extremism
Hostility
Militancy
Personality Development
Prejudice
Social Psychiatry

AUTHORITARIAN PARTY
1975-1979 00001

AUTHORITARIAN PERSONALITY
S-06-0528 1975 00005
BT Personality Type
RT Absolutism
Authoritarian Attitude
Authoritarianism
Autocrat
Dogmatism
Hostility
Imperial Presidency
Interpersonal Conflict
Intolerance
Personality Theory
Racial Prejudice

AUTHORITARIAN POLITICAL PARTY
S-28-0002 1979 00000
BT Political Party Type
RT Flangist Political Party
Military Political Party
Sector Based Political Party Type

AUTHORITARIAN REGIME
S-16-0134 1975 00035
BT Political Regime
NT Modernizing Authoritarian Regime
RT Absolute Monarch
Absolute Monarchy
Absolutism
Absolutist Government
Ancient Regime
Authoritarianism
Autocratic Government
Bonapartism
Centralized Government
Closed Leadership
Corporate Fascism
Dictatorial Regime
Falangism
Fascist Theory
Forced Requisitioning
Francoism
Imperial Presidency
Italian Fascism
National Socialism
One Political Party System
Political Repression
Revolutionary Directorate

AUTHORITARIANISM
S-38-0188 1975 00015
BT Ideologies
RT Absolute Monarch
Absolute Monarchy
Absolutism
Absolutist Government
Authoritarian Personality
Authoritarian Regime
Authority Mode
Authority Structure
Authority Theory
Authority Type
Autocrat
Bonapartism
Closed Society
Communist Government
Concentrated Power
Control Process
Despot
Dictator
Imperial Presidency
Militarism
Totalitarian Political System

AUTHORITARIANISM SCALE
S-24-0226 1975 00008
BT Scale Type
RT Absolutism
Aggression Scale
Alienation Scale
Anomie Scale
Attitude Cluster
Authoritarian Attitude
Political Tolerance

AUTHORITATIVE VALUE ALLOCATION
S-06-0608 1975 00002
BT Value Allocation
RT Authority
Authority Structure
Constitutional Authority
Goal Ambiguity
Goal Satisfaction
Goal Setting
Goal Specificity
System Analysis

AUTHORITIES
S-19-0066 1975 00000
BT Institutions
NT Interstate Authorities
Municipal Authorities
Public Authorities
RT Agencies
Commissions
Councils
Federal Commission
Government Enterprise

AUTHORITY
S-04-0001 1975 00012
NT Authority Mode
Authority Structure
Authority Type
RT Authoritative Value Allocation
Authority Theory
Basic Law
Government
Government Contract Theory
Leadership Authority Base
Legitimacy Theory
Moral Leadership
Obedience
Obligation Theory
Political Legitimacy Theory
Power Theory
Ruling Class
Social Contract Theory
Societal Contract Theory
Sovereignty
Theory

AUTHORITY FORECASTING
S-24-0011 1979 00000
BT Forecasting Methodology
RT Brainstorming
Delphi Technique
Divergence Mapping
Economic Forecasting
Policy Research
Political Forecasting
Scenario Construction
Scientific Research
Social Forecasting
Trend Analysis

AUTHORITY MODE
S-04-0002 1975 00002
BT Authority
NT Charismatic Authority
Derived Authority
Just Authority
Legal Rational Authority
Moral Authority
Scientific Authority
Traditional Authority
RT Authoritarianism
Authority Structure
Authority Type
Early Modern Theory Of The State
Leadership Authority Base
Moral Leadership
Moral Reasoning
Moral Theory
Political Legitimacy Theory
Religious Leadership
Weberian Analysis

AUTHORITY STRUCTURE
S-04-0010 1975 00014
BT Authority
NT Anarchy
Centralized Authority
Decentralized Authority
Delegated Authority
Diffuse Authority
Formal Authority
Hierarchical Authority
Independent Authority
Informal Authority
Integrated Authority
RT Authoritarianism
Authoritative Value Allocation
Authority Mode
Authority Theory
Authority Type
Constitution
Government
Government Characteristics
Institutions
Leadership Authority Base
Leadership Structure Type
Legitimacy Theory
Matriarchic Government
Moral Leadership
Moral Reasoning
National Sovereignty Theory
Sovereignty

AUTHORITY THEORY
S-38-0429 1975 00016
BT Political Philosophy Concept
RT Anarchism
Anarchy
Authoritarianism
Authority
Authority Structure
Centralized Authority
Consent Theory
Early Modern Theory Of The State
Legitimacy Theory
Mandate Of Heaven Theory
Moral Reasoning
Moral Theory
National Sovereignty Theory
Order Theory

Political Legitimacy Theory
Regime Type
Representation Theory
Roman Catholicism

AUTHORITY TYPE
S-04-0021 1975 00008
BT Authority
NT Parental Authority
Religious Authority
Secular Authority
RT Authoritarianism
Authority Mode
Authority Structure
Formal Authority
Government Characteristics
Government Type
Leadership Authority Base
Moral Reasoning
Moral Theory
Patriarchical Government
Religious Leadership

AUTHORIZATION PROCESS
S-31-0325 1975 00000
BT Decision Making Process
RT Allocation Process
Approval Process
Constitutional Authority
Economic Process
Implementation Process
Legislative Authorization
National Decision Making Process

AUTOBIOGRAPHY
S-18-0063 1979 00000
BT Monographs
RT Biographical Analysis
Biography
Career Analysis
Leadership Analysis
Political Autobiography
Political Biography
Political Fiction
Political Literature
Political Memoir

AUTOCORRELATION
S-24-0192 1975 00002
SN A measurement problem occurring in correlation analysis when change or time series studies requires that one deal with the same units at different time points.
BT Measurement Problem
RT Measurement Bias
Measurement Error
Random Error
Sampling Error
Statistical Data
Systematic Error

AUTOCRAT
S-32-0220 1975 00001
BT Politician
RT Absolute Monarch
Absolute Monarchy
Authoritarian Personality
Authoritarianism
Autocratic Government
Despot

AUTOCRATIC GOVERNMENT
S-16-0005 1975 00003
UF Autarchy
BT Government Type
RT Absolute Monarch
Absolute Monarchy
Absolutism
Absolutist Government
Authoritarian Regime
Autocrat
Centralized Government
Communist Government
Despotism
Dictatorship
Forced Requisitioning
Military Government
Tutelary Democracy

AUTOMATED PRODUCTION
S-31-0433 1975 00001
BT Production Process
RT Factory
Industrial Production
Labor Conflict
Technological Revolution
Technology

AUTOMATIC INTERACTION DETECTION
S-24-0040 1975 00000
SN Computer program using tree analysis to determine multivariate interrelationships.
BT Multivariate Analysis
RT Canonical Correlation Analysis
Covariance Analysis
Dimensional Analysis
Discriminant Analysis
Factor Analysis
Multiple Correlation Analysis
Multiple Regression Analysis
Partial Correlation Analysis
Path Analysis

AUTOMOBILE INDUSTRY
S-17-0075 1979 00000
BT Motor Vehicle Industry
RT Driver Licensing Policy
Motor Vehicle Insurance
Railway Industry
Shipping Industry
Transportation Policy
Transportation System
Trucking Industry

AVERAGE INCOME
S-06-0332 1975 00003
BT Income Measure
RT Disposable Income
Fixed Income
Income Policy
Median Income
Net Income
Tax Exempt Income

AVERAGE VOTER TURNOUT ELECTION
S-29-0181 1975 00001
BT Voter Turnout
RT Indirect Election
Low Turnout Election

AVOIDANCE BEHAVIOR
S-05-0027 1979 00000
BT Social Behavior
RT Accommodative Social Behavior
Administrative Behavior
Personal Behavior
Political Behavior
Psychological Theory
Psychology Discipline
Psychopathology
Sexual Behavior
Social Interaction Theory

AXIOLOGY
S-25-0034 1975 00001
SN Branch of philosophy dealing with values, motives, and ends of actions.
BT Ethical Theory
RT Bioethics
Emotive Ethical Theory
Ethical Relativism
Hedonism
Instrumentalism
Intuitionism
Metaethical Theory
Situational Ethics
Value System

AYATALLAH
S-32-0100 1979 00000
BT Religious Minister
RT Islamic Civilization
Islamic Society
Islamic Thought
Religious Elite
Religious Leader
Religious Leadership
Religious Politics
Religious Society
Teacher

BACKBENCHER
S-32-0148 1975 00003
BT Political Party Leader
RT Formal Political Party Leader
Frontbencher
Opposition Political Party Leader
Parliamentary Faction
Parliamentary Member
Political Party Cadre
Political Party Professional
Political Party Whip

BACKLASH VOTING
S-29-0144 1979 00000
BT Protest Voting
RT Bloc Voting
Minority Voter
Racial Politics
Racial Prejudice
Racial Voting
Racism
Voter Turnout

BACONIAN ANALYSIS
S-38-0517 1975 00000
SN Forms of inductive, empirical analysis associated with Francis Bacon.
BT Renaissance Political Thought
RT Cartesian Analysis
Inductive Method
Methodology
Rationality Theory
Scientific Research
Scientific Theory

BAD TIMES VOTER
1975-1979 00000

BAIL
S-31-0512 1975 00001
BT Pretrial Procedure
RT Arraignment
Bail Bond System
Bail Skipping
Detention
Detention Center
Justice System
Probation
Right To Bail

BAIL BOND SYSTEM
S-37-0090 1975 00000
BT Justice System
RT Bail
Bail Skipping
Court Procedure
Law Enforcement System
Pretrial Procedure
Pretrial Release
Prison
Probation
Right To Bail

BAIL SKIPPING
S-10-0003 1975 00000
BT Court Crime
RT Bail
Bail Bond System
Contempt Of Court
Jailing
Pretrial Release
Probation
Right To Bail

BAILIFF
S-36-0095 1975 00001
BT Court Official
RT Coroner
Government Employee
Judicial Administration

BALANCE OF PAYMENTS
S-06-0346 1975 00014
BT International Economic Characteristics
RT Balance Of Trade
Deflation
Foreign Trade Pattern
Trade Policy

BALANCE OF POWER
S-06-0664 1975 00057
BT International Political System Characteristics
NT Balance Of Terror
Balkanization
RT Arms Race
Balance Of Power Theory
Collective Security
International Law
International Relations Studies
Power Politics
Rapprochement
Sphere Of Influence

BALANCE OF POWER THEORY
S-38-0341 1975 00017
BT International Political Theory
RT Appeasement
Balance Of Power
Equilibrium Theory
Idealist Foreign Policy
Peaceful Coexistence
Power Measurement
Realist Foreign Policy

BALANCE OF TERROR
S-06-0665 1975 00008
BT Balance Of Power
NT Nuclear Parity
RT Global War Policy
Sphere Of Influence
Strategic Arms Reduction Policy

BALANCE OF TRADE
S-06-0347 1975 00010
BT International Economic Characteristics
RT Balance Of Payments
Foreign Trade Pattern
Government Economic Management
Trade Policy

BALANCED BUDGET
S-06-0248 1975 00001
BT Budget
RT Budget Cutting
Budget Discrepancy
Budget Formulation
Budget Planner
Internal Market

BALANCED ECONOMY
S-12-0010 1975 00001
BT Economy Type
RT Autarchic Economy
Barter Economy
Capital Investment Economy
Consumer Economy
Developed Economy
Dual Economy
Industrial Economy
Mixed Economic System
Mixed Economy
Modernizing Economy
Self Sufficient Economy
Welfare Economy

BALANCED FORCE
S-33-0008 1975 00004
BT Defense System
RT Arms Control Policy
Deterrence Policy
Military Establishment
Tactical Force

BALANCED FORCE REDUCTION POLICY
S-26-0055 1975 00006
BT Arms Reduction Policy
RT Nuclear Disarmament Policy
Peaceful Coexistence
Strategic Arms Limitation
Strategic Arms Race
Strategic Arms Reduction Policy

BALKANIZATION
S-06-0667 1975 00000
BT Balance Of Power
RT Divided Nation
Fragmentation
International Relations Studies
Nation Building
Nationalism
Regional Security

BALLISTIC MISSILE
S-33-0027 1975 00011
BT Missile
NT Antiballistic Missile
RT MARV
MIRV
Multiple Warhead Missile
Nuclear Weapon

BALLOT
S-29-0150 1975 00003
BT Voting Device
NT Australian Ballot
Long Ballot
Machine Ballot
Nonpartisan Ballot
Office Block Ballot
Paper Ballot
Political Party Column Ballot
Political Party List Ballot
Secret Ballot
Short Ballot
RT Ballot Box
Electoral Board
Electoral College
Electronic Roll Call Device
Presidential Nominating Process
Voting Device
Voting Machine

BALLOT BOX
S-29-0162 1975 00000
BT Voting Device
RT Ballot
Electronic Roll Call Device
Voting Device
Voting Machine

BANDWAGON EFFECT
S-29-0107 1975 00006
SN Tendency to vote for the candidate who appears most likely to win an election.
BT Electoral Outcome
RT Coattail Effect
Landslide Electoral Outcome
Majority Electoral Outcome
Presidential Coattail Effect
Vote Distribution

BANK NATIONALIZATION
S-31-0293 1975 00001
BT Nationalization Process
RT Bank Reserve
Basic Industry Nationalization
Industry Nationalization
Monetary Agency
Utility Nationalization

BANK RATE
USE Credit Policy

BANK RESERVE
S-06-0354 1975 00002
BT Money Creation
RT Bank Nationalization
Banking Agency
Budget Policy
Discount Rate
Monetary Agency
Monetary Economic Theory
Monetary Policy
Prime Loan Rate

BANKING AGENCY
S-19-0025 1975 00013
BT Monetary Agency
RT Bank Reserve
Banking Policy
Business Agency
Economic Institution
Money Demand
Money Supply
Prime Loan Rate

BANKING POLICY
S-26-0124 1975 00015
BT Monetary Policy
RT Banking Agency
Credit Policy
Deflation
Federal Reserve System
Government Economic Management
Monetary Economic Theory
Money Supply Policy

BANKRUPTCY LAW
S-21-0033 1975 00004
BT Economic Law
RT Consumer Protection Law
Legal Immunity
Property Rights
Tax Law
Tort

BAR ASSOCIATION
S-03-0053 1975 00002
BT Professional Organization
RT Grand Jury
Justice System
Law Enforcement Official
Law School
Lawyer
Occupational Interest Group

BARGAIN
USE Contract Type

BARGAINER
S-32-0005 1975 00001
BT Adjudicator
RT Arbitrator
Bargaining
Bargaining Theory
Mediator
Negotiation
Negotiator

BARGAINING
S-31-0228 1975 00022
BT Conflict Resolution
NT Bargaining Strategy Process
Economic Bargaining
Political Bargaining
RT Accommodation
Adjudication
Adjudicator
Agreement
Appeasement
Bargainer
Bargaining Theory
Conciliation
Decision Making Process
Declared War
Deescalation
Labor Boycott
Log Rolling
Mediation
Negotiation
Negotiator

BARGAINING STRATEGY PROCESS
S-31-0229 1975 00035
BT Bargaining
RT Economic Bargaining
Gaming
Negotiator
Policy Conflict
Political Bargaining

BARGAINING THEORY
S-38-0127 1975 00023
BT Formal Political Theory
RT Bargainer
Bargaining
Coalition Theory
Decision Making Theory
Economic Model
Game Theory
Negotiation
Policy Conflict
Political Bargaining

BARRISTER
S-36-0098 1975 00000
BT Court Attorney
RT Defense Attorney
Lawyer
Prosecuting Attorney
Solicitor

BARTER ECONOMIC SYSTEM
S-37-0011 1975 00000
BT Economic System
RT Barter Economy
Economic Bargaining

BARTER ECONOMY
S-12-0011 1975 00001
BT Economy Type
RT Agrarian Economy
Balanced Economy
Barter Economic System
Craft Economy
Dual Economy
Export Economy
Fascist Economy
Hunting And Trapping Economy
Market Economy
Nomadic Economy
Peasant Economy
Primitive Society
Subsistence Economy
Underdeveloped Economy

BASIC INDUSTRY NATIONALIZATION
S-31-0295 1975 00003
BT Industry Nationalization
RT Bank Nationalization
Big Business
Public Corporation
Socialist Economy
Utility Nationalization

BASIC LAW
S-21-0003 1975 00000
BT Law Type
NT City Charter
Constitution
RT Authority
Customary Law
Judicial Process
Judicial System
Law Formulation
Law System
Legal History
Natural Law
Procedural Law
Sacred Law
Sovereignty
Written Constitution

BASIC PERSONALITY
S-06-0529 1975 00006
BT Personality Type
RT Behavior Modification
Modal Personality
Personality Development

BASIC RESEARCH
S-24-0376 1975 00029
BT Research Orientation
RT Academic Elite
Advocacy Research
Applied Research
Applied Sociology
Concept Explication Research
Deductive Method
Descriptive Research
Experimental Research
Explanatory Research
Inductive Method
Policy Research
Predictive Research
Qualitative Research
Quantitative History
Quantitative Research
Research Management
Scientific Research
Theoretical Research

BAYESIAN ANALYSIS
S-24-0052 1975 00005
SN Statistical form of decision theory based on the measurement of subjective probabilities.
BT Probability Estimation
RT Subjective Probability Estimation

BEDROOM COMMUNITY
S-07-0051 1979 00000
BT Suburb
RT New Town
Suburban Environment
Suburban Migration
Suburban Population

BEHAVIOR
S-05-0001 1975 00006
NT Administrative Behavior
Animal Behavior
Economic Behavior
Personal Behavior
Political Behavior
Problem Solving Behavior
Social Behavior
RT Behavior Analysis
Behavioral Science
Behavioral Theory
Personality Development
Political Behavior Studies
Theory
Voting Behavior Analysis

BEHAVIOR ANALYSIS
S-09-0004 1975 00057
BT Contemporary Analytic Modes
RT Behavior
Contextual Analysis
Identity Analysis

Issue Salience
Motivational Analysis
Nonverbal Communication
Political Behavior
Political Behavior Studies
Political Psychology Analysis
Psychoanalysis
Rational Man Analysis
Situational Analysis
Sociological Analysis
Value Analysis
Voting Behavior Analysis

BEHAVIOR MODIFICATION
S-34-0006 1979 00000
BT Learning
RT Animal Behavior
Basic Personality
Behavioral Psychology
Behavioral Theory
Cooperative Behavior
Criminal Deterrence
Learning Psychology
Mental Health Policy
Personality Disorder
Psychological Behaviorism
Psychological Deprogramming
Psychological Programming
Rote Learning
Social Adjustment

BEHAVIORAL MEASUREMENT
S-24-0184 1975 00027
BT Measurement Object
RT Attitude Measurement
Change Measurement
Group Measurement
Individual Measurement
Perception Measurement

BEHAVIORAL PSYCHOLOGY
S-01-0169 1975 00036
BT Psychology Discipline
RT Animal Behavior
Behavior Modification
Behavioral Science Research
Cooperative Behavior
Coping Behavior
Freudian Psychology
Gestalt Psychology
Learning Psychology
Library Science Studies
Parapsychology
Pathological Behavior
Perception
Personality Development
Personality Theory
Political Behavior Studies
Political Sociology
Psycholinguistics
Psychological Anthropology
Psychological Behavioralism
Psychology Discipline
Psychopathology
Sexual Behavior
Social Pathology
Social Psychology
Sociolinguistics

BEHAVIORAL SCIENCE
S-01-0049 1975 00007
BT Academic Areas
RT Administrative Behavior
Administrative Science
Animal Behavior
Behavior
Behavioral Science Research
Comparative Sociology
Computer Science
Economics Discipline
Education Discipline
Gerontology
Group Theory
Individual Behavior
International Relations Studies
Mathematics Discipline
Methodological Individualism
Microeconomics
Personality Theory
Policy Science Studies
Political Behavior Studies
Political Psychology
Political Science Discipline
Political Science Methodology Studies
Psycholinguistics
Psychology Discipline
Psychopathology
Public Administration Studies
Social History
Social Psychology
Sociology Discipline

BEHAVIORAL SCIENCE RESEARCH
S-24-0396 1975 00026
BT Scientific Research
RT Animal Behavior
Behavioral Psychology
Behavioral Science
Behavioral Theory
Perception
Policy Science Studies

BEHAVIORAL THEORY
S-38-0019 1975 00019
BT Theory
RT Administrative Behavior
Animal Behavior
Behavior
Behavior Modification
Behavioral Science Research
Comtean Positivism
Contemporary Political Thought
Cooperative Behavior
Economic Behavior
Explanatory Political Theory
Legal Behavior
Legislative Behavior
Methodology
Organization Environment
Personality Theory
Political Behavior
Political Behaviorism
Small Group Behavior
Social Behavior
Sociology Of Knowledge

BELIEF MEASUREMENT
S-24-0181 1975 00029
BT Attitude Measurement
RT Affective Measurement
Belief System
Cognitive Measurement
Motivation Measurement

BELIEF SYSTEM
S-37-0002 1975 00074
BT System Type
NT Mass Belief System
RT Belief Measurement
Cognitive System
Cultural System
Militancy
Political Ideology
Social System
Value Analysis
Value System

BELLIGERENCE
S-06-0104 1975 00004
BT Aggressiveness
RT Aggression
Aggression Scale
Aggression Theory
Aggressiveness
Declared War
Militancy
War

BELLIGERENT
USE Aggressor State

BENCH TRIAL
S-31-0524 1975 00000
SN An adjudication proceeding in which the determination is made by a judge.
BT Public Trial
RT Civil Court
Jury Trial

BENEVOLENT DESPOT
S-32-0222 1975 00000
BT Despot
RT Benevolent Dictator
Benevolent Dictatorship
Guided Democracy Theory
Interim Government
Oriental Despot
Tsar

BENEVOLENT DESPOTISM
S-16-0142 1975 00000
BT Despotism
RT Benevolent Dictatorship
Despot
Oriental Despot
Oriental Despotism

BENEVOLENT DICTATOR
S-36-0050 1975 00000
BT Dictator
RT Benevolent Despot
Benevolent Dictatorship
Military Government
Military Governor
Monarch

BENEVOLENT DICTATORSHIP
S-16-0036 1975 00002
BT Dictatorship
RT Benevolent Despot
Benevolent Despotism
Benevolent Dictator
Military Governor
Modernizing Dictatorship
Monarch
Progressive Dictatorship

BENTHAMISM
S-38-0427 1975 00001
SN Utilitarian thought associated with Jeremy Bentham.
BT Utilitarianism
RT Distributive Justice Theory
Ethical Theory
Utilitarian Justice Theory
Utilitarianism

BERNSTEINIAN SOCIALISM
S-38-0294 1975 00001
SN The theory and practices associated with social democracy and the evolutionary path to socialism delineated by Eduard Bernstein.
BT Evolutionary Socialism
RT Democratic Socialist Revolution
Evolutionary Change
Fabian Socialism
Saint Simonianism
Social Democratic Movement
Socialist Political Party

BIAS
S-06-0120 1975 00028
BT Prejudice
RT Statistical Analysis

BIBLIOGRAPHIC CONTROL
S-18-0049 1979 00000
BT Bibliographic Service
RT Citation Analysis
Documentation Service
Government Information Service
Information Retrieval Program
Legislative Information Service
Private Information Service
Thesaurus

BIBLIOGRAPHIC SERVICE
S-18-0048 1975 00009
BT Information Service
NT Bibliographic Control
RT Abstracting
Abstracting Service
Citation Analysis
Documentation Service
Government Information Service
Information Network
Legislative Information Service
Machine Readable Information
Private Information Service
Thesaurus
University Information Service

BICAMERAL LEGISLATURE
S-19-0254 1975 00004
BT Legislature Type
RT Constitution
House Of Representatives
National Legislature
Representation Type
Senate
Subnational Legislature
Unicameral Legislature

BICULTURAL SOCIETY
S-35-0037 1975 00002
UF Biculturalism
BT Multicultural Society
RT Ethnic Conflict
Multiethnic Society
Multilingual Society
Multiracial Society
Plural Society
Social Stratification System

BICULTURALISM
USE Bicultural Society

BIENNIAL ELECTION
1975-1979 00000

BIG BUSINESS
S-19-0160 1975 00007
BT Business
RT Antitrust Law
Antitrust Policy
Basic Industry Nationalization
Business Studies
Capitalism
Corporate Economy
Ghetto Business
Monetary Institution
Power Elite
Small Business

BIGOTRY
S-06-0107 1975 00004
BT Intolerance
RT Hostility
Personality Development
Prejudice
Racial Attitude
Racial Intolerance
Racial Prejudice
White Militancy
Xenophobe

BILATERAL AID
S-06-0308 1975 00005
BT Foreign Aid
RT Bilateral Aid Policy
Bilateral State Agreement
Bilateral Treaty
Economic Aid Policy
Economic Alliance
Financial Aid
Multilateral Aid

BILATERAL AID POLICY
S-26-0256 1975 00005
BT Foreign Aid Policy
RT Bilateral Aid
Economic Aid Policy
Military Aid Policy
Multilateral Aid
Multilateral Aid Policy
Technical Aid Policy
Unilateral Aid Policy

BILATERAL FAMILY DESCENT PATTERN
S-20-0003 1975 00001
BT Family Descent Pattern
RT Communal Family
Cultural Anthropology
Linguistic Analysis
Matrilineal Family Descent Pattern
Patriarchal Kinship System
Patrilineal Family Descent Pattern

BILATERAL STATE AGREEMENT
S-02-0061 1975 00028
BT State Agreement Form
RT Bilateral Aid
DeFacto Recognition
DeJure Recognition
Executive Agreement
Multilateral Aid
Multilateral State Agreement
Mutual Deterrence Policy
Treaty Making

BILATERAL TREATY
S-02-0062 1975 00011
BT State Agreement Form
RT Bilateral Aid
Economic Aid Policy
Foreign Aid
Military Aid Policy
Military Assistance
Most Favored Nation Policy
Sphere Of Influence
Summit Diplomacy

BILINGUAL COMMUNITY
S-07-0035 1975 00002
BT Multilingual Community
RT Bilingualism
Integrated Community
Language Acquisition
Language Learning
Linguistic Assimilation
Multiethnic Community
Multilingual Community
Multilingual Society
Multiracial Community

BILINGUALISM
S-31-0815 1975 00015
BT Linguistic Integration
RT Assimilation
Bilingual Community
Ethnic Assimilation Theory
Language Acquisition
Language Learning
Psycholinguistics
Sociolinguistics

BILL DRAFTING
S-31-0583 1975 00002
BT Legislative Action
RT Legislative Amendment Process
Legislative Appropriation
Legislative Authorization
Legislative Bill Rejection
Legislative Calendar
Legislative Executive Relations

BILL OF ATTAINDER
S-15-0044 1975 00000
BT Defendants Rights
RT Constitutional Interpretation Theory
Double Jeopardy
Ex Post Facto Protection
Habeas Corpus
Judicial Procedure
Right Against Cruel And Unusual Punishment
Right To Due Process
Right To Equal Protection
Right To Speedy Trial
Right To Trial
Search And Seizure
Statute Of Limitations

BILL OF RIGHTS
S-21-0009 1975 00009
BT Constitutional Amendment
RT Constitutional Interpretation Theory
Ex Post Facto Protection
Judicial Process
Judicial System
Natural Law
Political Trial
Procedural Law

Right To Bear Arms
Search And Seizure

BINOMIAL TEST
S-24-0055 1975 00001
SN Significance test based on binomial distribution used when population sampled is composed of two classes or categories.
BT Statistical Significance Test
RT Chi Square Test
F Ratio
Interval Significance Test
Mann Whitney U Test
Nominal Significance Test
Ordinal Significance Test
Wald Wolfowitz Runs Test
Wilcoxian T Test

BIOETHICS
S-25-0035 1979 00000
BT Ethical Theory
RT Axiology
Biopolitics
Ethical Relativism
Research Ethics
Situational Ethics
Sociobiology

BIOGRAPHICAL ANALYSIS
S-09-0005 1975 00113
BT Contemporary Analytic Modes
NT Career Analysis
RT Autobiography
Class Analysis
Historical Analysis
Leadership Analysis
Political Biography
Situational Analysis
Socialization Analysis

BIOGRAPHY
S-18-0064 1979 00000
BT Monographs
RT Autobiography
Library
Newspapers
Political Autobiography
Political Biography
Political Fiction
Political Literature

BIOLOGICAL COMMUNITY
USE Ecosystem

BIOLOGICAL MODEL
S-24-0286 1975 00105
BT Natural Science Model
RT Biological Sciences
Ecological Model
Eugenics

BIOLOGICAL SCIENCES
S-01-0050 1979 00000
UF Biology
BT Academic Areas
NT Eugenics
RT Agricultural Science
Biological Model
Biological War
Biopolitics
Environmental Studies
Genetic Characteristics
Human Evolution
Human Geography
Natural Science Discipline
Physical Science
Psychology Discipline
Sociobiology

BIOLOGICAL WAR
S-08-0088 1979 00000
UF Biological Warfare
BT War
RT Biological Sciences
Biological Weapon
Chemical War
Genocide
Nuclear War

BIOLOGICAL WARFARE
1975-1979 00003
USE Biological War

BIOLOGICAL WEAPON
S-33-0020 1975 00005
BT Military Weapon
RT Biological War
Chemical Weapon
Defensive Weapon
Nuclear Weapon
Strategic Weapon
Tactical Weapon
Unconventional Weapon
War
War Atrocity

BIOLOGY
USE Biological Sciences

BIOPOLITICS
S-29-0005 1975 00000
SN Analysis framework which includes accounting of evolutionary trends using the biological metaphor.
BT Politics
RT Bioethics
Biological Sciences
Genetic Characteristics
Political Behavior

BIPARTISAN VOTING
S-31-0591 1975 00002
BT Legislative Voting
RT Censure Motion
Cloture
Discharge Petition
Nonpartisan Ballot
Voting
Voting Behavior

BIPOLAR INTERNATIONAL SYSTEM
S-37-0116 1975 00009
BT International Political System
NT Loose Bipolar International Political System
Tight Bipolar International Political System
RT Commonwealth International System
Hegemonic System
International System Polarization
Multipolar International Political System
Peaceful Coexistence
Regional International Political System

BIRTH CONTROL POLICY
S-26-0394 1975 00034
BT Population Policy
RT Abortion Law
Abortion Policy
Family Planning
Fertility Rate
Infant Mortality Rate

BIRTH RATE
S-06-0189 1975 00020
BT Demographic Profile
RT Abortion Law
Abortion Policy
Family Subsidization Policy
Fertility Rate
Population Management
Population Policy
Vital Statistics Data

BIVARIATE ANALYSIS
S-24-0033 1975 00014
BT Statistical Analysis
NT Correlation Analysis
RT Multivariate Analysis
Probability Estimation
Statistical Significance Test
Statistics Type
Univariate Analysis

BLACK ANCESTRY
S-06-0200 1975 00000
BT Ancestry
RT Black History
Black Identity
Black Political Thought
Black Studies
Ethnic Studies

BLACK BOURGEOISIE
S-06-0770 1975 00001
BT Bourgeoisie
RT Black Capitalism
Black Studies
Entrepreneur Class
Ethnic Community
Ghetto Business

BLACK CAPITALISM
S-37-0013 1975 00005
BT Capitalism
RT Black Bourgeoisie
Bourgeois Capitalism
Industrial Capitalism
Mature Capitalism
Mercantile Capitalism
Monopoly Capitalism
Private Sector
Warfare Capitalism

BLACK CULTURE
S-11-0016 1975 00014
BT Ethnic Culture
RT African Area Studies
Afro Asian Bloc
Black History
Black Studies
Community Culture
Cultural History
Ethnic Community
Urban Culture

BLACK EMANCIPATION
S-31-0146 1975 00003
BT Emancipation
NT Slavery Abolition
RT Black Studies
Womens Emancipation

BLACK GHETTO
S-07-0027 1975 00007
BT Ethnic Ghetto
RT Ethnic Community
Homogeneous Community

Housing Policy
Multiethnic Community
Segregation Policy

BLACK HISTORY
S-01-0100 1975 00024
BT History Discipline
RT African Area Studies
Black Ancestry
Black Culture
Black Studies
Cultural Anthropology
Cultural History
Ethnic Studies
Ethnology
Legal History
Oral History
Political Behavior Studies
Political History
Political Sociology
Urban History

BLACK IDENTITY
S-06-0384 1975 00014
BT Racial Identity
RT Black Ancestry
Black Insurrection
Black Militancy
Black Militant
Black Revolution
Black Studies
Cultural History
Ethnic Group Loyalty
Ethnicity
Identity Theory

BLACK INSURRECTION
S-08-0123 1975 00002
BT Racial Conflict
RT Black Identity
Black Liberation Movement
Black Militancy
Class Conflict
Internal War
Liberation Process
Militancy
Race Riot

BLACK LIBERATION MOVEMENT
S-27-0025 1975 00004
BT Liberation Movement
RT Black Insurrection
Black Separatist Movement
Ethnicity
National Liberation Movement
Peoples Liberation Movement
Womens Liberation Movement

BLACK MARKET
S-19-0180 1975 00003
BT Market
RT Consumer Market
Differentiated Market
Free Market
Marketplace
National Market
Stock Market
World Market

BLACK MILITANCY
S-06-0112 1975 00006
BT Racial Militancy
RT Black Identity
Black Insurrection
Black Militant
Black Panther
Black Studies
Ghetto Rioter
Racial Supremacy

BLACK MILITANT
S-32-0185 1975 00001
BT Militant
NT Black Muslim
Black Panther
RT Black Identity
Black Militancy
Black Studies

BLACK MUSLIM
S-32-0186 1975 00001
BT Black Militant
RT Black Nationalism
Pan Arabism
Pan Islamism

BLACK NATIONALISM
S-38-0264 1975 00007
BT Cultural Nationalism
RT Afro Asian Bloc
Black Muslim
Black Nationalist Movement
Black Political Thought
Cultural History
Ethnic Community
Identity Characteristics
Irredentism
Pan Africanism
Pan Arabism
Pan Islamism
Tribalism
Urban Government

BLACK NATIONALIST MOVEMENT
S-27-0035 1975 00004
BT Nationalist Movement
RT Black Nationalism
Black Panther
Black Separatist Movement
Black Studies
Ethnicity
Pan African Movement

BLACK PANTHER
S-32-0187 1975 00002
BT Black Militant
RT Black Militancy
Black Nationalist Movement
Ghetto Community

BLACK POLITICAL THOUGHT
S-38-0061 1975 00005
BT Contemporary Political Thought
RT Black Ancestry
Black Nationalism
Black Studies
Cultural History
Ethnic Ideology

BLACK PRESS
S-17-0021 1975 00001
BT Newspaper Industry
RT Black Studies
National Press
Political Literature
Radical Press
Underground Press

BLACK RACISM
S-38-0220 1975 00001
BT Racism
RT Antisemitism
Apartheid Theory
Attitude Characteristics
Black Studies
Ethnic Conflict
Institutional Racism
White Racism

BLACK REVOLUTION
S-08-0080 1975 00002
BT Racial Revolution
RT Black Identity
Bourgeois Revolution
Ghetto Rioter
Racial Conflict
Spontaneous Revolution

BLACK SEPARATIST MOVEMENT
S-27-0030 1975 00002
BT Separatist Movement
RT Black Liberation Movement
Black Nationalist Movement
Ethnic Community

BLACK STUDIES
S-01-0084 1975 00247
BT Ethnic Studies
RT American Indian Studies
Area Studies
Black Ancestry
Black Bourgeoisie
Black Culture
Black Emancipation
Black History
Black Identity
Black Militancy
Black Militant
Black Nationalist Movement
Black Political Thought
Black Press
Black Racism
Chicano Studies
Cultural Anthropology
Cultural History
Ethnic Community
Human Geography
Puerto Rican Studies

BLACK SUBURBAN COMMUNITY
S-07-0029 1975 00006
BT Suburban Ghetto Community
RT Ghetto Business
Homogeneous Community
Housing Policy
Integrated Community
Multiethnic Community
Population Concentration
Suburban Environment
Urban Ghetto Community

BLACK VOTER
S-32-0297 1975 00003
BT Voter
RT Black Voting
Class Voter
Ethnic Group Voting
Ethnic Voter
Minority Voter

BLACK VOTING
S-29-0134 1975 00008
BT Racial Voting
RT Black Voter
Class Voter
Ethnic Studies
Ethnic Voter
Ethnicity

Group Theory
Voting Behavior Analysis

BLACKLISTING POLICY
S-26-0235 1975 00000
BT Exclusionary Policy
RT Censorship Process
Quota Policy
Segregation Policy
Union

BLACKMAIL
S-10-0028 1975 00003
BT Individual Crime
RT Blackmailer
Economic Conspiracy
Extortion
Fraud
Kidnapping
Libel
Malpractice
Marital Offense
Military Espionage
Political Espionage
Slander

BLACKMAILER
S-36-0031 1975 00000
BT Personal Crime Criminal
RT Blackmail
Extortionist
Murderer
Slanderer
War Criminal

BLANKET PRIMARY
S-29-0064 1975 00000
SN Nominating election in which voters can vote across party lines for particular candidates.
BT Primary Election
RT Closed Primary
National Primary
Open Primary
Political Party Primary
Preference Primary

BLOC LEADER
S-32-0149 1975 00001
BT Political Party Leader
RT Local Elite
Political Party Professional

BLOC VOTING
S-29-0130 1975 00008
BT Group Voting
RT Backlash Voting
Ethnic Group Voting
Geographic Voting
Issue Politicization
Local Elite
Racial Voting
Regional Voting
Student Voting
Urban Voting
Voting Behavior Analysis
Voting Coalition

BLOCKADE POLICY
S-26-0185 1975 00005
BT Restrictive Trade Policy
RT Export Policy
Import Policy
International Sanction
Tariff Policy
War

BLUE COLLAR WORKER
S-32-0087 1975 00014
BT Industrial Worker
NT Semiskilled Worker
Skilled Worker
Unskilled Worker
RT Business
Factory
Occupational Identity
Occupational Role

BLUE LAW
S-21-0086 1979 00000
BT Social Law
RT Folkways
Gambling Law
Moral Authority
Pornography Law
Religious Authority
Traditional Authority

BOARD OF REGENTS
S-19-0033 1975 00000
BT Education Agency
RT Board Of Trustees
Education Accreditation Agency
Education Institution
Examination Agency
Higher Education
School Board

BOARD OF TRUSTEES
S-19-0034 1975 00000
BT Education Agency
RT Board Of Regents
Education Accreditation Agency
Education Institution
Examination Agency
Public Authorities
School Board

BODY POLITIC
USE Political System Type

BOLSHEVIK PARTY
1975-1979 00005

BOLSHEVIK POLITICAL PARTY
S-28-0012 1979 00000
BT Communist Political Party
RT Soviet Studies
Trotskyite Political Party

BOLSHEVIK REVOLUTION
S-08-0073 1975 00005
BT Communist Revolution
RT Bolshevism
Internal Conflict
Internal War
Marxism Leninism
National Political Revolution
Rebellion
Social Conflict
Struggle

BOLSHEVISM
S-38-0315 1975 00006
BT Marxism
RT Bolshevik Revolution
Castroism
Communism
Communist Government
Leninism
Maoism
Maoist
Maoist Political Party
Maoist Revolutionary
Marxism Leninism
One Political Party System
Polycentrism
Stalinism
Stalinist
Titoism
Trotskyism
Trotskyite Political Party

BOMB
S-33-0021 1979 00000
BT Military Weapon
RT Arms Industry
Munitions
Nuclear Weapon
Strategic Weapon
War Technology
Weapon

BONAPARTISM
S-22-0002 1979 00000
BT Leadership Type
RT Authoritarian Regime
Authoritarianism
Closed Leadership
Dictator
Dictatorship
National Leadership
Personalized Leadership

BOOK
USE Information Sources

BOOK ACQUISITION
USE Library

BOOK CENSORSHIP
S-31-0268 1975 00002
BT Published Media Censorship
RT Economic Exploitation
Information Manipulation
Journal Censorship
Periodical Publication Censorship
Scientific Report Censorship

BOOK CENSORSHIP AGENCY
1975-1979 00000

BOOK INDUSTRY
S-17-0018 1975 00013
BT Publication Industry
RT Documentation Service
Documents
Information Sources
Library Science Studies
Magazine Industry
News Agency
Newspaper Industry

BORDER CONFLICT
S-08-0099 1975 00007
BT Border War
RT Annexation
Border State
Conflict Model
National Political Division
Tactical War
Territory Jurisdiction
Undeclared War

BORDER STATE
S-16-0160 1975 00001
BT State Type
RT Border Conflict
Border War

BORDER WAR
S-08-0098 1975 00003
BT Limited War
NT Border Conflict
RT Border State
Brushfire War
Conflict Process
Tactical War

BOROUGH
S-24-0366 1979 00000
BT State Political Division
RT Borough Government
County
Legislative District
Township

BOROUGH GOVERNMENT
S-16-0100 1975 00000
BT Local Government
RT Borough
City Government
Mayor
Metropolitan Government
Municipal Authorities
Municipality
Provincial Government
State Government
Township Government
Urban Government
Wald Wolfowitz Runs Test
Wilcoxian T Test

BOSS POLITICS
S-29-0217 1975 00002
BT Partisan Politics
RT Local Political Boss
Machine Candidate
Machine Politics
One Political Party System
Patronage Bureaucracy
Patronage Politics
Political Boss
Political Patron

BOURGEOIS CAPITALISM
S-37-0014 1975 00002
BT Capitalism
RT Black Capitalism
Bourgeois Democracy
Bourgeois Dictatorship
Bourgeois Revolution
Bourgeois Society
Bourgeoisie
Industrial Capitalism
Marxism
Mature Capitalism
Mercantile Capitalism
Monopoly Capitalism
Private Sector
Warfare Capitalism
Welfare Capitalism

BOURGEOIS DEMOCRACY
S-16-0013 1975 00001
BT Democratic Government
RT Agrarian Democracy
Bourgeois Capitalism
Bourgeois Dictatorship
Bourgeois Revolution
Bourgeois Society
Bourgeoisie
Constitutional Democracy

BOURGEOIS DICTATORSHIP
S-16-0037 1975 00000
BT Dictatorship
RT Bourgeois Capitalism
Bourgeois Democracy
Bourgeois Revolution
Bourgeois Society
Bourgeoisie
Constitutional Dictatorship
Marxism Leninism

BOURGEOIS REVOLUTION
S-08-0076 1975 00006
BT Social Revolution
RT Black Revolution
Bourgeois Capitalism
Bourgeois Democracy
Bourgeois Dictatorship
Bourgeois Society
Bourgeoisie
Marxism
Marxism Leninism
Proletarian Revolution
Thermidor

BOURGEOIS SOCIETY
S-35-0010 1975 00004
BT Society Type Base
RT Affluent Society
Bourgeois Capitalism
Bourgeois Democracy
Bourgeois Dictatorship
Bourgeois Revolution
Bourgeoisie
Capitalist Society
Class Society
Feudal Society
Industrial Society
Marxism
Middle Class Values
Western Society

BOURGEOISIE
S-06-0769 1975 00005
BT Middle Class
NT Black Bourgeoisie
Petite Bourgeoisie
RT Bourgeois Capitalism
Bourgeois Democracy
Bourgeois Dictatorship
Bourgeois Revolution
Bourgeois Society
Capitalism
Entrepreneur Class
Entrepreneurship
Marxist Class Theory
Middle Class
Old Middle Class
Propertied Class

BRAINDRAIN
S-06-0235 1979 00000
BT Migration Pattern
RT Foreign Student
Immigration Pattern
Scientific Manpower Policy
Scientific Research
Scientist

BRAINSTORMING
S-24-0012 1979 00000
BT Forecasting Methodology
RT Authority Forecasting
Delphi Technique
Divergence Mapping
Economic Forecasting
Policy Evaluation Research
Policy Research
Political Forecasting
Predictive Research
Scenario Construction
Social Forecasting
Trend Analysis

BRAINWASHING
S-31-0304 1975 00003
BT Political Indoctrination
RT Ideological Indoctrination
Political Conditioning
Prisoner Of War Camp
Propaganda War
Psychological Programming
Psychological War

BRINKMANSHIP
S-26-0252 1975 00000
BT Foreign Policy
RT Cold War
Escalation
Gunboat Diplomacy
International Economic Boycott
International Sanction
Threat Indicator

BRITISH COMMONWEALTH AREA STUDIES
S-01-0040 1975 00010
BT Area Studies
RT Comparative Literature Studies
Comparative Political Studies
Comparative Sociology
Cultural Anthropology
Cultural History
Political Science Discipline
West European Area Studies

BROAD CONSTRUCTIONISM
S-38-0442 1975 00001
BT Constitutional Interpretation Theory
RT Constitution
Constitutional Democracy
Judicial Review
Strict Constructionism

BROADCAST ACCESS POLICY
S-26-0027 1975 00004
BT Broadcasting Policy
NT Equal Time Provision Policy
Fairness Doctrine
Prime Time Access Policy
RT Broadcast Censorship Policy
Broadcast Regulation Policy
Radio Policy
Television Policy

BROADCAST CENSORSHIP POLICY
S-26-0031 1975 00000
BT Broadcasting Policy
NT Broadcast Jamming Policy
RT Broadcast Access Policy
Broadcast Regulation Policy
Broadcasting Censorship
Prime Time Access Policy
Radio Policy
Television Policy

BROADCAST JAMMING POLICY
S-26-0032 1975 00000
BT Broadcast Censorship Policy
RT Broadcasting Censorship
Broadcasting Industry

BROADCAST REGULATION POLICY
S-26-0033 1975 00012
BT Broadcasting Policy
RT Broadcast Access Policy
Broadcast Censorship Policy
Broadcast Subsidization Policy
Broadcasting Censorship
Broadcasting Industry
Prime Time Access Policy
Radio Policy
Television Policy

BROADCAST SUBSIDIZATION POLICY
S-26-0034 1975 00002
BT Broadcasting Policy
RT Broadcast Regulation Policy
Broadcasting Industry
Radio Policy
Television Policy

BROADCASTER LICENSING POLICY
1975-1979 00002

BROADCASTER LISCENSING POLICY
USE Broadcasting Licensing Policy

BROADCASTING
S-31-0180 1975 00002
BT Mass Communication
NT Public Broadcasting
RT Broadcasting Industry
Broadcasting Policy
Equal Time Provision Policy
Fairness Doctrine
Media Access
Media Editorializing
News Conference
News Reporting
Newspaper Circulation
Public Broadcasting Policy
Radio Industry
Speeches

BROADCASTING AGENCY
S-19-0047 1975 00001
BT Communication Agency
RT Broadcasting Industry
Broadcasting Licensing Policy
Broadcasting Policy
News Reporting
Public Broadcasting Policy
Radio Censorship
Radio Policy

BROADCASTING CENSORSHIP
S-31-0277 1975 00001
BT Unpublished Media Censorship
NT Radio Censorship
Television Censorship
RT Broadcast Censorship Policy
Broadcast Jamming Policy
Broadcast Regulation Policy
Broadcasting Licensing Policy
Broadcasting Policy
Information Leaking
Media Access
Music Censorship
Political Censorship
Political Information Manipulation
Public Broadcasting Policy
Radio Policy
Theater Censorship

BROADCASTING INDUSTRY
S-17-0007 1975 00011
BT Communication Industry
NT Commercial Broadcasting Industry
Public Broadcasting Industry
Radio Industry
Television Industry
RT Broadcast Jamming Policy
Broadcast Regulation Policy
Broadcast Subsidization Policy
Broadcasting
Broadcasting Agency
Broadcasting Licensing Policy
Broadcasting Policy
Equal Time Provision Policy
Magazine Industry
News Agency
Public Broadcasting Policy
Publication Industry
Telecommunications Industry

BROADCASTING LICENSING POLICY
S-26-0035 1979 00000
UF Broadcaster Liscensing Policy
BT Broadcasting Policy
RT Broadcasting Agency
Broadcasting Censorship
Broadcasting Industry
Government Regulation
Mass Media Regulation Policy

BROADCASTING POLICY
S-26-0026 1975 00007
BT Mass Media Policy
NT Broadcast Access Policy
Broadcast Censorship Policy
Broadcast Regulation Policy
Broadcast Subsidization Policy
Broadcasting Licensing Policy
Public Broadcasting Policy
Radio Policy
Television Policy
RT Broadcasting
Broadcasting Agency
Broadcasting Censorship
Broadcasting Industry
Government Censorship Agency
Mass Media Access Policy
Mass Media Censorship Policy
Mass Media Licensing Policy
Mass Media Regulation Policy
Mass Media Subsidization Policy
Radio Censorship

BROKER
S-32-0006 1975 00002
BT Adjudicator
RT Arbitrator
Mediator
Moderator
Negotiator
Ombudsman

BROTHER
USE Family Role

BROTHERHOOD
S-06-0033 1975 00001
BT Group Solidarity
RT Caste Solidarity
Class Solidarity
Communal Solidarity
Gemeinschaft
Group Cohesion
Proletarian Unity
Social Solidarity

BRUSHFIRE WAR
S-08-0100 1975 00000
BT Limited War
RT Border War
Limited War
Tactical War

BUDDHISM
S-38-0554 1975 00015
BT Religious Thought
NT Lamaism
RT Confucianism
East Asian Area Studies
Eastern Culture
Eastern Political Thought
Islamic Thought
Judeo Christian Thought
Religious Movement
Shintoism
Taoism
Traditional Culture
Zoroastrianism

BUDGET
S-06-0247 1975 00015
BT Economic Characteristics
NT Balanced Budget
Budget Discrepancy
Capital Budget
RT Budget Agency
Budget Planner
Budget Policy
Budget Process
Budget Proposing
Budget Record
Budget Reviewing
Expenditure Record
Financial Record
Financing
Fiscal Management
Fiscal Planning
Government Economic Management
Government Economic Planning
Government Expenditure

BUDGET AGENCY
S-19-0023 1975 00010
BT Fiscal Agency
RT Appropriation Agency
Budget
Defense Appropriation
Economic Council
Interest Group
Military Budget
Monetary Agency
Public Treasury
Revenue Agency
Tax Agency

BUDGET AUDITING
S-31-0369 1975 00003
BT Budget Reviewing
RT Budget Cutting
Budget Estimation
Budget Planner

BUDGET CUTTING
S-31-0364 1975 00008
BT Budget Process
RT Balanced Budget
Budget Auditing
Budget Reviewing
Collective Policy Making
Tax Cut

BUDGET DEFICIT
S-06-0250 1975 00003
BT Budget Discrepancy
RT Budget Surplus
Expenditure Policy
Expenditure Record
Export Economy
Export Subsidization Policy
Financial Record
Government Borrowing
Government Expenditure

BUDGET DISCREPANCY
S-06-0249 1975 00001
BT Budget
NT Budget Deficit
Budget Surplus
RT Balanced Budget
Financial Record

BUDGET ESTIMATION
S-31-0366 1975 00010
BT Budget Formulation
RT Budget Auditing
Budget Proposing
Budget Reviewing
Capital Budget
Expenditure Record

BUDGET FORMULATION
S-31-0365 1975 00014
BT Budget Process
NT Budget Estimation
Budget Proposing
RT Balanced Budget
Budget Reviewing
Debt Ceiling Policy
Defense Authorization
Military Budget

BUDGET PLANNER
S-32-0132 1975 00005
BT Fiscal Planner
RT Balanced Budget
Budget
Budget Auditing
Fiscal Policy
Performance Budget
Social Planner

BUDGET POLICY
S-26-0094 1975 00021
BT Fiscal Policy
RT Bank Reserve
Budget
Budget Proposing
Budget Reviewing
Capital Formation Policy
Capital Investment Policy
Currency Revaluation Policy
Debt Ceiling Policy
Executive Budget
Executive Jurisdiction
Expenditure Policy
Fiscal Theory
Income Policy
Incremental Budget
Inflation Policy
Military Budget
Military Management
Monetary Policy
Monetary Process
Performance Budget
Public Debt Policy
Public Finance Policy
Revenue Policy
Tax Agency
Zero Based Budget

BUDGET PROCESS
S-31-0363 1979 00000
UF Budgetary Process
BT Economic Process
NT Budget Cutting
Budget Formulation
Budget Reviewing
RT Budget
Budget Proposing
Planning Policy

BUDGET PROPOSING
S-31-0367 1975 00002
BT Budget Formulation
RT Budget
Budget Estimation
Budget Policy
Budget Process
Budget Reviewing
Budget Surplus
Performance Budget
State Assembly

BUDGET RECORD
S-18-0012 1975 00007
BT Financial Record
RT Budget
Budget Reviewing
Budget Surplus
Capital Surplus
Expenditure Record
Income Record
Military Budget
Revenue Record

BUDGET REVIEWING
S-31-0368 1975 00009
BT Budget Process
NT Budget Auditing
RT Budget
Budget Cutting
Budget Estimation
Budget Formulation
Budget Policy
Budget Proposing
Budget Record
Budget Surplus
Capital Surplus
Performance Budget
Regulation Process
Regulatory Commission
Tax Agency

BUDGET SURPLUS
S-06-0251 1975 00001
BT Budget Discrepancy
RT Budget Deficit
Budget Proposing
Budget Record
Budget Reviewing
Public Debt Policy

BUDGETARY PROCESS
1975-1979 00041
USE Budget Process

BUFFER STATE
USE Neutralism

BUFFER ZONE THEORY
S-38-0348 1975 00001
BT Geopolitical Theory
RT Frontier Theory
Global War Policy
Heartland Theory
International Power Theory

BUILDING CODE
S-21-0051 1975 00002
BT Zoning Law
RT Housing Code
Housing Industry
Zoning Law

BUILDING DESIGN
USE Architectural Studies

BUILDING PROCESS
S-31-0046 1975 00003
BT Change Process
NT Community Building
Institution Building
Nation Building
RT Development Potential
Development Process
Housing Industry
Land Estate System

BUILDING SUPPLIES INDUSTRY
S-17-0028 1979 00000
BT Construction Industry
RT Housing Industry
Housing Policy
Lumber Industry
Production Industry
Ship Building Industry

BURDEN OF PROOF
S-15-0052 1975 00000
BT Right To Trial
RT Criminal Law System
Criminal Lawyer
Cross Examination
Defendants Rights
Evidence Admissibility
Ex Post Facto Protection
Fair Trial
Grand Jury Indictment
Habeas Corpus
Justice System
Right To Appeal
Right To Counsel
Right To Due Process
Right To Jury Trial
Right To Speedy Trial
Self Incrimination

BUREAU CHIEF
S-36-0004 1975 00000
BT Administrative Officer
RT Dean
Department Head
Executive Director

BUREAUCRACY
S-19-0070 1975 00033
BT Institutions
NT Economic Bureaucracy
Merit Bureaucracy
Public Bureaucracy

Religious Bureaucracy
RT Administrative Theory
Bureaucratic Characteristics
Bureaucratic Elite
Bureaucratic Theory
Interstate Authorities
Management
Organizations
Weberian Theory

BUREAUCRATIC AUTONOMY
S-06-0452 1975 00011
BT Bureaucratic Structural Characteristics
RT Bureaucratic Goal
Bureaucratic Hierarchy
Bureaucratic Theory
Government Bureaucracy

BUREAUCRATIC BEHAVIOR
S-05-0003 1975 00043
BT Administrative Behavior
RT Administrative Politics
Bureaucratic Leadership
Bureaucratic Politics
Bureaucratic Theory
Executive Behavior
Iron Law Of Oligarchy
Organization Behavior
Organization Rationality
Weberian Analysis

BUREAUCRATIC CAPABILITY CHARACTERISTICS
S-06-0445 1975 00010
BT Bureaucratic Characteristics
NT Bureaucratic Efficiency
RT Administrative Accountability
Administrative Discretion
Bureaucratic Elite
Bureaucratic Ethos
Bureaucratic Inertia
Bureaucratic Normative Characteristics
Bureaucratic Parallelism
Bureaucratic Rationality
Bureaucratic Rule
Bureaucratic Structural Characteristics
Bureaucratic Theory
Chief Executive Accountability
Executive Accountability

BUREAUCRATIC CHARACTERISTICS
S-06-0444 1975 00031
BT Administrative Characteristics
NT Bureaucratic Capability Characteristics
Bureaucratic Normative Characteristics
Bureaucratic Structural Characteristics
RT Administrative Capability Characteristics
Bureaucracy
Bureaucratic Elite
Bureaucratic Theory
Government Bureaucracy
Group Dynamics
Group Solidarity
Institutionalization
Organization Capability Characteristics
Organization Characteristics
Public Bureaucracy
Religious Bureaucracy

BUREAUCRATIC CONSERVATISM
S-38-0195 1979 00000
BT Conservatism
RT Bureaucratic Inertia
Bureaucratic Normative Characteristics
Bureaucratic Politics
Bureaucratic Society
Burkean Conservatism
Christian Conservatism
Neoconservatism
Status Quo Conservatism

BUREAUCRATIC EFFICIENCY
S-06-0446 1975 00010
BT Bureaucratic Capability Characteristics
RT Administrative Effectiveness
Administrative Efficiency
Bureaucratic Theory

BUREAUCRATIC ELITE
S-14-0016 1975 00019
BT Managerial Elite
RT Bureaucracy
Bureaucratic Capability Characteristics
Bureaucratic Characteristics
Bureaucratic Ethos
Bureaucratic Hierarchy
Bureaucratic Politics
Corporate Bureaucracy
Financial Elite
Iron Law Of Oligarchy
Military Elite
Public Bureaucracy

BUREAUCRATIC ETHOS
S-06-0448 1975 00005
BT Bureaucratic Normative Characteristics
RT Bureaucratic Capability Characteristics
Bureaucratic Elite
Bureaucratic Rationality
Bureaucratic Rule
Bureaucratic Theory

BUREAUCRATIC GOAL
S-06-0453 1975 00003
BT Bureaucratic Structural Characteristics
RT Administrative Normative Characteristics
Bureaucratic Autonomy
Bureaucratic Hierarchy

BUREAUCRATIC HIERARCHY
S-06-0454 1975 00005
BT Bureaucratic Structural Characteristics
NT Line Staff
RT Administrative Politics
Bureaucratic Autonomy
Bureaucratic Elite
Bureaucratic Goal
Bureaucratic Inertia
Bureaucratic Leadership
Bureaucratic Parallelism
Bureaucratic Rigidity
Governing Elite
Line Staff
Specialization Process

BUREAUCRATIC INERTIA
S-06-0456 1975 00007
BT Bureaucratic Structural Characteristics
RT Bureaucratic Capability Characteristics
Bureaucratic Conservatism
Bureaucratic Hierarchy
Bureaucratic Parallelism
Bureaucratic Rigidity

BUREAUCRATIC LEADERSHIP
S-22-0005 1975 00012
BT Administrative Leadership
RT Administrative Behavior
Administrative Leadership
Bureaucratic Behavior
Bureaucratic Hierarchy
Bureaucratic Politics
Bureaucratic Theory
Collective Leadership
Collegial Leadership
Ecclesiastical Leadership
National Leadership
Political Leadership
Political Party Leadership
Rational Legal Leadership
Totalitarian Leadership
Traditional Leadership

BUREAUCRATIC NORMATIVE CHARACTERISTICS
S-06-0447 1975 00009
BT Bureaucratic Characteristics
NT Bureaucratic Ethos
Bureaucratic Rationality
Bureaucratic Rule
RT Administrative Normative Characteristics
Administrative Science
Administrative Theory
Bureaucratic Capability Characteristics
Bureaucratic Conservatism
Bureaucratic Structural Characteristics
Executive Accountability

BUREAUCRATIC PARALLELISM
S-06-0457 1975 00000
SN Political arrangement in which two or more organizational units are charged with the same area of policy responsibility.
BT Bureaucratic Structural Characteristics
RT Administrative Theory
Bureaucratic Capability Characteristics
Bureaucratic Hierarchy
Bureaucratic Inertia
Bureaucratic Rigidity

BUREAUCRATIC POLITICS
S-29-0003 1975 00057
BT Administrative Politics
RT Administrative Development Theory
Administrative Leadership
Administrative Management
Bureaucratic Behavior
Bureaucratic Conservatism

Bureaucratic Elite
Bureaucratic Leadership
Bureaucratic Society
Interagency Rivalry
Legal Rational Authority
Technocracy
Weberian Theory

BUREAUCRATIC RATIONALITY
S-06-0449 1975 00003
BT Bureaucratic Normative Characteristics
RT Administrative Development Theory
Administrative Planning
Bureaucratic Capability Characteristics
Bureaucratic Ethos
Bureaucratic Rule

BUREAUCRATIC RIGIDITY
S-06-0458 1975 00010
BT Bureaucratic Structural Characteristics
RT Administrative Theory
Bureaucratic Hierarchy
Bureaucratic Inertia
Bureaucratic Parallelism

BUREAUCRATIC RULE
S-06-0450 1975 00004
BT Bureaucratic Normative Characteristics
RT Administrative Leadership
Administrative Theory
Administrative Tribunal
Bureaucratic Capability Characteristics
Bureaucratic Ethos
Bureaucratic Rationality
Bureaucratic Structural Characteristics

BUREAUCRATIC SOCIALIZATION
S-34-0033 1975 00004
BT Institutional Socialization
RT Administrative Accountability
Administrative Science
Administrative Theory
Bureaucratic Theory
Legislative Socialization

BUREAUCRATIC SOCIETY
S-35-0011 1975 00008
BT Society Type Base
RT Administrative Theory
Bureaucratic Conservatism
Bureaucratic Politics
Governing Elite
Meritocracy
Secular Society

BUREAUCRATIC STRUCTURAL CHARACTERISTICS
S-06-0451 1975 00015
BT Bureaucratic Characteristics
NT Bureaucratic Autonomy
Bureaucratic Goal
Bureaucratic Hierarchy
Bureaucratic Inertia
Bureaucratic Parallelism
Bureaucratic Rigidity
RT Administrative Accountability
Administrative Management
Administrative Policy Making
Bureaucratic Capability Characteristics
Bureaucratic Normative Characteristics
Bureaucratic Rule
Organization Cleavage Characteristics

BUREAUCRATIC THEORY
S-38-0040 1975 00021
BT Organization Theory
NT Iron Law Of Oligarchy
RT Administrative Behavior
Administrative Characteristics
Administrative Leadership
Administrative Theory
Bureaucracy
Bureaucratic Autonomy
Bureaucratic Behavior
Bureaucratic Capability Characteristics
Bureaucratic Characteristics
Bureaucratic Efficiency
Bureaucratic Ethos
Bureaucratic Leadership
Bureaucratic Socialization
Government Bureaucracy
Group Hierarchy
Hierarchical Authority
Institutions
Interagency Rivalry
International Government Bureaucracy
Iron Law Of Oligarchy
Local Government Bureaucracy
Modernizing Society
National Government Bureaucracy
Organization Behavior
Organization Effectiveness
Organization Efficiency
Organization Flexibility
Organization Hierarchy
Organization Rationality
Policy Incrementalism
Policy Output Scale
Political System Structural Characteristics
Social Organization Theory
Specialization Process
Weberian Analysis
Weberian Theory

BURGLER
USE Criminal

BURKEAN ANALYSIS
S-38-0388 1975 00002
BT Modern Political Thought
RT Burkean Conservatism
Common Wealth Theory
Representation

BURKEAN CONSERVATISM
S-38-0196 1975 00001
SN Analysis and beliefs associated with Edmund Burke's notions of tradition, history, organic class society and established religion as the pillars of stability in a society.
BT Conservatism
RT American Conservatism
Bureaucratic Conservatism
Burkean Analysis
Christian Conservatism
Classical Corporate Freedom Theory
Conservative Political Party
Conservative Regime
Equilibrium Theory
Neoconservatism
Objectivist Political Thought
Organic State Theory
Reactionary Conservatism
Status Quo Conservatism

BUSINESS
S-19-0159 1975 00015
BT Economic Institution
NT Big Business
Ghetto Business
Small Business
RT Blue Collar Worker
Business Agency
Business Contract
Business Management
Commerce
Commercial Occupation
Corporation
Enterprise
Factory
Farm Industry
Fiscal Institution
Labor Mediation
Labor Mediation Policy
Market
Monetary Institution
Prosperity
World Bank

BUSINESS ADMINISTRATION EDUCATION
S-13-0038 1979 00000
BT Professional Education
RT Business Agency
Business Management
Business Policy
Business Studies
Businessman
Management Training Program
Professional Occupational Role
Professional Socialization

BUSINESS ADMINSTRATION
USE Business Studies

BUSINESS AGENCY
S-19-0005 1975 00001
BT Agencies
NT Business Regulation Agency
RT Agricultural Agency
Banking Agency
Business
Business Administration Education
Business Contract
Business Economics
Business Studies
Commercial Sector
Consumer Agency
Consumption
Consumption Pattern
Fiscal Agency
International Economic Organization
International Trade Organization
Manufacturing Industry
Small Business
Small Businessman

BUSINESS CONTRACT
S-02-0038 1979 00000
BT Contract Type
RT Business
Business Agency
Business Income
Business Management
Business Policy
Business Studies
Contract Law
Corporation
Labor Management Contract

BUSINESS CREDIT POLICY
S-26-0012 1979 00000
BT Business Policy
RT Business Regulation Policy
Business Studies
Business Subsidization Policy
Consumer Credit Policy
Credit Policy
Food Policy

BUSINESS ECONOMICS
S-01-0060 1979 00000
BT Economics Discipline
RT Architectural Studies
Business Agency
Business Management
Business Policy
Business Studies
Consumer Economics
Econometrics
Industrial Economics
Institutional Economics
Labor Economics
Macroeconomics
Multinational Corporation
Regional Economics
Social Economics

BUSINESS ELITE
S-14-0005 1975 00011
BT Economic Elite
NT Commercial Elite
Corporate Elite
Financial Elite
RT Businessman
Commercial Elite
Decision Making Elite
Governing Elite
Management Characteristics
Managerial Elite
Political Elite
Private Monopoly

BUSINESS INCOME
S-06-0325 1975 00004
BT Income
NT Corporate Income
RT Business Contract
Farm Income
Foreign Income
Internal Market
Personal Income
Private Industry
Private Investment
Private Ownership
Profit Income
Unearned Income

BUSINESS LEADER
S-32-0051 1975 00003
BT Economic Leader
RT Artisan
Community Leader
Economic Decision Maker
Private Industry

BUSINESS MANAGEMENT
S-23-0010 1975 00030
UF Personnel Reocrds
Records Management
BT Economic Management
NT Corporate Management
RT Administrative Management
Business
Business Administration Education
Business Contract
Business Economics
Business Policy
Central Economic Management
Development Management
Fiscal Management
Industrial Management
International Economic Boycott
International Economic Management
Labor Management Relations Policy
Labor Mediation
Labor Mediation Policy
Monetary Management
National Economic Management
Personnel Management
Subnational Economic Management

BUSINESS POLICY
S-26-0011 1975 00017
BT Policy
NT Business Credit Policy
Business Regulation Policy
Business Subsidization Policy
RT Business Administration Education
Business Contract
Business Economics
Business Management
Business Price Support Policy
Business Studies
Businessman
Capitalist Economy
Consumer Industrial Policy
Consumer Policy
Consumer Protection Policy
Discount Rate
Economic Policy
Food Policy
Heavy Industrial Policy
Industrial Policy
Industry
International Economic Boycott
Labor Subsidization Policy
Light Industrial Policy
Market Freedom
Marketplace
Mixed Enterprise
Private Industry

BUSINESS PRICE SUPPORT POLICY
S-26-0129 1975 00000
BT Price Support Policy
RT Agricultural Price Support Policy
Business Policy
Government Economic Management
Private Capital
Private Industry
Private Investment

BUSINESS REGULATION AGENCY
S-19-0006 1975 00011
BT Business Agency
NT Antitrust Agency
RT Consumer Agency
Economic Control Agency
Economic Council
Environmental Agency
Fiscal Agency
Labor Management Relations Policy
Labor Mediation Policy
Labor Relations Agency
Planning Commission
Production Agency
Regulation Process
Regulatory Commission
Task Force

BUSINESS REGULATION POLICY
S-26-0013 1975 00052
BT Business Policy
NT Antitrust Policy
RT Air Fare Regulation Policy
Business Credit Policy
Business Subsidization Policy
Consumer Credit Policy
Government Economic Planning
Industrial Policy

BUSINESS STUDIES
S-01-0052 1979 00000
UF Business Adminstration
BT Academic Areas
NT Management Training Program
RT Big Business
Business Administration Education
Business Agency
Business Contract
Business Credit Policy
Business Economics
Business Policy
Businessman
Commerce
Commercial Occupation
Commercial Sector
Consumer Economics
Corporate Elite
Corporation
International Corporation
Management Characteristics
Market Research
Multinational Corporation
Small Business
World Commerce

BUSINESS SUBSIDIZATION POLICY
S-26-0015 1975 00006
BT Business Policy
RT Business Credit Policy
Business Regulation Policy
Government Economic Planning
Industrial Policy

BUSINESSMAN
S-32-0072 1975 00010
BT Commercial Occupation
NT Entrepreneur
Small Businessman
RT Business Administration Education
Business Elite
Business Policy

Business Studies
Corporate Elite
Financier
Speculator

BY ELECTION
S-29-0089 1975 00002
SN Special election held to fill a vacated office.
BT Special Election
RT Electoral Coalition
Electoral Data
Electoral Law
National Legislature
Political Party Convention

BYZANTINE CIVILIZATION
S-11-0005 1979 00000
BT Civilization
RT Ancient Civilization
Ancient Times
Eastern Civilization
Greek Civilization
Historical Analysis
History Discipline
Homogeneous Culture
Islamic Civilization
Political Culture
Roman Civilization

CABINET
S-19-0111 1975 00003
BT National Government Council
NT Cabinet Committee
Ministerial Committee
Shadow Cabinet
RT Cabinet Government
Cabinet Secretary
Council Of Ministers
Executive Government Institution
Minister
Ministerial Committee
Ministerial Responsibility
Parliamentary Government
Presidential Advisory Council
Privy Council

CABINET COMMITTEE
S-19-0112 1975 00000
BT Cabinet
RT Cabinet Member
Cabinet Secretary
Cabinet Undersecretary
Ministerial Committee
Parliamentary Government
Privy Council
Shadow Cabinet

CABINET COMMITTEE TYPE
1975-1979 00000

CABINET GOVERNMENT
S-16-0006 1975 00001
BT Government Type
RT Cabinet
Cabinet Instability
Cabinet Member
Cabinet Reorganization
Cabinet Secretary
Coalition Process
Council Of Ministers
Democratic Government
Minister
Ministerial Committee
Ministerial Responsibility
Parliamentary Democracy
Parliamentary Government

CABINET INSTABILITY
S-06-0694 1975 00002
BT Regime Instability
NT Ministerial Instability
RT Cabinet Government
Cabinet Reorganization
Government Dissolution Process
Government Instability
No Confidence Motion

CABINET MEMBER
S-36-0041 1975 00004
BT Government Official
NT International Commission Member
International Council Member
Minister
Privy Councilor
RT Cabinet Committee
Cabinet Government
Cabinet Secretary
Ministerial Responsibility
National Political Party Executive Member
Parliamentary Government

CABINET REORGANIZATION
S-31-0091 1975 00003
BT Executive Reorganization
RT Cabinet Government
Cabinet Instability
Congressional Reform
Government Dissolution Process
State House Of Representatives

CABINET SECRETARY
S-36-0045 1975 00004
BT Minister
NT Cabinet Undersecretary
RT Cabinet
Cabinet Committee
Cabinet Government
Cabinet Member
Privy Councilor

CABINET UNDERSECRETARY
S-36-0046 1975 00000
BT Cabinet Secretary
RT Cabinet Committee
Privy Councilor

CABLE TELEVISION
S-17-0012 1979 00000
BT Television Industry
RT Commercial Broadcasting Industry
Commercial Television
Public Broadcasting Industry
Public Television
State Controlled Television
Telecommunications Industry
Telephone Industry
Television Policy

CADRE PARTY
1975-1979 00000

CADRE POLITICAL PARTY
S-28-0059 1979 00000
SN Political party characterized by small active leadership group not concerned with mass membership base.
BT Structure Specific Political Party Type
RT Elite Political Party
Radical Political Party

CALCULATOR
USE Computer Equipment

CALCULUS
S-24-0024 1975 00001
BT Mathematical Analysis
RT Geometry
Linear Programming
Mathematics Discipline
Trigonometry

CALVINISM
S-38-0567 1975 00005
BT Protestantism
RT Anglicanism
Hussite Thought
Lutheranism
Protestant Sectarianism
Religious Identity
Religious Movement

CAMERA
1975-1979 00000

CAMERALISM
USE Mercantile Capitalism

CAMPAIGN ADVERTISING
1975-1979 00003

CAMPAIGN CONTRIBUTION
1975-1979 00007

CAMPAIGN CONTRIBUTOR
S-32-0170 1975 00006
BT Political Party Supporter
RT Patronage Worker
Political Party Campaign
Political Party Financial Record
Political Party Loyalist
Strong Political Party Identifier

CAMPAIGN FINANCE DISCLOSURE
1975-1979 00003
USE Election Campaign Financial Disclosure

CAMPAIGN FINANCING
1975-1979 00021

CAMPAIGN MANAGER
S-32-0150 1975 00001
BT Political Party Leader
RT Formal Political Party Leader
Local Political Elite
Political Party Advertising
Political Party Cadre
Political Party Campaign
Political Party Chief
Political Party Professional
Precinct Captain
Ward Chairperson

CAMPAIGN ORGANIZATION
1975-1979 00001

CAMPAIGN STRATEGY
1975-1979 00009

CAMPAIGN TACTICS
1975-1979 00001

CAMPAIGN WORKER
S-32-0175 1975 00004
BT Political Party Worker
RT Political Party Cadre
Political Party Loyalist
Strong Political Party Identifier

CAMPESINO
USE Farmer

CANAL
USE Water Transportation Industry

CANDIDATE IMAGE VOTER
S-32-0299 1975 00013
SN One whose vote is determined by perception of the qualities of an individual candidate.
BT Candidate Voter
RT Candidate Preference Voter
Voting
Voting Behavior

CANDIDATE ORIENTATION
S-32-0335 1975 00010
SN Electoral stance emphasizing characteristics of individual candidates.
BT Voter Orientation
RT Electoral Strategy
Issue Orientation
Political Party Orientation
Voting Behavior

CANDIDATE PREFERENCE VOTER
S-32-0300 1975 00022
BT Candidate Voter
RT Candidate Image Voter
Dark Horse Candidate
Voting
Voting Behavior

CANDIDATE SELECTION
S-31-0732 1975 00006
BT Selection Process
RT Delegate Selection
Electoral Opposition
Endorsement
Legislative Nominating Process
Machine Candidate
Nominating Process
Political Party Nominating Committee
Slate Making
Token Representation
Write In Voting

CANDIDATE VOTER
S-32-0298 1975 00009
BT Voter
NT Candidate Image Voter
Candidate Preference Voter
RT Dark Horse Candidate
Issue Voter
Lower House Member
Political Party Voter
Voting Behavior

CANON LAW
S-21-0082 1975 00000
BT Religious Law
RT Catholicism
Church Law
Church State Policy
Ecclesiastical Leadership
Papal Sovereignty
Thomism

CANONICAL CORRELATION ANALYSIS
S-24-0041 1975 00002
BT Multivariate Analysis
RT Analysis Of Variance
Automatic Interaction Detection
Cluster Analysis
Covariance Analysis
Factor Analysis
Multiple Regression Analysis

CANVASSING
S-29-0023 1975 00001
BT Election Campaign
RT Congressional Election Campaign
Election Campaign Tactics
Telephone Interview
Telephone Questionnaire

CAPITAL
S-06-0259 1975 00015
BT Economic Characteristics
NT Accumulated Capital
Assets
Capital Surplus
Foreign Capital
Investment Capital
Private Capital
Public Capital
RT Capital Investment Economy
Capitalist Economy
Fixed Assets
Money
National Currency
Private Investment

CAPITAL BUDGET
S-06-0252 1975 00000
BT Budget
NT Executive Budget
Incremental Budget
Military Budget
Performance Budget
Program Budget
Zero Based Budget
RT Budget Estimation
Capital Investment Economy
Performance Budget
Program Budget

CAPITAL FLOW
S-31-0391 1979 00000
UF Cash Flow
BT Investment
RT Capital Formation
Capital Formation Policy
Capital Growth Rate
Capital Surplus
Money
National Currency
Private Investment
Public Financing
Saving
Spending
World Bank

CAPITAL FORMATION
S-31-0392 1979 00000
UF Capitalization
BT Investment
RT Assets
Capital Flow
Capital Formation Policy
Capital Growth Rate
Capital Investment Policy
Capital Surplus
Private Investment
Public Financing
Public Investment
Public Saving
Saving
Spending

CAPITAL FORMATION POLICY
S-26-0095 1979 00000
BT Fiscal Policy
RT Antiinflation Policy
Budget Policy
Capital Flow
Capital Formation
Capital Investment Policy
Currency Revaluation Policy
Deflation Policy
Income Policy
Investment Policy

CAPITAL GROWTH RATE
S-06-0155 1975 00009
BT Economic Growth Rate
RT Capital Flow
Capital Formation
Capitalism
Economic Indicator
Monetary Economic Theory
Productivity Rate

CAPITAL INVESTMENT ECONOMY
S-12-0012 1979 00000
BT Economy Type
RT Balanced Economy
Capital
Capital Budget
Capital Investment Policy
Consumer Economy
Developed Economy
Dual Economy
Grants Economy
Industrial Economy
Investment
Investment Capital
Investment Policy
Market Economy
Mixed Economy
Modernizing Economy
Planned Economy
Private Investment
Self Sufficient Economy
Welfare Economy

CAPITAL INVESTMENT POLICY
S-26-0096 1979 00000
BT Fiscal Policy
RT Antiinflation Policy
Budget Policy
Capital Formation
Capital Formation Policy
Capital Investment Economy
Deflation Policy
Expenditure Policy
Income Policy
Investment
Investment Capital
Investment Policy

CAPITAL PUNISHMENT
S-31-0570 1975 00006
BT Criminal Punishment
RT Criminal Deterrence
Criminal Procedure Law
Criminology
Dean
Death Penalty Law
Life Sentence
Murder
Murderer
Penal Reform

Right Against Cruel And Unusual Punishment

CAPITAL SURPLUS
S-06-0263 1975 00007
BT Capital
RT Accumulated Capital
Assets
Budget Record
Budget Reviewing
Capital Flow
Capital Formation
Investment Capital
Private Capital
Public Capital

CAPITALISM
S-37-0012 1975 00029
BT Economic System
NT Black Capitalism
Bourgeois Capitalism
Industrial Capitalism
Mature Capitalism
Mercantile Capitalism
Monopoly Capitalism
State Capitalism
Warfare Capitalism
Welfare Capitalism
RT Big Business
Bourgeoisie
Capital Growth Rate
Capitalism Theory
Capitalist Class
Capitalist Economy
Capitalist Society
Economic Freedom
Free Enterprise System
Imperialist Economy
Marxist Capitalism Theory
Marxist Economic Determinism
Marxist Economic Theory
Marxist Immiseration Theory
Mercantile Economic System
Private Capital
Private Industry
Private Investment
Private Monopoly
Private Ownership
Profit Income
Protestant Ethic
Unearned Income

CAPITALISM THEORY
S-38-0107 1975 00022
BT Economic Theory
RT Capitalism
Classical Economic Theory
Consumerism
Economic Freedom
Free Enterprise System
Keynesian Economic Theory
Marxist Economic Theory
Mature Capitalism
Mercantile Economic Theory
Private Industry
Private Investment
Private Ownership
Profit Income

CAPITALIST CLASS
S-06-0763 1975 00001
BT Class Stratification Division
RT Capitalism
Capitalist Economy
Capitalist Society
Class Analysis
Entrepreneur
Entrepreneurship
Governing Elite
Private Ownership

CAPITALIST ECONOMY
S-12-0027 1975 00030
BT Market Economy
RT Business Policy
Capital
Capitalism
Capitalist Class
Commodity Market
Economic Cycle
Economic Freedom
Labor Surplus
Private Ownership
Profit Income
Socialist Market Economy
Unearned Income

CAPITALIST EMPIRE
S-16-0049 1975 00000
BT Empire
RT Colonial Empire
Communist Empire
Imperialist Economy
World Empire

CAPITALIST IMPERIALISM
S-37-0070 1975 00015
BT Economic Imperialism
RT Colony
Communist Imperialism
Economic Exploitation
Imperialist Economy
Leninist Imperialism Theory
Neoimperialism
Western Imperialism
Yankee Imperialism

CAPITALIST SOCIETY
S-35-0012 1975 00025
BT Society Type Base
RT Affluent Society
Bourgeois Society
Capitalism
Capitalist Class
Economic Freedom
Feudal Society
Industrial Society
Private Ownership

CAPITALIZATION
USE Capital Formation

CAREER ANALYSIS
S-09-0006 1979 00000
BT Biographical Analysis
RT Aggregate Data Analysis
Autobiography
Elite Analysis
Group Analysis
Historical Analysis
Leadership Analysis
Occupation Characteristics
Political Succession
Social Mobility
Structural Functional Analysis
Vertical Mobility

CARETAKER GOVERNMENT
S-16-0062 1979 00000
BT Interim Government
RT Colony
Empire
International Trusteeship
Mandate Territory
Military Coup
Protective Alliance
Protectorate

CARIBBEAN AREA STUDIES
S-01-0032 1975 00090
BT American Area Studies
RT Central American Area Studies
Comparative Analysis
Comparative Political Studies
Comparative Sociology
Cultural Anthropology
Latin American Area Studies
North American Area Studies

CARTEL
S-19-0164 1975 00025
BT Corporation
RT Antitrust Law
Antitrust Policy
Economic Conglomerate
Holding Company
International Corporation
Multinational Corporation
Private Monopoly
Public Corporation
Quasipublic Corporation

CARTESIAN ANALYSIS
S-38-0518 1975 00003
BT Renaissance Political Thought
RT Baconian Analysis
Philosophical Concept

CASE LAW
S-21-0021 1975 00000
BT Common Law
RT Adjudication
Civil Law System
Customary Law
Judge Made Law
Legal Studies

CASE STUDY
S-24-0400 1975 00100
BT Study Scope
NT Deviant Case Analysis
Ideal Case Analysis
RT Configurative Analysis
Ideographic Research
Participant Observation
Propositional Inventory
Quasiexperiment

CASH FLOW
USE Capital Flow

CASTE
USE Caste Society

CASTE DISSOLUTION
S-31-0772 1975 00000
BT Social Stratification Dissolution
RT Caste Maintenance
Caste Society
Class Dissolution
Ethnic Assimilation
Status Dissolution

Womens Liberation

CASTE FORMATION
S-31-0776 1975 00000
BT Social Stratification Formation
RT Caste Maintenance
Caste Society
Caste Solidarity
Class Formation
Ostracism
Status Formation

CASTE MAINTENANCE
S-31-0780 1975 00002
BT Social Stratification Maintenance
RT Caste Dissolution
Caste Formation
Caste Social System
Caste Society
Caste Solidarity
Class Maintenance
Ostracism
Status Maintenance

CASTE SOCIAL SYSTEM
S-37-0141 1975 00008
BT Social Stratification System
RT Caste Maintenance
Caste Society
Class Social System
Status Social System

CASTE SOCIETY
S-35-0013 1975 00007
UF Caste
BT Society Type Base
RT Aristocratic Class
Caste Dissolution
Caste Formation
Caste Maintenance
Caste Social System
Caste Solidarity
Caste Stratification Division
Clan Society
Class Stratification Division
Lower Caste
Peasant Organization
Religious Community
Segregated Community
Social Stratification System
Traditional Social Elite
Traditional Society
Tribal Society
Untouchables
Upper Caste

CASTE SOLIDARITY
S-06-0034 1975 00001
BT Group Solidarity
RT Brotherhood
Caste Formation
Caste Maintenance
Caste Society
Class Solidarity
Communal Solidarity
Ethnic Group Cohesion
Group Cohesion
Social Solidarity

CASTE STRATIFICATION DIVISION
S-06-0756 1975 00004
BT Social Stratification Division
NT Lower Caste
Middle Caste
Upper Caste
RT Caste Society
Class Stratification Division
Horizontal Stratification Division
Status Stratification Division
Vertical Stratification Division

CASTROISM
S-38-0316 1975 00006
BT Marxism
RT Bolshevism
Communism
Leninism
Liberation Movement
Maoism
Maoist
Maoist Political Party
Maoist Revolutionary
Marxism Leninism
Polycentrism
Stalinism
Stalinist
Titoism
Trotskyism
Yankee Imperialism

CASUISTRY
USE Moral Reasoning

CATASTROPHE ANALYSIS
S-09-0007 1979 00000
BT Contemporary Analytic Modes
RT Crisis
Crisis Management
Ecology Discipline
Ecology Movement
Epidemic
Natural Resource Management

CATASTROPHE INSURANCE
S-26-0300 1979 00000
BT Insurance
RT Accident Insurance
Catastrophe Insurance
Compulsory Insurance
Disability Insurance
Fire Insurance
Life Insurance
Malpractice Insurance
Motor Vehicle Industry
National Health Insurance
Natural Catastrophe
No Fault Insurance
Unemployment Insurance Policy

CATEGORICAL IMPERATIVE
USE Moral Authority

CATEGORY
USE Typology

CATHARSIS
S-31-0308 1979 00000
UF Personal Purge
BT Purge
RT Identity Analysis
Political Indoctrination
Political Purge
Political Self Criticism
Psychological Theory

CATHOLICISM
S-38-0562 1975 00013
BT Christian Thought
NT Eastern Orthodox Thought
Roman Catholicism
RT Augustinian Analysis
Canon Law
Papal Sovereignty
Protestantism
Religious Identity
Religious Movement
Scholastic Method
Scholasticism
Thomism
Trentine Doctrine

CAUCUS CHAIRPERSON
S-36-0265 1975 00000
BT Chairperson
RT Caucus Member
Caucus Staff Personnel

CAUCUS MEMBER
S-36-0262 1975 00000
BT Suborganization Official
NT Caucus Staff Personnel
RT Caucus Chairperson
Caucus Staff Personnel
Committee Member

CAUCUS STAFF PERSONNEL
S-36-0263 1975 00000
BT Caucus Member
RT Caucus Chairperson
Caucus Member

CAUDILLISM
S-38-0189 1975 00000
SN Political arrangement frequent in Latin America characterized by strong personalized leader.
BT Ideologies
RT Agrarianism
Corporatism
Militarism

CAUSAL ANALYSIS
S-24-0003 1979 00000
BT Analysis Methodology
RT Deductive Method
Economic Forecasting
Forecasting Methodology
Inductive Method
Mathematical Analysis
Political Forecasting
Predictive Research
Social Forecasting

CEASE DESIST ORDER
S-31-0479 1975 00000
BT Court Action
RT Acquittal
Consent Judgment
Conviction
Injunction
Obiter Dicta
Subpoena
Warrant
Writ Of Mandamus

CEASE FIRE POLICY
S-26-0327 1975 00001
BT Military Policy
RT Armistice Policy
Deescalation
Deescalation Policy
Demilitarization Policy
Demobilization Policy
Peace
War
War Policy

CELEBRITY
USE Social Elite

CELL LEADER
S-32-0151 1975 00000
BT Political Party Leader
RT Local Political Elite
Political Boss
Political Party Cadre
Political Party Professional

CENSORSHIP AGENCY
S-19-0008 1975 00000
UF Film Censorship Agency
Press Censorship Agency
Private Censorship Agency
Public Censorship Agency
BT Agencies
NT Government Censorship Agency
RT Censorship Process
Government Media Regulation Policy
Information Manipulation
Intelligence Agency
Music Censorship

CENSORSHIP PROCESS
S-31-0264 1975 00005
BT Control Process
NT Graphic Arts Censorship
Political Censorship
Published Media Censorship
Religious Censorship
Report Censorship
Unpublished Media Censorship
RT Academic Freedom
Blacklisting Policy
Censorship Agency
Government Media Regulation Policy
Repression Process

CENSURE MOTION
S-31-0592 1975 00000
BT Legislative Voting
NT No Confidence Motion
RT Bipartisan Voting
Cloture
Discharge Petition
Government Dissolution Process

CENSUS RECORD
S-18-0021 1975 00017
BT Administrative Record
RT Aggregate Data Statistics
Census Tract
Electoral History
Immigration Pattern
Population Composition
Population Distribution
Social Statistics

CENSUS TRACT
S-24-0360 1975 00007
BT City Unit
RT Census Record
City Unit
Demographic Characteristics
Demographic Indicator
Demographic Profile
Neighborhood
Street Block

CENTER PARTY
1975-1979 00000

CENTER PERIPHERY GOVERNMENT RELATIONS
S-31-0467 1979 00000
BT Intergovernmental Relations
RT Central Economic Planning
Centralized Authority
Centralized Government
City State Relations
Concentrated Power
Decentralized Authority
Decentralized Government
Federal City Relations
Federal State Relations

CENTER POLITICAL PARTY
S-28-0010 1979 00000
BT Ideological Spectrum Political Party Type
RT Centrist
Coalition Politics
Electoral Politics
Middle Class Political Party

CENTRAL AFRICAN AREA STUDIES
S-01-0026 1979 00000
BT African Area Studies
RT Cultural Anthropology
Demographic Studies
East African Area Studies
Geography Discipline
History Discipline
North African Area Studies
Political Science Discipline
South African Area Studies
West African Area Studies

CENTRAL AMERICAN AREA STUDIES
S-01-0033 1975 00088
BT American Area Studies
RT Caribbean Area Studies
Comparative Analysis
Comparative Political Studies
Comparative Sociology
Cultural Anthropology
Latin American Area Studies
North American Area Studies

CENTRAL BANKING SYSTEM
S-37-0035 1975 00003
BT Financial System
RT Federal Reserve System
Gold Reserve
Government Economic Management
International Banking System
Monetary Economic Theory
National Banking System
Subnational Banking System

CENTRAL CITY
S-07-0004 1979 00000
BT City
RT Decentralized City
Demographic Studies
Federated City
Inner City
Metropolitan City
Municipality
Urban Development Theory
Urban Geography
Urban Politics
Urban Sprawl

CENTRAL COMMITTEE
USE Political Party Central Committee

CENTRAL ECONOMIC MANAGEMENT
S-23-0012 1975 00007
BT Economic Management
NT Government Economic Management
RT Administrative Management
Business Management
Development Management
Fiscal Management
Forced Requisitioning
Government Economic Planning
Government Production Enterprise
International Economic Management
National Economic Management
Planned Economy
Subnational Economic Management

CENTRAL ECONOMIC PLANNING
S-31-0642 1975 00007
BT Economic Planning
NT Government Economic Planning
RT Center Periphery Government Relations
Fiscal Planning
Forced Requisitioning
Government Economic Management
National Economic Planning
Planned Economy

CENTRAL TENDENCY MEASURE
S-24-0070 1975 00002
BT Univariate Analysis
RT Dispersion Measure
Parameter Estimation
Population Estimation
Statistical Inference
Unbiased Estimation

CENTRALIZED AUTHORITY
S-04-0012 1975 00027
BT Authority Structure
RT Absolutism
Authority Theory
Center Periphery Government Relations
Centralized Government
Concentrated Power
Constitutional Authority
Formal Authority
Hierarchical Authority
Integrated Authority
One Political Party System
Political Authority
Sovereignty

CENTRALIZED GOVERNMENT
S-16-0007 1975 00027
BT Government Type
RT Absolutism
Absolutist Government
Authoritarian Regime
Autocratic Government
Center Periphery Government Relations
Centralized Authority
Communist Government
Despotism
Dictatorship
One Political Party System
Regulation Process

CENTRALIZED POLITICAL PARTY
S-06-0556 1975 00002
BT Political Party Centralization
RT Decentralized Political Party
Democratic Centralism
Political Party Central Committee
Political Party Organization

CENTRALLY PLANNED ECONOMY
S-12-0035 1979 00000
BT Planned Economy
NT Command Economy
RT Administrative Planning
Autarchic Economy
Collective Farm Economy
Collective Farming
Communist Economic System
Cooperative Farm Economy
Economic Control Agency
Economic Planning
Fascist Economy
Government Economic Planning
Industrial Economy
National Planner
Nationalized Economy
Planned Social Change
Socialist Economy
Socialist Market Economy
Totalitarian Political System

CENTRIST
S-32-0256 1975 00001
BT Spectrum Politicist
RT Center Political Party
Conservative
Leftist
Liberal
Political Neutralist
Political Radical

CERTIORARI
S-31-0480 1975 00000
BT Court Action
RT Consent Judgment
Injunction
Verdict
Warrant
Writ Of Mandamus

CHAIRPERSON
S-36-0264 1975 00000
BT Suborganization Official
NT Caucus Chairperson
Committee Chairperson
RT Committee Member

CHANCELLERY
S-19-0233 1975 00000
BT Executive Government Institution
RT Chancellor
Chief Executive Accountability
Chief Executive Advisor
Chief Executive Staff Personnel
Governorship
Plural Executive
Presidential Advisory Council

CHANCELLOR
S-36-0070 1975 00001
BT National Chief Government Executive
RT Chancellery
Chancellor Candidate
Chancellor Election
Chancellor Election Campaign
Chief Government Executive
Premier
President
Prime Minister

CHANCELLOR CAMPAIGN
1975-1979 00000

CHANCELLOR CANDIDATE
S-32-0230 1975 00000
BT National Chief Executive Candidate
RT Chancellor
Chancellor Election
Chancellor Election Campaign
Presidential Election
Prime Minister Election

CHANCELLOR ELECTION
S-29-0053 1975 00000
BT National Chief Executive Election
RT Chancellor
Chancellor Candidate
Chancellor Election Campaign
Presidential Election
Prime Minister Election

CHANCELLOR ELECTION CAMPAIGN
S-29-0026 1979 00000
BT National Chief Executive Election Campaign
RT Chancellor
Chancellor Candidate
Chancellor Election
Election Campaign Strategy
Election Campaign Tactics

CHANGE CHARACTERISTICS
S-06-0140 1975 00050
BT Characteristics
NT Development Characteristics
RT Change Measurement
Change Process
Economic Characteristics
Health Characteristics
Political System Characteristics
Social System Characteristics
System Characteristics

CHANGE INDICATOR
S-24-0257 1975 00010
BT Indicator
RT Development Index
Economic Indicator
Multiple Indicator
Political Indicator
Political Resource Indicator
Social Indicator

CHANGE MEASUREMENT
S-24-0185 1975 00013
BT Measurement Object
RT Attitude Measurement
Behavioral Measurement
Change Characteristics
Change Process
Development Index
Event Measurement
Group Measurement
Individual Measurement
Perception Measurement

CHANGE PROCESS
S-31-0045 1975 00086
BT Process
NT Building Process
Cultural Change Process
Development Process
Economic Change
Elite Change
Evolutionary Change
Institutional Change
Liberation Process
Political Change
RT Analytic Process
Change Characteristics
Change Measurement
Conflict Process
Control Process
Decision Making Process
Government Dissolution Process
Government Formation Process
Technological Development Theory

CHARACTER ASSASSINATION
S-10-0049 1979 00000
BT Slander
RT Libel
Political Conspiracy
Political Corruption

CHARACTERISTICS
S-06-0001 1975 00000
NT Association Characteristics
Attitude Characteristics
Change Characteristics
Demographic Characteristics
Economic Characteristics
Education Characteristics
Environmental Characteristics
Expertise
Genetic Characteristics
Government Characteristics
Health Characteristics
Identity Characteristics
Jurisdiction Characteristics
Language Characteristics
Legislative Characteristics
Management Characteristics
Military Characteristics
National Characteristics
Occupation Characteristics
Opportunity Characteristics
Personality Characteristics
Political Party Characteristics
System Characteristics
Technology
RT Agencies
Institutions
Process
Social Theory
Theory

CHARGE D'AFFAIRES
S-36-0122 1975 00000
BT Embassy Official
RT Ambassador
Consul General
Diplomat
Embassy Attache

CHARISMA
USE Charismatic Authority

CHARISMATIC AUTHORITY
S-04-0003 1975 00008
UF Charisma
BT Authority Mode
RT Charismatic Leader
Charismatic Leadership
Derived Authority
Legal Rational Authority
Moral Authority
Personalized Leadership

Political Authority
Prophetic Tradition
Religious Authority
Traditional Authority
Weberian Theory

CHARISMATIC LEADER
S-32-0057 1975 00006
BT Social Leader
RT Charismatic Authority
Charismatic Leadership
Cult Of Personality
Opinion Leader
Religious Leader

CHARISMATIC LEADERSHIP
S-22-0008 1975 00008
BT Personalized Leadership
RT Charismatic Authority
Charismatic Leader
Closed Leadership
National Leadership
Political Leadership
Prophetic Tradition
Totalitarian Leadership

CHARITABLE ORGANIZATION
S-03-0051 1979 00000
BT Philanthropic Organization
RT Charity
Education Grant
Government Grant
Grants
Nonprofit Institution
Private Sector
Public Policy Analysis
Tax Exempt Income
Taxation Policy
Welfare Policy

CHARITY
S-06-0504 1979 00000
BT Personality Characteristics
RT Altruism
Assertiveness
Charitable Organization
Courage
Creativity
Curiosity
Egocentrism
Empathy
Femininity
Gregariousness
Honesty
Masculinity
Optimism
Persistence

CHART
S-24-0131 1975 00000
BT Data Presentation Methodology
NT Curve
RT Curve
Diagram
Graph
Graph Analysis
Plot
Table

CHARTER CITY
1975-1979 00000

CHARTISM
S-38-0190 1975 00000
SN Nineteenth century English working class movement which developed People's Charter enunciating their principles.
BT Ideologies
RT Communalism
Egalitarianism
Populism

CHAUVINIST
S-32-0208 1975 00001
BT Political Role
NT Female Chauvinist
Jingoist
Male Chauvinist
National Chauvinist
Sexist
Xenophobe
RT Female Chauvinism
Male Chauvinism
Nationalism

CHECK AND BALANCE THEORY
S-38-0448 1975 00011
BT Constitutional Structural Theory
RT Congressional Executive Relations
Constitution
Equilibrium Theory
Executive Judicial Policy
Executive Legislative Policy
Extended Republic Theory
Informal Authority
Judicial Review
Separation Of Power Theory
State Rights Doctrine

CHEMICAL INDUSTRY
S-17-0002 1975 00005
BT Industry
NT Agrochemical Industry
Rubber Industry
Synthetics Industry
RT Chemical War
Chemical Weapon
Defense Industry
Heavy Industry
Manufacturing Industry
Oil Industry

CHEMICAL WAR
S-08-0089 1979 00000
UF Chemical Warfare
BT War
RT Biological War
Chemical Industry
Chemical Weapon
Nuclear War

CHEMICAL WARFARE
1975-1979 00001
USE Chemical War

CHEMICAL WEAPON
S-33-0022 1975 00004
BT Military Weapon
RT Biological Weapon
Chemical Industry
Chemical War
Defensive Weapon
Missile
Munitions
Nuclear Weapon
Strategic Weapon
Tactical Weapon
Unconventional Weapon
War Atrocity

CHI SQUARE TEST
S-24-0056 1975 00004
BT Statistical Significance Test
RT Binomial Test
F Ratio
Interval Significance Test
Mann Whitney U Test
Nominal Significance Test
Ordinal Significance Test
Wald Wolfowitz Runs Test
Wilcoxian T Test

CHICANO STUDIES
S-01-0085 1975 00053
BT Ethnic Studies
RT American Indian Studies
Area Studies
Black Studies
Comparative Analysis
Cultural Anthropology
Cultural History
Ethnic Community
Human Geography
Puerto Rican Studies

CHIEF EXECUTIVE ACCOUNTABILITY
S-06-0434 1975 00004
BT Executive Accountability
NT Presidential Accountability
RT Bureaucratic Capability Characteristics
Chancellery
Chief Executive Discretion
Chief Executive Prerogative
Chief Government Executive
Ministerial Responsibility
Presidential Advisor
Presidential Advisory Council

CHIEF EXECUTIVE ADVISOR
S-32-0013 1975 00002
BT Administrative Advisor
NT Presidential Advisor
RT Chancellery
Chief Executive Staff Personnel
Election Campaign Advisor
Presidential Advisory Council
Vice President

CHIEF EXECUTIVE DISCRETION
S-06-0439 1975 00001
BT Executive Discretion
NT Presidential Discretion
RT Chief Executive Accountability
Chief Executive Prerogative
Chief Government Executive
Independent Authority
Secret Diplomacy

CHIEF EXECUTIVE PREROGATIVE
S-06-0442 1975 00001
BT Executive Prerogative
RT Chief Executive Accountability
Chief Executive Discretion
Chief Government Executive
Independent Authority
Secret Diplomacy

CHIEF EXECUTIVE STAFF PERSONNEL
S-36-0011 1975 00002
BT Executive Staff Personnel
NT Presidential Staff Personnel

RT Chancellery
Chief Executive Advisor
Government Bureaucracy
Government Employee
Government Official
Vice President

CHIEF GOVERNMENT EXECUTIVE
S-36-0048 1975 00001
BT Government Official
NT Dictator
International Government Executive
Local Chief Government Executive
Military Governor
Monarch
National Chief Government Executive
Prefect
Subnational Chief Government Executive
RT Chancellor
Chief Executive Accountability
Chief Executive Discretion
Chief Executive Prerogative
National Chief Executive Primary
Plural Executive
Premier
President
Prime Minister
Prime Minister Candidate

CHIEF JUSTICE
S-36-0117 1975 00003
BT Supreme Court Justice
RT Constitutional Law
Judicial Administration
Judicial System
Legal System
National Judge
Supreme Court
Supreme Court Review

CHIEF MAGISTRATE
S-36-0114 1975 00000
BT Magistrate
RT Justice Of The Peace
Local Magistrate

CHILD
S-32-0036 1979 00000
BT Family Role
NT Exceptional Child
Handicapped Child
RT Child Care Service
Child Molestation
Child Psychology
Childhood
Childhood Political Socialization
Childhood Socialization
Childrens Rights
Day Care Center

CHILD CARE SERVICE
S-26-0367 1979 00000
UF Nursery School
BT Social Service
RT Child
Child Care Service
Child Molestation
Child Neglect
Childhood
Childrens Rights
Community Service
Day Care Center
Education Service
Exceptional Child
Family Service
Handicapped Child
Legal Service
Psychological Service

CHILD MOLESTATION
S-10-0046 1979 00000
BT Sex Crime
RT Assault
Child
Child Care Service
Child Neglect
Morals Offense
Violent Crime

CHILD NEGLECT
S-10-0029 1979 00000
BT Individual Crime
RT Assault
Child Care Service
Child Molestation
Childrens Rights
Handicapped Child

CHILD PSYCHOLOGY
S-01-0170 1979 00000
BT Psychology Discipline
RT Child
Child Rearing Practices
Childhood
Childhood Socialization
Childrens Rights
Exceptional Child
Gestalt Psychology

CHILD REARING PRACTICES
S-31-0197 1979 00000
BT Process
RT Child Psychology

CHILDHOOD
S-06-0182 1975 00082
BT Age
RT Adolescence
Child
Child Care Service
Child Psychology
Childrens Rights
Day Care Center
Exceptional Child
Infancy
Logic
Right To Education
Youth

CHILDHOOD POLITICAL SOCIALIZATION
S-34-0023 1975 00028
BT Childhood Socialization
RT Adolescent Political Socialization
Child
Youth
Youth Culture

CHILDHOOD SOCIALIZATION
S-34-0022 1975 00084
BT Group Socialization
NT Childhood Political Socialization
RT Adolescent Socialization
Child
Child Psychology
Cohort Group Socialization
Elite Socialization
Ethical Socialization
Exceptional Child
Family Socialization
Interest Group Socialization
Learning
Peer Group Socialization
Primary Group Socialization
Youth

CHILDRENS RIGHTS
S-15-0073 1979 00000
BT Social Rights
RT Child
Child Care Service
Child Neglect
Child Psychology
Childhood
Childrens Rights
Exceptional Child
Health Care Rights
Housing Rights
Income Rights
Marriage Rights
Right To Education
Sexual Freedom

CHILIASTIC MOVEMENT
S-27-0002 1975 00001
SN Movement whose belief predicts the arrival of a world savior.
BT Political Movement
RT Agrarian Movement
Christian Thought
Communal Movement
Eschatology
Millenarianism
Populist Movement
Sectarian Movement
Utopianism

CHINESE CULTURAL REVOLUTION
S-08-0065 1975 00014
BT Cultural Revolution
RT Ideological Struggle
Internal War
Maoism
Maoist
Maoist Political Party
Maoist Revolutionary
Permanent Revolution Theory
Political Revolution
Social Revolution
Spontaneous Revolution

CHRISTIAN CONSERVATISM
S-38-0197 1975 00002
BT Conservatism
RT American Conservatism
Bureaucratic Conservatism
Burkean Conservatism
Neoconservatism
Reactionary Conservatism
Religious Identity
Status Quo Conservatism

CHRISTIAN DEMOCRAT
S-32-0272 1975 00000
BT Democrat
RT Christian Democratic Movement
Christian Socialism
Christian Thought

CHRISTIAN DEMOCRATIC MOVEMENT
S-27-0011 1979 00000
BT Ideological Spectrum Political Movement
RT Christian Democrat
Christian Democratic Political Party
Christian Thought
Communist Movement
Democratic Political Party
Democratic Regime
Democratic Theory
Religious Authority

CHRISTIAN DEMOCRATIC PARTY
1975-1979 00011

CHRISTIAN DEMOCRATIC POLITICAL PARTY
S-28-0004 1979 00000
BT Democratic Political Party
RT Christian Democratic Movement
Liberal Democratic Political Party
Liberal Political Party
National Democratic Political Party

CHRISTIAN EXISTENTIALISM
S-38-0063 1975 00001
BT Existentialism
RT Christian Humanism
Christian Thought
Religious Thought

CHRISTIAN HUMANISM
S-38-0241 1975 00001
BT Humanism
RT Christian Existentialism
Christian Socialism
Christian Thought
Humanitarianism
Scientific Humanism
Socialist Humanism

CHRISTIAN SOCIALISM
S-38-0291 1975 00001
BT Socialist Theory
RT Agrarian Socialism
Aprista Socialism
Christian Democrat
Christian Humanism
Christian Thought
Democratic Socialism
Evolutionary Socialism
Guild Socialism
Humanitarianism
Marxism

CHRISTIAN THOUGHT
S-38-0561 1975 00020
BT Judeo Christian Thought
NT Catholicism
Protestantism
RT Chiliastic Movement
Christian Democrat
Christian Democratic Movement
Christian Existentialism
Christian Humanism
Christian Socialism
Erastianism
Gelasian Doctrine
Investiture Controversy
Religious Movement
Two Swords Theory

CHRONOLOGY
USE Longitudinal Analysis

CHURCH LAW
S-21-0083 1975 00001
BT Religious Law
RT Canon Law
Church State Policy
Ecclesiastical Leadership

CHURCH STATE POLICY
S-26-0398 1975 00005
BT Religious Policy
RT Canon Law
Church Law
Church State Separation Doctrine
Freedom Of Religion
Parochial School
Parochial School Subsidy
School Prayer Policy
Two Swords Theory

CHURCH STATE SEPARATION DOCTRINE
S-38-0449 1975 00004
BT Constitutional Structural Theory
RT Church State Policy
Judicial Review
Religious Politics
Separation Of Power Theory

CINEMA
USE Visual Arts

CINEMA CENSORSHIP
S-31-0282 1975 00001
BT Performing Arts Censorship
RT Television Censorship

CIRCUMSTANTIAL EVIDENCE
S-15-0055 1979 00000
BT Evidence Admissibility
RT Criminal Law System
Criminal Procedure Law
Right To Appeal
Right To Due Process
Right To Jury Trial

CITATION ANALYSIS
S-24-0080 1975 00002
SN A technique of bibliographic analysis whereby traditions and communities of intellectual interest and specializations are identified through calculations of the degrees to which authors reference each other's work.
BT Documentary Research
RT Abstracting Service
Bibliographic Control
Bibliographic Service
Indexing
Information Processing
Journal
Research Evaluation

CITIZEN
1975-1979 00001
USE Citizenship Status

CITIZEN PARTICIPATION
S-31-0704 1975 00125
BT Political Participation
RT Citizen To Citizen Diplomacy
Open University
Participatory Democracy
Participatory Democratic Theory
Participatory Management
Political Mobilization
Sunshine Law
Worker Management Participation

CITIZEN TO CITIZEN DIPLOMACY
S-31-0359 1975 00004
BT Person To Person Diplomacy
RT Citizen Participation
Dollar Diplomacy
Private Sector

CITIZENSHIP IMMUNITY
S-15-0016 1975 00000
BT Immunity
NT Citizenship Privilege
RT Citizenship Status
Diplomatic Immunity
Executive Immunity
Legal Immunity
Political Asylum
Social Rights

CITIZENSHIP PRIVILEGE
S-15-0017 1975 00003
BT Citizenship Immunity
RT Citizenship Status
Diplomatic Privilege
Independent Authority
Member Privilege
Native Born Citizen
Naturalized Citizen

CITIZENSHIP STATUS
S-36-0015 1975 00006
UF Citizen
Nationality
BT Status
NT Alien
Exile
Immigrant
Repatriate
Stateless Person
RT Citizenship Immunity
Citizenship Privilege
Refugee
Right To Bear Arms

CITY
S-07-0003 1975 00014
BT Community Type
NT Central City
Decentralized City
Federated City
Inner City
Metropolitan City
Municipality
Preindustrial City
Village
RT Economic Community
Federated City
Inner City
Megalopolis
Metropolitan City
Municipal Election
Slum Community
Slum Rehabilitation
Suburb
Urban Ghetto Community
Village
Village Community

CITY BLOCK
1975-1979 00001

CITY CHARTER
S-21-0004 1975 00000
BT Basic Law
NT Colonial Charter
RT Colonial Charter

CITY COUNCIL
S-19-0120 1975 00001
BT Local Government Council
RT Legislative Member
Local Chief Executive Election
Local Legislative Candidate
Local Legislative Election
Local Legislative Election Campaign
Local Legislative Leader
Local Legislative Speaker
Local Legislative Whip
Local Legislature
Local Planning Commission
Local Policy Making
Local Policy Planning
Local Political Elite
Local Primary
Mayor
Town Council
Village Council

CITY COUNCIL ELECTION
S-29-0102 1975 00006
BT Local Legislative Election
RT Local Legislative Election
Mayoralty Election

CITY COUNCIL GOVERNMENT
S-16-0102 1975 00001
BT City Government
RT City Councilman
City Manager Government
Council Manager Government
Local Policy Making
Local Political Division

CITY COUNCILMAN
S-36-0198 1975 00003
BT Local Legislative Member
RT Alderman
City Council Government
Legislative Member
Local Legislative Candidate
Local Legislative Leader
Local Legislative Whip
Local Legislature
Local Magistrate

CITY GOVERNMENT
S-16-0101 1975 00046
BT Local Government
NT City Council Government
City Manager Government
Commission Government
Council Manager Government
Strong Mayor Government
Weak Mayor Government
RT Borough Government
City State
City State Relations
County Government
Federal City Relations
Local Policy Making
Metropolitan Government
Municipal Court
Municipality
Provincial Government
Urban Government

CITY INCOME TAXATION
S-26-0150 1975 00000
BT Local Income Taxation
RT Property Taxation
School Taxation
Wage Taxation

CITY MANAGER
S-36-0083 1975 00013
BT Local Chief Government Executive
RT City Manager Government
Council Manager
Local Chief Executive Election
Local Policy Making
Mayor
Urban Policy Planning
Urban Politics Studies
Urban Studies

CITY MANAGER GOVERNMENT
S-16-0103 1975 00001
BT City Government
RT City Council Government
City Manager
Council Manager Government
County Manager Government
Local Policy Making
Weak Mayor Government

CITY PLANNER
S-32-0142 1975 00005
BT Local Planner
RT City Planning Commission
City Planning Policy
Local Policy Planning
New Town
Planned Economy
Urban Planner

CITY PLANNING COMMISSION
S-19-0099 1975 00001
BT Local Planning Commission
RT City Planner
City Planning Policy
City Policy Planning
Government Economic Planning
Local Government Council
Local Policy Planning
National Planning Commission
Subnational Government Council
Zoning Policy

CITY PLANNING POLICY
S-26-0352 1979 00000
BT Local Planning Policy
RT City Planner
City Planning Commission
Needs Assessment
Urban Politics Studies

CITY POLICY PLANNING
S-31-0665 1975 00017
BT Subnational Policy Planning
RT City Planning Commission
Local Policy Planning
New Town
Planned Economy
Rural Policy Planning
State Policy Planning
Subnational Policy Planning
Urban Design
Urban Policy Planning

CITY POLITICS
S-29-0236 1975 00022
BT Local Politics
RT City State Relations
Local Political Division
Metropolitan Politics
Urban Politics
Village Politics

CITY STATE
S-16-0161 1975 00000
BT State Type
RT City Government
City State Political System

CITY STATE POLITICAL SYSTEM
S-37-0107 1975 00001
BT Political System Type
RT Athenian Democratic Theory
City State

CITY STATE RELATIONS
S-31-0468 1979 00000
BT Intergovernmental Relations
RT Center Periphery Government Relations
City Government
City Politics
Federal City Relations
Federal State Relations
Police Community Relations
Policy Implementation
Policy Making Process
Revenue Sharing Policy
State Constitution
State Government

CITY TYPE
1975-1979 00005

CITY UNIT
S-24-0359 1975 00005
BT Local Political Division
NT Census Tract
Street Block
RT Census Tract
Demographic Indicator
Federated City
Metropolitan City
Neighborhood
Street Block

CIVIC ACTION MOVEMENT
S-27-0059 1975 00000
BT Social Movement
RT Civic Organization
Grass Roots Movement
Populist Movement

CIVIC COMPETENCE SCALE
S-24-0227 1975 00004
SN Means of measuring a person's political knowledge and efficacy.
BT Scale Type
RT Alienation Scale
Anomie Scale
Civic Culture
Efficacy Scale
Left Right Scale
Legitimacy Scale
Liberalism Conservatism Scale
Optimism Pessimism Scale

CIVIC CULTURE
S-11-0028 1975 00007
UF Civics
BT National Political Culture

NT Legalistic Political Culture
Parochial Political Culture
Pragmatic Political Culture
Secular Political Culture
Subject Participant Culture
Traditional Political Culture
RT Civic Competence Scale
Cultural History
Fragmented Political Culture
Generational Political Culture
Ideological Political Culture
Labor Discipline
Mass Culture
Modern Political Culture
Political Awareness
Pragmatic Political Culture
Secular Political Culture
Secular Society
Traditional Political Culture
Voluntarism Model

CIVIC CULTURE TYPE
1975-1979 00004

CIVIC EDUCATION
S-13-0005 1975 00008
BT Education Type
RT Adult Education
Continuing Education
Foreign Language Education
Humanistic Education
Ideological Education
Mass Education
Military Education
Political Education
Socialist Education

CIVIC ORGANIZATION
S-03-0037 1975 00011
BT Organizations
RT Civic Action Movement
Cooperatives
Cultural Organization
Ethnic Organization
Fraternal Organization
Voluntarism Model
Voluntary Association

CIVICS
USE Civic Culture

CIVIL AUTHORITY
S-04-0030 1975 00001
BT Government Authority
NT Education Compulsion Authority
Eminent Domain
Police Power
Tax Power
Testimony Compulsion Authority
RT Civil Military Authority
Civil Military Relations
Constitution
Constitutional Authority

CIVIL CODE
S-21-0018 1975 00003
BT Civil Law
RT Civil Court
Civil Law System
Civil Procedure Law
Codified Law
Probate Court
Statutory Law

CIVIL COURT
S-19-0128 1975 00005
BT Courts
NT Common Law Court
Family Court
Housing Court
Juvenile Court
Probate Court
RT Administrative Court
Bench Trial
Civil Code
Civil Lawyer
Constitutional Court
Justice Administration Agency
Justice Of The Peace
Local Court
Tax Court

CIVIL DEFENSE POLICY
S-26-0061 1975 00005
BT Defense Policy
RT Defensive Weapon
Deterrence Policy
Military Policy
Peace
Strategic Studies
War Policy

CIVIL DISOBEDIENCE
S-15-0068 1975 00014
BT Right Of Opposition
RT Civil Rights
Conscientious Objector
Protest
Protest Politics
Right Of Protest
Right Of Revolution
Right Of Secession

CIVIL LAW
S-21-0017 1975 00011
BT Law Type
NT Civil Code
RT Administrative Law
Civil Law System
Civil Lawyer
Civil Procedure Law
Comparative Law
Consumer Protection Law
Decriminalization
Environmental Law
Procedural Law
Property Law
Statutory Law
Tort

CIVIL LAW SYSTEM
S-37-0098 1975 00007
BT Law System
RT Administrative Law System
Case Law
Civil Code
Civil Law
Civil Military Relations
Codified Law
Common Law System
Constitutional Law System
Customary Law
International Law System
Law Type
Military Law System
Socialist Law System

CIVIL LAWYER
S-32-0094 1975 00004
BT Lawyer
RT Civil Court
Civil Law
Criminal Lawyer

CIVIL LIBERTY
S-15-0027 1975 00079
BT Political Liberty
NT Freedom Of Association
Freedom Of Press
Freedom Of Religion
Freedom Of Speech
Freedom Of Thought
Freedom Of Travel
Right Of Assembly
Right Of Petition
Right Of Privacy
Right To Bear Arms
RT Civil Liberty Liberalism
Civil Rights
Democratic Theory
Equal Opportunity
Equal Rights
Freedom
Freedom Of Inquiry
Human Rights
Political Asylum
Procedural Rights
Social Rights

CIVIL LIBERTY LIBERALISM
S-38-0250 1975 00003
BT Liberalism
RT Civil Liberty
Civil Rights Liberalism
Classical Liberalism
Economic Liberalism
Laissez Faire Liberalism
Liberty Theory
Nineteenth Century Liberalism
Political Liberty
Welfare Liberalism

CIVIL MILITARY AUTHORITY
S-04-0036 1975 00049
BT Government Authority
NT Conscription Power
War Power
RT Civil Authority
Civil Military Relations
Constitutional Authority

CIVIL MILITARY RELATIONS
S-31-0469 1979 00000
BT Intergovernmental Relations
RT Civil Authority
Civil Law System
Civil Military Authority
Military Agreement
Military Forces
Military Management
Military Policy
War Power

CIVIL PROCEDURE LAW
S-21-0077 1975 00003
BT Procedural Law
RT Civil Code
Civil Law
Criminal Procedure Law
Parliamentary Procedure Law

CIVIL RELIGION
S-04-0024 1979 00000
BT Religious Authority
RT Freedom Of Religion
Political Legitimacy Theory
Religious Authority
Religious Bureaucracy
Religious Education
Religious Group
Religious History
Religious Law
Religious Movement
Religious Politics
Religious Studies
Secular Authority
System Supports
Traditional Authority

CIVIL RIGHTS
S-15-0038 1975 00077
BT Political Liberty
NT Equal Rights
RT Civil Disobedience
Civil Liberty
Civil Rights Demonstration
Civil Rights Litigation
Civil Rights Movement
Defendants Rights
Freedom Of Association
Freedom Of Press
Freedom Of Religion
Freedom Of Speech
Freedom Of Travel
Human Rights
Human Rights Policy
Political Asylum
Procedural Rights
Progressive Politics
Public Trial
Right Of Assembly
Right Of Opposition
Right Of Petition
Right Of Privacy
Right Of Protest
Right Of Revolution
Right Of Secession
Right To Appeal
Right To Bear Arms
Secret Trial
Social Rights
Voting Rights

CIVIL RIGHTS DEMONSTRATING
1975-1979 00001

CIVIL RIGHTS DEMONSTRATION
S-08-0016 1975 00003
BT Demonstration
NT Sit In
RT Civil Rights
Civil Rights Leader
Civil Rights Movement
General Strike
Peace Demonstration
Protest
Rent Strike
Student Demonstration
Veterans Demonstration

CIVIL RIGHTS LEADER
S-32-0053 1975 00002
BT Political Leader
RT Activist
Civil Rights Demonstration
Civil Rights Movement
Social Leader

CIVIL RIGHTS LIBERALISM
S-38-0251 1975 00000
BT Liberalism
RT Civil Liberty Liberalism
Classical Liberalism
Economic Liberalism
Laissez Faire Liberalism
Liberty Theory
Nineteenth Century Liberalism
Political Liberty
Welfare Liberalism

CIVIL RIGHTS LITIGATION
S-31-0557 1975 00017
BT Litigation
RT Affirmative Action Employment Policy
Amicus Curiae
Civil Rights
Class Action Litigation
Constitutional Litigation
Consumer Protection Litigation

CIVIL RIGHTS MOVEMENT
S-27-0060 1975 00016
BT Social Movement
RT Civil Rights
Civil Rights Demonstration
Civil Rights Leader
Peace Movement
Protest Politics
Reform Movement
Social Movement

CIVIL SERVANT
S-36-0088 1975 00012
BT Government Official
NT International Civil Servant
National Civil Servant
Subnational Civil Servant
RT Ambassador
Civil Service Employee
Government Employee
International Civil Servant
National Civil Servant
Reappointment
Subnational Civil Servant

CIVIL SERVICE EMPLOYEE
S-32-0081 1975 00016
BT Government Employee
RT Civil Servant
Civil Service System
Civil Service Union
Government Bureaucracy

CIVIL SERVICE SYSTEM
S-26-0199 1975 00010
BT Employment Policy
RT Administrative Tribunal
Civil Service Employee
Civil Service Union
Merit Bureaucracy
Merit Policy
Patronage Policy
Tenure Policy

CIVIL SERVICE UNION
S-03-0066 1975 00003
BT Union
RT Civil Service Employee
Civil Service System
Government Employee
Labor Union
Public Employee Organization

CIVIL WAR
S-08-0048 1975 00037
BT Internal War
RT Guerrilla Activity
Guerrilla War
Ideological War
Mob Violence
National Liberation War
Partisan War
Political Violence
Religious War
Right Of Secession

CIVILIAN WEAPON
S-33-0017 1975 00004
BT Weapon
NT Handgun
RT Conventional Weapon
Crime
Gun Control Law
Military Weapon

CIVILIZATION
S-11-0002 1979 00000
BT Culture Type
NT African Civilization
Ancient Civilization
Byzantine Civilization
Eastern Civilization
Greek Civilization
Islamic Civilization
Roman Civilization
Western Civilization
RT Historical Analysis
History Discipline
Homogeneous Culture
Political Culture
Religious Culture
Secular Culture
Western Culture

CLAN KINSHIP SYSTEM
S-20-0019 1975 00001
BT Extended Kinship System
RT Extended Family
Kindred Family

CLAN ROLE
S-32-0034 1975 00003
BT Kinship Role
RT Extended Kinship System
Family Role
Patrilineal Family Descent Pattern

CLAN SOCIETY
S-35-0014 1975 00003
BT Society Type Base
RT Caste Society
Closed Society
Patrilineal Family Descent Pattern
Traditional Society
Tribal Society

CLASS ACTION LITIGATION
S-31-0558 1975 00005
BT Litigation
RT Amicus Curiae
Civil Rights Litigation

Constitutional Litigation
Consumer Protection Litigation
Damage Suit

CLASS ANALYSIS
S-09-0008 1975 00058
BT Contemporary Analytic Modes
RT Aristocracy Political Party
Biographical Analysis
Capitalist Class
Class Based Movement
Class Conflict
Class Equality
Class Inequality
Class Politics
Class Social System
Closed Class Social System
Contextual Analysis
Entrepreneur Class
Feudal Reaction Theory
Historical Sociology Analysis
Horizontal Cleavage
Horizontal Mobility
Horizontal Stratification Division
Ideological Conflict
Industrial Working Class
Intelligentsia
Landless Peasant Class
Landowning Class
Linguistic Analysis
Marxist Alienation Theory
Marxist Analysis
Marxist Sociology
Middle Class
Middle Class Movement
Middle Class Political Party
Nobility
Petite Bourgeoisie
Proletarian Movement
Propertied Class
Revisionist Historical Analysis
Ruling Class
Social Background
Social Class Identification
Social Class Origin
Society Type Base
Socioeconomic Background
Socioeconomic Data
Upper Caste
Upper Class
White Collar Worker

CLASS ANTAGONISM
S-08-0117 1975 00003
BT Class Conflict
RT Class Inequality
Class Polarization
Ethnic Conflict
Ethnic Group Conflict
Lower Class
Marxist Class Theory
Revolution

CLASS BASED COALITION
S-02-0015 1975 00001
BT Coalition Type
RT Democratic Coalition
Economic Coalition
Interest Group Coalition
Marxist Analysis
Marxist Class Theory
Political Coalition
Political Party Coalition
Voting Coalition

CLASS BASED MOVEMENT
S-27-0049 1979 00000
BT Sector Based Political Movement
NT Middle Class Movement
Proletarian Movement
Working Class Movement
RT Agrarian Movement
Class Analysis
Class Based Political Party
Class Conflict
Class Origin
Class Politics
Grass Roots Movement
Labor Political Party
Marxist Class Consciousness Theory
Populist Movement
Transnational Political Movement

CLASS BASED PARTY
1975-1979 00003

CLASS BASED POLITICAL PARTY
S-28-0036 1979 00000
BT Sector Based Political Party Type
NT Aristocracy Political Party
Labor Political Party
Middle Class Political Party
Peasant Political Party
Proletarian Political Party
RT Class Based Movement
Socialist Political Party

CLASS CONFLICT
S-08-0116 1975 00029
BT Group Conflict
NT Class Antagonism
RT Black Insurrection
Class Analysis
Class Based Movement
Class Struggle
Economic Conflict
Ethnic Conflict
General Strike
Ideological Conflict
Interparty Competition
Intraparty Competition
Labor Conflict
Marxist Analysis
Marxist Class Theory
Marxist Revolution Theory
Middle Class Movement
Mob Violence
Race Riot
Rebellion
Revolution
Social Cleavage

CLASS DISSOLUTION
S-31-0773 1975 00000
BT Social Stratification Dissolution
RT Caste Dissolution
Classless Society
Marxist Class Theory
Status Dissolution

CLASS EQUALITY
S-06-0729 1979 00000
BT Social Equality
RT Class Analysis
Economic Egalitarianism
Economic Equality
Education Equality
Egalitarianism
Income Equality
Political Equality
Racial Equality
Sex Equality
Socialist Theory
Status Equality

CLASS FORMATION
S-31-0777 1975 00011
BT Social Stratification Formation
RT Caste Formation
Marxist Class Theory
Middle Class Movement
Status Formation

CLASS INEQUALITY
S-06-0739 1975 00024
BT Social Inequality
RT Class Analysis
Class Antagonism
Economic Inequality
Economic Injustice
Education Inequality
Education Injustice
Equality Theory
Income Inequality
Marxist Class Theory
Political Inequality
Political Injustice
Racial Inequality
Racial Injustice
Sex Inequality
Sexual Injustice
Status Inequality

CLASS MAINTENANCE
S-31-0781 1975 00008
BT Social Stratification Maintenance
RT Caste Maintenance
Lower Class
Status Maintenance

CLASS ORIGIN
S-06-0201 1975 00012
BT Origin
NT Social Class Origin
RT Ancestry
Class Based Movement
Ethnic Origin
Population Attribute
Socioeconomic Background

CLASS POLARIZATION
S-08-0118 1975 00005
BT Group Conflict
RT Agitation Propaganda
Class Antagonism
Class Solidarity
Ethnic Conflict
Marxist Analysis
Nobility
Rebellion
Struggle

CLASS POLITICS
S-29-0006 1975 00013
BT Politics
RT Class Analysis
Class Based Movement
Class Social System
Class Society
Cultural Politics
Electoral Politics
Middle Class Movement

Middle Class Political Party
National Politics

CLASS REBELLION
S-08-0057 1975 00003
BT Social Rebellion
RT Class Struggle
Economic Rebellion
Group Conflict
Internal War
Marxist Class Theory
Mob Violence
Peasant Rebellion
Political Rebellion
Protest
Revolution
Slave Rebellion
Student Rebellion
War
Worker Rebellion

CLASS SOCIAL SYSTEM
S-37-0142 1975 00014
BT Social Stratification System
NT Closed Class Social System
Open Class Social System
RT Adolescent Socialization
Caste Social System
Class Analysis
Class Politics
Class Society
Lower Class
Society Type Base

CLASS SOCIETY
S-35-0015 1975 00008
BT Society Type Base
RT Bourgeois Society
Class Politics
Class Social System
Class Solidarity
Class Stratification Division
Classless Society
Industrial Society
Landless Peasant Class
Lower Class
Marxist Class Theory
Marxist Economic Theory
Marxist Ideology Explanation
Peasant Class
Peasant Society
Propertied Class
Squatter Society

CLASS SOLIDARITY
S-06-0035 1975 00004
BT Group Solidarity
NT Proletarian Unity
RT Brotherhood
Caste Solidarity
Class Polarization
Class Society
Class Stratification Division
Communal Solidarity
Ethnic Group Cohesion
Group Cohesion
Social Solidarity
Social Unity

CLASS STRATIFICATION DIVISION
S-06-0761 1975 00021
BT Social Stratification Division
NT Aristocratic Class
Capitalist Class
Entrepreneur Class
Landowning Class
Lower Class
Lumpen Proletariat
Middle Class
Nobility
Peasant Class
Propertied Class
Ruling Class
Upper Class
Working Class
RT Achieved Status
Caste Society
Caste Stratification Division
Class Society
Class Solidarity
Horizontal Stratification Division
Landowning Class
Lower Class
Lumpen Proletariat
Middle Class
Nobility
Peasant Class
Propertied Class
Ruling Class
Social Cleavage
Social Diversity
Social Prestige
Status Mobility
Status Stratification Division
Upper Class
Vertical Stratification Division

CLASS STRUGGLE
S-08-0127 1975 00005
BT Struggle
RT Class Conflict
Class Rebellion
Economic Conflict
Imperialist War
Internal War
Lower Class
Marxist Alienation Theory
Marxist Sociology
North South Conflict
Struggle
Worker Rebellion

CLASS VOTER
S-32-0301 1975 00006
BT Voter
NT Middle Class Voter
Upper Class Voter
Working Class Voter
RT Black Voter
Black Voting
Class Voting
Ethnic Voter
Group Benefits Voter
Voting

CLASS VOTING
S-29-0131 1975 00019
BT Group Voting
RT Age Group Voting
Class Voter
Electoral History
Geographic Voting
Protest Voting
Regional Voting
Student Voting
Urban Voting

CLASSICAL CORPORATE FREEDOM THEORY
S-38-0457 1975 00000
BT Freedom Theory
RT Burkean Conservatism
Freedom
Medieval Corporatism

CLASSICAL ECONOMIC THEORY
S-38-0108 1975 00021
BT Economic Theory
NT Laissez Faire Theory
Malthusian Theory
Ricardian Theory
RT Accumulated Capital
Capitalism Theory
Economic Incentive System
Keynesian Economic Theory
Laissez Faire Theory
Macroeconomics
Marxist Economic Theory
Mercantile Economic Theory
Neoclassical Economic Theory

CLASSICAL EDUCATION
S-13-0020 1979 00000
BT Humanities Education
RT Aesthetics
Artistic Elite
Classical Period
Humanistic Education
Liberal Arts Education
Religious Education
Teacher Education
Traditional Education

CLASSICAL LIBERALISM
S-38-0252 1975 00004
BT Liberalism
RT American Enlightenment Thought
Civil Liberty Liberalism
Civil Rights Liberalism
Economic Liberalism
Freedom
Humean Analysis
Laissez Faire Liberalism
Limited Government
Lockean Contractualism
Negative Freedom Theory
Nineteenth Century Liberalism
Welfare Liberalism

CLASSICAL NATURAL RIGHT DOCTRINE
S-38-0488 1975 00010
BT Natural Law Conventionalism Theory
RT Freedom
Great Chain Of Being Doctrine
Medieval Natural Law Theory
Right Reason Doctrine
Rights Of Man Doctrine
Roman Natural Law Theory
Scientific Natural Law Theory
Stoic Natural Law Theory

CLASSICAL PERIOD
S-06-0170 1979 00000
BT Historical Periods
RT Ancient Times
Antiquity
Archaeology
Aristotelian Thought
Classical Education
Classical Political Thought

Dark Ages
Platonic Political Thought
Socratic Political Thought

CLASSICAL POLITICAL THOUGHT
S-38-0047 1975 00008
BT Political Theory
NT Aristotelian Thought
Cynic Thought
Epicurean Thought
Neoplatonic Political Thought
Platonic Political Thought
Presocratic Political Thought
Pythagorean Thought
Roman Legal Thought
Skeptic Thought
Socratic Political Thought
Stoic Thought
Thucydidean Political Thought
RT Ancient History
Ancient Times
Classical Period
Customary Law
Greek Civilization
History Of Philosophy
Ideologies
Medieval Political Thought
Philosophical Concept
Political Philosophy Concept
Political Philosophy Studies
Renaissance Political Thought

CLASSIFICATION
S-24-0172 1975 00006
BT Nominal Measurement
NT Typology
RT Classification Process
Comparative Political Studies
Formalization
Historical Periods

CLASSIFICATION PROCESS
S-31-0006 1975 00021
BT Analytic Process
RT Aristotelian Thought
Classification
Formalization
Government Document Classification Policy
Government Secrecy Policy
Historical Periods
Typologizing

CLASSIFYING
1975-1979 00002

CLASSLESS SOCIETY
S-35-0016 1975 00001
BT Society Type Base
NT Communist Society
RT Class Dissolution
Class Society
Communism
Communist Society
Marxism
Utopianism

CLEAVAGE PROCESS
S-31-0788 1975 00017
SN The development of divisions within a social system.
BT Structural Process
NT Horizontal Cleavage
Vertical Cleavage
RT Alienation Process
Crisis
Factionalist
Fragmentation
Integration
Pluralistic Society
Polarization
Political Crisis

CLEMENCY
S-31-0538 1975 00002
BT Judicial Procedure
RT Amnesty
Appeal Procedure
Judicial Discretion

CLIENT
USE Clientelism

CLIENT NATION
S-16-0116 1975 00001
BT Nation Type
RT Aligned Nation
Client State
Clientelism
Debtor Nation
Dependent Nation
Divided Nation
Fourth World Nation
Nonaligned Nation
Third World Nation

CLIENT STATE
S-16-0162 1975 00002
BT State Type
RT Client Nation
Clientelism
Debtor Nation
Dependent Nation
Divided Nation
Fourth World Nation
Imperialism
Third World Nation

CLIENTELE INFORMATION POLICY
S-26-0286 1975 00002
BT Government Information Diffusion Policy
RT Consumer Information Policy
Information Manipulation
Information System

CLIENTELISM
S-38-0191 1975 00018
SN Political relationship characterized by personalized system of favors, service and obligation.
UF Client
BT Ideologies
RT Client Nation
Client State
Consumerism
Corporatism
Economic Ideology
Patron System
Pork Barrel

CLIMATOLOGY
S-01-0091 1979 00000
BT Physical Geography
RT Agronomy
Ecology Discipline
Environmental Studies
Natural Science Education
Natural Science Model
Scientific Research

CLINICAL PSYCHOLOGIST
S-32-0115 1979 00000
BT Psychologist
RT Clinical Psychology
Learning Psychologist
Psychiatry
Psychoanalysis
Psychological Behavioralism
Psychopathology
Social Psychologist

CLINICAL PSYCHOLOGY
S-01-0171 1979 00000
BT Psychology Discipline
RT Clinical Psychologist
Coping Behavior
Gestalt Psychology
Pathological Behavior
Personal Behavior
Psychological Service
Sexual Behavior

CLOSED CLASS SOCIAL SYSTEM
S-37-0143 1975 00002
BT Class Social System
RT Class Analysis
Open Class Social System

CLOSED LEADERSHIP
S-22-0014 1975 00001
BT Leadership Structure Type
RT Authoritarian Regime
Bonapartism
Charismatic Leadership
Closed Society
Ecclesiastical Leadership
Personalized Leadership
Political Leadership
Totalitarian Leadership
Traditional Leadership

CLOSED PRIMARY
S-29-0065 1975 00000
BT Primary Election
NT Partisan Primary
RT Blanket Primary
National Primary
Open Primary
Political Party Primary
Preference Primary

CLOSED QUESTIONNAIRE
S-24-0091 1975 00002
BT Questionnaire
RT Mail Questionnaire
Open Ended Questionnaire
Self Administered Questionnaire
Telephone Questionnaire

CLOSED SOCIETY
S-35-0032 1975 00004
BT Society Type Structure
NT Secret Society
RT Absolutism
Absolutist Government
Authoritarianism
Clan Society
Closed Leadership
Homogeneous Society
Imperial Presidency
Open Society
Religious Society
Secret Society
Traditional Society

CLOTHING INDUSTRY
S-17-0062 1979 00000
BT Textile Industry
RT Appliance Industry
Consumer Industry
Cottage Industry
Farm Industry
Light Industry
Paper Industry
Service Industry
Synthetics Industry

CLOTURE
S-31-0594 1975 00000
SN Parliamentary method of ending debate and forcing vote on an issue.
BT Legislative Voting
RT Bipartisan Voting
Censure Motion

CLUSTER ANALYSIS
S-24-0042 1975 00007
BT Multivariate Analysis
RT Aggregate Data Analysis
Canonical Correlation Analysis
Dimensional Analysis
Discriminant Analysis
Factor Analysis
Multiple Correlation Analysis
Partial Correlation Analysis

CLUSTER SAMPLING
S-24-0123 1975 00002
SN Sample design involving the selection of group rather than the individual as the sample unit.
BT Probability Sampling
RT Simple Random Sampling
Stratified Sampling
Systematic Sampling

COAL ENERGY
S-31-0120 1979 00000
BT Natural Resource Exploitation
RT Energy Management
Energy Policy
Energy Use Policy
Gas Energy
Geothermal Energy
Hydroelectric Energy
Nuclear Energy
Oil Energy
Solar Energy
Tidal Energy
Wind Energy

COAL INDUSTRY
S-17-0042 1979 00000
UF Coal Utility Industry
BT Extractive Industry
RT Electrical Industry
Nuclear Energy Industry
Solar Energy

COAL UTILITY INDUSTRY
1975-1979 00011
USE Coal Industry

COALITION CHANGE
S-31-0016 1975 00003
BT Coalition Process
NT Coalition Development
Coalition Structural Change
RT Coalition Development
Coalition Politics
Coalition Theory
Group Change

COALITION DEVELOPMENT
S-31-0017 1975 00014
BT Coalition Change
NT Coalition Formation
RT Coalition Change
Coalition Structural Change
Coalition Theory

COALITION DISINTEGRATION
S-31-0020 1975 00008
BT Coalition Structural Change
RT Coalition Dissolution
Coalition Theory
Government Instability

COALITION DISSOLUTION
S-31-0021 1975 00003
BT Coalition Structural Change
RT Coalition Disintegration
Government Dissolution Process
Ministerial Instability
Political Coalition
Political Party Alignment

COALITION FORMATION
S-31-0018 1975 00034
BT Coalition Development
RT Coalition Theory
Ecumenical Movement
Group Formation
Political Coalition
Political Party Alignment

COALITION GOVERNMENT
S-16-0008 1975 00016
BT Government Type
RT Coalition Politics
Coalition Theory
Coalition Type
Government Formation Process
Minority Government
Parliamentary Government
Political Coalition
Political Party Alignment

COALITION POLITICS
S-29-0007 1975 00019
BT Politics
RT Center Political Party
Coalition Change
Coalition Government
Coalition Process
Coalition Theory
Coalition Type
Electoral Politics
Government Formation Process
Political Coalition
Political Party Alignment
Primary Election

COALITION PROCESS
S-31-0015 1975 00019
BT Associational Process
NT Coalition Change
RT Alliance Process
Cabinet Government
Coalition Politics
Coalition Theory
Group Process
Political Coalition
Political Party Alignment

COALITION STRUCTURAL CHANGE
S-31-0019 1975 00004
BT Coalition Change
NT Coalition Disintegration
Coalition Dissolution
RT Coalition Development
Organization Structural Change

COALITION THEORY
S-38-0128 1975 00022
BT Formal Political Theory
NT Alliance Theory
RT Bargaining Theory
Coalition Change
Coalition Development
Coalition Disintegration
Coalition Formation
Coalition Government
Coalition Politics
Coalition Process
Coalition Type
International Alliance Theory
Mathematical Political Theory
Minimum Winning Coalition
Organization Formation
Political Coalition
Pork Barrel
Ruling Political Party
Security Community Theory

COALITION TYPE
S-02-0014 1975 00004
BT Agreement Type
NT Class Based Coalition
Economic Coalition
Multiethnic Coalition
Opinion Coalition
Political Coalition
Winning Coalition
RT Coalition Government
Coalition Politics
Coalition Theory
Contract Type
Interest Group Coalition
Legislative Coalition
Multiethnic Coalition
Opinion Coalition
Political Party Coalition
Protective Alliance
Voting Coalition
Winning Coalition

COAST GUARD
S-33-0059 1975 00004
BT Armed Forces
RT Admiralty
Army
Marines
Maritime Court
Merchant Marine
Navy
Professional Military Forces

COATTAIL EFFECT
S-29-0108 1975 00000
SN Electoral drawing power of a candidate enabling other candidates to share this electoral strength.
BT Electoral Outcome
NT Presidential Coattail Effect
RT Bandwagon Effect
Landslide Electoral Outcome
Majority Electoral Outcome
Vote Distribution

CODE ENFORCEMENT
S-31-0564 1975 00005
BT Law Enforcement
NT Equal Law Enforcement
RT Administrative Law
Equal Law Enforcement
National Law Enforcement

CODIFIED LAW
S-21-0100 1975 00014
BT Statutory Law
RT Civil Code
Civil Law System
Common Law
Jurisprudence
Law Administration
Legal Positivism

CODING
S-24-0253 1975 00019
BT Operationalization
RT Computer Processing
Data Format

COERCION
S-31-0233 1975 00017
BT Conflict Resolution
RT Appeasement
Collective Leadership
Collective Policy Making
Collegial Leadership
Governing Elite
Informal Power
Mediation
Negotiation
Political Power
Power Politics

COGNITIVE DEVELOPMENT
S-31-0083 1975 00066
BT Personality Development
RT Cognitive Model
Education Process
Learning
Logic
Perception Socialization
Personality Theory
Reality Construction

COGNITIVE DISSONANCE THEORY
S-38-0533 1975 00023
SN Approach to attitude change and consistency that emphasizes the effects of contradictions in a person's belief system.
BT Attitude Change Theory
RT Attitude Change Theory
Cognitive Measurement
Cognitive Model
Cognitive System
Learning Psychology
Perception
Personality Characteristics
Personality Development
Personality Theory
Psychological Behaviorism

COGNITIVE MEASUREMENT
S-24-0182 1975 00058
BT Attitude Measurement
RT Affective Measurement
Belief Measurement
Cognitive Dissonance Theory
Cognitive Model
Cognitive System
Motivation Measurement
Perception
Problem Solving Behavior
Reality Testing

COGNITIVE MODEL
S-24-0290 1975 00029
BT Social Science Model
RT Cognitive Development
Cognitive Dissonance Theory
Cognitive Measurement
Cognitive Theory
Communication Model
Perception
Personality Development

COGNITIVE SYSTEM
S-37-0004 1975 00015
UF Memory
BT System Type
RT Belief System
Cognitive Dissonance Theory
Cognitive Measurement
Cognitive Theory
Cultural System
Personality Development
Personality Theory
Social System
Value System

COGNITIVE THEORY
S-38-0535 1975 00035
BT Psychological Theory
RT Attitude Characteristics
Attribution Theory
Cognitive Model
Cognitive System
Cross Pressure Theory
Existential Psychologism
Gestalt Theory
Learning Psychology
Learning Theory
Motivation Theory
Perception
Psychological Behavioralism
Psychological Behaviorism
Psychopolitical Theory
Relative Deprivation Theory
Rote Learning
Stereotyping

COHORT ANALYSIS
S-24-0086 1975 00027
SN Examination of groups who are categorized according to a common characteristic.
BT Longitudinal Analysis
RT Cohort Group Socialization
Group Analysis
Group Composition

COHORT GROUP SOCIALIZATION
S-34-0024 1975 00008
BT Group Socialization
RT Adolescent Socialization
Adult Socialization
Childhood Socialization
Cohort Analysis
Elite Socialization
Family Socialization
Interest Group Socialization
Peer Group Socialization
Primary Group Socialization

COLD WAR
S-08-0090 1975 00048
BT War
RT Anticommunism
Brinkmanship
Economic Conflict
Global Politics
Global War Policy
Ideological Conflict
Institutional Conflict
International Relations Studies
International System Polarization
Limited War
Realist Foreign Policy
Undeclared War

COLLECTIVE ACTION THEORY
S-38-0587 1975 00029
BT Social Action Theory
RT Group Theory
Interest Group Theory
Public Good Theory
Social Choice Theory
Social Interaction Theory

COLLECTIVE BARGAINING POLICY
S-26-0316 1975 00018
BT Labor Management Relations Policy
NT Labor Mediation Policy
RT Compulsory Arbitration Policy
Labor Arbitration Policy
Labor Management Contract
Labor Mediation
Public Employee Union Policy
Right To Work Policy
Trade Union Policy

COLLECTIVE COMMUNITY
S-07-0018 1975 00003
BT Cooperative Community
RT Communal Community
Commune
Economic Community
Ethnic Ghetto
Homogeneous Community
Kibbutz
Language Community
Political Community
Red Commune
Rural Community
Utopian Community

COLLECTIVE FARM ECONOMY
S-12-0004 1975 00006
BT Farm Economy
RT Autarchic Economy
Centrally Planned Economy
Collective Farmer
Collective Farming
Communist Economic System
Family Farm Economy
Labor Intensive Economy
Planned Economy
Single Group Farm Economy
Socialist Economy
Socialist Market Economy
State Farm Economy

COLLECTIVE FARMER
S-32-0066 1975 00001
BT Farmer
RT Collective Farm Economy
Collective Farming
Private Farmer

Sharecropper
Tenant Farmer

COLLECTIVE FARMING
S-31-0428 1979 00000
UF Collectivized Farming
BT Farming
RT Centrally Planned Economy
Collective Farm Economy
Collective Farmer
Collective Ownership
Communist Economic System
Communist Studies
Planned Economy
Socialist Economy

COLLECTIVE LEADERSHIP
S-22-0015 1975 00003
BT Leadership Structure Type
RT Administrative Leadership
Bureaucratic Leadership
Coercion
Collegial Leadership
Communist Government
Democratic Leadership
Ecclesiastical Leadership
Governing Elite
Integrated Authority
National Leadership
Political Leadership
Political Party Leadership
Rational Legal Leadership
Small Group Leadership
Totalitarian Leadership

COLLECTIVE OWNERSHIP
S-37-0052 1975 00005
BT Property Ownership System
RT Absentee Landlord System
Collective Farming
Government Ownership
Land Tenure System
Marxism
Private Ownership

COLLECTIVE POLICY MAKING
S-31-0676 1975 00028
BT Policy Making Process
RT Budget Cutting
Coercion
Policy Format

COLLECTIVE SECURITY
S-06-0668 1975 00012
BT International Political System Characteristics
NT Regional Security
Supranational Security
RT Balance Of Power
Defense Alliance
Military Alliance
Peaceful Coexistence
Protective Alliance
Rapprochement
United Nations
Wartime Alliance

COLLECTIVIZED FARMING
1975-1979 00001
USE Collective Farming

COLLEGE
S-19-0203 1975 00048
BT Higher Education Institution
NT Community College
Junior College
Private College
State Supported College
RT Academic Community
Higher Education
Open University
Pedagogical Institute
State Supported College
University

COLLEGE TEACHER
USE Professor

COLLEGIAL DECISION MAKING
S-31-0326 1975 00006
BT Decision Making Process
RT Collegial Leadership
Committee Decision Making

COLLEGIAL LEADERSHIP
S-22-0016 1975 00000
BT Leadership Structure Type
RT Administrative Leadership
Bureaucratic Leadership
Coercion
Collective Leadership
Collegial Decision Making
Democratic Leadership
Ecclesiastical Leadership
Political Leadership
Small Group Leadership

COLONIAL CHARTER
S-21-0005 1975 00000
BT City Charter
RT City Charter
Colonial Court
Colony
Democratic Constitution
Government Document
Imperial Government

COLONIAL COURT
S-19-0134 1975 00001
BT Courts
RT Administrative Court
Colonial Charter
Colonial Empire
Colonial Ruler
Colony

COLONIAL DEVELOPMENT
S-31-0154 1975 00024
BT Colonization
RT Colonial Empire
Colonialism
Imperial Government
Imperialism
Modernization

COLONIAL EMPIRE
S-16-0050 1975 00015
BT Empire
RT Capitalist Empire
Colonial Court
Colonial Development
Colonial Ruler
Colonialism
Communist Empire
Imperial Government
Imperialism
Imperialism System
World Empire

COLONIAL RULER
S-36-0071 1975 00005
BT National Chief Government Executive
NT Governor General
RT Colonial Court
Colonial Empire
Imperial Government

COLONIALISM
S-38-0246 1975 00046
BT Imperialism
RT Colonial Development
Colonial Empire
Colonialist
Colony
Imperial Government
Imperialist Economy
Imperialist War
Neocolonialism
Neoimperialism
Open Door Policy
Plantation Economy
Proprietary Colony
Puppet Regime
Puppet State

COLONIALIST
S-32-0269 1975 00002
BT System Politicist
RT Colonialism
Colonization
Imperialist

COLONIZATION
S-31-0153 1975 00015
BT Extraterritorial Development
NT Colonial Development
RT Annexation
Colonialist
Decolonization
Secession

COLONY
S-16-0045 1975 00016
BT Extranational Government Structure
NT Former Colony
Proprietary Colony
RT Capitalist Imperialism
Caretaker Government
Colonial Charter
Colonial Court
Colonialism
Empire
Imperialism
Imperialism System
Mandate Territory
Open Door Policy
Protectorate

COMMAND ECONOMIC SYSTEM
S-37-0022 1975 00001
BT Economic System
RT Command Economy
Government Economic Management
Government Economic Planning
Government Production Enterprise
Totalitarian Political System

COMMAND ECONOMY
S-12-0036 1975 00003
BT Centrally Planned Economy
RT Command Economic System
Communist Economic System
Fascist Economy
Government Economic Management

Government Economic Planning
Government Production Enterprise
Imperialist Economy
Nationalized Economy
Planned Economy
Self Sufficient Economy
Totalitarian Political System
War Economy

COMMANDER IN CHIEF
S-36-0214 1975 00001
BT Military Officer
RT Commanding Officer
Joint Chiefs Of Staff

COMMANDING OFFICER
S-36-0215 1975 00014
BT Military Officer
RT Commander In Chief

COMMERCE
S-31-0372 1975 00005
BT Economic Relations
NT International Commerce
Interstate Commerce
Intrastate Commerce
World Commerce
RT Agricultural Advisory Board
Business
Business Studies
Commercial Agreement
Commercial Law
Commercial Sector
Commercial Treaty
Industrial Relations
Marketing
Trade
Trade Agency

COMMERCIAL AGREEMENT
S-02-0070 1975 00006
BT State Agreement Type
NT Commercial Treaty
RT Arms Sales
Commerce
Commercial Attache
Commercial Law
Contract Type
Economic Agreement
Economic Alliance
Interstate Authorities
Interstate Commerce Commission
Monetary Agreement
Protective Tariff
Trade Agreement

COMMERCIAL ATTACHE
S-36-0125 1979 00000
BT Embassy Attache
RT Commercial Agreement
Foreign Capital Market
Foreign Service Officer
International Commerce
Private Foreign Investment

COMMERCIAL BROADCASTING INDUSTRY
S-17-0008 1975 00012
BT Broadcasting Industry
RT Cable Television
Commercial Television
Public Broadcasting Industry
Public Television
Radio Industry
Television Industry

COMMERCIAL ELITE
S-14-0006 1975 00004
BT Business Elite
RT Business Elite
Corporate Elite
Decision Making Elite
Financial Elite
Governing Elite
Managerial Elite

COMMERCIAL LAW
S-21-0019 1975 00010
BT Law Type
RT Administrative Law System
Admiralty Law
Air Fare Regulation Policy
Airline Regulation Policy
Commerce
Commercial Agreement
Contract Law
Economic Law
Maritime Court
Maritime Law
Property Law
Zoning Law

COMMERCIAL OCCUPATION
S-32-0071 1975 00002
BT Occupational Role
NT Businessman
Financier
Speculator
RT Agricultural Occupation
Artisan
Business
Business Studies
Industrial Occupation
Occupation Characteristics
Professional Occupational Role

COMMERCIAL SECTOR
S-37-0028 1975 00014
BT Economic Sector
NT Free Trade Sector
RT Agricultural Sector
Business Agency
Business Studies
Commerce
Industrial Sector
Private Sector
Public Sector

COMMERCIAL TELEVISION
S-17-0013 1979 00000
BT Television Industry
RT Cable Television
Commercial Broadcasting Industry
Public Television
State Controlled Television
Telecommunications Industry
Television Policy

COMMERCIAL TREATY
S-02-0071 1975 00003
BT Commercial Agreement
RT Commerce
Contract Type
Economic Treaty
Government Economic Planning
Monetary Agreement

COMMISSION GOVERNMENT
S-16-0104 1975 00000
BT City Government
RT Local Policy Making
Strong Mayor Government
Weak Mayor Government

COMMISSION OF INQUIRY
S-19-0086 1975 00001
BT Investigation Commission
NT Legislative Commission Of Inquiry
Presidential Commission Of Inquiry
Royal Commission Of Inquiry
RT Congressional Hearing
Contempt Of Congress
Courts
Crime Commission
Federal Commission
Freedom Of Speech
Grand Jury Indictment
Grand Jury System
Investigation Commission
Legislative Commission
Presidential Commission
Regulatory Commission

COMMISSION RECORD
S-18-0008 1975 00001
BT Documents
RT Committee Record
Government Document
International Organization Record
Public Record

COMMISSIONS
S-19-0082 1975 00001
BT Institutions
NT Federal Commission
Investigation Commission
Legislative Commission
Planning Commission
Presidential Commission
Regulatory Commission
RT Agencies
Authorities
Councils

COMMITTEE CHAIRPERSON
S-36-0266 1975 00000
BT Chairperson
RT Committee Staff Personnel
Committee Staffing

COMMITTEE DECISION MAKING
S-31-0327 1975 00008
BT Decision Making Process
RT Collegial Decision Making
Committee Of The Whole
Congressional Hearing

COMMITTEE MEMBER
S-36-0267 1975 00004
BT Suborganization Official
NT Committee Staff Personnel
RT Caucus Member
Chairperson

COMMITTEE OF THE WHOLE
S-31-0614 1975 00000
SN Parliamentary device in which total body assumes the characteristics of a committee subunit.
BT Parliamentary Procedure
RT Committee Decision Making
Committee Rules
Congressional Procedure
Executive Session
Parliamentary Procedure

COMMITTEE RECORD
S-18-0009 1975 00002
BT Documents
RT Commission Record
Government Document
Political Party Record
Public Record

COMMITTEE RULES
S-31-0604 1975 00000
BT Legislative Procedure
RT Committee Of The Whole
Congressional Procedure
Legislative Calendar
Parliamentary Procedure

COMMITTEE STAFF PERSONNEL
S-36-0268 1975 00001
BT Committee Member
RT Committee Chairperson
Committee Staffing

COMMITTEE STAFFING
S-31-0605 1975 00000
BT Legislative Procedure
RT Ad Hoc Congressional Committee
Committee Chairperson
Committee Staff Personnel
Joint Congressional Committee
Parliamentary Procedure

COMMODITY MARKET
S-19-0181 1975 00020
BT Market
NT International Commodity Market
RT Capitalist Economy
Commodity Production
Consumer Market
Customs Union
Differentiated Market
Domestic Market
Financial Market
Marketplace
Mass Market
National Market
Stock Market
World Market

COMMODITY PRODUCTION
S-31-0435 1975 00013
BT Industrial Production
RT Advanced Industrial Society
Commodity Market
Consumer Industry
Mass Production

COMMON GOOD THEORY
S-38-0430 1975 00018
BT Political Philosophy Concept
NT Common Wealth Theory
General Interest Theory
General Will Theory
Public Interest Theory
RT Consensus Theory
Justice Theory
Legitimacy Theory
Political Legitimacy Theory
Public Good Theory
Public Interest

COMMON LAW
S-21-0020 1975 00011
BT Law Type
NT Case Law
Judge Made Law
RT Codified Law
Common Law Court
Common Law Procedure
Common Law System
Customary Law
Environmental Law
Negligence Law

COMMON LAW COURT
S-19-0129 1975 00000
BT Civil Court
RT Common Law
Common Law Procedure
Common Law System
Damage Suit
Family Court
Housing Court

COMMON LAW PROCEDURE
S-31-0539 1975 00000
BT Judicial Procedure
RT Common Law
Common Law Court
Comparative Law
Customary Law
Judicial Discretion

COMMON LAW SYSTEM
S-37-0099 1975 00006
BT Law System
RT Administrative Law System
Civil Law System
Common Law
Common Law Court
Constitutional Law System
Criminal Law System
Customary Law
International Law System
Judicial Process
Military Law System
Natural Law System
Pretrial Procedure
Procedural Due Process
Socialist Law System

COMMON MARKET
S-19-0183 1975 00020
BT Market
RT Common Market Area Studies
Differentiated Market
Economic Alliance
Economic Coalition
Economic Community
European Integration Theory
Extranational Bloc
Free Market
Multilateral Alliance
Multilateral Treaty
National Market
World Market

COMMON MARKET AREA STUDIES
S-01-0047 1975 00036
BT West European Area Studies
RT Common Market
Comparative Analysis
Comparative Political Studies
Comparative Sociology
Scandinavian Area Studies

COMMON WEALTH THEORY
S-38-0431 1975 00000
BT Common Good Theory
RT Burkean Analysis
Commonwealth Community Theory
Commonwealth International System
Distributive Justice Theory
Justice Theory

COMMONWEALTH COMMUNITY THEORY
S-38-0436 1975 00000
BT Community Philosophical Concept
RT Common Wealth Theory
Commonwealth International System

COMMONWEALTH INTERNATIONAL SYSTEM
S-37-0119 1975 00003
BT International Political System
RT Bipolar International System
Common Wealth Theory
Commonwealth Community Theory
International Economic Integration
Multipolar International Political System
Polycentric International Political System
Regional International Political System

COMMUNAL COMMUNITY
S-07-0019 1975 00010
BT Cooperative Community
NT Red Commune
RT Collective Community
Communal Movement
Commune
Economic Community
Ethnic Ghetto
Homogeneous Community
Language Community
Political Community
Rural Community
Squatter Community
Utopian Community

COMMUNAL FAMILY
S-20-0008 1975 00000
BT Family Type
RT Bilateral Family Descent Pattern
Communal Solidarity
Extended Family
Extended Kinship System
Intermarriage
Polygamy

COMMUNAL MOVEMENT
S-27-0061 1975 00002
BT Social Movement
RT Chiliastic Movement
Communal Community
Communal Politics
Communal Solidarity
Communalism
Communalist
Language Movement
Liberation Movement
Populist Movement

COMMUNAL POLITICS
S-29-0208 1975 00003
BT World Politics
RT Communal Movement
Communal Solidarity
Communalism
Communalist

COMMUNAL SOLIDARITY
S-06-0037 1975 00008
BT Group Solidarity
RT Brotherhood
Caste Solidarity

Class Solidarity
Communal Family
Communal Movement
Communal Politics
Communalism
Communalist
Gemeinschaft
Group Cohesion
Patrilineal Family Descent Pattern
Social Solidarity
Social Unity

COMMUNALISM
S-38-0192 1975 00005
BT Ideologies
RT Anarchosyndicalism
Chartism
Communal Movement
Communal Politics
Communal Solidarity
Communalist
Communist Society
Egalitarianism
Levellers Political Thought

COMMUNALIST
S-32-0270 1975 00001
BT System Politicist
RT Communal Movement
Communal Politics
Communal Solidarity
Communalism

COMMUNE
S-24-0362 1975 00007
BT Local Political Division
RT Collective Community
Communal Community
Economic Community
Kibbutz
Political Community
Red Commune

COMMUNICATION AGENCY
S-19-0046 1975 00004
BT Information Agency
NT Broadcasting Agency
Publication Agency
Telephone Agency
RT Communication Channel
Communication Field
Communication Industry
Communication Policy
Communication Process
Informal Power
International Communication

COMMUNICATION ANALYSIS
S-09-0009 1975 00053
BT Contemporary Analytic Modes
NT Mass Media Analysis
RT Communication Channel
Communication Field
Communication Flow
Communication Industry
Communication Model
Communication Process
Communication Theory
Contextual Analysis
International Communication
Leisure Time Analysis
Linguistic Analysis
Linguistic Theory
Mass Media Analysis
Mass Media Policy
Network Analysis
Nonverbal Communication
Remote Terminal
Sociological Analysis
Telecommunications Industry
Two Step Communication Flow

COMMUNICATION CHANNEL
S-31-0168 1975 00019
BT Communication Flow
RT Communication Agency
Communication Analysis
Communication Field
Communication Industry
Communication Model
Communication Policy
Communication Theory
Computer Network
Government Information Diffusion Policy
Telephone Agency
Two Step Communication Flow

COMMUNICATION FEEDBACK
S-06-0572 1979 00000
BT Feedback Loop
RT Communication Flow
Communication Policy
Communication Process
Functional Adaptation
Learning Feedback
Structural Adaptation
System Adaptive Capacity
System Maintenance Capacity
System Persistence Capacity

COMMUNICATION FIELD
S-31-0169 1975 00001
BT Communication Flow
RT Communication Agency
Communication Analysis
Communication Channel
Communication Industry
Communication Model
Communication Policy
Communication Theory
Two Step Communication Flow

COMMUNICATION FLOW
S-31-0167 1975 00024
BT Communication Process
NT Communication Channel
Communication Field
Two Step Communication Flow
RT Communication Analysis
Communication Feedback
Communication Model
Communication Theory
Computer Network
Information Acquisition
International Communication
Interpersonal Communication
Mass Communication
Mass Media Policy
Nonverbal Communication
Political Communication

COMMUNICATION INDUSTRY
S-17-0006 1975 00008
BT Industry
NT Broadcasting Industry
News Agency
Publication Industry
Telecommunications Industry
Telephone Industry
RT Advertising Industry
Communication Agency
Communication Analysis
Communication Channel
Communication Field
Communication Policy
Communication Process
Foreign Information Agency
Information Agency
International Communication
Mass Media Policy
Mass Media Regulation Policy
Mass Media Subsidization Policy
Telephone Agency

COMMUNICATION MODEL
S-24-0291 1975 00024
BT Social Science Model
RT Cognitive Model
Communication Analysis
Communication Channel
Communication Field
Communication Flow
Communication Process
Communication Theory
Cybernetic Model
Development Model
Information Dissemination
Interaction Model
International Communication
Nonverbal Communication

COMMUNICATION POLICY
S-26-0016 1975 00011
BT Policy
NT Individual Communication Policy
Mass Media Policy
RT Communication Agency
Communication Channel
Communication Feedback
Communication Field
Communication Industry
Communication Process
Foreign Information Agency
Information Dissemination
Information Policy
Magazine Industry
Mass Communication
Media Access
Media Editorializing
Telecommunications Industry
Telephone Agency

COMMUNICATION PROCESS
S-31-0166 1975 00067
BT Process
NT Communication Flow
Informal Communication
Information Acquisition
Information Dissemination
Information Explosion
Information Utilization
International Communication
Interpersonal Communication
Mass Communication
Nonverbal Communication
Political Party Advertising
RT Communication Agency
Communication Analysis
Communication Feedback

Communication Industry
Communication Model
Communication Policy
Communication Theory
Computer Network
Control Process
Education Process
Foreign Information Agency
Individual Communication Policy
Intelligence Agency
Interaction Analysis
Interaction Model
Knowledge Acquisition
Mass Media Policy
Postal Rate Policy

COMMUNICATION THEORY
S-38-0030 1975 00039
BT General System Theory
RT Anthropological Linguistic Theory
Communication Analysis
Communication Channel
Communication Field
Communication Flow
Communication Model
Communication Process
Computer Network
Critical Theory Analysis
Cybernetic Theory
Information Dissemination
Interaction Analysis
Interaction Model

COMMUNISM
S-38-0317 1975 00027
BT Marxism
NT International Communism
National Communism
Socialist Realism
RT Bolshevism
Castroism
Classless Society
Communist
Communist Government
Communist Studies
Eurocommunism
Evolutionary Marxism
Hegelian Marxism
Ideological Indoctrination
Leninism
Maoism
Marxism Leninism
Marxist Communism Theory
Marxist Revisionism
National Liberation Movement
Political Movement
Polycentrism
Proletarian Revolution
Stalinism
Stalinist
Titoism
Totalitarian Movement
Trotskyism
Trotskyite Political Party
Working Class Movement

COMMUNIST
S-32-0282 1975 00003
BT Socialist
NT Maoist
Stalinist
RT Communism
Communist Bloc
Communist Empire
Marxism
Marxist Communism Theory
Puppet State

COMMUNIST BLOC
S-02-0043 1975 00022
BT Extranational Bloc
RT Communist
Communist Empire
Communist Imperialism
International Bloc
International Communism
International Communist Movement
Political Front
Political Revolution
Polycentrism
Proletarian Revolution
Security Community
Western Bloc

COMMUNIST DEVIATIONISM
S-38-0328 1975 00009
BT Marxist Revisionism
RT Ideological Conflict
National Communism
Polycentrism
Trotskyite Political Party

COMMUNIST ECONOMIC SYSTEM
S-37-0023 1975 00037
BT Economic System
RT Centrally Planned Economy
Collective Farm Economy
Collective Farming
Command Economy
Communist Empire
Communist Society
Developing Economy
Government Economic Management
Internal Market
Marxist Economics
Mercantile Economic System
Multiple Year Economic Plan
National Communism
Nationalized Economy
Planned Economy
Socialist Economic Planning
Socialist Economic System
Socialist Economy
State Farm Economy
War Economy

COMMUNIST EDUCATION
S-13-0030 1979 00000
BT Political Education
RT Agitation Propaganda
Communist Society
Communist Studies
Fascist Education
Ideological Education
Ideologies
Political Socialization
Socialist Education

COMMUNIST EMPIRE
S-16-0051 1975 00002
BT Empire
RT Capitalist Empire
Colonial Empire
Communist
Communist Bloc
Communist Economic System
Communist Government
Communist Imperialism
East European Area Studies
Imperialism
Imperialism System
International Communism
International Communist Movement
Marxism Leninism
Russian Studies
Soviet And East European Area Studies
Soviet Studies
World Empire

COMMUNIST GOVERNMENT
S-16-0009 1975 00149
BT Government Type
RT Absolutist Government
Antifascism
Authoritarianism
Autocratic Government
Bolshevism
Centralized Government
Collective Leadership
Communism
Communist Empire
Communist Imperialism
Communist Revolution
Communist Society
International Communism
Maoism
Marxism
Marxism Leninism
Marxist Analysis
Marxist Political Thought
National Communism
Peoples Democratic State
Politburo Member
Totalitarian Dictatorship

COMMUNIST IMPERIALISM
S-37-0072 1975 00007
BT Political Imperialism
RT Capitalist Imperialism
Communist Bloc
Communist Empire
Communist Government
Containment Policy
Imperial Government
International Communism
Marxism Leninism
Marxist Analysis
Marxist Economics
Neoimperialism
Proletarian Internationalism
Totalitarian Dictatorship
Western Imperialism
Yankee Imperialism

COMMUNIST MOVEMENT
S-27-0012 1979 00000
BT Ideological Spectrum Political Movement
NT International Communist Movement
RT Christian Democratic Movement
Maoist Movement

COMMUNIST PARTY
1975-1979 00125

COMMUNIST PARTY MOVEMENT
1975-1979 00025

COMMUNIST POLITICAL PARTY
S-28-0011 1979 00000
BT Ideological Spectrum Political Party Type
NT Bolshevik Political Party
Maoist Political Party
Trotskyite Political Party
RT Maoism
Maoist
Maoist Political Party
Maoist Revolutionary
Political Party Congress
Proletarian Dictatorship
Proletarian Political Party
Radical Political Party
Socialist Political Party

COMMUNIST REVOLUTION
S-08-0072 1975 00026
BT Socialist Revolution
NT Bolshevik Revolution
RT Communist Government
Communist Society
Communist Studies
Democratic Socialist Revolution
Government Overthrow
Internal War
Maoist Revolutionary
Marxism
Marxist Revolution Theory
National Political Revolution
Social Revolution
Spontaneous Revolution
Technological Revolution
Thermidor
Working Class Emancipation

COMMUNIST SOCIETY
S-35-0017 1979 00000
BT Classless Society
RT Classless Society
Communalism
Communist Economic System
Communist Education
Communist Government
Communist Revolution
Communist Studies
Marxist Communism Theory
Marxist Theory
Soviet And East European Area Studies

COMMUNIST STUDIES
S-01-0054 1975 00074
BT Academic Areas
RT Collective Farming
Communism
Communist Education
Communist Revolution
Communist Society
Comparative Political Studies
Comparative Sociology
Cult Of Personality
East Asian Area Studies
East European Area Studies
International Communist Movement
International Relations Studies
Maoism
Maoist
Maoist Movement
Maoist Political Party
Maoist Revolutionary
Marxism
Marxism Leninism
Marxist Class Theory
Marxist Communism Theory
Marxist Existentialism
Marxist Revolution Theory
Marxist Sociology
Mobilization Policy
Peoples Democratic State
Political History
Political Purge
Political Refugee
Political Science Discipline
Political Self Criticism
Purge
Russian Studies
Soviet And East European Area Studies
Soviet Studies
Trotskyite Political Party

COMMUNITY BUILDING
S-31-0047 1975 00013
BT Building Process
RT Community Characteristics
Economic Community
Group Development
Institution Building
Nation Building

COMMUNITY CHARACTERISTICS
S-06-0003 1975 00034
BT Association Characteristics
NT Community Composition
Community Structural Characteristics
RT Community Building
Community Identity
Community Power Theory
Community Type
Cultural History
Group Characteristics
Organization Characteristics

COMMUNITY CLEAVAGE CHARACTERISTICS
S-06-0007 1975 00005
BT Community Structural Characteristics
RT Community Homogeneity
Community Power Theory
Community Size Characteristics
Organization Structural Characteristics
Pluralistic Society
Social Cleavage
Social Theory

COMMUNITY COLLEGE
S-19-0204 1975 00003
BT College
RT Higher Education
Junior College
Neighborhood School

COMMUNITY COMPOSITION
S-06-0004 1975 00010
BT Community Characteristics
NT Community Homogeneity
RT Community Culture
Community Identity
Community Philosophical Concept
Community Power Theory
Community Structural Characteristics
Community Type
Group Composition
Squatter Community

COMMUNITY CULTURE
S-11-0011 1975 00014
BT Culture Type
NT Village Culture
RT Black Culture
Community Composition
Community Identity
Community Philosophical Concept
Community Type
Ethnic Community
Ethnic Culture
Heterogeneous Culture
Homogeneous Culture
Mass Culture
Poverty Culture
Secular Culture
Squatter Community
Subculture
Traditional Culture
Urban Culture
Youth Culture

COMMUNITY DECISION MAKING
S-31-0333 1975 00024
BT Subnational Decision Making Process
RT Community Elite
Community Leader
Community Power Theory
Local Decision Making
Local Elite
Town Meeting
Township Government

COMMUNITY DESEGREGATION POLICY
S-26-0383 1975 00004
BT Desegregation Policy
RT Racial Integration
Racism
School Desegregation Policy

COMMUNITY ELITE
S-14-0039 1975 00004
BT Subnational Elite
RT Community Decision Making
Community Leader
Community Power Theory
Local Elite
Local Police Chief
Local Political Elite
Provincial Elite
Social Elite
Traditional Social Elite

COMMUNITY HOMOGENEITY
S-06-0005 1975 00003
BT Community Composition
RT Community Cleavage Characteristics
Community Power Theory
Community Size Characteristics
Community Structural Characteristics
Ethnic Community
Ghetto Community
Squatter Community

COMMUNITY IDENTITY
S-06-0378 1975 00011
BT Identity Characteristics
NT Community Interest
RT Afro Asian Bloc
Community Characteristics

Community Composition
Community Culture
Community Philosophical Concept
Cultural Identity
Ethnic Community
Ghetto Community
Group Characteristics
Identity Change
Identity Crisis
Language Loyalty
National Identity
Political Identity
Religious Identity
Social Identity

COMMUNITY INTEREST
S-06-0379 1975 00011
BT Community Identity
RT Economic Community
Interest Group
Interest Group Theory

COMMUNITY LEADER
S-32-0058 1975 00006
BT Social Leader
RT Business Leader
Community Decision Making
Community Elite
Community Power Theory
Local Elite
Opinion Leader
Religious Leader

COMMUNITY PHILOSOPHIC CONCEPT
1975-1979 00006
USE Community Philosophical Concept

COMMUNITY PHILOSOPHICAL CONCEPT
S-38-0435 1979 00000
UF Community Philosophic Concept
BT Political Philosophy Concept
NT Commonwealth Community Theory
Fraternity Theory
Organic State Theory
RT Community Composition
Community Culture
Community Identity
Contemporary Political Thought
Medieval Corporatism
Philosophical Concept
Political Philosophy Studies

COMMUNITY POWER THEORY
S-38-0163 1975 00017
BT Power Theory
RT Community Characteristics
Community Cleavage Characteristics
Community Composition
Community Decision Making
Community Elite
Community Homogeneity
Community Leader
Community Structural Characteristics
Community Type
Decision Making Theory
Elite Theory
Group Theory

COMMUNITY SERVICE
S-26-0368 1979 00000
BT Social Service
RT Child Care Service
Day Care Center
Education Service
Family Service
Health Service
Legal Service
Sanitation Industry
Service Industry Policy
Social Policy
Social Welfare Policy
Social Worker

COMMUNITY SIZE CHARACTERISTICS
S-06-0008 1975 00027
BT Community Structural Characteristics
RT Community Cleavage Characteristics
Community Homogeneity
Population Density

COMMUNITY STRUCTURAL CHARACTERISTICS
S-06-0006 1975 00013
BT Community Characteristics
NT Community Cleavage Characteristics
Community Size Characteristics
RT Community Composition
Community Homogeneity
Community Power Theory
Economic Community
Neighborhood
Organization Structural Characteristics

COMMUNITY TYPE
S-07-0001 1975 00008
NT Academic Community
City
Compound
Cooperative Community
Economic Community
Ethnic Community
Ghetto Community
Heterogeneous Community
Homogeneous Community
Neighborhood
Planned Community
Political Community
Religious Community
Reservation
Rural Community
Segregated Community
Slum Community
Squatter Community
Suburb
Town
Village Community
RT Community Characteristics
Community Composition
Community Culture
Community Power Theory
Economy Type

COMPACT
S-02-0035 1975 00000
BT Agreement Type
NT Interstate Compact
RT Alliance
Contract Type
Extranational Bloc
International Bloc
Marriage Contract
Security Community
State Agreement Declaration
State Agreement Type

COMPARATIVE ANALYSIS
S-24-0403 1975 00264
BT Study Scope
NT Cross Cultural Analysis
Cross Level Analysis
Cross National Analysis
International Analysis
Intracultural Analysis
RT Area Studies
Caribbean Area Studies
Central American Area Studies
Chicano Studies
Common Market Area Studies
Comparative Literature Studies
Comparative Political Studies
Comparative Sociology
Configurative Analysis
Cross Cultural Data
Cross Lagged Panel Analysis
Cultural Universalism
East European Area Studies
Historical Periods
Latin American Area Studies
Linkage Politics
Middle East Area Studies
North African Area Studies
North American Area Studies
Panel Analysis
Propositional Inventory
Russian Studies
Scandinavian Area Studies
South Asian Area Studies
Southeast Asian Area Studies
Soviet And East European Area Studies
Soviet Studies
Typologizing
West European Area Studies

COMPARATIVE LAW
S-01-0132 1979 00000
BT Legal Studies
RT Area Studies
Civil Law
Common Law Procedure
Constitutional Law System
Law Administration
Law Enforcement
Law Type
Legal History

COMPARATIVE LITERATURE STUDIES
S-01-0140 1979 00000
UF World Literature
BT Literature Studies
RT African Area Studies
American Area Studies
Asian Area Studies
British Commonwealth Area Studies
Comparative Analysis
Linguistics
Middle East Area Studies
Political Literature
Soviet And East European Area Studies
West European Area Studies

COMPARATIVE POLITICAL STUDIES
S-01-0157 1975 00069
BT Political Science Discipline
RT African Area Studies
American Area Studies

Area Studies
Asian Area Studies
British Commonwealth Area Studies
Caribbean Area Studies
Central American Area Studies
Classification
Common Market Area Studies
Communist Studies
Comparative Analysis
Comparative Sociology
Cross Cultural Analysis
Cross National Analysis
Cultural Anthropology
Cultural History
East Asian Area Studies
East European Area Studies
Economics Discipline
Ethnic Studies
Ethnology
History Discipline
International Relations Studies
Latin American Area Studies
Macrosociology
Middle East Area Studies
Nation Type
North African Area Studies
North American Area Studies
Policy Science Studies
Political Behavior Studies
Political Economy Studies
Political Geography
Political Science Methodology Studies
Political Sociology
Russian Studies
Scandinavian Area Studies
Social Anthropology
Social Psychology
South Asian Area Studies
Southeast Asian Area Studies
Soviet And East European Area Studies
Soviet Studies
West European Area Studies

COMPARATIVE SOCIOLOGY
S-01-0184 1975 00008
BT Sociology Discipline
RT African Area Studies
Applied Sociology
Area Studies
Asian Area Studies
Behavioral Science
British Commonwealth Area Studies
Caribbean Area Studies
Central American Area Studies
Common Market Area Studies
Communist Studies
Comparative Analysis
Comparative Political Studies
Cross Cultural Analysis
Cross Level Analysis
Cultural Anthropology
Cultural History
Demographic Studies
East Asian Area Studies
East European Area Studies
Economics Discipline
Ethnic Studies
Ethnography
Geography Discipline
Historical Sociology
History Discipline
Human Geography
Latin American Area Studies
Macrosociology
Middle East Area Studies
North African Area Studies
North American Area Studies
Policy Science Studies
Political Economy Studies
Political Geography
Political Sociology
Russian Studies
Social Anthropology
Social Classification
Social Pathology
Social Psychology
South Asian Area Studies
Southeast Asian Area Studies
Soviet And East European Area Studies
Soviet Studies
Urban Politics Studies
Urban Sociology
West European Area Studies

COMPENSATORY JUSTICE
S-38-0474 1979 00000
BT Justice Theory
RT Distributive Justice Theory
Egalitarian Justice Theory
Equity
Justice As Fairness Doctrine
Natural Justice Theory
Remedial Justice Theory
Utilitarian Justice Theory

COMPETITION
S-31-0199 1975 00029
BT Conflict Process
NT Direct Competition
Economic Competition
Elite Competition
External Competition
Foreign Competition
Formal Competition
Imperfect Competition
Indirect Competition
Internal Competition
International Competition
Perfect Competition
Political Competition
Political Party Competition
Unfair Competition
RT Exchange Theory
Social Darwinism

COMPOSITE SCALE
S-24-0204 1975 00000
SN Measuring technique which employs several indicators to describe a variable.
BT Scale Construction Methodology
RT Cross Cultural Index
Cumulative Scale
Guttman Scale
Likert Scale
Multidimensional Scale
Scalability Index
Semantic Differential
Thurstone Scale

COMPOUND
S-07-0016 1979 00000
BT Community Type
RT Cooperative Community
Ghetto Community
Inner City
Kibbutz
Reservation
Utopian Community

COMPULSORY ARBITRATION POLICY
S-26-0319 1975 00000
BT Labor Arbitration Policy
RT Arbitration
Collective Bargaining Policy
Labor Mediation Policy

COMPULSORY EDUCATION
S-13-0006 1975 00005
BT Education Type
RT Graduate School
Mass Education
Secondary Education
State Supported Higher Education
Traditional Education

COMPULSORY INSURANCE
S-26-0301 1979 00000
BT Insurance
RT Accident Insurance
Catastrophe Insurance
Fire Insurance
Life Insurance
Malpractice Insurance
Motor Vehicle Industry
Motor Vehicle Insurance
National Health Insurance
No Fault Insurance
Unemployment Insurance Policy

COMPULSORY VOTING
S-29-0123 1975 00000
BT Voting
RT Electoral Law

COMPUTER
USE Computer Processing

COMPUTER ASSISTED INSTRUCTION
S-31-0447 1975 00005
BT Education Process
RT Cybernetic Analysis
Programmed Instruction

COMPUTER EQUIPMENT
S-24-0328 1975 00007
UF Calculator
BT Data Processing Equipment
NT Input Output Device
RT Computer Network
Computer Program
Remote Terminal
Software
Unit Record Equipment

COMPUTER NETWORK
S-37-0076 1979 00000
BT Information System
RT Communication Channel
Communication Flow
Communication Process
Communication Theory
Computer Equipment
Cybernetic Analysis
Machine Readable Data

COMPUTER PROCESSING
S-24-0147 1975 00016
UF Computer
Direct Access Storage
Random Access Storage
BT Data Processing
RT Coding
Computer Programming
Cybernetic Analysis
Data Retrieval
Software

COMPUTER PROGRAM
S-24-0326 1975 00025
BT Computer Software
RT Computer Equipment
Computer Programming
Information Storage
Software

COMPUTER PROGRAMMING
S-24-0148 1975 00008
UF Assembler Language
BT Data Processing
RT Advanced Technology
Computer Processing
Computer Program
Machine Readable Information
Software

COMPUTER SCIENCE
S-01-0055 1975 00006
BT Academic Areas
RT Behavioral Science
Cybernetic Analysis
Data Processing Equipment
Econometrics
Engineering Discipline
Information Science
Library Science Studies
Logic
Machine Readable Data
Mathematics Discipline
Political Science Methodology Studies
Software

COMPUTER SIMULATION
S-24-0128 1975 00021
BT Simulation
RT Computer Simulation Model
Man Machine Simulation
Software

COMPUTER SIMULATION MODEL
S-24-0292 1975 00019
BT Social Science Model
RT Computer Simulation
Economic Development Model
Input Output Model
Probability Model

COMPUTER SOFTWARE
S-24-0325 1975 00002
BT Information Processing Equipment
NT Computer Program
RT Data Processing Equipment
Information Recording Equipment

COMTEAN POSITIVISM
S-38-0389 1975 00004
SN Auguste Comte's stage of socio-historical development in which man could discover and use invariable laws of society-social physics- to construct technocractic and harmonic world.
BT Modern Political Thought
RT Behavioral Theory
Empirical Theory
Reductionism

CONCENTRATED POWER
S-30-0002 1975 00008
BT Power Type
RT Absolutism
Authoritarianism
Center Periphery Government Relations
Centralized Authority
Dictatorship
Dispersed Power
Formal Power
Institutional Power
One Political Party System
Power Theory
Private Monopoly
State Power

CONCENTRATION CAMP
S-19-0296 1975 00002
BT Detention Center
RT Genocide
Political Prisoner
Preventive Detention
Prisoner
Prisoner Of War
Prisoner Of War Camp
Secret Police
Slave Labor Camp

CONCEPT EXPLICATION RESEARCH
S-24-0398 1979 00000
SN The clarification and specification of a theoretical construct.
UF Conceptual Explication Research
BT Theoretical Research
RT Analytic Process
Basic Research
Conceptual Equivalence
Explanatory Research
Interdisciplinary Research
Multiple Operationalization
Operationalization
Policy Research
Predictive Research
Qualitative Research
Quantitative History
Research Orientation
Scientific Research
Thesaurus

CONCEPTUAL EQUIVALENCE
S-24-0254 1975 00007
SN Cross-contextual identity of concepts.
BT Operationalization
NT Functional Equivalent
RT Concept Explication Research

CONCEPTUAL EXPLICATION RESEARCH
1975-1979 00225
USE Concept Explication Research

CONCILIAR MOVEMENT DOCTRINE
S-38-0382 1975 00000
BT Two Swords Theory
RT Papal Sovereignty
Religious Movement

CONCILIATION
S-31-0234 1975 00004
BT Conflict Resolution
RT Accommodation
Adjudication
Agreement
Appeasement
Bargaining
Decision Making Process
Declared War
Deescalation
Mediation
Negotiation

CONCORDANCE
USE Indexing

CONCUBINAGE
S-20-0009 1975 00000
BT Family Type
RT Polygamy

CONCURRENT MAJORITY THEORY
S-38-0084 1975 00000
SN Political doctrine that accords veto power to major groups involved in political process.
BT Democratic Theory
RT Athenian Democratic Theory
Democratic Elite Theory
General Will Democratic Theory
Interest Group Pluralism
Jacksonian Democratic Theory
Majoritarianism
Minority Rights Democratic Theory
Participatory Democratic Theory
Populist Democratic Theory
Procedural Democratic Theory
Republic Theory
Republican

CONFEDERAL GOVERNMENT
S-16-0058 1975 00004
BT Federal Government
RT Confederation Movement
Decentralized Government
State Rights Doctrine
Unitary Government

CONFEDERATION MOVEMENT
S-27-0003 1975 00004
BT Political Movement
RT Confederal Government
Decentralized Government
Federation Movement
Jeffersonian Democratic Theory
Majoritarianism
Minority Rights Democratic Theory
Participatory Democratic Theory
Populist Democratic Theory
Republic Theory
Separatist Movement
Socialist Democratic Theory

CONFIDENCE VOTING
S-29-0124 1975 00001
BT Voting
RT Government Dissolution Process
Government Formation Process
Legislative Dissolution
Legislative Voting
Parliament Cabinet Relations
Parliamentary Procedure

CONFIDENTIAL INFORMATION
S-18-0006 1975 00009
BT Information Sources
RT Documents
Intelligence Agency
Privileged Information
Spying
Surveillance

CONFIGURATIVE ANALYSIS
S-24-0409 1975 00002
BT Study Scope
RT Case Study
Comparative Analysis
Ideographic Research

CONFIRMATION
S-24-0141 1975 00003
BT Hypothesis Testing
RT Falsification
Replication

CONFIRMATION PROCESS
S-31-0328 1975 00001
BT Decision Making Process
RT Approval Process
Legislative Executive Relations

CONFISCATORY TAXATION
S-26-0140 1975 00001
BT Taxation Policy
RT Excise Taxation Policy
Import Duty
Income Taxation
Inheritance Taxation
Luxury Taxation
Tariff

CONFLICT
USE Conflict Type

CONFLICT CONTROL MANAGEMENT
S-23-0005 1975 00021
BT Conflict Management
RT Conflict Resolution
Conflict Resolution Theory
Conflict Theory
Crisis Management

CONFLICT FEDERALISM
S-37-0111 1975 00002
BT Federalism
RT Cooperative Federalism
New Federalism
State Rights Doctrine

CONFLICT INDICATOR
S-24-0262 1975 00013
BT Political Indicator
NT Threat Indicator
RT Political Instability Indicator
Political Resource Indicator

CONFLICT INTENSIFICATION
S-31-0216 1975 00010
BT Conflict Process
NT Escalation
Treaty Dissolution
RT Conflict Model
Crisis
International Crisis
Political Crisis
Treaty Dissolution
War

CONFLICT MANAGEMENT
S-23-0004 1975 00044
BT Management
NT Conflict Control Management
Crisis Management
RT Conflict Process
Conflict Resolution
Conflict Theory
Defense Management
Economic Management
Military Management

CONFLICT MODEL
S-24-0293 1975 00033
BT Social Science Model
RT Border Conflict
Conflict Intensification
Conflict Process
Conflict Theory
Conflict Type
Confrontation Politics
Consensus Model
Development Model
Endogenous System Stress

CONFLICT OF INTEREST
S-08-0024 1979 00000
BT Conflict Type
RT Crime
Institutional Conflict
Interpersonal Conflict
Organization Constraint
Social Conflict

CONFLICT PROCESS
S-31-0198 1975 00046
BT Process
NT Competition
Conflict Intensification
Conflict Resolution
Crisis
Dissent
RT Border War
Change Process
Conflict Management
Conflict Model
Conflict Theory
Conflict Type
Confrontation Politics
Decision Making Process
Interparty Competition
Legislative Process
Organization Conflict
Policy Making Process
Riot Theory
Social Cleavage

CONFLICT RESOLUTION
S-31-0220 1975 00051
BT Conflict Process
NT Accommodation
Adjudication
Agreement
Appeasement
Bargaining
Coercion
Conciliation
Deescalation
Mediation
Negotiation
RT Adversary System
Conflict Control Management
Conflict Management
Decision Making Process
International Law
Judicial Process
Summit Meeting

CONFLICT RESOLUTION THEORY
S-38-0123 1975 00033
BT Conflict Theory
RT Conflict Control Management
International Conflict
International Conflict Resolution Theory
Summit Meeting

CONFLICT THEORY
S-38-0121 1975 00070
BT Explanatory Political Theory
NT Aggression Theory
Conflict Resolution Theory
RT Conflict Control Management
Conflict Management
Conflict Model
Conflict Process
Conflict Type
Confrontation Politics
Crisis
Global War Policy
Group Representation Theory
Group Theory
Hobbesian Analysis
Ideology Explanatory Theory
International Politics
International Relations Studies
Intraparty Conflict
Marxist Class Theory
Marxist Revolution Theory
Organization Conflict
Political Crisis
Political Dissensus
Political Integration Theory
Power Politics
Power Theory
Revolution Theory
Social Cleavage
Treaty Breaking

CONFLICT TYPE
S-08-0001 1975 00012
UF Conflict
NT Aggression
Agitation
Conflict Of Interest
Cultural Conflict
Economic Conflict
Government Overthrow
Ideological Conflict
Institutional Conflict
Insurgency
Internal Conflict
International Conflict
Interpersonal Conflict
Social Conflict
Struggle
Violence
RT Conflict Model
Conflict Process
Conflict Theory
Riot Theory

CONFORMITY BEHAVIOR
S-05-0025 1975 00037
BT Accommodative Social Behavior
RT Adaptive Behavior
Coping Behavior
Habitual Behavior
Mass Behavior
Other Directed Personality

Other Directedness
Social Adjustment

CONFRONTATION POLITICS
S-29-0008 1975 00009
BT Politics
RT Conflict Model
Conflict Process
Conflict Theory
Electoral Politics
Power Politics
Protest

CONFUCIAN POLITICAL THEORY
S-38-0102 1975 00003
BT Eastern Political Thought
NT Mandate Of Heaven Theory
RT Confucianism
Mandate Of Heaven Theory
Neoconfucian Political Theory
Neoconfucianism

CONFUCIANISM
S-38-0556 1975 00013
BT Religious Thought
NT Neoconfucianism
RT Buddhism
Confucian Political Theory
Eastern Political Thought
Mandate Of Heaven Theory
Neoconfucianism
Shintoism
Taoism
Zoroastrianism

CONGLOMERATE
USE Corporation

CONGRESS
S-19-0257 1975 00059
BT National Legislature
NT Congressional System
House Of Representatives
Senate
RT Congressional Election Campaign
Congressional Leadership
Diet
National Assembly
Parliament
Parliamentary Leader
Peoples Assembly
Popular Assembly
Subnational Legislature

CONGRESSIONAL AGENCY
S-19-0259 1975 00005
BT Congressional System
RT Congressional Committee System
Congressional Delegation

CONGRESSIONAL AIDE
S-36-0206 1975 00002
BT Congressional Legislative Staff
RT Congressional Intern

CONGRESSIONAL CAMPAIGN
1975-1979 00004

CONGRESSIONAL CANDIDATE
S-32-0236 1975 00010
BT National Legislative Candidate
RT Congressional Election
Congressional Primary
Lower House Member

CONGRESSIONAL CAUCUS
S-19-0260 1975 00002
BT Congressional System
RT Congressional Committee System
Congressional Delegation

CONGRESSIONAL COMMITTEE
S-19-0262 1975 00014
BT Congressional Committee System
NT Ad Hoc Congressional Committee
Congressional Subcommittee
Joint Congressional Committee
Standing Congressional Committee
RT Senate House Conference Committee

CONGRESSIONAL COMMITTEE CHAIRPERSON
S-36-0149 1975 00002
BT National Legislative Committee Chairperson
RT Parliamentary Committee Chairperson

CONGRESSIONAL COMMITTEE SYSTEM
S-19-0261 1975 00014
BT Congressional System
NT Congressional Committee
Senate House Conference Committee
RT Congressional Agency
Congressional Caucus
Congressional Delegation
Congressional Seniority System
Parliamentary Committee

CONGRESSIONAL DELEGATION
S-19-0269 1975 00000
BT Congressional System
RT Ad Hoc Congressional Committee
Congressional Agency
Congressional Caucus
Congressional Committee System
Congressional Political Party
Congressional Seniority System
Joint Congressional Committee
Senate House Conference Committee

CONGRESSIONAL ELECTION
S-29-0058 1975 00031
BT National Legislative Election
RT Congressional Candidate
Parliamentary Election

CONGRESSIONAL ELECTION CAMPAIGN
S-29-0031 1979 00000
BT National Legislative Election Campaign
RT Canvassing
Congress
Congressional Political Party
Election Type
House Of Representatives
Parliamentary Election Campaign
Senate
Subnational Election Campaign

CONGRESSIONAL EXECUTIVE RELATIONS
S-31-0599 1975 00057
BT Legislative Executive Relations
RT Check And Balance Theory
Congressional Oversight
Parliament Cabinet Relations
State Of The Union

CONGRESSIONAL HEARING
S-31-0611 1975 00003
BT Legislative Hearing
NT Congressional Oversight
RT Commission Of Inquiry
Committee Decision Making
Congressional Investigation Committee
Contempt Of Congress

CONGRESSIONAL INFORMATION SYSTEM
1975-1979 00007

CONGRESSIONAL INTERN
S-36-0207 1975 00000
BT Congressional Legislative Staff
RT Congressional Aide
Economic Conflict
Global War Policy
Group Theory
Ideology Explanatory Theory
Marxist Class Theory

CONGRESSIONAL INVESTIGATION COMMITTEE
S-19-0088 1979 00000
UF Congressional Investigative Committee
BT Legislative Commission Of Inquiry
RT Congressional Hearing
Contempt Of Congress
Cross Examination
Federal Commission
Freedom Of Speech
Grand Jury Indictment
Legislative Commission
Self Defense

CONGRESSIONAL INVESTIGATIVE COMMITTEE
1975-1979 00003
USE Congressional Investigation Committee

CONGRESSIONAL LEADER
S-36-0180 1975 00001
BT National Legislative Leader
NT House Of Representatives Leader
Senate Leader
RT Congressional Political Party
Parliamentary Leader

CONGRESSIONAL LEADERSHIP
S-22-0023 1979 00000
BT Political Leadership
RT Congress
Executive Leadership
House Of Representatives
House Of Representatives Leader
House Of Representatives Speaker
Leadership Authority Base
Leadership Structure Type
Legislative Behavior
Legislative Power
National Leadership
Political Movement Leadership
Presidential Leadership
Senate

CONGRESSIONAL LEGISLATIVE STAFF
S-36-0205 1975 00003
BT National Legislative Staff
NT Congressional Aide
Congressional Intern
RT Parliamentary Legislative Staff

CONGRESSIONAL MEMBER
S-36-0189 1975 00026
BT National Legislative Member
NT Representative
Senator
RT Filibustering
Parliamentary Member

CONGRESSIONAL OVERSIGHT
S-31-0612 1975 00030
BT Congressional Hearing
RT Congressional Executive Relations

CONGRESSIONAL PARTY
1975-1979 00010

CONGRESSIONAL POLITICAL PARTY
S-28-0046 1979 00000
BT National Legislative Political Party
RT Congressional Delegation
Congressional Election Campaign
Congressional Leader
Congressional Procedure
Congressional Seniority System
Congressional Whip
Legislative Behavior
Parliamentary Political Party

CONGRESSIONAL PRIMARY
S-29-0073 1975 00000
BT National Legislative Primary
RT Congressional Candidate
Primary Election

CONGRESSIONAL PROCEDURE
S-31-0606 1975 00006
BT Legislative Procedure
NT Contempt Of Congress
Filibustering
RT Committee Of The Whole
Committee Rules
Congressional Political Party
Congressional System
Filibustering
Legislative Calendar
Legislative Hearing
Parliamentary Procedure
Parliamentary Procedure Law
Senatorial Courtesy

CONGRESSIONAL REFORM
S-31-0098 1975 00022
BT Legislative Reform
RT Apportionment Reform
Cabinet Reorganization
Executive Reorganization
Filibustering
Legislative Reorganization
Parliamentary Reform

CONGRESSIONAL RESEARCH SERVICE
1975-1979 00006

CONGRESSIONAL SENIORITY SYSTEM
S-19-0270 1975 00007
BT Congressional System
RT Congressional Committee System
Congressional Delegation
Congressional Political Party
Incumbent
Seniority
Standing Congressional Committee

CONGRESSIONAL SPEAKER
S-36-0161 1975 00000
BT National Legislative Speaker
NT House Of Representatives Speaker
Senate Speaker
RT Parliamentary Speaker

CONGRESSIONAL SUBCOMMITTEE
S-19-0264 1975 00003
BT Congressional Committee
RT Ad Hoc Congressional Committee
Joint Congressional Committee
Joint Standing Congressional Committee
Standing Congressional Committee

CONGRESSIONAL SYSTEM
S-19-0258 1975 00006
BT Congress
NT Congressional Agency
Congressional Caucus
Congressional Committee System
Congressional Delegation
Congressional Seniority System
RT Congressional Procedure
Filibustering
Law Formulation
Local Legislature
Provincial Parliament
Subnational Legislature

CONGRESSIONAL WHIP
S-36-0172 1975 00000
BT National Legislative Whip
RT Congressional Political Party
Parliamentary Whip

CONSCIENTIOUS OBJECTOR
S-32-0215 1975 00002
BT Political Role
RT Amnesty
Civil Disobedience
Draft Resistance
Pacifism
Peace Activist
Right Of Protest

CONSCRIPT
1975-1979 00000
USE Conscripted Armed Forces

CONSCRIPTED ARMED FORCES
S-33-0060 1975 00010
UF Conscript
BT Armed Forces
RT Army
Conscription Power
Draftee
Marines
Mass Militia Army
Mercenary Armed Forces
Military Forces
Military Mobilization
Military Recruit

CONSCRIPTION POWER
S-04-0037 1975 00000
UF Military Draft
BT Civil Military Authority
RT Conscripted Armed Forces
Draftee
War Power

CONSENSUAL NORMS
S-06-0718 1975 00005
BT Social Norms
RT Accommodative Social Behavior
Consensual Politics
Consensus Theory
Constraining Norms
Political Consensus
Social Adjustment

CONSENSUAL POLITICS
S-29-0009 1975 00007
BT Politics
RT Accommodative Social Behavior
Consensual Norms
Consensus Theory
Consociational Democracy
Electoral Politics
Political System Normative Characteristics

CONSENSUS MODEL
S-24-0294 1975 00013
BT Social Science Model
RT Assimilation Theory
Conflict Model
Consensus Theory
Equilibrium Model
Pluralist Model
Static Model

CONSENSUS THEORY
S-38-0439 1975 00006
BT Political Philosophy Concept
RT Accommodative Social Behavior
Common Good Theory
Consensual Norms
Consensual Politics
Consensus Model
Interaction Model
Order Theory

CONSENT JUDGMENT
S-31-0481 1975 00000
SN Decision by a court or administrative tribunal that is issued after negotiations and agreement by the affected parties.
BT Court Action
RT Acquittal
Cease Desist Order
Certiorari
Obiter Dicta
Subpoena
Verdict

CONSENT THEORY
S-38-0440 1975 00011
BT Political Philosophy Concept
RT Authority Theory
Hobbesian Absolutism
Hobbesian Analysis
Legitimacy Theory
Lockean Contractualism
Lockean Liberalism
Obligation Theory
Political Legitimacy Theory
Representation Theory
Rousseauian Analysis

CONSERVATION LAW
S-21-0054 1979 00000
BT Environmental Law
RT Environmental Agency
Environmental Management
Environmental Planning
Historical Preservation Law
Land Use Policy
Natural Resource Management
Natural Resource Policy

CONSERVATISM
S-38-0193 1975 00024
BT Ideologies
NT American Conservatism
Bureaucratic Conservatism
Burkean Conservatism
Christian Conservatism
Neoconservatism
Objectivist Political Thought
Reactionary Conservatism
Status Quo Conservatism
RT American Political Thought
Anticommunism
Conservative

Conservative Political Party
Conservative Regime
Traditional Authority
Traditional Culture
Traditional Social Elite

CONSERVATIVE
S-32-0257 1975 00003
BT Spectrum Politicist
RT American Political Thought
Centrist
Conservatism
Conservative Political Party
Extremist
Liberal

CONSERVATIVE PARTY
1975-1979 00009

CONSERVATIVE POLITICAL PARTY
S-28-0015 1979 00000
BT Ideological Spectrum Political Party Type
RT Burkean Conservatism
Conservatism
Conservative
Conservative Regime
Rightist Political Party
Status Quo Conservatism
Traditional Authority
Traditional Culture
Traditional Political Party

CONSERVATIVE REGIME
S-16-0136 1975 00002
BT Political Regime
RT Ancient Regime
Burkean Conservatism
Conservatism
Conservative Political Party
Elitism

CONSOCIATIONAL DEMOCRACY
S-16-0014 1975 00003
SN Political process characterized by sectoral organization and bargaining among sectoral elites.
BT Democratic Government
RT Consensual Politics
Constitutional Democracy
Federal Government
Majoritarian Democracy
Parliamentary Democracy
Participatory Democracy
Plebiscitary Democracy
Pluralist Democracy

CONSPICUOUS CONSUMPTION
S-06-0269 1975 00001
BT Consumption
RT Consumer Economics
Consumer Economy
Consumer Industry
Consumer Market
Consumption Pattern
Consumption Process
Domestic Consumption
Mass Consumption
Private Consumption
Prosperity
Public Consumption
Spending

CONSTABLE
S-36-0142 1975 00000
BT Local Police Official
RT Arraignment

CONSTANT SUM GAME THEORY
S-38-0133 1975 00001
BT Game Theory
RT Zero Sum Game Theory

CONSTITUENCY POLITICS
S-29-0010 1979 00000
BT Politics
RT Cultural Politics

CONSTITUENCY RELATIONS
S-31-0574 1975 00045
BT Legislative Process
RT Legislative Accountability
Legislative Role Orientation
Lobbying
Lobbying Tactic
Representation Type

CONSTITUENCY SIZE
S-29-0191 1975 00004
BT Electoral Unit
RT Electoral District
Local Election District

CONSTITUTION
S-21-0006 1975 00009
BT Basic Law
NT Constitutional Law
Democratic Constitution
National Constitution
State Constitution
Unwritten Constitution
Written Constitution
RT Authority Structure
Bicameral Legislature
Broad Constructionism
Check And Balance Theory
Civil Authority
Constitution Making
Constitutional Authority
Constitutional Law System
Constitutional Structural Theory
Formal Authority
Legislatures
Madisonian Thought
National Decision Making Process
Natural Law
Republican Constitutionalism
Statutory Law

CONSTITUTION AMENDMENT PROCESS
S-31-0578 1979 00000
UF Constitutional Amending Process
BT Constitutional Development
RT Constitution Making
Constitutional Amendment
Constitutional Authority
Constitutional Development
Constitutional Law System
Constitutional Revision
Formal Authority
Statutory Law

CONSTITUTION MAKING
S-31-0577 1975 00006
BT Constitutional Development
RT Constitution
Constitution Amendment Process
Constitutional Reform
Constitutional Revision
Interim Government
Madisonian Thought

CONSTITUTIONAL AMENDING PROCESS
1975-1979 00001
USE Constitution Amendment Process

CONSTITUTIONAL AMENDMENT
S-21-0008 1975 00012
BT Constitutional Law
NT Bill Of Rights
RT Constitution Amendment Process
Constitutional Democracy
Constitutional Development
Constitutional Interpretation Theory
Constitutional Reform
Constitutional Revision

CONSTITUTIONAL AUTHORITY
S-04-0028 1975 00015
BT Political Authority
RT Authoritative Value Allocation
Authorization Process
Centralized Authority
Civil Authority
Civil Military Authority
Constitution
Constitution Amendment Process
Decentralized Authority
Government Authority
Government Formation Process
Legal Rational Authority
Moral Authority

CONSTITUTIONAL CONVENTION
S-19-0103 1975 00003
BT Institutions
NT International Constitutional Convention
National Constitutional Convention
State Constitutional Convention
RT Delegation Member
State Constitutional Convention
Written Constitution

CONSTITUTIONAL CONVENTION DELEGATE SELECTION
S-31-0735 1975 00001
BT Convention Delegate Selection
RT Political Party Convention Delegate Selection

CONSTITUTIONAL COURT
S-19-0135 1975 00007
BT Courts
NT Appellate Court
District Court
Supreme Court
RT Civil Court
Constitutional Interpretation Theory
Constitutional Law
Criminal Court
Judicial Review

CONSTITUTIONAL DEMOCRACY
S-16-0015 1975 00016
BT Democratic Government
RT Bourgeois Democracy
Broad Constructionism
Consociational Democracy
Constitutional Amendment
Constitutional Dictatorship
Decentralized Government
Democratic Regime
Federal Government

Limited Government
Mixed Government
Parliamentary Democracy
Political Law
Representative Government
Socialist Government
Stable Democracy

CONSTITUTIONAL DEVELOPMENT
S-31-0576 1975 00019
BT Law Formulation
NT Constitution Amendment Process
Constitution Making
Constitutional Reform
Constitutional Revision
RT Constitution Amendment Process
Constitutional Amendment
Constitutional Interpretation Theory
Constitutional Structural Theory
State Constitutional Convention

CONSTITUTIONAL DICTATORSHIP
S-16-0038 1975 00000
BT Dictatorship
RT Bourgeois Dictatorship
Constitutional Democracy
Warfare State

CONSTITUTIONAL INTERPRETATION THEORY
S-38-0441 1975 00032
BT Political Philosophy Concept
NT Broad Constructionism
Constitutional Realism
Judicial Restraint Theory
Legalism
Strict Constructionism
RT Bill Of Attainder
Bill Of Rights
Constitutional Amendment
Constitutional Court
Constitutional Development
Constitutional Structural Theory

CONSTITUTIONAL JURISDICTION
S-06-0406 1975 00008
BT Court Jurisdiction
RT Appellate Jurisdiction
Constitutional Law
Constitutional Litigation
Original Jurisdiction

CONSTITUTIONAL LAW
S-21-0007 1975 00051
BT Constitution
NT Constitutional Amendment
RT Administrative Law
Chief Justice
Constitutional Court
Constitutional Jurisdiction
Constitutional Law System
Federal Constitution
Federal Judicial System
Human Rights Policy
Judicial Review
Legal Development
Legal History
Legal Jurisdiction
Legislative Jurisdiction
National Constitution
Presidential Accountability
Right To Due Process
Search And Seizure
State Constitution
State Constitutional Convention
Statutory Law
Supreme Court Review
Unwritten Constitution
Written Constitution

CONSTITUTIONAL LAW SYSTEM
S-37-0100 1975 00011
BT Law System
RT Administrative Law
Administrative Law System
Civil Law System
Common Law System
Comparative Law
Constitution
Constitution Amendment Process
Constitutional Law
Criminal Law System
Federal Constitution
International Law System
Judicial Review
Military Law
Military Law System
State Constitutional Convention
Supreme Court

CONSTITUTIONAL LITIGATION
S-31-0559 1975 00012
BT Litigation
RT Amicus Curiae
Civil Rights Litigation
Class Action Litigation
Constitutional Jurisdiction

CONSTITUTIONAL MONARCH
S-36-0056 1975 00002
BT Monarch
RT Absolute Monarch
Constitutional Monarchy

CONSTITUTIONAL MONARCHY
S-16-0074 1975 00002
BT Monarchy
RT Absolute Monarchy
Constitutional Monarch
Democratic Government
Limited Government
Limited Monarchy
Republican Monarchy

CONSTITUTIONAL REALISM
S-38-0443 1975 00000
BT Constitutional Interpretation Theory
RT Strict Constructionism

CONSTITUTIONAL REFORM
S-31-0579 1975 00012
BT Constitutional Development
RT Constitution Making
Constitutional Amendment
Constitutional Revision

CONSTITUTIONAL REVISION
S-31-0580 1975 00007
BT Constitutional Development
RT Constitution Amendment Process
Constitution Making
Constitutional Amendment
Constitutional Reform

CONSTITUTIONAL STRUCTURAL THEORY
S-38-0447 1975 00003
BT Political Philosophy Concept
NT Check And Balance Theory
Church State Separation Doctrine
Extended Republic Theory
Interposition Doctrine
Nullification Doctrine
Separation Of Power Theory
State Rights Doctrine
RT Constitution
Constitutional Development
Constitutional Interpretation Theory
Government Formation Process
Negative Freedom Theory
Republican Constitutionalism
Sovereignty Theory

CONSTRAINING NORMS
S-06-0719 1975 00012
BT Social Norms
RT Consensual Norms
Social Adjustment
Social Mores

CONSTRUCT VALIDITY
S-24-0165 1975 00020
BT Validity Measurement
RT Criterion Validity
Discriminant Validity
Face Validity

CONSTRUCTION INDUSTRY
S-17-0027 1975 00005
BT Industry
NT Building Supplies Industry
Housing Industry
Ship Building Industry
RT Defense Industry
Heavy Industry
Manufacturing Industry
Steel Industry

CONSUL GENERAL
S-36-0123 1975 00000
BT Embassy Official
RT Ambassador
Charge D'Affaires
Embassy Attache

CONSUMER
USE Consumerism

CONSUMER ACTIVIST
S-32-0182 1975 00004
BT Economic Activist
RT Consumer Behavior
Consumer Demonstration
Consumerism

CONSUMER ADVISORY BOARD
S-19-0011 1975 00001
BT Consumer Agency
RT Agricultural Advisory Board
Consumer Protection Agency

CONSUMER AGENCY
S-19-0010 1975 00000
BT Agencies
NT Consumer Advisory Board
Consumer Protection Agency
RT Agricultural Agency
Business Agency
Business Regulation Agency
Economic Control Agency
Environmental Advisory Agency
Environmental Agency
Price Control Agency
Price Control Law
Price Support Agency
Rationing Agency

CONSUMER BEHAVIOR
S-05-0008 1979 00000
BT Economic Behavior
RT Consumer Activist
Consumer Demonstration
Consumer Economy
Consumer Industry
Consumer Market
Consumer Policy
Consumerism
Consumption Pattern
Economic Behavior
Group Behavior

CONSUMER COOPERATIVE
1975-1979 00000
USE Marketing Cooperative

CONSUMER CREDIT POLICY
S-26-0045 1979 00000
BT Consumer Policy
RT Business Credit Policy
Business Regulation Policy
Consumer Protection Policy
Consumer Rights Movement
Consumerism
Credit Policy

CONSUMER DEMONSTRATION
S-08-0010 1975 00001
BT Economic Demonstration
RT Consumer Activist
Consumer Behavior
Consumer Interest Group
Consumer Producer Conflict
Consumerism
Rent Strike

CONSUMER ECONOMICS
S-01-0061 1975 00014
BT Economics Discipline
RT Business Economics
Business Studies
Conspicuous Consumption
Consumer Economy
Consumer Interest Group
Consumer Market
Consumerism
Consumption
Demand Analysis
Demand Elasticity
Econometrics
Economic Movement
Labor Economics
Regional Economics
Social Economics
Transportation Economics

CONSUMER ECONOMY
S-12-0013 1979 00000
BT Economy Type
RT Agrarian Economy
Balanced Economy
Capital Investment Economy
Conspicuous Consumption
Consumer Behavior
Consumer Economics
Consumerism
Cottage Industry Economy
Developed Economy
Developing Economy
Economic Community
Economic Movement
Hunting And Trapping Economy
Market Economy
Mixed Economy
Modernizing Economy
Public Consumption

CONSUMER INDUSTRIAL POLICY
S-26-0276 1975 00002
BT Industrial Policy
RT Business Policy
Consumer Policy
Economic Policy
Heavy Industrial Policy
Light Industrial Policy

CONSUMER INDUSTRY
S-17-0031 1975 00010
BT Industry
NT Dairy Industry
Farm Industry
Fishing Industry
RT Clothing Industry
Commodity Production
Conspicuous Consumption
Consumer Behavior
Consumption
Food Industry
Service Industry
Service Industry Policy
Synthetics Industry

CONSUMER INFORMATION POLICY
S-26-0287 1975 00011
BT Government Information Diffusion Policy
RT Clientele Information Policy
Consumer Interest Group

CONSUMER INTEREST GROUP
S-03-0015 1979 00000
BT Interest Group
RT Consumer Demonstration
Consumer Economics
Consumer Information Policy
Consumer Policy
Consumer Protection Litigation
Consumer Protection Policy
Consumerism

CONSUMER MARKET
S-19-0184 1975 00012
BT Market
RT Black Market
Commodity Market
Conspicuous Consumption
Consumer Behavior
Consumer Economics
Financial Market
Marketplace
Mass Market
National Market

CONSUMER POLICY
S-26-0044 1975 00009
BT Policy
NT Consumer Credit Policy
Consumer Protection Policy
RT Agricultural Policy
Business Policy
Consumer Behavior
Consumer Industrial Policy
Consumer Interest Group
Consumerism
Consumption

CONSUMER PRODUCER CONFLICT
S-08-0028 1975 00040
BT Economic Conflict
RT Consumer Demonstration
Economic Demonstration
Economic Rebellion
Group Conflict
Labor Conflict

CONSUMER PROTECTION AGENCY
S-19-0012 1975 00003
BT Consumer Agency
RT Consumer Advisory Board
Government Economic Management

CONSUMER PROTECTION LAW
S-21-0034 1979 00000
BT Economic Law
RT Antitrust Law
Bankruptcy Law
Civil Law
Consumer Rights Movement
Consumerism
Industrial Safety Law
Negligence Law

CONSUMER PROTECTION LITIGATION
S-31-0560 1975 00007
BT Litigation
RT Civil Rights Litigation
Class Action Litigation
Consumer Interest Group

CONSUMER PROTECTION POLICY
S-26-0046 1975 00013
BT Consumer Policy
RT Antitrust Agency
Business Policy
Consumer Credit Policy
Consumer Interest Group

CONSUMER RIGHTS MOVEMENT
S-27-0006 1979 00000
BT Economic Movement
RT Consumer Credit Policy
Consumer Protection Law
Consumerism
Trade Union Movement
Welfare Rights Movement

CONSUMERISM
S-38-0204 1975 00014
UF Consumer
BT Economic Ideology
RT Appliance Industry
Capitalism Theory
Clientelism
Consumer Activist
Consumer Behavior
Consumer Credit Policy
Consumer Demonstration
Consumer Economics
Consumer Economy
Consumer Interest Group
Consumer Policy
Consumer Protection Law
Consumer Rights Movement
Consumption
Economic Movement
Food Industry
Food Policy
Mass Consumption
Public Consumption

CONSUMPTION
S-06-0268 1975 00008
BT Economic Characteristics
NT Conspicuous Consumption
Consumption Pattern
Domestic Consumption
Energy Consumption
Mass Consumption
Private Consumption
Public Consumption
RT Business Agency
Consumer Economics
Consumer Industry
Consumer Policy
Consumerism
Consumption Process

CONSUMPTION PATTERN
S-06-0270 1975 00053
BT Consumption
RT Business Agency
Conspicuous Consumption
Consumer Behavior
Consumption Process
Domestic Consumption
Price Policy
Private Consumption
Production Process
Productivity Policy
Public Consumption

CONSUMPTION PROCESS
S-31-0370 1975 00011
BT Economic Process
RT Conspicuous Consumption
Consumption
Consumption Pattern
Export Market
Private Consumption
Spending

CONTAINMENT POLICY
S-26-0253 1975 00018
BT Foreign Policy
RT Anticommunism
Communist Imperialism
Convergence Theory
Expansionist Policy
Foreign Aid Policy
Intervention Policy

CONTEMPORARY ANALYTIC MODES
S-09-0001 1975 00004
NT Aggregate Data Analysis
Analysis Of Play
Behavior Analysis
Biographical Analysis
Catastrophe Analysis
Class Analysis
Communication Analysis
Contextual Analysis
Cost Benefit Analysis
Critical Theory Analysis
Cybernetic Analysis
Demand Analysis
Eastonian Analysis
Ecological Analysis
Elite Analysis
Graph Theory Analysis
Group Analysis
Historical Analysis
Ideal Type Analysis
Identity Analysis
Input Output Analysis
Interaction Analysis
Issue Analysis
Leadership Analysis
Leisure Time Analysis
Linguistic Analysis
Literature Analysis
Marginal Analysis
Marxist Analysis
Motivational Analysis
National Accounts Analysis
National Income Analysis
Network Analysis
Pluralist Analysis
Policy Analysis
Political Psychology Analysis
Psychoanalysis
Rational Man Analysis
Reductionist Analysis
Situational Analysis
Social Area Analysis
Socialization Analysis
Sociological Analysis
Spatial Analysis
Structural Functional Analysis
Survey Analysis
Transactional Analysis
Value Analysis
Voting Behavior Analysis
RT Analysis Methodology
Analytic Process
Contemporary Political Thought
Data Theory
Empirical Theory
Field Theory
Formal Political Theory
Futurology
Graph Theory Analysis
Modern Political Thought
Neoclassical Economic Theory
Neopositivism
Theory Of Causality

CONTEMPORARY POLITICAL THOUGHT
S-38-0060 1975 00002
BT Political Theory
NT Black Political Thought
Existentialism
Neohegelianism
Neomarxism
Ordinary Language Philosophy
Phenomenological Thought
Pragmatism
Progressivism
Radicalism
Straussian Thought
Structural Marxism
Teilhardean Thought
Utopianism
RT Behavioral Theory
Community Philosophical Concept
Contemporary Analytic Modes
Explanatory Political Theory
Ideologies
Medieval Political Thought
Modern Political Thought
Political Ideology
Political Philosophy Concept
Renaissance Political Thought

CONTEMPT OF CONGRESS
S-31-0607 1975 00001
BT Congressional Procedure
RT Commission Of Inquiry
Congressional Hearing
Congressional Investigation Committee
Prosecution Immunity

CONTEMPT OF COURT
S-10-0004 1975 00002
BT Court Crime
RT Bail Skipping
Court Procedure
Jury Tampering

CONTENT ANALYSIS
S-24-0379 1975 00106
BT Data Selection Orientation
RT Grammatical Analysis
Issue Intensity
Issue Salience
Linguistic Analysis
Mass Media Analysis

CONTESTED ELECTION
S-29-0043 1975 00001
BT Election Type
RT Initiative Election
Runoff Election
Special Election

CONTEXTUAL ANALYSIS
S-09-0011 1979 00000
BT Contemporary Analytic Modes
RT Behavior Analysis
Class Analysis
Communication Analysis
Cybernetic Analysis
Environmental Studies
Historical Analysis
Ideal Type Analysis
Issue Intensity
Issue Salience
Linguistic Analysis
Motivational Analysis
Organization Environment
Policy Analysis
Reductionist Analysis
Situational Analysis

CONTINGENCY THEORY
S-38-0045 1979 00000
BT Planning Theory
RT Administrative Planning
Economic Planning
Economic Policy
Forecasting Methodology
Futurology
Goal Setting
Modernization Theory
Organization Theory
Planning Policy
Planning Process
Planning Theory

CONTINUING EDUCATION
S-13-0007 1975 00006
BT Education Type
RT Adult Education
Alternative Education
Civic Education
Education Planning
Education Policy Making
Education Process
Higher Education

Public Education Policy
Secondary Education
Vocation Training Policy

CONTRACT
USE Contract Type

CONTRACT LAW
S-21-0023 1975 00012
BT Law Type
NT Negligence Law
Tort
RT Business Contract
Commercial Law
Contract Type
Economic Law
Marriage Contract
Patent Law
Property Law
Statutory Law

CONTRACT TYPE
S-02-0037 1979 00000
UF Bargain
Contract
BT Agreement Type
NT Business Contract
Labor Management Contract
Marriage Contract
RT Coalition Type
Commercial Agreement
Commercial Treaty
Compact
Contract Law
Political Front
World Commerce

CONTROL PROCESS
S-31-0263 1975 00085
BT Process
NT Censorship Process
Exploitation Process
Expropriation Process
Information Manipulation
Political Control
Purge
Regulation Process
Repression Process
RT Authoritarianism
Change Process
Communication Process
Control Theory
Decontrol Process
Destalinization Process
Nationalities Law
Political Purge

CONTROL THEORY
S-38-0164 1975 00019
BT Power Theory
RT Control Process
Power Type

CONTROL VARIABLE
S-24-0434 1975 00003
BT Intervening Variable
RT Exogenous Variable
Explanatory Variable

CONVENTION DELEGATE
S-32-0167 1975 00010
BT Delegate
RT Convention Delegate Selection
Delegate At Large
Favorite Son Candidate

CONVENTION DELEGATE SELECTION
S-31-0734 1975 00001
BT Delegate Selection
NT Constitutional Convention Delegate Selection
Political Party Convention Delegate Selection
RT Convention Delegate
Favorite Son Candidate
Slate Making

CONVENTIONAL WAR
S-08-0091 1975 00021
BT War
RT Conventional Weapon
Damage Limiting Strategy
Declared War
Just War
War By Proxy

CONVENTIONAL WEAPON
S-33-0023 1975 00016
BT Military Weapon
RT Civilian Weapon
Conventional War
Defensive Weapon
Handgun
Missile
Munitions
Nuclear Weapon
Strategic Weapon
Unconventional Weapon

CONVERGENCE THEORY
S-38-0036 1975 00010
SN Tendency toward similarity of structures among industrialized societies.
BT Modernization Theory
RT Containment Policy
Economic Development Theory
International Political Theory
International Relations Studies
Social Development Theory
Superpower Politics

CONVICTION
S-31-0482 1975 00003
BT Court Action
RT Acquittal
Cease Desist Order
Injunction
Life Sentence
Plea Bargaining
Subpoena
Verdict

COOPERATIVE BEHAVIOR
S-05-0026 1979 00000
BT Accommodative Social Behavior
RT Adaptive Behavior
Behavior Modification
Behavioral Psychology
Behavioral Theory
Cooperativism
Learning Psychology
Personality Characteristics
Psychological Programming
Psychology Discipline
Social Interaction Theory

COOPERATIVE COMMUNITY
S-07-0017 1975 00003
BT Community Type
NT Collective Community
Communal Community
Kibbutz
Utopian Community
RT Academic Community
Compound
Economic Community
Ghetto Community
Homogeneous Community
Integrated Community
New Town
Political Community
Squatter Community

COOPERATIVE FARM ECONOMY
S-12-0005 1975 00002
BT Farm Economy
RT Agricultural Cooperative
Centrally Planned Economy
Dairy Industry
Family Farm Economy
Farming
Labor Intensive Economy
Peasant Cooperative
Socialist Economy
Socialist Market Economy
State Farm Economy

COOPERATIVE FEDERALISM
S-37-0112 1975 00004
BT Federalism
RT Conflict Federalism
New Federalism

COOPERATIVES
S-03-0002 1975 00003
BT Associations
NT Agricultural Cooperative
Credit Cooperative
Housing Cooperative
Marketing Cooperative
Peasant Cooperative
Producer Cooperative
Village Cooperative
Worker Cooperative
RT Civic Organization
Cooperativism
Economic Community
Economic Interest Group
Peasant Organization
Social Group
Village Development
Worker Cooperative

COOPERATIVISM
S-38-0205 1975 00004
BT Economic Ideology
RT Cooperative Behavior
Cooperatives

COOPTATION
S-31-0742 1975 00001
SN Method of recruitment involving lateral rather than vertical movement into the group.
BT Recruitment Process
RT Elite Recruitment
Military Recruitment
Political Party Recruitment Pattern
Political Recruitment

COPING BEHAVIOR
S-05-0010 1979 00000
BT Personal Behavior
RT Adaptive Behavior
Behavioral Psychology
Clinical Psychology

Conformity Behavior
Pathological Behavior
Psychiatry
Psychoanalysis
Psychological Theory
Psychology Discipline
Psychopathology
Sexual Behavior
Social Adjustment
Social Psychiatry
Social Psychology

COPYRIGHT POLICY
S-26-0288 1975 00003
BT Government Information Diffusion Policy
RT Magazine Industry
Publication Industry

CORONER
S-36-0096 1975 00000
BT Court Official
RT Bailiff

CORPORATE BUREAUCRACY
S-19-0072 1975 00001
BT Economic Bureaucracy
RT Bureaucratic Elite
Corporate Management
Corporation

CORPORATE ECONOMY
S-12-0037 1975 00004
BT Planned Economy
NT Fascist Economy
RT Big Business
Corporate Farm Economy
Corporate Income
Corporate Power
Corporate State
Corporation
Nationalized Economy

CORPORATE ELITE
S-14-0007 1979 00000
BT Business Elite
RT Business Studies
Businessman
Commercial Elite
Decision Making Elite
Financial Elite
Managerial Elite
Multinational Corporation
Power Elite

CORPORATE FARM ECONOMY
S-31-0429 1975 00000
BT Farming
RT Corporate Economy
Farm Income
Farm Industry
Farm Production
Farming
Market Economy
Plantation Economy
Single Group Farm Economy
State Farm Economy

CORPORATE FARMING
1975-1979 00001

CORPORATE FASCISM
S-38-0225 1975 00000
BT Fascist Theory
RT Authoritarian Regime
Dictatorial Regime
Dictatorship
Falangism
Falangist
Fascist Movement
Francoism
Italian Fascism
National Socialism
Neofascism
Oligarchic Government
Peronism

CORPORATE INCOME
S-06-0326 1975 00007
BT Business Income
RT Corporate Economy
Family Income
Farm Income
Foreign Income
Personal Income

CORPORATE MANAGEMENT
S-23-0011 1975 00018
BT Business Management
RT Administrative Management
Corporate Bureaucracy
Corporation
Development Management
Industrial Management
International Economic Management
Personnel Management

CORPORATE POWER
S-30-0005 1975 00009
BT Economic Power
RT Corporate Economy
Countervailing Power
Economic Community
Economic Conglomerate
International Corporation

CORPORATE STATE
S-16-0163 1975 00003
BT State Type
RT Corporate Economy
Corporatism
Fascist Economy
Fascist Theory
Functional Representation Theory
Tutelary Democracy

CORPORATION
S-19-0163 1975 00028
UF Conglomerate
BT Economic Institution
NT Cartel
Economic Conglomerate
Holding Company
International Corporation
Public Corporation
Quasipublic Corporation
RT Business
Business Contract
Business Studies
Corporate Bureaucracy
Corporate Economy
Corporate Management
Corporation Lawyer
Corporatism
Economic Bureaucracy
Enterprise
Fiscal Institution
Monetary Institution
Multinational Organization
World Bank

CORPORATION LAWYER
S-32-0095 1975 00006
BT Lawyer
RT Corporation

CORPORATISM
S-38-0202 1975 00013
BT Ideologies
RT Absolutism
Caudillism
Clientelism
Corporate State
Corporation
Interest Group Theory
Medieval Corporatism
Syndicalism

CORRECTIONAL INSTITUTION
S-19-0292 1975 00012
BT Penal Institution
NT Jail
Juvenile Center
RT Law System
Prison
Prison Reform
Prison System

CORRELATION ANALYSIS
S-24-0034 1975 00084
BT Bivariate Analysis
NT Product Moment Correlation
Rank Order Correlation
Regression Analysis
RT Multivariate Analysis
Regression Analysis
Univariate Analysis

COSMOLOGY
S-25-0003 1975 00004
BT Philosophical Concept
RT Eschatology
History Of Philosophy
Metaphysics

COST BENEFIT ANALYSIS
S-09-0012 1975 00082
BT Contemporary Analytic Modes
RT Cost Effectiveness
Input Output Analysis
Marginal Analysis
National Accounts Analysis
National Income Analysis
Social Area Analysis
Value Analysis

COST EFFECTIVENESS
S-06-0157 1975 00056
BT Productivity Rate
RT Cost Benefit Analysis

COST OF LIVING INDEX
S-06-0287 1975 00001
BT Economic Index
RT Economic Growth Model
Economic Growth Rate
Economic Indicator
Fiscal Policy
Inflation Policy
Monetary Policy
Quality Of Life

COST SHARING
S-31-0401 1975 00005
BT Public Financing
RT Development Financing
Government Economic Management
Local Financing

COTTAGE INDUSTRY
S-17-0058 1975 00002
BT Light Industry
RT Clothing Industry
Cottage Industry Economy
Feudal Economic Stage
Production Process
Traditional Society
Transitional Society
Village Cooperative

COTTAGE INDUSTRY ECONOMY
S-12-0014 1979 00000
UF Cottage Industry Policy
BT Economy Type
NT Craft Economy
RT Agrarian Economy
Consumer Economy
Cottage Industry
Family Farm Economy
Farm Economy
Industrial Policy
Mixed Economy
Peasant Economy
Self Sufficient Economy
Subsistence Economy
Underdeveloped Economy

COTTAGE INDUSTRY POLICY
1975-1979 00000
USE Cottage Industry Economy

COUNCIL MANAGER
S-36-0084 1975 00000
BT Local Chief Government Executive
RT City Manager
Council Manager Government
Local Chief Executive Election
Mayor
Village Chief

COUNCIL MANAGER GOVERNMENT
S-16-0105 1975 00002
BT City Government
RT City Council Government
City Manager Government
Council Manager
Municipality
Strong Mayor Government
Weak Mayor Government

COUNCIL OF MINISTERS
S-19-0115 1975 00004
BT National Government Council
RT Cabinet
Cabinet Government
Executive Government Institution
Presidential Advisory Council
Privy Council
Shadow Cabinet

COUNCILS
S-19-0107 1975 00000
BT Institutions
NT Economic Council
International Government Council
National Government Council
Subnational Government Council
RT Agencies
Authorities
Commissions
Economic Institution
Executive Government Institution
Legislature Type

COUNTER CULTURE
S-11-0013 1975 00011
BT Culture Type
RT Counter Culture Ideology
Ethnic Culture
Heterogeneous Culture
Homogeneous Culture
Mass Culture
Political Culture
Poverty Culture
Religious Culture
Subculture
Urban Culture
Western Culture
Youth Culture

COUNTER CULTURE IDEOLOGY
S-38-0277 1975 00006
BT New Left
RT Anarchism
Anarchy
Counter Culture
New Left Militant
Nihilism
Student Activism
Student Radicalism

COUNTERDEMONSTRATOR
1975-1979 00000

COUNTERFORCE THEORY
S-38-0528 1979 00000
BT Strategic Theory
RT Assured Destruction Policy
Deterrence Policy
Massive Retaliation Policy
Second Strike Capability
Second Strike Policy
Strategic Studies

COUNTERINSURGENCY
S-08-0045 1975 00006
BT Insurgency
RT Government Overthrow
Internal War
Rebellion
Revolution
Struggle

COUNTERREVOLUTION
S-08-0063 1975 00007
BT Revolution
RT Anticommunism
Cultural Revolution
Dictatorship
Ecological Revolution
Fascist Theory
Feudal Reaction Theory
Government Overthrow
Internal War
Paramilitary Forces
Political Revolution
Reactionary Conservatism
Romanticism
Social Revolution
Spontaneous Revolution
Technological Revolution
Thermidor

COUNTERREVOLUTIONARY
1975-1979 00001

COUNTERVAILING POWER
S-30-0006 1975 00003
BT Economic Power
RT Corporate Power

COUNTY
S-24-0367 1975 00004
BT State Political Division
RT Borough
County Government
Legislative District
Township
Village

COUNTY GOVERNMENT
S-16-0089 1975 00014
BT Subnational Government
NT County Manager Government
RT City Government
County
County Level Court
County Manager Government
District Government Type
Local Government
Metropolitan Government
Provincial Government

COUNTY LEVEL COURT
S-19-0151 1975 00000
BT Local Court
RT County Government
County Manager Government
Customary Law
Jury System

COUNTY MANAGER GOVERNMENT
S-16-0090 1975 00000
BT County Government
RT City Manager Government
County Government
County Level Court
Local Government
Management
Management Characteristics
Manager
Metropolitan City
Provincial Government

COUP D'ETAT
S-08-0038 1975 00019
BT Government Overthrow
NT Military Coup
RT Economic Conflict
Elite Disintegration
Insurgency
Internal Conflict
Military Aggression
Military Coup
Mob Violence
Political Violence
Putsch
Rebellion
Revolution

COURAGE
S-06-0505 1979 00000
BT Personality Characteristics
RT Altruism
Ambivalence
Assertiveness
Charity
Creativity
Culture Shock
Curiosity
Egocentrism
Femininity
Gregariousness
Honesty
Imagination

Masculinity
Optimism
Persistence

COURT ACTION
S-31-0477 1975 00030
BT Judicial Process
NT Acquittal
Cease Desist Order
Certiorari
Consent Judgment
Conviction
Injunction
Life Sentence
Obiter Dicta
Subpoena
Verdict
Warrant
Writ Of Mandamus
RT Court Jurisdiction
Court Procedure
Criminal Punishment
Death Penalty Law
Judicial Decision Making
Judicial Procedure
Judicial Selection
Litigation
Municipal Court
Punishment

COURT ATTORNEY
S-36-0097 1975 00000
BT Court Official
NT Barrister
Defense Attorney
Prosecuting Attorney
Solicitor
RT Lawyer
Legal Advisor
Legal Service
Trial Court
Trial Procedure

COURT CRIME
S-10-0002 1975 00000
BT Crime
NT Bail Skipping
Contempt Of Court
Jury Tampering
Perjury
RT Court Procedure
Individual Crime
Recidivism
Religious Offense

COURT JURISDICTION
S-06-0404 1975 00012
BT Legal Jurisdiction
NT Appellate Jurisdiction
Constitutional Jurisdiction
Original Jurisdiction
RT Administrative Court
Court Action
Courts
Judicial Power
Judicial System
Municipal Court

COURT MARTIAL
S-31-0520 1975 00002
BT Military Trial
RT Martial Law
Military Prison
Punishment
War Crime Trial

COURT OFFICIAL
S-36-0093 1975 00002
BT Government Official
NT Amicus Curiae
Bailiff
Coroner
Court Attorney
Judge
Juror
RT Courts
Justice Of The Peace
Local Civil Servant
Municipal Court

COURT PROCEDURE
S-31-0490 1975 00008
BT Judicial Process
NT Post Trial Procedure
Pretrial Procedure
Trial
Trial Procedure
RT Adversary Process
Bail Bond System
Contempt Of Court
Court Action
Court Crime
Courts
Jury
Jury System
Law Enforcement
Litigation
Trial Procedure

COURT REFORM
S-31-0093 1975 00005
BT Judicial Reform
RT Penal Reform

COURT REPORT
S-18-0031 1975 00000
UF Legal Brief
BT Judicial Record
RT Court Transcript

COURT TRANSCRIPT
S-18-0032 1975 00002
BT Judicial Record
RT Court Report

COURTS
S-19-0124 1975 00006
BT Institutions
NT Administrative Court
Civil Court
Colonial Court
Constitutional Court
Criminal Court
International Court
Jury
Local Court
Maritime Court
Military Court
RT Commission Of Inquiry
Court Jurisdiction
Court Official
Court Procedure
Crime Commission
Investigation Commission
Judicial System
Jury System
Justice Administration Agency
Law System
Lawyer

COVARIANCE ANALYSIS
S-24-0043 1975 00006
BT Multivariate Analysis
RT Analysis Of Variance
Automatic Interaction Detection
Canonical Correlation Analysis
Dimensional Analysis
Discriminant Analysis
Factor Analysis
Multiple Correlation Analysis
Multiple Regression Analysis
Partial Correlation Analysis
Path Analysis

CRAFT ECONOMY
S-12-0015 1979 00000
UF Craft Guild
BT Cottage Industry Economy
RT Agrarian Economy
Barter Economy
Dual Economy
Farm Economy
Labor Intensive Economy
Medieval Corporatism
Mixed Economy
Nomadic Economy
Preindustrial Society
Self Sufficient Economy
Skilled Worker

CRAFT GUILD
1975-1979 00001
USE Craft Economy

CRAFT UNION
S-03-0067 1975 00000
BT Union
RT Industrial Union
Labor Union
Trade Union

CREATIVITY
S-06-0506 1979 00000
BT Personality Characteristics
RT Altruism
Ambivalence
Assertiveness
Charity
Courage
Curiosity
Egocentrism
Femininity
Gregariousness
Imagination
Masculinity
Optimism
Persistence

CREDIT COOPERATIVE
S-03-0004 1975 00003
BT Cooperatives
RT Agricultural Cooperative
Economic Interest Group
Housing Cooperative
Marketing Cooperative
Village Cooperative
Worker Cooperative

CREDIT POLICY
S-26-0125 1975 00015
UF Bank Rate
Loan
BT Monetary Policy
RT Banking Policy
Business Credit Policy
Consumer Credit Policy

Money Supply Policy
Tax Credit
Tax Rebate
World Bank

CRIME
S-10-0001 1975 00059
NT Court Crime
Crime Against Humanity
Crime Rate
Economic Crime
Individual Crime
Organized Crime
Piracy
Political Crime
Pornographic Crime
Recidivism
Religious Offense
Violent Crime
RT Civilian Weapon
Conflict Of Interest
Criminal Court
Criminal Law
Criminal Law System
Death Penalty Law
Illegal Abortion
Law Type
Psychological Aggression
Punishment

CRIME AGAINST HUMANITY
S-10-0007 1975 00002
BT Crime
NT Euthanasia
Genocide
War Crime
RT Murder
Organized Crime
Violent Crime
War Atrocity

CRIME COMMISSION
S-19-0092 1975 00001
BT Investigation Commission
RT Arraignment
Attorney General
Commission Of Inquiry
Courts

CRIME RATE
S-10-0013 1979 00000
BT Crime
RT Criminal
Criminal Law
Criminal Law System
Criminal Punishment
Criminology
Jail
Justice Administration
Law Enforcement System
Police
Recidivism

CRIMINAL
S-36-0028 1975 00026
UF Burgler
Felon
Robber
BT Status
NT Economic Criminal
Personal Crime Criminal
Political Criminal
War Criminal
RT Crime Rate
Criminal Court
Illegal Abortion
Prison
Prison System
Prisoner

CRIMINAL ABORTION
S-10-0030 1975 00002
BT Individual Crime
RT Illegal Abortion
Murder

CRIMINAL COURT
S-19-0142 1975 00005
BT Courts
NT Trial Court
RT Administrative Court
Constitutional Court
Crime
Criminal
Death Penalty Law
Grand Jury System
International Court
Jail
Justice Of The Peace
Local Court
Military Court
Penal Institution
Supreme Court

CRIMINAL DETERRENCE
S-26-0063 1979 00000
BT Deterrence Policy
RT Behavior Modification
Capital Punishment

CRIMINAL JUSTICE ADMINISTRATION
S-23-0031 1975 00033
BT Justice Administration
RT Criminal Law System
Death Penalty Law
Grand Jury Indictment
Grand Jury System
Jury System
Justice Administration Agency
Juvenile Center
Police Administration

CRIMINAL LAW
S-21-0026 1975 00025
BT Law Type
NT Death Penalty Law
Penal Law
RT Crime
Crime Rate
Criminal Law System
Criminal Punishment
Decriminalization
Grand Jury System
Illegal Abortion
Jury System
Procedural Law

CRIMINAL LAW SYSTEM
S-37-0101 1975 00014
BT Law System
RT Acquittal
Arraignment
Attorney General
Burden Of Proof
Circumstantial Evidence
Common Law System
Constitutional Law System
Crime
Crime Rate
Criminal Justice Administration
Criminal Law
Criminal Procedure Law
International Law System
Military Law System

CRIMINAL LAWYER
S-32-0096 1975 00004
BT Lawyer
RT Adversary System
Attorney General
Burden Of Proof
Civil Lawyer

CRIMINAL PRISON
S-19-0300 1975 00007
BT Prison
RT Jail
Juvenile Center
Law Enforcement Policy
Law Enforcement System
Military Prison
Murderer

CRIMINAL PROCEDURE LAW
S-21-0078 1975 00008
BT Procedural Law
RT Capital Punishment
Circumstantial Evidence
Civil Procedure Law
Criminal Law System
Penal Law

CRIMINAL PUNISHMENT
S-31-0569 1975 00033
BT Punishment
NT Capital Punishment
RT Court Action
Crime Rate
Criminal Law

CRIMINOLOGY
S-01-0185 1975 00018
BT Sociology Discipline
RT Applied Sociology
Capital Punishment
Crime Rate
Death Penalty Law
Decriminalization
Jury System
Legal Studies
Policy Science Studies
Psychological Anthropology
Psychopathology

CRISIS
S-31-0246 1979 00000
BT Conflict Process
NT Economic Crisis
Natural Catastrophe
Personality Crisis
Political Crisis
Social Crisis
RT Catastrophe Analysis
Cleavage Process
Conflict Intensification
Conflict Theory
Crisis Management
Economic Crisis
Escalation
Identity Crisis
International Crisis
Personality Crisis
Political Crisis

Political Instability
Social Crisis

CRISIS MANAGEMENT
S-23-0006 1979 00000
BT Conflict Management
RT Administrative Management
Catastrophe Analysis
Conflict Control Management
Crisis
Defense Management
Military Management
Political Crisis
Public Policy Management

CRITERION VALIDITY
S-24-0166 1975 00013
BT Validity Measurement
RT Construct Validity
Discriminant Validity
Face Validity

CRITICAL ELECTION
S-29-0044 1975 00005
BT Election Type
RT Deviating Election
Plebiscite Election
Political Party Realignment
Realigning Election
Reinstating Election

CRITICAL THEORY ANALYSIS
S-09-0013 1975 00019
BT Contemporary Analytic Modes
RT Communication Theory
Cultural Alienation
Dialectic
Eurocommunism
Hegelian Analysis
Left Hegelianism
Neomarxism
Policy Analysis

CROSS CULTURAL ANALYSIS
S-24-0404 1975 00253
BT Comparative Analysis
RT Comparative Political Studies
Comparative Sociology
Cross Cultural Data
Cross Cultural Index
Cross Level Analysis
Cross National Analysis
Cultural Group
Foreign Student
International Analysis
International Exchange Program
Intracultural Analysis
Public Opinion Survey

CROSS CULTURAL DATA
S-18-0096 1979 00000
UF Cross Cultural Survey
BT Survey Data
RT Comparative Analysis
Cross Cultural Analysis
Cultural Anthropology
Data Theory
Field Data
Political Statistics
Public Opinion Survey
Test Results

CROSS CULTURAL INDEX
S-24-0205 1975 00010
BT Scale Construction Methodology
RT Composite Scale
Cross Cultural Analysis
Cultural Development Policy
Scale Construction Methodology

CROSS CULTURAL SURVEY
1975-1979 00018
USE Cross Cultural Data

CROSS EXAMINATION
S-15-0053 1975 00000
BT Right To Trial
RT Burden Of Proof
Congressional Investigation Committee
Evidence Admissibility
Grand Jury Indictment
Right To Counsel
Right To Due Process
Right To Jury Trial
Right To Speedy Trial
Self Incrimination

CROSS LAGGED PANEL ANALYSIS
S-24-0089 1975 00000
SN Correlation analysis technique which enables one to separate and evaluate different interpretations of a causal relationship between two variables.
BT Time Series Analysis
RT Comparative Analysis
Cross Level Analysis
Panel Technique
Time Series Analysis

CROSS LEVEL ANALYSIS
S-24-0405 1975 00014
BT Comparative Analysis
RT Aggregate Data Analysis
Comparative Sociology
Cross Cultural Analysis
Cross Lagged Panel Analysis
Cross National Analysis
Interaction Analysis
International Analysis
Intracultural Analysis
Propositional Inventory

CROSS NATIONAL ANALYSIS
S-24-0406 1975 00198
BT Comparative Analysis
RT Aggregate Data Analysis
Comparative Political Studies
Cross Cultural Analysis
Cross Level Analysis
International Exchange Program

CROSS PRESSURE THEORY
S-38-0536 1975 00006
SN Assertion that overlapping group memberships tend to diminish intensity of commitment to any single issue or cause.
BT Psychological Theory
RT Achievement Theory
Cognitive Theory
Freudian Theory
Frustration Aggression Theory
Learning Theory
Multiple Group Membership
Overlapping Membership
Pluralist Group Theory
Psychological Behavioralism
Psychopolitical Theory

CROSS SECTIONAL ANALYSIS
S-24-0084 1975 00020
BT Observation Time
RT Longitudinal Analysis

CROWD BEHAVIOR
S-05-0033 1975 00008
BT Mass Behavior
RT Anomic Process
Deviant Behavior
Group Theory
Mass Behavior
Mob Violence
Riot Theory
Social Behavior

CULT OF PERSONALITY
S-31-0455 1979 00000
BT Elite Mass Relations
RT Charismatic Leader
Communist Studies
Elite Mass Relations
Leadership Analysis
Leadership Political Analysis
Leadership Psychological Analysis
Personality Theory
Personalized Leadership
Political Legitimacy Theory
Political Repression
Stalinism
Succession Struggle
Totalitarian Leadership
Totalitarian Political System

CULTURAL ADAPTATION
S-31-0051 1975 00029
BT Cultural Change Process
RT Acculturation
Acculturation Theory
Cultural Development Policy
Cultural Differentiation
Cultural History
Cultural Lag
Culture Shock
Ethnic Assimilation Theory

CULTURAL ADVISORY BOARD
S-19-0014 1975 00001
BT Cultural Agency
RT Arts Policy
Education Institution
Information Agency

CULTURAL AGENCY
S-19-0013 1975 00006
BT Agencies
NT Cultural Advisory Board
RT Cultural Group
Cultural Politics
Education Agency
Education Institution
Information Agency

CULTURAL AGGRESSION
S-08-0003 1975 00008
BT Aggression
RT Cultural Imperialism
Cultural Policy
Cultural Revolution
Ethnic Group Conflict
Interpersonal Conflict
Military Aggression
Psychological Aggression
Religious Conflict

Social Revolution

CULTURAL AGREEMENT
S-02-0072 1975 00003
BT State Agreement Type
NT Cultural Exchange Agreement
RT Cultural Development Policy
Education Agreement
Friendship Agreement

CULTURAL ALIENATION
S-06-0077 1975 00008
BT Alienation
RT Critical Theory Analysis
Cultural Group
Cultural Identity
Distrust
Estrangement
Normlessness
Political Alienation
Political Alienation Scale
Political Alienation Theory
Role Ambivalence

CULTURAL ANTHROPOLOGY
S-01-0009 1975 00040
BT Anthropology Discipline
NT Ethnography
Ethnolinguistics
Ethnology
Structural Linguistics
RT African Area Studies
American Area Studies
American Indian Studies
Anthropological Functionalism
Anthropological Linguistic Theory
Area Studies
Asian Area Studies
Bilateral Family Descent Pattern
Black History
Black Studies
British Commonwealth Area Studies
Caribbean Area Studies
Central African Area Studies
Central American Area Studies
Chicano Studies
Comparative Political Studies
Comparative Sociology
Cross Cultural Data
Cultural History
Demographic Studies
East African Area Studies
East Asian Area Studies
East European Area Studies
Ethnic Studies
Folk Literature
Latin American Area Studies
Macrosociology
North American Area Studies
Patrilineal Family
Physical Anthropology
Political Anthropology
Political Science Methodology Studies
Psychological Anthropology
Psychology Discipline
Russian Studies
Social Anthropology
Social Psychology
Sociolinguistics
South African Area Studies
South Asian Area Studies
Southeast Asian Area Studies
Soviet And East European Area Studies
Soviet Studies
West European Area Studies

CULTURAL ASSIMILATION
S-31-0798 1975 00034
BT Assimilation
RT Acculturation
Acculturation Theory
Cultural Evolutionism
Ethnic Assimilation
Ethnic Assimilation Theory
Linguistic Assimilation
Racial Assimilation

CULTURAL ATTACHE
S-36-0126 1975 00000
BT Embassy Attache
RT Economic Attache
Information Attache
Military Attache
Political Attache

CULTURAL CHANGE PROCESS
S-31-0050 1975 00054
BT Change Process
NT Cultural Adaptation
Cultural Differentiation
Cultural Lag
RT Anthropological Functionalism
Anthropological Linguistic Theory
Anthropology Discipline
Cultural Conflict
Cultural History
Development Process
Group Change

CULTURAL CLEAVAGE
S-06-0472 1975 00015
BT Cultural Diversity
RT Cultural Conflict
Cultural History
Cultural Variable
Ethnic Cleavage
Ethnic Diversity
Ethnic Heterogeneity
Fragmented Political Culture
Generation Gap
Linguistic Diversity
Multicultural Society
Racial Cleavage
Social Cleavage

CULTURAL CONFLICT
S-08-0025 1979 00000
BT Conflict Type
NT Religious Conflict
RT Cultural Change Process
Cultural Cleavage
Cultural Group Cohesion
Cultural History
Cultural Identity
Cultural Policy
Economic Conflict
Ideological Conflict
Institutional Conflict
Internal Conflict
Religious War
Social Conflict

CULTURAL DECISION MAKER
S-32-0027 1975 00003
BT Decision Maker
RT Economic Decision Maker
Organization Decision Maker
Political Decision Maker
Social Decision Maker

CULTURAL DETERMINISM
S-25-0011 1975 00010
BT Epistemology
RT Cultural Evolutionism
Cultural Relativism
Cultural Universalism

CULTURAL DEVELOPMENT POLICY
S-26-0080 1979 00000
BT Development Policy
NT Ethnic Heritage Policy
RT Cross Cultural Index
Cultural Adaptation
Cultural Agreement
Cultural Policy
Cultural System
Economic Development Policy
Political Development Policy
Social Development Policy

CULTURAL DIFFERENTIATION
S-31-0052 1975 00010
BT Cultural Change Process
RT Cultural Adaptation
Cultural Diversity
Cultural Lag
Ethnic Cleavage

CULTURAL DIVERSITY
S-06-0471 1975 00024
BT National Characteristics
NT Cultural Cleavage
Linguistic Diversity
Racial Diversity
RT Cultural Differentiation
Cultural Variable
Ethnic Diversity
Multicultural Society
National Self Determination
Pluralistic Society
Social Diversity
Social System Environment Characteristics

CULTURAL ELITE
S-14-0011 1975 00008
BT Intellectual Elite
NT Artistic Elite
Literary Elite
RT Academic Elite
Cultural History
Cultural Imperialism
Cultural Politics
Graduate School
Intelligentsia
Opinion Elite
Scientific Elite
Social Elite
Technological Elite

CULTURAL EVOLUTION
S-31-0064 1975 00014
BT Evolution
RT Anthropological Functionalism
Anthropological Linguistic Theory
Cultural Evolutionism
Cultural History
Genetic Evolution

Human Evolution
Natural Selection
Political Evolution
Social Evolution

CULTURAL EVOLUTIONISM
S-38-0007 1975 00002
BT Anthropological Theory
RT Acculturation Theory
Anthropological Functionalism
Anthropology Discipline
Antievolutionist Anthropological Theory
Cultural Assimilation
Cultural Determinism
Cultural Evolution
Cultural History
Cultural Relativism
Hydraulic Theory
Kinship Systematics Theory
Myth Analysis

CULTURAL EXCHANGE AGREEMENT
S-02-0073 1975 00042
BT Cultural Agreement
NT Cultural Exchange Treaty
RT Education Exchange Agreement
Friendship Treaty
International Exchange Program

CULTURAL EXCHANGE TREATY
S-02-0074 1975 00001
BT Cultural Exchange Agreement
RT Education Exchange Treaty
International Exchange Program

CULTURAL GROUP
S-03-0012 1979 00000
BT Groups
RT Cross Cultural Analysis
Cultural Agency
Cultural Alienation
Cultural History
Cultural Identity
Cultural Integration
Cultural Interest Group
Cultural Organization
Cultural Policy
Cultural Politics
Cultural System
Ethnic Group
Ethnic Studies
Group Theory
Interest Group
Nationality Group
Racial Group
Religious Group
Secondary Group
Social Group

CULTURAL GROUP COHESION
S-06-0041 1975 00007
BT Group Cohesion
RT Cultural Conflict
Cultural Identity
Ethnic Community
Ethnic Culture
Ethnic Group Cohesion
Language Loyalty

CULTURAL HISTORY
S-01-0101 1975 00209
BT History Discipline
RT Aesthetics
African Area Studies
Agricultural History
American Area Studies
American Indian Studies
Ancient History
Anthropological Theory
Art History
Asian Area Studies
Atomistic Family
Black Culture
Black History
Black Identity
Black Nationalism
Black Political Thought
Black Studies
British Commonwealth Area Studies
Chicano Studies
Civic Culture
Community Characteristics
Comparative Political Studies
Comparative Sociology
Cultural Adaptation
Cultural Anthropology
Cultural Change Process
Cultural Cleavage
Cultural Conflict
Cultural Elite
Cultural Evolution
Cultural Evolutionism
Cultural Group
Cultural Identity
Cultural Imperialism
Cultural Integration
Cultural Interest Group
Cultural Organization
Cultural Relativism
Cultural System
Cultural Universalism
Cultural Variable
Culture Type
East Asian Area Studies
East European Area Studies
Eastern Culture
Eastern Political Thought
Enculturation
Ethnic Culture
Ethnic Ideology
Ethnic Studies
Ethnicity
Ethnographic Data
Ethnography
Ethnology
Family Descent Pattern
Fine Arts
Historical Analysis
Human Geography
Ideographic Research
Institutional History
Intellectual History
Intracultural Analysis
Language Studies
Latin American Area Studies
Legal History
Myth Analysis
Mythology
National Character
North African Area Studies
North American Area Studies
Oral History
Progress
Puerto Rican Studies
Religious Culture
Religious History
Role Differentiation
Russian Studies
Social Anthropology
Social History
Social Psychology
Social System
South Asian Area Studies
Soviet And East European Area Studies
Soviet Studies
Technological Culture
Traditional Authority
Traditional Culture
Urban Culture
Urban History
Value Analysis
Value System
Village Culture
West European Area Studies
Western Culture
Youth Culture

CULTURAL IDENTITY
S-06-0380 1975 00055
BT Identity Characteristics
NT Ethnicity
Racial Identity
RT Anthropological Linguistic Theory
Community Identity
Cultural Alienation
Cultural Conflict
Cultural Group
Cultural Group Cohesion
Cultural History
Cultural Nationalism
Culture Type
Language Loyalty
Multicultural Society
National Identity
Pan Africanism
Pan Arabism
Pan Islamism
Pan Slav Movement
Pan Slavism
Social Identity

CULTURAL IMPERIALISM
S-37-0068 1975 00026
BT Imperialism System
RT Academic Imperialism
Cultural Aggression
Cultural Elite
Cultural History
Cultural Modernization
Economic Imperialism
Missionary
Neocolonialism
Political Imperialism
Political Persecution
Proprietary Colony

CULTURAL INTEGRATION
S-31-0802 1975 00019
BT Integration
RT Cultural Group
Cultural History
Ethnic Assimilation Theory
Functional Integration
Linguistic Integration

Racial Integration
Social Integration
Vertical Integration

CULTURAL INTEREST GROUP
S-03-0016 1975 00003
BT Interest Group
RT Association Interest Group
Cultural Group
Cultural History
Cultural Organization
Ethnic Community
Latent Interest Group
Political Interest Group

CULTURAL LAG
S-31-0053 1975 00002
BT Cultural Change Process
RT Cultural Adaptation
Cultural Differentiation
Cultural Modernization
Poverty Culture

CULTURAL MODERNIZATION
S-31-0078 1975 00022
BT Modernization
RT Cultural Imperialism
Cultural Lag
Culture Type
Economic Modernization
Institutional Innovation
Political Modernization
Social Modernization

CULTURAL NATIONALISM
S-38-0263 1975 00024
BT Nationalism
NT Black Nationalism
Irredentism
Pan Africanism
Pan Arabism
Pan Islamism
Pan Slavism
Tribalism
Zionism
RT Cultural Identity
Cultural Policy
Isolationism
Isolationist
National Identity Theory
Patriotism
Separatism
Zionism

CULTURAL ORGANIZATION
S-03-0038 1975 00007
BT Organizations
RT Civic Organization
Cultural Group
Cultural History
Cultural Interest Group
Ethnic Organization
Fraternal Organization
Professional Organization
Religious Organization
Voluntary Association
Youth Organization

CULTURAL POLICY
S-26-0047 1975 00010
UF Access To Culture
BT Policy
NT Arts Policy
Language Policy
RT Cultural Aggression
Cultural Conflict
Cultural Development Policy
Cultural Group
Cultural Nationalism
Cultural Politics
Cultural Revolution
Cultural System
Cultural Universalism
Education Policy
Information Policy

CULTURAL POLITICS
S-29-0011 1979 00000
BT Politics
RT Class Politics
Constituency Politics
Cultural Agency
Cultural Elite
Cultural Group
Cultural Policy
Cultural Variable
Electoral Participation
Informal Power

CULTURAL RELATIVISM
S-25-0012 1975 00009
BT Epistemology
RT Cultural Determinism
Cultural Evolutionism
Cultural History
Cultural Universalism
Ethical Relativism
Generation Gap
Social Diversity

CULTURAL REVOLUTION
S-08-0064 1975 00010
BT Revolution
NT Chinese Cultural Revolution
RT Afro Asian Bloc
Counterrevolution
Cultural Aggression
Cultural Policy
Cultural System
Internal War
Political Agitation
Political Revolution
Political Self Criticism
Religious Conflict
Social Revolution
Spontaneous Revolution
Technological Revolution

CULTURAL SYSTEM
S-37-0005 1975 00048
BT System Type
RT Belief System
Cognitive System
Cultural Development Policy
Cultural Group
Cultural History
Cultural Policy
Cultural Revolution
Cultural Universalism
Culture Type
Education System
Ethical Socialization
Extended Kinship System
Moral Learning
Multicultural Society

CULTURAL UNIVERSALISM
S-25-0013 1979 00000
BT Epistemology
RT Anthropology Discipline
Comparative Analysis
Cultural Determinism
Cultural History
Cultural Policy
Cultural Relativism
Cultural System
Cultural Variable
Human Nature Theory

CULTURAL VARIABLE
S-24-0446 1975 00038
BT Variable Substantive Content
RT Cultural Cleavage
Cultural Diversity
Cultural History
Cultural Politics
Cultural Universalism
Economic Variable
Historical Variable
Institutional Variable
Political Variable
Social Variable

CULTURE
USE Culture Type

CULTURE SHOCK
S-06-0507 1979 00000
BT Personality Characteristics
RT Acculturation
Ambivalence
Courage
Cultural Adaptation
Culture Type
Curiosity
Imagination
Personality Type

CULTURE TYPE
S-11-0001 1975 00007
UF Culture
NT Civilization
Community Culture
Counter Culture
Drug Culture
Ethnic Culture
Heterogeneous Culture
Homogeneous Culture
Mass Culture
Nonwestern Culture
Political Culture
Poverty Culture
Religious Culture
Secular Culture
Subculture
Technological Culture
Traditional Culture
Urban Culture
Western Culture
Work Culture
Youth Culture
RT Aesthetics
Cultural History
Cultural Identity
Cultural Modernization
Cultural System
Culture Shock

CUMULATIVE SCALE
S-24-0206 1975 00002
BT Scale Construction Methodology
RT Composite Scale
Factor Structure
Guttman Scale
Likert Scale
Measurement Level Scale
Multidimensional Scale
Scalability Index
Semantic Differential
Thurstone Scale

CUMULATIVE VOTING
S-29-0167 1975 00000
BT Voting Formulae
RT D'Hont Voting Method
Largest Average Voting Method
Largest Remainder Voting Method
List Voting
Single Transferable Vote

CURIOSITY
S-06-0508 1979 00000
BT Personality Characteristics
RT Altruism
Ambivalence
Assertiveness
Charity
Courage
Creativity
Culture Shock
Egocentrism
Empathy
Femininity
Gregariousness
Honesty
Imagination
Knowledge Production
Learning Theory
Masculinity
Optimism
Persistence

CURRENCY DEVALUATION POLICY
S-26-0112 1975 00007
UF Money Devaluation
BT Inflation Control Policy
RT Deflation Policy
Government Economic Management
Government Expenditure

CURRENCY REVALUATION POLICY
S-26-0098 1979 00000
BT Deflation Policy
RT Antiinflation Policy
Budget Policy
Capital Formation Policy
Expenditure Policy
Fiscal Policy
Investment Policy
Monetary Policy
Money Creation
Money Supply
National Currency

CURVE
S-24-0132 1975 00001
BT Chart
RT Chart
Diagram
Graph
Graph Analysis
Plot
Table

CUSTOM
USE Customary Law

CUSTOMARY LAW
S-21-0029 1975 00006
UF Custom
BT Law Type
RT Basic Law
Case Law
Civil Law System
Classical Political Thought
Common Law
Common Law Procedure
Common Law System
County Level Court
Eastern Culture
Eastern Legalist Theory
Environmental Law
Habitual Behavior
International Law
Legal Precedent
Natural Law
Primogeniture
Procedural Law
Stare Decisis
Traditional Society
Unwritten Constitution

CUSTOMS UNION
S-03-0041 1975 00001
BT International Economic Organization
RT Commodity Market
Economic Alliance
Economic Coalition
Economic Community
Economic Control Agency
Economic Institution
Economic Integration
Economic Interest Group
Extranational Bloc
Foreign Trade
Free Trade Policy
International Commodity Market
International Trade
Monetary Union
Payment Agreement
Trade Organization

CYBERNETIC ANALYSIS
S-09-0014 1975 00011
BT Contemporary Analytic Modes
RT Computer Assisted Instruction
Computer Network
Computer Processing
Computer Science
Contextual Analysis
Cybernetic Model
Cybernetic System
Cybernetic Theory
Decision Making Analysis
Demand Analysis
General System Theory
General Theory
Information Processing
Input Output Device
Input Output Model
Interaction Analysis
Social System Model
System Analysis
System Characteristics
System Outputs

CYBERNETIC MODEL
S-24-0295 1975 00014
BT Social Science Model
RT Communication Model
Cybernetic Analysis
Cybernetic System
Cybernetic Theory
Development Model
Equilibrium Model
Information Theory
Input Output Model

CYBERNETIC SYSTEM
S-37-0006 1975 00009
BT System Type
RT Cybernetic Analysis
Cybernetic Model
Cybernetic Theory
Economic System
Information Theory

CYBERNETIC THEORY
S-38-0031 1975 00008
BT General System Theory
RT Communication Theory
Cybernetic Analysis
Cybernetic Model
Cybernetic System
Econometrics

CYCLICAL EMPLOYMENT
S-06-0293 1975 00000
BT Employment Index
RT Depression
Economic Indicator
Seasonal Employment

CYNIC POLITICAL THOUGHT
1975-1979 00000

CYNIC THOUGHT
S-38-0049 1979 00000
SN Post-Socratic thought emphasizing independence, denial of convention and capacity to rise above circumstances.
BT Classical Political Thought
RT Ancient History
Epicurean Thought
Skeptic Thought
Stoic Thought

CYNICISM
S-06-0078 1975 00003
BT Alienation
NT Political Cynicism
RT Apathy
Cynicism Scale
Distrust
Efficacy Scale
Estrangement
Hostility
Inner Directedness
Political Alienation
Political Alienation Theory

CYNICISM SCALE
S-24-0228 1975 00000
BT Scale Type
RT Alienation Scale
Anomie Scale
Cynicism
Dogmatism Scale
Efficacy Scale
Frustration Scale
Liberalism Conservatism Scale
Optimism Pessimism Scale

Satisfaction Scale
Social Distance Scale
Social Frustration Scale
Stability Index
Support Opposition Scale

D'HONT VOTING METHOD
S-29-0168 1979 00000
SN Mathematical formulation for proportional representation based on the highest averages principle.
BT Voting Formulae
RT Cumulative Voting
Electoral Outcome
Largest Average Voting Method
List Voting
Multiple Member Districting
Single Transferable Vote

DAIRY INDUSTRY
S-17-0032 1975 00000
BT Consumer Industry
RT Agricultural Cooperative
Agricultural Production
Agricultural Science
Cooperative Farm Economy
Farm Industry
Farm Subsidy
Fishing Industry
Food Industry
Food Policy

DAMAGE LIMITING STRATEGY
S-26-0068 1975 00003
BT Nuclear Strategy
RT Conventional War
Military Planning
Military Science
Military Weapon
Nuclear Strike Policy
Strategic Studies

DAMAGE SUIT
S-31-0561 1975 00007
BT Litigation
RT Class Action Litigation
Common Law Court
Equity Law
Judicial Administration

DANCE
USE Visual Arts

DARK AGES
S-06-0171 1979 00000
BT Historical Periods
RT Ancient Times
Classical Period
Feudal Economic System
Feudal System
Medieval Ages
Renaissance

DARK HORSE CANDIDATE
S-32-0226 1975 00000
BT Political Candidate
RT Candidate Preference Voter
Candidate Voter
Election Campaign
Electoral Outcome
Favorite Son Candidate
National Candidate

DATA ARCHIVES
S-18-0004 1975 00013
BT Data Bank
RT Aggregate Data Analysis
Information System
Intelligence Agency
Machine Readable Data
Machine Readable Information
Statistical Data

DATA BANK
S-18-0003 1975 00014
BT Archives
NT Data Archives
RT Data Management
Data Processing
Data Retrieval
Data Storage
Information System
National Archives

DATA COLLECTION METHODOLOGY
S-24-0076 1975 00076
BT Methodology
NT Field Research
Nonreactive Observation
Observation Time
Questionnaire
Reactive Observation
Sampling Procedure
Simulation
RT Aggregate Data Analysis
Aggregate Data Statistics
Analysis Methodology
Data Presentation Methodology
Hypothesis Testing
Measurement
Research Design
Theoretical Framework

DATA FORMAT
S-24-0145 1979 00000
UF Data Formatting
BT Information Processing
RT Coding
Graph Theory Analysis

DATA FORMATTING
1975-1979 00006
USE Data Format

DATA MANAGEMENT
S-23-0027 1975 00014
BT Information Management
RT Data Bank
Economic Management
Government Document
Intelligence Agency

DATA PRESENTATION METHODOLOGY
S-24-0130 1975 00017
BT Methodology
NT Chart
Diagram
Graph
Plot
Table
RT Analysis Methodology
Analysis Of Variance
Data Collection Methodology
Hypothesis Testing
Information Processing
Measurement
Research Design
Statistics Discipline
Theoretical Framework

DATA PROCESSING
S-24-0146 1975 00007
BT Information Processing
NT Computer Processing
Computer Programming
RT Aggregate Data Statistics
Data Bank
Information Retrieval
Information Storage

DATA PROCESSING EQUIPMENT
S-24-0327 1975 00002
BT Information Processing Equipment
NT Computer Equipment
Unit Record Equipment
RT Computer Science
Computer Software
Information Recording Equipment

DATA RETRIEVAL
S-24-0150 1975 00006
BT Information Retrieval
RT Aggregate Data Analysis
Computer Processing
Data Bank
Question Formulation
Search Strategy Development

DATA SELECTION ORIENTATION
S-24-0377 1975 00009
BT Research Orientation
NT Aggregate Data Selection
Content Analysis
Demographic Analysis
Event Analysis
RT Advocacy Research
Descriptive Research
Experimental Research
Explanatory Research
Qualitative Research
Quantitative History
Quantitative Research
Theoretical Research

DATA STORAGE
S-24-0155 1975 00004
BT Information Storage
RT Abstracting
Aggregate Data Statistics
Data Bank
Indexing
Machine Readable Data
Machine Readable Information

DATA THEORY
S-38-0020 1975 00010
BT Theory
RT Contemporary Analytic Modes
Cross Cultural Data
Empirical Theory
Field Data
Formal Political Theory
Methodology
Scientific Theory
Theory Construction
Value Free Science Theory

DAY CARE CENTER
S-19-0157 1979 00000
BT Institutions
RT Child
Child Care Service
Childhood
Community Service
Family Service
Service Industry Policy

Social Policy

DAY LABORER
S-32-0091 1975 00000
BT Unskilled Worker
RT Agricultural Worker
Landless Peasant Class
Migrant Farming
Migrant Worker
Proletariat
Work Norm Policy
Working Conditions

DE FACTO RECOGNITION
1975-1979 00002

DE JURE RECOGNITION
1975-1979 00002

DEAN
S-36-0005 1975 00000
BT Administrative Officer
RT Administrative Officer
Bureau Chief
Capital Punishment
Department Head
Executive Director
Management
Murder
Penal Law
Penal Reform
Punishment
University

DEATH PENALTY LAW
S-21-0027 1979 00000
BT Criminal Law
RT Capital Punishment
Court Action
Crime
Criminal Court
Criminal Justice Administration
Criminology
Jail
Penal Law

DEBT CEILING POLICY
S-26-0134 1975 00000
BT Public Debt Policy
RT Budget Formulation
Budget Policy
Debt Financing
Deficit Financing
Deficit Spending
Deflation
Fiscal Policy
Monetary Policy

DEBT FINANCING
S-31-0402 1975 00005
BT Public Financing
NT National Debt Financing
War Debt Financing
RT Debt Ceiling Policy
Deferential Voter
Deficit Financing
Deficit Spending
Depression
Government Borrowing
Public Spending

DEBTOR NATION
S-16-0117 1975 00003
BT Nation Type
RT Aligned Nation
Client Nation
Client State
Dependent Nation
Government Borrowing
Public Spending

DECAY
S-31-0056 1975 00006
BT Development Process
NT Institutional Decay
Political Decay
Urban Decay
RT Alienation Process
Anarchy
Fragmentation
Political Corruption

DECENTRALIZED AUTHORITY
S-04-0013 1975 00039
BT Authority Structure
RT Anarchy
Center Periphery Government Relations
Constitutional Authority
Decentralized City
Decentralized Government
Decentralized Political Party
Delegated Authority
Diffuse Authority
Dispersed Power
Formal Authority
Hierarchical Authority
Independent Authority
Informal Authority
Polycentrism

DECENTRALIZED CITY
S-07-0005 1975 00008
BT City
RT Central City
Decentralized Authority
Decentralized Government
Federated City
Local Political Division
Metropolitan City
Metropolitan Government
Provincial Government
Urban Government

DECENTRALIZED GOVERNMENT
S-16-0010 1975 00027
BT Government Type
RT Center Periphery Government Relations
Confederal Government
Confederation Movement
Constitutional Democracy
Decentralized Authority
Decentralized City
Diffuse Authority
Dispersed Power
Federalism
Independent Authority
Limited Government
Local Political Division
Subnational Government

DECENTRALIZED POLITICAL PARTY
S-06-0559 1975 00001
BT Political Party Decentralization
RT Centralized Political Party
Decentralized Authority
Diffuse Authority
Dispersed Power
Mass Political Party
Political Party Organization

DECISION MAKER
S-32-0026 1975 00013
BT Roles
NT Cultural Decision Maker
Economic Decision Maker
Organization Decision Maker
Political Decision Maker
Social Decision Maker
RT Adjudicator
Decision Maker Perception
Decision Making Analysis
Decision Making Elite
Decision Making Process
Decision Making Theory
International Government Bureaucracy
Leader
Management
Manager
Planner
Policy Making Process
Political Leader
Politician

DECISION MAKER PERCEPTION
S-06-0094 1975 00094
BT Perception
RT Attitude Measurement
Decision Maker
Decision Making Analysis
Decision Making Theory
Information Processing
National Goal
National Image
National Interest
National Priority
Perception Measurement
Policy Making Process
Psychological Theory

DECISION MAKING ANALYSIS
S-24-0416 1975 00084
BT Microlevel Analysis
RT Cybernetic Analysis
Decision Maker
Decision Maker Perception
Decision Making Process
Decision Making Theory
Policy Analysis
Political Science Discipline
Public Choice Analysis
Voting Behavior Analysis

DECISION MAKING ELITE
S-14-0003 1975 00017
BT Elite Type
RT Attentive Public
Business Elite
Commercial Elite
Corporate Elite
Decision Maker
Decision Making Process
Decision Making Theory
Economic Elite
Elite Analysis
Elite Behavior
Elite Formation
Elite Mass Relations
Elite Norms
Elite Theory
Financial Elite
Foreign Policy Elite

Governing Elite
Leadership Analysis
Local Political Elite
Managerial Elite
Modernizing Elite
Pluralist Elite
Policy Making Process
Political Elite
Power Elite
Subnational Elite

DECISION MAKING PROCESS
S-31-0322 1975 00135
BT Process
NT Allocation Process
Approval Process
Authorization Process
Collegial Decision Making
Committee Decision Making
Confirmation Process
Implementation Process
International Decision Making Process
National Decision Making Process
Subnational Decision Making Process
Veto
RT Adjudication
Agreement
Analytic Process
Bargaining
Change Process
Conciliation
Conflict Process
Conflict Resolution
Decision Maker
Decision Making Analysis
Decision Making Elite
Decision Making Theory
Judging
Negotiation
Policy Making Process
Purge

DECISION MAKING THEORY
S-38-0124 1975 00069
BT Explanatory Political Theory
RT Administrative Behavior
Administrative Science
Analysis Framework
Analysis Methodology
Bargaining Theory
Community Power Theory
Decision Maker
Decision Maker Perception
Decision Making Analysis
Decision Making Elite
Decision Making Process
Elite Analysis
Goal Setting
International Decision Making Theory
Judging
Moral Choice
Planning Theory
Political Coalition
Power Theory
Public Choice Theory
Public Policy Analysis
Rational Choice Theory
Rational Model
Social Choice Theory
Transactional Theory
Voting Theory

DECLARED WAR
S-08-0092 1975 00000
BT War
RT Aggressor State
Arms Control Policy
Bargaining
Belligerence
Conciliation
Conventional War
Deescalation
Deescalation Policy
Mediation
Negotiation
War Policy
War Power
Weapon

DECOLONIZATION
S-31-0155 1975 00024
BT Extraterritorial Development
RT Annexation
Anticolonialism
Antiimperialism
Colonization
Decontrol Process
Dependent Nation
Former Colony
Independence Movement
National Self Determination
Nationalist Movement
Proprietary Colony
Right Of Secession
Secession

DECONTROL PROCESS
S-31-0342 1979 00000
BT Process
NT Denationalization Process
Deregulation Process
Destalinization Process
RT Control Process
Decolonization
Deregulation Process
Free Market
Government Deregulation
Political Control

DECRIMINALIZATION
S-21-0030 1979 00000
BT Law Type
RT Civil Law
Criminal Law
Criminology
Law Enforcement
Legal Studies
Penal Law
Public Policy Analysis

DEDUCTIVE METHOD
S-24-0004 1979 00000
BT Analysis Methodology
RT Applied Research
Basic Research
Causal Analysis
Hypothesis Testing
Inductive Method
Methodology
Moral Reasoning
Predictive Research
Qualitative Research
Scientific Research

DEESCALATION
S-31-0235 1975 00000
BT Conflict Resolution
RT Agreement
Appeasement
Bargaining
Cease Fire Policy
Conciliation
Declared War
Negotiation

DEESCALATION POLICY
S-26-0328 1975 00001
BT Military Policy
RT Arms Control Policy
Cease Fire Policy
Declared War
Demilitarization Policy
Demobilization Policy
East West Detente
Escalation Policy
Peaceful Coexistence
War Policy

DEFACTO RECOGNITION
S-31-0349 1979 00000
BT Diplomatic Recognition
RT Bilateral State Agreement
Diplomacy
Diplomatic History
Diplomatic Relations Normalization
International Law

DEFECTION
S-10-0058 1975 00000
BT Political Crime
NT Desertion
RT Illegal Immigration
Individual Crime
Political Espionage
Treason

DEFENDANTS RIGHTS
S-15-0043 1975 00011
BT Procedural Rights
NT Bill Of Attainder
Double Jeopardy
Habeas Corpus
Right Against Cruel And Unusual Punishment
Right To Bail
Right To Due Process
Right To Equal Protection
Right To Trial
Sanity Plea
Search And Seizure
Statute Of Limitations
RT Acquittal
Burden Of Proof
Civil Rights
Defender
Defense Attorney
Equal Rights
Jury Trial
Prosecution Immunity

DEFENDER
S-36-0100 1975 00001
BT Defense Attorney
NT Public Defender
RT Adversary Process
Attorney General
Defendants Rights
Defense Attorney

Lawyer
Solicitor

DEFENSE AGENCY
S-19-0059 1975 00010
BT Military Agency
NT Arms Control Agency
RT Armed Forces
Defense Appropriation
Defense Authorization
Defense Management
Defense Planning
Defense Policy
Defense System
Intelligence Agency
Military Agency
Military Intelligence Agency
Spying

DEFENSE ALLIANCE
S-02-0006 1975 00018
BT Military Alliance
NT Protective Alliance
RT Collective Security
Military Agreement
Military Treaty
Mutual Support Declaration
Nonaggression Agreement
Nonaggression Treaty
Regional Military Alliance
Security Community

DEFENSE APPROPRIATION
S-31-0638 1975 00004
BT Defense Planning
RT Appropriation Agency
Budget Agency
Defense Agency
Defense Authorization
Defense Policy
Defense Spending
Monetary Agency

DEFENSE ATTORNEY
S-36-0099 1975 00005
BT Court Attorney
NT Defender
RT Adversary Process
Barrister
Defendants Rights
Defender
Jury
Jury Trial
Lawyer
Prosecuting Attorney
Solicitor

DEFENSE AUTHORIZATION
S-31-0639 1975 00001
BT Defense Planning
RT Budget Formulation
Defense Agency
Defense Appropriation
Defense Planning
Defense Policy
Defense Spending

DEFENSE INDUSTRY
S-17-0035 1975 00004
BT Industry
NT Aerospace Industry
Arms Industry
RT Arms Sales
Chemical Industry
Construction Industry
Defense Management
Defense Planning
Defense Policy
Defense Spending
Military Policy
Protected Industry

DEFENSE MANAGEMENT
S-23-0007 1975 00009
BT Management
RT Conflict Management
Crisis Management
Defense Agency
Defense Industry
Defense Planning
Defense Policy
Defense System
Military Management
Military Planning
Military Reorganization Policy
Military Service Personnel

DEFENSE PLANNING
S-31-0637 1975 00014
BT Planning Process
NT Defense Appropriation
Defense Authorization
RT Administrative Planning
Defense Agency
Defense Authorization
Defense Industry
Defense Management
Defense Policy
Defense Spending
Defense System
Development Planning
Economic Planning
Global War Policy
Military Planning
Public Policy Planning
Social Planning
War Policy

DEFENSE POLICY
S-26-0050 1975 00115
BT Policy
NT Armistice Policy
Arms Control Policy
Civil Defense Policy
Deterrence Policy
Nuclear Strategy
Rearmament Policy
Strategic Policy
Truce
War Declaration Policy
RT Agreement Type
Defense Agency
Defense Appropriation
Defense Authorization
Defense Industry
Defense Management
Defense Planning
Defense Spending
Defense System
Mass Militia Army
Military Alliance
Military Policy
Protective Alliance
Strategic Policy
Strategic Studies

DEFENSE SPENDING
S-31-0415 1975 00059
BT Public Spending
RT Defense Appropriation
Defense Authorization
Defense Industry
Defense Planning
Defense Policy
Government Expenditure
War Debt Financing

DEFENSE SYSTEM
S-33-0007 1975 00024
BT National Security Forces
NT Balanced Force
Tactical Force
War Technology
RT Armed Forces
Defense Agency
Defense Management
Defense Planning
Defense Policy
Defensive Capability
Defensive Weapon
Military Alliance
Military Characteristics
Military Forces
Mutual Deterrence System
Mutual Support Declaration
Professional Military Forces
Regional Military Alliance
Reserve Military Forces
Security Community
Strategic Studies

DEFENSIVE CAPABILITY
S-06-0460 1975 00028
BT Military Characteristics
RT Arms Verification Policy
Defense System
Global War Policy
Military Intelligence
Military Size
Nuclear Capability
Nuclear Stockpiling
Offensive Capability
Retaliatory Capability

DEFENSIVE WEAPON
S-33-0024 1975 00004
BT Military Weapon
RT Biological Weapon
Chemical Weapon
Civil Defense Policy
Conventional Weapon
Defense System
Missile
Munitions
Nuclear Weapon
Strategic Weapon
Tactical Weapon
Test Ban Agreement
Unconventional Weapon

DEFERENCE
S-06-0096 1979 00000
BT Attitude Characteristics
RT Diffuse System Supports
Political Trust
Prejudice
Social Prestige
Social Stratification Maintenance
Tolerance

DEFERENTIAL VOTER
S-32-0305 1975 00002
SN Person who supports candidates or parties associated with high social status.
BT Voter
RT Apathetic Voter
Debt Financing
Deficit Financing
Deficit Spending
Depression
Government Borrowing
Government Expenditure
Marginal Voter
National Debt Financing
Public Spending
Voting Behavior

DEFICIT FINANCING
S-31-0405 1975 00001
BT Public Financing
RT Debt Ceiling Policy
Debt Financing
Deferential Voter
Deficit Spending
Depression
Government Borrowing
Government Economic Management
National Debt Financing
Public Financing
Public Spending

DEFICIT SPENDING
S-31-0416 1975 00000
BT Public Spending
RT Debt Ceiling Policy
Debt Financing
Deferential Voter
Deficit Financing
Government Expenditure
Public Finance Theory

DEFLATION
S-31-0136 1975 00003
BT Economic Change
RT Balance Of Payments
Banking Policy
Debt Ceiling Policy
Deflation Policy
Depression
Economic Depression
Economic Recession
Fiscal Policy
Inflation
Market
Monetary Policy
Money
Money Supply Policy
Price Fixing Policy
Price Freeze Policy
Price Policy

DEFLATION POLICY
S-26-0097 1975 00004
BT Fiscal Policy
NT Currency Revaluation Policy
RT Capital Formation Policy
Capital Investment Policy
Currency Devaluation Policy
Deflation
Discount Rate
Economic Stabilization Theory
Income Policy
Inflation Control Policy
Inflation Policy
Monetary Economic Theory
Monetary Policy
Revenue Policy
Wage Freeze Policy

DEGREE REQUIREMENT
S-24-0006 1979 00000
BT Education Testing
RT Accreditation Process
Education Policy
Literacy Test
Physiological Test
Psychological Test
Test Results

DEJURE RECOGNITION
S-31-0350 1979 00000
BT Diplomatic Recognition
RT Bilateral State Agreement
Diplomacy
Diplomatic History
Diplomatic Relations Normalization
International Law

DELEGATE
S-32-0166 1975 00002
BT Delegation Member
NT Convention Delegate
Delegate At Large
RT Political Party Cadre
Political Party Congress
Political Party Convention
Representation Theory

DELEGATE AT LARGE
S-32-0168 1975 00000
BT Delegate
RT Convention Delegate
Political Party Convention
Representative

DELEGATE REPRESENTATION THEORY
S-38-0503 1975 00001
SN Doctrine that legislators are chosen to reflect expressed wishes of their constituents.
BT Representation Theory
RT Delegated Authority
Group Representation Theory
Linkage Representation Theory
Representation
Territory Representation Theory
Trustee Representation Theory
Virtual Representation Theory

DELEGATE SELECTION
S-31-0733 1975 00001
BT Selection Process
NT Convention Delegate Selection
RT Appointment Process
Candidate Selection
Delegation Member
Endorsement
Legislative Nominating Process
Nominating Process
Recruitment Process
Representation
Slate Making
Territory Representation Theory
Trustee Representation Theory
Virtual Representation Theory

DELEGATED AUTHORITY
S-04-0014 1979 00000
BT Authority Structure
RT Decentralized Authority
Delegate Representation Theory
Diffuse Authority
Representation Theory
Representation Type

DELEGATION MEMBER
S-32-0165 1975 00002
BT Political Party Member
NT Delegate
RT Constitutional Convention
Delegate Selection
Political Party Convention

DELINQUENCY
USE Juvenile Delinquency

DELPHI TECHNIQUE
S-24-0013 1979 00000
BT Forecasting Methodology
RT Authority Forecasting
Brainstorming
Divergence Mapping
Economic Forecasting
Policy Evaluation Research
Policy Research
Political Forecasting
Predictive Research
Scenario Construction
Social Forecasting
Trend Analysis

DEMAND ANALYSIS
S-09-0015 1975 00032
BT Contemporary Analytic Modes
RT Agricultural Advisory Board
Consumer Economics
Cybernetic Analysis
Demand Elasticity
Eastonian Analysis
Input Output Analysis
Issue Intensity
Issue Salience

DEMAND CURVE
S-06-0288 1975 00006
BT Economic Index
NT Demand Elasticity
RT Economic Gain
Economic Loss
Economic Scarcity
Supply Curve
Supply Elasticity

DEMAND ELASTICITY
S-06-0289 1979 00000
BT Demand Curve
RT Consumer Economics
Demand Analysis
Economic Gain
Economic Loss
Economic Scarcity
Supply Elasticity

DEMILITARIZATION POLICY
S-26-0329 1975 00005
BT Military Policy
RT Cease Fire Policy
Deescalation Policy
Demobilization Policy
Military Reorganization Policy
Peace
Veteran

War Policy

DEMOBILIZATION POLICY
S-26-0330 1975 00000
BT Military Policy
RT Cease Fire Policy
Deescalation Policy
Demilitarization Policy
Military Reorganization Policy
Peace
Veteran
War Policy

DEMOCRACY
USE Democratic Political System

DEMOCRAT
S-32-0271 1975 00000
BT System Politicist
NT Christian Democrat
RT Democratic Constitution
Democratic Government
Democratic Political System
Democratic Theory

DEMOCRAT SOCIALIST
S-32-0285 1975 00000
BT Socialist
RT Democratic Socialism
Socialist Democracy
Socialist Democratic Theory
Socialist Government
Socialist Humanism

DEMOCRATIC CENTRALISM
S-38-0324 1975 00002
BT Leninism
RT Centralized Political Party

DEMOCRATIC COALITION
S-02-0020 1975 00001
BT Political Coalition
RT All Party Coalition
Class Based Coalition
Democratic Government
Democratic Theory
Diet
Governing Coalition
Intraparty Coalition
Legislative Coalition
Minimum Winning Coalition
Multiparty Coalition
Negative Coalition
Open Society
Political Coalition
Political Party Coalition
Voting Coalition
Winning Coalition

DEMOCRATIC CONSTITUTION
S-21-0010 1975 00000
BT Constitution
RT Colonial Charter
Democrat
Democratic Political System
Democratic Theory
International Constitutional Convention
National Constitution
Republican Constitutionalism
State Constitution
Unitary Constitution
Unwritten Constitution
Written Constitution

DEMOCRATIC ECONOMIC PLANNING
S-31-0644 1975 00000
BT Government Economic Planning
RT Administrative Management
Democratic Theory
Five Year Economic Planning
Socialist Economic Planning

DEMOCRATIC ELITE THEORY
S-38-0085 1975 00005
SN View that democracy is a system of government in which masses choose rulers from among competing elites and the elites are the real guardians of liberal values.
BT Democratic Theory
RT Athenian Democratic Theory
Concurrent Majority Theory
Economic Theory Of Democracy
Elite Theory
General Will Democratic Theory
Governing Elite
Guided Democracy Theory
Interest Group Pluralism
Majoritarianism
Minority Rights Democratic Theory
Participatory Democratic Theory
Pluralist Democracy
Pluralist Elite
Polyarchy
Populist Democratic Theory
Procedural Democratic Theory
Republic Theory

DEMOCRATIC GOVERNMENT
S-16-0011 1975 00024
BT Government Type
NT Agrarian Democracy
Bourgeois Democracy
Consociational Democracy
Constitutional Democracy
Developed Democracy
Direct Democracy
Elitist Democracy
Guided Democracy
Majoritarian Democracy
Mass Democracy
Parliamentary Democracy
Participatory Democracy
Plebiscitary Democracy
Pluralist Democracy
Political Party Democracy
Representative Democracy
Social Democracy
Socialist Democracy
Stable Democracy
Tutelary Democracy
RT Cabinet Government
Constitutional Monarchy
Democrat
Democratic Coalition
Democratic Leadership
Democratic Regime
Democratic Theory
Madisonian Thought
Minority Rights Democratic Theory
Parliamentary Government
Political Participation
Procedural Democratic Theory
Tutelary Democracy

DEMOCRATIC LEADERSHIP
S-22-0017 1975 00002
BT Leadership Structure Type
RT Collective Leadership
Collegial Leadership
Democratic Government
Democratic Political System
Democratic Regime
Elite Analysis
National Leadership
Open Leadership
Political Leadership
Political Party Leadership

DEMOCRATIC PARTY
1975-1979 00018

DEMOCRATIC POLITICAL PARTY
S-28-0003 1979 00000
BT Political Party Type
NT Christian Democratic Political Party
Liberal Democratic Political Party
National Democratic Political Party
Social Democratic Political Party
RT Christian Democratic Movement

DEMOCRATIC POLITICAL REVOLUTION
S-08-0069 1975 00001
BT Political Revolution
RT Democratic Socialist Revolution
Government Overthrow
National Political Revolution
Social Revolution
Socialist Revolution
Spontaneous Revolution
Technological Revolution
Thermidor

DEMOCRATIC POLITICAL SYSTEM
S-37-0108 1975 00036
UF Democracy
BT Political System Type
RT Democrat
Democratic Constitution
Democratic Leadership
Democratic Regime
Democratic Theory
Parliamentary Democracy
Participatory Democracy
Political Participation

DEMOCRATIC REGIME
S-16-0137 1975 00005
BT Political Regime
RT Agrarian Democracy
Christian Democratic Movement
Constitutional Democracy
Democratic Government
Democratic Leadership
Democratic Political System
Dictatorial Regime
Direct Democracy
Open Society
Open Society Theory
Parliamentary Democracy
Pluralist Democracy
Political Participation
Socialist Democracy

DEMOCRATIC SOCIALISM
S-38-0292 1975 00002
BT Socialist Theory
RT Agrarian Socialism
Aprista Socialism
Christian Socialism

Democrat Socialist
Eurocommunism
Evolutionary Socialism
Guild Socialism
Marxism
Marxist Theory
Social Democracy
Social Democratic Political Party
Socialist Political Party
Syndicalism

DEMOCRATIC SOCIALIST REVOLUTION
S-08-0074 1975 00000
BT Socialist Revolution
RT Bernsteinian Socialism
Communist Revolution
Democratic Political Revolution
Evolutionary Socialism
Government Overthrow
National Political Revolution
Social Revolution
Spontaneous Revolution
Struggle
Technological Revolution
Thermidor

DEMOCRATIC THEORY
S-38-0082 1975 00056
BT Political Theory
NT Athenian Democratic Theory
Concurrent Majority Theory
Democratic Elite Theory
Economic Theory Of Democracy
General Will Democratic Theory
Guided Democracy Theory
Industrial Democracy
Interest Group Pluralism
Jacksonian Democratic Theory
Jeffersonian Democratic Theory
Majoritarianism
Minority Rights Democratic Theory
Participatory Democratic Theory
Polyarchical Democratic Theory
Populist Democratic Theory
Procedural Democratic Theory
Republic Theory
Socialist Democratic Theory
RT American Enlightenment Thought
Anticolonialism
Antifascism
Antiimperialism
Antimilitarism
Christian Democratic Movement
Civil Liberty
Democrat
Democratic Coalition
Democratic Constitution
Democratic Economic Planning
Democratic Government
Democratic Political System
Developed Democracy
Liberalism
Minority Rights
Parliamentary Democracy
Participatory Management
Political Equality
Political Participation
Social Diversity
Social Equality
Socialist Theory

DEMOCRATIZATION
S-31-0791 1975 00019
BT Structural Process
RT Integration
Interim Government
Open Society
Open Society Theory
Participatory Democratic Theory
Popular Assembly

DEMOGRAPHIC ANALYSIS
S-24-0380 1975 00046
BT Data Selection Orientation
RT Demographic Characteristics
Demographic Studies
Ethnic Composition
Migration Pattern
Population Attribute
Population Composition
Population Concentration
Population Distribution
Population Growth

DEMOGRAPHIC CHARACTERISTICS
S-06-0179 1975 00057
BT Characteristics
NT Age
Demographic Indicator
Demographic Profile
Demographic Projection
Origin
Population Attribute
Population Composition
Population Distribution
Population Movement
RT Census Tract
Demographic Analysis
Demographic Studies
Education Characteristics
Health Characteristics
Language Characteristics
Occupation Characteristics
Social Diversity

DEMOGRAPHIC INDICATOR
S-06-0187 1975 00006
BT Demographic Characteristics
RT Age
Census Tract
City Unit
Demographic Profile
Demographic Studies
Fertility Rate
Population Attribute
Population Composition
Population Distribution
Statistical Analysis
Zero Population Growth

DEMOGRAPHIC PROFILE
S-06-0188 1975 00024
BT Demographic Characteristics
NT Birth Rate
Fertility Rate
Household Size
Illiteracy Rate
Life Expectancy
Literacy Rate
Mortality Rate
RT Age
Census Tract
Demographic Indicator
Demographic Studies
Population Attribute
Population Composition
Population Distribution
Population Identification

DEMOGRAPHIC PROJECTION
S-06-0197 1975 00014
BT Demographic Characteristics
RT Demographic Studies
Fertility Rate
Household Size
Illiteracy Rate
Life Expectancy
Mortality Rate
Population Attribute
Population Composition
Population Distribution
Population Growth

DEMOGRAPHIC STUDIES
S-01-0056 1975 00022
BT Academic Areas
RT Area Studies
Central African Area Studies
Central City
Comparative Sociology
Cultural Anthropology
Demographic Analysis
Demographic Characteristics
Demographic Indicator
Demographic Profile
Demographic Projection
Ecology Discipline
Economic History
Economics Discipline
Electoral History
Environmental Characteristics
Environmental Studies
Ethnography
Geography Discipline
Human Geography
Marginal Man Analysis
Physical Geography
Policy Science Studies
Political Geography
Political Science Discipline
Political Science Methodology Studies
Population Density
Population Growth
Social Anthropology
Social History
Sociology Discipline
Topography
Urban Geography

DEMONSTRATING
S-31-0254 1975 00000
BT Dissent
RT Demonstration
Draft Resistance
Mutiny
Protest
Resistance

DEMONSTRATION
S-08-0015 1975 00005
BT Political Agitation
NT Civil Rights Demonstration
General Strike
Peace Demonstration
Student Demonstration
Veterans Demonstration
Worker Demonstration

RT Demonstrating
Economic Agitation
Economic Demonstration
Jurisdiction Strike
Labor Boycott
Labor Conflict
Mob Violence
Mobilization Policy
Protest

DEMONSTRATOR
S-32-0180 1975 00001
BT Activist
RT Economic Activist
Peace Activist
Peaceful Protest
Political Activist
Protest
Rioter
Student Activist
War Protestor

DENATIONALIZATION
1975-1979 00000
USE Denationalization Process

DENATIONALIZATION PROCESS
S-31-0343 1979 00000
UF Denationalization
BT Decontrol Process
RT Deregulation Process
Destalinization Process
Economic Liberalism
Free Enterprise System
Free Market
Government Deregulation
Market System

DENOMINATIONAL SCHOOL
USE Religious School

DEPARTMENT HEAD
S-36-0006 1975 00000
BT Administrative Officer
RT Bureau Chief
Dean
Executive Director

DEPENDENT NATION
S-16-0118 1975 00068
BT Nation Type
RT Aligned Nation
Client Nation
Client State
Debtor Nation
Decolonization
Divided Nation
Economic Development Theory
Fourth World Nation
Preindustrial Society
Proxy War
Puppet Regime
Third World Nation
Underdeveloped Nation

DEPENDENT VARIABLE
S-24-0427 1975 00011
BT Variable Logical Status
RT Endogenous Variable
Exogenous Variable
Independent Variable
Interdependent Variable
Intervening Variable

DEPRESSED AREA
S-12-0017 1975 00004
BT Depressed Economy
RT Depression
Underdeveloped Economy

DEPRESSED ECONOMY
S-12-0016 1975 00005
BT Economy Type
NT Depressed Area
RT Depression
Nomadic Economy
Peasant Economy
Subsistence Economy
Underdeveloped Economy

DEPRESSION
S-31-0137 1975 00013
BT Economic Change
RT Cyclical Employment
Debt Financing
Deferential Voter
Deficit Financing
Deflation
Depressed Area
Depressed Economy
Economic Cycle
Economic Depression
Leninist Imperialism Theory
Market Economy
Marxist Economic Theory
Public Works Policy

DEPRIVATION
S-06-0126 1975 00008
BT Satisfaction
NT Relative Deprivation
RT Economic Deprivation
Poverty

DEPTH INTERVIEW
S-24-0108 1975 00000
BT Interview
RT Group Interview
Personal Interview
Telephone Interview

DEREGULATION PROCESS
S-31-0345 1979 00000
BT Decontrol Process
NT Government Deregulation
RT Decontrol Process
Denationalization Process

DERIVED AUTHORITY
S-04-0004 1975 00003
BT Authority Mode
RT Charismatic Authority
Informal Authority
Moral Authority
Traditional Authority

DESCRIPTIVE RESEARCH
S-24-0382 1975 00090
BT Research Orientation
NT Ideographic Research
RT Advocacy Research
Aggregate Data Analysis
Applied Research
Basic Research
Data Selection Orientation
Experimental Research
Explanatory Research
Historical Analysis
Ideographic Science
Inductive Method
Market Research
Policy Research
Predictive Research
Qualitative Research
Quantitative Research
Scientific Research
Theoretical Research

DESCRIPTIVE STATISTICS
S-24-0065 1975 00004
BT Statistics Type
RT Aggregate Data Statistics
Inferential Statistics
Nonparametric Statistics
Parametric Statistics
Statistics Discipline

DESEGREGATION POLICY
S-26-0382 1975 00020
BT Racial Policy
NT Community Desegregation Policy
School Desegregation Policy
RT Equal Opportunity
Ethnic Integration
Housing Integration
Multiracial Society
Racial Integration

DESERTION
S-10-0059 1975 00003
BT Defection
RT Amnesty
Individual Crime
Treason

DESPOT
S-32-0221 1975 00000
BT Politician
NT Benevolent Despot
Oriental Despot
RT Absolute Monarch
Absolute Monarchy
Absolutism
Authoritarianism
Autocrat
Benevolent Despotism
Despotism
Dictator
Dictatorship

DESPOTISM
S-16-0141 1975 00000
BT Rule Type
NT Benevolent Despotism
Oriental Despotism
RT Absolutism
Absolutist Government
Autocratic Government
Centralized Government
Despot
Dictatorship
Direct Rule
Indirect Rule
Military Directorate
One Political Party System
Revolutionary Directorate
Tyranny

DESTALINIZATION
1975-1979 00005
USE Destalinization Process

DESTALINIZATION PROCESS
S-31-0344 1979 00000
UF Destalinization
BT Decontrol Process

RT Control Process
Denationalization Process
Government Deregulation
Human Rights
Liberalism
Political Liberty
Stalinism

DETAINEE
S-36-0257 1975 00000
BT Prisoner
RT Hostage
Political Prisoner
Prisoner Of War

DETENTE
S-06-0675 1975 00031
BT Peaceful Coexistence
NT East West Detente
RT Disarmament
Disarmament Policy
East West Trade
Friendship Agreement
Military Agreement
Neutrality Treaty
Nuclear Parity
Peace Proposal

DETENTION
S-31-0513 1975 00001
BT Pretrial Procedure
NT Preventive Detention
RT Arraignment
Bail
Detention Center
Indictment
Pretrial Release

DETENTION CAMP
1975-1979 00001
USE Detention Center

DETENTION CENTER
S-19-0295 1979 00000
UF Detention Camp
BT Penal Institution
NT Concentration Camp
Prisoner Of War Camp
Slave Labor Camp
RT Arraignment
Bail
Detention
Indictment
Jail
Juvenile Center

DETERRENCE POLICY
S-26-0062 1975 00031
BT Defense Policy
NT Criminal Deterrence
Mutual Deterrence Policy
Nuclear Deterrence Policy
RT Arms Control Policy
Balanced Force
Civil Defense Policy
Counterforce Theory
Deterrence Theory
International Peacekeeping Forces
Military Policy
Nuclear Strategy
Rearmament Policy
War Declaration Policy

DETERRENCE THEORY
S-38-0342 1975 00027
BT International Political Theory
RT Deterrence Policy
Deterrent Weapon
Domino Theory
Foreign Policy Theory
Geopolitical Theory
International Alliance Theory
International Conflict Resolution Theory
International Decision Making Theory
International Field Theory
International Influence Theory
Realist Foreign Policy

DETERRENT WEAPON
S-33-0025 1975 00003
BT Military Weapon
RT Deterrence Theory
Second Strike Nuclear Weapon
Strategic Weapon
Tactical Weapon

DEVELOPED DEMOCRACY
S-16-0016 1975 00000
BT Democratic Government
RT Democratic Theory
Developed Economy
Developed Nation
Direct Democracy
Elitist Democracy
Participatory Democracy
Stable Democracy

DEVELOPED ECONOMY
S-12-0018 1975 00011
BT Economy Type
RT Balanced Economy
Capital Investment Economy
Consumer Economy
Developed Democracy
Developing Economy
Diversified Economic System
Industrial Association
Industrial Economy
Macroeconomics
Market Economy
Mixed Economy
Modernizing Economy
Regional Economics
Self Sufficient Economy
Welfare Economy

DEVELOPED NATION
S-16-0119 1975 00067
BT Nation Type
RT Developed Democracy
Developing Economy
Developing Nation
Development Policy
Development Theory
Rich Nation

DEVELOPING ECONOMY
S-12-0019 1975 00043
BT Economy Type
RT Communist Economic System
Consumer Economy
Developed Economy
Developed Nation
Developing Nation
Development Model
Development Policy
Economic Development Policy
Grants Economy
Industrial Economy
Macroeconomics
Market Economy
Mixed Economic System
Mixed Economy
Modernizing Economy
Regional Economics
Self Sufficient Economy
Socialist Market Economy

DEVELOPING NATION
S-16-0120 1975 00264
BT Nation Type
RT Developed Nation
Developing Economy
Developing Political System
Development Policy
Development Process
Development Theory
Modernizing Economy
Political Development Policy
Third World Nation
Underdeveloped Nation

DEVELOPING POLITICAL SYSTEM
S-37-0109 1975 00019
BT Political System Type
RT Developing Nation
Modernization
Modernization Theory
Political Development Policy
Political Development Theory
Transitional Political System

DEVELOPMENT CHARACTERISTICS
S-06-0141 1975 00046
BT Change Characteristics
NT Development Potential
Economic Development Characteristics
Historical Periods
Human Resources Development
Legal Development
Political Development
RT Development Model
Development Policy
Development Theory
Economic Characteristics
Political Development Policy
System Characteristics

DEVELOPMENT FINANCING
S-31-0406 1975 00029
BT Public Financing
RT Cost Sharing
Economy Pump Priming
Government Expenditure

DEVELOPMENT FUND
S-06-0301 1975 00017
BT Government Expenditure
RT Development Policy
Development Theory
Economy Pump Priming
Education Grant
Education Subsidy
Farm Subsidy
Government Grant
Government Loan
Government Research Support
Industrial Subsidy

DEVELOPMENT INDEX
S-24-0229 1975 00007
BT Scale Type
NT Economic Development Index
Political Development Index
Social Development Index
RT Change Indicator
Change Measurement
Development Model
Development Policy
Development Potential
Development Theory
Logic
Social Change Index
Stability Index
Urbanization Index

DEVELOPMENT MANAGEMENT
S-23-0008 1975 00036
BT Management
RT Administrative Management
Business Management
Central Economic Management
Corporate Management
Economic Management
Economy Pump Priming
Education Administration
Environmental Management
Fiscal Management
Monetary Management
Public Policy Management
Research Management

DEVELOPMENT MODEL
S-24-0296 1979 00000
BT Social Science Model
NT Economic Development Model
RT Communication Model
Conflict Model
Cybernetic Model
Developing Economy
Development Characteristics
Development Index
Development Planning
Development Policy
Development Theory
Econometric Model
Economic Growth Model
Economic Theory
Logic
Optimizing Model
Process Model
Social Development Policy
Social System Model

DEVELOPMENT PLANNING
S-31-0640 1975 00068
BT Planning Process
RT Administrative Planning
Defense Planning
Development Model
Economic Planning
Education Planning
Environmental Planning
Logic
Military Planning
Political Development Policy
Population Planning
Public Policy Planning
Social Planning

DEVELOPMENT POLICY
S-26-0079 1979 00000
BT Policy
NT Cultural Development Policy
Economic Development Policy
Political Development Policy
Social Development Policy
RT Agricultural Development
Developed Nation
Developing Economy
Developing Nation
Development Characteristics
Development Fund
Development Index
Development Model
Development Process
Economic Growth Policy
Education Development
Fiscal Policy
Political Development
Political Development Policy
Resource Development
Zero Based Budget

DEVELOPMENT POTENTIAL
S-06-0142 1975 00021
BT Development Characteristics
RT Building Process
Development Index
Development Process
Development Theory
Human Resources Development
Legal Development
Political Development

DEVELOPMENT PROCESS
S-31-0054 1975 00111
BT Change Process
NT Aging
Decay
Economic Development
Education Development
Evolution
Innovation
Institutional Development
Local Development
Modernization
Personality Development
Progress
Reform
Regional Development
Resource Development
Rural Development
Urban Development
RT Building Process
Cultural Change Process
Developing Nation
Development Policy
Development Potential
Economic Process
Modernity Scale
Policy Making Process
Political Development Policy
Political Party Innovation

DEVELOPMENT THEORY
S-38-0021 1975 00122
BT Theory
NT Administrative Development Theory
Economic Development Theory
Political Development Theory
Social Development Theory
Technological Development Theory
Urban Development Theory
RT Anthropological Theory
Developed Nation
Developing Nation
Development Characteristics
Development Fund
Development Index
Development Model
Development Potential
Economic Development Rate
Economic Development Stage
Economic Diversification
Economic Gain
Economic Scarcity
Economic Theory
Industrialization Level
Institutional Change
Macropolitical Theory
Modernization Theory
Nation Building Theory
Planning Theory
Political Development Policy
Post Industrial Society
Preindustrial Society
Progress Theory

DEVELOPMENTAL PSYCHOLOGY
S-01-0172 1979 00000
BT Psychology Discipline
RT Gestalt Psychology
Group Psychology
Logic
Parapsychology

DEVIANCE
USE Deviant Behavior

DEVIANT BEHAVIOR
S-05-0028 1975 00039
UF Deviance
BT Social Behavior
RT Crowd Behavior
Deviant Case Analysis
Mass Behavior
Personality Development
Personality Theory
Role Theory
Social Adjustment
Social Pathology
Social Psychiatry

DEVIANT CASE ANALYSIS
S-24-0401 1975 00001
BT Case Study
RT Deviant Behavior
Deviant Personality
Ideal Case Analysis

DEVIANT PERSONALITY
S-06-0530 1975 00007
BT Personality Type
RT Deviant Case Analysis
Pathological Behavior
Personality Disorder
Personality Theory
Social Psychiatry

DEVIATING ELECTION
S-29-0045 1975 00002
SN Vote result in which the dominant party is temporarily displaced.
BT Election Type
RT Critical Election
Election Turnout

Electoral Outcome
Electoral Participation
Maintaining Election

DHONDT VOTING METHOD
1975-1979 00000

DIAGRAM
S-24-0133 1975 00001
BT Data Presentation Methodology
NT Venn Diagram
RT Chart
Curve
Graph
Graph Analysis
Plot
Table

DIALECTIC
S-25-0014 1975 00010
BT Epistemology
RT Advocacy Research
Critical Theory Analysis
Dialectical Materialism
Hegelian Analysis
Marxism
Materialism
Socratic Political Thought

DIALECTICAL MATERIALISM
S-38-0310 1975 00004
BT Marxist Materialism
RT Dialectic
Marxism
Marxist Capitalism Theory
Marxist Class Theory
Marxist Economic Theory
Marxist Economics
Marxist Ideology Explanation
Marxist Theory
Materialism
Philosophical Materialism

DICTATOR
S-36-0049 1975 00003
BT Chief Government Executive
NT Benevolent Dictator
RT Absolute Monarchy
Absolutism
Authoritarianism
Bonapartism
Despot
Dictatorial Regime
Military Governor
Monarch
Proclamation
Stalinist
Warlord

DICTATORIAL REGIME
S-16-0138 1975 00008
BT Political Regime
RT Absolutism
Ancient Regime
Authoritarian Regime
Corporate Fascism
Democratic Regime
Dictator
Falangism
Francoism
Italian Fascism
Martial Law
Military Government
National Socialism
One Political Party System

DICTATORSHIP
S-16-0035 1975 00006
BT Government Type
NT Benevolent Dictatorship
Bourgeois Dictatorship
Constitutional Dictatorship
Military Dictatorship
Modernizing Dictatorship
Progressive Dictatorship
Proletarian Dictatorship
Totalitarian Dictatorship
RT Absolute Monarch
Absolute Monarchy
Absolutist Government
Autocratic Government
Bonapartism
Centralized Government
Concentrated Power
Corporate Fascism
Counterrevolution
Despot
Despotism
Elitist Democracy
Falangism
Fascist Theory
Francoism
Guided Democracy
National Socialism
Political Refugee
Tutelary Democracy

DICTATORSHIP OF PROLETARIAT
1975-1979 00005
USE Dictatorship Of The Proletariat

DICTATORSHIP OF THE PROLETARIAT
S-38-0299 1979 00000
UF Dictatorship Of Proletariat
BT Marxist Theory
RT Marxism Leninism
Marxist Alienation Theory
Marxist Capitalism Theory
Marxist Class Theory
Marxist Communism Theory
Marxist Economic Determinism
Marxist Economic Theory
Marxist Political Thought
Peoples Democratic State
Proletarian Internationalism
Proletarian Movement

DIET
S-19-0274 1975 00001
SN A national legislative body.
BT National Assembly
RT Congress
Democratic Coalition
Legislature Type
Peoples Assembly
Popular Assembly

DIFFERENTIAL CALCULUS
1975-1979 00000

DIFFERENTIAL EQUATION MODEL
S-24-0281 1975 00008
BT Mathematical Model
RT Economic Mathematical Model
Mathematics Discipline
Simultaneous Equation Model
Stochastic Model

DIFFERENTIATED MARKET
S-19-0185 1975 00001
BT Market
RT Black Market
Commodity Market
Common Market
Differentiated System
Financial Market
Free Market
Marketplace
Mass Market
National Market
Stock Market
World Market

DIFFERENTIATED SYSTEM
S-37-0007 1975 00003
BT System Type
NT Functional Differentiated System
Structural Differentiated System
RT Differentiated Market
Economic Development Theory
Social Mobility

DIFFUSE AUTHORITY
S-04-0015 1975 00000
BT Authority Structure
RT Anarchy
Decentralized Authority
Decentralized Government
Decentralized Political Party
Delegated Authority
Diffuse System Supports
Diffusion Model
Formal Authority
Hierarchical Authority
Independent Authority
Informal Authority

DIFFUSE SYSTEM SUPPORT
1975-1979 00034
USE Diffuse System Supports

DIFFUSE SYSTEM SUPPORTS
S-06-0594 1979 00000
SN General affect for a counrty's political institutions.
UF Diffuse System Support
BT System Supports
RT Deference
Diffuse Authority
Just Authority
Legitimacy Theory
Modern Political Culture
Political Culture
Political System Effectiveness
Specific System Supports

DIFFUSION MODEL
S-24-0298 1975 00029
BT Social Science Model
RT Atomistic Model
Diffuse Authority
Interaction Model
Process Model

DIGGERS POLITICAL THOUGHT
S-38-0520 1975 00000
SN Beliefs of seventeenth century English movement calling for all land to be commonly owned and administered.
BT Early Radical Thought
RT Early Republicanism
Levellers Political Thought
Radicalism

DIGNITY
USE Human Dignity Theory

DIMENSIONAL ANALYSIS
S-24-0044 1975 00004
BT Multivariate Analysis
RT Analysis Of Variance
Automatic Interaction Detection
Cluster Analysis
Covariance Analysis
Discriminant Analysis
Factor Analysis
Ideographic Science
Multiple Correlation Analysis
Multiple Regression Analysis
Partial Correlation Analysis
Path Analysis

DIPLOMACY
S-31-0347 1975 00071
BT Process
NT Diplomatic Recognition
Diplomatic Relations
Diplomatic Relations Break
Diplomatic Relations Normalization
Dollar Diplomacy
Executive Diplomacy
Gunboat Diplomacy
Person To Person Diplomacy
Secret Diplomacy
Summit Diplomacy
RT DeFacto Recognition
DeJure Recognition
Diplomat
Diplomatic History
Foreign Minister
International Adjudication
International Arbitration
International Conciliation
International Decision Making Process
International Negotiation
International Peace Negotiation
International Political Bargaining
Military History

DIPLOMAT
S-36-0119 1975 00013
BT Government Official
NT Embassy Official
Foreign Minister
Foreign Service Officer
RT Charge D'Affaires
Diplomacy
Diplomatic History
Diplomatic Immunity
Diplomatic Privilege
Diplomatic Recognition
Diplomatic Relations
Diplomatic Relations Break
Legislative Official
Mediator
Political Party Official

DIPLOMATIC HISTORY
S-01-0102 1979 00000
BT History Discipline
RT Ancient History
DeFacto Recognition
DeJure Recognition
Diplomacy
Diplomat
Diplomatic Recognition
Diplomatic Relations
Diplomatic Relations Normalization
Historical Analysis
Intellectual History
International Adjudication
International Arbitration
International Conciliation
International Decision Making Process
Legal History
Military History

DIPLOMATIC IMMUNITY
S-15-0018 1975 00001
BT Immunity
NT Diplomatic Privilege
RT Citizenship Immunity
Diplomat
Executive Immunity
Legal Immunity
Political Asylum
United Nations

DIPLOMATIC PRIVILEGE
S-15-0019 1975 00000
BT Diplomatic Immunity
RT Citizenship Privilege
Diplomat
International Law
Member Privilege

DIPLOMATIC RECOGNITION
S-31-0348 1975 00016
BT Diplomacy
NT DeFacto Recognition
DeJure Recognition
RT Diplomat
Diplomatic History
Diplomatic Relations
Diplomatic Relations Break
Diplomatic Relations Normalization
Person To Person Diplomacy
United Nations

DIPLOMATIC RELATIONS
S-31-0351 1975 00072
BT Diplomacy
RT Ambassador
Diplomat
Diplomatic History
Diplomatic Recognition
Diplomatic Relations Break
Diplomatic Relations Normalization
Executive Diplomacy
International Economic Relations
Summit Diplomacy
United Nations

DIPLOMATIC RELATIONS BREAK
S-31-0352 1975 00005
BT Diplomacy
RT Diplomat
Diplomatic Recognition
Diplomatic Relations
Economic Relations
Economic Retaliation
United Nations

DIPLOMATIC RELATIONS NORMALIZATION
S-31-0353 1979 00000
BT Diplomacy
RT DeFacto Recognition
DeJure Recognition
Diplomatic History
Diplomatic Recognition
Diplomatic Relations
Executive Diplomacy
International Economic Relations
International Law
Summit Diplomacy

DIRECT ACCESS STORAGE
USE Computer Processing

DIRECT COMPETITION
S-31-0200 1975 00000
BT Competition
RT Formal Competition
Imperfect Competition
Indirect Competition
Perfect Competition

DIRECT DEMOCRACY
S-16-0017 1975 00005
BT Democratic Government
RT Agrarian Democracy
Athenian Democratic Theory
Democratic Regime
Developed Democracy
Direct Rule
Initiative Election
Participatory Democracy
Plebiscitary Democracy
Plebiscite Election

DIRECT ELECTION
S-29-0046 1975 00003
BT Election Type
RT Electoral Procedure
Indirect Election
Initiative Election
Plebiscite Election

DIRECT RULE
S-16-0144 1975 00000
BT Rule Type
RT Despotism
Direct Democracy
Indirect Rule

DIRECT TAXATION
S-26-0141 1975 00001
BT Taxation Policy
RT Gift Taxation
Indirect Taxation
Progressive Taxation
Regressive Taxation

DIRECTORY
1975-1979 00000

DISABILITY INSURANCE
S-26-0302 1979 00000
BT Insurance
RT Accident Insurance
Catastrophe Insurance
Employment Policy

DISARMAMENT
S-06-0677 1975 00018
BT Peaceful Coexistence
RT Arms Control Policy
Detente
Rapprochement
Strategic Arms Limitation

DISARMAMENT AGREEMENT
S-02-0075 1975 00007
BT State Agreement Type
NT Disarmament Treaty
RT Arms Control Agreement
Nonaggression Agreement
Nuclear Nonproliferation Agreement
Strategic Arms Limitation

Strategic Arms Reduction Policy
Test Ban Agreement

DISARMAMENT POLICY
S-26-0058 1975 00001
BT Arms Control Policy
NT Nuclear Disarmament Policy
RT Arms Reduction Policy
Arms Verification Policy
Detente
Military Policy
Nuclear Weapon Nonproliferation Policy

DISARMAMENT TREATY
S-02-0076 1975 00001
BT Disarmament Agreement
RT Arms Control Treaty
Nuclear Nonproliferation Treaty
Strategic Arms Reduction Policy

DISCHARGE PETITION
S-31-0595 1975 00000
BT Legislative Voting
RT Bipartisan Voting
Censure Motion

DISCIPLINED TWO PARTY SYSTEM
S-37-0131 1975 00000
BT Two Political Party System
RT Responsible Two Party System

DISCOUNT RATE
S-06-0355 1975 00004
BT Money Creation
RT Bank Reserve
Business Policy
Deflation Policy
Prime Loan Rate

DISCOVERY
S-31-0439 1979 00000
BT Knowledge Production
RT Exploration
Explorer
Geographic Exploration
Geography Discipline
Prehistorical Times
Social Scientist

DISCRIMINANT ANALYSIS
S-24-0045 1975 00006
BT Multivariate Analysis
RT Analysis Of Variance
Automatic Interaction Detection
Cluster Analysis
Covariance Analysis
Dimensional Analysis
Discriminant Validity
Factor Analysis
Multiple Correlation Analysis
Partial Correlation Analysis
Path Analysis

DISCRIMINANT VALIDITY
S-24-0167 1975 00004
BT Validity Measurement
RT Construct Validity
Criterion Validity
Discriminant Analysis
Face Validity

DISCRIMINATION POLICY
S-26-0373 1975 00077
BT Social Policy
NT Racial Discrimination
Reverse Discrimination
Sex Discrimination
RT Disenfranchisement
Education Inequality
Equal Law Enforcement
Equal Rights
Ethnic Ghetto
Ethnic Policy
Housing Policy
Inequality
Intolerance
Job Discrimination
Literacy Test
Literacy Voting Test
Persecution
Religious Policy
Reverse Discrimination
Sexism
Untouchables
Urban Renewal Policy

DISEASE
S-06-0374 1979 00000
BT Health Characteristics
RT Alcoholism
Drug Addiction
Epidemic
Health Administration
Health Clinic
Health Education
Health Service
Morbidity Data
Public Health Institution

DISENFRANCHISEMENT
S-29-0116 1975 00000
BT Nonvoting
RT Discrimination Policy
Election Fraud
Eligible Voter
Literacy Voting Test
Poll Tax

DISPERSED POWER
S-30-0003 1975 00004
BT Power Type
RT Concentrated Power
Decentralized Authority
Decentralized Government
Decentralized Political Party
Formal Power
Informal Power

DISPERSION MEASURE
S-24-0071 1975 00000
BT Univariate Analysis
RT Central Tendency Measure
Population Estimation

DISPOSABLE INCOME
S-06-0333 1975 00000
BT Income Measure
RT Average Income
Economic Indicator
Fixed Assets
Fixed Income
Median Income
Net Income

DISSENT
S-31-0253 1975 00034
BT Conflict Process
NT Demonstrating
Mutiny
Protest
Resistance
RT Exile
Mutiny
New Left
New Left Militant
Political Party Dissident
Political Refugee
Protest
Resistance

DISSERTATION
1975-1979 00000
USE Thesis

DISTRIBUTIVE JUSTICE THEORY
S-38-0475 1975 00034
BT Justice Theory
RT Allocation Process
Aristotelian Thought
Benthamism
Common Wealth Theory
Compensatory Justice
Equity
Justice As Fairness Doctrine
Utilitarianism

DISTRICT ATTORNEY
S-36-0104 1975 00001
BT Attorney General
RT Magistrate
Military Prosecutor
Public Defender
Trial Court

DISTRICT COURT
S-19-0137 1975 00009
BT Constitutional Court
RT Appellate Court
Evidence Admissibility
National Supreme Court
Subnational Supreme Court
Supreme Court
Trial Court

DISTRICT GOVERNMENT TYPE
S-16-0091 1975 00001
BT Subnational Government
NT Fire District
Recreation District
School District
Sewer District
Transportation District
Water District
Zoning District
RT County Government
Districting
Local Government
Metropolitan Government
Municipality
Urban Government
Village

DISTRICT REPRESENTATION
S-31-0717 1975 00006
BT Representation Type
RT At Large Representation
Districting
Functional Representation
Geographic Representation
Minority Group Representation
Multiple Member District Representation
Multiple Member Districting
Proportional Representation
Single Member District Representation

Token Representation

DISTRICTING
S-31-0707 1975 00000
BT Apportionment
NT Gerrymandering
Legislative Districting
Legislative Redistricting
Multiple Member Districting
Single Member Districting
RT District Government Type
District Representation
Gerrymandering
National Political Division
One Man One Vote Representation

DISTRUST
S-06-0080 1975 00005
BT Alienation
NT Political Distrust
RT Cultural Alienation
Cynicism
Estrangement
Extremism
Paranoia
Personality Theory
Political Distrust

DIVERGENCE MAPPING
S-24-0014 1979 00000
BT Forecasting Methodology
RT Authority Forecasting
Brainstorming
Delphi Technique
Economic Forecasting
Policy Evaluation Research
Policy Research
Political Forecasting
Predictive Research
Scenario Construction
Social Forecasting
Trend Analysis

DIVERGENCE THEORY
S-38-0037 1975 00004
BT Modernization Theory
RT Economic Development Theory
Social Development Theory

DIVERSIFIED ECONOMIC SYSTEM
S-37-0024 1975 00001
BT Economic System
RT Advanced Industrial Society
Developed Economy

DIVIDED NATION
S-16-0121 1979 00000
BT Nation Type
RT Balkanization
Client Nation
Client State
Dependent Nation
Foreign Rule
Military Occupation
Underdeveloped Nation

DIVIDED SOVEREIGNTY
S-16-0153 1975 00003
BT Sovereignty
RT Limited Sovereignty
Popular Sovereignty
Territory Sovereignty

DIVINE JUSTICE THEORY
S-38-0476 1975 00000
BT Justice Theory
RT Religious Thought

DIVINE RIGHT THEORY
S-38-0391 1975 00002
BT Early Modern Theory Of The State
RT Legitimacy Theory
Mandate Of Heaven Theory
Organic State Theory

DIVISION OF LABOR
S-06-0276 1975 00020
BT Economic Characteristics
NT International Division Of Labor
National Division Of Labor
Socialist Division Of Labor
RT Labor Economics
Labor Intensive Economy
Labor Market
Marxist Alienation Theory
National Production

DIVORCE LAW
S-21-0092 1979 00000
BT Marital Law
RT Divorced
Family Law
Family Policy
Family Type
Gambling Law
Marital Law

DIVORCED
S-36-0228 1979 00000
BT Marital Status
RT Divorce Law
Marital Offense

DOCUMENTARY RESEARCH
S-24-0079 1975 00031
BT Nonreactive Observation
NT Citation Analysis
RT Government Document
Government Document Classification Policy
Library Research
Nonparticipant Observation
Propositional Inventory

DOCUMENTATION SERVICE
S-18-0050 1975 00002
BT Information Service
RT Abstracting
Abstracting Service
Archives
Bibliographic Control
Bibliographic Service
Book Industry
Documents
Government Document
Government Information Service
Intergovernmental Document
Judicial Record
Literature Review
Private Information Service
Statistical Data
Thesaurus
University Information Service

DOCUMENTS
S-18-0007 1975 00003
BT Information Sources
NT Commission Record
Committee Record
Employment Record
Financial Record
Government Document
International Organization Record
Political Party Record
Pronouncement
Public Record
RT Book Industry
Confidential Information
Documentation Service
Government Information Service
Legislative Information Service
Monographs
Newsletters
Newspapers
Private Information Service
Thesaurus
University Information Service

DOGMATISM
S-06-0097 1975 00009
BT Attitude Characteristics
RT Absolutism
Authoritarian Attitude
Authoritarian Personality
Dogmatism Scale
Extremism
Militancy

DOGMATISM SCALE
S-24-0233 1975 00001
BT Scale Type
RT Aggression Scale
Alienation Scale
Anomie Scale
Cynicism Scale
Dogmatism
Frustration Scale
Liberalism Conservatism Scale
Optimism Pessimism Scale
Social Distance Scale
Social Frustration Scale
Support Opposition Scale

DOLLAR DIPLOMACY
S-31-0354 1975 00001
BT Diplomacy
RT Citizen To Citizen Diplomacy
Executive Diplomacy
Gunboat Diplomacy

DOMESTIC CONSUMPTION
S-06-0271 1975 00003
BT Consumption
RT Conspicuous Consumption
Consumption Pattern
Economic Indicator
Mass Consumption
Private Consumption
Public Consumption

DOMESTIC INFORMATION POLICY
S-26-0281 1975 00003
BT Information Policy
NT Government Document Classification Policy
Government Information Diffusion Policy
Government Media Regulation Policy
RT Election Campaign Propaganda
Foreign Information Policy
Propaganda Policy

DOMESTIC INTERGOVERNMENTAL DOCUMENT
S-18-0026 1975 00003
BT Intergovernmental Document
RT Foreign Intergovernmental Document

DOMESTIC MARKET
S-19-0186 1975 00013
BT Market
RT Commodity Market
Financial Market
Free Market
Marketplace
Mass Market
Protective Tariff

DOMESTIC POLICY MAKING
S-31-0677 1975 00034
BT Policy Making Process
RT International Policy Making
National Policy Making

DOMINO THEORY
S-38-0343 1975 00005
BT International Political Theory
RT Deterrence Theory
Geopolitical Theory
Global War Policy
International Alliance Theory
International Conflict Resolution Theory
International Field Theory
International Influence Theory
International Integration Theory
International Organization Theory

DOUBLE JEOPARDY
S-15-0045 1975 00001
BT Defendants Rights
RT Bill Of Attainder
Habeas Corpus
Right Against Cruel And Unusual Punishment
Right To Due Process
Right To Equal Protection
Right To Jury Trial
Right To Speedy Trial
Right To Trial
Statute Of Limitations

DOWNWARD MOBILITY
S-06-0752 1975 00008
BT Vertical Mobility
RT Horizontal Mobility
Intergenerational Mobility
Social Stratification Formation
Upward Mobility

DRAFT RESISTANCE
S-31-0261 1975 00002
BT Resistance
RT Conscientious Objector
Demonstrating
Passive Resistance
Peace Activist

DRAFTEE
S-36-0218 1975 00000
BT Military Recruit
RT Conscripted Armed Forces
Conscription Power

DRIVER LICENSING POLICY
S-26-0406 1975 00000
BT Highway Safety Policy
RT Automobile Industry
Government Regulation
Testing
Transportation Policy

DRUG ABUSE
1975-1979 00048
USE Drug Addiction

DRUG ADDICTION
S-06-0375 1979 00000
UF Drug Abuse
BT Health Characteristics
RT Alcoholism
Disease
Drug Culture
Epidemic
Health Administration
Health Care Institution
Health Care Policy
Health Clinic
Health Service
Mental Health Policy
Public Health Institution
Public Health Policy

DRUG CONTROL POLICY
S-26-0377 1975 00032
BT Social Policy
RT Safety Policy
Social Resource Distribution Policy

DRUG CULTURE
S-11-0014 1975 00010
BT Culture Type
RT Drug Addiction
Poverty Culture
Subculture
Youth Culture

DUAL CITIZEN
S-36-0017 1975 00001
BT Alien
RT Native Born Citizen
Naturalized Citizen

DUAL ECONOMY
S-12-0020 1975 00004
BT Economy Type
RT Autarchic Economy
Balanced Economy
Barter Economy
Capital Investment Economy
Craft Economy
Mixed Economic System
Mixed Economy
Socialist Market Economy
Welfare Economy

DUMA
USE National Government Council

DURKHEIMIAN ANALYSIS
S-09-0067 1979 00000
BT Sociological Analysis
RT Marginal Man Analysis
Parsonsian Analysis
Social Theory
Weberian Analysis

DYNAMIC EQUILIBRIUM
S-06-0615 1975 00001
BT System Equilibrium
RT Homeostatic Equilibrium
System Performance

EARLY MODERN THEORY OF THE STATE
S-38-0390 1975 00001
BT Modern Political Thought
NT Divine Right Theory
Hobbesian Absolutism
Instrumental State Theory
Lockean Contractualism
Newtonian Mechanistic State Theory
Republican Constitutionalism
RT Authority Mode
Authority Theory
Early Republicanism
Organic State Theory

EARLY RADICAL THOUGHT
S-38-0519 1975 00000
BT Renaissance Political Thought
NT Diggers Political Thought
Early Republicanism
Levellers Political Thought
RT Early Republicanism
Extremism
Political Liberty
Radicalism
Republican Constitutionalism

EARLY REPUBLICANISM
S-38-0521 1975 00006
BT Early Radical Thought
RT Diggers Political Thought
Early Modern Theory Of The State
Early Radical Thought
Political Liberty
Radicalism
Republican Constitutionalism

EARTH SCIENCES
S-01-0057 1975 00001
UF Geology
BT Academic Areas
RT Agricultural Science
Ecological Analysis
Engineering Discipline
Environmental Studies
Natural Science Discipline
Physical Geography
Physical Science

EAST AFRICAN AREA STUDIES
S-01-0027 1979 00000
BT African Area Studies
RT Central African Area Studies
Cultural Anthropology
History Discipline
North African Area Studies
Political Science Discipline
Sociology Discipline
South African Area Studies
West African Area Studies

EAST ASIAN AREA STUDIES
S-01-0037 1975 00443
BT Asian Area Studies
RT Buddhism
Communist Studies
Comparative Political Studies
Comparative Sociology
Cultural Anthropology
Cultural History
Shintoism
South Asian Area Studies
Southeast Asian Area Studies

EAST EUROPEAN AREA STUDIES
S-01-0043 1979 00000
BT Soviet And East European Area Studies
RT Communist Empire
Communist Studies
Comparative Analysis
Comparative Political Studies
Comparative Sociology

Cultural Anthropology
Cultural History
Eastern Orthodox Thought
European Integration Theory
Marxism Leninism
Marxist Revolution Theory
Peoples Democratic State
Russian Studies
Soviet Studies
West European Area Studies

EAST WEST DETENTE
S-06-0676 1975 00076
BT Detente
RT Alliance
Alliance Process
Arms Control Agency
Deescalation Policy
Economic Bargaining
International System Polarization
Rapproachment
Sphere Of Influence
Summit Meeting

EAST WEST TRADE
S-31-0387 1975 00015
BT International Trade
RT Detente
Foreign Trade
International Capital Movement
International Commerce

EASTERN CIVILIZATION
S-11-0006 1979 00000
BT Civilization
RT African Civilization
Ancient Civilization
Byzantine Civilization
Greek Civilization
Historical Analysis
History Discipline
Homogeneous Culture
Islamic Civilization
Political Culture
Roman Civilization

EASTERN CULTURE
S-11-0022 1975 00019
BT Nonwestern Culture
RT Buddhism
Cultural History
Customary Law
Eastern Legalist Theory
Eastern Orthodox Thought
Eastern Political Thought
Hinduism
Political Culture
Western Culture

EASTERN LEGALIST THEORY
S-38-0104 1975 00002
BT Eastern Political Thought
RT Customary Law
Eastern Culture

EASTERN ORTHODOX THOUGHT
S-38-0563 1975 00004
BT Catholicism
RT East European Area Studies
Eastern Culture
Religious Culture
Religious Identity
Russian Studies
Soviet And East European Area Studies

EASTERN POLITICAL THOUGHT
S-38-0101 1975 00004
BT Political Theory
NT Confucian Political Theory
Eastern Legalist Theory
Neoconfucian Political Theory
RT Asian Area Studies
Buddhism
Confucianism
Cultural History
Eastern Culture
Nonwestern Culture
Nonwestern Society
Oriental Despotism
Presocratic Political Thought
Shintoism
Southeast Asian Area Studies
Zoroastrianism

EASTONIAN ANALYSIS
S-09-0016 1975 00005
SN A mode of political inquiry based on the application and refinement of general systems theory to the political realm.
BT Contemporary Analytic Modes
RT Demand Analysis
Ecological Analysis
General System Theory
Input Output Analysis
System Analysis
Value Allocation

ECCLESIASTICAL LEADERSHIP
S-22-0012 1975 00002
BT Religious Leadership
RT Bureaucratic Leadership
Canon Law
Church Law
Closed Leadership
Collective Leadership
Collegial Leadership
Moral Leadership
Personalized Leadership
Priest
Rabbi
Religious Authority
Religious Leader
Religious Thought
Traditional Leadership

ECOLOGICAL ANALYSIS
S-09-0017 1975 00022
UF Ecological Balance
BT Contemporary Analytic Modes
RT Air Pollution
Earth Sciences
Eastonian Analysis
Ecological Model
Ecology Movement
Ecosystem
Environmental Management
Environmental Planning
Pollution Policy
Spatial Analysis

ECOLOGICAL BALANCE
USE Ecological Analysis

ECOLOGICAL MODEL
S-24-0287 1975 00025
BT Natural Science Model
RT Air Pollution
Biological Model
Ecological Analysis
Ecology Discipline
Ecology Movement
Ecosystem

ECOLOGICAL REVOLUTION
S-08-0066 1975 00002
BT Revolution
NT Green Revolution
RT Air Pollution
Counterrevolution
Ecology Movement
Social Revolution
Spontaneous Revolution
Technological Revolution

ECOLOGY DISCIPLINE
S-01-0058 1975 00002
BT Academic Areas
RT Agricultural Science
Air Pollution
Anthropology Discipline
Catastrophe Analysis
Climatology
Demographic Studies
Ecological Model
Economic Geography
Ecosystem
Engineering Discipline
Environment Policy
Environmental Management
Environmental Planning
Environmental Studies
Geography Discipline
Natural Resource Policy
Natural Science Discipline
Noise Pollution
Physical Geography
Physical Science
Policy Science Studies
Political Science Discipline
Sociology Discipline
Topography
Waste Treatment Policy

ECOLOGY MOVEMENT
S-27-0004 1975 00009
BT Political Movement
RT Catastrophe Analysis
Ecological Analysis
Ecological Model
Ecological Revolution
Ecosystem
Environmental Agency
Fish And Wildlife Policy
Forest Land Policy
Green Revolution
Natural Resource Management
Natural Resource Policy
Pollution Policy
Reform Movement
Social Movement
Water Pollution Policy

ECONOMETRIC MODEL
S-24-0299 1975 00020
BT Social Science Model
RT Development Model
Econometrics
Economic Development Model
Economic Mathematical Model
Equilibrium Model
Growth Model

Input Output Model
Interaction Model
Neoclassical Economic Theory
Probability Model
Rational Choice Model

ECONOMETRICS
S-01-0062 1975 00003
BT Economics Discipline
RT Aggregate Data Analysis
Business Economics
Computer Science
Consumer Economics
Cybernetic Theory
Econometric Model
Economic Geography
Evolutionary Economics
Industrial Economics
Labor Economics
Mathematics Discipline
Political Economy Studies
Regional Economics
Social Economics
Sociology Discipline
Statistical Analysis
Transportation Economics
Urban Economics
Welfare Economics

ECONOMIC ACTIVIST
S-32-0181 1975 00000
BT Activist
NT Consumer Activist
RT Demonstrator
Economic Leader
Labor Boycott
Political Activist

ECONOMIC ADVISOR
S-32-0015 1975 00003
BT Advisor
RT Administrative Advisor
Economic Advisory Board
Education Advisor
Government Official
Legal Advisor
Military Advisor
Political Advisor
Science Advisor
Technical Advisor

ECONOMIC ADVISORY BOARD
S-19-0016 1975 00000
BT Economic Agency
RT Agricultural Advisory Board
Economic Advisor
Economic Control Agency
Economic Council
Economic Institution
Fiscal Agency
Labor Relations Agency
Planning Commission
Production Agency

ECONOMIC AGENCY
S-19-0015 1975 00009
BT Agencies
NT Economic Advisory Board
Economic Control Agency
Fiscal Agency
Labor Relations Agency
Production Agency
RT Economic Council
Economic Institution
Planning Commission
Welfare Agency

ECONOMIC AGITATION
S-08-0008 1975 00002
BT Agitation
NT Economic Demonstration
Labor Boycott
RT Agitation Propaganda
Demonstration
Economic Conflict
Economic Rebellion
Foreign Competition
Labor Conflict
Peasant Rebellion
Political Agitation
Political Rebellion
Political Violence
Protest Politics
Routinized Conflict
Social Conflict
Social Rebellion
Technological Revolution
Worker Rebellion

ECONOMIC AGREEMENT
S-02-0077 1975 00008
BT State Agreement Type
NT Economic Treaty
RT Commercial Agreement
Economic Alliance
Economic Dependency
Economic Relations
Monetary Agreement
Trade Agreement

ECONOMIC AID POLICY
S-26-0257 1975 00025
BT Foreign Aid Policy
RT Bilateral Aid
Bilateral Aid Policy
Bilateral Treaty
Farm Income
Grants Economy
Military Aid Policy
Multilateral Aid Policy
Technical Aid Policy
Technical Assistance
Unilateral Aid Policy
War Reparation Policy

ECONOMIC ALLIANCE
S-02-0003 1975 00012
BT Alliance
RT Bilateral Aid
Commercial Agreement
Common Market
Customs Union
Economic Agreement
Economic Coalition
Military Alliance

ECONOMIC ATTACHE
S-36-0127 1975 00000
BT Embassy Attache
RT Cultural Attache
Government Employee
Information Attache
Military Attache
Political Attache

ECONOMIC BACKGROUND
S-06-0209 1975 00024
BT Socioeconomic Background
RT Education Background
Population Attribute
Social Background
Social Class Origin

ECONOMIC BARGAINING
S-31-0230 1975 00013
BT Bargaining
RT Bargaining Strategy Process
Barter Economic System
East West Detente
Labor Arbitration
Political Bargaining

ECONOMIC BEHAVIOR
S-05-0007 1975 00042
BT Behavior
NT Consumer Behavior
RT Behavioral Theory
Consumer Behavior
Group Behavior
Habitual Behavior
Microeconomics
Political Behavior
Rational Man Analysis

ECONOMIC BRIBERY
S-10-0015 1975 00005
BT Economic Crime
RT Economic Conspiracy
Extortion
Fraud
Political Bribery
Political Fund Misuse
Political Graft
Spoils System
White Collar Crime

ECONOMIC BUREAUCRACY
S-19-0071 1975 00000
BT Bureaucracy
NT Corporate Bureaucracy
RT Antitrust Agency
Corporation
Economic Control Agency
Economic Council
Economic Elite
Governing Elite

ECONOMIC CHANGE
S-31-0135 1975 00046
BT Change Process
NT Deflation
Depression
Inflation
RT Institutional Development
Political Change
Social Change
Technological Change
Technological Progress

ECONOMIC CHARACTERISTICS
S-06-0246 1975 00024
BT Characteristics
NT Budget
Capital
Consumption
Division Of Labor
Economic Cycle
Economic Gain
Economic Index
Economic Loss
Economic Scarcity

Government Expenditure
Income
International Economic Characteristics
Money
RT Change Characteristics
Development Characteristics
Economic Development Theory
Economic Indicator
Economic System Characteristics
Economic Theory
Education Characteristics
Government Characteristics
Health Characteristics
Industrialization Level
Macroeconomics
Mass Production
Occupation Characteristics
Opportunity Characteristics
Regional Economic Development Level
System Characteristics

ECONOMIC COALITION
S-02-0016 1975 00000
BT Coalition Type
RT Class Based Coalition
Common Market
Customs Union
Economic Alliance
Economic Community
Interest Group Coalition
Political Coalition
Winning Coalition

ECONOMIC COMMUNITY
S-07-0023 1975 00007
BT Community Type
RT City
Collective Community
Common Market
Communal Community
Commune
Community Building
Community Interest
Community Structural Characteristics
Consumer Economy
Cooperative Community
Cooperatives
Corporate Power
Customs Union
Economic Coalition
Economic Council
Economic Index
Economic Movement
Economy Type
Kibbutz
Model City
Monetary Agreement
Monetary Union
Multilateral Treaty
New Town
Planned Economy
Political Community
Political Economy Studies
Red Commune
Regional Economics
Trade Bloc
Utopian Community

ECONOMIC COMPETITION
S-31-0201 1975 00035
BT Competition
RT Economic Competition Index
Economic Process
Foreign Competition
Industrial Espionage
International Competition
Unfair Competition

ECONOMIC COMPETITION INDEX
S-06-0290 1975 00001
BT Economic Index
RT Economic Competition
Economic Growth Index
Employment Index

ECONOMIC CONFLICT
S-08-0027 1975 00009
BT Conflict Type
NT Consumer Producer Conflict
Labor Conflict
RT Aggression
Class Conflict
Class Struggle
Cold War
Congressional Intern
Coup D'Etat
Cultural Conflict
Economic Agitation
Economic Rebellion
General Strike
Ideological Conflict
Insurgency
Internal Conflict
International Conflict
Marxist Economic Theory
Military Coup
Mob Violence
North South Conflict
Rebellion
Religious Conflict
Revolution
Routinized Conflict
Social Conflict
War By Proxy

ECONOMIC CONGLOMERATE
S-19-0165 1975 00002
BT Corporation
RT Cartel
Corporate Power
Holding Company
International Corporation
Public Corporation
Quasipublic Corporation

ECONOMIC CONSPIRACY
S-10-0016 1975 00000
BT Economic Crime
RT Blackmail
Economic Bribery
Economic Espionage
Economic Imperialism
Economic Sabotage
Extortion
Industrial Espionage
Organized Crime
Political Conspiracy
Political Fund Misuse
Property Crime
Tax Evasion
White Collar Crime

ECONOMIC CONTROL AGENCY
S-19-0017 1975 00006
BT Economic Agency
NT Price Control Agency
Price Support Agency
Rationing Agency
RT Antitrust Agency
Business Regulation Agency
Centrally Planned Economy
Consumer Agency
Customs Union
Economic Advisory Board
Economic Bureaucracy
Economic Council
Economic Institution
Fiscal Agency
Labor Relations Agency
Production Agency

ECONOMIC COUNCIL
S-19-0108 1975 00001
BT Councils
RT Antitrust Agency
Budget Agency
Business Regulation Agency
Economic Advisory Board
Economic Agency
Economic Bureaucracy
Economic Community
Economic Control Agency
Fiscal Agency
International Government Council
International Planning Commission
National Government Council
Planning Agency
Planning Commission
Public Treasury
Revenue Agency
Subnational Government Council

ECONOMIC CRIME
S-10-0014 1975 00005
BT Crime
NT Economic Bribery
Economic Conspiracy
Economic Espionage
Economic Sabotage
Fraud
Property Crime
Tax Evasion
White Collar Crime
RT Economic Criminal
Extortion
Malpractice
Political Bribery
Political Fund Misuse
Political Graft
Religious Offense
Violent Crime

ECONOMIC CRIMINAL
S-36-0029 1975 00002
BT Criminal
RT Economic Crime
Personal Crime Criminal
Political Criminal

ECONOMIC CRISIS
S-31-0247 1979 00000
BT Crisis
RT Crisis
Economic Cycle
Economic Theory

International Crisis
Natural Catastrophe
Political Crisis
Social Crisis

ECONOMIC CYCLE
S-06-0280 1975 00020
BT Economic Characteristics
NT Economic Depression
Economic Inflation
Economic Recovery
RT Capitalist Economy
Depression
Economic Crisis
Economic Development Theory
Economic Gain
Inflation
Supply Elasticity

ECONOMIC DECISION MAKER
S-32-0028 1975 00005
BT Decision Maker
RT Business Leader
Cultural Decision Maker
Economic Leader
Governing Elite
Organization Decision Maker
Political Decision Maker
Social Decision Maker

ECONOMIC DEMONSTRATION
S-08-0009 1975 00000
BT Economic Agitation
NT Consumer Demonstration
Rent Strike
RT Consumer Producer Conflict
Demonstration
Economic Espionage
Labor Boycott
Labor Conflict
Labor Strike
Lockout
Protest
Strike Breaking
Walkout

ECONOMIC DEPENDENCY
S-06-0621 1975 00062
BT Economic System Characteristics
RT Economic Agreement
Economic Deprivation
Economic Diversification
Economic Power Distribution
Economic Security
Economic Sovereignty
Economic Stratification
State Agreement Type

ECONOMIC DEPRESSION
S-06-0281 1975 00019
BT Economic Cycle
NT Economic Recession
RT Deflation
Depression
Economic Development Theory
Economic Inflation
Economic Recession
Economic Recovery
Inflation
Supply Elasticity

ECONOMIC DEPRIVATION
S-06-0622 1975 00017
BT Economic System Characteristics
RT Deprivation
Economic Dependency
Economic Injustice
Economic Power Distribution
Economic Recession
Economic Stratification
Marxist Alienation Theory

ECONOMIC DEVELOPMENT
S-31-0060 1975 00163
BT Development Process
NT Industrial Development
RT Economic Development Characteristics
Economic Development Level
Economic Development Model
Economic Development Policy
Economic Development Rate
Economic Development Theory
Economic Growth Model
Human Resources Development
Modernizing Economy
Modernizing Society
Post Industrial Economic Stage
Post Industrial Society
Preindustrial Society
Trickle Down Theory
Urban Decay

ECONOMIC DEVELOPMENT CHARACTERISTICS
S-06-0143 1975 00063
BT Development Characteristics
NT Economic Development Level
Economic Development Rate
Economic Development Stage
Entrepreneurship
RT Agricultural Development
Economic Development
Economic Development Policy
Economic Development Theory
Luddite Movement
Modernizing Economy
Political Development

ECONOMIC DEVELOPMENT INDEX
S-24-0230 1975 00009
BT Development Index
RT Economic Development Indicator
Economic Development Model
Economic Development Policy
Economic Development Rate
Economic Development Stage
Economic Development Theory
Economic Growth Model
Economic Theory
Modernizing Economy
Takeoff Stage

ECONOMIC DEVELOPMENT INDICATOR
S-24-0259 1975 00008
BT Economic Indicator
RT Economic Development Index
Economic Development Model
Economic Development Policy
Economic Development Theory
Per Capita Annual Income
Productivity Rate

ECONOMIC DEVELOPMENT LEVEL
S-06-0144 1975 00036
BT Economic Development Characteristics
NT Industrialization Level
Investment Ratio
National Economic Development Level
Regional Economic Development Level
RT Advanced Industrial Society
Economic Development
Economic Development Model
Economic Development Policy
Economic Development Rate
Economic Development Stage
Economic Development Theory
Economic Growth Rate
Economic Recession
Entrepreneurship
International Division Of Labor
Macroeconomics
Productivity Rate

ECONOMIC DEVELOPMENT MODEL
S-24-0297 1979 00000
BT Development Model
RT Computer Simulation Model
Econometric Model
Economic Development
Economic Development Index
Economic Development Indicator
Economic Development Level
Economic Development Policy
Economic Growth Model
Economic Mathematical Model
Equilibrium Model
Process Model
Rational Choice Model
Social System Model

ECONOMIC DEVELOPMENT POLICY
S-26-0082 1979 00000
BT Development Policy
RT Cultural Development Policy
Developing Economy
Economic Development
Economic Development Characteristics
Economic Development Index
Economic Development Indicator
Economic Development Level
Economic Development Model
Economic Development Stage
Political Development Policy
Social Development Policy

ECONOMIC DEVELOPMENT RATE
S-06-0152 1975 00022
BT Economic Development Characteristics
NT Economic Growth Rate
RT Development Theory
Economic Development
Economic Development Index
Economic Development Level
Economic Development Stage
Economy Pump Priming
Industrialization Level
Legal Development
Political Development
Subnational Economic Development Level

ECONOMIC DEVELOPMENT STAGE
S-06-0159 1975 00026
BT Economic Development Characteristics
NT Agricultural Economic Stage
Feudal Economic Stage
Industrial Economic Stage
Post Industrial Economic Stage
Pretakeoff Period
Takeoff Stage
RT Advanced Industrial Society
Development Theory
Economic Development Index
Economic Development Level
Economic Development Policy
Economic Development Rate
Economic Growth Rate
Economic Recession
Economic Theory
Entrepreneurship
Historical Periods
Industrialization Level
Legal Development
Political Development
Productivity Rate

ECONOMIC DEVELOPMENT THEORY
S-38-0023 1975 00117
BT Development Theory
NT Economic Growth Theory
RT Advanced Industrial Society
Convergence Theory
Dependent Nation
Differentiated System
Divergence Theory
Economic Characteristics
Economic Cycle
Economic Depression
Economic Development
Economic Development Characteristics
Economic Development Index
Economic Development Indicator
Economic Development Level
Economic History
Economic Integration
Economic System Characteristics
Economics Discipline
Gross National Product
Growth Model
International Economic System
Macroeconomics
National Division Of Labor
National Economic Development Level
New International Economic Order
Political Development Theory
Poor Nation
Post Industrial Economic Stage
Protected Industry
Social Development Theory
Technological Development Theory
Urban Development Theory

ECONOMIC DIVERSIFICATION
S-06-0623 1975 00005
BT Economic System Characteristics
NT Production Distribution
RT Development Theory
Economic Dependency
Economic Power Distribution
Economic Security
Economic Stratification

ECONOMIC EGALITARIANISM
S-38-0206 1975 00006
BT Economic Ideology
RT Class Equality
Economic Equality
Keynesian Economic Theory
Marxist Economic Theory
Political Equality
Social Equality
Status Equality

ECONOMIC ELITE
S-14-0004 1975 00007
BT Elite Type
NT Business Elite
RT Decision Making Elite
Economic Bureaucracy
Economic Leader
Elite Analysis
Entrepreneur Class
Financier
Governing Elite
Managerial Elite
Political Elite

ECONOMIC EQUALITY
S-06-0725 1979 00000
BT Equality
NT Income Equality
RT Class Equality
Economic Egalitarianism
Education Equality
Egalitarianism
Income Measure
New International Economic Order
Political Equality
Racial Equality
Sex Equality
Social Equality
Socialist Theory
Status Equality
Wage Level

ECONOMIC ESPIONAGE
S-10-0017 1975 00000
BT Economic Crime
NT Industrial Espionage
RT Economic Conspiracy
Economic Demonstration
Military Espionage
Organized Crime
Political Espionage
Property Crime
Robbery
White Collar Crime

ECONOMIC EXPLOITATION
S-31-0286 1975 00013
BT Exploitation Process
RT Book Censorship
Capitalist Imperialism
Economic Process
Marxist Alienation Theory
Political Exploitation
Racial Exploitation
Sex Exploitation

ECONOMIC FORECASTING
S-24-0015 1979 00000
BT Forecasting Methodology
RT Authority Forecasting
Brainstorming
Causal Analysis
Delphi Technique
Divergence Mapping
Economic Model
Mathematical Model
Policy Research
Political Forecasting
Predictive Research
Scenario Construction
Social Forecasting
Trend Analysis

ECONOMIC FREEDOM
S-15-0002 1975 00002
BT Freedom
NT Freedom Of Competition
Freedom Of Contract
Property Rights
Right To Job Security
RT Capitalism
Capitalism Theory
Capitalist Economy
Capitalist Society
Economic Freedom Theory
Economic Liberalism
Free Enterprise System
Freedom Theory
Laissez Faire Liberalism
Slavery Abolition

ECONOMIC FREEDOM THEORY
S-38-0458 1975 00002
BT Freedom Theory
RT Economic Freedom
Economic Mobilization
Free Enterprise System
Laissez Faire Liberalism
Negative Freedom Theory

ECONOMIC GAIN
S-06-0285 1979 00000
BT Economic Characteristics
RT Assets
Demand Curve
Demand Elasticity
Development Theory
Economic Cycle
Economic Incentive System
Economic Index
Economic Indicator
Economic Recovery
Profit Income
Unearned Income

ECONOMIC GEOGRAPHY
S-01-0088 1975 00015
BT Geography Discipline
RT Ecology Discipline
Econometrics
Economics Discipline
Human Geography
Industrial Psychology
Physical Geography
Political Economy Studies
Political Geography
Regional Economics
Urban Geography
Urban Politics Studies
Urban Sociology

ECONOMIC GROWTH INDEX
S-06-0291 1975 00006
BT Economic Index
RT Economic Competition Index
Economic Growth Policy
Economic Indicator
Employment Index
Industrial Working Class
Per Capita Income
Productivity Rate
Supply Elasticity
Trickle Down Theory

ECONOMIC GROWTH MODEL
S-24-0302 1979 00000
BT Growth Model
RT Cost Of Living Index
Development Model
Economic Development
Economic Development Index
Economic Development Model
Economic Mathematical Model
Economy Pump Priming
Optimizing Model
Probability Model
Process Model
Social Power Model
Social System Model

ECONOMIC GROWTH POLICY
S-26-0086 1975 00040
BT Economic Policy
NT Economic Program
RT Development Policy
Economic Growth Index
Economic Subsidization Policy
Economic Theory
Fiscal Policy
Investment Policy
Planning Theory
Price Support Policy
Productivity Policy
Trade Policy

ECONOMIC GROWTH RATE
S-06-0153 1975 00060
BT Economic Development Rate
NT Agricultural Growth Rate
Capital Growth Rate
Productivity Rate
RT Cost Of Living Index
Economic Development Level
Economic Development Stage
Economic Incentive System
Economic Indicator
Productivity Rate

ECONOMIC GROWTH THEORY
S-38-0024 1975 00041
BT Economic Development Theory
RT Fiscal Theory
Planning Theory
Social Development Theory
Technological Development Theory
Urban Development Theory

ECONOMIC HISTORY
S-01-0103 1975 00141
BT History Discipline
NT Agricultural History
Labor History
RT Ancient History
Demographic Studies
Economic Development Theory
Economics Discipline
Economy Type
Institutional History
Intellectual History
Labor History
Political History
Political Science Discipline
Social History
Sociology Discipline
Topography
Urban History

ECONOMIC IDEOLOGY
S-38-0203 1975 00011
BT Ideologies
NT Consumerism
Cooperativism
Economic Egalitarianism
Trickle Down Theory
RT Anarchosyndicalism
Clientelism
Economic Imperialism
Imperialism
Liberalism
Marxist Class Theory
Socialist Theory

ECONOMIC IMPERIALISM
S-37-0069 1975 00018
BT Imperialism System
NT Capitalist Imperialism
RT Academic Imperialism
Cultural Imperialism
Economic Conspiracy
Economic Ideology
Government Enterprise
Political Imperialism
War Reparation Policy

ECONOMIC INCENTIVE SYSTEM
S-37-0025 1975 00051
BT Economic System
RT Achievement Motivation
Classical Economic Theory
Economic Gain
Economic Growth Rate
Prestige Hierarchy
Wage Policy

ECONOMIC INDEX
S-06-0286 1975 00009
BT Economic Characteristics
NT Cost Of Living Index
Demand Curve
Economic Competition Index
Economic Growth Index
Employment Index
Industrial Index
Supply Curve
RT Aggregate Data Analysis
Aggregate Data Selection
Economic Community
Economic Gain
Macroeconomics

ECONOMIC INDICATOR
S-24-0258 1975 00007
BT Indicator
NT Economic Development Indicator
RT Capital Growth Rate
Change Indicator
Cost Of Living Index
Cyclical Employment
Disposable Income
Domestic Consumption
Economic Characteristics
Economic Gain
Economic Growth Index
Economic Growth Rate
Economic Theory
Gross National Product
Per Capita Income
Political Indicator
Social Indicator

ECONOMIC INEQUALITY
S-06-0735 1979 00000
BT Inequality
NT Income Inequality
RT Class Inequality
Economic Injustice
Education Inequality
Political Inequality
Political Injustice
Racial Inequality
Sex Inequality
Social Inequality
Status Inequality

ECONOMIC INFLATION
S-06-0283 1975 00075
BT Economic Cycle
RT Economic Depression
Economic Power Distribution
Economic Recession
Economic Recovery
Inflation Policy
Supply Elasticity

ECONOMIC INJUSTICE
S-06-0710 1979 00000
BT Social Injustice
RT Class Inequality
Economic Deprivation
Economic Inequality
Economic Power Distribution
Education Inequality
Education Injustice
Inequality
Justice Theory
Land Distribution
Monopoly
Political Injustice
Racial Inequality
Racial Injustice
Sex Inequality
Sexual Injustice
Social Inequality
Social Injustice
Status Inequality
Wage Level
Wealth Distribution

ECONOMIC INSTITUTION
S-19-0158 1975 00008
BT Institutions
NT Business
Corporation
Enterprise
Factory
Fiscal Institution
International Market
Market
Monetary Institution
RT Agencies
Banking Agency
Councils

Customs Union
Economic Advisory Board
Economic Agency
Economic Control Agency
Economy Type
Evolutionary Economics
Government Economic Planning
Institutional History
Military Industrial Complex
Production Agency
Public Treasury
Revenue Agency

ECONOMIC INTEGRATION
S-31-0803 1975 00007
BT Integration
NT Horizontal Economic Integration
International Economic Integration
National Economic Integration
Subnational Economic Integration
Vertical Economic Integration
RT Customs Union
Economic Development Theory
Economics Discipline
Horizontal Integration
Interaction Analysis

ECONOMIC INTEREST GROUP
S-03-0017 1975 00024
BT Interest Group
NT Industrial Association
RT Association Interest Group
Cooperatives
Credit Cooperative
Customs Union
Economic Organization
Industrial Association
International Economic Organization
Marketing Cooperative
Monetary Union
Occupational Interest Group
Policy Interest Group
Political Interest Group
Producer Cooperative
Public Employee Organization

ECONOMIC INTERFERENCE POLICY
S-26-0264 1975 00009
BT Interference Policy
RT Economic Law
Open Door Policy
Political Interference Policy
Political Intervention Policy

ECONOMIC LAW
S-21-0031 1975 00004
BT Law Type
NT Antitrust Law
Bankruptcy Law
Consumer Protection Law
Industrial Safety Law
Labor Law
Patent Law
Price Control Law
Property Law
Tax Code
Tax Law
Trade Union Law
Welfare Law
Zoning Law
RT Commercial Law
Contract Law
Economic Interference Policy
Equity Law
Legal History
Negligence Law
Social Law
Tort

ECONOMIC LEADER
S-32-0050 1975 00000
BT Leader
NT Business Leader
RT Economic Activist
Economic Decision Maker
Economic Elite
Elite Analysis
Political Leader
Social Leader

ECONOMIC LIBERALISM
S-38-0253 1975 00009
BT Liberalism
RT Civil Liberty Liberalism
Civil Rights Liberalism
Classical Liberalism
Denationalization Process
Economic Freedom
Freedom Of Competition
Government Deregulation
Laissez Faire Liberalism
Negative Freedom Theory
Nineteenth Century Liberalism
Welfare Liberalism

ECONOMIC LOSS
S-06-0298 1979 00000
BT Economic Characteristics
RT Demand Curve
Demand Elasticity
Economic Scarcity
Government Grant
Income Measure
Industrial Subsidy
Public Assistance
Subsidization Process

ECONOMIC MANAGEMENT
S-23-0009 1975 00019
BT Management
NT Business Management
Central Economic Management
Fiscal Management
Industrial Management
International Economic Management
Monetary Management
National Economic Management
Subnational Economic Management
RT Administrative Management
Conflict Management
Data Management
Development Management
Economic Relations
Economic Theory
Education Administration
Environmental Management
Participatory Management
PERT Analysis
Worker Management Participation
Worker Self Management

ECONOMIC MATHEMATICAL MODEL
S-24-0282 1979 00000
BT Mathematical Model
RT Differential Equation Model
Econometric Model
Economic Development Model
Economic Growth Model
Mathematical Analysis
Simultaneous Equation Model
Stochastic Model

ECONOMIC MOBILIZATION
S-31-0627 1975 00008
BT Mobilization Process
RT Economic Freedom Theory
Mass Mobilization
Military Mobilization
Political Mobilization
Political Movement
Social Mobilization
Worker Mobilization

ECONOMIC MODEL
S-38-0130 1975 00103
BT Formal Political Theory
RT Bargaining Theory
Economic Forecasting
Economic Statistics
Interaction Model
Macroeconomics
Methodology
Rational Choice Model
Rational Choice Theory
Rational Model
Statistical Analysis

ECONOMIC MODERNIZATION
S-31-0079 1975 00035
BT Modernization
RT Advanced Industrial Society
Cultural Modernization
Institutional Innovation
Modernization Theory
Modernizing Economy
Modernizing Ideology
Political Modernization
Social Modernization

ECONOMIC MOVEMENT
S-27-0005 1979 00000
BT Political Movement
NT Consumer Rights Movement
Trade Union Movement
Welfare Rights Movement
RT Consumer Economics
Consumer Economy
Consumerism
Economic Community
Economic Power
Economic Rebellion
Sector Based Political Movement
Separatist Movement
Tax Reform Movement

ECONOMIC ORGANIZATION
S-03-0039 1975 00008
BT Organizations
NT International Economic Organization
RT Economic Interest Group
Employer Organization
Industrial Union
International Organization
Labor Union
Occupational Interest Group
Professional Organization
Public Employee Organization
United Nations
Worker Organization

ECONOMIC PLAN
S-26-0088 1975 00009
BT Economic Program
NT Multiple Year Economic Plan
RT Economic Power
Government Economic Management
Government Economic Planning
Planification
Planning Policy
Power Of The Purse

ECONOMIC PLANNER
S-32-0130 1975 00003
BT Planner
NT Fiscal Planner
RT Economic Policy Making
Government Economic Planning
International Planner
National Planner
Planification
Planning Process
Political Planner
Social Planner
Subnational Planner

ECONOMIC PLANNING
S-31-0641 1975 00031
BT Planning Process
NT Central Economic Planning
Fiscal Planning
Industrial Economic Planning
International Economic Planning
National Economic Planning
Subnational Economic Planning
RT Administrative Planning
Centrally Planned Economy
Contingency Theory
Defense Planning
Development Planning
Economic Policy Making
Economic Program
Economic Recession
Economic Recovery
Education Planning
Environmental Planning
Financial Accounting
Government Economic Management
Gross National Product
Long Range Planning
Military Planning
Multiple Year Economic Plan
National Priority
Planification
Planned Economy
Planned Social Change
Planner
Population Planning
Public Policy Planning
Public Policy Studies
Short Range Planning
Social Engineering
Social Planning

ECONOMIC POLICY
S-26-0085 1975 00103
BT Policy
NT Economic Growth Policy
Economic Stabilization Policy
Economic Subsidization Policy
Fiscal Policy
Grants
International Economic Boycott
Investment Policy
Monetary Policy
Price Support Policy
Productivity Policy
Public Debt Policy
Public Finance Policy
Public Utility Regulation Policy
Revenue Policy
Trade Policy
RT Business Policy
Consumer Industrial Policy
Contingency Theory
Economic Policy Making
Economic Program
Economic Relations
Economy Type
Employment Policy
Government Economic Management
Government Economic Planning
Heavy Industrial Policy
Industrial Policy
Labor Policy
Labor Subsidization Policy
Light Industrial Policy
Multiple Year Economic Plan
Pension Law
Planning Policy
Public Finance Policy

ECONOMIC POLICY MAKING
S-31-0678 1975 00026
BT Policy Making Process
RT Economic Planner
Economic Planning
Economic Policy
Economic Power
Economic Process
Economic Program
Government Economic Management
Gross National Product
National Policy Making
Power Of The Purse

ECONOMIC POWER
S-30-0004 1975 00032
BT Power Type
NT Corporate Power
Countervailing Power
Power Of The Purse
RT Economic Movement
Economic Plan
Economic Policy Making
Formal Power
Institutional Power
Political Power

ECONOMIC POWER DISTRIBUTION
S-06-0625 1975 00039
BT Economic System Characteristics
NT Industrial Distribution
Land Distribution
Monopoly
Wealth Distribution
RT Economic Dependency
Economic Deprivation
Economic Diversification
Economic Inflation
Economic Injustice
Economic Security
Economic Sovereignty
Economic Stratification
Production Distribution
World Economy

ECONOMIC PROCESS
S-31-0362 1975 00007
BT Process
NT Budget Process
Consumption Process
Economic Relations
Economic Resource Allocation
Fiscal Process
Marketing
Production Process
RT Advanced Industrial Society
Allocation Process
Analytic Process
Authorization Process
Development Process
Economic Competition
Economic Exploitation
Economic Policy Making
Expropriation Process
Macroeconomics
Marketing
Prosperity

ECONOMIC PROGRAM
S-26-0087 1975 00008
BT Economic Growth Policy
NT Economic Plan
RT Economic Planning
Economic Policy
Economic Policy Making
Economic Recovery
Government Economic Management
Power Of The Purse

ECONOMIC REBELLION
S-08-0054 1975 00004
BT Rebellion
RT Class Rebellion
Consumer Producer Conflict
Economic Agitation
Economic Conflict
Economic Movement
Economic Sabotage
Institutional Conflict
Jurisdiction Strike
Labor Conflict
Labor Strike
Marxist Economic Theory
Marxist Revolution Theory
Mob Violence
Peasant Rebellion
Political Rebellion
Revolution
Slave Rebellion
Social Rebellion
Student Rebellion
Technological Revolution
War
Worker Rebellion

ECONOMIC RECESSION
S-06-0282 1975 00027
BT Economic Depression
RT Deflation
Economic Depression
Economic Deprivation
Economic Development Level
Economic Development Stage
Economic Inflation
Economic Planning
Economic Recovery

Fiscal Policy
Monetary Policy

ECONOMIC RECOVERY
S-06-0284 1975 00013
BT Economic Cycle
RT Economic Depression
Economic Gain
Economic Inflation
Economic Planning
Economic Program
Economic Recession
Economic Resource Allocation
Supply Elasticity

ECONOMIC RELATIONS
S-31-0371 1975 00018
BT Economic Process
NT Commerce
Industrial Relations
International Economic Relations
Trade
RT Diplomatic Relations Break
Economic Agreement
Economic Management
Economic Policy
Economic Sovereignty
International Economic Characteristics
International Economics
International Policy

ECONOMIC RESOURCE ALLOCATION
S-31-0388 1975 00061
BT Economic Process
NT Financing
Saving
Spending
RT Allocation Process
Economic Recovery
Gold Reserve
Government Expenditure
Spending
Wealth Distribution
Wealth Redistribution

ECONOMIC RETALIATION
S-31-0379 1975 00006
BT International Economic Relations
RT Diplomatic Relations Break
International Commerce
International Economic Interdependence
International Finance

ECONOMIC RIGHTS
USE Human Rights

ECONOMIC SABOTAGE
S-10-0019 1975 00002
BT Economic Crime
RT Economic Conspiracy
Economic Rebellion
Organized Crime
Political Sabotage
Property Crime
Tax Evasion
Vandalism
White Collar Crime

ECONOMIC SCARCITY
S-06-0299 1979 00000
BT Economic Characteristics
RT Demand Curve
Demand Elasticity
Development Theory
Economic Loss
Government Grant
Income Measure
Supply Curve

ECONOMIC SECTOR
S-37-0026 1975 00007
BT Economic System
NT Agricultural Sector
Commercial Sector
Industrial Sector
Private Sector
Public Sector
RT Financial System
Monetary System
Property Ownership System

ECONOMIC SECURITY
S-06-0643 1975 00010
BT Economic System Characteristics
RT Economic Dependency
Economic Diversification
Economic Power Distribution
Economic Sovereignty
Employment Characteristics
Government Economic Planning
Retirement
Right To Job Security

ECONOMIC SOVEREIGNTY
S-06-0644 1975 00009
BT Economic System Characteristics
RT Economic Dependency
Economic Power Distribution
Economic Relations
Economic Security
Economic Statistics
Employment Characteristics
Monopoly

ECONOMIC STABILIZATION POLICY
S-26-0090 1975 00011
BT Economic Policy
RT Economic Stabilization Theory
Economic Statistics
Government Economic Management
Government Economic Planning

ECONOMIC STABILIZATION THEORY
S-38-0112 1979 00000
BT Economic Theory
RT Deflation Policy
Economic Stabilization Policy
Fiscal Theory
Government Economic Management
Government Economic Planning
Inflation Control Policy
Inflation Policy
Monetary Economic Theory
Public Finance Theory

ECONOMIC STATISTICS
S-18-0081 1975 00007
BT Statistical Data
NT Wage Statistics
RT Aggregate Data Statistics
Economic Model
Economic Sovereignty
Economic Stabilization Policy
Economy Type
Employment Record
Field Data
Gross National Product
Mass Public Opinion
Per Capita Income
Political Statistics
Public Opinion Survey
Real Income
Social Statistics
Statistical Analysis
Statistical Table
Survey Data
Tariff Record

ECONOMIC STRATIFICATION
S-06-0645 1975 00012
BT Economic System Characteristics
RT Economic Dependency
Economic Deprivation
Economic Diversification
Economic Power Distribution
Economic System
Employment Characteristics
International Economic System
New International Economic Order
Wealth Distribution

ECONOMIC SUBSIDIZATION POLICY
S-26-0091 1975 00012
BT Economic Policy
RT Economic Growth Policy
Fiscal Policy
Government Economic Planning
Investment Policy
Price Control Law
Price Control Policy
Price Fixing Policy
Price Support Policy
Productivity Policy
Public Utility Regulation Policy
Trade Policy

ECONOMIC SYSTEM
S-37-0010 1975 00039
BT System Type
NT Barter Economic System
Capitalism
Command Economic System
Communist Economic System
Diversified Economic System
Economic Incentive System
Economic Sector
Feudal Economic System
Financial System
Free Enterprise System
Inheritance System
International Economic System
Market System
Mercantile Economic System
Mixed Economic System
Monetary System
Patron System
Property Ownership System
Socialist Economic System
RT Cybernetic System
Economic Stratification
Economy Type
Feudal Economic Stage
Imperialism System
Political System Type
Social System
Welfare System
World Economy

ECONOMIC SYSTEM CHARACTERISTICS
S-06-0620 1975 00067
BT System Characteristics
NT Economic Dependency
Economic Deprivation
Economic Diversification
Economic Power Distribution
Economic Security
Economic Sovereignty
Economic Stratification
Employment Characteristics
RT Analytic System Characteristics
Economic Characteristics
Economic Development Theory
Economy Type
International Economic Characteristics
International Economic System
Market System
New International Economic Order
Political System Characteristics
Social System Characteristics

ECONOMIC THEORY
S-38-0106 1979 00000
BT Political Theory
NT Capitalism Theory
Classical Economic Theory
Economic Stabilization Theory
Fiscal Theory
Keynesian Economic Theory
Marxist Economic Theory
Mercantile Economic Theory
Monetary Economic Theory
Neoclassical Economic Theory
Public Finance Theory
RT Development Model
Development Theory
Economic Characteristics
Economic Crisis
Economic Development Index
Economic Development Stage
Economic Growth Policy
Economic Indicator
Economic Management
Economics Discipline
Modernization Theory
Planning Theory
Progress Theory

ECONOMIC THEORY OF DEMOCRACY
S-38-0086 1975 00008
SN Description of democratic politics in which responsible political parties and rational voters are central elements.
BT Democratic Theory
RT Athenian Democratic Theory
Democratic Elite Theory
Guided Democracy Theory
Jacksonian Democratic Theory
Jeffersonian Democratic Theory
Participatory Democratic Theory
Populist Democratic Theory
Public Choice Theory
Rational Choice Model
Republic Theory
Socialist Democratic Theory

ECONOMIC TREATY
S-02-0078 1975 00002
BT Economic Agreement
RT Commercial Treaty
Protective Tariff
Trade Agreement

ECONOMIC VARIABLE
S-24-0447 1975 00025
BT Variable Substantive Content
RT Cultural Variable
Historical Variable
Institutional Variable
Political Variable
Social Variable

ECONOMICS DISCIPLINE
S-01-0059 1975 00023
BT Academic Areas
NT Business Economics
Consumer Economics
Econometrics
Evolutionary Economics
Industrial Economics
Institutional Economics
International Economics
Labor Economics
Macroeconomics
Microeconomics
Regional Economics
Social Economics
Transportation Economics
Urban Economics
Welfare Economics
RT Area Studies
Behavioral Science
Comparative Political Studies
Comparative Sociology
Demographic Studies
Economic Development Theory
Economic Geography
Economic History
Economic Integration
Economic Theory
Economist
Economy Type
Education Discipline
Engineering Discipline
Global Education
Historical Sociology
History Discipline
Industrial Sociology
Labor History
Management Training Program
Political Economy Studies
Political Science Discipline
Political Science Methodology Studies
Political Theory Studies
Social History
Sociology Discipline
South African Area Studies
Urban Politics Studies
West African Area Studies

ECONOMIST
S-32-0109 1979 00000
BT Social Scientist
RT Academic
Anthropologist
Economics Discipline
Geographer
Historian
Policy Scientist
Political Scientist
Professional Occupational Role
Public Policy Analysis
Social Psychologist
Sociologist

ECONOMY
1975-1979 00012
USE Economy Type

ECONOMY PUMP PRIMING
S-31-0417 1975 00001
BT Public Spending
RT Development Financing
Development Fund
Development Management
Economic Development Rate
Economic Growth Model
Government Expenditure
Government Grant
Public Investment

ECONOMY TYPE
S-12-0001 1979 00000
UF Economy
NT Agrarian Economy
Balanced Economy
Barter Economy
Capital Investment Economy
Consumer Economy
Cottage Industry Economy
Depressed Economy
Developed Economy
Developing Economy
Dual Economy
Export Economy
Grants Economy
Hunting And Trapping Economy
Industrial Economy
Labor Intensive Economy
Market Economy
Mixed Economy
Modernizing Economy
Nomadic Economy
Peasant Economy
Planned Economy
Self Sufficient Economy
Subsistence Economy
Underdeveloped Economy
War Economy
Welfare Economy
World Economy
RT Community Type
Economic Community
Economic History
Economic Institution
Economic Policy
Economic Statistics
Economic System
Economic System Characteristics
Economics Discipline
Government
Government Type
Ideal Type Analysis
Management
Planning Process
Society Type Base
Society Type Structure
System Type

ECOSYSTEM
S-37-0061 1975 00011
UF Biological Community
BT System Type
RT Air Pollution
Ecological Analysis
Ecological Model
Ecology Discipline
Ecology Movement
Energy Consumption
Environmental Management
Environmental Planning
Water Pollution
Water Pollution Policy

ECUMENICAL MOVEMENT
S-27-0065 1975 00000
BT Religious Movement
RT Coalition Formation
Religious Authority
Religious Community
Religious Group
Religious History
Religious Identity
Religious Studies
Transnational Political Movement

EDICT
1975-1979 00000

EDITORIAL CONTROL
S-31-0299 1975 00006
BT Information Manipulation
RT Journal Censorship
Mass Media Analysis
Mass Media Censorship Policy
Mass Media Regulation Policy
Media Access
Media Editorializing
Newspaper Censorship
Performing Arts Censorship
Periodical Publication Censorship
Unpublished Media Censorship

EDUCATION ACCREDITATION AGENCY
S-19-0035 1975 00001
BT Education Agency
RT Board Of Regents
Board Of Trustees
Education Institution
Examination Agency
Scholarship Agency
School Board

EDUCATION ACCREDITATION PROCESS
S-31-0003 1979 00000
BT Accreditation Process
RT Education Policy
Professional Accreditation Process
Professional Occupational Role
Professional School
Sociology Of The Professions
Testing

EDUCATION ADMINISTRATION
S-23-0020 1975 00048
BT Management
NT Higher Education Administration
RT Development Management
Economic Management
Education Advisor
Education Agency
Education Compulsion Authority
Education Exchange Treaty
Education Type
Health Administration
Law Administration
Public Policy Management
Research Management

EDUCATION ADVISOR
S-32-0016 1975 00004
BT Advisor
RT Administrative Advisor
Economic Advisor
Education Administration
Legal Advisor
School Teacher
Science Advisor
Technical Advisor

EDUCATION AGENCY
S-19-0032 1975 00013
BT Agencies
NT Board Of Regents
Board Of Trustees
Education Accreditation Agency
Examination Agency
Scholarship Agency
School Board
RT Academic Tenure Policy
Cultural Agency
Education Administration
Education Compulsion Authority
Education Institution
Education Planning
Education Psychology
Environmental Advisory Agency
Higher Education
Primary Education
Private Higher Education
Public Education Policy
Testing Agency
University Education

EDUCATION AGREEMENT
S-02-0079 1975 00001
BT State Agreement Type
NT Education Exchange Agreement
RT Cultural Agreement
Education Type
Foreign Student
Friendship Agreement

EDUCATION ASSOCIATION
S-03-0054 1979 00000
BT Professional Organization
RT Association Characteristics
Association Interest Group
Associational Process
Education Policy
High School
Professional Socialization
Teacher
Teacher Organization
University

EDUCATION BACKGROUND
S-06-0210 1975 00088
BT Socioeconomic Background
RT Economic Background
Population Attribute
Socioeconomic Background

EDUCATION CHARACTERISTICS
S-06-0361 1979 00000
BT Characteristics
NT Academic Specialization
RT Association Characteristics
Demographic Characteristics
Economic Characteristics
Education Curriculum
Education Planning
Education Policy
Education Policy Making
Education Socialization
Education System
Higher Education
Primary Education
Secondary Education
Technical Education

EDUCATION COMPULSION AUTHORITY
S-04-0031 1975 00002
BT Civil Authority
RT Education Administration
Education Agency
Education Policy Making
Education Politics
Right To Education

EDUCATION CURRICULUM
S-26-0190 1979 00000
BT Education Policy
RT Education Characteristics
Education Planning
Education Policy
Education Psychology
Instruction Methodology
Instructional Material
Learning Package
Political Education
Political Science Teaching
Teaching

EDUCATION DEVELOPMENT
S-31-0062 1975 00092
BT Development Process
RT Development Policy
Education Needs
Education Planner
Education Policy
Education Process
Urban Decay

EDUCATION DISCIPLINE
S-01-0077 1975 00013
BT Academic Areas
NT Education Philosophy
Education Psychology
RT Area Studies
Behavioral Science
Economics Discipline
Education Type
Graduate School
Learning Psychology
Learning Theory
Political Philosophy Studies
Political Science Discipline
Social Psychology
Sociology Discipline
Sociology Of Knowledge

EDUCATION EQUALITY
S-06-0730 1979 00000
BT Social Equality
RT Class Equality
Economic Equality
Education Opportunity
Education Type
Egalitarianism
Income Equality
Political Equality

Racial Equality
Sex Equality
Status Equality

EDUCATION EVALUATION
S-31-0691 1979 00000
BT Policy Evaluation
RT Education Policy
Education Policy Making
Education Process
Evaluating
Formative Evaluation
Learning
Normative Evaluation
Research Evaluation
Social Accounting
Summative Evaluation
Test Results

EDUCATION EXCHANGE AGREEMENT
S-02-0080 1975 00039
BT Education Agreement
NT Education Exchange Treaty
RT Cultural Exchange Agreement
Friendship Treaty
Government Grant
International Exchange Program

EDUCATION EXCHANGE TREATY
S-02-0081 1975 00001
BT Education Exchange Agreement
RT Cultural Exchange Treaty
Education Administration
Education Opportunity
Foreign Student
International Exchange Program
Person To Person Diplomacy

EDUCATION GRANT
S-26-0118 1979 00000
BT Grants
RT Charitable Organization
Development Fund
Education Planning
Education Policy Making
Education Subsidy
Government Grant
Government Research Support
Research And Development

EDUCATION INEQUALITY
S-06-0740 1975 00020
BT Social Inequality
RT Class Inequality
Discrimination Policy
Economic Inequality
Economic Injustice
Education Inequality
Education Injustice
Income Inequality
Political Inequality
Racial Inequality
Racial Injustice
Sex Inequality
Sexual Injustice
Status Inequality

EDUCATION INJUSTICE
S-06-0711 1979 00000
BT Social Injustice
RT Class Inequality
Economic Injustice
Education Inequality
Inequality
Political Injustice
Racial Inequality
Racial Injustice
Sex Inequality
Sexual Injustice
Social Inequality
Social Injustice
Status Inequality

EDUCATION INSTITUTION
S-19-0200 1975 00045
BT Institutions
NT Higher Education Institution
Neighborhood School
Primary School
Private School
Public School
Religious School
Secondary School
Urban School
Vocational Training School
RT Board Of Regents
Board Of Trustees
Cultural Advisory Board
Cultural Agency
Education Accreditation Agency
Education Agency
Education Needs
Education Planning
Education Policy
Education Policy Making
Education Politics
Education Type
Examination Agency
Institution Building
Institutional History
Primary Education
Private Education Policy
Private Higher Education
Private School Education
Private School Subsidy
Public Education Policy
Research Institution
School Desegregation Policy
Teacher Organization
University Education

EDUCATION NEEDS
S-26-0348 1979 00000
BT Needs Assessment
RT Education Development
Education Institution
Education Opportunity
Education Planning
Education Policy
Education Type
Population Planning

EDUCATION OPPORTUNITY
S-06-0496 1975 00056
UF Access To Education
Access To University
BT Opportunity Characteristics
RT Education Equality
Education Exchange Treaty
Education Needs
Education Policy
Job Dissatisfaction
School Integration

EDUCATION PHILOSOPHY
S-01-0078 1975 00075
BT Education Discipline
RT Education Psychology
Political Philosophy Studies
Social Philosophy

EDUCATION PLANNER
S-32-0139 1975 00006
BT Social Planner
RT Academic Areas
Education Development
Education Planning
National Planner
Primary School
Private School
Private University
Professional School
University

EDUCATION PLANNING
S-31-0654 1975 00056
UF Academic Management
BT Planning Process
NT Higher Education Planning
RT Academic Specialization
Continuing Education
Development Planning
Economic Planning
Education Agency
Education Characteristics
Education Curriculum
Education Grant
Education Institution
Education Needs
Education Planner
Education Policy
Education Politics
Education Psychology
Education Reform
Environmental Planning
Financial Accounting
Mass Education
Military Planning
Population Planning
Primary School
Private College
Private Education Policy
Private School
Private University
Professional School
Public Education Policy
Public Policy Planning
Right To Education
Scientific Manpower Policy
Social Planning
University Information Service

EDUCATION POLICY
S-26-0189 1975 00194
BT Policy
NT Education Curriculum
Higher Education Policy
Literacy Policy
Private Education Policy
Public Education Policy
Rehabilitation Education Policy
Vocation Training Policy
RT Academic Areas
Academic Tenure Policy
Admission Policy
Cultural Policy

Degree Requirement
Education Accreditation Process
Education Association
Education Characteristics
Education Curriculum
Education Development
Education Evaluation
Education Institution
Education Needs
Education Opportunity
Education Planning
Education Reform
Education Service
Education Subsidy
Employment Service
Ethical Socialization
Exceptional Child
Foreign Student
Higher Education
Higher Education Institution
Information Acquisition
Information Policy
Information Utilization
Knowledge Acquisition
Knowledge Production
Language Acquisition
Language Learning
Learning
Learning Feedback
Literacy Policy
Mass Education
Moral Learning
Nonprofit Institution
Open University
Private Education Policy
Public Education Policy
Rehabilitation Education Policy
Right To Education
Rote Learning
School Integration
School Taxation
Science Policy
Scientific Manpower Policy
Social Policy
Social Welfare Policy
Symbol Learning
Testing
Testing Agency
Verbal Learning
Veteran
Vocation Training Policy

EDUCATION POLICY MAKING
S-31-0679 1975 00059
BT Policy Making Process
RT Academic Elite
Academic Freedom
Academic Tenure Policy
Continuing Education
Education Characteristics
Education Compulsion Authority
Education Evaluation
Education Grant
Education Institution
Education Psychology
Local Policy Making
National Policy Making

EDUCATION POLITICS
S-29-0012 1975 00025
BT Politics
RT Academic Tenure Policy
Education Compulsion Authority
Education Institution
Education Planning
Education Process
Higher Education
Higher Education Institution
Mass Education

EDUCATION PROCESS
S-31-0446 1975 00093
BT Process
NT Computer Assisted Instruction
Instruction Methodology
Programmed Instruction
Teaching
RT Academic Areas
Cognitive Development
Communication Process
Continuing Education
Education Development
Education Evaluation
Education Politics
Education Reform
Education Socialization
Elementary Education
Graduate School
Higher Education
Higher Education Institution
Learning
Open University

EDUCATION PSYCHOLOGY
S-01-0079 1979 00000
BT Education Discipline
RT Education Agency
Education Curriculum
Education Philosophy
Education Planning
Education Policy Making
Language Learning
Learning Psychologist
Learning Psychology
Learning Theory
Progressive Education
Psychological Behavioralism
Psychological Behaviorism
Verbal Learning

EDUCATION REFORM
S-31-0088 1979 00000
BT Reform
RT Administrative Reform
Education Planning
Education Policy
Education Process
Executive Reform
Judicial Reform
Legislative Reform
Resource Development
University

EDUCATION RIGHTS
1975-1979 00014
USE Right To Education

EDUCATION SERVICE
S-26-0361 1979 00000
BT Service Policy
RT Adult Education
Child Care Service
Community Service
Education Policy
Employment Service
Health Service
Information Service
Legal Service
Medical Care Service
Psychological Service
Service Industry
Social Service

EDUCATION SOCIALIZATION
S-34-0037 1975 00045
BT Professional Socialization
RT Education Characteristics
Education Process
Learning Psychology
Learning Theory
Legal Socialization

EDUCATION SUBSIDY
S-06-0302 1975 00019
BT Government Expenditure
NT Parochial School Subsidy
Private School Subsidy
Vocational Subsidy
RT Development Fund
Education Grant
Education Policy
Government Grant
Government Loan
Government Research Support

EDUCATION SYSTEM
S-37-0062 1975 00102
BT System Type
RT Cultural System
Education Characteristics
Government
Information System
Social System
Value System

EDUCATION TESTING
S-24-0005 1979 00000
BT Analysis Methodology
NT Degree Requirement
Literacy Test
Physiological Test
Psychological Test
RT Aptitude Measurement
Intelligence Quotient
Test Results
Textbook
Verbal Learning

EDUCATION TYPE
S-13-0001 1975 00014
NT Adult Education
Alternative Education
Apprenticeship
Civic Education
Compulsory Education
Continuing Education
Foreign Language Education
Global Education
Higher Education
Humanities Education
Informal Education
Mass Education
Military Education
Natural Science Education
Outreach Education
Political Education

Primary Education
Private School Education
Professional Education
Progressive Education
Religious Education
Secondary Education
Self Taught Education
Sex Education
Technical Education
Traditional Education
RT Academic Specialization
Education Administration
Education Agreement
Education Discipline
Education Equality
Education Institution
Education Needs
Elite Type
Graduate School
Right To Education

EFFICACIOUS VOTER
S-32-0306 1975 00002
SN Voter with a high sense of political competence.
BT Voter
RT Political Efficacy

EFFICACY
S-06-0098 1975 00024
BT Attitude Characteristics
NT Political Efficacy
RT Alienation
Efficacy Scale
Satisfaction

EFFICACY SCALE
S-24-0234 1975 00011
BT Scale Type
RT Alienation Scale
Anomie Scale
Civic Competence Scale
Cynicism
Cynicism Scale
Efficacy
Frustration Scale
Legitimacy Scale
Optimism Pessimism Scale
Satisfaction
Satisfaction Scale
Social Distance Scale
Social Frustration Scale
Support Opposition Scale

EGALITARIAN JUSTICE THEORY
S-38-0477 1975 00004
BT Justice Theory
RT Compensatory Justice
Egalitarianism
Equality Theory
Equity
Levellers Political Thought
Rights Of Man Doctrine

EGALITARIANISM
S-38-0208 1975 00033
BT Ideologies
RT Chartism
Class Equality
Communalism
Economic Equality
Education Equality
Egalitarian Justice Theory
Equality
Equality Theory
Fraternity Theory
Humanism
Income Equality
Levellers Political Thought
Liberalism
Political Equality
Racial Equality
Sex Equality
Social Equality
Status Equality

EGOCENTRISM
S-06-0509 1979 00000
BT Personality Characteristics
RT Altruism
Ambivalence
Assertiveness
Charity
Courage
Creativity
Curiosity
Empathy
Femininity
Honesty
Imagination
Individualism Theory
Inner Directedness
Masculinity
Optimism
Persistence
Pessimism

ELECTION
USE Election Type

ELECTION CAMPAIGN
S-29-0014 1975 00017
BT Electoral Politics
NT Canvassing
Election Campaign Advertising
Election Campaign Financing
Election Campaign Organization
Election Campaign Strategy
National Election Campaign
Subnational Election Campaign
RT Dark Horse Candidate
Election Type
Electoral Competition
Electoral History
Electoral Outcome
Electoral Participation
Electoral Strategy
Electoral Unit
Favorite Son Candidate
Political Party Campaign
Primary Election
Reinstating Election
Voting Behavior

ELECTION CAMPAIGN ADVERTISING
S-29-0015 1979 00000
BT Election Campaign
RT Parliamentary Election Campaign
Political Party Campaign
Prime Time Access Policy

ELECTION CAMPAIGN ADVISOR
S-32-0020 1979 00000
BT Political Advisor
RT Chief Executive Advisor
Election Campaign Expenditure
Election Campaign Financing
Election Campaign Organization
Election Campaign Propaganda
Election Campaign Strategy
Election Campaign Tactics
Presidential Advisor

ELECTION CAMPAIGN CONTRIBUTION
S-29-0017 1979 00000
BT Election Campaign Financing
RT Election Campaign Expenditure
Election Campaign Financial Disclosure
Election Campaign Tactics
Political Party Financial Record

ELECTION CAMPAIGN EXPENDITURE
S-29-0018 1979 00000
BT Election Campaign Financing
RT Election Campaign Advisor
Election Campaign Contribution
Election Campaign Financing
Election Campaign Organization
Election Campaign Strategy
Election Campaign Tactics

ELECTION CAMPAIGN FINANCIAL DISCLOSURE
S-29-0019 1979 00000
UF Campaign Finance Disclosure
BT Election Campaign Financing
RT Election Campaign Contribution
Election Campaign Financing
Electoral Outcome
Government Regulation
Political Corruption
Political Party Financial Record

ELECTION CAMPAIGN FINANCING
S-29-0016 1979 00000
BT Election Campaign
NT Election Campaign Contribution
Election Campaign Expenditure
Election Campaign Financial Disclosure
RT Election Campaign Advisor
Election Campaign Expenditure
Election Campaign Financial Disclosure
Election Campaign Tactics
Political Party Financial Committee
Political Party Financial Record

ELECTION CAMPAIGN ORGANIZATION
S-29-0020 1979 00000
BT Election Campaign
RT Election Campaign Advisor
Election Campaign Expenditure
Election Campaign Tactics
Political Party Campaign

ELECTION CAMPAIGN PROPAGANDA
S-31-0190 1979 00000
BT Political Propaganda
RT Agitation
Domestic Information Policy
Election Campaign Advisor
Election Campaign Strategy
Election Campaign Tactics
Propaganda Policy

ELECTION CAMPAIGN STRATEGY
S-29-0021 1979 00000
BT Election Campaign
NT Election Campaign Tactics
RT Chancellor Election Campaign
Election Campaign Advisor
Election Campaign Expenditure

Election Campaign Propaganda
Mayoralty Election Campaign
Political Party Campaign

ELECTION CAMPAIGN TACTICS
S-29-0022 1979 00000
BT Election Campaign Strategy
RT Canvassing
Chancellor Election Campaign
Election Campaign Advisor
Election Campaign Contribution
Election Campaign Expenditure
Election Campaign Financing
Election Campaign Organization
Election Campaign Propaganda
Election Type
Parliamentary Election Campaign
Political Party Campaign

ELECTION FRAUD
S-10-0072 1975 00000
BT Political Fraud
NT Vote Fraud
RT Disenfranchisement
Fraud
Political Bribery
Political Fraud
Political Graft
Robbery

ELECTION TURNOUT
S-29-0179 1975 00004
BT Voting Result Interpretation
NT Voter Turnout
Voting Tactics
RT Deviating Election
Electoral Data
Electoral History
Favorite Son Candidate
Group Voting
Voting Behavior Analysis
Voting Data

ELECTION TYPE
S-29-0042 1975 00008
UF Election
BT Electoral Politics
NT Contested Election
Critical Election
Deviating Election
Direct Election
General Election
Indirect Election
Initiative Election
Maintaining Election
National Election
Nonpartisan Election
Open Primary
Partisan Election
Plebiscite Election
Preference Primary
Primary Election
Realigning Election
Reinstating Election
Runoff Election
Special Election
Subnational Election
Subnational Primary
RT Congressional Election Campaign
Election Campaign
Election Campaign Tactics
Electoral Competition
Electoral Outcome
Electoral Participation
Electoral Strategy
Electoral Unit
Incumbent
Parliamentary Election Campaign
Voting Behavior Analysis

ELECTORAL ALLIANCE
S-02-0004 1975 00004
BT Alliance
RT Electoral Coalition
Electoral Competition
Electoral Strategy
Electoral Tactics
National Front
Political Front
Political Party Electoral Competition
Primary Election

ELECTORAL BOARD
S-29-0185 1975 00000
BT Electoral Procedure
RT Ballot
Electoral College
Electoral Data
Electoral District
Electoral Law
Electoral Outcome
Voting Data

ELECTORAL COALITION
S-02-0021 1975 00011
BT Political Coalition
RT By Election
Electoral Alliance
Governing Coalition
Legislative Coalition
Opinion Coalition
Parliamentary Coalition
Parliamentary Election Campaign
Political Party Coalition
Popular Front
United Front
Voting Coalition
Winning Coalition

ELECTORAL COLLEGE
S-29-0186 1975 00002
BT Electoral Procedure
RT Ballot
Electoral Board
Electoral Strategy

ELECTORAL COMPETITION
S-29-0104 1975 00019
BT Electoral Politics
NT Political Party Electoral Competition
RT Election Campaign
Election Type
Electoral Alliance
Electoral Outcome
Electoral Participation
Electoral Strategy
Electoral Unit
Incumbent
Parliamentary Election Campaign

ELECTORAL DATA
S-18-0085 1975 00023
BT Political Statistics
RT Aggregate Data Analysis
Aggregate Data Selection
By Election
Election Turnout
Electoral Board
Electoral History
Macrolevel Analysis
Macropolitical Data
Mass Public Opinion
Voting Behavior Analysis
Voting Data

ELECTORAL DISTRICT
S-29-0192 1975 00005
BT Electoral Unit
NT Multimember District
Single Member District
RT Constituency Size
Electoral Board
Electoral Geography
Local Election District

ELECTORAL GEOGRAPHY
S-01-0094 1975 00003
BT Political Geography
RT Electoral District
Electoral History
Electoral Unit
Political Anthropology
Political Sociology
Voting
Voting Data

ELECTORAL HISTORY
S-01-0116 1975 00042
BT Political History
RT Census Record
Class Voting
Demographic Studies
Election Campaign
Election Turnout
Electoral Data
Electoral Geography
Political Behavior Studies
Political Geography
Political Sociology
Politics
Voting
Voting Data

ELECTORAL LAW
S-21-0068 1975 00016
BT Political Law
NT Suffrage Law
Voter Registration Law
RT Absentee Ballot
Absentee Voting
By Election
Compulsory Voting
Electoral Board
Eligible Voter

ELECTORAL OPPOSITION
S-06-0698 1975 00005
BT Political Opposition
RT Candidate Selection
Minority Political Party
Political Activist
Political Candidate
Political Opposition
Voting

ELECTORAL OUTCOME
S-29-0106 1975 00040
BT Electoral Politics
NT Bandwagon Effect
Coattail Effect
Landslide Electoral Outcome
Majority Electoral Outcome
Vote Distribution

RT D'Hont Voting Method
Dark Horse Candidate
Deviating Election
Election Campaign
Election Campaign Financial Disclosure
Election Type
Electoral Board
Electoral Competition
Electoral Participation
Electoral Strategy
Electoral Unit
Gubernatorial Election
Incumbent
Maintaining Election
National Chief Executive Primary
National Judicial Primary
Nonpartisan Election
Political Candidate
Voting Data
Voting Theory

ELECTORAL PARTICIPATION
S-29-0114 1975 00055
BT Electoral Politics
NT Nonvoting
Suffrage Extension
Voting
Voting Formulae
Voting Pattern
Voting Procedure
Voting Result Interpretation
RT Cultural Politics
Deviating Election
Election Campaign
Election Type
Electoral Competition
Electoral Outcome
Electoral Strategy
Eligible Voter
Parliamentary Election Campaign
Primary Election
Reinstating Election

ELECTORAL POLITICS
S-29-0013 1975 00046
BT Politics
NT Election Campaign
Election Type
Electoral Competition
Electoral Outcome
Electoral Participation
Electoral Procedure
Electoral Strategy
Electoral Unit
RT Center Political Party
Class Politics
Coalition Politics
Confrontation Politics
Consensual Politics
Eligible Voter
Incumbent
Parliamentary Politics
Partisan Politics
Political Candidate
Political Succession
Primary Election
Voting Behavior
Voting Behavior Analysis

ELECTORAL PROCEDURE
S-29-0184 1975 00016
BT Electoral Politics
NT Electoral Board
Electoral College
RT Direct Election
Electoral Strategy
Group Voting
Indirect Election
Voting Coalition

ELECTORAL STRATEGY
S-29-0187 1975 00008
BT Electoral Politics
NT Electoral Tactics
RT Candidate Orientation
Election Campaign
Election Type
Electoral Alliance
Electoral College
Electoral Competition
Electoral Outcome
Electoral Participation
Electoral Procedure
Parliamentary Election Campaign
Political Party Platform

ELECTORAL TACTICS
S-29-0188 1975 00001
BT Electoral Strategy
RT All Party Coalition
Electoral Alliance
Gerrymandering
National Front
Political Front
Popular Front
United Front

ELECTORAL UNIT
S-29-0190 1975 00002
BT Electoral Politics
NT Constituency Size
Electoral District
Local Election District
RT Election Campaign
Election Type
Electoral Competition
Electoral Geography
Electoral Outcome

ELECTRICAL INDUSTRY
S-17-0039 1979 00000
UF Electrical Utility Industry
BT Energy Industry
RT Coal Industry
Energy Consumption
Energy Use Policy
Extractive Industry
Gas Industry
Nuclear Energy Industry
Oil Industry
Ore Industry
Solar Energy

ELECTRICAL UTILITY INDUSTRY
1975-1979 00013
USE Electrical Industry

ELECTRONIC ROLL CALL DEVICE
S-29-0163 1975 00000
BT Voting Device
RT Ballot
Ballot Box
Voting Device
Voting Machine

ELEMENTARY EDUCATION
S-13-0035 1975 00020
BT Primary Education
RT Education Process
Private School Education
Secondary Education

ELIGIBLE VOTER
S-32-0307 1975 00000
BT Voter
NT Potential Voter
Registered Voter
RT Absentee Voter
Disenfranchisement
Electoral Law
Electoral Participation
Electoral Politics

ELITE
USE Elite Type

ELITE ANALYSIS
S-09-0018 1975 00062
BT Contemporary Analytic Modes
NT Elite Identification
RT Career Analysis
Decision Making Elite
Decision Making Theory
Democratic Leadership
Economic Elite
Economic Leader
Elite Behavior
Elite Change
Elite Circulation
Elite Mass Relations
Elite Perception
Elite Political Party
Elite Theory
Elite Type
Elitism
Foreign Policy Elite
Historical Sociology Analysis
Lasswellian Analysis
Leadership Analysis
Leadership Political Analysis
Leadership Psychological Analysis
Leadership Sociological Analysis
Leadership Type
Machiavellian Thought
Political Autobiography
Political Psychology Analysis
Political Style
Ruling Class
Ruling Political Party
Sociological Analysis
Technological Elite

ELITE BEHAVIOR
S-05-0014 1975 00015
BT Political Behavior
RT Decision Making Elite
Elite Analysis
Elite Change
Elite Formation
Elite Mass Relations
Elite Norms
Elite Perception
Elite Socialization
Elite Theory
Group Behavior
Legislative Behavior
Small Group Behavior

ELITE CHANGE
S-31-0139 1975 00021
BT Change Process
NT Elite Circulation
RT Elite Analysis
Elite Behavior
Elite Circulation
Elite Consolidation
Elite Disintegration
Elite Formation
Elite Norms
Governing Elite
Political Change

ELITE CIRCULATION
S-31-0140 1975 00011
BT Elite Change
RT Elite Analysis
Elite Change
Elite Consolidation
Elite Disintegration
Elite Formation
Elite Identification
Group Process
Leadership Type
Political Succession
Secession

ELITE COMPETITION
S-31-0202 1975 00018
BT Competition
RT Elite Mass Relations
Elite Norms
Open Leadership
Political Competition
Political Party Competition

ELITE COMPOSITION
S-06-0015 1975 00028
BT Group Composition
NT Elite Heterogeneity
Elite Homogeneity
RT Elite Identification
Elite Mass Relations
Elite Socialization
Elite Theory
Interlocking Group Membership
Leadership Type

ELITE CONSOLIDATION
S-31-0029 1975 00009
BT Group Consolidation
RT Elite Change
Elite Circulation
Elite Disintegration
Elite Formation
Elite Homogeneity

ELITE DISINTEGRATION
S-31-0031 1975 00001
BT Group Disintegration
RT Coup D'Etat
Elite Change
Elite Circulation
Elite Consolidation
Political Succession
Revolution
Ruling Class

ELITE FORMATION
S-31-0026 1975 00005
BT Group Formation
RT Decision Making Elite
Elite Behavior
Elite Change
Elite Circulation
Elite Consolidation
Governing Elite
Intellectual Elite
Leadership Type
Potential Elite

ELITE HETEROGENEITY
S-06-0016 1975 00007
BT Elite Composition
RT Elite Homogeneity
Elite Identification
Elite Theory

ELITE HOMOGENEITY
S-06-0017 1975 00008
BT Elite Composition
RT Elite Consolidation
Elite Heterogeneity
Elite Identification
Elite Recruitment
Elite Socialization
Elite Theory
Homogeneous Group Membership
Homogeneous Society

ELITE IDENTIFICATION
S-09-0019 1975 00006
BT Elite Analysis
NT Institutional Elite Identification
Issue Elite Identification
Reputational Elite Identification
RT Elite Circulation
Elite Composition
Elite Heterogeneity
Elite Homogeneity
Elite Type
Group Analysis
Leadership Analysis

ELITE MASS INTERACTION
1975-1979 00051
USE Elite Mass Relations

ELITE MASS RELATIONS
S-31-0454 1979 00000
UF Elite Mass Interaction
BT Process
NT Cult Of Personality
RT Cult Of Personality
Decision Making Elite
Elite Analysis
Elite Behavior
Elite Competition
Elite Composition
Elite Norms
Elite Perception
Elite Political Party
Elite Socialization
Iron Law Of Oligarchy
Mass Behavior
Plutocracy
Political Style

ELITE NORMS
S-06-0720 1979 00000
BT Social Norms
RT Decision Making Elite
Elite Behavior
Elite Change
Elite Competition
Elite Mass Relations
Elite Perception
Elite Socialization

ELITE PERCEPTION
S-24-0438 1979 00000
BT Group Perception
RT Elite Analysis
Elite Behavior
Elite Mass Relations
Elite Norms
Group Phenomena
Individual Perception
Individual Phenomena
Perception Measurement

ELITE POLITICAL PARTY
S-28-0060 1979 00000
BT Structure Specific Political Party Type
RT Cadre Political Party
Elite Analysis
Elite Mass Relations
Mass Political Party
National Legislative Political Party
Splinter Political Party
Third Political Party
Totalitarian Political Party

ELITE RECRUITMENT
S-31-0743 1975 00019
BT Recruitment Process
RT Cooptation
Elite Homogeneity
Military Recruitment
Nepotism
Political Gatekeeper
Political Opportunity Structure
Political Recruitment
Political Succession

ELITE SOCIALIZATION
S-34-0025 1975 00015
BT Group Socialization
RT Adult Socialization
Childhood Socialization
Cohort Group Socialization
Elite Behavior
Elite Composition
Elite Homogeneity
Elite Mass Relations
Elite Norms
Governing Elite
Interest Group Socialization
Peer Group Socialization

ELITE THEORY
S-38-0125 1975 00012
BT Explanatory Political Theory
RT Community Power Theory
Decision Making Elite
Democratic Elite Theory
Elite Analysis
Elite Behavior
Elite Composition
Elite Heterogeneity
Elite Homogeneity
Elite Type
Elitism
Group Theory
Interest Group Pluralism
Mass Society Theory
Polyarchical Democratic Theory

ELITE TYPE
S-14-0001 1975 00004
UF Elite
NT Academic Elite
Decision Making Elite
Economic Elite
Governing Elite
Intellectual Elite
Managerial Elite
Military Elite
Modernizing Elite
Opinion Elite
Pluralist Elite
Political Elite
Scientific Elite
Social Elite
Subnational Elite
Technological Elite
RT Education Type
Elite Analysis
Elite Identification
Elite Theory
Elitism
Gerontocracy
Institutional Elite Identification
Issue Elite Identification
Leadership Type
Political Science Discipline
Social System Characteristics
Theory

ELITISM
S-38-0209 1975 00005
BT Ideologies
RT Conservative Regime
Elite Analysis
Elite Theory
Elite Type
Fascist Theory
Leninism
Meritocracy
Militarism
Military Elite
Polyarchy
Reputational Elite Identification

ELITIST DEMOCRACY
S-16-0018 1975 00004
BT Democratic Government
RT Developed Democracy
Dictatorship
Guided Democracy
Oligarchic Government
Participatory Democracy
Plutocracy
Tutelary Democracy

EMANCIPATION
S-31-0145 1975 00001
BT Liberation Process
NT Black Emancipation
Womens Emancipation
Working Class Emancipation
RT Freedom
Human Dignity Theory
Revolutionary Change
Social Change
Working Class Emancipation

EMBASSY ATTACHE
S-36-0124 1975 00000
BT Embassy Official
NT Commercial Attache
Cultural Attache
Economic Attache
Information Attache
Military Attache
Political Attache
Scientific Attache
RT Ambassador
Charge D'Affaires
Consul General

EMBASSY OFFICIAL
S-36-0120 1975 00002
BT Diplomat
NT Ambassador
Charge D'Affaires
Consul General
Embassy Attache
RT Foreign Minister
Foreign Service Officer

EMERGENCY POWER
S-30-0012 1975 00012
BT Political Power
RT Executive Prerogative
Executive Privilege
Executive Pronouncement
Martial Law
Military Intervention Policy
Presidential Discretion
Proclamation
Pronouncement
Separation Of Power
State Power
War Power
Wartime Power

EMIGRATION PATTERN
S-06-0236 1975 00007
BT Migration Pattern
RT Emigration Policy
Emigration Process
Immigration Pattern
Internal Migration Pattern
Population Mobility

EMIGRATION POLICY
S-26-0390 1975 00003
BT Migration Policy
RT Emigration Pattern
Emigration Process
Population Management
Population Movement

EMIGRATION PROCESS
S-31-0619 1975 00007
BT Migration Process
RT Emigration Pattern
Emigration Policy
Emigre
Immigration Process
Internal Migration
Refugee Migration

EMIGRE
S-36-0022 1975 00005
BT Immigrant
RT Emigration Process
Geographic Origin
Immigration Policy
Immigration Process
Migration Process
Political Refugee
Refugee Migration

EMINENT DOMAIN
S-04-0032 1975 00001
BT Civil Authority
RT Eminent Domain Policy
Land Use Policy
Police Power
Property Law
Tax Power

EMINENT DOMAIN EXPROPRIATION
1975-1979 00001

EMINENT DOMAIN POLICY
S-26-0217 1975 00001
BT Public Land Use Policy
RT Eminent Domain
Government Regulation
Land Use Policy
Police Power
Property Law
Tax Power
Zoning Policy

EMOTIVE ETHICAL THEORY
S-25-0036 1975 00001
SN Assertion that ethical judgments are expressions of a person's emotions and feelings.
BT Ethical Theory
RT Axiology
Ethical Naturalism
Ethical Relativism
Hedonism
Instrumentalism
Intuitionism
Linguistic Ethical Theory
Metaethical Theory
Normative Analysis
Situational Ethics

EMPATHY
S-06-0510 1975 00008
BT Personality Characteristics
RT Altruism
Ambivalence
Assertiveness
Charity
Curiosity
Egocentrism
Femininity
Friendship
Gregariousness
Happiness
Honesty
Identity Characteristics
Imagination
Masculinity
Optimism
Other Directedness
Persistence
Pessimism
Submissiveness
Trust

EMPEROR
S-36-0057 1975 00006
BT Monarch
NT Kaiser
Khan
Shah
Sheik
Tsar

RT Abdication
Absolute Monarch
Absolute Monarchy
National Chief Government Executive

EMPIRE
S-16-0048 1975 00018
BT Extranational Government Structure
NT Capitalist Empire
Colonial Empire
Communist Empire
World Empire
RT Aligned Nation
Caretaker Government
Colony
Extranational Bloc
Extranational Commonwealth
Hostile Nation
Imperialism
Imperialism System
Indirect Rule
International Trusteeship
Mandate Territory
National Sovereignty Theory
Protectorate

EMPIRICAL THEORY
S-38-0578 1975 00014
BT Scientific Theory
RT Comtean Positivism
Contemporary Analytic Modes
Data Theory
Empiricism
Event
Mathematical Political Theory
Methodology
Neopositivism
Political Behaviorism

EMPIRICISM
S-25-0015 1975 00006
BT Epistemology
NT Holism
Methodological Individualism
Reductionism
RT Empirical Theory
Event
Logical Positivism
Materialism
Methodology
Neopositivism
Objectivism
Scientism

EMPLOYER ORGANIZATION
S-03-0043 1975 00000
BT Organizations
RT Economic Organization
Producer Cooperative
Professional Organization
Worker Organization

EMPLOYMENT
USE Employment Policy

EMPLOYMENT CHARACTERISTICS
S-06-0646 1975 00155
BT Economic System Characteristics
NT Full Employment
Labor Force
Labor Market
Labor Supply
Labor Surplus
Overemployment
Retirement
Underemployment
Unemployment
RT Economic Security
Economic Sovereignty
Economic Stratification
Job Discrimination
Job Preference
Job Satisfaction
Job Socialization
Occupation Characteristics

EMPLOYMENT INDEX
S-06-0292 1975 00008
BT Economic Index
NT Cyclical Employment
Seasonal Employment
RT Economic Competition Index
Economic Growth Index
Industrial Working Class

EMPLOYMENT OPPORTUNITY
S-06-0497 1975 00080
BT Opportunity Characteristics
RT Affirmative Action Employment Policy
Equal Employment Policy
Ethnic Policy
Feminism
Job Discrimination
Job Dissatisfaction
Job Preference
Job Satisfaction
Manpower Policy
Migration Process

EMPLOYMENT POLICY
S-26-0197 1975 00063
UF Employment
BT Policy
NT Affirmative Action Employment Policy
Civil Service System
Equal Employment Policy
Fair Employment Policy
Full Employment Policy
Manpower Policy
Merit Policy
Patronage Policy
Public Works Policy
Quota System Policy
Tenure Policy
Unemployment Policy
RT Disability Insurance
Economic Policy
Employment Record
Employment Service
Exclusionary Policy
Job Discrimination
Job Socialization
Job Training
Labor Management Contract
Manpower Policy
Manpower Training
Pension Law
Policy For Disadvantaged
Unemployment Insurance Policy
Veteran

EMPLOYMENT RECORD
S-18-0010 1975 00019
UF Absenteeism
BT Documents
RT Economic Statistics
Employment Policy
Expenditure Record

EMPLOYMENT SERVICE
S-26-0362 1979 00000
BT Service Policy
RT Education Policy
Education Service
Employment Policy
Health Service
Legal Service
Medical Care Service
Social Policy
Social Service

ENABLING LAW
S-21-0071 1975 00000
SN Statute authorizing the creation of a political or administrative unit.
BT Political Law
RT Historical Preservation Law
Home Rule Law
Sunset Law
Sunshine Law

ENCULTURATION
S-34-0003 1975 00004
BT Socialization
NT Americanization
RT Acculturation
Cultural History
Learning Theory
Political Socialization
Socialization Context
Socialization Type

ENCYCLOPEDIA
S-18-0044 1979 00000
BT Information Sources
RT Encyclopedist Thought
Essay
Information Service
Literature Review
Monographs
Textbook

ENCYCLOPEDIAST THOUGHT
1975-1979 00000

ENCYCLOPEDIST THOUGHT
S-38-0401 1979 00000
SN Views held by French editors of the 18th century Encyclopedia emphasizing importance of experimental method, practical side of science, and unity of arts and sciences.
BT Enlightenment Thought
RT Encyclopedia
French Revolutionary Thought
Philosophe Thought
Political Philosophy Studies

END OF IDEOLOGY ANALYSIS
S-38-0148 1975 00001
BT Ideology Explanatory Theory
RT Ideological Indoctrination
Ideological Polarization
Ideology Explanatory Theory
Legal Rational Authority
Post Industrial Society Theory

ENDOGENOUS SYSTEM DEMANDS
S-06-0591 1975 00006
BT System Demands
RT Endogenous System Stress
Interest Aggregation
Interest Articulation
Interest Group Coalition
Interest Group Politics
Interest Group Theory

ENDOGENOUS SYSTEM STRESS
S-06-0618 1975 00002
BT System Stress
RT Conflict Model
Endogenous System Demands
Exogenous System Stress
Social Stress

ENDOGENOUS VARIABLE
S-24-0428 1975 00003
BT Variable Logical Status
RT Dependent Variable
Exogenous Variable
Independent Variable
Interdependent Variable
Intervening Variable
Model City

ENDORSEMENT
S-31-0737 1975 00001
BT Selection Process
RT Appointment Process
Candidate Selection
Delegate Selection
Legislative Nominating Process
Recruitment Process
Slate Making
Social Role Process

ENERGY CONSUMPTION
S-06-0272 1975 00068
BT Consumption
RT Ecosystem
Electrical Industry
Energy Industry
Energy Policy
Energy Use Policy
Gas Industry
Nuclear Energy Industry
Solar Energy

ENERGY CRISIS
USE Energy Scarcity

ENERGY INDUSTRY
S-17-0038 1979 00000
UF Energy Utility Industry
BT Industry
NT Electrical Industry
Nuclear Energy Industry
RT Energy Consumption
Energy Use Policy
Extractive Industry
Gas Industry
Oil Industry
Ore Industry
Production Industry

ENERGY MANAGEMENT
S-23-0024 1979 00000
BT Natural Resource Management
RT Administrative Management
Coal Energy
Energy Scarcity
Energy Use Policy
Environmental Planning
Gas Energy
Industrial Management
Natural Resource Policy
Oil Energy
Radiation Level
Solar Energy
Wind Energy

ENERGY POLICY
S-26-0211 1979 00000
UF Fuel Technology
BT Policy
NT Energy Use Policy
RT Coal Energy
Energy Consumption
Energy Scarcity
Environment Policy
Gas Energy
Geothermal Energy
Hydroelectric Energy
Natural Resource Policy
Nuclear Energy
Oil Energy
Pollution Policy
Radiation Level
Solar Energy
Tidal Energy
Waste Treatment Policy
Wind Energy

ENERGY SCARCITY
S-31-0111 1979 00000
UF Energy Crisis
BT Scarcity
RT Energy Management
Energy Policy
Energy Use Policy
Food Scarcity
Housing Scarcity
Hunger
Labor Scarcity
Natural Resource Exploitation
Water Scarcity

ENERGY USE POLICY
S-26-0212 1975 00112
BT Energy Policy
RT Coal Energy
Electrical Industry
Energy Consumption
Energy Industry
Energy Management
Energy Scarcity
Environmental Pollution
Forest Land Policy
Gas Energy
Geothermal Energy
Nuclear Energy Industry
Oil Energy
Radiation Level
Solar Energy
Tidal Energy
Water Use Policy
Wind Energy

ENERGY UTILITY INDUSTRY
1975-1979 00022
USE Energy Industry

ENGINEER
S-32-0124 1975 00004
BT Technical Occupation
RT Engineering Discipline
Scientist
Technician

ENGINEERING DISCIPLINE
S-01-0080 1975 00003
BT Academic Areas
RT Computer Science
Earth Sciences
Ecology Discipline
Economics Discipline
Engineer
Mathematics Discipline
Natural Science Discipline
Physical Science
Public Administration Studies
Technical Occupation
Technocracy

ENLIGHTENED SELF INTEREST
S-06-0133 1975 00004
BT Self Interest
RT Enlightenment Thought
Inner Directedness
Political Trust
Psychological Freedom Theory

ENLIGHTENMENT LIBERALISM
S-38-0414 1975 00001
BT Liberal Political Thought
RT American Political Thought
Enlightenment Thought
Freedom

ENLIGHTENMENT THOUGHT
S-38-0397 1975 00019
BT Modern Political Thought
NT American Enlightenment Thought
Encyclopedist Thought
French Revolutionary Thought
Kantian Analysis
Philosophe Thought
Rousseauian Analysis
Voltairean Analysis
RT Enlightened Self Interest
Enlightenment Liberalism
Freedom

ENTERPRISE
S-19-0172 1975 00001
BT Economic Institution
NT Government Enterprise
Mixed Enterprise
RT Business
Corporation
Factory
Farm Economy
Farm Industry
Farm Production
Fiscal Institution
Market
Mixed Economy
Monetary Institution
Public Corporation
World Bank

ENTREPRENEUR
S-32-0073 1975 00010
BT Businessman
RT Capitalist Class
Entrepreneur Class
Factory
Financier
Private Sector

ENTREPRENEUR CLASS
S-06-0764 1975 00004
BT Class Stratification Division
RT Black Bourgeoisie
Bourgeoisie
Class Analysis
Economic Elite
Entrepreneur
Entrepreneurship
Financing
Landowning Class
Managerial Elite
Marxist Class Theory
Mercantile Economic System
Middle Class
Propertied Class
Ruling Class
Upper Class

ENTREPRENEURSHIP
S-06-0166 1979 00000
BT Economic Development Characteristics
RT Administrative Leadership
Bourgeoisie
Capitalist Class
Economic Development Level
Economic Development Stage
Entrepreneur Class
Financier
Industrial Economic Stage
Management Characteristics
Private Sector
Takeoff Stage

ENVIRONMENT POLICY
S-26-0213 1979 00000
UF Environmental Policy
BT Policy
NT Land Policy
Natural Resource Policy
Pollution Policy
Space Policy
RT Ecology Discipline
Energy Policy
Environmental Agency
Environmental Characteristics
Environmental Law
Environmental Studies
Lumber Industry
Resource Allocation
Resource Distribution
Resource Utilization

ENVIRONMENTAL ADVISORY AGENCY
S-19-0040 1975 00002
BT Environmental Agency
RT Consumer Agency
Education Agency
Environmental Control Agency
Planning Agency
Regulatory Agency Record

ENVIRONMENTAL AGENCY
S-19-0039 1975 00006
BT Agencies
NT Environmental Advisory Agency
Environmental Control Agency
RT Air Pollution Policy
Business Regulation Agency
Conservation Law
Consumer Agency
Ecology Movement
Environment Policy
Environmental Characteristics
Environmental Management
Environmental Planning
Environmental Studies
Green Revolution
Pollution Policy
Public Authorities
Soil Bank Policy
Stable Population

ENVIRONMENTAL CHARACTERISTICS
S-06-0363 1979 00000
BT Characteristics
NT Population Density
Quality Of Life
Radiation Level
RT Demographic Studies
Environment Policy
Environmental Agency
Environmental Law
Environmental Management
Environmental Planning
Environmental Pollution
Environmental Studies
Geography Discipline
System Analysis

ENVIRONMENTAL CONTROL AGENCY
S-19-0041 1975 00008
BT Environmental Agency
RT Air Pollution
Air Pollution Policy
Environmental Advisory Agency

ENVIRONMENTAL LAW
S-21-0053 1979 00000
BT Law Type
NT Conservation Law
Historical Preservation Law
RT Civil Law
Common Law
Customary Law
Environment Policy
Environmental Characteristics
Environmental Management
Environmental Planning
Environmental Studies
Labor Law
Natural Resource Management
Property Law

ENVIRONMENTAL MANAGEMENT
S-23-0022 1975 00033
BT Management
NT Natural Resource Management
RT. Air Pollution Policy
Conservation Law
Development Management
Ecological Analysis
Ecology Discipline
Economic Management
Ecosystem
Environmental Agency
Environmental Characteristics
Environmental Law
Environmental Studies
Health Administration

ENVIRONMENTAL PLANNING
S-31-0656 1975 00027
BT Planning Process
RT Administrative Planning
Air Pollution Policy
Conservation Law
Development Planning
Ecological Analysis
Ecology Discipline
Economic Planning
Ecosystem
Education Planning
Energy Management
Environmental Agency
Environmental Characteristics
Environmental Law
Environmental Studies
Mass Transit Policy
Military Planning
Natural Resource Policy
Pollution Policy
Population Management
Population Planning
Presidential Commission Of Inquiry
Public Policy Planning
Public Policy Studies
Social Planning
Water Pollution Policy

ENVIRONMENTAL POLICY
1975-1979 00053
USE Environment Policy

ENVIRONMENTAL POLLUTION
S-31-0103 1975 00022
BT Resource Development
NT Air Pollution
Noise Pollution
Water Pollution
RT Air Pollution Policy
Energy Use Policy
Environmental Characteristics
Extractive Industry
Mass Transit Policy
Noise Pollution Policy
Resource Allocation
Resource Distribution
Resource Utilization

ENVIRONMENTAL STUDIES
S-01-0081 1979 00000
BT Academic Areas
RT Agricultural Science
Architectural Studies
Biological Sciences
Climatology
Contextual Analysis
Demographic Studies
Earth Sciences
Ecology Discipline
Environment Policy
Environmental Agency
Environmental Characteristics
Environmental Law
Environmental Management
Environmental Planning
Interdisciplinary Studies
Legal Studies
Physical Anthropology
Physical Science
Regional Development
Regional Economics
Regional Planner
Social System Environment Characteristics
Topography

EPICUREAN POLITICAL THOUGHT
1975-1979 00000

EPICUREAN THOUGHT
S-38-0050 1979 00000
SN A post-Socratic doctrine that included social hedonism, utilitarian social relations and a contract theory of the state.
BT Classical Political Thought
RT Aristotelian Thought
Cynic Thought
Greek Civilization
Platonic Political Thought
Pythagorean Thought
Roman Civilization
Roman Legal Thought
Skeptic Thought
Socratic Political Thought
Stoic Thought
Thucydidean Political Thought

EPIDEMIC
S-06-0376 1979 00000
BT Health Characteristics
RT Alcoholism
Catastrophe Analysis
Disease
Drug Addiction
Health Administration
Health Care Agency
Health Care Institution
Health Care System
Health Service
Morbidity Data
Natural Catastrophe

EPISTEMOLOGY
S-25-0010 1975 00041
BT Metaphysics
NT Cultural Determinism
Cultural Relativism
Cultural Universalism
Dialectic
Empiricism
Essentialism
Historicism
Logical Positivism
Materialism
Neopositivism
Objectivism
Philosophical Idealism
Philosophical Realism
Scientific Determinism
Scientism
Subjectivism
Teleology
Verstehen Theory
RT Ethical Theory
Methodology
Ontology
Philosophy Discipline

EQUAL EMPLOYMENT POLICY
S-26-0200 1975 00023
BT Employment Policy
RT Affirmative Action Employment Policy
Employment Opportunity
Equal Rights
Fair Employment Law
Fair Employment Policy
Manpower Policy
Merit Policy
Public Works Policy
Quota System Policy
Sex Exploitation

EQUAL LAW ENFORCEMENT
S-31-0565 1975 00001
BT Code Enforcement
RT Code Enforcement
Discrimination Policy
Reverse Discrimination

EQUAL OPPORTUNITY
S-06-0498 1975 00041
BT Opportunity Characteristics
RT Affirmative Action Employment Policy
Civil Liberty
Desegregation Policy
Equal Rights
Equality Theory
Job Discrimination
Job Dissatisfaction
Procedural Rights

EQUAL RIGHTS
S-15-0039 1975 00021
BT Civil Rights
NT Minority Rights
Womens Rights
RT Civil Liberty
Defendants Rights
Discrimination Policy
Equal Employment Policy
Equal Opportunity
Procedural Rights
Reverse Discrimination
Womens Liberation

EQUAL TIME PROVISION POLICY
S-26-0028 1975 00003
BT Broadcast Access Policy
RT Broadcasting
Broadcasting Industry

EQUALITY
S-06-0724 1979 00000
BT Social System Structural Characteristics
NT Economic Equality
Political Equality
Social Equality
RT Egalitarianism
Equality Theory
Inequality
Judicial System
Justice Theory
Law Type

EQUALITY THEORY
S-38-0455 1975 00042
BT Political Philosophy Concept
RT Class Inequality
Egalitarian Justice Theory
Egalitarianism
Equal Opportunity
Equality
French Revolutionary Thought
Justice Theory
Levellers Political Thought
Political Opportunity Structure
Remedial Justice Theory
Rousseauian Analysis
Socratic Political Thought
Tocquevillian Analysis

EQUILIBRIUM MODEL
S-24-0300 1975 00009
BT Social Science Model
RT Consensus Model
Cybernetic Model
Econometric Model
Economic Development Model
Input Output Model
Interaction Model
Probability Model

EQUILIBRIUM THEORY
S-38-0032 1975 00009
BT General System Theory
RT Balance Of Power Theory
Burkean Conservatism
Check And Balance Theory
Group Theory
Pluralist Group Theory
Political System Theory
Social Integration Theory
System Characteristics

EQUITY
S-38-0478 1979 00000
BT Justice Theory
RT Compensatory Justice
Distributive Justice Theory
Egalitarian Justice Theory
Justice As Fairness Doctrine
Remedial Justice Theory

EQUITY LAW
S-21-0056 1975 00006
BT Law Type
RT Damage Suit
Economic Law
Historical Preservation Law
Natural Law System
Procedural Law

ERASTIANISM
S-38-0366 1975 00000
BT Medieval Political Thought
RT Christian Thought

ESCALATION
S-31-0217 1975 00000
BT Conflict Intensification
RT Brinkmanship
Crisis
Global War Policy
Political Crisis
Treaty Breaking
Treaty Dissolution

ESCALATION POLICY
S-26-0331 1975 00001
BT Military Policy
RT Armed Intervention Policy
Deescalation Policy
Reprisal Policy
War Policy

ESCHATOLOGY
S-25-0004 1975 00002
BT Philosophical Concept
NT Fatalism
Prophetic Tradition
RT Chiliastic Movement
Cosmology
Judeo Christian Thought
Millenarianism
Ontology
Religious Culture
Religious Fanaticism
Religious Thought

Transcendentalism
Utopianism

ESSAY
S-18-0043 1979 00000
BT Information Sources
RT Encyclopedia
Folk Literature
Humanistic Education
Humanities Discipline
Humanities Education
Political Literature

ESSENTIALISM
S-25-0019 1975 00001
BT Epistemology
RT Etymology
Historicism
Materialism

ESTRANGEMENT
S-06-0082 1975 00022
BT Alienation
NT Political Estrangement
RT Anomie
Cultural Alienation
Cynicism
Distrust
Marxist Alienation Theory
Marxist Class Theory
Ontological Existentialism
Political Alienation
Political Alienation Scale
Schizophrenia

ETHICAL NATURALISM
S-25-0037 1975 00006
SN Assertion that basic ethical principles are empirically true since they can be derived from empirical generalizations.
BT Ethical Theory
RT Emotive Ethical Theory
Ethical Relativism
Ethical Theory

ETHICAL RELATIVISM
S-25-0038 1975 00008
SN Assertion that ethical truth is relative to particular social conditions, historical phase, or cultural features.
BT Ethical Theory
RT Axiology
Bioethics
Cultural Relativism
Emotive Ethical Theory
Ethical Naturalism
Hedonism
Instrumentalism
Intuitionism
Linguistic Ethical Theory
Metaethical Theory
Normative Analysis
Situational Ethics

ETHICAL SOCIALIZATION
S-34-0040 1979 00000
BT Socialization Type
RT Adult Socialization
Childhood Socialization
Cultural System
Education Policy
Ethical Theory
Family Socialization
Moral Learning
Moral Theory
Professional Ethics
Professional Socialization

ETHICAL SUBJECTIVISM
1975-1979 00003

ETHICAL THEORY
S-25-0033 1975 00164
BT Metaphysics
NT Axiology
Bioethics
Emotive Ethical Theory
Ethical Naturalism
Ethical Relativism
Hedonism
Instrumentalism
Intuitionism
Linguistic Ethical Theory
Professional Ethics
Research Ethics
Situational Ethics
RT Benthamism
Epistemology
Ethical Naturalism
Ethical Socialization
Jurisprudence
Justice As Fairness Doctrine
Moral Learning
Nietzschean Analysis
Normative Analysis
Ontology
Utilitarianism

ETHNIC ASSIMILATION
S-31-0799 1975 00047
BT Assimilation
RT Adaptive Behavior
Caste Dissolution
Cultural Assimilation
Ethnic Assimilation Theory
Ethnic Cleavage
Ethnic Composition
Ethnic Group
Ethnic Group Loyalty
Ethnic Heritage Policy
Ethnic Heterogeneity
Ethnic Homogeneity
Ethnic Policy
Ethnic Politics
Ethnic Separatism
Ethnic Studies
Ethnicity
Ethnocentrism
Ethnographic Theory
Ethnography
Group Socialization
Linguistic Assimilation
Racial Assimilation

ETHNIC ASSIMILATION THEORY
S-38-0211 1975 00015
BT Ethnic Ideology
NT Racial Integration Theory
RT Acculturation
Americanization
Assimilation
Bilingualism
Cultural Adaptation
Cultural Assimilation
Cultural Integration
Ethnic Assimilation
Ethnic Cleavage
Ethnic Diversity
Ethnic Group
Ethnic Heterogeneity
Ethnic Homogeneity
Ethnic Integration
Ethnic Nationalism
Ethnic Particularism
Ethnic Politics
Ethnic Separatism
Ethnicity
Ethnocentrism
Linguistic Integration
Minority Law
Multiethnic Society
Multiethnic State
Multiracial Society
Nationality Group
Nationality Policy
Nationalization Process
Racial Assimilation
Racial Integration Theory
Racism
Social Integration
Urban Sociology

ETHNIC BACKGROUND
S-06-0204 1975 00016
BT Ethnic Origin
RT Ethnic Conflict
Ethnic Heritage Policy
Ethnic Studies
Ethnographic Theory
Family Planning
Multiethnic Community
Multiethnic Nation
Multiethnic State
Population Attribute
Racial Background

ETHNIC CLEAVAGE
S-06-0477 1975 00011
BT Ethnic Diversity
RT Cultural Cleavage
Cultural Differentiation
Ethnic Assimilation
Ethnic Assimilation Theory
Ethnic Heterogeneity
Ethnic Homogeneity
Racial Diversity
Social Cleavage

ETHNIC COMMUNITY
S-07-0024 1975 00062
BT Community Type
RT Association Interest Group
Black Bourgeoisie
Black Culture
Black Ghetto
Black Nationalism
Black Separatist Movement
Black Studies
Chicano Studies
Community Culture
Community Homogeneity
Community Identity
Cultural Group Cohesion
Cultural Interest Group
Ethnic Composition
Ethnic Conflict
Ethnic Culture
Ethnic Ghetto
Ethnic Group

Ethnic Heterogeneity
Ethnic Organization
Ethnology
Ghetto Community
Homogeneous Community
Language Community
Multiethnic Community
Political Geography
Racial Composition
Residential Pattern
Social Identity
Traditional Society

ETHNIC COMPOSITION
S-06-0221 1975 00028
BT Population Composition
RT Demographic Analysis
Ethnic Assimilation
Ethnic Community
Ethnic Group
Ethnic Group Voting
Ethnic Integration
Ethnic Organization
Ethnic Politics
Ethnic Studies
Ethnographic Theory
Multiethnic Nation
Multiethnic State
Nationality Composition
Population Attribute
Racial Composition
Religious Composition
Suburban Ghetto Community
Urban Ghetto Community

ETHNIC CONFLICT
S-06-0793 1975 00044
BT Social Stress
RT Bicultural Society
Black Racism
Class Antagonism
Class Conflict
Class Polarization
Ethnic Background
Ethnic Community
Ethnic Culture
Ethnic Diversity
Ethnic Ghetto
Ethnic Group Voting
Ethnic Heterogeneity
Ethnic Ideology
Ethnic Militancy
Ethnic Movement
Ethnic Nationalism
Ethnic Particularism
Ethnic Persecution
Ethnic Policy
Ethnic Politics
Ethnic Separatist Movement
Ethnicity
Ethnocentrism
Violence

ETHNIC CULTURE
S-11-0015 1975 00043
BT Culture Type
NT Black Culture
RT Community Culture
Counter Culture
Cultural Group Cohesion
Cultural History
Ethnic Community
Ethnic Conflict
Ethnic Group Conflict
Ethnic Heterogeneity
Ethnic Homogeneity
Ethnic Ideology
Ethnic Nationalism
Ethnic Studies
Ghetto Community
Political Culture
Poverty Culture
Religious Culture
Secular Culture
Subculture
Traditional Culture
Urban Culture
Western Culture
Youth Culture

ETHNIC DIVERSITY
S-06-0476 1975 00019
BT National Characteristics
NT Ethnic Cleavage
Ethnic Heterogeneity
Ethnic Homogeneity
RT Cultural Cleavage
Cultural Diversity
Ethnic Assimilation Theory
Ethnic Conflict
Ethnic Separatism
Ethnic Studies
Linguistic Diversity
National Self Determination
Racial Cleavage
Racial Diversity
Social Diversity

ETHNIC GHETTO
S-07-0026 1975 00008
BT Ghetto Community
NT Black Ghetto
RT Collective Community
Communal Community
Discrimination Policy
Ethnic Community
Ethnic Conflict
Ethnic Group
Ethnic Group Conflict
Ethnic Heritage Policy
Ethnocentrism
Homogeneous Community
Housing Policy
Integrated Community
Segregated Community
Suburban Ghetto Community
Urban Ghetto Community
Urbanization Pattern

ETHNIC GROUP
S-03-0025 1975 00156
BT Social Group
RT Cultural Group
Ethnic Assimilation
Ethnic Assimilation Theory
Ethnic Community
Ethnic Composition
Ethnic Ghetto
Ethnic Group Cohesion
Ethnic Group Loyalty
Ethnic Group Voting
Ethnic Heritage Policy
Face To Face Group
Ghetto Community
Group Composition
Kinship Group
Minority Group
Nationality Group
Racial Group
Reference Group
Religious Cult
Religious Group
Secondary Group

ETHNIC GROUP COHESION
S-06-0043 1975 00038
BT Minority Group Cohesion
RT Caste Solidarity
Class Solidarity
Cultural Group Cohesion
Ethnic Group
Ethnic Studies
Ethnocentrism
Ethnography
Social Solidarity

ETHNIC GROUP CONFLICT
S-08-0119 1979 00000
UF Ethnic Tension
BT Group Conflict
RT Class Antagonism
Cultural Aggression
Ethnic Culture
Ethnic Ghetto
Ethnic Militancy
Ethnic Nationalism
Ethnic Persecution
Ethnic Separatism
Ethnic Studies
Ethnocentrism
Ghetto Conflict
Ghetto Rioter

ETHNIC GROUP LOYALTY
S-06-0382 1975 00016
BT Ethnicity
RT Black Identity
Ethnic Assimilation
Ethnic Group
Ethnic Militancy
Ethnic Nationalism
Ethnic Particularism
Ethnic Separatism
Ethnocentrism
Group Theory
Language Loyalty
Minority Group
National Identity
Racial Identity

ETHNIC GROUP VOTING
S-29-0132 1975 00009
BT Group Voting
RT Age Group Voting
Black Voter
Bloc Voting
Ethnic Composition
Ethnic Conflict
Ethnic Group
Ethnic Policy
Ethnic Voter
Geographic Voting
Protest Voting
Racial Voting
Regional Voting
Religious Voting
Sex Group Voting

Student Voting
Suburban Voting
Urban Voting

ETHNIC HERITAGE POLICY
S-26-0081 1979 00000
BT Cultural Development Policy
RT Ethnic Assimilation
Ethnic Background
Ethnic Ghetto
Ethnic Group
Ethnic Origin
Ethnic Policy
Ethnic Studies
Ethnicity
Ethnocentrism
Ethnographic Data
Ethnographic Theory

ETHNIC HETEROGENEITY
S-06-0478 1975 00013
BT Ethnic Diversity
RT Cultural Cleavage
Ethnic Assimilation
Ethnic Assimilation Theory
Ethnic Cleavage
Ethnic Community
Ethnic Conflict
Ethnic Culture
Ethnic Homogeneity
Ethnic Separatism
Heterogeneous Community
Heterogeneous Culture
Heterogeneous Society
Linguistic Diversity
Racial Diversity

ETHNIC HOMOGENEITY
S-06-0479 1975 00009
BT Ethnic Diversity
RT Ethnic Assimilation
Ethnic Assimilation Theory
Ethnic Cleavage
Ethnic Culture
Ethnic Heterogeneity
Homogeneous Culture
Homogeneous Society
Urban Ghetto Community

ETHNIC IDEOLOGY
S-38-0210 1975 00008
BT Ideologies
NT Ethnic Assimilation Theory
Ethnic Nationalism
Ethnic Particularism
Ethnic Separatism
Ethnocentrism
Racism
RT Black Political Thought
Cultural History
Ethnic Conflict
Ethnic Culture
Ethnic Politics
Ethnicity
Ethnographic Theory
Gender Ideology

ETHNIC INTEGRATION
S-31-0811 1975 00025
BT Integration
RT Desegregation Policy
Ethnic Assimilation Theory
Ethnic Composition
Ethnic Policy
Ethnic Separatism
Ethnocentrism
Functional Integration
Group Cleavage Characteristics
Horizontal Integration
Linguistic Integration
Policy Development
Racial Integration
Social Integration
Urban Migration Pattern
Vertical Integration

ETHNIC MILITANCY
S-06-0110 1975 00001
BT Militancy
RT Ethnic Conflict
Ethnic Group Conflict
Ethnic Group Loyalty
Ethnic Politics
Ethnic Separatism
Ethnicity
Ghetto Rioter
Group Conflict
Urban Guerrilla
Urban Race Riot

ETHNIC MOVEMENT
S-27-0062 1975 00010
BT Social Movement
RT Ethnic Conflict
Ethnic Politics
Ethnic Separatism
Ethnic Studies
Ethnic Voter
Ethnicity

ETHNIC NATIONALISM
S-38-0213 1975 00035
BT Ethnic Ideology
RT Ethnic Assimilation Theory
Ethnic Conflict
Ethnic Culture
Ethnic Group Conflict
Ethnic Group Loyalty
Ethnic Particularism
Ethnic Policy
Ethnic Politics
Ethnic Separatism
Ethnicity
Ethnocentrism
National Identity
National Identity Theory
Racism
Xenophobe

ETHNIC ORGANIZATION
S-03-0044 1975 00016
BT Organizations
RT Civic Organization
Cultural Organization
Ethnic Community
Ethnic Composition
Ethnic Politics
Ethnic Studies
Ethnicity
Ethnocentrism
Ethnography
Fraternal Organization
Group Phenomena
Group Process
Interest Group
Social Group
Youth Organization

ETHNIC ORIGIN
S-06-0203 1975 00013
BT Origin
NT Ethnic Background
Racial Background
RT Ancestry
Class Origin
Ethnic Heritage Policy
Ethnocentrism
Ethnography
Ethnology
National Origin

ETHNIC PARTICULARISM
S-38-0214 1975 00004
BT Ethnic Ideology
RT Ethnic Assimilation Theory
Ethnic Conflict
Ethnic Group Loyalty
Ethnic Nationalism
Ethnic Politics
Ethnic Separatism
Ethnicity
Ethnocentrism
Racism

ETHNIC PERSECUTION
S-31-0314 1975 00017
BT Persecution
RT Ethnic Conflict
Ethnic Group Conflict
Ethnic Separatism
Ethnicity
Minority Persecution
Nationality Persecution
Political Persecution
Racial Persecution
Religious Persecution

ETHNIC POLICY
S-26-0378 1975 00021
BT Social Policy
NT Nationality Policy
Racial Policy
RT Discrimination Policy
Employment Opportunity
Ethnic Assimilation
Ethnic Conflict
Ethnic Group Voting
Ethnic Heritage Policy
Ethnic Integration
Ethnic Nationalism
Ethnic Separatism
Ethnocentrism
Face To Face Group
Integration
Military Integration Policy
Minority Rights
Nationality Group
Racial Persecution
Religious Policy
Reverse Discrimination
Urban Renewal Policy

ETHNIC POLITICS
S-29-0199 1975 00036
BT Politics
RT Ethnic Assimilation
Ethnic Assimilation Theory
Ethnic Composition
Ethnic Conflict
Ethnic Ideology
Ethnic Militancy

Ethnic Movement
Ethnic Nationalism
Ethnic Organization
Ethnic Particularism
Ethnic Separatism
Ethnic Separatist Movement
Ethnocentrism
Linkage Politics
Urban Politics Studies
Urban Race Riot
Urban Sociology

ETHNIC SEPARATISM
S-38-0215 1975 00012
BT Ethnic Ideology
RT Ethnic Assimilation
Ethnic Assimilation Theory
Ethnic Diversity
Ethnic Group Conflict
Ethnic Group Loyalty
Ethnic Heterogeneity
Ethnic Integration
Ethnic Militancy
Ethnic Movement
Ethnic Nationalism
Ethnic Particularism
Ethnic Persecution
Ethnic Policy
Ethnic Politics
Ethnic Separatist Movement
Ethnicity
Ethnocentrism
Racism
Separatist Movement

ETHNIC SEPARATIST MOVEMENT
S-27-0031 1975 00011
BT Separatist Movement
RT Ethnic Conflict
Ethnic Politics
Ethnic Separatism
Ethnocentrism
Group Conflict
Independence Movement
Liberation Movement
Nationalist Movement

ETHNIC STUDIES
S-01-0082 1975 00076
BT Academic Areas
NT American Indian Studies
Black Studies
Chicano Studies
Puerto Rican Studies
RT African Area Studies
American Area Studies
American Indian Studies
Anthropological Theory
Anthropology Discipline
Area Studies
Black Ancestry
Black History
Black Voting
Comparative Political Studies
Comparative Sociology
Cultural Anthropology
Cultural Group
Cultural History
Ethnic Assimilation
Ethnic Background
Ethnic Composition
Ethnic Culture
Ethnic Diversity
Ethnic Group Cohesion
Ethnic Group Conflict
Ethnic Heritage Policy
Ethnic Movement
Ethnic Organization
Ethnicity
Ethnographic Data
Ethnography
Ethnology
Geography Discipline
History Discipline
Identity Analysis
Identity Change
Identity Characteristics
Identity Theory
Intracultural Analysis
Linguistics
Multiethnic Community
Multiethnic Nation
Multiethnic Society
Multiethnic State
Multiracial Society
Nationalities Law
Nationality Composition
North African Area Studies
Political Behavior Studies
Political Science Discipline
Political Sociology
Psychology Discipline
Sociology Discipline
Urban Politics Studies

ETHNIC TENSION
1975-1979 00006
USE Ethnic Group Conflict

ETHNIC VOTER
S-32-0310 1975 00003
BT Voter
RT Black Voter
Black Voting
Class Voter
Ethnic Group Voting
Ethnic Movement
Ethnocentrism
Group Benefits Voter
Minority Voter
Urban Voting

ETHNICITY
S-06-0381 1975 00079
BT Cultural Identity
NT Ethnic Group Loyalty
RT African Area Studies
American Indian Studies
Black Identity
Black Liberation Movement
Black Nationalist Movement
Black Voting
Cultural History
Ethnic Assimilation
Ethnic Assimilation Theory
Ethnic Conflict
Ethnic Heritage Policy
Ethnic Ideology
Ethnic Militancy
Ethnic Movement
Ethnic Nationalism
Ethnic Organization
Ethnic Particularism
Ethnic Persecution
Ethnic Separatism
Ethnic Studies
Ethnocentrism
Ethnography
Ethnology
Identity Analysis
Identity Change
Identity Characteristics
Identity Theory
Minority Group Cohesion
Multiethnic Society
Racial Identity
Socialization Context

ETHNOCENTRISM
S-38-0216 1975 00014
BT Ethnic Ideology
RT Ethnic Assimilation
Ethnic Assimilation Theory
Ethnic Conflict
Ethnic Ghetto
Ethnic Group Cohesion
Ethnic Group Conflict
Ethnic Group Loyalty
Ethnic Heritage Policy
Ethnic Integration
Ethnic Nationalism
Ethnic Organization
Ethnic Origin
Ethnic Particularism
Ethnic Policy
Ethnic Politics
Ethnic Separatism
Ethnic Separatist Movement
Ethnic Voter
Ethnicity
Peasant Culture
Racism
Traditional Culture
Xenophobe

ETHNOGRAPHIC DATA
S-18-0089 1975 00036
BT Social Statistics
RT Anthropological Theory
Cultural History
Ethnic Heritage Policy
Ethnic Studies
Ethnography
Ethnology
Social Indicator
Statistical Table
Survey Data
Urban Geography
Urban Sociology
Vital Statistics Data

ETHNOGRAPHIC THEORY
S-38-0008 1975 00008
BT Anthropological Theory
RT Acculturation Theory
Anthropological Functionalism
Ethnic Assimilation
Ethnic Background
Ethnic Composition
Ethnic Heritage Policy
Ethnic Ideology
Ethnography
Ethnology
Geographic Determinism Theory
Group Theory
Kinship Systematics Theory

Structuralism

ETHNOGRAPHY
S-01-0010 1975 00026
BT Cultural Anthropology
RT Area Studies
Comparative Sociology
Cultural History
Demographic Studies
Ethnic Assimilation
Ethnic Group Cohesion
Ethnic Organization
Ethnic Origin
Ethnic Studies
Ethnicity
Ethnographic Data
Ethnographic Theory
Ethnolinguistics
Ethnology
Extended Kinship System
Human Geography
Social Anthropology

ETHNOLINGUISTICS
S-01-0011 1975 00017
BT Cultural Anthropology
RT Anthropological Linguistic Theory
Area Studies
Ethnography
Ethnology
Linguistic Analysis
Linguistic Assimilation
Linguistic Diversity
Linguistic Theory
Linguistics
Morphology
Mythology
Ordinary Language Philosophy
Psycholinguistics
Social Anthropology
Sociolinguistics
Structural Linguistics

ETHNOLOGY
S-01-0012 1975 00026
BT Cultural Anthropology
NT Mythology
RT Black History
Comparative Political Studies
Cultural History
Ethnic Community
Ethnic Origin
Ethnic Studies
Ethnicity
Ethnographic Data
Ethnographic Theory
Ethnography
Ethnolinguistics
Group Characteristics
Human Geography
Social Anthropology
Sociolinguistics

ETYMOLOGY
S-01-0136 1979 00000
SN The study of the origin and derivation of words.
BT Linguistics
RT Essentialism
Historicism
Materialism

EUGENICS
S-01-0051 1979 00000
UF Genetics
Genetics
BT Biological Sciences
RT Agronomy
Animal Husbandry
Biological Model
Genetic Characteristics
Horticulture
Human Evolution
Human Geography
Sociobiology

EUROCOMMUNISM
S-38-0223 1979 00000
BT Ideologies
RT Communism
Critical Theory Analysis
Democratic Socialism
Evolutionary Marxism
Evolutionary Socialism
Hegelian Marxism
Marxist Communism Theory
Marxist Existentialism
Marxist Revisionism
Neomarxism
Phenomenological Marxism
Socialist Humanism
Socialist Theory
Structural Marxism

EUROPEAN INTEGRATION THEORY
S-38-0357 1975 00016
BT International Integration Theory
RT Common Market
East European Area Studies
Free Trade Policy
Integration
International Commonwealth Theory
International Economic Organization Theory
International Regional Economic Integration
International Regional Political Integration
Multinational Security Forces
National Economic Integration
Political Unification
Russian Studies
Security Community Theory
Soviet And East European Area Studies
Soviet Studies
Supranational Integration
Trade Organization
West European Area Studies
Western Bloc

EUTHANASIA
S-10-0008 1979 00000
BT Crime Against Humanity
RT Gerontology
Individual Crime
Old Age

EVALUATING
S-31-0007 1979 00000
BT Analytic Process
RT Applied Research
Education Evaluation
Formative Evaluation
Judging
Needs Assessment
Normative Evaluation
Research Design
Research Evaluation
Summative Evaluation
Value Judgment

EVENT
S-24-0343 1975 00000
BT Analysis Unit
RT Empirical Theory
Empiricism
Event Analysis
Event Measurement
Research Unit

EVENT ANALYSIS
S-24-0381 1975 00043
BT Data Selection Orientation
RT Event
Event Measurement
Policy Analysis
Public Policy Analysis

EVENT MEASUREMENT
S-24-0186 1975 00001
BT Measurement Object
RT Change Measurement
Event
Event Analysis
Group Measurement
Policy Analysis

EVIDENCE ADMISSIBILITY
S-15-0054 1975 00003
BT Right To Trial
NT Circumstantial Evidence
RT Arbitrary Arrest
Arbitrary Imprisonment
Burden Of Proof
Cross Examination
District Court
Ex Post Facto Protection
Fair Trial
Grand Jury Indictment
Habeas Corpus
Judicial Procedure
Right To Appeal
Right To Counsel
Right To Due Process
Right To Jury Trial
Right To Speedy Trial
Search And Seizure
Self Incrimination
Wiretap Evidence Admissibility
Wiretapping Policy

EVOLUTION
S-31-0063 1975 00000
BT Development Process
NT Cultural Evolution
Genetic Evolution
Human Evolution
Political Evolution
Social Evolution
RT Evolutionary Change
Evolutionary Economics
Evolutionary Marxism
Evolutionary Socialism
Progress
Social Darwinism

EVOLUTIONARY CHANGE
S-31-0141 1975 00009
BT Change Process
NT Homeostatic Change
RT Bernsteinian Socialism
Evolution
Evolutionary Economics
Evolutionary Marxism
Evolutionary Socialism
Fabian Socialism
Genetic Characteristics
Innovation
Political Change
Political Party Ideology
Social Change
Social Darwinism
Technological Change

EVOLUTIONARY ECONOMICS
S-01-0063 1979 00000
BT Economics Discipline
RT Administrative Science
Econometrics
Economic Institution
Evolution
Evolutionary Change
Institution Building
Institutional Development
Institutional Economics
Institutional Innovation
Institutionalization

EVOLUTIONARY MARXISM
S-38-0321 1975 00002
BT Marxism
RT Communism
Eurocommunism
Evolution
Evolutionary Change
Hegelian Marxism
Leninism
Maoism
Marxism Leninism
Marxist Analysis
Marxist Economics
Marxist Revisionism
Polycentrism
Socialist Economic Planning
Socialist Political Party
Stalinism
Titoism

EVOLUTIONARY SOCIALISM
S-38-0293 1975 00002
BT Socialist Theory
NT Bernsteinian Socialism
Fabian Socialism
Saint Simonianism
RT Aprista Socialism
Christian Socialism
Democratic Socialism
Democratic Socialist Revolution
Eurocommunism
Evolution
Evolutionary Change
Guild Socialism
Marxism
Marxist Analysis
Marxist Theory
Social Change
Social Democratic Political Party
Social Evolution
Socialist Democracy
Socialist Economic System
Socialist Political Party
Syndicalism

EX POST FACTO PROTECTION
S-15-0056 1975 00000
SN Safeguards against unfair retroactive application of laws and judicial decisions.
BT Right To Trial
RT Arraignment
Bill Of Attainder
Bill Of Rights
Burden Of Proof
Evidence Admissibility
Grand Jury Indictment
Right To Appeal
Right To Counsel
Right To Due Process
Right To Jury Trial
Right To Speedy Trial
Self Incrimination

EXAMINATION
USE Testing

EXAMINATION AGENCY
S-19-0036 1975 00002
BT Education Agency
RT Board Of Regents
Board Of Trustees
Education Accreditation Agency
Education Institution
School Board

EXCEPTIONAL CHILD
S-32-0037 1979 00000
BT Child
RT Child Care Service
Child Psychology
Childhood
Childhood Socialization
Childrens Rights
Education Policy

EXCHANGE THEORY
S-38-0131 1975 00033
SN An approach to social behavior which focuses on the interpersonal transfer of things that are rewarding or costly.
BT Formal Political Theory
RT Competition
Interaction Analysis
Social Action Theory

EXCISE TAXATION
1975-1979 00001

EXCISE TAXATION POLICY
S-26-0142 1975 00001
BT Taxation Policy
RT Confiscatory Taxation
Gift Taxation
Import Duty
Inheritance Taxation
Luxury Taxation
Nuisance Taxation
Sales Taxation
Social Security Taxation
Tariff
Value Added Taxation

EXCLUSIONARY POLICY
S-26-0234 1975 00007
BT Policy
NT Blacklisting Policy
Quota Policy
Segregation Policy
RT Admission Policy
Employment Policy
Racism

EXECUTIVE ACCOUNTABILITY
S-06-0433 1975 00007
BT Administrative Accountability
NT Chief Executive Accountability
RT Bureaucratic Capability Characteristics
Bureaucratic Normative Characteristics
Executive Behavior
Executive Immunity
Government Accountability
Legislative Accountability
Ministerial Responsibility

EXECUTIVE AGREEMENT
S-02-0063 1975 00003
UF Presidential Agreement
BT State Agreement Form
RT Administrative Policy Making
Administrative Politics
Bilateral State Agreement
State Agreement Type

EXECUTIVE ASSISTANT
S-36-0008 1975 00001
BT Executive Director
RT Administrative Policy Making
Administrative Staff Personnel

EXECUTIVE BEHAVIOR
S-05-0004 1975 00013
BT Administrative Behavior
RT Administrative Leadership
Administrative Management
Bureaucratic Behavior
Executive Accountability
Executive Discretion
Executive Leadership
Executive Role Orientation
Organization Behavior

EXECUTIVE BUDGET
S-06-0253 1975 00002
BT Capital Budget
RT Administrative Management
Budget Policy
Executive Budget Proposal
Zero Based Budget

EXECUTIVE BUDGET PROPOSAL
S-26-0240 1975 00001
BT Executive Policy
RT Administrative Policy Making
Executive Budget
Executive Legislative Policy
Executive Pronouncement

EXECUTIVE COMMUNIQUE
S-26-0241 1975 00003
BT Executive Policy
RT Administrative Record
Executive Pardon
Executive Pronouncement
Executive Trial Balloon Policy
Presidential Policy

EXECUTIVE DIPLOMACY
S-31-0355 1975 00003
BT Diplomacy
NT Presidential Diplomacy
RT Administrative Politics
Diplomatic Relations
Diplomatic Relations Normalization
Dollar Diplomacy
Gunboat Diplomacy
International Decision Making Process
International Peace Negotiation
Secret Diplomacy
Summit Diplomacy

EXECUTIVE DIRECTOR
S-36-0007 1975 00001
BT Administrative Officer
NT Executive Assistant
RT Bureau Chief
Dean
Department Head
Executive Discretion

EXECUTIVE DISCRETION
S-06-0438 1975 00002
BT Administrative Discretion
NT Chief Executive Discretion
RT Administrative Policy Making
Administrative Politics
Executive Behavior
Executive Director
Executive Prerogative
Executive Privilege
Ministerial Responsibility

EXECUTIVE DISSOLUTION
S-31-0460 1975 00000
BT Government Dissolution Process
NT Abdication
Impeachment
Resignation
RT Executive Jurisdiction
Executive Leadership
Government Dissolution Process
Legislative Dissolution

EXECUTIVE GOVERNMENT INSTITUTION
S-19-0232 1975 00002
BT Institutions
NT Chancellery
Fascist Council
Governorship
Military Executive Council
Plural Executive
Premiership
Presidency
Secretariat
RT Cabinet
Council Of Ministers
Councils
Government Agency
International Government Council
National Government Council
Presidential Advisory Council
Presidential Commission
Presidential Task Force
Privy Council
Shadow Cabinet

EXECUTIVE IMMUNITY
S-15-0020 1975 00000
BT Immunity
RT Citizenship Immunity
Diplomatic Immunity
Executive Accountability
Executive Prerogative
Executive Privilege
Legal Immunity
Political Asylum
Trial System

EXECUTIVE JUDICIAL POLICY
S-26-0242 1975 00000
BT Executive Policy
RT Administrative Politics
Check And Balance Theory
Executive Jurisdiction
Executive Legislative Policy
Executive Pardon
Executive Pronouncement

EXECUTIVE JURISDICTION
S-06-0402 1975 00000
BT Jurisdiction Characteristics
RT Administrative Jurisdiction
Administrative Politics
Budget Policy
Executive Dissolution
Executive Judicial Policy
Legal Jurisdiction
Legislative Jurisdiction
Territory Jurisdiction
Union Jurisdiction

EXECUTIVE LEADERSHIP
S-22-0024 1979 00000
BT Political Leadership
NT Presidential Leadership
RT Congressional Leadership
Executive Behavior
Executive Dissolution
Executive Policy
Executive Power
Leadership Authority Base
Leadership Structure Type
National Leadership
Political Movement Leadership
Political Party Leadership

EXECUTIVE LEGISLATIVE POLICY
S-26-0243 1975 00003
BT Executive Policy
NT Presidential Legislative Program
RT Check And Balance Theory
Executive Budget Proposal
Executive Judicial Policy
Executive Pronouncement
Inaugural Address
Intergovernmental Relations
Legislative Executive Separation
Legislative Process
Presidential Policy

EXECUTIVE PARDON
S-26-0245 1975 00003
BT Executive Policy
RT Executive Communique
Executive Judicial Policy
Executive Pronouncement

EXECUTIVE POLICY
S-26-0239 1975 00007
BT Policy
NT Executive Budget Proposal
Executive Communique
Executive Judicial Policy
Executive Legislative Policy
Executive Pardon
Executive Pronouncement
Executive Trial Balloon Policy
Presidential Policy
RT Administrative Leadership
Administrative Politics
Executive Leadership

EXECUTIVE POLICY STATEMENT
1975-1979 00001

EXECUTIVE POWER
S-30-0013 1975 00014
BT Political Power
NT Presidential Power
RT Administrative Policy Making
Administrative Politics
Executive Leadership
Governing Elite
Judicial Power
Legislative Executive Separation
Legislative Power
Presidential Accountability
Separation Of Power

EXECUTIVE PREROGATIVE
S-06-0441 1975 00001
BT Administrative Discretion
NT Chief Executive Prerogative
RT Administrative Policy Making
Administrative Politics
Emergency Power
Executive Discretion
Executive Immunity
Executive Privilege
Presidential Discretion

EXECUTIVE PRIVILEGE
S-06-0443 1975 00003
BT Administrative Discretion
RT Emergency Power
Executive Discretion
Executive Immunity
Executive Prerogative
Ministerial Responsibility
Presidential Discretion

EXECUTIVE PRONOUNCEMENT
S-26-0246 1975 00000
BT Executive Policy
RT Emergency Power
Executive Budget Proposal
Executive Communique
Executive Judicial Policy
Executive Legislative Policy
Executive Pardon
Executive Trial Balloon Policy
Presidential Government
Presidential Policy

EXECUTIVE REFORM
S-31-0089 1975 00008
BT Reform
NT Executive Reorganization
RT Administrative Reform
Education Reform
Judicial Reform
Legislative Reform

EXECUTIVE REORGANIZATION
S-31-0090 1975 00011
BT Executive Reform
NT Cabinet Reorganization

RT Administrative Management
Administrative Politics
Congressional Reform

EXECUTIVE ROLE ORIENTATION
S-31-0765 1975 00007
BT Role Orientation
RT Administrative Theory
Executive Behavior
Judicial Role Orientation
Legislative Role Orientation
Political Role Orientation

EXECUTIVE SESSION
S-31-0615 1975 00000
BT Parliamentary Procedure
RT Committee Of The Whole
Legislative Behavior

EXECUTIVE STAFF PERSONNEL
S-36-0010 1975 00003
BT Administrative Staff Personnel
NT Chief Executive Staff Personnel
RT Judicial Staff Personnel
Legislative Staff Personnel

EXECUTIVE TRIAL BALLOON POLICY
S-26-0247 1975 00000
BT Executive Policy
RT Administrative Politics
Executive Communique
Executive Pronouncement
Presidential Policy

EXECUTIVE VETO
S-31-0336 1975 00001
BT Veto
NT Gubernatorial Veto
Presidential Veto
RT Administrative Politics
Item Veto
Pocket Veto
Security Council Veto

EXILE
S-36-0020 1979 00000
BT Citizenship Status
RT Dissent
Expatriate
Immigrant
Immigration Policy
Ostracism
Refugee
Religious Dissenter
Stateless Person

EXISTENTIAL PSYCHOLOGISM
S-38-0064 1975 00002
BT Existentialism
RT Alienation Process
Cognitive Theory
Gestalt Theory
Ontological Existentialism
Phenomenological Psychologism
Psychological Freedom Theory
Psychological Theory

EXISTENTIALISM
S-38-0062 1975 00004
BT Contemporary Political Thought
NT Christian Existentialism
Existential Psychologism
Marxist Existentialism
Ontological Existentialism
RT Hegelian Analysis
History Of Philosophy
Phenomenological Existentialism
Philosophical Concept

EXOGENOUS SYSTEM DEMANDS
S-06-0592 1975 00003
SN Demands made upon a system from outside its boundaries.
BT System Demands
RT Exogenous System Stress
Exogenous Variable
System Analysis
System Boundary

EXOGENOUS SYSTEM STRESS
S-06-0619 1975 00004
BT System Stress
RT Endogenous System Stress
Exogenous System Demands
Exogenous Variable

EXOGENOUS VARIABLE
S-24-0429 1975 00005
SN Variable external to those being examined.
BT Variable Logical Status
RT Control Variable
Dependent Variable
Endogenous Variable
Exogenous System Demands
Exogenous System Stress
Independent Variable
Interdependent Variable
Intervening Variable

EXPANSIONIST POLICY
S-26-0254 1975 00013
BT Foreign Policy
RT Containment Policy
Expansionist War
Imperialism
Interference Policy
Intervention Policy
Military Intervention Policy
Military Invasion

EXPANSIONIST WAR
S-08-0093 1975 00002
BT War
NT Imperialist War
RT Annexation
Expansionist Policy
Holy War
Ideological War
Imperialism
National Socialism
Political Revolution
Rebellion
Revolutionary War
Struggle

EXPATRIATE
S-36-0023 1975 00002
BT Immigrant
RT Exile
Refugee
Repatriate
Stateless Person

EXPENDITURE POLICY
S-26-0099 1975 00047
BT Fiscal Policy
NT Revenue Sharing Policy
RT Budget Deficit
Budget Policy
Capital Investment Policy
Currency Revaluation Policy
Expenditure Record
Government Economic Planning
Income Policy
Inflation
Inflation Policy
Monetary Policy
Public Debt Policy
Public Finance Theory
Revenue Policy

EXPENDITURE RECORD
S-18-0013 1975 00016
BT Financial Record
RT Budget
Budget Deficit
Budget Estimation
Budget Record
Employment Record
Expenditure Policy
Income Record
Political Party Financial Record
Revenue Record

EXPERIMENT
S-24-0421 1975 00013
BT Variable Control
RT Experimental Observation
Experimental Research
Field Theory
Nonexperiment
Quasiexperiment
Response Recording Equipment

EXPERIMENTAL OBSERVATION
S-24-0097 1975 00016
BT Reactive Observation
NT Gaming
Small Group Experiment
RT Experiment
Falsification
Interviewing Material
Participant Observation
Response Recording Equipment
Survey Research

EXPERIMENTAL RESEARCH
S-24-0384 1975 00122
BT Research Orientation
RT Applied Research
Basic Research
Data Selection Orientation
Descriptive Research
Experiment
Explanatory Research
Forecasting Methodology
Ideographic Research
Inductive Method
Predictive Research
Qualitative Research
Quantitative Research
Quasiexperimental Research
Research Institution
Research Laboratory
Response Recording Equipment
Scientific Research
Theoretical Research

EXPERT
S-36-0039 1979 00000
BT Status
RT Advisor
Expertise
Professional Education
Professional Occupational Role
Scientific Attache

EXPERTISE
S-06-0367 1979 00000
BT Characteristics
RT Administrative Science
Expert
Job Training
Management Characteristics
Management Training Program
Skill Acquisition
Skilled Worker

EXPLANATORY POLITICAL THEORY
S-38-0120 1975 00013
BT Political Theory
NT Conflict Theory
Decision Making Theory
Elite Theory
Formal Political Theory
Futurology
Group Theory
Ideology Explanatory Theory
Mass Society Theory
Micropolitical Theory
Nation State Explanatory Theory
Political Behaviorism
Political Integration Theory
Political System Theory
Post Industrial Society Theory
Power Theory
Public Choice Theory
Public Good Theory
Revolution Theory
Social Choice Theory
Structural Functional Political Theory
Transactional Theory
Voting Theory
RT Anthropological Theory
Behavioral Theory
Contemporary Political Thought
Explanatory Research
Explanatory Variable
General System Theory
Ideologies
International Political Theory
Macropolitical Theory
Modern Political Thought
Modernization Theory
Organization Theory
Political Philosophy Concept
Predictive Research
Psychological Theory

EXPLANATORY RESEARCH
S-24-0385 1975 00097
BT Research Orientation
NT Quasiexperimental Research
RT Applied Research
Basic Research
Concept Explication Research
Data Selection Orientation
Descriptive Research
Experimental Research
Explanatory Political Theory
Explanatory Variable
Falsification
Policy Research
Predictive Research
Propositional Inventory
Qualitative Research
Quantitative Research
Scientific Research
Theoretical Research
Theory Of Causality

EXPLANATORY VARIABLE
S-24-0431 1975 00010
BT Independent Variable
RT Control Variable
Explanatory Political Theory
Explanatory Research

EXPLOITATION
USE Exploitation Process

EXPLOITATION PROCESS
S-31-0285 1975 00015
UF Exploitation
BT Control Process
NT Economic Exploitation
Political Exploitation
Racial Exploitation
Sex Exploitation
RT Expropriation Process
Marxist Alienation Theory
Marxist Immiseration Theory
Marxist Labor Value Theory
Persecution
Political Control
Repression Process

EXPLORATION
S-31-0456 1979 00000
BT Process
NT Geographic Exploration
RT Archaeology
Discovery
Explorer
Geography Discipline
Physical Anthropology

EXPLORER
S-32-0032 1979 00000
BT Roles
RT Archaeology
Discovery
Exploration
Geographic Exploration
Geography Discipline
Physical Anthropology

EXPORT ECONOMY
S-12-0021 1975 00009
BT Economy Type
RT Barter Economy
Budget Deficit
Export Market
Imperialist Economy
Market Economy
Modernizing Economy
Plantation Economy

EXPORT MARKET
S-19-0187 1975 00013
BT Market
RT Consumption Process
Export Economy
Financial Market
Free Market
Marketplace
National Market
Protective Tariff

EXPORT POLICY
S-26-0186 1975 00055
BT Restrictive Trade Policy
RT Blockade Policy
Export Quota
Export Subsidization Policy
Gas Industry
Import Policy
Tariff Policy

EXPORT QUOTA
S-06-0348 1975 00004
BT International Economic Characteristics
RT Export Policy
Import Export Ratio
Import Quota

EXPORT SUBSIDIZATION POLICY
S-26-0181 1975 00002
BT Trade Policy
RT Budget Deficit
Export Policy
Free Trade Policy
Government Economic Planning
Most Favored Nation Policy
Restrictive Trade Policy

EXPROPRIATION PROCESS
S-31-0290 1975 00003
BT Control Process
NT Government Expropriation
RT Economic Process
Exploitation Process
Political Control
Regulation Process

EXTENDED FAMILY
S-20-0010 1975 00008
BT Family Type
RT Clan Kinship System
Communal Family
Extended Kinship System
Family Planning
Family Policy
Intermarriage
Kindred Family
Kinship Group
Sibling

EXTENDED KINSHIP SYSTEM
S-20-0018 1975 00001
BT Kinship System
NT Clan Kinship System
Matriarchal Kinship System
Patriarchal Kinship System
RT Ancestry
Clan Role
Communal Family
Cultural System
Ethnography
Extended Family
Kindred Family
Kinship Group
Kinship Role

EXTENDED REPUBLIC THEORY
S-38-0450 1975 00003
BT Constitutional Structural Theory
RT Check And Balance Theory
Madisonian Thought

EXTERNAL COMPETITION
S-31-0203 1975 00001
BT Competition
RT Internal Competition

EXTORTION
S-10-0031 1975 00001
BT Individual Crime
RT Blackmail
Economic Bribery
Economic Conspiracy

Economic Crime
Fraud
Kidnapping
Libel
Malpractice
Marital Offense
Police Brutality
Robbery
Slander
Tax Evasion
White Collar Crime

EXTORTIONIST
S-36-0032 1975 00000
BT Personal Crime Criminal
RT Blackmailer
Murderer
Slanderer
War Criminal

EXTRACTIVE INDUSTRY
S-17-0041 1975 00013
UF Mines
BT Industry
NT Coal Industry
Forestry Industry
Gas Industry
Oil Industry
Ore Industry
RT Electrical Industry
Energy Industry
Environmental Pollution
Mine Safety Policy
Natural Resource Policy
Oil Energy
Production Industry
Raw Material Production
Steel Industry

EXTRANATIONAL BLOC
S-02-0041 1975 00001
BT Agreement Type
NT Atlantic Community
Communist Bloc
Security Community
Third World Bloc
Western Bloc
RT Alliance
Common Market
Compact
Customs Union
Empire
Geopolitics
International Bloc
League Of Nations
Monetary Union
Multilateral State Agreement
Multipolar International Political System
National Region
Pan Africanism
Pan Arabism
Pan Islamism
Pan Slavism
Political Front
Popular Front
State Agreement Declaration
United Front
United Nations
World Alliance

EXTRANATIONAL COMMONWEALTH
S-16-0053 1975 00000
BT Extranational Government Structure
RT Empire
Extraparliamentary Politics
Former Colony
Global System
International Trusteeship
Western Bloc

EXTRANATIONAL GOVERNMENT STRUCTURE
S-16-0044 1975 00003
BT Government Type
NT Colony
Empire
Extranational Commonwealth
International Trusteeship
Mandate Territory
Protectorate
RT Foreign Rule
Indirect Rule
International Government
Military Occupation

EXTRAPARLIAMENTARY POLITICS
S-29-0200 1975 00000
BT Politics
RT Administrative Politics
Extranational Commonwealth
Parliament Cabinet Relations
Parliamentary Politics

EXTRATERRITORIAL DEVELOPMENT
S-31-0151 1975 00003
BT Political Change
NT Annexation
Colonization
Decolonization
Political Succession
Secession
RT Outer Space Law
Politicization

EXTREMISM
S-06-0100 1975 00001
BT Attitude Characteristics
NT Political Extremism
RT Aggressiveness
Alienation
Anticommunism
Authoritarian Attitude
Distrust
Dogmatism
Early Radical Thought
Extremist
Extremist Movement
McCarthyism
Militancy
Radicalism

EXTREMIST
S-32-0258 1975 00001
BT Spectrum Politicist
RT Conservative
Extremism
Leftist
Political Radical
Reactionary
Rightist

EXTREMIST MOVEMENT
S-27-0014 1975 00002
BT Ideological Spectrum Political Movement
NT Terrorist Movement
RT Extremism
Fascist Movement
Maoist Movement
Messianic Movement
Proletarian Movement
Radical Movement
Radical Student Movement
Revolutionary Movement

F RATIO
S-24-0057 1975 00000
SN Variance ratio calculated for the purpose of testing the viability of the null hypothesis.
BT Statistical Significance Test
RT Binomial Test
Chi Square Test
Interval Significance Test
Mann Whitney U Test
Nominal Significance Test
Ordinal Significance Test
Wald Wolfowitz Runs Test
Wilcoxian T Test

FABIAN SOCIALISM
S-38-0295 1975 00002
BT Evolutionary Socialism
RT Bernsteinian Socialism
Evolutionary Change
Socialist Democracy
Socialist Political Party

FACE TO FACE GROUP
S-03-0026 1975 00003
BT Social Group
NT Primary Group
RT Ethnic Group
Ethnic Policy
Group Cohesion
Group Consolidation
Group Theory
Interest Group
Kinship Group
Peer Group
Primary Group
Racial Group
Reference Group
Religious Cult
Religious Group
Small Group Behavior

FACE VALIDITY
S-24-0168 1975 00002
BT Validity Measurement
RT Construct Validity
Criterion Validity
Discriminant Validity

FACTIONALIST
S-32-0287 1975 00007
BT Separatist
RT Cleavage Process
Parliamentary Faction
Political Party Faction

FACTOR ANALYSIS
S-24-0046 1975 00021
BT Multivariate Analysis
RT Analysis Of Variance
Automatic Interaction Detection
Canonical Correlation Analysis
Cluster Analysis
Covariance Analysis
Dimensional Analysis

Discriminant Analysis
Factor Structure
Multiple Correlation Analysis
Multiple Regression Analysis
Partial Correlation Analysis
Path Analysis
Set Theory

FACTOR STRUCTURE
S-24-0207 1975 00005
BT Scale Construction Methodology
RT Cumulative Scale
Factor Analysis
Guttman Scale
Nominal Scale
Ordinal Scale
Ratio Scale
Scalability Index
Semantic Differential
Thurstone Scale
Unidimensional Scale

FACTORY
S-19-0177 1975 00005
BT Economic Institution
RT Automated Production
Blue Collar Worker
Business
Enterprise
Entrepreneur
Mixed Enterprise
Semiskilled Worker
Technician
Working Class
Working Conditions

FAIR EMPLOYMENT LAW
S-21-0038 1975 00005
BT Labor Law
RT Equal Employment Policy
Fair Employment Policy
Minimum Wage Law
Minimum Wage Policy
Pension Law
Right To Work Law

FAIR EMPLOYMENT POLICY
S-26-0201 1975 00004
BT Employment Policy
RT Admission Policy
Affirmative Action Employment Policy
Equal Employment Policy
Fair Employment Law
Manpower Policy

FAIR TRIAL
S-31-0518 1975 00003
BT Trial
RT Burden Of Proof
Evidence Admissibility
Justice Administration

FAIRNESS DOCTRINE
S-26-0029 1975 00001
BT Broadcast Access Policy
RT Broadcasting
Mass Communication
Mass Media Access Policy
Public Broadcasting Policy

FALANGISM
S-38-0226 1975 00000
SN Spanish fascist movement.
BT Fascist Theory
RT Authoritarian Regime
Corporate Fascism
Dictatorial Regime
Dictatorship
Falangist
Fascist Council
Fascist Movement
Flangist Political Party
Francoism
Italian Fascism
National Socialism
Neofascism
Oligarchic Government
One Political Party System
Peronism

FALANGIST
S-32-0274 1975 00000
BT Fascist
RT Corporate Fascism
Falangism
Fascist
Fascist Council
Fascist Movement
Fascist Theory
Francoism
National Socialist
National Socialist Political Party
Totalitarian Dictatorship
Totalitarian Political Party

FALSIFICATION
S-24-0142 1975 00002
BT Hypothesis Testing
RT Confirmation
Experimental Observation
Explanatory Research
Knowledge Production
Natural Experiment
Replication
Social Science Model
Sociology Of Science

FAMILY COURT
S-19-0130 1975 00001
BT Civil Court
RT Atomistic Family
Common Law Court
Housing Court

FAMILY DESCENT PATTERN
S-20-0002 1975 00018
BT Kinship
NT Bilateral Family Descent Pattern
Matrilineal Family Descent Pattern
Patrilineal Family Descent Pattern
RT Cultural History
Family Role
Family Socialization
Family Type
Kinship System
Marriage Type
Social Background

FAMILY FARM ECONOMY
S-12-0006 1975 00003
BT Farm Economy
RT Collective Farm Economy
Cooperative Farm Economy
Cottage Industry Economy
Plantation Economy
Self Sufficient Economy
Single Group Farm Economy
State Farm Economy

FAMILY INCOME
S-06-0327 1975 00020
BT Income
RT Corporate Income
Family Planning
Family Policy
Income Distribution
Income Measure
Personal Income
Profit Income
Tax Exempt Income
Unearned Income

FAMILY LAW
S-21-0087 1975 00010
UF Parent Responsibility
BT Social Law
RT Abortion Law
Divorce Law
Gambling Law
Marital Law
Miscegenation Law
Parental Authority
Polyandry

FAMILY PLANNING
S-31-0660 1975 00022
BT Population Planning
RT Abortion Law
Abortion Policy
Birth Control Policy
Ethnic Background
Extended Family
Family Income
Family Policy
Family Service
Family Type
Fertility Rate
Household Size
Malthusian Theory
Neighborhood Clinic
Parent
Polygamy
Population Policy
Service Policy
Zero Population Growth

FAMILY POLICY
S-26-0395 1975 00017
BT Population Policy
NT Family Subsidization Policy
RT Abortion Law
Abortion Policy
Divorce Law
Extended Family
Family Income
Family Planning
Family Political Socialization
Family Role
Family Service
Family Socialization
Family Type
Household Head
Housewife
Intermarriage
Marital Law
Monogamy
Parent
Parental Authority
Patrilineal Family

Service Policy

FAMILY POLITICAL SOCIALIZATION
S-34-0027 1975 00012
BT Family Socialization
RT Adolescent Political Socialization
Family Policy
Family Role
Kinship Group
Kinship Role

FAMILY ROLE
S-32-0035 1975 00065
UF Brother
Sister
BT Kinship Role
NT Child
Household Head
Housewife
Husband
Maternal Role
Parent
Paternal Role
Sibling
Wife
RT Clan Role
Family Descent Pattern
Family Policy
Family Political Socialization
Family Socialization
Family Type
Intragenerational Mobility
Marital Law
Marriage Contract
Matriarchal Family
Matriarchal Kinship System
Matrilineal Family Descent Pattern
Nuclear Family
Parental Authority
Patrilineal Family Descent Pattern
Polygamy
Sexism
Sibling
Single
Widow
Widower
Womens Studies

FAMILY SERVICE
S-26-0369 1979 00000
BT Social Service
RT Child Care Service
Community Service
Day Care Center
Family Planning
Family Policy
Service Industry Policy
Social Policy
Social Welfare Policy

FAMILY SOCIALIZATION
S-34-0026 1975 00030
BT Group Socialization
NT Family Political Socialization
RT Adolescent Socialization
Adult Socialization
Childhood Socialization
Cohort Group Socialization
Ethical Socialization
Family Descent Pattern
Family Policy
Family Role
Family Type
Kinship System
Matriarchal Family
Matriarchal Kinship System
Matrilineal Family Descent Pattern
Parental Authority
Peer Group
Peer Group Socialization
Primary Group Socialization
Role Differentiation
Sexism

FAMILY SUBSIDIZATION POLICY
S-26-0396 1975 00004
BT Family Policy
RT Birth Rate
Income Distribution

FAMILY TYPE
S-20-0006 1975 00063
BT Kinship
NT Atomistic Family
Communal Family
Concubinage
Extended Family
Kindred Family
Matriarchal Family
Nuclear Family
Paternalistic Family
Patrilineal Family
Stem Family
RT Divorce Law
Family Descent Pattern
Family Planning
Family Policy
Family Role
Family Socialization
Intragenerational Mobility
Kinship System
Marital Law
Sibling

FAR EAST STUDIES
USE Asian Area Studies

FARM COOPERATIVE
USE Agricultural Cooperative

FARM ECONOMY
S-12-0003 1975 00010
BT Agrarian Economy
NT Collective Farm Economy
Cooperative Farm Economy
Family Farm Economy
Plantation Economy
Single Group Farm Economy
State Farm Economy
RT Agrarian Movement
Agrarian Reform Policy
Agricultural Production
Agricultural Sector
Cottage Industry Economy
Craft Economy
Enterprise
Farm Income
Farm Industry
Farm Production
Farm Subsidy
Farmer
Farmer Union
Farming
Food Industry
Food Policy
Hunting And Trapping Economy
Labor Intensive Economy
Land Policy
Land Tenure System
Mixed Economy
Peasant Class
Peasant Cooperative
Peasant Economy
Rural Community
Seasonal Employment
Self Sufficient Economy
Subsistence Economy
Subsistence Farming
Tenant Farming
Underdeveloped Economy

FARM INCOME
S-06-0328 1975 00004
BT Income
RT Agrarian Reform Policy
Agricultural Price Support Policy
Business Income
Corporate Farm Economy
Corporate Income
Economic Aid Policy
Farm Economy
Farm Industry
Farm Production
Farmer Union
Farming
Income Measure
Land Policy
Price Support Policy
Profit Income
Unearned Income

FARM INDUSTRY
S-17-0033 1975 00006
BT Consumer Industry
RT Agricultural Occupation
Agricultural Policy
Agricultural Production
Agricultural Science
Agricultural Sector
Business
Clothing Industry
Corporate Farm Economy
Dairy Industry
Enterprise
Farm Economy
Farm Income
Farm Production
Farm Subsidy
Farming
Fishing Industry
Food Industry
Land Distribution
Land Policy
Land Pollution Policy
Land Tenure System
Market
Rural Development
Rural Policy Planning
Tenant Farming
Underdeveloped Economy

FARM PRODUCTION
S-31-0426 1975 00012
USE Agricultural Production
BT Agricultural Production
NT Farming
RT Agrarian Movement
Agrarian Reform Policy
Agricultural Cooperative

Corporate Farm Economy
Enterprise
Farm Economy
Farm Income
Farm Industry
Farm Subsidy
Farmer
International Commodity Market
Land Ownership Pattern
Land Policy
Production Agency
Seasonal Employment
Tenant Farmer

FARM SUBSIDY
S-06-0306 1975 00000
BT Government Expenditure
RT Agrarian Economy
Agrarian Reform Policy
Agrarianism
Agricultural Development
Agricultural Policy
Agricultural Price Support Policy
Dairy Industry
Development Fund
Farm Economy
Farm Industry
Farm Production
Farming
Government Agricultural Enterprise
Industrial Subsidy

FARM VOTER
S-32-0311 1975 00002
BT Voter
RT Agrarianism
Farmer
Rural Voter

FARMER
S-32-0065 1975 00010
UF Campesino
BT Agricultural Occupation
NT Collective Farmer
Private Farmer
Sharecropper
Tenant Farmer
RT Agrarian Democracy
Agrarianism
Agricultural Sector
Agricultural Worker
Agricultural Working Class
Farm Economy
Farm Production
Farm Voter
Farming
Migrant Population

FARMER UNION
S-03-0068 1975 00000
BT Union
RT Agrarian Democracy
Agrarian Movement
Agrarian Political Party
Agrarian Reform Movement
Agrarian Reform Policy
Agrarianism
Agricultural Sector
Agricultural Worker
Agricultural Working Class
Farm Economy
Farm Income
Peasant Organization

FARMING
S-31-0427 1975 00007
BT Farm Production
NT Collective Farming
Corporate Farm Economy
Migrant Farming
Subsistence Farming
Tenant Farming
RT Agrarian Economy
Agrarian Movement
Agricultural Agency
Agricultural Collectivization Policy
Agricultural History
Agricultural Occupation
Agricultural Policy
Agricultural Science
Agricultural Sector
Agricultural Worker
Agronomy
Animal Husbandry
Cooperative Farm Economy
Corporate Farm Economy
Farm Economy
Farm Income
Farm Industry
Farm Subsidy
Farmer
Government Agricultural Enterprise
Horticulture
National Production
Peasant Class
Private Rural Investment
Rural Environment

FASCIST
S-32-0273 1975 00001
BT System Politicist
NT Falangist
National Socialist
RT Falangist
Fascist Council
Fascist Economy
Fascist Education
Fascist Movement
Flangist Political Party
Imperialist

FASCIST COUNCIL
S-19-0234 1975 00000
BT Executive Government Institution
RT Absolutism
Anticommunism
Antisemitism
Falangism
Falangist
Fascist
Fascist Movement
Fascist Theory
Francoism
Military Executive Council
Oligarchic Government

FASCIST ECONOMY
S-12-0038 1979 00000
BT Corporate Economy
RT Absolutism
Autarchic Economy
Barter Economy
Centrally Planned Economy
Command Economy
Corporate State
Fascist
Fascist Political Party
Fascist Theory
Modernizing Economy
Nationalized Economy

FASCIST EDUCATION
S-13-0031 1979 00000
BT Political Education
RT Communist Education
Fascist
Fascist Movement
Ideological Education
Political Socialization

FASCIST MOVEMENT
S-27-0016 1975 00003
BT Ideological Spectrum Political Movement
RT Corporate Fascism
Extremist Movement
Falangism
Falangist
Fascist
Fascist Council
Fascist Education
Fascist Theory
Flangist Political Party
Francoism
National Socialism
National Socialist Political Party
Neofascism
Political Persecution
Populist Movement
Revolutionary Movement
Totalitarian Movement

FASCIST PARTY
1975-1979 00001

FASCIST POLITICAL PARTY
S-28-0016 1979 00000
BT Ideological Spectrum Political Party Type
NT Flangist Political Party
National Socialist Political Party
RT Fascist Economy

FASCIST THEORY
S-38-0224 1975 00003
BT Ideologies
NT Corporate Fascism
Falangism
Francoism
Italian Fascism
National Socialism
Neofascism
Peronism
RT Absolutism
Authoritarian Regime
Corporate State
Counterrevolution
Dictatorship
Elitism
Falangist
Fascist Council
Fascist Economy
Fascist Movement
Garrison State
Hegemonic One Party System
Mass Mobilization
Mass Society
Minority Persecution
National Socialist Political Party
One Political Party System

Paramilitary Forces
Totalitarian Dictatorship
Totalitarian Leadership

FATALISM
S-25-0005 1975 00004
BT Eschatology
RT Religious Thought

FATHER
S-32-0046 1975 00003
BT Paternal Role
RT Husband
Parent
Parental Authority
Paternal Role

FAVORITE SON CANDIDATE
S-32-0232 1975 00000
BT Presidential Candidate
RT Convention Delegate
Convention Delegate Selection
Dark Horse Candidate
Election Campaign
Election Turnout
Political Party Convention

FEDERAL CITY RELATIONS
S-31-0470 1979 00000
BT Intergovernmental Relations
RT Center Periphery Government Relations
City Government
City State Relations
Federal Government
Federal State Relations
Federalism
National Government
Police Community Relations

FEDERAL COMMISSION
S-19-0083 1975 00005
BT Commissions
NT Interstate Commerce Commission
RT Authorities
Commission Of Inquiry
Congressional Investigation Committee
Independent Regulatory Commission
International Planning Commission
Interstate Commerce
Interstate Commerce Commission
Legislative Commission
Municipal Authorities
Planning Commission
Presidential Commission
Public Authorities
Regulatory Commission

FEDERAL CONSTITUTION
S-21-0012 1975 00013
BT National Constitution
RT Constitutional Law
Constitutional Law System
Government Formation Process
New Federalism
Unitary Constitution

FEDERAL GOVERNMENT
S-16-0057 1975 00092
BT Government Type
NT Confederal Government
RT Consociational Democracy
Constitutional Democracy
Federal City Relations
Federal State Relations
Federal Taxation
Federated City
Federation Movement
Grant In Aid
Mixed Government
Multiethnic Nation
National Government
Republic
Unitary Government

FEDERAL GRANT IN AID
S-06-0316 1975 00026
UF Grant In Aid
BT Government Grant
RT Government Economic Planning
Government Loan
Industrial Subsidy

FEDERAL JUDICIAL SYSTEM
S-37-0084 1975 00012
BT National Judicial System
RT Constitutional Law
Justice Administration
National Judge
National Judicial Primary

FEDERAL RESERVE SYSTEM
S-37-0036 1975 00005
BT Financial System
RT Banking Policy
Central Banking System
Gold Reserve
Government Economic Planning
Intergovernmental Relations
International Banking System
National Banking System
Subnational Banking System

FEDERAL STATE RELATIONS
S-31-0471 1979 00000
BT Intergovernmental Relations
RT Center Periphery Government Relations
City State Relations
Federal City Relations
Federal Government
Federalism
National Government
Police Community Relations
State Government

FEDERAL STATE SEPARATION
S-30-0018 1975 00015
BT Separation Of Power
RT Federalism
Interstate Commerce
Judicial Power
Legislative Executive Separation

FEDERAL SYSTEM
1975-1979 00057
USE Federalism

FEDERAL TAXATION
S-26-0157 1975 00003
BT National Taxation
RT Federal Government
Gift Taxation
State Taxation
Subnational Taxation

FEDERALISM
S-37-0110 1979 00000
UF Federal System
BT Political System Type
NT Conflict Federalism
Cooperative Federalism
New Federalism
RT American Political Thought
Decentralized Government
Federal City Relations
Federal State Relations
Federal State Separation

FEDERATED CITY
S-07-0006 1975 00002
BT City
RT Central City
City
City Unit
Decentralized City
Federal Government
Metropolitan City
Metropolitan Government
Model City
Provincial Government
State Government
Urban Government

FEDERATION MOVEMENT
S-27-0009 1975 00002
BT Political Movement
RT Confederation Movement
Federal Government
Nationalist Movement

FEEDBACK LOOP
S-06-0571 1979 00000
BT Analytic System Characteristics
NT Communication Feedback
Learning Feedback
RT System Boundary
System Capacity
System Change
System Disequilibrium
System Function
System Inputs
System Outputs

FELON
USE Criminal

FEMALE CHAUVINISM
S-38-0237 1975 00000
BT Feminism
RT Chauvinist
Female Chauvinist
Female Voter
Ideological Struggle
Male Chauvinist
Sex Exploitation
Sex Inequality
Sex Role
Sexist
Womens Emancipation
Womens Liberation
Womens Liberation Movement
Womens Rights
Womens Studies

FEMALE CHAUVINIST
S-32-0209 1975 00000
BT Chauvinist
RT Female Chauvinism
Feminism
Male Chauvinist
Resistance
Sexist
Womens Liberation

FEMALE VOTER
S-32-0312 1975 00001
BT Voter
RT Female Chauvinism
Suffrage Equality
Suffrage Law
Suffragette
Womens Emancipation
Womens Liberation Movement

FEMININITY
S-06-0511 1979 00000
BT Personality Characteristics
RT Altruism
Ambivalence
Assertiveness
Charity
Courage
Creativity
Curiosity
Egocentrism
Empathy
Feminist Politics
Gregariousness
Honesty
Imagination
Masculinity
Optimism
Persistence
Sex Role
Womens Liberation Movement
Womens Studies

FEMINISM
S-38-0236 1975 00016
BT Sexism
NT Female Chauvinism
Womens Liberation
RT Employment Opportunity
Female Chauvinist
Identity Analysis
Identity Crisis
Male Chauvinism
Sex Inequality
Sex Persecution
Sex Role
Sexist
Social Movement
Suffrage Equality
Suffrage Law
Womens Emancipation
Womens Liberation Movement
Womens Rights
Womens Studies

FEMINIST POLITICS
S-29-0231 1979 00000
BT Sexual Politics
RT Femininity
Gay Politics
Group Politics
Power Politics
Protest Politics
Sex Role
Womens Liberation Movement
Womens Studies

FERTILITY RATE
S-06-0190 1975 00051
BT Demographic Profile
RT Birth Control Policy
Birth Rate
Demographic Indicator
Demographic Projection
Family Planning
Malthusian Theory

FEUDAL ECONOMIC STAGE
S-06-0161 1975 00003
BT Economic Development Stage
RT Agricultural Economic Stage
Cottage Industry
Economic System
Industrial Economic Stage
Pretakeoff Period

FEUDAL ECONOMIC SYSTEM
S-37-0033 1979 00000
UF Feudalist Economic System
BT Economic System
RT Dark Ages
Mercantile Economic System
Patron System

FEUDAL GOVERNMENT
S-16-0059 1975 00002
BT Government Type
RT Ancient Regime
Feudal Lord
Feudal Society
Feudal State

FEUDAL LORD
S-36-0078 1975 00002
BT Subnational Chief Government Executive
RT Aristocratic Class
Feudal Government
Feudal Society
Governor
Governor General
Local Chief Government Executive
Prefect
Prince

FEUDAL REACTION THEORY
S-38-0169 1975 00000
BT Revolution Theory
RT Class Analysis
Counterrevolution
Feudal Society
Feudal System
Rising Expectation Theory

FEUDAL SOCIETY
S-35-0018 1975 00010
BT Society Type Base
RT Aristocratic Class
Bourgeois Society
Capitalist Society
Feudal Government
Feudal Lord
Feudal Reaction Theory
Feudal State
Feudal System
Homogeneous Society
Medieval Corporatism
Nomadic Society
Peasant Class
Peasant Society
Preindustrial Society
Tribal Society

FEUDAL STATE
S-16-0164 1975 00003
BT State Type
RT Absolutism
Feudal Government
Feudal Society
Feudal System

FEUDAL SYSTEM
S-37-0114 1975 00014
BT Political System Type
RT Dark Ages
Feudal Reaction Theory
Feudal Society
Feudal State
Medieval Ages
Nobility
Traditional Political System

FEUDALIST ECONOMIC SYSTEM
1975-1979 00001
USE Feudal Economic System

FIELD DATA
S-18-0083 1979 00000
BT Statistical Data
RT Aggregate Data Analysis
Aggregate Data Statistics
Cross Cultural Data
Data Theory
Economic Statistics
Field Research
Field Theory
Political Statistics
Public Opinion Survey
Social Statistics
Survey Data
Thesis

FIELD RESEARCH
S-24-0077 1975 00027
BT Data Collection Methodology
RT Academic Imperialism
Academic Tenure Policy
Anthropological Theory
Anthropologist
Anthropology Discipline
Field Data
Nonreactive Observation
Questionnaire
Reactive Observation

FIELD THEORY
S-38-0583 1975 00001
BT Social Theory
RT Contemporary Analytic Modes
Experiment
Field Data
Role Theory
Social Action Theory
Social Learning Theory
Socialization Theory

FILIBUSTERING
S-31-0608 1975 00000
BT Congressional Procedure
RT Congressional Member
Congressional Procedure
Congressional Reform
Congressional System
Freedom Of Speech

FILM
USE Visual Arts

FILM CENSORSHIP AGENCY
1975-1979 00000
USE Censorship Agency

FINANCIAL ACCOUNTING
S-31-0692 1979 00000
UF Accountant
BT Policy Evaluation

RT Economic Planning
Education Planning
Fiscal Planning
Fiscal Process
Monetary Management
Monetary Process
National Policy Planning

FINANCIAL AID
S-06-0309 1975 00014
BT Foreign Aid
RT Bilateral Aid
Industrial Subsidy

FINANCIAL ELITE
S-14-0008 1979 00000
BT Business Elite
RT Bureaucratic Elite
Commercial Elite
Corporate Elite
Decision Making Elite
Financial System
Financier
Governing Elite
Managerial Elite
Policy Elite

FINANCIAL MARKET
S-19-0188 1975 00017
BT Market
NT Foreign Capital Market
RT Commodity Market
Consumer Market
Differentiated Market
Domestic Market
Export Market
Financial System
Financing
Gold Reserve
Marketplace
National Market
Prosperity
Stock Market
World Market

FINANCIAL RECORD
S-18-0011 1975 00007
BT Documents
NT Budget Record
Expenditure Record
Income Record
Political Party Financial Record
Revenue Record
RT Budget
Budget Deficit
Budget Discrepancy
Government Document

FINANCIAL SYSTEM
S-37-0034 1975 00013
BT Economic System
NT Central Banking System
Federal Reserve System
International Banking System
National Banking System
Subnational Banking System
RT Economic Sector
Financial Elite
Financial Market
Monetary System
Public Finance Policy

FINANCIER
S-32-0075 1975 00003
BT Commercial Occupation
NT Investor
RT Businessman
Economic Elite
Entrepreneur
Entrepreneurship
Financial Elite
Financing
Investor
Public Finance Policy
Speculator

FINANCING
S-31-0389 1975 00027
BT Economic Resource Allocation
NT Investment
RT Budget
Entrepreneur Class
Financial Market
Financier
Fiscal Process
Government Expropriation
Monetary Management
Monetary Policy
Money
Prime Loan Rate
Private Sector
Public Debt Policy
Public Saving
Saving
Speculator
Spending

FINE ARTS
S-01-0124 1979 00000
BT Humanities Discipline
NT Graphic Arts
Plastic Arts
Visual Arts
RT Aesthetics
Anthropology Discipline
Art History
Cultural History
Graphic Arts
Humanities Discipline
Literature Studies
Philosophy Discipline
Plastic Arts
Visual Arts

FINING
S-31-0502 1975 00000
BT Sentencing
RT Jailing
Probation

FIRE DISTRICT
S-16-0092 1975 00002
BT District Government Type
RT Recreation District
School District
Sewer District
Transportation District
Water District
Zoning District

FIRE INSURANCE
S-26-0303 1979 00000
BT Insurance
RT Accident Insurance
Catastrophe Insurance
Compulsory Insurance
Life Insurance
Malpractice Insurance
National Health Insurance
No Fault Insurance
Unemployment Insurance Policy

FIRST NUCLEAR STRIKE WEAPON
1975-1979 00001
USE First Strike Nuclear Weapon

FIRST STRIKE CAPABILITY
S-06-0464 1975 00005
BT Nuclear Capability
RT First Strike Nuclear Weapon
First Strike Policy
Global War Policy
Offensive Nuclear Capability
Second Strike Capability

FIRST STRIKE NUCLEAR WEAPON
S-33-0036 1979 00000
UF First Nuclear Strike Weapon
BT Nuclear Weapon
RT First Strike Capability
First Strike Policy
Missile
Second Strike Nuclear Weapon

FIRST STRIKE POLICY
S-26-0071 1975 00001
BT Nuclear Strike Policy
RT Aggressor State
First Strike Capability
First Strike Nuclear Weapon
Preemptive Attack Policy
Preventive Attack Policy
Second Strike Policy

FISCAL AGENCY
S-19-0021 1975 00004
BT Economic Agency
NT Appropriation Agency
Budget Agency
Monetary Agency
Public Treasury
Revenue Agency
Tax Agency
RT Business Agency
Business Regulation Agency
Economic Advisory Board
Economic Control Agency
Economic Council
Government Economic Planning
Planning Commission
Presidential Commission
Price Control Agency
Price Support Agency

FISCAL INSTITUTION
S-19-0178 1979 00000
BT Economic Institution
RT Business
Corporation
Enterprise
Institutional History
Market
Monetary Institution
Public Finance Policy
Public Finance Theory
World Bank

FISCAL MANAGEMENT
S-23-0014 1975 00019
BT Economic Management
RT Administrative Policy Making
Budget

Business Management
Central Economic Management
Development Management
Fiscal Theory
Zero Based Budget

FISCAL PLANNER
S-32-0131 1975 00001
BT Economic Planner
NT Budget Planner
RT Fiscal Planning
Government Economic Management
Government Economic Planning
Subnational Planner

FISCAL PLANNING
S-31-0647 1975 00010
BT Economic Planning
RT Budget
Central Economic Planning
Financial Accounting
Fiscal Planner
Fiscal Policy
Fiscal Process
Fiscal Theory
Long Range Planning
National Economic Planning
Short Range Planning

FISCAL POLICY
S-26-0092 1975 00045
BT Economic Policy
NT Antiinflation Policy
Budget Policy
Capital Formation Policy
Capital Investment Policy
Deflation Policy
Expenditure Policy
Income Policy
RT Budget Planner
Cost Of Living Index
Currency Revaluation Policy
Debt Ceiling Policy
Deflation
Development Policy
Economic Growth Policy
Economic Recession
Economic Subsidization Policy
Fiscal Planning
Fiscal Process
Fiscal Theory
Government Economic Management
Government Economic Planning
Inflation
Investment Policy
Keynesian Economic Theory
Price Support Policy
Private Saving
Public Finance Policy

FISCAL PROCESS
S-31-0420 1975 00019
BT Economic Process
NT Monetary Process
Subsidization Process
RT Allocation Process
Financial Accounting
Financing
Fiscal Planning
Fiscal Policy
Government Borrowing
Saving
Subsidization Process

FISCAL THEORY
S-38-0113 1979 00000
BT Economic Theory
RT Budget Policy
Economic Growth Theory
Economic Stabilization Theory
Fiscal Management
Fiscal Planning
Fiscal Policy
Government Economic Planning
Monetary Economic Theory
National Economic Management
Public Finance Theory
Taxation Policy

FISH AND WILDLIFE POLICY
S-26-0220 1975 00003
BT Natural Resource Policy
RT Ecology Movement
Fishing Industry
Forest Land Policy
Grazing Land Policy
Water Use Policy

FISHING INDUSTRY
S-17-0034 1975 00019
BT Consumer Industry
RT Dairy Industry
Farm Industry
Fish And Wildlife Policy
Food Industry

FIVE YEAR ECONOMIC PLANNING
S-31-0645 1975 00009
BT Government Economic Planning
RT Democratic Economic Planning
Socialist Economic Planning

FIXED ASSETS
S-06-0262 1979 00000
BT Assets
RT Accumulated Capital
Capital
Disposable Income
Fixed Income
Investment Policy
Machinery Industry
Net Income
Personal Income
Wealth Distribution

FIXED INCOME
S-06-0334 1975 00000
BT Income Measure
RT Average Income
Disposable Income
Fixed Assets
Median Income
Net Income
Personal Income

FIXED SUM GAMING
S-24-0099 1975 00000
SN Gaming context in which rewards and costs are given and static.
BT Gaming
RT N Person Gaming
Nonzero Sum Gaming
Prisoner Dilemma Gaming
Prisoner Dilemma Theory
Two Person Game Theory
Two Person Gaming
Variable Sum Gaming
Zero Sum Gaming

FLANGIST POLITICAL PARTY
S-28-0017 1979 00000
BT Fascist Political Party
RT Authoritarian Political Party
Falangism
Fascist
Fascist Movement
Francoism
Ideological Political Party
Neofascism
Totalitarian Political Party

FLOATING VOTER
S-32-0313 1975 00008
SN Voter who shifts support from one party to another in response to changing issues and candidates.
BT Voter
RT Floating Voting
Independent Voter

FLOATING VOTING
S-29-0125 1975 00005
BT Voting
RT Floating Voter
Independent Voting
Marginal Voter
Protest Voting

FLOOR LEADER
S-36-0157 1975 00001
BT Legislative Leader
RT Leader Of Opposition
Legislative Speaker
Legislative Whip
Majority Leader
Minority Leader
National Legislative Leader
National Legislative Speaker
Ranking Minority Member
Subnational Legislative Leader

FOLK LITERATURE
S-18-0045 1979 00000
BT Information Sources
RT Anthropology Discipline
Cultural Anthropology
Essay
Folkways
Humanistic Education
Humanities Discipline
Oral History

FOLKWAYS
S-06-0385 1975 00020
BT Identity Characteristics
RT Anthropological Theory
Anthropology Discipline
Blue Law
Folk Literature
Matrilineal Family Descent Pattern
Monogamy
Myth Analysis
Ritual
Taboo
Traditional Culture
Witchcraft

FOOD INDUSTRY
S-17-0048 1975 00071
BT Industry
RT Agricultural Advisory Board
Agricultural Production
Consumer Industry
Consumerism
Dairy Industry

Farm Economy
Farm Industry
Fishing Industry
Food Policy
Food Scarcity

FOOD POLICY
S-26-0009 1979 00000
BT Agricultural Policy
RT Agricultural Advisory Board
Agricultural Development
Agricultural Production
Agricultural Subsidization Policy
Business Credit Policy
Business Policy
Consumerism
Dairy Industry
Farm Economy
Food Industry
Food Scarcity
Forced Requisitioning
Soil Bank Policy

FOOD SCARCITY
S-31-0112 1979 00000
BT Scarcity
NT Hunger
Malnutrition
Starvation
RT Agricultural Development
Energy Scarcity
Food Industry
Food Policy
Labor Scarcity
Natural Resource Exploitation
Resource Allocation
Resource Distribution
Water Scarcity

FORCED REQUISITIONING
S-26-0010 1979 00000
BT Agricultural Policy
RT Agricultural Collectivization Policy
Agricultural Policy
Authoritarian Regime
Autocratic Government
Central Economic Management
Central Economic Planning
Food Policy
National Economic Planning
Totalitarian Political System

FORECASTING METHODOLOGY
S-24-0010 1979 00000
UF Futurible
BT Analysis Methodology
NT Authority Forecasting
Brainstorming
Delphi Technique
Divergence Mapping
Economic Forecasting
Political Forecasting
Scenario Construction
Social Forecasting
Trend Analysis
RT Causal Analysis
Contingency Theory
Experimental Research
Long Range Planning
Policy Evaluation Research
Policy Research
Predictive Research
Problem Solving Behavior
Quantitative Research
Research And Development

FOREIGN AFFAIRS AGENCY
S-19-0042 1975 00009
BT Agencies
NT Foreign Policy Advisory Board
RT Arms Control Agency
Government Employee
Information Agency
Intelligence Agency
Military Agency
Spying

FOREIGN AID
S-06-0307 1975 00037
BT Government Expenditure
NT Bilateral Aid
Financial Aid
Multilateral Aid
RT Bilateral Treaty
Foreign Aid Policy
Foreign Assistance
Foreign Policy
Government Loan
Grants Economy

FOREIGN AID POLICY
S-26-0255 1975 00033
BT Foreign Policy
NT Bilateral Aid Policy
Economic Aid Policy
Military Aid Policy
Multilateral Aid Policy
Technical Aid Policy
Unilateral Aid Policy
RT Containment Policy
Foreign Aid
Government Grant
Government Loan
Military Assistance

FOREIGN ASSISTANCE
S-06-0311 1975 00027
BT Government Expenditure
NT Military Assistance
Technical Assistance
Training Assistance
RT Foreign Aid
Foreign Policy
Government Grant
Government Loan

FOREIGN CAPITAL
S-06-0264 1975 00010
BT Capital
RT Assets
Foreign Capital Market
Foreign Investor
Foreign Subsidiary
Foreign Worker
Investment Capital

FOREIGN CAPITAL MARKET
S-19-0189 1975 00002
BT Financial Market
RT Commercial Attache
Foreign Capital
Foreign Investor
International Capital Movement

FOREIGN COMPETITION
S-31-0204 1975 00006
BT Competition
RT Economic Agitation
Economic Competition
Foreign Investor
Foreign Ownership

FOREIGN INCOME
S-06-0329 1975 00000
BT Income
RT Business Income
Corporate Income
Foreign Investor
Foreign Ownership
National Income
Profit Income
Trade
Unearned Income

FOREIGN INFORMATION AGENCY
S-19-0050 1975 00001
BT Information Agency
RT Communication Industry
Communication Policy
Communication Process
Foreign Information Policy
Foreign Policy Advisory Board
Informal Power
Intelligence Agency
Intergovernmental Document

FOREIGN INFORMATION POLICY
S-26-0291 1975 00007
BT Information Policy
RT Domestic Information Policy
Foreign Information Agency
Intelligence Agency
Propaganda Policy

FOREIGN INTERGOVERNMENTAL DOCUMENT
S-18-0027 1975 00001
BT Intergovernmental Document
NT Trade Document
Treaty Document
RT Domestic Intergovernmental Document
International Organization Record

FOREIGN INVESTOR
S-32-0077 1975 00006
BT Investor
RT Foreign Capital
Foreign Capital Market
Foreign Competition
Foreign Income
Foreign Ownership
Foreign Trade Pattern

FOREIGN LANGUAGE EDUCATION
S-13-0008 1979 00000
BT Education Type
RT Civic Education
Global Education
Humanities Discipline
Humanities Education
International Relations Studies
Language Studies
Linguistics

FOREIGN MARKET
1975-1979 00011

FOREIGN MINISTER
S-36-0132 1975 00003
BT Diplomat
RT Diplomacy
Embassy Official
Foreign Service Officer

FOREIGN OWNERSHIP
S-37-0053 1975 00008
BT Property Ownership System
RT Absentee Landlord System
Foreign Competition
Foreign Income
Foreign Investor
Foreign Subsidiary
Government Ownership
Private Ownership

FOREIGN POLICY
S-26-0251 1975 00532
BT Policy
NT Brinkmanship
Containment Policy
Expansionist Policy
Foreign Aid Policy
Intervention Policy
Open Door Policy
RT Agreement Type
Appeasement
Foreign Aid
Foreign Assistance
Foreign Policy Advisory Board
Foreign Policy Theory
International Organization Policy
International Policy
Isolationism
New International Economic Order
Realpolitik
Statecraft Theory
Strategic Policy
Treaty Document
World Politics

FOREIGN POLICY ADVISORY BOARD
S-19-0043 1975 00000
BT Foreign Affairs Agency
RT Foreign Information Agency
Foreign Policy
Foreign Policy Planner
Informal Power

FOREIGN POLICY ELITE
S-14-0026 1975 00035
BT Policy Elite
RT Attentive Public
Decision Making Elite
Elite Analysis
Foreign Policy Making
Foreign Policy Planner
Foreign Policy Theory
Opinion Elite

FOREIGN POLICY MAKING
S-31-0680 1975 00116
BT Policy Making Process
RT Foreign Policy Elite
Foreign Policy Planner
Foreign Policy Theory
Global War Policy
Idealist Foreign Policy
International Conflict
International Policy Making
National Policy Making
Protective Alliance
State Agreement Type

FOREIGN POLICY PLANNER
S-32-0137 1975 00007
BT Government Planner
RT Foreign Policy Advisory Board
Foreign Policy Elite
Foreign Policy Making
Idealist Foreign Policy
Intelligence Agency
International Planner
National Planner

FOREIGN POLICY THEORY
S-38-0344 1975 00123
BT International Political Theory
NT Idealist Foreign Policy
Realist Foreign Policy
RT Deterrence Theory
Foreign Policy
Foreign Policy Elite
Foreign Policy Making
Geopolitical Theory
Idealist Foreign Policy
International Alliance Theory
International Conflict Resolution Theory
International Decision Making Theory
International Field Theory
International Influence Theory
International Integration Theory
International Law Theory
International Organization Theory

FOREIGN RULE
S-16-0145 1975 00003
BT Rule Type
RT Divided Nation
Extranational Government Structure
Foreign Subsidiary
Imperialism
Imperialism System
Treaty Document

FOREIGN SERVICE OFFICER
S-36-0133 1975 00003
BT Diplomat
RT Ambassador
Commercial Attache
Embassy Official
Foreign Minister
Scientific Attache

FOREIGN STUDENT
S-32-0344 1979 00000
BT Student
RT Braindrain
Cross Cultural Analysis
Education Agreement
Education Exchange Treaty
Education Policy
International Exchange Program

FOREIGN SUBSIDIARY
S-19-0168 1975 00002
BT International Corporation
RT Foreign Capital
Foreign Ownership
Foreign Rule
Government Economic Planning
Holding Company

FOREIGN TRADE
S-31-0385 1975 00026
BT Trade
RT Customs Union
East West Trade
Foreign Trade Pattern
Gold Reserve
International Commerce
International Economic Interdependence
International Trade
Prosperity
Protective Tariff
World Commerce

FOREIGN TRADE PATTERN
S-06-0349 1975 00033
BT International Economic Characteristics
RT Balance Of Payments
Balance Of Trade
Foreign Investor
Foreign Trade
Import Export Ratio
Import Quota

FOREIGN WORKER
S-32-0079 1975 00003
BT Occupational Role
RT Agricultural Occupation
Foreign Capital
Industrial Occupation
Industrial Worker

FOREMAN
S-32-0085 1975 00000
BT Industrial Supervisor
RT Unionized Working Class

FOREST LAND POLICY
S-26-0221 1975 00004
BT Natural Resource Policy
RT Ecology Movement
Energy Use Policy
Fish And Wildlife Policy
Forestry Industry
Grazing Land Policy
Water Use Policy

FORESTRY INDUSTRY
S-17-0043 1975 00004
BT Extractive Industry
NT Lumber Industry
RT Forest Land Policy
Oil Industry
Ore Industry

FORMAL AUTHORITY
S-04-0016 1975 00003
BT Authority Structure
RT Authority Type
Centralized Authority
Constitution
Constitution Amendment Process
Decentralized Authority
Diffuse Authority
Hierarchical Authority
Independent Authority
Integrated Authority
Legal Rational Authority

FORMAL COMPETITION
S-31-0205 1975 00000
BT Competition
RT Direct Competition
Perfect Competition
Trade

FORMAL POLITICAL PARTY LEADER
S-32-0152 1975 00000
BT Political Party Leader
RT Backbencher
Campaign Manager
Frontbencher
Opposition Political Party Leader
Politburo Member
Political Boss
Political Candidate

Political Party Cadre
Political Party Chief
Political Party Professional
Political Party Whip
Ward Chairperson

FORMAL POLITICAL THEORY
S-38-0126 1975 00005
BT Explanatory Political Theory
NT Bargaining Theory
Coalition Theory
Economic Model
Exchange Theory
Game Theory
Mathematical Political Theory
Rational Model
Set Theory
RT Contemporary Analytic Modes
Data Theory
Formalization
Mathematical Analysis
Scientific Theory
Structural Functional Political Theory
Theoretical Range

FORMAL POWER
S-30-0008 1975 00001
BT Power Type
NT Institutional Power
RT Concentrated Power
Dispersed Power
Economic Power
Informal Power
Institutional Power
Political Power
Power Elite
Power Of The Purse
Power Theory
State Power

FORMALIZATION
S-31-0008 1975 00000
BT Analytic Process
RT Classification
Classification Process
Formal Political Theory
Mathematical Analysis
Typologizing

FORMATIVE EVALUATION
S-31-0693 1975 00010
SN Evaluation of a program with the aim of improving its performance.
BT Policy Evaluation
RT Education Evaluation
Evaluating
Management Information System
Normative Evaluation
Research Evaluation
Social Accounting
Summative Evaluation

FORMER COLONY
S-16-0046 1975 00017
BT Colony
RT Decolonization
Extranational Commonwealth
International Trusteeship
Mandate Territory
Neocolonialism
Proprietary Colony
Protectorate
Third World Nation

FOURTH WORLD NATION
S-16-0122 1979 00000
BT Nation Type
RT Aligned Nation
Client Nation
Client State
Dependent Nation
International Relations Studies
New International Economic Order
Nonaligned Nation
North South Conflict
Poor Nation
Power Theory
Scarcity
Third World Bloc
Third World Nation
United Nations

FRAGMENTATION
S-31-0792 1975 00016
BT Structural Process
NT Anomic Process
Political Fragmentation
Social Fragmentation
RT Alienation Process
Anarchy
Balkanization
Cleavage Process
Decay
Fragmented Political Culture
Integration
Vertical Cleavage

FRAGMENTED POLITICAL CULTURE
S-11-0035 1975 00006
SN Political system in which dissensus and cleavage predominate.
BT National Political Culture
RT Civic Culture
Cultural Cleavage
Fragmentation
Generational Political Culture
Modern Political Culture
Political Fragmentation
Popular Culture
Secular Political Culture
Traditional Political Culture

FRANCOISM
S-38-0227 1975 00001
BT Fascist Theory
RT Authoritarian Regime
Corporate Fascism
Dictatorial Regime
Dictatorship
Falangism
Falangist
Fascist Council
Fascist Movement
Flangist Political Party
Hegemonic One Party System
Italian Fascism
National Socialism
Neofascism
Oligarchic Government
One Political Party System
Peronism
Totalitarian Dictatorship
Totalitarian Leadership
Totalitarian Movement
Totalitarian Political System

FRATERNAL ORGANIZATION
S-03-0045 1975 00002
BT Organizations
RT Civic Organization
Cultural Organization
Ethnic Organization
Freemasonry
Interest Group
Peasant Organization
Secret Society
Social Group

FRATERNITY THEORY
S-38-0437 1975 00002
BT Community Philosophical Concept
RT Egalitarianism
French Revolutionary Thought
General Will Theory

FRAUD
S-10-0020 1975 00003
BT Economic Crime
RT Blackmail
Economic Bribery
Election Fraud
Extortion
Perjury
Political Fraud
Robbery
Tax Evasion
Vote Fraud
White Collar Crime

FREE ENTERPRISE SYSTEM
S-37-0040 1979 00000
BT Economic System
RT Capitalism
Capitalism Theory
Denationalization Process
Economic Freedom
Economic Freedom Theory
Government Deregulation
Individualism Model
Market Economy
Market Freedom
Market System
Private Ownership

FREE MARKET
S-19-0190 1975 00005
BT Market
RT Black Market
Common Market
Decontrol Process
Denationalization Process
Differentiated Market
Domestic Market
Export Market
Free Trade Sector
Internal Competition
Laissez Faire Theory
Marketplace
Mass Market
National Market
Stock Market
World Market

FREE MASONRY
S-38-0232 1975 00000
BT Ideologies
RT Freedom Of Speech
Religious Authority
Religious Movement
Religious Organization

FREE TRADE POLICY
S-26-0182 1975 00004
BT Trade Policy
RT Customs Union
European Integration Theory
Export Subsidization Policy
Free Trade Sector
Laissez Faire Liberalism
Laissez Faire Theory
Most Favored Nation Policy

FREE TRADE SECTOR
S-37-0029 1975 00002
BT Commercial Sector
RT Free Market
Free Trade Policy

FREEDOM
S-15-0001 1975 00010
NT Economic Freedom
Freedom Of Inquiry
Human Rights
Immunity
Political Liberty
RT Civil Liberty
Classical Corporate Freedom Theory
Classical Liberalism
Classical Natural Right Doctrine
Emancipation
Enlightenment Liberalism
Enlightenment Thought
Freedom And Necessity Doctrine
Freedom Theory
Liberal Political Party
Liberal Political Thought
Liberalism
Libertarianism
Liberty Theory
Moral Freedom Theory
Negative Freedom Theory
Nineteenth Century Liberalism
Political Freedom Theory
Political Opportunity Structure
Political Repression
Positive Freedom Theory
Psychological Freedom Theory
Rights Of Man Doctrine
Rousseauian Analysis
Theory
Tyrannicide
Womens Emancipation

FREEDOM AND NECESSITY DOCTRINE
S-38-0459 1975 00001
BT Freedom Theory
RT Freedom
Individual Freedom Theory

FREEDOM OF ASSOCIATION
S-15-0028 1975 00002
BT Civil Liberty
RT Civil Rights
Freedom Of Competition
Freedom Of Information
Freedom Of Inquiry
Freedom Of Press
Freedom Of Religion
Freedom Of Speech
Freedom Of Thought
Freedom Of Travel
Interest Group Politics
Procedural Rights
Right Of Assembly
Right Of Opposition
Right Of Petition
Right Of Privacy
Voting Rights

FREEDOM OF COMPETITION
S-15-0003 1975 00000
BT Economic Freedom
NT Market Freedom
RT Economic Liberalism
Freedom Of Association
Freedom Of Contract
Freedom Of Information
Freedom Of Inquiry
Internal Competition
Property Rights
Right To Job Security
Social Rights

FREEDOM OF CONTRACT
S-15-0005 1975 00002
BT Economic Freedom
NT Right To Strike
Right To Work
RT Freedom Of Competition
Labor Law
Property Rights
Social Rights

FREEDOM OF INFORMATION
S-15-0012 1975 00012
BT Freedom Of Inquiry
RT Academic Freedom
Freedom Of Association
Freedom Of Competition
Freedom Of Inquiry
Freedom Of Press
Freedom Of Religion
Freedom Of Speech
Human Rights
Information Sources
Liberty Theory
Scientific Freedom
Sunshine Law

FREEDOM OF INQUIRY
S-15-0010 1975 00005
BT Freedom
NT Academic Freedom
Freedom Of Information
Scientific Freedom
RT Civil Liberty
Freedom Of Association
Freedom Of Competition
Freedom Of Information
Freedom Of Press
Freedom Of Religion
Freedom Of Speech
Human Rights
Individualism Theory
Liberty Theory
Political Liberty
Social Rights

FREEDOM OF PRESS
S-15-0029 1975 00009
BT Civil Liberty
RT Academic Freedom
Civil Rights
Freedom Of Association
Freedom Of Information
Freedom Of Inquiry
Freedom Of Religion
Freedom Of Speech
Freedom Of Travel
Prime Time Access Policy
Procedural Rights
Right Of Assembly
Right Of Opposition
Right Of Petition
Right Of Privacy
Right Of Protest

FREEDOM OF RELIGION
S-15-0030 1975 00007
BT Civil Liberty
RT Church State Policy
Civil Religion
Civil Rights
Freedom Of Association
Freedom Of Information
Freedom Of Inquiry
Freedom Of Press
Freedom Of Speech
Freedom Of Travel
Human Rights
Liberty Theory
Procedural Rights
Religious Authority
Religious History
Right Of Assembly
Right Of Opposition
Right Of Petition
Right Of Privacy
School Prayer Policy

FREEDOM OF SPEECH
S-15-0031 1975 00017
BT Civil Liberty
RT Academic Freedom
Civil Rights
Commission Of Inquiry
Congressional Investigation Committee
Filibustering
Free Masonry
Freedom Of Association
Freedom Of Information
Freedom Of Inquiry
Freedom Of Press
Freedom Of Religion
Freedom Of Travel
Music Censorship
Political Tolerance
Prime Time Access Policy
Procedural Rights
Right Of Assembly
Right Of Opposition
Right Of Petition
Right Of Privacy
Right To Strike
School Prayer Policy
Sedition Law
Underground Political Party
Voting Rights
Wiretap Evidence Admissibility
Wiretapping Policy

FREEDOM OF THOUGHT
S-15-0032 1979 00000
BT Civil Liberty
RT Freedom Of Association

FREEDOM OF TRAVEL
S-15-0033 1975 00000
BT Civil Liberty
RT Civil Rights
Freedom Of Association
Freedom Of Press
Freedom Of Religion
Freedom Of Speech
Procedural Rights
Right Of Assembly
Right Of Opposition
Right Of Petition
Right Of Privacy

FREEDOM THEORY
S-38-0456 1975 00016
BT Political Philosophy Concept
NT Classical Corporate Freedom Theory
Economic Freedom Theory
Freedom And Necessity Doctrine
Individual Freedom Theory
Moral Freedom Theory
Negative Freedom Theory
Political Freedom Theory
Positive Freedom Theory
Psychological Freedom Theory
RT Economic Freedom
Freedom
Individualism Theory
Liberty Theory
Moral Choice
Moral Responsibility
Voluntarism

FREEMASONRY
S-35-0034 1979 00000
BT Secret Society
RT Fraternal Organization
Voluntary Association

FRENCH REVOLUTIONARY THOUGHT
S-38-0402 1975 00004
BT Enlightenment Thought
NT Jacobinism
RT Anticlericalism
Encyclopedist Thought
Equality Theory
Fraternity Theory

FREQUENCY TABLE
S-24-0139 1975 00002
BT Table
RT Aggregate Data Statistics
Scatter Plot

FREUDIAN PSYCHOLOGY
S-01-0173 1975 00008
BT Psychology Discipline
RT Behavioral Psychology
Gestalt Psychology
Ideographic Science
Jungian Theory
Learning Psychology
Logic
Parapsychology
Pathological Behavior
Personality Theory
Political Philosophy Studies
Political Psychology
Political Science Methodology Studies
Psychoanalysis
Psychological Anthropology
Psychology Discipline
Psychopathology
Sexual Behavior
Social Pathology
Social Psychology

FREUDIAN THEORY
S-38-0537 1975 00008
BT Psychological Theory
RT Alienation Psychological Theory
Attitude Change Theory
Cross Pressure Theory
Frustration Aggression Theory
Gestalt Theory
Identity Theory
Jungian Theory
Learning Theory
Motivation Theory
Pathological Behavior
Personality Theory
Psychological Behavioralism
Psychological Behaviorism
Psychopolitical Theory
Sexual Behavior

FRIENDSHIP
S-31-0756 1979 00000
BT Social Interaction
RT Empathy
Interpersonal Cooperation
Social Role Process
Social Stratification Formation
Social Stratification Maintenance
Trust

FRIENDSHIP AGREEMENT
S-02-0082 1975 00000
BT State Agreement Type
NT Friendship Treaty
RT Arms Control Agreement
Cultural Agreement
Detente
Education Agreement
Nonaggression Agreement
Peace
Peace Proposal

FRIENDSHIP TREATY
S-02-0083 1975 00001
BT Friendship Agreement
RT Cultural Exchange Agreement
Education Exchange Agreement
Nonaggression Treaty
Treaty Document

FRONTBENCHER
S-32-0153 1975 00000
BT Political Party Leader
RT Backbencher
Formal Political Party Leader
Parliamentary Leader
Parliamentary Member
Political Boss
Political Party Cadre
Political Party Chief
Political Party Professional
Political Party Whip

FRONTIER THEORY
S-38-0349 1975 00006
BT Geopolitical Theory
RT Buffer Zone Theory
Heartland Theory
Immigration Policy
Political Geography

FRUSTRATION AGGRESSION THEORY
S-38-0538 1975 00006
BT Psychological Theory
RT Achievement Theory
Alienation Psychological Theory
Cross Pressure Theory
Freudian Theory
Motivation Theory
Relative Deprivation Theory

FRUSTRATION SCALE
S-24-0235 1975 00003
BT Scale Type
RT Aggression Scale
Alienation Scale
Anomie Scale
Cynicism Scale
Dogmatism Scale
Efficacy Scale
Liberalism Conservatism Scale
Optimism Pessimism Scale
Satisfaction Scale
Social Frustration Scale
Voting Duty Scale

FUEL TECHNOLOGY
USE Energy Policy

FUEL UTILITY INDUSTRY
1975-1979 00015
USE Gas Industry

FULL EMPLOYMENT
S-06-0647 1975 00020
BT Employment Characteristics
RT Full Employment Policy
Government Economic Planning
Labor Force
Labor Market
Labor Supply
Labor Surplus
Overemployment
Structural Unemployment
Technological Unemployment
Underemployment
Unemployment

FULL EMPLOYMENT POLICY
S-26-0202 1975 00020
BT Employment Policy
RT Full Employment
Government Economic Management
Government Economic Planning
Manpower Policy
Public Works Policy
Unemployment Policy

FUNCTIONAL ADAPTATION
S-06-0581 1975 00008
BT System Adaptation
RT Adaptive Behavior
Communication Feedback
Functional Equivalent
Latent Function
Learning Feedback
Manifest Function
Social System
System Analysis
System Function

FUNCTIONAL DIFFERENTIATED SYSTEM
S-37-0008 1975 00007
BT Differentiated System
RT Functional Equivalent
Structural Differentiated System

FUNCTIONAL EQUIVALENT
S-24-0255 1975 00005
BT Conceptual Equivalence
RT Analytic System Characteristics
Functional Adaptation
Functional Differentiated System
Functional Integration
Indicator
Multiple Operationalization

FUNCTIONAL INTEGRATION
S-31-0812 1975 00004
BT Integration
RT Cultural Integration
Ethnic Integration
Functional Equivalent
Horizontal Integration
Linguistic Integration
Polarization
Policy Development
Racial Integration
Social Mobilization
Vertical Integration

FUNCTIONAL REPRESENTATION
S-31-0718 1975 00001
BT Representation Type
RT At Large Representation
District Representation
Functional Representation Theory
Geographic Representation
Indirect Representation
Interest Group Representation
Minority Group Representation
Multiple Member District Representation
Multiple Member Districting
Proportional Representation
Single Member District Representation

FUNCTIONAL REPRESENTATION THEORY
S-38-0504 1975 00000
BT Representation Theory
RT Corporate State
Functional Representation
Medieval Corporatism
Representation

FUNCTIONAL REQUISITE
1975-1979 00003

FUNCTIONAL REQUISITES
S-06-0611 1979 00000
SN A major task that must be performed if the system is to be sustained.
BT System Requisite
RT Manifest Function
Structural Requisites

FUNCTIONAL SPECIFICITY
S-06-0586 1975 00005
BT System Function
RT System Analysis

FUTURIBLE
1975-1979 00004
USE Forecasting Methodology

FUTUROLOGY
S-38-0142 1975 00043
BT Explanatory Political Theory
RT Advanced Technology
Contemporary Analytic Modes
Contingency Theory
Planning Theory

GAMBLING LAW
S-21-0088 1979 00000
BT Social Law
RT Abortion Law
Blue Law
Divorce Law
Family Law
Gambling Policy
Gun Control Law
Marital Law
Pornography Law

GAMBLING POLICY
S-26-0273 1979 00000
BT Policy
RT Gambling Law
Public Policy Analysis

GAME THEORY
S-38-0132 1975 00030
BT Formal Political Theory
NT Constant Sum Game Theory
N Person Game Theory
Prisoner Dilemma Theory
Two Person Game Theory
Zero Sum Game Theory
RT Bargaining Theory
Gaming
Man Machine Simulation
Mathematical Analysis
Mathematical Model
Mathematical Political Theory
Model Building
Rational Model
Simulation
Simulation Material
Variable Sum Gaming

GAMING
S-24-0098 1975 00051
BT Experimental Observation
NT Fixed Sum Gaming
N Person Gaming
Nonzero Sum Gaming
Prisoner Dilemma Gaming
Two Person Gaming
Variable Sum Gaming
Zero Sum Gaming
RT Bargaining Strategy Process
Game Theory
Learning Theory
Man Machine Simulation
Model Building
N Person Game Theory
Prisoner Dilemma Theory
Problem Solving Behavior
Simulation
Simulation Material
Small Group Experiment

GANDHIISM
S-38-0284 1975 00001
BT Nonviolent Resistance Theory
RT Pacifism
Passive Resistance

GARRISON STATE
S-16-0165 1975 00001
BT State Type
RT Fascist Theory
Lasswellian Analysis
Martial Law
Military Directorate
Military State
National Socialism
Warfare State

GAS ENERGY
S-31-0121 1979 00000
BT Natural Resource Exploitation
RT Coal Energy
Energy Management
Energy Policy
Energy Use Policy
Geothermal Energy
Hydroelectric Energy
Nuclear Energy
Oil Energy
Solar Energy
Tidal Energy
Wind Energy

GAS INDUSTRY
S-17-0045 1979 00000
UF Fuel Utility Industry
Gas Utility Industry
BT Extractive Industry
RT Electrical Industry
Energy Consumption
Energy Industry
Export Policy
Nuclear Energy Industry
Oil Industry
Ore Industry
Solar Energy

GAS UTILITY INDUSTRY
1975-1979 00004
USE Gas Industry

GAY LIBERATION
S-38-0234 1975 00003
BT Gender Ideology
RT Gay Politics
Sexism

GAY POLITICS
S-29-0232 1979 00000
BT Sexual Politics
RT Feminist Politics
Gay Liberation
Group Politics
National Politics
Protest Politics
Religious Politics

GELASIAN DOCTRINE
S-38-0383 1975 00000
SN View that relation between church and state is one of separate authorities but mutual interdependence.
BT Two Swords Theory
RT Christian Thought
Religious Movement

GEMEINSCHAFT
S-06-0038 1975 00001
SN Characterization of pre-industrial community in which there are strong emotional and kinship ties between members of the population.
BT Group Solidarity
RT Brotherhood
Communal Solidarity
Gesellschaft
Proletarian Unity
Social Solidarity
Social Unity
Verstehen Theory

GENDER IDEOLOGY
S-38-0233 1975 00004
SN Belief system based upon the importance of sexual characteristics, roles, or preferences as determinants of human behavior.
BT Ideologies
NT Gay Liberation
Sexism
RT Abortion Law
Ethnic Ideology
Sex Discrimination
Sex Role
Sexist

GENEALOGY
USE Social History

GENERAL ELECTION
S-29-0047 1975 00004
BT Election Type
RT Government Formation Process
Initiative Election
National Election
Voting

GENERAL INTEREST THEORY
S-38-0432 1975 00006
BT Common Good Theory
RT General Will Theory
Public Good Theory
Public Interest
Public Interest Theory
Value System

GENERAL STRIKE
S-08-0018 1975 00002
BT Demonstration
RT Civil Rights Demonstration
Class Conflict
Economic Conflict
Government Overthrow
Institutional Conflict
Insurgency
Labor Strike
Mob Violence
Peace Demonstration
Rebellion
Student Demonstration
Syndicalism
Veterans Demonstration
Worker Demonstration

GENERAL SYSTEM THEORY
S-38-0029 1975 00014
BT Theory
NT Communication Theory
Cybernetic Theory
Equilibrium Theory
RT Anthropological Theory
Cybernetic Analysis
Eastonian Analysis
Explanatory Political Theory
Macropolitical Theory
Political System Theory
Social Integration Theory
Social Theory
System Characteristics

GENERAL THEORY
S-38-0595 1975 00003
BT Theoretical Range
RT Cybernetic Analysis
Methodology
Middle Range Theory
Models
Philosophy Of Science Studies
Political Science Methodology Studies
System Characteristics
System Type

GENERAL WILL DEMOCRATIC THEORY
S-38-0087 1975 00001
BT Democratic Theory
RT Athenian Democratic Theory
Concurrent Majority Theory
Democratic Elite Theory
Guided Democracy Theory
Interest Group Pluralism
Jacksonian Democratic Theory
Jeffersonian Democratic Theory
Majoritarianism
Middle Range Theory
Minority Rights Democratic Theory
Participatory Democratic Theory
Populist Democratic Theory
Republic Theory
Socialist Democratic Theory

GENERAL WILL THEORY
S-38-0433 1975 00003
BT Common Good Theory
RT Fraternity Theory
General Interest Theory
Moral Freedom Theory
Obligation Theory
Public Interest Theory
Rousseauian Analysis
Sovereignty Theory

GENERATION GAP
S-11-0037 1975 00012
BT Generational Political Culture
RT Cultural Cleavage
Cultural Relativism
Generational Political Culture
Student Militancy

GENERATIONAL POLITICAL CULTURE
S-11-0036 1975 00013
BT National Political Culture
NT Generation Gap
RT Civic Culture
Fragmented Political Culture
Generation Gap
Modern Political Culture
Popular Culture
Pragmatic Political Culture
Secular Political Culture

GENETIC CHARACTERISTICS
S-06-0368 1975 00016
BT Characteristics
RT Biological Sciences
Biopolitics
Eugenics
Evolutionary Change
Genetic Evolution
Human Evolution
Social Evolution

GENETIC EVOLUTION
S-31-0065 1975 00007
BT Evolution
NT Natural Selection
RT Cultural Evolution
Genetic Characteristics
Human Evolution
Political Evolution
Social Evolution

GENETICS
USE Eugenics
Eugenics

GENOCIDE
S-10-0009 1975 00009
BT Crime Against Humanity
RT Biological War
Concentration Camp
International Law
Massacre
Murder
Political Crime
Racism
War Atrocity
War Crime

GEOGRAPHER
S-32-0110 1979 00000
BT Social Scientist
RT Academic
Anthropologist
Economist
Geopolitical Theory
Historian
Policy Scientist
Political Scientist
Sociologist

GEOGRAPHIC DETERMINISM THEORY
S-38-0009 1975 00006
SN An assertion that geographic location and environmental conditions are primary determinants of a locale's development.
BT Anthropological Theory
RT Ethnographic Theory
Geography Discipline
Hydraulic Theory

GEOGRAPHIC EXPLORATION
S-31-0457 1979 00000
BT Exploration
RT Discovery
Explorer
Geography Discipline

GEOGRAPHIC MOBILITY
S-06-0244 1975 00023
BT Population Mobility
RT Horizontal Mobility
Migration Pattern
Social Mobility
Vertical Mobility

GEOGRAPHIC ORIGIN
S-06-0206 1975 00002
BT Origin
RT Ancestry
Emigre
National Boundary
National Origin
Population Attribute

GEOGRAPHIC REPRESENTATION
S-31-0719 1975 00004
BT Representation Type
RT At Large Representation
District Representation
Functional Representation
Geography Discipline
Indirect Representation
Interest Group Representation
Minority Group Representation
Multimember District
Multiple Member Districting

Proportional Representation
Single Member District Representation
Token Representation

GEOGRAPHIC VOTING
S-29-0126 1979 00000
BT Voting
NT Regional Voting
RT Age Group Voting
Bloc Voting
Class Voting
Ethnic Group Voting
Racial Voting
Regional Voting
Religious Voting
Rural Voting
Sex Group Voting
Student Voting
Suburban Voting

GEOGRAPHY DISCIPLINE
S-01-0087 1975 00004
BT Academic Areas
NT Economic Geography
Human Geography
Physical Geography
Political Geography
Urban Geography
RT Agricultural Science
Archaeology
Area Studies
Central African Area Studies
Comparative Sociology
Demographic Studies
Discovery
Ecology Discipline
Environmental Characteristics
Ethnic Studies
Exploration
Explorer
Geographic Determinism Theory
Geographic Exploration
Geographic Representation
History Discipline
Ideographic Science
International Region
Middle East Area Studies
Military Science
National Boundary
National Political Division
Natural Science Discipline
North South Conflict
Physical Anthropology
Physical Science
Political Science Discipline
Population Identification
Scandinavian Area Studies
Social Anthropology
Sociology Discipline
South African Area Studies
Spatial Analysis
Spatial Model

GEOLOGY
USE Earth Sciences

GEOMETRY
S-24-0025 1975 00001
BT Mathematical Analysis
RT Calculus
Graph Analysis
Linear Programming
Mathematics Discipline
Trigonometry

GEOPOLITICAL THEORY
S-38-0347 1975 00007
BT International Political Theory
NT Buffer Zone Theory
Frontier Theory
Heartland Theory
RT Deterrence Theory
Domino Theory
Foreign Policy Theory
Geographer
Geopolitics
Global War Policy
International Alliance Theory
International Decision Making Theory
International Field Theory
International Influence Theory
International Integration Theory
Political Geography
Realist Foreign Policy

GEOPOLITICS
S-29-0201 1975 00016
BT Politics
RT Extranational Bloc
Geopolitical Theory
Global Politics
International Alliance Theory
International Power Theory
International Region
International Regional Conflict
Linkage Politics
Military Science
North South Conflict
Political Geography
Spatial Analysis
Spatial Model

GEOTHERMAL ENERGY
S-31-0122 1979 00000
BT Natural Resource Exploitation
RT Coal Energy
Energy Policy
Energy Use Policy
Gas Energy
Geothermal Energy
Hydroelectric Energy
Nuclear Energy
Nuclear Power
Oil Energy
Solar Energy
Tidal Energy
Wind Energy

GERIATRICS
USE Gerontology

GERMAN IDEALISM
S-38-0418 1975 00002
BT Modern Idealism
RT German Romanticism
Hegelian Analysis
Holism
Romanticism

GERMAN ROMANTICISM
S-38-0424 1975 00002
BT Romanticism
RT Aesthetics
German Idealism
Hegelian Analysis
Holism
Philosophical Idealism
Subjectivism

GERONTOCRACY
S-16-0060 1975 00000
SN A pattern of rule in which the elite are drawn from the older age groups.
BT Government Type
RT Age
Elite Type
Pension Law

GERONTOLOGY
S-01-0096 1979 00000
UF Geriatrics
BT Academic Areas
RT Age Group Voting
Anthropology Discipline
Behavioral Science
Euthanasia
Interdisciplinary Studies
Legal Studies
Old Age
Old Age Assistance Policy
Psychiatry
Right To Die
Social History
Sociology Discipline

GERRYMANDERING
S-31-0708 1975 00001
BT Districting
RT Districting
Electoral Tactics
Malapportionment
Multiple Member Districting
One Man One Vote Representation
Representation Theory
Representation Type

GESELLSCHAFT
S-06-0039 1975 00000
SN Characterization of a modern, industrialized society in which distance, manipulation, role playing and contract characterize interpersonal relationships.
BT Group Solidarity
RT Achieving Society
Gemeinschaft
Modern Ages
Society Type
Verstehen Theory
Weberian Analysis
Weberian Theory

GESTALT PSYCHOLOGY
S-01-0174 1979 00000
BT Psychology Discipline
RT Behavioral Psychology
Child Psychology
Clinical Psychology
Developmental Psychology
Freudian Psychology
Learning Psychology
Parapsychology
Psychiatry
Social Psychology

GESTALT THEORY
S-38-0539 1975 00002
BT Psychological Theory
RT Cognitive Theory
Existential Psychologism

Freudian Theory
Jungian Theory
Personality Theory
Psychological Behavioralism
Psychological Behaviorism
Psychopolitical Theory
Relative Deprivation Theory

GHETTO BUSINESS
S-19-0161 1975 00003
BT Business
RT Absentee Landlord System
Big Business
Black Bourgeoisie
Black Suburban Community

GHETTO COMMUNITY
S-07-0025 1975 00005
BT Community Type
NT Ethnic Ghetto
Suburban Ghetto Community
Urban Ghetto Community
RT Black Panther
Community Homogeneity
Community Identity
Compound
Cooperative Community
Ethnic Community
Ethnic Culture
Ethnic Group
Homogeneous Community
Housing Integration
Housing Policy
Immigration Pattern
Inner City
Language Community
Minority Group Cohesion
Segregated Community
Segregation Policy
Social Inequality
Squatter Community

GHETTO CONFLICT
S-08-0120 1979 00000
UF Ghetto Insurrection
BT Group Conflict
RT Ethnic Group Conflict
Ghetto Conflict
Ghetto Rioter
Inner City
Racial Exploitation
Segregated Community
Social Inequality

GHETTO INSURRECTION
1975-1979 00000
USE Ghetto Conflict

GHETTO RIOTER
S-32-0205 1975 00000
BT Rioter
RT Black Militancy
Black Revolution
Ethnic Group Conflict
Ethnic Militancy
Ghetto Conflict
Mob Violence
Protest
Rights Of Man Doctrine

GIFT TAXATION
S-26-0143 1975 00003
BT Taxation Policy
RT Direct Taxation
Excise Taxation Policy
Federal Taxation
Indirect Taxation
Inheritance Taxation
Luxury Taxation
Social Security Taxation

GINI CURVE
1975-1979 00001

GLOBAL EDUCATION
S-13-0009 1979 00000
BT Education Type
RT Area Studies
Economics Discipline
Foreign Language Education
Global Politics
Higher Education
Informal Education
International Relations Studies
Outreach Education
Political Science Discipline
Sociology Discipline
World Politics

GLOBAL POLITICS
S-29-0206 1975 00023
BT International Politics
RT Cold War
Geopolitics
Global Education
Global War Policy
Ideological Struggle
Ideological War
Imperialism
Imperialism System
Imperialist War
International Conflict
World Politics
World Region

GLOBAL SYSTEM
S-24-0351 1975 00093
BT Territory Classification
NT World Region
RT Aligned Nation
Extranational Commonwealth
Global War Policy
International Agency
International Bloc
International Commerce
International Commodity Market
International Communication
International Communism
International Corporation
International Court
International Economic Interdependence
International Government Council
International Law System
International Planning Commission
International Political System
International Politics
Military Alliance
Peace Treaty
World Economy
World Empire
World Law
World Market
World Politics
World War

GLOBAL WAR POLICY
S-26-0338 1975 00008
BT War Policy
RT Arms Race
Balance Of Terror
Buffer Zone Theory
Cold War
Conflict Theory
Congressional Intern
Defense Planning
Defensive Capability
Domino Theory
Escalation
First Strike Capability
Foreign Policy Making
Geopolitical Theory
Global Politics
Global System
Hostile Nation
Imperialism
Imperialist War
International Alliance Theory
International Policy Making
International Political System Characteristics
International Political Theory
International Politics
International Power Theory
International Relations Studies
Limited War Policy
Local War Policy
Military Aggression
Military Mobilization
Military Planning
Peoples War Policy
Power Politics
Protective Alliance
Strategic Studies
Strategic Theory
Total War Policy
War
War Economy
War Production
War Reparation Policy
World Politics

GOAL AMBIGUITY
S-06-0603 1975 00004
BT System Goal
RT Authoritative Value Allocation
Goal Specificity
System Analysis

GOAL SATISFACTION
S-06-0604 1975 00006
BT System Goal
RT Authoritative Value Allocation
Goal Setting
Living Conditions
Quality Of Life
Value Allocation

GOAL SETTING
S-06-0605 1975 00024
BT System Goal
RT Authoritative Value Allocation
Contingency Theory
Decision Making Theory
Goal Satisfaction
Goal Specificity
Planning Policy
Policy

Value Allocation

GOAL SPECIFICITY
S-06-0606 1975 00002
BT System Goal
RT Administrative Policy Making
Authoritative Value Allocation
Goal Ambiguity
Goal Setting
Value Allocation

GOLD RESERVE
S-06-0359 1975 00001
BT Money Supply
RT Central Banking System
Economic Resource Allocation
Federal Reserve System
Financial Market
Foreign Trade
Government Borrowing
International Banking System
International Economic Management
International Investment
National Currency

GOOD TIMES VOTER
1975-1979 00000

GOVERNING COALITION
S-02-0022 1975 00005
BT Political Coalition
RT All Party Coalition
Democratic Coalition
Electoral Coalition
Interest Group Coalition
Legislative Coalition
Multiparty Coalition
National Government
Opinion Coalition
Parliamentary Coalition
Political Party Coalition
Political Regime
Winning Coalition

GOVERNING ELITE
S-14-0009 1975 00023
BT Elite Type
RT Administrative Leadership
Aristocratic Class
Attentive Public
Bureaucratic Hierarchy
Bureaucratic Society
Business Elite
Capitalist Class
Coercion
Collective Leadership
Commercial Elite
Decision Making Elite
Democratic Elite Theory
Economic Bureaucracy
Economic Decision Maker
Economic Elite
Elite Change
Elite Formation
Elite Socialization
Executive Power
Financial Elite
Government Authority
Hierarchical Authority
International Government Executive
Leadership Sociological Analysis
Military Elite
Modernizing Elite
National Decision Making Process
National Government Bureaucracy
National Government Council
Opinion Elite
Pluralist Elite
Policy Elite
Political Decision Maker
Political Elite
Political Leadership
Political Regime
Power Elite
Power Politics
Social Elite
Subnational Elite
Upper Caste
Upper Class

GOVERNMENT
S-16-0001 1975 00017
NT Government Type
Nation Type
Regime Type
Rule Type
Sovereignty
State Type
RT Authority
Authority Structure
Economy Type
Education System
Government Agency
Government Authority
Government Characteristics
Government Employee
Government Formation Process
Government Political Party
Government Process
Governor
Governor General
Institution Building
International Government Council
International Government Executive
Management
National Government Council
Political Regime

GOVERNMENT ACCOUNTABILITY
S-06-0370 1979 00000
BT Government Characteristics
RT Administrative Accountability
Executive Accountability
Government Responsiveness
Legislative Accountability
Ministerial Responsibility
Presidential Accountability
Representative Democracy
Responsibility Doctrine

GOVERNMENT AGENCY
S-19-0044 1979 00000
BT Agencies
RT Executive Government Institution
Government
Government Authority
Government Bureaucracy
Government Employee
International Agency
Planning Agency
Welfare Agency

GOVERNMENT AGRICULTURAL ENTERPRISE
S-19-0174 1975 00003
BT Government Enterprise
RT Agricultural Advisory Board
Farm Subsidy
Farming
Government Economic Planning
Government Production Enterprise
Quasipublic Corporation

GOVERNMENT ARCHIVES
USE National Archives

GOVERNMENT AUTHORITY
S-04-0029 1975 00009
BT Political Authority
NT Civil Authority
Civil Military Authority
RT Constitutional Authority
Governing Elite
Government
Government Agency
Government Bureaucracy
Government Characteristics
Law Enforcement Official
Law Enforcement System

GOVERNMENT BORROWING
S-31-0407 1975 00001
BT Public Financing
RT Budget Deficit
Debt Financing
Debtor Nation
Deferential Voter
Deficit Financing
Fiscal Process
Gold Reserve
Government Enterprise
Local Financing
National Debt Financing
Public Spending
War Debt Financing

GOVERNMENT BUREAUCRACY
S-19-0075 1975 00034
BT Public Bureaucracy
NT International Government Bureaucracy
National Government Bureaucracy
Patronage Bureaucracy
Subnational Government Bureaucracy
RT Administrative Behavior
Administrative Jurisdiction
Bureaucratic Autonomy
Bureaucratic Characteristics
Bureaucratic Theory
Chief Executive Staff Personnel
Civil Service Employee
Government Agency
Government Authority
Legislative Official
Merit Bureaucracy
National Civil Servant
National Decision Making Process
Organization Theory
Political Regime
Political Sociology
Public Administration Studies
Public Authorities
Public Sector
Rational Legal Leadership

GOVERNMENT CENSORSHIP AGENCY
S-19-0009 1975 00003
BT Censorship Agency
RT Broadcasting Policy
Government Document Classification Policy

Government Propaganda
Government Report Censorship
Government Secrecy Policy
Intelligence Censorship
State Controlled Television

GOVERNMENT CHARACTERISTICS
S-06-0369 1979 00000
BT Characteristics
NT Government Accountability
Government Responsiveness
RT Authority Structure
Authority Type
Economic Characteristics
Government
Government Authority
Government Type
Jurisdiction Characteristics
Legislative Characteristics
Management Characteristics
National Characteristics
Political Party Characteristics
Political Regime
Political System Characteristics
Political System Structural Characteristics
Regime Type
Rule Type
System Characteristics

GOVERNMENT CONTRACT THEORY
S-38-0512 1975 00001
BT Social Contract Theory
RT Authority
Lockean Contractualism
Representation
Societal Contract Theory
State Of Nature Theory

GOVERNMENT DEREGULATION
S-31-0346 1979 00000
BT Deregulation Process
RT Decontrol Process
Denationalization Process
Destalinization Process
Economic Liberalism
Free Enterprise System
Market System

GOVERNMENT DISSOLUTION PROCESS
S-31-0459 1975 00002
BT Government Process
NT Executive Dissolution
Legislative Dissolution
RT Cabinet Instability
Cabinet Reorganization
Censure Motion
Change Process
Coalition Dissolution
Confidence Voting
Executive Dissolution
Government Formation Process
Government Instability
Government Process
Impeachment
Ministerial Instability
Political Instability
Prime Minister Election Campaign
Right Of Opposition

GOVERNMENT DOCUMENT
S-18-0019 1975 00007
BT Documents
NT Administrative Record
Intergovernmental Document
Judicial Record
Legislative Record
Licensing Record
RT Colonial Charter
Commission Record
Committee Record
Data Management
Documentary Research
Documentation Service
Financial Record
Government Information Service
Intelligence Censorship
International Organization Record
Legislative Information Service
Public Information Access Policy
Public Record
Publication Agency
Tariff Record
University Information Service

GOVERNMENT DOCUMENT CLASSIFICATION POLICY
S-26-0282 1975 00002
BT Domestic Information Policy
NT Government Secrecy Policy
RT Classification Process
Documentary Research
Government Censorship Agency
Government Report Censorship
Government Research Support
Intelligence Censorship
Military Intelligence
Privileged Information

GOVERNMENT ECONOMIC MANAGEMENT
S-23-0013 1975 00042
BT Central Economic Management
RT Appropriation Agency
Balance Of Trade
Banking Policy
Budget
Business Price Support Policy
Central Banking System
Central Economic Planning
Command Economic System
Command Economy
Communist Economic System
Consumer Protection Agency
Cost Sharing
Currency Devaluation Policy
Deficit Financing
Economic Plan
Economic Planning
Economic Policy
Economic Policy Making
Economic Program
Economic Stabilization Policy
Economic Stabilization Theory
Fiscal Planner
Fiscal Policy
Full Employment Policy
Government Enterprise
Industrial Policy
Investment Policy
Labor Policy
Money Supply Policy
National Accounts Analysis
National Banking System
National Debt Policy
National Economic Management
National Economic Planning
National Goal
National Income Analysis
National Income Taxation
Nationalized Economy
Nationalized Industry
Planification
Planned Economy
Planner
Planning Process
Price Policy
Public Spending
Public Works Policy
State Capitalism
Wage Policy

GOVERNMENT ECONOMIC PLANNING
S-31-0643 1975 00028
BT Central Economic Planning
NT Democratic Economic Planning
Five Year Economic Planning
Socialist Economic Planning
RT Appropriation Agency
Budget
Business Regulation Policy
Business Subsidization Policy
Central Economic Management
Centrally Planned Economy
City Planning Commission
Command Economic System
Command Economy
Commercial Treaty
Economic Institution
Economic Plan
Economic Planner
Economic Policy
Economic Security
Economic Stabilization Policy
Economic Stabilization Theory
Economic Subsidization Policy
Expenditure Policy
Export Subsidization Policy
Federal Grant In Aid
Federal Reserve System
Fiscal Agency
Fiscal Planner
Fiscal Policy
Fiscal Theory
Foreign Subsidiary
Full Employment
Full Employment Policy
Government Agricultural Enterprise
Government Enterprise
Government Expenditure
Inflation
Inflation Policy
International Economic Management
International Economics
Keynesian Economic Theory
Keynesian Economics
National Banking System
National Debt Policy
National Economic Management
National Economic Planning
National Goal

National Income
National Income Analysis
National Planner
National Planning Policy
National Tax Law
Nationalized Economy
Planner
Planning Agency
Planning Policy
Price Policy
Takeoff Stage

GOVERNMENT EMPLOYEE
S-32-0080 1975 00009
BT Occupational Role
NT Civil Service Employee
Patronage Worker
RT Administrative Staff Personnel
Bailiff
Chief Executive Staff Personnel
Civil Servant
Civil Service Union
Economic Attache
Foreign Affairs Agency
Government
Government Agency
Government Official
International Civil Servant
Presidential Appointment
Presidential Staff Personnel
State Legislative Staff
State Police

GOVERNMENT ENTERPRISE
S-19-0173 1975 00002
BT Enterprise
NT Government Agricultural Enterprise
Government Production Enterprise
RT Authorities
Economic Imperialism
Government Borrowing
Government Economic Management
Government Economic Planning
Government Expenditure
Government Expropriation
International Trade
Mixed Enterprise
Monetary Institution
Nation Building Theory
National Debt Financing
National Interest
Planned Economy
Planning Process
Public Authorities
Public Investment
Quasipublic Corporation
State Controlled Television

GOVERNMENT EXPENDITURE
S-06-0300 1975 00057
BT Economic Characteristics
NT Development Fund
Education Subsidy
Farm Subsidy
Foreign Aid
Foreign Assistance
Government Grant
Government Loan
Government Research Support
Industrial Subsidy
Public Assistance
Social Security
Unemployment Compensation
RT Budget
Budget Deficit
Currency Devaluation Policy
Defense Spending
Deferential Voter
Deficit Spending
Development Financing
Economic Resource Allocation
Economy Pump Priming
Government Economic Planning
Government Enterprise
National Policy Planning
Welfare State

GOVERNMENT EXPROPRIATION
S-31-0291 1975 00004
BT Expropriation Process
NT Nationalization Process
RT Financing
Government Enterprise
Nationalized Economy
Planned Economy
Planning Agency
Planning Policy
Political Control

GOVERNMENT EXTRACTIVE ENTERPRISE
1975-1979 00000

GOVERNMENT FORMATION PROCESS
S-31-0465 1975 00001
BT Government Process
RT Appointment Process
Change Process
Coalition Government
Coalition Politics
Confidence Voting
Constitutional Authority
Constitutional Structural Theory
Federal Constitution
General Election
Government
Government Dissolution Process
Prime Minister Election Campaign

GOVERNMENT GRANT
S-06-0315 1975 00015
BT Government Expenditure
NT Federal Grant In Aid
RT Charitable Organization
Development Fund
Economic Loss
Economic Scarcity
Economy Pump Priming
Education Exchange Agreement
Education Grant
Education Subsidy
Foreign Aid Policy
Foreign Assistance
Government Loan
Government Research Support
Grants Economy
Industrial Subsidy
Nonprofit Institution
PERT Analysis
Philanthropic Organization
Relocation Policy
Resource Distribution

GOVERNMENT INFORMATION DIFFUSION POLICY
S-26-0285 1975 00012
BT Domestic Information Policy
NT Clientele Information Policy
Consumer Information Policy
Copyright Policy
Science Information Policy
RT Communication Channel
Government Report Censorship
Government Secrecy Policy
Information Dissemination
Mass Media Analysis
Privileged Information
Public Information Access Policy
Report Censorship

GOVERNMENT INFORMATION SERVICE
S-18-0051 1979 00000
BT Information Service
NT Legislative Information Service
RT Abstracting Service
Archives
Bibliographic Control
Bibliographic Service
Documentation Service
Documents
Government Document
International Organization Record
Political Party Record
Private Information Service
Public Record
Statistical Data
Thesaurus
University Information Service

GOVERNMENT INSTABILITY
S-06-0692 1975 00019
BT Political Instability
RT Abdication
Cabinet Instability
Coalition Disintegration
Government Dissolution Process
Impeachment
Ministerial Instability
Minority Government
No Confidence Motion
Political Decay
Regime Instability

GOVERNMENT LOAN
S-06-0317 1975 00006
BT Government Expenditure
RT Development Fund
Education Subsidy
Federal Grant In Aid
Foreign Aid
Foreign Aid Policy
Foreign Assistance
Government Grant
Industrial Subsidy

GOVERNMENT MEDIA REGULATION POLICY
S-26-0290 1975 00002
BT Domestic Information Policy
RT Censorship Agency
Censorship Process
Government Propaganda
Ideological Indoctrination
Information Agency
Journal Censorship

Theater Censorship

GOVERNMENT OFFICIAL
S-36-0040 1975 00010
BT Status
NT Cabinet Member
Chief Government Executive
Civil Servant
Court Official
Diplomat
Incumbent
Law Enforcement Official
Legislative Official
Military Personnel
RT Administrative Personnel
Chief Executive Staff Personnel
Economic Advisor
Government Employee
Government Official
Political Official
Political Party Official
Public Authorities

GOVERNMENT OVERTHROW
S-08-0037 1975 00011
BT Conflict Type
NT Coup D'Etat
Putsch
RT Abdication
Communist Revolution
Counterinsurgency
Counterrevolution
Democratic Political Revolution
Democratic Socialist Revolution
General Strike
Insurgency
Internal War
National Political Revolution
Peasant Rebellion
Political Rebellion
Rebellion
Revolution
Revolutionary War
Social Conflict
Social Rebellion
Thermidor
War By Proxy

GOVERNMENT OWNERSHIP
S-37-0054 1975 00002
BT Property Ownership System
RT Collective Ownership
Foreign Ownership
Land Estate System
Land Tenure System
Primogeniture
Private Ownership

GOVERNMENT PARTY
1975-1979 00002

GOVERNMENT PLANNER
S-32-0136 1975 00004
BT Political Planner
NT Foreign Policy Planner
RT Administrative Planning
Government Process

GOVERNMENT POLITICAL PARTY
S-28-0043 1979 00000
BT Sector Based Political Party Type
RT Government
Legislative Political Party
National Political Party
Ruling Political Party

GOVERNMENT PROCESS
S-31-0458 1975 00021
BT Process
NT Government Dissolution Process
Government Formation Process
Intergovernmental Relations
RT Government
Government Dissolution Process
Government Planner
Influence Process
Judicial Process
Political Influence

GOVERNMENT PRODUCTION ENTERPRISE
S-19-0175 1975 00000
BT Government Enterprise
RT Central Economic Management
Command Economic System
Command Economy
Government Agricultural Enterprise
Oligopoly
Socialist Economy
War Economy

GOVERNMENT PROPAGANDA
S-31-0191 1975 00004
BT Political Propaganda
RT Government Censorship Agency
Government Media Regulation Policy
Government Secrecy Policy
Political Party Propaganda
War Propaganda

GOVERNMENT REGULATION
S-31-0311 1979 00000
BT Regulation Process
RT Arms Sales
Broadcasting Licensing Policy
Driver Licensing Policy
Election Campaign Financial Disclosure
Eminent Domain Policy
Highway Policy
Highway Safety Policy
Interstate Commerce Commission
Mine Safety Policy
Minimum Wage Policy
Noise Pollution
Postal Rate Policy
Poverty Program Spending
School Prayer Policy
Socialized Medicine System
Wiretap Evidence Admissibility
Wiretapping Policy

GOVERNMENT REPORT CENSORSHIP
S-31-0274 1975 00000
BT Report Censorship
RT Government Censorship Agency
Government Document Classification Policy
Government Information Diffusion Policy
Government Research Support
Government Secrecy Policy
Intelligence Censorship
Periodical Publication Censorship
Political Censorship
Public Broadcasting Industry
Unpublished Media Censorship

GOVERNMENT RESEARCH SUPPORT
S-06-0318 1975 00024
BT Government Expenditure
RT Development Fund
Education Grant
Education Subsidy
Government Document Classification Policy
Government Grant
Government Report Censorship
Government Secrecy Policy
Industrial Subsidy
Research Apparatus

GOVERNMENT RESPONSIVENESS
S-06-0371 1979 00000
BT Government Characteristics
RT Government Accountability
Legislative Accountability
Ministerial Responsibility
Representative Democracy
Responsibility Doctrine
Responsible Two Party System

GOVERNMENT SECRECY POLICY
S-26-0283 1975 00010
BT Government Document Classification Policy
NT Public Information Access Policy
RT Classification Process
Government Censorship Agency
Government Information Diffusion Policy
Government Propaganda
Government Report Censorship
Government Research Support
Intelligence Censorship
Spying

GOVERNMENT TYPE
S-16-0002 1975 00002
BT Government
NT Absolutist Government
Autarchic Government
Autocratic Government
Cabinet Government
Centralized Government
Coalition Government
Communist Government
Decentralized Government
Democratic Government
Dictatorship
Extranational Government Structure
Federal Government
Feudal Government
Gerontocracy
Interim Government
International Government
Limited Government
Matriarchic Government
Military Government
Minority Government
Mixed Government
Monarchy
National Government
Oligarchic Government
Parliamentary Government
Patriarchical Government
Plutocracy
Polyarchy
Presidential Government
Representative Government

Republic
Sheikdom
Socialist Government
Subnational Government
Unitary Government
RT Authority Type
Economy Type
Government Characteristics
Institution Building
Nation Type
Plebiscite Election
Political Party System
Political Regime
Regime Type
Rule Type
Society Type
Sovereignty
State Type
Two Political Party Democracy

GOVERNOR
S-36-0079 1975 00002
BT Subnational Chief Government Executive
NT State Governor
RT Feudal Lord
Government
Governor General
Governorship
Local Chief Government Executive
Prefect
Prince

GOVERNOR GENERAL
S-36-0072 1975 00000
BT Colonial Ruler
RT Feudal Lord
Government
Governor
Local Chief Government Executive
Prefect
Premier
Prince

GOVERNORSHIP
S-19-0235 1975 00000
BT Executive Government Institution
RT Chancellery
Governor
Premiership
Presidency
Secretariat

GRADUATE EDUCATION
S-13-0011 1975 00025
BT Higher Education
NT Political Science Training
RT Graduate School
Law School
Medical Education
Pedagogical Institute Education
Polytechnical Institute Education
Professional Education
State Supported Higher Education
University Education

GRADUATE SCHOOL
S-19-0213 1975 00007
BT University
RT Academy Of Science
Area Studies
Compulsory Education
Cultural Elite
Education Discipline
Education Process
Education Type
Graduate Education
Higher Education Administration
Higher Education Planning
Intellectual Elite
Law School
Military Education
Political Science Teaching
Political Science Training
Professional Education
Professional School
State Supported University
Student
University Education

GRADUATED TAXATION
S-26-0160 1975 00001
BT Progressive Taxation
RT Income Taxation
Progressive Taxation
Tax Reform Movement
Taxation Policy

GRAMMAR
S-06-0412 1979 00000
BT Language Characteristics
RT Language Learning
Semantics
Speech
Stylistics
Vocabulary

GRAMMATICAL ANALYSIS
S-09-0042 1979 00000
BT Linguistic Analysis
RT Content Analysis
Literature Analysis
Semantic Analysis
Verbal Analysis

GRAND COALITION
S-02-0028 1975 00001
BT All Party Coalition
RT Multiparty Coalition
Negative Coalition

GRAND JURY
S-19-0148 1975 00000
BT Jury
RT Bar Association
Grand Jury Indictment
Grand Jury System
Justice Administration Agency
Lawyer

GRAND JURY INDICTMENT
S-15-0057 1975 00000
BT Right To Trial
RT Appellate Court
Burden Of Proof
Commission Of Inquiry
Congressional Investigation Committee
Criminal Justice Administration
Cross Examination
Evidence Admissibility
Ex Post Facto Protection
Grand Jury
Grand Jury System
Habeas Corpus
Right To Appeal
Right To Counsel
Right To Due Process
Right To Jury Trial
Right To Speedy Trial
Self Incrimination

GRAND JURY SYSTEM
S-37-0091 1975 00000
BT Justice System
RT Adversary System
Commission Of Inquiry
Criminal Court
Criminal Justice Administration
Criminal Law
Grand Jury
Grand Jury Indictment
Law Enforcement System
Procedural Due Process
Right To Jury Trial
Right To Trial
Trial System

GRANT IN AID
S-26-0119 1979 00000
USE Federal Grant In Aid
BT Grants
RT Federal Government
Research And Development

GRANTS
S-26-0117 1979 00000
BT Economic Policy
NT Education Grant
Grant In Aid
Research Grant
RT Charitable Organization
Philanthropic Organization

GRANTS ECONOMY
S-12-0022 1979 00000
BT Economy Type
RT Capital Investment Economy
Developing Economy
Economic Aid Policy
Foreign Aid
Government Grant
Multilateral Aid Policy
Planned Economy
Technical Aid Policy
Welfare Economy

GRAPH
S-24-0135 1975 00002
BT Data Presentation Methodology
RT Chart
Curve
Diagram
Graph Analysis
Plot
Table

GRAPH ANALYSIS
S-24-0026 1979 00000
UF Graphic Analysis
BT Mathematical Analysis
RT Chart
Curve
Diagram
Geometry
Graph
Linear Programming

GRAPH THEORY ANALYSIS
S-09-0023 1979 00000
SN Mode of analysis that employs a formal mathematical system, often in conjunction with matrix algebra, for specifying relationships within a network of interrelated elements.

BT Contemporary Analytic Modes
RT Aggregate Data Analysis
Contemporary Analytic Modes
Data Format
Mathematical Analysis

GRAPHIC ANALYSIS
1975-1979 00009
USE Graph Analysis

GRAPHIC ARTS
S-01-0125 1979 00000
BT Fine Arts
RT Art History
Fine Arts
Humanities Discipline

GRAPHIC ARTS CENSORSHIP
S-31-0265 1975 00001
BT Censorship Process
RT Political Censorship
Published Media Censorship

GRASS ROOTS MOVEMENT
S-27-0055 1975 00004
BT Sector Based Political Movement
RT Agrarian Movement
Civic Action Movement
Class Based Movement
Populist Movement
Revolutionary Movement
Separatist Movement

GRAZING LAND POLICY
S-26-0222 1975 00001
BT Natural Resource Policy
RT Fish And Wildlife Policy
Forest Land Policy
Water Use Policy

GREAT CHAIN OF BEING DOCTRINE
S-38-0489 1975 00000
BT Natural Law Conventionalism Theory
RT Classical Natural Right Doctrine
Lockean Liberalism
Medieval Natural Law Theory
Metaphysics
Right Reason Doctrine
Rights Of Man Doctrine
Roman Natural Law Theory
Scientific Natural Law Theory
Stoic Natural Law Theory

GREEK CIVILIZATION
S-11-0007 1979 00000
BT Civilization
RT African Civilization
Ancient Civilization
Ancient Times
Antiquity
Byzantine Civilization
Classical Political Thought
Eastern Civilization
Epicurean Thought
Historical Analysis
History Discipline
Homogeneous Culture
Islamic Civilization
Political Culture
Roman Civilization
Socratic Political Thought
Western Civilization

GREEN REVOLUTION
S-08-0067 1975 00013
BT Ecological Revolution
RT Agrarian Reform Movement
Agrarian Socialism
Agrarian Syndicalism
Ecology Movement
Environmental Agency
Technological Revolution

GREGARIOUSNESS
S-06-0512 1979 00000
BT Personality Characteristics
RT Altruism
Assertiveness
Charity
Courage
Creativity
Curiosity
Empathy
Femininity
Honesty
Imagination
Masculinity
Optimism
Other Directedness
Persistence

GRIEVANCE PROCEDURE
S-31-0540 1975 00004
BT Judicial Procedure
RT Appeal Procedure
Judicial Review
Procedural Due Process

GROSS NATIONAL PRODUCT
S-31-0441 1975 00013
BT National Production
NT Per Capita Gross National Product
RT Economic Development Theory
Economic Indicator
Economic Planning
Economic Policy Making
Economic Statistics
Indicator
Industrial Economy
Real Income
Standard Of Living

GROUP ANALYSIS
S-09-0024 1975 00012
BT Contemporary Analytic Modes
NT Small Group Analysis
RT Analysis Methodology
Analysis Of Play
Career Analysis
Cohort Analysis
Elite Identification
Group Attitude
Group Characteristics
Group Psychology
Group Theory
Interaction Model
Interest Group Pluralism
Interest Group Politics
Leisure Time Analysis
Psychoanalysis
Small Group Analysis
Sociological Analysis
Womens Studies

GROUP ATTITUDE
S-06-0010 1975 00039
BT Group Characteristics
RT Attitude Characteristics
Group Analysis
Group Behavior
Interest Group
National Goal

GROUP BEHAVIOR
S-05-0029 1975 00030
BT Social Behavior
NT Small Group Behavior
RT Anthropology Discipline
Consumer Behavior
Economic Behavior
Elite Behavior
Group Attitude
Group Socialization
Group Theory
Interaction Analysis
Interaction Model
Interagency Rivalry
Interest Group Coalition
Interest Group Pluralism
Judicial Behavior
Legislative Behavior
Minority Group
Nonverbal Communication
Political Behavior
Social Behavior

GROUP BENEFITS VOTER
S-32-0314 1975 00003
SN A person who votes based upon calculations of the perceived rewards that will accrue to that person's group.
BT Voter
RT Class Voter
Ethnic Voter
Situation Of The Times Voter

GROUP CAPABILITY CHARACTERISTICS
S-06-0011 1975 00005
BT Group Characteristics
NT Group Effectiveness
Group Efficiency
RT Group Normative Characteristics
Interest Group Politics
Organization Capability Characteristics

GROUP CHANGE
S-31-0023 1975 00003
BT Group Process
NT Group Development
Group Structural Change
RT Coalition Change
Cultural Change Process
Group Innovation
Group Maintenance
Group Theory
Groups
Interest Group

GROUP CHARACTERISTICS
S-06-0009 1975 00015
BT Association Characteristics
NT Group Attitude
Group Capability Characteristics
Group Composition
Group Dynamics
Group Normative Characteristics
Group Solidarity
Group Status
Group Structural Characteristics
RT Community Characteristics
Community Identity
Ethnology
Group Analysis

Groups
Interest Group
Interest Group Pluralism
Interest Group Theory
Minority Group
Organization Characteristics
Political Party Characteristics
Reference Group Theory

GROUP CLEAVAGE CHARACTERISTICS
S-06-0048 1975 00009
BT Group Structural Characteristics
RT Ethnic Integration
Group Flexibility
Group Inertia
Group Size
Group Stability
Interest Group Coalition
Interest Group Pluralism
Organization Structural Characteristics
Political Party Factional Cleavage
Social Cleavage

GROUP COHESION
S-06-0040 1979 00000
UF Group Cohesiveness
BT Group Solidarity
NT Cultural Group Cohesion
Minority Group Cohesion
RT Brotherhood
Caste Solidarity
Class Solidarity
Communal Solidarity
Face To Face Group
Group Composition
Local Political Integration

GROUP COHESIVENESS
1975-1979 00024
USE Group Cohesion

GROUP COMPOSITION
S-06-0014 1975 00007
BT Group Characteristics
NT Elite Composition
Heterogeneous Group Membership
Homogeneous Group Membership
Interlocking Group Membership
Minority Group
Multiple Group Membership
Overlapping Membership
RT Cohort Analysis
Community Composition
Ethnic Group
Group Cohesion
Group Theory
Groups
Interest Group
Interest Group Coalition
Organization Cleavage Characteristics
Organization Pluralism
Organization Size
Political Party Composition

GROUP CONFLICT
S-08-0115 1975 00015
BT Social Conflict
NT Class Conflict
Class Polarization
Ethnic Group Conflict
Ghetto Conflict
Language Group Conflict
RT Class Rebellion
Consumer Producer Conflict
Ethnic Militancy
Ethnic Separatist Movement
Groups
Institutional Conflict
Interest Group
Organization Conflict
Peasant Rebellion
Political Rebellion
Political Violence
Rebellion
Revolution
Routinized Conflict
Sit In
Social Conflict
Social Rebellion
Struggle
Student Demonstration
War

GROUP CONSOLIDATION
S-31-0028 1975 00000
BT Group Structural Change
NT Elite Consolidation
RT Face To Face Group
Group Disintegration
Group Theory
Interaction Analysis
Interaction Model
Local Political Integration
Minority Group

GROUP CONSTRAINT
S-06-0026 1975 00001
BT Group Normative Characteristics
RT Group Discipline
Group Goal
Group Rationality
Group Theory
Organization Constraint

GROUP DEVELOPMENT
S-31-0024 1975 00005
BT Group Change
NT Group Formation
RT Community Building
Group Structural Change
Group Theory
Interaction Analysis
Interaction Model
Social Development Policy

GROUP DISCIPLINE
S-06-0027 1975 00001
BT Group Normative Characteristics
RT Group Constraint
Group Goal
Group Pluralism
Group Psychology
Group Rationality
Group Theory
Organization Constraint
Organization Normative Characteristics

GROUP DISINTEGRATION
S-31-0030 1975 00000
BT Group Structural Change
NT Elite Disintegration
RT Anomic Process
Anomie
Group Consolidation
Group Theory
Interaction Analysis
Interaction Model

GROUP DYNAMICS
S-06-0024 1975 00015
BT Group Characteristics
RT Bureaucratic Characteristics
Group Normative Characteristics
Group Psychology
Group Solidarity
Group Status
Group Theory
Interaction Analysis
Organization Pluralism

GROUP EFFECTIVENESS
S-06-0012 1975 00003
BT Group Capability Characteristics
RT Group Efficiency
Group Theory
Interest Group
Organization Efficiency

GROUP EFFICIENCY
S-06-0013 1975 00001
BT Group Capability Characteristics
RT Group Effectiveness
Group Theory
Interest Group
Organization Efficiency

GROUP FLEXIBILITY
S-06-0049 1975 00000
BT Group Structural Characteristics
RT Group Cleavage Characteristics
Group Hierarchy
Group Inertia
Group Size
Group Stability
Organization Flexibility

GROUP FORMATION
S-31-0025 1975 00008
BT Group Development
NT Elite Formation
RT Coalition Formation
Group Structural Change
Group Theory
Groups
Interaction Analysis
Interest Group
Interest Group Coalition

GROUP GOAL
S-06-0028 1975 00003
BT Group Normative Characteristics
RT Group Constraint
Group Discipline
Group Psychology
Group Rationality
Group Theory
Groups
Organization Goal
Organization Normative Characteristics

GROUP HIERARCHY
S-06-0050 1975 00004
BT Group Structural Characteristics
RT Administrative Politics
Bureaucratic Theory
Group Flexibility
Group Inertia
Group Size
Group Stability
Group Theory

Line Staff
Organization Constraint
Organization Hierarchy
Weberian Theory

GROUP INERTIA
S-06-0051 1975 00000
BT Group Structural Characteristics
RT Group Cleavage Characteristics
Group Flexibility
Group Hierarchy
Group Size
Group Stability
Group Theory
Organization Constraint
Organization Inertia

GROUP INNOVATION
S-31-0032 1975 00001
BT Group Process
RT Group Change
Group Maintenance
Group Theory

GROUP INTERVIEW
S-24-0109 1975 00000
BT Interview
RT Depth Interview
Group Theory
Personal Interview
Telephone Interview
Unstructured Interview

GROUP MAINTENANCE
S-31-0033 1975 00003
BT Group Process
RT Group Change
Group Innovation
Group Theory
Interaction Analysis
Interaction Model

GROUP MEASUREMENT
S-24-0187 1975 00001
BT Measurement Object
RT Attitude Measurement
Behavioral Measurement
Change Measurement
Event Measurement
Group Perception
Group Theory
Individual Measurement
Perception Measurement
Power Measurement

GROUP NORMATIVE CHARACTERISTICS
S-06-0025 1975 00015
BT Group Characteristics
NT Group Constraint
Group Discipline
Group Goal
Group Pluralism
Group Psychology
Group Rationality
RT Group Capability Characteristics
Group Dynamics
Group Theory
Organization Goal
Patriotism
Political Party Normative Characteristics

GROUP PERCEPTION
S-24-0437 1975 00032
BT Group Phenomena
NT Elite Perception
RT Group Measurement
Group Psychology
Group Theory
Interaction Analysis
Perception Measurement
Social Psychology

GROUP PHENOMENA
S-24-0436 1975 00001
BT Variable Phenomenological Status
NT Group Perception
RT Elite Perception
Ethnic Organization
Group Theory

GROUP PLURALISM
S-06-0029 1975 00002
BT Group Normative Characteristics
RT Group Discipline
Interest Group Representation
Organization Pluralism
Plural Society
Plural Voting
Pluralist Democracy

GROUP POLITICS
S-29-0202 1975 00005
BT Politics
NT Interest Group Politics
Language Group Politics
RT Feminist Politics
Gay Politics
Group Psychology
Group Theory
Group Voting
Interest Group
Interest Group Coalition
Interest Group Pluralism
Labor Politics
Linkage Politics
Lobbying Tactic
Minority Group
Partisan Politics
Partisan Primary
Protest Politics
Racial Politics
Religious Politics
Sexual Politics
Small Group Analysis
Sociology Discipline
Youth Politics

GROUP PROCESS
S-31-0022 1975 00006
BT Associational Process
NT Group Change
Group Innovation
Group Maintenance
Interest Aggregation
Interest Articulation
RT Alliance Process
Coalition Process
Elite Circulation
Ethnic Organization
Group Theory
Groups
Organization Process

GROUP PSYCHOLOGY
S-06-0030 1979 00000
BT Group Normative Characteristics
RT Developmental Psychology
Group Analysis
Group Discipline
Group Dynamics
Group Goal
Group Perception
Group Politics
Group Rationality
Political Psychology
Psychological Behaviorism
Psychological Theory
Psychology Discipline
Psychometric Model
Secret Society
Social Psychology

GROUP RATIONALITY
S-06-0031 1975 00003
BT Group Normative Characteristics
RT Group Constraint
Group Discipline
Group Goal
Group Psychology
Group Theory
Organization Normative Characteristics

GROUP REPRESENTATION THEORY
S-38-0505 1975 00004
BT Representation Theory
RT Conflict Theory
Delegate Representation Theory
Interest Group Politics
Linkage Representation Theory
Representation
Territory Representation Theory
Trustee Representation Theory
Virtual Representation Theory

GROUP SIZE
S-06-0052 1975 00015
BT Group Structural Characteristics
RT Group Cleavage Characteristics
Group Flexibility
Group Hierarchy
Group Inertia
Group Stability
Organization Size

GROUP SOCIALIZATION
S-34-0017 1975 00016
BT Socialization Context
NT Adolescent Socialization
Adult Socialization
Childhood Socialization
Cohort Group Socialization
Elite Socialization
Family Socialization
Interest Group Socialization
Job Socialization
Peer Group Socialization
Primary Group Socialization
RT Ethnic Assimilation
Group Behavior
Group Theory
Institutional Socialization
Interest Group
Professional Socialization
Socialization Type

GROUP SOLIDARITY
S-06-0032 1975 00006
BT Group Characteristics
NT Brotherhood
Caste Solidarity
Class Solidarity
Communal Solidarity
Gemeinschaft
Gesellschaft
Group Cohesion
Social Solidarity
RT Bureaucratic Characteristics
Group Dynamics
Interaction Analysis
Interest Group
Organization Cleavage Characteristics
Organization Goal
Organization Size
Patriotism
Political Party Discipline
Social Solidarity

GROUP STABILITY
S-06-0053 1975 00004
BT Group Structural Characteristics
RT Group Cleavage Characteristics
Group Flexibility
Group Hierarchy
Group Inertia
Group Size
Group Theory

GROUP STATUS
S-06-0046 1975 00010
BT Group Characteristics
RT Group Dynamics
Group Theory
Incumbent
Minority Group
Organization Status

GROUP STRUCTURAL CHANGE
S-31-0027 1975 00004
BT Group Change
NT Group Consolidation
Group Disintegration
RT Group Development
Group Formation
Group Theory
Interaction Analysis
Interaction Model

GROUP STRUCTURAL CHARACTERISTICS
S-06-0047 1975 00019
BT Group Characteristics
NT Group Cleavage Characteristics
Group Flexibility
Group Hierarchy
Group Inertia
Group Size
Group Stability
RT Group Theory
Heterogeneous Group Membership
Homogeneous Group Membership
Interlocking Group Membership
Leadership Structure Type
Organization Inertia
Organization Level
Organization Pluralism
Organization Size
Organization Structural Characteristics
Overlapping Membership
Political Party Structural Characteristics

GROUP THEORY
S-38-0143 1975 00009
BT Explanatory Political Theory
NT Interest Group Theory
Pluralist Group Theory
Reference Group Theory
RT Age Group Voting
Alienation Process
Association Characteristics
Behavioral Science
Black Voting
Collective Action Theory
Community Power Theory
Conflict Theory
Congressional Intern
Crowd Behavior
Cultural Group
Elite Theory
Equilibrium Theory
Ethnic Group Loyalty
Ethnographic Theory
Face To Face Group
Group Analysis
Group Behavior
Group Change
Group Composition
Group Consolidation
Group Constraint
Group Development
Group Discipline
Group Disintegration
Group Dynamics
Group Effectiveness
Group Efficiency
Group Formation
Group Goal
Group Hierarchy
Group Inertia
Group Innovation
Group Interview
Group Maintenance
Group Measurement
Group Normative Characteristics
Group Perception
Group Phenomena
Group Politics
Group Process
Group Rationality
Group Socialization
Group Stability
Group Status
Group Structural Change
Group Structural Characteristics
Group Voting
Groups
Integration
Interest Group
Interest Group Coalition
Interest Group Pluralism
Political Behavior
Political Psychology
Racial Group
Social Behavior
Social Group
Social Organization Theory
Social Psychology

GROUP VOTING
S-29-0128 1979 00000
BT Voting
NT Age Group Voting
Bloc Voting
Class Voting
Ethnic Group Voting
Racial Voting
Religious Voting
Rural Voting
Sex Group Voting
Student Voting
Suburban Voting
RT Election Turnout
Electoral Procedure
Group Politics
Group Theory
Urban Voting

GROUPS
S-03-0011 1975 00004
BT Associations
NT Cultural Group
Interest Group
Social Group
RT Group Change
Group Characteristics
Group Composition
Group Conflict
Group Formation
Group Goal
Group Process
Group Theory
Interest Group Politics
Organizations
Voluntary Association

GROWTH MODEL
S-24-0301 1975 00038
BT Social Science Model
NT Economic Growth Model
RT Econometric Model
Economic Development Theory
Malthusian Theory
Social System Model

GUARANTEED ANNUAL INCOME
S-06-0330 1975 00006
BT Income
RT Guaranteed Annual Income Policy
Income Measure

GUARANTEED ANNUAL INCOME POLICY
S-26-0105 1975 00006
BT Income Subsidy Policy
RT Guaranteed Annual Income
Income Maintenance Policy
Wage Policy
Welfare State

GUBERNATORIAL CANDIDATE
S-32-0243 1975 00001
BT State Chief Executive Candidate
RT Gubernatorial Election
Mayoralty Candidate
Subnational Chief Executive Election
Subnational Chief Executive Election Campaign
Subnational Chief Government Executive
Subnational Election Campaign

GUBERNATORIAL ELECTION
S-29-0095 1975 00008
BT Subnational Chief Executive Election
RT Electoral Outcome
Gubernatorial Candidate
Subnational Candidate
Subnational Chief Executive Candidate
Subnational Chief Executive Election Campaign
Subnational Chief Government Executive
Subnational Politics

GUBERNATORIAL VETO
S-31-0337 1975 00000
BT Executive Veto
RT Approval Process
Legislative Process
Presidential Veto

GUERRILLA
S-32-0197 1975 00003
BT Revolutionary
NT Urban Guerrilla
RT Guerrilla War
Insurrectionist
Internal Conflict
Maoist Revolutionary
War Criminal

GUERRILLA ACTIVITY
S-08-0050 1975 00016
BT Guerrilla War
RT Air Piracy
Armed Intervention Policy
Civil War
Ideological War
Maoism
Maoist
Militant
Military Intervention Policy
National Liberation War
Partisan War
Permanent Revolution Theory
Political Sabotage
Urban Guerrilla

GUERRILLA WAR
S-08-0049 1975 00018
BT Internal War
NT Guerrilla Activity
RT Armed Intervention Policy
Civil War
Guerrilla
Ideological War
Just War
Limited Military Aggression
Maoism
Maoist
Maoist Movement
Maoist Political Party
Maoist Revolutionary
Marxism Leninism
Military Forces
Military Intervention Policy
Military Invasion
National Liberation War
Partisan War
Political Agitator
Political Sabotage
Political Violence
Terrorism
Urban Guerrilla

GUIDED DEMOCRACY
S-16-0019 1975 00000
BT Democratic Government
RT Dictatorship
Elitist Democracy
Guided Democracy Theory
Interim Government
Tutelary Democracy

GUIDED DEMOCRACY THEORY
S-38-0088 1975 00001
BT Democratic Theory
RT Athenian Democratic Theory
Benevolent Despot
Democratic Elite Theory
Economic Theory Of Democracy
General Will Democratic Theory
Guided Democracy
Jacksonian Democratic Theory
Jeffersonian Democratic Theory
Majoritarianism
Participatory Democratic Theory
Populist Democratic Theory
Socialist Democratic Theory
Tutelary Democracy

GUIDED MISSILE
USE Missile

GUILD SOCIALISM
S-38-0297 1975 00000
BT Socialist Theory
RT Aprista Socialism
Christian Socialism
Democratic Socialism
Evolutionary Socialism
Marxism
Marxist Theory
Scientific Socialism
Syndicalism

GUN CONTROL LAW
S-21-0089 1975 00007
BT Social Law
RT Civilian Weapon
Gambling Law
Handgun
Pornography Law

GUNBOAT DIPLOMACY
S-31-0357 1975 00001
BT Diplomacy
RT Brinkmanship
Dollar Diplomacy
Executive Diplomacy
Presidential Diplomacy
Threat Indicator
Yankee Imperialism

GUTTMAN SCALE
S-24-0208 1975 00004
SN A cumulative and unidimensional scale, consisting of a small group of homogenous items ranging from least to most extreme that enables one to predict an individual's pattern on the basis of total score.
BT Scale Construction Methodology
RT Composite Scale
Cumulative Scale
Factor Structure
Likert Scale
Measurement Level Scale
Multidimensional Scale
Nominal Scale
Ordinal Scale
Ratio Scale
Scalability Index
Semantic Differential
Thurstone Scale
Unidimensional Scale

HABEAS CORPUS
S-15-0046 1975 00003
BT Defendants Rights
RT Arbitrary Arrest
Arbitrary Imprisonment
Bill Of Attainder
Burden Of Proof
Double Jeopardy
Evidence Admissibility
Grand Jury Indictment
Right Against Cruel And Unusual Punishment
Right To Appeal
Right To Due Process
Right To Equal Protection
Right To Jury Trial
Right To Speedy Trial
Right To Trial
Search And Seizure
Self Incrimination
Statute Of Limitations

HABITUAL BEHAVIOR
S-05-0031 1979 00000
BT Social Behavior
RT Accommodative Social Behavior
Administrative Behavior
Anthropology Discipline
Conformity Behavior
Customary Law
Economic Behavior
Mass Behavior
Obedience
Personal Behavior
Political Behavior
Ritual
Symbolic Action
System Supports

HAGIOLOGY
S-38-0377 1975 00001
SN Study of the lives and legends of the saints.
BT Scholasticism
RT Religious Authority
Religious History
Religious Studies
Scholastic Method

HALFWAY HOUSE
S-19-0243 1979 00000
BT Health Care Institution
RT Health Care Agency
Health Care Policy
Health Care Rights
Health Care System
Health Clinic
Hospital
Mental Health Policy
Mental Institution
Nursing Home
Private Hospital
Public Health Institution

HAMLET
S-07-0015 1975 00000
BT Village
RT Local Government
Preindustrial City
Village

HANDGUN
S-33-0018 1975 00003
BT Civilian Weapon
RT Conventional Weapon
Gun Control Law

HANDICAPPED
USE Policy For Disadvantaged

HANDICAPPED CHILD
S-32-0038 1979 00000
BT Child
RT Child Care Service
Child Neglect
Policy For Disadvantaged
Public Policy Analysis

HAPHAZARD SAMPLING
S-24-0119 1975 00000
BT Nonprobability Sampling
RT Purposive Sampling
Quota Sampling

HAPPINESS
S-06-0513 1979 00000
BT Personality Characteristics
RT Empathy
Honesty
Human Condition Theory
Imagination
Optimism
Virtue

HEALTH ADMINISTRATION
S-23-0025 1975 00010
BT Management
RT Disease
Drug Addiction
Education Administration
Environmental Management
Epidemic
Health Care Policy
Health Characteristics
Population Management
Public Health Policy
Public Policy Management
Research Management
Welfare Administration

HEALTH CARE AGENCY
S-19-0065 1975 00013
BT Welfare Agency
RT Epidemic
Halfway House
Health Care Institution
Health Care Policy
Medical Care Policy
Medical Care System
Municipal Authorities
Public Authorities
Public Health Institution

HEALTH CARE INSTITUTION
S-19-0242 1975 00016
BT Institutions
NT Halfway House
Health Clinic
Hospital
Mental Institution
Nursing Home
Public Health Institution
RT Agencies
Drug Addiction
Epidemic
Health Care Agency
Health Education
Medical Care Policy
Medical Care System
Welfare Agency

HEALTH CARE POLICY
S-26-0270 1979 00000
BT Policy
NT Medical Care Policy
Public Health Policy
RT Drug Addiction
Halfway House
Health Administration
Health Care Agency
Health Care Rights
Health Care System
Health Characteristics
Health Service
Medical Science
Mental Institution
National Health Insurance
Nursing Home
Private Hospital
Public Health Institution
Public Policy Analysis
Radiation Level

HEALTH CARE RIGHTS
S-15-0074 1975 00030
BT Social Rights
RT Abortion Law
Abortion Policy
Childrens Rights
Halfway House
Health Care Policy
Health Care System
Housing Rights
Income Rights
Marriage Rights
Medical Care System
Mental Institution
Nursing Home
Public Health Institution
Right To Die
Sexual Freedom

HEALTH CARE SYSTEM
S-37-0063 1975 00104
BT System Type
NT Medical Care System
RT Epidemic
Halfway House
Health Care Policy
Health Care Rights
Health Characteristics
Health Clinic
Health Education
Mental Health Policy
Mental Institution
Nursing Home
Private Hospital
Public Health Education
Public Health Institution
Public Health Policy

HEALTH CHARACTERISTICS
S-06-0372 1979 00000
BT Characteristics
NT Alcoholism
Disease
Drug Addiction
Epidemic
RT Change Characteristics
Demographic Characteristics
Economic Characteristics
Health Administration
Health Care Policy
Health Care System
Health Education
Health Service
Management Characteristics
Medical Education
Medical Science
Morbidity Data
National Characteristics
Personality Characteristics
System Characteristics

HEALTH CLINIC
S-19-0244 1975 00007
BT Health Care Institution
NT Neighborhood Clinic
RT Alcoholism
Disease
Drug Addiction
Halfway House
Health Care System
Hospital
Mental Institution
Nursing Home
Private Hospital
Public Health Institution

HEALTH EDUCATION
S-13-0039 1979 00000
BT Professional Education
NT Medical Education
Public Health Education
RT Disease
Health Care Institution
Health Care System
Health Characteristics
Legal Education

HEALTH SERVICE
S-26-0363 1979 00000
BT Service Policy
NT Medical Care Service
RT Community Service
Disease
Drug Addiction
Education Service
Employment Service
Epidemic
Health Care Policy
Health Characteristics
Information Service
Legal Service
Psychological Service
Sanitation Industry
Social Policy
Social Service

HEARTLAND THEORY
S-38-0350 1975 00000
BT Geopolitical Theory
RT Buffer Zone Theory
Frontier Theory

Political Geography

HEAVY INDUSTRIAL POLICY
S-26-0277 1975 00000
BT Industrial Policy
RT Business Policy
Consumer Industrial Policy
Economic Policy
Heavy Industry
Industrial Distribution
Industrial Economic Planning
Industrial Sector
Industry Nationalization
Light Industrial Policy
Service Industry Policy

HEAVY INDUSTRY
S-17-0053 1975 00001
BT Production Industry
NT Steel Industry
RT Chemical Industry
Construction Industry
Heavy Industrial Policy
Internal Market
Manufacturing Industry
Metallurgical Industry

HEDONISM
S-25-0039 1975 00001
BT Ethical Theory
RT Axiology
Emotive Ethical Theory
Ethical Relativism
Instrumentalism
Intuitionism
Linguistic Ethical Theory
Metaethical Theory
Situational Ethics

HEGELIAN ANALYSIS
S-38-0408 1975 00008
BT Modern Political Thought
NT Left Hegelianism
Right Hegelianism
RT Critical Theory Analysis
Dialectic
Existentialism
German Idealism
German Romanticism
Hegelian Marxism
Judeo Christian Thought
Kantian Analysis
Marxist Theory
Moral Freedom Theory
Neohegelianism
Phenomenological Thought
Philosophical Idealism
Positive Freedom Theory
Teleology

HEGELIAN MARXISM
S-38-0322 1975 00002
BT Marxism
RT Communism
Eurocommunism
Evolutionary Marxism
Hegelian Analysis
Left Hegelianism
Leninism
Maoism
Marxism Leninism
Marxist Revisionism
Polycentrism
Stalinism
Titoism
Trotskyism

HEGEMONIC ONE PARTY SYSTEM
S-37-0128 1975 00000
SN Political system in which the dominant party governs and permits the existence of subordinate parties.
BT One Political Party System
RT Fascist Theory
Francoism
Hegemonic System
Italian Fascism
Modified One Party System
National Socialism

HEGEMONIC SYSTEM
S-37-0120 1975 00008
SN A system in which one power predominates and cannot be effectively checked by subordinate powers.
BT International Political System
RT Bipolar International System
Hegemonic One Party System
Multipolar International Political System
Regional International Political System

HEREDITARY RULER
S-36-0063 1975 00002
BT Monarch
RT Absolute Monarch
Absolute Monarchy
Kaiser
Khan
King
Kinship Role
Political Succession
Queen
Regent
Shah
Sheik
Sheikdom
Sultan
Tsar

HERMENEUTICAL ANALYSIS
S-24-0020 1979 00000
BT Analysis Methodology
RT Analysis Methodology
Historical Analysis
Linguistic Analysis
Logical Analysis
Mathematical Analysis
Normative Analysis
Qualitative Analysis
Statistical Analysis

HETEROGENEOUS COMMUNITY
S-07-0031 1975 00001
BT Community Type
NT Integrated Community
Multiethnic Community
Multilingual Community
Multiracial Community
RT Academic Community
Ethnic Heterogeneity
Heterogeneous Culture
Heterogeneous Society
Integration

HETEROGENEOUS CULTURE
S-11-0017 1975 00007
BT Culture Type
RT Community Culture
Counter Culture
Ethnic Heterogeneity
Heterogeneous Community
Heterogeneous Society
Homogeneous Culture
Political Culture
Secular Culture
Technological Culture
Urban Culture
Western Culture
Youth Culture

HETEROGENEOUS GROUP MEMBERSHIP
S-06-0018 1975 00004
BT Group Composition
RT Group Structural Characteristics
Homogeneous Group Membership
Interlocking Group Membership
Multiple Group Membership
Organization Cleavage Characteristics
Overlapping Membership
Religious Affiliation
Social Stratification Division

HETEROGENEOUS SOCIETY
S-35-0035 1975 00007
BT Society Type Structure
NT Multicultural Society
Multiethnic Society
Multilingual Society
Multiracial Society
Plural Society
RT Atomistic Society
Ethnic Heterogeneity
Heterogeneous Community
Heterogeneous Culture
Open Society
Open Society Theory
Pluralistic Society
Social System

HIERARCHICAL AUTHORITY
S-04-0017 1975 00006
BT Authority Structure
RT Administrative Politics
Bureaucratic Theory
Centralized Authority
Decentralized Authority
Diffuse Authority
Formal Authority
Governing Elite
Hierarchical Integration
Independent Authority
Integrated Authority
Iron Law Of Oligarchy
King
Legal Rational Authority
Line Staff
Prestige Hierarchy
Social Theory

HIERARCHICAL INTEGRATION
S-31-0832 1975 00000
BT Vertical Integration
RT Administrative Theory
Hierarchical Authority
Hierarchical Model
Integrated Authority

Iron Law Of Oligarchy
Prestige Hierarchy
Specialization Process

HIERARCHICAL MODEL
S-24-0303 1975 00007
BT Social Science Model
RT Administrative Policy Making
Administrative Politics
Administrative Theory
Hierarchical Integration
Iron Law Of Oligarchy
Organization Model
Prestige Hierarchy
Social System Model
Structural Model

HIGH SCHOOL
S-19-0227 1975 00018
BT Secondary School
RT Education Association
Middle School
Secondary Education

HIGH TURNOUT ELECTION
S-29-0182 1975 00001
BT Voter Turnout
RT Local Legislative Election
Voting Behavior Analysis

HIGHER EDUCATION
S-13-0010 1975 00087
BT Education Type
NT Graduate Education
Pedagogical Institute Education
Polytechnical Institute Education
Private Higher Education
State Supported Higher Education
University Education
RT Academic
Academic Community
Academy Of Science
Board Of Regents
College
Community College
Continuing Education
Education Agency
Education Characteristics
Education Policy
Education Politics
Education Process
Global Education
Higher Education Administration
Higher Education Institution
Mass Education
Polytechnical Institute
Private College
Private University
Professional Education
Secondary Education
Teacher Education
Technical Education
Traditional Education
University

HIGHER EDUCATION ADMINISTRATION
S-23-0021 1975 00022
BT Education Administration
RT Academic Tenure Policy
Graduate School
Higher Education
Higher Education Institution
Information Management

HIGHER EDUCATION INSTITUTION
S-19-0201 1975 00050
BT Education Institution
NT Academy Of Science
College
Higher Party School
Military Institute
Pedagogical Institute
Polytechnical Institute
Professional School
University
RT Education Policy
Education Politics
Education Process
Higher Education
Higher Education Administration
Secondary School
Task Force

HIGHER EDUCATION PLANNING
S-31-0655 1975 00027
BT Education Planning
RT Academic Specialization
Academy Of Science
Graduate School
Higher Education Policy
Public Policy Planning
Social Planning

HIGHER EDUCATION POLICY
S-26-0191 1975 00078
BT Education Policy
RT Academic Specialization
Higher Education Planning
Literacy Policy
Private Education Policy
Public Education Policy
Rehabilitation Education Policy
Vocation Training Policy

HIGHER PARTY SCHOOL
S-19-0208 1975 00000
BT Higher Education Institution
RT Pedagogical Institute
University

HIGHJACKING
S-10-0032 1979 00000
BT Individual Crime
RT Kidnapping
Piracy
Political Conspiracy
Political Espionage
Terrorism
Terrorist

HIGHWAY INDUSTRY
1975-1979 00002

HIGHWAY POLICY
S-26-0421 1975 00007
BT Transportation Policy
RT Government Regulation
Highway Safety Policy
Mass Transit Policy
Transportation Industry

HIGHWAY SAFETY POLICY
S-26-0405 1975 00002
BT Traffic Safety Policy
NT Driver Licensing Policy
RT Air Safety Policy
Government Regulation
Highway Policy
Transportation Industry

HINDUISM
S-38-0558 1975 00011
BT Religious Thought
RT Asian Area Studies
Eastern Culture

HIPPIE MOVEMENT
S-27-0069 1975 00000
BT Youth Movement
RT Radical Student Movement
Youth Culture

HISTORIAN
S-32-0111 1979 00000
BT Social Scientist
RT Academic
Anthropologist
Economist
Geographer
Historical Periods
Historiography
History Discipline
Policy Scientist
Political Scientist
Social Scientist
Sociologist

HISTORICAL ANALYSIS
S-09-0026 1975 00224
BT Contemporary Analytic Modes
NT Historical Sociology Analysis
Revisionist Historical Analysis
RT African Civilization
Ancient Civilization
Ancient History
Art History
Biographical Analysis
Byzantine Civilization
Career Analysis
Civilization
Contextual Analysis
Cultural History
Descriptive Research
Diplomatic History
Eastern Civilization
Greek Civilization
Hermeneutical Analysis
Historical Sociology
Historicism
Historiography
History Discipline
Institutional History
Intellectual History
Islamic Civilization
Labor History
Leadership Analysis
Legal History
Normative Analysis
Psychohistory
Qualitative Analysis
Quantitative History
Roman Civilization
Situational Analysis
Social History
Sociological Analysis
Statistical Analysis

HISTORICAL MATERIALISM
S-38-0311 1975 00004
BT Marxist Materialism
RT Historical Sociology
Historical Sociology Analysis

HISTORICAL PERIODS
S-06-0167 1979 00000
BT Development Characteristics
NT Ancient Times
Classical Period
Dark Ages
Medieval Ages
Modern Ages
Prehistorical Times
Renaissance
RT Classification
Classification Process
Comparative Analysis
Economic Development Stage
Historian
History Discipline
Longitudinal Analysis
Typologizing

HISTORICAL PRESERVATION LAW
S-21-0055 1979 00000
BT Environmental Law
RT Conservation Law
Enabling Law
Equity Law
Home Rule Law
Land Use Policy
Natural Resource Management
Property Law

HISTORICAL SOCIOLOGY
S-01-0186 1975 00021
BT Sociology Discipline
RT Applied Sociology
Comparative Sociology
Economics Discipline
Historical Analysis
Historical Materialism
Historical Sociology Analysis
History Discipline
Labor History
Macrosociology
Marxist Sociology
Political Anthropology
Political Science Methodology Studies
Political Sociology
Social Anthropology
Social Pathology
Social Psychology
Social Theory

HISTORICAL SOCIOLOGY ANALYSIS
S-09-0027 1975 00018
BT Historical Analysis
RT Applied Sociology
Class Analysis
Elite Analysis
Historical Materialism
Historical Sociology
Ideal Case Analysis
Ideal Type Analysis
Labor History
Revisionist Historical Analysis
Situational Analysis
Weberian Analysis

HISTORICAL VARIABLE
S-24-0448 1975 00000
BT Variable Substantive Content
RT Cultural Variable
Economic Variable
Institutional Variable
Political Variable
Psychological Variable
Social Variable
Time Variable

HISTORICISM
S-25-0020 1975 00010
BT Epistemology
RT Essentialism
Etymology
Historical Analysis
Materialism
Revisionist Historical Analysis

HISTORIOGRAPHY
S-01-0106 1975 00129
BT History Discipline
RT Ancient History
Historian
Historical Analysis
History Of Philosophy
History Of Science
Institutional History
Intellectual History
Labor History
Legal History
Macropolitical Theory
Macrosociology
Marxist Revolution Theory
Oral History
Philosophy Discipline
Philosophy Of Science Studies
Political Behavior Studies
Political Science Methodology Studies
Political Theory Studies
Psychohistory
Quantitative History
Religious History
Revisionist Historical Analysis
Sociology Of Knowledge
Urban History

HISTORY DISCIPLINE
S-01-0097 1975 00028
BT Academic Areas
NT Ancient History
Art History
Black History
Cultural History
Diplomatic History
Economic History
Historiography
History Of Philosophy
History Of Science
Institutional History
Intellectual History
Legal History
Military History
Oral History
Political History
Psychohistory
Quantitative History
Religious History
Social History
Urban History
RT African Civilization
Ancient Civilization
Anthropology Discipline
Area Studies
Byzantine Civilization
Central African Area Studies
Civilization
Comparative Political Studies
Comparative Sociology
East African Area Studies
Eastern Civilization
Economics Discipline
Ethnic Studies
Geography Discipline
Greek Civilization
Historian
Historical Analysis
Historical Periods
Historical Sociology
Ideographic Science
Islamic Civilization
Longitudinal Analysis
Macrosociology
Middle East Area Studies
Political Science Discipline
Revisionist Historical Analysis
Roman Civilization
Sociology Discipline
Sociology Of Knowledge
Sociology Of Law
South African Area Studies
Thucydidean Political Thought
West African Area Studies
Western Civilization

HISTORY OF PHILOSOPHY
S-01-0107 1975 00019
UF Philosophical History
BT History Discipline
RT Ancient History
Aristotelian Thought
Art History
Classical Political Thought
Cosmology
Existentialism
Historiography
History Of Science
Intellectual History
Kantian Analysis
Marxist Sociology
Metaphysics
Philosophical Anthropology
Philosophical Concept
Philosophy Discipline
Philosophy Of Science Studies
Political Philosophy Concept
Political Philosophy Studies
Political Science Methodology Studies
Political Theory
Political Theory Studies
Pragmatism
Religious History
Scholastic Method
Scholasticism
Social Theory
Sociology Of Knowledge
Urban History
Voltairean Analysis

HISTORY OF SCIENCE
S-01-0108 1975 00019
UF Science History
BT History Discipline
NT History Of Technology
RT Historiography
History Of Philosophy
Intellectual History
Legal History
Macrosociology

Political Science Methodology Studies
Political Theory Studies
Quantitative History
Social Theory
Sociology Of Knowledge

HISTORY OF TECHNOLOGY
S-01-0109 1979 00000
UF Technological History
BT History Of Science
RT Agricultural History
Ancient History
Intellectual History
Labor History
Middle Level Technology
Technology Policy

HOBBESIAN ABSOLUTISM
S-38-0392 1975 00001
BT Early Modern Theory Of The State
RT Absolute Monarch
Absolutism
Consent Theory
Hobbesian Analysis
Instrumental State Theory
Newtonian Mechanistic State Theory
Order Theory
Possessive Individualism
Scientific Natural Law Theory
Social Contract Theory
State Of Nature Theory

HOBBESIAN ANALYSIS
S-38-0411 1975 00014
BT Modern Political Thought
RT Absolute Monarchy
Absolutism
Conflict Theory
Consent Theory
Hobbesian Absolutism
Modern Political Thought
Philosophical Materialism
Political Legitimacy Theory
Scientific Natural Law Theory
Sovereignty Theory
State Of Nature Theory

HOLDING COMPANY
S-19-0166 1975 00000
BT Corporation
RT Cartel
Economic Conglomerate
Foreign Subsidiary
International Corporation
Multinational Corporation

HOLISM
S-25-0016 1975 00004
SN Theory that entire entity as distinct from sum of its parts has an existence of its own.
BT Empiricism
RT German Idealism
German Romanticism
Methodological Individualism
Reductionism
Romanticism
Utopianism

HOLY WAR
S-08-0107 1975 00001
BT Religious War
RT Expansionist War
Just War
Pan Islamism
Peasant Rebellion
Political Rebellion
Religious Conflict
Social Rebellion
Undeclared War

HOME RULE
S-16-0146 1975 00004
BT Rule Type
RT Populism
Sovereign Nation
Sovereignty

HOME RULE LAW
S-21-0072 1975 00000
BT Political Law
RT Enabling Law
Historical Preservation Law
State Constitution
State Constitutional Convention
Sunset Law
Sunshine Law

HOMEOSTATIC CHANGE
S-31-0142 1975 00001
BT Evolutionary Change
RT Homeostatic Equilibrium
Institutional Change
Political Change
Social Change

HOMEOSTATIC EQUILIBRIUM
S-06-0616 1975 00004
SN A condition in which the system adjusts to extraordinary stress in such a way as to return itself to its original state of health and maintenance.
BT System Equilibrium
RT Dynamic Equilibrium
Homeostatic Change
Social System
System Performance

HOMOGENEOUS COMMUNITY
S-07-0037 1975 00003
BT Community Type
NT Language Community
RT Black Ghetto
Black Suburban Community
Collective Community
Communal Community
Cooperative Community
Ethnic Community
Ethnic Ghetto
Ghetto Community
Homogeneous Culture
Homogeneous Society
Integrated Community
Language Community
Model City
Suburban Ghetto Community
Town
Urban Ghetto Community

HOMOGENEOUS CULTURE
S-11-0018 1975 00004
BT Culture Type
RT Acculturation
African Civilization
Ancient Civilization
Byzantine Civilization
Civilization
Community Culture
Counter Culture
Eastern Civilization
Ethnic Homogeneity
Greek Civilization
Heterogeneous Culture
Homogeneous Community
Homogeneous Society
Islamic Civilization
Political Culture
Religious Cult
Roman Civilization
Village Culture
Western Civilization
Youth Culture

HOMOGENEOUS GROUP MEMBERSHIP
S-06-0019 1975 00004
BT Group Composition
RT Elite Homogeneity
Group Structural Characteristics
Heterogeneous Group Membership
Interlocking Group Membership
Minority Group
Overlapping Membership
Religious Affiliation
Religious Cult
Social Stratification Division

HOMOGENEOUS SOCIETY
S-35-0042 1975 00005
BT Society Type Structure
RT Assimilation Theory
Closed Society
Elite Homogeneity
Ethnic Homogeneity
Feudal Society
Homogeneous Community
Homogeneous Culture
Islamic Society
Mass Society
Nomadic Society
Religious Society
Social System
Tribal Society
Urban Society

HONESTY
S-06-0514 1979 00000
BT Personality Characteristics
RT Altruism
Ambivalence
Assertiveness
Charity
Courage
Curiosity
Egocentrism
Empathy
Femininity
Gregariousness
Happiness
Imagination
Masculinity
Moral Responsibility
Optimism
Persistence

HORIZONTAL CLEAVAGE
S-31-0789 1975 00000
BT Cleavage Process
RT Class Analysis
Horizontal Mobility
Horizontal Stratification Division

HORIZONTAL ECONOMIC INTEGRATION
S-31-0804 1979 00000
BT Economic Integration
RT International Economic Integration
National Economic Integration
Social Integration Theory
Subnational Economic Integration
Vertical Economic Integration

HORIZONTAL INTEGRATION
S-31-0813 1979 00000
BT Integration
RT Economic Integration
Ethnic Integration
Functional Integration
Linguistic Integration
Political Integration

HORIZONTAL MOBILITY
S-06-0748 1975 00004
BT Status Mobility
RT Class Analysis
Downward Mobility
Geographic Mobility
Horizontal Cleavage
Intergenerational Mobility
Intragenerational Mobility
Status Mobility
Upward Mobility
Vertical Mobility

HORIZONTAL STRATIFICATION DIVISION
S-06-0785 1975 00004
BT Social Stratification Division
RT Caste Stratification Division
Class Analysis
Class Stratification Division
Horizontal Cleavage

HORTICULTURE
S-01-0006 1979 00000
BT Agricultural Science
RT Agricultural Development
Agricultural Education
Agricultural Extension Service
Agricultural History
Agricultural Production
Agronomy
Animal Husbandry
Eugenics
Farming

HOSPITAL
S-19-0246 1975 00014
BT Health Care Institution
NT Private Hospital
Public Hospital
RT Halfway House
Health Clinic
Medical Care System
Mental Institution
Nursing Home
Public Health Institution

HOSTAGE
S-36-0258 1975 00001
BT Prisoner
RT Detainee
Political Prisoner
Prisoner Of War

HOSTILE NATION
S-16-0123 1975 00001
BT Nation Type
RT Aggressiveness
Aggressor State
Empire
Global War Policy
Hostility
War

HOSTILITY
S-06-0102 1975 00013
UF Animosity
BT Attitude Characteristics
NT Aggressiveness
RT Alienation
Authoritarian Attitude
Authoritarian Personality
Bigotry
Cynicism
Hostile Nation
Intolerance
Militancy
Personality Theory
Prejudice

HOUSE OF REPRESENTATIVES
S-19-0271 1979 00000
BT Congress
RT Bicameral Legislature
Congressional Election Campaign
Congressional Leadership
Legislative Behavior
Legislative History
Legislature Type
National Legislative Political Party
Unicameral Legislature

HOUSE OF REPRESENTATIVES LEADER
S-36-0181 1975 00003
BT Congressional Leader
RT Congressional Leadership
House Of Representatives Speaker
Senate Leader

HOUSE OF REPRESENTATIVES SPEAKER
S-36-0162 1975 00000
BT Congressional Speaker
RT Congressional Leadership
House Of Representatives Leader
Political Party Membership
Senate Speaker

HOUSEHOLD HEAD
S-32-0039 1975 00014
BT Family Role
RT Family Policy
Housewife
Husband
Maternal Role
Paternal Role
Wife

HOUSEHOLD SIZE
S-06-0191 1975 00019
BT Demographic Profile
RT Demographic Projection
Family Planning
Mortality Rate

HOUSEWIFE
S-32-0040 1975 00004
BT Family Role
RT Family Policy
Household Head
Maternal Role
Mother
Wife

HOUSING CODE
S-21-0052 1975 00005
BT Zoning Law
RT Absentee Landlord System
Architectural Studies
Building Code
Housing Court
Housing Industry
Housing Integration
Housing Rights

HOUSING COOPERATIVE
S-03-0005 1975 00002
BT Cooperatives
RT Credit Cooperative
Housing Court
Housing Industry

HOUSING COURT
S-19-0131 1975 00000
BT Civil Court
RT Common Law Court
Family Court
Housing Code
Housing Cooperative
Legislative Commission
Provincial Parliament

HOUSING INDUSTRY
S-17-0029 1975 00019
BT Construction Industry
RT Building Code
Building Process
Building Supplies Industry
Housing Code
Housing Cooperative
Housing Policy

HOUSING INTEGRATION
S-31-0828 1975 00007
BT Racial Integration
RT Desegregation Policy
Ghetto Community
Housing Code
Racial Assimilation
School Integration

HOUSING POLICY
S-26-0385 1975 00061
BT Social Policy
NT Open Housing Policy
Public Housing Policy
Relocation Policy
RT Architectural Studies
Black Ghetto
Black Suburban Community
Building Supplies Industry
Discrimination Policy
Ethnic Ghetto
Ghetto Community
Housing Industry
Housing Rights
Integration
Migration Policy
Planned Economy
Population Policy
Racial Integration
Residential Segregation
Service Policy
Social Resource Distribution Policy
Social Welfare Policy

Urban Renewal Policy

HOUSING RIGHTS
S-15-0075 1975 00007
BT Social Rights
RT Architectural Studies
Childrens Rights
Health Care Rights
Housing Code
Housing Policy
Income Rights
Marriage Rights

HOUSING SCARCITY
S-31-0116 1979 00000
BT Scarcity
RT Energy Scarcity
Labor Scarcity
Water Scarcity

HUMAN CONDITION THEORY
S-38-0468 1975 00017
BT Political Philosophy Concept
RT Happiness
Human Dignity Theory
Human Nature Theory
Human Needs Theory
Ontological Existentialism
Philosophical Anthropology
State Of Nature Theory

HUMAN DIGNITY THEORY
S-38-0469 1975 00029
UF Dignity
BT Political Philosophy Concept
RT Emancipation
Human Condition Theory
Humanism
Liberty Theory

HUMAN EVOLUTION
S-31-0067 1975 00013
BT Evolution
RT Biological Sciences
Cultural Evolution
Eugenics
Genetic Characteristics
Genetic Evolution
Natural Selection
Political Evolution
Social Evolution

HUMAN GEOGRAPHY
S-01-0089 1975 00012
BT Geography Discipline
RT American Indian Studies
Anthropology Discipline
Biological Sciences
Black Studies
Chicano Studies
Comparative Sociology
Cultural History
Demographic Studies
Economic Geography
Ethnography
Ethnology
Eugenics
Physical Anthropology
Physical Geography
Political Geography
Puerto Rican Studies
Social Anthropology
Urban Geography
Urban Sociology

HUMAN NATURE THEORY
S-38-0470 1975 00042
BT Political Philosophy Concept
RT Cultural Universalism
Human Condition Theory
Human Needs Theory
Individualism Theory
Life Satisfaction
Moral Learning
Philosophical Anthropology
Political Virtue
Sexual Freedom
State Of Nature Theory

HUMAN NEEDS THEORY
S-38-0540 1979 00000
BT Psychological Theory
RT Human Condition Theory
Human Nature Theory
Human Resources Development
Human Rights
Individualism Theory
Quality Of Life
Value Of Life

HUMAN RESOURCES DEVELOPMENT
S-06-0176 1979 00000
BT Development Characteristics
RT Development Potential
Economic Development
Human Needs Theory
Job Satisfaction
Learning Theory
Legal Development
Personnel Management
Political Development
Political Development Policy
Social Psychology

HUMAN RIGHTS
S-15-0014 1979 00000
UF Economic Rights
BT Freedom
RT Civil Liberty
Civil Rights
Destalinization Process
Freedom Of Information
Freedom Of Inquiry
Freedom Of Religion
Human Needs Theory
Human Rights Policy
Human Subject Rights
Immunity
Persecution
Political Liberty
Political Philosophy Studies
Political Repression
Political Tolerance
Procedural Rights
Progressive Politics
Right Of Opposition
Right To Strike
Sedition Law
Social Rights
Use Of Human Subjects
Voting Rights

HUMAN RIGHTS POLICY
S-26-0274 1979 00000
BT Policy
RT Civil Rights
Constitutional Law
Human Rights
Human Subject Rights
International Relations Studies
Political Liberty
Research Ethics

HUMAN SUBJECT RIGHTS
S-25-0046 1979 00000
BT Use Of Human Subjects
RT Human Rights
Human Rights Policy
Moral Reasoning
Research Center
Research Evaluation
Scientific Research
Situational Ethics

HUMANISM
S-38-0240 1975 00019
BT Ideologies
NT Christian Humanism
Humanitarianism
Scientific Humanism
Socialist Humanism
RT Egalitarianism
Human Dignity Theory
Individualism Theory

HUMANISTIC EDUCATION
S-13-0022 1975 00003
BT Liberal Arts Education
RT Aesthetics
Artistic Elite
Civic Education
Classical Education
Essay
Folk Literature
Humanistic Research
Humanities Discipline
Literature Review
Literature Studies
Novel
Poetry
Private College
Private Higher Education
Private School
Progressive Education
Religious Education
Self Taught Education
Short Story
Traditional Education
University
University Education

HUMANISTIC RESEARCH
S-24-0387 1975 00010
BT Research Orientation
RT Aesthetics
Humanistic Education
Humanities Discipline
Ideographic Research
Policy Research

HUMANITARIANISM
S-38-0242 1975 00020
BT Humanism
RT Christian Humanism
Christian Socialism
Scientific Humanism
Socialist Humanism

HUMANITIES DISCIPLINE
S-01-0123 1975 00019
BT Academic Areas
NT Fine Arts

RT Aesthetics
Art History
Artistic Elite
Arts Policy
Essay
Fine Arts
Folk Literature
Foreign Language Education
Graphic Arts
Humanistic Education
Humanistic Research
Language Studies
Liberal Arts Education
Literature Analysis
Literature Review
Literature Studies
Novel
Performing Arts Censorship
Plastic Arts
Poetry
Political Literature
Short Story
Sociology Of Art
Visual Arts

HUMANITIES EDUCATION
S-13-0019 1979 00000
BT Education Type
NT Classical Education
Liberal Arts Education
RT Artistic Elite
Essay
Foreign Language Education
Novel
Poetry
Religious Education
Short Story

HUMEAN ANALYSIS
S-38-0412 1975 00002
SN Theories and analyses associated with David Hume.
BT Modern Political Thought
RT Classical Liberalism

HUNGER
S-31-0113 1979 00000
BT Food Scarcity
RT Agricultural Development
Agricultural Production
Energy Scarcity
Malnutrition
Resource Allocation
Resource Distribution
Starvation

HUNTING AND FISHING SOCIETY
S-35-0019 1979 00000
BT Society Type Base
RT Agrarian Economy
Hunting And Trapping Economy
Nomadic Economy
Preindustrial Society
Primitive Society

HUNTING AND TRAPPING ECONOMY
S-12-0023 1979 00000
BT Economy Type
RT Agrarian Economy
Barter Economy
Consumer Economy
Farm Economy
Hunting And Fishing Society
Nomadic Economy
Preindustrial Society
Self Sufficient Economy
Trade
Trade Policy

HUSBAND
S-32-0041 1975 00016
BT Family Role
RT Father
Household Head
Marital Offense
Marriage Contract
Maternal Role
Paternal Role
Widower
Wife

HUSSITE THOUGHT
S-38-0568 1975 00000
SN Religious reformist and nationalistic movement dating back to the fourteenth century emphasizing supremacy of scriptures.
BT Protestantism
RT Anglicanism
Calvinism
Lutheranism
Protest
Protestant Sectarianism
Unitarianism

HYDRAULIC THEORY
S-38-0010 1975 00002
SN An approach to state formation and power that regards irrigation needs as the primary variable.
BT Anthropological Theory
RT Anthropological Functionalism
Cultural Evolutionism
Geographic Determinism Theory
Oriental Despotism

HYDROELECTRIC ENERGY
S-31-0123 1979 00000
BT Natural Resource Exploitation
RT Coal Energy
Energy Policy
Gas Energy
Geothermal Energy
Oil Energy
Solar Energy
Tidal Energy
Wind Energy

HYPOTHESIS TESTING
S-24-0140 1975 00077
UF Successive Appoximation
BT Methodology
NT Confirmation
Falsification
Replication
RT Data Collection Methodology
Data Presentation Methodology
Deductive Method
Indicator
Inductive Method
Literature Review
Measurement
Models
Propositional Inventory
Research Design
Test Results
Theoretical Framework
Thesis

HYSTERIA
S-06-0521 1975 00001
BT Personality Disorder
RT Personality Theory
Psychosis

IDEAL CASE ANALYSIS
S-24-0402 1975 00000
BT Case Study
RT Deviant Case Analysis
Historical Sociology Analysis
Ideal Type Analysis
Ideal Type Model
Weberian Analysis
Weberian Theory

IDEAL TYPE ANALYSIS
S-09-0029 1975 00006
BT Contemporary Analytic Modes
RT Contextual Analysis
Economy Type
Historical Sociology Analysis
Ideal Case Analysis
Ideal Type Model
Paradigm
Sociological Analysis
Weberian Analysis
Weberian Theory

IDEAL TYPE MODEL
S-24-0304 1975 00004
BT Social Science Model
RT Ideal Case Analysis
Ideal Type Analysis
Idealist Foreign Policy
Weberian Analysis
Weberian Theory

IDEALISM
USE Philosophical Idealism

IDEALIST FOREIGN POLICY
S-38-0345 1979 00000
BT Foreign Policy Theory
RT Balance Of Power Theory
Foreign Policy Making
Foreign Policy Planner
Foreign Policy Theory
Ideal Type Model
Policy Format
Realist Foreign Policy
Value Analysis

IDENTIFIER
USE Indexing

IDENTITY ANALYSIS
S-09-0030 1975 00041
BT Contemporary Analytic Modes
RT Behavior Analysis
Catharsis
Ethnic Studies
Ethnicity
Feminism
Identity Change
Identity Characteristics
Identity Theory
Political Psychology Analysis
Small Group Analysis
Social Psychiatry
Socialization Analysis
Value Analysis

IDENTITY CHANGE
S-06-0386 1975 00019
BT Identity Characteristics
RT Assimilation Theory
Community Identity
Ethnic Studies
Ethnicity
Identity Analysis

IDENTITY CHARACTERISTICS
S-06-0377 1975 00031
BT Characteristics
NT Community Identity
Cultural Identity
Folkways
Identity Change
Identity Crisis
Language Loyalty
National Identity
Occupational Identity
Political Identity
Religious Identity
Social Identity
RT Americanism
Attitude Characteristics
Attitude Cluster
Black Nationalism
Empathy
Ethnic Studies
Ethnicity
Identity Analysis
Identity Crisis
Identity Theory

IDENTITY CRISIS
S-06-0387 1975 00001
BT Identity Characteristics
RT Community Identity
Crisis
Feminism
Identity Characteristics
Identity Theory

IDENTITY THEORY
S-38-0541 1975 00031
BT Psychological Theory
RT Attitude Change Theory
Attribution Theory
Black Identity
Ethnic Studies
Ethnicity
Freudian Theory
Identity Analysis
Identity Characteristics
Identity Crisis
Learning Theory
Motivation Theory
Personality Crisis
Psychological Behavioralism
Psychological Behaviorism

IDEOGRAPHIC RESEARCH
S-24-0383 1975 00002
SN In-depth contextual analysis of specific cases and events.
BT Descriptive Research
RT Case Study
Configurative Analysis
Cultural History
Experimental Research
Humanistic Research
Quantitative Research
Study Scope

IDEOGRAPHIC SCIENCE
S-01-0147 1975 00002
BT Natural Science Discipline
RT Anthropology Discipline
Area Studies
Descriptive Research
Dimensional Analysis
Freudian Psychology
Geography Discipline
History Discipline
Natural Science Education
Political Science Discipline
Sociology Discipline
Study Scope

IDEOLOGICAL CONFLICT
S-08-0041 1975 00032
BT Conflict Type
RT Aggression
Agitation Propaganda
Class Analysis
Class Conflict
Cold War
Communist Deviationism
Cultural Conflict
Economic Conflict
Ideological Education
Ideological Struggle
Ideological War
Ideology Explanatory Theory
Imperialist War
Institutional Conflict
Insurgency
Marxist Ideology Explanation
Military Aggression
Military Coup
North South Conflict
Political Ideology
Political Purge
Rebellion
Religious Conflict
Religious War
Revolution
Social Conflict
Struggle
Succession Struggle
War By Proxy

IDEOLOGICAL EDUCATION
S-13-0032 1975 00004
BT Political Education
RT Alternative Education
Civic Education
Communist Education
Fascist Education
Ideological Conflict
Ideological Indoctrination
Ideological Polarization
Ideological Struggle
Ideology Explanatory Theory
Learning Theory
Military Education
Political Ideology
Socialist Education
Traditional Education

IDEOLOGICAL INDOCTRINATION
S-31-0305 1975 00005
BT Political Indoctrination
RT Brainwashing
Communism
End Of Ideology Analysis
Government Media Regulation Policy
Ideological Education
Ideological War
Polarization

IDEOLOGICAL MOVEMENT
1975-1979 00020
USE Ideological Spectrum Political Movement

IDEOLOGICAL PARTY
1975-1979 00005

IDEOLOGICAL POLARIZATION
S-31-0817 1975 00014
BT Polarization
RT Assimilation
End Of Ideology Analysis
Ideological Education
Ideological Political Culture
Ideological Struggle
Ideological Voter
Ideological War
Ideologue
Ideology Explanatory Theory
International System Polarization
Mannheim Ideology Explanation
Political Ideology
System Politicization

IDEOLOGICAL POLITICAL CULTURE
S-11-0038 1975 00012
BT National Political Culture
RT Civic Culture
Ideological Polarization
Ideology Explanatory Theory
Mannheim Ideology Explanation
Militancy
Modern Political Culture
National Socialism
Political Cynicism
Political Distrust
Political Extremism
Political Ideology
Pragmatic Political Culture
Secular Political Culture

IDEOLOGICAL POLITICAL PARTY
S-28-0008 1979 00000
BT Political Party Type
RT Flangist Political Party
Ideological Spectrum Political Party Type
Mannheim Ideology Explanation
Political Ideology
Radical Political Party
Sector Based Political Party Type

IDEOLOGICAL SPECTRUM POLITICAL MOVEMENT
S-27-0010 1979 00000
UF Ideological Movement
BT Political Movement
NT Christian Democratic Movement
Communist Movement
Extremist Movement
Fascist Movement
Maoist Movement
Radical Movement
Revolutionary Movement
Social Democratic Movement
RT Ideological Spectrum Political Party Type
Ideologies
Independence Movement

Messianic Movement
Nationalist Movement
Peace Movement
Political Ideology
Resistance Movement
Sector Based Political Movement

IDEOLOGICAL SPECTRUM POLITICAL PARTY TYPE
S-28-0009 1979 00000
BT Political Party Type
NT Center Political Party
Communist Political Party
Conservative Political Party
Fascist Political Party
Leftist Political Party
Liberal Political Party
Radical Political Party
Rightist Political Party
Socialist Political Party
RT Ideological Political Party
Ideological Spectrum Political Movement
Ideologies
Independence Movement
Nationalist Movement
Nationalist Political Party
Revolutionary Political Party
Sector Based Political Party Type
Structure Specific Political Party Type

IDEOLOGICAL STRUGGLE
S-08-0128 1975 00016
BT Struggle
RT Anticommunism
Chinese Cultural Revolution
Female Chauvinism
Global Politics
Ideological Conflict
Ideological Education
Ideological Polarization
Ideological Voter
Ideological War
Ideologue
Ideology Explanatory Theory
Marxist Ideology Explanation
North South Conflict
Political Agitation
Political Ideology
Revolution
Social Rebellion

IDEOLOGICAL VOTER
S-32-0315 1975 00015
BT Voter
RT Ideological Polarization
Ideological Struggle
Ideological War
Ideologue
Ideology Explanatory Theory
Partisan Image Voter
Protest Voter
Voter Orientation
Voting

IDEOLOGICAL WAR
S-08-0095 1975 00005
BT War
RT Civil War
Expansionist War
Global Politics
Guerrilla Activity
Guerrilla War
Ideological Conflict
Ideological Indoctrination
Ideological Polarization
Ideological Struggle
Ideological Voter
Ideologue
National Liberation War
Propaganda War
Psychological War
Rebellion
Revolutionary War
Undeclared War

IDEOLOGIES
S-38-0176 1975 00013
BT Political Theory
NT Absolutism
Agrarianism
Anarchism
Anarchosyndicalism
Anticlericalism
Anticolonialism
Anticommunism
Antifascism
Antiimperialism
Antimilitarism
Authoritarianism
Caudillism
Chartism
Clientelism
Communalism
Conservatism
Corporatism
Economic Ideology
Egalitarianism
Elitism
Ethnic Ideology
Eurocommunism
Fascist Theory
Free Masonry
Gender Ideology
Humanism
Imperialism
Liberalism
Libertarianism
Militarism
Millenarianism
Modernizing Ideology
Nationalism
New Left
Nihilism
Pacifism
Political Ideology
Populism
Social Darwinism
Socialist Theory
Syndicalism
Terrorism
Trade Unionism
RT Classical Political Thought
Communist Education
Contemporary Political Thought
Explanatory Political Theory
Ideological Spectrum Political Movement
Ideological Spectrum Political Party Type
Ideology Explanatory Theory
International Communist Movement
Mannheim Ideology Explanation
Modern Political Thought
Political Philosophy Concept
Progressive Politics
Psychological Theory
Renaissance Political Thought
Sector Based Political Movement
Social Theory
Stereotyping

IDEOLOGUE
S-32-0259 1975 00007
BT Spectrum Politicist
RT Ideological Polarization
Ideological Struggle
Ideological Voter
Ideological War
Mannheim Ideology Explanation
Political Radical
Reactionary
Rightist

IDEOLOGY EXPLANATORY THEORY
S-38-0147 1975 00023
BT Explanatory Political Theory
NT End Of Ideology Analysis
Mannheim Ideology Explanation
Marxist Ideology Explanation
RT Conflict Theory
Congressional Intern
End Of Ideology Analysis
Ideological Conflict
Ideological Education
Ideological Polarization
Ideological Political Culture
Ideological Struggle
Ideological Voter
Ideologies
Political Ideology
Revolution Theory

ILLEGAL ABORTION
S-10-0033 1979 00000
BT Individual Crime
RT Abortion Law
Crime
Criminal
Criminal Abortion
Criminal Law

ILLEGAL IMMIGRATION
S-10-0060 1979 00000
BT Political Crime
RT Defection
Immigration Pattern
Immigration Policy

ILLITERACY RATE
S-06-0192 1975 00006
BT Demographic Profile
RT Demographic Projection
Literacy Rate

IMAGINATION
S-06-0515 1979 00000
BT Personality Characteristics
RT Altruism
Assertiveness
Courage
Creativity
Culture Shock
Curiosity
Egocentrism
Empathy
Femininity

Gregariousness
Happiness
Honesty
Imagination
Learning Theory
Masculinity
Optimism
Persistence

IMMIGRANT
S-36-0021 1975 00049
BT Citizenship Status
NT Emigre
Expatriate
Refugee
RT Alien
Exile
Immigration Flow
Immigration Pattern
Immigration Policy
Immigration Process
Repatriate
Stateless Person

IMMIGRATION FLOW
S-06-0238 1975 00015
BT Immigration Pattern
RT Immigrant
Immigration Policy
Immigration Process
Internal Migration Pattern
Population Mobility
Population Transition

IMMIGRATION PATTERN
S-06-0237 1975 00028
BT Migration Pattern
NT Immigration Flow
RT Braindrain
Census Record
Emigration Pattern
Ghetto Community
Illegal Immigration
Immigrant
Immigration Policy
Immigration Process
Internal Migration Pattern
Migrant Population
Population Mobility
Population Transition

IMMIGRATION POLICY
S-26-0391 1975 00016
BT Migration Policy
RT Emigre
Exile
Frontier Theory
Illegal Immigration
Immigrant
Immigration Flow
Immigration Pattern
Immigration Process
Migrant Population
National Origin
Population Management
Relocation Policy

IMMIGRATION PROCESS
S-31-0620 1975 00010
BT Migration Process
RT Emigration Process
Emigre
Immigrant
Immigration Flow
Immigration Pattern
Immigration Policy
Internal Migration
Refugee Migration

IMMUNITY
S-15-0015 1975 00000
BT Freedom
NT Citizenship Immunity
Diplomatic Immunity
Executive Immunity
Legal Immunity
Legislative Immunity
Political Asylum
Prosecution Immunity
RT Human Rights
Political Liberty
Procedural Rights

IMPEACHMENT
S-31-0462 1975 00002
BT Executive Dissolution
RT Government Dissolution Process
Government Instability
Political Corruption
Political Crime

IMPERFECT COMPETITION
S-31-0206 1975 00001
BT Competition
RT Direct Competition

IMPERIAL GOVERNMENT
S-16-0064 1975 00017
BT International Government
RT Absolute Monarch
Colonial Charter
Colonial Development
Colonial Empire
Colonial Ruler
Colonialism
Communist Imperialism
Imperialism
Imperialism System
Imperialist
Imperialist Economy
Imperialist War
World Government

IMPERIAL PRESIDENCY
S-19-0240 1979 00000
BT Presidency
RT Authoritarian Personality
Authoritarian Regime
Authoritarianism
Closed Society
Power Abuse
Presidential Power

IMPERIALISM
S-38-0245 1975 00022
BT Ideologies
NT Colonialism
Neocolonialism
Neoimperialism
RT Anticolonialism
Client State
Colonial Development
Colonial Empire
Colony
Communist Empire
Economic Ideology
Empire
Expansionist Policy
Expansionist War
Foreign Rule
Global Politics
Global War Policy
Imperial Government
Imperialism System
Imperialist
Imperialist Economy
Imperialist War
Open Door Policy
Puppet Regime
Puppet State
Yankee Imperialism

IMPERIALISM SYSTEM
S-37-0066 1975 00011
BT System Type
NT Academic Imperialism
Cultural Imperialism
Economic Imperialism
Political Imperialism
RT Colonial Empire
Colony
Communist Empire
Economic System
Empire
Foreign Rule
Global Politics
Imperial Government
Imperialism
Imperialist
Imperialist Economy
Imperialist War
World Empire

IMPERIALIST
S-32-0276 1975 00000
BT System Politicist
RT Colonialist
Fascist
Imperial Government
Imperialism
Imperialism System
Imperialist Economy
Imperialist War

IMPERIALIST ECONOMY
S-12-0028 1975 00000
BT Market Economy
RT Capitalism
Capitalist Empire
Capitalist Imperialism
Colonialism
Command Economy
Export Economy
Imperial Government
Imperialism
Imperialism System
Imperialist
Imperialist War
International Economic Organization
Socialist Market Economy
World Market

IMPERIALIST WAR
S-08-0094 1975 00005
BT Expansionist War
RT Class Struggle
Colonialism
Global Politics
Global War Policy
Ideological Conflict
Imperial Government
Imperialism

Imperialism System
Imperialist
Imperialist Economy
Political Revolution
Proxy War
Psychological War
Rebellion
Revolution
Revolutionary War
Struggle

IMPLEMENTATION PROCESS
S-31-0329 1975 00017
BT Decision Making Process
RT Allocation Process
Approval Process
Authorization Process

IMPORT DUTY
S-26-0144 1975 00001
BT Taxation Policy
RT Confiscatory Taxation
Excise Taxation Policy
Luxury Taxation
Nuisance Taxation
Tariff

IMPORT EXPORT RATIO
S-06-0350 1975 00011
BT International Economic Characteristics
RT Export Quota
Foreign Trade Pattern
Import Quota

IMPORT POLICY
S-26-0187 1975 00041
BT Restrictive Trade Policy
RT Blockade Policy
Export Policy
Import Quota
Tariff Policy

IMPORT QUOTA
S-06-0351 1975 00007
BT International Economic Characteristics
RT Export Quota
Foreign Trade Pattern
Import Export Ratio
Import Policy
Protective Tariff

IMPOSED LEGAL SETTLEMENT
S-31-0496 1975 00000
BT Legal Settlement
RT Negotiated Legal Settlement

IMPRISONMENT
S-31-0492 1975 00003
BT Post Trial Procedure
NT Arbitrary Imprisonment
RT Internment
Presentence Investigation
Sentencing

INAUGURAL ADDRESS
S-26-0249 1975 00000
UF Inauguration
BT Presidential Policy
NT State Of The Union
RT Executive Legislative Policy
Presidential Legislative Program
Presidential Policy

INAUGURATION
USE Inaugural Address

INCENTIVE TAXATION
S-26-0152 1975 00007
BT Taxation Policy
RT Investment
Subsidization Process

INCENTIVE TAXATION POLICY
S-26-0145 1975 00011
BT Taxation Policy
RT Social Security Taxation
Value Added Taxation

INCOME
S-06-0324 1975 00037
BT Economic Characteristics
NT Business Income
Family Income
Farm Income
Foreign Income
Guaranteed Annual Income
Income Measure
National Income
Personal Income
Profit Income
Tax Exempt Income
Unearned Income
RT Assets
Income Policy
Income Rights
Income Taxation
Money

INCOME DISTRIBUTION
S-06-0635 1975 00090
BT Wealth Distribution
RT Family Income
Family Subsidization Policy
Income Elasticity
Income Inequality
Income Policy
Poverty
Prosperity
Subsistence Level
Wage Level
Wealth Distribution
Wealth Redistribution

INCOME ELASTICITY
S-06-0636 1979 00000
BT Wealth Distribution
RT Income Distribution
Income Policy
Wage Freeze Policy
Wage Level

INCOME EQUALITY
S-06-0726 1979 00000
BT Economic Equality
RT Class Equality
Education Equality
Egalitarianism
Income Maintenance Policy
Income Measure
Political Equality
Racial Equality
Sex Equality
Social Equality
Socialist Theory
Wage Freeze Policy
Wage Level

INCOME INEQUALITY
S-06-0736 1979 00000
BT Economic Inequality
RT Class Inequality
Education Inequality
Income Distribution
Income Measure
Political Inequality
Racial Inequality
Sex Inequality
Social Inequality
Status Inequality

INCOME MAINTENANCE POLICY
S-26-0102 1979 00000
BT Income Policy
RT Guaranteed Annual Income Policy
Income Equality
Income Measure
Income Redistribution Policy
Income Rights
Income Subsidy Policy
Wage Policy
Welfare Policy

INCOME MEASURE
S-06-0331 1975 00012
BT Income
NT Average Income
Disposable Income
Fixed Income
Median Income
Net Income
Real Income
RT Economic Equality
Economic Loss
Economic Scarcity
Family Income
Farm Income
Guaranteed Annual Income
Income Equality
Income Inequality
Income Maintenance Policy
Job Satisfaction
National Income
Profit Income
Standard Of Living
Unearned Income
Wage Freeze Policy
Wage Level

INCOME POLICY
S-26-0101 1975 00021
BT Fiscal Policy
NT Income Maintenance Policy
Income Redistribution Policy
Income Subsidy Policy
Inflation Control Policy
Inflation Policy
Price Control Policy
Price Fixing Policy
Price Freeze Policy
Price Policy
Wage Policy
RT Average Income
Budget Policy
Capital Formation Policy
Capital Investment Policy
Deflation Policy
Expenditure Policy
Income
Income Distribution

Income Elasticity
Inflation Policy
Monetary Policy
Public Debt Policy
Revenue Policy
Taxation Policy

INCOME RECORD
S-18-0014 1975 00009
BT Financial Record
RT Budget Record
Expenditure Record
Political Party Financial Record
Revenue Record

INCOME REDISTRIBUTION POLICY
S-26-0103 1975 00030
BT Income Policy
RT Income Maintenance Policy
Income Subsidy Policy
Income Taxation
Tax Reform Movement
Wage Policy
Wage Taxation

INCOME RIGHTS
S-15-0076 1975 00002
BT Social Rights
RT Childrens Rights
Health Care Rights
Housing Rights
Income
Income Maintenance Policy
Income Subsidy Policy
Marriage Rights
Unemployment Compensation

INCOME SUBSIDY POLICY
S-26-0104 1975 00011
BT Income Policy
NT Guaranteed Annual Income Policy
RT Income Maintenance Policy
Income Redistribution Policy
Income Rights
Wage Policy

INCOME TAXATION
S-26-0146 1975 00025
BT Taxation Policy
NT National Income Taxation
Subnational Income Taxation
RT Confiscatory Taxation
Graduated Taxation
Income
Income Redistribution Policy
Tariff
Tax Reform Movement
Wage Taxation

INCREMENTAL BUDGET
S-06-0254 1975 00005
UF Incremental Budgeting
BT Capital Budget
RT Budget Policy
Performance Budget
Program Budget
Zero Based Budget

INCREMENTAL BUDGETING
1975-1979 00005
USE Incremental Budget

INCUMBENT
S-36-0134 1979 00000
BT Government Official
RT Congressional Seniority System
Election Type
Electoral Competition
Electoral Outcome
Electoral Politics
Group Status
Political Role
Political Succession
Seniority

INDEPENDENCE MOVEMENT
S-27-0023 1975 00032
BT Political Movement
NT Liberation Movement
Separatist Movement
RT Decolonization
Ethnic Separatist Movement
Ideological Spectrum Political Movement
Ideological Spectrum Political Party Type
Liberation Movement
Nationalist Movement
Revolutionary Movement
Sector Based Political Movement
Social Movement
Terrorist Movement

INDEPENDENT AUTHORITY
S-04-0018 1975 00004
BT Authority Structure
RT Chief Executive Discretion
Chief Executive Prerogative
Citizenship Privilege
Decentralized Authority
Decentralized Government
Diffuse Authority
Formal Authority
Hierarchical Authority
Informal Authority
Integrated Authority

INDEPENDENT REGULATORY COMMISSION
S-19-0102 1975 00007
BT Regulatory Commission
RT Federal Commission
Planning Commission
Presidential Commission

INDEPENDENT VARIABLE
S-24-0430 1975 00015
BT Variable Logical Status
NT Explanatory Variable
RT Dependent Variable
Endogenous Variable
Exogenous Variable
Interdependent Variable
Intervening Variable

INDEPENDENT VOTER
S-32-0316 1975 00004
BT Voter
RT Floating Voter
Independent Voting
Informed Voter
Ticket Splitter

INDEPENDENT VOTING
S-29-0140 1975 00002
BT Voting
RT Floating Voting
Independent Voter
Ticket Splitter
Write In Voting

INDEXING
S-24-0156 1975 00009
UF Concordance
Identifier
Subject Indexing
BT Information Storage
RT Abstracting
Abstracting Service
Citation Analysis
Data Storage
Indicator
Microfilm Equipment
University Information Service

INDIAN STUDIES
USE American Indian Studies

INDICATOR
S-24-0256 1975 00012
BT Operationalization
NT Change Indicator
Economic Indicator
Multiple Indicator
Political Indicator
Social Indicator
RT Functional Equivalent
Gross National Product
Hypothesis Testing
Indexing
Measures
Scientific Research
Social Science Model

INDICTMENT
S-31-0515 1975 00000
BT Pretrial Procedure
RT Arraignment
Detention
Detention Center
Pretrial Release

INDIRECT COMPETITION
S-31-0207 1975 00000
BT Competition
RT Direct Competition
Perfect Competition

INDIRECT ELECTION
S-29-0048 1975 00000
BT Election Type
RT Average Voter Turnout Election
Direct Election
Electoral Procedure

INDIRECT REPRESENTATION
S-31-0720 1975 00000
BT Representation Type
RT At Large Representation
Functional Representation
Geographic Representation
Interest Group Representation
Minority Group Representation
Proportional Representation
Single Member District Representation

INDIRECT RULE
S-16-0147 1975 00001
BT Rule Type
RT Despotism
Direct Rule
Empire
Extranational Government Structure

INDIRECT TAXATION
S-26-0153 1975 00002
BT Taxation Policy
RT Direct Taxation
Gift Taxation
Regressive Taxation

INDIVIDUAL
S-24-0344 1975 00000
BT Analysis Unit
RT Attitude Characteristics
Individual Attitude
Individual Behavior

INDIVIDUAL ACCOMMODATION
USE Accommodative Social Behavior

INDIVIDUAL ADAPTATION
USE Adaptive Behavior

INDIVIDUAL ATTITUDE
S-24-0440 1975 00036
BT Individual Phenomena
RT Attitude Characteristics
Individual
Personality Development

INDIVIDUAL BEHAVIOR
S-24-0441 1975 00075
BT Individual Phenomena
RT Behavioral Science
Individual
Individual Perception
Micropolitical Thought
Nonverbal Communication
Personal Behavior
Personality Development
Reality Construction
Reality Testing

INDIVIDUAL COMMUNICATION POLICY
S-26-0017 1975 00007
BT Communication Policy
NT Postal Communication Policy
Postal Telephone Telegraph Policy
Telephone Policy
RT Communication Process
Mass Media Policy

INDIVIDUAL CRIME
S-10-0026 1975 00001
BT Crime
NT Assault
Blackmail
Child Neglect
Criminal Abortion
Extortion
Highjacking
Illegal Abortion
Juvenile Crime
Kidnapping
Libel
Malpractice
Marital Offense
Morals Offense
Murder
Police Brutality
Sex Crime
Slander
Street Crime
RT Court Crime
Defection
Desertion
Euthanasia
Recidivism
Religious Offense
Sedition
Treason
Tyrannicide
Violent Crime

INDIVIDUAL FREEDOM THEORY
S-38-0460 1975 00021
BT Freedom Theory
RT Freedom And Necessity Doctrine
Libertarianism
Moral Freedom Theory
Negative Freedom Theory
Ontological Existentialism
Political Freedom Theory
Positive Freedom Theory
Psychological Freedom Theory

INDIVIDUAL MEASUREMENT
S-24-0188 1975 00006
BT Measurement Object
RT Aptitude Measurement
Attitude Measurement
Behavioral Measurement
Change Measurement
Group Measurement
Intelligence Quotient
Perception Measurement
Power Measurement

INDIVIDUAL PERCEPTION
S-24-0442 1975 00165
BT Individual Phenomena
NT Reality Construction
Reality Testing
RT Elite Perception
Individual Behavior
Nonverbal Communication
Perception
Social Psychology

INDIVIDUAL PHENOMENA
S-24-0439 1975 00000
BT Variable Phenomenological Status
NT Individual Attitude
Individual Behavior
Individual Perception
RT Elite Perception
Personality Development

INDIVIDUALISM MODEL
S-24-0305 1979 00000
UF Individualistic Model
BT Social Science Model
RT Free Enterprise System

INDIVIDUALISM THEORY
S-38-0471 1975 00023
BT Political Philosophy Concept
NT Possessive Individualism
RT Egocentrism
Freedom Of Inquiry
Freedom Theory
Human Nature Theory
Human Needs Theory
Humanism
Liberty Theory
Pragmatism
Utilitarianism

INDIVIDUALISTIC MODEL
1975-1979 00013
USE Individualism Model

INDUCTIVE METHOD
S-24-0021 1979 00000
BT Analysis Methodology
RT Applied Research
Arms Verification Policy
Baconian Analysis
Basic Research
Causal Analysis
Deductive Method
Descriptive Research
Experimental Research
Hypothesis Testing
Methodology
Moral Reasoning

INDULGENCE
1975-1979 00001

INDUSTRIAL ASSOCIATION
S-03-0018 1979 00000
BT Economic Interest Group
RT Developed Economy
Economic Interest Group
Industrial Management
Industrial Policy
Industrial Sociology
Industry
Interest Group
Occupational Interest Group
Trade Organization

INDUSTRIAL CAPITALISM
S-37-0015 1975 00006
BT Capitalism
RT Black Capitalism
Bourgeois Capitalism
Industrial Economic Planning
Industrial Economic Stage
Industrial Economy
Industrial Management
Industrial Policy
Industrial Revolution
Industrial Sociology
Industry
Mature Capitalism
Mercantile Capitalism
Monopoly Capitalism
Private Sector
Warfare Capitalism
Welfare Capitalism

INDUSTRIAL DEMOCRACY
S-38-0089 1979 00000
BT Democratic Theory
RT Industrial Society
Participatory Democratic Theory
Populist Democratic Theory
Socialist Democratic Theory
Worker Self Management

INDUSTRIAL DEVELOPMENT
S-31-0061 1979 00000
BT Economic Development
RT Industrial Economic Stage
Industrial Economics
Industrial Index
Industrial Policy
Industrial Sector
Industry
Manufacturing Industry
Mass Production

INDUSTRIAL DISTRIBUTION
S-06-0626 1975 00004
BT Economic Power Distribution
RT Heavy Industrial Policy
Manufacturing Industry
Wealth Distribution

INDUSTRIAL ECONOMIC PLANNING
S-31-0648 1975 00001
BT Economic Planning
RT Heavy Industrial Policy
Industrial Capitalism
Industrial Management
Industrial Policy

INDUSTRIAL ECONOMIC STAGE
S-06-0162 1975 00005
BT Economic Development Stage
RT Advanced Industrial Society
Agricultural Economic Stage
Entrepreneurship
Feudal Economic Stage
Industrial Capitalism
Industrial Development
Industrial Policy
Industrial Sector

INDUSTRIAL ECONOMICS
S-01-0064 1979 00000
BT Economics Discipline
RT Business Economics
Econometrics
Industrial Development
Industrial Economy
Industrial Policy
Industrial Revolution
Industrial Society
Industrialization Level
Industry
Labor Economics
Macroeconomics
Microeconomics
Post Industrial Society
Social Economics
Transportation Economics
Urban Decay
Urban Economics
Urban History

INDUSTRIAL ECONOMY
S-12-0024 1975 00018
BT Economy Type
RT Balanced Economy
Capital Investment Economy
Centrally Planned Economy
Developed Economy
Developing Economy
Gross National Product
Industrial Capitalism
Industrial Economics
Industrial Management
Industrial Policy
Industrial Production
Industrial Revolution
Industrial Sector
Industrial Sociology
Industry
Mass Production
Urban Decay
Welfare Economy

INDUSTRIAL ESPIONAGE
S-10-0018 1975 00001
BT Economic Espionage
RT Economic Competition
Economic Conspiracy
Intelligence Censorship
Military Espionage
Organized Crime
Political Espionage
Property Crime
Robbery

INDUSTRIAL INDEX
S-06-0295 1979 00000
UF Industrialization Index
BT Economic Index
RT Industrial Development
Machinery Industry

INDUSTRIAL MANAGEMENT
S-23-0015 1975 00016
BT Economic Management
RT Business Management
Corporate Management
Energy Management
Industrial Association
Industrial Capitalism
Industrial Economic Planning
Industrial Economy
Industrial Policy
Industrial Production
Industrial Psychology
Industrial Sociology
Industry
Military Management

INDUSTRIAL OCCUPATION
S-32-0083 1975 00006
BT Occupational Role
NT Industrial Supervisor
Industrial Worker
RT Agricultural Occupation
Commercial Occupation
Foreign Worker
Industrial Working Class
Occupation Characteristics
Professional Occupational Role
White Collar Worker

INDUSTRIAL PLANT
USE Industry

INDUSTRIAL POLICY
S-26-0275 1975 00012
BT Policy
NT Consumer Industrial Policy
Heavy Industrial Policy
Light Industrial Policy
Service Industry Policy
RT Business Policy
Business Regulation Policy
Business Subsidization Policy
Cottage Industry Economy
Economic Policy
Government Economic Management
Industrial Association
Industrial Capitalism
Industrial Development
Industrial Economic Planning
Industrial Economic Stage
Industrial Economics
Industrial Economy
Industrial Management
Industrial Production
Industrial Revolution
Industrial Sector
Industrial Society
Industrial Sociology
Industry
Insurance
Manufacturing Industry
Nationalized Industry
Production Industry
Protected Industry
Public Utility Industry

INDUSTRIAL PRODUCTION
S-31-0434 1975 00017
BT Production Process
NT Commodity Production
Mass Production
Raw Material Production
RT Automated Production
Industrial Economy
Industrial Management
Industrial Policy
Industrial Revolution
Industrial Society
Industrial Sociology
Industry
Mine Safety Policy
National Production
War Production

INDUSTRIAL PSYCHOLOGY
S-01-0179 1975 00005
BT Social Psychology
RT Economic Geography
Industrial Management
Industrial Relations
Industrial Sociology
Industry
Urban Sociology

INDUSTRIAL RELATIONS
S-31-0377 1975 00015
BT Economic Relations
RT Commerce
Industrial Psychology
Industry
International Economic Relations
Mine Safety Policy
Modernization
Progress
Trade

INDUSTRIAL REVOLUTION
S-08-0077 1975 00007
BT Social Revolution
RT Industrial Capitalism
Industrial Economics
Industrial Economy
Industrial Policy
Industrial Production
Industrial Society
Industrial Sociology
Industry
Proletarian Revolution
Racial Revolution
Spontaneous Revolution
Technological Revolution
Technology

INDUSTRIAL SAFETY LAW
S-21-0035 1979 00000
BT Economic Law
NT Mine Safety Law

RT Consumer Protection Law
Industrial Safety Policy
Industry
Labor Law
Property Law
Welfare Law

INDUSTRIAL SAFETY POLICY
S-26-0401 1975 00007
BT Safety Policy
RT Industrial Safety Law
Mine Safety Law
Mine Safety Policy
Traffic Safety Policy

INDUSTRIAL SCHOOL
USE Vocational Training School

INDUSTRIAL SECTOR
S-37-0030 1975 00010
BT Economic Sector
RT Commercial Sector
Heavy Industrial Policy
Industrial Development
Industrial Economic Stage
Industrial Economy
Industrial Policy
Industrial Sociology
Industry
Public Sector
Urban Decay

INDUSTRIAL SOCIETY
S-35-0020 1975 00039
BT Society Type Base
NT Advanced Industrial Society
Post Industrial Society
RT Achieving Society
Advanced Technology
Bourgeois Society
Capitalist Society
Class Society
Industrial Democracy
Industrial Economics
Industrial Policy
Industrial Production
Industrial Revolution
Industrialization Level
Industry
Luddite Movement
Machinery Industry
Meritocracy
Modern Ages
Modernizing Society
Nuclear Family
Secular Society
Technocracy
Urban Decay
Urban Society
Western Society

INDUSTRIAL SOCIOLOGY
S-01-0187 1975 00014
BT Sociology Discipline
RT Applied Sociology
Economics Discipline
Industrial Association
Industrial Capitalism
Industrial Economy
Industrial Management
Industrial Policy
Industrial Production
Industrial Psychology
Industrial Revolution
Industrial Sector
Industrial Working Class
Industry
Macrosociology
Marxist Sociology
Policy Science Studies
Political Economy Studies
Political Sociology
Social Pathology
Urban Sociology

INDUSTRIAL SUBSIDY
S-06-0319 1975 00002
BT Government Expenditure
RT Development Fund
Economic Loss
Farm Subsidy
Federal Grant In Aid
Financial Aid
Government Grant
Government Loan
Government Research Support
Infant Industry
Protected Industry

INDUSTRIAL SUPERVISOR
S-32-0084 1975 00004
BT Industrial Occupation
NT Foreman
RT Industrial Worker

INDUSTRIAL UNION
S-03-0069 1975 00004
BT Union
RT Arbitration
Craft Union
Economic Organization
Labor Management Relations Policy
Labor Union
Producer Cooperative
Trade Union
Worker Cooperative

INDUSTRIAL WORKER
S-32-0086 1975 00022
BT Industrial Occupation
NT Blue Collar Worker
RT Foreign Worker
Foreman
Industrial Supervisor
Industrial Working Class
Working Class

INDUSTRIAL WORKING CLASS
S-06-0782 1975 00010
BT Working Class
RT Agricultural Working Class
Class Analysis
Economic Growth Index
Employment Index
Industrial Occupation
Industrial Sociology
Industrial Worker
Industrialization Level
Labor Conflict
Proletariat
Union Worker
Unionized Working Class

INDUSTRIALIZATION INDEX
1975-1979 00005
USE Industrial Index

INDUSTRIALIZATION LEVEL
S-06-0145 1975 00080
BT Economic Development Level
RT Development Theory
Economic Characteristics
Economic Development Rate
Economic Development Stage
Industrial Economics
Industrial Society
Industrial Working Class

INDUSTRY
S-17-0001 1975 00010
UF Industrial Plant
NT Chemical Industry
Communication Industry
Construction Industry
Consumer Industry
Defense Industry
Energy Industry
Extractive Industry
Food Industry
Infant Industry
Nationalized Industry
Private Industry
Production Industry
Protected Industry
Public Utility Industry
Service Industry
Transportation Industry
RT Business Policy
Industrial Association
Industrial Capitalism
Industrial Development
Industrial Economics
Industrial Economy
Industrial Management
Industrial Policy
Industrial Production
Industrial Psychology
Industrial Relations
Industrial Revolution
Industrial Safety Law
Industrial Sector
Industrial Society
Industrial Sociology
Labor Management Contract
Management
Mass Production

INDUSTRY NATIONALIZATION
S-31-0294 1975 00005
BT Nationalization Process
NT Basic Industry Nationalization
RT Bank Nationalization
Heavy Industrial Policy
Land Nationalization
Utility Nationalization

INEQUALITY
S-06-0734 1979 00000
BT Social System Structural Characteristics
NT Economic Inequality
Political Inequality
Social Inequality
RT Discrimination Policy
Economic Injustice
Education Injustice
Equality
Justice Theory
Political Injustice

Political Repression
Racial Injustice
Reverse Discrimination
Sex Exploitation
Social Injustice

INFANCY
S-06-0183 1975 00010
BT Age
RT Adolescence
Childhood

INFANT INDUSTRY
S-17-0049 1975 00001
BT Industry
RT Industrial Subsidy
Protective Tariff

INFANT MORTALITY RATE
S-06-0196 1975 00010
BT Mortality Rate
RT Birth Control Policy
Public Health Policy

INFERENTIAL STATISTICS
S-24-0066 1975 00003
BT Statistics Type
RT Descriptive Statistics
Nonparametric Statistics
Parametric Statistics
Statistics Discipline

INFLATION
S-31-0138 1975 00051
BT Economic Change
RT Deflation
Economic Cycle
Economic Depression
Expenditure Policy
Fiscal Policy
Government Economic Planning
Inflation Control Policy
Inflation Policy
Monetary Policy

INFLATION CONTROL POLICY
S-26-0111 1975 00027
BT Income Policy
NT Currency Devaluation Policy
RT Deflation Policy
Economic Stabilization Theory
Inflation

INFLATION POLICY
S-26-0110 1975 00021
BT Income Policy
RT Budget Policy
Cost Of Living Index
Deflation Policy
Economic Inflation
Economic Stabilization Theory
Expenditure Policy
Government Economic Planning
Income Policy
Inflation
Monetary Economic Theory
Monetary Policy
Public Debt Policy
Revenue Policy

INFLUENCE INDICATOR
S-24-0264 1975 00046
BT Political Indicator
RT Political Instability Indicator
Voting Indicator

INFLUENCE PROCESS
S-31-0473 1975 00107
BT Process
NT Political Influence
RT Government Process
Informal Authority
Informal Power

INFORMAL AUTHORITY
S-04-0019 1975 00003
BT Authority Structure
RT Check And Balance Theory
Decentralized Authority
Derived Authority
Diffuse Authority
Independent Authority
Influence Process

INFORMAL COMMUNICATION
S-31-0171 1975 00017
BT Communication Process
RT Information Dissemination
International Communication
Interpersonal Communication
Mass Communication
Nonverbal Communication
Political Communication
Political Indoctrination

INFORMAL EDUCATION
S-13-0023 1979 00000
BT Education Type
RT Adult Education
Global Education
Outreach Education
Skill Acquisition

INFORMAL POWER
S-30-0010 1975 00005
BT Power Type
RT Coercion
Communication Agency
Cultural Politics
Dispersed Power
Foreign Information Agency
Foreign Policy Advisory Board
Formal Power
Influence Process
Intelligence Agency
Intelligence Censorship

INFORMATION ACQUISITION
S-31-0172 1979 00000
BT Communication Process
NT Knowledge Acquisition
RT Communication Flow
Education Policy
Information Dissemination
Information Explosion
Information Sources
Information Theory
Information Utilization
Knowledge Production
Learning Theory
Sociology Of Knowledge

INFORMATION ADVISORY AGENCY
1975-1979 00000

INFORMATION AGENCY
S-19-0045 1975 00002
BT Agencies
NT Communication Agency
Foreign Information Agency
RT Communication Industry
Cultural Advisory Board
Cultural Agency
Foreign Affairs Agency
Government Media Regulation Policy
Information Science
Intelligence Agency
National Government Council
Spying

INFORMATION ATTACHE
S-36-0128 1975 00000
BT Embassy Attache
RT Cultural Attache
Economic Attache
Military Attache
Political Attache

INFORMATION DISSEMINATION
S-31-0174 1975 00040
BT Communication Process
RT Communication Model
Communication Policy
Communication Theory
Government Information Diffusion Policy
Informal Communication
Information Acquisition
Information Science
Information Theory
Information Utilization
International Communication
Interpersonal Communication
Knowledge Production
Library Science Studies
Mass Communication
Microfilm Equipment
Nonverbal Communication
Political Communication
Political Indoctrination
Political Party Advertising
Teaching

INFORMATION EXPLOSION
S-31-0175 1975 00005
BT Communication Process
RT Information Acquisition
Information Sources
Information System
Information Theory
Information Utilization
Knowledge Acquisition

INFORMATION LEAKING
S-31-0300 1975 00003
BT Information Manipulation
RT Broadcasting Censorship
Newspaper Censorship
Published Media Censorship
Report Censorship
Television Censorship

INFORMATION MANAGEMENT
S-23-0026 1975 00013
BT Management
NT Data Management
RT Higher Education Administration
Information Science
Information System
Information Theory
Intelligence Agency
Intelligence Censorship
Knowledge Production
Public Policy Management
Research Management

INFORMATION MANIPULATION
S-31-0298 1975 00008
BT Control Process
NT Editorial Control
Information Leaking
Media Access
RT Book Censorship
Censorship Agency
Clientele Information Policy
Intelligence Agency
Political Control

INFORMATION NETWORK
S-37-0077 1975 00017
BT Information System
RT Abstracting
Abstracting Service
Archives
Bibliographic Service
Information Retrieval Program
Information Retrieval System
Information Sources
Library Science Studies
Management Information System

INFORMATION POLICY
S-26-0280 1975 00014
BT Policy
NT Domestic Information Policy
Foreign Information Policy
Propaganda Policy
RT Agitation
Communication Policy
Cultural Policy
Education Policy
Information Science
Information System
Information Theory
Intelligence Censorship
Library Science Studies
Science Policy
Social Resource Distribution Policy

INFORMATION PROCESSING
S-24-0144 1975 00022
BT Methodology
NT Data Format
Data Processing
Information Retrieval
Information Storage
RT Citation Analysis
Cybernetic Analysis
Data Presentation Methodology
Decision Maker Perception
Information Processing Equipment
Information System
Information Theory
Knowledge Production
Microfilm Equipment
Remote Terminal

INFORMATION PROCESSING EQUIPMENT
S-24-0324 1975 00001
BT Research Apparatus
NT Computer Software
Data Processing Equipment
Information Recording Equipment
Laboratory
Simulation Material
RT Information Processing

INFORMATION RECORDING EQUIPMENT
S-24-0332 1975 00000
BT Information Processing Equipment
NT Interviewing Material
Microfilm Equipment
RT Computer Software
Data Processing Equipment

INFORMATION RETRIEVAL
S-24-0149 1975 00002
BT Information Processing
NT Data Retrieval
Question Formulation
Search Strategy Development
RT Abstracting Service
Archives
Data Processing
Information Storage

INFORMATION RETRIEVAL PROGRAM
S-18-0061 1975 00002
BT Software
RT Bibliographic Control
Information Network
Information Retrieval System
Management Information System
Statistical Data

INFORMATION RETRIEVAL SYSTEM
S-37-0078 1975 00006
BT Information System
RT Information Network
Information Retrieval Program
Information Theory
Management Information System

INFORMATION SCIENCE
S-01-0128 1975 00003
BT Academic Areas
RT Computer Science
Information Agency
Information Dissemination
Information Management
Information Policy
Information Service
Information Sources
Information System
Information Theory
Linguistics
Policy Science Studies
Political Science Discipline
Political Science Methodology Studies
Psychology Discipline
Sociology Discipline

INFORMATION SERVICE
S-18-0046 1975 00002
UF On Line Information System
BT Information Sources
NT Abstracting Service
Bibliographic Service
Documentation Service
Government Information Service
Private Information Service
University Information Service
RT Archives
Education Service
Encyclopedia
Health Service
Information Science
Information Sources
Information Theory
Information Utilization
Knowledge Production
Legal Service
Legislative Information Service
Library Science Studies
Service Industry
Social Policy
Social Service

INFORMATION SOURCES
S-18-0001 1975 00048
UF Book
NT Archives
Confidential Information
Documents
Encyclopedia
Essay
Folk Literature
Information Service
Journal
Library
Literature Review
Machine Readable Information
Monographs
Newsletters
Newspapers
Novel
Obituaries
Poetry
Political Film
Privileged Information
Short Story
Speeches
Statistical Data
Surveillance
Textbook
Thesaurus
Thesis
RT Book Industry
Freedom Of Information
Information Acquisition
Information Explosion
Information Network
Information Science
Information Service
Information Storage
Information System
Informed Voter
Instructional Material
Intelligence Agency
Library Science Studies
Propositional Inventory

INFORMATION STORAGE
S-24-0153 1975 00004
BT Information Processing
NT Abstracting
Data Storage
Indexing
RT Computer Program
Data Processing
Information Retrieval
Information Sources
Microfilm Equipment

INFORMATION SYSTEM
S-37-0075 1975 00027
BT System Type
NT Computer Network
Information Network
Information Retrieval System
Management Information System

RT Clientele Information Policy
Data Archives
Data Bank
Education System
Information Explosion
Information Management
Information Policy
Information Processing
Information Science
Information Sources
Information Theory
Information Utilization
Intelligence Agency
Library Science Studies
Surveillance

INFORMATION THEORY
S-38-0033 1979 00000
BT Theory
RT Cybernetic Model
Cybernetic System
Information Acquisition
Information Dissemination
Information Explosion
Information Management
Information Policy
Information Processing
Information Retrieval System
Information Science
Information Service
Information System

INFORMATION UTILIZATION
S-31-0176 1979 00000
BT Communication Process
RT Education Policy
Information Acquisition
Information Dissemination
Information Explosion
Information Service
Information System
Informed Voter
Learning Package
Management Information System
Sociology Of Knowledge

INFORMED VOTER
S-32-0317 1975 00008
BT Voter
RT Independent Voter
Information Sources
Information Utilization

INHERITANCE LAW
USE Inheritance System

INHERITANCE SYSTEM
S-37-0041 1979 00000
UF Inheritance Law
BT Economic System
RT Private Ownership
Probate Court
Property Ownership System
Unearned Income

INHERITANCE TAXATION
S-26-0154 1975 00003
BT Taxation Policy
RT Confiscatory Taxation
Excise Taxation Policy
Gift Taxation
Luxury Taxation
Nuisance Taxation
Social Security Taxation
Tariff

INITIATIVE ELECTION
S-29-0049 1979 00000
BT Election Type
RT Contested Election
Direct Democracy
Direct Election
General Election
Participatory Democracy
Popular Sovereignty
Representation Type

INJUNCTION
S-31-0483 1975 00003
BT Court Action
RT Cease Desist Order
Certiorari
Conviction
Life Sentence
Obiter Dicta
Right To Strike
Subpoena
Warrant
Writ Of Mandamus

INNER CITY
S-07-0007 1975 00014
BT City
RT Central City
City
Compound
Ghetto Community
Ghetto Conflict
Megalopolis
Metropolis
Municipality
Neighborhood
Outer City
Slum Rehabilitation
Squatter Community

INNER CITY SCHOOL
S-19-0230 1975 00009
BT Urban School
RT Neighborhood School
Primary Education
Secondary Education
Segregated Community
Segregation Policy

INNER DIRECTED PERSONALITY
S-06-0531 1975 00003
BT Personality Type
RT Inner Directedness
Other Directed Personality
Psychology Discipline
Rational Choice Theory

INNER DIRECTEDNESS
S-06-0105 1975 00003
BT Attitude Characteristics
RT Achievement Motivation
Cynicism
Egocentrism
Enlightened Self Interest
Inner Directed Personality
Other Directedness
Self Interest

INNOVATION
S-31-0070 1975 00060
BT Development Process
NT Institutional Innovation
Political Party Innovation
RT Evolutionary Change
Patent Law
Social Change
Technocracy
Technological Change
Technological Progress
Technology
Technology Development Policy

INPUT OUTPUT ANALYSIS
S-09-0031 1975 00016
BT Contemporary Analytic Modes
RT Cost Benefit Analysis
Demand Analysis
Eastonian Analysis
Input Output Device
Input Output Model
Interaction Analysis
Marginal Analysis
Marginal Utility Analysis
National Accounts Analysis
National Income Analysis

INPUT OUTPUT DEVICE
S-24-0329 1975 00000
BT Computer Equipment
NT Remote Terminal
RT Cybernetic Analysis
Input Output Analysis
Input Output Model
Unit Record Equipment

INPUT OUTPUT MODEL
S-24-0306 1975 00018
BT Social Science Model
RT Computer Simulation Model
Cybernetic Analysis
Cybernetic Model
Econometric Model
Equilibrium Model
Input Output Analysis
Input Output Device
Interaction Model

INSTITUTION BUILDING
S-31-0048 1975 00013
BT Building Process
RT Alliance
Association Characteristics
Associational Process
Community Building
Education Institution
Evolutionary Economics
Government
Government Type
Institutional History
National Characteristics
National Politics
Socialization
Society Type
System Characteristics
System Type

INSTITUTIONAL CHANGE
S-31-0143 1975 00040
BT Change Process
RT Administrative Science
Development Theory
Homeostatic Change
Institutional Development

INSTITUTIONAL CONFLICT
S-08-0042 1975 00005
BT Conflict Type
NT Routinized Conflict
RT Aggression
Cold War
Conflict Of Interest

Cultural Conflict
Economic Rebellion
General Strike
Group Conflict
Ideological Conflict
Institutional Decay
Institutions
Military Coup
Political Purge
Political Rebellion
Putsch
Rebellion
Social Conflict
Social Rebellion
Succession Struggle
War

INSTITUTIONAL DECAY
S-31-0057 1975 00008
BT Decay
RT Institutional Conflict
Institutional Development
Political Decay
Urban Decay

INSTITUTIONAL DEVELOPMENT
S-31-0073 1975 00044
BT Development Process
NT Institutionalization
RT Economic Change
Evolutionary Economics
Institutional Change
Institutional Decay
Institutional History
Institutions
Modernization
Modernizing Economy
Organization Development
Organization Formation
Reform

INSTITUTIONAL ECONOMICS
S-01-0065 1979 00000
BT Economics Discipline
RT Business Economics
Evolutionary Economics
Labor Economics
Neoclassical Economic Theory
Social Economics

INSTITUTIONAL ELITE IDENTIFICATION
S-09-0020 1975 00002
BT Elite Identification
RT Academic Elite
Elite Type
Issue Elite Identification
Leadership Analysis
Reputational Elite Identification

INSTITUTIONAL HISTORY
S-01-0110 1979 00000
BT History Discipline
RT Cultural History
Economic History
Economic Institution
Education Institution
Fiscal Institution
Historical Analysis
Historiography
Institution Building
Institutional Development
Institutional Innovation
Institutionalization
Intellectual History
Legal History
Military History
Political Science Methodology Studies
Psychohistory
Quantitative History
Research Institution
Social History
Urban History

INSTITUTIONAL INNOVATION
S-31-0071 1975 00023
BT Innovation
RT Cultural Modernization
Economic Modernization
Evolutionary Economics
Institutional History
Political Modernization
Political Party Innovation
Social Modernization

INSTITUTIONAL POWER
S-30-0009 1979 00000
UF Institutionalized Power
BT Formal Power
RT Concentrated Power
Economic Power
Formal Power
Institutionalization
Political Power
Power Elite
Power Politics
Power Theory

INSTITUTIONAL RACISM
S-38-0221 1979 00000
BT Racism
RT Apartheid Theory
Black Racism
Jim Crow Law
Racial Attitude
Racial Exploitation
Racial Inequality
Racial Prejudice
Racial Supremacy
Racist
White Racism

INSTITUTIONAL SOCIALIZATION
S-34-0032 1975 00010
BT Socialization Context
NT Bureaucratic Socialization
Legislative Socialization
Religious Socialization
RT Administrative Normative Characteristics
Administrative Science
Administrative Theory
Group Socialization
Institutions
Professional Socialization
Socialization Type

INSTITUTIONAL VARIABLE
S-24-0449 1975 00015
BT Variable Substantive Content
RT Cultural Variable
Economic Variable
Historical Variable
Institutions
Organization Variable
Political Variable
Psychological Variable
Social Variable

INSTITUTIONALIZATION
S-31-0074 1975 00029
BT Institutional Development
RT Administrative Development Theory
Bureaucratic Characteristics
Evolutionary Economics
Institutional History
Institutional Power
Institutions
International Communication
Modernization
Political Party Innovation
Political Party Institutionalization
Reform

INSTITUTIONALIZED POWER
1975-1979 00010
USE Institutional Power

INSTITUTIONALIZED RACISM
1975-1979 00012

INSTITUTIONS
S-19-0001 1975 00006
NT Agencies
Authorities
Bureaucracy
Commissions
Constitutional Convention
Councils
Courts
Day Care Center
Economic Institution
Education Institution
Executive Government Institution
Health Care Institution
Legislatures
Military Industrial Complex
Multinational Organization
Nonprofit Institution
Penal Institution
Police
Political Party Institution
Research Institution
Task Force
RT Authority Structure
Bureaucratic Theory
Characteristics
Institutional Conflict
Institutional Development
Institutional Socialization
Institutional Variable
Institutionalization
Integration
Organization Model
Political System Structural Characteristics
Process
Social System
Theory

INSTRUCTION METHODOLOGY
S-31-0448 1979 00000
BT Education Process
NT Instructional Material
RT Education Curriculum
Learning Theory
Programmed Instruction
Teaching

INSTRUCTIONAL MATERIAL
S-31-0449 1979 00000
BT Instruction Methodology
NT Learning Package
RT Education Curriculum
Information Sources
Learning Theory
Teaching
Textbook
Thesaurus

INSTRUMENTAL STATE THEORY
S-38-0393 1975 00001
BT Early Modern Theory Of The State
RT Hobbesian Absolutism
Lockean Contractualism
Newtonian Mechanistic State Theory

INSTRUMENTALISM
S-25-0040 1975 00005
BT Ethical Theory
RT Axiology
Emotive Ethical Theory
Ethical Relativism
Hedonism
Intuitionism
Linguistic Ethical Theory
Metaethical Theory
Situational Ethics

INSURANCE
S-26-0298 1979 00000
BT Policy
NT Accident Insurance
Catastrophe Insurance
Compulsory Insurance
Disability Insurance
Fire Insurance
Life Insurance
Malpractice Insurance
Motor Vehicle Insurance
National Health Insurance
No Fault Insurance
Unemployment Insurance Policy
RT Industrial Policy
Labor Policy
Welfare Policy
Welfare System

INSURGENCY
S-08-0044 1975 00015
BT Conflict Type
NT Counterinsurgency
RT Aggression
Coup D'Etat
Economic Conflict
General Strike
Government Overthrow
Ideological Conflict
Insurrectionist
Internal War
Military Aggression
Military Coup
Mob Violence
Political Violence
Psychological War
Putsch
Rebellion
Revolution
Revolutionary War
Social Conflict
Struggle
War By Proxy

INSURGENT
USE Rioter

INSURRECTIONIST
S-32-0199 1975 00002
BT Revolutionary
RT Guerrilla
Insurgency
Maoist Revolutionary

INTEGRAL CALCULUS
1975-1979 00000

INTEGRATED AUTHORITY
S-04-0020 1975 00001
BT Authority Structure
RT Absolute Monarchy
Absolutism
Centralized Authority
Collective Leadership
Formal Authority
Hierarchical Authority
Hierarchical Integration
Independent Authority
Integrated Community
Integration
National Political Integration
Police State

INTEGRATED COMMUNITY
S-07-0032 1975 00002
BT Heterogeneous Community
RT Bilingual Community
Black Suburban Community
Cooperative Community
Ethnic Ghetto
Homogeneous Community
Integrated Authority
Integration
Kibbutz
Language Community
Military Integration Policy
Multiracial Community
Suburban Ghetto Community
Utopian Community

INTEGRATION
S-31-0796 1975 00029
BT Structural Process
NT Assimilation
Cultural Integration
Economic Integration
Ethnic Integration
Functional Integration
Horizontal Integration
Linguistic Integration
Polarization
Political Integration
Racial Integration
Social Integration
Vertical Integration
RT Apartheid Theory
Cleavage Process
Democratization
Ethnic Policy
European Integration Theory
Fragmentation
Group Theory
Heterogeneous Community
Housing Policy
Institutions
Integrated Authority
Integrated Community
Interest Aggregation
Intermarriage
Internal Migration Pattern
Interstate Compact
Language Movement
Language Policy
Local Political Integration
Military Integration Policy

INTELLECTUAL ELITE
S-14-0010 1975 00028
BT Elite Type
NT Cultural Elite
Intelligentsia
RT Academic Elite
Attentive Public
Elite Formation
Graduate School
Intellectual History
Issue Elite Identification
Leadership Recruitment
Opinion Elite
Political Elite
Polytechnical Institute
Private College
Private University
Professor
Scientific Authority
Scientific Elite
Scientific Manpower Policy
Social Elite
Technological Elite

INTELLECTUAL HISTORY
S-01-0111 1979 00000
BT History Discipline
RT Ancient History
Art History
Cultural History
Diplomatic History
Economic History
Historical Analysis
Historiography
History Of Philosophy
History Of Science
History Of Technology
Institutional History
Intellectual Elite
Intelligentsia
Knowledge Production
Legal History
Oral History
Philosophical Idealism
Political History
Political Philosophy Studies
Psychohistory
Religious History
Social History
Social Philosophy
Sociology Of Knowledge

INTELLIGENCE AGENCY
S-19-0051 1975 00016
BT Agencies
NT Military Intelligence Agency
Secret Service
RT Censorship Agency
Communication Process
Confidential Information
Data Archives
Data Management
Defense Agency
Foreign Affairs Agency

Foreign Information Agency
Foreign Information Policy
Foreign Policy Planner
Informal Power
Information Agency
Information Management
Information Manipulation
Information Sources
Information System
Intelligence Censorship
Military Conspiracy
Military Espionage
Military Intelligence
National Security
National Security Forces
Political Informer
Secret Diplomacy
Supranational Security
Surveillance

INTELLIGENCE CENSORSHIP
S-31-0280 1975 00001
BT Unpublished Media Censorship
RT Government Censorship Agency
Government Document
Government Document Classification Policy
Government Report Censorship
Government Secrecy Policy
Industrial Espionage
Informal Power
Information Management
Information Policy
Intelligence Agency
Police State
Political Censorship
Political Information Manipulation
Public Information Access Policy
Publication Agency
Scientific Report Censorship
Secret Police
Secret Police Official
Spying

INTELLIGENCE QUOTIENT
S-24-0178 1979 00000
BT Aptitude Measurement
RT Affective Measurement
Attitude Measurement
Education Testing
Individual Measurement
Measurement Scale
Operationalization
Scale Type
Test Results

INTELLIGENTSIA
S-14-0014 1975 00014
BT Intellectual Elite
RT Academic Elite
Artistic Elite
Class Analysis
Cultural Elite
Intellectual History
Literary Elite
Modernizing Elite
Potential Elite
Scientific Elite
Scientific Manpower Policy
Technological Elite
Transitional Political Elite

INTERACTION ANALYSIS
S-09-0032 1975 00144
BT Contemporary Analytic Modes
RT Analysis Framework
Analysis Methodology
Analysis Of Play
Communication Process
Communication Theory
Cross Level Analysis
Cybernetic Analysis
Economic Integration
Exchange Theory
Group Behavior
Group Consolidation
Group Development
Group Disintegration
Group Dynamics
Group Formation
Group Maintenance
Group Perception
Group Solidarity
Group Structural Change
Input Output Analysis
Issue Salience
Linguistic Analysis
Network Analysis
Remote Terminal
Sociological Analysis

INTERACTION MODEL
S-24-0307 1975 00064
BT Social Science Model
RT Communication Model
Communication Process
Communication Theory
Consensus Theory
Diffusion Model
Econometric Model
Economic Model
Equilibrium Model
Group Analysis
Group Behavior
Group Consolidation
Group Development
Group Disintegration
Group Maintenance
Group Structural Change
Input Output Model
Psychometric Model
Social Integration Theory

INTERAGENCY RIVALRY
S-29-0004 1975 00003
BT Administrative Politics
RT Agencies
Bureaucratic Politics
Bureaucratic Theory
Group Behavior
Revenue Agency

INTERCODER RELIABILITY
S-24-0160 1975 00005
SN A measure of the extent to which different classifiers obtain same results.
BT Reliability Measurement
RT Internal Consistency Reliability
Interviewer Effect
Test Retest Reliability

INTERDEPENDENT VARIABLE
S-24-0432 1975 00005
BT Variable Logical Status
RT Dependent Variable
Endogenous Variable
Exogenous Variable
Independent Variable
Intervening Variable

INTERDISCIPLINARY RESEARCH
S-24-0388 1975 00029
BT Research Orientation
RT Academic Areas
Concept Explication Research

INTERDISCIPLINARY STUDIES
S-01-0129 1979 00000
BT Academic Areas
RT Environmental Studies
Gerontology

INTEREST AGGREGATION
S-31-0034 1975 00005
SN Process by which various political claims are combined into a more diffuse demand.
BT Group Process
RT Endogenous System Demands
Integration
Interest Articulation
Lobbying Tactic
System Analysis
System Demands

INTEREST ARTICULATION
S-31-0035 1975 00013
BT Group Process
RT Endogenous System Demands
Interest Aggregation
Lobbying Tactic
System Demands

INTEREST GROUP
S-03-0013 1975 00020
BT Groups
NT Association Interest Group
Consumer Interest Group
Cultural Interest Group
Economic Interest Group
Latent Interest Group
Occupational Interest Group
Political Interest Group
RT Budget Agency
Community Interest
Cultural Group
Ethnic Organization
Face To Face Group
Fraternal Organization
Group Attitude
Group Change
Group Characteristics
Group Composition
Group Conflict
Group Effectiveness
Group Efficiency
Group Formation
Group Politics
Group Socialization
Group Solidarity
Group Theory
Industrial Association
Interest Group Pluralism
Interest Group Politics
Interest Group Representation

Interest Group Theory
Lobbying Tactic
Nationality Group
Occupational Identity
Professional Organization
Racial Group
Reference Group
Religious Group
Secondary Group
Sector Based Political Movement
Social Group
Union
Veterans Organization
Worker Organization

INTEREST GROUP COALITION
S-02-0023 1975 00005
BT Political Coalition
RT Class Based Coalition
Coalition Type
Economic Coalition
Endogenous System Demands
Governing Coalition
Group Behavior
Group Cleavage Characteristics
Group Composition
Group Formation
Group Politics
Group Theory
Interest Group Politics
Interest Group Representation
Interest Group Theory
Minimum Winning Coalition
Multiethnic Coalition
Opinion Coalition
Political Party Coalition

INTEREST GROUP PLURALISM
S-38-0090 1975 00010
BT Democratic Theory
RT Concurrent Majority Theory
Democratic Elite Theory
Elite Theory
General Will Democratic Theory
Group Analysis
Group Behavior
Group Characteristics
Group Cleavage Characteristics
Group Politics
Group Theory
Interest Group
Interest Group Politics
Interest Group Representation
Jacksonian Democratic Theory
Jeffersonian Democratic Theory
Minority Rights Democratic Theory
Multiple Group Membership
Participatory Democratic Theory

INTEREST GROUP POLITICS
S-29-0203 1975 00079
BT Group Politics
RT Endogenous System Demands
Freedom Of Association
Group Analysis
Group Capability Characteristics
Group Representation Theory
Groups
Interest Group
Interest Group Coalition
Interest Group Pluralism
Interest Group Representation
Interest Group Socialization
Interest Group Theory
International Economic Boycott
Language Group Politics
Latent Interest Group
Lobbying Tactic
Lobbyist
One Political Party Democracy
Peasant Organization
Pork Barrel
Public Interest
Representation

INTEREST GROUP REPRESENTATION
S-31-0721 1975 00016
BT Representation Type
RT Functional Representation
Geographic Representation
Group Pluralism
Indirect Representation
Interest Group
Interest Group Coalition
Interest Group Pluralism
Interest Group Politics
Interest Group Theory
Minority Group Representation
New Middle Class
Political Party Secretariat
Political System Effectiveness
Political System Normative Characteristics

INTEREST GROUP SOCIALIZATION
S-34-0028 1975 00000
BT Group Socialization
RT Adolescent Socialization
Adult Socialization
Childhood Socialization
Cohort Group Socialization
Elite Socialization
Interest Group Politics
Interest Group Theory
Peer Group Socialization

INTEREST GROUP THEORY
S-38-0144 1975 00009
BT Group Theory
RT Association Interest Group
Collective Action Theory
Community Interest
Corporatism
Endogenous System Demands
Group Characteristics
Interest Group
Interest Group Coalition
Interest Group Politics
Interest Group Representation
Interest Group Socialization
Lobbying Tactic
Social Group

INTERFERENCE POLICY
S-26-0263 1975 00015
BT Intervention Policy
NT Economic Interference Policy
Political Interference Policy
RT Expansionist Policy
Military Intervention Policy
Political Intervention Policy

INTERGENERATIONAL MOBILITY
S-06-0749 1975 00019
BT Status Mobility
RT Downward Mobility
Horizontal Mobility
Intragenerational Mobility
Upward Mobility
Vertical Mobility

INTERGOVERNMENTAL DOCUMENT
S-18-0025 1975 00001
BT Government Document
NT Domestic Intergovernmental Document
Foreign Intergovernmental Document
RT Administrative Record
Documentation Service
Foreign Information Agency
International Organization Record
Legislative Information Service
Legislative Record
Parliamentary Paper
Regulatory Agency Record
White Paper

INTERGOVERNMENTAL RELATIONS
S-31-0466 1979 00000
BT Government Process
NT Center Periphery Government Relations
City State Relations
Civil Military Relations
Federal City Relations
Federal State Relations
Police Community Relations
RT Executive Legislative Policy
Federal Reserve System
Policy Implementation
Policy Making Process
Revenue Sharing Policy

INTERGROUP CONFLICT
1975-1979 00028
USE Internal Conflict

INTERIM GOVERNMENT
S-16-0061 1979 00000
BT Government Type
NT Caretaker Government
RT Benevolent Despot
Constitution Making
Democratization
Guided Democracy
Military Occupation
National Government

INTERLOCKING GROUP MEMBERSHIP
S-06-0020 1975 00006
BT Group Composition
RT Elite Composition
Group Structural Characteristics
Heterogeneous Group Membership
Homogeneous Group Membership
Kinship Group
Multiple Group Membership
Overlapping Membership
Social Stratification Division

INTERMARRIAGE
S-20-0023 1975 00007
BT Marriage Type
RT Apartheid Theory
Communal Family
Extended Family
Family Policy
Integration

INTERNAL COMPETITION
S-31-0208 1975 00003
BT Competition
RT External Competition
Free Market
Freedom Of Competition
Internal Consistency Reliability
Internal Market
International Competition
Intraparty Conflict

INTERNAL CONFLICT
S-08-0046 1979 00000
UF Intergroup Conflict
Intragroup Conflict
BT Conflict Type
NT Internal War
Rebellion
Revolution
RT Bolshevik Revolution
Coup D'Etat
Cultural Conflict
Economic Conflict
Guerrilla
Marxism
Organization Conflict
Revolution
Revolutionary Movement
Revolutionary War
Succession Struggle
War By Proxy

INTERNAL CONSISTENCY RELIABILITY
S-24-0161 1975 00010
BT Reliability Measurement
RT Intercoder Reliability
Internal Competition
Interviewer Effect
Test Retest Reliability

INTERNAL EXTERNAL REINFORCEMENT SCALE
S-24-0236 1975 00017
BT Scale Type
RT Social Distance Scale
Social Frustration Scale

INTERNAL MARKET
S-19-0195 1975 00003
BT National Market
RT Balanced Budget
Business Income
Communist Economic System
Heavy Industry
Internal Competition
Subnational Economic Planning

INTERNAL MIGRATION
S-31-0621 1975 00020
BT Migration Process
NT Rural Migration
Suburban Migration
Urban Migration
RT Emigration Process
Immigration Process
Internal Migration Pattern
Refugee Migration
Residential Pattern
Rural Migration Pattern

INTERNAL MIGRATION PATTERN
S-06-0239 1975 00020
BT Migration Pattern
NT Rural Migration Pattern
Suburban Migration Pattern
Urban Migration Pattern
RT Emigration Pattern
Immigration Flow
Immigration Pattern
Integration
Internal Migration
Population Mobility
Population Transition
Residence Requirement
Urban Migration

INTERNAL WAR
S-08-0047 1975 00017
BT Internal Conflict
NT Civil War
Guerrilla War
National Liberation War
RT Black Insurrection
Bolshevik Revolution
Chinese Cultural Revolution
Class Rebellion
Class Struggle
Communist Revolution
Counterinsurgency
Counterrevolution
Cultural Revolution
Government Overthrow
Insurgency
Military Coup
National Political Revolution
Political Rebellion
Political Violence
Putsch
Rebellion
Religious War
Revolution
Social Rebellion
Socialist Revolution
Spontaneous Revolution
Succession Struggle
Thermidor

INTERNATIONAL ADJUDICATION
S-31-0223 1975 00005
BT Adjudication
RT Diplomacy
Diplomatic History
International Conciliation
International Conference
International Decision Making Process
International Mediation
International Negotiation
International Peace Negotiation
International Political Bargaining
Treaty Making
World Court

INTERNATIONAL AGENCY
S-19-0054 1975 00028
BT Agencies
RT Administrative Policy Making
Global System
Government Agency
International Corporation
International Court
International Government Council
International Organization
International Planning Commission
Multinational Organization
United Nations

INTERNATIONAL ALLIANCE THEORY
S-38-0351 1975 00041
BT International Political Theory
RT Alliance Theory
Coalition Theory
Deterrence Theory
Domino Theory
Foreign Policy Theory
Geopolitical Theory
Geopolitics
Global War Policy
International Conflict Resolution Theory
International Decision Making Theory
International Field Theory
International Influence Theory
International Law Theory
International Organization Theory

INTERNATIONAL ANALYSIS
S-24-0407 1975 00068
BT Comparative Analysis
RT Cross Cultural Analysis
Cross Level Analysis
International Political System
International Regional Conflict
International Relations Studies
Intracultural Analysis

INTERNATIONAL ARBITRATION
S-31-0238 1975 00007
BT Arbitration
RT Arbitration
Diplomacy
Diplomatic History
International Crisis
International Influence Theory
International Integration Theory
International Law
International Law Theory
International Mediation
International Organization Theory
Labor Arbitration

INTERNATIONAL BANKING SYSTEM
S-37-0037 1975 00013
BT Financial System
RT Central Banking System
Federal Reserve System
Gold Reserve
National Banking System
Subnational Banking System

INTERNATIONAL BLOC
S-02-0051 1975 00007
BT Agreement Type
RT Alliance
Atlantic Community
Communist Bloc
Compact
Extranational Bloc
Global System
International Organization
League Of Nations
Multilateral Alliance
Political Front
Third World Bloc
World Alliance

INTERNATIONAL CAPITAL MOVEMENT
S-31-0380 1975 00012
BT International Economic Relations
RT East West Trade
Foreign Capital Market
International Economic Interdependence
International Finance
International Investment
Private Foreign Investment
Private Overseas Investment
Public Foreign Investment

INTERNATIONAL CIVIL SERVANT
S-36-0089 1975 00001
BT Civil Servant
RT Civil Servant
Government Employee
International Law
National Civil Servant
Subnational Civil Servant
United Nations

INTERNATIONAL COMMERCE
S-31-0373 1975 00027
BT Commerce
RT Commercial Attache
East West Trade
Economic Retaliation
Foreign Trade
Global System
International Organization
International Trade
Tourist Industry
World Commerce

INTERNATIONAL COMMISSION MEMBER
S-36-0042 1975 00004
BT Cabinet Member
RT United Nations

INTERNATIONAL COMMODITY MARKET
S-19-0182 1975 00029
BT Commodity Market
RT Customs Union
Farm Production
Global System
Multinational Organization
National Market

INTERNATIONAL COMMONWEALTH THEORY
S-38-0358 1975 00000
BT International Integration Theory
RT European Integration Theory
International Economic Organization Theory
Security Community Theory

INTERNATIONAL COMMUNICATION
S-31-0177 1975 00055
BT Communication Process
RT Communication Agency
Communication Analysis
Communication Flow
Communication Industry
Communication Model
Global System
Informal Communication
Information Dissemination
Institutionalization
Interpersonal Communication
Mass Communication
Nonverbal Communication
Political Communication

INTERNATIONAL COMMUNISM
S-38-0318 1975 00014
BT Communism
RT Communist Bloc
Communist Empire
Communist Government
Communist Imperialism
Global System
International Communist Movement
Popular Front

INTERNATIONAL COMMUNIST MOVEMENT
S-27-0013 1979 00000
UF International Communist Party Movement
BT Communist Movement
RT Communist Bloc
Communist Empire
Communist Studies
Ideologies
International Communism
International Organization
Messianic Movement
Radical Movement
Revolutionary Movement

INTERNATIONAL COMMUNIST PARTY MOVEMENT
1975-1979 00011
USE International Communist Movement

INTERNATIONAL COMPETITION
S-31-0209 1975 00025
BT Competition
RT Economic Competition
Internal Competition
Intervention Policy

INTERNATIONAL CONCILIATION
S-31-0224 1975 00030
BT Adjudication
RT Diplomacy
Diplomatic History
International Adjudication
International Conference
International Conflict
International Decision Making Process
International Law
International Mediation
International Negotiation
International Peace Negotiation
Summit Meeting
World Court

INTERNATIONAL CONFERENCE
S-03-0047 1979 00000
BT International Organization
NT Summit Meeting
RT International Adjudication
International Conciliation
International Negotiation
International Organization Policy
International Relations Studies
Summit Meeting
United Nations

INTERNATIONAL CONFLICT
S-08-0084 1979 00000
BT Conflict Type
NT International Regional Conflict
North South Conflict
War
RT Conflict Resolution Theory
Economic Conflict
Foreign Policy Making
Global Politics
International Conciliation
International Conflict Resolution Theory
International Crisis
International Decision Making Process
International Decision Making Theory
International Economics
International Peace
International Political System Characteristics
International Political Theory
International Power Theory
International Relations Studies
Military Science
Peace Studies
Proxy War
Strategic Studies
Threat Indicator
Treaty Breaking
World Politics

INTERNATIONAL CONFLICT RESOLUTION THEORY
S-38-0352 1975 00085
BT International Political Theory
RT Armistice Policy
Conflict Resolution Theory
Deterrence Theory
Domino Theory
Foreign Policy Theory
International Alliance Theory
International Conflict
International Crisis
International Decision Making Theory
International Field Theory
International Influence Theory
International Integration Theory
International Law
International Law Theory
International Organization Theory
Summit Meeting
United Nations
World Court

INTERNATIONAL CONSTITUTIONAL CONVENTION
S-19-0104 1975 00001
BT Constitutional Convention
RT Democratic Constitution
National Constitutional Convention
Presidential Commission Of Inquiry
United Nations

INTERNATIONAL CORPORATION
S-19-0167 1975 00019
BT Corporation
NT Foreign Subsidiary
Multinational Corporation
RT Business Studies
Cartel
Corporate Power
Economic Conglomerate
Global System
Holding Company
International Agency

International Law
Multinational Organization

INTERNATIONAL COUNCIL MEMBER
S-36-0043 1975 00001
BT Cabinet Member
RT International Government Executive
Privy Councilor

INTERNATIONAL COURT
S-19-0144 1975 00009
BT Courts
NT International Tribunal
World Court
RT Administrative Court
Anticolonialism
Criminal Court
Global System
International Agency
International Government Council
International Law
International Police
Maritime Court
Military Court
Supreme Court

INTERNATIONAL CRISIS
S-31-0251 1979 00000
BT Political Crisis
RT Conflict Intensification
Crisis
Economic Crisis
International Arbitration
International Conflict
International Conflict Resolution Theory
International Politics
Natural Catastrophe
Political Instability
Social Crisis
War
World Politics

INTERNATIONAL DECISION MAKING PROCESS
S-31-0330 1975 00028
BT Decision Making Process
RT Diplomacy
Diplomatic History
Executive Diplomacy
International Adjudication
International Conciliation
International Conflict
International Decision Making Theory
International Mediation
International Negotiation
International Peace Negotiation
National Decision Making Process
Subnational Decision Making Process

INTERNATIONAL DECISION MAKING THEORY
S-38-0353 1975 00022
BT International Political Theory
RT Decision Making Theory
Deterrence Theory
Foreign Policy Theory
Geopolitical Theory
International Alliance Theory
International Conflict
International Conflict Resolution Theory
International Decision Making Process
International Field Theory
International Influence Theory
International Integration Theory
International Law Theory
International Organization Theory
United Nations

INTERNATIONAL DIVISION OF LABOR
S-06-0277 1975 00003
BT Division Of Labor
RT Economic Development Level
National Division Of Labor
Socialist Division Of Labor

INTERNATIONAL ECONOMIC BOYCOTT
S-26-0121 1979 00000
BT Economic Policy
RT Brinkmanship
Business Management
Business Policy
Interest Group Politics
International Economic Relations
International Relations Studies
Labor Boycott
Trade Policy

INTERNATIONAL ECONOMIC CHARACTERISTICS
S-06-0345 1975 00062
BT Economic Characteristics
NT Balance Of Payments
Balance Of Trade
Export Quota
Foreign Trade Pattern
Import Export Ratio
Import Quota
RT Economic Relations
Economic System Characteristics
International Economic Development Level
International Economic System
Trade

INTERNATIONAL ECONOMIC DEVELOPMENT LEVEL
S-06-0149 1975 00006
BT Regional Economic Development Level
RT International Economic Characteristics
National Economic Development Level

INTERNATIONAL ECONOMIC INTEGRATION
S-31-0805 1975 00016
BT Economic Integration
NT International Regional Economic Integration
RT Commonwealth International System
Horizontal Economic Integration

INTERNATIONAL ECONOMIC INTERDEPENDENCE
S-31-0381 1975 00069
BT International Economic Relations
RT Economic Retaliation
Foreign Trade
Global System
International Capital Movement
International Finance
International Investment
International Trade
Public Foreign Investment
World Economy

INTERNATIONAL ECONOMIC MANAGEMENT
S-23-0016 1975 00021
BT Economic Management
RT Business Management
Central Economic Management
Corporate Management
Gold Reserve
Government Economic Planning
Monetary Management
National Economic Management
Subnational Economic Management

INTERNATIONAL ECONOMIC ORGANIZATION
S-03-0040 1975 00029
BT Economic Organization
NT Customs Union
Monetary Union
RT Business Agency
Economic Interest Group
Imperialist Economy
International Economic Organization Theory
International Labor Organization
International Law
International Market
International Trade Organization
Trade Bloc

INTERNATIONAL ECONOMIC ORGANIZATION THEORY
S-38-0359 1975 00010
BT International Integration Theory
RT European Integration Theory
International Commonwealth Theory
International Economic Organization
International Economic Planning
International Economics
Multinational Corporation
Multinational Organization Theory
Security Community Theory
United Nations

INTERNATIONAL ECONOMIC PLANNING
S-31-0649 1975 00017
BT Economic Planning
RT International Economic Organization Theory
International Market
National Economic Planning

INTERNATIONAL ECONOMIC RELATIONS
S-31-0378 1975 00184
BT Economic Relations
NT Economic Retaliation
International Capital Movement
International Economic Interdependence
International Finance
International Investment
RT Diplomatic Relations
Diplomatic Relations Normalization
Industrial Relations
International Economic Boycott
International Economic System
International Market
Trade
World Economy

INTERNATIONAL ECONOMIC SYSTEM
S-37-0042 1979 00000
BT Economic System
NT New International Economic Order
RT Economic Development Theory
Economic Stratification
Economic System Characteristics
International Economic Characteristics
International Economic Relations
International Influence Theory
International Market
International Organization
International Political System
International Power Theory

INTERNATIONAL ECONOMICS
S-01-0066 1975 00033
BT Economics Discipline
RT Economic Relations
Government Economic Planning
International Conflict
International Economic Organization Theory
International Relations Studies
Macroeconomics
Political Economy Studies
Regional Economics
Scarcity
Social Economics
Sociology Discipline
Trade
Trade Agency

INTERNATIONAL EXCHANGE PROGRAM
S-26-0295 1979 00000
BT International Policy
RT Cross Cultural Analysis
Cross National Analysis
Cultural Exchange Agreement
Cultural Exchange Treaty
Education Exchange Agreement
Education Exchange Treaty
Foreign Student

INTERNATIONAL FIELD THEORY
S-38-0354 1975 00002
SN A form of international analysis that focuses on the relative distances in analytical space of nations on attribute dimensions in explaining the behavior of nations.
BT International Political Theory
RT Deterrence Theory
Domino Theory
Foreign Policy Theory
Geopolitical Theory
International Alliance Theory
International Conflict Resolution Theory
International Decision Making Theory
International Influence Theory
International Integration Theory
International Law
International Law Theory
International Organization Theory
International Politics

INTERNATIONAL FINANCE
S-31-0382 1975 00012
BT International Economic Relations
RT Economic Retaliation
International Capital Movement
International Economic Interdependence
International Investment
Private Foreign Investment
Private Overseas Investment
Public Foreign Investment

INTERNATIONAL GOVERNMENT
S-16-0063 1975 00003
BT Government Type
NT Imperial Government
World Government
RT Extranational Government Structure
International Organization
National Government

INTERNATIONAL GOVERNMENT BUREAUCRACY
S-19-0076 1975 00001
BT Government Bureaucracy
RT Bureaucratic Theory
Decision Maker
Local Government Bureaucracy
National Government Bureaucracy
Subnational Government Bureaucracy
United Nations

INTERNATIONAL GOVERNMENT COUNCIL
S-19-0109 1975 00002
BT Councils
RT Economic Council
Executive Government Institution
Global System
Government
International Agency
International Court
International Tribunal
National Government Council
Subnational Government Council
World Court

INTERNATIONAL GOVERNMENT EXECUTIVE
S-36-0051 1975 00001
BT Chief Government Executive
RT Governing Elite
Government
International Council Member
National Chief Government Executive

INTERNATIONAL INFLUENCE THEORY
S-38-0355 1975 00123
BT International Political Theory
RT Deterrence Theory
Domino Theory
Foreign Policy Theory
Geopolitical Theory
International Alliance Theory
International Arbitration
International Conflict Resolution Theory
International Decision Making Theory
International Economic System
International Field Theory
International Integration Theory
International Law Theory
International Organization Theory
Intervention Policy
Realist Foreign Policy

INTERNATIONAL INTEGRATION THEORY
S-38-0356 1975 00019
BT International Political Theory
NT European Integration Theory
International Commonwealth Theory
International Economic Organization Theory
Security Community Theory
RT Domino Theory
Foreign Policy Theory
Geopolitical Theory
International Arbitration
International Conflict Resolution Theory
International Decision Making Theory
International Field Theory
International Influence Theory
International Law Theory
International Organization Theory
Multinational Organization Theory

INTERNATIONAL INVESTMENT
S-31-0383 1975 00014
BT International Economic Relations
RT Gold Reserve
International Capital Movement
International Economic Interdependence
International Finance
Private Foreign Investment
Private Overseas Investment
Public Foreign Investment

INTERNATIONAL JUDGE
S-36-0108 1975 00001
BT Judge
RT International Judicial System
International Law
National Judge
Subnational Judge
Supreme Court Justice
World Court

INTERNATIONAL JUDICIAL SYSTEM
S-37-0082 1975 00006
BT Judicial System
RT International Judge
International Law
National Judicial System
Subnational Judicial System
World Court

INTERNATIONAL LABOR ORGANIZATION
S-03-0063 1975 00005
BT Worker Organization
RT International Economic Organization
International Trade Organization
Labor Mediation
Union

INTERNATIONAL LAW
S-21-0057 1975 00068
BT Law Type
NT Law Of The Sea
World Law
RT Air Piracy
Annexation
Arms Control Agreement

Arms Control Treaty
Balance Of Power
Conflict Resolution
Customary Law
DeFacto Recognition
DeJure Recognition
Diplomatic Privilege
Diplomatic Relations Normalization
Genocide
International Arbitration
International Civil Servant
International Conciliation
International Conflict Resolution Theory
International Corporation
International Court
International Economic Organization
International Field Theory
International Judge
International Judicial System
International Law Enforcement
International Law Theory
International Organization
International Pacifism
International Peace
International Political System
International Sanction
International Tribunal
International Trusteeship
Prisoner Of War
Prisoner Of War Camp
Sea Piracy
Seabed Policy
Sovereignty
United Nations
War Criminal
World Court

INTERNATIONAL LAW ENFORCEMENT
S-31-0566 1975 00011
BT Law Enforcement
RT International Law
National Law Enforcement
Punishment
World Court
World Politics

INTERNATIONAL LAW SYSTEM
S-37-0102 1975 00010
BT Law System
RT Administrative Law System
Civil Law System
Common Law System
Constitutional Law System
Criminal Law System
Global System
International Organization
Law Type
Military Law System
Natural Law System
Socialist Law System
War Crime Trial
World Court

INTERNATIONAL LAW THEORY
S-38-0361 1975 00004
BT International Political Theory
RT Foreign Policy Theory
International Alliance Theory
International Arbitration
International Conflict Resolution Theory
International Decision Making Theory
International Field Theory
International Influence Theory
International Integration Theory
International Law
International Organization
International Organization Theory
Law Formulation
Law Type
World Court

INTERNATIONAL MARKET
S-19-0191 1979 00000
BT Economic Institution
NT Marketplace
Mass Market
National Market
Stock Market
World Market
RT International Economic Organization
International Economic Planning
International Economic Relations
International Economic System
International Policy Making
Market System

INTERNATIONAL MEDIATION
S-31-0240 1975 00021
BT Mediation
RT Arbitration
International Adjudication
International Arbitration
International Conciliation
International Decision Making Process
International Negotiation
International Peace Negotiation

INTERNATIONAL NEGOTIATION
S-31-0243 1975 00088
BT Negotiation
NT International Peace Negotiation
RT Diplomacy
International Adjudication
International Conciliation
International Conference
International Decision Making Process
International Mediation
International Organization Policy
International Political Bargaining
Summit Meeting
Treaty Making
World Court

INTERNATIONAL ORGANIZATION
S-03-0046 1979 00000
BT Organizations
NT International Conference
RT Economic Organization
International Agency
International Bloc
International Commerce
International Communist Movement
International Economic System
International Government
International Law
International Law System
International Law Theory
International Organization Policy
International Organization Theory
International Political System
International Relations Studies
New International Economic Order
Professional Organization
Seabed Policy
Trade Organization
United Nations

INTERNATIONAL ORGANIZATION POLICY
S-26-0296 1975 00115
BT International Policy
RT Foreign Policy
International Conference
International Negotiation
International Organization
International Organization Theory
United Nations

INTERNATIONAL ORGANIZATION RECORD
S-18-0039 1975 00041
BT Documents
RT Commission Record
Foreign Intergovernmental Document
Government Document
Government Information Service
Intergovernmental Document
Treaty Document
United Nations
University Information Service

INTERNATIONAL ORGANIZATION THEORY
S-38-0362 1975 00041
BT International Political Theory
RT Domino Theory
Foreign Policy Theory
International Alliance Theory
International Arbitration
International Conflict Resolution Theory
International Decision Making Theory
International Field Theory
International Influence Theory
International Integration Theory
International Law Theory
International Organization
International Organization Policy
Multinational Organization Theory
United Nations

INTERNATIONAL PACIFISM
S-38-0282 1975 00000
BT Pacifism
RT International Law
International Peace
Nonviolent Resistance Theory

INTERNATIONAL PARTY
1975-1979 00002

INTERNATIONAL PEACE
S-06-0672 1975 00027
BT Peace
RT Armistice Policy
International Conflict
International Law
International Pacifism
International Peace Negotiation
Limited Peace
Peace Activist
Strategic Arms Reduction Policy
United Nations

INTERNATIONAL PEACE NEGOTIATION
S-31-0244 1975 00020
BT International Negotiation
RT Appeasement
Diplomacy
Executive Diplomacy
International Adjudication
International Conciliation
International Decision Making Process
International Mediation
International Peace
International Political Bargaining
Treaty Making
United Nations

INTERNATIONAL PEACEKEEPING FORCES
S-33-0005 1975 00010
BT Peacekeeping Forces
RT Deterrence Policy
Multilateral Security Forces
Peace
United Nations

INTERNATIONAL PLANNER
S-32-0133 1975 00001
BT Planner
RT Economic Planner
Foreign Policy Planner
International Planning Commission
National Planner
Social Planner
Subnational Planner

INTERNATIONAL PLANNING COMMISSION
S-19-0095 1975 00010
BT Planning Commission
RT Economic Council
Federal Commission
Global System
International Agency
International Planner
Legislative Commission
Local Planning Commission
National Planning Commission
Presidential Commission
Subnational Planning Commission

INTERNATIONAL POLICE
S-19-0303 1975 00000
BT Police
RT International Court
International Police Official
International Tribunal
Military Police
National Police
Paramilitary Police
Private Police
Secret Police
Subnational Police
World Court

INTERNATIONAL POLICE OFFICIAL
S-36-0136 1975 00000
BT Law Enforcement Official
RT International Police
National Police Official
Secret Police Official
Subnational Police Official

INTERNATIONAL POLICY
S-26-0294 1975 00082
BT Policy
NT International Exchange Program
International Organization Policy
International Sanction
RT Agreement Type
Economic Relations
Foreign Policy
International Policy Making
International Political Theory
International Politics

INTERNATIONAL POLICY MAKING
S-31-0681 1975 00040
BT Policy Making Process
RT Domestic Policy Making
Foreign Policy Making
Global War Policy
International Market
International Policy
International Policy Planning
National Policy Making

INTERNATIONAL POLICY PLANNING
S-31-0662 1975 00019
BT Public Policy Planning
RT International Policy Making
National Policy Planning
Social Planning
Subnational Policy Planning

INTERNATIONAL POLITICAL BARGAINING
S-31-0232 1975 00036
BT Political Bargaining
RT Diplomacy
International Adjudication
International Negotiation
International Peace Negotiation
Intervention Policy

INTERNATIONAL POLITICAL INTEGRATION
S-31-0820 1975 00008
BT Political Integration
NT International Regional Political Integration
Supranational Integration
RT International Regional Conflict
National Political Integration
Political Unification
Subnational Political Integration

INTERNATIONAL POLITICAL PARTY
S-28-0024 1979 00000
BT Political Party Type
RT International Political Party Chairperson
International Political Party Committee Member
Structure Specific Political Party Type

INTERNATIONAL POLITICAL PARTY CHAIRPERSON
S-36-0235 1975 00000
BT International Political Party Executive Member
RT International Political Party
International Political Party Committee Member
International Political Party Executive Member
Political Party Secretariat

INTERNATIONAL POLITICAL PARTY COMMITTEE MEMBER
S-36-0236 1975 00000
BT International Political Party Executive Member
RT International Political Party
International Political Party Chairperson
International Political Party Executive Member
National Political Party Executive Member
Subnational Political Party Executive Member

INTERNATIONAL POLITICAL PARTY EXECUTIVE MEMBER
S-36-0234 1975 00000
BT Political Party Official
NT International Political Party Chairperson
International Political Party Committee Member
RT International Political Party Chairperson
International Political Party Committee Member
National Political Party Executive Member
Subnational Political Party Executive Member

INTERNATIONAL POLITICAL SYSTEM
S-37-0115 1975 00042
BT Political System Type
NT Bipolar International System
Commonwealth International System
Hegemonic System
Multipolar International Political System
Regional International Political System
RT Global System
International Analysis
International Economic System
International Law
International Organization
International Political System Characteristics
International Political Theory
International Politics

INTERNATIONAL POLITICAL SYSTEM CHARACTERISTICS
S-06-0659 1975 00109
BT Political System Characteristics
NT Arms Race
Balance Of Power
Collective Security
Peace
Peaceful Coexistence
Rapproachment
Sphere Of Influence
RT Global War Policy
International Conflict
International Political System
International Power Theory
International Regional Conflict
International Relations Studies
National Political System Characteristics
United Nations

World Politics

INTERNATIONAL POLITICAL THEORY
S-38-0340 1975 00035
BT Political Theory
NT Balance Of Power Theory
Deterrence Theory
Domino Theory
Foreign Policy Theory
Geopolitical Theory
International Alliance Theory
International Conflict Resolution Theory
International Decision Making Theory
International Field Theory
International Influence Theory
International Integration Theory
International Law Theory
International Organization Theory
RT Convergence Theory
Explanatory Political Theory
Global War Policy
International Conflict
International Policy
International Political System
International Politics
International Power Theory
International Sanction
Macropolitical Theory
Medieval International Theory
Multinational Organization Theory
World Politics

INTERNATIONAL POLITICS
S-29-0205 1975 00141
BT Politics
NT Global Politics
World Politics
RT Conflict Theory
Global System
Global War Policy
International Crisis
International Field Theory
International Policy
International Political System
International Political Theory
International Power Theory
International Sanction
Intervention Policy
Linkage Politics
National Politics
Threat Indicator

INTERNATIONAL POWER THEORY
S-38-0165 1975 00110
BT Power Theory
RT Alliance Theory
Buffer Zone Theory
Geopolitics
Global War Policy
International Conflict
International Economic System
International Political System Characteristics
International Political Theory
International Politics
International Relations Studies
International Sanction
Naval Power
Peace
Peace Studies
Policy Science Studies
Political Behavior Studies
Political Science Methodology Studies
Power Type
Realist Foreign Policy
Sea Power
Strategic Studies
World Politics

INTERNATIONAL REGION
S-24-0353 1979 00000
BT World Region
RT Geography Discipline
Geopolitics
International Regional Economic Integration
International Regional Political Integration
National Region
Regional Development
Regional International Political System
Regional Planning Policy

INTERNATIONAL REGIONAL CONFLICT
S-08-0085 1979 00000
BT International Conflict
RT Geopolitics
International Analysis
International Political Integration
International Political System Characteristics
International Regional Economic Integration
International Relations Studies
North South Conflict
Regional Development
Regional Economic Development Level
Regional International Political System
Regional Military Alliance
Regional Security
Strategic Studies

INTERNATIONAL REGIONAL ECONOMIC INTEGRATION
S-31-0806 1975 00034
BT International Economic Integration
RT European Integration Theory
International Region
International Regional Conflict
Regional Economics

INTERNATIONAL REGIONAL POLITICAL INTEGRATION
S-31-0821 1975 00026
BT International Political Integration
RT European Integration Theory
International Region
Supranational Integration

INTERNATIONAL RELATIONS STUDIES
S-01-0158 1975 00207
BT Political Science Discipline
RT Alliance Theory
Area Studies
Arms Race
Arms Verification Policy
Balance Of Power
Balkanization
Behavioral Science
Cold War
Communist Studies
Comparative Political Studies
Conflict Theory
Convergence Theory
Foreign Language Education
Fourth World Nation
Global Education
Global War Policy
Human Rights Policy
International Analysis
International Conference
International Conflict
International Economic Boycott
International Economics
International Organization
International Political System Characteristics
International Power Theory
International Regional Conflict
International System Polarization
Linguistics
Linkage Politics
Military Science
Peace
Peace Studies
Policy Science Studies
Political Behavior Studies
Political Economy Studies
Political Geography
Political Interference Policy
Political Intervention Policy
Political Science Methodology Studies
Political Sociology
Power Measurement
Rapproachment
Strategic Studies
Third World Nation
United Nations

INTERNATIONAL SANCTION
S-26-0297 1975 00012
BT International Policy
RT Arms Control Agreement
Blockade Policy
Brinkmanship
International Law
International Political Theory
International Politics
International Power Theory
International Trade
International Tribunal

INTERNATIONAL SYSTEM POLARIZATION
S-31-0818 1979 00000
BT Polarization
RT Bipolar International System
Cold War
East West Detente
Ideological Polarization
International Relations Studies

INTERNATIONAL TRADE
S-31-0386 1975 00071
BT Trade
NT East West Trade
RT Customs Union
Foreign Trade
Government Enterprise
International Commerce
International Economic Interdependence

International Sanction
International Trade Organization

INTERNATIONAL TRADE ORGANIZATION
S-03-0059 1975 00009
BT Trade Organization
NT Trade Bloc
RT Business Agency
International Economic Organization
International Labor Organization
International Trade

INTERNATIONAL TRIBUNAL
S-19-0145 1975 00001
BT International Court
RT International Government Council
International Law
International Police
International Sanction
Maritime Court
Military Court
War Atrocity
War Crime
War Crime Trial
World Court

INTERNATIONAL TRUSTEESHIP
S-16-0054 1975 00001
BT Extranational Government Structure
RT Caretaker Government
Empire
Extranational Commonwealth
Former Colony
International Law
Mandate Territory
Protectorate
United Nations

INTERNMENT
S-31-0494 1975 00000
BT Post Trial Procedure
RT Imprisonment
Parole
Presentence Investigation
Sentencing

INTERPARTY COMPETITION
S-31-0213 1975 00010
BT Political Party Competition
RT Class Conflict
Conflict Process
Intraparty Competition
Two Political Party Democracy
Voting

INTERPELLATION
S-31-0601 1975 00000
SN Interrogation of members of the executive by parliamentary members.
BT Parliament Cabinet Relations
NT Question Period
RT Question Time Debate

INTERPERSONAL COMMUNICATION
S-31-0178 1975 00136
BT Communication Process
RT Communication Flow
Informal Communication
Information Dissemination
International Communication
Interpersonal Cooperation
Mass Communication
Nonverbal Communication
Political Communication

INTERPERSONAL CONFLICT
S-08-0113 1979 00000
BT Conflict Type
RT Aggression
Authoritarian Personality
Conflict Of Interest
Cultural Aggression
Interpersonal Cooperation
Personality Disorder
Personality Theory
Personality Type
Psychological Aggression
Psychopathology
Social Conflict
Social Psychology

INTERPERSONAL COOPERATION
S-31-0755 1979 00000
BT Social Interaction
RT Friendship
Interpersonal Communication
Interpersonal Conflict
Nonverbal Communication
Social Role Process

INTERPOSITION DOCTRINE
S-38-0451 1975 00000
BT Constitutional Structural Theory
RT Right Of Secession
State Rights Doctrine

INTERRUPTED TIME SERIES ANALYSIS
1975-1979 00001

INTERSTATE AUTHORITIES
S-19-0067 1979 00000
UF Interstate Commission
BT Authorities
RT Bureaucracy
Commercial Agreement
Land Use Policy
Public Authorities
Subnational Government
Water Use Policy

INTERSTATE COMMERCE
S-31-0374 1975 00007
BT Commerce
RT Federal Commission
Federal State Separation
Interstate Compact
Intrastate Commerce

INTERSTATE COMMERCE COMMISSION
S-19-0084 1979 00000
BT Federal Commission
RT Commercial Agreement
Federal Commission
Government Regulation
Interstate Compact
Intrastate Commerce
Trade Agency
Trade Policy

INTERSTATE COMMISSION
1975-1979 00000
USE Interstate Authorities

INTERSTATE COMPACT
S-02-0036 1975 00000
BT Compact
RT Integration
Interstate Commerce
Interstate Commerce Commission
Multilateral Alliance
Multilateral Treaty

INTERVAL MEASUREMENT
S-24-0170 1975 00002
BT Measurement Level
RT Nominal Measurement
Ordinal Measurement
Ratio Scale Measurement

INTERVAL SCALE
S-24-0209 1975 00001
BT Scale Construction Methodology
RT Measurement Level Scale
Nominal Scale
Ordinal Scale
Ratio Scale
Unidimensional Scale

INTERVAL SIGNIFICANCE TEST
S-24-0058 1975 00000
SN Statistical test for determining the confidence intervals within which a parameter lies.
BT Statistical Significance Test
RT Binomial Test
Chi Square Test
F Ratio
Mann Whitney U Test
Nominal Significance Test
Ordinal Significance Test
Wald Wolfowitz Runs Test

INTERVENING VARIABLE
S-24-0433 1975 00008
BT Variable Logical Status
NT Control Variable
RT Dependent Variable
Endogenous Variable
Exogenous Variable
Independent Variable
Interdependent Variable

INTERVENTION POLICY
S-26-0262 1975 00058
BT Foreign Policy
NT Interference Policy
Military Intervention Policy
Political Intervention Policy
RT Containment Policy
Expansionist Policy
International Competition
International Influence Theory
International Political Bargaining
International Politics
Open Door Policy
Yankee Imperialism

INTERVIEW
S-24-0107 1975 00012
BT Reactive Observation
NT Depth Interview
Group Interview
Personal Interview
Structured Interview
Telephone Interview
Unstructured Interview
RT Interviewer Effect
Interviewing Material
Mail Questionnaire
Participant Observation
Survey Research

INTERVIEWER EFFECT
S-24-0162 1975 00021
BT Reliability Measurement
RT Attitude Measurement
Intercoder Reliability
Internal Consistency Reliability

Interview
Interviewing Material
Structured Interview
Test Retest Reliability

INTERVIEWING MATERIAL
S-24-0333 1975 00003
BT Information Recording Equipment
NT Response Recording Equipment
RT Experimental Observation
Interview
Interviewer Effect
Participant Observation
Questionnaire
Sampling Procedure
Survey Research

INTOLERANCE
S-06-0106 1975 00003
BT Attitude Characteristics
NT Bigotry
Racial Intolerance
RT Authoritarian Personality
Discrimination Policy
Hostility
Tolerance

INTRACULTURAL ANALYSIS
S-24-0408 1975 00004
BT Comparative Analysis
RT Cross Cultural Analysis
Cross Level Analysis
Cultural History
Ethnic Studies
International Analysis

INTRAGENERATIONAL MOBILITY
S-06-0750 1975 00008
BT Status Mobility
RT Family Role
Family Type
Horizontal Mobility
Intergenerational Mobility

INTRAGROUP CONFLICT
1975-1979 00003
USE Internal Conflict

INTRAPARTY ALIGNMENT
1975-1979 00002
USE Intraparty Coalition

INTRAPARTY COALITION
S-02-0029 1979 00000
UF Intraparty Alignment
BT Political Party Coalition
RT All Party Coalition
Democratic Coalition
Multiparty Coalition
Negative Coalition
Political Party Faction
Political Party Factional Cleavage

INTRAPARTY COMPETITION
S-31-0214 1975 00007
BT Political Party Competition
RT Class Conflict
Interparty Competition
Intraparty Conflict

INTRAPARTY CONFLICT
S-06-0551 1975 00008
BT Political Party Structural Characteristics
NT Political Party Factional Cleavage
RT Conflict Theory
Internal Competition
Intraparty Competition
Intraparty Democracy
Political Party Cohesion
Political Party Discipline
Political Party Faction

INTRAPARTY DEMOCRACY
S-06-0553 1975 00000
BT Political Party Structural Characteristics
RT Intraparty Conflict
Political Party Discipline
Political Party Norms

INTRASTATE COMMERCE
S-31-0375 1975 00000
BT Commerce
RT Interstate Commerce
Interstate Commerce Commission

INTUITIONISM
S-25-0041 1975 00002
BT Ethical Theory
RT Axiology
Emotive Ethical Theory
Ethical Relativism
Hedonism
Instrumentalism
Linguistic Ethical Theory
Metaethical Theory
Moral Theory
Situational Ethics

INVESTIGATION COMMISSION
S-19-0085 1979 00000
UF Investigative Commission
BT Commissions
NT Commission Of Inquiry
Crime Commission
RT Administrative Tribunal
Commission Of Inquiry
Courts
Judicial Administration Agency
Legislative Commission
Presidential Commission
Regulatory Commission
White Paper

INVESTIGATIVE COMMISSION
1975-1979 00008
USE Investigation Commission

INVESTITURE CONTROVERSY
S-38-0384 1975 00000
SN Eleventh century controversy between religious universalism and conceptions of territoriality of church.
BT Two Swords Theory
RT Christian Thought
Medieval State Theory
Monarchy

INVESTMENT
S-31-0390 1975 00026
BT Financing
NT Capital Flow
Capital Formation
Private Investment
Public Financing
Public Investment
RT Capital Investment Economy
Capital Investment Policy
Incentive Taxation
Investment Capital
Investment Ratio
Public Saving
Spending

INVESTMENT CAPITAL
S-06-0265 1975 00028
BT Capital
RT Accumulated Capital
Assets
Capital Investment Economy
Capital Investment Policy
Capital Surplus
Foreign Capital
Investment
Investment Ratio
Private Capital
Public Capital

INVESTMENT POLICY
S-26-0122 1975 00034
BT Economic Policy
RT Assets
Capital Formation Policy
Capital Investment Economy
Capital Investment Policy
Currency Revaluation Policy
Economic Growth Policy
Economic Subsidization Policy
Fiscal Policy
Fixed Assets
Government Economic Management
Public Finance Policy

INVESTMENT RATIO
S-06-0146 1975 00002
BT Economic Development Level
RT Investment
Investment Capital

INVESTOR
S-32-0076 1975 00001
BT Financier
NT Foreign Investor
RT Financier
Speculator

IRON LAW OF OLIGARCHY
S-38-0041 1975 00004
BT Bureaucratic Theory
RT Administrative Science
Bureaucratic Behavior
Bureaucratic Elite
Bureaucratic Theory
Elite Mass Relations
Hierarchical Authority
Hierarchical Integration
Hierarchical Model
Organization Behavior
Organization Model

IRREDENTISM
S-38-0265 1975 00002
BT Cultural Nationalism
RT Black Nationalism
Pan Africanism
Pan Arabism
Pan Islamism
Pan Slavism
Tribalism
Zionism

IRREGULAR FORCES
S-33-0042 1975 00000
BT National Security Forces
NT Irregular Military Forces
RT Military Forces
Paramilitary Forces
Paramilitary Police
Private Army
Professional Military Forces

IRREGULAR MILITARY FORCES
S-33-0043 1975 00000
BT Irregular Forces
NT Paramilitary Forces
Private Army
RT Military Establishment
Paramilitary Forces
Paramilitary Police
Private Army
Professional Military Forces
Secret Police

ISLAMIC CIVILIZATION
S-11-0008 1979 00000
BT Civilization
RT African Civilization
Ancient Civilization
Ayatallah
Byzantine Civilization
Eastern Civilization
Greek Civilization
Historical Analysis
History Discipline
Homogeneous Culture
Islamic Society
Pan Arab Movement
Religious Culture
Roman Civilization
Western Civilization

ISLAMIC SOCIETY
S-35-0048 1979 00000
BT Religious Society
RT Ayatallah
Homogeneous Society
Islamic Civilization
Islamic Thought
Medieval Islamic Thought
Middle East Area Studies
Nonwestern Society
Pan Islamism
Religious Community
Religious Culture

ISLAMIC THOUGHT
S-38-0559 1975 00019
BT Religious Thought
RT Arab Bloc
Ayatallah
Buddhism
Islamic Society
Judeo Christian Thought
Medieval Islamic Thought
Middle East Area Studies
Religious Culture
Religious Identity
Religious Movement
Shintoism
Taoism
Zoroastrianism

ISOLATIONISM
S-38-0272 1975 00016
BT Nationalism
RT Americanism
Cultural Nationalism
Foreign Policy
Isolationist
Neutralism
Patriotism
Separatism

ISOLATIONIST
S-32-0288 1975 00003
BT Separatist
RT Americanism
Cultural Nationalism
Isolationism
Separatism
Xenophobe

ISSUE ANALYSIS
S-09-0033 1975 00167
BT Contemporary Analytic Modes
NT Issue Intensity
Issue Salience
RT Issue Orientation
Issue Politicization
Issue Voter
Leadership Analysis
Social Area Analysis
Value Analysis
Voting Behavior Analysis

ISSUE ELITE IDENTIFICATION
S-09-0021 1975 00005
SN A procedure for determining the relevant decision makers in a specific policy area.
BT Elite Identification
RT Elite Type
Institutional Elite Identification
Intellectual Elite
Leadership Analysis
Reputational Elite Identification

ISSUE INTENSITY
S-09-0034 1979 00000
BT Issue Analysis
RT Content Analysis
Contextual Analysis
Demand Analysis
Issue Salience
Linguistic Analysis
Policy Analysis
Voting Behavior Analysis

ISSUE ORIENTATION
S-32-0336 1975 00037
BT Voter Orientation
RT Candidate Orientation
Issue Analysis
Neighborhood School
Political Party Orientation
Single Issue Voter
Voting Behavior

ISSUE POLITICIZATION
S-31-0159 1975 00016
BT Politicization
RT Bloc Voting
Issue Analysis
Issue Voter
Political Ideology
Single Issue Voter
System Politicization

ISSUE SALIENCE
S-09-0035 1979 00000
BT Issue Analysis
RT Behavior Analysis
Content Analysis
Contextual Analysis
Demand Analysis
Interaction Analysis
Issue Intensity
Voting Behavior Analysis

ISSUE VOTER
S-32-0318 1975 00025
BT Voter
NT Single Issue Voter
RT Candidate Voter
Issue Analysis
Issue Politicization
Marginal Voter
Minority Voter
Opinion Coalition
Voter Orientation
Voting

ITALIAN FASCISM
S-38-0228 1975 00006
BT Fascist Theory
RT Authoritarian Regime
Corporate Fascism
Dictatorial Regime
Falangism
Francoism
Hegemonic One Party System
National Socialism
Neofascism
One Political Party System
Peronism
Totalitarian Movement
Totalitarian Political System

ITEM VETO
S-31-0339 1975 00000
BT Veto
RT Executive Veto
Legislative Process
Presidential Veto

JACKSONIAN DEMOCRATIC THEORY
S-38-0091 1975 00002
BT Democratic Theory
RT Athenian Democratic Theory
Concurrent Majority Theory
Economic Theory Of Democracy
General Will Democratic Theory
Guided Democracy Theory
Interest Group Pluralism
Jeffersonian Democratic Theory
Majoritarianism
Participatory Democratic Theory
Populist Democratic Theory
Procedural Democratic Theory
Republic Theory

JACOBINISM
S-38-0403 1975 00001
BT French Revolutionary Thought
RT Revolution

JAIL
S-19-0293 1979 00000
BT Correctional Institution
RT Crime Rate
Criminal Court
Criminal Prison
Death Penalty Law
Detention Center
Juvenile Center
Military Prison
Prison
Prison Reform
Prison System
Punishment

JAILING
S-31-0503 1975 00001
BT Sentencing
RT Arbitrary Imprisonment
Bail Skipping
Fining
Probation

JEFFERSONIAN DEMOCRATIC THEORY
S-38-0092 1975 00002
BT Democratic Theory
RT Athenian Democratic Theory
Confederation Movement
Economic Theory Of Democracy
General Will Democratic Theory
Guided Democracy Theory
Interest Group Pluralism
Jacksonian Democratic Theory
Jeffersonian Thought
Majoritarianism
Minority Rights Democratic Theory
Participatory Democratic Theory
Populist Democratic Theory
Procedural Democratic Theory
Socialist Democratic Theory

JEFFERSONIAN THOUGHT
S-38-0399 1975 00002
BT American Enlightenment Thought
RT American Political Thought
Jeffersonian Democratic Theory
Madisonian Thought
State Rights Doctrine

JEOPARDY
S-31-0541 1975 00000
BT Judicial Procedure
RT Judicial Discretion
Procedural Due Process

JIM CROW LAW
S-21-0090 1975 00002
BT Social Law
RT Institutional Racism
Miscegenation Law
Racism
Segregation Policy
Segregationist

JINGOIST
S-32-0210 1975 00000
BT Chauvinist
RT National Chauvinist
Patriotism
Xenophobe

JOB DISCRIMINATION
S-06-0491 1979 00000
BT Occupation Characteristics
RT Affirmative Action Employment Policy
Discrimination Policy
Employment Characteristics
Employment Opportunity
Employment Policy
Equal Opportunity
Job Dissatisfaction
Job Preference
Job Satisfaction
Labor Market
Persecution
Racial Exploitation
Reverse Discrimination

JOB DISSATISFACTION
S-06-0492 1979 00000
BT Occupation Characteristics
RT Alienation
Education Opportunity
Employment Opportunity
Equal Opportunity
Job Discrimination
Job Preference
Job Satisfaction
Quality Of Life

JOB PREFERENCE
S-06-0493 1979 00000
BT Occupation Characteristics
RT Employment Characteristics
Employment Opportunity
Job Discrimination
Job Dissatisfaction
Job Satisfaction
Occupation Characteristics
Opportunity Characteristics
Personality Characteristics

JOB SATISFACTION
S-06-0494 1979 00000
BT Occupation Characteristics
RT Employment Characteristics
Employment Opportunity
Human Resources Development
Income Measure
Job Discrimination
Job Dissatisfaction
Job Preference
Occupation Characteristics
Personality Characteristics
Quality Of Life
Right To Job Security

JOB SOCIALIZATION
S-34-0029 1979 00000
BT Group Socialization
RT Employment Characteristics
Employment Policy
Job Training
Occupational Role
Skill Acquisition

JOB TRAINING
S-13-0051 1975 00037
BT Manpower Training
RT Affirmative Action Employment Policy
Employment Policy
Expertise
Job Socialization
Management Training Program
Military Training
Skill Acquisition
Training Assistance
Unemployed Person
Unemployment

JOINT CHIEFS OF STAFF
S-36-0216 1975 00000
BT Military Officer
RT Commander In Chief
Military Directorate
Military Officer
Military Planning
Military Policy

JOINT CONFERENCE COMMITTEE
1975-1979 00000
USE Joint Congressional Committee

JOINT CONGRESSIONAL COMMITTEE
S-19-0265 1979 00000
UF Joint Conference Committee
BT Congressional Committee
RT Ad Hoc Congressional Committee
Committee Staffing
Congressional Delegation
Congressional Subcommittee
Joint Standing Congressional Committee
Senate House Conference Committee
Standing Congressional Committee

JOINT STANDING COMMITTEE
1975-1979 00000
USE Joint Standing Congressional Committee

JOINT STANDING CONGRESSIONAL COMMITTEE
S-19-0267 1979 00000
UF Joint Standing Committee
BT Standing Congressional Committee
RT Ad Hoc Congressional Committee
Congressional Subcommittee
Joint Congressional Committee
Senate House Conference Committee

JOURNAL
S-18-0055 1979 00000
UF Magazine
Periodical
BT Information Sources
RT Citation Analysis
Knowledge Acquisition
Knowledge Production
Magazine Industry
Publication Agency
Publication Industry
Speeches

JOURNAL CENSORSHIP
S-31-0270 1975 00000
BT Periodical Publication Censorship
RT Book Censorship
Editorial Control
Government Media Regulation Policy
Newspaper Censorship

JUDAIC THOUGHT
S-38-0572 1975 00010
BT Judeo Christian Thought
RT Prophetic Tradition
Religious Culture
Religious Identity
Religious Movement

JUDEO CHRISTIAN THOUGHT
S-38-0560 1975 00003
BT Religious Thought
NT Christian Thought
Judaic Thought
RT Buddhism
Eschatology
Hegelian Analysis
Islamic Thought
Religious Culture
Right Hegelianism
Shintoism
Taoism
Zoroastrianism

JUDGE
S-36-0107 1975 00004
BT Court Official
NT International Judge
National Judge
Subnational Judge
Supreme Court Justice
RT Judging
Judicial Behavior
Judicial Decision Making
Judicial Discretion
Judicial Policy Making
Judicial Power
Judicial Procedure
Judicial Process
Judicial Retention
Judicial Role Orientation
Judicial Selection
Juror
Jury Tampering
Jury Trial
Justice Of The Peace
Law Enforcement Policy
Legal Behavior
National Judicial System

JUDGE MADE LAW
S-21-0022 1975 00004
BT Common Law
RT Case Law
Judicial Behavior
Judicial Decision Making
Judicial Discretion
Judicial Policy Making
Judicial Power
Judicial Procedure
Judicial Process
Legal Behavior
Legal Precedent
Procedural Law
Stare Decisis
Statutory Law

JUDGING
S-31-0009 1979 00000
BT Analytic Process
NT Value Judgment
RT Decision Making Process
Decision Making Theory
Evaluating
Judge
Judicial Administration
Judicial Behavior
Judicial Power
Judicial Procedure
Judicial Record
Judicial Restraint Theory
Judicial System
Justice System

JUDICIAL ADMINISTRATION
S-23-0029 1975 00004
BT Law Administration
RT Adjudication
Administrative Law
Bailiff
Chief Justice
Damage Suit
Judging
Judicial Administration Agency
Judicial Policy Making
Judicial Process
Judicial Role Orientation
Juror
Jury
Jury Selection
Jury System
Jury Trial
Justice Administration
Justice Administration Policy
Law System

JUDICIAL ADMINISTRATION AGENCY
S-19-0055 1975 00000
BT Agencies
NT Police Board
RT Adjudication
Investigation Commission
Judicial Administration
Justice Administration Agency
Justice As Fairness Doctrine
Law School

JUDICIAL APPOINTMENT
S-31-0554 1975 00001
BT Judicial Selection
RT Judicial Appointment Policy
Judicial Recruitment
Judicial Retention
Judicial Role Orientation
Judicial Selection
Senatorial Courtesy

JUDICIAL APPOINTMENT POLICY
S-26-0311 1975 00003
BT Justice Administration Policy
RT Judicial Appointment
Judicial Recruitment
Police Board Policy
Senatorial Courtesy

JUDICIAL BEHAVIOR
S-05-0015 1975 00030
BT Political Behavior
RT Adjudication
Adjudicator
Group Behavior
Judge
Judge Made Law
Judging
Judicial Decision Making
Judicial Policy Making
Judicial Retention
Legal Behavior

JUDICIAL DECISION MAKING
S-31-0534 1975 00039
BT Judicial Process
RT Adjudication
Adjudicator
Adversary Process
Court Action
Judge
Judge Made Law
Judicial Behavior
Judicial Procedure
Judicial Retention
Litigation

JUDICIAL DISCRETION
S-31-0542 1975 00010
BT Judicial Procedure
RT Amnesty
Attorney General
Clemency
Common Law Procedure
Jeopardy
Judge
Judge Made Law
Judicial Review
Justiciable Question
Legal Precedent
Probation
Stare Decisis

JUDICIAL POLICY MAKING
S-31-0682 1975 00076
BT Policy Making Process
RT Judge
Judge Made Law
Judicial Administration
Judicial Behavior
Judicial Power
Judicial Procedure
Judicial Process
Judicial Reform
Judicial Role Orientation
National Policy Making

JUDICIAL POWER
S-30-0015 1975 00018
BT Political Power
RT Court Jurisdiction
Executive Power
Federal State Separation
Judge
Judge Made Law
Judging
Judicial Policy Making
Judicial Role Orientation
Legislative Executive Separation
Legislative Power
Presidential Power
Separation Of Power

JUDICIAL PROCEDURE
S-31-0535 1975 00016
BT Judicial Process
NT Amnesty
Appeal Procedure
Clemency
Common Law Procedure
Grievance Procedure
Jeopardy
Judicial Discretion
Judicial Review
Justiciable Question
Legal Discrimination
Legal Precedent
Preemptory Challenge
Procedural Due Process
Substantive Due Process
RT Adjudication
Adversary Process
Bill Of Attainder
Court Action
Evidence Admissibility
Judge
Judge Made Law
Judging
Judicial Decision Making
Judicial Policy Making
Judicial Selection
Law Enforcement
Litigation

JUDICIAL PROCESS
S-31-0475 1975 00018
BT Process
NT Adversary Process
Court Action
Court Procedure
Judicial Decision Making
Judicial Procedure
Judicial Selection
Litigation
Public Order Maintenance
RT Adversary System
Basic Law
Bill Of Rights
Common Law System
Conflict Resolution
Government Process
Judge
Judge Made Law
Judicial Administration
Judicial Policy Making
Judicial System
Jurisdiction Characteristics
Jury System
Legislative Process
Original Jurisdiction

JUDICIAL RECORD
S-18-0030 1975 00012
BT Government Document
NT Court Report
Court Transcript
RT Administrative Record
Documentation Service
Judging
Legislative Information Service
Legislative Record
University Information Service

JUDICIAL RECRUITMENT
S-31-0747 1975 00004
BT Political Recruitment
RT Judicial Appointment
Judicial Appointment Policy
Leadership Recruitment
Legislative Recruitment
Political Party Recruitment

JUDICIAL REFORM
S-31-0092 1975 00011
BT Reform
NT Court Reform
Penal Reform
RT Administrative Reform
Education Reform
Executive Reform
Judicial Policy Making
Legislative Reform

JUDICIAL RESTRAINT THEORY
S-38-0444 1975 00005
BT Constitutional Interpretation Theory
RT Judging
Judicial Review
Legalism
Strict Constructionism

JUDICIAL RETENTION
S-31-0555 1975 00000
BT Judicial Selection
RT Judge
Judicial Appointment
Judicial Behavior
Judicial Decision Making
Judicial Selection

JUDICIAL REVIEW
S-31-0543 1975 00025
BT Judicial Procedure
NT Appellate Court Review
Supreme Court Review
RT Appeal Procedure
Appellate Court
Broad Constructionism
Check And Balance Theory
Church State Separation Doctrine
Constitutional Court
Constitutional Law
Constitutional Law System
Grievance Procedure
Judicial Discretion
Judicial Restraint Theory
Justiciable Question
Legal Precedent
Malapportionment
National Judicial System
National Supreme Court
Nullification Doctrine
Procedural Due Process
Right To Appeal
Separation Of Power Theory
Stare Decisis
Supreme Court Review

JUDICIAL ROLE ORIENTATION
S-31-0766 1975 00014
BT Role Orientation
RT Executive Role Orientation
Judge
Judicial Administration
Judicial Appointment
Judicial Policy Making
Judicial Power
Legislative Role Orientation
Political Role Orientation

JUDICIAL SELECTION
S-31-0553 1975 00002
BT Judicial Process
NT Judicial Appointment
Judicial Retention
RT Court Action
Judge
Judicial Appointment
Judicial Procedure
Judicial Retention
Judicial Staff Personnel

JUDICIAL STAFF PERSONNEL
S-36-0013 1975 00000
BT Administrative Staff Personnel
RT Executive Staff Personnel
Judicial Selection
Legislative Staff Personnel

JUDICIAL SYSTEM
S-37-0081 1975 00015
BT Legal System
NT International Judicial System
National Judicial System
Subnational Judicial System
RT Adversary Process
Basic Law
Bill Of Rights
Chief Justice
Court Jurisdiction
Courts
Equality
Judging
Judicial Process
Jury Trial
Justice System
Law System

JUNGIAN THEORY
S-38-0542 1979 00000
BT Psychological Theory
RT Freudian Psychology
Freudian Theory
Gestalt Theory
Personality Development
Personality Disorder
Psychological Aggression
Psychological Behaviorism
Psychopathology
Psychosis

JUNIOR COLLEGE
S-19-0205 1975 00002
BT College
RT Community College
Private College
State Supported College
University

JURISDICTION CHARACTERISTICS
S-06-0400 1975 00005
BT Characteristics
NT Administrative Jurisdiction
Executive Jurisdiction
Legal Jurisdiction
Legislative Jurisdiction
Territory Jurisdiction
Union Jurisdiction
RT Administrative Court
Government Characteristics
Judicial Process
Jurisprudence
Law System

JURISDICTION STRIKE
S-08-0031 1975 00000
BT Labor Strike
RT Demonstration
Economic Rebellion
Sit Down Strike
Strike Breaking
Walkout
Wildcat Strike

JURISPRUDENCE
S-25-0007 1975 00026
BT Philosophical Concept
NT Legal Positivism
RT Codified Law
Ethical Theory
Jurisdiction Characteristics
Justice As Fairness Doctrine
Law School
Law Type
Ontology
Sociology Of Law

JUROR
S-36-0118 1975 00001
BT Court Official
RT Judge
Judicial Administration
Jury
Jury Selection
Jury System
Jury Trial
Peoples Court

JURY
S-19-0147 1975 00003
BT Courts
NT Grand Jury
Trial Jury
RT Court Procedure
Defense Attorney
Judicial Administration
Juror
Jury Selection
Jury System
Jury Tampering
Jury Trial
Testimony
Trial Court

JURY SELECTION
S-31-0529 1975 00003
BT Trial Procedure
RT Judicial Administration
Juror
Jury
Jury System
Trial Strategy

JURY SYSTEM
S-37-0095 1975 00002
BT Trial System
RT County Level Court
Court Procedure
Courts
Criminal Justice Administration
Criminal Law
Criminology
Judicial Administration
Judicial Process
Juror
Jury
Jury Selection
Jury Tampering
Jury Trial

JURY TAMPERING
S-10-0005 1975 00000
BT Court Crime
RT Contempt Of Court
Judge
Jury
Jury System

JURY TRIAL
S-31-0525 1975 00000
BT Public Trial
RT Adversary System
Bench Trial
Defendants Rights
Defense Attorney
Judge
Judicial Administration
Judicial System
Juror
Jury
Jury System
Law System

JUST AUTHORITY
S-04-0005 1979 00000
BT Authority Mode
RT Diffuse System Supports
Just War
Justice Administration
Justice Administration Policy
Justice As Fairness Doctrine
Justice System
Legitimacy Theory
Liberty Theory
Political Authority
Political Legitimacy Theory
Remedial Justice Theory

JUST WAR
S-08-0096 1975 00003
BT War
RT Conventional War
Guerrilla War
Holy War
Just Authority
National Liberation War
Psychological War
Revolution
Revolutionary War
World War

JUSTICE ADMINISTRATION
S-23-0030 1975 00013
BT Law Administration
NT Criminal Justice Administration
Police Administration
RT Crime Rate
Fair Trial
Federal Judicial System
Judicial Administration
Just Authority
Justice Administration Policy
Justice As Fairness Doctrine
Justice System
Law System
Local Elite
Public Order Maintenance
Relative Justice Theory

JUSTICE ADMINISTRATION AGENCY
S-19-0057 1975 00004
BT Agencies
RT Administrative Court
Civil Court
Courts
Criminal Justice Administration
Grand Jury
Judicial Administration Agency
Justice Administration Policy
Law School
Local Court
Probate Court
Trial Jury

JUSTICE ADMINISTRATION POLICY
S-26-0310 1975 00010
BT Policy
NT Judicial Appointment Policy
Law Enforcement Policy
Police Board Policy
RT Judicial Administration
Just Authority
Justice Administration
Justice Administration Agency
Justice System
Law Enforcement Policy

JUSTICE AS FAIRNESS DOCTRINE
S-38-0479 1975 00007
BT Justice Theory
RT Compensatory Justice
Distributive Justice Theory
Equity
Ethical Theory
Judicial Administration Agency
Jurisprudence
Just Authority
Justice Administration
Justice System
Law System
Moral Freedom Theory
Relative Justice Theory
Remedial Justice Theory

JUSTICE OF THE PEACE
S-36-0112 1975 00000
BT Local Judge
RT Chief Magistrate
Civil Court
Court Official
Criminal Court
Judge
Local Court
Local Police
Magistrate
Police

JUSTICE SYSTEM
S-37-0088 1975 00014
BT Legal System
NT Adversary System
Bail Bond System
Grand Jury System
Law Enforcement System
Trial System
RT Bail
Bar Association
Burden Of Proof
Judging
Judicial System
Just Authority
Justice Administration
Justice Administration Policy
Justice As Fairness Doctrine
Justice Theory
Law System
Remedial Justice Theory

JUSTICE THEORY
S-38-0473 1975 00060
BT Political Philosophy Concept
NT Compensatory Justice
Distributive Justice Theory
Divine Justice Theory
Egalitarian Justice Theory
Equity
Justice As Fairness Doctrine
Natural Justice Theory
Relative Justice Theory
Remedial Justice Theory
Utilitarian Justice Theory
RT Common Good Theory
Common Wealth Theory
Economic Injustice
Equality
Equality Theory
Inequality
Justice System
Legitimacy Theory
Liberty Theory
Minority Rights
Moral Responsibility
Obligation Theory
Order Theory
Political Injustice
Political Man Theory
Political Virtue

JUSTICIABLE QUESTION
S-31-0546 1975 00002
BT Judicial Procedure
RT Judicial Discretion
Judicial Review
Legal Precedent
Procedural Due Process

JUVENILE CENTER
S-19-0294 1979 00000
BT Correctional Institution
RT Criminal Justice Administration
Criminal Prison
Detention Center
Jail
Juvenile Delinquency
Prison
Prison Reform
Prison System

JUVENILE COURT
S-19-0132 1975 00003
BT Civil Court
RT Juvenile Crime
Juvenile Delinquency

JUVENILE CRIME
S-10-0034 1975 00007
BT Individual Crime
NT Juvenile Delinquency
RT Juvenile Court
Juvenile Delinquency
Morals Offense
Street Crime

JUVENILE DELINQUENCY
S-10-0035 1975 00013
UF Delinquency
BT Juvenile Crime
RT Juvenile Center
Juvenile Court
Juvenile Crime
Morals Offense
Sex Crime
Street Crime

KAISER
S-36-0058 1975 00000
BT Emperor
RT Absolute Monarch
Absolute Monarchy
Hereditary Ruler
Khan
Queen
Regent
Sheik
Sultan
Tsar

KANTIAN ANALYSIS
S-38-0404 1975 00013
BT Enlightenment Thought
RT Hegelian Analysis
History Of Philosophy
Philosophical Concept
Positive Freedom Theory
Rousseauian Analysis

KEYNESIAN ECONOMIC THEORY
S-38-0114 1975 00009
BT Economic Theory
RT Capitalism Theory
Classical Economic Theory
Economic Egalitarianism
Fiscal Policy
Government Economic Planning
Keynesian Economics
Marxist Economic Theory
Mercantile Economic Theory
National Debt Financing
Public Debt Policy
Welfare State

KEYNESIAN ECONOMICS
S-01-0069 1975 00011
BT Macroeconomics
RT Government Economic Planning
Keynesian Economic Theory
Marxist Economics
Neoclassical Economic Theory

KHAN
S-36-0059 1975 00000
BT Emperor
RT Hereditary Ruler
Kaiser
King
Queen
Regent
Shah
Sultan
Tsar

KIBBUTZ
S-07-0021 1975 00007
BT Cooperative Community
RT Agrarian Economy
Agrarian Socialism
Collective Community
Commune
Compound
Economic Community
Integrated Community
Religious Community
Rural Community
Segregated Community
Utopian Community

KIBBUTZ MOVEMENT
1975-1979 00000

KIDNAPPING
S-10-0036 1979 00000
BT Individual Crime
RT Assault
Blackmail
Extortion
Highjacking
Murder
Piracy
Political Crime
Terrorism

KINDRED FAMILY
S-20-0011 1975 00000
BT Family Type
RT Ancestry
Clan Kinship System
Extended Family
Extended Kinship System

KING
S-36-0064 1975 00007
BT Monarch
RT Abdication
Absolute Monarch
Absolute Monarchy
Absolutist Government
Hereditary Ruler
Hierarchical Authority
Khan
Monarchy
Queen
Regent
Shah
Sheik
Sultan
Tsar

KINSHIP
S-20-0001 1975 00018
NT Family Descent Pattern
Family Type
Kinship System
Marriage Type
RT Ancestry
Kinship Group
Kinship Role
Kinship Systematics Theory
Structuralism
Tribal Political System
Tribal Politics
Tribal Society
Tribalism

KINSHIP GROUP
S-03-0028 1975 00016
BT Social Group
RT Association Characteristics
Ethnic Group
Extended Family
Extended Kinship System
Face To Face Group
Family Political Socialization
Interlocking Group Membership
Kinship
Kinship System
Nationality Group
Patriarchal Kinship System
Patrilineal Family
Reference Group
Village Chief
Village Politics

KINSHIP ROLE
S-32-0033 1975 00012
BT Roles
NT Clan Role
Family Role
RT Extended Kinship System
Family Political Socialization
Hereditary Ruler
Kinship
Peasant Organization
Role Theory
Tribal Politics
Tribal Society

KINSHIP SYSTEM
S-20-0017 1975 00033
BT Kinship
NT Extended Kinship System
RT Anthropological Theory
Family Descent Pattern
Family Socialization
Family Type
Kinship Group
Kinship Systematics Theory
Social System
Traditional Culture
Tribal Politics

KINSHIP SYSTEMATICS THEORY
S-38-0011 1975 00009

SN An approach to social identity and status by examining a person's relationship with the ancestors and descendants and other members of the extended family.
BT Anthropological Theory
RT Acculturation Theory
Cultural Evolutionism
Ethnographic Theory
Kinship
Kinship System
Structuralism

KNOWLEDGE ACQUISITION
S-31-0173 1979 00000
BT Information Acquisition
RT Communication Process
Education Policy
Information Explosion
Journal
Knowledge Production
Learning Theory
Magazine Industry
Sociology Of Knowledge

KNOWLEDGE PRODUCTION
S-31-0438 1979 00000
BT Production Process
NT Discovery
RT Curiosity
Education Policy
Falsification
Information Acquisition
Information Dissemination
Information Management
Information Processing
Information Service
Intellectual History
Journal
Knowledge Acquisition
Mannheim Ideology Explanation
Problem Solving Behavior
Scientific Research
Sociology Of Art
Sociology Of Knowledge
University

LABOR ARBITRATION
S-31-0239 1975 00003
BT Arbitration
RT Arbitration
Economic Bargaining
International Arbitration
Labor Arbitration Policy
Labor Boycott
Labor Law
Labor Management Relations Policy
Labor Mediation
Labor Negotiation
Labor Relations Agency

LABOR ARBITRATION POLICY
S-26-0318 1975 00002
BT Labor Management Relations Policy
NT Compulsory Arbitration Policy
RT Collective Bargaining Policy
Labor Arbitration
Labor Law
Labor Mediation Policy
Labor Negotiation
Labor Relations Agency
Public Employee Union Policy
Right To Work Policy

LABOR BOYCOTT
S-08-0012 1975 00001
BT Economic Agitation
RT Bargaining
Demonstration
Economic Activist
Economic Demonstration
International Economic Boycott
Labor Arbitration
Labor Conflict
Labor Law
Labor Negotiation
Labor Policy
Labor Strike
Worker Demonstration

LABOR CONFLICT
S-08-0029 1975 00014
BT Economic Conflict
NT Labor Strike
Lockout
Strike Breaking
RT Automated Production
Class Conflict
Consumer Producer Conflict
Demonstration
Economic Agitation
Economic Demonstration
Economic Rebellion
Industrial Working Class
Labor Boycott
Labor Management Contract
Labor Management Relations Policy
Labor Policy
Struggle
Worker Demonstration

LABOR DISCIPLINE
S-11-0051 1979 00000
BT Work Culture
RT Civic Culture
Labor Intensive Economy
Labor Law
Labor Policy
Labor Union
Protestant Ethic
Technological Culture
Work Ethic

LABOR ECONOMICS
S-01-0067 1979 00000
BT Economics Discipline
RT Business Economics
Consumer Economics
Division Of Labor
Econometrics
Industrial Economics
Institutional Economics
Labor Management Relations Policy
Labor Politics
Macroeconomics
Microeconomics
Social Economics
Trade Unionism
Urban Economics
Welfare Economics
Worker Organization

LABOR FORCE
S-06-0648 1979 00000
BT Employment Characteristics
RT Full Employment
Labor Market
Labor Supply
Labor Surplus
Manpower Policy
Overemployment
Retirement
Trade Union
Underemployment
Union Worker
Working Class

LABOR HISTORY
S-01-0105 1975 00061
BT Economic History
RT Administrative Science
Agricultural Science
Economic History
Economics Discipline
Historical Analysis
Historical Sociology
Historical Sociology Analysis
Historiography
History Of Technology
Labor Intensive Economy
Labor Law
Labor Mediation Policy
Labor Political Party
Labor Politics
Labor Strike
Labor Union
Middle Level Technology
Political History
Political Science Discipline
Social History
Sociology Discipline
Technology Policy
Technology Transfer

LABOR INTENSIVE ECONOMY
S-12-0025 1979 00000
BT Economy Type
RT Collective Farm Economy
Cooperative Farm Economy
Craft Economy
Division Of Labor
Farm Economy
Labor Discipline
Labor History
Labor Policy
Planned Economy
Plantation Economy
State Farm Economy
Subsistence Economy

LABOR LAW
S-21-0037 1975 00011
BT Economic Law
NT Fair Employment Law
Minimum Wage Law
Pension Law
Right To Work Law
RT Antitrust Law
Environmental Law
Freedom Of Contract
Industrial Safety Law
Labor Arbitration
Labor Arbitration Policy
Labor Boycott
Labor Discipline
Labor History
Labor Management Relations Policy
Labor Mediation
Labor Negotiation

Labor Policy
Legal History
Mine Safety Law
Right To Strike
Right To Work
Right To Work Law
Right To Work Policy
Tort
Trade Union Movement
Trade Union Policy
Work Norm Policy
Worker Management Participation
Worker Self Management
Working Conditions

LABOR MANAGEMENT CONTRACT
S-02-0039 1979 00000
BT Contract Type
RT Business Contract
Collective Bargaining Policy
Employment Policy
Industry
Labor Conflict
Labor Management Relations Policy
Labor Mediation
Labor Mediation Policy
Labor Negotiation
Wage Level

LABOR MANAGEMENT RELATIONS POLICY
S-26-0315 1975 00024
BT Labor Policy
NT Collective Bargaining Policy
Labor Arbitration Policy
Public Employee Union Policy
Right To Work Policy
Trade Union Policy
RT Business Management
Business Regulation Agency
Industrial Union
Labor Arbitration
Labor Conflict
Labor Economics
Labor Law
Labor Management Contract
Labor Negotiation
Labor Policy
Labor Politics
Labor Regulation Policy
Labor Relations Agency
Right To Work Law
Right To Work Policy
Strike Breaking
Walkout
Worker Management Participation
Worker Self Management

LABOR MARKET
S-06-0649 1979 00000
BT Employment Characteristics
RT Division Of Labor
Full Employment
Job Discrimination
Labor Force
Labor Supply
Labor Surplus
Overemployment
Retirement
Underemployment
Unemployment

LABOR MEDIATION
S-31-0241 1975 00003
BT Mediation
RT Arbitration
Business
Business Management
Collective Bargaining Policy
International Labor Organization
Labor Arbitration
Labor Law
Labor Management Contract
Labor Negotiation
Labor Politics
Labor Regulation Policy
Labor Relations Agency
Labor Strike
Labor Union
Subnational Economic Management

LABOR MEDIATION POLICY
S-26-0317 1975 00001
BT Collective Bargaining Policy
RT Business
Business Management
Business Regulation Agency
Compulsory Arbitration Policy
Labor Arbitration Policy
Labor History
Labor Management Contract
Labor Politics
Labor Relations Agency

LABOR NEGOTIATION
S-31-0245 1975 00007
BT Negotiation
RT Labor Arbitration
Labor Arbitration Policy
Labor Boycott
Labor Law
Labor Management Contract
Labor Management Relations Policy
Labor Mediation
Labor Policy
Labor Politics
Labor Regulation Policy
Labor Relations Agency
Labor Strike
Labor Union
Negotiator
Wage Level
Wage Policy
Working Conditions

LABOR PARTY
1975-1979 00009

LABOR POLICY
S-26-0314 1975 00026
BT Policy
NT Labor Management Relations Policy
Labor Regulation Policy
Labor Subsidization Policy
RT Economic Policy
Government Economic Management
Insurance
Labor Boycott
Labor Conflict
Labor Discipline
Labor Intensive Economy
Labor Law
Labor Management Relations Policy
Labor Negotiation
Labor Politics
Labor Scarcity

LABOR POLITICAL PARTY
S-28-0041 1979 00000
BT Class Based Political Party
NT Working Class Political Party
RT Aristocracy Political Party
Class Based Movement
Labor History
Leftist Political Party
Social Democratic Political Party
Socialist Political Party
Trade Union
Working Class Movement

LABOR POLITICS
S-29-0211 1975 00014
BT Politics
NT Trade Union Politics
RT Group Politics
Labor Economics
Labor History
Labor Management Relations Policy
Labor Mediation
Labor Mediation Policy
Labor Negotiation
Labor Policy
Labor Subsidization Policy
Linkage Politics
Working Class Movement

LABOR REGULATION POLICY
S-26-0323 1975 00007
BT Labor Policy
RT Labor Management Relations Policy
Labor Mediation
Labor Negotiation
Labor Subsidization Policy

LABOR RELATIONS AGENCY
S-19-0029 1975 00003
BT Economic Agency
RT Business Regulation Agency
Economic Advisory Board
Economic Control Agency
Labor Arbitration
Labor Arbitration Policy
Labor Management Relations Policy
Labor Mediation
Labor Mediation Policy
Labor Negotiation

LABOR SCARCITY
S-31-0117 1979 00000
BT Scarcity
RT Energy Scarcity
Food Scarcity
Housing Scarcity
Labor Policy
Resource Allocation
Resource Distribution
Water Scarcity

LABOR STRIKE
S-08-0030 1975 00018
BT Labor Conflict
NT Jurisdiction Strike
Sit Down Strike
Walkout
Wildcat Strike
RT Economic Demonstration
Economic Rebellion
General Strike
Labor Boycott
Labor History

Labor Mediation
Labor Negotiation
Lockout
Strike Breaking
Struggle
Union
Worker Demonstration

LABOR SUBSIDIZATION POLICY
S-26-0324 1975 00001
BT Labor Policy
RT Business Policy
Economic Policy
Labor Politics
Labor Regulation Policy
Subsidization Process

LABOR SUPPLY
S-06-0650 1979 00000
BT Employment Characteristics
RT Full Employment
Labor Force
Labor Market
Labor Surplus
Overemployment
Retirement
Underemployment
Unemployment

LABOR SURPLUS
S-06-0651 1979 00000
BT Employment Characteristics
RT Capitalist Economy
Full Employment
Labor Force
Labor Market
Labor Supply
Overemployment
Retirement
Underemployment

LABOR UNION
S-03-0070 1975 00036
BT Union
RT Civil Service Union
Craft Union
Economic Organization
Industrial Union
Labor Discipline
Labor History
Labor Mediation
Labor Negotiation
Producer Cooperative
Trade Union
Working Class Movement

LABORATORY
S-24-0336 1975 00000
BT Information Processing Equipment
NT Laboratory Equipment
Small Group Laboratory
RT Quasiexperiment

LABORATORY EQUIPMENT
S-24-0337 1975 00000
BT Laboratory
RT Small Group Laboratory

LAISSEZ FAIRE LIBERALISM
S-38-0254 1975 00009
BT Liberalism
RT Civil Liberty Liberalism
Civil Rights Liberalism
Classical Liberalism
Economic Freedom
Economic Freedom Theory
Economic Liberalism
Free Trade Policy
Limited Government
Lockean Contractualism
Negative Freedom Theory
Nineteenth Century Liberalism
Welfare Liberalism

LAISSEZ FAIRE THEORY
S-38-0109 1975 00006
BT Classical Economic Theory
RT Accumulated Capital
Classical Economic Theory
Free Market
Free Trade Policy
Limited Government
Malthusian Theory
Ricardian Theory

LAMA
S-32-0101 1979 00000
BT Religious Minister
RT Lamaism
Religious Elite
Religious Leader
Religious Politics
Religious Society
Teacher

LAMAISM
S-38-0555 1975 00001
BT Buddhism
RT Lama
Religious Leader
Religious Thought

LAND DISTRIBUTION
S-06-0627 1975 00021
BT Economic Power Distribution
NT Land Ownership Pattern
RT Economic Injustice
Farm Industry
Land Estate System
Land Nationalization
Land Policy
Land Reform Policy

LAND ESTATE SYSTEM
S-37-0055 1975 00010
BT Property Ownership System
RT Absentee Landlord System
Building Process
Government Ownership
Land Distribution
Land Tenure System
Primogeniture
Private Ownership
Property Rights

LAND NATIONALIZATION
S-31-0296 1975 00000
BT Nationalization Process
RT Agricultural Collectivization Policy
Industry Nationalization
Land Distribution
Land Ownership Pattern
Land Policy
Land Reform Policy
Land Use Policy
Utility Nationalization

LAND OWNERSHIP PATTERN
S-06-0628 1975 00037
BT Land Distribution
RT Absentee Landlord System
Agricultural Collectivization Policy
Farm Production
Land Nationalization
Land Reform Policy
Patron System
Squatter Society
Wealth Distribution

LAND POLICY
S-26-0214 1975 00027
BT Environment Policy
NT Land Use Policy
RT Farm Economy
Farm Income
Farm Industry
Farm Production
Land Distribution
Land Nationalization
Land Reform Policy
Natural Resource Policy
Pollution Policy

LAND POLLUTION POLICY
S-26-0226 1975 00001
BT Pollution Policy
RT Farm Industry
Land Use Policy
Noise Pollution Policy
Sanitation Policy
Water Pollution Policy

LAND REFORM POLICY
S-26-0005 1975 00025
BT Agrarian Reform Policy
RT Agrarian Reform Movement
Agrarian Socialism
Agrarian Syndicalism
Agricultural Policy
Agricultural Subsidization Policy
Land Distribution
Land Nationalization
Land Ownership Pattern
Land Policy
Land Use Policy
Maoism
Maoist
Maoist Political Party
Maoist Revolutionary

LAND TENURE SYSTEM
S-37-0056 1975 00021
BT Property Ownership System
RT Absentee Landlord System
Collective Ownership
Farm Economy
Farm Industry
Government Ownership
Land Estate System
Patron System
Primogeniture
Private Ownership
Slavery

LAND TRANSPORTATION INDUSTRY
S-17-0073 1975 00012
BT Transportation Industry
NT Motor Vehicle Industry
Railway Industry
RT Mass Transportation Industry
Transportation Policy
Water Transportation Industry

LAND USE POLICY
S-26-0215 1975 00068
BT Land Policy
NT Public Land Use Policy
Zoning Policy
RT Agricultural Development
Agricultural Subsidization Policy
Conservation Law
Eminent Domain
Eminent Domain Policy
Historical Preservation Law
Interstate Authorities
Land Nationalization
Land Pollution Policy
Land Reform Policy
Natural Resource Policy
Population Density
Property Law
Regional Economics
Residential Segregation
Scarcity
Spatial Analysis
Urban Sprawl

LANDLESS PEASANT CLASS
S-06-0776 1975 00006
BT Peasant Class
RT Absentee Landlord System
Class Analysis
Class Society
Day Laborer
Migrant Farming

LANDOWNING CLASS
S-06-0765 1975 00014
BT Class Stratification Division
RT Aristocratic Class
Class Analysis
Class Stratification Division
Entrepreneur Class
Nobility
Patron System
Peasant Class
Propertied Class
Ruling Class
Upper Class

LANDSLIDE ELECTORAL OUTCOME
S-29-0110 1975 00000
BT Electoral Outcome
RT Bandwagon Effect
Coattail Effect
Majority Electoral Outcome
Voting Data

LANGUAGE ACQUISITION
S-34-0007 1979 00000
BT Learning
NT Language Learning
RT Bilingual Community
Bilingualism
Education Policy
Language Characteristics
Language Learning
Language Policy
Language Studies
Learning Theory
Multilingual Society
Psycholinguistics
Symbol Learning
Verbal Learning
Vocabulary

LANGUAGE CHARACTERISTICS
S-06-0411 1979 00000
BT Characteristics
NT Grammar
Semantics
Speech
Stylistics
Vocabulary
RT Demographic Characteristics
Language Acquisition
Language Community
Language Learning
Language Loyalty
Language Policy
Linguistic Analysis
National Characteristics

LANGUAGE COMMUNITY
S-07-0038 1979 00000
BT Homogeneous Community
RT Collective Community
Communal Community
Ethnic Community
Ghetto Community
Homogeneous Community
Integrated Community
Language Characteristics
Language Group Conflict
Language Group Politics
Language Loyalty
Language Movement
Language Policy
Linguistic Analysis
Ordinary Language Philosophy
Sociolinguistics

LANGUAGE GROUP CONFLICT
S-08-0121 1975 00007
BT Group Conflict
RT Language Community
Language Group Politics
Language Policy
Linguistic Analysis
Racial Conflict
Struggle
War

LANGUAGE GROUP POLITICS
S-29-0204 1979 00000
BT Group Politics
RT Interest Group Politics
Language Community
Language Group Conflict
Language Loyalty
Language Movement

LANGUAGE LEARNING
S-34-0008 1979 00000
BT Language Acquisition
RT Bilingual Community
Bilingualism
Education Policy
Education Psychology
Grammar
Language Acquisition
Language Characteristics
Language Policy
Language Studies
Logic
Multilingual Society
Semantics
Speech
Stylistics
Symbol Learning
Verbal Learning
Vocabulary

LANGUAGE LOYALTY
S-06-0388 1975 00011
BT Identity Characteristics
RT Community Identity
Cultural Group Cohesion
Cultural Identity
Ethnic Group Loyalty
Language Characteristics
Language Community
Language Group Politics
Language Policy
Linguistic Analysis
Linguistic Theory
Racial Identity
Social Identity

LANGUAGE MOVEMENT
S-27-0063 1975 00004
BT Social Movement
RT Communal Movement
Integration
Language Community
Language Group Politics
Language Policy
Liberation Movement

LANGUAGE POLICY
S-26-0049 1975 00016
BT Cultural Policy
RT Integration
Language Acquisition
Language Characteristics
Language Community
Language Group Conflict
Language Learning
Language Loyalty
Language Movement
Language Studies

LANGUAGE STUDIES
S-01-0130 1979 00000
BT Academic Areas
RT Area Studies
Cultural History
Foreign Language Education
Humanities Discipline
Language Acquisition
Language Learning
Language Policy
Linguistic Analysis
Linguistics
Literature Studies

LARGE GROUP BEHAVIOR
1975-1979 00001

LARGEST AVERAGE VOTING METHOD
S-29-0169 1975 00000
BT Voting Formulae
RT Cumulative Voting
D'Hont Voting Method
Largest Remainder Voting Method
List Voting
Single Transferable Vote

LARGEST REMAINDER VOTING METHOD
S-29-0170 1975 00000
BT Voting Formulae
RT Cumulative Voting
Largest Average Voting Method
List Voting

Single Transferable Vote

LASSWELLIAN ANALYSIS
S-09-0058 1975 00001
BT Political Psychology Analysis
RT Elite Analysis
Garrison State
Leadership Political Analysis
Leadership Psychological Analysis
Political Psychology
Political Style

LATENT FUNCTION
S-06-0587 1975 00002
BT System Function
RT Functional Adaptation
Manifest Function
Structural Functional Analysis

LATENT GROUP
1975-1979 00000

LATENT INTEREST GROUP
S-03-0019 1975 00001
BT Interest Group
RT Association Interest Group
Cultural Interest Group
Interest Group Politics
Political Interest Group

LATIN AMERICAN AREA STUDIES
S-01-0034 1975 00395
UF South American Area Studies
South American Area Studies
BT American Area Studies
RT Caribbean Area Studies
Central American Area Studies
Comparative Analysis
Comparative Political Studies
Comparative Sociology
Cultural Anthropology
Cultural History
Latin American Bloc
North American Area Studies
Squatter Society

LATIN AMERICAN BLOC
S-02-0048 1975 00000
UF South American Bloc
BT Third World Bloc
RT Atlantic Community
Latin American Area Studies
Neutral Bloc
Security Community

LAW ADMINISTRATION
S-23-0028 1975 00006
BT Management
NT Judicial Administration
Justice Administration
RT Adjudication
Administrative Law
Codified Law
Comparative Law
Education Administration
Law Enforcement
Law Enforcement Official
Law Enforcement Policy
Law Enforcement System
Law System
Law Type
Legal Behavior
Public Policy Management

LAW ENFORCEMENT
S-31-0563 1975 00035
BT Public Order Maintenance
NT Code Enforcement
International Law Enforcement
National Law Enforcement
Punishment
Subnational Law Enforcement
RT Antitrust Law
Comparative Law
Court Procedure
Decriminalization
Judicial Procedure
Law Administration
Law Enforcement Official
Law Enforcement Policy
Law Enforcement System
Law System
Law Type
Legal History
Local Police
National Police Commissioner
Penal Institution
Police
Police Administration
Police Board
Police Board Policy
Police Power
Public Order Maintenance

LAW ENFORCEMENT OFFICIAL
S-36-0135 1975 00009
BT Government Official
NT International Police Official
National Police Official
Secret Police Official
Subnational Police Official
RT Bar Association
Government Authority
Law Administration
Law Enforcement
Law Enforcement System
Law System
Law Type
Local Elite
Police
Police Administration
Public Order Maintenance
Subnational Police

LAW ENFORCEMENT POLICY
S-26-0312 1975 00036
BT Justice Administration Policy
RT Criminal Prison
Judge
Justice Administration Policy
Law Administration
Law Enforcement
Law Enforcement System
Law System
Police
Police Administration
Police Board Policy
Public Order Maintenance

LAW ENFORCEMENT SYSTEM
S-37-0092 1975 00029
BT Justice System
NT Prison System
RT Administrative Law
Adversary System
Arrest
Bail Bond System
Crime Rate
Criminal Prison
Government Authority
Grand Jury System
Law Administration
Law Enforcement
Law Enforcement Official
Law Enforcement Policy
Penal Institution
Peoples Court
Police
Police Administration
Police Board
Trial System

LAW FORMULATION
S-31-0575 1975 00042
BT Legislative Process
NT Constitutional Development
Legislative Action
Treaty Ratification
RT Basic Law
Congressional System
International Law Theory
Law School
Law System
Law Type
Legal History
Legal System
Legislative Behavior
Legislative Executive Relations
Legislative Official
Legislative Procedure
Lobbying
Local Government Council
Political Culture
Sociology Of Law

LAW OF THE SEA
S-21-0058 1979 00000
BT International Law
RT Maritime Law
Natural Resource Management
Natural Resource Policy
Seabed Policy
World Law

LAW SCHOOL
S-19-0219 1975 00009
BT Professional School
RT Bar Association
Graduate Education
Graduate School
Judicial Administration Agency
Jurisprudence
Justice Administration Agency
Law Formulation
Law System
Lawyer
Legal Education
Legal Socialization
Legal Studies

LAW SYSTEM
S-37-0096 1975 00020
BT Legal System
NT Administrative Law System
Civil Law System
Common Law System
Constitutional Law System
Criminal Law System
International Law System

Military Law System
Natural Law System
Socialist Law System
RT Acquittal
Adjudication
Adversary Process
Advocacy Research
Appellate Court
Appellate Court Review
Appellate Jurisdiction
Basic Law
Correctional Institution
Courts
Judicial Administration
Judicial System
Jurisdiction Characteristics
Jury Trial
Justice Administration
Justice As Fairness Doctrine
Justice System
Law Administration
Law Enforcement
Law Enforcement Official
Law Enforcement Policy
Law Formulation
Law School
Law Type
Legal Behavior
Legal Development
Legal History
Legal Jurisdiction
Legal Service
Police Community Relations
Procedural Rights
Public Trial
Right To Counsel
Trial
Trial Court
Trial Procedure

LAW TYPE
S-21-0001 1975 00006
NT Administrative Law
Basic Law
Civil Law
Commercial Law
Common Law
Contract Law
Criminal Law
Customary Law
Decriminalization
Economic Law
Environmental Law
Equity Law
International Law
Maritime Law
Martial Law
Military Law
Natural Law
Outer Space Law
Political Law
Procedural Law
Sacred Law
Social Law
Socialist Law
Statutory Law
RT Appellate Jurisdiction
Civil Law System
Comparative Law
Crime
Equality
International Law System
International Law Theory
Jurisprudence
Law Administration
Law Enforcement
Law Enforcement Official
Law Formulation
Law System
Lawyer
Legal Positivism
Legal System
Legislature Type
Roman Legal Thought
Sociology Of Law
Trial
Trial Court

LAWYER
S-32-0093 1975 00020
BT Professional Occupational Role
NT Civil Lawyer
Corporation Lawyer
Criminal Lawyer
RT Bar Association
Barrister
Court Attorney
Courts
Defender
Defense Attorney
Grand Jury
Law School
Law Type
Legal Studies
Right To Counsel
Trial
Trial Court
Trial Jury
Trial Oral Argument
Trial Procedure
Trial Strategy

LEADER
S-32-0049 1975 00002
BT Roles
NT Economic Leader
Political Leader
Social Leader
RT Decision Maker
Leadership Analysis
Leadership Recruitment
Leadership Type
Lower House Speaker
Political Elite
Politician

LEADER OF OPPOSITION
S-36-0158 1975 00000
BT Legislative Leader
RT Floor Leader
Legislative Speaker
Legislative Whip
Majority Leader
Minority Leader
National Legislative Leader
Subnational Legislative Leader

LEADERSHIP ANALYSIS
S-09-0036 1975 00089
BT Contemporary Analytic Modes
NT Leadership Political Analysis
Leadership Psychological Analysis
Leadership Sociological Analysis
RT Autobiography
Biographical Analysis
Career Analysis
Cult Of Personality
Decision Making Elite
Elite Analysis
Elite Identification
Historical Analysis
Institutional Elite Identification
Issue Analysis
Issue Elite Identification
Leader
Leadership Authority Base
National Political Party Leader
Political Psychology Analysis
Political Purge
Political Style
Political Succession
Presidential Leadership
Presidential Legislative Program
Reputational Elite Identification
Social Leader
Sociological Analysis
Structural Functional Analysis

LEADERSHIP AUTHORITY BASE
S-22-0003 1979 00000
BT Leadership Type
NT Administrative Leadership
Moral Leadership
Personalized Leadership
Rational Legal Leadership
Traditional Leadership
RT Authority
Authority Mode
Authority Structure
Authority Type
Congressional Leadership
Executive Leadership
Leadership Analysis
Leadership Structure Type
National Leadership
National Political Party Leader
Political Leadership
Political Movement Leadership

LEADERSHIP POLITICAL ANALYSIS
S-09-0037 1975 00033
BT Leadership Analysis
RT Cult Of Personality
Elite Analysis
Lasswellian Analysis
Leadership Psychological Analysis
Leadership Sociological Analysis
Leadership Type
National Political Party Leader
Political Psychology Analysis

LEADERSHIP PSYCHOLOGICAL ANALYSIS
S-09-0038 1975 00025
BT Leadership Analysis
RT Cult Of Personality
Elite Analysis
Lasswellian Analysis
Leadership Political Analysis
Leadership Sociological Analysis
Leadership Type
Political Psychology Analysis
Political Style
Political Succession

LEADERSHIP RECRUITMENT
S-31-0748 1975 00008
BT Political Recruitment
RT Intellectual Elite
Judicial Recruitment
Leader
Legislative Recruitment
National Political Party Leader
Political Party Nominating Committee
Political Party Recruitment
Political Purge

LEADERSHIP SOCIOLOGICAL ANALYSIS
S-09-0039 1975 00022
BT Leadership Analysis
RT Elite Analysis
Governing Elite
Leadership Political Analysis
Leadership Psychological Analysis
Political Psychology Analysis
Political Succession

LEADERSHIP STRUCTURE TYPE
S-22-0013 1979 00000
BT Leadership Type
NT Closed Leadership
Collective Leadership
Collegial Leadership
Democratic Leadership
Open Leadership
Small Group Leadership
Totalitarian Leadership
RT Authority Structure
Congressional Leadership
Executive Leadership
Group Structural Characteristics
Leadership Authority Base
Moral Leadership
National Leadership
Personalized Leadership
Political Leadership
Political Movement Leadership
Rational Legal Leadership
Religious Leadership
Structural Functional Analysis
Structural Model
Structuralism
Traditional Leadership
Upper House Speaker

LEADERSHIP TYPE
S-22-0001 1975 00013
NT Bonapartism
Leadership Authority Base
Leadership Structure Type
National Leadership
Political Leadership
RT Elite Analysis
Elite Circulation
Elite Composition
Elite Formation
Elite Type
Leader
Leadership Political Analysis
Leadership Psychological Analysis
Municipal Election
National Political Party Leader
Political Succession
Upper House Speaker

LEAGUE OF NATIONS
S-02-0012 1975 00003
BT World Alliance
RT Extranational Bloc
International Bloc
Sovereignty
United Nations
World Court

LEARNING
S-34-0005 1979 00000
BT Socialization
NT Behavior Modification
Language Acquisition
Moral Learning
Nonverbal Learning
Rote Learning
Serial Learning
Skill Acquisition
Symbol Learning
Verbal Learning
RT Childhood Socialization
Cognitive Development
Education Evaluation
Education Policy
Education Process
Learning Feedback
Learning Psychology
Learning Theory
Socialization Type

LEARNING FEEDBACK
S-06-0573 1979 00000
BT Feedback Loop
RT Adaptive Behavior
Communication Feedback
Education Policy
Functional Adaptation
Learning
Learning Theory
Persistence
Structural Adaptation

LEARNING PACKAGE
S-31-0450 1979 00000
BT Instructional Material
RT Education Curriculum
Information Utilization
Learning Theory
Teaching

LEARNING PSYCHOLOGIST
S-32-0116 1979 00000
BT Psychologist
RT Clinical Psychologist
Education Psychology

LEARNING PSYCHOLOGY
S-01-0175 1975 00056
BT Psychology Discipline
RT Behavior Modification
Behavioral Psychology
Cognitive Dissonance Theory
Cognitive Theory
Cooperative Behavior
Education Discipline
Education Psychology
Education Socialization
Freudian Psychology
Gestalt Psychology
Learning
Logic
Nonverbal Learning
Parapsychology
Personality Development
Political Sociology
Psychological Anthropology
Psychological Programming
Rote Learning
Serial Learning
Skill Acquisition
Social Pathology
Social Psychology
Sociology Of Knowledge
Symbol Learning
Verbal Learning

LEARNING THEORY
S-38-0543 1975 00073
BT Psychological Theory
RT Acculturation
Achievement Theory
Adolescent Political Socialization
Adolescent Socialization
Adult Political Socialization
Adult Socialization
Alienation Psychological Theory
Attitude Change Theory
Attribution Theory
Cognitive Theory
Cross Pressure Theory
Curiosity
Education Discipline
Education Psychology
Education Socialization
Enculturation
Freudian Theory
Gaming
Human Resources Development
Identity Theory
Ideological Education
Imagination
Information Acquisition
Instruction Methodology
Instructional Material
Knowledge Acquisition
Language Acquisition
Learning
Learning Feedback
Learning Package
Logic
Moral Learning
Motivation Theory
Nonverbal Learning
Peer Group Socialization
Perception
Political Science Methodology Studies
Political Socialization
Psychological Behavioralism
Psychological Behaviorism
Psychological Deprogramming
Psychological Programming
Psychopolitical Theory
Role Acquisition
Role Socialization
Rote Learning
Serial Learning
Skill Acquisition
Social Conditioning
Socialization
Symbol Learning
Verbal Learning

LEFT HEGELIANISM
S-38-0409 1975 00000
BT Hegelian Analysis
RT Critical Theory Analysis
Hegelian Marxism
Neohegelianism
Neomarxism
Philosophical Materialism
Right Hegelianism

LEFT RIGHT SCALE
S-24-0237 1975 00001
BT Scale Type
RT Anomie Scale
Civic Competence Scale
Legitimacy Scale
Liberalism
Liberalism Conservatism Scale
Optimism Pessimism Scale
Satisfaction Scale
Social Change Index
Social Frustration Scale

LEFTIST
S-32-0260 1975 00006
BT Spectrum Politicist
RT Centrist
Extremist
Political Radical
Rightist

LEFTIST PARTY
1975-1979 00012

LEFTIST POLITICAL PARTY
S-28-0019 1979 00000
BT Ideological Spectrum Political Party Type
RT Labor Political Party
Radical Political Party

LEGAL ADVISOR
S-32-0017 1975 00003
BT Advisor
RT Administrative Advisor
Court Attorney
Economic Advisor
Education Advisor
Legal Behavior
Legal Education
Legal Socialization
Military Advisor
Political Advisor
Science Advisor
Technical Advisor

LEGAL BEHAVIOR
S-05-0016 1975 00007
BT Political Behavior
RT Behavioral Theory
Judge
Judge Made Law
Judicial Behavior
Law Administration
Law System
Legal Advisor
Legal Education
Legislative Behavior

LEGAL BRIEF
USE Court Report

LEGAL DEVELOPMENT
S-06-0177 1979 00000
BT Development Characteristics
RT Constitutional Law
Development Potential
Economic Development Rate
Economic Development Stage
Human Resources Development
Law System
Legal History
Legal System
Political Development
Political Development Policy

LEGAL DISCRIMINATION
S-31-0547 1975 00012
BT Judicial Procedure
RT Legal Immunity
Persecution
Procedural Due Process
Substantive Due Process

LEGAL EDUCATION
S-13-0042 1975 00006
BT Professional Education
RT Health Education
Law School
Legal Advisor
Legal Behavior
Legal History
Legal Malpractice
Legal Studies
Sociology Of Law
Technical Education
Traditional Education

LEGAL HISTORY
S-01-0112 1979 00000
BT History Discipline
RT Ancient History
Basic Law
Black History
Comparative Law
Constitutional Law
Cultural History
Diplomatic History
Economic Law
Historical Analysis
Historiography
History Of Science
Institutional History
Intellectual History
Labor Law
Law Enforcement
Law Formulation
Law System
Legal Development
Legal Education
Legalism
Political Law
Psychohistory

LEGAL IMMUNITY
S-15-0021 1975 00005
BT Immunity
RT Amnesty
Bankruptcy Law
Citizenship Immunity
Diplomatic Immunity
Executive Immunity
Legal Discrimination
Legislative Immunity
Political Asylum

LEGAL JURISDICTION
S-06-0403 1975 00015
BT Jurisdiction Characteristics
NT Court Jurisdiction
RT Administrative Jurisdiction
Constitutional Law
Executive Jurisdiction
Law System
Legal Settlement
Legislative Jurisdiction
Territory Jurisdiction

LEGAL MALPRACTICE
S-10-0039 1979 00000
BT Malpractice
RT Legal Education
Malfeasance
Medical Malpractice
Misfeasance

LEGAL POSITIVISM
S-25-0008 1975 00002
BT Jurisprudence
RT Codified Law
Law Type
Legal Studies
Logical Positivism
Sociology Of Law

LEGAL PRECEDENT
S-31-0548 1975 00005
BT Judicial Procedure
NT Stare Decisis
RT Customary Law
Judge Made Law
Judicial Discretion
Judicial Review
Justiciable Question
Substantive Due Process

LEGAL RATIONAL AUTHORITY
S-04-0006 1975 00003
BT Authority Mode
RT Bureaucratic Politics
Charismatic Authority
Constitutional Authority
End Of Ideology Analysis
Formal Authority
Hierarchical Authority
Merit Policy
Modern Political Culture
Moral Authority
Political Authority
Secular Authority
Technocratic Politics
Weberian Theory

LEGAL SERVICE
S-26-0365 1979 00000
BT Service Policy
RT Child Care Service
Community Service
Court Attorney
Education Service
Employment Service
Health Service
Information Service
Law System
Legal Studies
Legal System
Medical Care Service
Psychological Service
Service Industry Policy
Social Policy
Social Service

LEGAL SETTLEMENT
S-31-0495 1975 00009
BT Post Trial Procedure
NT Imposed Legal Settlement
Negotiated Legal Settlement

RT Legal Jurisdiction

LEGAL SOCIALIZATION
S-34-0038 1975 00001
BT Professional Socialization
RT Education Socialization
Law School
Legal Advisor

LEGAL STUDIES
S-01-0131 1975 00066
BT Academic Areas
NT Comparative Law
RT Administrative Law
Administrative Law System
Advocacy Research
Case Law
Criminology
Decriminalization
Environmental Studies
Gerontology
Law School
Lawyer
Legal Education
Legal Positivism
Legal Service
Policy Science Studies
Sociology Of Law

LEGAL SYSTEM
S-37-0080 1975 00034
BT System Type
NT Judicial System
Justice System
Law System
RT Chief Justice
Law Formulation
Law Type
Legal Development
Legal Service
Legalism
Legalistic Political Culture
Military Justice
Municipal Court
Police Community Relations
Political System Type

LEGALISM
S-38-0445 1975 00009
BT Constitutional Interpretation Theory
RT Judicial Restraint Theory
Legal History
Legal System
Legalistic Political Culture
Strict Constructionism

LEGALISTIC POLITICAL CULTURE
S-11-0029 1975 00000
BT Civic Culture
RT Legal System
Legalism
Modern Political Culture
Political Subculture
Pragmatic Political Culture
Secular Political Culture

LEGISLATING
1975-1979 00008
USE Legislative Action

LEGISLATING AMENDMENT PROCESS
USE Legislative Amendment Process

LEGISLATIVE ACCOUNTABILITY
S-06-0418 1979 00000
BT Legislative Characteristics
RT Administrative Accountability
Constituency Relations
Executive Accountability
Government Accountability
Government Responsiveness
Legislative Norms
Legislative Role Orientation
Ministerial Responsibility
Presidential Accountability
Representation Type
Responsibility Doctrine

LEGISLATIVE ACTION
S-31-0581 1979 00000
UF Legislating
BT Law Formulation
NT Adjournment Debate
Bill Drafting
Legislative Amendment Process
Legislative Appropriation
Legislative Authorization
Legislative Bill Rejection
Legislative Decision Making
Legislative Resolution
Legislative Voting
Question Time Debate
RT Legislative Behavior
Legislative Decision Making
Legislative Executive Relations
Legislative Hearing
Legislative Procedure
Voting Behavior

LEGISLATIVE AMENDING PROCESS
1975-1979 00006

LEGISLATIVE AMENDMENT PROCESS
S-31-0584 1979 00000
UF Legislating Amendment Process
BT Legislative Action
RT Bill Drafting
Legislative Appropriation
Legislative Authorization
Legislative Resolution
Legislative Voting

LEGISLATIVE APPROPRIATION
S-31-0585 1975 00012
BT Legislative Action
RT Appropriation Agency
Bill Drafting
Legislative Amendment Process
Legislative Authorization
Legislative Decision Making
Legislative Voting

LEGISLATIVE AUTHORIZATION
S-31-0586 1975 00004
BT Legislative Action
RT Authorization Process
Bill Drafting
Legislative Amendment Process
Legislative Appropriation
Legislative Bill Rejection
Legislative Characteristics
Legislative Decision Making

LEGISLATIVE BEHAVIOR
S-05-0017 1975 00051
BT Political Behavior
NT Legislative Voting Behavior
RT Adjournment Debate
Behavioral Theory
Congressional Leadership
Congressional Political Party
Elite Behavior
Executive Session
Group Behavior
House Of Representatives
Law Formulation
Legal Behavior
Legislative Action
Legislative Characteristics
Legislative Process
Legislative Role Orientation
Legislative Socialization
Legislative Voting Record
National Legislative Member
National Legislative Political Party
National Legislative Speaker
Proxy Voting
Roll Call Analysis
Senate

LEGISLATIVE BILL APPROVAL
1975-1979 00012

LEGISLATIVE BILL REJECTION
S-31-0587 1979 00000
BT Legislative Action
RT Bill Drafting
Legislative Authorization

LEGISLATIVE CALENDAR
S-31-0609 1975 00000
BT Legislative Procedure
RT Bill Drafting
Committee Rules
Congressional Procedure
Legislative Hearing
Parliamentary Procedure
Parliamentary Procedure Law
Parliamentary Speaker

LEGISLATIVE CHARACTERISTICS
S-06-0417 1975 00014
BT Characteristics
NT Legislative Accountability
Legislative Norms
RT Government Characteristics
Legislative Authorization
Legislative Behavior
Legislative Decision Making
Legislature Type
Legislatures
National Legislative Member
Political Party Characteristics
Senate

LEGISLATIVE COALITION
S-02-0024 1975 00010
BT Political Coalition
NT Parliamentary Coalition
RT All Party Coalition
Coalition Type
Democratic Coalition
Electoral Coalition
Governing Coalition
Minimum Winning Coalition
Multiparty Coalition
Negative Coalition
Opinion Coalition
Political Party Coalition
Voting Coalition
Winning Coalition

LEGISLATIVE COMMISSION
S-19-0093 1975 00005
BT Commissions
RT Commission Of Inquiry
Congressional Investigation Committee
Federal Commission
Housing Court
International Planning Commission
Investigation Commission
Legislative Commission Of Inquiry
Legislative Committee Chairperson
Lower House Member
National Planning Commission
Presidential Commission Of Inquiry
Provincial Parliament
Royal Commission Of Inquiry
Subnational Legislative Committee Chairperson

LEGISLATIVE COMMISSION OF INQUIRY
S-19-0087 1975 00001
BT Commission Of Inquiry
NT Congressional Investigation Committee
Parliamentary Commission Of Inquiry
RT Legislative Commission
Lower House Member
Presidential Commission Of Inquiry
Royal Commission Of Inquiry

LEGISLATIVE COMMITTEE CHAIRPERSON
S-36-0147 1975 00001
BT Legislative Official
NT National Legislative Committee Chairperson
Subnational Legislative Committee Chairperson
RT Legislative Commission
Legislative Committee Member
Legislative Leader
Legislative Member
Legislative Ombudsman
Legislative Staff

LEGISLATIVE COMMITTEE MEMBER
S-36-0154 1975 00005
BT Legislative Official
NT Ranking Minority Member
RT Legislative Committee Chairperson
Legislative Leader
Legislative Member
Legislative Ombudsman
Legislative Staff

LEGISLATIVE COMMITTEE STAFF
S-36-0203 1975 00001
BT Legislative Staff
RT National Legislative Staff
Subnational Legislative Staff

LEGISLATIVE COURTESY
S-06-0420 1975 00000
BT Legislative Norms
NT Senatorial Courtesy
RT Legislative Patriotism
Log Rolling
Seniority

LEGISLATIVE DEBATING
1975-1979 00002

LEGISLATIVE DECISION MAKING
S-31-0588 1975 00045
BT Legislative Action
RT Legislative Action
Legislative Appropriation
Legislative Authorization
Legislative Characteristics
Legislative Hearing
Legislative Resolution
Lower House Speaker
Question Time Debate

LEGISLATIVE DISSOLUTION
S-31-0464 1975 00000
BT Government Dissolution Process
RT Confidence Voting
Executive Dissolution

LEGISLATIVE DISTRICT
S-24-0368 1975 00007
BT State Political Division
RT Apportionment
Borough
County
Legislative Districting
Malapportionment
Township
Village

LEGISLATIVE DISTRICTING
S-31-0709 1975 00000
BT Districting
RT Apportionment
Legislative District
Malapportionment

LEGISLATIVE EXECUTIVE RELATIONS
S-31-0598 1975 00026
BT Legislative Process
NT Congressional Executive Relations
Parliament Cabinet Relations
RT Bill Drafting
Confirmation Process
Law Formulation
Legislative Action
Legislative Procedure
Lobbying
Lobbying Tactic
Veto

LEGISLATIVE EXECUTIVE SEPARATION
S-30-0019 1975 00004
BT Separation Of Power
RT Executive Legislative Policy
Executive Power
Federal State Separation
Judicial Power
Legislative Power

LEGISLATIVE HEARING
S-31-0610 1975 00000
BT Legislative Procedure
NT Congressional Hearing
RT Congressional Procedure
Legislative Action
Legislative Calendar
Legislative Decision Making
Legislative Record
Lobbying
National Legislative Staff
Parliamentary Committee

LEGISLATIVE HISTORY
S-01-0117 1975 00021
BT Political History
RT House Of Representatives
National Legislative Member
Political Behavior Studies
Political Psychology
Political Science Discipline
Political Sociology
Senate

LEGISLATIVE IMMUNITY
S-15-0022 1975 00000
BT Immunity
NT Member Privilege
RT Legal Immunity
Member Privilege
Political Asylum

LEGISLATIVE INFORMATION SERVICE
S-18-0052 1979 00000
BT Government Information Service
RT Abstracting Service
Archives
Bibliographic Control
Bibliographic Service
Documents
Government Document
Information Service
Intergovernmental Document
Judicial Record
Legislative Record
Political Party Record
Political Statistics
Public Record
Social Statistics
Statistical Data
Survey Data

LEGISLATIVE JURISDICTION
S-06-0408 1975 00003
BT Jurisdiction Characteristics
RT Administrative Jurisdiction
Constitutional Law
Executive Jurisdiction
Legal Jurisdiction
Territory Jurisdiction
Union Jurisdiction

LEGISLATIVE LEADER
S-36-0156 1975 00002
BT Legislative Official
NT Floor Leader
Leader Of Opposition
Legislative Speaker
Legislative Whip
Majority Leader
Minority Leader
National Legislative Leader
Subnational Legislative Leader
RT Legislative Committee Chairperson
Legislative Committee Member
Legislative Member
Legislative Ombudsman
Legislative Staff
Political Party Leader
Political Party Leadership

LEGISLATIVE MEMBER
S-36-0187 1975 00008
BT Legislative Official
NT National Legislative Member
Subnational Legislative Member

RT City Council
City Councilman
Legislative Committee Chairperson
Legislative Committee Member
Legislative Leader
Legislative Ombudsman
Legislative Staff
Local Decision Making
Local Government

LEGISLATIVE NOMINATING PROCESS
S-31-0739 1979 00000
BT Nominating Process
RT Appointment Process
Candidate Selection
Delegate Selection
Endorsement
National Legislature
Presidential Nominating Process

LEGISLATIVE NORMS
S-06-0419 1975 00005
BT Legislative Characteristics
NT Legislative Courtesy
Legislative Patriotism
Log Rolling
Pork Barrel
Seniority
RT Legislative Accountability
Legislative Procedure
Legislative Role Orientation
Legislative Socialization
Senatorial Courtesy

LEGISLATIVE OFFICIAL
S-36-0146 1975 00000
BT Government Official
NT Legislative Committee Chairperson
Legislative Committee Member
Legislative Leader
Legislative Member
Legislative Ombudsman
Legislative Staff
RT Diplomat
Government Bureaucracy
Law Formulation

LEGISLATIVE OMBUDSMAN
S-36-0201 1975 00001
BT Legislative Official
RT Legislative Committee Chairperson
Legislative Committee Member
Legislative Leader
Legislative Member
Legislative Staff

LEGISLATIVE PARTY
1975-1979 00013

LEGISLATIVE PATRIOTISM
S-06-0422 1975 00000
BT Legislative Norms
RT Legislative Courtesy
Seniority

LEGISLATIVE POLITICAL PARTY
S-28-0044 1979 00000
BT Sector Based Political Party Type
NT National Legislative Political Party
RT Government Political Party
Legislative Process
Legislative Socialization
Legislative Voting

LEGISLATIVE POWER
S-30-0016 1975 00025
BT Political Power
RT Congressional Leadership
Executive Power
Judicial Power
Legislative Executive Separation
National Legislative Political Party
Power Of The Purse
Presidential Power
Separation Of Power

LEGISLATIVE PROCEDURE
S-31-0603 1975 00005
BT Legislative Process
NT Committee Rules
Committee Staffing
Congressional Procedure
Legislative Calendar
Legislative Hearing
Parliamentary Procedure
RT Adjournment Debate
Law Formulation
Legislative Action
Legislative Executive Relations
Legislative Norms
Legislative Reform
Legislative Socialization
Lobbying
Policy Making Process
Senate Speaker
Seniority
Subnational Legislative Leader
Subnational Legislative Member
Subnational Legislative Speaker
Subnational Legislative Whip
Treaty Ratification

LEGISLATIVE PROCESS
S-31-0573 1975 00033
BT Process
NT Constituency Relations
Law Formulation
Legislative Executive Relations
Legislative Procedure
Lobbying
RT Conflict Process
Executive Legislative Policy
Gubernatorial Veto
Item Veto
Judicial Process
Legislative Behavior
Legislative Political Party
Legislative Socialization
Legislative Voting Behavior
Modern Political Culture
Pocket Veto
Policy Making Process
Presidential Veto
Senate House Conference Committee
Senator
Subnational Legislative Leader
Subnational Legislative Member
Subnational Legislative Speaker
Subnational Legislative Whip
Veto

LEGISLATIVE RECORD
S-18-0033 1975 00002
BT Government Document
NT Legislative Voting Record
Parliamentary Paper
RT Administrative Record
Intergovernmental Document
Judicial Record
Legislative Hearing
Legislative Information Service
Legislatures
National Legislative Staff
University Information Service

LEGISLATIVE RECRUITMENT
S-31-0749 1975 00008
BT Political Recruitment
RT Judicial Recruitment
Leadership Recruitment
Lower House Member
Political Party Recruitment

LEGISLATIVE REDISTRICTING
S-31-0710 1975 00001
BT Districting
RT Apportionment Reform
Malapportionment
Reapportionment

LEGISLATIVE REFORM
S-31-0096 1975 00018
BT Reform
NT Apportionment Reform
Congressional Reform
Legislative Reorganization
Parliamentary Reform
RT Administrative Reform
Education Reform
Executive Reform
Judicial Reform
Legislative Procedure

LEGISLATIVE REORGANIZATION
S-31-0099 1975 00011
BT Legislative Reform
RT Apportionment Reform
Congressional Reform
Parliamentary Reform

LEGISLATIVE RESOLUTION
S-31-0589 1975 00003
BT Legislative Action
RT Legislative Amendment Process
Legislative Decision Making
Legislative Voting

LEGISLATIVE ROLE ORIENTATION
S-31-0767 1975 00026
BT Role Orientation
RT Constituency Relations
Executive Role Orientation
Judicial Role Orientation
Legislative Accountability
Legislative Behavior
Legislative Norms
Legislative Socialization
National Legislative Member
Political Role Orientation
Representation Theory

LEGISLATIVE ROLL CALL RECORD
S-18-0035 1975 00006
BT Legislative Voting Record
RT Voting Data

LEGISLATIVE SOCIALIZATION
S-34-0034 1975 00002
BT Institutional Socialization
RT Bureaucratic Socialization
Legislative Behavior
Legislative Norms
Legislative Political Party
Legislative Procedure

Legislative Process
Legislative Role Orientation
National Legislative Member

LEGISLATIVE SPEAKER
S-36-0159 1975 00001
BT Legislative Leader
NT National Legislative Speaker
Subnational Legislative Speaker
RT Floor Leader
Leader Of Opposition
Legislative Whip
Majority Leader
Minority Leader
National Legislative Leader
Subnational Legislative Leader

LEGISLATIVE STAFF
S-36-0202 1975 00006
BT Legislative Official
NT Legislative Committee Staff
National Legislative Staff
Subnational Legislative Staff
RT Legislative Committee Chairperson
Legislative Committee Member
Legislative Leader
Legislative Member
Legislative Ombudsman

LEGISLATIVE STAFF PERSONNEL
S-36-0014 1975 00005
BT Administrative Staff Personnel
RT Executive Staff Personnel
Judicial Staff Personnel

LEGISLATIVE VOTING
S-31-0590 1975 00007
BT Legislative Action
NT Bipartisan Voting
Censure Motion
Cloture
Discharge Petition
RT Adjournment Debate
Confidence Voting
Legislative Amendment Process
Legislative Appropriation
Legislative Political Party
Legislative Resolution

LEGISLATIVE VOTING BEHAVIOR
S-05-0018 1975 00041
BT Legislative Behavior
RT Legislative Process
Legislative Voting Record
Voting Behavior

LEGISLATIVE VOTING INDICATOR
S-24-0269 1975 00005
BT Voting Indicator
RT Legislative Voting Record
Political Party Voting Indicator
Two Political Party Voting Indicator

LEGISLATIVE VOTING RECORD
S-18-0034 1975 00005
BT Legislative Record
NT Legislative Roll Call Record
RT Legislative Behavior
Legislative Voting Behavior
Legislative Voting Indicator
Voting Data

LEGISLATIVE WHIP
S-36-0170 1975 00001
BT Legislative Leader
NT National Legislative Whip
Subnational Legislative Whip
RT Floor Leader
Leader Of Opposition
Legislative Speaker
Majority Leader
Minority Leader
National Legislative Leader
National Legislative Whip
Subnational Legislative Leader

LEGISLATURE TYPE
S-19-0253 1975 00002
BT Legislatures
NT Bicameral Legislature
Unicameral Legislature
RT Councils
Diet
House Of Representatives
Law Type
Legislative Characteristics
National Legislature
Peoples Assembly
Senate
Subnational Legislature

LEGISLATURES
S-19-0252 1975 00015
BT Institutions
NT Legislature Type
National Legislature
Subnational Legislature
RT Constitution
Legislative Characteristics
Legislative Record
Lower House Member
Politicist
Senator
Separation Of Power

LEGITIMACY SCALE
S-24-0238 1975 00001
BT Scale Type
RT Alienation Scale
Anomie Scale
Civic Competence Scale
Efficacy Scale
Left Right Scale
Optimism Pessimism Scale
Satisfaction Scale
Support Opposition Scale

LEGITIMACY THEORY
S-38-0484 1975 00021
BT Political Philosophy Concept
NT Political Legitimacy Theory
RT Authority
Authority Structure
Authority Theory
Common Good Theory
Consent Theory
Diffuse System Supports
Divine Right Theory
Just Authority
Justice Theory
Liberty Theory
Lockean Liberalism
Mandate Of Heaven Theory
Natural Law Conventionalism Theory
Obedience
Obligation Theory
Order Theory
Political Man Theory
Social Contract Theory

LEISURE TIME ANALYSIS
S-09-0040 1979 00000
BT Contemporary Analytic Modes
RT Analysis Of Play
Communication Analysis
Group Analysis
Social Area Analysis
Sociology Discipline
Tourist Industry

LENINISM
S-38-0323 1975 00011
BT Marxism
NT Democratic Centralism
Leninist Imperialism Theory
RT Bolshevism
Castroism
Communism
Elitism
Evolutionary Marxism
Hegelian Marxism
Maoism
Maoist
Maoist Movement
Maoist Political Party
Maoist Revolutionary
Marxism Leninism
Marxist Revisionism
National Front
National Liberation Movement
National Liberation War
Polycentrism
Revolutionary Elite
Stalinism
Titoism
Trotskyism
Trotskyite Political Party

LENINIST IMPERIALISM THEORY
S-38-0325 1975 00002
BT Leninism
RT Antiimperialism
Capitalist Imperialism
Depression
Yankee Imperialism

LEVELLERS POLITICAL THOUGHT
S-38-0522 1975 00000
SN Beliefs associated with a faction in English Civil War calling for representative parliament, religious toleration and general economic levelling.
BT Early Radical Thought
RT Communalism
Diggers Political Thought
Egalitarian Justice Theory
Egalitarianism
Equality Theory
Radicalism

LIBEL
S-10-0037 1975 00001
BT Individual Crime
RT Blackmail
Character Assassination
Extortion
Perjury
Slander

LIBERAL
S-32-0261 1975 00005
BT Spectrum Politicist
RT Centrist
Conservative
Liberal Democratic Political Party
Liberal Political Party
Liberal Political Thought
Liberalism
New Left
Nineteenth Century Liberalism
Political Neutralist
Political Radical

LIBERAL ARTS EDUCATION
S-13-0021 1979 00000
BT Humanities Education
NT Humanistic Education
RT Artistic Elite
Classical Education
Humanities Discipline
Religious Education
Traditional Education
University

LIBERAL DEMOCRATIC PARTY
1975-1979 00004

LIBERAL DEMOCRATIC POLITICAL PARTY
S-28-0005 1979 00000
BT Democratic Political Party
RT Christian Democratic Political Party
Liberal
Liberal Political Thought
Liberalism
National Democratic Political Party
Social Democratic Political Party

LIBERAL PARTY
1975-1979 00004

LIBERAL POLITICAL PARTY
S-28-0020 1979 00000
BT Ideological Spectrum Political Party Type
RT Christian Democratic Political Party
Freedom
Liberal
Liberal Political Thought
Liberalism
Liberalism Conservatism Scale
National Democratic Political Party
Pluralist Analysis

LIBERAL POLITICAL THOUGHT
S-38-0413 1975 00017
BT Modern Political Thought
NT Enlightenment Liberalism
Lockean Liberalism
RT American Political Thought
Freedom
Liberal
Liberal Democratic Political Party
Liberal Political Party
Liberalism
Libertarianism
Liberty Theory
Pluralist Analysis

LIBERALISM
S-38-0249 1975 00033
BT Ideologies
NT Civil Liberty Liberalism
Civil Rights Liberalism
Classical Liberalism
Economic Liberalism
Laissez Faire Liberalism
Nineteenth Century Liberalism
Welfare Liberalism
RT Democratic Theory
Destalinization Process
Economic Ideology
Egalitarianism
Freedom
Left Right Scale
Liberal
Liberal Democratic Political Party
Liberal Political Party
Liberal Political Thought
Liberty Theory
Modernizing Ideology
Nationalism
Oxford Idealism

LIBERALISM CONSERVATISM SCALE
S-24-0239 1975 00014
BT Scale Type
RT Alienation Scale
American Conservatism
Anomie Scale
Civic Competence Scale
Cynicism Scale
Dogmatism Scale
Frustration Scale
Left Right Scale
Liberal Political Party
Optimism Pessimism Scale
Social Frustration Scale
Stability Index
Support Opposition Scale
Voting Duty Scale

LIBERATION FRONT
S-02-0053 1975 00006
BT Political Front
RT National Communism
National Front
Partisan War
Popular Front
United Front
Yankee Imperialism

LIBERATION MOVEMENT
S-27-0024 1975 00014
BT Independence Movement
NT Black Liberation Movement
National Liberation Movement
Peoples Liberation Movement
Womens Liberation Movement
RT Anticolonialism
Antiimperialism
Castroism
Communal Movement
Ethnic Separatist Movement
Independence Movement
Language Movement
Nationalism
Nationalist Movement
Proletarian Movement
Radical Movement
Resistance Movement
Revolutionary Movement
Separatist Movement
Social Movement
Sovereignty
Terrorism
Terrorist Movement

LIBERATION PROCESS
S-31-0144 1975 00008
BT Change Process
NT Emancipation
RT Anticolonialism
Antiimperialism
Black Insurrection
National Communism
Peoples Liberation Movement
Political Change
Revolutionary Change
Social Change

LIBERTARIANISM
S-38-0257 1975 00011
BT Ideologies
RT Anarchism
Freedom
Individual Freedom Theory
Liberal Political Thought
New Left

LIBERTY THEORY
S-38-0486 1975 00016
BT Political Philosophy Concept
RT Civil Liberty Liberalism
Civil Rights Liberalism
Freedom
Freedom Of Information
Freedom Of Inquiry
Freedom Of Religion
Freedom Theory
Human Dignity Theory
Individualism Theory
Just Authority
Justice Theory
Legitimacy Theory
Liberal Political Thought
Liberalism
Natural Law Conventionalism Theory
Obligation Theory
Slavery Abolition

LIBERUM VETO
1975-1979 00000

LIBRARY
S-18-0056 1975 00008
UF Book Acquisition
BT Information Sources
RT Archives
Biography
University Information Service

LIBRARY RESEARCH
S-24-0081 1975 00002
BT Nonreactive Observation
RT Documentary Research
Nonparticipant Observation

LIBRARY SCHOOL
USE Library Science Studies

LIBRARY SCIENCE STUDIES
S-01-0133 1979 00000
UF Library School
BT Academic Areas
RT Archives
Behavioral Psychology
Book Industry
Computer Science
Information Dissemination
Information Network
Information Policy
Information Service
Information Sources

Information System
Monographs
Newsletters
Newspapers

LICENSING RECORD
S-18-0038 1975 00003
BT Government Document
RT Administrative Record
Regulatory Agency Record
Tax Record

LIEUTENANT GOVERNOR
S-36-0081 1975 00000
BT State Governor
RT State Government
State Governor
State Politics
Subnational Chief Government Executive
Subnational Government
Subnational Government Bureaucracy
Subnational Government Council
Vice President

LIFE EXPECTANCY
S-06-0193 1975 00009
BT Demographic Profile
RT Demographic Projection
Life Satisfaction
Mortality Rate
Population Management
Population Planning

LIFE INSURANCE
S-26-0304 1979 00000
BT Insurance
RT Accident Insurance
Catastrophe Insurance
Compulsory Insurance
Fire Insurance
Malpractice Insurance
Motor Vehicle Industry
National Health Insurance
No Fault Insurance
Unemployment Insurance Policy

LIFE SATISFACTION
S-06-0128 1979 00000
BT Satisfaction
RT Human Nature Theory
Life Expectancy
Political Satisfaction
Quality Of Life

LIFE SENTENCE
S-31-0484 1975 00001
BT Court Action
RT Capital Punishment
Conviction
Injunction
Murder
Murderer
Obiter Dicta
Verdict
Warrant
Writ Of Mandamus

LIGHT INDUSTRIAL POLICY
S-26-0278 1975 00000
BT Industrial Policy
RT Business Policy
Consumer Industrial Policy
Economic Policy
Heavy Industrial Policy
Light Industry
Service Industry Policy

LIGHT INDUSTRY
S-17-0056 1975 00004
BT Manufacturing Industry
NT Appliance Industry
Cottage Industry
RT Clothing Industry
Light Industrial Policy
Machinery Industry
Mixed Enterprise
Paper Industry
Small Business
Synthetics Industry
Textile Industry

LIKERT SCALE
S-24-0210 1975 00006
BT Scale Construction Methodology
RT Composite Scale
Cumulative Scale
Guttman Scale
Measurement Level Scale
Multidimensional Scale
Nominal Scale
Ordinal Scale
Ratio Scale
Scalability Index
Semantic Differential
Thurstone Scale
Unidimensional Scale

LIMITED GOVERNMENT
S-16-0066 1979 00000
BT Government Type
RT Classical Liberalism
Constitutional Democracy
Constitutional Monarchy
Decentralized Government
Laissez Faire Liberalism
Laissez Faire Theory
Private Sector

LIMITED MILITARY AGGRESSION
S-08-0005 1975 00001
BT Military Aggression
RT Guerrilla War
Limited War

LIMITED MONARCHY
S-16-0075 1975 00001
BT Monarchy
RT Constitutional Monarchy
Mixed Government
Republican Monarchy

LIMITED PEACE
S-06-0673 1975 00004
BT Peace
RT International Peace
Limited War

LIMITED SOVEREIGNTY
S-16-0154 1975 00006
BT Sovereignty
RT Divided Sovereignty
Security Community
Subnational Government

LIMITED WAR
S-08-0097 1975 00010
BT War
NT Border War
Brushfire War
Tactical War
RT Brushfire War
Cold War
Limited Military Aggression
Limited Peace
Proxy War
War By Proxy

LIMITED WAR POLICY
S-26-0339 1975 00013
BT War Policy
RT Global War Policy
Local War Policy
Pacification Policy
Peoples War Policy
Total War Policy

LINE STAFF
S-06-0455 1975 00002
BT Bureaucratic Hierarchy
RT Bureaucratic Hierarchy
Group Hierarchy
Hierarchical Authority
Management
Manager
National Legislative Staff
Organization Characteristics
Organization Hierarchy
Presidential Staff Personnel
Public Administration Studies
Subnational Legislative Staff

LINEAR PROGRAMMING
S-24-0027 1975 00016
BT Mathematical Analysis
RT Calculus
Geometry
Graph Analysis
Trigonometry

LINGUISTIC ANALYSIS
S-09-0041 1975 00089
BT Contemporary Analytic Modes
NT Grammatical Analysis
Semantic Analysis
Verbal Analysis
RT Bilateral Family Descent Pattern
Class Analysis
Communication Analysis
Content Analysis
Contextual Analysis
Ethnolinguistics
Hermeneutical Analysis
Interaction Analysis
Issue Intensity
Language Characteristics
Language Community
Language Group Conflict
Language Loyalty
Language Studies
Linguistic Assimilation
Linguistic Ethical Theory
Linguistic Theory
Literature Analysis
Motivational Analysis
Political Psychology Analysis
Socialization Analysis
Sociolinguistics
Sociological Analysis
Wittgensteinian Thought

LINGUISTIC ASSIMILATION
S-31-0800 1975 00005
BT Assimilation
RT Bilingual Community
Cultural Assimilation
Ethnic Assimilation
Ethnolinguistics

Linguistic Analysis
Linguistic Theory
Racial Assimilation

LINGUISTIC DIVERSITY
S-06-0473 1975 00004
BT Cultural Diversity
RT Cultural Cleavage
Ethnic Diversity
Ethnic Heterogeneity
Ethnolinguistics
Social Diversity

LINGUISTIC ETHICAL THEORY
S-25-0042 1975 00005
BT Ethical Theory
RT Anthropological Linguistic Theory
Emotive Ethical Theory
Ethical Relativism
Hedonism
Instrumentalism
Intuitionism
Linguistic Analysis
Metaethical Theory
Ordinary Language Philosophy
Situational Ethics
Utilitarianism

LINGUISTIC INTEGRATION
S-31-0814 1975 00002
BT Integration
NT Bilingualism
RT Cultural Integration
Ethnic Assimilation Theory
Ethnic Integration
Functional Integration
Horizontal Integration
Polarization
Social Integration
Vertical Integration

LINGUISTIC THEORY
S-38-0034 1979 00000
BT Theory
RT Anthropological Linguistic Theory
Communication Analysis
Ethnolinguistics
Language Loyalty
Linguistic Analysis
Linguistic Assimilation
Linguistics
Literature Analysis

LINGUISTICS
S-01-0134 1975 00011
BT Academic Areas
NT Applied Linguistics
Etymology
Psycholinguistics
Sociolinguistics
RT Anthropological Linguistic Theory
Comparative Literature Studies
Ethnic Studies
Ethnolinguistics
Foreign Language Education
Information Science
International Relations Studies
Language Studies
Linguistic Theory
Literature Studies
Morphology
Political Science Methodology Studies
Psychology Discipline
Social Psychology
Sociology Discipline
Structural Linguistics

LINKAGE POLITICS
S-29-0213 1979 00000
BT Politics
RT Comparative Analysis
Ethnic Politics
Geopolitics
Group Politics
International Politics
International Relations Studies
Labor Politics
National Politics
Power Politics

LINKAGE REPRESENTATION THEORY
S-38-0506 1975 00007
BT Representation Theory
RT Delegate Representation Theory
Group Representation Theory
Territory Representation Theory
Trustee Representation Theory
Virtual Representation Theory

LIST VOTING
S-29-0171 1975 00001
BT Voting Formulae
RT Cumulative Voting
D'Hont Voting Method
Largest Average Voting Method
Largest Remainder Voting Method
Single Transferable Vote

LITERACY POLICY
S-26-0192 1975 00006
BT Education Policy
RT Education Policy
Higher Education Policy
Literacy Rate
Mass Education
Private Education Policy
Public Education Policy
Rehabilitation Education Policy
Vocation Training Policy

LITERACY RATE
S-06-0194 1975 00012
BT Demographic Profile
RT Illiteracy Rate
Literacy Policy
Literacy Test
Literacy Voting Test

LITERACY TEST
S-24-0007 1975 00002
BT Education Testing
RT Degree Requirement
Discrimination Policy
Literacy Rate
Physiological Test
Poll Tax
Psychological Test
Test Results
Voter Registration

LITERACY VOTING TEST
S-29-0175 1979 00000
BT Voting Procedure
RT Discrimination Policy
Disenfranchisement
Literacy Rate
Poll Tax
Voter Registration

LITERARY ELITE
S-14-0013 1975 00044
BT Cultural Elite
RT Academic Elite
Artistic Elite
Intelligentsia
Opinion Elite
Scientific Elite

LITERATURE ANALYSIS
S-09-0045 1979 00000
BT Contemporary Analytic Modes
RT Grammatical Analysis
Humanities Discipline
Linguistic Analysis
Linguistic Theory
Literature Studies
Political Literature
Semantic Analysis
Verbal Analysis

LITERATURE REVIEW
S-18-0057 1979 00000
BT Information Sources
RT Documentation Service
Encyclopedia
Humanistic Education
Humanities Discipline
Hypothesis Testing
Monographs
Thesaurus

LITERATURE STUDIES
S-01-0139 1979 00000
BT Academic Areas
NT Comparative Literature Studies
RT Area Studies
Fine Arts
Humanistic Education
Humanities Discipline
Language Studies
Linguistics
Literature Analysis
Political Literature

LITIGATION
S-31-0556 1975 00029
BT Judicial Process
NT Civil Rights Litigation
Class Action Litigation
Constitutional Litigation
Consumer Protection Litigation
Damage Suit
RT Adversary Process
Court Action
Court Procedure
Judicial Decision Making
Judicial Procedure

LIVING CONDITION
1975-1979 00005
USE Living Conditions

LIVING CONDITIONS
S-06-0702 1979 00000
UF Living Condition
BT Social System Environment Characteristics
RT Goal Satisfaction
Political Satisfaction
Population Density
Quality Of Life
Radiation Level
Satisfaction
Satisfaction Scale
Standard Of Living

Working Conditions

LOAN
USE Credit Policy

LOBBYING
S-31-0616 1975 00015
BT Legislative Process
NT Lobbying Tactic
RT Constituency Relations
Law Formulation
Legislative Executive Relations
Legislative Hearing
Legislative Procedure
Lobbying Tactic
Lobbyist
Veterans Organization

LOBBYING TACTIC
S-31-0617 1979 00000
UF Lobbyist Tactic
BT Lobbying
RT Constituency Relations
Group Politics
Interest Aggregation
Interest Articulation
Interest Group
Interest Group Politics
Interest Group Theory
Legislative Executive Relations
Lobbying
Lobbyist

LOBBYIST
S-32-0216 1975 00008
BT Political Role
RT Interest Group Politics
Lobbying
Lobbying Tactic
Trade Union

LOBBYIST TACTIC
1975-1979 00008
USE Lobbying Tactic

LOCAL CHIEF EXECUTIVE CANDIDATE
S-32-0240 1975 00000
BT Subnational Chief Executive Candidate
NT Mayoralty Candidate
RT State Chief Executive Candidate

LOCAL CHIEF EXECUTIVE ELECTION
S-29-0096 1975 00000
BT Subnational Chief Executive Election
NT Mayoralty Election
RT City Council
City Manager
Council Manager
Local Decision Making
Local Election Campaign
Mayor

LOCAL CHIEF EXECUTIVE ELECTION CAMPAIGN
S-29-0036 1975 00000
BT Subnational Chief Executive Election Campaign
NT Mayoralty Election Campaign
RT Local Judicial Election Campaign
Local Legislative Election Campaign

LOCAL CHIEF EXECUTIVE PRIMARY
S-29-0080 1975 00000
BT Subnational Chief Executive Primary
RT Local Judicial Primary
Local Legislative Primary
Presidential Primary

LOCAL CHIEF GOVERNMENT EXECUTIVE
S-36-0082 1975 00002
BT Chief Government Executive
NT City Manager
Council Manager
Mayor
Village Chief
RT Feudal Lord
Governor
Governor General
Prefect

LOCAL CIVIL SERVANT
S-36-0092 1975 00000
BT Subnational Civil Servant
RT Court Official
Local Government
Local Government Bureaucracy
Local Government Council

LOCAL COURT
S-19-0150 1975 00003
BT Courts
NT County Level Court
Municipal Court
Peoples Court
RT Administrative Court
Civil Court
Criminal Court
Justice Administration Agency
Justice Of The Peace
Probate Court
Trial Court

LOCAL DECISION MAKING
S-31-0334 1975 00018
BT Subnational Decision Making Process
RT Community Decision Making
Legislative Member
Local Chief Executive Election
Local Judicial System
Local Legislative Leader
Local Legislative Speaker
Local Legislative Whip
Local Legislature
Strong Mayor Government

LOCAL DEVELOPMENT
S-31-0075 1975 00018
BT Development Process
NT Village Development
RT Modernization
Municipal Reform Movement
Regional Development
Resource Development
Urban Development

LOCAL ECONOMIC DEVELOPMENT LEVEL
S-06-0151 1975 00006
BT Subnational Economic Development Level
RT National Economic Development Level
Regional Economic Development Level

LOCAL ECONOMIC INTEGRATION
S-31-0809 1975 00003
BT Subnational Economic Integration
RT Local Economic Planning

LOCAL ECONOMIC PLANNING
S-31-0652 1975 00005
BT Subnational Economic Planning
RT Local Economic Integration
State Economic Planning

LOCAL ELECTION
S-29-0091 1975 00003
BT Subnational Election
NT Municipal Election
RT Mayoralty Candidate
Provincial Election
Subnational Chief Executive Election
Subnational Judicial Election
Subnational Legislative Election

LOCAL ELECTION CAMPAIGN
S-29-0034 1975 00001
BT Subnational Election Campaign
RT Local Chief Executive Election
National Judicial Election Campaign
National Legislative Election Campaign
Subnational Chief Executive Election Campaign
Subnational Judicial Election Campaign
Subnational Legislative Election Campaign

LOCAL ELECTION DISTRICT
S-29-0195 1975 00002
BT Electoral Unit
NT Precinct
Ward
RT Constituency Size
Electoral District

LOCAL ELITE
S-14-0040 1975 00015
BT Subnational Elite
RT Attentive Public
Bloc Leader
Bloc Voting
Community Decision Making
Community Elite
Community Leader
Justice Administration
Law Enforcement Official
Local Policy Making
Local Policy Planning
Local Political Boss
Local Political Elite
Local Political Party Central Committee Member
Local Political Party Chairperson
Local Political Party Politburo Member
Provincial Elite
Social Elite
Subnational Elite
Township Government
Urban Government
Urban Politics

LOCAL FINANCING
S-31-0408 1975 00018
BT Public Financing
RT Cost Sharing
Government Borrowing
Local Taxation

LOCAL GOVERNMENT
S-16-0099 1975 00097
BT Subnational Government
NT Borough Government
City Government
Township Government
RT County Government
County Manager Government
District Government Type
Hamlet
Legislative Member
Local Civil Servant
Local Law Enforcement
Local Legislative Leader
Local Legislative Speaker
Local Legislative Whip
Local Legislature
Local Political Party
Local Taxation

LOCAL GOVERNMENT BUREAUCRACY
S-19-0080 1975 00010
BT Subnational Government Bureaucracy
RT Bureaucratic Theory
International Government Bureaucracy
Local Civil Servant
Local Policy Making
Local Political Boss
National Government Bureaucracy

LOCAL GOVERNMENT COUNCIL
S-19-0119 1975 00004
BT Subnational Government Council
NT City Council
Town Council
Village Council
RT City Planning Commission
Law Formulation
Local Civil Servant
Local Planning Commission
Local Policy Planning

LOCAL INCOME TAXATION
S-26-0149 1975 00001
BT Subnational Income Taxation
NT City Income Taxation
RT Tax Agency
Tax Code
Tax Power
Taxation Policy
Urban Politics Studies

LOCAL JUDGE
S-36-0111 1975 00003
BT Subnational Judge
NT Justice Of The Peace
RT Local Judicial Candidate
Local Judicial Election
Local Judicial System
Local Law Enforcement
Magistrate

LOCAL JUDICIAL CANDIDATE
S-32-0245 1975 00000
BT Subnational Judicial Candidate
RT Local Judge
Local Judicial Election
Local Judicial Election Campaign
Local Judicial System
Local Magistrate
State Judicial Candidate

LOCAL JUDICIAL ELECTION
S-29-0099 1975 00000
BT Subnational Judicial Election
RT Local Judge
Local Judicial Candidate
Local Judicial Election Campaign
Local Judicial System
Subnational Judicial Election Campaign

LOCAL JUDICIAL ELECTION CAMPAIGN
S-29-0039 1975 00000
BT Subnational Judicial Election Campaign
RT Local Chief Executive Election Campaign
Local Judicial Candidate
Local Judicial Election
Local Judicial System
Local Legislative Election Campaign

LOCAL JUDICIAL PRIMARY
S-29-0082 1975 00000
BT Subnational Judicial Primary
RT Local Chief Executive Primary
Local Legislative Primary

LOCAL JUDICIAL SYSTEM
S-37-0086 1975 00000
BT Subnational Judicial System
RT Local Decision Making
Local Judge
Local Judicial Candidate
Local Judicial Election
Local Judicial Election Campaign
Local Law Enforcement
Local Magistrate
State Judicial System

LOCAL LAW ENFORCEMENT
S-31-0572 1975 00002
BT Subnational Law Enforcement
RT Local Government
Local Judge
Local Judicial System
Local Magistrate
Local Police
National Law Enforcement
Police

LOCAL LEGISLATIVE CANDIDATE
S-32-0248 1979 00000
UF Local Legislator Candidate
BT Subnational Legislative Candidate
RT City Council
City Councilman
Local Legislative Election
Local Legislative Primary
State Legislative Candidate

LOCAL LEGISLATIVE COMMITTEE CHAIRPERSON
S-36-0152 1975 00000
BT Subnational Legislative Committee Chairperson
RT State Legislative Committee Chairperson

LOCAL LEGISLATIVE ELECTION
S-29-0101 1975 00002
BT Subnational Legislative Election
NT City Council Election
RT City Council
City Council Election
High Turnout Election
Local Legislative Candidate
Local Legislative Election Campaign
Local Legislature

LOCAL LEGISLATIVE ELECTION CAMPAIGN
S-29-0041 1975 00001
BT Subnational Legislative Election Campaign
RT City Council
Local Chief Executive Election Campaign
Local Judicial Election Campaign
Local Legislative Election

LOCAL LEGISLATIVE LEADER
S-36-0185 1975 00000
BT Subnational Legislative Leader
RT City Council
City Councilman
Local Decision Making
Local Government
State Legislative Leader

LOCAL LEGISLATIVE MEMBER
S-36-0196 1975 00001
BT Subnational Legislative Member
NT Alderman
City Councilman
RT State Legislative Election
State Legislative Member

LOCAL LEGISLATIVE PRIMARY
S-29-0084 1975 00000
BT Subnational Legislative Primary
RT Local Chief Executive Primary
Local Judicial Primary
Local Legislative Candidate

LOCAL LEGISLATIVE SPEAKER
S-36-0168 1975 00000
BT Subnational Legislative Speaker
RT City Council
Local Decision Making
Local Government
State Legislative Speaker

LOCAL LEGISLATIVE STAFF
S-36-0210 1975 00000
BT Subnational Legislative Staff
RT State Legislative Staff

LOCAL LEGISLATIVE WHIP
S-36-0175 1975 00000
BT Subnational Legislative Whip
RT City Council
City Councilman
Local Decision Making
Local Government
State Legislative Whip

LOCAL LEGISLATOR CANDIDATE
1975-1979 00000
USE Local Legislative Candidate

LOCAL LEGISLATURE
S-19-0282 1975 00001
BT Subnational Legislature
RT Alderman
City Council
City Councilman
Congressional System
Local Decision Making
Local Government
Local Legislative Election
Lower House Member
Municipal Election
Provincial Parliament
State Legislature
Strong Mayor Government

LOCAL MAGISTRATE
S-36-0115 1975 00002
BT Magistrate
RT Chief Magistrate
City Councilman
Local Judicial Candidate
Local Judicial System
Local Law Enforcement

LOCAL PARTY
1975-1979 00000

LOCAL PLANNER
S-32-0141 1975 00008
BT Subnational Planner
NT City Planner
Urban Planner
RT Local Policy Making
Local Policy Planning
Regional Planner
State Planner

LOCAL PLANNING COMMISSION
S-19-0098 1975 00002
BT Subnational Planning Commission
NT City Planning Commission
RT City Council
International Planning Commission
Local Government Council
Local Policy Making
Local Policy Planning
Subnational Government Council
Village Council

LOCAL PLANNING POLICY
S-26-0351 1975 00016
BT Subnational Planning Policy
NT City Planning Policy
RT Local Policy Making
Local Policy Planning
Local Political Party
Local Taxation
National Planning Policy
Needs Assessment
Regional Planning Policy
State Planning Policy

LOCAL POLICE
S-19-0310 1975 00030
BT Subnational Police
RT Justice Of The Peace
Law Enforcement
Local Law Enforcement
Police Board Policy
Police Community Relations
Police Power
Police State
Political Arrest
Preventive Detention
State Police

LOCAL POLICE CHIEF
S-36-0143 1975 00001
BT Local Police Official
RT Community Elite
Police
Police Board

LOCAL POLICE OFFICIAL
S-36-0141 1975 00002
BT Subnational Police Official
NT Constable
Local Police Chief
Sheriff
RT National Police Commissioner
Police
Police Board

LOCAL POLICY MAKING
S-31-0702 1975 00016
BT Subnational Policy Making
RT City Council
City Council Government
City Government
City Manager
City Manager Government
Commission Government
Education Policy Making
Local Elite
Local Government Bureaucracy
Local Planner
Local Planning Commission
Local Planning Policy
Local Political Boss
Local Political Elite
Local Political Party Central Committee Member
Local Political Party Chairperson
Local Political Party First Secretary
Local Politics
Metropolitan Politics
National Policy Making
Subnational Government Council
Subnational Planner
Town Council
Town Meeting
Township Government
Urban Government
Urban Planner
Urban Politics

LOCAL POLICY PLANNING
S-31-0666 1975 00029
BT Subnational Policy Planning
RT City Council
City Planner
City Planning Commission
City Policy Planning
Local Elite
Local Government Council
Local Planner
Local Planning Commission
Local Planning Policy
Local Political Boss
Local Political Party Central Committee Member
Local Political Party Chairperson
Local Political Party First Secretary
Local Political Party Politburo Member
Local Politics
Neighborhood School
Rural Policy Planning
State Policy Planning
Town Meeting
Township Government
Urban Design
Urban Government
Urban Planner
Urban Policy Planning
Village Politics

LOCAL POLITICAL BOSS
S-32-0054 1975 00000
BT Political Leader
RT Boss Politics
Local Elite
Local Government Bureaucracy
Local Policy Making
Local Policy Planning
Local Political Elite
Machine Candidate
Machine Politics
Political Role
Politician
Urban Government
Urban Politics
Weak Mayor Government

LOCAL POLITICAL DIVISION
S-24-0358 1975 00001
BT Subnational Political Division
NT City Unit
Commune
RT City Council Government
City Politics
Decentralized City
Decentralized Government
Province
State Political Division
Town
Town Meeting
Township Government
Urban Government
Village
Village Chief
Village Community
Ward
Weak Mayor Government

LOCAL POLITICAL ELITE
S-14-0023 1975 00026
BT Political Elite
RT Campaign Manager
Cell Leader
City Council
Community Elite
Decision Making Elite
Local Elite
Local Policy Making
Local Political Boss
Local Political Party Central Committee Member
Local Political Party Chairperson
Local Political Party Politburo Member
Magistrate
Mayor
Subnational Candidate
Subnational Elite
Subnational Judge
Town Council
Town Meeting
Township Government
Tribal Political System
Urban Government
Urban Politics

LOCAL POLITICAL INTEGRATION
S-31-0826 1975 00002
BT Subnational Political Integration
RT Assimilation
Group Cohesion
Group Consolidation
Integration

LOCAL POLITICAL PARTY
S-28-0054 1979 00000
BT Subnational Political Party
RT Local Government
Local Planning Policy
Metropolis

Provincial Political Party
State Political Party
Urban Politics Studies

LOCAL POLITICAL PARTY BOSS
1975-1979 00000

LOCAL POLITICAL PARTY CENTRAL COMMITTEE MEMBER
S-36-0249 1975 00000
BT Subnational Political Party Central Committee Member
RT Local Elite
Local Policy Making
Local Policy Planning
Local Political Elite
Local Politics

LOCAL POLITICAL PARTY CHAIRPERSON
S-36-0246 1975 00002
BT Subnational Political Party Chairperson
RT Local Elite
Local Policy Making
Local Policy Planning
Local Political Elite
Local Political Party Politburo Member
Subnational Political Party Central Committee Member
Subnational Political Party First Secretary

LOCAL POLITICAL PARTY FIRST SECRETARY
S-36-0254 1975 00001
BT Subnational Political Party First Secretary
RT Local Policy Making
Local Policy Planning
Regional Political Party First Secretary

LOCAL POLITICAL PARTY MACHINE
1975-1979 00001

LOCAL POLITICAL PARTY POLITBURO MEMBER
S-36-0251 1975 00000
BT Subnational Political Party Politburo Member
RT Local Elite
Local Policy Planning
Local Political Elite
Local Political Party Chairperson
Subnational Political Party Central Committee Member
Subnational Political Party First Secretary

LOCAL POLITICS
S-29-0235 1975 00033
BT Subnational Politics
NT City Politics
Metropolitan Politics
Urban Politics
Village Politics
RT Local Policy Making
Local Policy Planning
Local Political Party Central Committee Member
Local Taxation
Mayoralty Candidate
Mayoralty Election
Mayoralty Election Campaign
State Political Division

LOCAL PRIMARY
S-29-0078 1975 00000
BT Subnational Primary
RT City Council
Subnational Chief Executive Primary
Subnational Judicial Primary
Subnational Legislative Primary

LOCAL TAXATION
S-26-0167 1975 00009
BT Subnational Taxation
NT Municipal Taxation
RT Local Financing
Local Government
Local Planning Policy
Local Politics
School Taxation
State Taxation

LOCAL WAR POLICY
S-26-0340 1975 00002
BT War Policy
RT Global War Policy
Limited War Policy
Pacification Policy
Peoples War Policy
Total War Policy

LOCKEAN CONTRACTUALISM
S-38-0394 1975 00003
BT Early Modern Theory Of The State
RT American Political Thought
Classical Liberalism
Consent Theory
Government Contract Theory
Instrumental State Theory
Laissez Faire Liberalism
Lockean Liberalism
Possessive Individualism
Republican Constitutionalism
Social Contract Theory
Societal Contract Theory
State Of Nature Theory

LOCKEAN LIBERALISM
S-38-0415 1975 00009
BT Liberal Political Thought
RT Consent Theory
Great Chain Of Being Doctrine
Legitimacy Theory
Lockean Contractualism
Political Legitimacy Theory
Possessive Individualism
Property Rights

LOCKOUT
S-08-0035 1975 00000
BT Labor Conflict
RT Economic Demonstration
Labor Strike
Strike Breaking
Walkout
Worker Demonstration

LOG ROLLING
S-06-0423 1975 00004
BT Legislative Norms
RT Bargaining
Legislative Courtesy
Pork Barrel

LOGIC
S-01-0151 1979 00000
BT Philosophy Discipline
RT Childhood
Cognitive Development
Computer Science
Development Index
Development Model
Development Planning
Developmental Psychology
Freudian Psychology
Language Learning
Learning Psychology
Learning Theory
Logical Analysis
Moral Learning
Phenomenological Thought
Philosophy Of Action
Philosophy Of Mind
Philosophy Of Science Studies
Psychology Discipline
Qualitative Analysis
Social Learning Theory
Socialization
Sociology Of Knowledge
Verbal Learning
Wittgensteinian Thought

LOGICAL ANALYSIS
S-24-0022 1975 00007
BT Analysis Methodology
RT Hermeneutical Analysis
Logic
Logical Positivism
Mathematical Analysis

LOGICAL POSITIVISM
S-25-0021 1975 00009
BT Epistemology
RT Empiricism
Legal Positivism
Logical Analysis
Materialism
Neopositivism
Reductionism

LONG BALLOT
S-29-0152 1975 00001
BT Ballot
RT Australian Ballot
Machine Ballot
Nonpartisan Ballot
Office Block Ballot
Paper Ballot
Political Party Column Ballot
Political Party List Ballot
Secret Ballot
Short Ballot

LONG RANGE PLANNING
S-31-0657 1979 00000
BT Planning Process
RT Economic Planning
Fiscal Planning
Forecasting Methodology
National Economic Planning
National Planning Policy
Planning Process
Policy Making Process
Public Policy Planning
Short Range Planning
Social Planning

LONGITUDINAL ANALYSIS
S-24-0085 1975 00063
UF Chronology
BT Observation Time
NT Cohort Analysis
Panel Technique

Time Series Analysis
RT Cross Sectional Analysis
Historical Periods
History Discipline

LOOSE BIPOLAR INTERNATIONAL POLITICAL SYSTEM
S-37-0117 1975 00001
BT Bipolar International System
RT Tight Bipolar International Political System

LOW TURNOUT ELECTION
S-29-0183 1975 00000
BT Voter Turnout
RT Average Voter Turnout Election

LOWER CASTE
S-06-0757 1975 00001
BT Caste Stratification Division
NT Untouchables
RT Caste Society
Lower Class
Middle Caste
Upper Caste

LOWER CLASS
S-06-0766 1975 00012
BT Class Stratification Division
RT Class Antagonism
Class Maintenance
Class Social System
Class Society
Class Stratification Division
Class Struggle
Lower Caste
Lumpen Proletariat
Neighborhood Clinic
Peasant Class
Peasant Society
Racial Exploitation
Social Stratification System
Untouchables
Urban Migration
Working Class

LOWER HOUSE MEMBER
S-36-0193 1975 00002
BT Parliamentary Member
RT Candidate Voter
Congressional Candidate
Legislative Commission
Legislative Commission Of Inquiry
Legislative Recruitment
Legislatures
Local Legislature
Parliament
Politician
State Legislature
Subnational Legislative Election

LOWER HOUSE SPEAKER
S-36-0165 1975 00000
BT Parliamentary Speaker
RT Leader
Legislative Decision Making
Political Party Leader
Upper House Speaker

LUDDITE MOVEMENT
S-27-0032 1975 00000
SN Anti-machinery working class movement in early nineteenth century England.
BT Political Movement
RT Economic Development Characteristics
Industrial Society
Protest Politics
Social Protest
Working Class Movement

LUMBER INDUSTRY
S-17-0044 1979 00000
BT Forestry Industry
RT Building Supplies Industry
Environment Policy
Natural Resource Policy
Ship Building Industry

LUMPEN PROLETARIAT
S-06-0767 1975 00001
SN The section of the working class in classical Marxist analysis which was least employable and least likely to identify with the organized working class.
BT Class Stratification Division
RT Class Stratification Division
Lower Class
Marxist Class Theory
Working Class

LUTHERANISM
S-38-0569 1975 00000
BT Protestantism
RT Anglicanism
Augustinian Analysis
Calvinism
Hussite Thought
Protestant Sectarianism
Religious Identity
Religious Movement
Unitarianism

LUXURY TAXATION
S-26-0155 1975 00001
BT Taxation Policy
RT Confiscatory Taxation
Excise Taxation Policy
Gift Taxation
Import Duty
Inheritance Taxation
Nuisance Taxation
Property Taxation
Social Security Taxation
Tariff

MACHIAVELLIAN THOUGHT
S-38-0523 1975 00005
BT Renaissance Political Thought
RT Absolute Monarch
Elite Analysis
Renaissance State Theory
Statecraft Theory

MACHINE BALLOT
S-29-0153 1975 00000
BT Ballot
RT Australian Ballot
Long Ballot
Nonpartisan Ballot
Office Block Ballot
Paper Ballot
Political Party Column Ballot
Political Party List Ballot
Secret Ballot
Short Ballot
Voting Device
Voting Machine

MACHINE CANDIDATE
S-32-0227 1975 00000
BT Political Candidate
RT Boss Politics
Candidate Selection
Local Political Boss
Machine Politics
National Candidate
One Political Party Politics
Patronage Politics
Subnational Candidate

MACHINE POLITICS
S-29-0218 1975 00001
BT Partisan Politics
RT Boss Politics
Local Political Boss
Machine Candidate
Metropolitan Politics
Multiparty Politics
Patronage Politics

MACHINE READABLE DATA
S-18-0059 1975 00007
BT Machine Readable Information
RT Archives
Computer Network
Computer Science
Data Archives
Data Storage
Machine Readable Information
Software
Statistical Data

MACHINE READABLE INFORMATION
S-18-0058 1975 00002
BT Information Sources
NT Machine Readable Data
Software
RT Archives
Bibliographic Service
Computer Programming
Data Archives
Data Storage
Machine Readable Data
Statistical Data
University Information Service

MACHINERY INDUSTRY
S-17-0059 1979 00000
BT Manufacturing Industry
RT Appliance Industry
Fixed Assets
Industrial Index
Industrial Society
Light Industry
Paper Industry
Textile Industry

MACRO LEVEL ANALYSIS
1975-1979 00004
USE Macrolevel Analysis

MACRO POLITICAL DATA
1975-1979 00001
USE Macropolitical Data

MACRO POLITICAL THEORY
1975-1979 00003
USE Macropolitical Theory

MACROECONOMICS
S-01-0068 1975 00010
BT Economics Discipline
NT Keynesian Economics
Marxist Economics
RT Business Economics
Classical Economic Theory

Developed Economy
Developing Economy
Economic Characteristics
Economic Development Level
Economic Development Theory
Economic Index
Economic Model
Economic Process
Industrial Economics
International Economics
Labor Economics
Macrolevel Analysis
Macropolitical Data
Macropolitical Theory
Macrosociology
Malthusian Theory
Market Economy
Market Model
Marxist Economic Theory
Mercantile Economic Theory
Ricardian Theory
Transportation Economics
Urban Economics
Welfare Economics

MACROLEVEL ANALYSIS
S-24-0413 1979 00000
UF Macro Level Analysis
BT Theoretical Framework
NT System Analysis
RT Electoral Data
Macroeconomics
Macrolevel Analysis
Macropolitical Data
Macropolitical Theory
Macrosociology
Microlevel Analysis

MACROPOLITICAL DATA
S-18-0086 1979 00000
UF Macro Political Data
BT Political Statistics
RT Electoral Data
Macroeconomics
Macrolevel Analysis
Macropolitical Theory
Macrosociology

MACROPOLITICAL THEORY
S-38-0363 1979 00000
UF Macro Political Theory
BT Political Theory
RT Development Theory
Explanatory Political Theory
General System Theory
Historiography
International Political Theory
Macroeconomics
Macrolevel Analysis
Macropolitical Data
Macrosociology
Modernization Theory
Organization Theory
Planning Theory
Political Philosophy Studies

MACROSOCIOLOGY
S-01-0188 1975 00010
BT Sociology Discipline
RT Applied Sociology
Comparative Political Studies
Comparative Sociology
Cultural Anthropology
Historical Sociology
Historiography
History Discipline
History Of Science
Industrial Sociology
Macroeconomics
Macrolevel Analysis
Macropolitical Data
Macropolitical Theory
Marxist Sociology
Political Sociology
Social Anthropology
Social Pathology
Social Psychology
Social System
Social System Characteristics
Urban Sociology

MACROTHESAURUS
USE Thesaurus

MADISONIAN THOUGHT
S-38-0400 1975 00002
BT American Enlightenment Thought
RT American Political Thought
Constitution
Constitution Making
Democratic Government
Extended Republic Theory
Jeffersonian Thought
Republican Constitutionalism
Separation Of Power Theory

MAGAZINE
USE Journal

MAGAZINE INDUSTRY
S-17-0019 1975 00008
BT Publication Industry
RT Advertising Industry
Book Industry
Broadcasting Industry
Communication Policy
Copyright Policy
Journal
Knowledge Acquisition
National Press
News Agency
Newspaper Industry
Publication Agency
Telecommunications Industry

MAGIC
S-38-0013 1975 00008
BT Myth Analysis
RT Primitive Society
Shamanism
Superstition
Taboo
Witchcraft

MAGISTRATE
S-36-0113 1975 00000
BT Subnational Judge
NT Chief Magistrate
Local Magistrate
RT Arraignment
District Attorney
Justice Of The Peace
Local Judge
Local Political Elite
Urban Politics Studies

MAIL QUESTIONNAIRE
S-24-0092 1975 00012
BT Questionnaire
RT Closed Questionnaire
Interview
Open Ended Questionnaire
Self Administered Questionnaire
Telephone Questionnaire

MAINTAINING ELECTION
S-29-0050 1975 00001
BT Election Type
RT Deviating Election
Electoral Outcome
Reinstating Election

MAJOR PARTY
1975-1979 00000

MAJOR POLITICAL PARTY
S-28-0025 1979 00000
BT Political Party Type
RT Majoritarian Democracy
Majority Electoral Outcome
Majority Leader
Majority Political Party
Ruling Political Party
Structure Specific Political Party Type

MAJORITARIAN DEMOCRACY
S-16-0020 1975 00007
BT Democratic Government
RT Consociational Democracy
Major Political Party
Majoritarianism
Majority Electoral Outcome
Majority Political Party
Mass Democracy
Multiparty Democracy
Parliamentary Democracy
Participatory Democracy
Plebiscitary Democracy

MAJORITARIANISM
S-38-0093 1975 00008
BT Democratic Theory
RT Absolute Majority Electoral Outcome
Athenian Democratic Theory
Concurrent Majority Theory
Confederation Movement
Democratic Elite Theory
General Will Democratic Theory
Guided Democracy Theory
Jacksonian Democratic Theory
Jeffersonian Democratic Theory
Majoritarian Democracy
Minimum Winning Coalition
Participatory Democratic Theory
Plebiscitary Democracy
Populist Democratic Theory
Procedural Democratic Theory
Representation
Republic Theory

MAJORITY ELECTORAL OUTCOME
S-29-0111 1975 00012
BT Electoral Outcome
NT Absolute Majority Electoral Outcome
RT Bandwagon Effect
Coattail Effect
Landslide Electoral Outcome
Major Political Party
Majoritarian Democracy
Majority Leader
Majority Political Party

Plebiscitary Democracy
Vote Distribution

MAJORITY LEADER
S-36-0177 1975 00001
BT Legislative Leader
RT Floor Leader
Leader Of Opposition
Legislative Speaker
Legislative Whip
Major Political Party
Majority Electoral Outcome
Majority Political Party
Minority Leader
National Legislative Leader
National Legislative Whip
Political Leader
Political Leadership
Subnational Legislative Leader

MAJORITY PARTY
1975-1979 00006

MAJORITY POLITICAL PARTY
S-28-0026 1979 00000
BT Political Party Type
RT Major Political Party
Majoritarian Democracy
Majority Electoral Outcome
Majority Leader
Ruling Political Party
Sector Based Political Party Type

MALAPPORTIONMENT
S-31-0713 1975 00001
BT Apportionment
RT Gerrymandering
Judicial Review
Legislative District
Legislative Districting
Legislative Redistricting
Voting Data

MALE CHAUVINISM
S-38-0239 1975 00002
BT Sexism
RT Chauvinist
Feminism
Male Chauvinist
Patriarchal Kinship System
Patriarchical Government
Sex Role
Sexist
Womens Emancipation
Womens Liberation Movement

MALE CHAUVINIST
S-32-0211 1975 00001
BT Chauvinist
RT Female Chauvinism
Female Chauvinist
Male Chauvinism
Sex Role
Sexism
Sexist
Womens Emancipation

MALFEASANCE
S-10-0061 1975 00000
BT Political Crime
RT Legal Malpractice
Malpractice
Medical Malpractice
Misfeasance
Political Conspiracy
Political Corruption
Political Fraud
Power Abuse

MALNUTRITION
S-31-0114 1979 00000
BT Food Scarcity
RT Agricultural Development
Hunger
Resource Allocation
Resource Distribution
Starvation
Water Scarcity

MALPRACTICE
S-10-0038 1979 00000
BT Individual Crime
NT Legal Malpractice
Medical Malpractice
RT Blackmail
Economic Crime
Extortion
Malfeasance
Misfeasance
Political Crime
Political Fraud
Professional Occupational Role

MALPRACTICE INSURANCE
S-26-0305 1979 00000
BT Insurance
RT Accident Insurance
Catastrophe Insurance
Compulsory Insurance
Fire Insurance
Life Insurance
Motor Vehicle Industry

MALTHUSIAN THEORY
S-38-0110 1975 00002
BT Classical Economic Theory
RT Family Planning
Fertility Rate
Growth Model
Laissez Faire Theory
Macroeconomics
Population Growth
Population Transition
Ricardian Theory

MAN MACHINE SIMULATION
S-24-0129 1975 00002
BT Simulation
RT Advanced Technology
Computer Simulation
Game Theory
Gaming
Rational Model
Rationality Theory
Simulation Material

MANAGEMENT
S-23-0001 1975 00032
NT Administrative Management
Conflict Management
Defense Management
Development Management
Economic Management
Education Administration
Environmental Management
Health Administration
Information Management
Law Administration
Military Management
Participatory Management
Population Management
Public Policy Management
Research Management
Welfare Administration
RT Bureaucracy
County Manager Government
Dean
Decision Maker
Economy Type
Government
Industry
Line Staff
Management Characteristics
Management Information System
Manager
Managerial Elite
Organization Decision Maker
Organization Development
Organization Effectiveness
Organization Efficiency
Organization Flexibility
Organization Goal
Organization Hierarchy
Organizations
Policy
Policy Implementation
Policy Making Process

MANAGEMENT CHARACTERISTICS
S-06-0426 1975 00032
BT Characteristics
NT Administrative Characteristics
RT Administrative Planning
Administrative Science
Business Elite
Business Studies
County Manager Government
Entrepreneurship
Expertise
Government Characteristics
Health Characteristics
Management
Management Information System
Management Training Program
Manager
Organization Capability Characteristics
Organization Characteristics

MANAGEMENT INFORMATION SYSTEM
S-37-0079 1975 00005
BT Information System
RT Formative Evaluation
Information Network
Information Retrieval Program
Information Retrieval System
Information Utilization
Management
Management Characteristics
Manager
Organization Effectiveness
Organization Efficiency
Planning Process
Planning Theory
Summative Evaluation

MANAGEMENT SCIENCE
USE Administrative Science

MANAGEMENT TRAINING PROGRAM
S-01-0053 1979 00000
BT Business Studies
RT Administrative Management
Administrative Planning
Administrative Policy Making
Administrative Science
Business Administration Education
Economics Discipline
Expertise
Job Training
Management Characteristics
Public Administration Studies
Training Assistance
Vocation Training Policy

MANAGER
S-32-0097 1975 00010
BT Professional Occupational Role
NT White Collar Worker
RT County Manager Government
Decision Maker
Line Staff
Management
Management Characteristics
Management Information System
Managerial Elite
Organization Decision Maker
Organization Development
Organization Effectiveness
Organization Efficiency
Policy Implementation
Policy Making Process

MANAGERIAL ELITE
S-14-0015 1975 00007
BT Elite Type
NT Bureaucratic Elite
RT Business Elite
Commercial Elite
Corporate Elite
Decision Making Elite
Economic Elite
Entrepreneur Class
Financial Elite
Management
Manager
Political Elite
Power Elite
Scientific Elite
Technological Elite

MANDATE OF HEAVEN THEORY
S-38-0103 1975 00000
BT Confucian Political Theory
RT Authority Theory
Confucian Political Theory
Confucianism
Divine Right Theory
Legitimacy Theory
Religious Authority
Representation Theory
Sovereignty Theory

MANDATE TERRITORY
S-16-0055 1975 00002
BT Extranational Government Structure
RT Caretaker Government
Colony
Empire
Former Colony
International Trusteeship
Popular Sovereignty
Protectorate
Territory Classification
Territory Jurisdiction
Territory Sovereignty
United Nations

MANDATORY ASSOCIATION
1975-1979 00000

MANIFEST FUNCTION
S-06-0588 1975 00000
BT System Function
RT Annexation
Functional Adaptation
Functional Requisites
Latent Function

MANN WHITNEY U TEST
S-24-0059 1979 00000
SN Nonparametric measure of signficance for use with ordinal data involving two samples.
BT Statistical Significance Test
RT Binomial Test
Chi Square Test
F Ratio
Interval Significance Test
Nominal Significance Test
Ordinal Significance Test

MANN WHITNEY V TEST
1975-1979 00000

MANNHEIM IDEOLOGY EXPLANATION
S-38-0149 1975 00002
SN Assertion that explanations of social reality are class or group bound and only free floating intellectuals can overcome this determinism.
BT Ideology Explanatory Theory
RT Ideological Polarization
Ideological Political Culture
Ideological Political Party
Ideologies
Ideologue
Knowledge Production
Marxist Ideology Explanation
Sociology Of Knowledge

MANPOWER POLICY
S-26-0203 1975 00049
BT Employment Policy
RT Employment Opportunity
Employment Policy
Equal Employment Policy
Fair Employment Policy
Full Employment Policy
Labor Force
Manpower Training
Merit Policy
Occupation Characteristics
Professional Education
Public Works Policy
Quota System Policy
Unemployment Policy

MANPOWER TRAINING
S-13-0050 1979 00000
BT Technical Education
NT Job Training
Vocational Education
RT Employment Policy
Manpower Policy
Occupation Characteristics
Professional Education

MANUFACTURING INDUSTRY
S-17-0055 1975 00037
BT Production Industry
NT Light Industry
Machinery Industry
Paper Industry
Textile Industry
RT Business Agency
Chemical Industry
Construction Industry
Heavy Industry
Industrial Development
Industrial Distribution
Industrial Policy
Metallurgical Industry

MAOISM
S-38-0326 1975 00045
BT Marxism
RT Agrarian Socialism
Bolshevism
Castroism
Chinese Cultural Revolution
Communism
Communist Government
Communist Political Party
Communist Studies
Evolutionary Marxism
Guerrilla Activity
Guerrilla War
Hegelian Marxism
Land Reform Policy
Leninism
Maoist
Maoist Movement
Maoist Political Party
Maoist Revolutionary
Marxism Leninism
Marxist Analysis
Marxist Economics
Marxist Revisionism
Marxist Sociology
Partisan War
Peasant Mobilization
Peoples Army
Peoples War Policy
Polycentrism
Proletarian Cultural Revolution Movement
Red Commune
Revolutionary War
Spontaneous Revolution
Stalinism
Titoism
Totalitarian Dictatorship
Totalitarian Leadership
Totalitarian Movement
Totalitarian Political System
Trotskyism

MAOIST
S-32-0283 1975 00001
BT Communist
RT Bolshevism
Castroism
Chinese Cultural Revolution
Communist Political Party
Communist Studies
Guerrilla Activity
Guerrilla War
Land Reform Policy

Leninism
Maoism
Maoist Movement
Maoist Political Party
Maoist Revolutionary
Marxism Leninism
Marxist Analysis
Marxist Economics
Marxist Sociology
Peasant Mobilization
Polycentrism
Proletarian Cultural Revolution Movement
Red Commune
Stalinism
Stalinist
Totalitarian Dictatorship
Totalitarian Leadership
Totalitarian Movement
Totalitarian Political System

MAOIST MOVEMENT
S-27-0017 1975 00004
BT Ideological Spectrum Political Movement
RT Agrarian Movement
Communist Movement
Communist Studies
Extremist Movement
Guerrilla War
Leninism
Maoism
Maoist
Maoist Political Party
Maoist Revolutionary
Marxism Leninism
Messianic Movement
Revolutionary Change
Revolutionary Movement
Terrorist Movement
Totalitarian Movement

MAOIST PARTY
1975-1979 00000

MAOIST POLITICAL PARTY
S-28-0013 1979 00000
BT Communist Political Party
RT Bolshevism
Castroism
Chinese Cultural Revolution
Communist Political Party
Communist Studies
Guerrilla War
Land Reform Policy
Leninism
Maoism
Maoist
Maoist Movement
Maoist Revolutionary
Marxism Leninism
Marxist Analysis
Marxist Economics
Marxist Sociology
Peasant Mobilization
Polycentrism
Proletarian Cultural Revolution Movement
Red Commune
Stalinism
Totalitarian Dictatorship
Totalitarian Leadership
Totalitarian Movement
Totalitarian Political System

MAOIST REVOLUTIONARY
S-32-0200 1975 00004
BT Revolutionary
RT Bolshevism
Castroism
Chinese Cultural Revolution
Communist Political Party
Communist Revolution
Communist Studies
Guerrilla
Guerrilla War
Insurrectionist
Land Reform Policy
Leninism
Maoism
Maoist
Maoist Movement
Maoist Political Party
Marxism Leninism
Marxist Analysis
Marxist Economics
Marxist Sociology
Peasant Mobilization
Permanent Revolution Theory
Polycentrism
Proletarian Cultural Revolution Movement
Red Commune
Revolution Theory
Stalinism
Totalitarian Dictatorship
Totalitarian Leadership
Totalitarian Movement
Totalitarian Political System

MARGINAL ANALYSIS
S-09-0046 1975 00003
BT Contemporary Analytic Modes
NT Marginal Utility Analysis
RT Cost Benefit Analysis
Input Output Analysis
Marginal Man Analysis
Marginal Utility Analysis
Microeconomics
National Accounts Analysis
National Income Analysis

MARGINAL MAN ANALYSIS
S-09-0068 1979 00000
BT Sociological Analysis
RT Demographic Studies
Durkheimian Analysis
Marginal Analysis
Marginal Voter
Parsonsian Analysis
Social System Structural Characteristics
Squatter Community
Structural Functional Analysis
Weberian Analysis

MARGINAL UTILITY ANALYSIS
S-09-0047 1975 00014
BT Marginal Analysis
RT Input Output Analysis
Marginal Analysis
Microeconomics
National Accounts Analysis
National Income Analysis
Public Policy Analysis

MARGINAL VOTER
S-32-0320 1975 00001
BT Voter
RT Alienated Voter
Apathetic Voter
Deferential Voter
Floating Voting
Issue Voter
Marginal Man Analysis
Political Efficacy
Protest Voter
Voter Orientation
Voter Turnout
Voting
Voting Behavior

MARINE
S-36-0222 1975 00000
BT Military Service Personnel
RT Pilot
Sailor
Soldier

MARINES
S-33-0061 1975 00013
BT Armed Forces
RT Admiralty
Air Force
Army
Coast Guard
Conscripted Armed Forces
Mercenary Armed Forces
Navy
Peoples Army
Professional Military Forces
Reserve Military Forces
Voluntary Armed Forces

MARITAL LAW
S-21-0091 1979 00000
BT Social Law
NT Divorce Law
RT Divorce Law
Family Law
Family Policy
Family Role
Family Type
Gambling Law
Marital Status

MARITAL OFFENSE
S-10-0041 1979 00000
BT Individual Crime
RT Blackmail
Divorced
Extortion
Husband
Marital Status
Married
Morals Offense
Sex Crime
Wife

MARITAL STATUS
S-36-0227 1979 00000
BT Status
NT Divorced
Married
Single
Widow
Widower
RT Marital Law
Marital Offense
Marriage Contract

Marriage Rights

MARITIME COURT
S-19-0154 1975 00000
BT Courts
RT Admiralty Law
Coast Guard
Commercial Law
International Court
International Tribunal
Maritime Law
Navy
Piracy

MARITIME LAW
S-21-0060 1975 00032
BT Law Type
RT Admiralty Law
Commercial Law
Law Of The Sea
Maritime Court

MARKET
S-19-0179 1975 00010
BT Economic Institution
NT Black Market
Commodity Market
Common Market
Consumer Market
Differentiated Market
Domestic Market
Export Market
Financial Market
Free Market
RT Business
Deflation
Enterprise
Farm Industry
Fiscal Institution
Market Model
Marketing
Mixed Enterprise
Monetary Institution
World Bank

MARKET ECONOMY
S-12-0026 1975 00031
UF Market Value
BT Economy Type
NT Capitalist Economy
Imperialist Economy
Socialist Market Economy
RT Barter Economy
Capital Investment Economy
Consumer Economy
Corporate Farm Economy
Depression
Developed Economy
Developing Economy
Export Economy
Free Enterprise System
Macroeconomics
Market Model
Market Research
Market System
Mercantile Capitalism
Mercantile Economic System
Mercantile Economic Theory
Modernizing Economy
Welfare Economy

MARKET FREEDOM
S-15-0004 1975 00010
BT Freedom Of Competition
RT Business Policy
Free Enterprise System
Market Model
Market System
Marketplace
Martial Law
Military Directorate
Military Occupation
Military Police
Military Prison
Right To Strike
Right To Work

MARKET MODEL
S-24-0308 1975 00040
BT Social Science Model
RT Macroeconomics
Market
Market Economy
Market Freedom
Market Research
Market System
Marketing
Marketing Cooperative
Marketplace

MARKET RESEARCH
S-24-0389 1979 00000
BT Research Orientation
RT Business Studies
Descriptive Research
Market Economy
Market Model
Market System
Marketing
Marketplace
Policy Research
Quantitative Research
Research And Development
Theoretical Research

MARKET SYSTEM
S-37-0044 1979 00000
BT Economic System
RT Denationalization Process
Economic System Characteristics
Free Enterprise System
Government Deregulation
International Market
Market Economy
Market Freedom
Market Model
Market Research
Marketing
Socialist Market Economy

MARKET VALUE
USE Market Economy

MARKETING
S-31-0423 1979 00000
BT Economic Process
RT Advertising Industry
Commerce
Economic Process
Market
Market Model
Market Research
Market System
Production Process
Research And Development

MARKETING COOPERATIVE
S-03-0006 1975 00001
UF Consumer Cooperative
BT Cooperatives
RT Agricultural Cooperative
Credit Cooperative
Economic Interest Group
Market Model
Marketplace
Peasant Cooperative
Producer Cooperative
Trade Organization
Worker Cooperative

MARKETPLACE
S-19-0192 1975 00010
BT International Market
RT Artisan
Black Market
Business Policy
Commodity Market
Consumer Market
Differentiated Market
Domestic Market
Export Market
Financial Market
Free Market
Market Freedom
Market Model
Market Research
Marketing Cooperative
Mass Market
Self Sufficient Economy

MARRIAGE CONTRACT
S-02-0040 1979 00000
BT Contract Type
RT Compact
Contract Law
Family Role
Husband
Marital Status
Marriage Type
Married
Wife

MARRIAGE RIGHTS
S-15-0077 1979 00000
BT Social Rights
RT Childrens Rights
Health Care Rights
Housing Rights
Income Rights
Marital Status
Marriage Type
Right To Education
Sexual Freedom

MARRIAGE TYPE
S-20-0022 1975 00074
BT Kinship
NT Intermarriage
Monogamy
Polygamy
RT Family Descent Pattern
Marriage Contract
Marriage Rights
Married
Monogamy
Polyandry

MARRIED
S-36-0229 1979 00000
BT Marital Status
RT Marital Offense
Marriage Contract
Marriage Type
Single

MARTIAL LAW
S-21-0061 1975 00008
BT Law Type
RT Court Martial
Dictatorial Regime
Emergency Power
Garrison State
Market Freedom
Military Dictatorship
Military Justice
Military Law
Military Law System
Military Occupation
Military Police
Military State
Military Trial
Military Tribunal
Police State

MARV
S-33-0030 1979 00000
BT Multiple Warhead Missile
RT Arms Control Policy
Assured Destruction Policy
Ballistic Missile
Missile
Nuclear Arms Race
Nuclear Weapon
Offensive Weapon System
Strategic Arms Limitation
Strategic Weapon
Weapon Delivery System

MARXISM
S-38-0314 1975 00028
BT Socialist Theory
NT Bolshevism
Castroism
Communism
Evolutionary Marxism
Hegelian Marxism
Leninism
Maoism
Marxism Leninism
Marxist Revisionism
Polycentrism
Stalinism
Titoism
Trotskyism
RT Agrarian Socialism
Aprista Socialism
Bourgeois Capitalism
Bourgeois Revolution
Bourgeois Society
Christian Socialism
Classless Society
Collective Ownership
Communist
Communist Government
Communist Revolution
Communist Studies
Democratic Socialism
Dialectic
Dialectical Materialism
Evolutionary Socialism
Guild Socialism
Internal Conflict
Marxism Leninism
Marxist Analysis
Marxist Capitalism Theory
Marxist Class Consciousness Theory
Marxist Communism Theory
Marxist Materialism
Marxist Political Thought
Marxist Revolution Theory
Marxist Sociology
Marxist Theory
National Liberation Movement
Neomarxism
Phenomenological Marxism
Praxis
Proletarian Dictatorship
Proletarian Movement
Proletarian Political Party
Proletarian Socialist Movement
Proletariat
Scientific Socialism
Soviet Studies
Structural Marxism
Syndicalism

MARXISM LENINISM
S-38-0329 1975 00021
BT Marxism
RT Bolshevik Revolution
Bolshevism
Bourgeois Dictatorship
Bourgeois Revolution
Castroism
Communism
Communist Empire
Communist Government
Communist Imperialism
Communist Studies
Dictatorship Of The Proletariat
East European Area Studies
Evolutionary Marxism
Guerrilla War
Hegelian Marxism
Leninism
Maoism
Maoist
Maoist Movement
Maoist Political Party
Maoist Revolutionary
Marxism
Marxist Analysis
Marxist Class Theory
Marxist Communism Theory
Marxist Revisionism
Marxist Revolution Theory
Partisan War
Peoples Democratic State
Political Revolution
Polycentrism
Proletarian Dictatorship
Proletarian Political Party
Russian Studies
Soviet Studies
Stalinism
Titoism
Trotskyism

MARXIST ALIENATION THEORY
S-38-0300 1975 00004
BT Marxist Theory
RT Alienation
Alienation Process
Anomie
Class Analysis
Class Struggle
Dictatorship Of The Proletariat
Division Of Labor
Economic Deprivation
Economic Exploitation
Estrangement
Exploitation Process
Marxist Analysis
Marxist Class Theory
Marxist Communism Theory
Marxist Economic Determinism
Marxist Existentialism
Marxist Immiseration Theory
Marxist Materialism
Marxist Revisionism
Marxist Revolution Theory
Marxist Sociology
Political Alienation
Political Estrangement
Political Powerlessness
Praxis
Proletariat
Social Psychology

MARXIST ANALYSIS
S-09-0048 1975 00026
BT Contemporary Analytic Modes
RT Class Analysis
Class Based Coalition
Class Conflict
Class Polarization
Communist Government
Communist Imperialism
Evolutionary Marxism
Evolutionary Socialism
Maoism
Maoist
Maoist Political Party
Maoist Revolutionary
Marxism
Marxism Leninism
Marxist Alienation Theory
Marxist Class Theory
Marxist Communism Theory
Marxist Economic Determinism
Marxist Economic Theory
Marxist Economics
Marxist Materialism
Marxist Political Thought
Marxist Revisionism
Marxist Revolution Theory
Marxist Sociology
Marxist Theory
Revisionist Historical Analysis

MARXIST CAPITALISM THEORY
S-38-0301 1975 00017
BT Marxist Theory
RT Capitalism
Dialectical Materialism
Dictatorship Of The Proletariat
Marxism
Marxist Class Theory
Marxist Communism Theory

Marxist Economic Determinism
Marxist Labor Value Theory
Marxist Materialism
Mature Capitalism

MARXIST CLASS CONSCIOUSNESS THEORY
S-38-0303 1975 00018
BT Marxist Class Theory
NT Proletarian Internationalism
RT Class Based Movement
Marxism
Marxist Communism Theory
Marxist Ideology Explanation
Marxist Immiseration Theory
Marxist Labor Value Theory
Marxist Political Thought
Marxist Sociology
Working Class Movement

MARXIST CLASS THEORY
S-38-0302 1975 00008
BT Marxist Theory
NT Marxist Class Consciousness Theory
Marxist Immiseration Theory
RT Bourgeoisie
Class Antagonism
Class Based Coalition
Class Conflict
Class Dissolution
Class Formation
Class Inequality
Class Rebellion
Class Society
Communist Studies
Conflict Theory
Congressional Intern
Dialectical Materialism
Dictatorship Of The Proletariat
Economic Ideology
Entrepreneur Class
Estrangement
Lumpen Proletariat
Marxism Leninism
Marxist Alienation Theory
Marxist Analysis
Marxist Capitalism Theory
Marxist Communism Theory
Marxist Economic Determinism
Marxist Economics
Marxist Existentialism
Marxist Ideology Explanation
Marxist Labor Value Theory
Marxist Materialism
Praxis
Proletarian Internationalism
Proletarian Revolution
Working Class
Working Class Movement

MARXIST COMMUNISM THEORY
S-38-0306 1975 00007
BT Marxist Theory
RT Communism
Communist
Communist Society
Communist Studies
Dictatorship Of The Proletariat
Eurocommunism
Marxism
Marxism Leninism
Marxist Alienation Theory
Marxist Analysis
Marxist Capitalism Theory
Marxist Class Consciousness Theory
Marxist Class Theory
Marxist Economic Determinism
Marxist Economic Theory
Marxist Economics
Marxist Ideology Explanation
Marxist Immiseration Theory
Marxist Materialism
Marxist Political Thought
Praxis
Working Class Movement

MARXIST ECONOMIC DETERMINISM
S-38-0307 1975 00008
BT Marxist Theory
RT Capitalism
Dictatorship Of The Proletariat
Marxist Alienation Theory
Marxist Analysis
Marxist Capitalism Theory
Marxist Class Theory
Marxist Communism Theory
Marxist Immiseration Theory
Marxist Labor Value Theory
Marxist Materialism

MARXIST ECONOMIC THEORY
S-38-0115 1975 00009
BT Economic Theory
RT Capitalism
Capitalism Theory
Class Society
Classical Economic Theory
Depression
Dialectical Materialism
Dictatorship Of The Proletariat
Economic Conflict
Economic Egalitarianism
Economic Rebellion
Keynesian Economic Theory
Macroeconomics
Marxist Analysis
Marxist Communism Theory
Marxist Economics
Marxist Labor Value Theory
Mercantile Economic Theory
Scientific Socialism

MARXIST ECONOMICS
S-01-0070 1975 00004
BT Macroeconomics
RT Communist Economic System
Communist Imperialism
Dialectical Materialism
Evolutionary Marxism
Keynesian Economics
Maoism
Maoist
Maoist Political Party
Maoist Revolutionary
Marxist Analysis
Marxist Class Theory
Marxist Communism Theory
Marxist Economic Theory
Marxist Labor Value Theory
Marxist Sociology
Scientific Socialism
Socialist Theory

MARXIST EXISTENTIALISM
S-38-0065 1975 00001
BT Existentialism
RT Communist Studies
Eurocommunism
Marxist Alienation Theory
Marxist Class Theory
Marxist Materialism
Marxist Revisionism
Neomarxism
Political Philosophy Studies
Praxis

MARXIST IDEOLOGY EXPLANATION
S-38-0150 1975 00010
BT Ideology Explanatory Theory
RT Class Society
Dialectical Materialism
Ideological Conflict
Ideological Struggle
Mannheim Ideology Explanation
Marxist Class Consciousness Theory
Marxist Class Theory
Marxist Communism Theory
Marxist Theory
Sociology Of Knowledge

MARXIST IMMISERATION THEORY
S-38-0305 1975 00001
SN Assertion in classical Marxist analysis that the recurring economic crises of capitalism increasingly depress the standard of living
of the working class.
BT Marxist Class Theory
RT Capitalism
Exploitation Process
Marxist Alienation Theory
Marxist Class Consciousness Theory
Marxist Communism Theory
Marxist Economic Determinism
Standard Of Living
Working Class Movement

MARXIST LABOR VALUE THEORY
S-38-0308 1975 00004
BT Marxist Theory
RT Exploitation Process
Marxist Capitalism Theory
Marxist Class Consciousness Theory
Marxist Class Theory
Marxist Economic Determinism
Marxist Economic Theory
Marxist Economics
Marxist Materialism
Marxist Revisionism

MARXIST MATERIALISM
S-38-0309 1975 00003
BT Marxist Theory
NT Dialectical Materialism
Historical Materialism
RT Marxism
Marxist Alienation Theory
Marxist Analysis
Marxist Capitalism Theory
Marxist Class Theory
Marxist Communism Theory
Marxist Economic Determinism
Marxist Existentialism
Marxist Labor Value Theory
Materialism
Structural Marxism

MARXIST POLITICAL THOUGHT
S-38-0416 1975 00009
BT Modern Political Thought
RT Communist Government
Dictatorship Of The Proletariat
Marxism
Marxist Analysis
Marxist Class Consciousness Theory
Marxist Communism Theory
Marxist Revolution Theory
Marxist Theory
Political Alienation Theory
Political Revolution
Progress Theory
Proletarian Revolution
Socialist Theory

MARXIST REVISIONISM
S-38-0327 1975 00009
BT Marxism
NT Communist Deviationism
RT Communism
Eurocommunism
Evolutionary Marxism
Hegelian Marxism
Leninism
Maoism
Marxism Leninism
Marxist Alienation Theory
Marxist Analysis
Marxist Existentialism
Marxist Labor Value Theory
Marxist Sociology
Neomarxism
Polycentrism
Revisionist Historical Analysis
Stalinism
Titoism
Trotskyism

MARXIST REVOLUTION THEORY
S-38-0312 1979 00000
BT Marxist Theory
RT Class Conflict
Communist Revolution
Communist Studies
Conflict Theory
East European Area Studies
Economic Rebellion
Historiography
Marxism
Marxism Leninism
Marxist Alienation Theory
Marxist Analysis
Marxist Political Thought
Marxist Sociology
Peasant Rebellion
Revolution
Revolutionary
Revolutionary Change
Revolutionary Elite
Revolutionary Movement
Revolutionary Political Party
Soviet Studies

MARXIST SOCIOLOGY
S-01-0189 1975 00014
BT Sociology Discipline
RT Class Analysis
Class Struggle
Communist Studies
Historical Sociology
History Of Philosophy
Industrial Sociology
Macrosociology
Maoism
Maoist
Maoist Political Party
Maoist Revolutionary
Marxism
Marxist Alienation Theory
Marxist Analysis
Marxist Class Consciousness Theory
Marxist Economics
Marxist Revisionism
Marxist Revolution Theory
Marxist Theory
Political Sociology
Rural Sociology
Social Pathology
Social Psychology
Soviet And East European Area Studies
Soviet Studies

MARXIST THEORY
S-38-0298 1975 00050
BT Socialist Theory
NT Dictatorship Of The Proletariat
Marxist Alienation Theory
Marxist Capitalism Theory
Marxist Class Theory
Marxist Communism Theory
Marxist Economic Determinism
Marxist Labor Value Theory
Marxist Materialism
Marxist Revolution Theory
Praxis
RT Agrarian Socialism
Aprista Socialism
Communist Society
Democratic Socialism
Dialectical Materialism
Evolutionary Socialism
Guild Socialism
Hegelian Analysis
Marxism
Marxist Analysis
Marxist Ideology Explanation
Marxist Political Thought
Marxist Sociology
Neomarxism
Phenomenological Marxism
Scientific Socialism
Structural Marxism

MASCULINITY
S-06-0516 1979 00000
BT Personality Characteristics
RT Altruism
Ambivalence
Assertiveness
Charity
Courage
Creativity
Curiosity
Egocentrism
Empathy
Femininity
Gregariousness
Honesty
Imagination
Optimism
Persistence

MASS BEHAVIOR
S-05-0032 1975 00022
BT Social Behavior
NT Crowd Behavior
RT Accommodative Social Behavior
Adaptive Behavior
Administrative Behavior
Conformity Behavior
Crowd Behavior
Deviant Behavior
Elite Mass Relations
Habitual Behavior
Mass Mobilization
Mass Political Party
Mass Revolutionary Movement
Mass Society
Mass Society Theory
Mobilization Policy
Mobilization Process
Political Behavior
Political Participation
Social Interaction Theory
Voting Behavior

MASS BELIEF SYSTEM
S-37-0003 1979 00000
BT Belief System
RT Mass Public Opinion
Mass Society
Political Ideology
Political Socialization
Political Value Acquisition
Public Opinion Survey
Value Analysis
Value System

MASS COMMUNICATION
S-31-0179 1975 00017
BT Communication Process
NT Broadcasting
Media Editorializing
News Conference
News Flow
News Reporting
Newspaper Circulation
RT Communication Flow
Communication Policy
Fairness Doctrine
Informal Communication
Information Dissemination
International Communication
Interpersonal Communication
Mass Society Theory
Nonverbal Communication
Political Communication
Political Party Advertising

MASS CONSUMPTION
S-06-0273 1975 00003
BT Consumption
RT Conspicuous Consumption
Consumerism
Domestic Consumption
Mass Production
Mass Society
Private Consumption
Private Sector
Public Consumption

MASS CULTURE
S-11-0019 1979 00000
BT Culture Type
NT Popular Culture
RT Civic Culture
Community Culture
Counter Culture
Mass Education
Mass Mobilization
Mass Political Party
Mass Society
Political Culture

MASS DEMOCRACY
S-16-0021 1975 00006
BT Democratic Government
RT Agrarian Democracy
Majoritarian Democracy
Mass Education
Mass Society
Participatory Democracy
Pluralist Democracy
Representation Theory
Representative Government

MASS EDUCATION
S-13-0024 1975 00012
BT Education Type
RT Alternative Education
Civic Education
Compulsory Education
Education Planning
Education Policy
Education Politics
Higher Education
Literacy Policy
Mass Culture
Mass Democracy
Mass Society
Military Education
Political Education
Public School
State Supported Higher Education
Urban Education

MASS MARKET
S-19-0193 1975 00003
BT International Market
RT Commodity Market
Consumer Market
Differentiated Market
Domestic Market
Free Market
Marketplace
National Market
World Market

MASS MEDIA ACCESS POLICY
S-26-0039 1975 00009
BT Mass Media Policy
RT Broadcasting Policy
Fairness Doctrine
Mass Media Censorship Policy
Mass Media Licensing Policy
Mass Media Policy
Mass Media Regulation Policy
Mass Media Subsidization Policy

MASS MEDIA ANALYSIS
S-09-0010 1975 00076
BT Communication Analysis
RT Communication Analysis
Content Analysis
Editorial Control
Government Information Diffusion Policy
Mass Media Policy
Network Analysis

MASS MEDIA CENSORSHIP POLICY
S-26-0040 1975 00003
BT Mass Media Policy
RT Broadcasting Policy
Editorial Control
Mass Media Access Policy
Mass Media Licensing Policy
Mass Media Regulation Policy
Mass Media Subsidization Policy

MASS MEDIA LICENSING POLICY
S-26-0041 1975 00000
BT Mass Media Policy
RT Broadcasting Policy
Mass Media Access Policy
Mass Media Censorship Policy
Mass Media Regulation Policy
Mass Media Subsidization Policy

MASS MEDIA POLICY
S-26-0025 1975 00017
BT Communication Policy
NT Broadcasting Policy
Mass Media Access Policy
Mass Media Censorship Policy
Mass Media Licensing Policy
Mass Media Regulation Policy
Mass Media Subsidization Policy
RT Communication Analysis
Communication Flow
Communication Industry
Communication Process
Individual Communication Policy
Mass Media Access Policy
Mass Media Analysis

MASS MEDIA REGULATION POLICY
S-26-0042 1975 00005
BT Mass Media Policy
RT Broadcasting Licensing Policy
Broadcasting Policy
Communication Industry
Editorial Control
Mass Media Access Policy
Mass Media Censorship Policy
Mass Media Licensing Policy
Mass Media Subsidization Policy

MASS MEDIA SUBSIDIZATION POLICY
S-26-0043 1975 00002
BT Mass Media Policy
RT Broadcasting Policy
Communication Industry
Mass Media Access Policy
Mass Media Censorship Policy
Mass Media Licensing Policy
Mass Media Regulation Policy

MASS MILITIA ARMY
S-33-0054 1975 00004
BT Army Organization
RT Conscripted Armed Forces
Defense Policy
Mass Mobilization
Mass Society
National Guard
Regular Army
Standing Army
War Policy

MASS MOBILIZATION
S-31-0628 1975 00018
BT Mobilization Process
RT Economic Mobilization
Fascist Theory
Mass Behavior
Mass Culture
Mass Militia Army
Mass Public Opinion
Military Mobilization
National Socialism
Political Mobilization
Political Movement Leadership
Social Mobilization
Worker Mobilization

MASS PARTY
1975-1979 00001

MASS POLITICAL PARTY
S-28-0061 1979 00000
BT Structure Specific Political Party Type
RT Decentralized Political Party
Elite Political Party
Mass Behavior
Mass Culture
National Socialist Political Party
Political Movement Leadership
Proletarian Political Party

MASS PRODUCTION
S-31-0436 1975 00002
BT Industrial Production
RT Commodity Production
Economic Characteristics
Industrial Development
Industrial Economy
Industry
Mass Consumption

MASS PUBLIC OPINION
S-18-0098 1979 00000
BT Public Opinion Survey
RT Aggregate Data Statistics
Economic Statistics
Electoral Data
Mass Belief System
Mass Mobilization
Policy Public Opinion Linkage
Political Socialization
Political Statistics
Public Opinion Indicator
Public Opinion Leader
Social Statistics

MASS REVOLUTIONARY MOVEMENT
S-27-0021 1975 00004
BT Revolutionary Movement
RT Mass Behavior
Mass Society
Mass Society Theory
Proletarian Movement
Revolution
Revolution Theory

MASS SOCIETY
S-35-0023 1975 00011
BT Society Type Base
NT Atomistic Society
RT Atomistic Family
Atomistic Model
Fascist Theory
Homogeneous Society
Mass Behavior
Mass Belief System

Mass Consumption
Mass Culture
Mass Democracy
Mass Education
Mass Militia Army
Mass Revolutionary Movement
Mass Society Theory
McCarthyism
National Socialism
Normlessness
Political Mobilization

MASS SOCIETY THEORY
S-38-0151 1975 00009
SN It has two usages. One refers to the levelling and the loss of standards of excellence in all dimensions of social action as the lower classes come to participate in the decision-making processes of society. The other refers to the threats to democractic stability posed by an atomized citizenry inadequately protected from elite manipulation and mobilization.
BT Explanatory Political Theory
RT Anomic Process
Atomistic Family
Atomistic Society
Elite Theory
Mass Behavior
Mass Communication
Mass Revolutionary Movement
Mass Society

MASS TRANSIT POLICY
S-26-0422 1975 00013
BT Transportation Policy
NT Air Transportation Policy
Railroad Policy
Urban Transit Policy
RT Environmental Planning
Environmental Pollution
Highway Policy
Mass Transportation Industry
Transportation Economics
Transportation Policy
Transportation System

MASS TRANSPORTATION INDUSTRY
S-17-0078 1975 00006
BT Transportation Industry
RT Air Transportation Industry
Land Transportation Industry
Mass Transit Policy
Motor Vehicle Industry
Transportation System
Trucking Industry
Water Transportation Industry

MASSACRE
S-10-0011 1975 00001
BT War Crime
RT Genocide
Military Conspiracy
Murder
War Atrocity

MASSIVE RETALIATION POLICY
S-26-0069 1979 00000
UF Massive Retaliation Strategy
BT Nuclear Strategy
RT Counterforce Theory

MASSIVE RETALIATION STRATEGY
1975-1979 00006
USE Massive Retaliation Policy

MATCHING CASE
S-24-0424 1975 00000
BT Quasiexperiment
RT Quasiexperimental Research

MATERIALISM
S-25-0022 1975 00006
BT Epistemology
NT Philosophical Materialism
RT Dialectic
Dialectical Materialism
Empiricism
Essentialism
Etymology
Historicism
Logical Positivism
Marxist Materialism
Neopositivism
Objectivism
Philosophical Realism
Scientific Determinism

MATERNAL ROLE
S-32-0042 1975 00010
BT Family Role
NT Mother
RT Household Head
Housewife
Husband
Matriarchal Family
Matrilineal Family Descent Pattern
Paternal Role
Sex Role
Sibling
Wife
Womens Rights

MATHEMATICAL ANALYSIS
S-24-0023 1975 00012
BT Analysis Methodology
NT Calculus
Geometry
Graph Analysis
Linear Programming
Model Building
Trigonometry
RT Causal Analysis
Economic Mathematical Model
Formal Political Theory
Formalization
Game Theory
Graph Theory Analysis
Hermeneutical Analysis
Logical Analysis
Mathematical Model
Mathematical Political Theory
Mathematics Discipline
Measurement Problem
Measurement Procedure
Measurement Scale
Measures
Probability Model
Set Theory
Statistical Analysis
Statistics Discipline

MATHEMATICAL MODEL
S-24-0280 1975 00106
BT Models
NT Differential Equation Model
Economic Mathematical Model
Simultaneous Equation Model
Stochastic Model
RT Economic Forecasting
Game Theory
Mathematical Analysis
Mathematical Political Theory
Mathematics Discipline
Measurement Problem
Measurement Procedure
Measurement Scale
Measures
Natural Science Model
Probability Model
Social Science Model

MATHEMATICAL POLITICAL THEORY
S-38-0138 1975 00005
BT Formal Political Theory
RT Coalition Theory
Empirical Theory
Game Theory
Mathematical Analysis
Mathematical Model
Mathematics Discipline
Models
Rational Model
Set Theory

MATHEMATICS DISCIPLINE
S-01-0141 1975 00001
BT Academic Areas
RT Behavioral Science
Calculus
Computer Science
Differential Equation Model
Econometrics
Engineering Discipline
Geometry
Mathematical Analysis
Mathematical Model
Mathematical Political Theory
Political Science Methodology Studies
Trigonometry

MATRIARCHAL FAMILY
S-20-0012 1975 00004
BT Family Type
RT Family Role
Family Socialization
Maternal Role
Matriarchal Kinship System
Matrilineal Family Descent Pattern
Serial Monogamy
Sex Role
Womens Rights

MATRIARCHAL KINSHIP SYSTEM
S-20-0020 1975 00003
BT Extended Kinship System
RT Family Role
Family Socialization
Matriarchal Family
Matriarchic Government
Matrilineal Family Descent Pattern
Sex Role
Womens Rights

MATRIARCHIC GOVERNMENT
S-16-0067 1975 00000
BT Government Type
RT Authority Structure
Matriarchal Kinship System
Matrilineal Family Descent Pattern
Patriarchical Government
Sex Role

MATRILINEAL FAMILY DESCENT PATTERN
S-20-0004 1975 00003
BT Family Descent Pattern
RT Anthropological Theory
Bilateral Family Descent Pattern
Family Role
Family Socialization
Folkways
Maternal Role
Matriarchal Family
Matriarchal Kinship System
Matriarchic Government
Sex Role

MATURE CAPITALISM
S-37-0016 1975 00004
BT Capitalism
RT Advanced Industrial Society
Black Capitalism
Bourgeois Capitalism
Capitalism Theory
Industrial Capitalism
Marxist Capitalism Theory
Mercantile Capitalism
Monopoly Capitalism
Private Sector
Technological Culture
Warfare Capitalism
Welfare Capitalism

MAYOR
S-36-0085 1975 00005
BT Local Chief Government Executive
RT Borough Government
City Council
City Manager
Council Manager
Local Chief Executive Election
Local Political Elite
Mayoralty Candidate
Mayoralty Election
Mayoralty Election Campaign
Village Chief

MAYORALTY CAMPAIGN
1975-1979 00001

MAYORALTY CANDIDATE
S-32-0241 1975 00002
BT Local Chief Executive Candidate
RT Gubernatorial Candidate
Local Election
Local Politics
Mayor
Mayoralty Election
Mayoralty Election Campaign

MAYORALTY ELECTION
S-29-0097 1975 00004
BT Local Chief Executive Election
RT City Council Election
Local Politics
Mayor
Mayoralty Candidate
Mayoralty Election Campaign

MAYORALTY ELECTION CAMPAIGN
S-29-0037 1979 00000
BT Local Chief Executive Election Campaign
RT Election Campaign Strategy
Local Politics
Mayor
Mayoralty Candidate
Mayoralty Election

MCCARTHYISM
S-38-0184 1975 00003
SN Anti-communist movement in the United States in the 1950s.
BT Anticommunism
RT American Conservatism
Americanism
Anticommunism
Extremism
Mass Society
Reactionary Conservatism

MEASUREMENT
S-24-0157 1975 00023
BT Methodology
NT Measurement Evaluation
Measurement Level
Measurement Object
Measurement Problem
Measurement Procedure
Measurement Scale
Operationalization
RT Analysis Methodology
Aptitude Measurement
Data Collection Methodology
Data Presentation Methodology
Hypothesis Testing
Measurement Bias
Measurement Error
Measurement Evaluation
Measurement Object
Measurement Procedure
Measurement Scale
Measures
Nonmetric Multidimensional Scale
Reliability Measurement
Research Design
Statistical Data

MEASUREMENT BIAS
S-24-0193 1975 00045
BT Measurement Problem
NT Response Bias
RT Autocorrelation
Measurement
Measurement Error
Measurement Evaluation
Measurement Level
Measurement Problem
Missing Data
Random Error
Reliability Measurement
Sampling Error
Systematic Error

MEASUREMENT ERROR
S-24-0195 1975 00031
BT Measurement Problem
RT Autocorrelation
Measurement
Measurement Bias
Missing Data
Random Error
Sampling Error
Systematic Error

MEASUREMENT EVALUATION
S-24-0158 1975 00105
BT Measurement
NT Reliability Measurement
Validity Measurement
RT Aptitude Measurement
Measurement
Measurement Bias
Measurement Level
Measurement Object
Measurement Problem
Measurement Procedure
Measurement Scale
Measures
Power Measurement
Research Evaluation

MEASUREMENT LEVEL
S-24-0169 1975 00003
BT Measurement
NT Interval Measurement
Nominal Measurement
Ordinal Measurement
Ratio Scale Measurement
RT Aptitude Measurement
Measurement Bias
Measurement Evaluation
Measurement Object
Measurement Problem
Measurement Procedure
Measurement Scale
Power Measurement
Statistical Data

MEASUREMENT LEVEL SCALE
S-24-0211 1975 00001
BT Scale Construction Methodology
RT Cumulative Scale
Guttman Scale
Interval Scale
Likert Scale
Measurement Object
Multidimensional Scale
Nominal Scale
Ordinal Scale
Ratio Scale
Scalability Index
Semantic Differential
Thurstone Scale
Unidimensional Scale

MEASUREMENT OBJECT
S-24-0176 1975 00001
BT Measurement
NT Aptitude Measurement
Attitude Measurement
Behavioral Measurement
Change Measurement
Event Measurement
Group Measurement
Individual Measurement
Perception Measurement
Power Measurement
RT Measurement
Measurement Evaluation
Measurement Level
Measurement Level Scale
Measurement Problem
Measurement Procedure
Measurement Scale

Measures

MEASUREMENT PROBLEM
S-24-0191 1975 00053
BT Measurement
NT Autocorrelation
Measurement Bias
Measurement Error
Missing Data
Random Error
Sampling Error
Systematic Error
RT Aptitude Measurement
Mathematical Analysis
Mathematical Model
Measurement Bias
Measurement Evaluation
Measurement Level
Measurement Object
Measurement Procedure
Measurement Scale
Measures
Power Measurement
Statistical Data

MEASUREMENT PROCEDURE
S-24-0201 1975 00084
BT Measurement
RT Mathematical Analysis
Mathematical Model
Measurement
Measurement Evaluation
Measurement Level
Measurement Object
Measurement Problem
Measurement Scale
Measures
Operationalization
Power Measurement
Probability Model
Statistics Discipline

MEASUREMENT SCALE
S-24-0202 1975 00018
BT Measurement
NT Scale Construction Methodology
Scale Type
RT Aptitude Measurement
Intelligence Quotient
Mathematical Analysis
Mathematical Model
Measurement
Measurement Evaluation
Measurement Level
Measurement Object
Measurement Problem
Measurement Procedure
Power Measurement

MEASURES
S-24-0277 1975 00003
BT Operationalization
RT Indicator
Mathematical Analysis
Mathematical Model
Measurement
Measurement Evaluation
Measurement Object
Measurement Problem
Measurement Procedure
Multiple Operationalization
Probability Model
Statistical Data
Statistics Discipline

MEDIA ACCESS
S-31-0301 1975 00013
BT Information Manipulation
RT Broadcasting
Broadcasting Censorship
Communication Policy
Editorial Control
Media Editorializing
Newspaper Censorship
Published Media Censorship
Radio Censorship
Television Censorship

MEDIA EDITORIALIZING
S-31-0182 1975 00010
BT Mass Communication
RT Broadcasting
Communication Policy
Editorial Control
Media Access
News Conference
News Flow
News Reporting
Newspaper Censorship
Newspaper Circulation

MEDIAN INCOME
S-06-0335 1975 00002
BT Income Measure
RT Average Income
Disposable Income
Fixed Income
Net Income
Per Capita Income
Personal Income

MEDIATION
S-31-0236 1975 00011
BT Conflict Resolution
NT Arbitration
International Mediation
Labor Mediation
RT Accommodation
Adjudication
Agreement
Appeasement
Bargaining
Coercion
Conciliation
Declared War
Mediator
Negotiation

MEDIATOR
S-32-0007 1975 00001
BT Adjudicator
RT Arbitrator
Bargainer
Broker
Diplomat
Mediation
Moderator
Negotiator
Ombudsman

MEDICAL ASSOCIATION
S-03-0055 1975 00005
BT Professional Organization
RT Association Interest Group
Medical Care Policy
Medical Care System
Medical Education
Occupational Interest Group
Physician

MEDICAL CARE POLICY
S-26-0271 1975 00082
BT Health Care Policy
RT Health Care Agency
Health Care Institution
Medical Association
Medical Care Service
Medical Care System
Medical Science
Mental Institution
National Health Insurance
Old Age Assistance Policy
Physician
Private Hospital
Public Health Education
Public Health Policy
Public Policy Analysis
Right To Die
Socialized Medicine System

MEDICAL CARE SERVICE
S-26-0364 1979 00000
BT Health Service
RT Education Service
Employment Service
Legal Service
Medical Care Policy
Medical Science
Physician
Private Hospital
Social Policy
Social Service

MEDICAL CARE SYSTEM
S-37-0064 1975 00056
BT Health Care System
NT Socialized Medicine System
RT Health Care Agency
Health Care Institution
Health Care Rights
Hospital
Medical Association
Medical Care Policy
Medical Education
Medical Science
Mental Institution
Private Hospital
Public Health Education

MEDICAL EDUCATION
S-13-0040 1975 00012
BT Health Education
RT Graduate Education
Health Characteristics
Medical Association
Medical Care System
Medical Malpractice
Medical Science
Physician
Public Health Education
Socialized Medicine System

MEDICAL MALPRACTICE
S-10-0040 1979 00000
BT Malpractice
RT Legal Malpractice
Malfeasance
Medical Education
Misfeasance

MEDICAL SCIENCE
S-01-0142 1979 00000
BT Academic Areas
NT Psychiatry
RT Health Care Policy
Health Characteristics
Medical Care Policy
Medical Care Service
Medical Care System
Medical Education
Natural Science Education

MEDIEVAL AGES
S-06-0172 1979 00000
BT Historical Periods
RT Ancient Times
Dark Ages
Feudal System
Medieval International Theory
Medieval Islamic Thought
Medieval Natural Law Theory
Medieval Political Thought
Medieval State Theory
Renaissance

MEDIEVAL CORPORATISM
S-38-0367 1975 00002
BT Medieval Political Thought
RT Classical Corporate Freedom Theory
Community Philosophical Concept
Corporatism
Craft Economy
Feudal Society
Functional Representation Theory
Medieval International Theory
Medieval Islamic Thought
Medieval Natural Law Theory
Medieval State Theory
Organic State Theory
Social Contract Theory
Two Swords Theory

MEDIEVAL INTERNATIONAL THEORY
S-38-0368 1975 00000
BT Medieval Political Thought
RT International Political Theory
Medieval Ages
Medieval Corporatism
Medieval State Theory
Two Swords Theory

MEDIEVAL ISLAMIC THOUGHT
S-38-0369 1975 00003
BT Medieval Political Thought
RT Aristotelian Thought
Islamic Society
Islamic Thought
Medieval Ages
Medieval Corporatism
Medieval Natural Law Theory
Neoplatonic Political Thought
Two Swords Theory

MEDIEVAL NATURAL LAW THEORY
S-38-0490 1975 00002
BT Natural Law Conventionalism Theory
RT Aristotelian Thought
Classical Natural Right Doctrine
Great Chain Of Being Doctrine
Medieval Ages
Medieval Corporatism
Medieval Islamic Thought
Right Reason Doctrine
Roman Natural Law Theory
Scientific Natural Law Theory
Stoic Natural Law Theory
Thomism

MEDIEVAL POLITICAL THOUGHT
S-38-0364 1975 00000
BT Political Theory
NT Augustinian Analysis
Erastianism
Medieval Corporatism
Medieval International Theory
Medieval Islamic Thought
Medieval State Theory
Monasticism
Nominalism
Quietistic Thought
Scholasticism
Thomism
Trentine Doctrine
Two Swords Theory
RT Classical Political Thought
Contemporary Political Thought
Medieval Ages
Political Philosophy Concept
Renaissance Political Thought

MEDIEVAL STATE THEORY
S-38-0370 1975 00002
BT Medieval Political Thought
RT Investiture Controversy
Medieval Ages
Medieval Corporatism
Medieval International Theory
Statecraft Theory
Thomism
Two Swords Theory

MEGALOPOLIS
S-07-0009 1975 00004
BT Metropolitan City
RT City
Inner City
Metropolis
Municipality
Neighborhood
Outer City
Suburb
Urban Development
Urban Politics Studies
Urban Studies

MEMBER PRIVILEGE
S-15-0023 1975 00000
BT Legislative Immunity
RT Citizenship Privilege
Diplomatic Privilege
Legislative Immunity

MEMORY
USE Cognitive System

MENTAL HEALTH POLICY
S-26-0410 1975 00046
BT Social Welfare Policy
RT Alcoholism
Behavior Modification
Drug Addiction
Halfway House
Health Care System
Mental Institution
Old Age Assistance Policy
Personality Disorder
Psychotherapy

MENTAL INSTITUTION
S-19-0249 1979 00000
BT Health Care Institution
RT Halfway House
Health Care Policy
Health Care Rights
Health Care System
Health Clinic
Hospital
Medical Care Policy
Medical Care System
Mental Health Policy
Personality Disorder
Public Health Institution

MERCANTILE CAPITALISM
S-37-0017 1975 00003
UF Cameralism
BT Capitalism
RT Black Capitalism
Bourgeois Capitalism
Industrial Capitalism
Market Economy
Mature Capitalism
Mercantile Economic System
Mercantile Economic Theory
Monopoly Capitalism
Private Sector
Warfare Capitalism
Welfare Capitalism

MERCANTILE ECONOMIC SYSTEM
S-37-0045 1975 00006
BT Economic System
RT Capitalism
Communist Economic System
Entrepreneur Class
Feudal Economic System
Market Economy
Mercantile Capitalism
Mercantile Economic Theory
Mixed Economic System
Socialist Economic System

MERCANTILE ECONOMIC THEORY
S-38-0116 1975 00002
BT Economic Theory
RT Capitalism Theory
Classical Economic Theory
Keynesian Economic Theory
Macroeconomics
Market Economy
Marxist Economic Theory
Mercantile Capitalism
Mercantile Economic System

MERCENARY
S-36-0219 1975 00001
BT Military Recruit
RT Mercenary Armed Forces
Volunteer

MERCENARY ARMED FORCES
S-33-0062 1975 00001
BT Armed Forces
RT Admiralty
Air Force
Army
Conscripted Armed Forces
Marines
Mercenary
Professional Military Forces
Voluntary Armed Forces

MERCHANT MARINE
S-33-0063 1979 00000
BT Armed Forces
RT Coast Guard
Naval Forces
Shipping Industry

MERIT BUREAUCRACY
S-19-0073 1979 00000
BT Bureaucracy
RT Civil Service System
Government Bureaucracy
Merit Policy
Meritocracy
Public Bureaucracy
Test Results

MERIT POLICY
S-26-0204 1975 00004
BT Employment Policy
RT Civil Service System
Equal Employment Policy
Legal Rational Authority
Manpower Policy
Merit Bureaucracy
Meritocracy
Testing

MERITOCRACY
S-35-0004 1975 00005
BT Society Type
RT Academic Elite
Achievement Theory
Achieving Society
Bureaucratic Society
Elitism
Industrial Society
Merit Bureaucracy
Merit Policy
Modernizing Society
Secular Society
Technocracy
Western Society

MERTONIAN ANALYSIS
1975-1979 00001

MESSIANIC MOVEMENT
S-27-0033 1975 00001
SN Movement organized around the belief that a savior will deliver mankind from evil or suffering.
BT Political Movement
RT Extremist Movement
Ideological Spectrum Political Movement
International Communist Movement
Maoist Movement
Millenarianism
Totalitarian Movement
Utopianism

METAETHICAL THEORY
S-25-0048 1975 00002
SN Frameworks which categorize ethical theory and examine the logic or meaning of the terms of moral discourse.
BT Metaphysics
NT Moral Theory
RT Axiology
Emotive Ethical Theory
Ethical Relativism
Hedonism
Instrumentalism
Intuitionism
Linguistic Ethical Theory
Nietzschean Analysis
Normative Analysis
Ontology
Ordinary Language Philosophy
Professional Ethics
Situational Ethics

METALLURGICAL INDUSTRY
S-17-0063 1979 00000
BT Production Industry
RT Heavy Industry
Manufacturing Industry
Steel Industry

METAPHYSICS
S-25-0009 1975 00016
BT Philosophical Concept
NT Epistemology
Ethical Theory
Metaethical Theory
Ontology
Voluntarism
RT Aesthetics
Cosmology
Great Chain Of Being Doctrine
History Of Philosophy
Philosophy Discipline

METHODOLOGICAL INDIVIDUALISM
S-25-0017 1975 00001
BT Empiricism
RT Behavioral Science
Holism
Methodology
Reductionism
Research Design
Research Orientation
Theoretical Framework

METHODOLOGY
S-24-0001 1975 00104
NT Analysis Methodology
Data Collection Methodology
Data Presentation Methodology
Hypothesis Testing
Information Processing
Measurement
Models
Research Apparatus
Research Design
Research Orientation
Study Scope
Theoretical Framework
RT Anthropological Functionalism
Attitude Change Theory
Baconian Analysis
Behavioral Theory
Data Theory
Deductive Method
Economic Model
Empirical Theory
Empiricism
Epistemology
General Theory
Inductive Method
Methodological Individualism
Middle Range Theory
Political Philosophy Concept
Political Science Methodology Studies
Political Theory
Small Group Analysis
Theory Construction

METROPOLIS
S-07-0010 1975 00003
BT Metropolitan City
RT Inner City
Local Political Party
Megalopolis
Metropolitan Politics
Municipality
Neighborhood
Outer City
Urban Development Theory
Urban Society

METROPOLITAN CITY
S-07-0008 1975 00035
BT City
NT Megalopolis
Metropolis
Outer City
RT Central City
City
City Unit
County Manager Government
Decentralized City
Federated City
Metropolitan Government
Metropolitan Growth Pattern
Metropolitan Politics
Model City
Municipality
Urban Government
Urban Politics Studies

METROPOLITAN GOVERNMENT
S-16-0109 1975 00016
BT Subnational Government
NT Provincial Government
RT Borough Government
City Government
County Government
Decentralized City
District Government Type
Federated City
Metropolitan City
Metropolitan Politics
Public Administration Studies
Urban Government

METROPOLITAN GROWTH PATTERN
S-06-0226 1975 00024
BT Population Distribution
RT Metropolitan City
Population Concentration
Residential Pattern
Urbanization Pattern

METROPOLITAN POLITICS
S-29-0237 1975 00012
BT Local Politics
RT City Politics
Local Policy Making
Machine Politics
Metropolis
Metropolitan City
Metropolitan Government
Urban Politics
Urban Politics Studies
Village Politics

MICRO LEVEL ANALYSIS
1975-1979 00003
USE Microlevel Analysis

MICRO POLITICAL THEORY
1975-1979 00002
USE Micropolitical Theory

MICRO POLITICAL THOUGHT
1975-1979 00000
USE Micropolitical Thought

MICROECONOMICS
S-01-0071 1975 00008
BT Economics Discipline
RT Behavioral Science
Economic Behavior
Industrial Economics
Labor Economics
Marginal Analysis
Marginal Utility Analysis
Political Behavior Studies
Social Pathology
Urban Economics

MICROFILM EQUIPMENT
S-24-0335 1975 00001
BT Information Recording Equipment
RT Indexing
Information Dissemination
Information Processing
Information Storage

MICROLEVEL ANALYSIS
S-24-0415 1979 00000
UF Micro Level Analysis
BT Theoretical Framework
NT Decision Making Analysis
Public Choice Analysis
Role Analysis
RT Macrolevel Analysis
Micropolitical Theory
Micropolitical Thought
Variable

MICROPOLITICAL THEORY
S-38-0152 1979 00000
UF Micro Political Theory
BT Explanatory Political Theory
RT Microlevel Analysis
Micropolitical Thought
Theoretical Range

MICROPOLITICAL THOUGHT
S-38-0385 1979 00000
UF Micro Political Thought
BT Political Theory
RT Individual Behavior
Microlevel Analysis
Micropolitical Theory
Theoretical Range

MIDDLE AGE
S-06-0184 1975 00004
BT Age
RT Aging
Old Age

MIDDLE CASTE
S-06-0759 1975 00000
BT Caste Stratification Division
RT Lower Caste
Middle Caste
Middle Class
Social Stratification Division
Upper Caste

MIDDLE CLASS
S-06-0768 1975 00017
BT Class Stratification Division
NT Bourgeoisie
New Middle Class
Old Middle Class
RT Bourgeoisie
Class Analysis
Class Stratification Division
Entrepreneur Class
Middle Caste
Middle Class Political Party
Middle Class Values
Middle Class Voter
Petite Bourgeoisie
Propertied Class
Ruling Class
Social Stratification Division
Upper Class
Working Class

MIDDLE CLASS MOVEMENT
S-27-0050 1979 00000
UF Middle Class Suburban Movement
BT Class Based Movement
RT Class Analysis
Class Conflict
Class Formation
Class Politics
Middle Class Political Party
Proletarian Movement
Working Class Movement

MIDDLE CLASS PARTY
1975-1979 00000

MIDDLE CLASS POLITICAL PARTY
S-28-0038 1979 00000
BT Class Based Political Party
RT Aristocracy Political Party
Center Political Party
Class Analysis
Class Politics
Middle Class
Middle Class Movement
Middle Class Values

MIDDLE CLASS SUBURBAN MOVEMENT
1975-1979 00001
USE Middle Class Movement

MIDDLE CLASS VALUES
S-06-0715 1975 00024
BT Social Mores
RT Bourgeois Society
Middle Class
Middle Class Political Party
Middle Class Voter
Value Analysis

MIDDLE CLASS VOTER
S-32-0302 1975 00000
BT Class Voter
RT Middle Class
Middle Class Values
Upper Class Voter
Working Class Voter

MIDDLE EAST AREA STUDIES
S-01-0041 1975 00302
BT Area Studies
RT Arab Bloc
Comparative Analysis
Comparative Literature Studies
Comparative Political Studies
Comparative Sociology
Geography Discipline
History Discipline
Islamic Society
Islamic Thought
National Region
Oil Energy
Pan Islamism
Political Science Discipline
Shah
Sheik
Sociology Discipline

MIDDLE LEVEL TECHNOLOGY
S-06-0801 1975 00012
BT Technology
RT Advanced Technology
History Of Technology
Labor History
Technological Obsolescence
Technology Policy
Technology Transfer
Technology Transfer Policy
Wind Energy

MIDDLE RANGE THEORY
S-38-0596 1975 00004
BT Theoretical Range
RT General Theory
General Will Democratic Theory
Methodology
Research Orientation
Sociology Discipline
Theoretical Framework

MIDDLE SCHOOL
S-19-0228 1975 00002
BT Secondary School
RT High School
Primary Education

MIGRANT FARMING
S-31-0430 1975 00001
BT Farming
RT Day Laborer
Landless Peasant Class
Migrant Population
Migrant Worker
Migration Pattern
Migration Policy
Migration Process
Subsistence Farming
Tenant Farming

MIGRANT POPULATION
S-06-0213 1975 00012
BT Population Attribute
RT Farmer
Immigration Pattern
Immigration Policy
Migrant Farming
Migrant Worker
Migration Pattern
Migration Policy
Population Density
Rural Population
Urban Population

MIGRANT WORKER
S-32-0064 1975 00016
BT Agricultural Worker
RT Agricultural Worker
Day Laborer
Migrant Farming
Migrant Population
Migration Pattern
Migration Policy
Migration Process

MIGRATION PATTERN
S-06-0234 1975 00026
BT Population Movement
NT Braindrain
Emigration Pattern
Immigration Pattern
Internal Migration Pattern
RT Demographic Analysis
Geographic Mobility
Migrant Farming
Migrant Population
Migrant Worker
Migration Policy
Migration Process
Population Growth
Population Mobility
Population Transition

MIGRATION POLICY
S-26-0389 1975 00008
BT Social Policy
NT Emigration Policy
Immigration Policy
RT Housing Policy
Migrant Farming
Migrant Population
Migrant Worker
Migration Pattern
Migration Process
Population Transition

MIGRATION PROCESS
S-31-0618 1975 00028
BT Process
NT Emigration Process
Immigration Process
Internal Migration
Refugee Migration
RT Emigre
Employment Opportunity
Migrant Farming
Migrant Worker
Migration Pattern
Migration Policy
Relocation Policy

MILITANCY
S-06-0109 1975 00011
BT Attitude Characteristics
NT Ethnic Militancy
Racial Militancy
Student Militancy
RT Activist
Aggressiveness
Alienation
Authoritarian Attitude
Belief System
Belligerence
Black Insurrection
Dogmatism
Extremism
Hostility
Ideological Political Culture

MILITANT
S-32-0184 1975 00002
BT Political Activist
NT Black Militant
New Left Militant
Student Militant
RT Guerrilla Activity
Political Agitator
Political Conspirator
Political Party Activist
Political Party Dissident
Revolutionary
Right Wing Activist
Terrorist

MILITARISM
S-38-0258 1975 00009
BT Ideologies
RT Armed Intervention Policy
Authoritarianism
Caudillism
Elitism
Military Industrial Complex
Military Mind

MILITARY ADVISOR
S-32-0018 1975 00002
BT Advisor
RT Administrative Advisor
Economic Advisor
Legal Advisor
Military Agency
Military Attache
Military Education
Military Elite
Military Forces
Political Advisor
Science Advisor
Technical Advisor

MILITARY AGENCY
S-19-0058 1975 00005
BT Agencies
NT Defense Agency
RT Army Organization
Defense Agency
Foreign Affairs Agency
Military Advisor
Military Attache
Military Characteristics
Military Court
Military Executive Council
Military Institute
Military Intelligence Agency
Military Prison
Navy

MILITARY AGGRESSION
S-08-0004 1975 00009
BT Aggression
NT Limited Military Aggression
RT Annexation
Armed Intervention Policy
Coup D'Etat
Cultural Aggression
Global War Policy
Ideological Conflict
Insurgency
Military Characteristics
Military Coup
Military Invasion
Military Political Party
Psychological Aggression
Putsch
Rebellion
Revolution
War

MILITARY AGREEMENT
S-02-0084 1975 00006
BT State Agreement Type
NT Military Treaty
RT Civil Military Relations
Defense Alliance
Detente
Military Alliance
Military Assistance
Military Planning
Military Policy
Neutrality Agreement
Nonaggression Agreement
Strategic Studies
Summit Meeting

MILITARY AID POLICY
S-26-0258 1975 00023
BT Foreign Aid Policy
RT Bilateral Aid Policy
Bilateral Treaty
Economic Aid Policy
Military Policy
Multilateral Aid Policy
Technical Aid Policy
Unilateral Aid Policy

MILITARY AIRCRAFT
S-33-0033 1975 00032
BT Munitions
RT Air Force
Aircraft Industry
Arms Industry
Warship

MILITARY ALLIANCE
S-02-0005 1975 00031
BT Alliance
NT Defense Alliance
Regional Military Alliance
RT Arms Race
Collective Security
Defense Policy
Defense System
Economic Alliance
Global System
Military Agreement
Multilateral Alliance
Multilateral State Agreement
Mutual Support Declaration
Neutrality Agreement
Nonaggression Agreement
Peace Treaty
Security Community
Strategic Arms Race
Test Ban Agreement
Wartime Alliance
World Alliance

MILITARY ASSISTANCE
S-06-0312 1975 00026
BT Foreign Assistance
RT Bilateral Treaty
Foreign Aid Policy
Military Agreement
Military Policy
Technical Assistance
Training Assistance

MILITARY ATTACHE
S-36-0129 1975 00001
BT Embassy Attache
RT Cultural Attache
Economic Attache
Information Attache
Military Advisor
Military Agency
Political Attache

MILITARY BUDGET
S-06-0255 1979 00000
BT Capital Budget
RT Armed Forces
Budget Agency
Budget Formulation
Budget Policy
Budget Record
Military Management
Military Personnel
Military Planning
Standing Army
Strategic Studies

MILITARY CHARACTERISTICS
S-06-0459 1975 00026
BT Characteristics
NT Defensive Capability
Military Intelligence
Military Size
Nuclear Capability
Offensive Capability
Retaliatory Capability
Strategic Advantage
RT Army Organization
Defense System
Military Agency
Military Aggression
Military Education
Military Elite
Military Establishment
Military Forces
Military Intervention Policy
Military Policy
Military Political Party
Military State
National Security

MILITARY CONSPIRACY
S-10-0062 1975 00002
BT Political Crime
RT Intelligence Agency
Massacre
Military Coup
Military Dictatorship
Military Directorate
Military Espionage
Political Espionage
War Crime

MILITARY COUP
S-08-0039 1975 00029
BT Coup D'Etat
RT Caretaker Government
Coup D'Etat
Economic Conflict
Ideological Conflict
Institutional Conflict
Insurgency
Internal War
Military Aggression
Military Conspiracy
Military Court
Military Dictatorship
Military Directorate
Military Government
Military Intervention Policy
Military Officer
Military Political Party
Political Violence
Putsch
Rebellion
Revolution

MILITARY COURT
S-19-0155 1975 00000
BT Courts
NT Military Tribunal
RT Adjudication
Administrative Court
Criminal Court
International Court
International Tribunal
Military Agency
Military Coup
Military Police
Military Policy
Military Trial

MILITARY DICTATORSHIP
S-16-0039 1975 00009
BT Dictatorship
RT Martial Law
Military Conspiracy
Military Coup
Military Directorate
Military Elite
Military Government
Military Intervention Policy
Military Occupation
Military Political Party
Military State
Tyranny

MILITARY DIRECTORATE
S-16-0148 1975 00004
BT Rule Type
RT Despotism
Garrison State
Joint Chiefs Of Staff
Market Freedom
Military Conspiracy
Military Coup
Military Dictatorship
Military Elite
Military Establishment
Military Executive Council
Military Government
Military Intervention Policy
Military Political Party
Military State
Military Tribunal
Tyranny

MILITARY DRAFT
USE Conscription Power

MILITARY EDUCATION
S-13-0025 1975 00015
BT Education Type
NT Military Training
RT Civic Education
Graduate School
Ideological Education
Mass Education
Military Advisor
Military Characteristics
Military History
Military Institute
Military Law System
Military Management
Military Mind
Military Policy
Military Reorganization Policy
Military Science
Military Service Personnel
Officer Corps
Political Education
Technical Education

MILITARY ELITE
S-14-0017 1975 00023
BT Elite Type
RT Army Organization
Bureaucratic Elite
Elitism
Governing Elite
Military Advisor
Military Characteristics
Military Dictatorship
Military Directorate
Military Establishment
Military Government
Political Elite
Potential Elite
Power Elite
Transitional Political Elite

MILITARY ESPIONAGE
S-10-0063 1975 00001
BT Political Crime
RT Blackmail
Economic Espionage
Industrial Espionage
Intelligence Agency
Military Conspiracy
War Crime

MILITARY ESTABLISHMENT
S-33-0048 1975 00022
BT Military Forces
NT Armed Forces
RT Arms Industry
Balanced Force
Irregular Military Forces
Military Characteristics
Military Directorate
Military Elite
Military Government
Military Governor
Military Policy
Military State
Nuclear Power
Professional Military Forces
Reserve Military Forces
Tactical Force

MILITARY EXECUTIVE COUNCIL
S-19-0236 1975 00001
BT Executive Government Institution
RT Fascist Council
Military Agency
Military Directorate
Military Forces
Military Governor

MILITARY FORCES
S-33-0047 1975 00073
BT National Security Forces
NT Military Establishment
Professional Military Forces
Reserve Military Forces
RT Civil Military Relations
Conscripted Armed Forces
Defense System
Guerrilla War
Irregular Forces
Military Advisor
Military Characteristics
Military Executive Council

Military Mobilization
Military Officer
Military Personnel
Military Policy
Military Recruitment
Military Size

MILITARY GOVERNMENT
S-16-0068 1975 00053
BT Government Type
NT Military Occupation
RT Absolutist Government
Autocratic Government
Benevolent Dictator
Dictatorial Regime
Military Coup
Military Dictatorship
Military Directorate
Military Elite
Military Establishment
Military Management
Military Occupation
Military Policy
Military State
Military Tribunal
Puppet Regime
Tyranny

MILITARY GOVERNOR
S-36-0052 1975 00000
BT Chief Government Executive
NT Warlord
RT Benevolent Dictator
Benevolent Dictatorship
Dictator
Military Establishment
Military Executive Council
Military Intervention Policy
Military Occupation
Military Officer

MILITARY HISTORY
S-01-0113 1975 00100
BT History Discipline
RT Ancient History
Diplomacy
Diplomatic History
Institutional History
Military Education
Military Institute
Military Justice
Military Management
Military Science
Peace Studies
Political Geography
Political History
Strategic Studies

MILITARY INDUSTRIAL COMPLEX
S-19-0288 1975 00004
BT Institutions
RT Arms Industry
Economic Institution
Militarism
Multinational Organization
Navy
Yankee Imperialism

MILITARY INSTITUTE
S-19-0209 1975 00003
BT Higher Education Institution
RT Military Agency
Military Education
Military History
Military Intelligence Agency
Military Mind
Military Reorganization Policy
Military Science
Military Training
Officer Corps
Polytechnical Institute
Professional Military Forces
Professional Socialization

MILITARY INTEGRATION POLICY
S-26-0333 1975 00002
BT Military Reorganization Policy
RT Ethnic Policy
Integrated Community
Integration
Military Reform Policy

MILITARY INTELLIGENCE
S-06-0461 1975 00018
BT Military Characteristics
RT Defensive Capability
Government Document Classification Policy
Intelligence Agency
Military Management
Surveillance

MILITARY INTELLIGENCE AGENCY
S-19-0052 1975 00000
BT Intelligence Agency
RT Defense Agency
Military Agency
Military Institute
Secret Service
Spying

MILITARY INTERVENTION POLICY
S-26-0266 1975 00051
BT Intervention Policy
NT Military Invasion
RT Emergency Power
Expansionist Policy
Guerrilla Activity
Guerrilla War
Interference Policy
Military Characteristics
Military Coup
Military Dictatorship
Military Directorate
Military Governor
Military Invasion
Military Occupation
Military State
Political Interference Policy
Political Intervention Policy
War Policy

MILITARY INVASION
S-26-0267 1979 00000
BT Military Intervention Policy
RT Expansionist Policy
Guerrilla War
Military Aggression
Military Intervention Policy
Political Interference Policy
Political Intervention Policy
War
War Policy

MILITARY JUSTICE
S-15-0066 1975 00002
BT Procedural Rights
RT Acquittal
Legal System
Martial Law
Military History
Military Law
Military Law System
Military Occupation
Military Prosecutor
Military Tribunal

MILITARY LAW
S-21-0062 1975 00005
BT Law Type
NT Uniform Code Of Military Justice
RT Constitutional Law System
Martial Law
Military Justice
Military Law System
Military Occupation
Military Planning
Military Police
Military Policy
Military Prison
Military Prosecutor
Military Tribunal
War Policy

MILITARY LAW SYSTEM
S-37-0103 1975 00004
BT Law System
RT Administrative Law System
Civil Law System
Common Law System
Constitutional Law System
Criminal Law System
International Law System
Martial Law
Military Education
Military Justice
Military Law
Military Prison
Military Tribunal

MILITARY MANAGEMENT
S-23-0033 1975 00030
BT Management
RT Admiralty
Army Organization
Budget Policy
Civil Military Relations
Conflict Management
Crisis Management
Defense Management
Industrial Management
Military Budget
Military Education
Military Government
Military History
Military Intelligence
Military Planning
Military Policy
Military Reform Policy
Military Science
Military Size

MILITARY MIND
S-06-0115 1975 00007
BT Attitude Characteristics
RT Militarism
Military Education
Military Institute
Military Personnel
Military Policy
Military Training
Professional Military Forces

Professional Socialization

MILITARY MOBILIZATION
S-31-0629 1975 00014
BT Mobilization Process
RT Conscripted Armed Forces
Economic Mobilization
Global War Policy
Mass Mobilization
Military Forces
Military Personnel
Military Planning
Military Policy
Political Mobilization
Social Mobilization
Worker Mobilization

MILITARY OCCUPATION
S-16-0069 1979 00000
BT Military Government
RT Divided Nation
Extranational Government Structure
Interim Government
Market Freedom
Martial Law
Military Dictatorship
Military Government
Military Governor
Military Intervention Policy
Military Justice
Military Law
Military Tribunal
Protectorate
War

MILITARY OFFICER
S-36-0213 1975 00034
BT Military Personnel
NT Commander In Chief
Commanding Officer
Joint Chiefs Of Staff
RT Administrative Personnel
Joint Chiefs Of Staff
Military Coup
Military Forces
Military Governor
Military Recruit
Military Service Personnel
Officer Corps

MILITARY PARTY
1975-1979 00003

MILITARY PERSONNEL
S-36-0212 1975 00025
BT Government Official
NT Military Officer
Military Recruit
Military Service Personnel
RT Administrative Personnel
Military Budget
Military Forces
Military Mind
Military Mobilization
Military Training
Naval Power
Weapon

MILITARY PLANNING
S-31-0658 1975 00030
BT Planning Process
RT Administrative Planning
Army Organization
Damage Limiting Strategy
Defense Management
Defense Planning
Development Planning
Economic Planning
Education Planning
Environmental Planning
Global War Policy
Joint Chiefs Of Staff
Military Agreement
Military Budget
Military Law
Military Management
Military Mobilization
Military Policy
Military Science
Military Size
Officer Corps
Public Policy Planning
Security Forces
Standing Army

MILITARY POLICE
S-19-0304 1975 00000
BT Police
RT International Police
Market Freedom
Martial Law
Military Court
Military Law
Military Trial
National Police
Private Police
Secret Police
Subnational Police

MILITARY POLICY
S-26-0325 1975 00167
BT Policy
NT Armed Intervention Policy
Cease Fire Policy
Deescalation Policy
Demilitarization Policy
Demobilization Policy
Escalation Policy
Military Reorganization Policy
Mobilization Policy
Reprisal Policy
War Policy
RT Agreement Type
Armistice Policy
Arms Control Policy
Arms Industry
Arms Inspection Policy
Arms Reduction Policy
Army Organization
Civil Defense Policy
Civil Military Relations
Defense Industry
Defense Policy
Deterrence Policy
Disarmament Policy
Joint Chiefs Of Staff
Military Agreement
Military Aid Policy
Military Assistance
Military Characteristics
Military Court
Military Education
Military Establishment
Military Forces
Military Government
Military Law
Military Management
Military Mind
Military Mobilization
Military Planning
Military Recruitment
Military Science
Military Size
Military Weapon
Nuclear Strategy
Nuclear Weapon Nonproliferation Policy
Officer Corps
Professional Military Forces
Rearmament Policy
Security Forces
Standing Army
Strategic Policy
Superpower Politics
War Technology
Wartime Propaganda Policy

MILITARY POLITICAL PARTY
S-28-0048 1979 00000
BT Sector Based Political Party Type
RT Authoritarian Political Party
Military Aggression
Military Characteristics
Military Coup
Military Dictatorship
Military Directorate
Military State
Monarchist Political Party
Nationalist Political Party
Rightist Political Party

MILITARY PRISON
S-19-0301 1975 00000
BT Prison
RT Court Martial
Criminal Prison
Jail
Market Freedom
Military Agency
Military Law
Military Law System
Military Prosecutor
Military Trial
Military Tribunal
Punishment

MILITARY PROSECUTOR
S-36-0105 1975 00000
BT Attorney General
RT District Attorney
Military Justice
Military Law
Military Prison
Military Trial
Military Tribunal
Trial Court

MILITARY RECRUIT
S-36-0217 1975 00000
BT Military Personnel
NT Draftee
Mercenary
Volunteer
RT Conscripted Armed Forces
Military Officer
Military Recruitment
Professional Military Forces
Voluntary Armed Forces
Volunteer

MILITARY RECRUITMENT
S-31-0744 1975 00025
BT Recruitment Process
RT Cooptation
Elite Recruitment
Military Forces
Military Policy
Military Recruit
Military Science
Military Service Personnel
Nepotism
Political Recruitment

MILITARY REFORM POLICY
S-26-0334 1975 00015
BT Military Reorganization Policy
RT Military Integration Policy
Military Management
Military Reorganization Policy
War Policy

MILITARY REORGANIZATION POLICY
S-26-0332 1975 00012
BT Military Policy
NT Military Integration Policy
Military Reform Policy
RT Defense Management
Demilitarization Policy
Demobilization Policy
Military Education
Military Institute
Military Reform Policy
Military Science
Military Training
War Policy

MILITARY SCIENCE
S-01-0145 1975 00019
UF Military Studies
BT Academic Areas
RT Arms Verification Policy
Damage Limiting Strategy
Geography Discipline
Geopolitics
International Conflict
International Relations Studies
Military Education
Military History
Military Institute
Military Management
Military Planning
Military Policy
Military Recruitment
Military Reorganization Policy
Military Training
Military Weapon
Peace Studies
Policy Science Studies
Political Science Discipline
Strategic Studies

MILITARY SERVICE PERSONNEL
S-36-0221 1975 00020
BT Military Personnel
NT Marine
Pilot
Sailor
Soldier
Veteran
RT Defense Management
Military Education
Military Officer
Military Recruitment
Military Size
Military Training

MILITARY SIZE
S-06-0462 1975 00005
BT Military Characteristics
RT Defensive Capability
Military Forces
Military Management
Military Planning
Military Policy
Military Service Personnel
Retaliatory Capability
Strategic Advantage
Strategic Studies

MILITARY STATE
S-16-0166 1975 00004
BT State Type
RT Aggressor State
Garrison State
Martial Law
Military Characteristics
Military Dictatorship
Military Directorate
Military Establishment
Military Government
Military Intervention Policy
Military Political Party
Tyranny
Warfare State

MILITARY STUDIES
USE Military Science

MILITARY SYSTEM
1975-1979 00023

MILITARY TRAINING
S-13-0026 1975 00032
BT Military Education
RT Job Training
Military Institute
Military Mind
Military Personnel
Military Reorganization Policy
Military Science
Military Service Personnel
Officer Corps
Professional Socialization
Technical Education
Vocational Education

MILITARY TREATY
S-02-0085 1975 00004
BT Military Agreement
RT Aligned Nation
Alliance
Alliance Theory
Defense Alliance
Neutrality Treaty
Nonaggression Treaty
Security Community Theory

MILITARY TRIAL
S-31-0519 1975 00000
BT Trial
NT Court Martial
War Crime Trial
RT Martial Law
Military Court
Military Police
Military Prison
Military Prosecutor
Peoples Court
Trial Court

MILITARY TRIBUNAL
S-19-0156 1975 00001
BT Military Court
RT Martial Law
Military Directorate
Military Government
Military Justice
Military Law
Military Law System
Military Occupation
Military Prison
Military Prosecutor
Peoples Court
Trial Court

MILITARY WEAPON
S-33-0019 1975 00021
BT Weapon
NT Biological Weapon
Bomb
Chemical Weapon
Conventional Weapon
Defensive Weapon
Deterrent Weapon
RT Arms Industry
Civilian Weapon
Damage Limiting Strategy
Military Policy
Military Science
Multinational Security Forces

MILLENARIANISM
S-38-0259 1975 00005
BT Ideologies
RT Chiliastic Movement
Eschatology
Messianic Movement
Prophetic Tradition
Religious Community
Religious Culture
Religious Fanaticism
Religious Movement

MINE SAFETY LAW
S-21-0036 1979 00000
BT Industrial Safety Law
RT Industrial Safety Policy
Labor Law
Property Law
Safety Policy

MINE SAFETY POLICY
S-26-0402 1975 00000
BT Safety Policy
RT Extractive Industry
Government Regulation
Industrial Production
Industrial Relations
Industrial Safety Policy

MINES
USE Extractive Industry

MINIMUM WAGE LAW
S-21-0039 1975 00001
BT Labor Law
RT Fair Employment Law
Minimum Wage Policy
Pension Law
Right To Work Law
Wage Stabilization Policy

MINIMUM WAGE POLICY
S-26-0107 1975 00003
BT Wage Policy
RT Fair Employment Law
Government Regulation
Minimum Wage Law
Pension Law
Wage Stabilization Policy

MINIMUM WINNING COALITION
S-02-0034 1975 00004
BT Winning Coalition
RT Coalition Theory
Democratic Coalition
Interest Group Coalition
Legislative Coalition
Majoritarianism
Negative Coalition
Parliamentary Coalition
Voting Coalition

MINISTER
S-36-0044 1975 00002
BT Cabinet Member
NT Cabinet Secretary
RT Cabinet
Cabinet Government
Privy Council
Privy Councilor

MINISTERIAL COMMITTEE
S-19-0113 1975 00001
BT Cabinet
RT Cabinet
Cabinet Committee
Cabinet Government
Parliament Cabinet Relations

MINISTERIAL INSTABILITY
S-06-0695 1975 00000
BT Cabinet Instability
RT Coalition Dissolution
Government Dissolution Process
Government Instability
No Confidence Motion

MINISTERIAL RESPONSIBILITY
S-06-0436 1975 00000
BT Administrative Accountability
RT Cabinet
Cabinet Government
Cabinet Member
Chief Executive Accountability
Executive Accountability
Executive Discretion
Executive Privilege
Government Accountability
Government Responsiveness
Legislative Accountability
Parliament Cabinet Relations

MINOR PARTY
1975-1979 00003

MINOR POLITICAL PARTY
S-28-0027 1979 00000
BT Political Party Type
RT Minority Political Party
Opposition Political Party
Third Political Party

MINORITY COALITION
1975-1979 00000

MINORITY GOVERNMENT
S-16-0070 1975 00003
BT Government Type
RT Coalition Government
Government Instability
Minority Group Representation
Minority Law
Multiethnic Nation
Multiethnic State
Parliamentary Government

MINORITY GROUP
S-06-0021 1979 00000
BT Group Composition
RT Ethnic Group
Ethnic Group Loyalty
Group Behavior
Group Characteristics
Group Consolidation
Group Politics
Group Status
Homogeneous Group Membership
Minority Group Cohesion
Minority Group Representation
Racial Group
Secondary Group
Token Representation

MINORITY GROUP COHESION
S-06-0042 1975 00009
BT Group Cohesion
NT Ethnic Group Cohesion
RT Ethnicity
Ghetto Community
Minority Group
Minority Group Representation
Minority Political Party
Minority Rights
Minority Voter

MINORITY GROUP REPRESENTATION
S-31-0722 1975 00030
BT Representation Type
RT At Large Representation
District Representation
Functional Representation
Geographic Representation
Indirect Representation
Interest Group Representation
Minority Government
Minority Group
Minority Group Cohesion
Minority Political Party
Minority Rights
Multimember District
Multiple Member District Representation
Multiple Member Districting
Proportional Representation

MINORITY LAW
S-21-0093 1975 00001
BT Social Law
RT Ethnic Assimilation Theory
Minority Government
Minority Persecution
Minority Political Party
Minority Rights
Nationalities Law
Representation Theory
Social Rights

MINORITY LEADER
S-36-0178 1975 00001
BT Legislative Leader
RT Floor Leader
Leader Of Opposition
Legislative Speaker
Legislative Whip
Majority Leader
Minority Political Party
National Legislative Leader
National Legislative Whip
Subnational Legislative Leader

MINORITY PARTY
1975-1979 00004

MINORITY PERSECUTION
S-31-0315 1975 00008
BT Persecution
RT Ethnic Persecution
Fascist Theory
Minority Law
Minority Rights
National Socialism
Nationality Persecution
Political Persecution
Racial Persecution
Religious Persecution
Sex Persecution

MINORITY POLITICAL PARTY
S-28-0049 1979 00000
BT Sector Based Political Party Type
RT Electoral Opposition
Minor Political Party
Minority Group Cohesion
Minority Group Representation
Minority Law
Minority Leader
Minority Rights Democratic Theory
Minority Voter
Splinter Political Party

MINORITY RIGHTS
S-15-0040 1975 00016
BT Equal Rights
RT Democratic Theory
Ethnic Policy
Justice Theory
Minority Group Cohesion
Minority Group Representation
Minority Law
Minority Persecution
Minority Rights Democratic Theory
Procedural Democratic Theory
Racial Equality
Racial Injustice
Womens Rights

MINORITY RIGHTS DEMOCRATIC THEORY
S-38-0094 1975 00001
BT Democratic Theory
RT Athenian Democratic Theory
Concurrent Majority Theory
Confederation Movement
Democratic Elite Theory
Democratic Government
General Will Democratic Theory
Interest Group Pluralism
Jeffersonian Democratic Theory
Minority Political Party
Minority Rights
Participatory Democratic Theory
Populist Democratic Theory
Procedural Democratic Theory
Republic Theory
Social Democracy
Socialist Democratic Theory

MINORITY VOTER
S-32-0321 1975 00002
BT Voter
RT Backlash Voting
Black Voter
Ethnic Voter
Issue Voter
Minority Group Cohesion
Minority Political Party
Voter Turnout
Voting Data
Voting Pattern
Voting Result Interpretation

MIRV
S-33-0031 1979 00000
BT Multiple Warhead Missile
RT Arms Control Policy
Assured Destruction Policy
Ballistic Missile
Missile
Nuclear Arms Race
Nuclear Weapon
Offensive Weapon System
Strategic Arms Limitation
Strategic Weapon
Weapon Delivery System

MISCEGENATION LAW
S-21-0094 1975 00000
BT Social Law
RT Family Law
Jim Crow Law
Pornography Law
Segregation Policy
Separatism

MISFEASANCE
S-10-0064 1975 00000
BT Political Crime
RT Legal Malpractice
Malfeasance
Malpractice
Medical Malpractice
Political Conspiracy
Political Corruption
Political Fraud
Power Abuse

MISSILE
S-33-0026 1975 00015
UF Guided Missile
BT Weapon
NT Ballistic Missile
Multiple Warhead Missile
RT Chemical Weapon
Conventional Weapon
Defensive Weapon
First Strike Nuclear Weapon
MARV
MIRV
Munitions
Nuclear Weapon
Second Strike Nuclear Weapon
Strategic Weapon
Tactical Weapon

MISSING DATA
S-24-0196 1975 00007
BT Measurement Problem
RT Measurement Bias
Measurement Error
Random Error
Sampling Error
Systematic Error

MISSIONARY
S-32-0102 1979 00000
BT Religious Minister
RT Cultural Imperialism
Religious Education
Religious Group
Religious Leader
Religious Minister
Religious Organization

MIXED ECONOMIC SYSTEM
S-37-0046 1975 00002
BT Economic System
RT Balanced Economy
Developing Economy
Dual Economy
Mercantile Economic System
Mixed Economy
Mixed Enterprise
Mixed Government
Socialist Economic System

MIXED ECONOMY
S-12-0030 1975 00004
BT Economy Type
RT Agrarian Economy
Balanced Economy
Capital Investment Economy
Consumer Economy
Cottage Industry Economy
Craft Economy
Developed Economy
Developing Economy
Dual Economy
Enterprise
Farm Economy
Mixed Economic System
Modernizing Economy
Welfare Economy

MIXED ENTERPRISE
S-19-0176 1975 00000
BT Enterprise
RT Business Policy
Factory
Government Enterprise
Light Industry
Market
Mixed Economic System

MIXED GOVERNMENT
S-16-0071 1975 00002
BT Government Type
RT Constitutional Democracy
Federal Government
Limited Monarchy
Mixed Economic System
Pluralist Democracy

MOB VIOLENCE
S-08-0131 1975 00010
BT Violence
RT Civil War
Class Conflict
Class Rebellion
Coup D'Etat
Crowd Behavior
Demonstration
Economic Conflict
Economic Rebellion
General Strike
Ghetto Rioter
Insurgency
Mobilization Policy
Peasant Rebellion
Political Rebellion
Psychological Aggression
Putsch
Rebellion
Revolution
Revolutionary War
Slave Rebellion
Social Rebellion
Struggle
Student Rebellion

MOBILIZATION POLICY
S-26-0335 1975 00002
BT Military Policy
RT Communist Studies
Demonstration
Mass Behavior
Mob Violence
Mobilization Process
Political Rebellion
Social Role Process

MOBILIZATION PROCESS
S-31-0626 1975 00029
BT Process
NT Economic Mobilization
Mass Mobilization
Military Mobilization
Peasant Mobilization
Political Mobilization
Social Mobilization
Worker Mobilization
RT Mass Behavior
Mobilization Policy
Social Role Process

MODAL PERSONALITY
S-06-0532 1975 00002
BT Personality Type
RT Basic Personality
Psychohistory

MODEL BUILDING
S-24-0028 1975 00096
BT Mathematical Analysis
RT Administrative Planning
Game Theory
Gaming
Models

MODEL CITY
S-07-0041 1979 00000
BT Planned Community
RT Economic Community
Endogenous Variable
Federated City
Homogeneous Community
Metropolitan City
Neighborhood
New Town
Planned Community
Urban Policy Planning
Urban Renewal Policy

MODELS
S-24-0279 1975 00095
BT Methodology
NT Mathematical Model
Natural Science Model
Social Science Model
RT Analysis Methodology
General Theory
Hypothesis Testing

Mathematical Political Theory
Model Building
Research Design

MODERATOR
S-32-0008 1975 00000
BT Adjudicator
RT Arbitrator
Broker
Mediator
Negotiator
Ombudsman

MODERN AGES
S-06-0175 1979 00000
BT Historical Periods
RT Gesellschaft
Industrial Society
Modern Political Culture
Modern Political Thought
Modernization
Modernization Theory
Modernizing Economy
Modernizing Ideology
Modernizing Society

MODERN IDEALISM
S-38-0417 1975 00000
BT Modern Political Thought
NT German Idealism
Oxford Idealism
Transcendentalism
RT Modern Political Culture
Modern Political Thought
Neohegelianism

MODERN POLITICAL CULTURE
S-11-0024 1975 00003
BT Political Culture
NT Political Professionalization
Political Secularization
RT Civic Culture
Diffuse System Supports
Fragmented Political Culture
Generational Political Culture
Ideological Political Culture
Legal Rational Authority
Legalistic Political Culture
Legislative Process
Modern Ages
Modern Idealism
Modernizing Economy
Political Value Acquisition
Popular Culture
Pragmatic Political Culture
Secular Political Culture
Secular Society
Specific System Supports
Subject Participant Culture

MODERN POLITICAL THOUGHT
S-38-0386 1975 00003
BT Political Theory
NT American Political Thought
Burkean Analysis
Comtean Positivism
Early Modern Theory Of The State
Enlightenment Thought
Hegelian Analysis
Hobbesian Analysis
Humean Analysis
Liberal Political Thought
Marxist Political Thought
Modern Idealism
Nietzschean Analysis
Progress Theory
Romanticism
Tocquevillian Analysis
Utilitarianism
RT Contemporary Analytic Modes
Contemporary Political Thought
Explanatory Political Theory
Hobbesian Analysis
Ideologies
Modern Ages
Modern Idealism
Nation State Explanatory Theory
Political Philosophy Concept
Teilhardean Thought

MODERNITY SCALE
S-24-0240 1975 00010
SN Means of measuring characteristics presumed to be part of modern society, such as openess to innovation.
USE Modernization Scale
BT Scale Type
RT Development Process
Modernization
Progress

MODERNIZATION
S-31-0077 1975 00090
BT Development Process
NT Cultural Modernization
Economic Modernization
Political Modernization
Social Modernization
RT Advanced Technology
Colonial Development
Developing Political System
Industrial Relations
Institutional Development
Institutionalization
Local Development
Modern Ages
Modernity Scale
Progress
Urban Decay

MODERNIZATION SCALE
S-24-0241 1979 00000
UF Modernity Scale
BT Scale Type
RT Modernizing Economy

MODERNIZATION THEORY
S-38-0035 1975 00060
BT Theory
NT Convergence Theory
Divergence Theory
RT Contingency Theory
Developing Political System
Development Theory
Economic Modernization
Economic Theory
Explanatory Political Theory
Macropolitical Theory
Modern Ages
Modernizing Economy
Modernizing Ideology
Modernizing Political System
Nation Building Theory
Political Modernization
Political Theory
Progress Theory
Progressivism
Technocratic Politics

MODERNIZING AUTHORITARIAN REGIME
S-16-0135 1975 00006
BT Authoritarian Regime
RT Modernizing Dictatorship
Modernizing Political System
Progressive Dictatorship
Technocracy

MODERNIZING DICTATORSHIP
S-16-0040 1975 00002
BT Dictatorship
RT Benevolent Dictatorship
Modernizing Authoritarian Regime
Modernizing Elite
Modernizing Political System
National Socialism
Progressive Dictatorship

MODERNIZING ECONOMY
S-12-0031 1979 00000
BT Economy Type
RT Balanced Economy
Capital Investment Economy
Consumer Economy
Developed Economy
Developing Economy
Developing Nation
Economic Development
Economic Development Characteristics
Economic Development Index
Economic Modernization
Export Economy
Fascist Economy
Institutional Development
Market Economy
Mixed Economy
Modern Ages
Modern Political Culture
Modernization Scale
Modernization Theory
Modernizing Political System
Modernizing Society
Planned Economy
Political Development
Socialist Market Economy
Welfare Economy

MODERNIZING ELITE
S-14-0018 1975 00005
BT Elite Type
RT Academic Elite
Decision Making Elite
Governing Elite
Intelligentsia
Modernizing Dictatorship
Modernizing Political Elite
Opinion Elite
Policy Elite
Political Elite
Potential Elite
Revolutionary Elite
Scientific Elite
Technological Elite
Transitional Political Elite

MODERNIZING IDEOLOGY
S-38-0260 1975 00019
BT Ideologies
RT Economic Modernization
Liberalism
Modern Ages
Modernization Theory
Political Modernization
Socialist Theory

MODERNIZING POLITICAL ELITE
S-14-0024 1975 00007
BT Political Elite
RT Modernizing Elite
Modernizing Political System
Modernizing Social Elite
Nation Building
Potential Elite
Revolutionary Elite
Transitional Political Elite

MODERNIZING POLITICAL SYSTEM
S-37-0124 1979 00000
BT Political System Type
RT Modernization Theory
Modernizing Authoritarian Regime
Modernizing Dictatorship
Modernizing Economy
Modernizing Political Elite
Modernizing Society
Political Development
Political Development Theory

MODERNIZING SOCIAL ELITE
S-14-0035 1975 00004
BT Social Elite
RT Modernizing Political Elite
Potential Elite
Religious Elite
Revolutionary Elite
Technological Elite
Traditional Social Elite

MODERNIZING SOCIETY
S-35-0005 1975 00019
BT Society Type
RT Achieving Society
Affluent Society
Bureaucratic Theory
Economic Development
Industrial Society
Meritocracy
Modern Ages
Modernizing Economy
Modernizing Political System
Secular Society
Social Development Theory
Transitional Society
Urban Society
Western Society

MODIFIED ONE PARTY SYSTEM
S-37-0129 1975 00000
BT One Political Party System
RT Hegemonic One Party System

MONARCH
S-36-0054 1975 00003
BT Chief Government Executive
NT Absolute Monarch
Constitutional Monarch
Emperor
Hereditary Ruler
King
Prince
Queen
Regent
Sultan
RT Benevolent Dictator
Benevolent Dictatorship
Dictator

MONARCHIST PARTY
1975-1979 00001

MONARCHIST POLITICAL PARTY
S-28-0028 1979 00000
BT Political Party Type
RT Military Political Party

MONARCHY
S-16-0072 1975 00013
BT Government Type
NT Absolute Monarchy
Constitutional Monarchy
Limited Monarchy
Republican Monarchy
RT Abdication
Absolute Monarch
Investiture Controversy
King
Queen
Royalist
Royalist State Theory
Sheikdom

MONASTICISM
S-38-0371 1975 00001
BT Medieval Political Thought
RT Religious Community
Scholasticism

MONETARY AGENCY
S-19-0024 1975 00002
BT Fiscal Agency
NT Banking Agency
RT Appropriation Agency
Bank Nationalization
Bank Reserve
Budget Agency
Defense Appropriation
Monetary Institution
Public Treasury
Revenue Agency
Tax Agency

MONETARY AGREEMENT
S-02-0086 1975 00001
BT State Agreement Type
RT Commercial Agreement
Commercial Treaty
Economic Agreement
Economic Community
Monetary Exchange System

MONETARY ECONOMIC THEORY
S-38-0117 1979 00000
BT Economic Theory
RT Bank Reserve
Banking Policy
Capital Growth Rate
Central Banking System
Deflation Policy
Economic Stabilization Theory
Fiscal Theory
Inflation Policy
Monetary Process
Money Supply Policy

MONETARY EXCHANGE SYSTEM
S-37-0048 1975 00012
BT Monetary System
RT Monetary Agreement
Monetary Policy
Monetary Process
Money

MONETARY INSTITUTION
S-19-0198 1979 00000
BT Economic Institution
NT World Bank
RT Big Business
Business
Corporation
Enterprise
Fiscal Institution
Government Enterprise
Market
Monetary Agency
Monetary Management
Monetary Policy
Public Corporation

MONETARY MANAGEMENT
S-23-0017 1975 00005
BT Economic Management
RT Administrative Management
Business Management
Development Management
Financial Accounting
Financing
International Economic Management
Monetary Institution
Money
National Economic Management
Subnational Economic Management

MONETARY POLICY
S-26-0123 1975 00027
BT Economic Policy
NT Banking Policy
Credit Policy
Money Supply Policy
RT Bank Reserve
Budget Policy
Cost Of Living Index
Currency Revaluation Policy
Debt Ceiling Policy
Deflation
Deflation Policy
Economic Recession
Expenditure Policy
Financing
Income Policy
Inflation
Inflation Policy
Monetary Exchange System
Monetary Institution
Monetary Process
National Banking System
Prime Loan Rate
Private Saving
Private Spending
Public Debt Policy
Public Finance Policy
Revenue Policy
Tax Cut
World Bank

MONETARY PROCESS
S-31-0421 1975 00006
BT Fiscal Process
RT Budget Policy
Financial Accounting
Monetary Economic Theory
Monetary Exchange System
Monetary Policy

Monetary System
Public Financing
Public Spending
Saving
Subsidization Process
Welfare Spending
World Bank

MONETARY SYSTEM
S-37-0047 1975 00026
BT Economic System
NT Monetary Exchange System
RT Economic Sector
Financial System
Monetary Process
Monetary Union
Money
Property Ownership System

MONETARY UNION
S-03-0042 1975 00003
BT International Economic Organization
RT Customs Union
Economic Community
Economic Interest Group
Extranational Bloc
Monetary System
Trade Organization

MONEY
S-06-0352 1975 00009
BT Economic Characteristics
NT Money Creation
Money Demand
Money Supply
RT Capital
Capital Flow
Deflation
Financing
Income
Monetary Exchange System
Monetary Management
Monetary System
National Currency
Private Spending

MONEY CREATION
S-06-0353 1975 00004
BT Money
NT Bank Reserve
Discount Rate
Prime Loan Rate
RT Currency Revaluation Policy
Money Demand
Money Supply
National Currency

MONEY DEMAND
S-06-0357 1975 00004
BT Money
RT Banking Agency
Money Creation
Money Supply
National Currency

MONEY DEVALUATION
USE Currency Devaluation Policy

MONEY SUPPLY
S-06-0358 1975 00006
BT Money
NT Gold Reserve
National Currency
RT Banking Agency
Currency Revaluation Policy
Money Creation
Money Demand

MONEY SUPPLY POLICY
S-26-0126 1975 00004
BT Monetary Policy
RT Banking Policy
Credit Policy
Deflation
Government Economic Management
Monetary Economic Theory
National Currency

MONK
S-32-0103 1979 00000
BT Religious Minister
RT Religious Education
Religious Group
Religious Leader
Religious Minister
Religious Organization

MONOGAMY
S-20-0024 1975 00001
BT Marriage Type
NT Serial Monogamy
RT Atomistic Family
Family Policy
Folkways
Marriage Type
Nuclear Family

MONOGRAPHS
S-18-0062 1975 00001
BT Information Sources
NT Autobiography
Biography
Political Literature
RT Documents
Encyclopedia
Library Science Studies
Literature Review
Newsletters
Thesis
University Information Service

MONOPOLY
S-06-0629 1975 00010
BT Economic Power Distribution
NT Oligopoly
Perfect Monopoly
Private Monopoly
Public Monopoly
RT Antitrust Law
Antitrust Policy
Economic Injustice
Economic Sovereignty
Nationalized Industry

MONOPOLY CAPITALISM
S-37-0018 1975 00002
BT Capitalism
RT Black Capitalism
Bourgeois Capitalism
Industrial Capitalism
Mature Capitalism
Mercantile Capitalism
Private Sector
Warfare Capitalism
Welfare Capitalism

MORAL AUTHORITY
S-04-0007 1975 00026
UF Categorical Imperative
BT Authority Mode
RT Blue Law
Charismatic Authority
Constitutional Authority
Derived Authority
Legal Rational Authority
Moral Leadership
Moral Responsibility
Moral Theory
Relative Justice Theory
Religious Authority
Religious Studies
Theocratic Authority
Traditional Authority

MORAL CHOICE
S-38-0462 1979 00000
BT Moral Freedom Theory
RT Decision Making Theory
Freedom Theory
Moral Learning
Moral Responsibility
Moral Theory
Rational Choice Model
Value Analysis
Value System

MORAL FREEDOM THEORY
S-38-0461 1975 00014
BT Freedom Theory
NT Moral Choice
Moral Responsibility
RT Freedom
General Will Theory
Hegelian Analysis
Individual Freedom Theory
Justice As Fairness Doctrine
Positive Freedom Theory
Rousseauian Analysis
Socratic Political Thought

MORAL LEADERSHIP
S-22-0006 1979 00000
BT Leadership Authority Base
RT Authority
Authority Mode
Authority Structure
Ecclesiastical Leadership
Leadership Structure Type
Moral Authority
Personalized Leadership
Religious Authority
Religious Leadership
Traditional Leadership

MORAL LEARNING
S-34-0009 1979 00000
BT Learning
RT Cultural System
Education Policy
Ethical Socialization
Ethical Theory
Human Nature Theory
Learning Theory
Logic
Moral Choice
Personal Behavior
Socialization Theory
Symbol Learning
Value System

MORAL REASONING
S-25-0050 1979 00000
UF Casuistry
BT Moral Theory
RT Authority Mode
Authority Structure

Authority Theory
Authority Type
Deductive Method
Human Subject Rights
Inductive Method
Use Of Human Subjects

MORAL RESPONSIBILITY
S-38-0463 1979 00000
BT Moral Freedom Theory
RT Freedom Theory
Honesty
Justice Theory
Moral Authority
Moral Choice
Moral Theory
Political Virtue
Responsibility Doctrine
Socratic Political Thought

MORAL THEORY
S-25-0049 1979 00000
BT Metaethical Theory
NT Moral Reasoning
RT Authority Mode
Authority Theory
Authority Type
Ethical Socialization
Intuitionism
Moral Authority
Moral Choice
Moral Responsibility
Professional Ethics
Religious Authority
Research Ethics
Straussian Thought
Use Of Human Subjects

MORALS OFFENSE
S-10-0042 1975 00005
BT Individual Crime
RT Child Molestation
Juvenile Crime
Juvenile Delinquency
Marital Offense
Pornographic Crime
Pornography Law
Rape
Sex Crime
Street Crime

MORBIDITY DATA
S-18-0090 1975 00025
BT Social Statistics
RT Disease
Epidemic
Health Characteristics
Obituaries
Social Indicator
Socioeconomic Data
Statistical Table
Vital Statistics Data

MORPHOLOGY
S-01-0016 1975 00006
BT Structural Linguistics
RT Anthropological Linguistic Theory
Ethnolinguistics
Linguistics

MORTALITY RATE
S-06-0195 1975 00023
BT Demographic Profile
NT Infant Mortality Rate
RT Demographic Projection
Household Size
Life Expectancy

MOST DIFFERENT SYSTEM DESIGN
S-24-0370 1975 00001
BT Research Design
RT Most Similar System Design
Social Science Model

MOST FAVORED NATION POLICY
S-26-0183 1975 00007
BT Trade Policy
RT Bilateral Treaty
Export Subsidization Policy
Free Trade Policy
Restrictive Trade Policy

MOST SIMILAR SYSTEM DESIGN
S-24-0371 1975 00001
BT Research Design
RT Most Different System Design

MOTHER
S-32-0043 1975 00015
BT Maternal Role
RT Housewife
Parent
Parental Authority
Wife

MOTIVATION MEASUREMENT
S-24-0183 1975 00016
BT Attitude Measurement
RT Affective Measurement
Belief Measurement
Cognitive Measurement
Motivational Analysis
Personality Theory

MOTIVATION THEORY
S-38-0544 1975 00067
BT Psychological Theory
RT Achievement Theory
Aggression Theory
Alienation Psychological Theory
Attitude Change Theory
Attitude Characteristics
Attribution Theory
Cognitive Theory
Freudian Theory
Frustration Aggression Theory
Identity Theory
Learning Theory
Motivational Analysis
Personality Development
Psychological Behavioralism
Psychological Behaviorism
Psychopolitical Theory

MOTIVATIONAL ANALYSIS
S-09-0049 1979 00000
BT Contemporary Analytic Modes
RT Behavior Analysis
Contextual Analysis
Linguistic Analysis
Motivation Measurement
Motivation Theory
Pluralist Analysis
Policy Analysis
Political Psychology Analysis
Psychoanalysis
Situational Analysis
Sociological Analysis

MOTOR VEHICLE INDUSTRY
S-17-0074 1975 00005
BT Land Transportation Industry
NT Automobile Industry
Trucking Industry
RT Catastrophe Insurance
Compulsory Insurance
Life Insurance
Malpractice Insurance
Mass Transportation Industry
Motor Vehicle Insurance
National Health Insurance
No Fault Insurance
Railway Industry
Shipping Industry
Transportation Policy
Unemployment Policy

MOTOR VEHICLE INSURANCE
S-26-0306 1979 00000
BT Insurance
RT Accident Insurance
Automobile Industry
Compulsory Insurance
Motor Vehicle Industry
No Fault Insurance
Trucking Industry

MULTICULTURAL SOCIETY
S-35-0036 1979 00000
BT Heterogeneous Society
NT Bicultural Society
RT Cultural Cleavage
Cultural Diversity
Cultural Identity
Cultural System
Multiethnic Society
Multiethnic State
Multilingual Community
Multilingual Society
Multiracial Society
Plural Society
Society Type Structure

MULTIDIMENSIONAL SCALE
S-24-0212 1975 00021
BT Scale Construction Methodology
NT Nonmetric Multidimensional Scale
RT Composite Scale
Cumulative Scale
Guttman Scale
Likert Scale
Measurement Level Scale
Nominal Scale
Ordinal Scale
Ratio Scale
Scalability Index
Semantic Differential
Thurstone Scale

MULTIETHNIC COALITION
S-02-0017 1975 00000
BT Coalition Type
RT Coalition Type
Interest Group Coalition
Political Coalition
Political Party Coalition
Voting Coalition
Winning Coalition

MULTIETHNIC COMMUNITY
S-07-0033 1975 00002
BT Heterogeneous Community
RT Bilingual Community
Black Ghetto
Black Suburban Community
Ethnic Background
Ethnic Community
Ethnic Studies
Multilingual Community
Multiracial Community
Suburban Ghetto Community
Urban Ghetto Community

MULTIETHNIC NATION
S-16-0124 1975 00009
BT Nation Type
RT Ethnic Background
Ethnic Composition
Ethnic Studies
Federal Government
Minority Government

MULTIETHNIC SOCIETY
S-35-0038 1975 00012
BT Heterogeneous Society
RT Bicultural Society
Ethnic Assimilation Theory
Ethnic Studies
Ethnicity
Multicultural Society
Multiethnic State
Multilingual Society
Multiracial Society
Plural Society

MULTIETHNIC STATE
S-16-0167 1975 00012
BT State Type
RT Ethnic Assimilation Theory
Ethnic Background
Ethnic Composition
Ethnic Studies
Minority Government
Multicultural Society
Multiethnic Society

MULTILATERAL AID
S-06-0310 1975 00002
BT Foreign Aid
RT Bilateral Aid
Bilateral Aid Policy
Bilateral State Agreement

MULTILATERAL AID POLICY
S-26-0259 1975 00005
BT Foreign Aid Policy
RT Bilateral Aid Policy
Economic Aid Policy
Grants Economy
Military Aid Policy
Technical Aid Policy
Unilateral Aid Policy

MULTILATERAL ALLIANCE
S-02-0009 1975 00006
BT Alliance
RT Common Market
International Bloc
Interstate Compact
Military Alliance
Multilateral State Agreement
Protective Alliance
Regional Military Alliance
World Alliance

MULTILATERAL SECURITY FORCES
S-33-0003 1975 00001
BT Multinational Security Forces
RT International Peacekeeping Forces
Peacekeeping Forces

MULTILATERAL STATE AGREEMENT
S-02-0064 1975 00016
BT State Agreement Form
RT Bilateral State Agreement
Extranational Bloc
Military Alliance
Multilateral Alliance
State Agreement Type

MULTILATERAL TREATY
S-02-0065 1975 00004
BT State Agreement Form
RT Common Market
Economic Community
Interstate Compact
State Agreement Type

MULTILINGUAL COMMUNITY
S-07-0034 1975 00001
BT Heterogeneous Community
NT Bilingual Community
RT Bilingual Community
Multicultural Society
Multiethnic Community
Multiracial Community

MULTILINGUAL SOCIETY
S-35-0039 1975 00002
BT Heterogeneous Society
RT Bicultural Society
Bilingual Community
Language Acquisition
Language Learning
Multicultural Society
Multiethnic Society
Multiracial Society
Plural Society

MULTIMEMBER DISTRICT
S-29-0193 1975 00001
BT Electoral District
RT Geographic Representation
Minority Group Representation
Proportional Representation
Representative Democracy
Single Member District

MULTINATIONAL CORPORATION
S-19-0169 1975 00065
BT International Corporation
RT Business Economics
Business Studies
Cartel
Corporate Elite
Holding Company
International Economic Organization Theory
Multinational Organization
Public Corporation
Quasipublic Corporation

MULTINATIONAL ORGANIZATION
S-19-0289 1975 00009
BT Institutions
RT Corporation
International Agency
International Commodity Market
International Corporation
Military Industrial Complex
Multinational Corporation
Multinational Organization Theory

MULTINATIONAL ORGANIZATION THEORY
S-38-0042 1975 00009
BT Organization Theory
RT International Economic Organization Theory
International Integration Theory
International Organization Theory
International Political Theory
Multinational Organization
United Nations

MULTINATIONAL SECURITY FORCES
S-33-0002 1975 00005
BT Security Forces
NT Multilateral Security Forces
Peacekeeping Forces
RT European Integration Theory
Military Weapon
National Security Forces

MULTIPARTY COALITION
S-02-0030 1975 00005
BT Political Party Coalition
RT All Party Coalition
Democratic Coalition
Governing Coalition
Grand Coalition
Intraparty Coalition
Legislative Coalition
Parliamentary Coalition
Voting Coalition

MULTIPARTY DEMOCRACY
S-16-0025 1975 00002
BT Political Party Democracy
RT Majoritarian Democracy
One Political Party Democracy
Two Political Party Democracy

MULTIPARTY POLITICS
S-29-0219 1975 00005
BT Partisan Politics
RT Machine Politics
Multiparty System

MULTIPARTY SYSTEM
S-37-0126 1975 00009
BT Political Party System
RT Multiparty Politics
Two Political Party System

MULTIPLE CORRELATION ANALYSIS
S-24-0047 1975 00006
BT Multivariate Analysis
RT Analysis Of Variance
Automatic Interaction Detection
Cluster Analysis
Covariance Analysis
Dimensional Analysis
Discriminant Analysis
Factor Analysis
Multiple Regression Analysis
Partial Correlation Analysis
Path Analysis

MULTIPLE FAMILY DWELLING
S-06-0229 1975 00001
BT Residential Pattern
RT Single Family Dwelling

MULTIPLE GROUP MEMBERSHIP
S-06-0022 1975 00001
BT Group Composition
RT Cross Pressure Theory
Heterogeneous Group Membership
Interest Group Pluralism
Interlocking Group Membership

Overlapping Membership

MULTIPLE INDICATOR
S-24-0260 1975 00000
BT Indicator
RT Change Indicator
Operationalization
Social Science Model
Statistical Data

MULTIPLE MEMBER DISTRICT REPRESENTATION
S-31-0723 1975 00000
BT Representation Type
RT District Representation
Functional Representation
Minority Group Representation
Multiple Member Districting
Proportional Representation

MULTIPLE MEMBER DISTRICTING
S-31-0711 1975 00000
BT Districting
RT D'Hont Voting Method
District Representation
Functional Representation
Geographic Representation
Gerrymandering
Minority Group Representation
Multiple Member District Representation
Proportional Representation

MULTIPLE OPERATIONALIZATION
S-24-0278 1975 00001
BT Operationalization
RT Concept Explication Research
Functional Equivalent
Measures
Research And Development
Research Design

MULTIPLE REGRESSION ANALYSIS
S-24-0048 1975 00017
BT Multivariate Analysis
RT Analysis Of Variance
Automatic Interaction Detection
Canonical Correlation Analysis
Covariance Analysis
Dimensional Analysis
Factor Analysis
Multiple Correlation Analysis
Partial Correlation Analysis
Path Analysis

MULTIPLE WARHEAD MISSILE
S-33-0029 1975 00002
BT Missile
NT MARV
MIRV
RT Ballistic Missile
Nuclear Weapon

MULTIPLE YEAR ECONOMIC PLAN
S-26-0089 1975 00004
BT Economic Plan
RT Communist Economic System
Economic Planning
Economic Policy
Planification

MULTIPOLAR INTERNATIONAL POLITICAL SYSTEM
S-37-0121 1975 00016
BT International Political System
NT Polycentric International Political System
RT Bipolar International System
Commonwealth International System
Extranational Bloc
Hegemonic System
Regional International Political System

MULTIRACIAL COMMUNITY
S-07-0036 1975 00004
BT Heterogeneous Community
RT Bilingual Community
Integrated Community
Multiethnic Community
Multilingual Community

MULTIRACIAL SOCIETY
S-35-0040 1975 00002
BT Heterogeneous Society
RT Bicultural Society
Desegregation Policy
Ethnic Assimilation Theory
Ethnic Studies
Multicultural Society
Multiethnic Society
Multilingual Society

MULTIVARIATE ANALYSIS
S-24-0038 1975 00046
BT Statistical Analysis
NT Analysis Of Variance
Automatic Interaction Detection
Canonical Correlation Analysis
Cluster Analysis
Covariance Analysis
Dimensional Analysis
Discriminant Analysis
Factor Analysis
Multiple Correlation Analysis
Multiple Regression Analysis
Partial Correlation Analysis
Path Analysis
RT Bivariate Analysis
Correlation Analysis
Probability Estimation
Product Moment Correlation
Regression Analysis
Statistical Significance Test
Statistics Type
Univariate Analysis

MUNICIPAL AUTHORITIES
S-19-0068 1975 00008
BT Authorities
RT Borough Government
Federal Commission
Health Care Agency
Municipal Election
Public Authorities
Subnational Legislature
Transportation Agency

MUNICIPAL COURT
S-19-0152 1975 00000
BT Local Court
RT City Government
Court Action
Court Jurisdiction
Court Official
Legal System

MUNICIPAL ELECTION
S-29-0092 1975 00005
BT Local Election
RT City
Leadership Type
Local Legislature
Municipal Authorities
Municipal Reform Movement
Municipality
Urban Politics

MUNICIPAL REFORM MOVEMENT
S-27-0043 1975 00016
BT Reform Movement
RT Local Development
Municipal Election
Tax Reform Movement

MUNICIPAL TAXATION
S-26-0168 1975 00003
BT Local Taxation
RT State Taxation

MUNICIPALITY
S-07-0012 1975 00012
BT City
RT Borough Government
Central City
City Government
Council Manager Government
District Government Type
Inner City
Megalopolis
Metropolis
Metropolitan City
Municipal Election
Neighborhood
Outer City
School District
Urban Government

MUNITIONS
S-33-0032 1975 00000
BT Weapon
NT Military Aircraft
Warship
RT Bomb
Chemical Weapon
Conventional Weapon
Defensive Weapon
Missile
Nuclear Weapon

MURDER
S-10-0043 1975 00008
BT Individual Crime
RT Assassination
Assault
Capital Punishment
Crime Against Humanity
Criminal Abortion
Dean
Genocide
Kidnapping
Life Sentence
Massacre
Murderer
Tyrannicide

MURDERER
S-36-0033 1975 00000
BT Personal Crime Criminal
RT Blackmailer
Capital Punishment
Criminal Prison
Extortionist
Life Sentence
Murder
War Criminal

MUSIC CENSORSHIP
S-31-0283 1975 00000
BT Performing Arts Censorship
RT Broadcasting Censorship
Censorship Agency
Freedom Of Speech
Radio Censorship
Television Censorship

MUTINY
S-31-0255 1975 00001
BT Dissent
RT Demonstrating
Dissent
Piracy
Protest
Resistance

MUTUAL DETERRENCE POLICY
S-26-0064 1975 00010
BT Deterrence Policy
RT Bilateral State Agreement
Nuclear Deterrence Policy
Strategic Arms Race

MUTUAL DETERRENCE SYSTEM
S-33-0011 1975 00003
BT War Technology
RT Arms Control Policy
Defense System
Nuclear Power
Offensive Weapon System

MUTUAL SUPPORT DECLARATION
S-02-0058 1975 00000
BT State Agreement Declaration
RT Defense Alliance
Defense System
Military Alliance
Unilateral Declaration
War Policy
World Alliance

MYTH ANALYSIS
S-38-0012 1975 00024
BT Anthropological Theory
NT Magic
Shamanism
Superstition
Taboo
Witchcraft
RT Anthropological Functionalism
Anthropological Linguistic Theory
Cultural Evolutionism
Cultural History
Folkways
Structuralism

MYTHOLOGY
S-01-0013 1975 00005
BT Ethnology
NT Ritual
RT Cultural History
Ethnolinguistics
Oral History
Political Theory Studies
Social Anthropology
Sociology Of Knowledge

N PERSON GAME THEORY
S-38-0134 1975 00007
BT Game Theory
RT Gaming
N Person Gaming
Two Person Game Theory

N PERSON GAMING
S-24-0100 1975 00010
BT Gaming
RT Fixed Sum Gaming
N Person Game Theory

NATION
S-24-0356 1975 00001
BT National Political Division
RT Nation Type
National Government
Regime Type
State Type
Subnational Political Division

NATION BUILDING
S-31-0049 1975 00033
BT Building Process
RT Assimilation
Balkanization
Community Building
Modernizing Political Elite
Nation Building Theory
National Identity
National Identity Theory
National Prestige
Nationalism
Nationalist Movement
Nationality Policy
Political Value Acquisition
Potential Elite
Racial Pride

NATION BUILDING THEORY
S-38-0154 1975 00016
BT Nation State Explanatory Theory
RT Development Theory
Government Enterprise
Modernization Theory
Nation Building
National Image
Political Development Theory

NATION STATE
S-16-0168 1975 00011
BT State Type
RT Nation State Explanatory Theory
Nation Type
National Boundary
National Goal
National Government
National Sovereignty Theory
Nationalist Political Party
Puppet State

NATION STATE EXPLANATORY THEORY
S-38-0153 1975 00007
BT Explanatory Political Theory
NT Nation Building Theory
National Identity Theory
National Sovereignty Theory
Statecraft Theory
RT Modern Political Thought
Nation State
National Characteristics
Nationalist Movement

NATION TYPE
S-16-0114 1975 00003
BT Government
NT Aligned Nation
Client Nation
Debtor Nation
Dependent Nation
Developed Nation
Developing Nation
Divided Nation
Fourth World Nation
Hostile Nation
Multiethnic Nation
Nonaligned Nation
Poor Nation
Rich Nation
Sovereign Nation
Third World Nation
Underdeveloped Nation
RT Comparative Political Studies
Government Type
Nation
Nation State
National Goal
National Politics
National Priority
Regime Type
Rule Type
State Type

NATIONAL ACCOUNTS ANALYSIS
S-09-0050 1975 00000
BT Contemporary Analytic Modes
RT Cost Benefit Analysis
Government Economic Management
Input Output Analysis
Marginal Analysis
Marginal Utility Analysis
National Income Analysis

NATIONAL ARCHIVES
S-18-0005 1975 00001
UF Government Archives
BT Archives
RT Archives
Data Bank

NATIONAL ASSEMBLY
S-19-0273 1975 00003
BT National Legislature
NT Diet
Peoples Assembly
Popular Assembly
RT Congress
Parliament
Representative Government

NATIONAL BANKING SYSTEM
S-37-0038 1975 00005
BT Financial System
RT Central Banking System
Federal Reserve System
Government Economic Management
Government Economic Planning
International Banking System
Monetary Policy
Subnational Banking System

NATIONAL BOUNDARY
S-06-0480 1975 00011
BT National Characteristics
RT Geographic Origin
Geography Discipline
Nation State
National Characteristics
National Political Division
National Security
National Self Determination

NATIONAL CANDIDATE
S-32-0228 1975 00002
BT Political Candidate
NT National Chief Executive Candidate
National Judicial Candidate
National Legislative Candidate
RT Dark Horse Candidate
Machine Candidate
Subnational Candidate

NATIONAL CHARACTER
S-06-0481 1975 00015
BT National Characteristics
RT Attitude Cluster
Cultural History
National Goal
National Image
National Interest
National Political Culture
Nationalism
Political Psychology
Social Diversity

NATIONAL CHARACTERISTICS
S-06-0470 1975 00004
BT Characteristics
NT Cultural Diversity
Ethnic Diversity
National Boundary
National Character
National Image
National Interest
National Self Determination
Social Diversity
RT Americanism
Government Characteristics
Health Characteristics
Institution Building
Language Characteristics
Nation State Explanatory Theory
National Boundary
Nationalism

NATIONAL CHAUVINIST
S-32-0212 1975 00002
BT Chauvinist
RT Jingoist
National Prestige
Patriotism
Political Psychology
Xenophobe

NATIONAL CHIEF EXECUTIVE CANDIDATE
S-32-0229 1975 00001
BT National Candidate
NT Chancellor Candidate
Presidential Candidate
Prime Minister Candidate
RT National Judicial Candidate
National Legislative Candidate
Subnational Chief Executive Candidate

NATIONAL CHIEF EXECUTIVE ELECTION
S-29-0052 1975 00010
BT National Election
NT Chancellor Election
Presidential Election
Prime Minister Election
RT National Judicial Election
National Legislative Election

NATIONAL CHIEF EXECUTIVE ELECTION CAMPAIGN
S-29-0025 1975 00003
BT National Election Campaign
NT Chancellor Election Campaign
Presidential Election Campaign
Prime Minister Election Campaign
RT National Chief Government Executive
National Judicial Election Campaign
National Legislative Election Campaign
Nuclear Deterrence Policy
Subnational Chief Executive Election Campaign
Subnational Judicial Election Campaign
Subnational Legislative Election Campaign

NATIONAL CHIEF EXECUTIVE PRIMARY
S-29-0069 1975 00001
BT National Primary
NT Presidential Primary
RT Chief Government Executive
Electoral Outcome
National Chief Government Executive
National Legislative Election Campaign
Nominating Process
Presidential Candidate

NATIONAL CHIEF GOVERNMENT EXECUTIVE
S-36-0069 1975 00007
BT Chief Government Executive
NT Chancellor
Colonial Ruler
Premier
President
Prime Minister
RT Emperor
International Government Executive
National Chief Executive Election Campaign
National Chief Executive Primary
Subnational Chief Government Executive

NATIONAL CIVIL SERVANT
S-36-0090 1975 00006
BT Civil Servant
RT Civil Servant
Government Bureaucracy
International Civil Servant
Subnational Civil Servant

NATIONAL COMMUNISM
S-38-0319 1975 00018
BT Communism
RT Communist Deviationism
Communist Economic System
Communist Government
Liberation Front
Liberation Process
National Front
National Liberation Movement

NATIONAL CONSTITUTION
S-21-0011 1975 00009
BT Constitution
NT Federal Constitution
Unitary Constitution
RT Constitutional Law
Democratic Constitution
New Federalism
Republican Constitutionalism
State Constitution
Unwritten Constitution
Written Constitution

NATIONAL CONSTITUTIONAL CONVENTION
S-19-0105 1975 00001
BT Constitutional Convention
RT International Constitutional Convention

NATIONAL CURRENCY
S-06-0360 1975 00002
BT Money Supply
RT Capital
Capital Flow
Currency Revaluation Policy
Gold Reserve
Money
Money Creation
Money Demand
Money Supply Policy

NATIONAL DEBT FINANCING
S-31-0403 1975 00000
BT Debt Financing
RT Deferential Voter
Deficit Financing
Government Borrowing
Government Enterprise
Keynesian Economic Theory
War Debt Financing

NATIONAL DEBT POLICY
S-26-0135 1975 00001
BT Public Debt Policy
RT Government Economic Management
Government Economic Planning
Revenue Policy

NATIONAL DECISION MAKING PROCESS
S-31-0331 1975 00009
BT Decision Making Process
RT Approval Process
Authorization Process
Constitution
Governing Elite
Government Bureaucracy
International Decision Making Process
National Goal
Subnational Decision Making Process

NATIONAL DEMOCRATIC PARTY
1975-1979 00001

NATIONAL DEMOCRATIC POLITICAL PARTY
S-28-0006 1979 00000
BT Democratic Political Party
RT Christian Democratic Political Party
Liberal Democratic Political Party
Liberal Political Party
Social Democratic Political Party

NATIONAL DIVISION OF LABOR
S-06-0278 1975 00000
BT Division Of Labor
RT Economic Development Theory
International Division Of Labor
National Economic Integration
Socialist Division Of Labor

NATIONAL ECONOMIC DEVELOPMENT LEVEL
S-06-0147 1975 00007
BT Economic Development Level
RT Economic Development Theory
International Economic Development Level
Local Economic Development Level
Regional Economic Development Level

NATIONAL ECONOMIC INTEGRATION
S-31-0807 1975 00002
BT Economic Integration
RT European Integration Theory
Horizontal Economic Integration
National Division Of Labor

NATIONAL ECONOMIC MANAGEMENT
S-23-0018 1975 00033
BT Economic Management
RT Business Management
Central Economic Management
Fiscal Theory
Government Economic Management
Government Economic Planning
International Economic Management
Monetary Management
National Socialism
Planification
Subnational Economic Management

NATIONAL ECONOMIC PLANNING
S-31-0650 1975 00033
BT Economic Planning
RT Central Economic Planning
Fiscal Planning
Forced Requisitioning
Government Economic Management
Government Economic Planning
International Economic Planning
Long Range Planning
National Goal
Subnational Economic Planning

NATIONAL ELECTION
S-29-0051 1975 00018
BT Election Type
NT National Chief Executive Election
National Judicial Election
National Legislative Election
RT General Election
Plebiscite Election
Subnational Election
Voter Qualification
Voting Behavior Analysis

NATIONAL ELECTION CAMPAIGN
S-29-0024 1975 00006
BT Election Campaign
NT National Chief Executive Election Campaign
National Judicial Election Campaign
National Legislative Election Campaign
RT Subnational Election Campaign

NATIONAL FRONT
S-02-0054 1975 00001
BT Political Front
RT Electoral Alliance
Electoral Tactics
Leninism
Liberation Front
National Communism
Popular Front
Revolution Theory
United Front

NATIONAL GOAL
S-06-0484 1975 00033
BT National Interest
NT National Priority
National Security
RT Decision Maker Perception
Government Economic Management
Government Economic Planning
Group Attitude
Nation State
Nation Type
National Character
National Decision Making Process
National Economic Planning
National Priority
Political History
State Of The Union
Value System

NATIONAL GOVERNMENT
S-16-0077 1975 00016
BT Government Type
RT Federal City Relations
Federal Government
Federal State Relations
Governing Coalition
Interim Government
International Government
Nation
Nation State
Parliamentary Government
Subnational Government
Unitary Government

NATIONAL GOVERNMENT BUREAUCRACY
S-19-0077 1975 00050
BT Government Bureaucracy
RT Bureaucratic Theory
Governing Elite
International Government Bureaucracy
Local Government Bureaucracy
Subnational Government Bureaucracy

NATIONAL GOVERNMENT COUNCIL
S-19-0110 1975 00002
UF Duma
BT Councils
NT Cabinet
Council Of Ministers
Presidential Advisory Council
Privy Council
RT Economic Council
Executive Government Institution
Governing Elite
Government
Information Agency
International Government Council
Subnational Government Council

NATIONAL GUARD
S-33-0055 1975 00002
BT Army Organization
RT Mass Militia Army
Regular Army
Standing Army

NATIONAL HEALTH INSURANCE
S-26-0307 1975 00021
BT Insurance
RT Catastrophe Insurance
Compulsory Insurance
Fire Insurance
Health Care Policy
Life Insurance
Medical Care Policy
Motor Vehicle Industry
Public Health Policy
Unemployment Insurance Policy

NATIONAL IDENTITY
S-06-0389 1975 00038
BT Identity Characteristics
NT National Pride
RT Community Identity
Cultural Identity
Ethnic Group Loyalty
Ethnic Nationalism
Nation Building
National Identity Theory
Nationalism
Nationalist Political Party
Political Psychology
Racial Identity
Religious Identity
Social Identity

NATIONAL IDENTITY THEORY
S-38-0155 1975 00010
BT Nation State Explanatory Theory
RT Cultural Nationalism
Ethnic Nationalism
Nation Building
National Identity
National Prestige
National Pride
Nationalism
Nationalist
Nationalist Movement
Nationality Composition

NATIONAL IMAGE
S-06-0482 1975 00011
BT National Characteristics
RT Decision Maker Perception
Nation Building Theory
National Character
National Interest
National Political Culture
National Self Determination
Political Psychology

NATIONAL INCOME
S-06-0338 1975 00003
BT Income
NT Per Capita Income
RT Foreign Income
Government Economic Planning
Income Measure
National Income Analysis
Personal Income
Profit Income

NATIONAL INCOME ANALYSIS
S-09-0051 1975 00008
BT Contemporary Analytic Modes
RT Cost Benefit Analysis
Government Economic Management
Government Economic Planning
Input Output Analysis
Marginal Analysis
Marginal Utility Analysis
National Accounts Analysis
National Income

NATIONAL INCOME TAXATION
S-26-0147 1975 00008
BT Income Taxation
RT Government Economic Management
Taxation Policy

NATIONAL INTEREST
S-06-0483 1975 00042
BT National Characteristics
NT National Goal
RT Decision Maker Perception
Government Enterprise
National Character
National Image
National Self Determination
Nationalism
Social Diversity

NATIONAL JUDGE
S-36-0109 1975 00002
BT Judge
RT Appointment Process
Chief Justice
Federal Judicial System
International Judge
National Judicial Primary
National Judicial System
National Supreme Court
Subnational Judge
Supreme Court Justice
Supreme Court Review

NATIONAL JUDICIAL CANDIDATE
S-32-0234 1975 00000
BT National Candidate
RT National Chief Executive Candidate
National Judicial Primary
National Judicial System
National Legislative Candidate
Subnational Judicial Candidate

NATIONAL JUDICIAL ELECTION
S-29-0056 1975 00000
BT National Election
RT National Chief Executive Election
National Legislative Election

NATIONAL JUDICIAL ELECTION CAMPAIGN
S-29-0029 1975 00000
BT National Election Campaign
RT Local Election Campaign
National Chief Executive Election Campaign
National Legislative Election Campaign
Subnational Chief Executive Election Campaign
Subnational Judicial Election Campaign
Subnational Legislative Election Campaign

NATIONAL JUDICIAL PRIMARY
S-29-0071 1975 00000
BT National Primary
RT Electoral Outcome
Federal Judicial System
National Judge
National Judicial Candidate
National Judicial System
Subnational Judicial Election Campaign

NATIONAL JUDICIAL SYSTEM
S-37-0083 1975 00001
BT Judicial System
NT Federal Judicial System
RT International Judicial System
Judge
Judicial Review
National Judge
National Judicial Candidate
National Judicial Primary
National Law Enforcement
National Supreme Court
Supreme Court

NATIONAL LAW ENFORCEMENT
S-31-0567 1975 00001
BT Law Enforcement
RT Code Enforcement
International Law Enforcement
Local Law Enforcement
National Judicial System
Punishment
Subnational Law Enforcement

NATIONAL LEADERSHIP
S-22-0021 1975 00001
BT Leadership Type
RT Administrative Leadership
Bonapartism
Bureaucratic Leadership
Charismatic Leadership
Collective Leadership
Congressional Leadership
Democratic Leadership
Executive Leadership
Leadership Authority Base
Leadership Structure Type
National Legislative Member
National Legislative Speaker
Open Leadership
Personalized Leadership
Political Leadership
Political Movement Leadership
Political Party Leadership
Presidential Leadership
Rational Legal Leadership
Totalitarian Leadership
Traditional Leadership
Upper House Speaker

NATIONAL LEGISLATIVE CANDIDATE
S-32-0235 1979 00000
UF National Legislator Candidate
BT National Candidate
NT Congressional Candidate
Parliamentary Candidate
RT National Chief Executive Candidate
National Judicial Candidate
Subnational Legislative Candidate

NATIONAL LEGISLATIVE COMMITTEE CHAIRPERSON
S-36-0148 1975 00000
BT Legislative Committee Chairperson
NT Congressional Committee Chairperson
Parliamentary Committee Chairperson
RT Subnational Legislative Committee Chairperson

NATIONAL LEGISLATIVE ELECTION
S-29-0057 1975 00009
BT National Election
NT Congressional Election
Parliamentary Election
RT National Chief Executive Election
National Judicial Election
National Legislative Member
National Legislative Political Party
National Legislature

NATIONAL LEGISLATIVE ELECTION CAMPAIGN
S-29-0030 1975 00002
BT National Election Campaign
NT Congressional Election Campaign
Parliamentary Election Campaign
RT Local Election Campaign
National Chief Executive Election Campaign
National Chief Executive Primary
National Judicial Election Campaign
National Legislative Primary
Subnational Chief Executive Election Campaign
Subnational Judicial Election Campaign
Subnational Legislative Election Campaign

NATIONAL LEGISLATIVE LEADER
S-36-0179 1975 00001
BT Legislative Leader
NT Congressional Leader
Parliamentary Leader
RT Floor Leader
Leader Of Opposition
Legislative Speaker
Legislative Whip
Majority Leader
Minority Leader
National Legislative Member
National Legislative Primary
Opposition Political Party Leader
Subnational Legislative Leader

NATIONAL LEGISLATIVE MEMBER
S-36-0188 1975 00004
BT Legislative Member
NT Congressional Member
Parliamentary Member
RT Legislative Behavior
Legislative Characteristics
Legislative History
Legislative Role Orientation
Legislative Socialization
National Leadership
National Legislative Election
National Legislative Leader
National Legislative Primary
National Legislature
Subnational Legislative Member

NATIONAL LEGISLATIVE POLITICAL PARTY
S-28-0045 1979 00000
BT Legislative Political Party
NT Congressional Political Party
Parliamentary Political Party
RT Elite Political Party
House Of Representatives
Legislative Behavior
Legislative Power
National Legislative Election
National Legislature
National Political Party
Senate

NATIONAL LEGISLATIVE PRIMARY
S-29-0072 1975 00000
BT National Primary
NT Congressional Primary
RT National Legislative Election Campaign
National Legislative Leader
National Legislative Member

NATIONAL LEGISLATIVE SPEAKER
S-36-0160 1975 00000
BT Legislative Speaker
NT Congressional Speaker
Parliamentary Speaker
RT Floor Leader
Legislative Behavior
National Leadership
National Legislative Whip
Subnational Legislative Speaker

NATIONAL LEGISLATIVE STAFF
S-36-0204 1975 00000
BT Legislative Staff
NT Congressional Legislative Staff
Parliamentary Legislative Staff
RT Legislative Committee Staff
Legislative Hearing
Legislative Record
Line Staff

NATIONAL LEGISLATIVE WHIP
S-36-0171 1975 00000
BT Legislative Whip
NT Congressional Whip
Parliamentary Whip
RT Legislative Whip
Majority Leader
Minority Leader
National Legislative Speaker

NATIONAL LEGISLATOR CANDIDATE
1975-1979 00000
USE National Legislative Candidate

NATIONAL LEGISLATURE
S-19-0256 1975 00019
BT Legislatures
NT Congress
National Assembly
Parliament
Parliamentary Committee System
RT Bicameral Legislature
By Election
Legislative Nominating Process
Legislature Type
National Legislative Election
National Legislative Member
National Legislative Political Party
Representation Type
Unicameral Legislature

NATIONAL LIBERATION MOVEMENT
S-27-0026 1975 00021
BT Liberation Movement
RT Black Liberation Movement
Communism
Leninism
Marxism
National Communism
National Self Determination
Nationalism
Peoples Liberation Movement
Revolution

NATIONAL LIBERATION WAR
S-08-0051 1975 00020
BT Internal War
NT Partisan War
RT Civil War
Guerrilla Activity
Guerrilla War
Ideological War
Just War
Leninism
Psychological War
Revolution Theory

NATIONAL MARKET
S-19-0194 1975 00003
BT International Market
NT Internal Market
RT Black Market
Commodity Market
Common Market
Consumer Market
Differentiated Market
Export Market
Financial Market
Free Market
International Commodity Market
Mass Market
World Market

NATIONAL ORIGIN
S-06-0207 1975 00002
BT Origin
RT Ethnic Origin
Geographic Origin
Immigration Policy

NATIONAL PARTY
1975-1979 00000

NATIONAL PLANNER
S-32-0134 1975 00000
BT Planner
RT Centrally Planned Economy
Economic Planner
Education Planner
Foreign Policy Planner
Government Economic Planning
International Planner
Social Planner
Subnational Planner

NATIONAL PLANNING COMMISSION
S-19-0096 1975 00001
BT Planning Commission
RT City Planning Commission
International Planning Commission
Legislative Commission
Presidential Commission
Presidential Task Force
Subnational Planning Commission

NATIONAL PLANNING POLICY
S-26-0346 1975 00007
BT Planning Policy
RT Administrative Planning
Apportionment Reform
Government Economic Planning
Local Planning Policy
Long Range Planning
Needs Assessment
Regional Planning Policy
State Planning Policy
Subnational Planning Policy

NATIONAL POLICE
S-19-0305 1975 00006
BT Police
RT International Police
Military Police
National Police Commissioner
Paramilitary Police
Private Police
Secret Police
Subnational Police

NATIONAL POLICE COMMISSIONER
S-36-0138 1975 00000
BT National Police Official
RT Law Enforcement
Local Police Official
National Police

NATIONAL POLICE OFFICIAL
S-36-0137 1975 00000
BT Law Enforcement Official
NT National Police Commissioner
RT International Police Official
Secret Police Official
Subnational Police Official

NATIONAL POLICY MAKING
S-31-0683 1975 00020
BT Policy Making Process
RT Administrative Policy Making
Domestic Policy Making
Economic Policy Making
Education Policy Making
Foreign Policy Making
International Policy Making
Judicial Policy Making
Local Policy Making

NATIONAL POLICY PLANNING
S-31-0663 1975 00025
BT Public Policy Planning
RT Financial Accounting
Government Expenditure
International Policy Planning
National Priority
Presidential Legislative Program
Presidential Task Force
Subnational Policy Planning

NATIONAL POLITICAL CULTURE
S-11-0027 1975 00014
BT Political Culture
NT Civic Culture
Fragmented Political Culture
Generational Political Culture
Ideological Political Culture
Political Subculture
RT Attitude Characteristics
Attitude Cluster
National Character
National Image
Political Psychology

NATIONAL POLITICAL DIVISION
S-24-0355 1975 00000
BT National Region
NT Nation
RT Border Conflict
Districting
Geography Discipline
National Boundary
Subnational Political Division

NATIONAL POLITICAL INTEGRATION
S-31-0823 1975 00011
BT Political Integration
RT Integrated Authority
International Political Integration
Political Unification
Subnational Political Integration

NATIONAL POLITICAL PARTY
S-28-0052 1979 00000
BT Political Party Type
NT Subnational Political Party
RT Government Political Party
National Legislative Political Party
National Political Party Leader
Nationalities Law
Structure Specific Political Party Type
Subnational Political Party

NATIONAL POLITICAL PARTY CENTRAL COMMITTEE MEMBER
S-36-0240 1975 00004
BT National Political Party Committee Member
RT National Political Party First Secretary
National Political Party Politburo Member

NATIONAL POLITICAL PARTY CHAIRPERSON
S-36-0238 1975 00000
BT National Political Party Executive Member
RT National Political Party Committee Member
National Political Party Politburo Member
National Political Party Secretary

NATIONAL POLITICAL PARTY COMMITTEE MEMBER
S-36-0239 1975 00000
BT National Political Party Executive Member
NT National Political Party Central Committee Member
RT National Political Party Chairperson
National Political Party Politburo Member
National Political Party Secretary

NATIONAL POLITICAL PARTY EXECUTIVE MEMBER
S-36-0237 1975 00001
BT Political Party Official
NT National Political Party Chairperson
National Political Party Committee Member
National Political Party Politburo Member
National Political Party Secretary
RT Cabinet Member
International Political Party Committee Member
International Political Party Executive Member
Political Party National Committee
Subnational Political Party Executive Member

NATIONAL POLITICAL PARTY FIRST SECRETARY
S-36-0243 1975 00002
BT National Political Party Secretary
RT National Political Party Central Committee Member
Political Party Chief
Political Party Membership

NATIONAL POLITICAL PARTY LEADER
S-32-0157 1975 00002
BT Political Boss
RT Leadership Analysis
Leadership Authority Base
Leadership Political Analysis
Leadership Recruitment
Leadership Type
National Political Party
Parliamentary Speaker
Political Party Chief

NATIONAL POLITICAL PARTY POLITBURO MEMBER
S-36-0241 1975 00000
BT National Political Party Executive Member
RT National Political Party Central Committee Member
National Political Party Chairperson
National Political Party Committee Member
National Political Party Secretary

NATIONAL POLITICAL PARTY SECRETARY
S-36-0242 1975 00000
BT National Political Party Executive Member
NT National Political Party First Secretary
RT National Political Party Chairperson
National Political Party Committee Member
National Political Party Politburo Member

NATIONAL POLITICAL REVOLUTION
S-08-0070 1975 00020
BT Political Revolution
RT Bolshevik Revolution
Communist Revolution
Democratic Political Revolution
Democratic Socialist Revolution
Government Overthrow
Internal War
Revolution Theory
Social Revolution
Socialist Revolution
Spontaneous Revolution
Thermidor

NATIONAL POLITICAL SYSTEM CHARACTERISTICS
S-06-0681 1975 00011
BT Political System Characteristics
RT International Political System Characteristics
Nationalism
Political System Theory

NATIONAL POLITICS
S-29-0214 1975 00015
BT Politics
RT Class Politics
Gay Politics
Institution Building
International Politics
Linkage Politics
Nation Type
Parliamentary Politics
Political Behavior
Political Party Membership
Representation Type
Sexual Politics

NATIONAL PRESS
S-17-0022 1975 00009
BT Newspaper Industry
RT Black Press
Magazine Industry
News Conference
Radical Press
Telecommunications Industry
Underground Press

NATIONAL PRESTIGE
S-06-0391 1975 00003
BT National Pride
RT Nation Building
National Chauvinist
National Identity Theory
National Pride
Nationalism
Political Identity

NATIONAL PRIDE
S-06-0390 1975 00009
BT National Identity
NT National Prestige
RT National Identity Theory
National Prestige
Nationalism
Political Identity

NATIONAL PRIMARY
S-29-0068 1975 00000
BT Primary Election
NT National Chief Executive Primary
National Judicial Primary
National Legislative Primary
RT Blanket Primary
Closed Primary
Open Primary
Preference Primary

NATIONAL PRIORITY
S-06-0485 1975 00017
BT National Goal
RT Decision Maker Perception
Economic Planning
Nation Type
National Goal
National Policy Planning
National Security
State Of The Union
Value System

NATIONAL PRODUCTION
S-31-0440 1975 00002
BT Production Process
NT Gross National Product
Standard Of Living
RT Agricultural Production
Division Of Labor
Farming
Industrial Production

War Production

NATIONAL REGION
S-24-0354 1975 00054
BT World Region
NT National Political Division
Subnational Political Division
RT Extranational Bloc
International Region
Middle East Area Studies

NATIONAL SECURITY
S-06-0486 1975 00118
BT National Goal
RT Intelligence Agency
Military Characteristics
National Boundary
National Priority
National Security Forces
Surveillance

NATIONAL SECURITY FORCES
S-33-0006 1975 00006
BT Security Forces
NT Defense System
Irregular Forces
Military Forces
RT Intelligence Agency
Multinational Security Forces
National Security
Strategic Studies

NATIONAL SELF DETERMINATION
S-06-0487 1979 00000
BT National Characteristics
RT Cultural Diversity
Decolonization
Ethnic Diversity
National Boundary
National Image
National Interest
National Liberation Movement
Nationalism
Patriotism

NATIONAL SOCIALISM
S-38-0229 1975 00013
BT Fascist Theory
RT Authoritarian Regime
Corporate Fascism
Dictatorial Regime
Dictatorship
Expansionist War
Falangism
Fascist Movement
Francoism
Garrison State
Hegemonic One Party System
Ideological Political Culture
Italian Fascism
Mass Mobilization
Mass Society
Minority Persecution
Modernizing Dictatorship
National Economic Management
National Socialist Political Party
Paramilitary Organization
Peronism
Political Persecution
Racial Persecution
Racial Politics
Racial Supremacy
Slave Labor Camp
Totalitarian Dictatorship
Totalitarian Leadership
Totalitarian Movement
Totalitarian Political System

NATIONAL SOCIALIST
S-32-0275 1975 00001
BT Fascist
RT Falangist
National Socialist Political Party

NATIONAL SOCIALIST PARTY
1975-1979 00003

NATIONAL SOCIALIST POLITICAL PARTY
S-28-0018 1979 00000
BT Fascist Political Party
RT Falangist
Fascist Movement
Fascist Theory
Mass Political Party
National Socialism
National Socialist
Totalitarian Movement
Totalitarian Political Party

NATIONAL SOVEREIGNTY THEORY
S-38-0156 1975 00008
BT Nation State Explanatory Theory
RT Authority Structure
Authority Theory
Empire
Nation State
Nationalism
Sovereign Nation
Sovereignty
Sovereignty Theory

NATIONAL SUPREME COURT
S-19-0139 1975 00050
BT Supreme Court
RT District Court
Judicial Review
National Judge
National Judicial System
State Supreme Court
Subnational Supreme Court

NATIONAL TAX LAW
S-21-0047 1975 00003
BT Tax Law
RT Government Economic Planning
National Taxation
Progressive Taxation
Regressive Taxation
Tax Code
Taxation Policy

NATIONAL TAXATION
S-26-0156 1975 00001
BT Taxation Policy
NT Federal Taxation
RT National Tax Law
Progressive Taxation
Regressive Taxation
State Taxation
Subnational Taxation
Taxation Policy

NATIONALISM
S-38-0261 1975 00077
BT Ideologies
NT Americanism
Cultural Nationalism
Isolationism
Neutralism
Patriotism
Separatism
RT Antiimperialism
Balkanization
Chauvinist
Liberalism
Liberation Movement
Nation Building
National Character
National Characteristics
National Identity
National Identity Theory
National Interest
National Liberation Movement
National Political System Characteristics
National Prestige
National Pride
National Self Determination
National Sovereignty Theory
Nationalist
Nationalist Movement
Nationalist Political Party
Nationality Composition
Pan Slav Movement
Peoples Liberation Movement
Plebiscite Election
Populism
Racial Pride
Socialist Theory

NATIONALIST
S-32-0277 1975 00004
BT System Politicist
RT National Identity Theory
Nationalism
Nationalist Movement
Nationalist Political Party
Nationality Composition
Nationality Group
Nationality Policy

NATIONALIST MOVEMENT
S-27-0034 1975 00017
BT Political Movement
NT Black Nationalist Movement
Pan African Movement
Pan Arab Movement
Pan Slav Movement
Zionist Movement
RT Decolonization
Ethnic Separatist Movement
Federation Movement
Ideological Spectrum Political Movement
Ideological Spectrum Political Party Type
Independence Movement
Liberation Movement
Nation Building
Nation State Explanatory Theory
National Identity Theory
Nationalism
Nationalist
Pan Slav Movement
Sector Based Political Movement
Sector Based Political Party Type
Separatist Movement
Social Movement

NATIONALIST PARTY
1975-1979 00005

NATIONALIST POLITICAL PARTY
S-28-0029 1979 00000
BT Political Party Type
RT Ideological Spectrum Political Party Type
Military Political Party
Nation State
National Identity
Nationalism
Nationalist

NATIONALITIES LAW
S-21-0095 1975 00002
BT Social Law
RT Control Process
Ethnic Studies
Minority Law
National Political Party
Nationality Group
Nationality Persecution
Nationality Policy
Nationalization Process

NATIONALITY
USE Citizenship Status

NATIONALITY COMPOSITION
S-06-0222 1975 00004
BT Population Composition
RT Ethnic Composition
Ethnic Studies
National Identity Theory
Nationalism
Nationalist
Nationality Group
Racial Composition
Religious Composition

NATIONALITY GROUP
S-03-0029 1975 00007
BT Social Group
RT Cultural Group
Ethnic Assimilation Theory
Ethnic Group
Ethnic Policy
Interest Group
Kinship Group
Nationalist
Nationalities Law
Nationality Composition
Racial Group
Reference Group
Religious Cult
Religious Group
Secondary Group

NATIONALITY PERSECUTION
S-31-0316 1975 00001
BT Persecution
RT Ethnic Persecution
Minority Persecution
Nationalities Law
Political Persecution
Racial Persecution
Religious Persecution
Xenophobe

NATIONALITY POLICY
S-26-0379 1975 00015
BT Ethnic Policy
RT Ethnic Assimilation Theory
Nation Building
Nationalist
Nationalities Law
Political Integration Theory

NATIONALIZATION PROCESS
S-31-0292 1975 00010
BT Government Expropriation
NT Bank Nationalization
Industry Nationalization
Land Nationalization
Utility Nationalization
RT Ethnic Assimilation Theory
Nationalities Law
Nationalized Industry
Socialist Theory

NATIONALIZED ECONOMY
S-12-0039 1975 00001
BT Planned Economy
RT Centrally Planned Economy
Command Economy
Communist Economic System
Corporate Economy
Fascist Economy
Government Economic Management
Government Economic Planning
Government Expropriation
Socialist Economy
Socialist Theory

NATIONALIZED INDUSTRY
S-17-0050 1975 00003
BT Industry
RT Government Economic Management
Industrial Policy
Monopoly
Nationalization Process
Protected Industry
Public Utility Industry
Television Industry

NATIVE BORN CITIZEN
S-36-0018 1975 00001
BT Alien
RT Citizenship Privilege
Dual Citizen
Naturalized Citizen

NATURAL CATASTROPHE
S-31-0248 1979 00000
BT Crisis
RT Catastrophe Insurance
Economic Crisis
Epidemic
International Crisis
Political Crisis
Social Crisis

NATURAL EXPERIMENT
S-24-0425 1975 00000
BT Quasiexperiment
RT Falsification
Natural Science Model
Quasiexperiment
Social Science Model
Sociology Of Science

NATURAL JUSTICE THEORY
S-38-0480 1975 00001
BT Justice Theory
RT Compensatory Justice
Natural Law Conventionalism Theory
Platonic Political Thought

NATURAL LAW
S-21-0064 1975 00011
BT Law Type
RT Basic Law
Bill Of Rights
Constitution
Customary Law
Religious Law
Sacred Law
Socialist Legality

NATURAL LAW CONVENTIONALISM THEORY
S-38-0487 1975 00001
BT Political Philosophy Concept
NT Classical Natural Right Doctrine
Great Chain Of Being Doctrine
Medieval Natural Law Theory
Right Reason Doctrine
Rights Of Man Doctrine
Roman Natural Law Theory
Scientific Natural Law Theory
Stoic Natural Law Theory
RT Legitimacy Theory
Liberty Theory
Natural Justice Theory
Obligation Theory
Order Theory
Political Man Theory
Right Of Revolution
Right Reason Doctrine
Rights Of Man Doctrine

NATURAL LAW SYSTEM
S-37-0104 1975 00000
BT Law System
RT Common Law System
Equity Law
International Law System
Socialist Law System

NATURAL RESOURCE EXPLOITATION
S-31-0119 1975 00048
BT Resource Utilization
NT Coal Energy
Gas Energy
Geothermal Energy
Hydroelectric Energy
Nuclear Energy
Oil Energy
Solar Energy
Tidal Energy
Wind Energy
RT Energy Scarcity
Food Scarcity
Natural Resource Management

NATURAL RESOURCE MANAGEMENT
S-23-0023 1975 00067
BT Environmental Management
NT Energy Management
RT Air Pollution Policy
Catastrophe Analysis
Conservation Law
Ecology Movement
Environmental Law
Historical Preservation Law
Law Of The Sea
Natural Resource Exploitation
Population Management
Public Policy Management

NATURAL RESOURCE POLICY
S-26-0219 1975 00058
BT Environment Policy
NT Fish And Wildlife Policy
Forest Land Policy
Grazing Land Policy
Water Use Policy

RT Archaeology
Conservation Law
Ecology Discipline
Ecology Movement
Energy Management
Energy Policy
Environmental Planning
Extractive Industry
Land Policy
Land Use Policy
Law Of The Sea
Lumber Industry
Oil Energy
Pollution Policy
Raw Material Production
Seabed Policy
Solar Energy
Space Policy
Tidal Energy
Wind Energy

NATURAL SCIENCE DISCIPLINE
S-01-0146 1975 00010
BT Academic Areas
NT Ideographic Science
Physical Science
RT Agricultural Science
Archaeology
Biological Sciences
Earth Sciences
Ecology Discipline
Engineering Discipline
Geography Discipline
Natural Science Education
Psychology Discipline

NATURAL SCIENCE EDUCATION
S-13-0027 1979 00000
BT Education Type
RT Climatology
Ideographic Science
Medical Science
Natural Science Discipline
Physical Science
Research Institution
Scientism
Topography

NATURAL SCIENCE MODEL
S-24-0285 1975 00019
BT Models
NT Biological Model
Ecological Model
RT Climatology
Mathematical Model
Natural Experiment
Philosophy Of Science Studies
Scientism
Social Science Model
Theory Construction
Theory Of Causality
Topography

NATURAL SELECTION
S-31-0066 1975 00001
BT Genetic Evolution
RT Cultural Evolution
Human Evolution
Social Darwinism

NATURALIZED CITIZEN
S-36-0019 1975 00003
BT Alien
RT Citizenship Privilege
Dual Citizen
Native Born Citizen

NAVAL FORCES
S-33-0065 1975 00069
BT Navy
NT Naval Power
RT Merchant Marine
Professional Military Forces
Reserve Military Forces

NAVAL POWER
S-33-0066 1975 00022
BT Naval Forces
NT Sea Power
RT International Power Theory
Military Personnel
Navy
Sailor
Strategic Studies

NAVY
S-33-0064 1975 00077
BT Armed Forces
NT Naval Forces
RT Admiralty
Army
Coast Guard
Marines
Maritime Court
Military Agency
Military Industrial Complex
Naval Power
Professional Military Forces
Reserve Military Forces
Sailor
Sea Power
Warship

NEEDS ASSESSMENT
S-26-0347 1979 00000
BT Planning Policy
NT Education Needs
RT City Planning Policy
Evaluating
Local Planning Policy
National Planning Policy
Policy Evaluation Research
Regional Planning Policy
Research And Development
Research Evaluation
State Planning Policy

NEGATIVE COALITION
S-02-0031 1975 00000
BT Political Party Coalition
RT Democratic Coalition
Grand Coalition
Intraparty Coalition
Legislative Coalition
Minimum Winning Coalition
Parliamentary Coalition
Voting Coalition

NEGATIVE FREEDOM THEORY
S-38-0464 1975 00004
BT Freedom Theory
RT Classical Liberalism
Constitutional Structural Theory
Economic Freedom Theory
Economic Liberalism
Freedom
Individual Freedom Theory
Laissez Faire Liberalism
Nineteenth Century Liberalism
Positive Freedom Theory

NEGATIVE LIBERTARIANISM
1975-1979 00000

NEGATIVE VOTING ABSTENTION
S-29-0118 1975 00000
SN The practice of not voting because of apathy or uninvolvement.
BT Voting Abstention
RT Apathetic Voter
Voter Orientation
Voter Turnout
Voting Behavior
Voting Behavior Analysis
Voting Theory

NEGLIGENCE LAW
S-21-0024 1979 00000
BT Contract Law
RT Common Law
Consumer Protection Law
Economic Law
Property Law
Tort
Zoning Law

NEGOTIATED LEGAL SETTLEMENT
S-31-0497 1975 00003
BT Legal Settlement
NT Plea Bargaining
RT Imposed Legal Settlement

NEGOTIATION
S-31-0242 1975 00020
BT Conflict Resolution
NT International Negotiation
Labor Negotiation
RT Accommodation
Adjudication
Agreement
Appeasement
Bargainer
Bargaining
Bargaining Theory
Coercion
Conciliation
Decision Making Process
Declared War
Deescalation
Mediation
Negotiator

NEGOTIATOR
S-32-0009 1975 00006
BT Adjudicator
RT Arbitrator
Bargainer
Bargaining
Bargaining Strategy Process
Broker
Labor Negotiation
Mediator
Moderator
Negotiation
Ombudsman

NEIGHBORHOOD
S-07-0039 1975 00016
UF Neighborhood Community
BT Community Type
RT Census Tract
City Unit

Community Structural Characteristics
Inner City
Megalopolis
Metropolis
Model City
Municipality
Outer City
Police Community Relations
Suburb

NEIGHBORHOOD CLINIC
S-19-0245 1975 00000
BT Health Clinic
RT Family Planning
Lower Class
Nursing Home
Public Health Institution
Public Hospital

NEIGHBORHOOD COMMUNITY
1975-1979 00032
USE Neighborhood

NEIGHBORHOOD SCHOOL
S-19-0220 1975 00012
BT Education Institution
RT Community College
Inner City School
Issue Orientation
Local Policy Planning
Open University
School Integration
Urban School

NEOCLASSICAL ECONOMIC THEORY
S-38-0118 1979 00000
BT Economic Theory
RT Classical Economic Theory
Contemporary Analytic Modes
Econometric Model
Institutional Economics
Keynesian Economics
Welfare Economics

NEOCOLONIALISM
S-38-0247 1975 00012
BT Imperialism
RT Colonialism
Cultural Imperialism
Former Colony
Neoimperialism
Yankee Imperialism

NEOCONFUCIAN POLITICAL THEORY
S-38-0105 1975 00000
BT Eastern Political Thought
RT Confucian Political Theory
Neoconfucianism
Religious Culture
Religious Thought

NEOCONFUCIANISM
S-38-0557 1975 00002
BT Confucianism
RT Confucian Political Theory
Confucianism
Neoconfucian Political Theory
Religious Culture

NEOCONSERVATISM
S-38-0198 1975 00001
BT Conservatism
RT American Conservatism
Bureaucratic Conservatism
Burkean Conservatism
Christian Conservatism
Objectivist Political Thought
Reactionary Conservatism
Status Quo Conservatism

NEOFASCISM
S-38-0230 1975 00000
BT Fascist Theory
RT Corporate Fascism
Falangism
Fascist Movement
Flangist Political Party
Francoism
Italian Fascism
Peronism

NEOHEGELIANISM
S-38-0067 1975 00001
BT Contemporary Political Thought
RT Hegelian Analysis
Left Hegelianism
Modern Idealism
Neomarxism

NEOIMPERIALISM
S-38-0248 1975 00002
BT Imperialism
RT Capitalist Imperialism
Colonialism
Communist Imperialism
Neocolonialism
Western Imperialism
Yankee Imperialism

NEOMARXISM
S-38-0068 1975 00005
BT Contemporary Political Thought
RT Critical Theory Analysis
Eurocommunism
Left Hegelianism
Marxism
Marxist Existentialism
Marxist Revisionism
Marxist Theory
Neohegelianism
New Left
New Left Militant
Phenomenological Marxism
Socialist Humanism
Structural Marxism

NEOPLATONIC POLITICAL THOUGHT
S-38-0051 1975 00000
BT Classical Political Thought
RT Augustinian Analysis
Medieval Islamic Thought
Organic State Theory
Platonic Political Thought
Skeptic Thought
Stoic Thought

NEOPOSITIVISM
S-25-0024 1975 00000
BT Epistemology
RT Contemporary Analytic Modes
Empirical Theory
Empiricism
Logical Positivism
Materialism
Objectivism
Scientism

NEPOTISM
S-31-0745 1975 00001
BT Recruitment Process
RT Elite Recruitment
Military Recruitment
Patronage Politics
Political Recruitment

NET INCOME
S-06-0336 1975 00000
BT Income Measure
RT Average Income
Disposable Income
Fixed Assets
Fixed Income
Median Income
Personal Income
Taxation Policy

NETWORK ANALYSIS
S-09-0052 1975 00022
SN An examination of the interaction and communication patterns among individuals and groups.
BT Contemporary Analytic Modes
RT Communication Analysis
Interaction Analysis
Mass Media Analysis
Policy Analysis
Remote Terminal
Social Area Analysis

NEUROSIS
S-06-0522 1975 00005
BT Personality Disorder
RT Paranoia
Pathological Behavior
Psychiatry
Psychology Discipline
Psychosis
Psychotherapy

NEUTRAL BLOC
S-02-0049 1975 00002
BT Third World Bloc
RT Afro Asian Bloc
Arab Bloc
Latin American Bloc
Neutralism
Security Community

NEUTRALISM
S-38-0273 1975 00007
UF Buffer State
BT Nationalism
RT Isolationism
Neutral Bloc
Patriotism
Separatism

NEUTRALITY AGREEMENT
S-02-0087 1975 00001
BT State Agreement Type
NT Neutrality Treaty
RT Military Agreement
Military Alliance
Wartime Alliance
World Alliance

NEUTRALITY TREATY
S-02-0088 1975 00000
BT Neutrality Agreement
RT Detente
Military Treaty
Peaceful Coexistence

NEW FEDERALISM
S-37-0113 1975 00015
BT Federalism
RT Conflict Federalism
Cooperative Federalism
Federal Constitution
National Constitution
State Rights Doctrine

NEW INTERNATIONAL ECONOMIC ORDER
S-37-0043 1979 00000
BT International Economic System
RT Economic Development Theory
Economic Equality
Economic Stratification
Economic System Characteristics
Foreign Policy
Fourth World Nation
International Organization
Resource Utilization
Third World Bloc
World Economy

NEW LEFT
S-38-0276 1979 00000
UF New Leftism
BT Ideologies
NT Counter Culture Ideology
Student Activism
Student Radicalism
RT Dissent
Liberal
Libertarianism
Neomarxism
New Left Militant
Phenomenological Marxism
Radicalism
Revolution Theory
Student Protest

NEW LEFT MILITANT
S-32-0188 1975 00001
BT Militant
RT Counter Culture Ideology
Dissent
Neomarxism
New Left
Radical Movement
Radicalism
Student Protest

NEW LEFTISM
1975-1979 00006
USE New Left

NEW MIDDLE CLASS
S-06-0772 1975 00002
BT Middle Class
RT Interest Group Representation
White Collar Worker

NEW TOWN
S-07-0042 1979 00000
BT Planned Community
RT Bedroom Community
City Planner
City Policy Planning
Cooperative Community
Economic Community
Model City
Planned Community
Social Planner
Subnational Planning Policy
Town
Urban Development Theory
Urban Policy Planning

NEW VOTER
S-32-0322 1975 00001
BT Voter
RT Voting Behavior Analysis
Youth Voter

NEWS AGENCY
S-17-0016 1975 00004
BT Communication Industry
RT Book Industry
Broadcasting Industry
Magazine Industry
Publication Industry
Telecommunications Industry

NEWS CONFERENCE
S-31-0183 1975 00002
BT Mass Communication
RT Broadcasting
Media Editorializing
National Press
News Flow
News Reporting
Political Information Manipulation

NEWS COVERAGE
S-31-0186 1975 00030
BT News Reporting
RT News Flow
Newspaper Circulation
Newspaper Industry

NEWS FLOW
S-31-0184 1975 00006
BT Mass Communication
RT Media Editorializing
News Conference
News Coverage
News Reporting
Newspaper Circulation
Newspaper Industry

NEWS REPORTING
S-31-0185 1975 00030
BT Mass Communication
NT News Coverage
RT Broadcasting
Broadcasting Agency
Media Editorializing
News Conference
News Flow
Newspaper Circulation
Newspaper Industry
Public Broadcasting

NEWSLETTERS
S-18-0070 1975 00000
BT Information Sources
RT Documents
Library Science Studies
Monographs
Newspapers

NEWSPAPER CENSORSHIP
S-31-0271 1975 00002
BT Periodical Publication Censorship
RT Editorial Control
Information Leaking
Journal Censorship
Media Access
Media Editorializing
Newspaper Industry
Political Information Manipulation

NEWSPAPER CIRCULATION
S-31-0187 1975 00001
BT Mass Communication
RT Broadcasting
Media Editorializing
News Coverage
News Flow
News Reporting
Newspaper Industry

NEWSPAPER INDUSTRY
S-17-0020 1975 00017
BT Publication Industry
NT Black Press
National Press
Radical Press
Underground Press
RT Book Industry
Magazine Industry
News Coverage
News Flow
News Reporting
Newspaper Censorship
Newspaper Circulation
Newspapers

NEWSPAPERS
S-18-0071 1975 00020
BT Information Sources
RT Biography
Documents
Library Science Studies
Newsletters
Newspaper Industry
Public Record

NEWTONIAN MECHANISTIC STATE THEORY
S-38-0395 1975 00000
BT Early Modern Theory Of The State
RT Hobbesian Absolutism
Instrumental State Theory

NIETZSCHEAN ANALYSIS
S-38-0421 1975 00005
BT Modern Political Thought
RT Ethical Theory
Metaethical Theory
Nihilism

NIHILISM
S-38-0280 1975 00004
BT Ideologies
RT Anarchism
Anarchist
Anarchosyndicalism
Counter Culture Ideology
Nietzschean Analysis

NINETEENTH CENTURY LIBERALISM
S-38-0255 1975 00001
BT Liberalism
RT Civil Liberty Liberalism
Civil Rights Liberalism
Classical Liberalism
Economic Liberalism
Freedom
Laissez Faire Liberalism
Liberal
Negative Freedom Theory
Welfare Liberalism

NO CONFIDENCE MOTION
S-31-0593 1975 00000
SN A parliamentary maneuver to bring about a vote on the legitimacy of the incumbent executive.
BT Censure Motion
RT Cabinet Instability
Government Instability
Ministerial Instability
Parliamentary Procedure
Political Instability
Prime Minister Election Campaign

NO FAULT INSURANCE
S-26-0308 1979 00000
BT Insurance
RT Accident Insurance
Catastrophe Insurance
Compulsory Insurance
Fire Insurance
Life Insurance
Motor Vehicle Industry
Motor Vehicle Insurance

NOBILITY
S-06-0774 1975 00014
USE Aristocratic Class
BT Class Stratification Division
RT Aristocratic Class
Class Analysis
Class Polarization
Class Stratification Division
Feudal System
Landowning Class
Peasant Class
Propertied Class
Ruling Class
Social Prestige
Upper Class

NOISE POLLUTION
S-31-0105 1975 00004
BT Environmental Pollution
RT Ecology Discipline
Government Regulation
Noise Pollution Policy
Quality Of Life
Water Pollution

NOISE POLLUTION POLICY
S-26-0227 1975 00003
BT Pollution Policy
RT Environmental Pollution
Land Pollution Policy
Noise Pollution
Sanitation Policy
Water Pollution Policy

NOMADIC CULTURE
S-11-0046 1975 00003
BT Traditional Culture
RT Nomadic Economy
Nomadic Society
Peasant Culture

NOMADIC ECONOMY
S-12-0032 1975 00002
BT Economy Type
RT Agrarian Economy
Barter Economy
Craft Economy
Depressed Economy
Hunting And Fishing Society
Hunting And Trapping Economy
Nomadic Culture
Peasant Economy
Subsistence Economy
Underdeveloped Economy

NOMADIC SOCIETY
S-35-0025 1975 00003
BT Society Type Base
RT Feudal Society
Homogeneous Society
Nomadic Culture
Nonwestern Society
Peasant Society
Primitive Society
Tribal Society

NOMINAL MEASUREMENT
S-24-0171 1975 00002
BT Measurement Level
NT Classification
RT Interval Measurement
Ordinal Measurement
Ratio Scale Measurement

NOMINAL SCALE
S-24-0214 1975 00001
BT Scale Construction Methodology
RT Factor Structure
Guttman Scale
Interval Scale
Likert Scale
Measurement Level Scale
Multidimensional Scale
Ordinal Scale
Ratio Scale
Scalability Index
Semantic Differential
Thurstone Scale
Unidimensional Scale

NOMINAL SIGNIFICANCE TEST
S-24-0060 1975 00002
BT Statistical Significance Test
RT Binomial Test
Chi Square Test
F Ratio
Interval Significance Test
Mann Whitney U Test
Ordinal Significance Test
Wald Wolfowitz Runs Test
Wilcoxian T Test

NOMINALISM
S-38-0372 1975 00001
BT Medieval Political Thought
RT Scholasticism

NOMINATING PROCESS
S-31-0738 1979 00000
UF Nomination Process
BT Selection Process
NT Legislative Nominating Process
Presidential Nominating Process
RT Candidate Selection
Delegate Selection
National Chief Executive Primary
Slate Making
Social Role Process

NOMINATION PROCESS
1975-1979 00006
USE Nominating Process

NONAGGRESSION AGREEMENT
S-02-0089 1975 00001
BT State Agreement Type
NT Nonaggression Treaty
RT Defense Alliance
Disarmament Agreement
Friendship Agreement
Military Agreement
Military Alliance
Peace Treaty

NONAGGRESSION TREATY
S-02-0090 1975 00001
BT Nonaggression Agreement
RT Arms Control Treaty
Defense Alliance
Friendship Treaty
Military Treaty
Peace Treaty
Peaceful Coexistence

NONALIGNED NATION
S-16-0125 1975 00015
BT Nation Type
RT Aligned Nation
Client Nation
Fourth World Nation
Political Neutralist
Sovereign Nation
Third World Nation

NONEXPERIMENT
S-24-0422 1975 00000
BT Variable Control
RT Experiment
Quasiexperiment

NONMETRIC MULTIDIMENSIONAL SCALE
S-24-0213 1975 00004
BT Multidimensional Scale
RT Measurement

NONPARAMETRIC STATISTICS
S-24-0067 1975 00001
BT Statistics Type
RT Descriptive Statistics
Inferential Statistics
Parametric Statistics

NONPARTICIPANT OBSERVATION
S-24-0082 1975 00002
BT Nonreactive Observation
RT Documentary Research
Library Research

NONPARTISAN BALLOT
S-29-0154 1975 00000
BT Ballot
RT Bipartisan Voting
Long Ballot
Machine Ballot
Office Block Ballot
Paper Ballot
Political Party Column Ballot
Political Party List Ballot
Short Ballot

NONPARTISAN ELECTION
S-29-0060 1975 00005
BT Election Type
RT Electoral Outcome
Nonpartisan Primary
Partisan Election

NONPARTISAN PRIMARY
S-29-0075 1975 00000
BT Open Primary
RT Nonpartisan Election
Partisan Primary

NONPROBABILITY SAMPLING
S-24-0118 1975 00000
BT Sampling Procedure
NT Haphazard Sampling
Purposive Sampling
Quota Sampling
RT Area Sampling

NONPROFIT INSTITUTION
S-19-0290 1979 00000
BT Institutions
RT Charitable Organization
Education Policy
Government Grant
Taxation Policy

NONREACTIVE OBSERVATION
S-24-0078 1975 00000
BT Data Collection Methodology
NT Documentary Research
Library Research
Nonparticipant Observation
RT Field Research
Questionnaire
Reactive Observation

NONVERBAL COMMUNICATION
S-31-0188 1975 00048
BT Communication Process
NT Political Communication
Political Propaganda
RT Behavior Analysis
Communication Analysis
Communication Flow
Communication Model
Group Behavior
Individual Behavior
Individual Perception
Informal Communication
Information Dissemination
International Communication
Interpersonal Communication
Interpersonal Cooperation
Mass Communication
Political Communication

NONVERBAL LEARNING
S-34-0010 1979 00000
BT Learning
RT Learning Psychology
Learning Theory
Symbol Learning
Verbal Learning

NONVIOLENT RESISTANCE THEORY
S-38-0283 1975 00004
BT Pacifism
NT Gandhiism
RT International Pacifism

NONVOTER
S-32-0323 1975 00000
BT Voter
RT Alienated Voter
Apathetic Voter
Nonvoting
Voting Abstention

NONVOTING
S-29-0115 1975 00001
BT Electoral Participation
NT Disenfranchisement
Voting Abstention
RT Nonvoter
Political Powerlessness
Voting

NONWESTERN CULTURE
S-11-0021 1975 00009
BT Culture Type
NT Eastern Culture
RT Eastern Political Thought
North African Area Studies
Oral History
Oriental Despot
Oriental Despotism
Religious Culture
Secular Culture
Taoism
Traditional Culture
Village Culture

NONWESTERN SOCIETY
S-35-0006 1975 00006
BT Society Type
RT Eastern Political Thought
Islamic Society
Nomadic Society
Oriental Despot
Oriental Despotism
Peasant Society
Primitive Society

NONZERO SUM GAMING
S-24-0101 1975 00001
BT Gaming
RT Fixed Sum Gaming
Prisoner Dilemma Gaming
Two Person Gaming
Variable Sum Gaming
Zero Sum Gaming

NORMATIVE ANALYSIS
S-24-0030 1975 00039
BT Analysis Methodology
RT Analysis Framework
Emotive Ethical Theory
Ethical Relativism
Ethical Theory
Hermeneutical Analysis
Historical Analysis
Metaethical Theory
Qualitative Analysis

NORMATIVE EVALUATION
S-31-0694 1975 00034
BT Policy Evaluation
RT Education Evaluation
Evaluating
Formative Evaluation
Objectivism
Research Evaluation
Social Accounting
Summative Evaluation

NORMLESSNESS
S-06-0084 1975 00008
BT Alienation
NT Political Normlessness
RT Ambivalence
Anomic Process
Anomie
Anomie Scale
Apathy
Atomistic Society
Cultural Alienation
Mass Society
Political Alienation
Political Alienation Scale
Political Alienation Theory

NORTH AFRICAN AREA STUDIES
S-01-0028 1975 00055
BT African Area Studies
RT Central African Area Studies
Comparative Analysis
Comparative Political Studies
Comparative Sociology
Cultural History
East African Area Studies
Ethnic Studies
Nonwestern Culture
South African Area Studies
West African Area Studies

NORTH AMERICAN AREA STUDIES
S-01-0035 1975 00172
BT American Area Studies
RT Caribbean Area Studies
Central American Area Studies
Comparative Analysis
Comparative Political Studies
Comparative Sociology
Cultural Anthropology
Cultural History
Latin American Area Studies

NORTH SOUTH CONFLICT
S-08-0086 1979 00000
BT International Conflict
RT Class Struggle
Economic Conflict
Fourth World Nation
Geography Discipline
Geopolitics
Ideological Conflict
Ideological Struggle
International Regional Conflict
Regional Development
Regional Security
United Nations

NOVEL
S-18-0072 1979 00000
BT Information Sources
RT Humanistic Education
Humanities Discipline
Humanities Education
Poetry
Political Fiction
Political Memoir
Short Story

NUCLEAR ARMS RACE
S-06-0661 1975 00026
BT Arms Race
RT MARV
MIRV
Strategic Arms Race
Strategic Arms Reduction Policy

NUCLEAR CAPABILITY
S-06-0463 1975 00036
BT Military Characteristics
NT First Strike Capability
Offensive Nuclear Capability
Second Strike Capability
RT Defensive Capability
Retaliatory Capability
Strategic Advantage

NUCLEAR DETERRENCE POLICY
S-26-0065 1975 00024
BT Deterrence Policy
RT Mutual Deterrence Policy
National Chief Executive Election Campaign
Strategic Arms Limitation

NUCLEAR DISARMAMENT POLICY
S-26-0059 1975 00018
BT Disarmament Policy
RT Balanced Force Reduction Policy
Peaceful Coexistence
Strategic Arms Reduction Policy

NUCLEAR ENERGY
S-31-0124 1979 00000
BT Natural Resource Exploitation
RT Coal Energy
Energy Policy
Gas Energy

Geothermal Energy
Oil Energy
Solar Energy
Tidal Energy
Wind Energy

NUCLEAR ENERGY INDUSTRY
S-17-0040 1979 00000
BT Energy Industry
RT Coal Industry
Electrical Industry
Energy Consumption
Energy Use Policy
Gas Industry
Nuclear Power
Oil Industry
Ore Industry
Radiation Level
Solar Energy

NUCLEAR FAMILY
S-20-0013 1975 00025
BT Family Type
RT Atomistic Family
Atomistic Society
Family Role
Industrial Society
Monogamy
Sibling
Stem Family

NUCLEAR NONPROLIFERATION AGREEMENT
S-02-0091 1975 00013
BT State Agreement Type
NT Nuclear Nonproliferation Treaty
RT Disarmament Agreement
Peaceful Coexistence
Strategic Arms Limitation
Test Ban Agreement

NUCLEAR NONPROLIFERATION TREATY
S-02-0092 1975 00019
BT Nuclear Nonproliferation Agreement
RT Disarmament Treaty
Strategic Arms Limitation
Test Ban Treaty

NUCLEAR PARITY
S-06-0666 1975 00009
BT Balance Of Terror
RT Detente
Nuclear Weapon Proliferation
Strategic Arms Limitation

NUCLEAR POWER
S-33-0012 1975 00079
BT War Technology
RT Geothermal Energy
Military Establishment
Mutual Deterrence System
Nuclear Energy Industry
Offensive Weapon System
Radiation Level

NUCLEAR STOCKPILING
S-33-0037 1979 00000
BT Nuclear Weapon
RT Arms Control Agreement
Defensive Capability
Nuclear Strategy
Nuclear Weapon Proliferation
Preemptive Attack Policy
Preventive Attack Policy
Second Strike Policy
Strategic Studies

NUCLEAR STRATEGY
S-26-0066 1975 00038
BT Defense Policy
NT Assured Destruction Policy
Damage Limiting Strategy
Massive Retaliation Policy
Nuclear Strike Policy
RT Arms Control Policy
Deterrence Policy
Military Policy
Nuclear Stockpiling
Rearmament Policy
Strategic Arms Race
War Declaration Policy

NUCLEAR STRIKE POLICY
S-26-0070 1975 00014
BT Nuclear Strategy
NT First Strike Policy
Preemptive Attack Policy
Preventive Attack Policy
Second Strike Policy
RT Damage Limiting Strategy
Strategic Advantage

NUCLEAR WAR
S-08-0102 1975 00022
BT War
RT Biological War
Chemical War
Offensive Nuclear Capability
Total War
World War

NUCLEAR WEAPON
S-33-0035 1975 00039
BT Weapon
NT First Strike Nuclear Weapon
Nuclear Stockpiling
Second Strike Nuclear Weapon
RT Antiballistic Missile
Ballistic Missile
Biological Weapon
Bomb
Chemical Weapon
Conventional Weapon
Defensive Weapon
MARV
MIRV
Missile
Multiple Warhead Missile
Munitions
Strategic Weapon
Tactical Weapon
Unconventional Weapon
War

NUCLEAR WEAPON NONPROLIFERATION POLICY
S-26-0060 1975 00027
BT Arms Control Policy
RT Arms Control Policy
Arms Inspection Policy
Arms Reduction Policy
Disarmament Policy
Military Policy
Strategic Arms Limitation

NUCLEAR WEAPON PROLIFERATION
S-06-0662 1975 00069
BT Arms Race
RT Nuclear Parity
Nuclear Stockpiling
Strategic Arms Race
Strategic Arms Reduction Policy

NUISANCE TAXATION
S-26-0158 1975 00000
BT Taxation Policy
RT Excise Taxation Policy
Import Duty
Inheritance Taxation
Luxury Taxation
Property Taxation
Sales Taxation
Social Security Taxation
Tariff

NULLIFICATION DOCTRINE
S-38-0452 1975 00000
BT Constitutional Structural Theory
RT Judicial Review

NURSERY SCHOOL
USE Child Care Service

NURSING HOME
S-19-0250 1979 00000
BT Health Care Institution
RT Halfway House
Health Care Policy
Health Care Rights
Health Care System
Health Clinic
Hospital
Neighborhood Clinic
Private Hospital
Public Hospital

OBEDIENCE
S-05-0019 1979 00000
BT Political Behavior
RT Authority
Habitual Behavior
Legitimacy Theory
Obligation Theory
Political Legitimacy Theory
Socratic Political Thought

OBITER DICTA
S-31-0485 1975 00000
SN Supplementary opinions by judges on matters of the case not essential to the judicial decision.
BT Court Action
RT Cease Desist Order
Consent Judgment
Injunction
Life Sentence
Subpoena
Verdict
Warrant
Writ Of Mandamus

OBITUARIES
S-18-0073 1975 00000
BT Information Sources
RT Morbidity Data
Vital Statistics Data

OBJECTIVELY DERIVED STATUS
S-06-0789 1979 00000
BT Status Stratification Division
RT Achieved Status
Ascribed Status
Social Background
Status Stratification Division
Subjectively Derived Status
Vertical Stratification Division

OBJECTIVISM
S-25-0025 1975 00003
SN Doctrine that objects external to cognition are primary.
BT Epistemology
RT Empiricism
Materialism
Neopositivism
Normative Evaluation
Objectivist Political Thought
Scientism

OBJECTIVIST POLITICAL THOUGHT
S-38-0199 1975 00000
BT Conservatism
RT American Conservatism
Burkean Conservatism
Neoconservatism
Objectivism
Reactionary Conservatism
Status Quo Conservatism

OBLIGATION THEORY
S-38-0496 1975 00034
BT Political Philosophy Concept
RT Authority
Consent Theory
General Will Theory
Justice Theory
Legitimacy Theory
Liberty Theory
Natural Law Conventionalism Theory
Obedience
Order Theory
Political Legitimacy Theory
Political Virtue
Socratic Political Thought

OBSERVATION TIME
S-24-0083 1975 00000
BT Data Collection Methodology
NT Cross Sectional Analysis
Longitudinal Analysis
RT Reactive Observation

OCCUPATION CHARACTERISTICS
S-06-0490 1979 00000
BT Characteristics
NT Job Discrimination
Job Dissatisfaction
Job Preference
Job Satisfaction
RT Agricultural Occupation
Career Analysis
Commercial Occupation
Demographic Characteristics
Economic Characteristics
Employment Characteristics
Industrial Occupation
Job Preference
Job Satisfaction
Manpower Policy
Manpower Training
Occupational Role
Right To Job Security
Social Stratification System
Technical Occupation

OCCUPATIONAL IDENTITY
S-06-0392 1975 00044
BT Identity Characteristics
RT Blue Collar Worker
Interest Group
Professional Organization
Social Class Identification
Social Identity

OCCUPATIONAL INTEREST GROUP
S-03-0020 1975 00005
BT Interest Group
RT Association Interest Group
Bar Association
Economic Interest Group
Economic Organization
Industrial Association
Medical Association
Occupational Role
Policy Interest Group
Political Interest Group
Professional Organization
Social Group
Teacher Organization

OCCUPATIONAL ROLE
S-32-0061 1975 00141
BT Roles
NT Agricultural Occupation
Artisan
Commercial Occupation
Foreign Worker
Government Employee
Industrial Occupation
Professional Occupational Role
Unemployed Person
Union Worker
RT Blue Collar Worker
Job Socialization
Occupation Characteristics
Occupational Interest Group

OCEAN FLOOR
USE Seabed Policy

OFFENSIVE CAPABILITY
S-06-0467 1975 00019
BT Military Characteristics
RT Defensive Capability
Offensive Weapon System
Strategic Studies

OFFENSIVE NUCLEAR CAPABILITY
S-06-0465 1975 00006
BT Nuclear Capability
RT First Strike Capability
Nuclear War
Second Strike Capability

OFFENSIVE WEAPON SYSTEM
S-33-0013 1975 00007
BT War Technology
NT Weapon Delivery System
RT Armed Forces
MARV
MIRV
Mutual Deterrence System
Nuclear Power
Offensive Capability

OFFICE BLOCK BALLOT
S-29-0155 1975 00000
BT Ballot
RT Australian Ballot
Long Ballot
Machine Ballot
Nonpartisan Ballot
Paper Ballot
Political Party Column Ballot
Political Party List Ballot
Secret Ballot
Short Ballot

OFFICER CORPS
S-33-0057 1975 00023
BT Regular Army
RT Armed Forces
Military Education
Military Institute
Military Officer
Military Planning
Military Policy
Military Training

OIL ENERGY
S-31-0125 1979 00000
BT Natural Resource Exploitation
RT Coal Energy
Energy Management
Energy Policy
Energy Use Policy
Extractive Industry
Gas Energy
Geothermal Energy
Hydroelectric Energy
Middle East Area Studies
Natural Resource Policy
Nuclear Energy
Solar Energy
Tidal Energy

OIL INDUSTRY
S-17-0046 1975 00131
BT Extractive Industry
RT Chemical Industry
Electrical Industry
Energy Industry
Forestry Industry
Gas Industry
Nuclear Energy Industry
Ore Industry
Solar Energy

OLD AGE
S-06-0185 1975 00021
BT Age
RT Euthanasia
Gerontology
Middle Age
Old Age Assistance Policy

OLD AGE ASSISTANCE POLICY
S-26-0411 1975 00010
BT Social Welfare Policy
RT Gerontology
Medical Care Policy
Mental Health Policy
Old Age
Poverty Policy
Public Health Policy
Retirement
Social Security Policy
Welfare Policy

OLD MIDDLE CLASS
S-06-0773 1975 00001
BT Middle Class
RT Ancient Regime
Bourgeoisie
Propertied Class

OLIGARCHIC GOVERNMENT
S-16-0078 1975 00002
BT Government Type
RT Corporate Fascism
Elitist Democracy
Falangism
Fascist Council
Francoism

Polyarchy
Technocracy

OLIGOPOLY
S-06-0630 1975 00007
BT Monopoly
RT Government Production Enterprise
Perfect Monopoly
Population Distribution
Private Monopoly

OMBUDSMAN
S-32-0010 1975 00004
BT Adjudicator
RT Arbitrator
Broker
Mediator
Moderator
Negotiator

ON LINE INFORMATION SYSTEM
USE Information Service

ON VIEW ARREST
S-31-0509 1975 00000
BT Arrest
RT Arbitrary Arrest
Political Arrest
Warrant Arrest

ONE MAN ONE VOTE REPRESENTATION
S-31-0724 1975 00002
BT Representation Type
RT Districting
Gerrymandering
Organization Theory
Representation Theory
Supreme Court

ONE PARTY DEMOCRACY
1975-1979 00000

ONE PARTY POLITICS
1975-1979 00009

ONE PARTY SYSTEM
1975-1979 00013

ONE POLITICAL PARTY DEMOCRACY
S-16-0026 1979 00000
BT Political Party Democracy
RT Interest Group Politics
Multiparty Democracy
One Political Party Politics
Representation Theory
Two Political Party Democracy

ONE POLITICAL PARTY POLITICS
S-29-0220 1979 00000
BT Partisan Politics
RT Machine Candidate
One Political Party Democracy

ONE POLITICAL PARTY SYSTEM
S-37-0127 1979 00000
BT Political Party System
NT Hegemonic One Party System
Modified One Party System
RT Absolutist Government
Authoritarian Regime
Bolshevism
Boss Politics
Centralized Authority
Centralized Government
Concentrated Power
Despotism
Dictatorial Regime
Falangism
Fascist Theory
Francoism
Italian Fascism
Totalitarian Dictatorship
Totalitarian Political System
Two Political Party System

ONTOLOGICAL EXISTENTIALISM
S-38-0066 1975 00003
BT Existentialism
RT Estrangement
Existential Psychologism
Human Condition Theory
Individual Freedom Theory
Political Freedom Theory

ONTOLOGY
S-25-0051 1979 00000
BT Metaphysics
RT Epistemology
Eschatology
Ethical Theory
Jurisprudence
Metaethical Theory

OPEN CLASS SOCIAL SYSTEM
S-37-0144 1975 00004
BT Class Social System
RT Closed Class Social System
Social Mobility

OPEN DOOR POLICY
S-26-0269 1975 00000
BT Foreign Policy
RT Colonialism
Colony
Economic Interference Policy
Imperialism
Intervention Policy
Political Interference Policy
Political Intervention Policy

OPEN ENDED QUESTIONNAIRE
S-24-0093 1975 00002
BT Questionnaire
RT Closed Questionnaire
Mail Questionnaire
Self Administered Questionnaire
Telephone Questionnaire

OPEN HOUSING POLICY
S-26-0386 1975 00004
BT Housing Policy
RT Relocation Policy

OPEN LEADERSHIP
S-22-0018 1975 00000
BT Leadership Structure Type
RT Democratic Leadership
Elite Competition
National Leadership
Open Society
Political Leadership

OPEN PRIMARY
S-29-0074 1975 00001
BT Election Type
NT Nonpartisan Primary
RT Blanket Primary
Closed Primary
National Primary
Political Party Primary
Preference Primary

OPEN SOCIETY
S-35-0043 1975 00004
BT Society Type Structure
RT Closed Society
Democratic Coalition
Democratic Regime
Democratization
Heterogeneous Society
Open Leadership
Open Society Theory
Plural Society
Social Democracy

OPEN SOCIETY THEORY
S-38-0497 1975 00003
BT Political Philosophy Concept
RT Democratic Regime
Democratization
Heterogeneous Society
Open Society
Plural Society
Social Democracy

OPEN UNIVERSITY
S-19-0214 1979 00000
BT University
RT Citizen Participation
College
Education Policy
Education Process
Neighborhood School
Private University
Public University
Urban School

OPERATIONALIZATION
S-24-0252 1975 00025
SN Process of establishing empirical indicators for a variable or concept.
BT Measurement
NT Coding
Conceptual Equivalence
Indicator
Measures
Multiple Operationalization
RT Applied Research
Concept Explication Research
Intelligence Quotient
Measurement Procedure
Multiple Indicator

OPINION CHANGE
S-34-0042 1975 00032
BT Opinion Socialization
RT Attitude Change Theory
Attitude Cluster
Attitude Measurement
Opinion Formation
Opinion Stability
Political Orientation Development
Political Value Acquisition

OPINION COALITION
S-02-0018 1975 00000
BT Coalition Type
RT Attitude Cluster
Attitude Measurement
Coalition Type
Electoral Coalition
Governing Coalition
Interest Group Coalition
Issue Voter
Legislative Coalition
Political Coalition
Voting Coalition
Winning Coalition

OPINION ELITE
S-14-0019 1975 00002
BT Elite Type
NT Attentive Public

RT Cultural Elite
Foreign Policy Elite
Governing Elite
Intellectual Elite
Literary Elite
Modernizing Elite
Opinion Formation
Opinion Leader
Opinion Socialization
Policy Elite
Social Elite

OPINION FORMATION
S-34-0043 1975 00040
BT Opinion Socialization
RT Opinion Change
Opinion Elite
Opinion Stability
Political Orientation Development
Political Value Acquisition

OPINION LEADER
S-32-0059 1975 00006
BT Social Leader
NT Public Opinion Leader
RT Charismatic Leader
Community Leader
Opinion Elite
Parliamentary Speaker
Religious Leader

OPINION SOCIALIZATION
S-34-0041 1975 00009
BT Socialization Type
NT Opinion Change
Opinion Formation
Opinion Stability
RT Attentive Public
Opinion Elite
Perception Socialization
Political Orientation Development
Political Socialization
Political Value Acquisition
Role Socialization
Social Conditioning

OPINION STABILITY
S-34-0044 1975 00013
BT Opinion Socialization
RT Opinion Change
Opinion Formation
Political Orientation Development
Political Value Acquisition

OPPORTUNITY CHARACTERISTICS
S-06-0495 1975 00022
BT Characteristics
NT Education Opportunity
Employment Opportunity
Equal Opportunity
RT Affirmative Action Employment Policy
Ambition
Economic Characteristics
Job Preference

OPPOSITION PARTY
1975-1979 00009

OPPOSITION POLITICAL PARTY
S-28-0030 1979 00000
BT Political Party Type
RT Minor Political Party
Political Opposition
Political Tolerance

OPPOSITION POLITICAL PARTY LEADER
S-32-0154 1975 00002
BT Political Party Leader
RT Backbencher
Formal Political Party Leader
National Legislative Leader
Political Opposition
Political Party Cadre
Political Party Chief

OPPRESSION
USE Power Abuse

OPTIMISM
S-06-0517 1979 00000
BT Personality Characteristics
RT Altruism
Ambivalence
Assertiveness
Charity
Courage
Creativity
Curiosity
Egocentrism
Empathy
Femininity
Gregariousness
Happiness
Honesty
Imagination
Masculinity
Persistence
Pessimism

OPTIMISM PESSIMISM SCALE
S-24-0242 1975 00003
BT Scale Type
RT Alienation Scale
Anomie Scale
Civic Competence Scale
Cynicism Scale
Dogmatism Scale
Efficacy Scale
Frustration Scale
Left Right Scale
Legitimacy Scale
Liberalism Conservatism Scale
Satisfaction Scale
Social Frustration Scale
Support Opposition Scale

OPTIMIZING MODEL
S-24-0309 1975 00053
BT Social Science Model
RT Development Model
Economic Growth Model
Rational Choice Model

ORAL HISTORY
S-01-0114 1975 00011
BT History Discipline
RT Ancient History
Black History
Cultural History
Folk Literature
Historiography
Intellectual History
Mythology
Nonwestern Culture
Political History
Psychohistory
Religious History
Ritual
Sociolinguistics

ORDER THEORY
S-38-0498 1975 00014
BT Political Philosophy Concept
RT Authority Theory
Consensus Theory
Hobbesian Absolutism
Justice Theory
Legitimacy Theory
Natural Law Conventionalism Theory
Obligation Theory
Platonic Political Thought
Power Type
Socratic Political Thought

ORDINAL MEASUREMENT
S-24-0174 1975 00005
BT Measurement Level
RT Interval Measurement
Nominal Measurement
Ratio Scale Measurement

ORDINAL SCALE
S-24-0215 1975 00004
BT Scale Construction Methodology
RT Factor Structure
Guttman Scale
Interval Scale
Likert Scale
Measurement Level Scale
Multidimensional Scale
Nominal Scale
Ratio Scale
Scalability Index
Semantic Differential
Thurstone Scale
Unidimensional Scale

ORDINAL SIGNIFICANCE TEST
S-24-0061 1975 00000
BT Statistical Significance Test
RT Binomial Test
Chi Square Test
F Ratio
Interval Significance Test
Mann Whitney U Test
Nominal Significance Test
Wald Wolfowitz Runs Test
Wilcoxian T Test

ORDINARY LANGUAGE PHILOSOPHY
S-38-0069 1975 00007
BT Contemporary Political Thought
NT Wittgensteinian Thought
RT Ethnolinguistics
Language Community
Linguistic Ethical Theory
Metaethical Theory
Philosophical Concept

ORE INDUSTRY
S-17-0047 1975 00006
BT Extractive Industry
RT Electrical Industry
Energy Industry
Forestry Industry
Gas Industry
Nuclear Energy Industry
Oil Industry
Solar Energy

ORGANIC STATE THEORY
S-38-0438 1975 00006
BT Community Philosophical Concept
RT Burkean Conservatism
Divine Right Theory
Early Modern Theory Of The State
Medieval Corporatism
Neoplatonic Political Thought
Platonic Political Thought
Political System Theory

ORGANIZATION BEHAVIOR
S-05-0005 1975 00062
BT Administrative Behavior
RT Administrative Development Theory
Administrative Theory
Bureaucratic Behavior
Bureaucratic Theory
Executive Behavior
Iron Law Of Oligarchy
Organization Conflict
Organization Theory

ORGANIZATION CAPABILITY CHARACTERISTICS
S-06-0055 1975 00015
BT Organization Characteristics
NT Organization Effectiveness
Organization Efficiency
RT Bureaucratic Characteristics
Group Capability Characteristics
Management Characteristics
Organization Environment
Organization Normative Characteristics
Organization Structural Characteristics
Youth Organization

ORGANIZATION CHANGE
S-31-0037 1975 00051
BT Organization Process
NT Organization Development
Organization Structural Change
RT Administrative Development Theory
Organization Formation
Organization Innovation
Organization Maintenance

ORGANIZATION CHARACTERISTICS
S-06-0054 1975 00051
BT Association Characteristics
NT Organization Capability Characteristics
Organization Composition
Organization Environment
Organization Normative Characteristics
Organization Status
Organization Structural Characteristics
RT Administrative Science
Administrative Theory
Bureaucratic Characteristics
Community Characteristics
Group Characteristics
Line Staff
Management Characteristics
Organization Membership
Organization Theory
Political Party Characteristics
System Characteristics

ORGANIZATION CLEAVAGE CHARACTERISTICS
S-06-0068 1975 00009
BT Organization Structural Characteristics
NT Organization Conflict
RT Bureaucratic Structural Characteristics
Group Composition
Group Solidarity
Heterogeneous Group Membership
Organization Hierarchy
Organization Level
Organization Pluralism
Political Party Factional Cleavage
Social Cleavage

ORGANIZATION COMPOSITION
S-06-0058 1975 00007
BT Organization Characteristics
NT Organization Membership
RT Organization Environment
Organization Goal
Organization Hierarchy
Organization Membership
Organization Pluralism
Organization Size
Organization Status
Organization Structural Characteristics
Organization Theory
Political Party Composition

ORGANIZATION CONFLICT
S-06-0069 1979 00000
BT Organization Cleavage Characteristics
RT Conflict Process
Conflict Theory
Group Conflict
Internal Conflict
Organization Behavior
Organization Goal
Organization Process
Organization Structural Change
Organization Theory
Role Conflict
Social Conflict

ORGANIZATION CONSOLIDATION
S-31-0041 1975 00005
BT Organization Structural Change
RT Organization Disintegration
Organization Formation

ORGANIZATION CONSTRAINT
S-06-0062 1975 00011
BT Organization Normative Characteristics
RT Conflict Of Interest
Group Constraint
Group Discipline
Group Hierarchy
Group Inertia
Organization Formation
Organization Inertia

ORGANIZATION DECISION MAKER
S-32-0029 1975 00014
BT Decision Maker
RT Cultural Decision Maker
Economic Decision Maker
Management
Manager
Organization Membership
Political Decision Maker
Social Decision Maker

ORGANIZATION DEVELOPMENT
S-31-0038 1975 00048
BT Organization Change
NT Organization Formation
RT Administrative Development Theory
Institutional Development
Management
Manager
Organization Formation
Organization Structural Change

ORGANIZATION DISINTEGRATION
S-31-0042 1975 00009
BT Organization Structural Change
RT Anomie
Anomie Scale
Organization Consolidation

ORGANIZATION EFFECTIVENESS
S-06-0056 1975 00049
BT Organization Capability Characteristics
RT Bureaucratic Theory
Management
Management Information System
Manager
Organization Efficiency

ORGANIZATION EFFICIENCY
S-06-0057 1975 00013
BT Organization Capability Characteristics
RT Bureaucratic Theory
Group Effectiveness
Group Efficiency
Management
Management Information System
Manager
Organization Effectiveness

ORGANIZATION ENVIRONMENT
S-06-0060 1979 00000
BT Organization Characteristics
RT Administrative Behavior
Administrative Science
Administrative Theory
Analytic System Characteristics
Behavioral Theory
Contextual Analysis
Organization Capability Characteristics
Organization Composition
Organization Normative Characteristics
Organization Structural Characteristics
System Analysis

ORGANIZATION FLEXIBILITY
S-06-0070 1975 00007
BT Organization Structural Characteristics
RT Bureaucratic Theory
Group Flexibility
Management
Organization Hierarchy
Organization Inertia
Organization Membership
Organization Size

ORGANIZATION FORMATION
S-31-0039 1975 00012
BT Organization Development
RT Administrative Development Theory
Coalition Theory
Institutional Development
Organization Change
Organization Consolidation
Organization Constraint
Organization Development
Organization Innovation
Organization Structural Change

ORGANIZATION GOAL
S-06-0063 1975 00018
BT Organization Normative Characteristics
RT Group Goal
Group Normative Characteristics
Group Solidarity
Management
Organization Composition
Organization Conflict
Organization Rationality

ORGANIZATION HIERARCHY
S-06-0071 1975 00023
BT Organization Structural Characteristics
RT Bureaucratic Theory
Group Hierarchy
Line Staff
Management
Organization Cleavage Characteristics
Organization Composition
Organization Flexibility
Organization Inertia
Organization Level
Organization Size
Weberian Analysis

ORGANIZATION INERTIA
S-06-0072 1975 00002
BT Organization Structural Characteristics
RT Group Inertia
Group Structural Characteristics
Organization Constraint
Organization Flexibility
Organization Hierarchy

ORGANIZATION INNOVATION
S-31-0043 1975 00029
BT Organization Process
RT Administrative Development Theory
Organization Change
Organization Formation
Organization Maintenance
Organization Structural Change
Technological Change

ORGANIZATION LEVEL
S-06-0073 1975 00001
BT Organization Structural Characteristics
RT Group Structural Characteristics
Organization Cleavage Characteristics
Organization Hierarchy
Organization Size

ORGANIZATION MAINTENANCE
S-31-0044 1975 00008
BT Organization Process
RT Organization Change
Organization Innovation

ORGANIZATION MEMBERSHIP
S-06-0059 1975 00016
BT Organization Composition
RT Organization Characteristics
Organization Composition
Organization Decision Maker
Organization Flexibility
Organization Size
Organization Status
Recruitment Process
Religious Affiliation

ORGANIZATION MODEL
S-24-0310 1975 00029
BT Social Science Model
RT Administrative Science
Hierarchical Model
Institutions
Iron Law Of Oligarchy
Social Power Model

ORGANIZATION NORMATIVE CHARACTERISTICS
S-06-0061 1975 00019
BT Organization Characteristics
NT Organization Constraint
Organization Goal
Organization Pluralism
Organization Rationality
RT Group Discipline
Group Goal
Group Rationality
Organization Capability Characteristics
Organization Environment
Organization Structural Characteristics
Political Party Normative Characteristics
Professional Organization
Youth Organization

ORGANIZATION PLURALISM
S-06-0064 1975 00007
BT Organization Normative Characteristics
RT Group Composition
Group Dynamics
Group Pluralism
Group Structural Characteristics
Organization Cleavage Characteristics
Organization Composition
Organization Structural Characteristics

ORGANIZATION PROCESS
S-31-0036 1975 00018
BT Associational Process
NT Organization Change
Organization Innovation
Organization Maintenance
RT Group Process
Organization Conflict
Professional Organization

ORGANIZATION RATIONALITY
S-06-0065 1975 00009
BT Organization Normative Characteristics
RT Bureaucratic Behavior
Bureaucratic Theory
Organization Goal

ORGANIZATION SIZE
S-06-0074 1975 00017
BT Organization Structural Characteristics
RT Group Composition
Group Size
Group Solidarity
Group Structural Characteristics
Organization Composition
Organization Flexibility
Organization Hierarchy
Organization Level
Organization Membership

ORGANIZATION STATUS
S-06-0066 1975 00003
BT Organization Characteristics
RT Group Status
Organization Composition
Organization Membership

ORGANIZATION STRUCTURAL CHANGE
S-31-0040 1975 00022
BT Organization Change
NT Organization Consolidation
Organization Disintegration
RT Coalition Structural Change
Organization Conflict
Organization Development
Organization Formation
Organization Innovation

ORGANIZATION STRUCTURAL CHARACTERISTICS
S-06-0067 1975 00078
BT Organization Characteristics
NT Organization Cleavage Characteristics
Organization Flexibility
Organization Hierarchy
Organization Inertia
Organization Level
Organization Size
RT Community Cleavage Characteristics
Community Structural Characteristics
Group Cleavage Characteristics
Group Structural Characteristics
Organization Capability Characteristics
Organization Composition
Organization Environment
Organization Normative Characteristics
Organization Pluralism
Political Party Structural Characteristics

ORGANIZATION THEORY
S-38-0038 1975 00096
BT Theory
NT Administrative Theory
Bureaucratic Theory
Multinational Organization Theory
Social Organization Theory
RT Administrative Development Theory
Administrative Science
Contingency Theory
Explanatory Political Theory
Government Bureaucracy
Macropolitical Theory
One Man One Vote Representation
Organization Behavior
Organization Characteristics

Organization Composition
Organization Conflict
Organizations

ORGANIZATION VARIABLE
S-24-0453 1975 00008
BT Social Variable
RT Institutional Variable

ORGANIZATIONS
S-03-0036 1975 00009
BT Associations
NT Civic Organization
Cultural Organization
Economic Organization
Employer Organization
Ethnic Organization
Fraternal Organization
International Organization
Peasant Organization
Philanthropic Organization
Professional Organization
Religious Organization
Trade Organization
Veterans Organization
Worker Organization
RT Bureaucracy
Groups
Management
Organization Theory
Policy Interest Group
Voluntary Association

ORGANIZED CRIME
S-10-0051 1975 00002
BT Crime
RT Assassination
Crime Against Humanity
Economic Conspiracy
Economic Espionage
Economic Sabotage
Industrial Espionage
Pornographic Crime
Robbery

ORGANIZED POLITICAL VIOLENCE
1975-1979 00009

ORIENTAL DESPOT
S-32-0223 1975 00000
BT Despot
RT Benevolent Despot
Benevolent Despotism
Nonwestern Culture
Nonwestern Society
Oriental Despotism

ORIENTAL DESPOTISM
S-16-0143 1975 00002
BT Despotism
RT Benevolent Despotism
Eastern Political Thought
Hydraulic Theory
Nonwestern Culture
Nonwestern Society
Oriental Despot
Warlord

ORIGIN
S-06-0198 1975 00002
BT Demographic Characteristics
NT Ancestry
Class Origin
Ethnic Origin
Geographic Origin
National Origin
Socioeconomic Background
RT Population Attribute
Population Composition

ORIGINAL JURISDICTION
S-06-0407 1975 00000
BT Court Jurisdiction
RT Appellate Jurisdiction
Constitutional Jurisdiction
Judicial Process

OSTRACISM
S-31-0753 1979 00000
BT Social Process
RT Caste Formation
Caste Maintenance
Exile
Selection Process
Social Role Process
Social Stratification Formation
Social Stratification Maintenance
Social Stratification Process

OTHER DIRECTED PERSONALITY
S-06-0533 1975 00002
BT Personality Type
RT Conformity Behavior
Inner Directed Personality
Other Directedness

OTHER DIRECTEDNESS
S-06-0116 1975 00002
BT Attitude Characteristics
RT Altruism
Conformity Behavior
Empathy
Gregariousness
Inner Directedness
Other Directed Personality
Tolerance
Trust

OUTER CITY
S-07-0011 1975 00002
BT Metropolitan City
RT Inner City
Megalopolis
Metropolis
Municipality
Neighborhood
Suburb

OUTER SPACE LAW
S-21-0065 1975 00005
BT Law Type
RT Extraterritorial Development

OUTREACH EDUCATION
S-13-0028 1979 00000
BT Education Type
RT Adult Education
Global Education
Informal Education
Professional Education
Teacher Education

OVER SPECIALIZATION
S-31-0834 1979 00000
BT Specialization Process
RT Professional Education
Professional Politician
Professional School

OVEREMPLOYMENT
S-06-0652 1975 00000
BT Employment Characteristics
RT Full Employment
Labor Force
Labor Market
Labor Supply
Labor Surplus
Underemployment
Unemployment

OVERLAPPING MEMBERSHIP
S-06-0023 1975 00002
BT Group Composition
RT Cross Pressure Theory
Group Structural Characteristics
Heterogeneous Group Membership
Homogeneous Group Membership
Interlocking Group Membership
Multiple Group Membership
Social Stratification Division

OXFORD IDEALISM
S-38-0419 1975 00000
SN English nineteenth century neo-Hegelian thought emphasizing positive freedom and the state as a moral entity.
BT Modern Idealism
RT Liberalism
Philosophical Idealism

PACIFICATION POLICY
S-26-0341 1975 00001
BT War Policy
RT Limited War Policy
Local War Policy
War Reparation Policy

PACIFISM
S-38-0281 1975 00003
BT Ideologies
NT International Pacifism
Nonviolent Resistance Theory
RT Antimilitarism
Antiwar Movement
Conscientious Objector
Gandhiism
Peace
Peace Activist
Peaceful Protest

PAINTING
USE Visual Arts

PAN AFRICAN MOVEMENT
S-27-0036 1975 00004
BT Nationalist Movement
RT Black Nationalist Movement
Pan Arab Movement

PAN AFRICANISM
S-38-0266 1975 00007
BT Cultural Nationalism
RT Black Nationalism
Cultural Identity
Extranational Bloc
Irredentism
Pan Arabism
Pan Islamism

PAN ARAB MOVEMENT
S-27-0037 1975 00002
BT Nationalist Movement
RT Islamic Civilization
Pan African Movement
Pan Slav Movement
Supranational Security

PAN ARABISM
S-38-0267 1975 00003
BT Cultural Nationalism
RT Black Muslim
Black Nationalism

Cultural Identity
Extranational Bloc
Irredentism
Pan Africanism
Pan Islamism

PAN ISLAMISM
S-38-0268 1975 00001
BT Cultural Nationalism
RT Arab Bloc
Black Muslim
Black Nationalism
Cultural Identity
Extranational Bloc
Holy War
Irredentism
Islamic Society
Middle East Area Studies
Pan Africanism
Pan Arabism
Religious Culture
Religious Movement

PAN SLAV MOVEMENT
S-27-0038 1975 00000
BT Nationalist Movement
RT Cultural Identity
Nationalism
Nationalist Movement
Pan Arab Movement
Pan Slavism
Religious Culture
Religious Movement

PAN SLAVISM
S-38-0269 1975 00002
BT Cultural Nationalism
RT Cultural Identity
Extranational Bloc
Irredentism
Pan Slav Movement

PANEL ANALYSIS
S-24-0410 1975 00010
BT Study Scope
RT Comparative Analysis
Panel Technique

PANEL TECHNIQUE
S-24-0087 1975 00002
BT Longitudinal Analysis
RT Cross Lagged Panel Analysis
Panel Analysis
Time Series Analysis

PAPAL SOVEREIGNTY
S-16-0155 1975 00001
BT Sovereignty
RT Canon Law
Catholicism
Conciliar Movement Doctrine
Roman Catholicism
Territory Sovereignty

PAPER BALLOT
S-29-0156 1975 00000
BT Ballot
NT Absentee Ballot
RT Long Ballot
Machine Ballot
Nonpartisan Ballot
Office Block Ballot
Political Party Column Ballot
Political Party List Ballot
Secret Ballot
Short Ballot

PAPER INDUSTRY
S-17-0060 1979 00000
BT Manufacturing Industry
RT Clothing Industry
Light Industry
Machinery Industry
Textile Industry

PARADIGM
S-24-0372 1975 00041
SN Framework for identifying and organizing the basic units of explanation in a subject area.
BT Research Design
RT Analysis Framework
Ideal Type Analysis
Parameter Estimation
Social Science Model

PARAMETER ESTIMATION
S-24-0073 1975 00006
BT Population Estimation
RT Central Tendency Measure
Paradigm
Statistical Inference
Unbiased Estimation

PARAMETRIC STATISTICS
S-24-0068 1975 00003
BT Statistics Type
RT Descriptive Statistics
Inferential Statistics
Nonparametric Statistics

PARAMILITARY FORCES
S-33-0044 1975 00005
BT Irregular Military Forces
NT Paramilitary Organization
RT Armed Forces
Counterrevolution
Fascist Theory
Irregular Forces
Irregular Military Forces
Paramilitary Police
Private Army
Professional Military Forces

PARAMILITARY ORGANIZATION
S-33-0045 1975 00001
BT Paramilitary Forces
RT National Socialism
Private Army
Right To Bear Arms

PARAMILITARY POLICE
S-19-0306 1975 00000
BT Police
RT International Police
Irregular Forces
Irregular Military Forces
National Police
Paramilitary Forces
Private Police
Secret Police
Subnational Police

PARANOIA
S-06-0524 1975 00006
BT Psychosis
RT Distrust
Neurosis
Psychology Discipline
Schizophrenia

PARAPSYCHOLOGY
S-01-0176 1979 00000
BT Psychology Discipline
RT Behavioral Psychology
Developmental Psychology
Freudian Psychology
Gestalt Psychology
Learning Psychology
Philosophy Of Science Studies
Psychiatry
Psychology Discipline
Psychopathology
Social Psychiatry

PARENT
S-32-0044 1979 00000
BT Family Role
RT Anthropology Discipline
Family Planning
Family Policy
Father
Mother
Paternal Role

PARENT RESPONSIBILITY
USE Family Law

PARENTAL AUTHORITY
S-04-0022 1975 00023
BT Authority Type
RT Family Law
Family Policy
Family Role
Family Socialization
Father
Mother
Traditional Authority

PARLIAMENT
S-19-0277 1975 00007
BT National Legislature
RT Congress
Lower House Member
National Assembly
Parliamentary Democracy
Parliamentary Government
Parliamentary Leader
Parliamentary Speaker
Popular Assembly

PARLIAMENT CABINET RELATIONS
S-31-0600 1975 00001
BT Legislative Executive Relations
NT Interpellation
RT Confidence Voting
Congressional Executive Relations
Extraparliamentary Politics
Ministerial Committee
Ministerial Responsibility
Question Period

PARLIAMENTARY CAMPAIGN
1975-1979 00002

PARLIAMENTARY CANDIDATE
S-32-0237 1975 00001
BT National Legislative Candidate
RT Parliamentary Election

PARLIAMENTARY COALITION
S-02-0025 1975 00004
BT Legislative Coalition
RT All Party Coalition
Electoral Coalition
Governing Coalition
Minimum Winning Coalition
Multiparty Coalition
Negative Coalition

Parliamentary Faction
Political Party Coalition
Voting Coalition
Winning Coalition

PARLIAMENTARY COMMISSION OF INQUIRY
S-19-0089 1975 00000
BT Legislative Commission Of Inquiry
RT Parliamentary Committee
Parliamentary Paper
Presidential Commission Of Inquiry
Royal Commission Of Inquiry
White Paper

PARLIAMENTARY COMMITTEE
S-19-0279 1975 00004
BT Parliamentary Committee System
RT Congressional Committee System
Legislative Hearing
Parliamentary Commission Of Inquiry
Parliamentary Committee Chairperson
Parliamentary Committee System
Parliamentary Legislative Staff

PARLIAMENTARY COMMITTEE CHAIRPERSON
S-36-0150 1975 00000
BT National Legislative Committee Chairperson
RT Congressional Committee Chairperson
Parliamentary Committee

PARLIAMENTARY COMMITTEE SYSTEM
S-19-0278 1979 00000
BT National Legislature
NT Parliamentary Committee
Parliamentary Faction
RT Parliamentary Government
Parliamentary Politics
Parliamentary Procedure

PARLIAMENTARY DEMOCRACY
S-16-0022 1975 00005
BT Democratic Government
RT Cabinet Government
Consociational Democracy
Constitutional Democracy
Democratic Political System
Democratic Regime
Democratic Theory
Majoritarian Democracy
Parliament
Parliamentary Government
Representative Democracy

PARLIAMENTARY ELECTION
S-29-0059 1975 00017
BT National Legislative Election
RT Congressional Election
Parliamentary Candidate
Parliamentary Leader

PARLIAMENTARY ELECTION CAMPAIGN
S-29-0032 1979 00000
BT National Legislative Election Campaign
RT Congressional Election Campaign
Election Campaign Advertising
Election Campaign Tactics
Election Type
Electoral Coalition
Electoral Competition
Electoral Participation
Electoral Strategy
Parliamentary Political Party
Parliamentary Politics
Voting Behavior Analysis

PARLIAMENTARY FACTION
S-19-0280 1975 00001
BT Parliamentary Committee System
RT Backbencher
Factionalist
Parliamentary Coalition
Parliamentary Opposition

PARLIAMENTARY GOVERNMENT
S-16-0079 1975 00007
BT Government Type
RT Cabinet
Cabinet Committee
Cabinet Government
Cabinet Member
Coalition Government
Democratic Government
Minority Government
National Government
Parliament
Parliamentary Committee System
Parliamentary Democracy
Parliamentary Procedure Law
Parliamentary Speaker
Upper House Member

PARLIAMENTARY LEADER
S-36-0183 1975 00004
BT National Legislative Leader
RT Congress
Congressional Leader
Frontbencher
Parliament
Parliamentary Election

PARLIAMENTARY LEGISLATIVE STAFF
S-36-0208 1975 00000
BT National Legislative Staff
RT Congressional Legislative Staff
Parliamentary Committee

PARLIAMENTARY MEMBER
S-36-0192 1975 00006
BT National Legislative Member
NT Lower House Member
Upper House Member
RT Backbencher
Congressional Member
Frontbencher

PARLIAMENTARY OPPOSITION
S-06-0699 1975 00002
BT Political Opposition
RT Parliamentary Faction
Parliamentary Whip
Question Period
Shadow Cabinet

PARLIAMENTARY PAPER
S-18-0036 1975 00000
BT Legislative Record
NT White Paper
RT Intergovernmental Document
Parliamentary Commission Of Inquiry

PARLIAMENTARY PARTY
1975-1979 00008

PARLIAMENTARY POLITICAL PARTY
S-28-0047 1979 00000
BT National Legislative Political Party
RT Congressional Political Party
Parliamentary Election Campaign
Parliamentary Whip

PARLIAMENTARY POLITICS
S-29-0215 1975 00015
BT Politics
RT Electoral Politics
Extraparliamentary Politics
National Politics
Parliamentary Committee System
Parliamentary Election Campaign
Parliamentary Procedure Law
Political Coalition
Prime Minister Election Campaign

PARLIAMENTARY PROCEDURE
S-31-0613 1975 00000
BT Legislative Procedure
NT Committee Of The Whole
Executive Session
RT Committee Of The Whole
Committee Rules
Committee Staffing
Confidence Voting
Congressional Procedure
Legislative Calendar
No Confidence Motion
Parliamentary Committee System
Parliamentary Procedure Law
Parliamentary Speaker
Pork Barrel
Senatorial Courtesy

PARLIAMENTARY PROCEDURE LAW
S-21-0079 1975 00000
BT Procedural Law
RT Civil Procedure Law
Congressional Procedure
Legislative Calendar
Parliamentary Government
Parliamentary Politics
Parliamentary Procedure
Parliamentary Speaker
Parliamentary Whip

PARLIAMENTARY REFORM
S-31-0100 1975 00001
BT Legislative Reform
RT Apportionment Reform
Congressional Reform
Legislative Reorganization

PARLIAMENTARY SPEAKER
S-36-0164 1975 00000
BT National Legislative Speaker
NT Lower House Speaker
Upper House Speaker
RT Congressional Speaker
Legislative Calendar
National Political Party Leader
Opinion Leader
Parliament
Parliamentary Government
Parliamentary Procedure
Parliamentary Procedure Law

PARLIAMENTARY WHIP
S-36-0173 1975 00000
BT National Legislative Whip
RT Congressional Whip
Parliamentary Opposition
Parliamentary Political Party
Parliamentary Procedure Law

PAROCHIAL PARTICIPANT CULTURE
1975-1979 00002

PAROCHIAL POLITICAL CULTURE
S-11-0030 1979 00000
SN Orientation towards politics in which neither participation nor sense of political efficacy is strong.
BT Civic Culture
RT Political Subculture

PAROCHIAL SCHOOL
S-19-0225 1975 00004
BT Religious School
RT Church State Policy
Parochial School Subsidy
Private School
Religious Authority
Religious Organization

PAROCHIAL SCHOOL SUBSIDY
S-06-0303 1975 00000
BT Education Subsidy
RT Church State Policy
Parochial School
Private School Subsidy

PAROLE
S-31-0499 1975 00005
BT Post Trial Procedure
RT Internment
Prison Reform
Sentencing

PARSONIAN ANALYSIS
1975-1979 00006

PARSONIAN SOCIOLOGY
1975-1979 00006

PARSONSIAN ANALYSIS
S-09-0069 1979 00000
BT Sociological Analysis
RT Durkheimian Analysis
Marginal Man Analysis
Parsonsian Sociology

PARSONSIAN SOCIOLOGY
S-01-0190 1979 00000
BT Sociology Discipline
RT Parsonsian Analysis
Social Action Theory
Social Science Model
Social Theory
Sociology Of The Professions

PARTIAL CORRELATION ANALYSIS
S-24-0049 1975 00011
BT Multivariate Analysis
RT Analysis Of Variance
Automatic Interaction Detection
Cluster Analysis
Covariance Analysis
Dimensional Analysis
Discriminant Analysis
Factor Analysis
Multiple Correlation Analysis
Multiple Regression Analysis
Path Analysis

PARTICIPANT OBSERVATION
S-24-0114 1975 00009
BT Reactive Observation
RT Anthropological Theory
Case Study
Experimental Observation
Interview
Interviewing Material
Survey Research

PARTICIPATORY DEMOCRACY
S-16-0023 1975 00011
BT Democratic Government
RT Citizen Participation
Consociational Democracy
Democratic Political System
Developed Democracy
Direct Democracy
Elitist Democracy
Initiative Election
Majoritarian Democracy
Mass Democracy
Participatory Democratic Theory
Political Participation
Representative Democracy

PARTICIPATORY DEMOCRATIC THEORY
S-38-0095 1975 00008
BT Democratic Theory
RT Athenian Democratic Theory
Citizen Participation
Concurrent Majority Theory
Confederation Movement
Democratic Elite Theory
Democratization
Economic Theory Of Democracy
General Will Democratic Theory
Guided Democracy Theory
Industrial Democracy
Interest Group Pluralism
Jacksonian Democratic Theory
Jeffersonian Democratic Theory
Majoritarianism
Minority Rights Democratic Theory
Participatory Democracy
Political Participation
Populist Democratic Theory
Republic Theory
Socialist Democratic Theory

PARTICIPATORY MANAGEMENT
S-23-0034 1975 00024
BT Management
NT Worker Management Participation
RT Citizen Participation
Democratic Theory
Economic Management
Personnel Management
Political Participation
Socialist Democratic Theory
Worker Self Management

PARTISAN ELECTION
S-29-0061 1975 00004
BT Election Type
RT Nonpartisan Election
Political Party Primary
Primary Election

PARTISAN IMAGE VOTER
S-32-0325 1975 00017
BT Political Party Voter
RT Ideological Voter
Straight Party Voter

PARTISAN POLITICS
S-29-0216 1975 00017
BT Politics
NT Boss Politics
Machine Politics
Multiparty Politics
One Political Party Politics
Patronage Politics
Two Political Party Politics
RT Electoral Politics
Group Politics
Partisan Primary
Political Party Cohesion
Political Party Electoral Competition
Political Party Identification
Primary Election
Racial Politics
Religious Politics
Sexual Politics

PARTISAN PRIMARY
S-29-0066 1975 00000
BT Closed Primary
NT Political Party Primary
RT Group Politics
Nonpartisan Primary
Partisan Politics
Political Party Cohesion
Political Party Electoral Competition
Political Party Primary

PARTISAN WAR
S-08-0052 1975 00001
BT National Liberation War
RT Civil War
Guerrilla Activity
Guerrilla War
Liberation Front
Maoism
Marxism Leninism
Political Violence
Psychological War

PARTY DEMOCRACY
1975-1979 00002

PARTY SYSTEM
1975-1979 00027
USE Political Party System

PASSIVE RESISTANCE
S-31-0262 1975 00000
BT Resistance
RT Draft Resistance
Gandhiism

PATENT LAW
S-21-0042 1975 00004
BT Economic Law
RT Advanced Technology
Contract Law
Innovation
Technological Development Theory
Technological Progress

PATERNAL ROLE
S-32-0045 1975 00004
BT Family Role
NT Father
RT Father
Household Head
Husband

Maternal Role
Parent

PATERNALISTIC FAMILY
S-20-0014 1975 00003
BT Family Type
RT Patriarchal Kinship System
Patriarchical Government
Patrilineal Family
Traditional Culture

PATH ANALYSIS
S-24-0050 1975 00024
BT Multivariate Analysis
RT Analysis Of Variance
Automatic Interaction Detection
Covariance Analysis
Dimensional Analysis
Discriminant Analysis
Factor Analysis
Multiple Correlation Analysis
Multiple Regression Analysis
Partial Correlation Analysis

PATHOLOGICAL BEHAVIOR
S-05-0011 1979 00000
BT Personal Behavior
RT Behavioral Psychology
Clinical Psychology
Coping Behavior
Deviant Personality
Freudian Psychology
Freudian Theory
Neurosis
Psychiatry
Psychoanalysis
Psychological Theory
Psychology Discipline
Psychopathology
Psychosis
Sexual Behavior
Social Psychiatry
Social Psychology

PATRIARCHAL KINSHIP SYSTEM
S-20-0021 1975 00005
BT Extended Kinship System
RT Bilateral Family Descent Pattern
Kinship Group
Male Chauvinism
Paternalistic Family
Patriarchical Government
Patrilineal Family

PATRIARCHIC GOVERNMENT
1975-1979 00002
USE Patriarchical Government

PATRIARCHICAL GOVERNMENT
S-16-0080 1979 00000
UF Patriarchic Government
BT Government Type
RT Authority Type
Male Chauvinism
Matriarchic Government
Paternalistic Family
Patriarchal Kinship System
Sex Role

PATRILINEAL FAMILY
S-20-0015 1975 00001
BT Family Type
RT Cultural Anthropology
Family Policy
Kinship Group
Paternalistic Family
Patriarchal Kinship System
Serial Monogamy

PATRILINEAL FAMILY DESCENT PATTERN
S-20-0005 1975 00006
BT Family Descent Pattern
RT Bilateral Family Descent Pattern
Clan Role
Clan Society
Communal Solidarity
Family Role

PATRIOTISM
S-38-0274 1975 00007
BT Nationalism
RT Americanism
Cultural Nationalism
Group Normative Characteristics
Group Solidarity
Isolationism
Jingoist
National Chauvinist
National Self Determination
Neutralism
Veterans Organization

PATRON SYSTEM
S-37-0049 1979 00000
BT Economic System
RT Clientelism
Feudal Economic System
Land Ownership Pattern
Land Tenure System
Landowning Class
Patronage Bureaucracy
Patronage Politics

PATRONAGE BUREAUCRACY
S-19-0078 1979 00000
BT Government Bureaucracy
RT Boss Politics
Patron System
Political Appointee
Political Boss
Political Broker
Political Corruption
Political Graft
Political Influence
Political Party Loyalty
Spoils Politics
Spoils System

PATRONAGE POLICY
S-26-0205 1975 00001
BT Employment Policy
RT Civil Service System
Patronage Politics
Patronage Worker
Quota System Policy
Spoils Politics
Spoils System

PATRONAGE POLITICS
S-29-0221 1975 00010
BT Partisan Politics
RT Boss Politics
Machine Candidate
Machine Politics
Nepotism
Patron System
Patronage Policy
Patronage Worker

PATRONAGE WORKER
S-32-0082 1975 00001
BT Government Employee
RT Campaign Contributor
Patronage Policy
Patronage Politics

PATTERN MAINTENANCE
S-06-0600 1975 00001
BT System Maintenance
RT Social System
Structural Adaptation
System Analysis
System Maintenance Capacity

PAYMENT AGREEMENT
S-02-0093 1975 00009
BT State Agreement Type
RT Customs Union

PEACE
S-06-0671 1975 00014
BT International Political System Characteristics
NT International Peace
Limited Peace
RT Agreement
Armistice Policy
Arms Control Policy
Arms Reduction Policy
Cease Fire Policy
Civil Defense Policy
Demilitarization Policy
Demobilization Policy
Friendship Agreement
International Peacekeeping Forces
International Power Theory
International Relations Studies
Pacifism
Peace Activist
Peace Demonstration
Peace Proposal
Peace Studies
Peace Treaty
Political Neutralist
Rapproachment
Truce

PEACE ACTIVIST
S-32-0190 1975 00001
BT Political Activist
RT Antiwar Movement
Conscientious Objector
Demonstrator
Draft Resistance
International Peace
Pacifism
Peace
Peace Demonstration
Peace Movement
Peace Proposal
Peace Studies
Peace Treaty
Peaceful Protest
Student Demonstration

PEACE DEMONSTRATION
S-08-0019 1975 00000
BT Demonstration
RT Civil Rights Demonstration
General Strike
Peace
Peace Activist
Peaceful Protest

Sit In
Social Revolution
Veterans Demonstration
Worker Demonstration

PEACE MOVEMENT
S-27-0040 1975 00002
BT Political Movement
NT Antiwar Movement
RT Civil Rights Movement
Ideological Spectrum Political Movement
Peace Activist
Peaceful Protest
Reform Movement
Resistance Movement
Social Movement

PEACE PROPOSAL
S-02-0094 1975 00011
BT State Agreement Type
RT Detente
Friendship Agreement
Peace
Peace Activist
Peace Studies
Peaceful Protest

PEACE STUDIES
S-01-0149 1975 00044
BT Academic Areas
RT International Conflict
International Power Theory
International Relations Studies
Military History
Military Science
Peace
Peace Activist
Peace Proposal
Peaceful Coexistence
Political Geography
Political Science Discipline
Social Pathology
Sociology Discipline
Strategic Studies

PEACE TREATY
S-02-0095 1975 00005
BT State Agreement Type
RT Arms Control Treaty
Global System
Military Alliance
Nonaggression Agreement
Nonaggression Treaty
Peace
Peace Activist
Peaceful Coexistence

PEACEFUL COEXISTENCE
S-06-0674 1975 00018
BT International Political System Characteristics
NT Detente
Disarmament
Strategic Arms Limitation
RT Arms Control Treaty
Balance Of Power Theory
Balanced Force Reduction Policy
Bipolar International System
Collective Security
Deescalation Policy
Neutrality Treaty
Nonaggression Treaty
Nuclear Disarmament Policy
Nuclear Nonproliferation Agreement
Peace Studies
Peace Treaty
Rapproachment

PEACEFUL PROTEST
S-31-0257 1975 00004
BT Protest
RT Demonstrator
Pacifism
Peace Activist
Peace Demonstration
Peace Movement
Peace Proposal
Protest Politics

PEACEKEEPING FORCES
S-33-0004 1975 00004
BT Multinational Security Forces
NT International Peacekeeping Forces
RT Multilateral Security Forces
United Nations

PEASANT CLASS
S-06-0775 1975 00025
BT Class Stratification Division
NT Landless Peasant Class
RT Agrarian Movement
Agrarian Political Party
Class Society
Class Stratification Division
Farm Economy
Farming
Feudal Society
Landowning Class
Lower Class
Nobility
Peasant Economy
Propertied Class
Traditional Culture

PEASANT COOPERATIVE
S-03-0007 1975 00002
BT Cooperatives
RT Agricultural Cooperative
Cooperative Farm Economy
Farm Economy
Marketing Cooperative
Peasant Organization
Producer Cooperative
Village Cooperative
Worker Cooperative

PEASANT CULTURE
S-11-0047 1975 00028
BT Traditional Culture
RT Ethnocentrism
Nomadic Culture
Traditional Political Culture
Village Culture

PEASANT ECONOMY
S-12-0033 1975 00026
BT Economy Type
RT Agrarian Economy
Barter Economy
Cottage Industry Economy
Depressed Economy
Farm Economy
Nomadic Economy
Peasant Class
Peasant Society
Subsistence Economy
Underdeveloped Economy

PEASANT MOBILIZATION
S-31-0630 1979 00000
BT Mobilization Process
RT Maoism
Maoist
Maoist Political Party
Maoist Revolutionary
Political Mobilization

PEASANT ORGANIZATION
S-03-0049 1975 00006
BT Organizations
RT Caste Society
Cooperatives
Farmer Union
Fraternal Organization
Interest Group Politics
Kinship Role
Peasant Cooperative
Religious Organization

PEASANT PARTY
1975-1979 00001

PEASANT POLITICAL PARTY
S-28-0039 1979 00000
BT Class Based Political Party
RT Agrarian Political Party
Aristocracy Political Party

PEASANT REBELLION
S-08-0058 1975 00029
BT Social Rebellion
RT Class Rebellion
Economic Agitation
Economic Rebellion
Government Overthrow
Group Conflict
Holy War
Marxist Revolution Theory
Mob Violence
Peasant Society
Political Rebellion
Revolution
Student Rebellion
Worker Rebellion

PEASANT SOCIETY
S-35-0026 1975 00048
BT Society Type Base
RT Agrarian Movement
Agrarian Political Party
Class Society
Feudal Society
Lower Class
Nomadic Society
Nonwestern Society
Peasant Economy
Peasant Rebellion
Primitive Society
Squatter Community
Squatter Society
Traditional Society
Tribal Society

PEASANTRY MOBILIZATION
1975-1979 00016

PEDAGOGICAL INSTITUTE
S-19-0210 1975 00001
BT Higher Education Institution
RT Academic Community
Academy Of Science
College
Higher Party School
University

PEDAGOGICAL INSTITUTE EDUCATION
S-13-0013 1975 00002
BT Higher Education
NT Teacher Education
RT Graduate Education
Teacher Education
Traditional Education
University Education

PEER GROUP
S-03-0035 1975 00008
BT Secondary Group
RT Adolescence
Face To Face Group
Family Socialization
Peer Group Socialization
Primary Group Socialization
Professional Organization
Racial Group
Reference Group
Religious Group

PEER GROUP SOCIALIZATION
S-34-0030 1975 00016
BT Group Socialization
RT Adolescent Socialization
Adult Political Socialization
Adult Socialization
Childhood Socialization
Cohort Group Socialization
Elite Socialization
Family Socialization
Interest Group Socialization
Learning Theory
Peer Group
Primary Group Socialization

PENAL INSTITUTION
S-19-0291 1975 00011
BT Institutions
NT Correctional Institution
Detention Center
Prison
RT Criminal Court
Law Enforcement
Law Enforcement System
Police
Prison Reform
Recidivism

PENAL LAW
S-21-0028 1975 00003
BT Criminal Law
RT Amnesty
Criminal Procedure Law
Dean
Death Penalty Law
Decriminalization
Penal Reform
Recidivism
Uniform Code Of Military Justice

PENAL REFORM
S-31-0094 1975 00020
BT Judicial Reform
NT Prison Reform
RT Capital Punishment
Court Reform
Dean
Penal Law
Recidivism
Uniform Code Of Military Justice

PENSION LAW
S-21-0040 1975 00003
BT Labor Law
RT Economic Policy
Employment Policy
Fair Employment Law
Gerontocracy
Minimum Wage Law
Minimum Wage Policy
Quality Of Life

PEOPLES ARMY
S-33-0068 1975 00010
BT Armed Forces
RT Admiralty
Army
Maoism
Marines
Voluntary Armed Forces

PEOPLES ASSEMBLY
S-19-0275 1975 00000
BT National Assembly
RT Congress
Diet
Legislature Type
Peoples Democratic State
Popular Assembly

PEOPLES COURT
S-19-0153 1975 00000
BT Local Court
RT Juror
Law Enforcement System
Military Trial
Military Tribunal

PEOPLES DEMOCRATIC STATE
S-16-0169 1975 00000
BT State Type
RT Communist Government
Communist Studies
Dictatorship Of The Proletariat
East European Area Studies
Marxism Leninism
Peoples Assembly
Puppet State
Revolution
Tutelary Democracy

PEOPLES LIBERATION MOVEMENT
S-27-0027 1975 00001
BT Liberation Movement
RT Black Liberation Movement
Liberation Process
National Liberation Movement
Nationalism
Revolution

PEOPLES WAR POLICY
S-26-0342 1975 00003
BT War Policy
RT Global War Policy
Limited War Policy
Local War Policy
Maoism
Total War Policy

PER CAPITA ANNUAL INCOME
S-06-0340 1975 00004
BT Per Capita Income
RT Economic Development Indicator
Personal Income

PER CAPITA GROSS NATIONAL PRODUCT
S-31-0442 1975 00002
BT Gross National Product
RT Per Capita Income
Standard Of Living

PER CAPITA INCOME
S-06-0339 1975 00013
BT National Income
NT Per Capita Annual Income
RT Economic Growth Index
Economic Indicator
Economic Statistics
Median Income
Per Capita Gross National Product
Personal Income
Quality Of Life

PERCEPTION
S-06-0093 1975 00046
BT Attitude Cluster
NT Decision Maker Perception
RT Behavioral Psychology
Behavioral Science Research
Cognitive Dissonance Theory
Cognitive Measurement
Cognitive Model
Cognitive Theory
Individual Perception
Learning Theory
Perception Measurement
Perception Socialization
Social Psychology

PERCEPTION MEASUREMENT
S-24-0189 1975 00108
BT Measurement Object
RT Attitude Measurement
Behavioral Measurement
Change Measurement
Decision Maker Perception
Elite Perception
Group Measurement
Group Perception
Individual Measurement
Perception
Reality Construction
Reality Testing
Social Psychology
Stereotyping

PERCEPTION SOCIALIZATION
S-34-0045 1975 00024
BT Socialization Type
RT Cognitive Development
Opinion Socialization
Perception
Political Orientation Development
Political Value Acquisition
Social Conditioning

PERFECT COMPETITION
S-31-0210 1975 00001
BT Competition
RT Direct Competition
Formal Competition
Indirect Competition
Unfair Competition

PERFECT MONOPOLY
S-06-0631 1975 00001
BT Monopoly
RT Oligopoly
Private Monopoly
Public Monopoly

PERFORMANCE BUDGET
S-06-0256 1975 00008
BT Capital Budget
RT Budget Planner
Budget Policy
Budget Proposing
Budget Reviewing
Capital Budget
Incremental Budget
Program Budget
Zero Based Budget

PERFORMING ARTS CENSORSHIP
S-31-0281 1975 00000
BT Unpublished Media Censorship
NT Cinema Censorship
Music Censorship
Theater Censorship
RT Editorial Control
Humanities Discipline
Published Media Censorship

PERIODICAL
USE Journal

PERIODICAL PUBLICATION CENSORSHIP
S-31-0269 1975 00000
BT Published Media Censorship
NT Journal Censorship
Newspaper Censorship
RT Book Censorship
Editorial Control
Government Report Censorship
Scientific Report Censorship

PERJURY
S-10-0006 1975 00001
BT Court Crime
RT Fraud
Libel
Slander

PERMANENT REVOLUTION THEORY
S-38-0170 1975 00002
BT Revolution Theory
RT Chinese Cultural Revolution
Guerrilla Activity
Maoist Revolutionary
Trotskyism
Trotskyite Political Party

PERONISM
S-38-0231 1975 00007
BT Fascist Theory
RT Corporate Fascism
Falangism
Francoism
Italian Fascism
National Socialism
Neofascism

PERSECUTION
S-31-0313 1975 00001
BT Repression Process
NT Ethnic Persecution
Minority Persecution
Nationality Persecution
Political Persecution
Racial Persecution
Religious Persecution
Sex Persecution
RT Antisemitism
Discrimination Policy
Exploitation Process
Human Rights
Job Discrimination
Legal Discrimination
Purge
Racial Discrimination

PERSISTENCE
S-06-0526 1979 00000
BT Personality Characteristics
RT Altruism
Ambivalence
Assertiveness
Charity
Courage
Creativity
Curiosity
Egocentrism
Empathy
Femininity
Gregariousness
Honesty
Imagination
Learning Feedback
Masculinity
Optimism

PERSON TO PERSON DIPLOMACY
S-31-0358 1975 00007
BT Diplomacy
NT Citizen To Citizen Diplomacy
RT Diplomatic Recognition
Education Exchange Treaty

PERSONAL BEHAVIOR
S-05-0009 1975 00018
BT Behavior
NT Coping Behavior
Pathological Behavior
Sexual Behavior
RT Avoidance Behavior
Clinical Psychology
Habitual Behavior
Individual Behavior
Moral Learning
Personality Characteristics
Personality Theory
Psychiatry
Psychological Theory
Psychology Discipline
Sexual Behavior
Social Adjustment
Social Behavior
Social Psychiatry
Social Psychology

PERSONAL CRIME CRIMINAL
S-36-0030 1975 00004
BT Criminal
NT Blackmailer
Extortionist
Murderer
Slanderer
RT Economic Criminal
Political Criminal
War Criminal

PERSONAL INCOME
S-06-0341 1975 00029
BT Income
RT Business Income
Corporate Income
Family Income
Fixed Assets
Fixed Income
Median Income
National Income
Net Income
Per Capita Annual Income
Per Capita Income
Profit Income
Unearned Income

PERSONAL INTERVIEW
S-24-0110 1975 00010
BT Interview
RT Depth Interview
Group Interview
Telephone Interview
Unstructured Interview

PERSONAL PURGE
USE Catharsis

PERSONALITY CHARACTERISTICS
S-06-0499 1975 00132
BT Characteristics
NT Altruism
Ambivalence
Assertiveness
Charity
Courage
Creativity
Culture Shock
Curiosity
Egocentrism
Empathy
Femininity
Gregariousness
Happiness
Honesty
Imagination
Masculinity
Optimism
Persistence
Personality Disorder
Personality Type
Pessimism
Virtue
RT Attitude Characteristics
Cognitive Dissonance Theory
Cooperative Behavior
Health Characteristics
Job Preference
Job Satisfaction
Personal Behavior
Personality Theory
Psychohistory
Psychological Theory
Social Psychiatry

PERSONALITY CRISIS
S-31-0249 1979 00000
BT Crisis
RT Crisis
Identity Theory
Personality Type
Psychoanalysis

PERSONALITY DEVELOPMENT
S-31-0082 1975 00026
BT Development Process
NT Cognitive Development
RT Achievement Motivation
Authoritarian Attitude
Basic Personality
Behavior
Behavioral Psychology
Bigotry
Cognitive Dissonance Theory

Cognitive Model
Cognitive System
Deviant Behavior
Individual Attitude
Individual Behavior
Individual Phenomena
Jungian Theory
Learning Psychology
Motivation Theory
Psychohistory
Psychopathology
Social Development Policy
Social Learning Theory
Socialization

PERSONALITY DISORDER
S-06-0520 1975 00015
BT Personality Characteristics
NT Hysteria
Neurosis
Psychosis
RT Behavior Modification
Deviant Personality
Interpersonal Conflict
Jungian Theory
Mental Health Policy
Mental Institution
Personality Type
Psychological Variable
Psychopathology
Social Pathology
Social Psychiatry

PERSONALITY THEORY
S-38-0545 1975 00057
BT Psychological Theory
RT Alienation Psychological Theory
Attribution Theory
Authoritarian Personality
Behavioral Psychology
Behavioral Science
Behavioral Theory
Cognitive Development
Cognitive Dissonance Theory
Cognitive System
Cult Of Personality
Deviant Behavior
Deviant Personality
Distrust
Freudian Psychology
Freudian Theory
Gestalt Theory
Hostility
Hysteria
Interpersonal Conflict
Motivation Measurement
Personal Behavior
Personality Characteristics
Personality Type
Psychology Discipline
Psychopathology
Psychopolitical Theory
Psychosis
Schizophrenia
Social Psychiatry
Socialization

PERSONALITY TYPE
S-06-0527 1975 00017
BT Personality Characteristics
NT Authoritarian Personality
Basic Personality
Deviant Personality
Inner Directed Personality
Modal Personality
Other Directed Personality
RT Culture Shock
Interpersonal Conflict
Personality Crisis
Personality Disorder
Personality Theory

PERSONALIZED LEADERSHIP
S-22-0007 1975 00017
BT Leadership Authority Base
NT Charismatic Leadership
RT Bonapartism
Charismatic Authority
Closed Leadership
Cult Of Personality
Ecclesiastical Leadership
Leadership Structure Type
Moral Leadership
National Leadership
Political Leadership
Political Party Leadership
Political Succession
Religious Leadership
Totalitarian Leadership
Traditional Leadership

PERSONNEL MANAGEMENT
S-23-0003 1975 00034
UF Personnel Promotion
Personnel Selection
BT Administrative Management
RT Business Management
Corporate Management
Human Resources Development
Participatory Management

PERSONNEL PROMOTION
USE Personnel Management

PERSONNEL RECORDS
USE Business Management

PERSONNEL SELECTION
USE Personnel Management

PERT ANALYSIS
S-09-0055 1979 00000
BT Policy Analysis
RT Analysis Methodology
Economic Management
Government Grant
Policy Evaluation Research
Policy Incrementalism
Policy Output Scale
Policy Research
Predictive Research
Qualitative Analysis
Research Management
Statistical Analysis
Trend Analysis

PESSIMISM
S-06-0534 1979 00000
BT Personality Characteristics
RT Alienation
Ambivalence
Apathy
Egocentrism
Empathy
Optimism
Psychological Variable

PETITE BOURGEOISIE
S-06-0771 1975 00004
BT Bourgeoisie
RT Class Analysis
Middle Class
Propertied Class

PHENOMENOLOGICAL EXISTENTIALISM
S-38-0072 1975 00005
BT Phenomenological Thought
RT Existentialism
Phenomenological Psychologism

PHENOMENOLOGICAL MARXISM
S-38-0073 1975 00002
BT Phenomenological Thought
RT Eurocommunism
Marxism
Marxist Theory
Neomarxism
New Left

PHENOMENOLOGICAL PSYCHOLOGISM
S-38-0074 1975 00002
BT Phenomenological Thought
RT Existential Psychologism
Phenomenological Existentialism
Psychological Theory
Psychology Discipline

PHENOMENOLOGICAL THOUGHT
S-38-0071 1975 00014
BT Contemporary Political Thought
NT Phenomenological Existentialism
Phenomenological Marxism
Phenomenological Psychologism
RT Hegelian Analysis
Logic
Philosophical Concept

PHILANTHROPIC ORGANIZATION
S-03-0050 1979 00000
BT Organizations
NT Charitable Organization
RT Government Grant
Grants
Private Sector
Public Policy Analysis
Research Council
Research Grant
Tax Exempt Income
Taxation Policy

PHILOSOPHE THOUGHT
S-38-0405 1975 00000
SN Views held by French enlightenment thinkers emphasizing individual freedom and attacks on organized religion.
BT Enlightenment Thought
RT Encyclopedist Thought
Rousseauian Analysis
Voltairean Analysis

PHILOSOPHIC ANTHROPOLOGY
1975-1979 00004
USE Philosophical Anthropology

PHILOSOPHICAL ANTHROPOLOGY
S-01-0017 1979 00000
SN Examination of the historical unfolding of human nature and its potentials in a social philosophy.
UF Philosophic Anthropology
BT Anthropology Discipline

RT Anthropological Theory
History Of Philosophy
Human Condition Theory
Human Nature Theory
Philosophy Discipline
Political Philosophy Studies
Psychological Anthropology
Social Philosophy

PHILOSOPHICAL CONCEPT
S-25-0001 1975 00008
NT Aesthetics
Cosmology
Eschatology
Jurisprudence
Metaphysics
RT Cartesian Analysis
Classical Political Thought
Community Philosophical Concept
Existentialism
History Of Philosophy
Kantian Analysis
Ordinary Language Philosophy
Phenomenological Thought
Philosophy Discipline
Political Philosophy Concept
Political Theory
Theory
Value Free Science Theory
Wittgensteinian Thought

PHILOSOPHICAL HISTORY
USE History Of Philosophy

PHILOSOPHICAL IDEALISM
S-25-0026 1975 00010
UF Idealism
BT Epistemology
RT German Romanticism
Hegelian Analysis
Intellectual History
Oxford Idealism
Platonic Political Thought
Romanticism

PHILOSOPHICAL MATERIALISM
S-25-0023 1975 00004
BT Materialism
RT Dialectical Materialism
Hobbesian Analysis
Left Hegelianism
Scientific Determinism

PHILOSOPHICAL REALISM
S-25-0027 1975 00003
BT Epistemology
RT Materialism
Scientific Determinism
Scientific Theory
Scientism

PHILOSOPHY DISCIPLINE
S-01-0150 1975 00010
BT Academic Areas
NT Logic
Philosophy Of Action
Philosophy Of Mind
Philosophy Of Science Studies
Social Philosophy
RT Epistemology
Fine Arts
Historiography
History Of Philosophy
Metaphysics
Philosophical Anthropology
Philosophical Concept
Political Philosophy Studies
Political Theory Studies
Sociology Discipline
Sociology Of Knowledge
Socratic Political Thought

PHILOSOPHY OF ACTION
S-01-0152 1979 00000
BT Philosophy Discipline
RT Logic
Symbolic Action

PHILOSOPHY OF MIND
S-01-0153 1979 00000
BT Philosophy Discipline
RT Logic
Symbolic Action

PHILOSOPHY OF SCIENCE STUDIES
S-01-0154 1975 00070
BT Philosophy Discipline
RT General Theory
Historiography
History Of Philosophy
Logic
Natural Science Model
Parapsychology
Political Science Methodology Studies
Sociology Of Knowledge
Theory Of Causality

PHYSICAL ANTHROPOLOGY
S-01-0018 1975 00005
BT Anthropology Discipline
RT Cultural Anthropology
Environmental Studies
Exploration
Explorer
Geography Discipline
Human Geography
Physical Geography
Topography

PHYSICAL GEOGRAPHY
S-01-0090 1975 00003
BT Geography Discipline
NT Climatology
Topography
RT Area Studies
Demographic Studies
Earth Sciences
Ecology Discipline
Economic Geography
Human Geography
Physical Anthropology
Physical Science
Political Geography
Rural Sociology
Urban Geography
Urban Sociology

PHYSICAL SCIENCE
S-01-0148 1975 00007
BT Natural Science Discipline
RT Biological Sciences
Earth Sciences
Ecology Discipline
Engineering Discipline
Environmental Studies
Geography Discipline
Natural Science Education
Physical Geography

PHYSICIAN
S-32-0106 1975 00036
BT Professional Occupational Role
RT Medical Association
Medical Care Policy
Medical Care Service
Medical Education
Professional Socialization

PHYSIOLOGICAL TEST
S-24-0008 1979 00000
BT Education Testing
RT Degree Requirement
Literacy Test
Psychological Test
Test Results

PILOT
S-36-0223 1975 00003
BT Military Service Personnel
RT Air Piracy
Marine
Sailor
Soldier

PIRACY
S-10-0052 1975 00000
BT Crime
NT Air Piracy
Sea Piracy
RT Highjacking
Kidnapping
Maritime Court
Mutiny
Political Crime
War Crime

PLANIFICATION
S-31-0636 1975 00001
SN Approach to multi-year economic planning that emphasizes mutual cooperation and participation of the government and economic units in a country.
BT Administrative Planning
RT Economic Plan
Economic Planner
Economic Planning
Government Economic Management
Multiple Year Economic Plan
National Economic Management
Planner
Public Policy Planning
Public Policy Studies
Social Planning

PLANNED COMMUNITY
S-07-0040 1979 00000
BT Community Type
NT Model City
New Town
RT Model City
New Town
Planned Social Change
Planner
Planning Agency

PLANNED ECONOMY
S-12-0034 1975 00004
BT Economy Type
NT Centrally Planned Economy
Corporate Economy
Nationalized Economy
Socialist Economy
RT Autarchic Economy
Autarchic Government

Capital Investment Economy
Central Economic Management
Central Economic Planning
City Planner
City Policy Planning
Collective Farm Economy
Collective Farming
Command Economy
Communist Economic System
Economic Community
Economic Planning
Government Economic Management
Government Enterprise
Government Expropriation
Grants Economy
Housing Policy
Labor Intensive Economy
Modernizing Economy
Planning Agency
Political Community
Regional Economics
Social Planning
Socialist Market Economy
State Farm Economy
Town
Underdeveloped Economy
Urban Development Theory
Urban Policy Planning
Utopian Community
Village Community
War Economy
Welfare Economy

PLANNED SOCIAL CHANGE
S-31-0163 1975 00015
BT Social Change
RT Centrally Planned Economy
Economic Planning
Planned Community
Planner
Reform

PLANNER
S-32-0129 1975 00007
BT Roles
NT Economic Planner
International Planner
National Planner
Political Planner
Social Planner
Subnational Planner
RT Decision Maker
Economic Planning
Government Economic Management
Government Economic Planning
Planification
Planned Community
Planned Social Change
Urban Policy Planning

PLANNING AGENCY
S-19-0061 1975 00010
BT Agencies
RT Economic Council
Environmental Advisory Agency
Government Agency
Government Economic Planning
Government Expropriation
Planned Community
Planned Economy
Planning Commission
Research Institution

PLANNING COMMISSION
S-19-0094 1975 00002
BT Commissions
NT International Planning Commission
National Planning Commission
Subnational Planning Commission
RT Administrative Planning
Business Regulation Agency
Economic Advisory Board
Economic Agency
Economic Council
Federal Commission
Fiscal Agency
Independent Regulatory Commission
Planning Agency
Presidential Commission
Price Control Agency
Regulation Process
Regulatory Commission

PLANNING POLICY
S-26-0345 1975 00009
BT Policy
NT National Planning Policy
Needs Assessment
Research And Development
Subnational Planning Policy
RT Administrative Planning
Budget Process
Contingency Theory
Economic Plan
Economic Policy
Goal Setting
Government Economic Planning
Government Expropriation

PLANNING PROCESS
S-31-0634 1975 00040
BT Process
NT Administrative Planning
Defense Planning
Development Planning
Economic Planning
Education Planning
Environmental Planning
Long Range Planning
Military Planning
Population Planning
Public Policy Planning
Short Range Planning
Social Planning
RT Contingency Theory
Economic Planner
Economy Type
Government Economic Management
Government Enterprise
Long Range Planning
Management Information System
Policy Making Process
Short Range Planning

PLANNING THEORY
S-38-0044 1975 00040
BT Theory
NT Contingency Theory
RT Contingency Theory
Decision Making Theory
Development Theory
Economic Growth Policy
Economic Growth Theory
Economic Theory
Futurology
Macropolitical Theory
Management Information System

PLANTATION ECONOMY
S-12-0007 1975 00009
BT Farm Economy
RT Absentee Landlord System
Colonialism
Corporate Farm Economy
Export Economy
Family Farm Economy
Labor Intensive Economy
Rubber Industry
Self Sufficient Economy
Single Group Farm Economy
State Farm Economy
Subsistence Economy

PLASTIC ARTS
S-01-0126 1979 00000
BT Fine Arts
RT Art History
Fine Arts
Humanities Discipline

PLATONIC POLITICAL THOUGHT
S-38-0052 1975 00015
BT Classical Political Thought
RT Ancient History
Aristotelian Thought
Augustinian Analysis
Classical Period
Epicurean Thought
Natural Justice Theory
Neoplatonic Political Thought
Order Theory
Organic State Theory
Philosophical Idealism
Presocratic Political Thought
Pythagorean Thought
Skeptic Thought
Stoic Thought

PLEA BARGAINING
S-31-0498 1975 00005
BT Negotiated Legal Settlement
RT Acquittal
Conviction
Pretrial Procedure
Prosecution Immunity
Sentencing

PLEBISCITARY DEMOCRACY
S-16-0028 1975 00000
SN Form of democractic rule in which leaders frequently request approval of policy goals through referenda.
BT Democratic Government
RT Consociational Democracy
Direct Democracy
Majoritarian Democracy
Majoritarianism
Majority Electoral Outcome
Representative Democracy

PLEBISCITE ELECTION
S-29-0062 1979 00000
BT Election Type
RT Critical Election
Direct Democracy
Direct Election
Government Type
National Election
Nationalism
Regime Type

PLOT
S-24-0136 1975 00000
BT Data Presentation Methodology
NT Scatter Plot
RT Chart
Curve
Diagram
Graph
Table

PLURAL EXECUTIVE
S-19-0237 1975 00000
BT Executive Government Institution
RT Chancellery
Chief Government Executive
Plural Voting
Secretariat

PLURAL SOCIETY
S-35-0041 1975 00004
BT Heterogeneous Society
RT Bicultural Society
Group Pluralism
Multicultural Society
Multiethnic Society
Multilingual Society
Open Society
Open Society Theory
Plural Voting

PLURAL VOTING
S-29-0141 1975 00002
SN A method of voting in which the elector casts more than one vote, normally indicating a party and a candidate choice.
BT Voting
RT Group Pluralism
Plural Executive
Plural Society
Voting Behavior
Voting Behavior Analysis

PLURALIST ANALYSIS
S-09-0053 1975 00007
BT Contemporary Analytic Modes
RT Liberal Political Party
Liberal Political Thought
Motivational Analysis
Pluralist Democracy
Pluralist Group Theory
Policy Analysis
Sociological Analysis
Structural Functional Analysis

PLURALIST DEMOCRACY
S-16-0029 1975 00016
BT Democratic Government
RT Consociational Democracy
Democratic Elite Theory
Democratic Regime
Group Pluralism
Mass Democracy
Mixed Government
Pluralist Analysis
Pluralist Group Theory
Pluralistic Society
Political Party Competition
Procedural Democratic Theory
Representative Democracy

PLURALIST ELITE
S-14-0021 1975 00005
BT Elite Type
RT Decision Making Elite
Democratic Elite Theory
Governing Elite
Pluralist Group Theory
Policy Elite
Political Elite
Political Party Competition
Polyarchical Democratic Theory
Revolutionary Elite
Subnational Elite
Transitional Political Elite

PLURALIST GROUP THEORY
S-38-0145 1975 00002
BT Group Theory
RT Cross Pressure Theory
Equilibrium Theory
Pluralist Analysis
Pluralist Democracy
Pluralist Elite
Pluralistic Society
Social Integration Theory

PLURALIST MODEL
S-24-0311 1975 00012
BT Social Science Model
RT Consensus Model
Social System Model
Voluntarism Model

PLURALIST SOCIETY
1975-1979 00022
USE Pluralistic Society

PLURALISTIC SOCIETY
S-35-0044 1979 00000
UF Pluralist Society
BT Society Type Structure
RT Cleavage Process
Community Cleavage Characteristics
Cultural Diversity
Heterogeneous Society
Pluralist Democracy
Pluralist Group Theory
Pluralistic Society
Social System Structural Characteristics
Subculture

PLUTOCRACY
S-16-0081 1975 00000
SN Form of government in which the wealthy rule.
BT Government Type
RT Elite Mass Relations
Elitist Democracy
Policy Elite
Political Elite
Social Elite

POCKET VETO
S-31-0340 1975 00000
BT Veto
RT Administrative Discretion
Executive Veto
Legislative Process

POETRY
S-18-0074 1979 00000
BT Information Sources
RT Humanistic Education
Humanities Discipline
Humanities Education
Novel
Short Story

POLARIZATION
S-31-0816 1975 00011
BT Integration
NT Ideological Polarization
International System Polarization
RT Cleavage Process
Functional Integration
Ideological Indoctrination
Linguistic Integration
Policy Development
Social Integration

POLICE
S-19-0302 1975 00029
BT Institutions
NT International Police
Military Police
National Police
Paramilitary Police
Private Police
Secret Police
Subnational Police
RT Crime Rate
Justice Of The Peace
Law Enforcement
Law Enforcement Official
Law Enforcement Policy
Law Enforcement System
Local Law Enforcement
Local Police Chief
Local Police Official
Penal Institution
Police Community Relations
Prison
Public Order Maintenance
Secret Service

POLICE ADMINISTRATION
S-23-0032 1975 00009
BT Justice Administration
RT Criminal Justice Administration
Law Enforcement
Law Enforcement Official
Law Enforcement Policy
Law Enforcement System
Police Brutality
Police Community Relations

POLICE BOARD
S-19-0056 1975 00000
BT Judicial Administration Agency
RT Law Enforcement
Law Enforcement System
Local Police Chief
Local Police Official
Police Board Policy

POLICE BOARD POLICY
S-26-0313 1975 00000
BT Justice Administration Policy
RT Judicial Appointment Policy
Law Enforcement
Law Enforcement Policy
Local Police
Police Board
Police Community Relations

POLICE BRUTALITY
S-10-0044 1979 00000
BT Individual Crime
RT Assault
Extortion
Police Administration
Police Power

Police State

POLICE COMMUNITY RELATIONS
S-31-0472 1979 00000
BT Intergovernmental Relations
RT City State Relations
Federal City Relations
Federal State Relations
Law System
Legal System
Local Police
Neighborhood
Police
Police Administration
Police Board Policy
Public Order Maintenance
State Police

POLICE POWER
S-04-0033 1975 00005
BT Civil Authority
RT Eminent Domain
Eminent Domain Policy
Law Enforcement
Local Police
Police Brutality
Police State
Policy Enforcement
Public Order Maintenance

POLICE STATE
S-16-0170 1975 00000
BT State Type
RT Integrated Authority
Intelligence Censorship
Local Police
Martial Law
Police Brutality
Police Power
Puppet Regime
Puppet State
Totalitarian Dictatorship

POLICY
S-26-0001 1975 00017
NT Admission Policy
Agricultural Policy
Business Policy
Communication Policy
Consumer Policy
Cultural Policy
Defense Policy
Development Policy
Economic Policy
Education Policy
Employment Policy
Energy Policy
Environment Policy
Exclusionary Policy
Executive Policy
Foreign Policy
Gambling Policy
Health Care Policy
Human Rights Policy
Industrial Policy
Information Policy
Insurance
International Policy
Justice Administration Policy
Labor Policy
Military Policy
Planning Policy
Political Party Policy
Science Policy
Seabed Policy
Service Policy
Social Policy
Technology Policy
Transportation Policy
RT Goal Setting
Management
Policy Analysis
Policy Science Studies
Process
Public Choice Analysis
Racial Prejudice
Theory
Value Analysis

POLICY ANALYSIS
S-09-0054 1975 00157
BT Contemporary Analytic Modes
NT PERT Analysis
Public Policy Analysis
RT Contextual Analysis
Critical Theory Analysis
Decision Making Analysis
Event Analysis
Event Measurement
Issue Intensity
Motivational Analysis
Network Analysis
Pluralist Analysis
Policy
Policy Science Studies
Policy Scientist
Psychoanalysis
Public Choice Analysis
Public Policy Management
Situational Analysis
Sociological Analysis
Value Analysis

POLICY ARTICULATION
S-31-0684 1975 00027
BT Policy Making Process
RT Policy Conflict
Policy Development
Policy Enforcement
Policy Evaluation
Policy Format
Policy Implementation
Policy Incrementalism
Policy Output Scale

POLICY COMPLIANCE
S-31-0685 1979 00000
BT Policy Making Process
RT Policy Enforcement

POLICY CONFLICT
S-31-0686 1975 00033
BT Policy Making Process
RT Bargaining Strategy Process
Bargaining Theory
Policy Articulation
Policy Development
Policy Enforcement
Policy Evaluation
Policy Format
Policy Implementation

POLICY DEVELOPMENT
S-31-0687 1975 00145
BT Policy Making Process
NT Policy Public Opinion Linkage
RT Ethnic Integration
Functional Integration
Polarization
Policy Articulation
Policy Conflict
Policy Enforcement
Policy Evaluation
Policy Format
Policy Implementation
Policy Incrementalism
Policy Output Scale
Political Development Policy

POLICY ELITE
S-14-0025 1975 00032
BT Political Elite
NT Foreign Policy Elite
RT Financial Elite
Governing Elite
Modernizing Elite
Opinion Elite
Pluralist Elite
Plutocracy
Potential Elite
Power Elite

POLICY ENFORCEMENT
S-31-0689 1979 00000
BT Policy Making Process
RT Police Power
Policy Articulation
Policy Compliance
Policy Conflict
Policy Development
Policy Evaluation
Policy Implementation

POLICY EVALUATION
S-31-0690 1975 00687
BT Policy Making Process
NT Education Evaluation
Financial Accounting
Formative Evaluation
Normative Evaluation
Research Evaluation
Social Accounting
Summative Evaluation
RT Policy Articulation
Policy Conflict
Policy Development
Policy Enforcement
Policy Format
Policy Implementation
Policy Incrementalism
Policy Public Opinion Linkage
Short Range Planning

POLICY EVALUATION RESEARCH
S-24-0391 1975 00093
BT Policy Research
RT Applied Anthropology
Applied Research
Brainstorming
Delphi Technique
Divergence Mapping
Forecasting Methodology
Needs Assessment
PERT Analysis
Policy Public Opinion Linkage
Policy Science Studies
Policy Scientist
Political Forecasting
Research And Development

Scenario Construction
Social Forecasting
Trend Analysis

POLICY FOR DISADVANTAGED
S-26-0392 1979 00000
UF Handicapped
BT Social Policy
RT Employment Policy
Handicapped Child
Public Policy Analysis
Safety Policy
Service Policy
Social Service
Social Welfare Policy

POLICY FORMAT
S-31-0698 1975 00103
BT Policy Making Process
RT Collective Policy Making
Idealist Foreign Policy
Policy Articulation
Policy Conflict
Policy Development
Policy Evaluation
Policy Implementation
Policy Incrementalism
Policy Output Scale
Policy Public Opinion Linkage

POLICY IMPLEMENTATION
S-31-0699 1975 00112
BT Policy Making Process
RT Administrative Policy Making
City State Relations
Intergovernmental Relations
Management
Manager
Policy Articulation
Policy Conflict
Policy Development
Policy Enforcement
Policy Evaluation
Policy Format
Policy Incrementalism
Service Delivery System
Short Range Planning

POLICY INCREMENTALISM
S-31-0700 1975 00012
BT Policy Making Process
RT Administrative Policy Making
Administrative Science
Bureaucratic Theory
PERT Analysis
Policy Articulation
Policy Development
Policy Evaluation
Policy Format
Policy Implementation
Policy Output Scale

POLICY INTEREST GROUP
S-03-0022 1975 00046
BT Political Interest Group
RT Association Interest Group
Economic Interest Group
Occupational Interest Group
Organizations
Policy Public Opinion Linkage
Social Group

POLICY MAKING PROCESS
S-31-0674 1975 00215
BT Process
NT Administrative Policy Making
Collective Policy Making
Domestic Policy Making
Economic Policy Making
Education Policy Making
Foreign Policy Making
International Policy Making
Judicial Policy Making
National Policy Making
Policy Articulation
Policy Compliance
Policy Conflict
Policy Development
Policy Enforcement
Policy Evaluation
Policy Format
Policy Implementation
Policy Incrementalism
Subnational Policy Making
RT Analytic Process
City State Relations
Conflict Process
Decision Maker
Decision Maker Perception
Decision Making Elite
Decision Making Process
Development Process
Intergovernmental Relations
Legislative Procedure
Legislative Process
Long Range Planning
Management
Manager
Planning Process
Policy Public Opinion Linkage
Short Range Planning
Social Interaction
Structural Process

POLICY OUTPUT INDEX
1975-1979 00054
USE Policy Output Scale

POLICY OUTPUT SCALE
S-24-0243 1979 00000
UF Policy Output Index
BT Scale Type
RT Bureaucratic Theory
PERT Analysis
Policy Articulation
Policy Development
Policy Format
Policy Incrementalism
Policy Public Opinion Linkage
Public Policy Analysis

POLICY PUBLIC OPINION LINKAGE
S-31-0688 1979 00000
SN The relationship between mass opinion and governmental policy outputs.
BT Policy Development
RT Mass Public Opinion
Policy Evaluation
Policy Evaluation Research
Policy Format
Policy Interest Group
Policy Making Process
Policy Output Scale
Policy Research
Policy Science Studies
Policy Scientist
Public Opinion Indicator
Public Opinion Survey

POLICY RESEARCH
S-24-0390 1975 00321
BT Research Orientation
NT Policy Evaluation Research
RT Academic Specialization
Applied Anthropology
Applied Linguistics
Applied Research
Applied Sociology
Authority Forecasting
Basic Research
Brainstorming
Concept Explication Research
Delphi Technique
Descriptive Research
Divergence Mapping
Economic Forecasting
Explanatory Research
Forecasting Methodology
Humanistic Research
Market Research
PERT Analysis
Policy Public Opinion Linkage
Policy Science Studies
Policy Scientist
Political Forecasting
Predictive Research
Public Policy Studies
Qualitative Research
Quantitative Research
Scenario Construction
Scientific Research
Social Forecasting
Trend Analysis

POLICY SCIENCE STUDIES
S-01-0159 1975 00128
BT Political Science Discipline
RT Administrative Science
Applied Anthropology
Applied Research
Behavioral Science
Behavioral Science Research
Comparative Political Studies
Comparative Sociology
Criminology
Demographic Studies
Ecology Discipline
Industrial Sociology
Information Science
International Power Theory
International Relations Studies
Legal Studies
Military Science
Policy
Policy Analysis
Policy Evaluation Research
Policy Public Opinion Linkage
Policy Research
Political Behavior Studies
Political Economy Studies
Political Science Methodology Studies
Public Administration Studies
Public Choice Analysis
Public Policy Analysis

Public Policy Studies
Quality Of Life
Social Psychology
Strategic Studies
Urban Politics Studies
Urban Sociology

POLICY SCIENTIST
S-32-0112 1975 00011
BT Social Scientist
RT Academic
Anthropologist
Economist
Geographer
Historian
Policy Analysis
Policy Evaluation Research
Policy Public Opinion Linkage
Policy Research
Political Science Methodology Studies
Political Scientist
Public Administration Studies
Sociologist

POLITBURO MEMBER
S-32-0155 1975 00001
BT Political Party Leader
RT Communist Government
Formal Political Party Leader
Political Party Chief
Political Party Leadership
Political Party Professional

POLITICAL ACTIVIST
S-32-0183 1975 00025
BT Activist
NT Militant
Peace Activist
Political Agitator
Political Conspirator
Political Party Activist
Political Party Dissident
Political Party Follower
Revolutionary
Right Wing Activist
Suffragette
Terrorist
RT Activist
Attentive Public
Demonstrator
Economic Activist
Electoral Opposition
Political Party Leader
Politician
Praxis
Protest Politics
Right Of Opposition
Right Wing Activist
Rights Of Man Doctrine
Rioter

POLITICAL ADVERTISING
S-31-0195 1975 00000
BT Political Communication
RT Advertising Industry
Political Propaganda

POLITICAL ADVISOR
S-32-0019 1975 00002
BT Advisor
NT Election Campaign Advisor
RT Administrative Advisor
Economic Advisor
Legal Advisor
Military Advisor
Science Advisor
Technical Advisor

POLITICAL AGITATION
S-08-0013 1975 00000
BT Agitation
NT Agitation Propaganda
Demonstration
RT Cultural Revolution
Economic Agitation
Ideological Struggle
Political Violence
Protest Politics
Psychological War
Rebellion
Revolution
Social Conflict
Social Rebellion

POLITICAL AGITATOR
S-32-0191 1975 00000
UF Agitator
BT Political Activist
RT Guerrilla War
Militant
Political Conspirator
Political Party Activist
Political Party Dissident
Protest Politics
Revolutionary
Right Wing Activist
Terrorist

POLITICAL ALIENATION
S-06-0086 1975 00024
BT Alienation
RT Cultural Alienation
Cynicism
Estrangement
Marxist Alienation Theory
Normlessness
Political Apathy
Political Cynicism
Political Efficacy
Political Estrangement
Political Powerlessness
Protest Politics

POLITICAL ALIENATION SCALE
S-24-0224 1975 00003
BT Alienation Scale
RT Cultural Alienation
Estrangement
Normlessness
Political Apathy
Political Cynicism

POLITICAL ALIENATION THEORY
S-38-0499 1975 00008
BT Political Philosophy Concept
RT Cultural Alienation
Cynicism
Marxist Political Thought
Normlessness
Political Apathy
Political Cynicism
Political Powerlessness
Protest Politics
Social Contract Theory

POLITICAL ANTHROPOLOGY
S-01-0019 1975 00005
BT Anthropology Discipline
RT Cultural Anthropology
Electoral Geography
Historical Sociology
Political Behavior Studies
Political Geography
Political History
Political Psychology
Political Science Discipline
Political Science Methodology Studies
Political Sociology
Social Anthropology

POLITICAL APATHY
S-06-0091 1975 00016
BT Apathy
RT Political Alienation
Political Alienation Scale
Political Alienation Theory
Political Cynicism
Political Distrust
Political Efficacy
Political Estrangement
Political Normlessness
Political Powerlessness

POLITICAL APPOINTEE
S-32-0251 1975 00001
BT Political Official
RT Patronage Bureaucracy
Spoils Politics

POLITICAL ARREST
S-31-0510 1975 00000
BT Arrest
RT Arbitrary Arrest
Local Police
On View Arrest
Warrant Arrest

POLITICAL ASSASSIN
S-36-0036 1975 00000
BT Political Criminal
RT Assassination
Political Crime
Terrorism
Traitor

POLITICAL ASYLUM
S-15-0024 1979 00000
BT Immunity
RT Citizenship Immunity
Civil Liberty
Civil Rights
Diplomatic Immunity
Executive Immunity
Legal Immunity
Legislative Immunity
Political Liberty
Prosecution Immunity

POLITICAL ATTACHE
S-36-0130 1975 00000
BT Embassy Attache
RT Cultural Attache
Economic Attache
Information Attache
Military Attache

POLITICAL ATTITUDE
S-06-0117 1979 00000
UF Public Attitude
BT Attitude Characteristics
RT Attentive Public
Attitude Change Theory

Attitude Cluster
Political Awareness
Political Socialization
Political Trust
Survey Analysis
Survey Data
Survey Research
Trust

POLITICAL AUTHORITY
S-04-0027 1975 00013
BT Secular Authority
NT Constitutional Authority
Government Authority
RT Absolutism
Centralized Authority
Charismatic Authority
Just Authority
Legal Rational Authority
Political Legitimacy Theory
Sovereignty
Weberian Theory

POLITICAL AUTOBIOGRAPHY
S-18-0067 1975 00004
BT Political Biography
RT Autobiography
Biography
Elite Analysis
Political Fiction
Political Memoir

POLITICAL AWARENESS
S-06-0118 1975 00029
BT Attitude Characteristics
RT Civic Culture
Political Attitude
Political Efficacy
Political Estrangement
Political Satisfaction
Political Trust
Subject Participant Culture

POLITICAL BARGAINING
S-31-0231 1975 00007
BT Bargaining
NT International Political Bargaining
RT Bargaining Strategy Process
Bargaining Theory
Economic Bargaining

POLITICAL BEHAVIOR
S-05-0013 1975 00049
BT Behavior
NT Elite Behavior
Judicial Behavior
Legal Behavior
Legislative Behavior
Obedience
Voting Behavior
RT Avoidance Behavior
Behavior Analysis
Behavioral Theory
Biopolitics
Economic Behavior
Group Behavior
Group Theory
Habitual Behavior
Mass Behavior
National Politics
Political Behavior Studies
Political Behaviorism
Politics
Problem Solving Behavior

POLITICAL BEHAVIOR STUDIES
S-01-0160 1975 00040
BT Political Science Discipline
RT Administrative Science
Behavior
Behavior Analysis
Behavioral Psychology
Behavioral Science
Black History
Comparative Political Studies
Electoral History
Ethnic Studies
Historiography
International Power Theory
International Relations Studies
Legislative History
Microeconomics
Policy Science Studies
Political Anthropology
Political Behavior
Political Geography
Political History
Political Philosophy Studies
Political Science Methodology Studies
Political Sociology
Political Theory Studies
Psychopathology
Social Psychology
Sociology Of Law
Survey Research
Voting

POLITICAL BEHAVIORALISM
1975-1979 00008

POLITICAL BEHAVIORISM
S-38-0158 1979 00000
BT Explanatory Political Theory
RT Behavioral Theory
Empirical Theory
Political Behavior
Structural Functional Political Theory
Transactional Theory
Voting Theory

POLITICAL BIOGRAPHY
S-18-0066 1975 00082
BT Political Literature
NT Political Autobiography
RT Autobiography
Biographical Analysis
Biography
Political Fiction
Political Memoir

POLITICAL BOSS
S-32-0156 1975 00000
BT Political Party Leader
NT National Political Party Leader
RT Boss Politics
Cell Leader
Formal Political Party Leader
Frontbencher
Patronage Bureaucracy
Political Party Cadre
Political Party Chief
Political Party Machine
Political Party Professional
Political Party Whip
Precinct Captain
Ward Chairperson

POLITICAL BRIBERY
S-10-0067 1975 00002
BT Political Corruption
RT Economic Bribery
Economic Crime
Election Fraud
Political Fraud
Spoils System
Vote Fraud

POLITICAL BROKER
S-32-0224 1975 00005
BT Politician
RT Patronage Bureaucracy
Political Candidate
Political Gatekeeper
Political Influence
Political Informer
Political Patron
Professional Politician

POLITICAL CAMPAIGN ADVERTISING
1975-1979 00010

POLITICAL CAMPAIGN ADVISOR
1975-1979 00000

POLITICAL CAMPAIGN PROPAGANDA
1975-1979 00001

POLITICAL CANDIDATE
S-32-0225 1975 00009
BT Politician
NT Dark Horse Candidate
Machine Candidate
National Candidate
Subnational Candidate
RT Electoral Opposition
Electoral Outcome
Electoral Politics
Formal Political Party Leader
Political Broker
Political Leader
Political Party Activist
Political Party Cadre
Political Party Chief
Political Party Professional
Precinct Captain
Recruitment Process

POLITICAL CENSORSHIP
S-31-0266 1975 00004
BT Censorship Process
RT Broadcasting Censorship
Government Report Censorship
Graphic Arts Censorship
Intelligence Censorship
Published Media Censorship
Religious Censorship

POLITICAL CHANGE
S-31-0150 1975 00076
BT Change Process
NT Extraterritorial Development
Politicization
Revolutionary Change
Social Change
Technological Change
Urbanization Process
RT Economic Change
Elite Change
Evolutionary Change
Homeostatic Change
Liberation Process
Political Development Theory
Political Evolution
Progressive Politics

Revolutionary Change
Social Change

POLITICAL CLUB
S-03-0023 1975 00000
BT Political Interest Group
RT Political Informer
Secret Society
Social Group

POLITICAL COALITION
S-02-0019 1979 00000
BT Coalition Type
NT Democratic Coalition
Electoral Coalition
Governing Coalition
Interest Group Coalition
Legislative Coalition
Political Party Coalition
Voting Coalition
RT Class Based Coalition
Coalition Dissolution
Coalition Formation
Coalition Government
Coalition Politics
Coalition Process
Coalition Theory
Decision Making Theory
Democratic Coalition
Economic Coalition
Multiethnic Coalition
Opinion Coalition
Parliamentary Politics
Political Front
Pork Barrel
United Front
Winning Coalition

POLITICAL COMMUNICATION
S-31-0194 1975 00019
BT Nonverbal Communication
NT Political Advertising
RT Communication Flow
Informal Communication
Information Dissemination
International Communication
Interpersonal Communication
Mass Communication
Nonverbal Communication
Political Party Advertising

POLITICAL COMMUNITY
S-07-0043 1975 00008
BT Community Type
RT Collective Community
Communal Community
Commune
Cooperative Community
Economic Community
Planned Economy
Squatter Community
Suburb
Town
Utopian Community
Village Community

POLITICAL COMPETITION
S-31-0211 1975 00014
BT Competition
RT Elite Competition
Political Opportunity Structure
Political Party Competition
Two Political Party Democracy

POLITICAL CONDITIONING
S-34-0051 1975 00000
BT Social Conditioning
RT Brainwashing
Political Indoctrination
Political Value Acquisition
Stereotyping

POLITICAL CONSENSUS
S-06-0689 1975 00010
BT Political System Structural Characteristics
RT Consensual Norms

POLITICAL CONSPIRACY
S-10-0065 1975 00002
BT Political Crime
RT Character Assassination
Economic Conspiracy
Highjacking
Malfeasance
Misfeasance
Political Conspirator
Political Corruption
Political Espionage
Political Fraud
Political Sabotage
Sedition
Treason

POLITICAL CONSPIRATOR
S-32-0192 1975 00001
BT Political Activist
RT Militant
Political Agitator
Political Conspiracy
Political Party Dissident
Revolutionary
Right Wing Activist
Terrorist

POLITICAL CONTROL
S-31-0302 1975 00028
BT Control Process
NT Political Indoctrination
Political Self Criticism
RT Decontrol Process
Exploitation Process
Expropriation Process
Government Expropriation
Information Manipulation
Political Persecution
Political Repression
Political Socialization
Purge
Repression Process

POLITICAL CORRUPTION
S-10-0066 1975 00023
BT Political Crime
NT Political Bribery
Political Graft
Spoils System
RT Character Assassination
Decay
Election Campaign Financial Disclosure
Impeachment
Malfeasance
Misfeasance
Patronage Bureaucracy
Political Conspiracy
Political Espionage
Political Fraud
Political Sabotage
Power Of The Purse

POLITICAL CRIME
S-10-0055 1975 00004
BT Crime
NT Assassination
Defection
Illegal Immigration
Malfeasance
Military Conspiracy
Military Espionage
Misfeasance
Political Conspiracy
Political Corruption
Political Espionage
Political Fraud
Political Sabotage
Sedition
Treason
RT Air Piracy
Genocide
Impeachment
Kidnapping
Malpractice
Piracy
Political Assassin
Political Informer
Power Abuse
Purge
Religious Offense
Sea Piracy
Sedition Law
Traitor
War Crime

POLITICAL CRIMINAL
S-36-0035 1975 00000
BT Criminal
NT Political Assassin
Traitor
RT Economic Criminal
Personal Crime Criminal
War Criminal

POLITICAL CRISIS
S-31-0250 1979 00000
BT Crisis
NT International Crisis
RT Cleavage Process
Conflict Intensification
Conflict Theory
Crisis
Crisis Management
Economic Crisis
Escalation
Natural Catastrophe
Political Instability
Political Legitimacy Theory
Political Succession
Social Crisis

POLITICAL CULTURE
S-11-0023 1975 00055
BT Culture Type
NT Modern Political Culture
National Political Culture
RT African Civilization
Ancient Civilization
Byzantine Civilization
Civilization
Counter Culture
Diffuse System Supports

Eastern Civilization
Eastern Culture
Ethnic Culture
Greek Civilization
Heterogeneous Culture
Homogeneous Culture
Law Formulation
Mass Culture
Political Socialization
Political System Type
Religious Culture
Roman Civilization
Secular Culture
System Politicization
Technological Culture
Traditional Culture
Western Civilization
Western Culture
Youth Culture

POLITICAL CYNICISM
S-06-0079 1975 00011
BT Cynicism
RT Ideological Political Culture
Political Alienation
Political Alienation Scale
Political Alienation Theory
Political Apathy
Political Distrust
Political Estrangement
Political Powerlessness

POLITICAL DECAY
S-31-0058 1975 00014
BT Decay
RT Government Instability
Institutional Decay
Urban Decay

POLITICAL DECISION MAKER
S-32-0030 1975 00010
BT Decision Maker
RT Cultural Decision Maker
Economic Decision Maker
Governing Elite
Organization Decision Maker
Political Leader
Political Role
Politician
Public Opinion Leader
Social Decision Maker

POLITICAL DEVELOPMENT
S-06-0178 1979 00000
BT Development Characteristics
RT Development Policy
Development Potential
Economic Development Characteristics
Economic Development Rate
Economic Development Stage
Human Resources Development
Legal Development
Modernizing Economy
Modernizing Political System
Political Development Policy
Political Development Theory
Social Development Policy

POLITICAL DEVELOPMENT INDEX
S-24-0231 1975 00010
BT Development Index
RT Political Development Policy
Political Development Theory
Political Resource Indicator

POLITICAL DEVELOPMENT POLICY
S-26-0083 1979 00000
BT Development Policy
RT Cultural Development Policy
Developing Nation
Developing Political System
Development Characteristics
Development Planning
Development Policy
Development Process
Development Theory
Economic Development Policy
Human Resources Development
Legal Development
Policy Development
Political Development
Political Development Index
Political Development Policy
Social Development Policy

POLITICAL DEVELOPMENT THEORY
S-38-0025 1975 00064
BT Development Theory
RT Administrative Development Theory
Autarchic Government
Developing Political System
Economic Development Theory
Modernizing Political System
Nation Building Theory
Political Change
Political Development
Political Development Index
Political System Type
Political Theory
Social Development Theory
Takeoff Stage
Technological Development Theory

POLITICAL DISSENSUS
S-06-0690 1975 00008
BT Political System Structural Characteristics
RT Conflict Theory
Political Distrust
Political Instability
Political Opposition

POLITICAL DISTRUST
S-06-0081 1975 00024
BT Distrust
RT Distrust
Ideological Political Culture
Political Apathy
Political Cynicism
Political Dissensus
Political Estrangement

POLITICAL ECONOMY STUDIES
S-01-0161 1975 00042
BT Political Science Discipline
RT Area Studies
Comparative Political Studies
Comparative Sociology
Econometrics
Economic Community
Economic Geography
Economics Discipline
Industrial Sociology
International Economics
International Relations Studies
Policy Science Studies
Political Geography
Political History
Political Science Methodology Studies

POLITICAL EDUCATION
S-13-0029 1975 00003
BT Education Type
NT Communist Education
Fascist Education
Ideological Education
Socialist Education
RT Civic Education
Education Curriculum
Mass Education
Military Education
Political Science Training

POLITICAL EFFICACY
S-06-0099 1975 00046
BT Efficacy
RT Activist
Efficacious Voter
Marginal Voter
Political Alienation
Political Apathy
Political Awareness
Political Powerlessness
Political Satisfaction
Political Secularization
Political Trust
Secular Political Culture
Subject Participant Culture

POLITICAL ELITE
S-14-0022 1975 00042
BT Elite Type
NT Local Political Elite
Modernizing Political Elite
Policy Elite
Potential Elite
Power Elite
Provincial Elite
Revolutionary Elite
Traditional Political Elite
Transitional Political Elite
RT Business Elite
Decision Making Elite
Economic Elite
Governing Elite
Intellectual Elite
Leader
Managerial Elite
Military Elite
Modernizing Elite
Pluralist Elite
Plutocracy
Purge
Social Elite

POLITICAL EQUALITY
S-06-0727 1979 00000
BT Equality
RT Class Equality
Democratic Theory
Economic Egalitarianism
Economic Equality
Education Equality
Egalitarianism
Income Equality
Racial Equality
Sex Equality
Social Equality
Socialist Theory
Status Equality

POLITICAL ESPIONAGE
S-10-0070 1975 00004
BT Political Crime
RT Blackmail
Defection
Economic Espionage
Highjacking
Industrial Espionage
Military Conspiracy
Political Conspiracy
Political Corruption
Political Record Falsification
Political Sabotage
Sedition

POLITICAL ESTRANGEMENT
S-06-0083 1975 00015
BT Estrangement
RT Marxist Alienation Theory
Political Alienation
Political Apathy
Political Awareness
Political Cynicism
Political Distrust
Political Normlessness

POLITICAL EVOLUTION
S-31-0068 1975 00005
BT Evolution
RT Cultural Evolution
Genetic Evolution
Human Evolution
Political Change
Political Party Innovation
Social Evolution

POLITICAL EXPLOITATION
S-31-0287 1975 00000
BT Exploitation Process
RT Economic Exploitation
Political Persecution
Racial Exploitation
Sex Exploitation

POLITICAL EXTREMISM
S-06-0101 1975 00003
BT Extremism
RT Ideological Political Culture
Radicalism
Terrorism
Terrorist

POLITICAL FICTION
S-18-0068 1975 00007
BT Political Literature
RT Autobiography
Biography
Novel
Political Autobiography
Political Biography
Political Memoir

POLITICAL FILM
S-18-0075 1975 00001
BT Information Sources
RT Political Literature
Visual Arts

POLITICAL FORECASTING
S-24-0016 1979 00000
BT Forecasting Methodology
RT Authority Forecasting
Brainstorming
Causal Analysis
Delphi Technique
Divergence Mapping
Economic Forecasting
Policy Evaluation Research
Policy Research
Political Science Methodology Studies
Predictive Research
Scenario Construction
Social Forecasting
Trend Analysis

POLITICAL FRAGMENTATION
S-31-0794 1979 00000
BT Fragmentation
RT Alienation Process
Anomic Process
Anomie
Fragmented Political Culture
Social Fragmentation

POLITICAL FRAUD
S-10-0071 1975 00002
BT Political Crime
NT Election Fraud
Political Fund Misuse
Political Information Manipulation
Political Record Falsification
RT Election Fraud
Fraud
Malfeasance
Malpractice
Misfeasance
Political Bribery
Political Conspiracy
Political Corruption
Political Graft
Power Abuse
Vote Fraud

POLITICAL FREEDOM THEORY
S-38-0465 1975 00009
BT Freedom Theory
RT Freedom
Individual Freedom Theory
Ontological Existentialism
Slavery Abolition

POLITICAL FRONT
S-02-0052 1975 00001
BT Agreement Type
NT Liberation Front
National Front
Popular Front
United Front
RT Alliance
Atlantic Community
Communist Bloc
Contract Type
Electoral Alliance
Electoral Tactics
Extranational Bloc
International Bloc
Political Coalition
Security Community
Third World Bloc

POLITICAL FUND MISUSE
S-10-0074 1975 00001
BT Political Fraud
RT Economic Bribery
Economic Conspiracy
Economic Crime
Political Graft
Property Crime
Spoils System

POLITICAL GATEKEEPER
S-32-0217 1975 00001
BT Political Role
RT Elite Recruitment
Political Broker
Political Influence
Politician

POLITICAL GEOGRAPHY
S-01-0093 1975 00014
BT Geography Discipline
NT Electoral Geography
RT Area Studies
Comparative Political Studies
Comparative Sociology
Demographic Studies
Economic Geography
Electoral History
Ethnic Community
Frontier Theory
Geopolitical Theory
Geopolitics
Heartland Theory
Human Geography
International Relations Studies
Military History
Peace Studies
Physical Geography
Political Anthropology
Political Behavior Studies
Political Economy Studies
Political History
Political Science Discipline
Political Sociology
Statistical Analysis
Strategic Studies
Urban Geography
Urban Politics Studies
Urban Sociology
World Region

POLITICAL GRAFT
S-10-0068 1975 00002
BT Political Corruption
RT Economic Bribery
Economic Crime
Election Fraud
Patronage Bureaucracy
Political Fraud
Political Fund Misuse
Spoils System
Vote Fraud

POLITICAL HISTORY
S-01-0115 1975 00511
BT History Discipline
NT Electoral History
Legislative History
RT Ancient History
Black History
Communist Studies
Economic History
Intellectual History
Labor History
Military History
National Goal
Oral History
Political Anthropology
Political Behavior Studies
Political Economy Studies
Political Geography
Political Psychology

Political Science Discipline
Political Sociology
Religious History
Social History
Urban History
Urban Politics Studies

POLITICAL IDENTITY
S-06-0393 1975 00008
BT Identity Characteristics
NT Political Party Identification
RT Community Identity
National Prestige
National Pride
Political Socialization

POLITICAL IDEOLOGY
S-38-0285 1979 00000
BT Ideologies
RT Belief System
Contemporary Political Thought
Ideological Conflict
Ideological Education
Ideological Polarization
Ideological Political Culture
Ideological Political Party
Ideological Spectrum Political Movement
Ideological Struggle
Ideology Explanatory Theory
Issue Politicization
Mass Belief System
Political Philosophy Concept
Political Philosophy Studies
Politicization
System Politicization

POLITICAL IMPERIALISM
S-37-0071 1975 00005
BT Imperialism System
NT Communist Imperialism
Western Imperialism
Yankee Imperialism
RT Academic Imperialism
Cultural Imperialism
Economic Imperialism

POLITICAL INDICATOR
S-24-0261 1975 00003
BT Indicator
NT Conflict Indicator
Influence Indicator
Political Instability Indicator
Political Resource Indicator
Public Opinion Indicator
Voting Indicator
RT Change Indicator
Economic Indicator
Social Indicator

POLITICAL INDOCTRINATION
S-31-0303 1975 00003
BT Political Control
NT Brainwashing
Ideological Indoctrination
RT Catharsis
Informal Communication
Information Dissemination
Political Conditioning
Political Persecution
Political Self Criticism

POLITICAL INEQUALITY
S-06-0737 1979 00000
BT Inequality
RT Class Inequality
Economic Inequality
Education Inequality
Income Inequality
Political Injustice
Racial Inequality
Sex Inequality
Social Inequality
Social Injustice

POLITICAL INFLUENCE
S-31-0474 1975 00046
BT Influence Process
RT Government Process
Patronage Bureaucracy
Political Broker
Political Gatekeeper
Political Interest Group
Spoils System

POLITICAL INFORMATION MANIPULATION
S-10-0075 1975 00002
BT Political Fraud
RT Broadcasting Censorship
Intelligence Censorship
News Conference
Newspaper Censorship
Political Propaganda
Political Record Falsification
Political Sabotage

POLITICAL INFORMER
S-32-0218 1975 00001
BT Political Role
RT Intelligence Agency
Political Broker
Political Club
Political Crime
Secret Society

POLITICAL INJUSTICE
S-06-0686 1979 00000
BT Political System Normative Characteristics
RT Class Inequality
Economic Inequality
Economic Injustice
Education Injustice
Inequality
Justice Theory
Political Inequality
Racial Injustice
Relative Justice Theory
Sexual Injustice
Social Inequality
Social Injustice
Status Inequality

POLITICAL INSTABILITY
S-06-0691 1975 00051
BT Political System Structural Characteristics
NT Government Instability
Regime Instability
RT Crisis
Government Dissolution Process
International Crisis
No Confidence Motion
Political Crisis
Political Dissensus

POLITICAL INSTABILITY INDICATOR
S-24-0265 1975 00004
BT Political Indicator
RT Conflict Indicator
Influence Indicator
Voting Indicator

POLITICAL INTEGRATION
S-31-0819 1975 00029
BT Integration
NT International Political Integration
National Political Integration
Political Unification
Subnational Political Integration
RT Horizontal Integration
Political Integration Theory

POLITICAL INTEGRATION THEORY
S-38-0159 1975 00017
BT Explanatory Political Theory
RT Conflict Theory
Nationality Policy
Political Integration
Political System Theory
System Integration

POLITICAL INTEREST GROUP
S-03-0021 1975 00013
BT Interest Group
NT Policy Interest Group
Political Club
RT Association Interest Group
Cultural Interest Group
Economic Interest Group
Latent Interest Group
Occupational Interest Group
Political Influence
Social Group

POLITICAL INTERFERENCE POLICY
S-26-0265 1979 00000
BT Interference Policy
RT Economic Interference Policy
International Relations Studies
Military Intervention Policy
Military Invasion
Open Door Policy
Political Intervention Policy
Political Power
Power Theory
World Politics

POLITICAL INTERVENTION POLICY
S-26-0268 1979 00000
BT Intervention Policy
RT Economic Interference Policy
Interference Policy
International Relations Studies
Military Intervention Policy
Military Invasion
Open Door Policy
Political Interference Policy
Political Power
Power Theory

POLITICAL LAW
S-21-0066 1975 00001
BT Law Type
NT Admiralty Law
Electoral Law
Enabling Law
Home Rule Law
Sedition Law
Sunset Law
Sunshine Law

RT Constitutional Democracy
Legal History
Procedural Law
Social Law
Socialist Law

POLITICAL LEADER
S-32-0052 1975 00021
BT Leader
NT Civil Rights Leader
Local Political Boss
Titular Leader
RT Decision Maker
Economic Leader
Majority Leader
Political Candidate
Political Decision Maker
Politician
Public Opinion Leader
Social Leader
Town Council

POLITICAL LEADERSHIP
S-22-0022 1975 00056
BT Leadership Type
NT Congressional Leadership
Executive Leadership
Political Movement Leadership
Political Party Leadership
RT Administrative Leadership
Bureaucratic Leadership
Charismatic Leadership
Closed Leadership
Collective Leadership
Collegial Leadership
Democratic Leadership
Governing Elite
Leadership Authority Base
Leadership Structure Type
Majority Leader
National Leadership
Open Leadership
Personalized Leadership
Political Party Leadership
Political Purge
Purge
Rational Legal Leadership
Small Group Leadership
Totalitarian Leadership
Traditional Leadership
Upper House Speaker

POLITICAL LEGITIMACY THEORY
S-38-0485 1975 00038
BT Legitimacy Theory
RT Authority
Authority Mode
Authority Theory
Civil Religion
Common Good Theory
Consent Theory
Cult Of Personality
Hobbesian Analysis
Just Authority
Lockean Liberalism
Obedience
Obligation Theory
Political Authority
Political Crisis
Political Socialization
Political Virtue
Representation
Social Contract Theory
System Politicization

POLITICAL LIBERTY
S-15-0026 1975 00008
BT Freedom
NT Civil Liberty
Civil Rights
Procedural Rights
Right Of Opposition
Social Rights
Voting Rights
RT Civil Liberty Liberalism
Civil Rights Liberalism
Destalinization Process
Early Radical Thought
Early Republicanism
Freedom Of Inquiry
Human Rights
Human Rights Policy
Immunity
Political Asylum

POLITICAL LITERATURE
S-18-0065 1975 00052
BT Monographs
NT Political Biography
Political Fiction
Political Memoir
RT Autobiography
Biography
Black Press
Comparative Literature Studies
Essay
Humanities Discipline
Literature Analysis
Literature Studies
Political Film
Textbook

POLITICAL MAN THEORY
S-38-0500 1975 00001
BT Political Philosophy Concept
RT Aristotelian Thought
Justice Theory
Legitimacy Theory
Natural Law Conventionalism Theory
Political Virtue

POLITICAL MEMOIR
S-18-0069 1975 00004
BT Political Literature
RT Autobiography
Novel
Political Autobiography
Political Biography
Political Fiction

POLITICAL MOBILIZATION
S-31-0631 1979 00000
BT Mobilization Process
RT Citizen Participation
Economic Mobilization
Mass Mobilization
Mass Society
Military Mobilization
Peasant Mobilization
Social Mobilization
Worker Mobilization

POLITICAL MODERNIZATION
S-31-0080 1975 00024
BT Modernization
RT Cultural Modernization
Economic Modernization
Institutional Innovation
Modernization Theory
Modernizing Ideology
Social Modernization

POLITICAL MOVEMENT
S-27-0001 1975 00012
NT Chiliastic Movement
Confederation Movement
Ecology Movement
Economic Movement
Federation Movement
Ideological Spectrum Political Movement
Independence Movement
Luddite Movement
Messianic Movement
Nationalist Movement
Peace Movement
Reform Movement
Resistance Movement
Sector Based Political Movement
Social Movement
Totalitarian Movement
RT Communism
Economic Mobilization
Political Movement Leadership

POLITICAL MOVEMENT LEADERSHIP
S-22-0026 1979 00000
BT Political Leadership
RT Congressional Leadership
Executive Leadership
Leadership Authority Base
Leadership Structure Type
Mass Mobilization
Mass Political Party
National Leadership
Political Movement
Political Party Leadership
Presidential Leadership

POLITICAL NEUTRALIST
S-32-0262 1975 00000
BT Spectrum Politicist
RT Centrist
Liberal
Nonaligned Nation
Peace
Political Radical

POLITICAL NORMLESSNESS
S-06-0085 1975 00002
BT Normlessness
RT Alienation Psychological Theory
Political Apathy
Political Estrangement
Political Psychology

POLITICAL OFFICIAL
S-32-0250 1975 00002
BT Politician
NT Political Appointee
RT Government Official
Professional Politician

POLITICAL OPPORTUNITY STRUCTURE
S-06-0696 1975 00009
BT Political System Structural Characteristics
RT Elite Recruitment
Equality Theory
Freedom
Political Competition

POLITICAL OPPOSITION
S-06-0697 1975 00017
BT Political System Structural Characteristics
NT Electoral Opposition
Parliamentary Opposition
RT Electoral Opposition
Opposition Political Party
Opposition Political Party Leader
Political Dissensus
Political Refugee
Political Tolerance
Protest Politics
Refugee
Right Of Opposition
Support Opposition Scale

POLITICAL ORIENTATION DEVELOPMENT
S-34-0047 1975 00029
BT Political Socialization
RT Opinion Change
Opinion Formation
Opinion Socialization
Opinion Stability
Perception Socialization
Political Value Acquisition
Role Acquisition
Role Socialization
Social Conditioning

POLITICAL PARTICIPATION
S-31-0703 1979 00000
BT Process
NT Citizen Participation
RT Democratic Government
Democratic Political System
Democratic Regime
Democratic Theory
Mass Behavior
Participatory Democracy
Participatory Democratic Theory
Participatory Management
Political Socialization
System Politicization
Voting

POLITICAL PARTY ACTIVIST
S-32-0193 1975 00009
BT Political Activist
RT Militant
Political Agitator
Political Candidate
Political Party Cadre
Political Party Dissident
Political Party Follower
Political Party Loyalist
Political Party Member

POLITICAL PARTY ADVERTISING
S-31-0196 1975 00000
BT Communication Process
RT Campaign Manager
Information Dissemination
Mass Communication
Political Communication
Political Party Propaganda

POLITICAL PARTY AFFILIATION
S-06-0541 1975 00020
BT Political Party Membership
RT Political Party Electoral Strength
Political Party Identification
Political Party Loyalty
Political Party Loyalty Intensity
Political Party Recruitment Pattern
Political Socialization

POLITICAL PARTY ALIGNMENT
S-06-0554 1979 00000
BT Political Party Structural Characteristics
RT Coalition Dissolution
Coalition Formation
Coalition Government
Coalition Politics
Coalition Process
Political Party Coalition
Political Party Cohesion
Political Party Decentralization
Political Party Faction
Political Party Hierarchy
Political Party Type

POLITICAL PARTY BUREAUCRACY
S-06-0564 1975 00003
BT Political Party Organization
RT Political Party Centralization
Political Party Decentralization
Political Party Hierarchy
Political Party Institution
Political Party Machine

POLITICAL PARTY CADRE
S-32-0158 1975 00007
BT Political Party Leader
RT Backbencher
Campaign Manager
Campaign Worker
Cell Leader
Delegate
Formal Political Party Leader
Frontbencher
Opposition Political Party Leader
Political Boss
Political Candidate
Political Party Activist
Political Party Chief
Political Party Loyalist
Political Party Professional
Political Party Supporter
Political Party Whip
Political Party Worker
Precinct Captain
Precinct Worker
Rank And File Member
Ward Chairperson

POLITICAL PARTY CAMPAIGN
S-19-0313 1979 00000
BT Political Party Institution
RT Campaign Contributor
Campaign Manager
Election Campaign
Election Campaign Advertising
Election Campaign Organization
Election Campaign Strategy
Election Campaign Tactics
Political Party Caucus
Political Party Committee
Political Party Convention

POLITICAL PARTY CAMPAIGN ORGANIZATION
1975-1979 00002

POLITICAL PARTY CAPABILITY CHARACTERISTICS
S-06-0536 1975 00017
BT Political Party Characteristics
RT Political Party Composition
Political Party Normative Characteristics
Political Party Program
Political Party Structural Characteristics

POLITICAL PARTY CAUCUS
S-19-0314 1975 00001
BT Political Party Institution
RT Political Party Campaign
Political Party Central Committee
Political Party Committee
Political Party Convention
Political Party Secretariat

POLITICAL PARTY CENSORSHIP AGENCY
1975-1979 00000

POLITICAL PARTY CENTRAL COMMITTEE
S-19-0316 1975 00001
UF Central Committee
BT Political Party Committee
RT Centralized Political Party
Political Party Caucus
Political Party Congress
Political Party Convention
Political Party Politburo
Political Party Secretariat

POLITICAL PARTY CENTRALIZATION
S-06-0555 1975 00002
BT Political Party Structural Characteristics
NT Centralized Political Party
RT Political Party Bureaucracy
Political Party Decentralization
Political Party Hierarchy
Political Party Institution
Political Party Institutionalization
Political Party Machine

POLITICAL PARTY CHARACTERISTICS
S-06-0535 1975 00024
BT Characteristics
NT Political Party Capability Characteristics
Political Party Composition
Political Party Normative Characteristics
Political Party Structural Characteristics
RT Government Characteristics
Group Characteristics
Legislative Characteristics
Organization Characteristics
Political Party System

POLITICAL PARTY CHIEF
S-32-0159 1975 00000
BT Political Party Leader
RT Campaign Manager
Formal Political Party Leader
Frontbencher
National Political Party First Secretary
National Political Party Leader
Opposition Political Party Leader
Politburo Member
Political Boss

Political Candidate
Political Party Cadre
Political Party Leadership
Political Party Organization
Political Party Professional
Political Party Secretariat
Political Party Whip
Ward Chairperson

POLITICAL PARTY COALITION
S-02-0026 1975 00018
BT Political Coalition
NT All Party Coalition
Intraparty Coalition
Multiparty Coalition
Negative Coalition
RT Class Based Coalition
Coalition Type
Democratic Coalition
Electoral Coalition
Governing Coalition
Interest Group Coalition
Legislative Coalition
Multiethnic Coalition
Parliamentary Coalition
Political Party Alignment
Voting Coalition
Voting Tactics
Winning Coalition

POLITICAL PARTY COHESION
S-06-0557 1975 00016
BT Political Party Structural Characteristics
RT Intraparty Conflict
Partisan Politics
Partisan Primary
Political Party Alignment
Political Party Discipline
Political Party Hierarchy
Political Party Loyalty
Political Party Realignment

POLITICAL PARTY COLUMN BALLOT
S-29-0158 1975 00000
SN Ballot form in which candidate choices are grouped according to party affiliation.
BT Ballot
RT Australian Ballot
Long Ballot
Machine Ballot
Nonpartisan Ballot
Office Block Ballot
Paper Ballot
Political Party List Ballot
Secret Ballot
Short Ballot

POLITICAL PARTY COMMITTEE
S-19-0315 1975 00000
BT Political Party Institution
NT Political Party Central Committee
Political Party Executive Committee
Political Party Financial Committee
Political Party National Committee
Political Party Politburo
Political Party Secretariat
Political Party State Committee
RT Political Party Campaign
Political Party Caucus
Political Party Convention

POLITICAL PARTY COMPETITION
S-31-0212 1975 00029
BT Competition
NT Interparty Competition
Intraparty Competition
RT Elite Competition
Pluralist Democracy
Pluralist Elite
Political Competition

POLITICAL PARTY COMPOSITION
S-06-0537 1975 00004
BT Political Party Characteristics
NT Political Party Constituency
Political Party Membership
RT Group Composition
Organization Composition
Political Party Capability Characteristics
Political Party Congress
Political Party Faction

POLITICAL PARTY CONGRESS
S-06-0565 1975 00007
BT Political Party Organization
RT Communist Political Party
Delegate
Political Party Central Committee
Political Party Composition
Political Party Convention

POLITICAL PARTY CONSTITUENCY
S-06-0538 1975 00004
BT Political Party Composition
NT Political Party Electoral Strength
RT Political Party Membership
Political Party Realignment

POLITICAL PARTY CONVENTION
S-19-0323 1975 00013
BT Political Party Institution
RT Appointment Process
By Election
Delegate
Delegate At Large
Delegation Member
Favorite Son Candidate
Political Party Campaign
Political Party Caucus
Political Party Central Committee
Political Party Committee
Political Party Congress
Political Party Convention Delegate Selection
Political Party Executive Committee
Political Party Financial Committee
Political Party National Committee
Political Party Nominating Committee
Presidential Nominating Process

POLITICAL PARTY CONVENTION DELEGATE SELECTION
S-31-0736 1975 00004
BT Convention Delegate Selection
RT Constitutional Convention Delegate Selection
Political Party Convention

POLITICAL PARTY DECENTRALIZATION
S-06-0558 1975 00002
BT Political Party Structural Characteristics
NT Decentralized Political Party
RT Political Party Alignment
Political Party Bureaucracy
Political Party Centralization
Political Party Hierarchy
Political Party Institutionalization
Political Party Organization

POLITICAL PARTY DEMOCRACY
S-16-0024 1979 00000
BT Democratic Government
NT Multiparty Democracy
One Political Party Democracy
Two Political Party Democracy
RT Political Party System

POLITICAL PARTY DISCIPLINE
S-06-0544 1975 00001
BT Political Party Normative Characteristics
RT Group Solidarity
Intraparty Conflict
Intraparty Democracy
Political Party Cohesion
Political Party Dissident
Political Party Institution
Political Party Institutionalization
Political Party Loyalty
Political Party Machine
Political Party Norms

POLITICAL PARTY DISSIDENT
S-32-0194 1975 00003
BT Political Activist
RT Dissent
Militant
Political Agitator
Political Conspirator
Political Party Activist
Political Party Discipline
Political Party Faction
Right Wing Activist

POLITICAL PARTY ELECTORAL COMPETITION
S-29-0105 1975 00018
BT Electoral Competition
RT Electoral Alliance
Partisan Politics
Partisan Primary
Political Party National Committee

POLITICAL PARTY ELECTORAL STRENGTH
S-06-0539 1975 00038
BT Political Party Constituency
RT Political Party Affiliation
Political Party Membership
Political Party Recruitment Pattern

POLITICAL PARTY EXECUTIVE COMMITTEE
S-19-0317 1975 00003
BT Political Party Committee
RT Political Party Convention
Political Party Financial Committee
Political Party Leader
Political Party Leadership
Political Party National Committee
Political Party Politburo
Political Party Secretariat
Political Party State Committee

POLITICAL PARTY FACTION
S-06-0560 1975 00014
BT Political Party Structural Characteristics
RT Factionalist
Intraparty Coalition
Intraparty Conflict
Political Party Alignment
Political Party Composition
Political Party Dissident
Political Party Factional Cleavage

POLITICAL PARTY FACTIONAL CLEAVAGE
S-06-0552 1975 00026
BT Intraparty Conflict
RT Group Cleavage Characteristics
Intraparty Coalition
Organization Cleavage Characteristics
Political Party Faction
Political Party Realignment

POLITICAL PARTY FINANCE COMMITTEE
1975-1979 00001
USE Political Party Financial Committee

POLITICAL PARTY FINANCE RECORD
1975-1979 00002
USE Political Party Financial Record

POLITICAL PARTY FINANCIAL COMMITTEE
S-19-0318 1979 00000
UF Political Party Finance Committee
BT Political Party Committee
RT Election Campaign Financing
Political Party Convention
Political Party Executive Committee
Political Party Financial Record
Political Party National Committee
Political Party State Committee

POLITICAL PARTY FINANCIAL RECORD
S-18-0015 1979 00000
UF Political Party Finance Record
BT Financial Record
RT Campaign Contributor
Election Campaign Contribution
Election Campaign Financial Disclosure
Election Campaign Financing
Expenditure Record
Income Record
Political Party Financial Committee
Revenue Record

POLITICAL PARTY FOLLOWER
S-32-0195 1975 00005
BT Political Activist
RT Political Party Activist
Political Party Loyalist
Political Party Member
Political Party Orientation
Political Party Supporter

POLITICAL PARTY HIERARCHY
S-06-0561 1975 00003
BT Political Party Structural Characteristics
RT Political Party Alignment
Political Party Bureaucracy
Political Party Centralization
Political Party Cohesion
Political Party Decentralization
Political Party Institution
Political Party Institutionalization
Political Party Machine
Political Party Organization

POLITICAL PARTY IDENTIFICATION
S-06-0394 1975 00040
BT Political Identity
RT Partisan Politics
Political Party Affiliation
Political Party Loyalty
Political Party Loyalty Intensity
Political Party Program
Political Party Recruitment Pattern
Political Party Ticket Voting
Political Socialization
Split Ticket Voting

POLITICAL PARTY IDEOLOGY
S-06-0545 1975 00044
BT Political Party Normative Characteristics
RT Evolutionary Change
Political Party Manifesto
Political Party Norms
Political Party Platform
Political Party Policy
Political Party Program

POLITICAL PARTY INNOVATION
S-31-0072 1979 00000
BT Innovation
RT Development Process
Institutional Innovation
Institutionalization
Political Evolution
Political Party System

POLITICAL PARTY INSTITUTION
S-19-0312 1975 00000
BT Institutions
NT Political Party Campaign
Political Party Caucus
Political Party Committee
Political Party Convention
RT Agencies
Political Party Bureaucracy
Political Party Centralization
Political Party Discipline
Political Party Hierarchy
Political Party Institutionalization
Political Party Machine
Political Party Organization
Task Force

POLITICAL PARTY INSTITUTIONALIZATION
S-06-0562 1975 00006
BT Political Party Structural Characteristics
RT Institutionalization
Political Party Centralization
Political Party Decentralization
Political Party Discipline
Political Party Hierarchy
Political Party Institution
Political Party Machine
Political Party Organization
Political Party Realignment

POLITICAL PARTY LEADER
S-32-0147 1975 00007
BT Political Party Role
NT Backbencher
Bloc Leader
Campaign Manager
Cell Leader
Formal Political Party Leader
Frontbencher
Opposition Political Party Leader
Politburo Member
Political Boss
Political Party Cadre
Political Party Chief
Political Party Professional
Political Party Whip
Precinct Captain
Ward Chairperson
RT Legislative Leader
Lower House Speaker
Political Activist
Political Party Executive Committee
Political Party Leadership
Political Party Official
Political Party Secretariat
Politician

POLITICAL PARTY LEADERSHIP
S-22-0027 1975 00031
BT Political Leadership
RT Bureaucratic Leadership
Collective Leadership
Democratic Leadership
Executive Leadership
Legislative Leader
National Leadership
Personalized Leadership
Politburo Member
Political Leadership
Political Movement Leadership
Political Party Chief
Political Party Executive Committee
Political Party Leader
Political Party Official
Political Party Secretariat
Presidential Leadership
Small Group Leadership
Totalitarian Leadership
Traditional Leadership

POLITICAL PARTY LIST BALLOT
S-29-0159 1975 00000
BT Ballot
RT Australian Ballot
Long Ballot
Machine Ballot
Nonpartisan Ballot
Office Block Ballot
Paper Ballot
Political Party Column Ballot
Secret Ballot
Short Ballot

POLITICAL PARTY LOYALIST
S-32-0171 1975 00011
BT Political Party Supporter
RT Campaign Contributor
Campaign Worker
Political Party Activist
Political Party Cadre
Political Party Follower
Political Party Voter
Political Socialization
Strong Political Party Identifier
Weak Political Party Identifier

POLITICAL PARTY LOYALTY
S-06-0546 1975 00020
BT Political Party Normative Characteristics
NT Political Party Loyalty Intensity
RT Patronage Bureaucracy
Political Party Affiliation
Political Party Cohesion
Political Party Discipline
Political Party Identification
Political Party Program

POLITICAL PARTY LOYALTY INTENSITY
S-06-0547 1975 00006
BT Political Party Loyalty
RT Political Party Affiliation
Political Party Identification

POLITICAL PARTY MACHINE
S-06-0566 1975 00000
BT Political Party Organization
RT Political Boss
Political Party Bureaucracy
Political Party Centralization
Political Party Discipline
Political Party Hierarchy
Political Party Institution
Political Party Institutionalization

POLITICAL PARTY MANIFESTO
S-06-0548 1975 00000
BT Political Party Normative Characteristics
RT Political Party Ideology
Political Party Norms
Political Party Platform
Political Party Program

POLITICAL PARTY MEMBER
S-32-0164 1975 00005
BT Political Party Role
NT Delegation Member
Political Party Supporter
Political Party Worker
Rank And File Member
RT Political Party Activist
Political Party Follower
Politician

POLITICAL PARTY MEMBERSHIP
S-06-0540 1975 00009
BT Political Party Composition
NT Political Party Affiliation
Political Party Recruitment Pattern
RT House Of Representatives Speaker
National Political Party First Secretary
National Politics
Political Party Constituency
Political Party Electoral Strength
Political Party Orientation
Political Party Program
Political Party State Committee

POLITICAL PARTY NATIONAL COMMITTEE
S-19-0319 1979 00000
BT Political Party Committee
RT National Political Party Executive Member
Political Party Convention
Political Party Electoral Competition
Political Party Executive Committee
Political Party Financial Committee
Political Party Normative Characteristics
Political Party Organization

POLITICAL PARTY NOMINATING COMMITTEE
S-06-0567 1975 00000
BT Political Party Organization
RT Candidate Selection
Leadership Recruitment
Political Party Convention

POLITICAL PARTY NORMATIVE CHARACTERISTICS
S-06-0543 1975 00015
BT Political Party Characteristics
NT Political Party Discipline
Political Party Ideology
Political Party Loyalty
Political Party Manifesto
Political Party Norms
RT Group Normative Characteristics
Organization Normative Characteristics
Political Party Capability Characteristics
Political Party National Committee
Political Party Politburo
Political Party Program
Political Party Structural Characteristics

POLITICAL PARTY NORMS
S-06-0549 1975 00001
BT Political Party Normative Characteristics
RT Intraparty Democracy
Political Party Discipline
Political Party Ideology
Political Party Manifesto
Political Party Platform
Political Party Policy
Political Party Politburo
Political Party Program

POLITICAL PARTY OFFICIAL
S-36-0233 1975 00002
BT Status
NT International Political Party Executive Member
National Political Party Executive Member
Subnational Political Party Executive Member
RT Administrative Personnel
Diplomat
Government Official
Political Party Leader
Political Party Leadership
Suborganization Official

POLITICAL PARTY ORGANIZATION
S-06-0563 1975 00017
BT Political Party Structural Characteristics
NT Political Party Bureaucracy
Political Party Congress
Political Party Machine
Political Party Nominating Committee
RT Centralized Political Party
Decentralized Political Party
Political Party Chief
Political Party Decentralization
Political Party Hierarchy
Political Party Institution
Political Party Institutionalization
Political Party National Committee
Political Party Secretariat
Political Party System
Youth Organization

POLITICAL PARTY ORIENTATION
S-32-0337 1975 00021
BT Voter Orientation
RT Candidate Orientation
Issue Orientation
Political Party Follower
Political Party Membership
Political Socialization
Strong Political Party Identifier
Weak Political Party Identifier

POLITICAL PARTY PLATFORM
S-26-0356 1975 00004
BT Political Party Policy
RT Electoral Strategy
Political Party Ideology
Political Party Manifesto
Political Party Norms
Political Party Program

POLITICAL PARTY POLICY
S-26-0355 1975 00031
BT Policy
NT Political Party Platform
Political Party Program
RT Political Party Ideology
Political Party Norms
Political Party Propaganda

POLITICAL PARTY POLITBURO
S-19-0320 1975 00005
BT Political Party Committee
RT Political Party Central Committee
Political Party Executive Committee
Political Party Normative Characteristics
Political Party Norms
Political Party Secretariat
Political Party State Committee

POLITICAL PARTY PRIMARY
S-29-0067 1975 00003
BT Partisan Primary
RT Blanket Primary
Closed Primary
Open Primary
Partisan Election
Partisan Primary
Primary Election

POLITICAL PARTY PROFESSIONAL
S-32-0160 1975 00004
BT Political Party Leader
RT Backbencher
Bloc Leader
Campaign Manager
Cell Leader
Formal Political Party Leader
Frontbencher
Politburo Member
Political Boss
Political Candidate
Political Party Cadre
Political Party Chief
Political Party Secretariat
Political Party Whip
Political Party Worker
Politician
Precinct Captain

Precinct Worker
Ward Chairperson

POLITICAL PARTY PROGRAM
S-26-0357 1975 00011
BT Political Party Policy
RT Political Party Capability Characteristics
Political Party Identification
Political Party Ideology
Political Party Loyalty
Political Party Manifesto
Political Party Membership
Political Party Normative Characteristics
Political Party Norms
Political Party Platform

POLITICAL PARTY PROPAGANDA
S-31-0192 1975 00002
BT Political Propaganda
RT Government Propaganda
Political Party Advertising
Political Party Policy

POLITICAL PARTY REALIGNMENT
S-06-0568 1975 00020
BT Political Party Structural Characteristics
RT Critical Election
Political Party Cohesion
Political Party Constituency
Political Party Factional Cleavage
Political Party Institutionalization

POLITICAL PARTY RECORD
S-18-0040 1975 00004
BT Documents
RT Committee Record
Government Information Service
Legislative Information Service

POLITICAL PARTY RECRUITMENT
S-31-0750 1975 00008
BT Political Recruitment
RT Judicial Recruitment
Leadership Recruitment
Legislative Recruitment

POLITICAL PARTY RECRUITMENT PATTERN
S-06-0542 1975 00012
BT Political Party Membership
RT Cooptation
Political Party Affiliation
Political Party Electoral Strength
Political Party Identification
Recruitment Process

POLITICAL PARTY ROLE
S-32-0146 1975 00028
BT Roles
NT Political Party Leader
Political Party Member
RT Political Role
Politician
Role Socialization

POLITICAL PARTY SECRETARIAT
S-19-0321 1975 00002
BT Political Party Committee
RT Interest Group Representation
International Political Party Chairperson
Political Party Caucus
Political Party Central Committee
Political Party Chief
Political Party Executive Committee
Political Party Leader
Political Party Leadership
Political Party Organization
Political Party Politburo
Political Party Professional
Political Party State Committee
Political Party Structural Characteristics

POLITICAL PARTY STATE COMMITTEE
S-19-0322 1975 00000
BT Political Party Committee
RT Political Party Executive Committee
Political Party Financial Committee
Political Party Membership
Political Party Politburo
Political Party Secretariat
Political Party Structural Characteristics

POLITICAL PARTY STRUCTURAL CHARACTERISTICS
S-06-0550 1975 00016
BT Political Party Characteristics
NT Intraparty Conflict
Intraparty Democracy
Political Party Alignment
Political Party Centralization
Political Party Cohesion
Political Party Decentralization
Political Party Faction
Political Party Hierarchy
Political Party Institutionalization
Political Party Organization
Political Party Realignment
RT Group Structural Characteristics
Organization Structural Characteristics
Political Party Capability Characteristics
Political Party Normative Characteristics
Political Party Secretariat
Political Party State Committee

POLITICAL PARTY SUPPORTER
S-32-0169 1975 00022
BT Political Party Member
NT Campaign Contributor
Political Party Loyalist
Strong Political Party Identifier
Weak Political Party Identifier
RT Political Party Cadre
Political Party Follower
Political Party Worker
Rank And File Member

POLITICAL PARTY SYSTEM
S-37-0125 1979 00000
UF Party System
BT Political System Type
NT Multiparty System
One Political Party System
Two Political Party System
RT Government Type
Political Party Characteristics
Political Party Democracy
Political Party Innovation
Political Party Organization
Political Party Type

POLITICAL PARTY TICKET VOTING
S-29-0142 1975 00010
BT Voting
RT Political Party Identification
Straight Ticket Voting

POLITICAL PARTY TYPE
S-28-0001 1975 00005
NT Authoritarian Political Party
Democratic Political Party
Ideological Political Party
Ideological Spectrum Political Party Type
International Political Party
Major Political Party
Majority Political Party
Minor Political Party
Monarchist Political Party
National Political Party
Nationalist Political Party
Opposition Political Party
Republican Political Party
Revolutionary Political Party
Ruling Political Party
Sector Based Political Party Type
Separatist Political Party
Structure Specific Political Party Type
Underground Political Party
RT Political Party Alignment
Political Party System
Politics
Rank And File Member
Theory

POLITICAL PARTY VOTER
S-32-0324 1975 00031
BT Voter
NT Partisan Image Voter
Straight Party Voter
RT Candidate Voter
Political Party Loyalist
Political Socialization
Voter Orientation

POLITICAL PARTY VOTING INDICATOR
S-24-0270 1975 00017
BT Voting Indicator
RT Absentee Voting
Legislative Voting Indicator

POLITICAL PARTY WHIP
S-32-0161 1975 00000
BT Political Party Leader
RT Backbencher
Formal Political Party Leader
Frontbencher
Political Boss
Political Party Cadre
Political Party Chief
Political Party Professional

POLITICAL PARTY WORKER
S-32-0174 1975 00002
BT Political Party Member
NT Campaign Worker
Precinct Worker
RT Political Party Cadre
Political Party Professional
Political Party Supporter
Rank And File Member

POLITICAL PATRON
S-32-0252 1975 00002
SN Political figure who personally represents and protects client groups.
BT Politician
RT Boss Politics
Political Broker
Professional Politician
Spoils Politics

POLITICAL PERSECUTION
S-31-0317 1975 00002
BT Persecution
RT Cultural Imperialism
Ethnic Persecution
Fascist Movement
Minority Persecution
National Socialism
Nationality Persecution
Political Control
Political Exploitation
Political Indoctrination
Political Repression
Racial Persecution
Religious Persecution
Sex Persecution

POLITICAL PHILOSOPHY CONCEPT
S-38-0428 1975 00056
BT Political Theory
NT Authority Theory
Common Good Theory
Community Philosophical Concept
Consensus Theory
Consent Theory
Constitutional Interpretation Theory
Constitutional Structural Theory
Equality Theory
Freedom Theory
Human Condition Theory
Human Dignity Theory
Human Nature Theory
Individualism Theory
Justice Theory
Legitimacy Theory
Liberty Theory
Natural Law Conventionalism Theory
Obligation Theory
Open Society Theory
Order Theory
Political Alienation Theory
Political Man Theory
Rationality Theory
Representation Theory
Responsibility Doctrine
Social Contract Theory
Sovereignty Theory
RT Classical Political Thought
Contemporary Political Thought
Explanatory Political Theory
History Of Philosophy
Ideologies
Medieval Political Thought
Methodology
Modern Political Thought
Philosophical Concept
Political Ideology
Political Philosophy Studies

POLITICAL PHILOSOPHY STUDIES
S-01-0162 1975 00084
BT Political Science Discipline
RT Classical Political Thought
Community Philosophical Concept
Education Discipline
Education Philosophy
Encyclopedist Thought
Freudian Psychology
History Of Philosophy
Human Rights
Intellectual History
Macropolitical Theory
Marxist Existentialism
Philosophical Anthropology
Philosophy Discipline
Political Behavior Studies
Political Ideology
Political Philosophy Concept
Political Science Methodology Studies
Political Theory
Political Theory Studies
Political Virtue
Social Anthropology
Social Philosophy
Social Psychology
Sociology Of Knowledge
Socratic Political Thought

POLITICAL PLANNER
S-32-0135 1975 00000
BT Planner
NT Government Planner
RT Economic Planner
Social Planner

POLITICAL POWER
S-30-0011 1975 00026
BT Power Type
NT Emergency Power
Executive Power
Judicial Power
Legislative Power
Separation Of Power
RT Coercion
Economic Power
Formal Power
Institutional Power
Political Interference Policy
Political Intervention Policy
Political Resource Indicator
Power Measurement
Power Of The Purse
Power Theory

POLITICAL POWERLESSNESS
S-06-0088 1975 00013
BT Powerlessness
RT Marxist Alienation Theory
Nonvoting
Political Alienation
Political Alienation Theory
Political Apathy
Political Cynicism
Political Efficacy

POLITICAL PRISONER
S-36-0259 1975 00000
BT Prisoner
RT Concentration Camp
Detainee
Hostage
Prisoner Of War

POLITICAL PROFESSIONALIZATION
S-11-0025 1975 00002
BT Modern Political Culture
RT Political Subculture
Pragmatic Political Culture

POLITICAL PROPAGANDA
S-31-0189 1975 00006
BT Nonverbal Communication
NT Election Campaign Propaganda
Government Propaganda
Political Party Propaganda
War Propaganda
RT Political Advertising
Political Information Manipulation
Political Record Falsification

POLITICAL PSYCHOLOGY
S-01-0180 1975 00013
BT Social Psychology
RT Behavioral Science
Freudian Psychology
Group Psychology
Group Theory
Lasswellian Analysis
Legislative History
National Character
National Chauvinist
National Identity
National Image
National Political Culture
Political Anthropology
Political History
Political Normlessness
Political Science Methodology Studies
Political Sociology
Psychological Anthropology
Psychopathology
Social Pathology

POLITICAL PSYCHOLOGY ANALYSIS
S-09-0057 1975 00012
BT Contemporary Analytic Modes
NT Lasswellian Analysis
RT Behavior Analysis
Elite Analysis
Identity Analysis
Leadership Analysis
Leadership Political Analysis
Leadership Psychological Analysis
Leadership Sociological Analysis
Linguistic Analysis
Motivational Analysis
Political Style
Psychoanalysis
Psychopolitical Theory

POLITICAL PURGE
S-31-0309 1979 00000
BT Purge
RT Catharsis
Communist Studies
Control Process
Ideological Conflict
Institutional Conflict
Leadership Analysis
Leadership Recruitment
Political Leadership
Political Revolution
Political Succession
Rebellion
Succession Struggle

POLITICAL RADICAL
S-32-0263 1975 00009
BT Spectrum Politicist
RT Centrist
Extremist
Ideologue
Leftist
Liberal
Political Neutralist
Reactionary
Rightist

POLITICAL REBELLION
S-08-0055 1975 00015
BT Rebellion
RT Antiimperialism
Class Rebellion
Economic Agitation
Economic Rebellion
Government Overthrow
Group Conflict
Holy War
Institutional Conflict
Internal War
Mob Violence
Mobilization Policy
Peasant Rebellion
Political Violence
Revolution
Slave Rebellion
Social Rebellion
Struggle
Student Rebellion
War

POLITICAL RECORD FALSIFICATION
S-10-0076 1975 00000
BT Political Fraud
RT Political Espionage
Political Information Manipulation
Political Propaganda
Political Sabotage

POLITICAL RECRUITER
1975-1979 00000

POLITICAL RECRUITMENT
S-31-0746 1975 00009
BT Recruitment Process
NT Judicial Recruitment
Leadership Recruitment
Legislative Recruitment
Political Party Recruitment
RT Cooptation
Elite Recruitment
Military Recruitment
Nepotism
Presidential Appointment

POLITICAL REFUGEE
S-36-0025 1975 00004
BT Refugee
RT Communist Studies
Dictatorship
Dissent
Emigre
Political Opposition
Totalitarian Political System

POLITICAL REGIME
S-16-0132 1975 00006
BT Regime Type
NT Ancient Regime
Authoritarian Regime
Conservative Regime
Democratic Regime
Dictatorial Regime
Puppet Regime
RT Governing Coalition
Governing Elite
Government
Government Bureaucracy
Government Characteristics
Government Type
Rule Type
State Type

POLITICAL REPRESSION
S-31-0321 1979 00000
BT Repression Process
RT Absolutist Government
Authoritarian Regime
Cult Of Personality
Freedom
Human Rights
Inequality
Political Control
Political Persecution
Repression Process
Totalitarian Dictatorship
Tyranny
Underground Political Party

POLITICAL RESOURCE INDICATOR
S-24-0266 1975 00003
BT Political Indicator
RT Change Indicator
Conflict Indicator
Political Development Index
Political Power
Public Opinion Indicator
Stability Index
Voting Indicator

POLITICAL REVOLUTION
S-08-0068 1975 00020
BT Revolution
NT Democratic Political Revolution
National Political Revolution
Socialist Revolution
RT Chinese Cultural Revolution
Communist Bloc
Counterrevolution
Cultural Revolution
Expansionist War
Imperialist War
Marxism Leninism
Marxist Political Thought
Political Purge
Political Violence
Religious Conflict
Social Revolution
Spontaneous Revolution
Student Rebellion
Succession Struggle
Technological Revolution
Thermidor

POLITICAL ROLE
S-32-0178 1975 00028
BT Roles
NT Activist
Chauvinist
Conscientious Objector
Lobbyist
Political Gatekeeper
Political Informer
Politician
Politicist
Separatist
Voter
RT Incumbent
Local Political Boss
Political Decision Maker
Political Party Role
Professional Politician
Public Opinion Leader
Titular Leader

POLITICAL ROLE ORIENTATION
S-31-0768 1975 00012
BT Role Orientation
RT Executive Role Orientation
Judicial Role Orientation
Legislative Role Orientation
Role Socialization
Role Specialization

POLITICAL SABOTAGE
S-10-0077 1975 00005
BT Political Crime
RT Economic Sabotage
Guerrilla Activity
Guerrilla War
Political Conspiracy
Political Corruption
Political Espionage
Political Information Manipulation
Political Record Falsification
Sedition

POLITICAL SATISFACTION
S-06-0129 1975 00015
BT Satisfaction
RT Life Satisfaction
Living Conditions
Political Awareness
Political Efficacy
Quality Of Life
Secular Political Culture

POLITICAL SCIENCE DISCIPLINE
S-01-0156 1975 00028
BT Academic Areas
NT Comparative Political Studies
International Relations Studies
Policy Science Studies
Political Behavior Studies
Political Economy Studies
Political Philosophy Studies
Political Science Methodology Studies
Political Theory Studies
Public Administration Studies
Public Policy Studies
Urban Politics Studies
RT Administrative Science
African Area Studies
American Area Studies
Anthropology Discipline
Area Studies
Asian Area Studies
Behavioral Science
British Commonwealth Area Studies
Central African Area Studies
Communist Studies
Decision Making Analysis
Demographic Studies
East African Area Studies
Ecology Discipline
Economic History
Economics Discipline
Education Discipline

Elite Type
Ethnic Studies
Geography Discipline
Global Education
History Discipline
Ideographic Science
Information Science
Labor History
Legislative History
Middle East Area Studies
Military Science
Peace Studies
Political Anthropology
Political Geography
Political History
Political Scientist
Political Sociology
Psychology Discipline
Public Policy Studies
Russian Studies
Scandinavian Area Studies
Social History
Social Pathology
Social Psychology
Sociology Discipline
South African Area Studies
Soviet And East European Area Studies
Soviet Studies
Strategic Studies
West African Area Studies
West European Area Studies

POLITICAL SCIENCE METHODOLOGY STUDIES
S-01-0163 1975 00052
BT Political Science Discipline
RT Administrative Science
Anthropology Discipline
Behavioral Science
Comparative Political Studies
Computer Science
Cultural Anthropology
Demographic Studies
Economics Discipline
Freudian Psychology
General Theory
Historical Sociology
Historiography
History Of Philosophy
History Of Science
Information Science
Institutional History
International Power Theory
International Relations Studies
Learning Theory
Linguistics
Mathematics Discipline
Methodology
Philosophy Of Science Studies
Policy Science Studies
Policy Scientist
Political Anthropology
Political Behavior Studies
Political Economy Studies
Political Forecasting
Political Philosophy Studies
Political Psychology
Political Theory Studies
Psycholinguistics
Psychology Discipline
Social Anthropology
Social Pathology
Social Psychology
Sociolinguistics
Sociology Discipline
Sociology Of Knowledge
Strategic Studies

POLITICAL SCIENCE TEACHING
S-31-0453 1975 00011
BT Teaching
RT Education Curriculum
Graduate School
Simulation Material
Teacher Education
Textbook

POLITICAL SCIENCE TRAINING
S-13-0012 1975 00002
BT Graduate Education
RT Graduate School
Political Education
Politics
Professional Education
Professional Socialization

POLITICAL SCIENTIST
S-32-0113 1975 00005
BT Social Scientist
RT Academic
Anthropologist
Economist
Geographer
Historian
Policy Scientist
Political Science Discipline
Social Psychologist
Sociologist

POLITICAL SECULARIZATION
S-11-0026 1975 00001
BT Modern Political Culture
RT Political Efficacy
Political Subculture
Sectarian
Sectarian Movement
Secular Society

POLITICAL SELF CRITICISM
S-31-0306 1975 00000
BT Political Control
RT Catharsis
Communist Studies
Cultural Revolution
Political Indoctrination
Political Socialization
Political System Normative Characteristics
Political Trial

POLITICAL SOCIALIZATION
S-34-0046 1975 00051
BT Socialization Type
NT Political Orientation Development
Political Value Acquisition
RT Acculturation
Communist Education
Enculturation
Fascist Education
Learning Theory
Mass Belief System
Mass Public Opinion
Opinion Socialization
Political Attitude
Political Control
Political Culture
Political Identity
Political Legitimacy Theory
Political Participation
Political Party Affiliation
Political Party Identification
Political Party Loyalist
Political Party Orientation
Political Party Voter
Political Self Criticism
Socialization Analysis
Socialization Context
Socialization Type

POLITICAL SOCIOLOGY
S-01-0191 1975 00009
BT Sociology Discipline
RT Applied Sociology
Area Studies
Behavioral Psychology
Black History
Comparative Political Studies
Comparative Sociology
Electoral Geography
Electoral History
Ethnic Studies
Government Bureaucracy
Historical Sociology
Industrial Sociology
International Relations Studies
Learning Psychology
Legislative History
Macrosociology
Marxist Sociology
Political Anthropology
Political Behavior Studies
Political Geography
Political History
Political Psychology
Political Science Discipline
Primary Group
Psychology Discipline
Social Anthropology
Social Pathology
Social Psychology
Urban Sociology
Womens Studies

POLITICAL STATISTICS
S-18-0084 1975 00000
BT Statistical Data
NT Electoral Data
Macropolitical Data
Voting Data
RT Aggregate Data Analysis
Aggregate Data Statistics
Area Sampling
Cross Cultural Data
Economic Statistics
Field Data
Legislative Information Service
Mass Public Opinion
Private Information Service
Public Opinion Survey
Social Statistics
Survey Data

POLITICAL STYLE
S-06-0687 1975 00015
BT Political System Normative Characteristics
RT Elite Analysis
Elite Mass Relations
Lasswellian Analysis
Leadership Analysis
Leadership Psychological Analysis
Political Psychology Analysis
Sociological Analysis
Symbolic Politics

POLITICAL SUBCULTURE
S-11-0039 1979 00000
BT National Political Culture
RT Legalistic Political Culture
Parochial Political Culture
Political Professionalization
Political Secularization
Political System Effectiveness

POLITICAL SUCCESSION
S-31-0156 1979 00000
BT Extraterritorial Development
RT Career Analysis
Electoral Politics
Elite Circulation
Elite Disintegration
Elite Recruitment
Hereditary Ruler
Incumbent
Leadership Analysis
Leadership Psychological Analysis
Leadership Sociological Analysis
Leadership Type
Personalized Leadership
Political Crisis
Political Purge
Succession Struggle
Totalitarian Leadership

POLITICAL SYSTEM
1975-1979 00026
USE Political System Type

POLITICAL SYSTEM CAPABILITY CHARACTERISTICS
S-06-0682 1975 00017
BT Political System Characteristics
NT Political System Effectiveness
Political System Efficiency
RT Political System Normative Characteristics
Political System Structural Characteristics

POLITICAL SYSTEM CHARACTERISTICS
S-06-0658 1975 00054
BT System Characteristics
NT International Political System Characteristics
National Political System Characteristics
Political System Capability Characteristics
Political System Normative Characteristics
Political System Structural Characteristics
RT Analytic System Characteristics
Change Characteristics
Economic System Characteristics
Government Characteristics
Representation Type
Social System Characteristics
System Analysis
System Politicization

POLITICAL SYSTEM EFFECTIVENESS
S-06-0683 1975 00011
BT Political System Capability Characteristics
RT Diffuse System Supports
Interest Group Representation
Political Subculture
Political System Efficiency
Political System Structural Characteristics
Political System Theory
Social System Structural Characteristics

POLITICAL SYSTEM EFFICIENCY
S-06-0684 1975 00002
BT Political System Capability Characteristics
RT Political System Effectiveness
Political System Theory
Political System Type
System Function
System Inputs
System Persistence Capacity

POLITICAL SYSTEM NORMATIVE CHARACTERISTICS
S-06-0685 1975 00007
BT Political System Characteristics
NT Political Injustice
Political Style
RT Consensual Politics
Interest Group Representation
Political Self Criticism
Political System Capability Characteristics
Political System Structural Characteristics
System Politicization

POLITICAL SYSTEM STRUCTURAL CHARACTERISTICS
S-06-0688 1975 00052
BT Political System Characteristics
NT Political Consensus
Political Dissensus
Political Instability
Political Opportunity Structure
Political Opposition
RT Bureaucratic Theory
Government Characteristics
Institutions
Political System Capability Characteristics
Political System Effectiveness
Political System Normative Characteristics
Social System Structural Characteristics

POLITICAL SYSTEM THEORY
S-38-0160 1975 00050
BT Explanatory Political Theory
RT Equilibrium Theory
General System Theory
National Political System Characteristics
Organic State Theory
Political Integration Theory
Political System Effectiveness
Political System Efficiency
Structural Functional Political Theory
System Characteristics
System Equilibrium
Transactional Theory

POLITICAL SYSTEM TYPE
S-37-0106 1979 00000
UF Body Politic
Political System
Polity
BT System Type
NT City State Political System
Democratic Political System
Developing Political System
Federalism
Feudal System
International Political System
Modernizing Political System
Political Party System
Totalitarian Political System
Traditional Political System
Transitional Political System
Tribal Political System
RT Economic System
Legal System
Political Culture
Political Development Theory
Political System Efficiency
Social System
Value System

POLITICAL THEORY
S-38-0046 1975 00027
BT Theory
NT Classical Political Thought
Contemporary Political Thought
Democratic Theory
Eastern Political Thought
Economic Theory
Explanatory Political Theory
Ideologies
International Political Theory
Macropolitical Theory
Medieval Political Thought
Micropolitical Thought
Modern Political Thought
Political Philosophy Concept
Renaissance Political Thought
Strategic Theory
RT Anthropological Theory
History Of Philosophy
Methodology
Modernization Theory
Philosophical Concept
Political Development Theory
Political Philosophy Studies
Politics
Power Politics
Psychological Theory
Qualitative Research
Social Theory

POLITICAL THEORY STUDIES
S-01-0164 1975 00022
BT Political Science Discipline
RT Administrative Theory
Economics Discipline
Historiography

History Of Philosophy
History Of Science
Mythology
Philosophy Discipline
Political Behavior Studies
Political Philosophy Studies
Political Science Methodology Studies
Psychology Discipline
Sacred Law
Social Anthropology
Sociology Discipline
Sociology Of Knowledge
Theory

POLITICAL TOLERANCE
S-06-0136 1975 00007
BT Tolerance
RT Authoritarianism Scale
Freedom Of Speech
Human Rights
Opposition Political Party
Political Opposition
Political Trust
Pragmatic Political Culture
Right Of Assembly

POLITICAL TRIAL
S-31-0522 1975 00001
BT Trial
RT Bill Of Rights
Political Self Criticism
Trial Procedure
Trial Strategy
Trial System

POLITICAL TRUST
S-06-0139 1979 00000
BT Trust
RT Deference
Enlightened Self Interest
Political Attitude
Political Awareness
Political Efficacy
Political Tolerance
Political Virtue
Quality Of Life
Tolerance

POLITICAL UNIFICATION
S-31-0824 1975 00025
BT Political Integration
RT European Integration Theory
International Political Integration
National Political Integration
Subnational Political Integration

POLITICAL VALUE ACQUISITION
S-34-0048 1975 00020
BT Political Socialization
RT Mass Belief System
Modern Political Culture
Nation Building
Opinion Change
Opinion Formation
Opinion Socialization
Opinion Stability
Perception Socialization
Political Conditioning
Political Orientation Development
Role Socialization
Social Conditioning

POLITICAL VARIABLE
S-24-0450 1975 00010
BT Variable Substantive Content
RT Cultural Variable
Economic Variable
Historical Variable
Institutional Variable
Psychological Variable
Social Variable
Time Variable

POLITICAL VIOLENCE
S-08-0132 1975 00039
BT Violence
RT Aggression
Civil War
Coup D'Etat
Economic Agitation
Group Conflict
Guerrilla War
Insurgency
Internal War
Military Coup
Partisan War
Political Agitation
Political Rebellion
Political Revolution
Psychological Aggression
Putsch
Racial Conflict
Rebellion
Revolution
Revolutionary War
Riot Theory
Social Conflict
Spontaneous Revolution
Struggle
Student Riot
Terrorism
Violence
War

POLITICAL VIRTUE
S-06-0519 1979 00000
BT Virtue
RT Human Nature Theory
Justice Theory
Moral Responsibility
Obligation Theory
Political Legitimacy Theory
Political Man Theory
Political Philosophy Studies
Political Trust

POLITICIAN
S-32-0219 1975 00003
BT Political Role
NT Autocrat
Despot
Political Broker
Political Candidate
Political Official
Political Patron
Professional Politician
RT Activist
Decision Maker
Leader
Local Political Boss
Lower House Member
Political Activist
Political Decision Maker
Political Gatekeeper
Political Leader
Political Party Leader
Political Party Member
Political Party Professional
Political Party Role

POLITICIST
S-32-0254 1975 00001
SN A person characterized by high level of political activity related to his political belief system.
BT Political Role
NT Spectrum Politicist
System Politicist
RT Legislatures
Politicization

POLITICIZATION
S-31-0158 1975 00023
BT Political Change
NT Issue Politicization
System Politicization
RT Extraterritorial Development
Political Ideology
Politicist
Revolutionary Change

POLITICS
S-29-0001 1975 00009
NT Administrative Politics
Biopolitics
Class Politics
Coalition Politics
Confrontation Politics
Consensual Politics
Constituency Politics
Cultural Politics
Education Politics
Electoral Politics
Ethnic Politics
Extraparliamentary Politics
Geopolitics
Group Politics
International Politics
Labor Politics
Linkage Politics
National Politics
Parliamentary Politics
Partisan Politics
Power Politics
Progressive Politics
Protest Politics
Racial Politics
Religious Politics
Sexual Politics
Spoils Politics
Subnational Politics
Symbolic Politics
Technocratic Politics
Transitional Politics
Youth Politics
RT Electoral History
Political Behavior
Political Party Type
Political Science Training
Political Theory
Process
Theory

POLITY
USE Political System Type

POLL
1975-1979 00004

POLL TAX
S-29-0176 1975 00000
BT Voting Procedure
RT Disenfranchisement
Literacy Test
Literacy Voting Test
Public Opinion Survey
Voter Registration

POLLING PLACE
S-29-0197 1975 00000
BT Precinct
RT Precinct
Precinct Captain
Voter Registration
Voting Device

POLLUTION POLICY
S-26-0224 1975 00015
BT Environment Policy
NT Air Pollution Policy
Land Pollution Policy
Noise Pollution Policy
Sanitation Policy
Water Pollution Policy
RT Air Pollution
Ecological Analysis
Ecology Movement
Energy Policy
Environmental Agency
Environmental Planning
Land Policy
Natural Resource Policy
Space Policy

POLYANDRY
S-20-0027 1975 00000
SN Practice of having two or more husbands.
BT Polygamy
RT Anthropological Functionalism
Family Law
Marriage Type
Polygyny

POLYARACHIC DEMOCRATIC THEORY
USE Polyarchical Democratic Theory

POLYARCHAL DEMOCRATIC THEORY
1975-1979 00002

POLYARCHICAL DEMOCRATIC THEORY
S-38-0096 1979 00000
SN The view that democracy can be realized provided that there are institutional guarantees that promote consent and political equality which in turn
prevent the emergence of a hegemonic elite.
UF Polyarachic Democratic Theory
BT Democratic Theory
RT Elite Theory
Pluralist Elite
Polyarchy

POLYARCHY
S-16-0082 1975 00003
BT Government Type
RT Democratic Elite Theory
Elitism
Oligarchic Government
Polyarchical Democratic Theory

POLYCENTRIC INTERNATIONAL POLITICAL SYSTEM
S-37-0122 1975 00002
BT Multipolar International Political System
RT Commonwealth International System

POLYCENTRISM
S-38-0330 1975 00005
SN Condition in which power is dispersed and institutionally located in many autonomous structures.
BT Marxism
RT Bolshevism
Castroism
Communism
Communist Bloc
Communist Deviationism
Decentralized Authority
Evolutionary Marxism
Hegelian Marxism
Leninism
Maoism
Maoist
Maoist Political Party
Maoist Revolutionary
Marxism Leninism
Marxist Revisionism
Stalinism
Titoism
Trotskyism
Trotskyite Political Party

POLYGAMY
S-20-0026 1975 00001
BT Marriage Type
NT Polyandry
Polygyny
RT Communal Family
Concubinage
Family Planning
Family Role

POLYGYNY
S-20-0028 1975 00001
BT Polygamy
RT Anthropological Functionalism
Polyandry

POLYTECHNICAL INSTITUTE
S-19-0211 1975 00000
BT Higher Education Institution
RT Higher Education
Intellectual Elite
Military Institute
Vocational Training School

POLYTECHNICAL INSTITUTE EDUCATION
S-13-0015 1975 00000
BT Higher Education
RT Graduate Education
Professional Education
Technical Education
Technology
University Education

POOR NATION
S-16-0126 1975 00031
BT Nation Type
RT Economic Development Theory
Fourth World Nation
Third World Nation
Underdeveloped Nation

POPULAR ASSEMBLY
S-19-0276 1975 00000
BT National Assembly
RT Congress
Democratization
Diet
Parliament
Peoples Assembly
Representation Theory

POPULAR CULTURE
S-11-0020 1979 00000
BT Mass Culture
RT Fragmented Political Culture
Generational Political Culture
Modern Political Culture
Subculture

POPULAR FRONT
S-02-0055 1975 00002
BT Political Front
RT Antifascism
Electoral Coalition
Electoral Tactics
Extranational Bloc
International Communism
Liberation Front
National Front
United Front

POPULAR SOVEREIGNTY
S-16-0156 1975 00003
BT Sovereignty
RT Divided Sovereignty
Initiative Election
Mandate Territory
Territory Sovereignty

POPULATION ATTRIBUTE
S-06-0212 1975 00037
BT Demographic Characteristics
NT Migrant Population
Population Growth
Rural Population
Stable Population
Suburban Population
Urban Population
RT Age
Ancestry
Class Origin
Demographic Analysis
Demographic Indicator
Demographic Profile
Demographic Projection
Economic Background
Education Background
Ethnic Background
Ethnic Composition
Geographic Origin
Origin
Population Density
Socioeconomic Background

POPULATION COMPOSITION
S-06-0220 1975 00036
BT Demographic Characteristics
NT Ethnic Composition
Nationality Composition
Racial Composition
Religious Composition
RT Age
Census Record
Demographic Analysis

Demographic Indicator
Demographic Profile
Demographic Projection
Origin
Population Distribution
Population Growth
Population Identification
Population Movement

POPULATION CONCENTRATION
S-06-0227 1975 00056
BT Population Distribution
RT Black Suburban Community
Demographic Analysis
Metropolitan Growth Pattern
Residential Pattern

POPULATION DENSITY
S-06-0364 1979 00000
BT Environmental Characteristics
RT Community Size Characteristics
Demographic Studies
Land Use Policy
Living Conditions
Migrant Population
Population Attribute
Population Movement
Population Policy
Quality Of Life
Radiation Level
Rural Population
Stable Population
Suburban Population
Urban Politics Studies
Urban Population
Urban Population Area

POPULATION DISTRIBUTION
S-06-0225 1975 00047
BT Demographic Characteristics
NT Metropolitan Growth Pattern
Population Concentration
Residential Pattern
Urbanization Pattern
RT Age
Census Record
Demographic Analysis
Demographic Indicator
Demographic Profile
Demographic Projection
Oligopoly
Population Composition
Population Identification
Population Movement

POPULATION ESTIMATION
S-24-0072 1975 00016
BT Univariate Analysis
NT Parameter Estimation
Statistical Inference
Unbiased Estimation
RT Central Tendency Measure
Dispersion Measure
Zero Population Growth

POPULATION GROWTH
S-06-0214 1979 00000
BT Population Attribute
NT Zero Population Growth
RT Demographic Analysis
Demographic Projection
Demographic Studies
Malthusian Theory
Migration Pattern
Population Composition
Population Mobility
Population Planning

POPULATION IDENTIFICATION
S-24-0346 1975 00002
BT Social Classification
NT Rural Population Area
Suburban Population Area
Urban Population Area
RT Demographic Profile
Geography Discipline
Population Composition
Population Distribution
Rural Population Area
Suburban Population Area
Urban Population Area

POPULATION MANAGEMENT
S-23-0037 1975 00015
BT Management
RT Birth Rate
Emigration Policy
Environmental Planning
Health Administration
Immigration Policy
Life Expectancy
Natural Resource Management
Public Policy Management
Welfare Administration
Zero Population Growth

POPULATION MOBILITY
S-06-0243 1975 00008
BT Population Movement
NT Geographic Mobility
RT Emigration Pattern
Immigration Flow
Immigration Pattern
Internal Migration Pattern
Migration Pattern
Population Growth
Population Transition

POPULATION MOVEMENT
S-06-0233 1975 00013
BT Demographic Characteristics
NT Migration Pattern
Population Mobility
Population Transition
RT Emigration Policy
Population Composition
Population Density
Population Distribution
Population Policy
Stable Population
Urbanization Pattern

POPULATION PLANNING
S-31-0659 1975 00020
BT Planning Process
NT Family Planning
RT Development Planning
Economic Planning
Education Needs
Education Planning
Environmental Planning
Life Expectancy
Population Growth
Population Transition
Public Policy Planning
Social Engineering
Social Planning
Zero Population Growth

POPULATION POLICY
S-26-0393 1975 00046
BT Social Policy
NT Birth Control Policy
Family Policy
RT Birth Rate
Family Planning
Housing Policy
Population Density
Population Movement
Population Transition
Religious Policy
Service Policy
Social Resource Distribution Policy
Social Welfare Policy
Stable Population

POPULATION TRANSITION
S-06-0245 1979 00000
BT Population Movement
RT Immigration Flow
Immigration Pattern
Internal Migration Pattern
Malthusian Theory
Migration Pattern
Migration Policy
Population Mobility
Population Planning
Population Policy

POPULISM
S-38-0286 1975 00013
BT Ideologies
RT Agrarianism
Chartism
Home Rule
Nationalism
Populist Movement

POPULIST DEMOCRATIC THEORY
S-38-0097 1975 00001
BT Democratic Theory
RT Athenian Democratic Theory
Concurrent Majority Theory
Confederation Movement
Democratic Elite Theory
Economic Theory Of Democracy
General Will Democratic Theory
Guided Democracy Theory
Industrial Democracy
Jacksonian Democratic Theory
Jeffersonian Democratic Theory
Majoritarianism
Minority Rights Democratic Theory
Participatory Democratic Theory
Republic Theory
Socialist Democratic Theory

POPULIST MOVEMENT
S-27-0056 1975 00004
BT Sector Based Political Movement
RT Agrarian Movement
Agrarian Reform Movement
Chiliastic Movement
Civic Action Movement
Class Based Movement
Communal Movement
Fascist Movement
Grass Roots Movement
Populism
Radical Movement
Reform Movement
Sectarian Movement

PORK BARREL
S-06-0424 1975 00001
BT Legislative Norms
RT Clientelism
Coalition Theory
Interest Group Politics
Log Rolling
Parliamentary Procedure
Political Coalition

PORNOGRAPHIC CRIME
S-10-0080 1979 00000
BT Crime
RT Morals Offense
Organized Crime
Sex Crime
Sex Role
Sexism

PORNOGRAPHY LAW
S-21-0096 1979 00000
BT Social Law
RT Blue Law
Gambling Law
Gun Control Law
Miscegenation Law
Morals Offense
Sex Crime

POSITIVE FREEDOM THEORY
S-38-0466 1975 00002
BT Freedom Theory
RT Freedom
Hegelian Analysis
Individual Freedom Theory
Kantian Analysis
Moral Freedom Theory
Negative Freedom Theory
Rousseauian Analysis

POSITIVE VOTING ABSTENTION
S-29-0119 1975 00000
SN Conscious decision not to vote on the ground that alternatives presented do not reflect meaningful choice.
BT Voting Abstention
RT Apathetic Voter
Protest Politics
System Politicist

POSSESSIVE INDIVIDUALISM
S-38-0472 1975 00007
BT Individualism Theory
RT Atomistic Society
Hobbesian Absolutism
Lockean Contractualism
Lockean Liberalism
Utilitarianism

POST INDUSTRIAL ECONOMIC STAGE
S-06-0163 1975 00003
BT Economic Development Stage
RT Advanced Industrial Society
Economic Development
Economic Development Theory

POST INDUSTRIAL SOCIETY
S-35-0022 1975 00015
BT Industrial Society
RT Advanced Industrial Society
Development Theory
Economic Development
Industrial Economics
Technocracy
Technology

POST INDUSTRIAL SOCIETY THEORY
S-38-0161 1975 00013
BT Explanatory Political Theory
RT Advanced Industrial Society
End Of Ideology Analysis
Structural Functional Political Theory

POST TRIAL PROCEDURE
S-31-0491 1975 00000
BT Court Procedure
NT Imprisonment
Internment
Legal Settlement
Parole
Presentence Investigation
Sentencing
RT Pretrial Procedure
Trial
Trial Procedure

POSTAL CENSORSHIP POLICY
1975-1979 00000

POSTAL COMMUNICATION POLICY
S-26-0018 1975 00002
BT Individual Communication Policy
RT Postal Rate Policy
Postal Telephone Telegraph Policy
Telephone Policy

POSTAL RATE POLICY
S-26-0020 1975 00000
BT Postal Telephone Telegraph Policy
RT Communication Process
Government Regulation
Postal Communication Policy
Postal Telephone Telegraph Policy
Price Policy

POSTAL TELEPHONE TELEGRAPH POLICY
S-26-0019 1975 00000
BT Individual Communication Policy
NT Postal Rate Policy
RT Postal Communication Policy
Postal Rate Policy
Telephone Policy

POTENTIAL ELITE
S-14-0027 1975 00002
BT Political Elite
RT Attentive Public
Elite Formation
Intelligentsia
Military Elite
Modernizing Elite
Modernizing Political Elite
Modernizing Social Elite
Nation Building
Policy Elite
Power Elite
Revolutionary Elite
Transitional Political Elite

POTENTIAL ELITE GROUP
1975-1979 00002

POTENTIAL VOTER
S-32-0308 1975 00000
BT Eligible Voter
RT Registered Voter

POVERTY
S-06-0637 1975 00043
BT Wealth Distribution
RT Deprivation
Income Distribution
Poverty Program Spending
Squatter Community
Squatter Society
Subsistence Level

POVERTY CULTURE
S-11-0040 1975 00017
BT Culture Type
RT Community Culture
Counter Culture
Cultural Lag
Drug Culture
Ethnic Culture
Poverty Program Spending
Village Culture

POVERTY POLICY
S-26-0412 1975 00037
BT Social Welfare Policy
RT Old Age Assistance Policy

POVERTY PROGRAM SPENDING
S-31-0418 1975 00015
BT Public Spending
RT Government Regulation
Poverty
Poverty Culture
Social Welfare Policy
Welfare State

POWER ABUSE
S-29-0224 1979 00000
UF Oppression
BT Power Politics
RT Imperial Presidency
Malfeasance
Misfeasance
Political Crime
Political Fraud
Power Theory
Realpolitik

POWER ELITE
S-14-0028 1975 00007
BT Political Elite
RT Big Business
Corporate Elite
Decision Making Elite
Formal Power
Governing Elite
Institutional Power
Managerial Elite
Military Elite
Policy Elite
Potential Elite
Revolutionary Elite
Social Elite
Transitional Political Elite

POWER MEASUREMENT
S-24-0190 1979 00000
BT Measurement Object
RT Balance Of Power Theory
Group Measurement
Individual Measurement
International Relations Studies
Measurement Evaluation
Measurement Level
Measurement Problem
Measurement Procedure
Measurement Scale
Political Power
Power Theory
Power Type

POWER OF THE PURSE
S-30-0007 1975 00000
BT Economic Power
RT Economic Plan
Economic Policy Making
Economic Program
Formal Power
Legislative Power
Political Corruption
Political Power

POWER POLITICS
S-29-0223 1975 00020
BT Politics
NT Power Abuse
Realpolitik
RT Arms Race
Balance Of Power
Coercion
Conflict Theory
Confrontation Politics
Feminist Politics
Global War Policy
Governing Elite
Institutional Power
Linkage Politics
Political Theory
Realist Foreign Policy
Spoils Politics
Symbolic Politics

POWER THEORY
S-38-0162 1975 00048
BT Explanatory Political Theory
NT Community Power Theory
Control Theory
International Power Theory
RT Aggression Theory
Authority
Concentrated Power
Conflict Theory
Decision Making Theory
Formal Power
Fourth World Nation
Institutional Power
Political Interference Policy
Political Intervention Policy
Political Power
Power Abuse
Power Measurement
Power Type
Public Choice Theory
Realpolitik
Structural Functional Political Theory
Transactional Theory

POWER TYPE
S-30-0001 1975 00007
NT Concentrated Power
Dispersed Power
Economic Power
Formal Power
Informal Power
Political Power
State Power
Wartime Power
RT Control Theory
International Power Theory
Order Theory
Power Measurement
Power Theory
Realpolitik
Separation Of Power Theory
Sovereignty Theory

POWERLESSNESS
S-06-0087 1975 00012
BT Alienation
NT Political Powerlessness
RT Apathy
Social Theory

PRAGMATIC POLITICAL CULTURE
S-11-0031 1975 00003
BT Civic Culture
RT Accommodative Social Behavior
Civic Culture
Generational Political Culture
Ideological Political Culture
Legalistic Political Culture
Modern Political Culture
Political Professionalization
Political Tolerance
Pragmatism
Secular Political Culture
Subject Participant Culture
Work Culture

PRAGMATISM
S-38-0075 1975 00010
BT Contemporary Political Thought
RT History Of Philosophy
Individualism Theory
Pragmatic Political Culture

PRAXIOLOGY
1975-1979 00008
USE Praxis

PRAXIS
S-38-0313 1979 00000
UF Praxiology
BT Marxist Theory
RT Marxism
Marxist Alienation Theory
Marxist Class Theory
Marxist Communism Theory
Marxist Existentialism
Political Activist
Revolution Theory
Revolutionary Change

PRECINCT
S-29-0196 1975 00002
BT Local Election District
NT Polling Place
RT Polling Place
Ward

PRECINCT CAPTAIN
S-32-0162 1975 00000
BT Political Party Leader
RT Campaign Manager
Political Boss
Political Candidate
Political Party Cadre
Political Party Professional
Polling Place
Ward Chairperson

PRECINCT WORKER
S-32-0176 1975 00000
BT Political Party Worker
RT Political Party Cadre
Political Party Professional
Ward Chairperson

PREDICTIVE RESEARCH
S-24-0392 1975 00065
BT Research Orientation
RT Applied Research
Basic Research
Brainstorming
Causal Analysis
Concept Explication Research
Deductive Method
Delphi Technique
Descriptive Research
Divergence Mapping
Economic Forecasting
Experimental Research
Explanatory Political Theory
Explanatory Research
Forecasting Methodology
PERT Analysis
Policy Research
Political Forecasting
Qualitative Research
Quantitative History
Quantitative Research
Scenario Construction
Scientific Research
Social Forecasting
Theoretical Research
Trend Analysis

PREDISPOSITION
1975-1979 00001

PREEMPTIVE ATTACK POLICY
S-26-0072 1975 00008
BT Nuclear Strike Policy
RT First Strike Policy
Nuclear Stockpiling
Preventive Attack Policy
Second Strike Policy

PREEMPTORY CHALLENGE
S-31-0550 1975 00000
BT Judicial Procedure
RT Procedural Due Process

PREFECT
S-36-0087 1975 00001
BT Chief Government Executive
RT Feudal Lord•
Governor
Governor General
Local Chief Government Executive
Prince
Regional Political Party First Secretary

PREFERENCE PRIMARY
S-29-0076 1975 00002
BT Election Type
RT Blanket Primary
Closed Primary
National Primary
Open Primary

PREHISTORICAL TIMES
S-06-0173 1979 00000
BT Historical Periods
RT Ancient Times
Antiquity
Archaeology
Discovery

PREINDUSTRIAL CITY
S-07-0013 1975 00002
BT City
RT Hamlet
Village

PREINDUSTRIAL SOCIETY
S-35-0046 1975 00010
BT Traditional Society
RT Advanced Industrial Society
Craft Economy
Dependent Nation
Development Theory
Economic Development
Feudal Society
Hunting And Fishing Society
Hunting And Trapping Economy

PREJUDICE
S-06-0119 1975 00017
BT Attitude Characteristics
NT Bias
RT Authoritarian Attitude
Bigotry
Deference
Hostility

PRELAPSARIAN THEORY
1975-1979 00000

PREMIER
S-36-0073 1975 00001
BT National Chief Government Executive
RT Chancellor
Chief Government Executive
Governor General
President
Prime Minister
Prime Minister Candidate

PREMIERSHIP
S-19-0238 1975 00000
BT Executive Government Institution
RT Governorship
Presidency
Secretariat

PRESENTENCE INVESTIGATION
S-31-0500 1975 00000
BT Post Trial Procedure
RT Imprisonment
Internment
Sentencing

PRESIDENCY
S-19-0239 1975 00044
BT Executive Government Institution
NT Imperial Presidency
RT Governorship
Premiership
President
Presidential Candidate
Presidential Government
Presidential Leadership
Presidential Nominating Process
Presidential Policy
Presidential Primary
Presidential Staff Personnel
Secretariat

PRESIDENT
S-36-0074 1975 00036
BT National Chief Government Executive
NT Vice President
RT Chancellor
Chief Government Executive
Premier
Presidency
Presidential Candidate
Presidential Government
Presidential Leadership
Presidential Nominating Process
Presidential Policy
Presidential Staff Personnel
Prime Minister
Prime Minister Candidate
Proclamation

PRESIDENTIAL ACCOUNTABILITY
S-06-0435 1975 00013
BT Chief Executive Accountability
RT Constitutional Law
Executive Power
Government Accountability
Legislative Accountability
Presidential Discretion

PRESIDENTIAL ADVISOR
S-32-0014 1975 00004
BT Chief Executive Advisor
RT Chief Executive Accountability
Election Campaign Advisor
Vice President

PRESIDENTIAL ADVISORY COUNCIL
S-19-0116 1975 00006
BT National Government Council
RT Cabinet
Chancellery
Chief Executive Accountability
Chief Executive Advisor
Council Of Ministers
Executive Government Institution
Privy Council

PRESIDENTIAL AGREEMENT
USE Executive Agreement

PRESIDENTIAL APPOINTMENT
S-31-0730 1975 00005
BT Appointment Process
RT Government Employee
Political Recruitment
Reappointment
Senatorial Courtesy

PRESIDENTIAL CAMPAIGN
1975-1979 00014

PRESIDENTIAL CANDIDATE
S-32-0231 1975 00019
BT National Chief Executive Candidate
NT Favorite Son Candidate
RT National Chief Executive Primary
Presidency
President
Presidential Leadership
Presidential Nominating Process
Presidential Primary
Prime Minister Candidate

PRESIDENTIAL COATTAIL EFFECT
S-29-0109 1975 00004
BT Coattail Effect
RT Bandwagon Effect
Voting Behavior

PRESIDENTIAL COMMISSION
S-19-0100 1975 00003
BT Commissions
RT Commission Of Inquiry
Executive Government Institution
Federal Commission
Fiscal Agency
Independent Regulatory Commission
International Planning Commission
Investigation Commission
National Planning Commission
Planning Commission
Presidential Commission Of Inquiry

PRESIDENTIAL COMMISSION OF INQUIRY
S-19-0090 1975 00002
BT Commission Of Inquiry
RT Environmental Planning
International Constitutional Convention
Legislative Commission
Legislative Commission Of Inquiry
Parliamentary Commission Of Inquiry
Presidential Commission
Royal Commission Of Inquiry

PRESIDENTIAL DIPLOMACY
S-31-0356 1975 00006
BT Executive Diplomacy
RT Gunboat Diplomacy
Presidential Government
Presidential Legislative Program
Presidential Task Force
Secret Diplomacy
Summit Diplomacy

PRESIDENTIAL DISCRETION
S-06-0440 1975 00002
BT Chief Executive Discretion
RT Emergency Power
Executive Prerogative
Executive Privilege
Presidential Accountability

PRESIDENTIAL ELECTION
S-29-0054 1975 00056
BT National Chief Executive Election
RT Chancellor Candidate
Chancellor Election
Prime Minister Election

PRESIDENTIAL ELECTION CAMPAIGN
S-29-0027 1979 00000
BT National Chief Executive Election Campaign
RT Presidential Primary

PRESIDENTIAL GOVERNMENT
S-16-0083 1975 00008
BT Government Type
RT Executive Pronouncement
Presidency
President
Presidential Diplomacy
Presidential Policy
Representative Government

PRESIDENTIAL LEADERSHIP
S-22-0025 1979 00000
BT Executive Leadership
RT Congressional Leadership
Leadership Analysis
National Leadership
Political Movement Leadership
Political Party Leadership
Presidency
President
Presidential Candidate
Presidential Legislative Program
Presidential Power
Presidential Task Force

PRESIDENTIAL LEGISLATIVE PROGRAM
S-26-0244 1975 00007
BT Executive Legislative Policy
RT Inaugural Address
Leadership Analysis

National Policy Planning
Presidential Diplomacy
Presidential Leadership
Presidential Policy

PRESIDENTIAL NOMINATING PROCESS
S-31-0740 1975 00010
BT Nominating Process
RT Ballot
Legislative Nominating Process
Political Party Convention
Presidency
President
Presidential Candidate
Presidential Primary

PRESIDENTIAL POLICY
S-26-0248 1979 00000
UF Presidential Policy Message
BT Executive Policy
NT Inaugural Address
RT Executive Communique
Executive Legislative Policy
Executive Pronouncement
Executive Trial Balloon Policy
Inaugural Address
Presidency
President
Presidential Government
Presidential Legislative Program
Presidential Power

PRESIDENTIAL POLICY MESSAGE
1975-1979 00003
USE Presidential Policy

PRESIDENTIAL POWER
S-30-0014 1975 00073
BT Executive Power
RT Imperial Presidency
Judicial Power
Legislative Power
Presidential Leadership
Presidential Policy
Presidential Task Force
Separation Of Power
State Of The Union
State Power
Wartime Power

PRESIDENTIAL PREROGATIVE
1975-1979 00013

PRESIDENTIAL PRIMARY
S-29-0070 1975 00008
BT National Chief Executive Primary
RT Local Chief Executive Primary
Presidency
Presidential Candidate
Presidential Election Campaign
Presidential Nominating Process

PRESIDENTIAL STAFF PERSONNEL
S-36-0012 1975 00013
BT Chief Executive Staff Personnel
RT Government Employee
Line Staff
Presidency
President
Public Administration Studies
Vice President

PRESIDENTIAL TASK FORCE
S-19-0330 1975 00001
BT Task Force
RT Executive Government Institution
National Planning Commission
National Policy Planning
Presidential Diplomacy
Presidential Leadership
Presidential Power

PRESIDENTIAL VETO
S-31-0338 1975 00004
BT Executive Veto
RT Gubernatorial Veto
Item Veto
Legislative Process

PRESOCRATIC POLITICAL THOUGHT
S-38-0053 1975 00001
BT Classical Political Thought
RT Ancient History
Eastern Political Thought
Platonic Political Thought
Pythagorean Thought
Stoic Thought
Thucydidean Political Thought

PRESS CENSORSHIP AGENCY
1975-1979 00000
USE Censorship Agency

PRESTIGE HIERARCHY
S-06-0744 1979 00000
BT Social System Structural Characteristics
NT Social Prestige
RT Achieved Status
Ascribed Status
Economic Incentive System
Hierarchical Authority
Hierarchical Integration
Hierarchical Model
Status Stratification Division
Subjectively Derived Status
Vertical Stratification Division

PRETAKEOFF PERIOD
S-06-0164 1975 00001
BT Economic Development Stage
RT Agricultural Economic Stage
Feudal Economic Stage

PRETRIAL PROCEDURE
S-31-0505 1975 00003
BT Court Procedure
NT Arraignment
Arrest
Bail
Detention
Indictment
Pretrial Release
RT Bail Bond System
Common Law System
Plea Bargaining
Post Trial Procedure

PRETRIAL RELEASE
S-31-0516 1975 00000
BT Pretrial Procedure
RT Arraignment
Bail Bond System
Bail Skipping
Detention
Indictment

PREVENTIVE ATTACK POLICY
S-26-0073 1975 00000
BT Nuclear Strike Policy
RT First Strike Policy
Nuclear Stockpiling
Preemptive Attack Policy
Second Strike Policy

PREVENTIVE DETENTION
S-31-0514 1975 00001
BT Detention
RT Arrest
Concentration Camp
Local Police

PRICE CONTROL AGENCY
S-19-0018 1975 00003
BT Economic Control Agency
RT Consumer Agency
Fiscal Agency
Planning Commission
Price Control Law
Price Fixing Policy
Price Support Agency
Rationing Agency

PRICE CONTROL LAW
S-21-0043 1975 00004
BT Economic Law
RT Consumer Agency
Economic Subsidization Policy
Price Control Agency
Price Control Policy
Price Fixing Policy
Price Freeze Policy
Price Support Agency
Welfare Law

PRICE CONTROL POLICY
S-26-0114 1975 00022
BT Income Policy
RT Economic Subsidization Policy
Price Control Law
Price Fixing Policy
Price Freeze Policy
Price Support Agency
Price Support Policy

PRICE FIXING POLICY
S-26-0115 1975 00015
BT Income Policy
RT Deflation
Economic Subsidization Policy
Price Control Agency
Price Control Law
Price Control Policy
Price Freeze Policy
Price Support Agency

PRICE FREEZE POLICY
S-26-0116 1979 00000
UF Price Freezing Policy
BT Income Policy
RT Deflation
Price Control Law
Price Control Policy
Price Fixing Policy

PRICE FREEZING POLICY
1975-1979 00004
USE Price Freeze Policy

PRICE POLICY
S-26-0113 1975 00052
BT Income Policy
RT Consumption Pattern
Deflation
Government Economic Management
Government Economic Planning
Postal Rate Policy
Wage Freeze Policy

PRICE SUPPORT AGENCY
S-19-0019 1975 00000
BT Economic Control Agency
RT Consumer Agency
Fiscal Agency
Price Control Agency
Price Control Law
Price Control Policy
Price Fixing Policy
Rationing Agency

PRICE SUPPORT POLICY
S-26-0127 1975 00001
BT Economic Policy
NT Agricultural Price Support Policy
Business Price Support Policy
RT Economic Growth Policy
Economic Subsidization Policy
Farm Income
Fiscal Policy
Price Control Policy

PRIEST
S-32-0104 1979 00000
BT Religious Minister
RT Ecclesiastical Leadership
Religious Education
Religious Elite
Religious Leader
Religious Policy
Religious Role
Teacher

PRIMARY EDUCATION
S-13-0034 1975 00007
BT Education Type
NT Elementary Education
RT Education Agency
Education Characteristics
Education Institution
Inner City School
Middle School
Primary School
Private School Education
Secondary Education

PRIMARY ELECTION
S-29-0063 1975 00009
BT Election Type
NT Blanket Primary
Closed Primary
National Primary
RT Coalition Politics
Congressional Primary
Election Campaign
Electoral Alliance
Electoral Participation
Electoral Politics
Partisan Election
Partisan Politics
Political Party Primary

PRIMARY GROUP
S-03-0027 1975 00005
BT Face To Face Group
RT Face To Face Group
Political Sociology

PRIMARY GROUP SOCIALIZATION
S-34-0031 1975 00009
BT Group Socialization
RT Adolescent Socialization
Adult Political Socialization
Adult Socialization
Childhood Socialization
Cohort Group Socialization
Family Socialization
Peer Group
Peer Group Socialization

PRIMARY SCHOOL
S-19-0221 1975 00016
BT Education Institution
RT Education Planner
Education Planning
Primary Education
Public School
Secondary School
Urban School

PRIME LOAN RATE
S-06-0356 1975 00000
BT Money Creation
RT Bank Reserve
Banking Agency
Discount Rate
Financing
Monetary Policy

PRIME MINISTER
S-36-0076 1975 00010
BT National Chief Government Executive
RT Chancellor
Chief Government Executive
Premier
President
Prime Minister Candidate
Prime Minister Election Campaign
Proclamation

PRIME MINISTER CAMPAIGN
1975-1979 00000

PRIME MINISTER CANDIDATE
S-32-0233 1975 00001
BT National Chief Executive Candidate
RT Chief Government Executive
Premier
President
Presidential Candidate
Prime Minister
Prime Minister Election
Prime Minister Election Campaign

PRIME MINISTER ELECTION
S-29-0055 1975 00000
BT National Chief Executive Election
RT Chancellor Candidate
Chancellor Election
Presidential Election
Prime Minister Candidate
Prime Minister Election Campaign

PRIME MINISTER ELECTION CAMPAIGN
S-29-0028 1979 00000
BT National Chief Executive Election Campaign
RT Government Dissolution Process
Government Formation Process
No Confidence Motion
Parliamentary Politics
Prime Minister
Prime Minister Candidate
Prime Minister Election

PRIME TIME ACCESS POLICY
S-26-0030 1979 00000
UF Prime Time Access Rule
BT Broadcast Access Policy
RT Broadcast Censorship Policy
Broadcast Regulation Policy
Election Campaign Advertising
Freedom Of Press
Freedom Of Speech

PRIME TIME ACCESS RULE
1975-1979 00000
USE Prime Time Access Policy

PRIMITIVE SOCIETY
S-35-0007 1975 00015
BT Society Type
RT Barter Economy
Hunting And Fishing Society
Magic
Nomadic Society
Nonwestern Society
Peasant Society
Traditional Society
Tribalism

PRIMOGENITURE
S-37-0057 1975 00000
BT Property Ownership System
RT Customary Law
Government Ownership
Land Estate System
Land Tenure System
Private Ownership
Slavery

PRINCE
S-36-0065 1975 00004
BT Monarch
RT Absolute Monarchy
Feudal Lord
Governor
Governor General
Prefect

PRISON
S-19-0299 1975 00010
BT Penal Institution
NT Criminal Prison
Military Prison
RT Bail Bond System
Correctional Institution
Criminal
Jail
Juvenile Center
Police

PRISON REFORM
S-31-0095 1975 00006
BT Penal Reform
RT Correctional Institution
Jail
Juvenile Center
Parole
Penal Institution
Prison System
Punishment

PRISON SYSTEM
S-37-0093 1975 00012
BT Law Enforcement System
RT Correctional Institution
Criminal
Jail
Juvenile Center
Prison Reform
Prisoner

PRISONER
S-36-0256 1975 00012
BT Status
NT Detainee
Hostage
Political Prisoner
Prisoner Of War

RT Concentration Camp
Criminal
Prison System

PRISONER DILEMMA GAMING
S-24-0102 1975 00013
BT Gaming
RT Fixed Sum Gaming
Nonzero Sum Gaming
Two Person Game Theory
Two Person Gaming
Variable Sum Gaming
Zero Sum Gaming

PRISONER DILEMMA THEORY
S-38-0135 1975 00013
BT Game Theory
RT Fixed Sum Gaming
Gaming
Variable Sum Gaming
Zero Sum Gaming

PRISONER OF WAR
S-36-0260 1975 00006
BT Prisoner
RT Concentration Camp
Detainee
Hostage
International Law
Political Prisoner
Prisoner Of War Camp
War Criminal
World Court

PRISONER OF WAR CAMP
S-19-0297 1975 00001
BT Detention Center
RT Brainwashing
Concentration Camp
International Law
Prisoner Of War
Secret Police
Slave Labor Camp

PRIVATE ARMY
S-33-0046 1975 00000
BT Irregular Military Forces
RT Irregular Forces
Irregular Military Forces
Paramilitary Forces
Paramilitary Organization

PRIVATE BUREAUCRACY
1975-1979 00002

PRIVATE CAPITAL
S-06-0266 1975 00004
BT Capital
RT Assets
Business Price Support Policy
Capital Surplus
Capitalism
Investment Capital
Public Capital

PRIVATE CENSORSHIP AGENCY
1975-1979 00000
USE Censorship Agency

PRIVATE COLLEGE
S-19-0206 1975 00003
BT College
RT Academic Tenure Policy
Education Planning
Higher Education
Humanistic Education
Intellectual Elite
Junior College
State Supported College
University

PRIVATE CONSUMPTION
S-06-0274 1975 00001
BT Consumption
RT Conspicuous Consumption
Consumption Pattern
Consumption Process
Domestic Consumption
Mass Consumption
Public Consumption

PRIVATE EDUCATION POLICY
S-26-0193 1975 00003
BT Education Policy
RT Education Institution
Education Planning
Education Policy
Higher Education Policy
Literacy Policy
Public Education Policy
Vocation Training Policy

PRIVATE FARMER
S-32-0067 1975 00000
BT Farmer
RT Collective Farmer
Sharecropper
Tenant Farmer

PRIVATE FOREIGN INVESTMENT
S-31-0394 1975 00027
BT Private Investment
NT Private Overseas Investment
RT Commercial Attache
International Capital Movement
International Finance
International Investment
Private Industrial Investment
Private Rural Investment
Public Foreign Investment
Yankee Imperialism

PRIVATE HIGHER EDUCATION
S-13-0016 1975 00006
BT Higher Education
RT Education Agency
Education Institution
Humanistic Education
State Supported Higher Education
Traditional Education
University Education

PRIVATE HOSPITAL
S-19-0247 1979 00000
BT Hospital
RT Halfway House
Health Care Policy
Health Care System
Health Clinic
Medical Care Policy
Medical Care Service
Medical Care System
Nursing Home
Public Health Institution
Public Hospital

PRIVATE INDUSTRIAL INVESTMENT
S-31-0396 1975 00008
BT Private Investment
RT Private Foreign Investment

PRIVATE INDUSTRY
S-17-0051 1975 00012
BT Industry
RT Business Income
Business Leader
Business Policy
Business Price Support Policy
Capitalism
Capitalism Theory

PRIVATE INFORMATION SERVICE
S-18-0053 1979 00000
BT Information Service
RT Abstracting Service
Archives
Bibliographic Control
Bibliographic Service
Documentation Service
Documents
Government Information Service
Political Statistics
Private Sector
Public Record
Social Statistics
Statistical Data
University Information Service

PRIVATE INVESTMENT
S-31-0393 1975 00013
BT Investment
NT Private Foreign Investment
Private Industrial Investment
Private Rural Investment
RT Business Income
Business Price Support Policy
Capital
Capital Flow
Capital Formation
Capital Investment Economy
Capitalism
Capitalism Theory
Private Spending
Public Investment

PRIVATE MONOPOLY
S-06-0632 1975 00001
BT Monopoly
RT Business Elite
Capitalism
Cartel
Concentrated Power
Oligopoly
Perfect Monopoly
Public Monopoly

PRIVATE OVERSEAS INVESTMENT
S-31-0395 1975 00004
BT Private Foreign Investment
RT International Capital Movement
International Finance
International Investment

PRIVATE OWNERSHIP
S-37-0058 1975 00017
BT Property Ownership System
RT Business Income
Capitalism
Capitalism Theory
Capitalist Class
Capitalist Economy
Capitalist Society
Collective Ownership
Foreign Ownership
Free Enterprise System
Government Ownership
Inheritance System
Land Estate System
Land Tenure System
Primogeniture
Propertied Class

Slavery

PRIVATE POLICE
S-19-0307 1975 00000
BT Police
RT International Police
Military Police
National Police
Paramilitary Police
Secret Police
Subnational Police

PRIVATE RURAL INVESTMENT
S-31-0397 1975 00000
BT Private Investment
RT Farming
Private Foreign Investment
Rural Community
Rural Development
Rural Environment
Rural Policy Planning

PRIVATE SAVING
S-31-0410 1979 00000
BT Saving
RT Fiscal Policy
Monetary Policy
Public Saving
Spending

PRIVATE SCHOOL
S-19-0222 1975 00003
BT Education Institution
RT Education Planner
Education Planning
Humanistic Education
Parochial School
Public School
Religious School

PRIVATE SCHOOL EDUCATION
S-13-0036 1975 00002
BT Education Type
RT Education Institution
Elementary Education
Primary Education
Progressive Education
Secondary Education

PRIVATE SCHOOL SUBSIDY
S-06-0304 1975 00001
BT Education Subsidy
RT Education Institution
Parochial School Subsidy

PRIVATE SECTOR
S-37-0031 1975 00046
BT Economic Sector
RT Agricultural Sector
Black Capitalism
Bourgeois Capitalism
Charitable Organization
Citizen To Citizen Diplomacy
Commercial Sector
Entrepreneur
Entrepreneurship
Financing
Industrial Capitalism
Limited Government
Mass Consumption
Mature Capitalism
Mercantile Capitalism
Monopoly Capitalism
Philanthropic Organization
Private Information Service
Private Spending
Public Sector
Warfare Capitalism

PRIVATE SPENDING
S-31-0413 1975 00000
BT Spending
RT Monetary Policy
Money
Private Investment
Private Sector
Resource Allocation
Resource Distribution

PRIVATE UNIVERSITY
S-19-0215 1975 00005
BT University
RT Academic Tenure Policy
Education Planner
Education Planning
Higher Education
Intellectual Elite
Open University
Professional School

PRIVILEGED INFORMATION
S-18-0076 1975 00002
BT Information Sources
RT Confidential Information
Government Document Classification Policy
Government Information Diffusion Policy

PRIVY COUNCIL
S-19-0117 1975 00002
BT National Government Council
RT Cabinet
Cabinet Committee
Council Of Ministers
Executive Government Institution
Minister
Presidential Advisory Council
Shadow Cabinet

PRIVY COUNCILOR
S-36-0047 1975 00001
SN A highly placed personal adviser to the head of government.
BT Cabinet Member
RT Cabinet Secretary
Cabinet Undersecretary
International Council Member
Minister

PROBABILITY ESTIMATION
S-24-0051 1975 00027
BT Statistical Analysis
NT Bayesian Analysis
Subjective Probability Estimation
RT Bivariate Analysis
Multivariate Analysis
Probability Model
Probability Sampling
Statistical Significance Test
Statistics Type
Univariate Analysis

PROBABILITY MODEL
S-24-0312 1979 00000
BT Social Science Model
RT Computer Simulation Model
Econometric Model
Economic Growth Model
Equilibrium Model
Mathematical Analysis
Mathematical Model
Measurement Procedure
Measures
Probability Estimation
Probability Sampling
Social Statistics
Statistical Analysis

PROBABILITY SAMPLING
S-24-0122 1975 00001
BT Sampling Procedure
NT Cluster Sampling
Simple Random Sampling
Stratified Sampling
Systematic Sampling
RT Area Sampling
Probability Estimation
Probability Model
Statistical Analysis

PROBATE COURT
S-19-0133 1975 00001
BT Civil Court
RT Administrative Court
Civil Code
Inheritance System
Justice Administration Agency
Local Court

PROBATION
S-31-0504 1975 00000
BT Sentencing
RT Bail
Bail Bond System
Bail Skipping
Fining
Jailing
Judicial Discretion
Punishment
Sentencing

PROBLEM SOLVING BEHAVIOR
S-05-0021 1979 00000
BT Behavior
RT Applied Anthropology
Applied Sociology
Cognitive Measurement
Forecasting Methodology
Gaming
Knowledge Production
Political Behavior
Public Administration Studies
Public Policy Studies
Research And Development
Simulation
Sociology Of Knowledge

PROCEDURAL DEMOCRACY
1975-1979 00003
USE Procedural Democratic Theory

PROCEDURAL DEMOCRATIC THEORY
S-38-0098 1979 00000
UF Procedural Democracy
BT Democratic Theory
RT Concurrent Majority Theory
Democratic Elite Theory
Democratic Government
Jacksonian Democratic Theory
Jeffersonian Democratic Theory
Majoritarianism
Minority Rights
Minority Rights Democratic Theory
Pluralist Democracy
Procedural Due Process
Procedural Law

Procedural Rights

PROCEDURAL DUE PROCESS
S-31-0551 1975 00006
BT Judicial Procedure
RT Appeal Procedure
Common Law System
Grand Jury System
Grievance Procedure
Jeopardy
Judicial Review
Justiciable Question
Legal Discrimination
Preemptory Challenge
Procedural Democratic Theory
Substantive Due Process

PROCEDURAL LAW
S-21-0076 1975 00002
BT Law Type
NT Civil Procedure Law
Criminal Procedure Law
Parliamentary Procedure Law
RT Basic Law
Bill Of Rights
Civil Law
Criminal Law
Customary Law
Equity Law
Judge Made Law
Political Law
Procedural Democratic Theory

PROCEDURAL RIGHTS
S-15-0042 1975 00009
BT Political Liberty
NT Defendants Rights
Military Justice
RT Civil Liberty
Civil Rights
Equal Opportunity
Equal Rights
Freedom Of Association
Freedom Of Press
Freedom Of Religion
Freedom Of Speech
Freedom Of Travel
Human Rights
Immunity
Law System
Procedural Democratic Theory
Right Of Assembly
Right Of Opposition
Right Of Petition
Right Of Privacy
Right Of Protest
Right To Bear Arms

PROCESS
S-31-0001 1975 00002
NT Accreditation Process
Analytic Process
Associational Process
Change Process
Child Rearing Practices
Communication Process
Conflict Process
Control Process
Decision Making Process
Decontrol Process
Diplomacy
Economic Process
Education Process
Elite Mass Relations
Exploration
Government Process
Influence Process
Judicial Process
Legislative Process
Migration Process
Mobilization Process
Planning Process
Policy Making Process
Political Participation
Representation
Selection Process
Social Process
Social Stratification Process
Sports
Structural Process
RT Characteristics
Institutions
Policy
Politics
Process Model
Roles

PROCESS MODEL
S-24-0313 1975 00022
BT Social Science Model
RT Development Model
Diffusion Model
Economic Development Model
Economic Growth Model
Process
Social Power Model
Social System Model

PROCLAMATION
S-18-0022 1975 00001
BT Administrative Record
RT Dictator
Emergency Power
President
Prime Minister
Pronouncement
State Of The Union
Veto Message

PRODUCER COOPERATIVE
S-03-0008 1975 00005
BT Cooperatives
RT Agricultural Cooperative
Economic Interest Group
Employer Organization
Industrial Union
Labor Union
Marketing Cooperative
Peasant Cooperative
Trade Union

PRODUCER DEMONSTRATION
1975-1979 00000

PRODUCT MOMENT CORRELATION
S-24-0035 1975 00008
BT Correlation Analysis
RT Multivariate Analysis
Rank Order Correlation
Regression Analysis
Univariate Analysis

PRODUCTION AGENCY
S-19-0030 1975 00003
BT Economic Agency
NT Trade Agency
RT Business Regulation Agency
Economic Advisory Board
Economic Control Agency
Economic Institution
Farm Production

PRODUCTION DISTRIBUTION
S-06-0624 1975 00008
BT Economic Diversification
RT Economic Power Distribution
Production Industry

PRODUCTION INDUSTRY
S-17-0052 1975 00003
BT Industry
NT Heavy Industry
Manufacturing Industry
Metallurgical Industry
RT Aircraft Industry
Appliance Industry
Building Supplies Industry
Energy Industry
Extractive Industry
Industrial Policy
Production Distribution
Ship Building Industry

PRODUCTION PROCESS
S-31-0424 1975 00044
BT Economic Process
NT Agricultural Production
Automated Production
Industrial Production
Knowledge Production
National Production
Subsistence Production
War Production
RT Consumption Pattern
Cottage Industry
Marketing
Worker Productivity

PRODUCTION QUOTA
S-26-0131 1975 00002
BT Productivity Policy
RT Work Norm Policy

PRODUCTIVITY POLICY
S-26-0130 1975 00018
BT Economic Policy
NT Production Quota
Work Norm Policy
RT Antitrust Agency
Consumption Pattern
Economic Growth Policy
Economic Subsidization Policy

PRODUCTIVITY RATE
S-06-0156 1975 00036
BT Economic Growth Rate
NT Cost Effectiveness
Worker Productivity
RT Agricultural Growth Rate
Capital Growth Rate
Economic Development Indicator
Economic Development Level
Economic Development Stage
Economic Growth Index
Economic Growth Rate

PROFESSIONAL ACCREDITATION PROCESS
S-31-0004 1979 00000
BT Accreditation Process
RT Education Accreditation Process
Professional Education
Professional Occupational Role
Professional School

Testing

PROFESSIONAL ATHLETE
S-32-0025 1979 00000
BT Athlete
RT Amateur Athlete
Amateur Sports
Professional Sports
Sports

PROFESSIONAL EDUCATION
S-13-0037 1975 00041
BT Education Type
NT Business Administration Education
Health Education
Legal Education
RT Adult Education
Apprenticeship
Expert
Graduate Education
Graduate School
Higher Education
Manpower Policy
Manpower Training
Outreach Education
Over Specialization
Political Science Training
Polytechnical Institute Education
Professional Accreditation Process
Public Health Policy
Sociology Of The Professions
State Supported Higher Education
Teacher Education
Technical Education

PROFESSIONAL ETHICS
S-25-0043 1979 00000
BT Ethical Theory
RT Ethical Socialization
Metaethical Theory
Moral Theory
Professional Socialization
Research Ethics
Sociology Of The Professions

PROFESSIONAL MILITARY FORCES
S-33-0070 1975 00027
BT Military Forces
RT Admiralty
Armed Forces
Army
Army Organization
Coast Guard
Defense System
Irregular Forces
Irregular Military Forces
Marines
Mercenary Armed Forces
Military Establishment
Military Institute
Military Mind
Military Policy
Military Recruit
Naval Forces
Navy
Paramilitary Forces
Reserve Military Forces
Tactical Force

PROFESSIONAL OCCUPATIONAL ROLE
S-32-0092 1975 00158
UF Specialist
BT Occupational Role
NT Lawyer
Manager
Physician
Religious Minister
Social Scientist
Social Worker
Sociologist
Teacher
Technical Occupation
RT Academic Specialization
Accreditation Process
Artisan
Business Administration Education
Commercial Occupation
Economist
Education Accreditation Process
Expert
Industrial Occupation
Malpractice
Professional Accreditation Process
Sheriff
Sociology Of The Professions
Specialization Process

PROFESSIONAL ORGANIZATION
S-03-0052 1975 00017
BT Organizations
NT Bar Association
Education Association
Medical Association
Teacher Organization
RT Cultural Organization
Economic Organization
Employer Organization
Interest Group
International Organization
Occupational Identity
Occupational Interest Group
Organization Normative Characteristics
Organization Process
Peer Group
Professional Socialization
Social Group
Sociology Of The Professions

PROFESSIONAL POLITICIAN
S-32-0253 1975 00005
BT Politician
RT Over Specialization
Political Broker
Political Official
Political Patron
Political Role

PROFESSIONAL SCHOOL
S-19-0218 1975 00015
BT Higher Education Institution
NT Law School
RT Accreditation Process
Education Accreditation Process
Education Planner
Education Planning
Graduate School
Over Specialization
Private University
Professional Accreditation Process
Professional Socialization
Sociology Of The Professions
State Supported University
Vocational Training School

PROFESSIONAL SOCIALIZATION
S-34-0036 1975 00023
BT Socialization Context
NT Education Socialization
Legal Socialization
RT Academic Specialization
Business Administration Education
Education Association
Ethical Socialization
Group Socialization
Institutional Socialization
Military Institute
Military Mind
Military Training
Physician
Political Science Training
Professional Ethics
Professional Organization
Professional School
Public Health Education
Socialization Type

PROFESSIONAL SPORTS
S-31-0785 1979 00000
BT Sports
RT Amateur Athlete
Amateur Sports
Athlete
Professional Athlete

PROFESSOR
S-32-0121 1975 00025
UF Academician
College Teacher
BT Teacher
RT Academic
Academic Areas
Intellectual Elite
School Teacher
University

PROFIT INCOME
S-06-0342 1979 00000
BT Income
RT Business Income
Capitalism
Capitalism Theory
Capitalist Economy
Economic Gain
Family Income
Farm Income
Foreign Income
Income Measure
National Income
Personal Income
Protestant Ethic
Tax Exempt Income
Unearned Income

PROGRAM BUDGET
S-06-0257 1975 00009
BT Capital Budget
RT Capital Budget
Incremental Budget
Performance Budget

PROGRAMMED INSTRUCTION
S-31-0451 1975 00011
BT Education Process
RT Computer Assisted Instruction
Instruction Methodology

PROGRESS
S-31-0084 1975 00002
BT Development Process
NT Technological Progress
RT Cultural History
Evolution
Industrial Relations
Modernity Scale
Modernization
Progressivism
Reform

PROGRESS THEORY
S-38-0422 1975 00014
BT Modern Political Thought
RT Development Theory
Economic Theory
Marxist Political Thought
Modernization Theory
Progressive Politics
Progressivism

PROGRESSIVE DICTATORSHIP
S-16-0041 1975 00000
BT Dictatorship
RT Benevolent Dictatorship
Modernizing Authoritarian Regime
Modernizing Dictatorship

PROGRESSIVE EDUCATION
S-13-0043 1975 00007
BT Education Type
RT Alternative Education
Education Psychology
Humanistic Education
Private School Education
Progressivism
Sex Education
Traditional Education
Urban Education

PROGRESSIVE POLITICS
S-29-0226 1975 00001
BT Politics
RT Civil Rights
Human Rights
Ideologies
Political Change
Progress Theory
Progressivism
Protest Politics

PROGRESSIVE TAXATION
S-26-0159 1975 00005
BT Taxation Policy
NT Graduated Taxation
RT Direct Taxation
Graduated Taxation
National Tax Law
National Taxation
Regressive Taxation
State Income Taxation
Subnational Income Taxation

PROGRESSIVISM
S-38-0076 1975 00006
BT Contemporary Political Thought
RT Modernization Theory
Progress
Progress Theory
Progressive Education
Progressive Politics

PROLETARIAN CULTURAL REVOLUTION MOVEMENT
S-27-0052 1975 00006
BT Proletarian Movement
RT Maoism
Maoist
Maoist Political Party
Maoist Revolutionary
Proletarian Political Party
Proletarian Socialist Movement
Working Class
Working Class Movement

PROLETARIAN DICTATORSHIP
S-16-0042 1975 00001
BT Dictatorship
RT Communist Political Party
Marxism
Marxism Leninism
Proletarian Movement
Proletarian Revolution
Proletarian Unity
Working Class Movement

PROLETARIAN INTERNATIONALISM
S-38-0304 1979 00000
BT Marxist Class Consciousness Theory
RT Communist Imperialism
Dictatorship Of The Proletariat
Marxist Class Theory
Proletarian Revolution
Proletarian Socialist Movement
Proletarian Unity
Trotskyism

PROLETARIAN MOVEMENT
S-27-0051 1975 00001
BT Class Based Movement
NT Proletarian Cultural Revolution Movement
Proletarian Socialist Movement
RT Class Analysis
Dictatorship Of The Proletariat
Extremist Movement
Liberation Movement
Marxism
Mass Revolutionary Movement
Middle Class Movement
Proletarian Dictatorship
Proletarian Political Party
Proletarian Revolution
Proletarian Unity
Proletariat
Radical Movement
Revolutionary Movement
Working Class Movement

PROLETARIAN POLITICAL PARTY
S-28-0040 1979 00000
BT Class Based Political Party
RT Aristocracy Political Party
Communist Political Party
Marxism
Marxism Leninism
Mass Political Party
Proletarian Cultural Revolution Movement
Proletarian Movement
Proletarian Socialist Movement
Proletarian Unity
Working Class Movement
Working Class Political Party

PROLETARIAN REVOLUTION
S-08-0078 1975 00005
BT Social Revolution
RT Bourgeois Revolution
Communism
Communist Bloc
Industrial Revolution
Marxist Class Theory
Marxist Political Thought
Proletarian Dictatorship
Proletarian Internationalism
Proletarian Movement
Racial Revolution
Spontaneous Revolution
Technological Revolution
Worker Demonstration

PROLETARIAN SOCIALIST MOVEMENT
S-27-0053 1975 00003
BT Proletarian Movement
RT Marxism
Proletarian Cultural Revolution Movement
Proletarian Internationalism
Proletarian Political Party
Socialist Revolution
Working Class Movement

PROLETARIAN UNITY
S-06-0036 1975 00001
BT Class Solidarity
RT Brotherhood
Gemeinschaft
Proletarian Dictatorship
Proletarian Internationalism
Proletarian Movement
Proletarian Political Party
Proletarian Unity
Social Solidarity

PROLETARIAT
S-06-0783 1975 00003
BT Working Class
RT Agricultural Working Class
Day Laborer
Industrial Working Class
Marxism
Marxist Alienation Theory
Proletarian Movement
Unionized Working Class

PROLETARIAT INTERNATIONALISM
1975-1979 00002

PRONOUNCEMENT
S-18-0041 1975 00000
BT Documents
RT Emergency Power
Proclamation
Veto Message

PROPAGANDA POLICY
S-26-0292 1975 00001
BT Information Policy
NT Wartime Propaganda Policy
RT Agitation
Agitation Propaganda
Domestic Information Policy
Election Campaign Propaganda
Foreign Information Policy

PROPAGANDA WAR
S-08-0105 1975 00001
BT Psychological War
RT Brainwashing
Ideological War
Revolutionary War

Total War

PROPERTIED CLASS
S-06-0777 1975 00003
BT Class Stratification Division
RT Aristocratic Class
Bourgeoisie
Class Analysis
Class Society
Class Stratification Division
Entrepreneur Class
Landowning Class
Middle Class
Nobility
Old Middle Class
Peasant Class
Petite Bourgeoisie
Private Ownership
Property Ownership System
Ruling Class
Upper Class

PROPERTY CRIME
S-10-0021 1975 00008
BT Economic Crime
NT Robbery
Vandalism
RT Economic Conspiracy
Economic Espionage
Economic Sabotage
Industrial Espionage
Political Fund Misuse
Robbery
Street Crime

PROPERTY LAW
S-21-0044 1979 00000
BT Economic Law
RT Civil Law
Commercial Law
Contract Law
Eminent Domain
Eminent Domain Policy
Environmental Law
Historical Preservation Law
Industrial Safety Law
Land Use Policy
Mine Safety Law
Negligence Law
Tax Code
Tax Law
Tort

PROPERTY OWNERSHIP SYSTEM
S-37-0050 1975 00025
BT Economic System
NT Absentee Landlord System
Collective Ownership
Foreign Ownership
Government Ownership
Land Estate System
Land Tenure System
Primogeniture
Private Ownership
Slavery
RT Economic Sector
Inheritance System
Monetary System
Propertied Class
Property Rights

PROPERTY RIGHTS
S-15-0008 1975 00034
BT Economic Freedom
RT Bankruptcy Law
Freedom Of Competition
Freedom Of Contract
Land Estate System
Lockean Liberalism
Property Ownership System
Right To Job Security

PROPERTY TAXATION
S-26-0161 1975 00028
BT Taxation Policy
RT City Income Taxation
Luxury Taxation
Nuisance Taxation
Tax Assessment
Tax Reform Movement
Value Added Taxation
Wage Taxation

PROPERTY VOTING QUALIFICATION
S-15-0084 1975 00000
BT Voter Qualification
RT Registration Requirement
Residence Requirement
Voting Age Requirement

PROPHETIC TRADITION
S-25-0006 1975 00001
BT Eschatology
RT Charismatic Authority
Charismatic Leadership
Judaic Thought
Millenarianism
Utopianism

PROPORTIONAL REPRESENTATION
S-31-0725 1975 00004
BT Representation Type
RT At Large Representation
District Representation
Functional Representation
Geographic Representation
Indirect Representation
Minority Group Representation
Multimember District
Multiple Member District Representation
Multiple Member Districting
Representation Theory
Single Member District Representation

PROPOSITIONAL INVENTORY
S-24-0411 1979 00000
BT Study Scope
RT Case Study
Comparative Analysis
Cross Level Analysis
Documentary Research
Explanatory Research
Hypothesis Testing
Information Sources
Research Orientation
Validity Measurement

PROPRIETARY COLONY
S-16-0047 1975 00000
BT Colony
RT Colonialism
Cultural Imperialism
Decolonization
Former Colony

PROSECUTING ATTORNEY
S-36-0102 1975 00004
BT Court Attorney
NT Attorney General
RT Barrister
Defense Attorney
Solicitor

PROSECUTION IMMUNITY
S-15-0025 1975 00002
BT Immunity
RT Contempt Of Congress
Defendants Rights
Plea Bargaining
Political Asylum
Self Incrimination
Testimony

PROSPERITY
S-06-0638 1975 00005
BT Wealth Distribution
RT Affluent Society
Business
Conspicuous Consumption
Economic Process
Financial Market
Foreign Trade
Income Distribution
Rich Nation
Small Business

PROTECTED INDUSTRY
S-17-0064 1975 00002
BT Industry
RT Defense Industry
Economic Development Theory
Industrial Policy
Industrial Subsidy
Nationalized Industry
Protective Tariff

PROTECTIVE ALLIANCE
S-02-0007 1975 00009
BT Defense Alliance
RT Caretaker Government
Coalition Type
Collective Security
Defense Policy
Foreign Policy Making
Global War Policy
Multilateral Alliance
Protectorate
Regional Security
Security Community

PROTECTIVE TARIFF
S-26-0171 1975 00006
BT Tariff
RT Autarchic Economy
Commercial Agreement
Domestic Market
Economic Treaty
Export Market
Foreign Trade
Import Quota
Infant Industry
Protected Industry
Trade Agreement
Trade Organization

PROTECTORATE
S-16-0056 1975 00004
BT Extranational Government Structure
RT Caretaker Government
Colony
Empire

Former Colony
International Trusteeship
Mandate Territory
Military Occupation
Protective Alliance

PROTEST
S-31-0256 1975 00019
BT Dissent
NT Peaceful Protest
Social Protest
Student Protest
RT Agitation
Agitation Propaganda
Civil Disobedience
Civil Rights Demonstration
Class Rebellion
Confrontation Politics
Demonstrating
Demonstration
Demonstrator
Dissent
Economic Demonstration
Ghetto Rioter
Hussite Thought
Mutiny
Protest Politics
Protest Voter
Protest Voting
Racial Militancy
Resistance
Right Of Petition
Right Of Protest
Right Of Revolution
Rights Of Man Doctrine
Rioter

PROTEST POLITICS
S-29-0227 1975 00024
BT Politics
RT Activist
Antiwar Movement
Civil Disobedience
Civil Rights Movement
Economic Agitation
Feminist Politics
Gay Politics
Group Politics
Luddite Movement
Peaceful Protest
Political Activist
Political Agitation
Political Agitator
Political Alienation
Political Alienation Theory
Political Opposition
Positive Voting Abstention
Progressive Politics
Protest
Protest Voter
Racial Politics
Religious Politics
Right Of Protest
Sexual Politics
Social Conflict
Social Deviance
Social Protest
Social Rebellion
Student Activism
Student Activist
Student Demonstration
Student Militancy
Student Protest
Student Rebellion
Terrorism
War Protestor
Youth Politics

PROTEST VOTER
S-32-0327 1975 00003
BT Voter
RT Alienated Voter
Ideological Voter
Marginal Voter
Protest
Protest Politics
Protest Voting
Racial Voting
Right Of Protest
Social Protest

PROTEST VOTING
S-29-0143 1975 00002
BT Voting
NT Backlash Voting
RT Age Group Voting
Class Voting
Ethnic Group Voting
Floating Voting
Protest
Protest Voter
Racial Voting
Religious Voting
Sex Group Voting
Student Voting

PROTESTANT ETHIC
S-11-0052 1979 00000
BT Work Culture
RT Capitalism
Labor Discipline
Profit Income
Protestant Sectarianism
Protestantism
Western Culture
Work Ethic

PROTESTANT SECTARIANISM
S-38-0570 1975 00005
BT Protestantism
RT Anabaptism
Anglicanism
Calvinism
Hussite Thought
Lutheranism
Protestant Ethic
Religious Culture
Religious Identity
Religious Movement
Unitarianism

PROTESTANTISM
S-38-0565 1975 00013
BT Christian Thought
NT Anglicanism
Calvinism
Hussite Thought
Lutheranism
Protestant Sectarianism
Unitarianism
RT Catholicism
Protestant Ethic
Quietistic Thought
Religious Culture
Religious Identity
Religious Movement
Right Hegelianism

PROVINCE
S-24-0363 1975 00002
BT Subnational Political Division
RT Local Political Division
State Political Division

PROVINCIAL ELECTION
S-29-0093 1975 00001
BT Subnational Election
RT Local Election
Subnational Chief Executive Election
Subnational Judicial Candidate
Subnational Judicial Election
Subnational Legislative Election

PROVINCIAL ELITE
S-14-0029 1975 00004
BT Political Elite
RT Community Elite
Local Elite
Provincial Government
Social Elite
Subnational Elite
Urban Politics Studies

PROVINCIAL GOVERNMENT
S-16-0110 1975 00014
BT Metropolitan Government
RT Borough Government
City Government
County Government
County Manager Government
Decentralized City
Federated City
Provincial Elite
State Government
State Governor

PROVINCIAL PARLIAMENT
S-19-0283 1975 00000
BT Subnational Legislature
RT Congressional System
Housing Court
Legislative Commission
Local Legislature
Provincial Political Party
State Assembly
State House Of Representatives
State Legislature
State Senate

PROVINCIAL PARTY
1975-1979 00003

PROVINCIAL POLITICAL PARTY
S-28-0055 1979 00000
BT Subnational Political Party
RT Local Political Party
Provincial Parliament
State Legislature

PROXY VOTING
S-29-0145 1975 00000
BT Voting
RT Absentee Voting
Legislative Behavior
Voting Data

PROXY WAR
S-08-0103 1979 00000
BT War
RT Dependent Nation
Imperialist War
International Conflict
Limited War
Superpower Politics

War Policy

PSYCHIATRY
S-01-0143 1979 00000
BT Medical Science
NT Social Psychiatry
RT Clinical Psychologist
Coping Behavior
Gerontology
Gestalt Psychology
Neurosis
Parapsychology
Pathological Behavior
Personal Behavior
Psychohistory
Sexual Behavior

PSYCHOANALYSIS
S-09-0059 1979 00000
BT Contemporary Analytic Modes
NT Psychotherapy
RT Behavior Analysis
Clinical Psychologist
Coping Behavior
Freudian Psychology
Group Analysis
Motivational Analysis
Pathological Behavior
Personality Crisis
Policy Analysis
Political Psychology Analysis
Psychohistory
Psychological Service
Psychologist
Psychology Discipline
Psychopathology
Psychopolitical Theory
Psychosis
Sexual Behavior

PSYCHOHISTORY
S-01-0118 1979 00000
BT History Discipline
RT Historical Analysis
Historiography
Institutional History
Intellectual History
Legal History
Modal Personality
Oral History
Personality Characteristics
Personality Development
Psychiatry
Psychoanalysis
Psychology Discipline
Psychopathology
Social History
Social Psychiatry

PSYCHOLINGUISTICS
S-01-0137 1975 00013
BT Linguistics
RT Behavioral Psychology
Behavioral Science
Bilingualism
Ethnolinguistics
Language Acquisition
Political Science Methodology Studies
Psychology Discipline
Social Behavior
Social Pathology
Sociolinguistics
Structural Linguistics

PSYCHOLOGICAL AGGRESSION
S-08-0006 1975 00008
BT Aggression
RT Aggression Scale
Aggressiveness
Agitation Propaganda
Crime
Cultural Aggression
Interpersonal Conflict
Jungian Theory
Military Aggression
Mob Violence
Political Violence
Psychological Behaviorism
Psychological Theory
Psychological War
Psychology Discipline
Religious Conflict
Social Psychiatry
Spontaneous Revolution
Struggle

PSYCHOLOGICAL ANTHROPOLOGY
S-01-0020 1975 00000
BT Anthropology Discipline
RT Adaptive Behavior
Animal Behavior
Anthropological Functionalism
Behavioral Psychology
Criminology
Cultural Anthropology
Freudian Psychology
Learning Psychology
Philosophical Anthropology
Political Psychology
Psychology Discipline
Psychopathology
Social Pathology

PSYCHOLOGICAL BEHAVIORALISM
S-38-0546 1975 00008
BT Psychological Theory
RT Behavioral Psychology
Clinical Psychologist
Cognitive Theory
Cross Pressure Theory
Education Psychology
Freudian Theory
Gestalt Theory
Identity Theory
Learning Theory
Motivation Theory
Psychological Behaviorism
Psychopolitical Theory
Relative Deprivation Theory

PSYCHOLOGICAL BEHAVIORISM
S-38-0547 1975 00001
SN Early analysis in which stimulus and response (without the intervening organism) are the two variables used in explanation of behavior.
BT Psychological Theory
NT Psychological Programming
RT Behavior Modification
Cognitive Dissonance Theory
Cognitive Theory
Education Psychology
Freudian Theory
Gestalt Theory
Group Psychology
Identity Theory
Jungian Theory
Learning Theory
Motivation Theory
Psychological Aggression
Psychological Behavioralism
Psychologist
Psychopolitical Theory
Relative Deprivation Theory

PSYCHOLOGICAL DEPROGRAMMING
S-38-0549 1979 00000
BT Psychological Programming
RT Behavior Modification
Learning Theory
Religious Cult
Religious Education

PSYCHOLOGICAL FREEDOM THEORY
S-38-0467 1975 00001
BT Freedom Theory
RT Enlightened Self Interest
Existential Psychologism
Freedom
Individual Freedom Theory
Utilitarianism

PSYCHOLOGICAL PROGRAMMING
S-38-0548 1979 00000
BT Psychological Behaviorism
NT Psychological Deprogramming
RT Behavior Modification
Brainwashing
Cooperative Behavior
Learning Psychology
Learning Theory
Religious Cult
Religious Education

PSYCHOLOGICAL SERVICE
S-26-0370 1979 00000
BT Service Policy
RT Child Care Service
Clinical Psychology
Education Service
Health Service
Legal Service
Psychoanalysis
Psychologist
Psychology Discipline
Social Service
Social Welfare Policy

PSYCHOLOGICAL TEST
S-24-0009 1979 00000
BT Education Testing
RT Degree Requirement
Literacy Test
Physiological Test
Psychologist

PSYCHOLOGICAL THEORY
S-38-0529 1975 00063
BT Theory
NT Achievement Theory
Alienation Psychological Theory
Attitude Change Theory
Attribution Theory
Cognitive Theory
Cross Pressure Theory
Freudian Theory
Frustration Aggression Theory
Gestalt Theory
Human Needs Theory
Identity Theory
Jungian Theory

Learning Theory
Motivation Theory
Personality Theory
Psychological Behavioralism
Psychological Behaviorism
Psychopolitical Theory
Relative Deprivation Theory
RT Adaptive Behavior
Aggression Scale
Anthropological Theory
Avoidance Behavior
Catharsis
Coping Behavior
Decision Maker Perception
Existential Psychologism
Explanatory Political Theory
Group Psychology
Ideologies
Pathological Behavior
Personal Behavior
Personality Characteristics
Phenomenological Psychologism
Political Theory
Psychological Aggression
Psychologist
Psychology Discipline
Sexual Behavior

PSYCHOLOGICAL VARIABLE
S-24-0451 1975 00019
BT Variable Substantive Content
RT Historical Variable
Institutional Variable
Personality Disorder
Pessimism
Political Variable
Psychology Discipline
Social Variable

PSYCHOLOGICAL WAR
S-08-0104 1975 00008
BT War
NT Propaganda War
RT Brainwashing
Ideological War
Imperialist War
Insurgency
Just War
National Liberation War
Partisan War
Political Agitation
Psychological Aggression
Revolution
Struggle
Terrorism
War Propaganda

PSYCHOLOGIST
S-32-0114 1979 00000
BT Social Scientist
NT Clinical Psychologist
Learning Psychologist
Social Psychologist
RT Academic
Anthropologist
Psychoanalysis
Psychological Behaviorism
Psychological Service
Psychological Test
Psychological Theory
Psychology Discipline
Social Scientist
Social Worker

PSYCHOLOGY DISCIPLINE
S-01-0168 1975 00011
BT Academic Areas
NT Behavioral Psychology
Child Psychology
Clinical Psychology
Developmental Psychology
Freudian Psychology
Gestalt Psychology
Learning Psychology
Parapsychology
Psychopathology
Social Psychology
RT Acculturation
Administrative Science
Adolescent Political Socialization
Adolescent Socialization
Animal Behavior
Avoidance Behavior
Behavioral Psychology
Behavioral Science
Biological Sciences
Cooperative Behavior
Coping Behavior
Cultural Anthropology
Ethnic Studies
Freudian Psychology
Group Psychology
Information Science
Inner Directed Personality
Linguistics
Logic
Natural Science Discipline
Neurosis
Paranoia
Parapsychology
Pathological Behavior
Personal Behavior
Personality Theory
Phenomenological Psychologism
Political Science Discipline
Political Science Methodology Studies
Political Sociology
Political Theory Studies
Psychoanalysis
Psychohistory
Psycholinguistics
Psychological Aggression
Psychological Anthropology
Psychological Service
Psychological Theory
Psychological Variable
Psychologist
Psychopathology
Sexual Behavior
Social Anthropology
Social Pathology
Sociolinguistics
Sociology Discipline

PSYCHOMETRIC MODEL
S-24-0314 1975 00005
BT Social Science Model
RT Group Psychology
Interaction Model
Rational Choice Model

PSYCHOPATHOLOGY
S-01-0177 1975 00056
BT Psychology Discipline
RT Avoidance Behavior
Behavioral Psychology
Behavioral Science
Clinical Psychologist
Coping Behavior
Criminology
Freudian Psychology
Interpersonal Conflict
Jungian Theory
Parapsychology
Pathological Behavior
Personality Development
Personality Disorder
Personality Theory
Political Behavior Studies
Political Psychology
Psychoanalysis
Psychohistory
Psychological Anthropology
Psychology Discipline
Sexual Behavior
Social Pathology
Social Psychiatry

PSYCHOPOLITICAL THEORY
S-38-0550 1975 00007
BT Psychological Theory
RT Achievement Theory
Aggression Theory
Alienation Psychological Theory
Attitude Change Theory
Attribution Theory
Cognitive Theory
Cross Pressure Theory
Freudian Theory
Gestalt Theory
Learning Theory
Motivation Theory
Personality Theory
Political Psychology Analysis
Psychoanalysis
Psychological Behavioralism
Psychological Behaviorism
Relative Deprivation
Relative Deprivation Theory
Social Psychiatry

PSYCHOSIS
S-06-0523 1975 00013
BT Personality Disorder
NT Paranoia
Schizophrenia
RT Hysteria
Jungian Theory
Neurosis
Pathological Behavior
Personality Theory
Psychoanalysis
Social Psychiatry

PSYCHOTHERAPY
S-09-0060 1979 00000
BT Psychoanalysis
RT Mental Health Policy
Neurosis

PUBLIC ADMINISTRATION STUDIES
S-01-0165 1975 00212
BT Political Science Discipline
RT Administrative Behavior
Administrative Characteristics
Administrative Law
Administrative Management
Administrative Planning
Administrative Policy Making
Administrative Politics
Administrative Science
Administrative Theory
Behavioral Science
Engineering Discipline
Government Bureaucracy
Line Staff
Management Training Program
Metropolitan Government
Policy Science Studies
Policy Scientist
Presidential Staff Personnel
Problem Solving Behavior
Public Finance Theory
Public Policy Studies
Sociology Discipline
Urban Sociology

PUBLIC ASSISTANCE
S-06-0320 1975 00013
BT Government Expenditure
NT Welfare
RT Economic Loss
Social Security
Unemployment Compensation
Unemployment Insurance Policy
Unemployment Policy
Welfare State

PUBLIC ATTITUDE
USE Political Attitude

PUBLIC AUTHORITIES
S-19-0069 1975 00005
BT Authorities
RT Administrative Management
Board Of Trustees
Environmental Agency
Federal Commission
Government Bureaucracy
Government Enterprise
Government Official
Health Care Agency
Interstate Authorities
Municipal Authorities
Welfare Agency

PUBLIC BROADCASTING
S-31-0181 1975 00003
BT Broadcasting
RT News Reporting

PUBLIC BROADCASTING INDUSTRY
S-17-0009 1975 00006
BT Broadcasting Industry
RT Cable Television
Commercial Broadcasting Industry
Government Report Censorship
Public Television
Radio Industry
State Controlled Television
Telecommunications Industry
Television Industry

PUBLIC BROADCASTING POLICY
S-26-0036 1975 00003
BT Broadcasting Policy
RT Broadcasting
Broadcasting Agency
Broadcasting Censorship
Broadcasting Industry
Fairness Doctrine

PUBLIC BUREAUCRACY
S-19-0074 1975 00031
BT Bureaucracy
NT Government Bureaucracy
RT Bureaucratic Characteristics
Bureaucratic Elite
Merit Bureaucracy
Religious Bureaucracy

PUBLIC CAPITAL
S-06-0267 1975 00005
BT Capital
RT Assets
Capital Surplus
Investment Capital
Private Capital

PUBLIC CENSORSHIP AGENCY
1975-1979 00000
USE Censorship Agency

PUBLIC CHOICE ANALYSIS
S-24-0417 1975 00022
BT Microlevel Analysis
RT Decision Making Analysis
Policy
Policy Analysis
Policy Science Studies
Social Choice Theory
Voting
Voting Abstention

PUBLIC CHOICE THEORY
S-38-0166 1975 00037
BT Explanatory Political Theory
RT Decision Making Theory
Economic Theory Of Democracy
Power Theory
Public Good Theory
Rational Choice Theory
Social Choice Theory
Voting Theory

PUBLIC CONSUMPTION
S-06-0275 1975 00001
BT Consumption
RT Conspicuous Consumption
Consumer Economy
Consumerism
Consumption Pattern
Domestic Consumption
Mass Consumption
Private Consumption

PUBLIC CORPORATION
S-19-0170 1975 00009
BT Corporation
RT Basic Industry Nationalization
Cartel
Economic Conglomerate
Enterprise
Monetary Institution
Multinational Corporation
Quasipublic Corporation

PUBLIC DEBT POLICY
S-26-0133 1975 00003
BT Economic Policy
NT Debt Ceiling Policy
National Debt Policy
RT Budget Policy
Budget Surplus
Expenditure Policy
Financing
Income Policy
Inflation Policy
Keynesian Economic Theory
Monetary Policy
Revenue Policy

PUBLIC DEFENDER
S-36-0101 1975 00001
BT Defender
RT District Attorney
Solicitor

PUBLIC EDUCATION POLICY
S-26-0194 1975 00040
BT Education Policy
RT Continuing Education
Education Agency
Education Institution
Education Planning
Education Policy
Higher Education Policy
Literacy Policy
Private Education Policy
Rehabilitation Education Policy
Vocation Training Policy

PUBLIC EMPLOYEE ORGANIZATION
S-03-0064 1975 00004
BT Worker Organization
NT Union
RT Civil Service Union
Economic Interest Group
Economic Organization
Union

PUBLIC EMPLOYEE UNION POLICY
S-26-0320 1975 00011
BT Labor Management Relations Policy
RT Collective Bargaining Policy
Labor Arbitration Policy
Right To Work Policy
Trade Union Policy

PUBLIC FINANCE POLICY
S-26-0136 1979 00000
BT Economic Policy
RT Budget Policy
Economic Policy
Financial System
Financier
Fiscal Institution
Fiscal Policy
Investment Policy
Monetary Policy
Public Finance Theory
Public Financing

PUBLIC FINANCE THEORY
S-38-0119 1979 00000
BT Economic Theory
RT Deficit Spending
Economic Stabilization Theory
Expenditure Policy
Fiscal Institution
Fiscal Theory
Public Administration Studies
Public Finance Policy

Public Financing
Public Policy Analysis
Public Spending

PUBLIC FINANCING
S-31-0400 1975 00041
BT Investment
NT Cost Sharing
Debt Financing
Deficit Financing
Development Financing
Government Borrowing
Local Financing
RT Capital Flow
Capital Formation
Deficit Financing
Monetary Process
Public Finance Policy
Public Finance Theory
Public Saving
Public Spending

PUBLIC FOREIGN INVESTMENT
S-31-0399 1979 00000
BT Public Investment
RT International Capital Movement
International Economic Interdependence
International Finance
International Investment
Private Foreign Investment

PUBLIC GOOD THEORY
S-38-0167 1979 00000
BT Explanatory Political Theory
RT Collective Action Theory
Common Good Theory
General Interest Theory
Public Choice Theory
Public Interest Theory
Social Choice Theory

PUBLIC HEALTH EDUCATION
S-13-0041 1979 00000
BT Health Education
RT Health Care System
Medical Care Policy
Medical Care System
Medical Education
Professional Socialization
Public Health Policy
Technical Education

PUBLIC HEALTH INSTITUTION
S-19-0251 1979 00000
UF Public Health Service
BT Health Care Institution
RT Alcoholism
Disease
Drug Addiction
Halfway House
Health Care Agency
Health Care Policy
Health Care Rights
Health Care System
Health Clinic
Hospital
Mental Institution
Neighborhood Clinic
Private Hospital
Public Hospital

PUBLIC HEALTH POLICY
S-26-0272 1975 00056
BT Health Care Policy
RT Abortion Law
Abortion Policy
Drug Addiction
Health Administration
Health Care System
Infant Mortality Rate
Medical Care Policy
National Health Insurance
Old Age Assistance Policy
Professional Education
Public Health Education
Public Health Policy

PUBLIC HEALTH SERVICE
1975-1979 00015
USE Public Health Institution

PUBLIC HOSPITAL
S-19-0248 1975 00006
BT Hospital
RT Neighborhood Clinic
Nursing Home
Private Hospital
Public Health Institution

PUBLIC HOUSING POLICY
S-26-0387 1979 00000
BT Housing Policy
RT Relocation Policy

PUBLIC INFORMATION ACCESS POLICY
S-26-0284 1975 00009
BT Government Secrecy Policy
RT Government Document
Government Information Diffusion Policy
Intelligence Censorship

PUBLIC INTEREST
S-06-0722 1975 00022
BT Social Utility
RT Common Good Theory
General Interest Theory
Interest Group Politics
Social Choice Theory

PUBLIC INTEREST THEORY
S-38-0434 1975 00015
BT Common Good Theory
RT General Interest Theory
General Will Theory
Public Good Theory

PUBLIC INVESTMENT
S-31-0398 1979 00000
BT Investment
NT Public Foreign Investment
RT Capital Formation
Economy Pump Priming
Government Enterprise
Private Investment
Public Spending

PUBLIC LAND USE POLICY
S-26-0216 1975 00013
BT Land Use Policy
NT Eminent Domain Policy
RT Zoning Policy

PUBLIC MONOPOLY
S-06-0633 1975 00003
BT Monopoly
RT Perfect Monopoly
Private Monopoly

PUBLIC OPINION INDICATOR
S-24-0267 1975 00040
BT Political Indicator
RT Mass Public Opinion
Policy Public Opinion Linkage
Political Resource Indicator
Public Opinion Survey
Voting Indicator
Voting Turnout Indicator

PUBLIC OPINION LEADER
S-32-0060 1975 00008
BT Opinion Leader
RT Mass Public Opinion
Political Decision Maker
Political Leader
Political Role

PUBLIC OPINION SURVEY
S-18-0097 1975 00088
BT Survey Data
NT Mass Public Opinion
RT Aggregate Data Statistics
Cross Cultural Analysis
Cross Cultural Data
Economic Statistics
Field Data
Mass Belief System
Policy Public Opinion Linkage
Political Statistics
Poll Tax
Public Opinion Indicator
Socioeconomic Data
Test Results
Vital Statistics Data

PUBLIC ORDER MAINTENANCE
S-31-0562 1975 00006
BT Judicial Process
NT Law Enforcement
RT Justice Administration
Law Enforcement
Law Enforcement Official
Law Enforcement Policy
Police
Police Community Relations
Police Power
Status Quo Conservatism

PUBLIC POLICY ANALYSIS
S-09-0056 1975 00247
BT Policy Analysis
RT Applied Sociology
Charitable Organization
Decision Making Theory
Decriminalization
Economist
Event Analysis
Gambling Policy
Handicapped Child
Health Care Policy
Marginal Utility Analysis
Medical Care Policy
Philanthropic Organization
Policy For Disadvantaged
Policy Output Scale
Policy Science Studies
Public Finance Theory
Public Policy Studies
Public Television
Scarcity
Service Delivery System
Spatial Analysis

State Controlled Television

PUBLIC POLICY MANAGEMENT
S-23-0038 1975 00070
BT Management
RT Administrative Leadership
Administrative Planning
Administrative Policy Making
Crisis Management
Development Management
Education Administration
Health Administration
Information Management
Law Administration
Natural Resource Management
Policy Analysis
Population Management
Public Policy Studies

PUBLIC POLICY PLANNING
S-31-0661 1975 00072
BT Planning Process
NT International Policy Planning
National Policy Planning
Subnational Policy Planning
RT Administrative Planning
Defense Planning
Development Planning
Economic Planning
Education Planning
Environmental Planning
Higher Education Planning
Long Range Planning
Military Planning
Planification
Population Planning
Public Policy Studies
Short Range Planning
Social Engineering
Social Planning

PUBLIC POLICY STUDIES
S-01-0166 1979 00000
BT Political Science Discipline
RT Administrative Policy Making
Applied Anthropology
Applied Sociology
Economic Planning
Environmental Planning
Planification
Policy Research
Policy Science Studies
Political Science Discipline
Problem Solving Behavior
Public Administration Studies
Public Policy Analysis
Public Policy Management
Public Policy Planning
Service Delivery System
Social Engineering
Social Planning

PUBLIC RECORD
S-18-0042 1975 00007
BT Documents
RT Commission Record
Committee Record
Government Document
Government Information Service
Legislative Information Service
Newspapers
Private Information Service
University Information Service

PUBLIC SAVING
S-31-0411 1979 00000
BT Saving
RT Capital Formation
Financing
Investment
Private Saving
Public Financing
Spending

PUBLIC SCHOOL
S-19-0223 1975 00032
BT Education Institution
RT Mass Education
Primary School
Private School
Secondary School

PUBLIC SECTOR
S-37-0032 1975 00036
BT Economic Sector
RT Agricultural Sector
Commercial Sector
Government Bureaucracy
Industrial Sector
Private Sector

PUBLIC SPENDING
S-31-0414 1975 00013
BT Spending
NT Defense Spending
Deficit Spending
Economy Pump Priming
Poverty Program Spending
Welfare Spending
RT Debt Financing
Debtor Nation
Deferential Voter
Deficit Financing
Government Borrowing
Government Economic Management
Monetary Process
Public Finance Theory
Public Financing
Public Investment
Unemployment

PUBLIC TELEVISION
S-17-0014 1979 00000
BT Television Industry
RT Cable Television
Commercial Broadcasting Industry
Commercial Television
Public Broadcasting Industry
Public Policy Analysis
State Controlled Television
Telecommunications Industry
Television Policy

PUBLIC TREASURY
S-19-0026 1975 00002
BT Fiscal Agency
RT Budget Agency
Economic Council
Economic Institution
Monetary Agency
Revenue Agency

PUBLIC TRIAL
S-31-0523 1975 00001
BT Trial
NT Bench Trial
Jury Trial
RT Adversary Process
Adversary System
Civil Rights
Law System
Trial Jury
Trial Procedure
Trial System

PUBLIC UNIVERSITY
S-19-0216 1979 00000
BT University
NT State Supported University
RT Open University

PUBLIC UTILITY INDUSTRY
S-17-0065 1975 00006
BT Industry
RT Industrial Policy
Nationalized Industry

PUBLIC UTILITY REGULATION POLICY
S-26-0137 1975 00005
BT Economic Policy
RT Economic Subsidization Policy

PUBLIC WORKS POLICY
S-26-0206 1975 00011
BT Employment Policy
RT Depression
Equal Employment Policy
Full Employment Policy
Government Economic Management
Manpower Policy

PUBLICATION AGENCY
S-19-0048 1975 00001
BT Communication Agency
RT Government Document
Intelligence Censorship
Journal
Magazine Industry

PUBLICATION INDUSTRY
S-17-0017 1975 00019
BT Communication Industry
NT Book Industry
Magazine Industry
Newspaper Industry
RT Advertising Industry
Broadcasting Industry
Copyright Policy
Journal
News Agency
Telecommunications Industry

PUBLISHED MEDIA CENSORSHIP
S-31-0267 1975 00003
BT Censorship Process
NT Book Censorship
Periodical Publication Censorship
RT Graphic Arts Censorship
Information Leaking
Media Access
Performing Arts Censorship
Political Censorship
Report Censorship
Television Censorship
Unpublished Media Censorship

PUERTO RICAN STUDIES
S-01-0086 1975 00005
BT Ethnic Studies
RT American Indian Studies
Area Studies
Black Studies
Chicano Studies
Cultural History
Human Geography

PUNISHMENT
S-31-0568 1975 00022
BT Law Enforcement
NT Criminal Punishment
RT Court Action
Court Martial
Crime
Dean
International Law Enforcement
Jail
Military Prison
National Law Enforcement
Prison Reform
Probation
Recidivism

PUPPET REGIME
S-16-0139 1975 00000
BT Political Regime
RT Colonialism
Dependent Nation
Imperialism
Military Government
Police State
Puppet State

PUPPET STATE
S-16-0171 1975 00000
BT State Type
RT Colonialism
Communist
Imperialism
Nation State
Peoples Democratic State
Police State
Puppet Regime

PURGE
S-31-0307 1979 00000
BT Control Process
NT Catharsis
Political Purge
RT Communist Studies
Decision Making Process
Persecution
Political Control
Political Crime
Political Elite
Political Leadership
Repression Process
Succession Struggle
Totalitarian Political System

PURPOSIVE SAMPLING
S-24-0120 1975 00001
BT Nonprobability Sampling
RT Haphazard Sampling
Quota Sampling

PUTSCH
S-08-0040 1975 00000
SN A sudden revolt or uprising against political authority.
BT Government Overthrow
RT Coup D'Etat
Institutional Conflict
Insurgency
Internal War
Military Aggression
Military Coup
Mob Violence
Political Violence
Rebellion
Revolution

PYTHAGOREAN POLITICAL THOUGHT
1975-1979 00000

PYTHAGOREAN THOUGHT
S-38-0054 1979 00000
SN Pre-Socratic doctrines that saw universe as ordered by various mathematical ratios.
BT Classical Political Thought
RT Aristotelian Thought
Epicurean Thought
Platonic Political Thought
Presocratic Political Thought
Socratic Political Thought

QUALITATIVE ANALYSIS
S-24-0031 1975 00008
BT Analysis Methodology
RT Hermeneutical Analysis
Historical Analysis
Logic
Normative Analysis
PERT Analysis

QUALITATIVE RESEARCH
S-24-0393 1975 00004
BT Research Orientation
RT Advocacy Research
Applied Research
Basic Research
Concept Explication Research
Data Selection Orientation
Deductive Method
Descriptive Research
Experimental Research
Explanatory Research
Policy Research
Political Theory
Predictive Research
Quantitative Research
Scientific Research
Theoretical Research

QUALITY OF LIFE
S-06-0365 1979 00000
BT Environmental Characteristics
RT Cost Of Living Index
Goal Satisfaction
Human Needs Theory
Job Dissatisfaction
Job Satisfaction
Life Satisfaction
Living Conditions
Noise Pollution
Pension Law
Per Capita Income
Policy Science Studies
Political Satisfaction
Political Trust
Population Density
Radiation Level
Real Income
Satisfaction
Satisfaction Scale
Standard Of Living
Working Conditions

QUANTITATIVE HISTORY
S-01-0119 1979 00000
BT History Discipline
RT Applied Research
Basic Research
Concept Explication Research
Data Selection Orientation
Historical Analysis
Historiography
History Of Science
Institutional History
Predictive Research
Quantitative Research
Quasiexperiment
Scientific Research
Social History
Statistics Discipline
Urban History

QUANTITATIVE RESEARCH
S-24-0394 1975 00029
BT Research Orientation
RT Applied Anthropology
Applied Linguistics
Applied Research
Applied Sociology
Basic Research
Data Selection Orientation
Descriptive Research
Experimental Research
Explanatory Research
Forecasting Methodology
Ideographic Research
Market Research
Policy Research
Predictive Research
Qualitative Research
Quantitative History
Scientific Research
Theoretical Research

QUASIEXPERIMENT
S-24-0423 1975 00009
SN A research design that incorporates the features of a classical experiment without having the same level of control over relevant variables.
BT Variable Control
NT Matching Case
Natural Experiment
RT Case Study
Experiment
Laboratory
Natural Experiment
Nonexperiment
Quantitative History
Quasiexperimental Research
Question Formulation

QUASIEXPERIMENTAL RESEARCH
S-24-0386 1975 00017
BT Explanatory Research
RT Experimental Research
Matching Case
Quasiexperiment

QUASIPUBLIC CORPORATION
S-19-0171 1975 00007
BT Corporation
RT Cartel
Economic Conglomerate
Government Agricultural Enterprise
Government Enterprise
Multinational Corporation
Public Corporation

QUEEN
S-36-0066 1975 00000
BT Monarch
RT Hereditary Ruler
Kaiser

Khan
King
Monarchy
Regent
Shah
Sheik
Sultan
Tsar

QUESTION FORMULATION
S-24-0151 1975 00001
BT Information Retrieval
RT Data Retrieval
Quasiexperiment
Questionnaire
Survey Data
Survey Research

QUESTION PERIOD
S-31-0602 1975 00000
BT Interpellation
RT Parliament Cabinet Rèlations
Parliamentary Opposition
Question Time Debate

QUESTION TIME DEBATE
S-31-0596 1975 00000
BT Legislative Action
RT Interpellation
Legislative Decision Making
Question Period

QUESTIONNAIRE
S-24-0090 1975 00025
BT Data Collection Methodology
NT Closed Questionnaire
Mail Questionnaire
Open Ended Questionnaire
Self Administered Questionnaire
Telephone Questionnaire
RT Field Research
Interviewing Material
Nonreactive Observation
Question Formulation
Reactive Observation
Sampling Procedure

QUIETISTIC THOUGHT
S-38-0373 1975 00000
BT Medieval Political Thought
NT Anabaptism
Antitrinitarianism
RT Protestantism

QUOTA POLICY
S-26-0236 1975 00004
BT Exclusionary Policy
RT Blacklisting Policy
Residential Segregation
Segregation Policy

QUOTA SAMPLING
S-24-0121 1975 00000
BT Nonprobability Sampling
RT Haphazard Sampling
Purposive Sampling

QUOTA SYSTEM POLICY
S-26-0207 1975 00003
BT Employment Policy
RT Affirmative Action Employment Policy
Equal Employment Policy
Manpower Policy
Patronage Policy

RABBI
S-32-0105 1979 00000
BT Religious Minister
RT Ecclesiastical Leadership
Religious Education
Religious Elite
Religious Leader
Religious Policy
Religious Role
Teacher

RACE RIOT
S-08-0124 1975 00004
BT Racial Conflict
NT Urban Race Riot
RT Black Insurrection
Class Conflict
Racial Cleavage
Racism
Segregation Policy
Struggle

RACIAL ASSIMILATION
S-31-0801 1975 00010
BT Assimilation
RT Cultural Assimilation
Ethnic Assimilation
Ethnic Assimilation Theory
Housing Integration
Linguistic Assimilation
Racial Attitude
Racial Cleavage
Racial Composition
Racial Integration Theory

RACIAL ATTITUDE
S-06-0121 1975 00046
BT Attitude Characteristics
NT Racial Prejudice
Racial Pride
Racial Supremacy
RT Bigotry
Institutional Racism
Racial Assimilation
Racial Identity
Racial Injustice
Racial Intolerance
Racial Militancy
Racial Policy
Racial Tension
Racial Tolerance
Racism
Racist

RACIAL BACKGROUND
S-06-0205 1975 00038
BT Ethnic Origin
RT Ancestry
Ethnic Background

RACIAL CLEAVAGE
S-06-0475 1975 00013
BT Racial Diversity
RT Cultural Cleavage
Ethnic Diversity
Race Riot
Racial Assimilation
Racial Conflict
Racial Tension
Racist
Social Cleavage

RACIAL COMPOSITION
S-06-0223 1975 00033
BT Population Composition
RT Ethnic Community
Ethnic Composition
Nationality Composition
Racial Assimilation
Racial Integration
Religious Composition
Token Representation

RACIAL CONFLICT
S-08-0122 1975 00021
BT Social Conflict
NT Black Insurrection
Race Riot
RT Black Revolution
Language Group Conflict
Political Violence
Racial Cleavage
Racial Tension
Racism
Racist
Rebellion
Revolution
Sit In
Struggle
War

RACIAL DISCRIMINATION
S-26-0374 1979 00000
BT Discrimination Policy
RT Persecution
Residential Segregation
Reverse Discrimination
Sex Discrimination

RACIAL DIVERSITY
S-06-0474 1975 00006
BT Cultural Diversity
NT Racial Cleavage
RT Ethnic Cleavage
Ethnic Diversity
Ethnic Heterogeneity
Racial Group
Racial Politics
Social Diversity

RACIAL EQUALITY
S-06-0731 1979 00000
BT Social Equality
RT Class Equality
Economic Equality
Education Equality
Egalitarianism
Income Equality
Minority Rights
Political Equality
Sex Equality
Status Equality

RACIAL EXPLOITATION
S-31-0288 1975 00005
BT Exploitation Process
RT Economic Exploitation
Ghetto Conflict
Institutional Racism
Job Discrimination
Lower Class
Political Exploitation
Racial Inequality
Racial Injustice
Racial Persecution
Racial Policy

Racial Politics
Racial Tension
Racism
Sex Exploitation

RACIAL GROUP
S-03-0030 1975 00049
BT Social Group
RT Cultural Group
Ethnic Group
Face To Face Group
Group Theory
Interest Group
Minority Group
Nationality Group
Peer Group
Racial Diversity
Racial Identity
Racial Politics
Racial Pride
Reference Group
Religious Group
Religious Organization

RACIAL IDENTITY
S-06-0383 1975 00023
BT Cultural Identity
NT Black Identity
RT Ethnic Group Loyalty
Ethnicity
Language Loyalty
National Identity
Racial Attitude
Racial Group
Racial Inequality
Racial Militancy
Racial Policy
Racial Pride
Racial Supremacy
Racial Tolerance
Social Identity

RACIAL INEQUALITY
S-06-0741 1975 00044
BT Social Inequality
RT Class Inequality
Economic Inequality
Economic Injustice
Education Inequality
Education Injustice
Income Inequality
Institutional Racism
Political Inequality
Racial Exploitation
Racial Identity
Racial Injustice
Racial Policy
Racial Prejudice
Racial Tension
Racism
Sex Inequality
Sexual Injustice
Social Injustice
Status Inequality

RACIAL INJUSTICE
S-06-0712 1975 00006
BT Social Injustice
RT Class Inequality
Economic Injustice
Education Inequality
Education Injustice
Inequality
Minority Rights
Political Injustice
Racial Attitude
Racial Exploitation
Racial Inequality
Racial Persecution
Racial Policy
Sex Inequality
Sexual Injustice
Social Inequality
Social Injustice
Status Inequality
Womens Rights

RACIAL INTEGRATION
S-31-0827 1975 00032
BT Integration
NT Housing Integration
School Integration
RT Community Desegregation Policy
Cultural Integration
Desegregation Policy
Ethnic Integration
Functional Integration
Housing Policy
Racial Composition
Racial Integration Theory
Racial Policy
Racial Politics
Social Integration
Vertical Integration

RACIAL INTEGRATION THEORY
S-38-0212 1975 00019
BT Ethnic Assimilation Theory
RT Ethnic Assimilation Theory
Racial Assimilation
Racial Integration

RACIAL INTOLERANCE
S-06-0108 1975 00003
BT Intolerance
RT Bigotry
Racial Attitude
Racial Prejudice
Racial Supremacy
Racial Tolerance
Racism
Racist

RACIAL MILITANCY
S-06-0111 1975 00001
BT Militancy
NT Black Militancy
White Militancy
RT Activist
Protest
Racial Attitude
Racial Identity
Racial Supremacy

RACIAL PERSECUTION
S-31-0318 1975 00006
BT Persecution
RT Apartheid
Ethnic Persecution
Ethnic Policy
Minority Persecution
National Socialism
Nationality Persecution
Political Persecution
Racial Exploitation
Racial Injustice
Racial Policy
Racial Politics
Religious Persecution

RACIAL POLICY
S-26-0380 1975 00020
BT Ethnic Policy
NT Apartheid
Desegregation Policy
RT Racial Attitude
Racial Exploitation
Racial Identity
Racial Inequality
Racial Injustice
Racial Integration
Racial Persecution
Racial Politics
Racial Prejudice
Racial Pride
Racial Voting
Racism
Racist
Separatism

RACIAL POLITICS
S-29-0228 1975 00020
BT Politics
RT Backlash Voting
Group Politics
National Socialism
Partisan Politics
Protest Politics
Racial Diversity
Racial Exploitation
Racial Group
Racial Integration
Racial Persecution
Racial Policy
Racial Pride
Racial Voting
Religious Politics
Sexual Politics
Youth Politics

RACIAL PREJUDICE
S-06-0122 1975 00026
BT Racial Attitude
RT Authoritarian Personality
Backlash Voting
Bigotry
Institutional Racism
Policy
Racial Inequality
Racial Intolerance
Racial Policy
Racism

RACIAL PRIDE
S-06-0123 1975 00002
BT Racial Attitude
RT Nation Building
Nationalism
Racial Group
Racial Identity
Racial Policy
Racial Politics
Racial Revolution
Racial Voting

RACIAL REVOLUTION
S-08-0079 1975 00000
BT Social Revolution
NT Black Revolution
RT Industrial Revolution
Proletarian Revolution

Racial Pride
Racism
Sit In
Social Conflict
Spontaneous Revolution

RACIAL SUPREMACY
S-06-0124 1975 00002
BT Racial Attitude
RT Black Militancy
Institutional Racism
National Socialism
Racial Identity
Racial Intolerance
Racial Militancy
Racism
White Militancy
White Racism

RACIAL TENSION
S-06-0794 1975 00016
BT Social Stress
RT Racial Attitude
Racial Cleavage
Racial Conflict
Racial Exploitation
Racial Inequality
Racial Tolerance
Violence

RACIAL TOLERANCE
S-06-0137 1975 00008
BT Tolerance
RT Racial Attitude
Racial Identity
Racial Intolerance
Racial Tension

RACIAL VOTING
S-29-0133 1975 00007
BT Group Voting
NT Black Voting
RT Age Group Voting
Backlash Voting
Bloc Voting
Ethnic Group Voting
Geographic Voting
Protest Voter
Protest Voting
Racial Policy
Racial Politics
Racial Pride
Regional Voting
Religious Voting
Sex Group Voting
Student Voting
Suburban Voting
Urban Voting

RACISM
S-38-0217 1975 00039
BT Ethnic Ideology
NT Antisemitism
Apartheid Theory
Black Racism
Institutional Racism
White Racism
RT Apartheid
Backlash Voting
Community Desegregation Policy
Ethnic Assimilation Theory
Ethnic Nationalism
Ethnic Particularism
Ethnic Separatism
Ethnocentrism
Exclusionary Policy
Genocide
Jim Crow Law
Race Riot
Racial Attitude
Racial Conflict
Racial Exploitation
Racial Inequality
Racial Intolerance
Racial Policy
Racial Prejudice
Racial Revolution
Racial Supremacy
Racist
Residential Segregation
Segregation Policy
White Militancy

RACIST
S-32-0292 1975 00002
BT Segregationist
RT Institutional Racism
Racial Attitude
Racial Cleavage
Racial Conflict
Racial Intolerance
Racial Policy
Racism

RADIATION LEVEL
S-06-0366 1979 00000
UF Radioactive Fallout
Radioactive Pollution
Radioactive Wastes
BT Environmental Characteristics
RT Energy Management
Energy Policy
Energy Use Policy
Health Care Policy
Living Conditions
Nuclear Energy Industry
Nuclear Power
Population Density
Quality Of Life
Regulatory Agency Record

RADICAL MOVEMENT
S-27-0018 1975 00012
BT Ideological Spectrum Political Movement
NT Radical Student Movement
RT Extremist Movement
International Communist Movement
Liberation Movement
New Left Militant
Populist Movement
Proletarian Movement
Radical Political Party
Radicalism
Revolutionary Movement
Separatist Movement
Terrorist Movement
Totalitarian Movement

RADICAL PARTY
1975-1979 00005

RADICAL POLITICAL PARTY
S-28-0021 1979 00000
BT Ideological Spectrum Political Party Type
RT Cadre Political Party
Communist Political Party
Ideological Political Party
Leftist Political Party
Radical Movement
Radical Press
Radical Student Movement
Radicalism
Revolutionary Movement
Underground Political Party

RADICAL PRESS
S-17-0023 1975 00001
BT Newspaper Industry
RT Black Press
National Press
Radical Political Party
Radicalism
Underground Political Party
Underground Press

RADICAL STUDENT MOVEMENT
S-27-0019 1975 00006
BT Radical Movement
RT Extremist Movement
Hippie Movement
Radical Political Party
Radicalism
Student
Youth Movement
Youth Organization

RADICALISM
S-38-0077 1975 00024
BT Contemporary Political Thought
RT Diggers Political Thought
Early Radical Thought
Early Republicanism
Extremism
Levellers Political Thought
New Left
New Left Militant
Political Extremism
Radical Movement
Radical Political Party
Radical Press
Radical Student Movement
System Politicization
Underground Political Party
Underground Press

RADIO CENSORSHIP
S-31-0278 1975 00001
BT Broadcasting Censorship
RT Broadcasting Agency
Broadcasting Policy
Media Access
Music Censorship
Radio Industry
Television Censorship
Theater Censorship

RADIO INDUSTRY
S-17-0010 1975 00009
BT Broadcasting Industry
RT Broadcasting
Commercial Broadcasting Industry
Public Broadcasting Industry
Radio Censorship
Radio Policy
Telecommunications Industry
Television Industry

RADIO POLICY
S-26-0037 1975 00004
BT Broadcasting Policy
RT Broadcast Access Policy
Broadcast Censorship Policy
Broadcast Regulation Policy
Broadcast Subsidization Policy
Broadcasting Agency
Broadcasting Censorship
Radio Industry

RADIOACTIVE FALLOUT
USE Radiation Level

RADIOACTIVE POLLUTION
USE Radiation Level

RADIOACTIVE WASTES
USE Radiation Level

RAILROAD POLICY
S-26-0426 1975 00008
BT Mass Transit Policy
RT Air Transportation Policy
Railway Industry
Urban Transit Policy

RAILWAY INDUSTRY
S-17-0077 1975 00013
BT Land Transportation Industry
RT Automobile Industry
Motor Vehicle Industry
Railroad Policy
Shipping Industry
Transportation Policy
Trucking Industry

RANDOM ACCESS STORAGE
USE Computer Processing

RANDOM ERROR
S-24-0197 1975 00001
BT Measurement Problem
RT Autocorrelation
Measurement Bias
Measurement Error
Missing Data
Sampling Error
Systematic Error

RANK AND FILE MEMBER
S-32-0177 1975 00000
BT Political Party Member
RT Political Party Cadre
Political Party Supporter
Political Party Type
Political Party Worker
Union

RANK ORDER CORRELATION
S-24-0036 1975 00005
BT Correlation Analysis
RT Product Moment Correlation
Ratio Scale
Ratio Scale Measurement

RANKING MINORITY MEMBER
S-36-0155 1975 00000
BT Legislative Committee Member
RT Floor Leader

RAPE
S-10-0047 1979 00000
BT Sex Crime
RT Assault
Morals Offense
Sex Role
Violent Crime

RAPPROACHMENT
S-06-0679 1979 00000
BT International Political System Characteristics
RT Balance Of Power
Collective Security
Disarmament
East West Detente
International Relations Studies
Peace
Peaceful Coexistence

RATIO SCALE
S-24-0216 1975 00000
BT Scale Construction Methodology
RT Factor Structure
Guttman Scale
Interval Scale
Likert Scale
Measurement Level Scale
Multidimensional Scale
Nominal Scale
Ordinal Scale
Rank Order Correlation
Ratio Scale Measurement
Scalability Index
Semantic Differential
Thurstone Scale
Unidimensional Scale

RATIO SCALE MEASUREMENT
S-24-0175 1975 00002
BT Measurement Level
RT Interval Measurement
Nominal Measurement
Ordinal Measurement
Rank Order Correlation
Ratio Scale

RATIONAL CHOICE MODEL
S-24-0315 1975 00039
BT Social Science Model
RT Econometric Model
Economic Development Model
Economic Model
Economic Theory Of Democracy
Moral Choice
Optimizing Model
Psychometric Model
Rational Choice Theory
Rational Man Analysis
Rational Model
Rationality Theory

RATIONAL CHOICE THEORY
S-38-0140 1975 00037
BT Rational Model
RT Decision Making Theory
Economic Model
Inner Directed Personality
Public Choice Theory
Rational Choice Model
Rational Man Analysis
Rationality Theory
Social Choice Theory

RATIONAL LEGAL LEADERSHIP
S-22-0009 1975 00000
BT Leadership Authority Base
RT Administrative Leadership
Bureaucratic Leadership
Collective Leadership
Government Bureaucracy
Leadership Structure Type
National Leadership
Political Leadership
Totalitarian Leadership
Weberian Analysis
Weberian Theory

RATIONAL MAN ANALYSIS
S-09-0061 1975 00010
BT Contemporary Analytic Modes
RT Behavior Analysis
Economic Behavior
Rational Choice Model
Rational Choice Theory
Rational Model
Rationality Theory
Reductionist Analysis

RATIONAL MODEL
S-38-0139 1975 00023
BT Formal Political Theory
NT Rational Choice Theory
RT Atomistic Model
Decision Making Theory
Economic Model
Game Theory
Man Machine Simulation
Mathematical Political Theory
Rational Choice Model
Rational Man Analysis
Rationality Theory

RATIONALITY THEORY
S-38-0501 1975 00026
BT Political Philosophy Concept
RT Baconian Analysis
Man Machine Simulation
Rational Choice Model
Rational Choice Theory
Rational Man Analysis
Rational Model

RATIONING AGENCY
S-19-0020 1975 00000
BT Economic Control Agency
RT Consumer Agency
Price Control Agency
Price Support Agency

RAW MATERIAL PRODUCTION
S-31-0437 1975 00019
BT Industrial Production
RT Extractive Industry
Natural Resource Policy

REACTIONARY
S-32-0264 1975 00001
BT Spectrum Politicist
RT Extremist
Ideologue
Political Radical
Reactionary Conservatism
Rightist

REACTIONARY CONSERVATISM
S-38-0200 1975 00000
BT Conservatism
RT American Conservatism
Burkean Conservatism
Christian Conservatism
Counterrevolution
McCarthyism
Neoconservatism
Objectivist Political Thought
Reactionary
Status Quo Conservatism

REACTIVE OBSERVATION
S-24-0096 1975 00002
BT Data Collection Methodology
NT Experimental Observation
Interview
Participant Observation
Survey Research
RT Field Research
Nonreactive Observation
Observation Time
Questionnaire
Sampling Procedure

REAL INCOME
S-06-0337 1975 00004
BT Income Measure
RT Economic Statistics
Gross National Product
Quality Of Life
Socioeconomic Data

REALIGNING ELECTION
S-29-0085 1975 00010
BT Election Type
RT Critical Election
Voting

REALIST FOREIGN POLICY
S-38-0346 1979 00000
BT Foreign Policy Theory
RT Balance Of Power Theory
Cold War
Deterrence Theory
Geopolitical Theory
Idealist Foreign Policy
International Influence Theory
International Power Theory
Power Politics
Realpolitik
Superpower Politics

REALITY CONSTRUCTION
S-24-0443 1979 00000
BT Individual Perception
RT Cognitive Development
Individual Behavior
Perception Measurement
Reality Testing

REALITY TESTING
S-24-0444 1979 00000
BT Individual Perception
RT Cognitive Measurement
Individual Behavior
Perception Measurement
Reality Construction

REALPOLITIK
S-29-0225 1975 00002
SN Approach to foreign policy that emphasizes power considerations rather than psychological or value considerations.
BT Power Politics
RT Foreign Policy
Power Abuse
Power Theory
Power Type
Realist Foreign Policy

REAPPOINTMENT
S-31-0731 1975 00000
BT Appointment Process
RT Civil Servant
Presidential Appointment

REAPPORTIONMENT
S-31-0714 1975 00002
BT Apportionment
RT Apportionment Reform
Legislative Redistricting

REARMAMENT POLICY
S-26-0075 1975 00000
BT Defense Policy
RT Arms Control Policy
Deterrence Policy
Military Policy
Nuclear Strategy

REBELLION
S-08-0053 1975 00013
BT Internal Conflict
NT Economic Rebellion
Political Rebellion
Social Rebellion
Student Rebellion
Worker Rebellion
RT Bolshevik Revolution
Class Conflict
Class Polarization
Counterinsurgency
Coup D'Etat
Economic Conflict
Expansionist War
General Strike
Government Overthrow
Group Conflict
Ideological Conflict
Ideological War
Imperialist War
Institutional Conflict
Insurgency
Internal War
Military Aggression
Military Coup
Mob Violence
Political Agitation
Political Purge
Political Violence
Putsch
Racial Conflict
Religious Conflict
Religious War
Revolution
Revolutionary War
Routinized Conflict
Struggle
Succession Struggle
Thermidor
Urban Race Riot
Violence
War

RECIDIVISM
S-10-0081 1979 00000
BT Crime
RT Court Crime
Crime Rate
Individual Crime
Penal Institution
Penal Law
Penal Reform
Punishment

RECORDS MANAGEMENT
USE Business Management

RECREATION
USE Analysis Of Play

RECREATION DISTRICT
S-16-0093 1975 00005
BT District Government Type
RT Analysis Of Play
Fire District
School District
Sewer District
Transportation District
Water District
Zoning District

RECRUITMENT PROCESS
S-31-0741 1975 00028
BT Selection Process
NT Cooptation
Elite Recruitment
Military Recruitment
Nepotism
Political Recruitment
RT Appointment Process
Delegate Selection
Endorsement
Organization Membership
Political Candidate
Political Party Recruitment Pattern
Slate Making
Social Role Process
Testing Agency

RED COMMUNE
S-07-0020 1975 00004
BT Communal Community
RT Agricultural Collectivization Policy
Collective Community
Commune
Economic Community
Maoism
Maoist
Maoist Political Party
Maoist Revolutionary

REDUCTIONISM
S-25-0018 1975 00003
BT Empiricism
RT Comtean Positivism
Holism
Logical Positivism
Methodological Individualism
Reductionist Analysis

REDUCTIONIST ANALYSIS
S-09-0062 1975 00000
BT Contemporary Analytic Modes
RT Analysis Methodology
Contextual Analysis
Rational Man Analysis
Reductionism
Revisionist Historical Analysis

REFERENCE GROUP
S-03-0031 1975 00011
BT Social Group
RT Ethnic Group
Face To Face Group
Interest Group
Kinship Group
Nationality Group
Peer Group
Racial Group
Religious Cult

Religious Group
Secondary Group

REFERENCE GROUP THEORY
S-38-0146 1975 00012
BT Group Theory
RT Group Characteristics
Social Learning Theory
Socialization Theory

REFORM
S-31-0086 1975 00129
BT Development Process
NT Administrative Reform
Education Reform
Executive Reform
Judicial Reform
Legislative Reform
RT Institutional Development
Institutionalization
Planned Social Change
Progress
Reform Movement
Technological Progress
Urban Development

REFORM MOVEMENT
S-27-0042 1975 00030
BT Political Movement
NT Municipal Reform Movement
Tax Reform Movement
RT Civil Rights Movement
Ecology Movement
Peace Movement
Populist Movement
Reform
Separatist Movement
Social Movement

REFORMATION THEORY
S-38-0524 1975 00001
BT Renaissance Political Thought
RT Religious Culture
Religious Movement

REFUGEE
S-36-0024 1975 00008
BT Immigrant
NT Political Refugee
RT Citizenship Status
Exile
Expatriate
Political Opposition
Refugee Migration

REFUGEE MIGRATION
S-31-0625 1975 00005
BT Migration Process
RT Emigration Process
Emigre
Immigration Process
Internal Migration
Refugee

REGENT
S-36-0067 1975 00000
BT Monarch
RT Abdication
Hereditary Ruler
Kaiser
Khan
King
Queen
Shah
Sheik
Sultan
Tsar

REGIME INSTABILITY
S-06-0693 1975 00017
BT Political Instability
NT Cabinet Instability
RT Government Instability
Regime Type

REGIME TYPE
S-16-0131 1975 00010
BT Government
NT Political Regime
RT Authority Theory
Government Characteristics
Government Type
Nation
Nation Type
Plebiscite Election
Regime Instability
Rule Type
Ruling Political Party
State Type

REGIONAL CONFLICT
1975-1979 00039

REGIONAL DEVELOPMENT
S-31-0101 1975 00046
BT Development Process
RT Environmental Studies
International Region
International Regional Conflict
Local Development
North South Conflict
Regional Economics
Resource Development
Rural Development
Urban Development
Urban Redevelopment

REGIONAL ECONOMIC DEVELOPMENT LEVEL
S-06-0148 1975 00018
BT Economic Development Level
NT International Economic Development Level
Subnational Economic Development Level
RT Economic Characteristics
International Regional Conflict
Local Economic Development Level
National Economic Development Level
Regional Economics

REGIONAL ECONOMICS
S-01-0072 1979 00000
BT Economics Discipline
RT Business Economics
Consumer Economics
Developed Economy
Developing Economy
Econometrics
Economic Community
Economic Geography
Environmental Studies
International Economics
International Regional Economic Integration
Land Use Policy
Planned Economy
Regional Development
Regional Economic Development Level
Regional Planner
Regional Planning Policy
Social Economics
Transportation Economics

REGIONAL INTERNATIONAL POLITICAL SYSTEM
S-37-0123 1975 00059
BT International Political System
RT Bipolar International System
Commonwealth International System
Hegemonic System
International Region
International Regional Conflict
Multipolar International Political System

REGIONAL MILITARY ALLIANCE
S-02-0008 1975 00032
BT Military Alliance
RT Defense Alliance
Defense System
International Regional Conflict
Multilateral Alliance
Wartime Alliance

REGIONAL PLANNER
S-32-0144 1975 00007
BT Subnational Planner
RT Environmental Studies
Local Planner
Regional Economics
Regional Planning Policy
State Planner

REGIONAL PLANNING POLICY
S-26-0353 1975 00017
BT Subnational Planning Policy
RT Administrative Planning
International Region
Local Planning Policy
National Planning Policy
Needs Assessment
Regional Economics
Regional Planner
State Planning Policy

REGIONAL POLITICAL PARTY FIRST SECRETARY
S-36-0255 1975 00002
BT Subnational Political Party First Secretary
RT Local Political Party First Secretary
Prefect

REGIONAL SECURITY
S-06-0669 1975 00033
BT Collective Security
RT Balkanization
International Regional Conflict
North South Conflict
Protective Alliance
Sphere Of Influence

REGIONAL STUDIES
USE Area Studies

REGIONAL VOTING
S-29-0127 1979 00000
BT Geographic Voting
RT Age Group Voting
Bloc Voting
Class Voting
Ethnic Group Voting
Geographic Voting
Racial Voting
Religious Voting

Rural Voting
Sex Group Voting
Suburban Voting

REGISTERED VOTER
S-32-0309 1975 00000
BT Eligible Voter
RT Potential Voter
Registration Requirement
Voter Registration

REGISTRATION REQUIREMENT
S-15-0085 1975 00000
BT Voter Qualification
RT Property Voting Qualification
Registered Voter
Residence Requirement
Voting Age Requirement

REGRESSION ANALYSIS
S-24-0037 1975 00053
BT Correlation Analysis
RT Correlation Analysis
Multivariate Analysis
Product Moment Correlation
Statistical Analysis

REGRESSIVE TAXATION
S-26-0162 1975 00003
BT Taxation Policy
RT Direct Taxation
Indirect Taxation
National Tax Law
National Taxation
Progressive Taxation
State Taxation
Subnational Taxation

REGRESSIVE TAXATION POLICY
1975-1979 00000

REGULAR ARMY
S-33-0056 1975 00003
BT Army Organization
NT Officer Corps
RT Mass Militia Army
National Guard
Standing Army

REGULATION PROCESS
S-31-0310 1979 00000
BT Control Process
NT Government Regulation
RT Budget Reviewing
Business Regulation Agency
Centralized Government
Expropriation Process
Planning Commission
Regulatory Commission

REGULATORY AGENCY RECORD
S-18-0023 1975 00004
BT Administrative Record
RT Environmental Advisory Agency
Intergovernmental Document
Licensing Record
Radiation Level
Tariff Record
Tax Record

REGULATORY COMMISSION
S-19-0101 1975 00022
BT Commissions
NT Independent Regulatory Commission
RT Air Fare Regulation Policy
Airline Regulation Policy
Budget Reviewing
Business Regulation Agency
Commission Of Inquiry
Federal Commission
Investigation Commission
Planning Commission
Regulation Process
Transportation Agency

REHABILITATION EDUCATION POLICY
S-26-0195 1975 00031
BT Education Policy
RT Education Policy
Higher Education Policy
Literacy Policy
Public Education Policy
Vocation Training Policy

REINSTATING ELECTION
S-29-0086 1975 00002
BT Election Type
RT Critical Election
Election Campaign
Electoral Participation
Maintaining Election
Voting Result Interpretation

RELATIVE DEPRIVATION
S-06-0127 1975 00012
BT Deprivation
RT Psychopolitical Theory
Relative Deprivation Theory

RELATIVE DEPRIVATION THEORY
S-38-0551 1975 00007
BT Psychological Theory
RT Achievement Theory
Alienation Psychological Theory
Attitude Change Theory
Cognitive Theory
Frustration Aggression Theory
Gestalt Theory
Psychological Behavioralism
Psychological Behaviorism
Psychopolitical Theory
Relative Deprivation

RELATIVE JUSTICE THEORY
S-38-0481 1975 00001
BT Justice Theory
RT Justice Administration
Justice As Fairness Doctrine
Moral Authority
Political Injustice

RELIABILITY MEASUREMENT
S-24-0159 1975 00020
BT Measurement Evaluation
NT Intercoder Reliability
Internal Consistency Reliability
Interviewer Effect
Test Retest Reliability
RT Measurement
Measurement Bias
Social Science Model
Statistical Data
Statistics Discipline
Validity Measurement

RELIGIOUS AFFILIATION
S-06-0396 1979 00000
BT Religious Identity
RT Heterogeneous Group Membership
Homogeneous Group Membership
Organization Membership
Religious Authority
Religious Community
Religious Group
Religious Identity
Religious Minister
Sociology Of Religion

RELIGIOUS AUTHORITY
S-04-0023 1975 00005
BT Authority Type
NT Civil Religion
Theocratic Authority
RT Antitrinitarianism
Arab Bloc
Atheism
Augustinian Analysis
Blue Law
Charismatic Authority
Christian Democratic Movement
Civil Religion
Ecclesiastical Leadership
Ecumenical Movement
Free Masonry
Freedom Of Religion
Hagiology
Mandate Of Heaven Theory
Moral Authority
Moral Leadership
Moral Theory
Parochial School
Religious Affiliation
Religious Censorship
Religious Community
Religious Conflict
Religious Cult
Religious Culture
Religious Elite
Religious Fundamentalism
Religious History
Religious Law
Religious Leader
Religious Leadership
Religious Minister
Religious Movement
Religious Offense
Religious Organization
Religious Persecution
Religious Policy
Religious Politics
Religious School
Religious Socialization
Religious Society
Religious Studies
Religious War
Sociology Of Religion
Traditional Authority
Traditional Political Culture

RELIGIOUS BUREAUCRACY
S-19-0081 1975 00002
BT Bureaucracy
RT Augustinian Analysis
Bureaucratic Characteristics
Civil Religion
Public Bureaucracy
Religious Fundamentalism
Religious History

RELIGIOUS CENSORSHIP
S-31-0272 1975 00000
BT Censorship Process
RT Political Censorship
Religious Authority
Religious Conflict
Religious Culture
Religious Dissenter

Religious Fundamentalism
Religious Offense

RELIGIOUS COMMUNITY
S-07-0044 1975 00009
BT Community Type
RT Caste Society
Ecumenical Movement
Islamic Society
Kibbutz
Millenarianism
Monasticism
Religious Affiliation
Religious Authority
Religious Culture
Religious Education
Religious Elite
Religious Group
Religious Identity
Religious Minister
Religious Movement
Religious Policy
Religious School
Religious Socialization
Religious Society
Religious Studies
Religious Thought
Segregated Community
Sociology Of Religion
Utopian Community

RELIGIOUS COMPOSITION
S-06-0224 1975 00006
BT Population Composition
RT Ethnic Composition
Nationality Composition
Racial Composition

RELIGIOUS CONFLICT
S-08-0026 1975 00016
BT Cultural Conflict
RT Cultural Aggression
Cultural Revolution
Economic Conflict
Holy War
Ideological Conflict
Political Revolution
Psychological Aggression
Rebellion
Religious Authority
Religious Censorship
Religious Elite
Religious Fanaticism
Religious Identity
Religious Movement
Religious Policy
Religious Political Party
Religious Politics
Religious Studies
Religious War
Social Conflict
Social Revolution
Struggle

RELIGIOUS CULT
S-03-0033 1979 00000
BT Religious Group
RT Ethnic Group
Face To Face Group
Homogeneous Culture
Homogeneous Group Membership
Nationality Group
Psychological Deprogramming
Psychological Programming
Reference Group
Religious Authority
Religious Culture
Religious Movement
Secret Society

RELIGIOUS CULTURE
S-11-0041 1975 00064
BT Culture Type
RT Civilization
Counter Culture
Cultural History
Eastern Orthodox Thought
Eschatology
Ethnic Culture
Islamic Civilization
Islamic Society
Islamic Thought
Judaic Thought
Judeo Christian Thought
Millenarianism
Neoconfucian Political Theory
Neoconfucianism
Nonwestern Culture
Pan Islamism
Pan Slav Movement
Political Culture
Protestant Sectarianism
Protestantism
Reformation Theory
Religious Authority
Religious Censorship
Religious Community
Religious Cult
Religious Fundamentalism
Religious Group
Religious Movement
Religious Policy
Religious Politics
Religious Studies
Religious Thought
Roman Catholicism
Shintoism
Sociology Of Religion
Subculture
Traditional Culture
Unitarianism
Village Culture
Zionism

RELIGIOUS DISSENTER
S-32-0341 1975 00002
BT Religious Role
RT Exile
Religious Censorship
Religious Elite
Religious Fanaticism

RELIGIOUS EDUCATION
S-13-0044 1979 00000
BT Education Type
RT Civil Religion
Classical Education
Humanistic Education
Humanities Education
Liberal Arts Education
Missionary
Monk
Priest
Psychological Deprogramming
Psychological Programming
Rabbi
Religious Community
Religious Group
Religious Law
Religious Policy
Religious School
Religious Studies

RELIGIOUS ELITE
S-14-0036 1975 00008
BT Social Elite
RT Ayatallah
Lama
Modernizing Social Elite
Priest
Rabbi
Religious Authority
Religious Community
Religious Conflict
Religious Dissenter
Religious Law
Religious Leader
Religious Organization
Religious Policy
Religious Politics
Traditional Political Elite
Traditional Social Elite

RELIGIOUS FANATICISM
S-06-0397 1975 00004
BT Religious Identity
RT Eschatology
Millenarianism
Religious Conflict
Religious Dissenter
Religious War

RELIGIOUS FUNDAMENTALISM
S-38-0573 1979 00000
BT Religious Thought
RT Religious Authority
Religious Bureaucracy
Religious Censorship
Religious Culture
Religious Organization
Religious Policy
Religious Politics
Traditional Authority

RELIGIOUS GROUP
S-03-0032 1975 00041
BT Social Group
NT Religious Cult
RT Anglicanism
Civil Religion
Cultural Group
Ecumenical Movement
Ethnic Group
Face To Face Group
Interest Group
Missionary
Monk
Nationality Group
Peer Group
Racial Group
Reference Group
Religious Affiliation
Religious Community
Religious Culture
Religious Education
Religious History
Religious Identity
Religious Leadership

Religious Minister
Religious Organization
Religious Political Party
Secondary Group
Sociology Of Religion

RELIGIOUS HISTORY
S-01-0120 1979 00000
BT History Discipline
RT Ancient History
Art History
Civil Religion
Cultural History
Ecumenical Movement
Freedom Of Religion
Hagiology
Historiography
History Of Philosophy
Intellectual History
Oral History
Political History
Religious Authority
Religious Bureaucracy
Religious Group
Religious Policy
Religious Society
Religious Studies
Social History
Sociology Of Religion

RELIGIOUS IDENTITY
S-06-0395 1975 00049
BT Identity Characteristics
NT Religious Affiliation
Religious Fanaticism
RT Calvinism
Catholicism
Christian Conservatism
Community Identity
Eastern Orthodox Thought
Ecumenical Movement
Islamic Thought
Judaic Thought
Lutheranism
National Identity
Protestant Sectarianism
Protestantism
Religious Affiliation
Religious Community
Religious Conflict
Religious Group
Religious Movement
Roman Catholicism
Shintoism
Social Identity
Zionism

RELIGIOUS LAW
S-21-0081 1975 00003
BT Sacred Law
NT Canon Law
Church Law
RT Augustinian Analysis
Civil Religion
Natural Law
Religious Authority
Religious Education
Religious Elite
Religious Offense
Religious Policy
Religious Politics
Religious Studies
Religious Thought

RELIGIOUS LEADER
S-32-0340 1975 00013
BT Religious Role
RT Ayatallah
Charismatic Leader
Community Leader
Ecclesiastical Leadership
Lama
Lamaism
Missionary
Monk
Opinion Leader
Priest
Rabbi
Religious Authority
Religious Elite
Religious Leadership
Religious Organization
Religious Policy
Religious Politics
Religious Role
Religious Socialization

RELIGIOUS LEADERSHIP
S-22-0011 1979 00000
BT Traditional Leadership
NT Ecclesiastical Leadership
RT Authority Mode
Authority Type
Ayatallah
Leadership Structure Type
Moral Leadership
Personalized Leadership
Religious Authority
Religious Group
Religious Leader
Religious Movement
Religious Policy
Religious Political Party
Religious Politics

RELIGIOUS MINISTER
S-32-0099 1979 00000
BT Professional Occupational Role
NT Ayatallah
Lama
Missionary
Monk
Priest
Rabbi
RT Missionary
Monk
Religious Affiliation
Religious Authority
Religious Community
Religious Group
Religious Movement
Religious Society

RELIGIOUS MOVEMENT
S-27-0064 1975 00027
BT Social Movement
NT Ecumenical Movement
RT Buddhism
Calvinism
Catholicism
Christian Thought
Civil Religion
Conciliar Movement Doctrine
Free Masonry
Gelasian Doctrine
Islamic Thought
Judaic Thought
Lutheranism
Millenarianism
Pan Islamism
Pan Slav Movement
Protestant Sectarianism
Protestantism
Reformation Theory
Religious Authority
Religious Community
Religious Conflict
Religious Cult
Religious Culture
Religious Identity
Religious Leadership
Religious Minister
Religious Offense
Religious Organization
Religious Policy
Religious Political Party
Religious Politics
Religious School
Religious Socialization
Religious War
Roman Catholicism
Sectarian Movement
Sociology Of Religion
Zionism
Zionist Movement
Zoroastrianism

RELIGIOUS OFFENSE
S-10-0082 1979 00000
BT Crime
RT Court Crime
Economic Crime
Individual Crime
Political Crime
Religious Authority
Religious Censorship
Religious Law
Religious Movement
Religious Politics

RELIGIOUS ORGANIZATION
S-03-0057 1975 00017
BT Organizations
RT Cultural Organization
Free Masonry
Missionary
Monk
Parochial School
Peasant Organization
Racial Group
Religious Authority
Religious Elite
Religious Fundamentalism
Religious Group
Religious Leader
Religious Movement
Religious Policy
Religious Political Party
Religious Politics
Religious Socialization
Secondary Group
Youth Organization

RELIGIOUS PARTY
1975-1979 00001

RELIGIOUS PERSECUTION
S-31-0319 1975 00010
BT Persecution
RT Ethnic Persecution
Minority Persecution
Nationality Persecution
Political Persecution
Racial Persecution
Religious Authority
Religious Policy
Religious Politics

RELIGIOUS POLICY
S-26-0397 1975 00011
BT Social Policy
NT Church State Policy
School Prayer Policy
RT Discrimination Policy
Ethnic Policy
Population Policy
Priest
Rabbi
Religious Authority
Religious Community
Religious Conflict
Religious Culture
Religious Education
Religious Elite
Religious Fundamentalism
Religious History
Religious Law
Religious Leader
Religious Leadership
Religious Movement
Religious Organization
Religious Persecution
Religious Political Party
Religious Politics
Religious Role
Religious School
Religious Socialization
Religious Studies
Religious Thought
Religious War

RELIGIOUS POLITICAL PARTY
S-28-0051 1979 00000
BT Traditional Political Party
RT Religious Conflict
Religious Group
Religious Leadership
Religious Movement
Religious Organization
Religious Policy
Religious Politics
Religious Society

RELIGIOUS POLITICS
S-29-0229 1975 00018
BT Politics
RT Ayatallah
Church State Separation Doctrine
Civil Religion
Gay Politics
Group Politics
Lama
Partisan Politics
Protest Politics
Racial Politics
Religious Authority
Religious Conflict
Religious Culture
Religious Elite
Religious Fundamentalism
Religious Law
Religious Leader
Religious Leadership
Religious Movement
Religious Offense
Religious Organization
Religious Persecution
Religious Policy
Religious Political Party
Religious Role
Religious Socialization
Religious Thought
Religious War
Sexual Politics
Theocratic Authority
Youth Politics

RELIGIOUS ROLE
S-32-0339 1975 00008
BT Roles
NT Religious Dissenter
Religious Leader
RT Priest
Rabbi
Religious Leader
Religious Policy
Religious Politics
Religious School
Religious War

RELIGIOUS SCHOOL
S-19-0224 1975 00001
UF Denominational School
BT Education Institution
NT Parochial School
RT Private School
Religious Authority
Religious Community
Religious Education
Religious Movement
Religious Policy
Religious Role
Religious Socialization
Religious Studies
Religious Thought

RELIGIOUS SOCIALIZATION
S-34-0035 1979 00000
BT Institutional Socialization
RT Religious Authority
Religious Community
Religious Leader
Religious Movement
Religious Organization
Religious Policy
Religious Politics
Religious School

RELIGIOUS SOCIETY
S-35-0047 1979 00000
BT Traditional Society
NT Islamic Society
RT Ayatallah
Closed Society
Homogeneous Society
Lama
Religious Authority
Religious Community
Religious History
Religious Minister
Religious Political Party
Secular Society

RELIGIOUS STUDIES
S-01-0181 1979 00000
BT Academic Areas
RT Civil Religion
Ecumenical Movement
Hagiology
Moral Authority
Religious Authority
Religious Community
Religious Conflict
Religious Culture
Religious Education
Religious History
Religious Law
Religious Policy
Religious School

RELIGIOUS THOUGHT
S-38-0552 1975 00037
BT Theory
NT Atheism
Buddhism
Confucianism
Hinduism
Islamic Thought
Judeo Christian Thought
Religious Fundamentalism
Shintoism
Taoism
Zoroastrianism
RT Christian Existentialism
Divine Justice Theory
Ecclesiastical Leadership
Eschatology
Fatalism
Lamaism
Neoconfucian Political Theory
Religious Community
Religious Culture
Religious Law
Religious Policy
Religious Politics
Religious School
Sacred Law
Theocratic Authority
Trentine Doctrine

RELIGIOUS VOTING
S-29-0135 1975 00008
BT Group Voting
RT Age Group Voting
Ethnic Group Voting
Geographic Voting
Protest Voting
Racial Voting
Regional Voting
Sex Group Voting

RELIGIOUS WAR
S-08-0106 1979 00000
BT War
NT Holy War
RT Civil War
Cultural Conflict
Ideological Conflict
Internal War
Rebellion
Religious Authority
Religious Conflict

Religious Fanaticism
Religious Movement
Religious Policy
Religious Politics
Religious Role
Social Conflict
Theocratic Authority

RELOCATION POLICY
S-26-0388 1975 00003
BT Housing Policy
RT Government Grant
Immigration Policy
Migration Process
Open Housing Policy
Public Housing Policy
Repatriate

REMEDIAL JUSTICE THEORY
S-38-0482 1975 00002
BT Justice Theory
RT Aristotelian Thought
Compensatory Justice
Equality Theory
Equity
Just Authority
Justice As Fairness Doctrine
Justice System

REMOTE TERMINAL
S-24-0330 1975 00000
BT Input Output Device
RT Communication Analysis
Computer Equipment
Information Processing
Interaction Analysis
Network Analysis

RENAISSANCE
S-06-0174 1979 00000
BT Historical Periods
RT Dark Ages
Medieval Ages
Renaissance Political Thought

RENAISSANCE POLITICAL THOUGHT
S-38-0516 1975 00003
BT Political Theory
NT Baconian Analysis
Cartesian Analysis
Early Radical Thought
Machiavellian Thought
Reformation Theory
Renaissance State Theory
Royalist State Theory
RT Classical Political Thought
Contemporary Political Thought
Ideologies
Medieval Political Thought
Renaissance
Renaissance State Theory
Royalist
Royalist State Theory

RENAISSANCE STATE THEORY
S-38-0525 1975 00001
BT Renaissance Political Thought
RT Absolute Monarch
Machiavellian Thought
Renaissance Political Thought
Royalist
Royalist State Theory
State Type

RENT STRIKE
S-08-0011 1975 00000
BT Economic Demonstration
RT Civil Rights Demonstration
Consumer Demonstration

REPATRIATE
S-36-0026 1975 00000
BT Citizenship Status
RT Alien
Expatriate
Immigrant
Relocation Policy
Stateless Person

REPLICATION
S-24-0143 1975 00014
BT Hypothesis Testing
RT Confirmation
Falsification

REPORT CENSORSHIP
S-31-0273 1975 00000
BT Censorship Process
NT Government Report Censorship
Scientific Report Censorship
RT Government Information Diffusion Policy
Information Leaking
Published Media Censorship
Unpublished Media Censorship

REPOSITORY
USE Archives

REPRESENTATION
S-31-0705 1975 00019
BT Process
NT Apportionment
Representation Type
RT Burkean Analysis
Delegate Representation Theory
Delegate Selection
Functional Representation Theory
Government Contract Theory
Group Representation Theory
Interest Group Politics
Majoritarianism
Political Legitimacy Theory
Representation Theory
Representative
Representative Democracy
Representative Government
Responsibility Doctrine

REPRESENTATION THEORY
S-38-0502 1975 00016
BT Political Philosophy Concept
NT Delegate Representation Theory
Functional Representation Theory
Group Representation Theory
Linkage Representation Theory
Territory Representation Theory
Trustee Representation Theory
Virtual Representation Theory
RT Apportionment
Authority Theory
Consent Theory
Delegate
Delegated Authority
Gerrymandering
Legislative Role Orientation
Mandate Of Heaven Theory
Mass Democracy
Minority Law
One Man One Vote Representation
One Political Party Democracy
Popular Assembly
Proportional Representation
Representation
Representation Type
Representative
Representative Democracy
Representative Government
Responsibility Doctrine
Sovereignty Theory
Token Representation

REPRESENTATION TYPE
S-31-0715 1975 00008
BT Representation
NT At Large Representation
District Representation
Functional Representation
Geographic Representation
Indirect Representation
Interest Group Representation
Minority Group Representation
Multiple Member District Representation
One Man One Vote Representation
Proportional Representation
Single Member District Representation
Token Representation
RT Bicameral Legislature
Constituency Relations
Delegated Authority
Gerrymandering
Initiative Election
Legislative Accountability
National Legislature
National Politics
Political System Characteristics
Representation Theory
Representative
Representative Democracy
Representative Government

REPRESENTATIVE
S-36-0190 1975 00004
BT Congressional Member
RT Delegate At Large
Representation
Representation Theory
Representation Type
Senator

REPRESENTATIVE DEMOCRACY
S-16-0030 1975 00008
BT Democratic Government
RT Government Accountability
Government Responsiveness
Multimember District
Parliamentary Democracy
Participatory Democracy
Plebiscitary Democracy
Pluralist Democracy
Representation
Representation Theory
Representation Type
Representative Government
Republic
Republican Political Party

REPRESENTATIVE GOVERNMENT
S-16-0084 1975 00008
BT Government Type
RT Constitutional Democracy
Mass Democracy
National Assembly
Presidential Government
Representation
Representation Theory
Representation Type
Representative Democracy
Republican Monarchy

REPRESSION PROCESS
S-31-0312 1975 00033
BT Control Process
NT Persecution
Political Repression
RT Censorship Process
Exploitation Process
Political Control
Political Repression
Purge
Reprisal Policy

REPRISAL POLICY
S-26-0336 1975 00001
BT Military Policy
RT Armed Intervention Policy
Escalation Policy
Repression Process
War Policy

REPUBLIC
S-16-0085 1975 00002
BT Government Type
RT Federal Government
Representative Democracy
Republic Theory
Republican
Republican Constitutionalism
Republican Political Party

REPUBLIC THEORY
S-38-0099 1975 00004
BT Democratic Theory
RT Athenian Democratic Theory
Concurrent Majority Theory
Confederation Movement
Democratic Elite Theory
Economic Theory Of Democracy
General Will Democratic Theory
Jacksonian Democratic Theory
Majoritarianism
Minority Rights Democratic Theory
Participatory Democratic Theory
Populist Democratic Theory
Republic
Republican
Socialist Democratic Theory

REPUBLICAN
S-32-0278 1975 00002
BT System Politicist
RT Concurrent Majority Theory
Republic
Republic Theory
Republican Constitutionalism
Republican Monarchy
Republican Political Party

REPUBLICAN CONSTITUTIONALISM
S-38-0396 1975 00009
BT Early Modern Theory Of The State
RT Constitution
Constitutional Structural Theory
Democratic Constitution
Early Radical Thought
Early Republicanism
Lockean Contractualism
Madisonian Thought
National Constitution
Republic
Republican
Republican Political Party

REPUBLICAN MONARCHY
S-16-0076 1975 00001
BT Monarchy
RT Absolute Monarchy
Constitutional Monarchy
Limited Monarchy
Representative Government
Republican

REPUBLICAN PARTY
1975-1979 00015

REPUBLICAN POLITICAL PARTY
S-28-0031 1979 00000
BT Political Party Type
RT Representative Democracy
Republic
Republican
Republican Constitutionalism

REPUTATIONAL ELITE IDENTIFICATION
S-09-0022 1975 00009
BT Elite Identification
RT Elitism
Institutional Elite Identification
Issue Elite Identification
Leadership Analysis

RESEARCH AND DEVELOPMENT
S-26-0349 1979 00000
BT Planning Policy
RT Academic
Advanced Technology
Applied Anthropology
Applied Linguistics
Applied Sociology
Education Grant
Forecasting Methodology
Grant In Aid
Market Research
Marketing
Multiple Operationalization
Needs Assessment
Policy Evaluation Research
Problem Solving Behavior
Research Center
Research Grant
Research Institution
Research Management
Research Unit
Technological Change
Technology

RESEARCH APPARATUS
S-24-0323 1975 00007
BT Methodology
NT Information Processing Equipment
RT Government Research Support
Research Center
Research Design
Research Orientation

RESEARCH CENTER
S-19-0327 1975 00008
BT Research Unit
RT Academic Areas
Applied Research
Human Subject Rights
Research And Development
Research Apparatus
Research Council
Research Laboratory
Research Management

RESEARCH COUNCIL
S-19-0325 1975 00004
BT Research Institution
RT Applied Research
Philanthropic Organization
Research Center
Research Laboratory
Research Management
Research Unit
Use Of Human Subjects

RESEARCH DESIGN
S-24-0340 1975 00105
BT Methodology
NT Analysis Framework
Most Different System Design
Most Similar System Design
Paradigm
RT Analysis Methodology
Analytic Process
Data Collection Methodology
Data Presentation Methodology
Evaluating
Hypothesis Testing
Measurement
Methodological Individualism
Models
Multiple Operationalization
Research Apparatus
Research Evaluation
Research Orientation
Study Scope
Theoretical Framework

RESEARCH ETHICS
S-25-0044 1979 00000
BT Ethical Theory
NT Use Of Human Subjects
RT Bioethics
Human Rights Policy
Moral Theory
Professional Ethics
Research Institution
Scientific Research
Situational Ethics
University

RESEARCH EVALUATION
S-31-0695 1975 00775
BT Policy Evaluation
RT Applied Research
Citation Analysis
Education Evaluation
Evaluating
Formative Evaluation
Human Subject Rights
Measurement Evaluation
Needs Assessment
Normative Evaluation
Research Design
Summative Evaluation

RESEARCH GRANT
S-26-0120 1979 00000
BT Grants
RT Philanthropic Organization
Research And Development
Research Institution
Research Management
Research Unit

RESEARCH INSTITUTION
S-19-0324 1975 00017
BT Institutions
NT Research Council
Research Unit
RT Academic Areas
Academic Community
Academy Of Science
Education Institution
Experimental Research
Institutional History
Natural Science Education
Planning Agency
Research And Development
Research Ethics
Research Grant
Research Laboratory
Task Force
University
University Information Service

RESEARCH LABORATORY
S-19-0328 1975 00002
BT Research Unit
RT Applied Research
Experimental Research
Research Center
Research Council
Research Institution
Response Recording Equipment
Use Of Human Subjects

RESEARCH MANAGEMENT
S-23-0039 1979 00000
BT Management
RT Administrative Management
Applied Research
Basic Research
Development Management
Education Administration
Health Administration
Information Management
PERT Analysis
Research And Development
Research Center
Research Council
Research Grant
Research Unit
Scientific Research

RESEARCH ORIENTATION
S-24-0373 1975 00171
BT Methodology
NT Advocacy Research
Applied Research
Basic Research
Data Selection Orientation
Descriptive Research
Experimental Research
Explanatory Research
Humanistic Research
Interdisciplinary Research
Market Research
Policy Research
Predictive Research
Qualitative Research
Quantitative Research
Scientific Research
Theoretical Research
RT Analytic Process
Concept Explication Research
Methodological Individualism
Middle Range Theory
Propositional Inventory
Research Apparatus
Research Design
Study Scope
Theoretical Framework

RESEARCH UNIT
S-19-0326 1975 00011
BT Research Institution
NT Research Center
Research Laboratory
RT Analysis Unit
Event
Research And Development
Research Council
Research Grant
Research Management
Use Of Human Subjects

RESERVATION
S-07-0045 1979 00000
BT Community Type
RT American Indian Studies
Compound
Squatter Community

RESERVE MILITARY FORCES
S-33-0071 1975 00010
BT Military Forces
RT Armed Forces
Army
Defense System
Marines
Military Establishment
Naval Forces
Navy
Professional Military Forces
Tactical Force

RESIDENCE REQUIREMENT
S-15-0086 1975 00003
BT Voter Qualification
RT Internal Migration Pattern
Property Voting Qualification
Registration Requirement
Residential Segregation
Voting Age Requirement

RESIDENTIAL PATTERN
S-06-0228 1975 00064
BT Population Distribution
NT Multiple Family Dwelling
Single Family Dwelling
RT Ethnic Community
Internal Migration
Metropolitan Growth Pattern
Population Concentration
Residential Segregation

RESIDENTIAL SEGREGATION
S-26-0238 1979 00000
BT Segregation Policy
RT Housing Policy
Land Use Policy
Quota Policy
Racial Discrimination
Racism
Residence Requirement
Residential Pattern

RESIGNATION
S-31-0463 1975 00001
BT Executive Dissolution
RT Abdication

RESISTANCE
S-31-0260 1975 00006
BT Dissent
NT Draft Resistance
Passive Resistance
RT Demonstrating
Dissent
Female Chauvinist
Mutiny
Protest

RESISTANCE MOVEMENT
S-27-0045 1975 00010
BT Political Movement
RT Ideological Spectrum Political Movement
Liberation Movement
Peace Movement
Separatist Movement

RESOURCE ALLOCATION
S-31-0107 1975 00061
BT Resource Development
RT Environment Policy
Environmental Pollution
Food Scarcity
Hunger
Labor Scarcity
Malnutrition
Private Spending
Resource Distribution
Scarcity
Starvation
Water Scarcity

RESOURCE DEVELOPMENT
S-31-0102 1975 00041
BT Development Process
NT Environmental Pollution
Resource Allocation
Resource Distribution
Resource Utilization
RT Development Policy
Education Reform
Local Development
Regional Development
Scarcity
Urban Decay

RESOURCE DISTRIBUTION
S-31-0108 1975 00069
BT Resource Development
RT Environment Policy
Environmental Pollution
Food Scarcity
Government Grant
Hunger
Labor Scarcity
Malnutrition
Private Spending
Resource Allocation
Resource Utilization
Scarcity
Starvation
Water Scarcity

RESOURCE UTILIZATION
S-31-0109 1975 00059
BT Resource Development
NT Natural Resource Exploitation
Scarcity
RT Agricultural Development
Environment Policy
Environmental Pollution
New International Economic Order
Resource Distribution

RESPONSE BIAS
S-24-0194 1975 00030
BT Measurement Bias
RT Sampling Bias

RESPONSE RECORDING EQUIPMENT
S-24-0334 1975 00001
BT Interviewing Material
RT Experiment
Experimental Observation
Experimental Research
Research Laboratory

RESPONSIBILITY DOCTRINE
S-38-0510 1975 00010
SN An approach to representation which emphasizes the weighing and evaluation of constituency opinions as a basis for developing a position on policy issues.
BT Political Philosophy Concept
RT Government Accountability
Government Responsiveness
Legislative Accountability
Moral Responsibility
Representation
Representation Theory

RESPONSIBLE TWO PARTY SYSTEM
S-37-0132 1975 00006
BT Two Political Party System
RT Disciplined Two Party System
Government Responsiveness
Two Political Party System

RESTRICTIVE TRADE POLICY
S-26-0184 1975 00026
BT Trade Policy
NT Blockade Policy
Export Policy
Import Policy
Tariff Policy
RT Export Subsidization Policy
Most Favored Nation Policy

RETALIATORY CAPABILITY
S-06-0468 1975 00005
BT Military Characteristics
RT Defensive Capability
Military Size
Nuclear Capability
Strategic Advantage
Strategic Studies

RETIREMENT
S-06-0653 1979 00000
BT Employment Characteristics
RT Economic Security
Labor Force
Labor Market
Labor Supply
Labor Surplus
Old Age Assistance Policy

REVENUE AGENCY
S-19-0027 1975 00003
BT Fiscal Agency
RT Appropriation Agency
Budget Agency
Economic Council
Economic Institution
Interagency Rivalry
Monetary Agency
Public Treasury
Tax Agency

REVENUE POLICY
S-26-0138 1975 00020
BT Economic Policy
NT Taxation Policy
RT Budget Policy
Deflation Policy
Expenditure Policy
Income Policy
Inflation Policy
Monetary Policy
National Debt Policy
Public Debt Policy
Revenue Sharing Policy
Tax Credit
Tax Cut

REVENUE RECORD
S-18-0016 1975 00004
BT Financial Record
NT Tariff Record
Tax Record
RT Budget Record
Expenditure Record
Income Record
Political Party Financial Record

REVENUE SHARING POLICY
S-26-0100 1975 00034
BT Expenditure Policy
RT City State Relations
Intergovernmental Relations
Revenue Policy

REVERSE DISCRIMINATION
S-26-0375 1979 00000
BT Discrimination Policy
RT Discrimination Policy
Equal Law Enforcement
Equal Rights
Ethnic Policy
Inequality
Job Discrimination
Racial Discrimination
Sex Discrimination

REVISIONIST HISTORICAL ANALYSIS
S-09-0028 1975 00011
SN A reexamination of assumptions, methods, and theories used in analyzing historical topics.
BT Historical Analysis
RT Class Analysis
Historical Sociology Analysis
Historicism
Historiography
History Discipline
Marxist Analysis
Marxist Revisionism
Reductionist Analysis
Situational Analysis

REVOLUTION
S-08-0062 1975 00028
BT Internal Conflict
NT Counterrevolution
Cultural Revolution
Ecological Revolution
Political Revolution
Social Revolution
Spontaneous Revolution
Technological Revolution
Thermidor
RT Class Antagonism
Class Conflict
Class Rebellion
Counterinsurgency
Coup D'Etat
Economic Conflict
Economic Rebellion
Elite Disintegration
Government Overthrow
Group Conflict
Ideological Conflict
Ideological Struggle
Imperialist War
Insurgency
Internal Conflict
Internal War
Jacobinism
Just War
Marxist Revolution Theory
Mass Revolutionary Movement
Military Aggression
Military Coup
Mob Violence
National Liberation Movement
Peasant Rebellion
Peoples Democratic State
Peoples Liberation Movement
Political Agitation
Political Rebellion
Political Violence
Psychological War
Putsch
Racial Conflict
Rebellion
Revolution Theory
Revolutionary
Revolutionary Change
Revolutionary Elite
Revolutionary Movement
Revolutionary War
Rising Expectation Theory
Routinized Conflict
Social Rebellion
Soviet Studies
Violence
War

REVOLUTION THEORY
S-38-0168 1975 00048
BT Explanatory Political Theory
NT Feudal Reaction Theory
Permanent Revolution Theory
Rising Expectation Theory
RT Conflict Theory
Ideology Explanatory Theory
Maoist Revolutionary
Mass Revolutionary Movement
National Front
National Liberation War

National Political Revolution
New Left
Praxis
Revolution
Revolutionary
Revolutionary Change
Revolutionary Elite
Revolutionary Movement
Right Of Revolution
Rising Expectation Theory
Social Revolution
Soviet Studies

REVOLUTIONARY
S-32-0196 1975 00010
BT Political Activist
NT Guerrilla
Insurrectionist
Maoist Revolutionary
RT Marxist Revolution Theory
Militant
Political Agitator
Political Conspirator
Revolution
Revolution Theory
Revolutionary Change
Revolutionary Elite
Revolutionary Movement
Right Wing Activist
Terrorist

REVOLUTIONARY CHANGE
S-31-0161 1975 00031
BT Political Change
RT Emancipation
Liberation Process
Maoist Movement
Marxist Revolution Theory
Political Change
Politicization
Praxis
Revolution
Revolution Theory
Revolutionary
Revolutionary Elite
Revolutionary Movement
Revolutionary War
Riot Theory
Social Change
Social Revolution
Socialist Revolution
Technological Change
Terrorism

REVOLUTIONARY DIRECTORATE
S-16-0149 1975 00001
BT Rule Type
RT Authoritarian Regime
Despotism
Revolutionary Elite

REVOLUTIONARY ELITE
S-14-0030 1975 00008
BT Political Elite
RT Leninism
Marxist Revolution Theory
Modernizing Elite
Modernizing Political Elite
Modernizing Social Elite
Pluralist Elite
Potential Elite
Power Elite
Revolution
Revolution Theory
Revolutionary
Revolutionary Change
Revolutionary Directorate
Revolutionary Movement
Revolutionary War

REVOLUTIONARY MOVEMENT
S-27-0020 1975 00040
BT Ideological Spectrum Political Movement
NT Mass Revolutionary Movement
RT Extremist Movement
Fascist Movement
Grass Roots Movement
Independence Movement
Internal Conflict
International Communist Movement
Liberation Movement
Maoist Movement
Marxist Revolution Theory
Proletarian Movement
Radical Movement
Radical Political Party
Revolution
Revolution Theory
Revolutionary
Revolutionary Change
Revolutionary Elite
Revolutionary War
Separatist Movement
Socialist Revolution
Soviet Studies
Terrorism
Terrorist Movement
Transitional Political Elite
Underground Political Party

REVOLUTIONARY PARTY
1975-1979 00004

REVOLUTIONARY POLITICAL PARTY
S-28-0032 1979 00000
BT Political Party Type
RT Ideological Spectrum Political Party Type
Marxist Revolution Theory
Soviet Studies
Underground Political Party

REVOLUTIONARY WAR
S-08-0108 1975 00020
BT War
RT Expansionist War
Government Overthrow
Ideological War
Imperialist War
Insurgency
Internal Conflict
Just War
Maoism
Mob Violence
Political Violence
Propaganda War
Rebellion
Revolution
Revolutionary Change
Revolutionary Elite
Revolutionary Movement

RICARDIAN THEORY
S-38-0111 1975 00003
SN Approach to economic and social analysis associated with the classic liberalism of David Ricardo.
BT Classical Economic Theory
RT Laissez Faire Theory
Macroeconomics
Malthusian Theory

RICH NATION
S-16-0127 1975 00012
BT Nation Type
RT Advanced Industrial Society
Developed Nation
Prosperity

RIGHT AGAINST CRUEL AND UNUSUAL PUNISHMENT
S-15-0047 1975 00002
BT Defendants Rights
RT Bill Of Attainder
Capital Punishment
Double Jeopardy
Habeas Corpus
Right To Due Process
Right To Equal Protection
Right To Jury Trial
Right To Speedy Trial
Right To Trial
Sanity Plea
Search And Seizure
Statute Of Limitations

RIGHT HEGELIANISM
S-38-0410 1975 00000
BT Hegelian Analysis
RT Judeo Christian Thought
Left Hegelianism
Protestantism

RIGHT OF ASSEMBLY
S-15-0034 1975 00002
BT Civil Liberty
RT Civil Rights
Freedom Of Association
Freedom Of Press
Freedom Of Religion
Freedom Of Speech
Freedom Of Travel
Political Tolerance
Procedural Rights
Right Of Opposition
Right Of Petition
Right Of Privacy
Right Of Protest
Right To Strike
Voting Rights

RIGHT OF OPPOSITION
S-15-0067 1975 00001
BT Political Liberty
NT Civil Disobedience
Right Of Protest
Right Of Revolution
Right Of Secession
RT Civil Rights
Freedom Of Association
Freedom Of Press
Freedom Of Religion
Freedom Of Speech
Freedom Of Travel
Government Dissolution Process
Human Rights

Political Activist
Political Opposition
Procedural Rights
Right Of Assembly
Right Of Petition
Right Of Privacy
Right Of Protest
Right Of Revolution
Voting Rights

RIGHT OF PETITION
S-15-0035 1975 00001
BT Civil Liberty
RT Civil Rights
Freedom Of Association
Freedom Of Press
Freedom Of Religion
Freedom Of Speech
Freedom Of Travel
Procedural Rights
Protest
Right Of Assembly
Right Of Opposition
Right Of Privacy
Voting Rights

RIGHT OF PRIVACY
S-15-0036 1975 00031
BT Civil Liberty
RT Civil Rights
Freedom Of Association
Freedom Of Press
Freedom Of Religion
Freedom Of Speech
Freedom Of Travel
Procedural Rights
Right Of Assembly
Right Of Opposition
Right Of Petition

RIGHT OF PROTEST
S-15-0069 1975 00003
BT Right Of Opposition
RT Civil Disobedience
Civil Rights
Conscientious Objector
Freedom Of Press
Procedural Rights
Protest
Protest Politics
Protest Voter
Right Of Assembly
Right Of Opposition
Right Of Revolution
Right Of Secession
Right To Strike

RIGHT OF REVOLUTION
S-15-0070 1975 00000
BT Right Of Opposition
RT Civil Disobedience
Civil Rights
Natural Law Conventionalism Theory
Protest
Revolution Theory
Right Of Opposition
Right Of Protest
Right Of Secession

RIGHT OF SECESSION
S-15-0071 1975 00001
BT Right Of Opposition
RT Civil Disobedience
Civil Rights
Civil War
Decolonization
Interposition Doctrine
Right Of Protest
Right Of Revolution
Sea Power

RIGHT REASON DOCTRINE
S-38-0491 1975 00000
BT Natural Law Conventionalism Theory
RT Classical Natural Right Doctrine
Great Chain Of Being Doctrine
Medieval Natural Law Theory
Natural Law Conventionalism Theory
Rights Of Man Doctrine
Roman Natural Law Theory
Scientific Natural Law Theory
Stoic Natural Law Theory

RIGHT TO APPEAL
S-15-0058 1975 00000
BT Right To Trial
RT Appellate Court
Burden Of Proof
Circumstantial Evidence
Civil Rights
Evidence Admissibility
Ex Post Facto Protection
Grand Jury Indictment
Habeas Corpus
Judicial Review
Right To Counsel
Right To Due Process
Right To Jury Trial
Right To Speedy Trial
Right To Trial
Secret Trial
Self Incrimination

RIGHT TO BAIL
S-15-0048 1975 00000
BT Defendants Rights
RT Bail
Bail Bond System
Bail Skipping
Right To Due Process
Right To Equal Protection
Right To Trial
Secret Trial

RIGHT TO BEAR ARMS
S-15-0037 1975 00002
BT Civil Liberty
RT Bill Of Rights
Citizenship Status
Civil Rights
Paramilitary Organization
Procedural Rights

RIGHT TO COUNSEL
S-15-0059 1975 00003
BT Right To Trial
RT Amicus Curiae
Burden Of Proof
Cross Examination
Evidence Admissibility
Ex Post Facto Protection
Grand Jury Indictment
Law System
Lawyer
Right To Appeal
Right To Trial

RIGHT TO DIE
S-15-0078 1979 00000
BT Social Rights
RT Gerontology
Health Care Rights
Medical Care Policy

RIGHT TO DUE PROCESS
S-15-0049 1975 00011
BT Defendants Rights
RT Arbitrary Arrest
Arbitrary Imprisonment
Bill Of Attainder
Burden Of Proof
Circumstantial Evidence
Constitutional Law
Cross Examination
Double Jeopardy
Evidence Admissibility
Ex Post Facto Protection
Grand Jury Indictment
Habeas Corpus
Right Against Cruel And Unusual Punishment
Right To Appeal
Right To Bail
Right To Equal Protection
Right To Strike
Right To Trial
Sanity Plea
Search And Seizure
Self Incrimination
Stare Decisis
Statute Of Limitations

RIGHT TO EDUCATION
S-15-0079 1979 00000
UF Education Rights
BT Social Rights
RT Childhood
Childrens Rights
Education Compulsion Authority
Education Planning
Education Policy
Education Type
Marriage Rights

RIGHT TO EQUAL PROTECTION
S-15-0050 1975 00014
BT Defendants Rights
RT Bill Of Attainder
Double Jeopardy
Habeas Corpus
Right Against Cruel And Unusual Punishment
Right To Bail
Right To Due Process
Right To Trial
Sanity Plea
Search And Seizure
Statute Of Limitations

RIGHT TO JOB SECURITY
S-15-0009 1979 00000
BT Economic Freedom
RT Economic Security
Freedom Of Competition
Job Satisfaction
Occupation Characteristics
Property Rights
Right To Work
Social Security
Welfare System

RIGHT TO JURY TRIAL
S-15-0060 1975 00000
BT Right To Trial
RT Burden Of Proof
Circumstantial Evidence
Cross Examination
Double Jeopardy
Evidence Admissibility
Ex Post Facto Protection
Grand Jury Indictment
Grand Jury System
Habeas Corpus
Right Against Cruel And Unusual Punishment
Right To Appeal
Right To Trial
Trial System

RIGHT TO SPEEDY TRIAL
S-15-0061 1975 00000
BT Right To Trial
RT Bill Of Attainder
Burden Of Proof
Cross Examination
Double Jeopardy
Evidence Admissibility
Ex Post Facto Protection
Grand Jury Indictment
Habeas Corpus
Right Against Cruel And Unusual Punishment
Right To Appeal
Right To Trial

RIGHT TO STRIKE
S-15-0006 1975 00000
BT Freedom Of Contract
RT Freedom Of Speech
Human Rights
Injunction
Labor Law
Market Freedom
Right Of Assembly
Right Of Protest
Right To Due Process
Right To Work
Social Rights

RIGHT TO TRIAL
S-15-0051 1975 00000
BT Defendants Rights
NT Burden Of Proof
Cross Examination
Evidence Admissibility
Ex Post Facto Protection
Grand Jury Indictment
Right To Appeal
Right To Counsel
Right To Jury Trial
Right To Speedy Trial
Self Incrimination
RT Bill Of Attainder
Double Jeopardy
Grand Jury System
Habeas Corpus
Right Against Cruel And Unusual Punishment
Right To Appeal
Right To Bail
Right To Counsel
Right To Due Process
Right To Equal Protection
Right To Jury Trial
Right To Speedy Trial
Sanity Plea
Search And Seizure
Secret Trial
Self Incrimination
Statute Of Limitations
Trial System

RIGHT TO WORK
S-15-0007 1975 00004
BT Freedom Of Contract
RT Labor Law
Market Freedom
Right To Job Security
Right To Strike

RIGHT TO WORK LAW
S-21-0041 1975 00002
BT Labor Law
RT Fair Employment Law
Labor Law
Labor Management Relations Policy
Minimum Wage Law
Right To Work Policy

RIGHT TO WORK POLICY
S-26-0321 1975 00003
BT Labor Management Relations Policy
RT Collective Bargaining Policy
Labor Arbitration Policy
Labor Law
Labor Management Relations Policy
Public Employee Union Policy
Right To Work Law
Trade Union Policy
Work Ethic

RIGHT WING ACTIVIST
S-32-0201 1975 00001
BT Political Activist
RT Anticommunism
Militant
Political Activist
Political Agitator
Political Conspirator
Political Party Dissident
Revolutionary
Terrorist

RIGHTIST
S-32-0265 1975 00003
BT Spectrum Politicist
RT Extremist
Ideologue
Leftist
Political Radical
Reactionary
Spectrum Politicist

RIGHTIST PARTY ▲
1975-1979 00006

RIGHTIST POLITICAL PARTY
S-28-0022 1979 00000
BT Ideological Spectrum Political Party Type
RT Conservative Political Party
Military Political Party

RIGHTS OF MAN DOCTRINE
S-38-0492 1975 00019
BT Natural Law Conventionalism Theory
RT Classical Natural Right Doctrine
Egalitarian Justice Theory
Freedom
Ghetto Rioter
Great Chain Of Being Doctrine
Natural Law Conventionalism Theory
Political Activist
Protest
Right Reason Doctrine
Roman Natural Law Theory
Scientific Natural Law Theory
Student Activist
War Protestor

RIOT THEORY
S-38-0584 1979 00000
BT Social Theory
RT Conflict Process
Conflict Type
Crowd Behavior
Political Violence
Revolutionary Change
Violence

RIOTER
S-32-0204 1975 00001
UF Insurgent
BT Activist
NT Ghetto Rioter
RT Activist
Demonstrator
Political Activist
Protest
Student Activist
War Protestor

RISING EXPECTATION THEORY
S-38-0171 1975 00008
BT Revolution Theory
RT Feudal Reaction Theory
Revolution
Revolution Theory
Social Anthropology

RITUAL
S-01-0014 1975 00019
BT Mythology
RT Folkways
Habitual Behavior
Oral History
Social Anthropology

ROBBER
USE Criminal

ROBBERY
S-10-0022 1975 00003
BT Property Crime
RT Assault
Economic Espionage
Election Fraud
Extortion
Fraud
Industrial Espionage
Organized Crime
Property Crime
Street Crime
Tax Evasion
Vandalism

ROLE ACQUISITION
S-31-0758 1979 00000
BT Social Role Process
RT Learning Theory
Political Orientation Development
Role Allocation
Role Analysis
Role Differentiation
Role Expectation
Role Orientation
Role Performance

Role Specialization

ROLE ALLOCATION
S-31-0759 1975 00031
BT Social Role Process
RT Role Acquisition
Role Analysis
Role Conflict
Role Differentiation
Role Expectation
Role Orientation
Role Performance
Role Theory
Sex Role

ROLE AMBIVALENCE
S-06-0502 1975 00013
BT Ambivalence
RT Anomie
Cultural Alienation
Role Analysis
Role Conflict

ROLE ANALYSIS
S-24-0418 1975 00108
BT Microlevel Analysis
RT Role Acquisition
Role Allocation
Role Ambivalence
Role Conflict
Role Differentiation
Role Expectation
Role Orientation
Role Performance
Role Socialization
Role Specialization
Roles
Social Psychology

ROLE CONFLICT
S-31-0760 1975 00012
BT Social Role Process
RT Organization Conflict
Role Allocation
Role Ambivalence
Role Analysis
Role Differentiation
Role Expectation
Role Orientation
Role Performance
Role Socialization
Role Specialization
Role Theory
Roles
Sexism
Social Psychology

ROLE DIFFERENTIATION
S-31-0761 1975 00026
BT Social Role Process
NT Role Specialization
RT Cultural History
Family Socialization
Role Acquisition
Role Allocation
Role Analysis
Role Conflict
Role Expectation
Role Orientation
Role Performance
Role Socialization
Sex Role

ROLE EXPECTATION
S-31-0763 1975 00041
BT Social Role Process
RT Role Acquisition
Role Allocation
Role Analysis
Role Conflict
Role Differentiation
Role Orientation
Role Performance

ROLE ORIENTATION
S-31-0764 1975 00044
BT Social Role Process
NT Executive Role Orientation
Judicial Role Orientation
Legislative Role Orientation
Political Role Orientation
RT Role Acquisition
Role Allocation
Role Analysis
Role Conflict
Role Differentiation
Role Expectation
Role Performance

ROLE PERFORMANCE
S-31-0769 1975 00087
BT Social Role Process
RT Role Acquisition
Role Allocation
Role Analysis
Role Conflict
Role Differentiation
Role Expectation
Role Orientation
Social Interaction

ROLE SOCIALIZATION
S-34-0049 1975 00028
BT Socialization Type
RT Learning Theory
Opinion Socialization
Political Orientation Development
Political Party Role
Political Role Orientation
Political Value Acquisition
Role Analysis
Role Conflict
Role Differentiation
Role Theory
Sex Role
Social Conditioning

ROLE SPECIALIZATION
S-31-0762 1975 00019
BT Role Differentiation
RT Political Role Orientation
Role Acquisition
Role Analysis
Role Conflict
Role Theory
Roles

ROLE THEORY
S-38-0585 1975 00033
BT Social Theory
RT Anthropological Functionalism
Assimilation Theory
Deviant Behavior
Field Theory
Kinship Role
Role Allocation
Role Conflict
Role Socialization
Role Specialization
Roles
Social Action Theory
Social Integration Theory
Social Learning Theory
Social Pathology
Social Psychology
Socialization Theory
Structuralism
Weberian Theory

ROLES
S-32-0001 1975 00006
NT Academic
Adjudicator
Advisor
Athlete
Decision Maker
Explorer
Kinship Role
Leader
Occupational Role
Planner
Political Party Role
Political Role
Religious Role
Sex Role
Student
RT Process
Role Analysis
Role Conflict
Role Specialization
Role Theory

ROLL CALL ANALYSIS
S-09-0077 1975 00023
BT Voting Behavior Analysis
RT Legislative Behavior
Spatial Voting Analysis
Voting Data

ROMAN CATHOLICISM
S-38-0564 1975 00027
BT Catholicism
RT Augustinian Analysis
Authority Theory
Papal Sovereignty
Religious Culture
Religious Identity
Religious Movement
Thomism
Trentine Doctrine

ROMAN CIVILIZATION
S-11-0009 1979 00000
BT Civilization
RT African Civilization
Ancient Civilization
Ancient Times
Antiquity
Byzantine Civilization
Eastern Civilization
Epicurean Thought
Greek Civilization
Historical Analysis
History Discipline
Homogeneous Culture
Islamic Civilization
Political Culture
Roman Legal Thought
Roman Natural Law Theory
Western Civilization

ROMAN LEGAL THOUGHT
S-38-0055 1975 00004
BT Classical Political Thought
RT Epicurean Thought
Law Type
Roman Civilization
Roman Natural Law Theory

ROMAN NATURAL LAW THEORY
S-38-0493 1975 00001
BT Natural Law Conventionalism Theory
RT Classical Natural Right Doctrine
Great Chain Of Being Doctrine
Medieval Natural Law Theory
Right Reason Doctrine
Rights Of Man Doctrine
Roman Civilization
Roman Legal Thought
Scientific Natural Law Theory
Stoic Natural Law Theory

ROMANTICISM
S-38-0423 1979 00000
BT Modern Political Thought
NT German Romanticism
RT Aesthetics
Counterrevolution
German Idealism
Holism
Philosophical Idealism
Subjectivism

ROTE LEARNING
S-34-0011 1979 00000
BT Learning
RT Behavior Modification
Cognitive Theory
Education Policy
Learning Psychology
Learning Theory
Serial Learning
Skill Acquisition

ROUSSEAUIAN ANALYSIS
S-38-0406 1975 00012
BT Enlightenment Thought
RT Consent Theory
Equality Theory
Freedom
General Will Theory
Kantian Analysis
Moral Freedom Theory
Philosophe Thought
Positive Freedom Theory
State Of Nature Theory
Voltairean Analysis

ROUTINIZED CONFLICT
S-08-0043 1975 00002
BT Institutional Conflict
RT Economic Agitation
Economic Conflict
Group Conflict
Rebellion
Revolution
Struggle
War

ROYAL COMMISSION OF INQUIRY
S-19-0091 1975 00002
BT Commission Of Inquiry
RT Legislative Commission
Legislative Commission Of Inquiry
Parliamentary Commission Of Inquiry
Presidential Commission Of Inquiry

ROYALIST
S-32-0279 1975 00000
BT System Politicist
RT Absolute Monarch
Monarchy
Renaissance Political Thought
Renaissance State Theory
Royalist State Theory
State Type

ROYALIST STATE THEORY
S-38-0526 1975 00000
BT Renaissance Political Thought
RT Absolute Monarch
Monarchy
Renaissance Political Thought
Renaissance State Theory
Royalist
State Type

RUBBER INDUSTRY
S-17-0004 1979 00000
BT Chemical Industry
RT Agrochemical Industry
Plantation Economy
Synthetics Industry

RULE TYPE
S-16-0140 1975 00004
BT Government
NT Despotism
Direct Rule
Foreign Rule
Home Rule
Indirect Rule
Military Directorate
Revolutionary Directorate
Technocracy
Tyranny
RT Government Characteristics
Government Type
Nation Type
Political Regime
Regime Type
Ruling Political Party
Society Type
State Type

RULING CLASS
S-06-0778 1975 00004
BT Class Stratification Division
RT Aristocratic Class
Authority
Class Analysis
Class Stratification Division
Elite Analysis
Elite Disintegration
Entrepreneur Class
Landowning Class
Middle Class
Nobility
Propertied Class
Social Prestige
Upper Class

RULING PARTY
1975-1979 00011

RULING POLITICAL PARTY
S-28-0033 1979 00000
BT Political Party Type
RT Coalition Theory
Elite Analysis
Government Political Party
Major Political Party
Majority Political Party
Regime Type
Rule Type

RUNOFF ELECTION
S-29-0087 1975 00002
BT Election Type
RT Contested Election
Special Election

RURAL COMMUNITY
S-07-0046 1975 00049
BT Community Type
RT Agricultural Occupation
Collective Community
Communal Community
Farm Economy
Kibbutz
Private Rural Investment
Rural Development
Rural Environment
Town
Utopian Community
Village Community

RURAL DEVELOPMENT
S-31-0129 1975 00061
BT Development Process
NT Agricultural Development
RT Farm Industry
Private Rural Investment
Regional Development
Rural Community
Rural Environment
Rural Migration
Urban Development

RURAL ENVIRONMENT
S-06-0703 1975 00020
BT Social System Environment Characteristics
RT Farming
Private Rural Investment
Rural Community
Rural Development
Suburban Environment
Urban Environment

RURAL MIGRATION
S-31-0622 1975 00019
BT Internal Migration
RT Rural Development
Rural Migration Pattern
Rural Population
Rural Population Area
Suburban Migration
Urban Migration

RURAL MIGRATION PATTERN
S-06-0240 1975 00004
BT Internal Migration Pattern
RT Internal Migration
Rural Migration
Rural Population
Rural Population Area
Suburban Migration Pattern
Urban Migration Pattern

RURAL POLICY PLANNING
S-31-0667 1975 00008
BT Subnational Policy Planning
RT City Policy Planning
Farm Industry
Local Policy Planning
Private Rural Investment
Rural Population
Rural Population Area

State Policy Planning
Urban Design
Urban Policy Planning

RURAL POPULATION
S-06-0216 1975 00023
BT Population Attribute
RT Migrant Population
Population Density
Rural Migration
Rural Migration Pattern
Rural Policy Planning
Suburban Population
Urban Population

RURAL POPULATION AREA
S-24-0347 1975 00025
BT Population Identification
RT Population Identification
Rural Migration
Rural Migration Pattern
Rural Policy Planning
Suburban Population Area
Urban Population Area

RURAL SOCIOLOGY
S-01-0192 1975 00012
BT Sociology Discipline
RT Agricultural Occupation
Agricultural Science
Applied Sociology
Marxist Sociology
Physical Geography
Social Action Theory
Social Anthropology
Social Psychology

RURAL VOTER
S-32-0328 1975 00004
BT Voter
RT Farm Voter
Rural Voting
Suburban Voter

RURAL VOTING
S-29-0136 1975 00008
BT Group Voting
RT Age Group Voting
Geographic Voting
Regional Voting
Rural Voter
Suburban Voting
Urban Voting

RUSSIAN STUDIES
S-01-0044 1979 00000
BT Soviet And East European Area Studies
RT Communist Empire
Communist Studies
Comparative Analysis
Comparative Political Studies
Comparative Sociology
Cultural Anthropology
Cultural History
East European Area Studies
Eastern Orthodox Thought
European Integration Theory
Marxism Leninism
Political Science Discipline
Soviet Studies

SACRED LAW
S-21-0080 1975 00002
BT Law Type
NT Religious Law
RT Basic Law
Natural Law
Political Theory Studies
Religious Thought
Taboo

SAFETY MEASURES
USE Safety Policy

SAFETY POLICY
S-26-0400 1975 00011
UF Safety Measures
BT Social Policy
NT Industrial Safety Policy
Mine Safety Policy
Traffic Safety Policy
RT Drug Control Policy
Mine Safety Law
Policy For Disadvantaged

SAILOR
S-36-0224 1975 00004
BT Military Service Personnel
RT Marine
Naval Power
Navy
Pilot
Soldier

SAINT SIMONIANISM
S-38-0296 1975 00004
SN Doctrine calling for the reorganization of society in which scientific and technocratic experts would rule through scientific production.
BT Evolutionary Socialism
RT Bernsteinian Socialism
Socialist Democracy
Socialist Humanism
Socialist Theory

SALES TAXATION
S-26-0163 1975 00004
BT Taxation Policy
RT Excise Taxation Policy
Nuisance Taxation
Tariff
Value Added Taxation
Wage Taxation

SAMPLING BIAS
S-24-0199 1975 00005
BT Sampling Error
RT Response Bias
Sampling Procedure

SAMPLING ERROR
S-24-0198 1975 00007
BT Measurement Problem
NT Sampling Bias
RT Autocorrelation
Measurement Bias
Measurement Error
Missing Data
Random Error

SAMPLING PROCEDURE
S-24-0116 1975 00018
BT Data Collection Methodology
NT Area Sampling
Nonprobability Sampling
Probability Sampling
RT Interviewing Material
Questionnaire
Reactive Observation
Sampling Bias

SANITATION INDUSTRY
S-17-0068 1975 00003
BT Service Industry
RT Community Service
Health Service
Social Service

SANITATION POLICY
S-26-0228 1975 00001
BT Pollution Policy
RT Land Pollution Policy
Noise Pollution Policy
Waste Treatment Policy
Water Pollution Policy

SANITY PLEA
S-15-0063 1975 00001
BT Defendants Rights
RT Right Against Cruel And Unusual Punishment
Right To Due Process
Right To Equal Protection
Right To Trial

SATISFACTION
S-06-0125 1975 00040
BT Attitude Characteristics
NT Deprivation
Life Satisfaction
Political Satisfaction
RT Efficacy
Efficacy Scale
Living Conditions
Quality Of Life
Satisfaction Scale
Trust

SATISFACTION SCALE
S-24-0244 1975 00017
BT Scale Type
RT Alienation Scale
Anomie Scale
Cynicism Scale
Efficacy Scale
Frustration Scale
Left Right Scale
Legitimacy Scale
Living Conditions
Optimism Pessimism Scale
Quality Of Life
Satisfaction
Social Change Index
Social Distance Scale
Social Frustration Scale
Stability Index
Support Opposition Scale
Voting Duty Scale

SAVING
S-31-0409 1979 00000
BT Economic Resource Allocation
NT Private Saving
Public Saving
RT Capital Flow
Capital Formation
Financing
Fiscal Process
Monetary Process
Spending

SCALABILITY INDEX
S-24-0217 1975 00003
BT Scale Construction Methodology
RT Composite Scale
Cumulative Scale
Factor Structure
Guttman Scale
Likert Scale
Measurement Level Scale
Multidimensional Scale
Nominal Scale
Ordinal Scale
Ratio Scale
Semantic Differential
Thurstone Scale
Unidimensional Scale

SCALE CONSTRUCTION METHODOLOGY
S-24-0203 1975 00026
BT Measurement Scale
NT Composite Scale
Cross Cultural Index
Cumulative Scale
Factor Structure
Guttman Scale
Interval Scale
Likert Scale
Measurement Level Scale
Multidimensional Scale
Nominal Scale
Ordinal Scale
Ratio Scale
Scalability Index
Semantic Differential
Thurstone Scale
Unidimensional Scale
RT Cross Cultural Index
Scale Type
Social Science Model
Statistical Data

SCALE TYPE
S-24-0221 1975 00007
BT Measurement Scale
NT Aggression Scale
Alienation Scale
Anomie Scale
Authoritarianism Scale
Civic Competence Scale
Cynicism Scale
Development Index
Dogmatism Scale
Efficacy Scale
Frustration Scale
Internal External Reinforcement Scale
Left Right Scale
Legitimacy Scale
Liberalism Conservatism Scale
Modernity Scale
Modernization Scale
Optimism Pessimism Scale
Policy Output Scale
Satisfaction Scale
Social Change Index
Social Distance Scale
Social Frustration Scale
Stability Index
Support Opposition Scale
Urbanization Index
Voting Duty Scale
RT Aggression Scale
Intelligence Quotient
Scale Construction Methodology

SCANDINAVIAN AREA STUDIES
S-01-0048 1975 00039
BT West European Area Studies
RT Common Market Area Studies
Comparative Analysis
Comparative Political Studies
Geography Discipline
Political Science Discipline

SCARCITY
S-31-0110 1979 00000
BT Resource Utilization
NT Energy Scarcity
Food Scarcity
Housing Scarcity
Labor Scarcity
Water Scarcity
RT Fourth World Nation
International Economics
Land Use Policy
Public Policy Analysis
Resource Allocation
Resource Development
Resource Distribution
Third World Nation

SCATTER PLOT
S-24-0137 1975 00000
BT Plot
RT Frequency Table
Venn Diagram

SCENARIO CONSTRUCTION
S-24-0017 1979 00000
BT Forecasting Methodology
RT Authority Forecasting
Brainstorming
Delphi Technique
Divergence Mapping
Economic Forecasting
Policy Evaluation Research
Policy Research
Political Forecasting
Predictive Research
Social Forecasting
Trend Analysis

SCHIZOPHRENIA
S-06-0525 1975 00034
BT Psychosis
RT Estrangement
Paranoia
Personality Theory

SCHOLARSHIP AGENCY
S-19-0037 1975 00008
BT Education Agency
RT Education Accreditation Agency
School Board

SCHOLASTIC METHOD
S-38-0378 1975 00001
BT Scholasticism
RT Catholicism
Hagiology
History Of Philosophy

SCHOLASTICISM
S-38-0376 1975 00002
BT Medieval Political Thought
NT Hagiology
Scholastic Method
RT Catholicism
History Of Philosophy
Monasticism
Nominalism

SCHOOL BOARD
S-19-0038 1975 00007
BT Education Agency
RT Board Of Regents
Board Of Trustees
Education Accreditation Agency
Examination Agency
Scholarship Agency

SCHOOL DESEGREGATION POLICY
S-26-0384 1975 00048
BT Desegregation Policy
RT Community Desegregation Policy
Education Institution
School Integration

SCHOOL DISTRICT
S-16-0094 1975 00019
BT District Government Type
RT Fire District
Municipality
Recreation District
Sewer District
Transportation District
Water District
Zoning District

SCHOOL INTEGRATION
S-31-0829 1975 00026
BT Racial Integration
RT Education Opportunity
Education Policy
Housing Integration
Neighborhood School
School Desegregation Policy

SCHOOL PRAYER POLICY
S-26-0399 1975 00001
BT Religious Policy
RT Church State Policy
Freedom Of Religion
Freedom Of Speech
Government Regulation

SCHOOL TAXATION
S-26-0164 1975 00003
BT Taxation Policy
RT City Income Taxation
Education Policy
Local Taxation
Subnational Taxation

SCHOOL TEACHER
S-32-0122 1975 00025
BT Teacher
RT Education Advisor
Professor

SCIENCE ADVISOR
S-32-0021 1975 00017
BT Advisor
RT Administrative Advisor
Economic Advisor
Education Advisor
Legal Advisor
Military Advisor
Political Advisor
Science Information Policy
Science Policy
Technical Advisor

SCIENCE HISTORY
USE History Of Science

SCIENCE INFORMATION POLICY
S-26-0289 1975 00008
BT Government Information Diffusion Policy
RT Academy Of Science
Science Advisor
Science Policy
Scientific Authority
Scientific Elite

SCIENCE POLICY
S-26-0359 1975 00041
BT Policy
RT Education Policy
Information Policy
Science Advisor
Science Information Policy
Scientific Attache
Scientific Authority
Scientific Elite
Scientific Manpower Policy

SCIENTIFIC ATTACHE
S-36-0131 1979 00000
BT Embassy Attache
RT Expert
Foreign Service Officer
Science Policy
Technical Advisor

SCIENTIFIC AUTHORITY
S-04-0008 1979 00000
BT Authority Mode
RT Intellectual Elite
Science Information Policy
Science Policy
Scientific Elite
Sociology Of Science

SCIENTIFIC DETERMINISM
S-25-0028 1975 00004
BT Epistemology
RT Materialism
Philosophical Materialism
Philosophical Realism
Scientism

SCIENTIFIC ELITE
S-14-0033 1975 00007
BT Elite Type
RT Academic Elite
Cultural Elite
Intellectual Elite
Intelligentsia
Literary Elite
Managerial Elite
Modernizing Elite
Science Information Policy
Science Policy
Scientific Authority
Sociology Of Science
Technological Elite

SCIENTIFIC FREEDOM
S-15-0013 1975 00007
BT Freedom Of Inquiry
RT Academic Freedom
Freedom Of Information
Scientific Research
Scientist

SCIENTIFIC HUMANISM
S-38-0243 1975 00001
BT Humanism
RT Christian Humanism
Humanitarianism
Socialist Humanism

SCIENTIFIC MANPOWER POLICY
S-26-0408 1975 00002
BT Social Resource Distribution Policy
RT Braindrain
Education Planning
Education Policy
Intellectual Elite
Intelligentsia
Science Policy
Scientific Research
Technological Elite

SCIENTIFIC NATURAL LAW THEORY
S-38-0494 1975 00001
BT Natural Law Conventionalism Theory
RT Classical Natural Right Doctrine
Great Chain Of Being Doctrine
Hobbesian Absolutism
Hobbesian Analysis
Medieval Natural Law Theory
Right Reason Doctrine
Rights Of Man Doctrine
Roman Natural Law Theory
Stoic Natural Law Theory

SCIENTIFIC REPORT CENSORSHIP
S-31-0275 1975 00000
BT Report Censorship
RT Book Censorship
Intelligence Censorship
Periodical Publication Censorship
Unpublished Media Censorship

SCIENTIFIC RESEARCH
S-24-0395 1975 00084
BT Research Orientation
NT Behavioral Science Research
RT Applied Research
Authority Forecasting
Baconian Analysis
Basic Research
Braindrain
Climatology
Concept Explication Research
Deductive Method
Descriptive Research
Experimental Research
Explanatory Research
Human Subject Rights
Indicator
Knowledge Production
Policy Research
Predictive Research
Qualitative Research
Quantitative History
Quantitative Research
Research Ethics
Research Management
Scientific Freedom
Scientific Manpower Policy
Scientific Theory
Scientist
Sociology Of Science
Theoretical Research
Topography
Use Of Human Subjects

SCIENTIFIC SOCIALISM
S-38-0334 1975 00003
BT Socialist Theory
RT Guild Socialism
Marxism
Marxist Economic Theory
Marxist Economics
Marxist Theory
Structural Marxism

SCIENTIFIC THEORY
S-38-0577 1975 00019
BT Theory
NT Empirical Theory
Theory Of Causality
Value Free Science Theory
RT Baconian Analysis
Data Theory
Formal Political Theory
Philosophical Realism
Scientific Research
Scientist
Sociology Of Science
Theoretical Range
Theory Construction

SCIENTISM
S-25-0029 1975 00012
SN Assertion that all experiences can be explained by means of empirical definitions of rationality and truth.
BT Epistemology
RT Empiricism
Natural Science Education
Natural Science Model
Neopositivism
Objectivism
Philosophical Realism
Scientific Determinism
Sociology Of Science

SCIENTIST
S-32-0125 1975 00024
BT Technical Occupation
RT Braindrain
Engineer
Scientific Freedom
Scientific Research
Scientific Theory
Sociology Of Science
Technician

SCULPTURE
USE Visual Arts

SEA PIRACY
S-10-0054 1975 00000
BT Piracy
RT International Law
Political Crime
Sea Power

SEA POWER
S-33-0067 1975 00017
BT Naval Power
RT International Power Theory
Navy
Right Of Secession
Sea Piracy
Secessionist
Warship

SEABED POLICY
S-26-0358 1979 00000
UF Ocean Floor
BT Policy
RT International Law
International Organization
Law Of The Sea
Natural Resource Policy

SEAMAN
USE Armed Forces

SEARCH AND SEIZURE
S-15-0064 1975 00002
BT Defendants Rights
RT Bill Of Attainder
Bill Of Rights
Constitutional Law
Evidence Admissibility
Habeas Corpus
Right Against Cruel And Unusual Punishment
Right To Due Process
Right To Equal Protection
Right To Trial
Trial System
Wiretap Evidence Admissibility
Wiretapping Policy

SEARCH STRATEGY DEVELOPMENT
S-24-0152 1975 00004
BT Information Retrieval
RT Data Retrieval

SEASONAL EMPLOYMENT
S-06-0294 1975 00000
BT Employment Index
RT Cyclical Employment
Farm Economy
Farm Production

SECESSION
S-31-0157 1975 00007
BT Extraterritorial Development
RT Annexation
Colonization
Decolonization
Elite Circulation
Secessionist

SECESSIONIST
S-32-0289 1975 00004
BT Separatist
RT Sea Power
Secession
Sectionalist

SECOND NUCLEAR STRIKE WEAPON
1975-1979 00001
USE Second Strike Nuclear Weapon

SECOND STRIKE CAPABILITY
S-06-0466 1975 00004
BT Nuclear Capability
RT Counterforce Theory
First Strike Capability
Offensive Nuclear Capability
Second Strike Policy

SECOND STRIKE NUCLEAR WEAPON
S-33-0038 1979 00000
UF Second Nuclear Strike Weapon
BT Nuclear Weapon
RT Deterrent Weapon
First Strike Nuclear Weapon
Missile
Strategic Studies
Strategic Weapon
War

SECOND STRIKE POLICY
S-26-0074 1975 00001
BT Nuclear Strike Policy
RT Counterforce Theory
First Strike Policy
Nuclear Stockpiling
Preemptive Attack Policy
Preventive Attack Policy
Second Strike Capability

SECONDARY EDUCATION
S-13-0045 1975 00017
BT Education Type
RT Compulsory Education
Continuing Education
Education Characteristics
Elementary Education
High School
Higher Education
Inner City School
Primary Education
Private School Education
Sex Education
Technical Education
Traditional Education

SECONDARY GROUP
S-03-0034 1975 00000
BT Social Group
NT Peer Group
RT Cultural Group
Ethnic Group
Interest Group
Minority Group
Nationality Group
Reference Group
Religious Group
Religious Organization

SECONDARY SCHOOL
S-19-0226 1975 00020
BT Education Institution
NT High School
Middle School
RT Higher Education Institution
Primary School
Public School
Vocational Training School

SECRET ASSOCIATION
1975-1979 00000

SECRET BALLOT
S-29-0160 1975 00000
BT Ballot
RT Australian Ballot
Long Ballot
Machine Ballot
Office Block Ballot
Paper Ballot
Political Party Column Ballot
Political Party List Ballot
Short Ballot

SECRET DIPLOMACY
S-31-0360 1975 00002
BT Diplomacy
RT Chief Executive Discretion
Chief Executive Prerogative
Executive Diplomacy
Intelligence Agency
Presidential Diplomacy
Spying
Summit Diplomacy
Surveillance

SECRET POLICE
S-19-0308 1975 00002
BT Police
RT Concentration Camp
Intelligence Censorship
International Police
Irregular Military Forces
Military Police
National Police
Paramilitary Police
Prisoner Of War Camp
Private Police
Secret Police Official
Secret Trial
Slave Labor Camp

SECRET POLICE OFFICIAL
S-36-0139 1975 00000
BT Law Enforcement Official
RT Intelligence Censorship
International Police Official
National Police Official
Secret Police
Subnational Police Official

SECRET SERVICE
S-19-0053 1975 00002
BT Intelligence Agency
RT Military Intelligence Agency
Police
Surveillance

SECRET SOCIETY
S-35-0033 1975 00002
BT Closed Society
NT Freemasonry
RT Associational Process
Closed Society
Fraternal Organization
Group Psychology
Political Club
Political Informer
Religious Cult
Voluntary Association

SECRET TRIAL
S-31-0526 1975 00000
BT Trial
NT Star Chamber Proceeding
RT Civil Rights
Right To Appeal
Right To Bail
Right To Trial
Secret Police

SECRETARIAT
S-19-0241 1975 00002
BT Executive Government Institution
RT Governorship
Plural Executive
Premiership
Presidency

SECTARIAN
S-32-0280 1975 00001
BT System Politicist
RT Anticleric
Political Secularization
Sectarian Movement
Secular Society

SECTARIAN MOVEMENT
S-27-0066 1975 00002
BT Social Movement
RT Anabaptism
Atheism
Chiliastic Movement

Political Secularization
Populist Movement
Religious Movement
Sectarian
Secular Political Culture
Secular Society

SECTIONAL CONFLICT
1975-1979 00007

SECTIONALIST
S-32-0290 1975 00000
BT Separatist
RT Secessionist

SECTOR BASED POLITICAL MOVEMENT
S-27-0046 1979 00000
BT Political Movement
NT Agrarian Movement
Class Based Movement
Grass Roots Movement
Populist Movement
Transnational Political Movement
RT Economic Movement
Ideological Spectrum Political Movement
Ideologies
Independence Movement
Interest Group
Nationalist Movement
Sector Based Political Party Type
Social Movement

SECTOR BASED POLITICAL PARTY TYPE
S-28-0034 1979 00000
BT Political Party Type
NT Agrarian Political Party
Class Based Political Party
Government Political Party
Legislative Political Party
Military Political Party
Minority Political Party
Traditional Political Party
RT Authoritarian Political Party
Ideological Political Party
Ideological Spectrum Political Party Type
Majority Political Party
Nationalist Movement
Sector Based Political Movement
Secular Political Culture
Secular Society
Structure Specific Political Party Type

SECULAR AUTHORITY
S-04-0026 1975 00001
BT Authority Type
NT Political Authority
RT Civil Religion
Legal Rational Authority
Secular Culture
Secular Society

SECULAR CULTURE
S-11-0042 1975 00008
BT Culture Type
RT Civilization
Community Culture
Ethnic Culture
Heterogeneous Culture
Nonwestern Culture
Political Culture
Secular Authority
Secular Society
Technological Culture
Youth Culture

SECULAR POLITICAL CULTURE
S-11-0032 1975 00002
BT Civic Culture
RT Civic Culture
Fragmented Political Culture
Generational Political Culture
Ideological Political Culture
Legalistic Political Culture
Modern Political Culture
Political Efficacy
Political Satisfaction
Pragmatic Political Culture
Sectarian Movement
Sector Based Political Party Type
Secular Society
Technological Culture

SECULAR SOCIETY
S-35-0008 1975 00006
BT Society Type
RT Achieving Society
Affluent Society
Atheism
Bureaucratic Society
Civic Culture
Industrial Society
Meritocracy
Modern Political Culture
Modernizing Society
Political Secularization
Religious Society
Sectarian
Sectarian Movement
Sector Based Political Party Type
Secular Authority
Secular Culture
Secular Political Culture
Social Modernization
Transitional Society
Urban Society
Western Society

SECURITY COMMUNITY
S-02-0044 1975 00010
BT Extranational Bloc
RT Afro Asian Bloc
Arab Bloc
Atlantic Community
Communist Bloc
Compact
Defense Alliance
Defense System
Latin American Bloc
Limited Sovereignty
Military Alliance
Neutral Bloc
Political Front
Protective Alliance
Security Community Theory
Security Forces
Third World Bloc
Western Bloc

SECURITY COMMUNITY THEORY
S-38-0360 1975 00005
BT International Integration Theory
RT Alliance Theory
Coalition Theory
European Integration Theory
International Commonwealth Theory
International Economic Organization Theory
Military Treaty
Security Community
Security Forces

SECURITY COUNCIL VETO
S-31-0341 1975 00000
BT Veto
RT Executive Veto
United Nations

SECURITY FORCES
S-33-0001 1975 00005
NT Multinational Security Forces
National Security Forces
RT Military Planning
Military Policy
Security Community
Security Community Theory
Strategic Studies
United Nations
Weapon
Weapon Delivery Subsystem

SEDITION
S-10-0078 1975 00001
BT Political Crime
RT Individual Crime
Political Conspiracy
Political Espionage
Political Sabotage
Sedition Law
Treason
War Crime

SEDITION LAW
S-21-0073 1975 00000
BT Political Law
RT Freedom Of Speech
Human Rights
Political Crime
Sedition

SEGREGATED COMMUNITY
S-07-0047 1975 00017
BT Community Type
RT Apartheid
Apartheid Theory
Caste Society
Ethnic Ghetto
Ghetto Community
Ghetto Conflict
Inner City School
Kibbutz
Religious Community
Segregation Policy
Suburban Ghetto Community
Urban Ghetto Community

SEGREGATION POLICY
S-26-0237 1975 00018
BT Exclusionary Policy
NT Residential Segregation
RT Apartheid
Apartheid Theory
Black Ghetto
Blacklisting Policy
Ghetto Community
Inner City School
Jim Crow Law
Miscegenation Law
Quota Policy

Race Riot
Racism
Segregated Community
Separatism

SEGREGATIONIST
S-32-0291 1975 00001
BT Separatist
NT Racist
RT Apartheid Theory
Jim Crow Law

SELECTION PROCESS
S-31-0728 1975 00024
BT Process
NT Appointment Process
Candidate Selection
Delegate Selection
Endorsement
Nominating Process
Recruitment Process
Slate Making
RT Ostracism
Social Interaction
Social Role Process
Social Stratification Process
Structural Process
Token Representation

SELF ADMINISTERED QUESTIONNAIRE
S-24-0094 1975 00004
BT Questionnaire
RT Closed Questionnaire
Mail Questionnaire
Open Ended Questionnaire
Telephone Questionnaire

SELF DEFENSE
S-31-0532 1975 00003
BT Trial Strategy
RT Congressional Investigation Committee
Self Incrimination
Testimony

SELF INCRIMINATION
S-15-0062 1975 00002
BT Right To Trial
RT Burden Of Proof
Cross Examination
Evidence Admissibility
Ex Post Facto Protection
Grand Jury Indictment
Habeas Corpus
Prosecution Immunity
Right To Appeal
Right To Due Process
Right To Trial
Self Defense

SELF INTEREST
S-06-0130 1975 00032
BT Attitude Characteristics
NT Achievement Motivation
Ambition
Enlightened Self Interest
RT Inner Directedness

SELF SUFFICIENT ECONOMY
S-12-0041 1975 00009
BT Economy Type
NT Autarchic Economy
RT Agrarian Economy
Balanced Economy
Capital Investment Economy
Command Economy
Cottage Industry Economy
Craft Economy
Developed Economy
Developing Economy
Family Farm Economy
Farm Economy
Hunting And Trapping Economy
Marketplace
Plantation Economy
Underdeveloped Economy

SELF TAUGHT EDUCATION
S-13-0046 1975 00001
BT Education Type
RT Alternative Education
Apprenticeship
Humanistic Education

SEMANTIC ANALYSIS
S-09-0043 1979 00000
BT Linguistic Analysis
RT Grammatical Analysis
Literature Analysis
Semantic Analysis
Verbal Analysis

SEMANTIC DIFFERENTIAL
S-24-0218 1975 00011
SN Scale in which one locates an object by attributing to it characteristics associated with opposite word pairs.
BT Scale Construction Methodology
RT Composite Scale
Cumulative Scale
Factor Structure
Guttman Scale
Likert Scale
Measurement Level Scale
Multidimensional Scale
Nominal Scale
Ordinal Scale
Ratio Scale
Scalability Index
Thurstone Scale
Unidimensional Scale

SEMANTICS
S-06-0413 1979 00000
BT Language Characteristics
RT Grammar
Language Learning
Speech
Stylistics
Vocabulary

SEMISKILLED WORKER
S-32-0088 1975 00003
BT Blue Collar Worker
RT Factory
Skilled Worker
Unskilled Worker
Working Class

SENATE
S-19-0272 1979 00000
BT Congress
RT Bicameral Legislature
Congressional Election Campaign
Congressional Leadership
Legislative Behavior
Legislative Characteristics
Legislative History
Legislature Type
National Legislative Political Party
Unicameral Legislature
Upper House Member

SENATE HOUSE CONFERENCE COMMITTEE
S-19-0268 1975 00002
BT Congressional Committee System
RT Ad Hoc Congressional Committee
Congressional Committee
Congressional Delegation
Joint Congressional Committee
Joint Standing Congressional Committee
Legislative Process
Standing Congressional Committee

SENATE LEADER
S-36-0182 1975 00003
BT Congressional Leader
RT House Of Representatives Leader

SENATE SPEAKER
S-36-0163 1975 00000
BT Congressional Speaker
RT House Of Representatives Speaker
Legislative Procedure

SENATOR
S-36-0191 1975 00012
BT Congressional Member
RT Legislative Process
Legislatures
Representative

SENATORIAL COURTESY
S-06-0421 1975 00000
BT Legislative Courtesy
RT Congressional Procedure
Judicial Appointment
Judicial Appointment Policy
Legislative Norms
Parliamentary Procedure
Presidential Appointment

SENIOR CITIZEN MOVEMENT
S-27-0067 1979 00000
BT Social Movement
RT Tax Reform Movement

SENIORITY
S-06-0425 1975 00005
BT Legislative Norms
RT Congressional Seniority System
Incumbent
Legislative Courtesy
Legislative Patriotism
Legislative Procedure

SENTENCING
S-31-0501 1975 00015
BT Post Trial Procedure
NT Fining
Jailing
Probation
RT Arbitrary Imprisonment
Imprisonment
Internment
Parole
Plea Bargaining
Presentence Investigation
Probation

SEPARATION OF POWER
S-30-0017 1975 00026
BT Political Power
NT Federal State Separation
Legislative Executive Separation
RT American Political Thought
Emergency Power

Executive Power
Judicial Power
Legislative Power
Legislatures
Presidential Power
Separation Of Power Theory

SEPARATION OF POWER THEORY
S-38-0453 1975 00011
BT Constitutional Structural Theory
RT Check And Balance Theory
Church State Separation Doctrine
Judicial Review
Madisonian Thought
Power Type
Separation Of Power
State Rights Doctrine

SEPARATISM
S-38-0275 1975 00009
BT Nationalism
RT Cultural Nationalism
Isolationism
Isolationist
Miscegenation Law
Neutralism
Racial Policy
Segregation Policy
Separatist
Separatist Movement

SEPARATIST
S-32-0286 1975 00002
BT Political Role
NT Factionalist
Isolationist
Secessionist
Sectionalist
Segregationist
RT Separatism
Separatist Movement

SEPARATIST MOVEMENT
S-27-0029 1979 00000
BT Independence Movement
NT Black Separatist Movement
Ethnic Separatist Movement
RT Confederation Movement
Economic Movement
Ethnic Separatism
Grass Roots Movement
Liberation Movement
Nationalist Movement
Radical Movement
Reform Movement
Resistance Movement
Revolutionary Movement
Separatism
Separatist
Separatist Political Party
Terrorist Movement
Welfare Rights Movement

SEPARATIST PARTY
1975-1979 00002

SEPARATIST POLITICAL PARTY
S-28-0057 1979 00000
BT Political Party Type
RT Separatist Movement

SERIAL LEARNING
S-34-0012 1979 00000
BT Learning
RT Learning Psychology
Learning Theory
Rote Learning

SERIAL MONOGAMY
S-20-0025 1975 00000
SN Marriage system which permits one spouse and requires termination of first marriage before second spouse is taken.
BT Monogamy
RT Matriarchal Family
Patrilineal Family

SERVICE DELIVERY SYSTEM
S-37-0137 1979 00000
BT System Type
NT Agricultural Extension Service
RT Adult Education
Policy Implementation
Public Policy Analysis
Public Policy Studies
Service Policy
Social Policy
Welfare Policy

SERVICE INDUSTRY
S-17-0066 1979 00000
BT Industry
NT Advertising Industry
Sanitation Industry
Tourist Industry
RT Clothing Industry
Consumer Industry
Education Service
Information Service
Service Industry Policy
Service Policy
Telecommunications Industry
Transportation Industry

SERVICE INDUSTRY POLICY
S-26-0279 1979 00000
BT Industrial Policy
RT Community Service
Consumer Industry
Day Care Center
Family Service
Heavy Industrial Policy
Legal Service
Light Industrial Policy
Service Industry
Service Policy
Social Service

SERVICE POLICY
S-26-0360 1979 00000
BT Policy
NT Education Service
Employment Service
Health Service
Legal Service
Psychological Service
Social Service
RT Family Planning
Family Policy
Housing Policy
Policy For Disadvantaged
Population Policy
Service Delivery System
Service Industry
Service Industry Policy
Social Policy

SET THEORY
S-38-0141 1975 00003
BT Formal Political Theory
RT Factor Analysis
Mathematical Analysis
Mathematical Political Theory

SEWER DISTRICT
S-16-0095 1975 00000
BT District Government Type
RT Fire District
Recreation District
School District
Transportation District
Water District
Zoning District

SEX CRIME
S-10-0045 1975 00012
BT Individual Crime
NT Child Molestation
Rape
RT Assault
Juvenile Delinquency
Marital Offense
Morals Offense
Pornographic Crime
Pornography Law

SEX DISCRIMINATION
S-26-0376 1979 00000
BT Discrimination Policy
RT Gender Ideology
Racial Discrimination
Reverse Discrimination
Sex Exploitation
Sex Inequality
Sex Persecution
Sexism
Sexist
Sexual Injustice
Sexual Politics
Womens Liberation Movement

SEX EDUCATION
S-13-0047 1979 00000
BT Education Type
RT Progressive Education
Secondary Education
Sex Role
Sexism
Technical Education

SEX EQUALITY
S-06-0732 1979 00000
BT Social Equality
RT Class Equality
Economic Equality
Education Equality
Egalitarianism
Income Equality
Political Equality
Racial Equality
Sex Exploitation
Sex Role
Status Equality
Womens Liberation Movement

SEX EXPLOITATION
S-31-0289 1979 00000
UF Sexual Exploitation
BT Exploitation Process
RT Economic Exploitation
Equal Employment Policy
Female Chauvinism
Inequality

Political Exploitation
Racial Exploitation
Sex Discrimination
Sex Equality
Sex Role
Sexism
Womens Liberation Movement

SEX GROUP VOTING
S-29-0137 1975 00003
BT Group Voting
RT Age Group Voting
Ethnic Group Voting
Geographic Voting
Protest Voting
Racial Voting
Regional Voting
Religious Voting
Sex Role
Sexism
Sexist
Student Voting

SEX INEQUALITY
S-06-0742 1975 00044
BT Social Inequality
RT Class Inequality
Economic Inequality
Economic Injustice
Education Inequality
Education Injustice
Female Chauvinism
Feminism
Income Inequality
Political Inequality
Racial Inequality
Racial Injustice
Sex Discrimination
Sex Persecution
Sex Role
Sexism
Sexist
Sexual Injustice
Status Inequality
Wife

SEX PERSECUTION
S-31-0320 1975 00006
BT Persecution
RT Feminism
Minority Persecution
Political Persecution
Sex Discrimination
Sex Inequality
Sexism

SEX ROLE
S-32-0342 1975 00228
BT Roles
RT Female Chauvinism
Femininity
Feminism
Feminist Politics
Gender Ideology
Male Chauvinism
Male Chauvinist
Maternal Role
Matriarchal Family
Matriarchal Kinship System
Matriarchic Government
Matrilineal Family Descent Pattern
Patriarchical Government
Pornographic Crime
Rape
Role Allocation
Role Differentiation
Role Socialization
Sex Education
Sex Equality
Sex Exploitation
Sex Group Voting
Sex Inequality
Sexism
Sexual Behavior
Sexual Freedom
Sexual Injustice
Sexual Politics
Suffrage Law
Womens Emancipation
Womens Liberation
Womens Studies

SEXISM
S-38-0235 1975 00033
BT Gender Ideology
NT Feminism
Male Chauvinism
RT Discrimination Policy
Family Role
Family Socialization
Gay Liberation
Male Chauvinist
Pornographic Crime
Role Conflict
Sex Discrimination
Sex Education
Sex Exploitation
Sex Group Voting
Sex Inequality
Sex Persecution
Sex Role
Sexist
Sexual Behavior
Sexual Freedom
Sexual Injustice
Sexual Politics
Suffrage Equality
Suffrage Extension
Suffrage Law
Token Representation

SEXIST
S-32-0213 1975 00001
BT Chauvinist
RT Female Chauvinism
Female Chauvinist
Feminism
Gender Ideology
Male Chauvinism
Male Chauvinist
Sex Discrimination
Sex Group Voting
Sex Inequality
Sexism
Suffrage Law

SEXUAL BEHAVIOR
S-05-0012 1979 00000
BT Personal Behavior
RT Accommodative Social Behavior
Avoidance Behavior
Behavioral Psychology
Clinical Psychology
Coping Behavior
Freudian Psychology
Freudian Theory
Pathological Behavior
Personal Behavior
Psychiatry
Psychoanalysis
Psychological Theory
Psychology Discipline
Psychopathology
Sex Role
Sexism
Social Interaction Theory
Social Psychiatry
Social Psychology

SEXUAL EXPLOITATION
1975-1979 00006
USE Sex Exploitation

SEXUAL FREEDOM
S-15-0080 1979 00000
BT Social Rights
RT Childrens Rights
Health Care Rights
Human Nature Theory
Marriage Rights
Sex Role
Sexism

SEXUAL INJUSTICE
S-06-0713 1979 00000
BT Social Injustice
RT Class Inequality
Economic Injustice
Education Inequality
Education Injustice
Political Injustice
Racial Inequality
Racial Injustice
Sex Discrimination
Sex Inequality
Sex Role
Sexism
Social Inequality
Social Injustice
Status Inequality

SEXUAL POLITICS
S-29-0230 1979 00000
BT Politics
NT Feminist Politics
Gay Politics
RT Group Politics
National Politics
Partisan Politics
Protest Politics
Racial Politics
Religious Politics
Sex Discrimination
Sex Role
Sexism
Youth Politics

SHADOW CABINET
S-19-0114 1975 00000
BT Cabinet
RT Cabinet Committee
Council Of Ministers
Executive Government Institution
Parliamentary Opposition
Privy Council

SHAH
S-36-0060 1975 00002
BT Emperor
RT Hereditary Ruler
Khan
King
Middle East Area Studies
Queen
Regent
Sheik
Sultan
Tsar

SHAMANISM
S-38-0014 1975 00002
SN Belief that an individual possesses unusual and supernatural healing powers.
BT Myth Analysis
RT Magic
Superstition
Taboo
Witchcraft

SHARECROPPER
S-32-0068 1975 00003
BT Farmer
RT Collective Farmer
Private Farmer
Tenant Farmer
Tenant Farming

SHEIK
S-36-0061 1975 00001
BT Emperor
RT Absolute Monarchy
Hereditary Ruler
Kaiser
King
Middle East Area Studies
Queen
Regent
Shah
Sheikdom
Sultan
Tsar

SHEIKDOM
S-16-0086 1975 00001
BT Government Type
RT Hereditary Ruler
Monarchy
Sheik
Sultan

SHERIFF
S-36-0144 1975 00001
BT Local Police Official
RT Professional Occupational Role

SHINTOISM
S-38-0574 1975 00000
BT Religious Thought
RT Buddhism
Confucianism
East Asian Area Studies
Eastern Political Thought
Islamic Thought
Judeo Christian Thought
Religious Culture
Religious Identity
Taoism
Zoroastrianism

SHIP BUILDING INDUSTRY
S-17-0030 1979 00000
BT Construction Industry
RT Building Supplies Industry
Lumber Industry
Production Industry
Shipping Industry

SHIPPING INDUSTRY
S-17-0080 1979 00000
BT Water Transportation Industry
RT Air Transportation Industry
Automobile Industry
Merchant Marine
Motor Vehicle Industry
Railway Industry
Ship Building Industry
Transportation Policy
Trucking Industry

SHORT BALLOT
S-29-0161 1975 00000
BT Ballot
RT Australian Ballot
Long Ballot
Machine Ballot
Nonpartisan Ballot
Office Block Ballot
Paper Ballot
Political Party Column Ballot
Political Party List Ballot
Secret Ballot

SHORT RANGE PLANNING
S-31-0671 1979 00000
BT Planning Process
RT Economic Planning
Fiscal Planning
Long Range Planning
Planning Process
Policy Evaluation
Policy Implementation
Policy Making Process
Public Policy Planning

SHORT STORY
S-18-0077 1979 00000
BT Information Sources
RT Humanistic Education
Humanities Discipline
Humanities Education
Novel
Poetry

SIBLING
S-32-0047 1975 00000
BT Family Role
RT Extended Family
Family Role
Family Type
Maternal Role
Nuclear Family

SIMPLE RANDOM SAMPLING
S-24-0124 1975 00005
BT Probability Sampling
RT Cluster Sampling
Stratified Sampling
Systematic Sampling

SIMULATION
S-24-0127 1975 00048
BT Data Collection Methodology
NT Computer Simulation
Man Machine Simulation
RT Game Theory
Gaming
Problem Solving Behavior
Simulation Material

SIMULATION MATERIAL
S-24-0339 1975 00007
BT Information Processing Equipment
RT Game Theory
Gaming
Man Machine Simulation
Political Science Teaching
Simulation

SIMULTANEOUS EQUATION MODEL
S-24-0283 1975 00007
BT Mathematical Model
RT Differential Equation Model
Economic Mathematical Model

SINGLE
S-36-0230 1979 00000
BT Marital Status
RT Family Role
Married
Widow
Widower

SINGLE FAMILY DWELLING
S-06-0230 1975 00001
BT Residential Pattern
RT Multiple Family Dwelling

SINGLE GROUP FARM ECONOMY
S-12-0008 1975 00001
BT Farm Economy
RT Collective Farm Economy
Corporate Farm Economy
Family Farm Economy
Plantation Economy
State Farm Economy

SINGLE ISSUE VOTER
S-32-0319 1975 00002
BT Issue Voter
RT Issue Orientation
Issue Politicization

SINGLE MEMBER DISTRICT
S-29-0194 1975 00002
BT Electoral District
RT Absolute Majority Electoral Outcome
Multimember District
Single Member District Representation

SINGLE MEMBER DISTRICT REPRESENTATION
S-31-0726 1975 00001
BT Representation Type
RT At Large Representation
District Representation
Functional Representation
Geographic Representation
Indirect Representation
Proportional Representation
Single Member District
Single Member Districting

SINGLE MEMBER DISTRICTING
S-31-0712 1975 00000
BT Districting
RT Single Member District Representation

SINGLE TRANSFERABLE VOTE
S-29-0172 1975 00001
BT Voting Formulae
RT Cumulative Voting
D'Hont Voting Method
Largest Average Voting Method
Largest Remainder Voting Method

List Voting

SISTER
USE Family Role

SIT DOWN STRIKE
S-08-0032 1975 00000
BT Labor Strike
RT Jurisdiction Strike
Sit In
Strike Breaking
Union
Walkout
Wildcat Strike

SIT IN
S-08-0017 1975 00000
BT Civil Rights Demonstration
RT Group Conflict
Peace Demonstration
Racial Conflict
Racial Revolution
Sit Down Strike
Social Rebellion
Student Demonstration
Veterans Demonstration

SITUATION OF THE TIMES VOTER
S-32-0329 1975 00002
BT Voter
RT Group Benefits Voter
Situational Analysis
Voter Orientation

SITUATIONAL ANALYSIS
S-09-0063 1979 00000
BT Contemporary Analytic Modes
RT Behavior Analysis
Biographical Analysis
Contextual Analysis
Historical Analysis
Historical Sociology Analysis
Motivational Analysis
Policy Analysis
Revisionist Historical Analysis
Situation Of The Times Voter
Sociological Analysis

SITUATIONAL ETHICS
S-25-0047 1975 00025
BT Ethical Theory
RT Axiology
Bioethics
Emotive Ethical Theory
Ethical Relativism
Hedonism
Human Subject Rights
Instrumentalism
Intuitionism
Linguistic Ethical Theory
Metaethical Theory
Research Ethics
Use Of Human Subjects

SKEPTIC POLITICAL THOUGHT
1975-1979 00000

SKEPTIC THOUGHT
S-38-0056 1979 00000
SN Post-Socractic doctrines which asserted that the only knowable thing is one's inner feelings and hence one should avoid judgment on all matters since there
is no objective good.
BT Classical Political Thought
RT Cynic Thought
Epicurean Thought
Neoplatonic Political Thought
Platonic Political Thought
Socratic Political Thought
Stoic Thought

SKILL ACQUISITION
S-34-0013 1979 00000
UF Aptitude
BT Learning
RT Apprenticeship
Expertise
Informal Education
Job Socialization
Job Training
Learning Psychology
Learning Theory
Rote Learning
Symbol Learning
Technical Education
Verbal Learning

SKILLED WORKER
S-32-0089 1975 00010
BT Blue Collar Worker
RT Craft Economy
Expertise
Semiskilled Worker
Unskilled Worker

SLANDER
S-10-0048 1975 00000
BT Individual Crime
NT Character Assassination
RT Blackmail
Extortion
Libel
Perjury
Slanderer

SLANDERER
S-36-0034 1975 00000
BT Personal Crime Criminal
RT Blackmailer
Extortionist
Slander
War Criminal

SLATE MAKING
S-31-0751 1975 00000
BT Selection Process
RT Appointment Process
Candidate Selection
Convention Delegate Selection
Delegate Selection
Endorsement
Nominating Process
Recruitment Process

SLAVE LABOR CAMP
S-19-0298 1975 00000
BT Detention Center
RT Concentration Camp
National Socialism
Prisoner Of War Camp
Secret Police

SLAVE REBELLION
S-08-0059 1975 00002
BT Social Rebellion
RT Class Rebellion
Economic Rebellion
Mob Violence
Political Rebellion
Slave Society
Slavery
Student Rebellion
Worker Rebellion

SLAVE SOCIETY
S-35-0027 1975 00008
BT Society Type Base
RT Slave Rebellion
Slavery

SLAVERY
S-37-0059 1975 00033
BT Property Ownership System
RT Absentee Landlord System
Land Tenure System
Primogeniture
Private Ownership
Slave Rebellion
Slave Society
Slavery Abolition

SLAVERY ABOLITION
S-31-0147 1975 00009
BT Black Emancipation
RT Economic Freedom
Liberty Theory
Political Freedom Theory
Slavery
Social Protest

SLUM COMMUNITY
S-07-0048 1975 00005
BT Community Type
RT City
Slum Rehabilitation
Urban Politics Studies

SLUM REHABILITATION
S-31-0134 1975 00003
BT Urban Renewal
RT City
Inner City
Slum Community
Urban Planner
Urban Policy Planning
Urban Politics Studies
Urban Redevelopment

SMALL BUSINESS
S-19-0162 1975 00011
BT Business
RT Big Business
Business Agency
Business Studies
Light Industry
Prosperity
Small Businessman

SMALL BUSINESSMAN
S-32-0074 1975 00003
BT Businessman
RT Artisan
Business Agency
Small Business

SMALL GROUP ANALYSIS
S-09-0025 1975 00015
BT Group Analysis
RT Group Analysis
Group Politics
Identity Analysis
Methodology
Small Group Behavior
Small Group Experiment
Small Group Laboratory

SMALL GROUP BEHAVIOR
S-05-0030 1975 00026
BT Group Behavior
RT Behavioral Theory
Elite Behavior
Face To Face Group
Small Group Analysis
Small Group Experiment
Small Group Leadership

SMALL GROUP EXPERIMENT
S-24-0106 1979 00000
UF Small Group Experimentation
BT Experimental Observation
RT Gaming
Small Group Analysis
Small Group Behavior

SMALL GROUP EXPERIMENTATION
1975-1979 00033
USE Small Group Experiment

SMALL GROUP LABORATORY
S-24-0338 1975 00010
BT Laboratory
RT Laboratory Equipment
Small Group Analysis

SMALL GROUP LEADERSHIP
S-22-0019 1975 00004
BT Leadership Structure Type
RT Collective Leadership
Collegial Leadership
Political Leadership
Political Party Leadership
Small Group Behavior
Traditional Leadership

SOCIAL ACCOUNTING
S-31-0696 1975 00003
BT Policy Evaluation
RT Education Evaluation
Formative Evaluation
Normative Evaluation
Summative Evaluation

SOCIAL ACTION THEORY
S-38-0586 1975 00032
BT Social Theory
NT Collective Action Theory
Social Interaction Theory
RT Assimilation Theory
Exchange Theory
Field Theory
Parsonsian Sociology
Role Theory
Rural Sociology
Social Anthropology
Social Integration Theory
Social Learning Theory
Socialization Theory
Symbolic Action
System Characteristics
System Equilibrium
Weberian Theory

SOCIAL ADJUSTMENT
S-34-0052 1979 00000
BT Social Conditioning
RT Accommodative Social Behavior
Acculturation
Adaptive Behavior
Behavior Modification
Conformity Behavior
Consensual Norms
Constraining Norms
Coping Behavior
Deviant Behavior
Personal Behavior
Social Behavior
Social Norms
System Adaptive Capacity

SOCIAL ANTHROPOLOGY
S-01-0021 1975 00031
BT Anthropology Discipline
RT African Area Studies
Area Studies
Comparative Political Studies
Comparative Sociology
Cultural Anthropology
Cultural History
Demographic Studies
Ethnography
Ethnolinguistics
Ethnology
Geography Discipline
Historical Sociology
Human Geography
Macrosociology
Mythology
Political Anthropology
Political Philosophy Studies
Political Science Methodology Studies
Political Sociology
Political Theory Studies
Psychology Discipline
Rising Expectation Theory
Ritual
Rural Sociology
Social Action Theory
Social Psychology

SOCIAL AREA ANALYSIS
S-09-0064 1975 00001
BT Contemporary Analytic Modes
RT Analysis Of Play
Area Sampling
Cost Benefit Analysis
Issue Analysis
Leisure Time Analysis
Network Analysis
Socialization Analysis
Spatial Analysis

SOCIAL BACKGROUND
S-06-0211 1975 00046
BT Socioeconomic Background
RT Class Analysis
Economic Background
Family Descent Pattern
Objectively Derived Status
Social Class Origin
Subjectively Derived Status

SOCIAL BEHAVIOR
S-05-0022 1975 00066
BT Behavior
NT Accommodative Social Behavior
Avoidance Behavior
Deviant Behavior
Group Behavior
Habitual Behavior
Mass Behavior
Symbolic Action
RT Administrative Behavior
Behavioral Theory
Crowd Behavior
Group Behavior
Group Theory
Personal Behavior
Psycholinguistics
Social Adjustment
Social Change
Social Norms
Social Role Process
Social Theory

SOCIAL CHANGE
S-31-0162 1975 00121
BT Political Change
NT Planned Social Change
RT Atomistic Family
Economic Change
Emancipation
Evolutionary Change
Evolutionary Socialism
Homeostatic Change
Innovation
Liberation Process
Political Change
Revolutionary Change
Social Behavior
Social Change Index
Social Stability
Technological Change
Urbanization Process

SOCIAL CHANGE INDEX
S-24-0245 1975 00007
BT Scale Type
RT Development Index
Left Right Scale
Satisfaction Scale
Social Change
Social Conflict
Social Distance Scale
Social Frustration Scale
Stability Index
Urbanization Index

SOCIAL CHOICE THEORY
S-38-0172 1979 00000
BT Explanatory Political Theory
RT Collective Action Theory
Decision Making Theory
Public Choice Analysis
Public Choice Theory
Public Good Theory
Public Interest
Rational Choice Theory

SOCIAL CLASS IDENTIFICATION
S-06-0399 1975 00013
BT Social Identity
RT Class Analysis
Occupational Identity
Social Class Origin
Social Classification

SOCIAL CLASS ORIGIN
S-06-0202 1975 00026
BT Class Origin
RT Class Analysis
Economic Background
Social Background
Social Class Identification

SOCIAL CLASSIFICATION
S-24-0345 1975 00004
BT Analysis Unit
NT Population Identification
RT Comparative Sociology
Social Class Identification

SOCIAL CLEAVAGE
S-06-0489 1975 00014
BT Social Diversity
RT Class Conflict
Class Stratification Division
Community Cleavage Characteristics
Conflict Process
Conflict Theory
Cultural Cleavage
Ethnic Cleavage
Group Cleavage Characteristics
Organization Cleavage Characteristics
Racial Cleavage
Social Conflict
Social Diversity
Social System
Social System Structural Characteristics
Sociology Discipline

SOCIAL CLEAVAGE INDICATOR
S-24-0274 1975 00005
BT Social Indicator
RT Social Theory
Sociometric Indicator
Stress Indicator

SOCIAL CONDITIONING
S-34-0050 1975 00002
BT Socialization Type
NT Political Conditioning
Social Adjustment
Stereotyping
RT Learning Theory
Opinion Socialization
Perception Socialization
Political Orientation Development
Political Value Acquisition
Role Socialization
Social System

SOCIAL CONFLICT
S-08-0114 1975 00029
BT Conflict Type
NT Group Conflict
Racial Conflict
RT Aggression
Aggression Theory
Agitation
Bolshevik Revolution
Conflict Of Interest
Cultural Conflict
Economic Agitation
Economic Conflict
Government Overthrow
Group Conflict
Ideological Conflict
Institutional Conflict
Insurgency
Interpersonal Conflict
Organization Conflict
Political Agitation
Political Violence
Protest Politics
Racial Revolution
Religious Conflict
Religious War
Social Change Index
Social Cleavage
Social Instability
Social Revolution
Struggle
War
Wildcat Strike

SOCIAL CONTRACT THEORY
S-38-0511 1975 00009
BT Political Philosophy Concept
NT Government Contract Theory
Societal Contract Theory
State Of Nature Theory
RT Authority
Hobbesian Absolutism
Legitimacy Theory
Lockean Contractualism
Medieval Corporatism
Political Alienation Theory
Political Legitimacy Theory

SOCIAL CRISIS
S-31-0252 1979 00000
BT Crisis
RT Crisis
Economic Crisis
International Crisis
Natural Catastrophe
Political Crisis
Social Instability
Social System Normative Characteristics
Social System Structural Characteristics

SOCIAL CRITICISM
S-06-0795 1975 00007
BT Social Stress
RT Social Disorder
Social Instability

SOCIAL DARWINISM
S-38-0287 1975 00005
BT Ideologies
RT Competition
Evolution
Evolutionary Change
Natural Selection

SOCIAL DECISION MAKER
S-32-0031 1975 00004
BT Decision Maker
RT Cultural Decision Maker
Economic Decision Maker
Organization Decision Maker
Political Decision Maker
Social Leader

SOCIAL DEMOCRACY
S-16-0031 1975 00002
BT Democratic Government
RT Democratic Socialism
Minority Rights Democratic Theory
Open Society
Open Society Theory
Social Democratic Movement
Social Democratic Political Party
Social Policy
Socialist Democracy
Socialist Government
Socialist Political Party

SOCIAL DEMOCRATIC MOVEMENT
S-27-0022 1975 00002
BT Ideological Spectrum Political Movement
RT Bernsteinian Socialism
Social Democracy
Social Democratic Political Party
Social Movement

SOCIAL DEMOCRATIC PARTY
1975-1979 00006

SOCIAL DEMOCRATIC POLITICAL PARTY
S-28-0007 1979 00000
BT Democratic Political Party
RT Democratic Socialism
Evolutionary Socialism
Labor Political Party
Liberal Democratic Political Party
National Democratic Political Party
Social Democracy
Social Democratic Movement
Socialist Democracy
Socialist Democratic Theory
Socialist Government
Socialist Political Party

SOCIAL DEVELOPMENT INDEX
S-24-0232 1975 00008
BT Development Index
RT Social Development Policy
Social Development Theory

SOCIAL DEVELOPMENT POLICY
S-26-0084 1979 00000
BT Development Policy
RT Cultural Development Policy
Development Model
Economic Development Policy
Group Development
Personality Development
Political Development
Political Development Policy
Social Development Index
Social Development Policy
Social Development Theory

SOCIAL DEVELOPMENT THEORY
S-38-0026 1975 00054
BT Development Theory
RT Administrative Development Theory
Convergence Theory
Divergence Theory
Economic Development Theory
Economic Growth Theory
Modernizing Society
Political Development Theory
Social Development Index
Social Development Policy
Technological Development Theory
Urban Development Theory

SOCIAL DEVIANCE
S-06-0796 1975 00021
BT Social Stress
RT Protest Politics
Social Disorder
Social Instability
Violence

SOCIAL DISORDER
S-06-0797 1975 00013
BT Social Stress
RT Social Criticism
Social Deviance
Social Instability
Violence

SOCIAL DISTANCE SCALE
S-24-0246 1975 00025
BT Scale Type
RT Alienation Scale
Anomie Scale
Cynicism Scale
Dogmatism Scale

Efficacy Scale
Internal External Reinforcement Scale
Satisfaction Scale
Social Change Index
Social Frustration Scale
Stability Index
Support Opposition Scale

SOCIAL DISTANCE THEORY
S-38-0589 1979 00000
BT Social Theory
RT Alienation
Ascribed Status
Social Interaction Theory
Social Stratification Process
Status Maintenance
Status Social System

SOCIAL DIVERSITY
S-06-0488 1975 00003
BT National Characteristics
NT Social Cleavage
RT Class Stratification Division
Cultural Diversity
Cultural Relativism
Democratic Theory
Demographic Characteristics
Ethnic Diversity
Linguistic Diversity
National Character
National Interest
Racial Diversity
Social Cleavage
Social System Structural Characteristics
Social Theory

SOCIAL ECONOMICS
S-01-0073 1979 00000
BT Economics Discipline
RT Business Economics
Consumer Economics
Econometrics
Industrial Economics
Institutional Economics
International Economics
Labor Economics
Regional Economics
Social Policy
Transportation Economics
Urban Economics
Welfare Economics

SOCIAL ELITE
S-14-0034 1975 00011
UF Celebrity
BT Elite Type
NT Modernizing Social Elite
Religious Elite
Traditional Social Elite
RT Academic Elite
Community Elite
Cultural Elite
Governing Elite
Intellectual Elite
Local Elite
Opinion Elite
Plutocracy
Political Elite
Power Elite
Provincial Elite
Upper Class

SOCIAL ENGINEERING
S-31-0673 1975 00005
BT Social Planning
RT Administrative Planning
Economic Planning
Population Planning
Public Policy Planning
Public Policy Studies
Subnational Policy Planning

SOCIAL EQUALITY
S-06-0728 1979 00000
BT Equality
NT Class Equality
Education Equality
Racial Equality
Sex Equality
Status Equality
RT Democratic Theory
Economic Egalitarianism
Economic Equality
Egalitarianism
Income Equality
Political Equality
Social Theory
Socialist Theory

SOCIAL EVOLUTION
S-31-0069 1975 00008
BT Evolution
RT Cultural Evolution
Evolutionary Socialism
Genetic Characteristics
Genetic Evolution
Human Evolution
Political Evolution

SOCIAL FORECASTING
S-24-0018 1979 00000
BT Forecasting Methodology
RT Authority Forecasting
Brainstorming
Causal Analysis
Delphi Technique
Divergence Mapping
Economic Forecasting
Policy Evaluation Research
Policy Research
Political Forecasting
Predictive Research
Scenario Construction
Social Theory
Trend Analysis

SOCIAL FRAGMENTATION
S-31-0795 1975 00013
BT Fragmentation
RT Anomie
Political Fragmentation
Social Group

SOCIAL FRUSTRATION SCALE
S-24-0247 1975 00000
BT Scale Type
RT Aggression Scale
Alienation Scale
Anomie Scale
Cynicism Scale
Dogmatism Scale
Efficacy Scale
Frustration Scale
Internal External Reinforcement Scale
Left Right Scale
Liberalism Conservatism Scale
Optimism Pessimism Scale
Satisfaction Scale
Social Change Index
Social Distance Scale
Stability Index
Support Opposition Scale

SOCIAL GOAL
S-06-0708 1975 00012
BT Social System Normative Characteristics
RT Social Mores
Social Norms
Social Policy
Social Utility

SOCIAL GROUP
S-03-0024 1975 00012
BT Groups
NT Ethnic Group
Face To Face Group
Kinship Group
Nationality Group
Racial Group
Reference Group
Religious Group
Secondary Group
RT Association Interest Group
Cooperatives
Cultural Group
Ethnic Organization
Fraternal Organization
Group Theory
Interest Group
Interest Group Theory
Occupational Interest Group
Policy Interest Group
Political Club
Political Interest Group
Professional Organization
Social Fragmentation
Social Policy
Social System
Social Theory

SOCIAL HISTORY
S-01-0121 1975 00359
UF Genealogy
BT History Discipline
RT Ancient History
Anthropology Discipline
Behavioral Science
Cultural History
Demographic Studies
Economic History
Economics Discipline
Gerontology
Historical Analysis
Institutional History
Intellectual History
Labor History
Political History
Political Science Discipline
Psychohistory
Quantitative History
Religious History
Sociology Discipline
Urban Decay

SOCIAL IDENTITY
S-06-0398 1975 00017
BT Identity Characteristics
NT Social Class Identification
RT Community Identity
Cultural Identity
Ethnic Community
Language Loyalty
National Identity
Occupational Identity
Racial Identity
Religious Identity
Social Theory

SOCIAL INDICATOR
S-24-0273 1975 00010
BT Indicator
NT Social Cleavage Indicator
Sociometric Indicator
Stress Indicator
RT Analysis Unit
Change Indicator
Economic Indicator
Ethnographic Data
Morbidity Data
Political Indicator
Social Psychological Data
Statistical Analysis
Statistical Table
Survey Data
Vital Statistics Data
Wage Statistics

SOCIAL INEQUALITY
S-06-0738 1975 00051
BT Inequality
NT Class Inequality
Education Inequality
Racial Inequality
Sex Inequality
Status Inequality
RT Economic Inequality
Economic Injustice
Education Injustice
Ghetto Community
Ghetto Conflict
Income Inequality
Political Inequality
Political Injustice
Racial Injustice
Sexual Injustice
Social Injustice
Social Mobility
Social Stratification Division
Social Stress

SOCIAL INJUSTICE
S-06-0709 1979 00000
BT Social System Normative Characteristics
NT Economic Injustice
Education Injustice
Racial Injustice
Sexual Injustice
RT Economic Injustice
Education Injustice
Inequality
Political Inequality
Political Injustice
Racial Inequality
Racial Injustice
Sexual Injustice
Social Inequality
Status Inequality

SOCIAL INSTABILITY
S-06-0798 1975 00024
BT Social Stress
RT Social Conflict
Social Crisis
Social Criticism
Social Deviance
Social Disorder
Social Revolution
Violence

SOCIAL INTEGRATION
S-31-0830 1975 00030
BT Integration
RT Adaptive Behavior
Cultural Integration
Ethnic Assimilation Theory
Ethnic Integration
Linguistic Integration
Polarization
Racial Integration
Social Integration Theory
Social Interaction Theory
Social Policy
Specialization Process
Vertical Integration

SOCIAL INTEGRATION THEORY
S-38-0590 1975 00022
BT Social Theory
RT Annexation
Assimilation Theory
Equilibrium Theory
General System Theory
Horizontal Economic Integration
Interaction Model
Pluralist Group Theory
Role Theory
Social Action Theory
Social Integration
Social Learning Theory
Social Organization Theory
Socialization Theory
System Characteristics
System Equilibrium

SOCIAL INTERACTION
S-31-0754 1979 00000
BT Social Process
NT Friendship
Interpersonal Cooperation
RT Policy Making Process
Role Performance
Selection Process
Social Role Process
Social Stratification Dissolution
Social Stratification Formation
Social Stratification Maintenance
Social Stratification Process
Structural Process

SOCIAL INTERACTION THEORY
S-38-0588 1975 00231
BT Social Action Theory
RT Avoidance Behavior
Collective Action Theory
Cooperative Behavior
Mass Behavior
Sexual Behavior
Social Distance Theory
Social Integration

SOCIAL LAW
S-21-0084 1975 00007
BT Law Type
NT Abortion Law
Blue Law
Family Law
Gambling Law
Gun Control Law
Jim Crow Law
Marital Law
Minority Law
Miscegenation Law
Nationalities Law
Pornography Law
RT Economic Law
Political Law
Social System
Social Theory
Sociology Discipline
Welfare Law

SOCIAL LEADER
S-32-0056 1975 00003
BT Leader
NT Charismatic Leader
Community Leader
Opinion Leader
RT Civil Rights Leader
Economic Leader
Leadership Analysis
Political Leader
Social Decision Maker
Social Policy

SOCIAL LEARNING THEORY
S-38-0591 1975 00034
BT Social Theory
RT Acculturation Theory
Adaptive Behavior
Assimilation Theory
Field Theory
Logic
Personality Development
Reference Group Theory
Role Theory
Social Action Theory
Social Integration Theory
Socialization Theory

SOCIAL MOBILITY
S-06-0746 1975 00089
BT Social System Structural Characteristics
NT Status Mobility
RT Ambition
Career Analysis
Differentiated System
Geographic Mobility
Open Class Social System
Social Inequality
Social Prestige
Social Stability
Social Stratification Division

SOCIAL MOBILIZATION
S-31-0632 1975 00026
BT Mobilization Process
RT Economic Mobilization
Functional Integration
Mass Mobilization
Military Mobilization
Political Mobilization
Worker Mobilization

SOCIAL MODERNIZATION
S-31-0081 1975 00040
BT Modernization
RT Cultural Modernization
Economic Modernization
Institutional Innovation
Political Modernization
Secular Society

SOCIAL MORES
S-06-0714 1975 00023
BT Social System Normative Characteristics
NT Middle Class Values
Socially Desirable Behavior
RT Constraining Norms
Social Goal
Social Norms
Social Psychology
Social System
Social Theory
Social Utility
Value Analysis

SOCIAL MOVEMENT
S-27-0058 1975 00032
BT Political Movement
NT Civic Action Movement
Civil Rights Movement
Communal Movement
Ethnic Movement
Language Movement
Religious Movement
Sectarian Movement
Senior Citizen Movement
Youth Movement
RT Civil Rights Movement
Ecology Movement
Feminism
Independence Movement
Liberation Movement
Nationalist Movement
Peace Movement
Reform Movement
Sector Based Political Movement
Social Democratic Movement
Social System
Social Theory

SOCIAL NORMS
S-06-0717 1975 00050
BT Social System Normative Characteristics
NT Consensual Norms
Constraining Norms
Elite Norms
RT Social Adjustment
Social Behavior
Social Goal
Social Mores
Social Policy
Socially Desirable Behavior

SOCIAL ORGANIZATION THEORY
S-38-0043 1975 00042
BT Organization Theory
RT Administrative Science
Bureaucratic Theory
Group Theory
Social Integration Theory
Societal Contract Theory

SOCIAL PATHOLOGY
S-01-0193 1975 00011
BT Sociology Discipline
RT Anomic Process
Anomie
Applied Sociology
Behavioral Psychology
Comparative Sociology
Deviant Behavior
Freudian Psychology
Historical Sociology
Industrial Sociology
Learning Psychology
Macrosociology
Marxist Sociology
Microeconomics
Peace Studies
Personality Disorder
Political Psychology
Political Science Discipline
Political Science Methodology Studies
Political Sociology
Psycholinguistics
Psychological Anthropology
Psychology Discipline
Psychopathology
Role Theory
Social Policy
Social Psychology
Sociobiology
Sociology Of The Professions

SOCIAL PHILOSOPHY
S-01-0155 1975 00021
BT Philosophy Discipline
RT Education Philosophy
Intellectual History
Philosophical Anthropology
Political Philosophy Studies
Social Psychiatry
Social System
Social Theory
Sociology Discipline

SOCIAL PLANNER
S-32-0138 1975 00000
BT Planner
NT Education Planner
RT Budget Planner
Economic Planner
International Planner
National Planner
New Town
Political Planner
Social Planning
Subnational Planner

SOCIAL PLANNING
S-31-0672 1975 00010
BT Planning Process
NT Social Engineering
RT Administrative Planning
Defense Planning
Development Planning
Economic Planning
Education Planning
Environmental Planning
Higher Education Planning
International Policy Planning
Long Range Planning
Planification
Planned Economy
Population Planning
Public Policy Planning
Public Policy Studies
Social Planner
Subnational Policy Planning

SOCIAL POLICY
S-26-0371 1975 00052
BT Policy
NT Abortion Policy
Discrimination Policy
Drug Control Policy
Ethnic Policy
Housing Policy
Migration Policy
Policy For Disadvantaged
Population Policy
Religious Policy
Safety Policy
Social Resource Distribution Policy
Social Welfare Policy
Urban Renewal Policy
RT Community Service
Day Care Center
Education Policy
Employment Service
Family Service
Health Service
Information Service
Legal Service
Medical Care Service
Service Delivery System
Service Policy
Social Democracy
Social Economics
Social Goal
Social Group
Social Integration
Social Leader
Social Norms
Social Pathology
Social Power Model
Social Service
Social Theory

SOCIAL POWER MODEL
S-24-0316 1975 00017
BT Social Science Model
RT Economic Growth Model
Organization Model
Process Model
Social Policy

SOCIAL PRESTIGE
S-06-0745 1979 00000
BT Prestige Hierarchy
RT Class Stratification Division
Deference
Nobility
Ruling Class
Social Mobility
Social Stratification Division
Status Mobility
Status Stratification Division
Upper Class

SOCIAL PROCESS
S-31-0752 1979 00000
BT Process
NT Ostracism
Social Interaction
Social Role Process

RT Social Role Process
Social Stratification Formation
Social Stratification Maintenance
Social Stratification Process
Status Maintenance

SOCIAL PROTEST
S-31-0258 1975 00016
BT Protest
RT Luddite Movement
Protest Politics
Protest Voter
Slavery Abolition
Student Protest

SOCIAL PSYCHIATRY
S-01-0144 1979 00000
BT Psychiatry
RT Alienation Psychological Theory
Authoritarian Attitude
Coping Behavior
Deviant Behavior
Deviant Personality
Identity Analysis
Parapsychology
Pathological Behavior
Personal Behavior
Personality Characteristics
Personality Disorder
Personality Theory
Psychohistory
Psychological Aggression
Psychopathology
Psychopolitical Theory
Psychosis
Sexual Behavior
Social Philosophy

SOCIAL PSYCHOLOGICAL DATA
S-18-0091 1975 00036
BT Social Statistics
RT Social Indicator
Socioeconomic Data
Statistical Table
Survey Data
Vital Statistics Data

SOCIAL PSYCHOLOGIST
S-32-0117 1979 00000
BT Psychologist
RT Anthropologist
Clinical Psychologist
Economist
Political Scientist
Social Psychology
Social Worker
Sociologist

SOCIAL PSYCHOLOGY
S-01-0178 1975 00131
BT Psychology Discipline
NT Industrial Psychology
Political Psychology
RT Administrative Science
Anthropology Discipline
Behavioral Psychology
Behavioral Science
Comparative Political Studies
Comparative Sociology
Coping Behavior
Cultural Anthropology
Cultural History
Education Discipline
Freudian Psychology
Gestalt Psychology
Group Perception
Group Psychology
Group Theory
Historical Sociology
Human Resources Development
Individual Perception
Interpersonal Conflict
Learning Psychology
Linguistics
Macrosociology
Marxist Alienation Theory
Marxist Sociology
Pathological Behavior
Perception
Perception Measurement
Personal Behavior
Policy Science Studies
Political Behavior Studies
Political Philosophy Studies
Political Science Discipline
Political Science Methodology Studies
Political Sociology
Role Analysis
Role Conflict
Role Theory
Rural Sociology
Sexual Behavior
Social Anthropology
Social Mores
Social Pathology
Social Psychologist
Social System
Sociology Discipline
Stress Indicator

SOCIAL REBELLION
S-08-0056 1975 00009
BT Rebellion
NT Class Rebellion
Peasant Rebellion
Slave Rebellion
RT Economic Agitation
Economic Rebellion
Government Overthrow
Group Conflict
Holy War
Ideological Struggle
Institutional Conflict
Internal War
Mob Violence
Political Agitation
Political Rebellion
Protest Politics
Revolution
Sit In
Struggle
Student Rebellion
War

SOCIAL RESOURCE DISTRIBUTION POLICY
S-26-0407 1975 00018
BT Social Policy
NT Scientific Manpower Policy
RT Drug Control Policy
Housing Policy
Information Policy
Population Policy
Social Welfare Policy
Urban Renewal Policy

SOCIAL REVOLUTION
S-08-0075 1975 00013
BT Revolution
NT Bourgeois Revolution
Industrial Revolution
Proletarian Revolution
Racial Revolution
RT Chinese Cultural Revolution
Communist Revolution
Counterrevolution
Cultural Aggression
Cultural Revolution
Democratic Political Revolution
Democratic Socialist Revolution
Ecological Revolution
National Political Revolution
Peace Demonstration
Political Revolution
Religious Conflict
Revolution Theory
Revolutionary Change
Social Conflict
Social Instability
Social Rights
Socialist Revolution
Spontaneous Revolution
Struggle
Student Rebellion
Technological Revolution
Thermidor

SOCIAL RIGHTS
S-15-0072 1975 00032
BT Political Liberty
NT Childrens Rights
Health Care Rights
Housing Rights
Income Rights
Marriage Rights
Right To Die
Right To Education
Sexual Freedom
RT Citizenship Immunity
Civil Liberty
Civil Rights
Freedom Of Competition
Freedom Of Contract
Freedom Of Inquiry
Human Rights
Minority Law
Right To Strike
Social Revolution
Social Role Process
Unemployment Policy
Voting Rights

SOCIAL ROLE PROCESS
S-31-0757 1975 00028
BT Social Process
NT Role Acquisition
Role Allocation
Role Conflict
Role Differentiation
Role Expectation
Role Orientation
Role Performance
RT Analytic Process
Atomistic Family
Endorsement
Friendship
Interpersonal Cooperation

Mobilization Policy
Mobilization Process
Nominating Process
Ostracism
Recruitment Process
Selection Process
Social Behavior
Social Interaction
Social Process
Social Rights
Social Science Model
Social Stratification Process
Specialization Process
Structural Process

SOCIAL SCIENCE MODEL
S-24-0288 1975 00047
BT Models
NT Atomistic Model
Cognitive Model
Communication Model
Computer Simulation Model
Conflict Model
Consensus Model
Cybernetic Model
Development Model
Diffusion Model
Econometric Model
Equilibrium Model
Growth Model
Hierarchical Model
Ideal Type Model
Individualism Model
Input Output Model
Interaction Model
Market Model
Optimizing Model
Organization Model
Pluralist Model
Probability Model
Process Model
Psychometric Model
Rational Choice Model
Social Power Model
Social System Model
Spatial Model
Static Model
Structural Model
Teleological Model
Voluntarism Model
RT Falsification
Indicator
Mathematical Model
Most Different System Design
Multiple Indicator
Natural Experiment
Natural Science Model
Paradigm
Parsonsian Sociology
Reliability Measurement
Scale Construction Methodology
Social Role Process

SOCIAL SCIENTIST
S-32-0107 1975 00049
BT Professional Occupational Role
NT Anthropologist
Economist
Geographer
Historian
Policy Scientist
Political Scientist
Psychologist
RT Discovery
Historian
Psychologist
Sociology Of Science
Teacher

SOCIAL SECURITY
S-06-0322 1975 00005
BT Government Expenditure
RT Public Assistance
Right To Job Security
Unemployment Compensation
Welfare

SOCIAL SECURITY POLICY
S-26-0413 1975 00016
BT Social Welfare Policy
RT Old Age Assistance Policy

SOCIAL SECURITY TAXATION
S-26-0165 1975 00004
BT Taxation Policy
RT Excise Taxation Policy
Gift Taxation
Incentive Taxation Policy
Inheritance Taxation
Luxury Taxation
Nuisance Taxation
Unemployment Compensation
Value Added Taxation

SOCIAL SERVICE
S-26-0366 1979 00000
BT Service Policy
NT Child Care Service
Community Service
Family Service
RT Education Service
Employment Service
Health Service
Information Service
Legal Service
Medical Care Service
Policy For Disadvantaged
Psychological Service
Sanitation Industry
Service Industry Policy
Social Policy

SOCIAL SOLIDARITY
S-06-0044 1975 00006
BT Group Solidarity
NT Social Unity
RT Brotherhood
Caste Solidarity
Class Solidarity
Communal Solidarity
Ethnic Group Cohesion
Gemeinschaft
Group Solidarity
Proletarian Unity

SOCIAL STABILITY
S-06-0754 1975 00019
BT Social System Structural Characteristics
RT Anomic Process
Social Change
Social Mobility
Social Stress
Social System
Status Quo Conservatism

SOCIAL STATISTICS
S-18-0088 1975 00003
BT Statistical Data
NT Ethnographic Data
Morbidity Data
Social Psychological Data
Socioeconomic Data
Vital Statistics Data
RT Aggregate Data Analysis
Aggregate Data Statistics
Analysis Of Variance
Census Record
Economic Statistics
Field Data
Legislative Information Service
Mass Public Opinion
Political Statistics
Private Information Service
Probability Model
Statistical Table
Survey Data

SOCIAL STRATIFICATION DISSOLUTION
S-31-0771 1975 00003
BT Social Stratification Process
NT Caste Dissolution
Class Dissolution
Status Dissolution
RT Social Interaction
Social Stratification Formation
Social Stratification Maintenance

SOCIAL STRATIFICATION DIVISION
S-06-0755 1975 00014
BT Social System Structural Characteristics
NT Caste Stratification Division
Class Stratification Division
Horizontal Stratification Division
Status Stratification Division
Vertical Stratification Division
RT Area Sampling
Heterogeneous Group Membership
Homogeneous Group Membership
Interlocking Group Membership
Middle Caste
Middle Class
Overlapping Membership
Social Inequality
Social Mobility
Social Prestige
Social Stress
Subjectively Derived Status

SOCIAL STRATIFICATION FORMATION
S-31-0775 1975 00008
BT Social Stratification Process
NT Caste Formation
Class Formation
Status Formation
RT Downward Mobility
Friendship
Ostracism
Social Interaction
Social Process
Social Stratification Dissolution
Social Stratification Maintenance
Status Maintenance

SOCIAL STRATIFICATION MAINTENANCE
S-31-0779 1975 00012
BT Social Stratification Process
NT Caste Maintenance
Class Maintenance
Status Maintenance
RT Deference
Friendship
Ostracism
Social Interaction
Social Process
Social Stratification Dissolution
Social Stratification Formation

SOCIAL STRATIFICATION PROCESS
S-31-0770 1975 00029
BT Process
NT Social Stratification Dissolution
Social Stratification Formation
Social Stratification Maintenance
RT Ostracism
Selection Process
Social Distance Theory
Social Interaction
Social Process
Social Role Process
Structural Process

SOCIAL STRATIFICATION SYSTEM
S-37-0140 1975 00042
BT Social System
NT Caste Social System
Class Social System
Status Social System
RT Bicultural Society
Caste Society
Lower Class
Occupation Characteristics
Society Type Base

SOCIAL STRESS
S-06-0792 1975 00030
BT Social System Structural Characteristics
NT Ethnic Conflict
Racial Tension
Social Criticism
Social Deviance
Social Disorder
Social Instability
RT Atomistic Family
Endogenous System Stress
Social Inequality
Social Stability
Social Stratification Division
Stress Indicator

SOCIAL SYSTEM
S-37-0139 1975 00019
BT System Type
NT Social Stratification System
RT Analytic System Characteristics
Associational Process
Belief System
Cognitive System
Cultural History
Economic System
Education System
Functional Adaptation
Heterogeneous Society
Homeostatic Equilibrium
Homogeneous Society
Institutions
Kinship System
Macrosociology
Pattern Maintenance
Political System Type
Social Cleavage
Social Conditioning
Social Group
Social Law
Social Mores
Social Movement
Social Philosophy
Social Psychology
Social Stability
Social System Characteristics
Social System Model
Social Theory
Sociobiology
Value System

SOCIAL SYSTEM CHARACTERISTICS
S-06-0700 1975 00060
BT System Characteristics
NT Social System Environment Characteristics
Social System Normative Characteristics
Social System Structural Characteristics
RT Analytic System Characteristics
Change Characteristics
Economic System Characteristics
Elite Type
Macrosociology
Political System Characteristics
Social System
Social Theory
Sociological Analysis

SOCIAL SYSTEM ENVIRONMENT CHARACTERISTICS
S-06-0701 1975 00038
BT Social System Characteristics
NT Living Conditions
Rural Environment
Suburban Environment
Urban Environment
Working Conditions
RT Cultural Diversity
Environmental Studies
Social System Normative Characteristics
Social System Structural Characteristics

SOCIAL SYSTEM MODEL
S-24-0317 1975 00016
BT Social Science Model
RT Cybernetic Analysis
Development Model
Economic Development Model
Economic Growth Model
Growth Model
Hierarchical Model
Pluralist Model
Process Model
Social System
Social Theory

SOCIAL SYSTEM NORMATIVE CHARACTERISTICS
S-06-0707 1975 00039
BT Social System Characteristics
NT Social Goal
Social Injustice
Social Mores
Social Norms
Social Utility
RT Social Crisis
Social System Environment Characteristics
Social System Structural Characteristics
Value Analysis

SOCIAL SYSTEM STRUCTURAL CHARACTERISTICS
S-06-0723 1975 00075
BT Social System Characteristics
NT Equality
Inequality
Prestige Hierarchy
Social Mobility
Social Stability
Social Stratification Division
Social Stress
RT Marginal Man Analysis
Pluralistic Society
Political System Effectiveness
Political System Structural Characteristics
Social Cleavage
Social Crisis
Social Diversity
Social System Environment Characteristics
Social System Normative Characteristics
Society Type Base
Society Type Structure

SOCIAL THEORY
S-38-0581 1975 00062
BT Theory
NT Assimilation Theory
Field Theory
Riot Theory
Role Theory
Social Action Theory
Social Distance Theory
Social Integration Theory
Social Learning Theory
Socialization Theory
Weberian Theory
RT Anthropological Theory Characteristics
Community Cleavage Characteristics
Durkheimian Analysis
General System Theory
Hierarchical Authority
Historical Sociology
History Of Philosophy
History Of Science
Ideologies
Parsonsian Sociology
Political Theory
Powerlessness
Social Behavior
Social Cleavage Indicator
Social Diversity

Social Equality
Social Forecasting
Social Group
Social Identity
Social Law
Social Mores
Social Movement
Social Philosophy
Social Policy
Social System
Social System Characteristics
Social System Model
Society Type Base
Sociobiology
Sociolinguistics
Sociological Analysis
Sociology Discipline
Theory Construction

SOCIAL UNITY
S-06-0045 1975 00010
BT Social Solidarity
RT Class Solidarity
Communal Solidarity
Gemeinschaft

SOCIAL UTILITY
S-06-0721 1975 00015
BT Social System Normative Characteristics
NT Public Interest
RT Social Goal
Social Mores

SOCIAL VARIABLE
S-24-0452 1975 00007
BT Variable Substantive Content
NT Organization Variable
RT Cultural Variable
Economic Variable
Historical Variable
Institutional Variable
Political Variable
Psychological Variable
Time Variable

SOCIAL WELFARE POLICY
S-26-0409 1975 00062
BT Social Policy
NT Mental Health Policy
Old Age Assistance Policy
Poverty Policy
Social Security Policy
Welfare Policy
RT Community Service
Education Policy
Family Service
Housing Policy
Policy For Disadvantaged
Population Policy
Poverty Program Spending
Psychological Service
Social Resource Distribution Policy
Unemployment Insurance Policy

SOCIAL WORKER
S-32-0118 1979 00000
BT Professional Occupational Role
RT Anthropologist
Community Service
Psychologist
Social Psychologist
Urban Politics Studies

SOCIALIST
S-32-0281 1975 00015
BT System Politicist
NT Communist
Democrat Socialist
RT Socialist Democracy
Socialist Democratic Theory
Socialist Division Of Labor

SOCIALIST DEMOCRACY
S-16-0032 1975 00008
BT Democratic Government
RT Democrat Socialist
Democratic Regime
Evolutionary Socialism
Fabian Socialism
Saint Simonianism
Social Democracy
Social Democratic Political Party
Socialist
Socialist Democratic Theory
Socialist Government

SOCIALIST DEMOCRATIC THEORY
S-38-0100 1975 00003
BT Democratic Theory
RT Athenian Democratic Theory
Confederation Movement
Democrat Socialist
Economic Theory Of Democracy
General Will Democratic Theory
Guided Democracy Theory
Industrial Democracy
Jeffersonian Democratic Theory
Minority Rights Democratic Theory
Participatory Democratic Theory
Participatory Management
Populist Democratic Theory
Republic Theory
Social Democratic Political Party
Socialist
Socialist Democracy

SOCIALIST DIVISION OF LABOR
S-06-0279 1975 00000
BT Division Of Labor
RT International Division Of Labor
National Division Of Labor
Socialist

SOCIALIST ECONOMIC PLANNING
S-31-0646 1975 00008
BT Government Economic Planning
RT Communist Economic System
Democratic Economic Planning
Evolutionary Marxism
Five Year Economic Planning
Socialist Economic System
Socialist Economy

SOCIALIST ECONOMIC SYSTEM
S-37-0060 1975 00012
BT Economic System
RT Communist Economic System
Evolutionary Socialism
Mercantile Economic System
Mixed Economic System
Socialist Economic Planning
Socialist Economy
Socialist Government
Socialist Law
Worker Self Management

SOCIALIST ECONOMY
S-12-0040 1975 00017
BT Planned Economy
RT Autarchic Economy
Basic Industry Nationalization
Centrally Planned Economy
Collective Farm Economy
Collective Farming
Communist Economic System
Cooperative Farm Economy
Government Production Enterprise
Nationalized Economy
Socialist Economic Planning
Socialist Economic System
Socialist Government
State Farm Economy

SOCIALIST EDUCATION
S-13-0033 1975 00007
BT Political Education
RT Civic Education
Communist Education
Ideological Education

SOCIALIST GOVERNMENT
S-16-0087 1975 00018
BT Government Type
RT Constitutional Democracy
Democrat Socialist
Social Democracy
Social Democratic Political Party
Socialist Democracy
Socialist Economic System
Socialist Economy
Socialist Law
Socialist Legality
Socialist Political Party
Socialist Revolution
Socialist Theory

SOCIALIST HUMANISM
S-38-0244 1975 00002
BT Humanism
RT Christian Humanism
Democrat Socialist
Eurocommunism
Humanitarianism
Neomarxism
Saint Simonianism
Scientific Humanism
Worker Self Management

SOCIALIST LAW
S-21-0097 1975 00001
BT Law Type
NT Socialist Legality
RT Political Law
Socialist Economic System
Socialist Government
Socialist Law System
Socialist Realism

SOCIALIST LAW SYSTEM
S-37-0105 1975 00002
BT Law System
RT Civil Law System
Common Law System
International Law System
Natural Law System
Socialist Law
Socialist Legality
Socialist Realism

SOCIALIST LEGALITY
S-21-0098 1975 00000
BT Socialist Law
RT Natural Law
Socialist Government
Socialist Law System
Stalinism

SOCIALIST MARKET ECONOMY
S-12-0029 1979 00000
BT Market Economy
RT Agrarian Socialism
Capitalist Economy
Centrally Planned Economy
Collective Farm Economy
Cooperative Farm Economy
Developing Economy
Dual Economy
Imperialist Economy
Market System
Modernizing Economy
Planned Economy
Socialist Theory

SOCIALIST PARTY
1975-1979 00027

SOCIALIST POLITICAL PARTY
S-28-0023 1979 00000
BT Ideological Spectrum Political Party Type
RT Aprista Socialism
Bernsteinian Socialism
Class Based Political Party
Communist Political Party
Democratic Socialism
Evolutionary Marxism
Evolutionary Socialism
Fabian Socialism
Labor Political Party
Social Democracy
Social Democratic Political Party
Socialist Government
Socialist Theory

SOCIALIST REALISM
S-38-0320 1975 00006
SN Doctrine that requires expressions of art to act in the service of socialist goals and principles.
BT Communism
RT Aesthetics
Socialist Law
Socialist Law System

SOCIALIST REVOLUTION
S-08-0071 1975 00011
BT Political Revolution
NT Communist Revolution
Democratic Socialist Revolution
RT Agrarian Movement
Agrarian Socialism
Democratic Political Revolution
Internal War
National Political Revolution
Proletarian Socialist Movement
Revolutionary Change
Revolutionary Movement
Social Revolution
Socialist Government
Socialist Theory
Spontaneous Revolution
Technological Revolution
Thermidor

SOCIALIST THEORY
S-38-0288 1975 00027
BT Ideologies
NT Agrarian Socialism
Aprista Socialism
Christian Socialism
Democratic Socialism
Evolutionary Socialism
Guild Socialism
Marxism
Marxist Theory
Scientific Socialism
Utopian Socialism
RT Antifascism
Antiimperialism
Class Equality
Democratic Theory
Economic Equality
Economic Ideology
Eurocommunism
Income Equality
Marxist Economics
Marxist Political Thought
Modernizing Ideology
Nationalism
Nationalization Process
Nationalized Economy
Political Equality
Saint Simonianism
Social Equality
Socialist Government
Socialist Market Economy
Socialist Political Party
Socialist Revolution
Utopian Socialism
Working Class Voter

SOCIALIZATION
S-34-0001 1975 00036
NT Acculturation
Enculturation
Learning
Socialization Context
Socialization Type
RT Institution Building
Learning Theory
Logic
Personality Development
Personality Theory
Socialization Analysis
Socialization Theory
Socially Desirable Behavior Theory
Youth Culture

SOCIALIZATION ANALYSIS
S-09-0065 1975 00025
BT Contemporary Analytic Modes
RT Adaptive Behavior
Biographical Analysis
Identity Analysis
Linguistic Analysis
Political Socialization
Social Area Analysis
Socialization
Socialization Context
Socialization Theory
Sociological Analysis
Value Analysis

SOCIALIZATION CONTEXT
S-34-0016 1975 00019
BT Socialization
NT Group Socialization
Institutional Socialization
Professional Socialization
RT Acculturation
Enculturation
Ethnicity
Political Socialization
Socialization Analysis
Socialization Theory
Socialization Type

SOCIALIZATION THEORY
S-38-0592 1975 00029
BT Social Theory
RT Acculturation Theory
Assimilation Theory
Field Theory
Moral Learning
Reference Group Theory
Role Theory
Social Action Theory
Social Integration Theory
Social Learning Theory
Socialization
Socialization Analysis
Socialization Context

SOCIALIZATION TYPE
S-34-0039 1975 00001
BT Socialization
NT Ethical Socialization
Opinion Socialization
Perception Socialization
Political Socialization
Role Socialization
Social Conditioning
RT Acculturation
Adaptive Behavior
Americanization
Enculturation
Group Socialization
Institutional Socialization
Learning
Political Socialization
Professional Socialization
Socialization Context
Status
Value Analysis

SOCIALIZED MEDICINE SYSTEM
S-37-0065 1975 00003
BT Medical Care System
RT Government Regulation
Medical Care Policy
Medical Education

SOCIALLY DESIRABLE BEHAVIOR
S-06-0716 1975 00010
BT Social Mores
RT Social Norms
Socialization

SOCIETAL CONTRACT THEORY
S-38-0513 1975 00002
BT Social Contract Theory
RT Authority
Government Contract Theory
Lockean Contractualism
Social Organization Theory
Society Type
State Of Nature Theory

SOCIETY TYPE
S-35-0001 1975 00010
NT Achieving Society
Affluent Society
Meritocracy
Modernizing Society
Nonwestern Society
Primitive Society
Secular Society
Society Type Base
Society Type Structure
Traditional Society
Transitional Society
Western Society
RT Gesellschaft
Government Type
Institution Building
Rule Type
Societal Contract Theory

SOCIETY TYPE BASE
S-35-0009 1979 00000
BT Society Type
NT Bourgeois Society
Bureaucratic Society
Capitalist Society
Caste Society
Clan Society
Class Society
Classless Society
Feudal Society
Hunting And Fishing Society
Industrial Society
Mass Society
Nomadic Society
Peasant Society
Slave Society
Squatter Society
Tribal Society
Urban Society
RT Class Analysis
Class Social System
Economy Type
Social Stratification System
Social System Structural Characteristics
Social Theory
Status Social System

SOCIETY TYPE STRUCTURE
S-35-0031 1979 00000
BT Society Type
NT Closed Society
Heterogeneous Society
Homogeneous Society
Open Society
Pluralistic Society
RT Economy Type
Multicultural Society
Social System Structural Characteristics

SOCIOBIOLOGY
S-01-0194 1979 00000
BT Sociology Discipline
RT Applied Sociology
Bioethics
Biological Sciences
Eugenics
Social Pathology
Social System
Social Theory

SOCIOECONOMIC BACKGROUND
S-06-0208 1975 00119
BT Origin
NT Economic Background
Education Background
Social Background
RT Class Analysis
Class Origin
Education Background
Population Attribute
Socioeconomic Data

SOCIOECONOMIC DATA
S-18-0092 1975 00035
BT Social Statistics
RT Class Analysis
Morbidity Data
Public Opinion Survey
Real Income
Social Psychological Data
Socioeconomic Background

SOCIOLINGUISTICS
S-01-0138 1975 00038
BT Linguistics
RT Anthropological Linguistic Theory
Anthropology Discipline
Applied Linguistics
Behavioral Psychology
Bilingualism
Cultural Anthropology
Ethnolinguistics
Ethnology
Language Community
Linguistic Analysis
Oral History
Political Science Methodology Studies
Psycholinguistics
Psychology Discipline
Social Theory
Sociology Discipline
Structural Linguistics

SOCIOLOGICAL ANALYSIS
S-09-0066 1979 00000
BT Contemporary Analytic Modes
NT Durkheimian Analysis
Marginal Man Analysis
Parsonsian Analysis
Weberian Analysis
RT Anthropology Discipline
Behavior Analysis
Communication Analysis
Elite Analysis
Group Analysis
Historical Analysis
Ideal Type Analysis
Interaction Analysis
Leadership Analysis
Linguistic Analysis
Motivational Analysis
Pluralist Analysis
Policy Analysis
Political Style
Situational Analysis
Social System Characteristics
Social Theory
Socialization Analysis
Sociology Discipline
Spatial Analysis

SOCIOLOGIST
S-32-0119 1979 00000
BT Professional Occupational Role
RT Economist
Geographer
Historian
Policy Scientist
Political Scientist
Social Psychologist

SOCIOLOGY DISCIPLINE
S-01-0182 1975 00042
BT Academic Areas
NT Applied Sociology
Comparative Sociology
Criminology
Historical Sociology
Industrial Sociology
Macrosociology
Marxist Sociology
Parsonsian Sociology
Political Sociology
Rural Sociology
Social Pathology
Sociobiology
Sociology Of Art
Sociology Of Knowledge
Sociology Of Law
Sociology Of Religion
Sociology Of Science
Sociology Of The Professions
Sociology Of Work
Urban Sociology
RT Administrative Science
Analysis Of Play
Anthropology Discipline
Applied Sociology
Area Studies
Behavioral Science
Demographic Studies
East African Area Studies
Ecology Discipline
Econometrics
Economic History
Economics Discipline
Education Discipline
Ethnic Studies
Geography Discipline
Gerontology
Global Education
Group Politics
History Discipline
Ideographic Science
Information Science
International Economics
Labor History
Leisure Time Analysis
Linguistics
Middle East Area Studies
Middle Range Theory
Peace Studies
Philosophy Discipline
Political Science Discipline
Political Science Methodology Studies
Political Theory Studies
Psychology Discipline
Public Administration Studies
Social Cleavage
Social History
Social Law

Social Philosophy
Social Psychology
Social Theory
Sociolinguistics
Sociological Analysis
West African Area Studies
Womens Studies

SOCIOLOGY OF ART
S-01-0195 1979 00000
BT Sociology Discipline
RT Aesthetics
Arts Policy
Humanities Discipline
Knowledge Production
Sociology Of Knowledge
Sociology Of Law
Sociology Of Religion
Sociology Of Science
Sociology Of The Professions
Sociology Of Work
Visual Arts

SOCIOLOGY OF KNOWLEDGE
S-01-0196 1975 00149
BT Sociology Discipline
RT Applied Sociology
Behavioral Theory
Education Discipline
Historiography
History Discipline
History Of Philosophy
History Of Science
Information Acquisition
Information Utilization
Intellectual History
Knowledge Acquisition
Knowledge Production
Learning Psychology
Logic
Mannheim Ideology Explanation
Marxist Ideology Explanation
Mythology
Philosophy Discipline
Philosophy Of Science Studies
Political Philosophy Studies
Political Science Methodology Studies
Political Theory Studies
Problem Solving Behavior
Sociology Of Art
Sociology Of Religion
Sociology Of The Professions

SOCIOLOGY OF LAW
S-01-0197 1975 00022
BT Sociology Discipline
RT Administrative Law System
History Discipline
Jurisprudence
Law Formulation
Law Type
Legal Education
Legal Positivism
Legal Studies
Political Behavior Studies
Sociology Of Art
Sociology Of Religion

SOCIOLOGY OF RELIGION
S-01-0198 1979 00000
BT Sociology Discipline
RT Religious Affiliation
Religious Authority
Religious Community
Religious Culture
Religious Group
Religious History
Religious Movement
Sociology Of Art
Sociology Of Knowledge
Sociology Of Law
Sociology Of Science
Sociology Of The Professions
Sociology Of Work

SOCIOLOGY OF SCIENCE
S-01-0199 1979 00000
BT Sociology Discipline
RT Falsification
Natural Experiment
Scientific Authority
Scientific Elite
Scientific Research
Scientific Theory
Scientism
Scientist
Social Scientist
Sociology Of Art
Sociology Of Religion

SOCIOLOGY OF THE PROFESSIONS
S-01-0200 1979 00000
BT Sociology Discipline
RT Accreditation Process
Education Accreditation Process
Parsonsian Sociology
Professional Education
Professional Ethics
Professional Occupational Role
Professional Organization
Professional School
Social Pathology
Sociology Of Art
Sociology Of Knowledge
Sociology Of Religion
Sociology Of Work

SOCIOLOGY OF WORK
S-01-0201 1979 00000
BT Sociology Discipline
RT Sociology Of Art
Sociology Of Religion
Sociology Of The Professions

SOCIOMETRIC INDICATOR
S-24-0275 1975 00024
BT Social Indicator
RT Social Cleavage Indicator

SOCRATIC POLITICAL THOUGHT
S-38-0057 1979 00000
BT Classical Political Thought
RT Classical Period
Dialectic
Epicurean Thought
Equality Theory
Greek Civilization
Moral Freedom Theory
Moral Responsibility
Obedience
Obligation Theory
Order Theory
Philosophy Discipline
Political Philosophy Studies
Pythagorean Thought
Skeptic Thought
Stoic Thought

SOFTWARE
S-18-0060 1975 00001
BT Machine Readable Information
NT Information Retrieval Program
RT Computer Equipment
Computer Processing
Computer Program
Computer Programming
Computer Science
Computer Simulation
Machine Readable Data

SOIL BANK POLICY
S-26-0008 1975 00000
BT Agricultural Subsidization Policy
RT Agricultural Price Support Policy
Agricultural Production
Environmental Agency
Food Policy

SOIL SCIENCE
USE Agronomy

SOLAR ENERGY
S-31-0126 1979 00000
BT Natural Resource Exploitation
RT Advanced Technology
Coal Energy
Coal Industry
Electrical Industry
Energy Consumption
Energy Management
Energy Policy
Energy Use Policy
Gas Energy
Gas Industry
Geothermal Energy
Hydroelectric Energy
Natural Resource Policy
Nuclear Energy
Nuclear Energy Industry
Oil Energy
Oil Industry
Ore Industry
Technology
Tidal Energy
Wind Energy

SOLDIER
S-36-0225 1975 00012
BT Military Service Personnel
RT Army
Marine
Pilot
Sailor

SOLICITOR
S-36-0106 1975 00000
BT Court Attorney
RT Attorney General
Barrister
Defender
Defense Attorney
Prosecuting Attorney
Public Defender

SOUTH AFRICAN AREA STUDIES
S-01-0029 1979 00000
BT African Area Studies
RT Anthropology Discipline
Central African Area Studies
Cultural Anthropology
East African Area Studies
Economics Discipline
Geography Discipline

History Discipline
North African Area Studies
Political Science Discipline
South African Area Studies
West African Area Studies

SOUTH AMERICAN AREA STUDIES
USE Latin American Area Studies
Latin American Area Studies

SOUTH AMERICAN BLOC
USE Latin American Bloc

SOUTH ASIAN AREA STUDIES
S-01-0038 1975 00189
BT Asian Area Studies
RT Comparative Analysis
Comparative Political Studies
Comparative Sociology
Cultural Anthropology
Cultural History
East Asian Area Studies
Southeast Asian Area Studies

SOUTHEAST ASIAN AREA STUDIES
S-01-0039 1975 00211
BT Asian Area Studies
RT Comparative Analysis
Comparative Political Studies
Comparative Sociology
Cultural Anthropology
East Asian Area Studies
Eastern Political Thought
South Asian Area Studies

SOVEREIGN NATION
S-16-0128 1975 00003
BT Nation Type
RT Home Rule
National Sovereignty Theory
Nonaligned Nation
Sovereignty
Sovereignty Theory
Third World Nation

SOVEREIGNTY
S-16-0152 1975 00017
BT Government
NT Divided Sovereignty
Limited Sovereignty
Papal Sovereignty
Popular Sovereignty
Territory Sovereignty
RT Authority
Authority Structure
Basic Law
Centralized Authority
Government Type
Home Rule
International Law
League Of Nations
Liberation Movement
National Sovereignty Theory
Political Authority
Sovereign Nation
Sovereignty Theory
State Type

SOVEREIGNTY THEORY
S-38-0515 1975 00017
BT Political Philosophy Concept
RT Constitutional Structural Theory
General Will Theory
Hobbesian Analysis
Mandate Of Heaven Theory
National Sovereignty Theory
Power Type
Representation Theory
Sovereign Nation
Sovereignty
United Nations

SOVIET AND EAST EUROPEAN AREA STUDIES
S-01-0042 1975 00727
BT Area Studies
NT East European Area Studies
Russian Studies
Soviet Studies
RT Communist Empire
Communist Society
Communist Studies
Comparative Analysis
Comparative Literature Studies
Comparative Political Studies
Comparative Sociology
Cultural Anthropology
Cultural History
Eastern Orthodox Thought
European Integration Theory
Marxist Sociology
Political Science Discipline
West European Area Studies

SOVIET STUDIES
S-01-0045 1979 00000
BT Soviet And East European Area Studies
RT Bolshevik Political Party
Communist Empire
Communist Studies
Comparative Analysis
Comparative Political Studies
Comparative Sociology
Cultural Anthropology
Cultural History
East European Area Studies
European Integration Theory
Marxism
Marxism Leninism
Marxist Revolution Theory
Marxist Sociology
Political Science Discipline
Revolution
Revolution Theory
Revolutionary Movement
Revolutionary Political Party
Russian Studies

SPACE EXPLORATION POLICY
S-26-0231 1975 00006
BT Space Policy
RT Aerospace Industry
Space Use Policy

SPACE POLICY
S-26-0230 1975 00005
BT Environment Policy
NT Space Exploration Policy
Space Use Policy
Waste Treatment Policy
RT Natural Resource Policy
Pollution Policy

SPACE USE POLICY
S-26-0232 1975 00011
BT Space Policy
RT Space Exploration Policy

SPATIAL ANALYSIS
S-09-0071 1975 00049
BT Contemporary Analytic Modes
RT Ecological Analysis
Geography Discipline
Geopolitics
Land Use Policy
Public Policy Analysis
Social Area Analysis
Sociological Analysis
Spatial Model
Statistical Analysis
Structural Functional Analysis
Urban Geography

SPATIAL MODEL
S-24-0318 1975 00039
BT Social Science Model
RT Geography Discipline
Geopolitics
Spatial Analysis
Spatial Voting Analysis
Statistical Analysis

SPATIAL VOTING ANALYSIS
S-09-0078 1975 00002
BT Voting Behavior Analysis
RT Roll Call Analysis
Spatial Model

SPECIAL ELECTION
S-29-0088 1975 00001
BT Election Type
NT By Election
RT Contested Election
Runoff Election
Voting

SPECIALIST
USE Professional Occupational Role

SPECIALIZATION PROCESS
S-31-0833 1979 00000
BT Structural Process
NT Over Specialization
RT Bureaucratic Hierarchy
Bureaucratic Theory
Hierarchical Integration
Professional Occupational Role
Social Integration
Social Role Process

SPECIFIC SYSTEM SUPPORT
1975-1979 00049
USE Specific System Supports

SPECIFIC SYSTEM SUPPORTS
S-06-0595 1979 00000
UF Specific System Support
BT System Supports
RT Diffuse System Supports
Modern Political Culture
System Boundary
System Capacity
System Change
System Integration
System Maintenance
System Outputs

SPECTRUM POLITICIST
S-32-0255 1975 00000
SN One whose political stance and activism can be identified on the existing political continuum in a specific country.
BT Politicist
NT Centrist
Conservative

Extremist
Ideologue
Leftist
Liberal
Political Neutralist
Political Radical
Reactionary
Rightist
RT Rightist
System Politicist

SPECULATOR
S-32-0078 1975 00002
BT Commercial Occupation
RT Businessman
Financier
Financing
Investor

SPEECH
S-06-0414 1979 00000
BT Language Characteristics
RT Grammar
Language Learning
Semantics
Stylistics
Vocabulary

SPEECHES
S-18-0078 1975 00005
BT Information Sources
RT Broadcasting
Journal
State Of The Union

SPENDING
S-31-0412 1975 00011
BT Economic Resource Allocation
NT Private Spending
Public Spending
RT Capital Flow
Capital Formation
Conspicuous Consumption
Consumption Process
Economic Resource Allocation
Financing
Investment
Private Saving
Public Saving
Saving

SPHERE OF INFLUENCE
S-06-0680 1975 00010
BT International Political System Characteristics
RT Balance Of Power
Balance Of Terror
Bilateral Treaty
East West Detente
Regional Security

SPLINTER PARTY
1975-1979 00000

SPLINTER POLITICAL PARTY
S-28-0062 1979 00000
BT Structure Specific Political Party Type
RT Elite Political Party
Minority Political Party

SPLIT TICKET VOTING
S-29-0146 1975 00004
BT Voting
RT Political Party Identification

SPOILS POLITICS
S-29-0233 1975 00000
BT Politics
RT Patronage Bureaucracy
Patronage Policy
Political Appointee
Political Patron
Power Politics
Spoils System
Symbolic Politics

SPOILS SYSTEM
S-10-0069 1975 00002
BT Political Corruption
RT Economic Bribery
Patronage Bureaucracy
Patronage Policy
Political Bribery
Political Fund Misuse
Political Graft
Political Influence
Spoils Politics

SPONTANEOUS REVOLUTION
S-08-0081 1975 00000
BT Revolution
RT Black Revolution
Chinese Cultural Revolution
Communist Revolution
Counterrevolution
Cultural Revolution
Democratic Political Revolution
Democratic Socialist Revolution
Ecological Revolution
Industrial Revolution
Internal War
Maoism
National Political Revolution
Political Revolution
Political Violence
Proletarian Revolution
Psychological Aggression
Racial Revolution
Social Revolution
Socialist Revolution
Struggle
Student Rebellion
Technological Revolution

SPORTS
S-31-0783 1979 00000
BT Process
NT Amateur Sports
Professional Sports
RT Amateur Athlete
Analysis Of Play
Athlete
Professional Athlete

SPYING
S-18-0101 1979 00000
BT Surveillance
RT Confidential Information
Defense Agency
Foreign Affairs Agency
Government Secrecy Policy
Information Agency
Intelligence Censorship
Military Intelligence Agency
Secret Diplomacy

SQUATTER COMMUNITY
S-07-0049 1979 00000
BT Community Type
RT Communal Community
Community Composition
Community Culture
Community Homogeneity
Cooperative Community
Ghetto Community
Inner City
Marginal Man Analysis
Peasant Society
Political Community
Poverty
Reservation
Urban Migration Pattern

SQUATTER SOCIETY
S-35-0028 1979 00000
BT Society Type Base
RT Class Society
Land Ownership Pattern
Latin American Area Studies
Peasant Society
Poverty
Urban Ghetto Community

STABILITY INDEX
S-24-0248 1975 00003
BT Scale Type
RT Alienation Scale
Anomie Scale
Cynicism Scale
Development Index
Liberalism Conservatism Scale
Political Resource Indicator
Satisfaction Scale
Social Change Index
Social Distance Scale
Social Frustration Scale
Support Opposition Scale
Urbanization Index
Voting Duty Scale

STABLE DEMOCRACY
S-16-0033 1975 00004
BT Democratic Government
RT Constitutional Democracy
Developed Democracy

STABLE POPULATION
S-06-0217 1975 00002
BT Population Attribute
RT Environmental Agency
Population Density
Population Movement
Population Policy

STALINISM
S-38-0331 1975 00019
BT Marxism
RT Bolshevism
Castroism
Communism
Cult Of Personality
Destalinization Process
Evolutionary Marxism
Hegelian Marxism
Leninism
Maoism
Maoist
Maoist Political Party
Maoist Revolutionary
Marxism Leninism

Marxist Revisionism
Polycentrism
Socialist Legality
Stalinist
Titoism
Trotskyism
Trotskyite Political Party

STALINIST
S-32-0284 1975 00000
BT Communist
RT Bolshevism
Castroism
Communism
Dictator
Maoist
Stalinism
Totalitarian Political System

STALINIZATION
1975-1979 00002

STANDARD OF LIVING
S-31-0443 1975 00011
BT National Production
RT Gross National Product
Income Measure
Living Conditions
Marxist Immiseration Theory
Per Capita Gross National Product
Quality Of Life

STANDING ARMY
S-33-0058 1975 00001
BT Army Organization
RT Mass Militia Army
Military Budget
Military Planning
Military Policy
National Guard
Regular Army
Strategic Studies
Strategic Theory

STANDING COMMITTEE
1975-1979 00000

STANDING CONGRESSIONAL COMMITTEE
S-19-0266 1979 00000
BT Congressional Committee
NT Joint Standing Congressional Committee
RT Ad Hoc Congressional Committee
Congressional Seniority System
Congressional Subcommittee
Joint Congressional Committee
Senate House Conference Committee

STAR CHAMBER PROCEEDING
S-31-0527 1975 00000
BT Secret Trial
RT State Political Division
Trial Oral Argument

STARE DECISIS
S-31-0549 1975 00002
SN Common law principle which holds that previous judicial decisions should serve as guides and precedents for later cases involving similar situations.
BT Legal Precedent
RT Customary Law
Judge Made Law
Judicial Discretion
Judicial Review
Right To Due Process

STARVATION
S-31-0115 1979 00000
BT Food Scarcity
RT Agricultural Development
Hunger
Malnutrition
Resource Allocation
Resource Distribution

STATE
S-24-0364 1975 00000
BT Subnational Political Division
RT State Agreement Type
State Constitution
State Government
State Judicial System
State Legislature
State Political Division
State Politics
State Power

STATE AGREEMENT DECLARATION
S-02-0057 1975 00003
BT Agreement Type
NT Mutual Support Declaration
Unilateral Declaration
RT Alliance
Compact
Extranational Bloc
State Agreement Form
State Agreement Type

STATE AGREEMENT FORM
S-02-0060 1975 00001
BT Agreement Type
NT Bilateral State Agreement
Bilateral Treaty
Executive Agreement
Multilateral State Agreement
Multilateral Treaty
RT Alliance
State Agreement Declaration
State Agreement Type
World Alliance

STATE AGREEMENT TYPE
S-02-0066 1975 00002
BT Agreement Type
NT Arms Control Agreement
Arms Sales
Commercial Agreement
Cultural Agreement
Disarmament Agreement
Economic Agreement
Education Agreement
Friendship Agreement
Military Agreement
Monetary Agreement
Neutrality Agreement
Nonaggression Agreement
Nuclear Nonproliferation Agreement
Payment Agreement
Peace Proposal
Peace Treaty
Test Ban Agreement
Trade Agreement
RT Alliance
Compact
Economic Dependency
Executive Agreement
Foreign Policy Making
Multilateral State Agreement
Multilateral Treaty
State
State Agreement Declaration
State Agreement Form
World Alliance

STATE ASSEMBLY
S-19-0285 1975 00003
BT State Legislature
RT Budget Proposing
Provincial Parliament
State House Of Representatives
State Senate

STATE CAPITALISM
S-37-0019 1975 00003
BT Capitalism
RT Government Economic Management

STATE CHIEF EXECUTIVE CANDIDATE
S-32-0242 1975 00000
BT Subnational Chief Executive Candidate
NT Gubernatorial Candidate
RT Local Chief Executive Candidate

STATE CONSTITUTION
S-21-0014 1975 00002
BT Constitution
RT City State Relations
Constitutional Law
Democratic Constitution
Home Rule Law
National Constitution
State
Unwritten Constitution
Written Constitution

STATE CONSTITUTIONAL CONVENTION
S-19-0106 1975 00005
BT Constitutional Convention
RT Constitutional Convention
Constitutional Development
Constitutional Law
Constitutional Law System
Home Rule Law
Written Constitution

STATE CONTROLLED TELEVISION
S-17-0015 1979 00000
BT Television Industry
RT Cable Television
Commercial Television
Government Censorship Agency
Government Enterprise
Public Broadcasting Industry
Public Policy Analysis
Public Television
State Power
Telecommunications Industry

STATE ECONOMIC PLANNING
S-31-0653 1975 00006
BT Subnational Economic Planning
RT Local Economic Planning

STATE FARM ECONOMY
S-12-0009 1975 00002
BT Farm Economy
RT Collective Farm Economy
Communist Economic System
Cooperative Farm Economy
Corporate Farm Economy
Family Farm Economy
Labor Intensive Economy
Planned Economy
Plantation Economy
Single Group Farm Economy

Socialist Economy

STATE GOVERNMENT
S-16-0111 1975 00098
BT Subnational Government
RT Borough Government
City State Relations
Federal State Relations
Federated City
Lieutenant Governor
Provincial Government
State

STATE GOVERNOR
S-36-0080 1975 00006
BT Governor
NT Lieutenant Governor
RT Lieutenant Governor
Provincial Government
Subnational Chief Executive Candidate
Subnational Chief Executive Election
Subnational Chief Government Executive
Subnational Election

STATE HOUSE OF REPRESENTATIVES
S-19-0286 1975 00006
BT State Legislature
RT Cabinet Reorganization
Provincial Parliament
State Assembly

STATE INCOME TAXATION
S-26-0151 1975 00000
BT Subnational Income Taxation
RT Progressive Taxation
State Planning Policy
State Politics
State Power
Subnational Income Taxation
Taxation Policy

STATE INDUSTRY
1975-1979 00000

STATE JUDICIAL CANDIDATE
S-32-0246 1975 00001
BT Subnational Judicial Candidate
RT Local Judicial Candidate
State Judicial System

STATE JUDICIAL SYSTEM
S-37-0087 1975 00009
BT Subnational Judicial System
RT Local Judicial System
State
State Judicial Candidate

STATE LEGISLATIVE CANDIDATE
S-32-0249 1979 00000
UF State Legislator Cadidate
BT Subnational Legislative Candidate
RT Local Legislative Candidate
State Legislative Election
State Legislative Leader
State Legislative Member
State Politics

STATE LEGISLATIVE COMMITTEE CHAIRPERSON
S-36-0153 1975 00000
BT Subnational Legislative Committee Chairperson
RT Local Legislative Committee Chairperson

STATE LEGISLATIVE ELECTION
S-29-0103 1975 00003
BT Subnational Legislative Election
RT Local Legislative Member
State Legislative Candidate
State Legislative Leader
State Legislative Member
State Senator

STATE LEGISLATIVE LEADER
S-36-0186 1975 00001
BT Subnational Legislative Leader
RT Local Legislative Leader
State Legislative Candidate
State Legislative Election
State Legislative Member
State Political Party
State Senator

STATE LEGISLATIVE MEMBER
S-36-0199 1975 00014
BT Subnational Legislative Member
NT State Senator
RT Local Legislative Member
State Legislative Candidate
State Legislative Election
State Legislative Leader
State Senator

STATE LEGISLATIVE SPEAKER
S-36-0169 1975 00001
BT Subnational Legislative Speaker
RT Local Legislative Speaker
State Legislature
State Political Party

STATE LEGISLATIVE STAFF
S-36-0211 1975 00004
BT Subnational Legislative Staff
RT Government Employee
Local Legislative Staff
State Legislature

STATE LEGISLATIVE WHIP
S-36-0176 1975 00000
BT Subnational Legislative Whip
RT Local Legislative Whip
State Legislature
State Political Division
State Political Party
State Politics

STATE LEGISLATOR CADIDATE
USE State Legislative Candidate

STATE LEGISLATOR CANDIDATE
1975-1979 00001

STATE LEGISLATURE
S-19-0284 1975 00041
BT Subnational Legislature
NT State Assembly
State House Of Representatives
State Senate
RT Local Legislature
Lower House Member
Provincial Parliament
Provincial Political Party
State
State Legislative Speaker
State Legislative Staff
State Legislative Whip
State Political Division
State Political Party
State Politics
State Senator

STATE OF NATURE THEORY
S-38-0514 1975 00004
BT Social Contract Theory
RT Government Contract Theory
Hobbesian Absolutism
Hobbesian Analysis
Human Condition Theory
Human Nature Theory
Lockean Contractualism
Rousseauian Analysis
Societal Contract Theory

STATE OF THE UNION
S-26-0250 1979 00000
BT Inaugural Address
RT Congressional Executive Relations
National Goal
National Priority
Presidential Power
Proclamation
Speeches

STATE PARTY
1975-1979 00008

STATE PLANNER
S-32-0145 1975 00002
BT Subnational Planner
RT Administrative Planning
Local Planner
Regional Planner
State Planning Policy
State Policy Planning

STATE PLANNING POLICY
S-26-0354 1975 00003
BT Subnational Planning Policy
RT Local Planning Policy
National Planning Policy
Needs Assessment
Regional Planning Policy
State Income Taxation
State Planner
State Policy Planning
Subnational Income Taxation

STATE POLICE
S-19-0311 1975 00001
BT Subnational Police
RT Government Employee
Local Police
Police Community Relations
State Police Official

STATE POLICE OFFICIAL
S-36-0145 1975 00000
BT Subnational Police Official
RT State Police

STATE POLICY PLANNING
S-31-0668 1975 00019
BT Subnational Policy Planning
RT City Policy Planning
Local Policy Planning
Rural Policy Planning
State Planner
State Planning Policy
Urban Design
Urban Policy Planning

STATE POLITICAL DIVISION
S-24-0365 1975 00000
BT Subnational Political Division
NT Borough
County
Legislative District
Township

RT Local Political Division
Local Politics
Province
Star Chamber Proceeding
State
State Legislative Whip
State Legislature
State Political Party
State Politics

STATE POLITICAL PARTY
S-28-0056 1979 00000
BT Subnational Political Party
RT Local Political Party
State Legislative Leader
State Legislative Speaker
State Legislative Whip
State Legislature
State Political Division
Subnational Decision Making Process
Subnational Election
Subnational Election Campaign
Subnational Government

STATE POLITICS
S-29-0241 1975 00021
BT Subnational Politics
RT Lieutenant Governor
State
State Income Taxation
State Legislative Candidate
State Legislative Whip
State Legislature
State Political Division
Subnational Income Taxation

STATE POWER
S-30-0020 1975 00009
BT Power Type
RT Concentrated Power
Emergency Power
Formal Power
Presidential Power
State
State Controlled Television
State Income Taxation
Subnational Income Taxation

STATE RIGHTS DOCTRINE
S-38-0454 1975 00004
BT Constitutional Structural Theory
RT Check And Balance Theory
Confederal Government
Conflict Federalism
Interposition Doctrine
Jeffersonian Thought
New Federalism
Separation Of Power Theory

STATE SENATE
S-19-0287 1975 00002
BT State Legislature
RT Provincial Parliament
State Assembly

STATE SENATOR
S-36-0200 1975 00001
BT State Legislative Member
RT State Legislative Election
State Legislative Leader
State Legislative Member
State Legislature
Subnational Legislative Election
Subnational Legislative Leader
Subnational Legislative Member

STATE SUPPORTED COLLEGE
S-19-0207 1975 00001
BT College
RT College
Junior College
Private College
State Supported Higher Education
University

STATE SUPPORTED HIGHER EDUCATION
S-13-0017 1975 00004
BT Higher Education
RT Compulsory Education
Graduate Education
Mass Education
Private Higher Education
Professional Education
State Supported College
State Supported University
Technical Education
Traditional Education
University Education

STATE SUPPORTED UNIVERSITY
S-19-0217 1975 00002
BT Public University
RT Graduate School
Professional School
State Supported Higher Education

STATE SUPREME COURT
S-19-0141 1975 00007
BT Subnational Supreme Court
RT National Supreme Court

STATE TAXATION
S-26-0169 1975 00004
BT Subnational Taxation
RT Federal Taxation
Local Taxation
Municipal Taxation
National Taxation
Regressive Taxation

STATE TYPE
S-16-0158 1975 00010
BT Government
NT Aggressor State
Border State
City State
Client State
Corporate State
Feudal State
Garrison State
Military State
Multiethnic State
Nation State
Peoples Democratic State
Police State
Puppet State
Warfare State
Welfare State
RT Aggressor State
Government Type
Nation
Nation Type
Political Regime
Regime Type
Renaissance State Theory
Royalist
Royalist State Theory
Rule Type
Sovereignty

STATECRAFT THEORY
S-38-0157 1975 00001
BT Nation State Explanatory Theory
RT Absolute Monarch
Aristotelian Thought
Foreign Policy
Machiavellian Thought
Medieval State Theory

STATELESS PERSON
S-36-0027 1975 00000
UF Statelessness
BT Citizenship Status
RT Alien
Alienation Process
Exile
Expatriate
Immigrant
Repatriate

STATELESSNESS
USE Stateless Person

STATIC MODEL
S-24-0319 1975 00005
BT Social Science Model
RT Consensus Model
Structural Model

STATISTICAL ANALYSIS
S-24-0032 1975 00054
BT Analysis Methodology
NT Bivariate Analysis
Multivariate Analysis
Probability Estimation
Statistical Significance Test
Statistics Type
Univariate Analysis
RT Aggregate Data Analysis
Aggregate Data Statistics
Analytic Process
Bias
Demographic Indicator
Econometrics
Economic Model
Economic Statistics
Hermeneutical Analysis
Historical Analysis
Mathematical Analysis
PERT Analysis
Political Geography
Probability Model
Probability Sampling
Regression Analysis
Social Indicator
Spatial Analysis
Spatial Model
Statistical Data
Statistical Table
Statistics Discipline
Theory Of Causality
Voting Data

STATISTICAL DATA
S-18-0079 1975 00010
BT Information Sources
NT Aggregate Data Statistics
Economic Statistics
Field Data
Political Statistics
Social Statistics
Statistical Table
Survey Data
Test Results

RT Aggregate Data Analysis
Aggregate Data Selection
Autocorrelation
Data Archives
Documentation Service
Government Information Service
Information Retrieval Program
Legislative Information Service
Machine Readable Data
Machine Readable Information
Measurement
Measurement Level
Measurement Problem
Measures
Multiple Indicator
Private Information Service
Reliability Measurement
Scale Construction Methodology
Statistical Analysis
Statistical Inference
Statistics Discipline
Street Block
Threat Indicator
University Information Service

STATISTICAL INFERENCE
S-24-0074 1975 00013
BT Population Estimation
RT Central Tendency Measure
Parameter Estimation
Statistical Data
Statistical Significance Test
Statistics Discipline
Theory Of Causality
Unbiased Estimation

STATISTICAL SIGNIFICANCE TEST
S-24-0054 1975 00007
BT Statistical Analysis
NT Binomial Test
Chi Square Test
F Ratio
Interval Significance Test
Mann Whitney U Test
Nominal Significance Test
Ordinal Significance Test
Wald Wolfowitz Runs Test
Wilcoxian T Test
RT Analysis Of Variance
Bivariate Analysis
Multivariate Analysis
Probability Estimation
Statistical Inference
Statistics Type
Univariate Analysis

STATISTICAL TABLE
S-18-0094 1975 00003
BT Statistical Data
RT Aggregate Data Statistics
Economic Statistics
Ethnographic Data
Morbidity Data
Social Indicator
Social Psychological Data
Social Statistics
Statistical Analysis
Statistics Type
Vital Statistics Data

STATISTICS DISCIPLINE
S-01-0203 1979 00000
BT Academic Areas
RT Data Presentation Methodology
Descriptive Statistics
Inferential Statistics
Mathematical Analysis
Measurement Procedure
Measures
Quantitative History
Reliability Measurement
Statistical Analysis
Statistical Data
Statistical Inference
Theoretical Range

STATISTICS TYPE
S-24-0064 1975 00002
BT Statistical Analysis
NT Descriptive Statistics
Inferential Statistics
Nonparametric Statistics
Parametric Statistics
RT Aggregate Data Statistics
Analysis Of Variance
Bivariate Analysis
Multivariate Analysis
Probability Estimation
Statistical Significance Test
Statistical Table

STATUS
S-36-0001 1975 00028
NT Administrative Personnel
Citizenship Status
Criminal
Expert
Government Official
Marital Status
Political Party Official
Prisoner
Suborganization Official
RT Socialization Type
Theory

STATUS DISSOLUTION
S-31-0774 1975 00004
BT Social Stratification Dissolution
RT Caste Dissolution
Class Dissolution
Status Social System

STATUS EQUALITY
S-06-0733 1979 00000
BT Social Equality
RT Achieved Status
Ascribed Status
Class Equality
Economic Egalitarianism
Economic Equality
Education Equality
Egalitarianism
Political Equality
Racial Equality
Sex Equality
Status Social System
Status Stratification Division

STATUS FORMATION
S-31-0778 1975 00012
BT Social Stratification Formation
RT Caste Formation
Class Formation
Status Social System

STATUS INEQUALITY
S-06-0743 1975 00033
BT Social Inequality
RT Class Inequality
Economic Inequality
Economic Injustice
Education Inequality
Education Injustice
Income Inequality
Political Injustice
Racial Inequality
Racial Injustice
Sex Inequality
Sexual Injustice
Social Injustice

STATUS MAINTENANCE
S-31-0782 1975 00014
BT Social Stratification Maintenance
RT Caste Maintenance
Class Maintenance
Social Distance Theory
Social Process
Social Stratification Formation
Status Quo Conservatism
Status Social System

STATUS MOBILITY
S-06-0747 1975 00039
BT Social Mobility
NT Horizontal Mobility
Intergenerational Mobility
Intragenerational Mobility
Vertical Mobility
RT Ambition
Class Stratification Division
Horizontal Mobility
Social Prestige
Status Social System
Status Stratification Division
Vertical Mobility

STATUS QUO CONSERVATISM
S-38-0201 1979 00000
BT Conservatism
RT Bureaucratic Conservatism
Burkean Conservatism
Christian Conservatism
Conservative Political Party
Neoconservatism
Objectivist Political Thought
Public Order Maintenance
Reactionary Conservatism
Social Stability
Status Maintenance

STATUS SOCIAL SYSTEM
S-37-0145 1975 00029
BT Social Stratification System
NT Achieved Status System
Ascribed Status System
RT Caste Social System
Social Distance Theory
Society Type Base
Status Dissolution
Status Equality
Status Formation
Status Maintenance
Status Mobility
Status Stratification Division

STATUS STRATIFICATION DIVISION
S-06-0786 1975 00037
BT Social Stratification Division
NT Achieved Status
Ascribed Status
Objectively Derived Status
Subjectively Derived Status
RT Caste Stratification Division
Class Stratification Division
Objectively Derived Status
Prestige Hierarchy
Social Prestige
Status Equality
Status Mobility
Status Social System
Stratified Sampling
Subjectively Derived Status

STATUTE OF LIMITATIONS
S-15-0065 1975 00001
BT Defendants Rights
RT Bill Of Attainder
Double Jeopardy
Habeas Corpus
Right Against Cruel And Unusual Punishment
Right To Due Process
Right To Equal Protection
Right To Trial

STATUTORY LAW
S-21-0099 1975 00019
BT Law Type
NT Codified Law
RT Civil Code
Civil Law
Constitution
Constitution Amendment Process
Constitutional Law
Contract Law
Judge Made Law
Written Constitution

STEEL INDUSTRY
S-17-0054 1975 00005
BT Heavy Industry
RT Construction Industry
Extractive Industry
Metallurgical Industry

STEM FAMILY
S-20-0016 1975 00002
BT Family Type
RT Atomistic Family
Nuclear Family

STEREOTYPING
S-34-0053 1975 00054
BT Social Conditioning
RT Attribution Theory
Cognitive Theory
Ideologies
Perception Measurement
Political Conditioning

STOCHASTIC MODEL
S-24-0284 1975 00029
BT Mathematical Model
RT Differential Equation Model
Economic Mathematical Model

STOCK MARKET
S-19-0196 1975 00004
BT International Market
RT Black Market
Commodity Market
Differentiated Market
Financial Market
Free Market
World Market

STOIC NATURAL LAW THEORY
S-38-0495 1975 00000
BT Natural Law Conventionalism Theory
RT Classical Natural Right Doctrine
Great Chain Of Being Doctrine
Medieval Natural Law Theory
Right Reason Doctrine
Roman Natural Law Theory
Scientific Natural Law Theory

STOIC POLITICAL THOUGHT
1975-1979 00002

STOIC THOUGHT
S-38-0058 1979 00000
BT Classical Political Thought
RT Aristotelian Thought
Cynic Thought
Epicurean Thought
Neoplatonic Political Thought
Platonic Political Thought
Presocratic Political Thought
Skeptic Thought
Socratic Political Thought

STRAIGHT PARTY VOTER
S-32-0326 1975 00004
BT Political Party Voter
RT Partisan Image Voter
Straight Ticket Voting

STRAIGHT TICKET VOTING
S-29-0147 1975 00006
BT Voting
RT Political Party Ticket Voting
Straight Party Voter

STRATEGIC ADVANTAGE
S-06-0469 1975 00028
BT Military Characteristics
RT Antiballistic Missile
Arms Control Policy
Military Size
Nuclear Capability
Nuclear Strike Policy
Retaliatory Capability
Strategic Theory

STRATEGIC ARMS LIMITATION
S-06-0678 1975 00049
BT Peaceful Coexistence
RT Arms Control Agency
Arms Control Agreement
Arms Control Policy
Arms Control Treaty
Arms Inspection Policy
Arms Reduction Policy
Balanced Force Reduction Policy
Disarmament
Disarmament Agreement
MARV
MIRV
Nuclear Deterrence Policy
Nuclear Nonproliferation Agreement
Nuclear Nonproliferation Treaty
Nuclear Parity
Nuclear Weapon Nonproliferation Policy
Strategic Studies

STRATEGIC ARMS RACE
S-06-0663 1975 00017
BT Arms Race
RT Antiballistic Missile
Arms Control Agency
Arms Inspection Policy
Arms Reduction Policy
Balanced Force Reduction Policy
Military Alliance
Mutual Deterrence Policy
Nuclear Arms Race
Nuclear Strategy
Nuclear Weapon Proliferation
Strategic Studies
Strategic Theory

STRATEGIC ARMS REDUCTION POLICY
S-26-0056 1975 00022
BT Arms Reduction Policy
RT Arms Control Agency
Arms Control Agreement
Arms Control Policy
Arms Control Treaty
Arms Inspection Policy
Arms Race
Balance Of Terror
Balanced Force Reduction Policy
Disarmament Agreement
Disarmament Treaty
International Peace
Nuclear Arms Race
Nuclear Disarmament Policy
Nuclear Weapon Proliferation

STRATEGIC POLICY
S-26-0076 1979 00000
BT Defense Policy
RT Defense Policy
Foreign Policy
Military Policy
Strategic Studies
Strategic Theory
War Policy

STRATEGIC STUDIES
S-01-0204 1975 00109
BT Academic Areas
RT Arms Industry
Arms Verification Policy
Civil Defense Policy
Counterforce Theory
Damage Limiting Strategy
Defense Policy
Defense System
Global War Policy
International Conflict
International Power Theory
International Regional Conflict
International Relations Studies
Military Agreement
Military Budget
Military History
Military Science
Military Size
National Security Forces
Naval Power
Nuclear Stockpiling
Offensive Capability
Peace Studies
Policy Science Studies
Political Geography
Political Science Discipline

Political Science Methodology Studies
Retaliatory Capability
Second Strike Nuclear Weapon
Security Forces
Standing Army
Strategic Arms Limitation
Strategic Arms Race
Strategic Policy
Strategic Theory

STRATEGIC THEORY
S-38-0527 1975 00088
BT Political Theory
NT Counterforce Theory
RT Global War Policy
Standing Army
Strategic Advantage
Strategic Arms Race
Strategic Policy
Strategic Studies
Strategic Weapon

STRATEGIC WEAPON
S-33-0039 1975 00023
BT Weapon
RT Biological Weapon
Bomb
Chemical Weapon
Conventional Weapon
Defensive Weapon
Deterrent Weapon
MARV
MIRV
Missile
Nuclear Weapon
Second Strike Nuclear Weapon
Strategic Theory
Tactical Weapon
Unconventional Weapon

STRATIFIED SAMPLING
S-24-0125 1975 00001
SN Sample design in which population is divided into relevant groups and individuals from these groups are sampled.
BT Probability Sampling
RT Cluster Sampling
Simple Random Sampling
Status Stratification Division
Systematic Sampling

STRAUSSIAN ANALYSIS
1975-1979 00000
USE Straussian Thought

STRAUSSIAN THOUGHT
S-38-0078 1979 00000
SN Idealistic method of interpreting political philosophy texts and history of political philosophy associated with Leo Strauss.
UF Straussian Analysis
BT Contemporary Political Thought
RT Moral Theory
Traditional Authority

STREET BLOCK
S-24-0361 1975 00000
BT City Unit
RT Census Tract
City Unit
Statistical Data
Voting Data

STREET CRIME
S-10-0050 1975 00001
BT Individual Crime
RT Assault
Juvenile Crime
Juvenile Delinquency
Morals Offense
Property Crime
Robbery
Vandalism
Violent Crime

STRESS INDICATOR
S-24-0276 1975 00005
BT Social Indicator
RT Social Cleavage Indicator
Social Psychology
Social Stress

STRICT CONSTRUCTIONISM
S-38-0446 1975 00003
BT Constitutional Interpretation Theory
RT Broad Constructionism
Constitutional Realism
Judicial Restraint Theory
Legalism

STRIKE BREAKING
S-08-0036 1975 00002
BT Labor Conflict
RT Economic Demonstration
Jurisdiction Strike
Labor Management Relations Policy
Labor Strike
Lockout
Sit Down Strike
Wildcat Strike

STRONG MAYOR GOVERNMENT
S-16-0106 1975 00002
BT City Government
RT Commission Government
Council Manager Government
Local Decision Making
Local Legislature
Weak Mayor Government

STRONG POLITICAL PARTY IDENTIFIER
S-32-0172 1975 00003
BT Political Party Supporter
RT Campaign Contributor
Campaign Worker
Political Party Loyalist
Political Party Orientation
Weak Political Party Identifier

STRUCTURAL ADAPTATION
S-06-0582 1975 00013
BT System Adaptation
RT Adaptive Behavior
Communication Feedback
Learning Feedback
Pattern Maintenance
Structural Differentiated System
Structural Requisites
System Analysis

STRUCTURAL DIFFERENTIATED SYSTEM
S-37-0009 1975 00007
BT Differentiated System
RT Functional Differentiated System
Structural Adaptation
Structural Functional Analysis

STRUCTURAL FUNCTIONAL ANALYSIS
S-09-0072 1975 00030
BT Contemporary Analytic Modes
RT Career Analysis
Latent Function
Leadership Analysis
Leadership Structure Type
Marginal Man Analysis
Pluralist Analysis
Spatial Analysis
Structural Differentiated System
Structural Functional Political Theory
Structural Model
Structural Process
Structural Requisites
Structure Specific Political Party Type
Weberian Analysis

STRUCTURAL FUNCTIONAL POLITICAL THEORY
S-38-0173 1975 00000
BT Explanatory Political Theory
RT Anthropological Functionalism
Formal Political Theory
Political Behaviorism
Political System Theory
Post Industrial Society Theory
Power Theory
Structural Functional Analysis
Structural Model
Structural Process
Structural Requisites
Structuralism

STRUCTURAL LINGUISTICS
S-01-0015 1975 00021
SN An approach to linguistic inquiry which analyzes the organization and components of language and the relations between language and culture.
BT Cultural Anthropology
NT Morphology
RT Anthropological Linguistic Theory
Anthropological Theory
Ethnolinguistics
Linguistics
Psycholinguistics
Sociolinguistics

STRUCTURAL MARXISM
S-38-0079 1975 00002
BT Contemporary Political Thought
RT Anthropological Functionalism
Eurocommunism
Marxism
Marxist Materialism
Marxist Theory
Neomarxism
Scientific Socialism
Structuralism

STRUCTURAL MODEL
S-24-0320 1975 00023
BT Social Science Model
RT Analytic Process
Hierarchical Model
Leadership Structure Type
Static Model
Structural Functional Analysis
Structural Functional Political Theory

Structural Requisites

STRUCTURAL PROCESS
S-31-0786 1975 00001
BT Process
NT Alienation Process
Cleavage Process
Democratization
Fragmentation
Integration
Specialization Process
RT Analytic Process
Policy Making Process
Selection Process
Social Interaction
Social Role Process
Social Stratification Process
Structural Functional Analysis
Structural Functional Political Theory
Structural Requisites
Structure Specific Political Party Type

STRUCTURAL REQUISITE
1975-1979 00000

STRUCTURAL REQUISITES
S-06-0612 1979 00000
BT System Requisite
RT Functional Requisites
Structural Adaptation
Structural Functional Analysis
Structural Functional Political Theory
Structural Model
Structural Process
System Equilibrium
System Goal
System Maintenance
System Performance
System Stability
System Stress

STRUCTURAL UNEMPLOYMENT
S-06-0656 1975 00006
BT Unemployment
RT Full Employment
Technological Unemployment
Unemployed Person

STRUCTURAL VIOLENCE
1975-1979 00025

STRUCTURALISM
S-38-0018 1975 00009
BT Anthropological Theory
RT Aesthetics
Anthropological Functionalism
Anthropological Linguistic Theory
Ethnographic Theory
Kinship
Kinship Systematics Theory
Leadership Structure Type
Myth Analysis
Role Theory
Structural Functional Political Theory
Structural Marxism
Structure Specific Political Party Type

STRUCTURE SPECIFIC POLITICAL PARTY TYPE
S-28-0058 1979 00000
BT Political Party Type
NT Cadre Political Party
Elite Political Party
Mass Political Party
Splinter Political Party
Third Political Party
Totalitarian Political Party
RT Ideological Spectrum Political Party Type
International Political Party
Major Political Party
National Political Party
Sector Based Political Party Type
Structural Functional Analysis
Structural Process
Structuralism

STRUCTURED INTERVIEW
S-24-0111 1975 00000
BT Interview
RT Attitude Measurement
Interviewer Effect
Survey Research

STRUGGLE
S-08-0126 1975 00003
BT Conflict Type
NT Class Struggle
Ideological Struggle
Succession Struggle
RT Aggression
Agitation
Bolshevik Revolution
Class Polarization
Class Struggle
Counterinsurgency
Democratic Socialist Revolution
Expansionist War
Group Conflict
Ideological Conflict
Imperialist War
Insurgency
Labor Conflict
Labor Strike
Language Group Conflict
Mob Violence
Political Rebellion
Political Violence
Psychological Aggression
Psychological War
Race Riot
Racial Conflict
Rebellion
Religious Conflict
Routinized Conflict
Social Conflict
Social Rebellion
Social Revolution
Spontaneous Revolution
Student Rebellion
Thermidor
War
Worker Rebellion

STUDENT
S-32-0343 1975 00124
BT Roles
NT Foreign Student
RT Graduate School
Radical Student Movement
Student Activism
Student Activist
Student Riot
Student Voting
Youth Culture

STUDENT ACTIVISM
S-38-0278 1975 00014
BT New Left
RT Activist
Counter Culture Ideology
Protest Politics
Student
Student Radicalism
Youth Organization

STUDENT ACTIVIST
S-32-0206 1975 00004
BT Activist
RT Activist
Demonstrator
Protest Politics
Rights Of Man Doctrine
Rioter
Student
Student Radicalism
Student Riot
War Protestor

STUDENT DEMONSTRATION
S-08-0020 1975 00004
BT Demonstration
NT Student Riot
RT Civil Rights Demonstration
General Strike
Group Conflict
Peace Activist
Protest Politics
Sit In
Student Rebellion
Veterans Demonstration
Worker Demonstration

STUDENT MILITANCY
S-06-0114 1975 00004
BT Militancy
RT Activist
Generation Gap
Protest Politics
Student Militant

STUDENT MILITANT
S-32-0189 1975 00002
BT Militant
RT Student Militancy
Student Protest
Student Radicalism
Student Rebellion

STUDENT PROTEST
S-31-0259 1975 00007
BT Protest
RT New Left
New Left Militant
Protest Politics
Social Protest
Student Militant
Student Radicalism
Student Rebellion
Student Riot
Student Voter
Student Voting

STUDENT RADICALISM
S-38-0279 1975 00005
BT New Left
RT Counter Culture Ideology
Student Activism
Student Activist
Student Militant
Student Protest

STUDENT REBELLION
S-08-0060 1975 00006
BT Rebellion
RT Class Rebellion
Economic Rebellion
Mob Violence
Peasant Rebellion
Political Rebellion
Political Revolution
Protest Politics
Slave Rebellion
Social Rebellion
Social Revolution
Spontaneous Revolution
Struggle
Student Demonstration
Student Militant
Student Protest
Student Riot
Youth Culture

STUDENT RIOT
S-08-0021 1979 00000
BT Student Demonstration
RT Political Violence
Student
Student Activist
Student Protest
Student Rebellion

STUDENT VOTER
S-32-0330 1975 00002
BT Voter
RT Absentee Voting
Student Protest
Student Voting
Youth Voter

STUDENT VOTING
S-29-0138 1975 00000
BT Group Voting
RT Age Group Voting
Bloc Voting
Class Voting
Ethnic Group Voting
Geographic Voting
Protest Voting
Racial Voting
Sex Group Voting
Student
Student Protest
Student Voter
Suburban Voting
Youth Culture

STUDY SCOPE
S-24-0399 1975 00004
BT Methodology
NT Case Study
Comparative Analysis
Configurative Analysis
Panel Analysis
Propositional Inventory
RT Ideographic Research
Ideographic Science
Research Design
Research Orientation
Theoretical Framework

STYLISTICS
S-06-0415 1979 00000
BT Language Characteristics
RT Grammar
Language Learning
Semantics
Speech
Vocabulary

SUBCULTURE
S-11-0043 1979 00000
BT Culture Type
RT Community Culture
Counter Culture
Drug Culture
Ethnic Culture
Pluralistic Society
Popular Culture
Religious Culture
Urban Culture

SUBGROUP VOTING
1975-1979 00000

SUBJECT INDEXING
USE Indexing

SUBJECT PARTICIPANT CULTURE
S-11-0033 1975 00002
BT Civic Culture
RT Modern Political Culture
Political Awareness
Political Efficacy
Pragmatic Political Culture
Traditional Political Culture

SUBJECTIVE PROBABILITY ESTIMATION
S-24-0053 1975 00004
BT Probability Estimation
RT Bayesian Analysis

SUBJECTIVELY DERIVED STATUS
S-06-0790 1979 00000
BT Status Stratification Division
RT Achieved Status
Ascribed Status
Objectively Derived Status
Prestige Hierarchy
Social Background
Social Stratification Division
Status Stratification Division
Vertical Stratification Division

SUBJECTIVISM
S-25-0030 1975 00005
SN Doctrine that all knowledge is limited to experience of the self.
BT Epistemology
RT German Romanticism
Romanticism

SUBMISSIVENESS
S-06-0134 1975 00001
BT Attitude Characteristics
RT Alienation
Apathy
Empathy

SUBNATIONAL BANKING SYSTEM
S-37-0039 1975 00000
BT Financial System
RT Central Banking System
Federal Reserve System
International Banking System
National Banking System

SUBNATIONAL CANDIDATE
S-32-0238 1975 00000
BT Political Candidate
NT Subnational Chief Executive Candidate
Subnational Judicial Candidate
Subnational Legislative Candidate
RT Gubernatorial Election
Local Political Elite
Machine Candidate
National Candidate

SUBNATIONAL CHIEF EXECUTIVE CANDIDATE
S-32-0239 1975 00000
BT Subnational Candidate
NT Local Chief Executive Candidate
State Chief Executive Candidate
RT Gubernatorial Election
National Chief Executive Candidate
State Governor
Subnational Judicial Candidate
Subnational Legislative Candidate

SUBNATIONAL CHIEF EXECUTIVE ELECTION
S-29-0094 1975 00000
BT Subnational Election
NT Gubernatorial Election
Local Chief Executive Election
RT Gubernatorial Candidate
Local Election
Provincial Election
State Governor
Subnational Judicial Candidate
Subnational Judicial Election
Subnational Legislative Election

SUBNATIONAL CHIEF EXECUTIVE ELECTION CAMPAIGN
S-29-0035 1975 00000
BT Subnational Election Campaign
NT Local Chief Executive Election Campaign
RT Gubernatorial Candidate
Gubernatorial Election
Local Election Campaign
National Chief Executive Election Campaign
National Judicial Election Campaign
National Legislative Election Campaign
Subnational Judicial Election Campaign
Subnational Legislative Election Campaign

SUBNATIONAL CHIEF EXECUTIVE PRIMARY
S-29-0079 1975 00001
BT Subnational Primary
NT Local Chief Executive Primary
RT Local Primary

SUBNATIONAL CHIEF GOVERNMENT EXECUTIVE
S-36-0077 1975 00002
BT Chief Government Executive
NT Feudal Lord
Governor
RT Gubernatorial Candidate
Gubernatorial Election
Lieutenant Governor
National Chief Government Executive

State Governor

SUBNATIONAL CIVIL SERVANT
S-36-0091 1975 00001
BT Civil Servant
NT Local Civil Servant
RT Civil Servant
International Civil Servant
National Civil Servant

SUBNATIONAL CONSTITUTIONAL CONVENTION
1975-1979 00000

SUBNATIONAL DECISION MAKING PROCESS
S-31-0332 1975 00004
BT Decision Making Process
NT Community Decision Making
Local Decision Making
RT International Decision Making Process
National Decision Making Process
State Political Party
Town Meeting

SUBNATIONAL ECONOMIC DEVELOPMENT LEVEL
S-06-0150 1975 00005
BT Regional Economic Development Level
NT Local Economic Development Level
RT Economic Development Rate

SUBNATIONAL ECONOMIC INTEGRATION
S-31-0808 1975 00000
BT Economic Integration
NT Local Economic Integration
RT Horizontal Economic Integration

SUBNATIONAL ECONOMIC MANAGEMENT
S-23-0019 1975 00003
BT Economic Management
RT Business Management
Central Economic Management
International Economic Management
Labor Mediation
Monetary Management
National Economic Management

SUBNATIONAL ECONOMIC PLANNING
S-31-0651 1975 00000
BT Economic Planning
NT Local Economic Planning
State Economic Planning
RT Internal Market
National Economic Planning

SUBNATIONAL ELECTION
S-29-0090 1975 00003
BT Election Type
NT Local Election
Provincial Election
Subnational Chief Executive Election
Subnational Judicial Election
Subnational Legislative Election
RT National Election
State Governor
State Political Party
Subnational Political Party
Subnational Primary

SUBNATIONAL ELECTION CAMPAIGN
S-29-0033 1975 00001
BT Election Campaign
NT Local Election Campaign
Subnational Chief Executive Election Campaign
Subnational Judicial Election Campaign
Subnational Legislative Election Campaign
RT Congressional Election Campaign
Gubernatorial Candidate
National Election Campaign
State Political Party
Subnational Policy Planning
Subnational Political Party
Subnational Politics
Subnational Primary

SUBNATIONAL ELITE
S-14-0038 1975 00001
BT Elite Type
NT Community Elite
Local Elite
RT Decision Making Elite
Governing Elite
Local Elite
Local Political Elite
Pluralist Elite
Provincial Elite
Subnational Political Party

SUBNATIONAL GOVERNMENT
S-16-0088 1975 00014
BT Government Type
NT County Government
District Government Type
Local Government
Metropolitan Government
State Government
Urban Government
RT Decentralized Government
Interstate Authorities
Lieutenant Governor
Limited Sovereignty
National Government
State Political Party
Subnational Political Party

SUBNATIONAL GOVERNMENT BUREAUCRACY
S-19-0079 1975 00007
BT Government Bureaucracy
NT Local Government Bureaucracy
RT Administrative Officer
Administrative Personnel
International Government Bureaucracy
Lieutenant Governor
National Government Bureaucracy

SUBNATIONAL GOVERNMENT COUNCIL
S-19-0118 1975 00001
BT Councils
NT Local Government Council
RT City Planning Commission
Economic Council
International Government Council
Lieutenant Governor
Local Planning Commission
Local Policy Making
National Government Council
Subnational Planning Commission

SUBNATIONAL INCOME TAXATION
S-26-0148 1975 00000
BT Income Taxation
NT Local Income Taxation
State Income Taxation
RT Progressive Taxation
State Income Taxation
State Planning Policy
State Politics
State Power
Taxation Policy

SUBNATIONAL JUDGE
S-36-0110 1975 00001
BT Judge
NT Local Judge
Magistrate
RT International Judge
Local Political Elite
National Judge
Supreme Court Justice

SUBNATIONAL JUDICIAL CANDIDATE
S-32-0244 1975 00000
BT Subnational Candidate
NT Local Judicial Candidate
State Judicial Candidate
RT National Judicial Candidate
Provincial Election
Subnational Chief Executive Candidate
Subnational Chief Executive Election
Subnational Legislative Candidate
Subnational Legislative Election

SUBNATIONAL JUDICIAL ELECTION
S-29-0098 1975 00001
BT Subnational Election
NT Local Judicial Election
RT Local Election
Provincial Election
Subnational Chief Executive Election
Subnational Legislative Election

SUBNATIONAL JUDICIAL ELECTION CAMPAIGN
S-29-0038 1975 00000
BT Subnational Election Campaign
NT Local Judicial Election Campaign
RT Local Election Campaign
Local Judicial Election
National Chief Executive Election Campaign
National Judicial Election Campaign
National Judicial Primary
National Legislative Election Campaign
Subnational Chief Executive Election Campaign
Subnational Legislative Election Campaign

SUBNATIONAL JUDICIAL PRIMARY
S-29-0081 1975 00000
BT Subnational Primary
NT Local Judicial Primary
RT Local Primary
Subnational Legislative Primary

SUBNATIONAL JUDICIAL SYSTEM
S-37-0085 1975 00000
BT Judicial System
NT Local Judicial System
State Judicial System
RT International Judicial System
Subnational Supreme Court

SUBNATIONAL LAW ENFORCEMENT
S-31-0571 1975 00001
BT Law Enforcement
NT Local Law Enforcement
RT National Law Enforcement

SUBNATIONAL LEGISLATIVE CANDIDATE
S-32-0247 1979 00000
BT Subnational Candidate
NT Local Legislative Candidate
State Legislative Candidate
RT National Legislative Candidate
Subnational Chief Executive Candidate
Subnational Judicial Candidate
Subnational Legislative Member
Subnational Legislature

SUBNATIONAL LEGISLATIVE COMMITTEE CHAIRPERSON
S-36-0151 1975 00000
BT Legislative Committee Chairperson
NT Local Legislative Committee Chairperson
State Legislative Committee Chairperson
RT Legislative Commission
National Legislative Committee Chairperson

SUBNATIONAL LEGISLATIVE ELECTION
S-29-0100 1975 00003
BT Subnational Election
NT Local Legislative Election
State Legislative Election
RT Local Election
Lower House Member
Provincial Election
State Senator
Subnational Chief Executive Election
Subnational Judicial Candidate
Subnational Judicial Election

SUBNATIONAL LEGISLATIVE ELECTION CAMPAIGN
S-29-0040 1975 00000
BT Subnational Election Campaign
NT Local Legislative Election Campaign
RT Local Election Campaign
National Chief Executive Election Campaign
National Judicial Election Campaign
National Legislative Election Campaign
Subnational Chief Executive Election Campaign
Subnational Judicial Election Campaign

SUBNATIONAL LEGISLATIVE LEADER
S-36-0184 1975 00001
BT Legislative Leader
NT Local Legislative Leader
State Legislative Leader
RT Floor Leader
Leader Of Opposition
Legislative Procedure
Legislative Process
Legislative Speaker
Legislative Whip
Majority Leader
Minority Leader
National Legislative Leader
State Senator

SUBNATIONAL LEGISLATIVE MEMBER
S-36-0195 1975 00002
BT Legislative Member
NT Local Legislative Member
State Legislative Member
RT Legislative Procedure
Legislative Process
National Legislative Member
State Senator
Subnational Legislative Candidate

SUBNATIONAL LEGISLATIVE PRIMARY
S-29-0083 1975 00000
BT Subnational Primary
NT Local Legislative Primary
RT Local Primary
Subnational Judicial Primary

SUBNATIONAL LEGISLATIVE SPEAKER
S-36-0167 1975 00001
BT Legislative Speaker
NT Local Legislative Speaker
State Legislative Speaker
RT Legislative Procedure
Legislative Process
National Legislative Speaker

SUBNATIONAL LEGISLATIVE STAFF
S-36-0209 1975 00002
BT Legislative Staff
NT Local Legislative Staff
State Legislative Staff
RT Legislative Committee Staff
Line Staff
Subnational Policy Making
Subnational Policy Planning
Subnational Politics
Suborganization Official

SUBNATIONAL LEGISLATIVE WHIP
S-36-0174 1975 00000
BT Legislative Whip
NT Local Legislative Whip
State Legislative Whip
RT Legislative Procedure
Legislative Process
Suborganization Official

SUBNATIONAL LEGISLATOR CANDIDATE
1975-1979 00001

SUBNATIONAL LEGISLATURE
S-19-0281 1975 00007
BT Legislatures
NT Local Legislature
Provincial Parliament
State Legislature
RT Bicameral Legislature
Congress
Congressional System
Legislature Type
Municipal Authorities
Subnational Legislative Candidate
Subnational Political Party
Unicameral Legislature

SUBNATIONAL PARTY
1975-1979 00000

SUBNATIONAL PLANNER
S-32-0140 1975 00004
BT Planner
NT Local Planner
Regional Planner
State Planner
RT Economic Planner
Fiscal Planner
International Planner
Local Policy Making
National Planner
Social Planner

SUBNATIONAL PLANNING COMMISSION
S-19-0097 1975 00002
BT Planning Commission
NT Local Planning Commission
RT International Planning Commission
National Planning Commission
Subnational Government Council

SUBNATIONAL PLANNING POLICY
S-26-0350 1975 00003
BT Planning Policy
NT Local Planning Policy
Regional Planning Policy
State Planning Policy
RT National Planning Policy
New Town
Subnational Policy Making

SUBNATIONAL POLICE
S-19-0309 1975 00004
BT Police
NT Local Police
State Police
RT International Police
Law Enforcement Official
Military Police
National Police
Paramilitary Police
Private Police
Subnational Police Official

SUBNATIONAL POLICE OFFICIAL
S-36-0140 1975 00001
BT Law Enforcement Official
NT Local Police Official
State Police Official
RT International Police Official
National Police Official
Secret Police Official
Subnational Police

SUBNATIONAL POLICY MAKING
S-31-0701 1975 00009
BT Policy Making Process
NT Local Policy Making
RT Subnational Legislative Staff
Subnational Planning Policy
Subnational Politics

SUBNATIONAL POLICY PLANNING
S-31-0664 1975 00005
BT Public Policy Planning
NT City Policy Planning
Local Policy Planning
Rural Policy Planning
State Policy Planning
Urban Policy Planning
RT City Policy Planning
International Policy Planning
National Policy Planning
Social Engineering
Social Planning
Subnational Election Campaign
Subnational Legislative Staff

SUBNATIONAL POLITICAL DIVISION
S-24-0357 1975 00001
BT National Region
NT Local Political Division
Province
State
State Political Division
RT Nation
National Political Division
Subnational Political Integration
Subnational Politics

SUBNATIONAL POLITICAL INTEGRATION
S-31-0825 1975 00002
BT Political Integration
NT Local Political Integration
RT International Political Integration
National Political Integration
Political Unification
Subnational Political Division

SUBNATIONAL POLITICAL PARTY
S-28-0053 1979 00000
BT National Political Party
NT Local Political Party
Provincial Political Party
State Political Party
RT National Political Party
Subnational Election
Subnational Election Campaign
Subnational Elite
Subnational Government
Subnational Legislature

SUBNATIONAL POLITICAL PARTY CENTRAL COMMITTEE MEMBER
S-36-0248 1975 00000
BT Subnational Political Party Committee Member
NT Local Political Party Central Committee Member
RT Local Political Party Chairperson
Local Political Party Politburo Member
Subnational Political Party First Secretary

SUBNATIONAL POLITICAL PARTY CHAIRPERSON
S-36-0245 1975 00000
BT Subnational Political Party Executive Member
NT Local Political Party Chairperson
RT Subnational Political Party Committee Member
Subnational Political Party Politburo Member
Subnational Political Party Secretary
Suborganization Official

SUBNATIONAL POLITICAL PARTY COMMITTEE MEMBER
S-36-0247 1975 00000
BT Subnational Political Party Executive Member
NT Subnational Political Party Central Committee Member
RT Subnational Political Party Chairperson
Subnational Political Party Politburo Member
Subnational Political Party Secretary

SUBNATIONAL POLITICAL PARTY EXECUTIVE MEMBER
S-36-0244 1975 00000
BT Political Party Official
NT Subnational Political Party Chairperson
Subnational Political Party Committee Member
Subnational Political Party Politburo Member
Subnational Political Party Secretary
RT International Political Party Committee Member
International Political Party Executive Member
National Political Party Executive Member
Suborganization Official

SUBNATIONAL POLITICAL PARTY FIRST SECRETARY
S-36-0253 1975 00001
BT Subnational Political Party Secretary
NT Local Political Party First Secretary
Regional Political Party First Secretary
RT Local Political Party Chairperson
Local Political Party Politburo Member
Subnational Political Party Central Committee Member

SUBNATIONAL POLITICAL PARTY POLITBURO MEMBER
S-36-0250 1975 00000
BT Subnational Political Party Executive Member
NT Local Political Party Politburo Member
RT Subnational Political Party Chairperson
Subnational Political Party Committee Member
Subnational Political Party Secretary

SUBNATIONAL POLITICAL PARTY SECRETARY
S-36-0252 1975 00001
BT Subnational Political Party Executive Member
NT Subnational Political Party First Secretary
RT Subnational Political Party Chairperson
Subnational Political Party Committee Member
Subnational Political Party Politburo Member

SUBNATIONAL POLITICS
S-29-0234 1975 00007
BT Politics
NT Local Politics
State Politics
Tribal Politics
RT Gubernatorial Election
Subnational Election Campaign
Subnational Legislative Staff
Subnational Policy Making
Subnational Political Division
Subnational Primary

SUBNATIONAL PRIMARY
S-29-0077 1975 00001
BT Election Type
NT Local Primary
Subnational Chief Executive Primary
Subnational Judicial Primary
Subnational Legislative Primary
RT Subnational Election
Subnational Election Campaign
Subnational Politics

SUBNATIONAL SUPREME COURT
S-19-0140 1975 00000
BT Supreme Court
NT State Supreme Court
RT District Court
National Supreme Court
Subnational Judicial System

SUBNATIONAL TAXATION
S-26-0166 1975 00001
BT Taxation Policy
NT Local Taxation
State Taxation
RT Federal Taxation
National Taxation
Regressive Taxation
School Taxation

SUBORGANIZATION OFFICIAL
S-36-0261 1975 00000
BT Status
NT Caucus Member
Chairperson
Committee Member
RT Political Party Official
Subnational Legislative Staff
Subnational Legislative Whip
Subnational Political Party Chairperson
Subnational Political Party Executive Member

SUBPOENA
S-31-0486 1975 00000
BT Court Action
RT Cease Desist Order
Consent Judgment
Conviction
Injunction
Obiter Dicta
Verdict
Warrant
Writ Of Mandamus

SUBSAHARAN AFRICAN AREA STUDIES
1975-1979 00249

SUBSIDIZATION PROCESS
S-31-0422 1975 00008
BT Fiscal Process
RT Economic Loss
Fiscal Process
Incentive Taxation
Labor Subsidization Policy
Monetary Process

SUBSISTENCE ECONOMY
S-12-0043 1975 00013
BT Economy Type
RT Agrarian Economy
Barter Economy
Cottage Industry Economy
Depressed Economy
Farm Economy
Labor Intensive Economy
Nomadic Economy

Peasant Economy
Plantation Economy
Subsistence Level
Underdeveloped Economy

SUBSISTENCE FARMING
S-31-0431 1975 00010
BT Farming
RT Farm Economy
Migrant Farming
Subsistence Level
Subsistence Production
Tenant Farming

SUBSISTENCE LEVEL
S-06-0639 1975 00005
BT Wealth Distribution
RT Income Distribution
Poverty
Subsistence Economy
Subsistence Farming
Subsistence Wage Level

SUBSISTENCE PRODUCTION
S-31-0444 1975 00004
BT Production Process
RT Subsistence Farming

SUBSISTENCE WAGE LEVEL
S-06-0641 1975 00003
BT Wage Level
RT Subsistence Level
Wealth Distribution
Wealth Redistribution

SUBSTANTIVE DUE PROCESS
S-31-0552 1975 00007
BT Judicial Procedure
RT Legal Discrimination
Legal Precedent
Procedural Due Process

SUBURB
S-07-0050 1975 00010
BT Community Type
NT Bedroom Community
RT City
Megalopolis
Neighborhood
Outer City
Political Community
Suburban Environment
Town
Village Community

SUBURBAN ENVIRONMENT
S-06-0704 1975 00006
BT Social System Environment Characteristics
RT Bedroom Community
Black Suburban Community
Rural Environment
Suburb
Suburban Migration
Suburban Politics
Suburban Population Area
Suburban Voter
Suburban Voting
Urban Environment

SUBURBAN GHETTO COMMUNITY
S-07-0028 1975 00001
BT Ghetto Community
NT Black Suburban Community
RT Ethnic Composition
Ethnic Ghetto
Homogeneous Community
Integrated Community
Multiethnic Community
Segregated Community
Suburban Migration
Suburban Migration Pattern
Urban Ghetto Community

SUBURBAN MIGRATION
S-31-0623 1975 00007
BT Internal Migration
RT Bedroom Community
Rural Migration
Suburban Environment
Suburban Ghetto Community
Suburban Migration Pattern
Suburban Politics
Suburban Population

SUBURBAN MIGRATION PATTERN
S-06-0241 1975 00009
BT Internal Migration Pattern
RT Rural Migration Pattern
Suburban Ghetto Community
Suburban Migration
Suburban Politics
Urban Migration Pattern

SUBURBAN POLITICS
S-29-0239 1975 00005
BT Urban Politics
RT Suburban Environment
Suburban Migration
Suburban Migration Pattern
Suburban Population

SUBURBAN POPULATION
S-06-0218 1975 00002
BT Population Attribute
RT Bedroom Community
Population Density
Rural Population
Suburban Migration
Suburban Politics
Urban Population

SUBURBAN POPULATION AREA
S-24-0348 1975 00005
BT Population Identification
RT Population Identification
Rural Population Area
Suburban Environment
Urban Population Area

SUBURBAN VOTER
S-32-0331 1975 00001
BT Voter
RT Rural Voter
Suburban Environment
Urban Voter

SUBURBAN VOTING
S-29-0139 1975 00001
BT Group Voting
RT Age Group Voting
Ethnic Group Voting
Geographic Voting
Racial Voting
Regional Voting
Rural Voting
Student Voting
Suburban Environment
Urban Voting

SUCCESSION STRUGGLE
S-08-0129 1975 00037
BT Struggle
RT Cult Of Personality
Ideological Conflict
Institutional Conflict
Internal Conflict
Internal War
Political Purge
Political Revolution
Political Succession
Purge
Rebellion

SUCCESSIVE APPOXIMATION
USE Hypothesis Testing

SUFFRAGE EQUALITY
S-15-0082 1975 00004
BT Voting Rights
RT Female Voter
Feminism
Sexism
Voter Qualification
Womens Emancipation
Womens Liberation Movement

SUFFRAGE EXTENSION
S-29-0120 1975 00001
BT Electoral Participation
RT Sexism
Womens Liberation Movement

SUFFRAGE LAW
S-21-0069 1975 00002
BT Electoral Law
RT Female Voter
Feminism
Sex Role
Sexism
Sexist
Suffragette
Voter Registration Law
Womens Liberation Movement
Womens Rights

SUFFRAGETTE
S-32-0202 1975 00001
BT Political Activist
RT Female Voter
Suffrage Law
Womens Emancipation
Womens Liberation Movement
Womens Rights
Womens Studies

SULTAN
S-36-0068 1975 00001
BT Monarch
RT Hereditary Ruler
Kaiser
Khan
King
Queen
Regent
Shah
Sheik
Sheikdom
Tsar

SUMMATIVE EVALUATION
S-31-0697 1975 00012
SN Evaluation of a program with the aim of determining whether it should be continued or terminated.
BT Policy Evaluation
RT Education Evaluation
Evaluating
Formative Evaluation
Management Information System
Normative Evaluation
Research Evaluation

Social Accounting

SUMMIT DIPLOMACY
S-31-0361 1975 00003
BT Diplomacy
RT Bilateral Treaty
Diplomatic Relations
Diplomatic Relations Normalization
Executive Diplomacy
Presidential Diplomacy
Secret Diplomacy

SUMMIT MEETING
S-03-0048 1979 00000
BT International Conference
RT Conflict Resolution
Conflict Resolution Theory
East West Detente
International Conciliation
International Conference
International Conflict Resolution Theory
International Negotiation
Military Agreement
Superpower Politics
Treaty Making

SUNSET LAW
S-21-0074 1979 00000
BT Political Law
RT Enabling Law
Home Rule Law
Sunshine Law

SUNSHINE LAW
S-21-0075 1979 00000
BT Political Law
RT Citizen Participation
Enabling Law
Freedom Of Information
Home Rule Law
Sunset Law

SUPERPOWER POLITICS
S-29-0209 1975 00189
BT World Politics
RT Convergence Theory
Military Policy
Proxy War
Realist Foreign Policy
Summit Meeting
Transnational Politics
War

SUPERSTITION
S-38-0015 1975 00003
BT Myth Analysis
RT Magic
Shamanism
Taboo
Witchcraft

SUPPLY CURVE
S-06-0296 1975 00010
BT Economic Index
NT Supply Elasticity
RT Demand Curve
Economic Scarcity
Supply Elasticity

SUPPLY ELASTICITY
S-06-0297 1979 00000
BT Supply Curve
RT Demand Curve
Demand Elasticity
Economic Cycle
Economic Depression
Economic Growth Index
Economic Inflation
Economic Recovery
Supply Curve

SUPPORT OPPOSITION SCALE
S-24-0249 1975 00003
BT Scale Type
RT Alienation Scale
Anomie Scale
Cynicism Scale
Dogmatism Scale
Efficacy Scale
Legitimacy Scale
Liberalism Conservatism Scale
Optimism Pessimism Scale
Political Opposition
Satisfaction Scale
Social Distance Scale
Social Frustration Scale
Stability Index
Voting Duty Scale

SUPRANATIONAL INTEGRATION
S-31-0822 1975 00007
BT International Political Integration
RT European Integration Theory
International Regional Political Integration
Supranational Security

SUPRANATIONAL SECURITY
S-06-0670 1975 00015
BT Collective Security
RT Intelligence Agency
Pan Arab Movement
Supranational Integration

SUPREME COURT
S-19-0138 1975 00061
BT Constitutional Court
NT National Supreme Court
Subnational Supreme Court
RT Appellate Court
Chief Justice
Constitutional Law System
Criminal Court
District Court
International Court
National Judicial System
One Man One Vote Representation
Supreme Court Review

SUPREME COURT JUSTICE
S-36-0116 1975 00013
BT Judge
NT Chief Justice
RT International Judge
National Judge
Subnational Judge

SUPREME COURT REVIEW
S-31-0545 1975 00007
BT Judicial Review
RT Appellate Court Review
Chief Justice
Constitutional Law
Judicial Review
National Judge
Supreme Court

SURVEILLANCE
S-18-0100 1979 00000
BT Information Sources
NT Spying
RT Confidential Information
Information System
Intelligence Agency
Military Intelligence
National Security
Secret Diplomacy
Secret Service
Validity Measurement

SURVEY ANALYSIS
S-09-0073 1975 00034
BT Contemporary Analytic Modes
RT Aggregate Data Analysis
Political Attitude
Survey Data
Voting Behavior Analysis

SURVEY DATA
S-18-0095 1975 00033
BT Statistical Data
NT Cross Cultural Data
Public Opinion Survey
RT Aggregate Data Statistics
Economic Statistics
Ethnographic Data
Field Data
Legislative Information Service
Political Attitude
Political Statistics
Question Formulation
Social Indicator
Social Psychological Data
Social Statistics
Survey Analysis

SURVEY RESEARCH
S-24-0115 1975 00104
BT Reactive Observation
RT Experimental Observation
Interview
Interviewing Material
Participant Observation
Political Attitude
Political Behavior Studies
Question Formulation
Structured Interview

SYMBOL LEARNING
S-34-0014 1979 00000
BT Learning
RT Education Policy
Language Acquisition
Language Learning
Learning Psychology
Learning Theory
Moral Learning
Nonverbal Learning
Skill Acquisition
Verbal Learning

SYMBOLIC ACTION
S-05-0034 1979 00000
BT Social Behavior
RT Habitual Behavior
Philosophy Of Action
Philosophy Of Mind
Social Action Theory
Symbolic Politics

SYMBOLIC POLITICS
S-29-0243 1975 00032
SN Emphasis on the role of substitute objects that evoke desired political responses.
BT Politics
RT Political Style
Power Politics

Spoils Politics
Symbolic Action

SYNDICALISM
S-38-0336 1975 00003
SN Doctrine that councils of workers should own the means of production and this should be achieved through general strikes and spontaneous and terroristic revolutionary activities.
BT Ideologies
NT Agrarian Syndicalism
RT Anarchism
Anarchosyndicalism
Aprista Socialism
Corporatism
Democratic Socialism
Evolutionary Socialism
General Strike
Guild Socialism
Marxism
Trade Union Movement
Trade Unionism

SYNTHETICS INDUSTRY
S-17-0005 1979 00000
BT Chemical Industry
RT Agrochemical Industry
Clothing Industry
Consumer Industry
Light Industry
Rubber Industry

SYSTEM ADAPTATION
S-06-0580 1975 00012
BT System Change
NT Functional Adaptation
Structural Adaptation
RT System Adaptive Capacity
System Analysis
System Innovation
System Performance
System Stability

SYSTEM ADAPTIVE CAPACITY
S-06-0576 1975 00009
BT System Capacity
RT Communication Feedback
Social Adjustment
System Adaptation
System Maintenance
System Performance
System Stability

SYSTEM ANALYSIS
S-24-0414 1975 00037
BT Macrolevel Analysis
RT Analytic Process
Analytic System Characteristics
Authoritative Value Allocation
Cybernetic Analysis
Eastonian Analysis
Environmental Characteristics
Exogenous System Demands
Functional Adaptation
Functional Specificity
Goal Ambiguity
Interest Aggregation
Organization Environment
Pattern Maintenance
Political System Characteristics
Structural Adaptation
System Adaptation
System Change
System Characteristics
System Demands
System Disequilibrium
System Function
System Goal
System Innovation
System Inputs
System Integration
System Interdependence
System Maintenance
System Maintenance Capacity
System Outputs
System Performance
System Persistence Capacity
System Requisite
System Stability
System Supports
System Type
Value Allocation

SYSTEM BOUNDARY
S-06-0574 1975 00012
BT Analytic System Characteristics
RT Exogenous System Demands
Feedback Loop
Specific System Supports
System Change
System Function
System Interdependence
System Maintenance
System Requisite
System Stress

SYSTEM CAPACITY
S-06-0575 1975 00006
BT Analytic System Characteristics
NT System Adaptive Capacity
System Maintenance Capacity
System Persistence Capacity
RT Feedback Loop
Specific System Supports
System Change
System Function
System Innovation
System Integration
System Maintenance
System Outputs
System Performance
System Stress

SYSTEM CHANGE
S-06-0579 1975 00018
BT Analytic System Characteristics
NT System Adaptation
System Innovation
RT Feedback Loop
Specific System Supports
System Analysis
System Boundary
System Capacity
System Disequilibrium
System Inputs
System Persistence Capacity
System Stress

SYSTEM CHARACTERISTICS
S-06-0569 1975 00008
BT Characteristics
NT Analytic System Characteristics
Economic System Characteristics
Political System Characteristics
Social System Characteristics
RT Change Characteristics
Cybernetic Analysis
Development Characteristics
Economic Characteristics
Equilibrium Theory
General System Theory
General Theory
Government Characteristics
Health Characteristics
Institution Building
Organization Characteristics
Political System Theory
Social Action Theory
Social Integration Theory
System Analysis
System Equilibrium
System Independence
System Type

SYSTEM DEMANDS
S-06-0590 1975 00011
BT System Inputs
NT Endogenous System Demands
Exogenous System Demands
RT Interest Aggregation
Interest Articulation
System Analysis
System Equilibrium
System Independence
System Supports

SYSTEM DISEQUILIBRIUM
S-06-0584 1975 00004
BT Analytic System Characteristics
RT Feedback Loop
System Analysis
System Change
System Inputs
System Persistence Capacity
System Stress

SYSTEM EQUILIBRIUM
S-06-0614 1975 00006
BT System Stability
NT Dynamic Equilibrium
Homeostatic Equilibrium
RT Political System Theory
Social Action Theory
Social Integration Theory
Structural Requisites
System Characteristics
System Demands
System Function
System Goal
System Independence
System Performance

SYSTEM FUNCTION
S-06-0585 1975 00003
BT Analytic System Characteristics
NT Functional Specificity
Latent Function
Manifest Function
RT Feedback Loop
Functional Adaptation
Political System Efficiency
System Analysis
System Boundary
System Capacity
System Equilibrium
System Goal
System Independence
System Interdependence

SYSTEM GOAL
S-06-0602 1975 00001
BT System Outputs
NT Goal Ambiguity
Goal Satisfaction
Goal Setting
Goal Specificity
Value Allocation
RT Structural Requisites
System Analysis
System Equilibrium
System Function
System Maintenance

SYSTEM INDEPENDENCE
S-06-0598 1975 00002
BT System Interdependence
RT System Characteristics
System Demands
System Equilibrium
System Function
System Interdependence
System Maintenance Capacity
System Performance

SYSTEM INNOVATION
S-06-0583 1975 00009
BT System Change
RT System Adaptation
System Analysis
System Capacity
System Outputs
System Performance

SYSTEM INPUTS
S-06-0589 1975 00002
BT Analytic System Characteristics
NT System Demands
System Supports
RT Feedback Loop
Political System Efficiency
System Analysis
System Change
System Disequilibrium
System Outputs
System Performance
System Stress

SYSTEM INTEGRATION
S-06-0596 1975 00004
BT Analytic System Characteristics
RT Political Integration Theory
Specific System Supports
System Analysis
System Capacity
System Stability

SYSTEM INTERDEPENDENCE
S-06-0597 1975 00026
BT Analytic System Characteristics
NT System Independence
RT System Analysis
System Boundary
System Function
System Independence

SYSTEM MAINTENANCE
S-06-0599 1975 00016
BT Analytic System Characteristics
NT Pattern Maintenance
RT Specific System Supports
Structural Requisites
System Adaptive Capacity
System Analysis
System Boundary
System Capacity
System Goal
System Maintenance Capacity
System Persistence Capacity
System Supports

SYSTEM MAINTENANCE CAPACITY
S-06-0577 1975 00007
BT System Capacity
RT Communication Feedback
Pattern Maintenance
System Analysis
System Independence
System Maintenance
System Stability

SYSTEM OUTPUTS
S-06-0601 1975 00008
BT Analytic System Characteristics
NT System Goal
System Performance
System Requisite
System Stability
System Stress
RT Cybernetic Analysis
Feedback Loop
Specific System Supports
System Analysis
System Capacity
System Innovation
System Inputs

SYSTEM PERFORMANCE
S-06-0609 1975 00026
BT System Outputs
RT Dynamic Equilibrium
Homeostatic Equilibrium
Structural Requisites
System Adaptation
System Adaptive Capacity
System Analysis
System Capacity
System Equilibrium
System Independence
System Innovation
System Inputs
System Requisite
System Stability
System Stress

SYSTEM PERSISTENCE CAPACITY
S-06-0578 1975 00005
BT System Capacity
RT Communication Feedback
Political System Efficiency
System Analysis
System Change
System Disequilibrium
System Maintenance
System Stability

SYSTEM POLITICIST
S-32-0266 1975 00000
SN One whose political stance and activism is based on beliefs of how public power should be legitimately organized in a particular society.
BT Politicist
NT Anarchist
Anticleric
Colonialist
Communalist
Democrat
Fascist
Imperialist
Nationalist
Republican
Royalist
Sectarian
Socialist
RT Positive Voting Abstention
Spectrum Politicist
System Politicization
System Stress

SYSTEM POLITICIZATION
S-31-0160 1979 00000
UF Systemic Politicization
BT Politicization
RT Ideological Polarization
Issue Politicization
Political Culture
Political Ideology
Political Legitimacy Theory
Political Participation
Political System Characteristics
Political System Normative Characteristics
Radicalism
System Politicist

SYSTEM REQUISITE
S-06-0610 1979 00000
BT System Outputs
NT Functional Requisites
Structural Requisites
RT System Analysis
System Boundary
System Performance
System Stability

SYSTEM REQUISITES
1975-1979 00001

SYSTEM STABILITY
S-06-0613 1975 00040
BT System Outputs
NT System Equilibrium
RT Structural Requisites
System Adaptation
System Adaptive Capacity
System Analysis
System Integration
System Maintenance Capacity
System Performance
System Persistence Capacity
System Requisite
System Stress

SYSTEM STRESS
S-06-0617 1975 00005
BT System Outputs
NT Endogenous System Stress
Exogenous System Stress
RT Structural Requisites
System Boundary
System Capacity
System Change
System Disequilibrium
System Inputs
System Performance
System Politicist
System Stability

SYSTEM SUPPORTS
S-06-0593 1975 00020
BT System Inputs
NT Diffuse System Supports
Specific System Supports

RT Civil Religion
Habitual Behavior
System Analysis
System Demands
System Maintenance

SYSTEM TYPE
S-37-0001 1975 00002
NT Belief System
Cognitive System
Cultural System
Cybernetic System
Differentiated System
Economic System
Ecosystem
Education System
Health Care System
Imperialism System
Information System
Legal System
Political System Type
Service Delivery System
Social System
Transportation System
Value System
Welfare System
RT Economy Type
General Theory
Institution Building
System Analysis
System Characteristics
Theory

SYSTEMATIC ERROR
S-24-0200 1975 00004
BT Measurement Problem
RT Autocorrelation
Measurement Bias
Measurement Error
Missing Data
Random Error

SYSTEMATIC SAMPLING
S-24-0126 1975 00000
BT Probability Sampling
RT Cluster Sampling
Simple Random Sampling
Stratified Sampling

SYSTEMIC POLITICIZATION
1975-1979 00004
USE System Politicization

TABLE
S-24-0138 1975 00000
BT Data Presentation Methodology
NT Frequency Table
RT Chart
Curve
Diagram
Graph
Plot

TABOO
S-38-0016 1975 00003
BT Myth Analysis
RT Folkways
Magic
Sacred Law
Shamanism
Superstition
Witchcraft

TACTICAL FORCE
S-33-0009 1975 00019
BT Defense System
RT Armed Forces
Balanced Force
Military Establishment
Professional Military Forces
Reserve Military Forces
Tactical War
Tactical Weapon
War Technology

TACTICAL WAR
S-08-0101 1979 00000
BT Limited War
RT Border Conflict
Border War
Brushfire War
Tactical Force
Tactical Weapon
War By Proxy
War Technology

TACTICAL WEAPON
S-33-0040 1975 00016
BT Weapon
RT Biological Weapon
Chemical Weapon
Defensive Weapon
Deterrent Weapon
Missile
Nuclear Weapon
Strategic Weapon
Tactical Force
Tactical War
Unconventional Weapon

TAKEOFF STAGE
S-06-0165 1975 00000
BT Economic Development Stage
RT Economic Development Index
Entrepreneurship
Government Economic Planning
Political Development Theory

TAOISM
S-38-0575 1975 00001
BT Religious Thought
RT Buddhism
Confucianism
Islamic Thought
Judeo Christian Thought
Nonwestern Culture
Shintoism
Zoroastrianism

TARIFF
S-26-0170 1975 00001
BT Taxation Policy
NT Protective Tariff
RT Confiscatory Taxation
Excise Taxation Policy
Import Duty
Income Taxation
Inheritance Taxation
Luxury Taxation
Nuisance Taxation
Sales Taxation

TARIFF AGENCY
1975-1979 00000

TARIFF POLICY
S-26-0188 1975 00012
BT Restrictive Trade Policy
RT Blockade Policy
Export Policy
Import Policy

TARIFF RECORD
S-18-0017 1975 00000
BT Revenue Record
RT Economic Statistics
Government Document
Regulatory Agency Record
Tax Record
Trade Document

TARIFF UNION
1975-1979 00000

TASK FORCE
S-19-0329 1975 00001
BT Institutions
NT Presidential Task Force
RT Business Regulation Agency
Higher Education Institution
Political Party Institution
Research Institution

TAX AGENCY
S-19-0028 1975 00001
BT Fiscal Agency
RT Appropriation Agency
Budget Agency
Budget Policy
Budget Reviewing
Local Income Taxation
Monetary Agency
Revenue Agency
Tax Code
Tax Law
Tax Power
Tax Record
Taxation Policy

TAX ASSESSMENT
S-26-0172 1979 00000
BT Taxation Policy
RT Property Taxation
Tax Base
Tax Code
Tax Evasion
Tax Power
Tax Reform Movement
Tax Shelter
Taxation Policy

TAX BASE
S-26-0175 1979 00000
BT Taxation Policy
RT Tax Assessment
Tax Code
Tax Court
Tax Credit
Tax Law
Tax Record
Tax Shelter
Taxation Policy

TAX CODE
S-21-0045 1975 00004
BT Economic Law
RT Local Income Taxation
National Tax Law
Property Law
Tax Agency
Tax Assessment
Tax Base
Tax Court
Tax Evasion
Tax Law
Tax Power

Taxation Policy

TAX COURT
S-19-0127 1975 00000
BT Administrative Court
RT Civil Court
Tax Base
Tax Code
Tax Evasion
Tax Law

TAX CREDIT
S-26-0173 1979 00000
BT Taxation Policy
RT Credit Policy
Revenue Policy
Tax Base
Tax Cut
Tax Rebate
Tax Shelter

TAX CUT
S-26-0174 1979 00000
BT Taxation Policy
RT Budget Cutting
Monetary Policy
Revenue Policy
Tax Credit
Tax Rebate
Tax Shelter

TAX EVASION
S-10-0024 1975 00001
BT Economic Crime
RT Economic Conspiracy
Economic Sabotage
Extortion
Fraud
Robbery
Tax Assessment
Tax Code
Tax Court
White Collar Crime

TAX EXEMPT INCOME
S-06-0343 1975 00009
BT Income
RT Average Income
Charitable Organization
Family Income
Philanthropic Organization
Profit Income
Tax Law
Taxation Policy

TAX LAW
S-21-0046 1975 00014
BT Economic Law
NT National Tax Law
RT Antitrust Law
Bankruptcy Law
Property Law
Tax Agency
Tax Base
Tax Code
Tax Court
Tax Exempt Income
Tax Power
Tax Record
Tax Reform Movement
Taxation Policy

TAX POWER
S-04-0034 1975 00006
BT Civil Authority
RT Eminent Domain
Eminent Domain Policy
Local Income Taxation
Tax Agency
Tax Assessment
Tax Code
Tax Law
Taxation Policy

TAX REBATE
S-26-0176 1979 00000
BT Taxation Policy
RT Credit Policy
Tax Credit
Tax Cut
Tax Shelter

TAX RECORD
S-18-0018 1975 00001
BT Revenue Record
RT Licensing Record
Regulatory Agency Record
Tariff Record
Tax Agency
Tax Base
Tax Law

TAX REFORM MOVEMENT
•S-27-0044 1979 00000
BT Reform Movement
RT Economic Movement
Graduated Taxation
Income Redistribution Policy
Income Taxation
Municipal Reform Movement
Property Taxation
Senior Citizen Movement
Tax Assessment
Tax Law
Wage Taxation

TAX SHELTER
S-26-0177 1979 00000
BT Taxation Policy
RT Tax Assessment
Tax Base
Tax Credit
Tax Cut
Tax Rebate

TAXATION
1975-1979 00032

TAXATION POLICY
S-26-0139 1975 00080
BT Revenue Policy
NT Confiscatory Taxation
Direct Taxation
Excise Taxation Policy
Gift Taxation
Import Duty
Incentive Taxation
Incentive Taxation Policy
Income Taxation
Indirect Taxation
Inheritance Taxation
Luxury Taxation
National Taxation
Nuisance Taxation
Progressive Taxation
Property Taxation
Regressive Taxation
Sales Taxation
School Taxation
Social Security Taxation
Subnational Taxation
Tariff
Tax Assessment
Tax Base
Tax Credit
Tax Cut
Tax Rebate
Tax Shelter
Value Added Taxation
Wage Taxation
RT Charitable Organization
Fiscal Theory
Graduated Taxation
Income Policy
Local Income Taxation
National Income Taxation
National Tax Law
National Taxation
Net Income
Nonprofit Institution
Philanthropic Organization
State Income Taxation
Subnational Income Taxation
Tax Agency
Tax Assessment
Tax Base
Tax Code
Tax Exempt Income
Tax Law
Tax Power

TEACHER
S-32-0120 1975 00033
BT Professional Occupational Role
NT Professor
School Teacher
RT Academic
Ayatallah
Education Association
Lama
Priest
Rabbi
Social Scientist
Teacher Organization
Textbook

TEACHER EDUCATION
S-13-0014 1979 00000
BT Pedagogical Institute Education
RT Classical Education
Higher Education
Outreach Education
Pedagogical Institute Education
Political Science Teaching
Professional Education
Teacher Organization

TEACHER ORGANIZATION
S-03-0056 1975 00003
BT Professional Organization
RT Education Association
Education Institution
Occupational Interest Group
Teacher
Teacher Education

TEACHING
S-31-0452 1979 00000
BT Education Process
NT Political Science Teaching

RT Education Curriculum
Information Dissemination
Instruction Methodology
Instructional Material
Learning Package

TECHNICAL ADVISOR
S-32-0022 1975 00006
BT Advisor
RT Administrative Advisor
Economic Advisor
Education Advisor
Legal Advisor
Military Advisor
Political Advisor
Science Advisor
Scientific Attache

TECHNICAL AID POLICY
S-26-0260 1975 00012
BT Foreign Aid Policy
RT Bilateral Aid Policy
Economic Aid Policy
Grants Economy
Military Aid Policy
Multilateral Aid Policy
Technical Assistance
Technician
Trickle Down Theory
Unilateral Aid Policy

TECHNICAL ASSISTANCE
S-06-0313 1975 00024
BT Foreign Assistance
RT Economic Aid Policy
Military Assistance
Technical Aid Policy
Training Assistance

TECHNICAL EDUCATION
S-13-0048 1975 00011
BT Education Type
NT Agricultural Education
Manpower Training
RT Academic Specialization
Adult Education
Alternative Education
Apprenticeship
Education Characteristics
Higher Education
Legal Education
Military Education
Military Training
Polytechnical Institute Education
Professional Education
Public Health Education
Secondary Education
Sex Education
Skill Acquisition
State Supported Higher Education
Technical Occupation
Technician
Technocracy

TECHNICAL OCCUPATION
S-32-0123 1975 00001
BT Professional Occupational Role
NT Engineer
Scientist
Technician
RT Engineering Discipline
Occupation Characteristics
Technical Education
Technocracy

TECHNICIAN
S-32-0126 1975 00001
BT Technical Occupation
RT Engineer
Factory
Scientist
Technical Aid Policy
Technical Education
Technocracy
Technological Unemployment
Technology

TECHNOCRACY
S-16-0150 1975 00020
BT Rule Type
RT Advanced Technology
Bureaucratic Politics
Engineering Discipline
Industrial Society
Innovation
Meritocracy
Modernizing Authoritarian Regime
Oligarchic Government
Post Industrial Society
Technical Education
Technical Occupation
Technician
Technocratic Politics
Technological Change
Technological Culture
Technological Development Theory
Technological Elite
Technological Obsolescence
Technological Revolution
Technology
Technology Policy
Technology Transfer

TECHNOCRATIC POLITICS
S-29-0244 1975 00008
BT Politics
RT Legal Rational Authority
Modernization Theory
Technocracy
Technological Change
Technological Culture
Technological Development Theory
Technological Elite
Technological Progress
Technology
Technology Policy
Technology Transfer Policy
Transitional Politics
Weberian Analysis

TECHNOLOGICAL CHANGE
S-31-0164 1975 00050
BT Political Change
RT Economic Change
Evolutionary Change
Innovation
Organization Innovation
Research And Development
Revolutionary Change
Social Change
Technocracy
Technocratic Politics
Technological Elite
Technological Progress
Technological Revolution
Technology
Technology Policy

Weberian Analysis
Weberian Theory

TECHNOLOGICAL CULTURE
S-11-0044 1975 00014
BT Culture Type
RT Cultural History
Heterogeneous Culture
Labor Discipline
Mature Capitalism
Political Culture
Secular Culture
Secular Political Culture
Technocracy
Technocratic Politics
Technological Elite
Technological Progress
Technological Revolution
Technology
Technology Policy
Technology Transfer Policy
Urban Culture
Western Culture
Western Society
Work Culture
Youth Culture

TECHNOLOGICAL DEVELOPMENT THEORY
S-38-0027 1975 00034
BT Development Theory
RT Administrative Development Theory
Advanced Industrial Society
Change Process
Economic Development Theory
Economic Growth Theory
Patent Law
Political Development Theory
Social Development Theory
Technocracy
Technocratic Politics
Technological Elite
Technological Progress
Technological Revolution
Technology
Technology Development Policy
Urban Development Theory
Weberian Analysis

TECHNOLOGICAL ELITE
S-14-0041 1975 00004
BT Elite Type
RT Academic Elite
Cultural Elite
Elite Analysis
Intellectual Elite
Intelligentsia
Managerial Elite
Modernizing Elite
Modernizing Social Elite
Scientific Elite
Scientific Manpower Policy
Technocracy
Technocratic Politics
Technological Change
Technological Culture
Technological Development Theory
Technological Progress
Technology

TECHNOLOGICAL HISTORY
USE History Of Technology

TECHNOLOGICAL OBSOLESCENCE
S-06-0802 1975 00001
BT Technology
RT Advanced Industrial Society
Advanced Technology
Middle Level Technology
Technocracy
Technology Transfer

TECHNOLOGICAL PROGRESS
S-31-0085 1975 00051
BT Progress
RT Economic Change
Innovation
Patent Law
Reform
Technocratic Politics
Technological Change
Technological Culture
Technological Development Theory
Technological Elite
Technological Revolution
Technology Development Policy

TECHNOLOGICAL REVOLUTION
S-08-0082 1975 00008
BT Revolution
RT Automated Production
Communist Revolution
Counterrevolution
Cultural Revolution
Democratic Political Revolution
Democratic Socialist Revolution
Ecological Revolution
Economic Agitation
Economic Rebellion
Green Revolution
Industrial Revolution
Political Revolution
Proletarian Revolution
Social Revolution
Socialist Revolution
Spontaneous Revolution
Technocracy
Technological Change
Technological Culture
Technological Development Theory
Technological Progress
Technology
Technology Development Policy
Technology Policy
Technology Transfer Policy

TECHNOLOGICAL UNEMPLOYMENT
S-06-0657 1975 00002
SN Unemployment due to displacement of certain occupations by technology.
BT Unemployment
RT Full Employment
Structural Unemployment
Technician
Unemployment Policy

TECHNOLOGY
S-06-0799 1975 00053
BT Characteristics
NT Advanced Technology
Middle Level Technology
Technological Obsolescence
Technology Transfer
RT Advanced Industrial Society
Automated Production
Industrial Revolution
Innovation
Polytechnical Institute Education
Post Industrial Society
Research And Development
Solar Energy
Technician
Technocracy
Technocratic Politics
Technological Change
Technological Culture
Technological Development Theory
Technological Elite
Technological Revolution

TECHNOLOGY CONSTRAINT POLICY
S-26-0417 1979 00000
BT Technology Policy
RT Technology Development Policy
Technology Transfer Policy

TECHNOLOGY DEVELOPMENT POLICY
S-26-0418 1979 00000
BT Technology Policy
RT Innovation
Technological Development Theory
Technological Progress
Technological Revolution
Technology Constraint Policy
Technology Transfer Policy

TECHNOLOGY POLICY
S-26-0416 1979 00000
BT Policy
NT Technology Constraint Policy
Technology Development Policy
Technology Transfer Policy
RT Advanced Industrial Society
Advanced Technology
History Of Technology
Labor History
Middle Level Technology
Technocracy
Technocratic Politics
Technological Change
Technological Culture
Technological Revolution

TECHNOLOGY TRANSFER
S-06-0803 1975 00086
BT Technology
RT Advanced Technology
Labor History
Middle Level Technology
Technocracy
Technological Obsolescence
Technology Transfer Policy

TECHNOLOGY TRANSFER POLICY
S-26-0419 1979 00000
BT Technology Policy
RT Advanced Technology
Middle Level Technology
Technocratic Politics
Technological Culture
Technological Revolution
Technology Constraint Policy
Technology Development Policy
Technology Transfer

TEILHARDEAN THOUGHT
S-38-0080 1975 00000
SN Thought associated with Pierre Teilhard de Chardin which merges science and theology in a theory of progress energized by love.
BT Contemporary Political Thought
RT Modern Political Thought

TELECOMMUNICATIONS INDUSTRY
S-17-0025 1975 00015
BT Communication Industry
RT Broadcasting Industry
Cable Television
Commercial Television
Communication Analysis
Communication Policy
Magazine Industry
National Press
News Agency
Public Broadcasting Industry
Public Television
Publication Industry
Radio Industry
Service Industry
State Controlled Television
Telephone Agency
Telephone Industry

TELEOLOGICAL MODEL
S-24-0321 1975 00005
BT Social Science Model
RT Aristotelian Thought
Teleology

TELEOLOGY
S-25-0031 1975 00003
SN Doctrine that posits purpose, design, and final ends are inherent in nature and must be taken into account in explanation.
BT Epistemology
RT Aristotelian Thought
Hegelian Analysis
Teleological Model

TELEPHONE AGENCY
S-19-0049 1975 00001
BT Communication Agency
RT Communication Channel
Communication Industry
Communication Policy
Telecommunications Industry
Telephone Allocation Policy
Telephone Industry
Telephone Policy

TELEPHONE ALLOCATION POLICY
S-26-0022 1975 00000
BT Telephone Policy
RT Allocation Process
Telephone Agency
Telephone Industry
Wiretapping Policy

TELEPHONE INDUSTRY
S-17-0026 1975 00003
BT Communication Industry
RT Cable Television
Telecommunications Industry
Telephone Agency
Telephone Allocation Policy
Telephone Policy

TELEPHONE INTERVIEW
S-24-0112 1975 00004
BT Interview
RT Canvassing
Depth Interview
Group Interview
Personal Interview
Unstructured Interview

TELEPHONE POLICY
S-26-0021 1975 00001
BT Individual Communication Policy
NT Telephone Allocation Policy
Wiretapping Policy
RT Postal Communication Policy
Postal Telephone Telegraph Policy
Telephone Agency
Telephone Industry

TELEPHONE QUESTIONNAIRE
S-24-0095 1975 00001
BT Questionnaire
RT Canvassing
Closed Questionnaire
Mail Questionnaire
Open Ended Questionnaire
Self Administered Questionnaire

TELEVISION CENSORSHIP
S-31-0279 1975 00004
BT Broadcasting Censorship
RT Cinema Censorship
Information Leaking
Media Access
Music Censorship
Published Media Censorship
Radio Censorship
Theater Censorship

TELEVISION INDUSTRY
S-17-0011 1975 00095
BT Broadcasting Industry
NT Cable Television
Commercial Television
Public Television
State Controlled Television
RT Commercial Broadcasting Industry
Nationalized Industry
Public Broadcasting Industry
Radio Industry
Television Policy

TELEVISION POLICY
S-26-0038 1975 00030
BT Broadcasting Policy
RT Broadcast Access Policy
Broadcast Censorship Policy
Broadcast Regulation Policy
Broadcast Subsidization Policy
Cable Television
Commercial Television
Public Television
Television Industry

TENANT FARMER
S-32-0069 1975 00004
BT Farmer
RT Agricultural Advisory Board
Collective Farmer
Farm Production
Private Farmer
Sharecropper
Tenant Farming

TENANT FARMING
S-31-0432 1975 00003
BT Farming
RT Agricultural Advisory Board
Farm Economy
Farm Industry
Migrant Farming
Sharecropper
Subsistence Farming
Tenant Farmer

TENURE POLICY
S-26-0208 1975 00003
BT Employment Policy
NT Academic Tenure Policy
RT Academic Elite
Civil Service System
Unemployment Policy

TERRITORY CLASSIFICATION
S-24-0350 1975 00001
BT Analysis Unit
NT Global System
RT Apportionment Reform
Area Studies
Mandate Territory

TERRITORY JURISDICTION
S-06-0409 1975 00030
BT Jurisdiction Characteristics
RT Administrative Jurisdiction
Border Conflict
Executive Jurisdiction
Legal Jurisdiction
Legislative Jurisdiction
Mandate Territory
Territory Sovereignty

TERRITORY REPRESENTATION THEORY
S-38-0507 1975 00000
BT Representation Theory
RT Delegate Representation Theory
Delegate Selection
Group Representation Theory
Linkage Representation Theory
Trustee Representation Theory

TERRITORY SOVEREIGNTY
S-16-0157 1975 00024
BT Sovereignty
RT Divided Sovereignty
Mandate Territory
Papal Sovereignty
Popular Sovereignty
Territory Jurisdiction

TERRORISM
S-38-0338 1979 00000
BT Ideologies
RT Guerrilla War
Highjacking
Kidnapping
Liberation Movement
Political Assassin
Political Extremism
Political Violence
Protest Politics
Psychological War
Revolutionary Change
Revolutionary Movement
Terrorist Movement
Violence

TERRORIST
S-32-0203 1975 00032
BT Political Activist
RT Air Piracy
Highjacking
Militant
Political Agitator
Political Conspirator
Political Extremism
Revolutionary
Right Wing Activist
Terrorist Movement

TERRORIST MOVEMENT
S-27-0015 1979 00000
BT Extremist Movement
RT Independence Movement
Liberation Movement
Maoist Movement
Radical Movement
Revolutionary Movement
Separatist Movement
Terrorism
Terrorist

TEST BAN AGREEMENT
S-02-0096 1975 00005
BT State Agreement Type
NT Test Ban Treaty
RT Arms Control Agreement
Arms Control Policy
Arms Inspection Policy
Defensive Weapon
Disarmament Agreement
Military Alliance
Nuclear Nonproliferation Agreement

TEST BAN TREATY
S-02-0097 1975 00007
BT Test Ban Agreement
RT Arms Control Policy
Arms Control Treaty
Arms Inspection Policy
Nuclear Nonproliferation Treaty

TEST RESULTS
S-18-0099 1979 00000
BT Statistical Data
RT Aptitude Measurement
Cross Cultural Data
Degree Requirement
Education Evaluation
Education Testing
Hypothesis Testing
Intelligence Quotient
Literacy Test
Merit Bureaucracy
Physiological Test
Public Opinion Survey
Test Retest Reliability
Testing
Testing Agency

TEST RETEST RELIABILITY
S-24-0163 1975 00002
BT Reliability Measurement
RT Intercoder Reliability
Internal Consistency Reliability
Interviewer Effect
Test Results

TESTIMONY
S-31-0533 1975 00003
BT Trial Strategy
RT Jury
Prosecution Immunity

Self Defense
Testimony Compulsion Authority

TESTIMONY COMPULSION AUTHORITY
S-04-0035 1975 00000
BT Civil Authority
RT Testimony

TESTING
S-31-0011 1979 00000
UF Examination
BT Analytic Process
RT Accreditation Process
Driver Licensing Policy
Education Accreditation Process
Education Policy
Merit Policy
Professional Accreditation Process
Test Results
Testing Agency

TESTING AGENCY
S-19-0062 1979 00000
BT Agencies
RT Education Agency
Education Policy
Recruitment Process
Test Results
Testing

TEXTBOOK
S-18-0102 1979 00000
BT Information Sources
RT Education Testing
Encyclopedia
Instructional Material
Political Literature
Political Science Teaching
Teacher
Thesaurus
Thesis

TEXTILE INDUSTRY
S-17-0061 1979 00000
BT Manufacturing Industry
NT Clothing Industry
RT Light Industry
Machinery Industry
Paper Industry

THEATER CENSORSHIP
S-31-0284 1979 00000
BT Performing Arts Censorship
RT Aesthetics
Broadcasting Censorship
Government Media Regulation Policy
Radio Censorship
Television Censorship

THEATRE
USE Visual Arts

THEATRE CENSORSHIP
1975-1979 00001

THEOCRATIC AUTHORITY
S-04-0025 1975 00003
BT Religious Authority
RT Moral Authority
Religious Politics
Religious Thought
Religious War
Weberian Analysis

THEORETICAL FRAMEWORK
S-24-0412 1975 00095
BT Methodology
NT Macrolevel Analysis
Microlevel Analysis
Variable
RT Analysis Methodology
Data Collection Methodology
Data Presentation Methodology
Hypothesis Testing
Methodological Individualism
Middle Range Theory
Research Design
Research Orientation
Study Scope
Theoretical Range
Theory

THEORETICAL RANGE
S-38-0594 1975 00004
BT Theory
NT General Theory
Middle Range Theory
RT Formal Political Theory
Micropolitical Theory
Micropolitical Thought
Scientific Theory
Statistics Discipline
Theoretical Framework
Theoretical Research
Theory
Theory Construction

THEORETICAL RESEARCH
S-24-0397 1975 00130
BT Research Orientation
NT Concept Explication Research
RT Advocacy Research
Applied Research
Basic Research
Data Selection Orientation
Descriptive Research
Experimental Research
Explanatory Research
Market Research
Predictive Research
Qualitative Research
Quantitative Research
Scientific Research
Theoretical Range
Theory

THEORY
S-38-0001 1975 00017
NT Anthropological Theory
Behavioral Theory
Data Theory
Development Theory
General System Theory
Information Theory
Linguistic Theory
Modernization Theory
Organization Theory
Planning Theory
Political Theory
Psychological Theory
Religious Thought
Scientific Theory
Social Theory
Theoretical Range
Theory Construction
RT Academic Areas
Authority
Behavior
Characteristics
Elite Type
Freedom
Institutions
Philosophical Concept
Policy
Political Party Type
Political Theory Studies
Politics
Socialization
Status
System Type
Theoretical Framework
Theoretical Range
Theoretical Research
Theory Construction

THEORY CONSTRUCTION
S-38-0597 1975 00066
BT Theory
RT Data Theory
Methodology
Natural Science Model
Scientific Theory
Social Theory
Theoretical Range
Theory

THEORY OF CAUSALITY
S-38-0579 1979 00000
BT Scientific Theory
RT Contemporary Analytic Modes
Explanatory Research
Natural Science Model
Philosophy Of Science Studies
Statistical Analysis
Statistical Inference

THERMIDOR
S-08-0083 1975 00001
SN That phase of a revolutionary process in which reaction and opposition become manifest and organized.
BT Revolution
RT Bourgeois Revolution
Communist Revolution
Counterrevolution
Democratic Political Revolution
Democratic Socialist Revolution
Government Overthrow
Internal War
National Political Revolution
Political Revolution
Rebellion
Social Revolution
Socialist Revolution
Struggle

THESAURUS
S-18-0103 1979 00000
UF Macrothesaurus
BT Information Sources
RT Bibliographic Control
Bibliographic Service
Concept Explication Research
Documentation Service
Documents
Government Information Service
Instructional Material
Literature Review
Textbook

THESIS
S-18-0104 1975 00000
UF Dissertation
BT Information Sources

RT Field Data
Hypothesis Testing
Monographs
Textbook

THIRD PARTY
1975-1979 00004

THIRD POLITICAL PARTY
S-28-0063 1979 00000
BT Structure Specific Political Party Type
RT Elite Political Party
Minor Political Party

THIRD WORLD BLOC
S-02-0045 1975 00066
BT Extranational Bloc
NT Afro Asian Bloc
Arab Bloc
Latin American Bloc
Neutral Bloc
RT Atlantic Community
Fourth World Nation
International Bloc
New International Economic Order
Political Front
Security Community
Third World Nation

THIRD WORLD NATION
S-16-0129 1979 00000
BT Nation Type
RT Aligned Nation
Client Nation
Client State
Dependent Nation
Developing Nation
Former Colony
Fourth World Nation
International Relations Studies
Nonaligned Nation
Poor Nation
Scarcity
Sovereign Nation
Third World Bloc
United Nations

THOMISM
S-38-0379 1975 00002
SN Theory associated directly with or analytically traceable to Thomas Aquinas.
BT Medieval Political Thought
RT Aristotelian Thought
Canon Law
Catholicism
Medieval Natural Law Theory
Medieval State Theory
Roman Catholicism

THREAT INDICATOR
S-24-0263 1975 00010
BT Conflict Indicator
RT Arms Verification Policy
Brinkmanship
Gunboat Diplomacy
International Conflict
International Politics
Statistical Data
War

THUCYDIDEAN POLITICAL THOUGHT
S-38-0059 1975 00001
SN Form of political-historical analysis associated with Thucydides.
BT Classical Political Thought
RT Ancient History
Epicurean Thought
History Discipline
Presocratic Political Thought

THURSTONE SCALE
S-24-0219 1975 00001
BT Scale Construction Methodology
RT Composite Scale
Cumulative Scale
Factor Structure
Guttman Scale
Likert Scale
Measurement Level Scale
Multidimensional Scale
Nominal Scale
Ordinal Scale
Ratio Scale
Scalability Index
Semantic Differential
Unidimensional Scale

TICKET SPLITTER
S-32-0332 1975 00000
BT Voter
RT Independent Voter
Independent Voting

TIDAL ENERGY
S-31-0127 1979 00000
BT Natural Resource Exploitation
RT Advanced Technology
Coal Energy
Energy Policy
Energy Use Policy
Gas Energy
Geothermal Energy
Hydroelectric Energy
Natural Resource Policy
Nuclear Energy
Oil Energy
Solar Energy
Water Use Policy
Wind Energy

TIGHT BIPOLAR INTERNATIONAL POLITICAL SYSTEM
S-37-0118 1975 00001
BT Bipolar International System
RT Loose Bipolar International Political System

TIME SERIES ANALYSIS
S-24-0088 1975 00012
SN The analysis of temporally ordered data through the making of observations at regular intervals.
BT Longitudinal Analysis
NT Cross Lagged Panel Analysis
RT Cross Lagged Panel Analysis
Panel Technique

TIME VARIABLE
S-24-0454 1975 00050
BT Variable Substantive Content
RT Historical Variable
Political Variable
Social Variable

TITOISM
S-38-0332 1975 00001
SN Doctrines of communist development, rule and workers management associated with Joseph Tito.
BT Marxism
RT Bolshevism
Castroism
Communism
Evolutionary Marxism
Hegelian Marxism
Leninism
Maoism
Marxism Leninism
Marxist Revisionism
Polycentrism
Stalinism
Trotskyism

TITULAR LEADER
S-32-0055 1975 00000
BT Political Leader
RT Political Role

TOCQUEVILLIAN ANALYSIS
S-38-0425 1975 00002
BT Modern Political Thought
RT Equality Theory

TOKEN REPRESENTATION
S-31-0727 1979 00000
BT Representation Type
RT Candidate Selection
District Representation
Geographic Representation
Minority Group
Racial Composition
Representation Theory
Selection Process
Sexism

TOLERANCE
S-06-0135 1975 00013
BT Attitude Characteristics
NT Political Tolerance
Racial Tolerance
RT Altruism
Deference
Intolerance
Other Directedness
Political Trust
Trust

TOPOGRAPHY
S-01-0092 1979 00000
BT Physical Geography
RT Agronomy
Demographic Studies
Ecology Discipline
Economic History
Environmental Studies
Natural Science Education
Natural Science Model
Physical Anthropology
Scientific Research

TORT
S-21-0025 1979 00000
BT Contract Law
RT Bankruptcy Law
Civil Law
Economic Law
Labor Law
Negligence Law
Property Law

TOTAL WAR
S-08-0109 1975 00001
BT War
NT World War
RT Nuclear War
Propaganda War

TOTAL WAR POLICY
S-26-0343 1975 00001
BT War Policy
RT Global War Policy
Limited War Policy
Local War Policy
Peoples War Policy
War Reparation Policy

TOTALITARIAN DICTATORSHIP
S-16-0043 1975 00004
BT Dictatorship
RT Absolutism
Absolutist Government
Communist Government
Communist Imperialism
Falangist
Fascist Theory
Francoism
Maoism
Maoist
Maoist Political Party
Maoist Revolutionary
National Socialism
One Political Party System
Police State
Political Repression
Totalitarian Leadership
Totalitarian Movement
Tyranny

TOTALITARIAN LEADERSHIP
S-22-0020 1975 00005
BT Leadership Structure Type
RT Absolutism
Administrative Leadership
Bureaucratic Leadership
Charismatic Leadership
Closed Leadership
Collective Leadership
Cult Of Personality
Fascist Theory
Francoism
Maoism
Maoist
Maoist Political Party
Maoist Revolutionary
National Leadership
National Socialism
Personalized Leadership
Political Leadership
Political Party Leadership
Political Succession
Rational Legal Leadership
Totalitarian Dictatorship
Totalitarian Movement
Totalitarian Political System

TOTALITARIAN MOVEMENT
S-27-0070 1975 00001
BT Political Movement
RT Communism
Fascist Movement
Francoism
Italian Fascism
Maoism
Maoist
Maoist Movement
Maoist Political Party
Maoist Revolutionary
Messianic Movement
National Socialism
National Socialist Political Party
Radical Movement
Totalitarian Dictatorship
Totalitarian Leadership
Totalitarian Political System

TOTALITARIAN PARTY
1975-1979 00001

TOTALITARIAN POLITICAL PARTY
S-28-0064 1979 00000
BT Structure Specific Political Party Type
RT Elite Political Party
Falangist
Flangist Political Party
National Socialist Political Party

TOTALITARIAN POLITICAL SYSTEM
S-37-0133 1975 00018
BT Political System Type
RT Absolute Monarch
Absolute Monarchy
Absolutism
Absolutist Government
Authoritarianism
Centrally Planned Economy
Command Economic System
Command Economy
Cult Of Personality
Forced Requisitioning
Francoism
Italian Fascism
Maoism
Maoist
Maoist Political Party
Maoist Revolutionary
National Socialism
One Political Party System
Political Refugee
Purge
Stalinist
Totalitarian Leadership
Totalitarian Movement

TOURISM
USE Tourist Industry

TOURIST INDUSTRY
S-17-0069 1975 00011
UF Tourism
BT Service Industry
RT Analysis Of Play
International Commerce
Leisure Time Analysis

TOWN
S-07-0052 1975 00005
BT Community Type
RT Homogeneous Community
Local Political Division
New Town
Planned Economy
Political Community
Rural Community
Suburb
Town Council
Town Meeting
Township
Township Government
Village Community

TOWN COUNCIL
S-19-0121 1975 00000
BT Local Government Council
NT Town Meeting
RT City Council
Local Policy Making
Local Political Elite
Political Leader
Town
Township
Township Government
Village Council

TOWN MEETING
S-19-0122 1975 00000
BT Town Council
RT Community Decision Making
Local Policy Making
Local Policy Planning
Local Political Division
Local Political Elite
Subnational Decision Making Process
Town

TOWNSHIP
S-24-0369 1975 00001
BT State Political Division
RT Borough
County
Legislative District
Town
Town Council
Township Government
Village

TOWNSHIP GOVERNMENT
S-16-0108 1975 00001
BT Local Government
RT Borough Government
Community Decision Making
Local Elite
Local Policy Making
Local Policy Planning
Local Political Division
Local Political Elite
Town
Town Council
Township

TRADE
S-31-0384 1975 00029
BT Economic Relations
NT Foreign Trade
International Trade
RT Commerce
Foreign Income
Formal Competition
Hunting And Trapping Economy
Industrial Relations
International Economic Characteristics
International Economic Relations
International Economics
Trade Agency

TRADE AGENCY
S-19-0031 1975 00001
BT Production Agency
RT Commerce
International Economics
Interstate Commerce Commission
Trade

Trade Agreement
Trade Organization

TRADE AGREEMENT
S-02-0098 1975 00006
BT State Agreement Type
RT Commercial Agreement
Economic Agreement
Economic Treaty
Protective Tariff
Trade Agency
World Commerce

TRADE BLOC
S-03-0060 1975 00011
BT International Trade Organization
RT Atlantic Community
Economic Community
International Economic Organization

TRADE DOCUMENT
S-18-0028 1975 00000
BT Foreign Intergovernmental Document
RT Tariff Record
Treaty Document

TRADE ORGANIZATION
S-03-0058 1975 00001
BT Organizations
NT International Trade Organization
RT Customs Union
European Integration Theory
Industrial Association
International Organization
Marketing Cooperative
Monetary Union
Protective Tariff
Trade Agency

TRADE POLICY
S-26-0180 1975 00047
BT Economic Policy
NT Export Subsidization Policy
Free Trade Policy
Most Favored Nation Policy
Restrictive Trade Policy
RT Balance Of Payments
Balance Of Trade
Economic Growth Policy
Economic Subsidization Policy
Hunting And Trapping Economy
International Economic Boycott
Interstate Commerce Commission
World Commerce

TRADE UNION
S-03-0071 1975 00011
BT Union
RT Craft Union
Industrial Union
Labor Force
Labor Political Party
Labor Union
Lobbyist
Producer Cooperative
Trade Union Politics
Union Worker
Unionized Working Class

TRADE UNION LAW
S-21-0048 1975 00002
BT Economic Law
RT Trade Union Movement

TRADE UNION MOVEMENT
S-27-0007 1975 00017
BT Economic Movement
RT Consumer Rights Movement
Labor Law
Syndicalism
Trade Union Law
Trade Union Politics
Trade Unionism
Worker Organization

TRADE UNION POLICY
S-26-0322 1975 00013
BT Labor Management Relations Policy
RT Collective Bargaining Policy
Labor Law
Public Employee Union Policy
Right To Work Policy

TRADE UNION POLITICS
S-29-0212 1975 00010
BT Labor Politics
RT Trade Union
Trade Union Movement
Worker Organization

TRADE UNIONISM
S-38-0339 1975 00011
BT Ideologies
RT Labor Economics
Syndicalism
Trade Union Movement

TRADITIONAL AUTHORITY
S-04-0009 1975 00009
BT Authority Mode
RT Absolute Monarch
Absolutism
Ascribed Status
Blue Law
Charismatic Authority
Civil Religion
Conservatism
Conservative Political Party
Cultural History
Derived Authority
Moral Authority
Parental Authority
Religious Authority
Religious Fundamentalism
Straussian Thought
Traditional Culture
Traditional Leadership
Traditional Political Party

TRADITIONAL CULTURE
S-11-0045 1975 00053
BT Culture Type
NT Nomadic Culture
Peasant Culture
RT Buddhism
Community Culture
Conservatism
Conservative Political Party
Cultural History
Ethnic Culture
Ethnocentrism
Folkways
Kinship System
Nonwestern Culture
Paternalistic Family
Peasant Class
Political Culture
Religious Culture
Traditional Authority
Traditional Education
Traditional Political Culture
Traditional Political Party
Traditional Political System
Traditional Society
Village Culture

TRADITIONAL EDUCATION
S-13-0053 1975 00007
BT Education Type
NT Urban Education
RT Academic Areas
Academic Specialization
Classical Education
Compulsory Education
Higher Education
Humanistic Education
Ideological Education
Legal Education
Liberal Arts Education
Pedagogical Institute Education
Private Higher Education
Progressive Education
Secondary Education
State Supported Higher Education
Traditional Culture

TRADITIONAL LEADERSHIP
S-22-0010 1975 00003
BT Leadership Authority Base
NT Religious Leadership
RT Absolute Monarch
Administrative Leadership
Bureaucratic Leadership
Closed Leadership
Ecclesiastical Leadership
Leadership Structure Type
Moral Leadership
National Leadership
Personalized Leadership
Political Leadership
Political Party Leadership
Small Group Leadership
Traditional Authority
Traditional Political Party
Traditional Political System
Traditional Society

TRADITIONAL PARTY
1975-1979 00000

TRADITIONAL POLITICAL CULTURE
S-11-0034 1975 00007
BT Civic Culture
RT Civic Culture
Fragmented Political Culture
Peasant Culture
Religious Authority
Subject Participant Culture
Traditional Culture
Traditional Political Party
Traditional Political System
Traditional Society

TRADITIONAL POLITICAL ELITE
S-14-0031 1975 00003
BT Political Elite
RT Ascribed Status
Religious Elite
Traditional Political Party
Traditional Social Elite
Transitional Political Elite

TRADITIONAL POLITICAL PARTY
S-28-0050 1979 00000
BT Sector Based Political Party Type
NT Religious Political Party
RT Conservative Political Party
Traditional Authority
Traditional Culture
Traditional Leadership
Traditional Political Culture
Traditional Political Elite
Traditional Political System
Traditional Social Elite
Traditional Society
Transitional Political Elite
Village Politics

TRADITIONAL POLITICAL SYSTEM
S-37-0134 1975 00004
BT Political System Type
RT Feudal System
Traditional Culture
Traditional Leadership
Traditional Political Culture
Traditional Political Party
Traditional Social Elite
Traditional Society
Tribal Political System
Village Politics

TRADITIONAL SOCIAL ELITE
S-14-0037 1975 00005
BT Social Elite
RT Ascribed Status
Caste Society
Community Elite
Conservatism
Modernizing Social Elite
Religious Elite
Traditional Political Elite
Traditional Political Party
Traditional Political System
Traditional Society

TRADITIONAL SOCIETY
S-35-0045 1975 00048
BT Society Type
NT Preindustrial Society
Religious Society
RT Ascribed Status
Caste Society
Clan Society
Closed Society
Cottage Industry
Customary Law
Ethnic Community
Peasant Society
Primitive Society
Traditional Culture
Traditional Leadership
Traditional Political Culture
Traditional Political Party
Traditional Political System
Traditional Social Elite
Untouchables
Village Community

TRAFFIC SAFETY POLICY
S-26-0403 1975 00008
BT Safety Policy
NT Air Safety Policy
Highway Safety Policy
RT Industrial Safety Policy

TRAINING ASSISTANCE
S-06-0314 1975 00016
BT Foreign Assistance
RT Job Training
Management Training Program
Military Assistance
Technical Assistance

TRAITOR
S-36-0037 1975 00000
BT Political Criminal
RT Political Assassin
Political Crime
Treason

TRANSACTIONAL ANALYSIS
S-09-0074 1975 00012
BT Contemporary Analytic Modes
RT Transactional Theory
Value Analysis

TRANSACTIONAL THEORY
S-38-0174 1975 00001
BT Explanatory Political Theory
RT Decision Making Theory
Political Behaviorism
Political System Theory
Power Theory
Transactional Analysis

TRANSCENDENTALISM
S-38-0420 1975 00001
BT Modern Idealism
RT Eschatology

TRANSITIONAL POLITICAL ELITE
S-14-0032 1975 00003
BT Political Elite
RT Intelligentsia
Military Elite
Modernizing Elite
Modernizing Political Elite
Pluralist Elite
Potential Elite
Power Elite
Revolutionary Movement
Traditional Political Elite
Traditional Political Party
Transitional Politics
Transitional Society

TRANSITIONAL POLITICAL SYSTEM
S-37-0135 1975 00013
BT Political System Type
RT Developing Political System
Transitional Politics
Transitional Society

TRANSITIONAL POLITICS
S-29-0245 1975 00012
BT Politics
RT Technocratic Politics
Transitional Political Elite
Transitional Political System
Transitional Society

TRANSITIONAL SOCIETY
S-35-0049 1975 00019
BT Society Type
RT Cottage Industry
Modernizing Society
Secular Society
Transitional Political Elite
Transitional Political System
Transitional Politics

TRANSNATIONAL POLITICAL MOVEMENT
S-27-0057 1975 00001
BT Sector Based Political Movement
RT Class Based Movement
Ecumenical Movement
Transnational Politics

TRANSNATIONAL POLITICS
S-29-0210 1975 00004
BT World Politics
RT Superpower Politics
Transnational Political Movement

TRANSPORTATION AGENCY
S-19-0063 1975 00007
BT Agencies
RT Municipal Authorities
Regulatory Commission
Transportation System

TRANSPORTATION DISTRICT
S-16-0096 1975 00002
BT District Government Type
RT Fire District
Recreation District
School District
Sewer District
Water District
Zoning District

TRANSPORTATION ECONOMICS
S-01-0074 1979 00000
BT Economics Discipline
RT Consumer Economics
Econometrics
Industrial Economics
Macroeconomics
Mass Transit Policy
Regional Economics
Social Economics
Transportation Policy
Transportation System
Urban Economics
Urban Transit Policy

TRANSPORTATION INDUSTRY
S-17-0070 1975 00016
BT Industry
NT Air Transportation Industry
Land Transportation Industry
Mass Transportation Industry
Water Transportation Industry
RT Highway Policy
Highway Safety Policy
Service Industry
Transportation System

TRANSPORTATION POLICY
S-26-0420 1975 00024
BT Policy
NT Highway Policy
Mass Transit Policy
RT Automobile Industry
Driver Licensing Policy
Land Transportation Industry
Mass Transit Policy
Motor Vehicle Industry
Railway Industry
Shipping Industry
Transportation Economics
Transportation System
Trucking Industry

TRANSPORTATION SYSTEM
S-37-0148 1979 00000
BT System Type
RT Air Transportation Industry
Air Transportation Policy
Automobile Industry
Mass Transit Policy
Mass Transportation Industry
Transportation Agency
Transportation Economics
Transportation Industry
Transportation Policy

TREASON
S-10-0079 1975 00002
BT Political Crime
RT Defection
Desertion
Individual Crime
Political Conspiracy
Sedition
Traitor
War Crime

TREATY BREAKING
S-31-0219 1975 00003
BT Treaty Dissolution
RT Conflict Theory
Escalation
International Conflict
Treaty Dissolution
Treaty Making
War

TREATY DISSOLUTION
S-31-0218 1975 00000
BT Conflict Intensification
NT Treaty Breaking
RT Conflict Intensification
Escalation
Treaty Breaking

TREATY DOCUMENT
S-18-0029 1975 00001
BT Foreign Intergovernmental Document
RT Foreign Policy
Foreign Rule
Friendship Treaty
International Organization Record
Trade Document

TREATY MAKING
S-31-0226 1975 00015
BT Agreement
RT Atlantic Community
Bilateral State Agreement
International Adjudication
International Negotiation
International Peace Negotiation
Summit Meeting
Treaty Breaking
World Court

TREATY RATIFICATION
S-31-0597 1975 00004
BT Law Formulation
RT Legislative Procedure

TREND ANALYSIS
S-24-0019 1979 00000
BT Forecasting Methodology
RT Authority Forecasting
Brainstorming
Delphi Technique
Divergence Mapping
Economic Forecasting
PERT Analysis
Policy Evaluation Research
Policy Research
Political Forecasting
Predictive Research
Scenario Construction
Social Forecasting

TRENTINE DOCTRINE
S-38-0380 1975 00000
BT Medieval Political Thought
RT Catholicism
Religious Thought
Roman Catholicism

TRIAL
S-31-0517 1975 00001
BT Court Procedure
NT Fair Trial
Military Trial
Political Trial
Public Trial
Secret Trial
RT Adversary Process
Adversary System
Law System
Law Type
Lawyer
Post Trial Procedure
Trial Court
Trial Jury
Trial System

TRIAL COURT
S-19-0143 1975 00003
BT Criminal Court
RT Adversary Process
Adversary System
Appellate Court
Court Attorney
District Attorney
District Court
Jury
Law System
Law Type
Lawyer
Local Court
Military Prosecutor
Military Trial
Military Tribunal
Trial
Trial Jury
Trial Procedure
Trial System

TRIAL JURY
S-19-0149 1975 00000
BT Jury
RT Adversary System
Justice Administration Agency
Lawyer
Public Trial
Trial
Trial Court
Trial Procedure
Trial Strategy

TRIAL ORAL ARGUMENT
S-31-0530 1975 00000
BT Trial Procedure
RT Lawyer
Star Chamber Proceeding

TRIAL PROCEDURE
S-31-0528 1975 00003
BT Court Procedure
NT Jury Selection
Trial Oral Argument
Trial Strategy
RT Court Attorney
Court Procedure
Law System
Lawyer
Political Trial
Post Trial Procedure
Public Trial
Trial Court
Trial Jury
Trial System

TRIAL STRATEGY
S-31-0531 1975 00000
BT Trial Procedure
NT Self Defense
Testimony
RT Adversary System
Jury Selection
Lawyer
Political Trial
Trial Jury

TRIAL SYSTEM
S-37-0094 1975 00002
BT Justice System
NT Jury System
RT Adversary Process
Adversary System
Executive Immunity
Grand Jury System
Law Enforcement System
Political Trial
Public Trial
Right To Jury Trial
Right To Trial
Search And Seizure
Trial
Trial Court
Trial Procedure

TRIBAL POLITICAL SYSTEM
S-37-0136 1975 00013
BT Political System Type
RT Kinship
Local Political Elite
Traditional Political System
Tribal Politics
Tribal Society
Tribalism

TRIBAL POLITICS
S-29-0242 1975 00010
BT Subnational Politics
RT Kinship
Kinship Role
Kinship System
Tribal Political System
Tribal Society
Tribalism

TRIBAL SOCIETY
S-35-0029 1975 00044
BT Society Type Base
RT Caste Society
Clan Society
Feudal Society
Homogeneous Society
Kinship

Kinship Role
Nomadic Society
Peasant Society
Tribal Political System
Tribal Politics
Tribalism

TRIBALISM
S-38-0270 1975 00005
BT Cultural Nationalism
RT Black Nationalism
Irredentism
Kinship
Primitive Society
Tribal Political System
Tribal Politics
Tribal Society

TRICKLE DOWN THEORY
S-38-0207 1979 00000
BT Economic Ideology
RT Economic Development
Economic Growth Index
Technical Aid Policy

TRIGONOMETRY
S-24-0029 1975 00000
BT Mathematical Analysis
RT Calculus
Geometry
Linear Programming
Mathematics Discipline

TROTSKYISM
S-38-0333 1975 00016
BT Marxism
RT Bolshevism
Castroism
Communism
Hegelian Marxism
Leninism
Maoism
Marxism Leninism
Marxist Revisionism
Permanent Revolution Theory
Polycentrism
Proletarian Internationalism
Stalinism
Titoism
Trotskyite Political Party

TROTSKYITE PARTY
1975-1979 00000

TROTSKYITE POLITICAL PARTY
S-28-0014 1979 00000
BT Communist Political Party
RT Bolshevik Political Party
Bolshevism
Communism
Communist Deviationism
Communist Studies
Leninism
Permanent Revolution Theory
Polycentrism
Stalinism
Trotskyism

TRUCE
S-26-0077 1975 00000
BT Defense Policy
RT Armistice Policy
Arms Control Policy
Peace
War Declaration Policy

TRUCKING INDUSTRY
S-17-0076 1979 00000
BT Motor Vehicle Industry
RT Air Transportation Industry
Automobile Industry
Mass Transportation Industry
Motor Vehicle Insurance
Railway Industry
Shipping Industry
Transportation Policy

TRUST
S-06-0138 1979 00000
BT Attitude Characteristics
NT Political Trust
RT Empathy
Friendship
Other Directedness
Political Attitude
Satisfaction
Tolerance

TRUSTEE REPRESENTATION THEORY
S-38-0508 1975 00001
SN Doctrine that legislators are selected to exercise their best independent judgments on behalf of their constituency.
BT Representation Theory
RT Delegate Representation Theory
Delegate Selection
Group Representation Theory
Linkage Representation Theory
Territory Representation Theory
Virtual Representation Theory

TSAR
S-36-0062 1975 00004
BT Emperor
RT Absolutism
Benevolent Despot
Hereditary Ruler
Kaiser
Khan
King
Queen
Regent
Shah
Sheik
Sultan

TUTELARY DEMOCRACY
S-16-0034 1975 00000
BT Democratic Government
RT Absolutism
Absolutist Government
Autocratic Government
Corporate State
Democratic Government
Dictatorship
Elitist Democracy
Guided Democracy
Guided Democracy Theory
Peoples Democratic State

TWO PARTY DEMOCRACY
1975-1979 00001

TWO PARTY POLITICS
1975-1979 00003

TWO PARTY SYSTEM
1975-1979 00010

TWO PARTY VOTING INDICATOR
1975-1979 00001

TWO PERSON GAME THEORY
S-38-0136 1975 00006
BT Game Theory
RT Fixed Sum Gaming
N Person Game Theory
Prisoner Dilemma Gaming
Two Person Gaming

TWO PERSON GAMING
S-24-0103 1975 00013
BT Gaming
RT Fixed Sum Gaming
Nonzero Sum Gaming
Prisoner Dilemma Gaming
Two Person Game Theory
Variable Sum Gaming
Zero Sum Gaming

TWO POLITICAL PARTY DEMOCRACY
S-16-0027 1979 00000
BT Political Party Democracy
RT Government Type
Interparty Competition
Multiparty Democracy
One Political Party Democracy
Political Competition
Two Political Party Politics
Two Political Party System

TWO POLITICAL PARTY POLITICS
S-29-0222 1979 00000
BT Partisan Politics
RT Two Political Party Democracy
Two Political Party System
Two Political Party Voting Indicator

TWO POLITICAL PARTY SYSTEM
S-37-0130 1979 00000
BT Political Party System
NT Disciplined Two Party System
Responsible Two Party System
RT Multiparty System
One Political Party System
Responsible Two Party System
Two Political Party Democracy
Two Political Party Politics
Two Political Party Voting Indicator

TWO POLITICAL PARTY VOTING INDICATOR
S-24-0271 1979 00000
BT Voting Indicator
RT Legislative Voting Indicator
Two Political Party Politics
Two Political Party System
Voting Data
Voting Result Interpretation
Voting Theory
Voting Turnout Indicator

TWO STEP COMMUNICATION FLOW
S-31-0170 1975 00001
BT Communication Flow
RT Communication Analysis
Communication Channel
Communication Field

TWO SWORDS THEORY
S-38-0381 1975 00000
BT Medieval Political Thought
NT Conciliar Movement Doctrine
Gelasian Doctrine
Investiture Controversy
RT Christian Thought
Church State Policy

Medieval Corporatism
Medieval International Theory
Medieval Islamic Thought
Medieval State Theory

TYPOLOGIZING
S-31-0012 1975 00011
BT Analytic Process
RT Analysis Framework
Classification Process
Comparative Analysis
Formalization
Historical Periods
Typology

TYPOLOGY
S-24-0173 1975 00022
UF Category
BT Classification
RT Aggregate Data Statistics
Typologizing

TYRANNICIDE
S-10-0057 1975 00000
BT Assassination
RT Freedom
Individual Crime
Murder
Tyranny

TYRANNY
S-16-0151 1975 00003
BT Rule Type
RT Absolute Monarch
Absolute Monarchy
Absolutism
Absolutist Government
Aggression
Despotism
Military Dictatorship
Military Directorate
Military Government
Military State
Political Repression
Totalitarian Dictatorship
Tyrannicide

UNBIASED ESTIMATION
S-24-0075 1975 00007
BT Population Estimation
RT Central Tendency Measure
Parameter Estimation
Statistical Inference

UNCONVENTIONAL WEAPON
S-33-0041 1975 00001
BT Weapon
RT Biological Weapon
Chemical Weapon
Conventional Weapon
Defensive Weapon
Nuclear Weapon
Strategic Weapon
Tactical Weapon

UNDECLARED WAR
S-08-0111 1975 00002
BT War
RT Armed Intervention Policy
Border Conflict
Cold War
Holy War
Ideological War

UNDERDEVELOPED ECONOMY
S-12-0044 1975 00030
BT Economy Type
RT Agrarian Economy
Barter Economy
Cottage Industry Economy
Depressed Area
Depressed Economy
Farm Economy
Farm Industry
Nomadic Economy
Peasant Economy
Planned Economy
Self Sufficient Economy
Subsistence Economy

UNDERDEVELOPED NATION
S-16-0130 1975 00073
BT Nation Type
RT Dependent Nation
Developing Nation
Divided Nation
Poor Nation

UNDEREMPLOYMENT
S-06-0654 1975 00015
BT Employment Characteristics
RT Full Employment
Labor Force
Labor Market
Labor Supply
Labor Surplus
Overemployment
Unemployment
Unemployment Policy

UNDERGROUND PARTY
1975-1979 00000

UNDERGROUND POLITICAL PARTY
S-28-0065 1979 00000
BT Political Party Type
RT Freedom Of Speech
Political Repression
Radical Political Party
Radical Press
Radicalism
Revolutionary Movement
Revolutionary Political Party
Underground Press

UNDERGROUND PRESS
S-17-0024 1975 00001
BT Newspaper Industry
RT Black Press
National Press
Radical Press
Radicalism
Underground Political Party

UNEARNED INCOME
S-06-0344 1979 00000
BT Income
RT Business Income
Capitalism
Capitalist Economy
Economic Gain
Family Income
Farm Income
Foreign Income
Income Measure
Inheritance System
Personal Income
Profit Income

UNEMPLOYED PERSON
S-32-0127 1975 00009
BT Occupational Role
RT Job Training
Structural Unemployment
Unemployment
Unemployment Compensation
Unemployment Insurance Policy
Unemployment Policy
Welfare
Welfare Agency

UNEMPLOYMENT
S-06-0655 1975 00063
BT Employment Characteristics
NT Structural Unemployment
Technological Unemployment
RT Full Employment
Job Training
Labor Market
Labor Supply
Overemployment
Public Spending
Underemployment
Unemployed Person
Unemployment Insurance Policy
Unemployment Policy
Welfare Administration
Welfare Agency
Welfare Policy
Welfare State

UNEMPLOYMENT COMPENSATION
S-06-0323 1975 00005
BT Government Expenditure
RT Income Rights
Public Assistance
Social Security
Social Security Taxation
Unemployed Person
Unemployment Insurance Policy
Unemployment Policy
Welfare
Welfare Administration
Welfare Capitalism
Welfare State
Welfare System

UNEMPLOYMENT INSURANCE POLICY
S-26-0309 1975 00004
BT Insurance
RT Catastrophe Insurance
Compulsory Insurance
Employment Policy
Fire Insurance
Life Insurance
National Health Insurance
Public Assistance
Social Welfare Policy
Unemployed Person
Unemployment
Unemployment Compensation
Unemployment Policy
Welfare
Welfare Agency
Welfare Spending

UNEMPLOYMENT POLICY
S-26-0210 1975 00024
BT Employment Policy
RT Full Employment Policy
Manpower Policy
Motor Vehicle Industry

Public Assistance
Social Rights
Technological Unemployment
Tenure Policy
Underemployment
Unemployed Person
Unemployment
Unemployment Compensation
Unemployment Insurance Policy
Vocational Education
Welfare Administration
Welfare Agency
Welfare Policy

UNFAIR COMPETITION
S-31-0215 1975 00000
BT Competition
RT Economic Competition
Perfect Competition

UNICAMERAL LEGISLATURE
S-19-0255 1975 00001
BT Legislature Type
RT Bicameral Legislature
House Of Representatives
National Legislature
Senate
Subnational Legislature

UNIDIMENSIONAL SCALE
S-24-0220 1975 00005
BT Scale Construction Methodology
RT Factor Structure
Guttman Scale
Interval Scale
Likert Scale
Measurement Level Scale
Nominal Scale
Ordinal Scale
Ratio Scale
Scalability Index
Semantic Differential
Thurstone Scale

UNIFORM CODE OF MILITARY JUSTICE
S-21-0063 1975 00000
BT Military Law
RT Penal Law
Penal Reform

UNILATERAL AID POLICY
S-26-0261 1975 00000
BT Foreign Aid Policy
RT Bilateral Aid Policy
Economic Aid Policy
Military Aid Policy
Multilateral Aid Policy
Technical Aid Policy
Unilateral Declaration

UNILATERAL DECLARATION
S-02-0059 1975 00003
BT State Agreement Declaration
RT Mutual Support Declaration
Unilateral Aid Policy

UNION
S-03-0065 1975 00015
BT Public Employee Organization
NT Civil Service Union
Craft Union
Farmer Union
Industrial Union
Labor Union
Trade Union
RT Blacklisting Policy
Interest Group
International Labor Organization
Labor Strike
Public Employee Organization
Rank And File Member
Sit Down Strike
Union Jurisdiction

UNION JURISDICTION
S-06-0410 1975 00000
BT Jurisdiction Characteristics
RT Administrative Jurisdiction
Executive Jurisdiction
Legislative Jurisdiction
Union
Union Worker

UNION WORKER
S-32-0128 1979 00000
UF Unionized Worker
BT Occupational Role
RT Industrial Working Class
Labor Force
Trade Union
Union Jurisdiction
Unionized Working Class

UNIONIZED WORKER
1975-1979 00002
USE Union Worker

UNIONIZED WORKING CLASS
S-06-0784 1975 00003
BT Working Class
RT Agricultural Working Class
Foreman
Industrial Working Class
Proletariat
Trade Union
Union Worker

UNIT RECORD EQUIPMENT
S-24-0331 1975 00000
BT Data Processing Equipment
RT Computer Equipment
Input Output Device

UNITARIANISM
S-38-0571 1975 00000
BT Protestantism
RT Anglicanism
Hussite Thought
Lutheranism
Protestant Sectarianism
Religious Culture

UNITARY CONSTITUTION
S-21-0013 1975 00001
BT National Constitution
RT Democratic Constitution
Federal Constitution
Unitary Government

UNITARY GOVERNMENT
S-16-0113 1975 00002
BT Government Type
RT Confederal Government
Federal Government
National Government
Unitary Constitution

UNITED FRONT
S-02-0056 1975 00006
BT Political Front
RT All Party Coalition
Electoral Coalition
Electoral Tactics
Extranational Bloc
Liberation Front
National Front
Political Coalition
Popular Front

UNITED NATIONS
S-02-0013 1975 00106
BT World Alliance
RT Collective Security
Diplomatic Immunity
Diplomatic Recognition
Diplomatic Relations
Diplomatic Relations Break
Economic Organization
Extranational Bloc
Fourth World Nation
International Agency
International Civil Servant
International Commission Member
International Conference
International Conflict Resolution Theory
International Constitutional Convention
International Decision Making Theory
International Economic Organization Theory
International Government Bureaucracy
International Law
International Organization
International Organization Policy
International Organization Record
International Organization Theory
International Peace
International Peace Negotiation
International Peacekeeping Forces
International Political System Characteristics
International Relations Studies
International Trusteeship
League Of Nations
Mandate Territory
Multinational Organization Theory
North South Conflict
Peacekeeping Forces
Security Council Veto
Security Forces
Sovereignty Theory
Third World Nation
World Alliance
World Court
World Government
World Law
World Politics

UNIVARIATE ANALYSIS
S-24-0069 1975 00002
BT Statistical Analysis
NT Central Tendency Measure
Dispersion Measure
Population Estimation
RT Bivariate Analysis
Correlation Analysis
Multivariate Analysis
Probability Estimation
Product Moment Correlation
Statistical Significance Test

UNIVERSITY
S-19-0212 1975 00080
BT Higher Education Institution
NT Graduate School
Open University
Private University
Public University
RT Academic
Academic Areas
Academic Community
Academy Of Science
College
Dean
Education Association
Education Planner
Education Reform
Higher Education
Higher Party School
Humanistic Education
Junior College
Knowledge Production
Liberal Arts Education
Pedagogical Institute
Private College
Professor
Research Ethics
Research Institution
State Supported College
University Education

UNIVERSITY ADMISSION
USE Admission Policy

UNIVERSITY EDUCATION
S-13-0018 1975 00051
BT Higher Education
RT Academic
Academic Community
Education Agency
Education Institution
Graduate Education
Graduate School
Humanistic Education
Pedagogical Institute Education
Polytechnical Institute Education
Private Higher Education
State Supported Higher Education
University

UNIVERSITY INFORMATION SERVICE
S-18-0054 1979 00000
BT Information Service
RT Abstracting Service
Academic Areas
Archives
Bibliographic Service
Documentation Service
Documents
Education Planning
Government Document
Government Information Service
Indexing
International Organization Record
Judicial Record
Legislative Record
Library
Machine Readable Information
Monographs
Private Information Service
Public Record
Research Institution
Statistical Data

UNPUBLISHED MEDIA CENSORSHIP
S-31-0276 1975 00000
BT Censorship Process
NT Broadcasting Censorship
Intelligence Censorship
Performing Arts Censorship
RT Editorial Control
Government Report Censorship
Published Media Censorship
Report Censorship
Scientific Report Censorship

UNSKILLED WORKER
S-32-0090 1975 00007
BT Blue Collar Worker
NT Day Laborer
RT Semiskilled Worker
Skilled Worker

UNSTRUCTURED INTERVIEW
S-24-0113 1975 00000
BT Interview
RT Group Interview
Personal Interview
Telephone Interview

UNTOUCHABLES
S-06-0758 1975 00000
BT Lower Caste
RT Caste Society
Discrimination Policy
Lower Class
Traditional Society

UNWRITTEN CONSTITUTION
S-21-0015 1975 00000
BT Constitution
RT Constitutional Law
Customary Law
Democratic Constitution
National Constitution
State Constitution
Written Constitution

UPPER CASTE
S-06-0760 1975 00001
BT Caste Stratification Division
RT Caste Society
Class Analysis
Governing Elite
Lower Caste
Middle Caste

UPPER CLASS
S-06-0779 1975 00004
BT Class Stratification Division
RT Aristocratic Class
Class Analysis
Class Stratification Division
Entrepreneur Class
Governing Elite
Landowning Class
Middle Class
Nobility
Propertied Class
Ruling Class
Social Elite
Social Prestige
Upper Class Voter

UPPER CLASS VOTER
S-32-0303 1975 00001
BT Class Voter
RT Middle Class Voter
Upper Class
Working Class Voter

UPPER HOUSE MEMBER
S-36-0194 1975 00000
BT Parliamentary Member
RT Parliamentary Government
Senate

UPPER HOUSE SPEAKER
S-36-0166 1975 00000
BT Parliamentary Speaker
RT Leadership Structure Type
Leadership Type
Lower House Speaker
National Leadership
Political Leadership

UPWARD MOBILITY
S-06-0753 1975 00030
BT Vertical Mobility
RT Ambition
Downward Mobility
Horizontal Mobility
Intergenerational Mobility

URBAN CONFLICT
1975-1979 00019

URBAN CULTURE
S-11-0048 1975 00029
BT Culture Type
RT Black Culture
Community Culture
Counter Culture
Cultural History
Ethnic Culture
Heterogeneous Culture
Subculture
Technological Culture
Urban History
Urban Politics Studies
Western Culture
Work Culture
Youth Culture

URBAN DECAY
S-31-0059 1979 00000
BT Decay
RT Economic Development
Education Development
Industrial Economics
Industrial Economy
Industrial Sector
Industrial Society
Institutional Decay
Modernization
Political Decay
Resource Development
Social History
Urban Design
Urban Development
Urban Sprawl
Urbanization Index

URBAN DESIGN
S-31-0670 1979 00000
BT Urban Policy Planning
RT Architectural Studies
City Policy Planning
Local Policy Planning
Rural Policy Planning
State Policy Planning
Urban Decay
Urban Politics
Urban Sprawl

URBAN DEVELOPMENT
S-31-0131 1975 00099
BT Development Process
NT Urban Redevelopment
RT Local Development
Megalopolis
Reform
Regional Development
Rural Development
Urban Decay
Urban Development Theory
Urban Economics
Urban History
Urban Sprawl

URBAN DEVELOPMENT THEORY
S-38-0028 1975 00060
BT Development Theory
RT Administrative Development Theory
Central City
Economic Development Theory
Economic Growth Theory
Metropolis
New Town
Planned Economy
Social Development Theory
Technological Development Theory
Urban Development
Urbanization Process

URBAN ECONOMICS
S-01-0075 1979 00000
BT Economics Discipline
RT Econometrics
Industrial Economics
Labor Economics
Macroeconomics
Microeconomics
Social Economics
Transportation Economics
Urban Development
Urban Environment
Urban Geography
Urban History
Urban Planner
Urban Policy Planning
Urban Renewal
Urbanization Pattern
Urbanization Process

URBAN EDUCATION
S-13-0054 1979 00000
BT Traditional Education
RT Mass Education
Progressive Education
Urban Ghetto Community
Urban Policy Planning
Urban Politics
Urban Politics Studies
Urban Population
Urban School
Urbanization Process

URBAN ENVIRONMENT
S-06-0705 1975 00058
BT Social System Environment Characteristics
RT Rural Environment
Suburban Environment
Urban Economics

URBAN GEOGRAPHY
S-01-0095 1975 00028
BT Geography Discipline
RT Central City
Demographic Studies
Economic Geography
Ethnographic Data
Human Geography
Physical Geography
Political Geography
Spatial Analysis
Urban Economics
Urban History
Urban Politics Studies
Urban Sociology
Urban Sprawl

URBAN GHETTO COMMUNITY
S-07-0030 1975 00014
BT Ghetto Community
RT Black Suburban Community
City
Ethnic Composition
Ethnic Ghetto
Ethnic Homogeneity
Homogeneous Community
Multiethnic Community
Segregated Community
Squatter Society
Suburban Ghetto Community
Urban Education
Urban Sprawl

URBAN GOVERNMENT
S-16-0112 1975 00059
BT Subnational Government
RT Black Nationalism
Borough Government
City Government
Decentralized City
District Government Type
Federated City
Local Elite
Local Policy Making
Local Policy Planning
Local Political Boss
Local Political Division
Local Political Elite
Metropolitan City
Metropolitan Government
Municipality
Urban Politics
Urban Politics Studies

URBAN GUERRILLA
S-32-0198 1975 00002
BT Guerrilla
RT Ethnic Militancy
Guerrilla Activity
Guerrilla War

URBAN HISTORY
S-01-0122 1979 00000
BT History Discipline
RT Architectural Studies
Black History
Cultural History
Economic History
Historiography
History Of Philosophy
Industrial Economics
Institutional History
Political History
Quantitative History
Urban Culture
Urban Development
Urban Economics
Urban Geography
Urban Politics
Urban Society
Urban Sociology
Urbanization Pattern
Urbanization Process

URBAN MIGRATION
S-31-0624 1975 00034
BT Internal Migration
RT Internal Migration Pattern
Lower Class
Rural Migration

URBAN MIGRATION PATTERN
S-06-0242 1975 00023
BT Internal Migration Pattern
RT Ethnic Integration
Rural Migration Pattern
Squatter Community
Suburban Migration Pattern

URBAN PLANNER
S-32-0143 1975 00008
BT Local Planner
RT Administrative Planning
City Planner
Local Policy Making
Local Policy Planning
Slum Rehabilitation
Urban Economics
Urban Politics Studies
Waste Treatment Policy

URBAN POLICY PLANNING
S-31-0669 1975 00065
BT Subnational Policy Planning
NT Urban Design
RT Architectural Studies
City Manager
City Policy Planning
Local Policy Planning
Model City
New Town
Planned Economy
Planner
Rural Policy Planning
Slum Rehabilitation
State Policy Planning
Urban Economics
Urban Education
Urban Politics Studies

URBAN POLITICS
S-29-0238 1975 00060
BT Local Politics
NT Suburban Politics
RT Architectural Studies
Central City
City Politics
Local Elite
Local Policy Making
Local Political Boss
Local Political Elite
Metropolitan Politics
Municipal Election
Urban Design
Urban Education
Urban Government
Urban History

Urban Politics Studies
Urban Race Riot
Urban Society
Urban Sociology
Urban Sprawl

URBAN POLITICS STUDIES
S-01-0167 1975 00047
BT Political Science Discipline
RT City Manager
City Planning Policy
Comparative Sociology
Economic Geography
Economics Discipline
Ethnic Politics
Ethnic Studies
Local Income Taxation
Local Political Party
Magistrate
Megalopolis
Metropolitan City
Metropolitan Politics
Policy Science Studies
Political Geography
Political History
Population Density
Provincial Elite
Slum Community
Slum Rehabilitation
Social Worker
Urban Culture
Urban Education
Urban Geography
Urban Government
Urban Planner
Urban Policy Planning
Urban Politics
Urban Race Riot
Urban Society
Urban Sociology
Waste Treatment Policy

URBAN POPULATION
S-06-0219 1975 00041
BT Population Attribute
RT Architectural Studies
Migrant Population
Population Density
Rural Population
Suburban Population
Urban Education
Urban Population Area

URBAN POPULATION AREA
S-24-0349 1975 00044
BT Population Identification
RT Population Density
Population Identification
Rural Population Area
Suburban Population Area
Urban Population

URBAN RACE RIOT
S-08-0125 1979 00000
BT Race Riot
RT Ethnic Militancy
Ethnic Politics
Rebellion
Urban Politics
Urban Politics Studies
Urban Society
Urban Sociology

URBAN REDEVELOPMENT
S-31-0132 1975 00012
BT Urban Development
NT Urban Renewal
RT Architectural Studies
Regional Development
Slum Rehabilitation
Village Development

URBAN RENEWAL
S-31-0133 1975 00010
BT Urban Redevelopment
NT Slum Rehabilitation
RT Architectural Studies
Urban Economics
Urban Renewal Policy

URBAN RENEWAL POLICY
S-26-0415 1975 00011
BT Social Policy
RT Discrimination Policy
Ethnic Policy
Housing Policy
Model City
Social Resource Distribution Policy
Urban Renewal

URBAN RIOT
1975-1979 00007

URBAN SCHOOL
S-19-0229 1975 00021
BT Education Institution
NT Inner City School
RT Neighborhood School
Open University
Primary School
Urban Education

URBAN SOCIETY
S-35-0030 1975 00052
BT Society Type Base
RT Achieving Society
Affluent Society
Homogeneous Society
Industrial Society
Metropolis
Modernizing Society
Secular Society
Urban History
Urban Politics
Urban Politics Studies
Urban Race Riot
Urban Sociology
Western Society

URBAN SOCIOLOGY
S-01-0202 1975 00050
BT Sociology Discipline
RT Comparative Sociology
Economic Geography
Ethnic Assimilation Theory
Ethnic Politics
Ethnographic Data
Human Geography
Industrial Psychology
Industrial Sociology
Macrosociology
Physical Geography
Policy Science Studies
Political Geography
Political Sociology
Public Administration Studies
Urban Geography
Urban History
Urban Politics
Urban Politics Studies
Urban Race Riot
Urban Society

URBAN SPRAWL
S-06-0232 1979 00000
BT Urbanization Pattern
RT Central City
Land Use Policy
Urban Decay
Urban Design
Urban Development
Urban Geography
Urban Ghetto Community
Urban Politics

URBAN STUDIES
S-01-0205 1979 00000
BT Academic Areas
RT City Manager
Megalopolis

URBAN TRANSIT POLICY
S-26-0427 1975 00021
BT Mass Transit Policy
RT Railroad Policy
Transportation Economics

URBAN VOTER
S-32-0333 1975 00005
BT Voter
RT Suburban Voter
Urban Voting

URBAN VOTING
S-29-0148 1975 00009
BT Voting
RT Age Group Voting
Bloc Voting
Class Voting
Ethnic Group Voting
Ethnic Voter
Group Voting
Racial Voting
Rural Voting
Suburban Voting
Urban Voter
Voting Behavior Analysis

URBANIZATION INDEX
S-24-0250 1975 00015
BT Scale Type
RT Development Index
Social Change Index
Stability Index
Urban Decay
Urbanization Pattern
Voting Duty Scale

URBANIZATION PATTERN
S-06-0231 1975 00028
BT Population Distribution
NT Urban Sprawl
RT Ethnic Ghetto
Metropolitan Growth Pattern
Population Movement
Urban Economics
Urban History
Urbanization Index
Urbanization Process

URBANIZATION PROCESS
S-31-0165 1975 00056
BT Political Change
RT Social Change
Urban Development Theory
Urban Economics
Urban Education

Urban History
Urbanization Pattern

USE OF HUMAN SUBJECTS
S-25-0045 1979 00000
BT Research Ethics
NT Human Subject Rights
RT Human Rights
Moral Reasoning
Moral Theory
Research Council
Research Laboratory
Research Unit
Scientific Research
Situational Ethics

UTILITARIAN JUSTICE THEORY
S-38-0483 1975 00003
BT Justice Theory
RT Benthamism
Compensatory Justice
Utilitarianism

UTILITARIANISM
S-38-0426 1975 00016
BT Modern Political Thought
NT Benthamism
RT Benthamism
Distributive Justice Theory
Ethical Theory
Individualism Theory
Linguistic Ethical Theory
Possessive Individualism
Psychological Freedom Theory
Utilitarian Justice Theory

UTILITY NATIONALIZATION
S-31-0297 1975 00000
BT Nationalization Process
RT Bank Nationalization
Basic Industry Nationalization
Industry Nationalization
Land Nationalization

UTOPIAN COMMUNITY
S-07-0022 1975 00003
BT Cooperative Community
RT Collective Community
Communal Community
Compound
Economic Community
Integrated Community
Kibbutz
Planned Economy
Political Community
Religious Community
Rural Community
Utopian Socialism
Utopianism

UTOPIAN SOCIALISM
S-38-0335 1975 00003
BT Socialist Theory
RT Socialist Theory
Utopian Community
Utopianism

UTOPIANISM
S-38-0081 1975 00007
BT Contemporary Political Thought
RT Chiliastic Movement
Classless Society
Eschatology
Holism
Messianic Movement
Prophetic Tradition
Utopian Community
Utopian Socialism

VALIDITY MEASUREMENT
S-24-0164 1975 00024
BT Measurement Evaluation
NT Construct Validity
Criterion Validity
Discriminant Validity
Face Validity
RT Propositional Inventory
Reliability Measurement
Surveillance

VALUE ADDED TAXATION
S-26-0178 1975 00001
BT Taxation Policy
RT Excise Taxation Policy
Incentive Taxation Policy
Property Taxation
Sales Taxation
Social Security Taxation

VALUE ALLOCATION
S-06-0607 1975 00007
BT System Goal
NT Authoritative Value Allocation
RT Eastonian Analysis
Goal Satisfaction
Goal Setting
Goal Specificity
System Analysis

VALUE ANALYSIS
S-09-0075 1975 00118
BT Contemporary Analytic Modes
RT Analysis Framework
Analytic Process
Behavior Analysis
Belief System
Cost Benefit Analysis
Cultural History
Idealist Foreign Policy
Identity Analysis
Issue Analysis
Mass Belief System
Middle Class Values
Moral Choice
Policy
Policy Analysis
Social Mores
Social System Normative Characteristics
Socialization Analysis
Socialization Type
Transactional Analysis
Value Free Science Theory

VALUE FREE SCIENCE THEORY
S-38-0580 1975 00023
BT Scientific Theory
RT Data Theory
Philosophical Concept
Value Analysis
Value System
Weberian Analysis
Weberian Theory

VALUE JUDGMENT
S-31-0010 1979 00000
BT Judging
RT Evaluating

VALUE OF LIFE
S-37-0150 1979 00000
BT Value System
RT Human Needs Theory

VALUE SYSTEM
S-37-0149 1975 00131
BT System Type
NT Value Of Life
RT Axiology
Belief System
Cognitive System
Cultural History
Education System
General Interest Theory
Mass Belief System
Moral Choice
Moral Learning
National Goal
National Priority
Political System Type
Social System
Value Free Science Theory

VANDALISM
S-10-0023 1975 00001
BT Property Crime
RT Assault
Economic Sabotage
Robbery
Street Crime

VARIABLE
S-24-0419 1975 00016
BT Theoretical Framework
NT Variable Control
Variable Logical Status
Variable Phenomenological Status
Variable Substantive Content
RT Microlevel Analysis

VARIABLE CONTROL
S-24-0420 1975 00007
BT Variable
NT Experiment
Nonexperiment
Quasiexperiment
RT Variable Logical Status
Variable Phenomenological Status
Variable Substantive Content

VARIABLE LOGICAL STATUS
S-24-0426 1975 00020
BT Variable
NT Dependent Variable
Endogenous Variable
Exogenous Variable
Independent Variable
Interdependent Variable
Intervening Variable
RT Variable Control
Variable Phenomenological Status
Variable Substantive Content

VARIABLE PHENOMENOLOGICAL STATUS
S-24-0435 1975 00001
BT Variable
NT Group Phenomena
Individual Phenomena
RT Variable Control
Variable Logical Status
Variable Substantive Content

VARIABLE SUBSTANTIVE CONTENT
S-24-0445 1975 00004
BT Variable
NT Cultural Variable
Economic Variable
Historical Variable
Institutional Variable
Political Variable
Psychological Variable
Social Variable
Time Variable
RT Variable Control
Variable Logical Status
Variable Phenomenological Status

VARIABLE SUM GAMING
S-24-0104 1975 00000
BT Gaming
RT Fixed Sum Gaming
Game Theory
Nonzero Sum Gaming
Prisoner Dilemma Gaming
Prisoner Dilemma Theory
Two Person Gaming
Zero Sum Gaming

VENN DIAGRAM
S-24-0134 1975 00000
BT Diagram
RT Scatter Plot

VERBAL ANALYSIS
S-09-0044 1979 00000
BT Linguistic Analysis
RT Grammatical Analysis
Literature Analysis
Semantic Analysis

VERBAL LEARNING
S-34-0015 1979 00000
BT Learning
RT Education Policy
Education Psychology
Education Testing
Language Acquisition
Language Learning
Learning Psychology
Learning Theory
Logic
Nonverbal Learning
Skill Acquisition
Symbol Learning

VERDICT
S-31-0487 1975 00000
BT Court Action
RT Acquittal
Certiorari
Consent Judgment
Conviction
Life Sentence
Obiter Dicta
Subpoena
Warrant
Writ Of Mandamus

VERSTEHEN THEORY
S-25-0032 1975 00006
SN Doctrine of explanation which emphasizes sympathetic understanding of a historical configuration as the basis of explaining it.
BT Epistemology
RT Gemeinschaft
Gesellschaft
Weberian Analysis
Weberian Theory

VERTICAL CLEAVAGE
S-31-0790 1975 00001
BT Cleavage Process
RT Fragmentation
Vertical Integration
Weberian Analysis

VERTICAL ECONOMIC INTEGRATION
S-31-0810 1979 00000
BT Economic Integration
RT Horizontal Economic Integration

VERTICAL INTEGRATION
S-31-0831 1975 00000
BT Integration
NT Hierarchical Integration
RT Cultural Integration
Ethnic Integration
Functional Integration
Linguistic Integration
Racial Integration
Social Integration
Vertical Cleavage

VERTICAL MOBILITY
S-06-0751 1975 00005
BT Status Mobility
NT Downward Mobility
Upward Mobility
RT Career Analysis
Geographic Mobility
Horizontal Mobility
Intergenerational Mobility
Status Mobility

VERTICAL STRATIFICATION DIVISION
S-06-0791 1975 00005
BT Social Stratification Division
RT Caste Stratification Division
Class Stratification Division
Objectively Derived Status
Prestige Hierarchy
Subjectively Derived Status

VETERAN
S-36-0226 1975 00015
BT Military Service Personnel
RT Demilitarization Policy
Demobilization Policy
Education Policy
Employment Policy
Veterans Demonstration
Veterans Organization

VETERANS DEMONSTRATION
S-08-0022 1975 00000
BT Demonstration
RT Civil Rights Demonstration
General Strike
Peace Demonstration
Sit In
Student Demonstration
Veteran
Worker Demonstration

VETERANS ORGANIZATION
S-03-0061 1975 00000
BT Organizations
RT Interest Group
Lobbying
Patriotism
Veteran
Youth Organization

VETO
S-31-0335 1975 00002
BT Decision Making Process
NT Executive Veto
Item Veto
Pocket Veto
Security Council Veto
RT Approval Process
Legislative Executive Relations
Legislative Process
Veto Message

VETO MESSAGE
S-18-0024 1975 00000
BT Administrative Record
RT Proclamation
Pronouncement
Veto

VICE PRESIDENT
S-36-0075 1975 00004
BT President
RT Chief Executive Advisor
Chief Executive Staff Personnel
Lieutenant Governor
Presidential Advisor
Presidential Staff Personnel

VILLAGE
S-07-0014 1975 00007
BT City
NT Hamlet
RT City
County
District Government Type
Hamlet
Legislative District
Local Political Division
Preindustrial City
Township
Village Chief
Village Culture

VILLAGE CHIEF
S-36-0086 1975 00002
BT Local Chief Government Executive
RT Council Manager
Kinship Group
Local Political Division
Mayor
Village
Village Community

VILLAGE COMMUNITY
S-07-0053 1975 00018
BT Community Type
RT City
Local Political Division
Planned Economy
Political Community
Rural Community
Suburb
Town
Traditional Society
Village Chief
Village Cooperative
Village Culture

VILLAGE COOPERATIVE
S-03-0009 1975 00001
BT Cooperatives
RT Agricultural Cooperative
Cottage Industry
Credit Cooperative
Peasant Cooperative
Village Community

Village Culture
Village Development

VILLAGE COUNCIL
S-19-0123 1975 00000
BT Local Government Council
RT City Council
Local Planning Commission
Town Council
Village Development

VILLAGE CULTURE
S-11-0012 1975 00012
BT Community Culture
RT Cultural History
Homogeneous Culture
Nonwestern Culture
Peasant Culture
Poverty Culture
Religious Culture
Traditional Culture
Village
Village Community
Village Cooperative

VILLAGE DEVELOPMENT
S-31-0076 1975 00007
BT Local Development
RT Cooperatives
Urban Redevelopment
Village Cooperative
Village Council
Village Politics

VILLAGE POLITICS
S-29-0240 1975 00010
BT Local Politics
RT City Politics
Kinship Group
Local Policy Planning
Metropolitan Politics
Traditional Political Party
Traditional Political System
Village Development

VIOLENCE
S-08-0130 1979 00000
BT Conflict Type
NT Mob Violence
Political Violence
RT Aggression
Ethnic Conflict
Political Violence
Racial Tension
Rebellion
Revolution
Riot Theory
Social Deviance
Social Disorder
Social Instability
Terrorism
Violent Crime
War

VIOLENT CRIME
S-10-0083 1979 00000
BT Crime
RT Assault
Child Molestation
Crime Against Humanity
Economic Crime
Individual Crime
Rape
Street Crime
Violence

VIRTUAL REPRESENTATION THEORY
S-38-0509 1975 00001
SN View that political representation should be based on the representative discerning the true interests of the represented even though the represented are not aware of their true interests.
BT Representation Theory
RT Delegate Representation Theory
Delegate Selection
Group Representation Theory
Linkage Representation Theory
Trustee Representation Theory

VIRTUE
S-06-0518 1979 00000
BT Personality Characteristics
NT Political Virtue
RT Happiness

VISUAL ARTS
S-01-0127 1979 00000
UF Cinema
Dance
Film
Painting
Sculpture
Theatre
BT Fine Arts
RT Art History
Fine Arts
Humanities Discipline
Political Film
Sociology Of Art

VITAL STATISTICS DATA
S-18-0093 1975 00006
BT Social Statistics
RT Birth Rate
Ethnographic Data
Morbidity Data
Obituaries
Public Opinion Survey
Social Indicator
Social Psychological Data
Statistical Table

VOCABULARY
S-06-0416 1979 00000
BT Language Characteristics
RT Grammar
Language Acquisition
Language Learning
Semantics
Speech
Stylistics

VOCATION TRAINING POLICY
S-26-0196 1975 00005
BT Education Policy
RT Continuing Education
Education Policy
Higher Education Policy
Literacy Policy
Management Training Program
Private Education Policy
Public Education Policy
Rehabilitation Education Policy
Vocational Subsidy

VOCATIONAL EDUCATION
S-13-0052 1975 00012
BT Manpower Training
RT Academic Specialization
Apprenticeship
Military Training
Unemployment Policy
Vocational Training School

VOCATIONAL SUBSIDY
S-06-0305 1975 00001
BT Education Subsidy
RT Vocation Training Policy

VOCATIONAL TRAINING SCHOOL
S-19-0231 1975 00000
UF Industrial School
BT Education Institution
RT Polytechnical Institute
Professional School
Secondary School
Vocational Education

VOLTAIREAN ANALYSIS
S-38-0407 1975 00000
SN Theories and method of, for example, belief analysis associated with work of Voltaire.
BT Enlightenment Thought
RT History Of Philosophy
Philosophe Thought
Rousseauian Analysis

VOLUNTARISM
S-25-0052 1975 00010
BT Metaphysics
RT Freedom Theory
Voluntarism Model
Volunteer

VOLUNTARISM MODEL
S-24-0322 1975 00003
BT Social Science Model
RT Civic Culture
Civic Organization
Pluralist Model
Voluntarism
Volunteer

VOLUNTARY ARMED FORCES
S-33-0069 1975 00030
BT Armed Forces
RT Marines
Mercenary Armed Forces
Military Recruit
Peoples Army
Volunteer

VOLUNTARY ASSOCIATION
S-03-0073 1975 00030
BT Associations
RT Association Interest Group
Civic Organization
Cultural Organization
Freemasonry
Groups
Organizations
Secret Society
Volunteer

VOLUNTEER
S-36-0220 1975 00003
BT Military Recruit
RT Mercenary
Military Recruit
Voluntarism
Voluntarism Model
Voluntary Armed Forces
Voluntary Association

VOTE DISTRIBUTION
S-29-0113 1975 00000
BT Electoral Outcome
RT Bandwagon Effect
Coattail Effect
Majority Electoral Outcome
Voter
Voting Behavior Analysis
Voting Data

VOTE FRAUD
S-10-0073 1975 00000
BT Election Fraud
RT Fraud
Political Bribery
Political Fraud
Political Graft

VOTER
S-32-0293 1975 00008
BT Political Role
NT Absentee Voter
Alienated Voter
Apathetic Voter
Black Voter
Candidate Voter
Class Voter
Deferential Voter
Efficacious Voter
Eligible Voter
Ethnic Voter
Farm Voter
Female Voter
Floating Voter
Group Benefits Voter
Ideological Voter
Independent Voter
Informed Voter
Issue Voter
Marginal Voter
Minority Voter
New Voter
Nonvoter
Political Party Voter
Protest Voter
Rural Voter
Situation Of The Times Voter
Student Voter
Suburban Voter
Ticket Splitter
Urban Voter
Voter Orientation
Youth Voter
RT Vote Distribution
Voter Orientation
Voter Qualification
Voter Registration
Voter Turnout
Voting Rights
Voting Tactics

VOTER ORIENTATION
S-32-0334 1975 00052
BT Voter
NT Candidate Orientation
Issue Orientation
Political Party Orientation
RT Ideological Voter
Issue Voter
Marginal Voter
Negative Voting Abstention
Political Party Voter
Situation Of The Times Voter
Voter
Voting Behavior

VOTER QUALIFICATION
S-15-0083 1975 00000
BT Voting Rights
NT Property Voting Qualification
Registration Requirement
Residence Requirement
Voting Age Requirement
RT Absentee Voter
Absentee Voting
National Election
Suffrage Equality
Voter
Voter Registration
Voter Registration Law

VOTER REGISTRATION
S-29-0177 1975 00004
BT Voting Procedure
RT Literacy Test
Literacy Voting Test
Poll Tax
Polling Place
Registered Voter
Voter
Voter Qualification
Voter Registration Law

VOTER REGISTRATION LAW
S-21-0070 1975 00000
BT Electoral Law
RT Suffrage Law
Voter Qualification
Voter Registration

VOTER TURNOUT
S-29-0180 1975 00025
BT Election Turnout
NT Average Voter Turnout Election
High Turnout Election
Low Turnout Election
RT Backlash Voting
Marginal Voter
Minority Voter
Negative Voting Abstention
Voter
Voting Behavior
Voting Behavior Analysis
Voting Data

VOTING
S-29-0121 1975 00013
BT Electoral Participation
NT Absentee Voting
Compulsory Voting
Confidence Voting
Floating Voting
Geographic Voting
Group Voting
Independent Voting
Plural Voting
Political Party Ticket Voting
Protest Voting
Proxy Voting
Split Ticket Voting
Straight Ticket Voting
Urban Voting
Voting Device
Write In Voting
RT Bipartisan Voting
Candidate Image Voter
Candidate Preference Voter
Class Voter
Electoral Geography
Electoral History
Electoral Opposition
General Election
Ideological Voter
Interparty Competition
Issue Voter
Marginal Voter
Nonvoting
Political Behavior Studies
Political Participation
Public Choice Analysis
Realigning Election
Special Election
Voting Behavior Analysis
Voting Data
Voting Formulae
Voting Pattern
Voting Procedure
Voting Result Interpretation
Voting Theory

VOTING ABSTENTION
S-29-0117 1975 00000
BT Nonvoting
NT Negative Voting Abstention
Positive Voting Abstention
RT Nonvoter
Public Choice Analysis
Voting Behavior Analysis
Voting Data
Voting Theory

VOTING AGE
1975-1979 00000
USE Voting Age Requirement

VOTING AGE REQUIREMENT
S-15-0087 1979 00000
UF Voting Age
BT Voter Qualification
RT Property Voting Qualification
Registration Requirement
Residence Requirement

VOTING BEHAVIOR
S-05-0020 1975 00102
BT Political Behavior
RT Bipartisan Voting
Candidate Image Voter
Candidate Orientation
Candidate Preference Voter
Candidate Voter
Deferential Voter
Election Campaign
Electoral Politics
Issue Orientation
Legislative Action
Legislative Voting Behavior
Marginal Voter
Mass Behavior
Negative Voting Abstention
Plural Voting
Presidential Coattail Effect
Voter Orientation
Voter Turnout
Voting Behavior Analysis
Voting Theory

VOTING BEHAVIOR ANALYSIS
S-09-0076 1975 00072
BT Contemporary Analytic Modes
NT Roll Call Analysis
Spatial Voting Analysis
RT Absentee Voting
Aggregate Data Analysis
Behavior
Behavior Analysis
Black Voting
Bloc Voting
Decision Making Analysis
Election Turnout
Election Type
Electoral Data
Electoral Politics
High Turnout Election
Issue Analysis
Issue Intensity
Issue Salience
National Election
Negative Voting Abstention
New Voter
Parliamentary Election Campaign
Plural Voting
Survey Analysis
Urban Voting
Vote Distribution
Voter Turnout
Voting
Voting Abstention
Voting Behavior
Voting Coalition
Voting Pattern
Voting Result Interpretation
Voting Theory

VOTING COALITION
S-02-0032 1975 00007
BT Political Coalition
RT All Party Coalition
Bloc Voting
Class Based Coalition
Coalition Type
Democratic Coalition
Electoral Coalition
Electoral Procedure
Legislative Coalition
Minimum Winning Coalition
Multiethnic Coalition
Multiparty Coalition
Negative Coalition
Opinion Coalition
Parliamentary Coalition
Political Party Coalition
Voting Behavior Analysis
Voting Tactics
Winning Coalition

VOTING DATA
S-18-0087 1975 00020
BT Political Statistics
RT Election Turnout
Electoral Board
Electoral Data
Electoral Geography
Electoral History
Electoral Outcome
Landslide Electoral Outcome
Legislative Roll Call Record
Legislative Voting Record
Malapportionment
Minority Voter
Proxy Voting
Roll Call Analysis
Statistical Analysis
Street Block
Two Political Party Voting Indicator
Vote Distribution
Voter Turnout
Voting
Voting Abstention
Voting Formulae
Voting Pattern
Voting Procedure
Voting Turnout Indicator

VOTING DEVICE
S-29-0149 1975 00002
BT Voting
NT Ballot
Ballot Box
Electronic Roll Call Device
Voting Machine
RT Ballot
Ballot Box
Electronic Roll Call Device
Machine Ballot
Polling Place

VOTING DUTY SCALE
S-24-0251 1975 00000
BT Scale Type
RT Frustration Scale
Liberalism Conservatism Scale
Satisfaction Scale
Stability Index
Support Opposition Scale
Urbanization Index

VOTING FORMULAE
S-29-0166 1975 00004
BT Electoral Participation
NT Cumulative Voting
D'Hont Voting Method
Largest Average Voting Method
Largest Remainder Voting Method
List Voting
Single Transferable Vote
RT Voting
Voting Data
Voting Pattern
Voting Procedure

VOTING INDICATOR
S-24-0268 1975 00014
BT Political Indicator
NT Legislative Voting Indicator
Political Party Voting Indicator
Two Political Party Voting Indicator
Voting Turnout Indicator
RT Influence Indicator
Political Instability Indicator
Political Resource Indicator
Public Opinion Indicator

VOTING MACHINE
S-29-0164 1975 00000
BT Voting Device
RT Ballot
Ballot Box
Electronic Roll Call Device
Machine Ballot

VOTING PATTERN
S-29-0173 1975 00034
BT Electoral Participation
RT Minority Voter
Voting
Voting Behavior Analysis
Voting Data
Voting Formulae
Voting Procedure
Voting Turnout Indicator

VOTING PROCEDURE
S-29-0174 1975 00007
BT Electoral Participation
NT Literacy Voting Test
Poll Tax
Voter Registration
RT Voting
Voting Data
Voting Formulae
Voting Pattern
Voting Result Interpretation
Voting Turnout Indicator

VOTING RESULT INTERPRETATION
S-29-0178 1975 00056
BT Electoral Participation
NT Election Turnout
RT Minority Voter
Reinstating Election
Two Political Party Voting Indicator
Voting
Voting Behavior Analysis
Voting Procedure

VOTING RIGHTS
S-15-0081 1975 00005
BT Political Liberty
NT Suffrage Equality
Voter Qualification
RT Absentee Ballot
Absentee Voting
Civil Rights
Freedom Of Association
Freedom Of Speech
Human Rights
Right Of Assembly
Right Of Opposition
Right Of Petition
Social Rights
Voter

VOTING TACTICS
S-29-0189 1975 00001
BT Election Turnout
RT Political Party Coalition
Voter
Voting Coalition
Voting Theory

VOTING THEORY
S-38-0175 1975 00037
BT Explanatory Political Theory
RT Decision Making Theory
Electoral Outcome
Negative Voting Abstention
Political Behaviorism
Public Choice Theory
Two Political Party Voting Indicator
Voting
Voting Abstention
Voting Behavior
Voting Behavior Analysis
Voting Tactics

VOTING TURNOUT INDICATOR
S-24-0272 1975 00010
BT Voting Indicator
RT Public Opinion Indicator
Two Political Party Voting Indicator
Voting Data
Voting Pattern
Voting Procedure

WAGE CONTROL LAW
1975-1979 00009

WAGE FREEZE POLICY
S-26-0109 1975 00001
BT Wage Policy
RT Deflation Policy
Income Elasticity
Income Equality
Income Measure
Price Policy
Wage Level
Wage Statistics

WAGE LEVEL
S-06-0640 1975 00048
BT Wealth Distribution
NT Subsistence Wage Level
RT Economic Equality
Economic Injustice
Income Distribution
Income Elasticity
Income Equality
Income Measure
Labor Management Contract
Labor Negotiation
Wage Freeze Policy
Wage Policy

WAGE POLICY
S-26-0106 1975 00037
BT Income Policy
NT Minimum Wage Policy
Wage Freeze Policy
Wage Stabilization Policy
RT Economic Incentive System
Government Economic Management
Guaranteed Annual Income Policy
Income Maintenance Policy
Income Redistribution Policy
Income Subsidy Policy
Labor Negotiation
Wage Level

WAGE STABILIZATION POLICY
S-26-0108 1975 00004
BT Wage Policy
RT Minimum Wage Law
Minimum Wage Policy
Wage Statistics

WAGE STATISTICS
S-18-0082 1975 00019
BT Economic Statistics
RT Social Indicator
Wage Freeze Policy
Wage Stabilization Policy

WAGE TAXATION
S-26-0179 1975 00003
BT Taxation Policy
RT City Income Taxation
Income Redistribution Policy
Income Taxation
Property Taxation
Sales Taxation
Tax Reform Movement

WALD WOLFOWITZ RUNS TEST
S-24-0062 1975 00000
SN Nonparametric measure of statistical significance.
BT Statistical Significance Test
RT Binomial Test
Borough Government
Chi Square Test
F Ratio
Interval Significance Test
Nominal Significance Test
Ordinal Significance Test
Wilcoxian T Test

WALKOUT
S-08-0033 1975 00000
BT Labor Strike
RT Economic Demonstration
Jurisdiction Strike
Labor Management Relations Policy
Lockout
Sit Down Strike
Wildcat Strike

WAR
S-08-0087 1975 00075
BT International Conflict
NT Biological War
Chemical War
Cold War
Conventional War
Declared War
Expansionist War
Ideological War
Just War
Limited War
Nuclear War
Proxy War
Psychological War
Religious War
Revolutionary War
Total War
Undeclared War
War By Proxy
RT Aggression
Aggression Theory
Aggressor State
Belligerence
Biological Weapon
Blockade Policy
Cease Fire Policy
Class Rebellion
Conflict Intensification
Economic Rebellion
Global War Policy
Group Conflict
Hostile Nation
Institutional Conflict
International Crisis
Language Group Conflict
Military Aggression
Military Invasion
Military Occupation
Nuclear Weapon
Political Rebellion
Political Violence
Racial Conflict
Rebellion
Revolution
Routinized Conflict
Second Strike Nuclear Weapon
Social Conflict
Social Rebellion
Struggle
Superpower Politics
Threat Indicator
Treaty Breaking
Violence
War Policy
Warfare State
Wartime Alliance
Wartime Power

WAR ATROCITY
S-10-0012 1975 00002
BT War Crime
RT Biological Weapon
Chemical Weapon
Crime Against Humanity
Genocide
International Tribunal
Massacre
War Crime Trial
War Criminal

WAR BY PROXY
S-08-0112 1979 00000
BT War
RT Conventional War
Economic Conflict
Government Overthrow
Ideological Conflict
Insurgency
Internal Conflict
Limited War
Tactical War

WAR CRIME
S-10-0010 1975 00003
BT Crime Against Humanity
NT Massacre
War Atrocity
RT Genocide
International Tribunal
Military Conspiracy
Military Espionage
Piracy
Political Crime
Sedition
Treason
War Crime Trial
War Criminal

WAR CRIME TRIAL
S-31-0521 1975 00001
BT Military Trial
RT Court Martial
International Law System
International Tribunal
War Atrocity
War Crime
War Criminal

WAR CRIMINAL
S-36-0038 1975 00004
BT Criminal
RT Blackmailer
Extortionist
Guerrilla
International Law
Murderer
Personal Crime Criminal
Political Criminal
Prisoner Of War
Slanderer

War Atrocity
War Crime
War Crime Trial

WAR DEBT FINANCING
S-31-0404 1975 00002
BT Debt Financing
RT Defense Spending
Government Borrowing
National Debt Financing
War Production

WAR DECLARATION POLICY
S-26-0078 1975 00002
BT Defense Policy
RT Armistice Policy
Deterrence Policy
Nuclear Strategy
Truce
War Power

WAR ECONOMY
S-12-0045 1975 00009
BT Economy Type
RT Command Economy
Communist Economic System
Global War Policy
Government Production Enterprise
Planned Economy
War Policy
War Power
War Production
Warfare Capitalism
Warfare State
Wartime Power

WAR POLICY
S-26-0337 1975 00056
BT Military Policy
NT Global War Policy
Limited War Policy
Local War Policy
Pacification Policy
Peoples War Policy
Total War Policy
War Reparation Policy
RT Armed Intervention Policy
Cease Fire Policy
Civil Defense Policy
Declared War
Deescalation Policy
Defense Planning
Demilitarization Policy
Demobilization Policy
Escalation Policy
Mass Militia Army
Military Intervention Policy
Military Invasion
Military Law
Military Reform Policy
Military Reorganization Policy
Mutual Support Declaration
Proxy War
Reprisal Policy
Strategic Policy
War
War Economy
War Power
War Propaganda
Warfare State
Warlord
Wartime Alliance
Wartime Power

WAR POWER
S-04-0038 1975 00007
BT Civil Military Authority
RT Civil Military Relations
Conscription Power
Declared War
Emergency Power
War Declaration Policy
War Economy
War Policy
Warfare State
Warlord
Wartime Power

WAR PRODUCTION
S-31-0445 1975 00003
BT Production Process
RT Global War Policy
Industrial Production
National Production
War Debt Financing
War Economy

WAR PROPAGANDA
S-31-0193 1975 00002
BT Political Propaganda
RT Government Propaganda
Psychological War
War Policy
Wartime Propaganda Policy

WAR PROTESTOR
S-32-0207 1975 00001
BT Activist
RT Activist
Demonstrator
Protest Politics
Rights Of Man Doctrine
Rioter
Student Activist

WAR REPARATION POLICY
S-26-0344 1979 00000
BT War Policy
RT Economic Aid Policy
Economic Imperialism
Global War Policy
Pacification Policy
Total War Policy

WAR TECHNOLOGY
S-33-0010 1975 00037
BT Defense System
NT Mutual Deterrence System
Nuclear Power
Offensive Weapon System
Weapon
RT Bomb
Military Policy
Tactical Force
Tactical War

WARD
S-29-0198 1975 00000
BT Local Election District
RT Local Political Division
Precinct
Ward Chairperson

WARD CHAIRPERSON
S-32-0163 1975 00001
BT Political Party Leader
RT Campaign Manager
Formal Political Party Leader
Political Boss
Political Party Cadre
Political Party Chief
Political Party Professional
Precinct Captain
Precinct Worker
Ward

WARFARE CAPITALISM
S-37-0020 1975 00001
BT Capitalism
RT Black Capitalism
Bourgeois Capitalism
Industrial Capitalism
Mature Capitalism
Mercantile Capitalism
Monopoly Capitalism
Private Sector
War Economy
Welfare Capitalism

WARFARE STATE
S-16-0172 1975 00001
BT State Type
RT Aggression
Aggression Scale
Aggression Theory
Aggressor State
Constitutional Dictatorship
Garrison State
Military State
War
War Economy
War Policy
War Power
Warlord
Wartime Power

WARLORD
S-36-0053 1975 00003
BT Military Governor
RT Dictator
Oriental Despotism
War Policy
War Power
Warfare State
Wartime Power

WARRANT
S-31-0488 1975 00000
BT Court Action
RT Cease Desist Order
Certiorari
Injunction
Life Sentence
Obiter Dicta
Subpoena
Verdict
Writ Of Mandamus

WARRANT ARREST
S-31-0511 1975 00000
BT Arrest
RT Arbitrary Arrest
On View Arrest
Political Arrest

WARSHIP
S-33-0034 1975 00020
BT Munitions
RT Military Aircraft
Navy
Sea Power

WARTIME ALLIANCE
S-02-0010 1975 00004
BT Alliance
RT Collective Security
Military Alliance

Neutrality Agreement
Regional Military Alliance
War
War Policy

WARTIME POWER
S-30-0021 1975 00001
BT Power Type
RT Emergency Power
Presidential Power
War
War Economy
War Policy
War Power
Warfare State
Warlord
Wartime Propaganda Policy

WARTIME PROPAGANDA POLICY
S-26-0293 1975 00002
BT Propaganda Policy
RT Military Policy
War Propaganda
Wartime Power

WASTE TREATMENT POLICY
S-26-0233 1979 00000
BT Space Policy
RT Ecology Discipline
Energy Policy
Sanitation Policy
Urban Planner
Urban Politics Studies
Water Pollution Policy

WATER DISTRICT
S-16-0097 1975 00000
BT District Government Type
RT Fire District
Recreation District
School District
Sewer District
Transportation District

WATER POLLUTION
S-31-0106 1975 00011
BT Environmental Pollution
RT Ecosystem
Noise Pollution
Water Pollution Policy
Water Transportation Industry

WATER POLLUTION POLICY
S-26-0229 1975 00017
BT Pollution Policy
RT Air Pollution Policy
Ecology Movement
Ecosystem
Environmental Planning
Land Pollution Policy
Noise Pollution Policy
Sanitation Policy
Waste Treatment Policy
Water Pollution
Water Transportation Industry
Water Use Policy

WATER SCARCITY
S-31-0118 1979 00000
BT Scarcity
RT Energy Scarcity
Food Scarcity
Housing Scarcity
Labor Scarcity
Malnutrition
Resource Allocation
Resource Distribution
Water Use Policy

WATER TRANSPORTATION INDUSTRY
S-17-0079 1975 00017
UF Canal
BT Transportation Industry
NT Shipping Industry
RT Land Transportation Industry
Mass Transportation Industry
Water Pollution
Water Pollution Policy
Water Use Policy

WATER USE POLICY
S-26-0223 1975 00064
BT Natural Resource Policy
RT Energy Use Policy
Fish And Wildlife Policy
Forest Land Policy
Grazing Land Policy
Interstate Authorities
Tidal Energy
Water Pollution Policy
Water Scarcity
Water Transportation Industry

WEAK MAYOR GOVERNMENT
S-16-0107 1975 00001
BT City Government
RT City Manager Government
Commission Government
Council Manager Government
Local Political Boss
Local Political Division
Strong Mayor Government

WEAK POLITICAL PARTY IDENTIFIER
S-32-0173 1975 00002
BT Political Party Supporter
RT Political Party Loyalist
Political Party Orientation
Strong Political Party Identifier

WEALTH DISTRIBUTION
S-06-0634 1975 00048
BT Economic Power Distribution
NT Income Distribution
Income Elasticity
Poverty
Prosperity
Subsistence Level
Wage Level
Wealth Redistribution
RT Economic Injustice
Economic Resource Allocation
Economic Stratification
Fixed Assets
Income Distribution
Industrial Distribution
Land Ownership Pattern
Subsistence Wage Level

WEALTH REDISTRIBUTION
S-06-0642 1975 00026
BT Wealth Distribution
RT Economic Resource Allocation
Income Distribution
Subsistence Wage Level

WEAPON
S-33-0016 1975 00007
BT War Technology
NT Civilian Weapon
Military Weapon
Missile
Munitions
Nuclear Weapon
Strategic Weapon
Tactical Weapon
Unconventional Weapon
RT Armed Forces
Arms Sales
Bomb
Declared War
Military Personnel
Security Forces
Weapon Delivery Subsystem
Weapon Delivery System

WEAPON DELIVERY SUBSYSTEM
S-33-0015 1975 00001
BT Weapon Delivery System
RT Armed Forces
Security Forces
Weapon

WEAPON DELIVERY SYSTEM
S-33-0014 1975 00018
BT Offensive Weapon System
NT Weapon Delivery Subsystem
RT Armed Forces
MARV
MIRV
Weapon

WEAPONS SALES
USE Arms Sales

WEBERIAN ANALYSIS
S-09-0070 1975 00020
BT Sociological Analysis
RT Administrative Theory
Authority Mode
Bureaucratic Behavior
Bureaucratic Theory
Durkheimian Analysis
Gesellschaft
Historical Sociology Analysis
Ideal Case Analysis
Ideal Type Analysis
Ideal Type Model
Marginal Man Analysis
Organization Hierarchy
Rational Legal Leadership
Structural Functional Analysis
Technocratic Politics
Technological Change
Technological Development Theory
Theocratic Authority
Value Free Science Theory
Verstehen Theory
Vertical Cleavage
Weberian Theory

WEBERIAN THEORY
S-38-0593 1975 00023
SN Form of socio-historical analysis of authority configurations associated with Max Weber.
BT Social Theory
RT Administrative Science
Bureaucracy
Bureaucratic Politics
Bureaucratic Theory
Charismatic Authority
Gesellschaft
Group Hierarchy
Ideal Case Analysis
Ideal Type Analysis

Ideal Type Model
Legal Rational Authority
Political Authority
Rational Legal Leadership
Role Theory
Social Action Theory
Technological Change
Value Free Science Theory
Verstehen Theory
Weberian Analysis

WELFARE
S-06-0321 1975 00017
BT Public Assistance
RT Social Security
Unemployed Person
Unemployment Compensation
Unemployment Insurance Policy
Welfare Administration
Welfare Agency
Welfare Law
Welfare Policy
Welfare State

WELFARE ADMINISTRATION
S-23-0040 1975 00013
BT Management
RT Health Administration
Population Management
Unemployment
Unemployment Compensation
Unemployment Policy
Welfare
Welfare Agency
Welfare Economics
Welfare Policy
Welfare Spending
Welfare State
Welfare System

WELFARE AGENCY
S-19-0064 1975 00015
BT Agencies
NT Health Care Agency
RT Economic Agency
Government Agency
Health Care Institution
Public Authorities
Unemployed Person
Unemployment
Unemployment Insurance Policy
Unemployment Policy
Welfare
Welfare Administration

WELFARE CAPITALISM
S-37-0021 1975 00004
BT Capitalism
RT Bourgeois Capitalism
Industrial Capitalism
Mature Capitalism
Mercantile Capitalism
Monopoly Capitalism
Unemployment Compensation
Warfare Capitalism
Welfare Economics
Welfare Liberalism

WELFARE CLASS MOVEMENT
1975-1979 00001

WELFARE ECONOMICS
S-01-0076 1975 00018
BT Economics Discipline
RT Econometrics
Labor Economics
Macroeconomics
Neoclassical Economic Theory
Social Economics
Welfare Administration
Welfare Capitalism
Welfare Liberalism
Welfare Spending
Welfare System

WELFARE ECONOMY
S-12-0046 1979 00000
BT Economy Type
RT Balanced Economy
Capital Investment Economy
Developed Economy
Dual Economy
Grants Economy
Industrial Economy
Market Economy
Mixed Economy
Modernizing Economy
Planned Economy
Welfare Policy
Welfare State
Welfare System

WELFARE LAW
S-21-0049 1975 00003
BT Economic Law
RT Industrial Safety Law
Price Control Law
Social Law
Welfare
Welfare Policy
Welfare Rights Movement
Welfare State

WELFARE LIBERALISM
S-38-0256 1975 00002
BT Liberalism
RT Civil Liberty Liberalism
Civil Rights Liberalism
Classical Liberalism
Economic Liberalism
Laissez Faire Liberalism
Nineteenth Century Liberalism
Welfare Capitalism
Welfare Economics
Welfare State

WELFARE POLICY
S-26-0414 1975 00024
BT Social Welfare Policy
RT Charitable Organization
Income Maintenance Policy
Insurance
Old Age Assistance Policy
Service Delivery System
Unemployment
Unemployment Policy
Welfare
Welfare Administration
Welfare Economy
Welfare Law
Welfare Spending
Welfare State
Welfare System

WELFARE RIGHTS MOVEMENT
S-27-0008 1975 00001
BT Economic Movement
RT Consumer Rights Movement
Separatist Movement
Welfare Law

WELFARE SPENDING
S-31-0419 1975 00013
BT Public Spending
RT Monetary Process
Unemployment Insurance Policy
Welfare Administration
Welfare Economics
Welfare Policy

WELFARE STATE
S-16-0173 1975 00012
BT State Type
RT Government Expenditure
Guaranteed Annual Income Policy
Keynesian Economic Theory
Poverty Program Spending
Public Assistance
Unemployment
Unemployment Compensation
Welfare
Welfare Administration
Welfare Economy
Welfare Law
Welfare Liberalism
Welfare Policy
Welfare System

WELFARE SYSTEM
S-37-0151 1975 00025
BT System Type
RT Economic System
Insurance
Right To Job Security
Unemployment Compensation
Welfare Administration
Welfare Economics
Welfare Economy
Welfare Policy
Welfare State

WEST AFRICAN AREA STUDIES
S-01-0030 1979 00000
BT African Area Studies
RT Anthropology Discipline
Central African Area Studies
East African Area Studies
Economics Discipline
History Discipline
North African Area Studies
Political Science Discipline
Sociology Discipline
South African Area Studies

WEST EUROPEAN AREA STUDIES
S-01-0046 1975 00799
BT Area Studies
NT Common Market Area Studies
Scandinavian Area Studies
RT Atlantic Community
British Commonwealth Area Studies
Comparative Analysis
Comparative Literature Studies
Comparative Political Studies
Comparative Sociology
Cultural Anthropology
Cultural History
East European Area Studies

European Integration Theory
Political Science Discipline
Soviet And East European Area Studies
Western Bloc
Western Culture
Western Society

WESTERN BLOC
S-02-0050 1975 00010
BT Extranational Bloc
RT Afro Asian Bloc
Atlantic Community
Communist Bloc
European Integration Theory
Extranational Commonwealth
Security Community
West European Area Studies

WESTERN CIVILIZATION
S-11-0010 1979 00000
BT Civilization
RT Greek Civilization
History Discipline
Homogeneous Culture
Islamic Civilization
Political Culture
Roman Civilization
Western Culture
Western Society

WESTERN CULTURE
S-11-0049 1975 00048
BT Culture Type
RT Civilization
Counter Culture
Cultural History
Eastern Culture
Ethnic Culture
Heterogeneous Culture
Political Culture
Protestant Ethic
Technological Culture
Urban Culture
West European Area Studies
Western Civilization
Work Culture
Youth Culture

WESTERN IMPERIALISM
S-37-0073 1975 00019
BT Political Imperialism
RT Capitalist Imperialism
Communist Imperialism
Neoimperialism
Yankee Imperialism

WESTERN SOCIETY
S-35-0050 1975 00016
BT Society Type
RT Achieving Society
Affluent Society
Bourgeois Society
Industrial Society
Meritocracy
Modernizing Society
Secular Society
Technological Culture
Urban Society
West European Area Studies
Western Civilization

WHITE COLLAR CRIME
S-10-0025 1975 00002
BT Economic Crime
RT Economic Bribery
Economic Conspiracy
Economic Espionage
Economic Sabotage
Extortion
Fraud
Tax Evasion
White Collar Worker

WHITE COLLAR WORKER
S-32-0098 1975 00006
BT Manager
RT Class Analysis
Industrial Occupation
New Middle Class
White Collar Crime

WHITE MILITANCY
S-06-0113 1975 00000
BT Racial Militancy
RT Bigotry
Racial Supremacy
Racism
White Racism

WHITE PAPER
S-18-0037 1975 00003
SN Investigatory reports developed by commission of inquiry empowered by a legislature.
BT Parliamentary Paper
RT Administrative Record
Intergovernmental Document
Investigation Commission
Parliamentary Commission Of Inquiry

WHITE RACISM
S-38-0222 1975 00017
BT Racism
RT Antisemitism
Apartheid
Apartheid Theory
Black Racism
Institutional Racism
Racial Supremacy
White Militancy

WIDOW
S-36-0231 1979 00000
BT Marital Status
RT Family Role
Single
Widower
Wife

WIDOWER
S-36-0232 1979 00000
BT Marital Status
RT Family Role
Husband
Single
Widow

WIFE
S-32-0048 1975 00020
BT Family Role
RT Household Head
Housewife
Husband
Marital Offense
Marriage Contract
Maternal Role
Mother
Sex Inequality
Widow
Womens Emancipation
Womens Liberation
Womens Liberation Movement
Womens Rights
Womens Studies

WILCOXIAN T TEST
S-24-0063 1979 00000
BT Statistical Significance Test
RT Binomial Test
Borough Government
Chi Square Test
F Ratio
Nominal Significance Test
Ordinal Significance Test
Wald Wolfowitz Runs Test

WILCOXON T TEST
1975-1979 00000

WILDCAT STRIKE
S-08-0034 1975 00000
BT Labor Strike
RT Jurisdiction Strike
Sit Down Strike
Social Conflict
Strike Breaking
Walkout

WIND ENERGY
S-31-0128 1979 00000
BT Natural Resource Exploitation
RT Coal Energy
Energy Management
Energy Policy
Energy Use Policy
Gas Energy
Geothermal Energy
Hydroelectric Energy
Middle Level Technology
Natural Resource Policy
Nuclear Energy
Solar Energy
Tidal Energy

WINNING COALITION
S-02-0033 1975 00003
BT Coalition Type
NT Minimum Winning Coalition
RT Coalition Type
Democratic Coalition
Economic Coalition
Electoral Coalition
Governing Coalition
Legislative Coalition
Multiethnic Coalition
Opinion Coalition
Parliamentary Coalition
Political Coalition
Political Party Coalition
Voting Coalition

WIRETAP EVIDENCE ADMISSIBILITY
S-26-0024 1975 00000
BT Wiretapping Policy
RT Evidence Admissibility
Freedom Of Speech
Government Regulation
Search And Seizure
Wiretapping Policy

WIRETAPPING POLICY
S-26-0023 1975 00005
BT Telephone Policy
NT Wiretap Evidence Admissibility
RT Evidence Admissibility
Freedom Of Speech
Government Regulation
Search And Seizure
Telephone Allocation Policy
Wiretap Evidence Admissibility

WITCHCRAFT
S-38-0017 1975 00002
BT Myth Analysis
RT Folkways
Magic
Shamanism
Superstition
Taboo

WITTGENSTEINIAN THOUGHT
S-38-0070 1975 00000
BT Ordinary Language Philosophy
RT Linguistic Analysis
Logic
Philosophical Concept

WOMENS EMANCIPATION
S-31-0148 1975 00012
BT Emancipation
RT Black Emancipation
Female Chauvinism
Female Voter
Feminism
Freedom
Male Chauvinism
Male Chauvinist
Sex Role
Suffrage Equality
Suffragette
Wife
Working Class Emancipation

WOMENS LIBERATION
S-38-0238 1975 00012
BT Feminism
RT Caste Dissolution
Equal Rights
Female Chauvinism
Female Chauvinist
Sex Role
Wife
Womens Liberation Movement
Womens Rights
Womens Studies

WOMENS LIBERATION MOVEMENT
S-27-0028 1975 00019
BT Liberation Movement
RT Black Liberation Movement
Female Chauvinism
Female Voter
Femininity
Feminism
Feminist Politics
Male Chauvinism
Sex Discrimination
Sex Equality
Sex Exploitation
Suffrage Equality
Suffrage Extension
Suffrage Law
Suffragette
Wife
Womens Liberation
Womens Studies

WOMENS RIGHTS
S-15-0041 1975 00020
BT Equal Rights
RT Abortion Law
Abortion Policy
Affirmative Action Employment Policy
Female Chauvinism
Feminism
Maternal Role
Matriarchal Family
Matriarchal Kinship System
Minority Rights
Racial Injustice
Suffrage Law
Suffragette
Wife
Womens Liberation

WOMENS STUDIES
S-01-0206 1975 00188
BT Academic Areas
RT Family Role
Female Chauvinism
Femininity
Feminism
Feminist Politics
Group Analysis
Political Sociology
Sex Role
Sociology Discipline
Suffragette
Wife
Womens Liberation
Womens Liberation Movement

WORK CULTURE
S-11-0050 1979 00000
BT Culture Type
NT Labor Discipline
Protestant Ethic
Work Ethic
RT Pragmatic Political Culture
Technological Culture
Urban Culture
Western Culture
Work Norm Policy
Worker Productivity

WORK ETHIC
S-11-0053 1979 00000
BT Work Culture
RT Labor Discipline
Protestant Ethic
Right To Work Policy
Work Norm Policy

WORK NORM POLICY
S-26-0132 1975 00009
BT Productivity Policy
RT Day Laborer
Labor Law
Production Quota
Work Culture
Work Ethic
Worker Productivity

WORKER COOPERATIVE
S-03-0010 1975 00002
BT Cooperatives
RT Cooperatives
Credit Cooperative
Industrial Union
Marketing Cooperative
Peasant Cooperative
Worker Organization

WORKER DEMONSTRATION
S-08-0023 1975 00000
BT Demonstration
RT General Strike
Labor Boycott
Labor Conflict
Labor Strike
Lockout
Peace Demonstration
Proletarian Revolution
Student Demonstration
Veterans Demonstration
Worker Rebellion

WORKER MANAGEMENT PARTICIPATION
S-23-0035 1975 00040
BT Participatory Management
NT Worker Self Management
RT Citizen Participation
Economic Management
Labor Law
Labor Management Relations Policy

WORKER MOBILIZATION
S-31-0633 1975 00006
BT Mobilization Process
RT Economic Mobilization
Mass Mobilization
Military Mobilization
Political Mobilization
Social Mobilization

WORKER ORGANIZATION
S-03-0062 1975 00003
BT Organizations
NT International Labor Organization
Public Employee Organization
RT Economic Organization
Employer Organization
Interest Group
Labor Economics
Trade Union Movement
Trade Union Politics
Worker Cooperative
Worker Self Management
Working Class Movement
Youth Organization

WORKER PRODUCTIVITY
S-06-0158 1975 00044
BT Productivity Rate
RT Production Process
Work Culture
Work Norm Policy
Worker Self Management
Working Conditions

WORKER REBELLION
S-08-0061 1975 00005
BT Rebellion
RT Class Rebellion
Class Struggle
Economic Agitation
Economic Rebellion
Peasant Rebellion
Slave Rebellion
Struggle
Worker Demonstration
Working Class Movement

WORKER SELF MANAGEMENT
S-23-0036 1975 00018
BT Worker Management Participation
RT Administrative Management
Economic Management
Industrial Democracy
Labor Law
Labor Management Relations Policy
Participatory Management
Socialist Economic System
Socialist Humanism
Worker Organization
Worker Productivity

WORKING CLASS
S-06-0780 1975 00034
BT Class Stratification Division
NT Agricultural Working Class
Industrial Working Class
Proletariat
Unionized Working Class
RT Factory
Industrial Worker
Labor Force
Lower Class
Lumpen Proletariat
Marxist Class Theory
Middle Class
Proletarian Cultural Revolution Movement
Semiskilled Worker
Working Class Movement
Working Class Voter

WORKING CLASS EMANCIPATION
S-31-0149 1975 00000
BT Emancipation
RT Communist Revolution
Emancipation
Womens Emancipation
Working Class Movement
Working Class Voter

WORKING CLASS MOVEMENT
S-27-0054 1975 00010
BT Class Based Movement
RT Communism
Labor Political Party
Labor Politics
Labor Union
Luddite Movement
Marxist Class Consciousness Theory
Marxist Class Theory
Marxist Communism Theory
Marxist Immiseration Theory
Middle Class Movement
Proletarian Cultural Revolution Movement
Proletarian Dictatorship
Proletarian Movement
Proletarian Political Party
Proletarian Socialist Movement
Worker Organization
Worker Rebellion
Working Class
Working Class Emancipation

WORKING CLASS PARTY
1975-1979 00003

WORKING CLASS POLITICAL PARTY
S-28-0042 1979 00000
BT Labor Political Party
RT Aristocracy Political Party
Proletarian Political Party

WORKING CLASS VOTER
S-32-0304 1975 00008
BT Class Voter
RT Middle Class Voter
Socialist Theory
Upper Class Voter
Working Class
Working Class Emancipation

WORKING CONDITION
1975-1979 00037
USE Working Conditions

WORKING CONDITIONS
S-06-0706 1979 00000
UF Working Condition
BT Social System Environment Characteristics
RT Day Laborer
Factory
Labor Law
Labor Negotiation
Living Conditions
Quality Of Life
Worker Productivity
Working Conditions

WORLD ALLIANCE
S-02-0011 1975 00003
BT Alliance
NT League Of Nations
United Nations
RT Extranational Bloc
International Bloc
Military Alliance
Multilateral Alliance
Mutual Support Declaration
Neutrality Agreement
State Agreement Form
State Agreement Type
United Nations

WORLD BANK
S-19-0199 1979 00000
BT Monetary Institution
RT Business
Capital Flow
Corporation
Credit Policy
Enterprise
Fiscal Institution
Market
Monetary Policy
Monetary Process

WORLD COMMERCE
S-31-0376 1975 00003
BT Commerce
RT Business Studies
Contract Type
Foreign Trade
International Commerce
Trade Agreement
Trade Policy
World Market

WORLD COURT
S-19-0146 1975 00002
BT International Court
RT International Adjudication
International Conciliation
International Conflict Resolution Theory
International Government Council
International Judge
International Judicial System
International Law
International Law Enforcement
International Law System
International Law Theory
International Negotiation
International Police
International Tribunal
League Of Nations
Prisoner Of War
Treaty Making
United Nations
World Law
World Politics

WORLD ECONOMY
S-12-0047 1979 00000
BT Economy Type
RT Economic Power Distribution
Economic System
Global System
International Economic Interdependence
International Economic Relations
New International Economic Order

WORLD EMPIRE
S-16-0052 1975 00000
BT Empire
RT Capitalist Empire
Colonial Empire
Communist Empire
Global System
Imperialism System
World Government

WORLD GOVERNMENT
S-16-0065 1975 00006
BT International Government
RT Imperial Government
United Nations
World Empire

WORLD LAW
S-21-0059 1975 00002
BT International Law
RT Global System
Law Of The Sea
United Nations
World Court
World Politics

WORLD LITERATURE
USE Comparative Literature Studies

WORLD MARKET
S-19-0197 1975 00014
BT International Market
RT Black Market
Commodity Market
Common Market
Differentiated Market
Financial Market
Free Market
Global System
Imperialist Economy
Mass Market
National Market
Stock Market
World Commerce

WORLD POLITICS
S-29-0207 1975 00028
BT International Politics
NT Communal Politics
Superpower Politics
Transnational Politics
RT Foreign Policy
Global Education
Global Politics
Global System
Global War Policy
International Conflict
International Crisis
International Law Enforcement
International Political System Characteristics
International Political Theory
International Power Theory
Political Interference Policy
United Nations
World Court
World Law

WORLD REGION
S-24-0352 1975 00017
BT Global System
NT International Region
National Region
RT Global Politics
Political Geography

WORLD WAR
S-08-0110 1975 00047
BT Total War
RT Armed Intervention Policy
Global System
Just War
Nuclear War

WRIT OF MANDAMUS
S-31-0489 1975 00000
BT Court Action
RT Acquittal
Cease Desist Order
Certiorari
Injunction
Life Sentence
Obiter Dicta
Subpoena
Verdict
Warrant

WRITE IN VOTING
S-29-0165 1975 00000
BT Voting
RT Candidate Selection
Independent Voting

WRITTEN CONSTITUTION
S-21-0016 1975 00001
BT Constitution
RT Basic Law
Constitutional Convention
Constitutional Law
Democratic Constitution
National Constitution
State Constitution
State Constitutional Convention
Statutory Law
Unwritten Constitution

XENOPHOBE
S-32-0214 1975 00000
BT Chauvinist
RT Bigotry
Ethnic Nationalism
Ethnocentrism
Isolationist
Jingoist
National Chauvinist
Nationality Persecution

YANKEE IMPERIALISM
S-37-0074 1975 00007
BT Political Imperialism
RT Capitalist Imperialism
Castroism
Communist Imperialism
Gunboat Diplomacy
Imperialism
Intervention Policy
Leninist Imperialism Theory
Liberation Front
Military Industrial Complex
Neocolonialism
Neoimperialism
Private Foreign Investment
Western Imperialism

YOUNG VOTER
1975-1979 00002
USE Youth Voter

YOUTH
S-06-0186 1975 00038
BT Age
RT Adolescence
Childhood
Childhood Political Socialization
Childhood Socialization
Youth Culture
Youth Movement
Youth Organization
Youth Politics
Youth Voter

YOUTH CULTURE
S-11-0054 1975 00009
BT Culture Type
RT Adolescence
Adolescent Political Socialization
Adolescent Socialization
Childhood Political Socialization
Community Culture
Counter Culture
Cultural History
Drug Culture
Ethnic Culture
Heterogeneous Culture
Hippie Movement
Homogeneous Culture
Political Culture
Secular Culture
Socialization
Student
Student Rebellion
Student Voting
Technological Culture
Urban Culture
Western Culture
Youth
Youth Movement
Youth Organization
Youth Politics

YOUTH MOVEMENT
S-27-0068 1975 00007
BT Social Movement
NT Hippie Movement
RT Adolescent Political Socialization
Adolescent Socialization
Radical Student Movement
Youth
Youth Culture
Youth Organization
Youth Politics
Youth Voter

YOUTH ORGANIZATION
S-03-0072 1979 00000
BT Associations
RT Association Characteristics
Associational Process
Cultural Organization
Ethnic Organization
Organization Capability Characteristics
Organization Normative Characteristics
Political Party Organization
Radical Student Movement
Religious Organization
Student Activism
Veterans Organization
Worker Organization
Youth
Youth Culture
Youth Movement
Youth Politics

YOUTH POLITICS
S-29-0246 1975 00011
BT Politics
RT Adolescence
Adolescent Political Socialization
Adolescent Socialization
Group Politics
Protest Politics
Racial Politics
Religious Politics
Sexual Politics
Youth
Youth Culture
Youth Movement
Youth Organization
Youth Voter

YOUTH VOTER
S-32-0338 1979 00000
UF Young Voter
BT Voter
RT Adolescence
New Voter
Student Voter
Youth
Youth Movement
Youth Politics

ZERO BASED BUDGET
S-06-0258 1979 00000
BT Capital Budget
RT Budget Policy
Development Policy
Executive Budget
Fiscal Management
Incremental Budget
Performance Budget

ZERO POPULATION GROWTH
S-06-0215 1979 00000
BT Population Growth
RT Demographic Indicator
Family Planning

Population Estimation
Population Management
Population Planning

ZERO SUM GAME THEORY
S-38-0137 1975 00005
BT Game Theory
RT Constant Sum Game Theory
Zero Sum Gaming

ZERO SUM GAMING
S-24-0105 1975 00004
BT Gaming
RT Fixed Sum Gaming
Nonzero Sum Gaming
Prisoner Dilemma Gaming
Prisoner Dilemma Theory
Two Person Gaming
Variable Sum Gaming
Zero Sum Game Theory

ZIONISM
S-38-0271 1975 00011
BT Cultural Nationalism
RT Cultural Nationalism
Irredentism
Religious Culture
Religious Identity
Religious Movement
Zionist Movement

ZIONIST MOVEMENT
S-27-0039 1975 00015
BT Nationalist Movement
RT Religious Movement
Zionism

ZONING DISTRICT
S-16-0098 1975 00000
BT District Government Type
RT Fire District
Recreation District
School District
Sewer District
Transportation District
Zoning Law

ZONING LAW
S-21-0050 1975 00003
BT Economic Law
NT Building Code
Housing Code
RT Building Code
Commercial Law
Negligence Law
Zoning District
Zoning Policy

ZONING POLICY
S-26-0218 1975 00012
BT Land Use Policy
RT City Planning Commission
Eminent Domain Policy
Public Land Use Policy
Zoning Law

ZOROASTRIANISM
S-38-0576 1975 00001
SN Ancient religion which believed in an eternal struggle between cosmic forces of good and evil.
BT Religious Thought
RT Buddhism
Confucianism
Eastern Political Thought
Islamic Thought
Judeo Christian Thought
Religious Movement
Shintoism
Taoism

GEOGRAPHICAL TERMINOLOGY

GEOGRAPHICAL TERMINOLOGY

AFGHANISTAN
G-08-0002 1975 00006
BT Middle East

AFRICA
G-01-0001 1975 00253
NT Central Africa
East Africa
North Africa
South Africa
West Africa

AFRICA SOUTH OF SAHARA
1975-1979 00140
USE Central Africa
East Africa
South Africa
West Africa

ALBANIA
G-06-0003 1975 00007
BT Eastern Europe

ALGERIA
G-01-0018 1975 00011
BT North Africa

AMERICA
G-02-0001 1975 02955
NT Caribbean Islands
Central America
North America
South America

AMERICAN SAMOA
G-09-0022 1979 00000
BT Polynesia

AMIRANTE ISLAND
G-07-0002 1979 00000
BT Indian Ocean Region

ANDAMAN ISLAND
G-07-0003 1979 00000
BT Indian Ocean Region

ANDORRA
G-06-0015 1975 00000
BT Western Europe

ANGOLA
G-01-0025 1975 00025
BT South Africa

ANTARCTIC REGIONS
G-10-0002 1979 00000
UF Antarctica
BT Polar Regions

ANTARCTICA
1975-1979 00003
USE Antarctic Regions

ANTIGUA
G-02-0003 1975 00000
BT Caribbean Islands

ARAB REPUBLIC OF EGYPT
USE Egypt

ARCTIC REGIONS
G-10-0003 1979 00000
BT Polar Regions

ARGENTINA
G-02-0042 1975 00031
BT South America

ASCENSION ISLAND
G-04-0002 1979 00000
BT Atlantic Ocean Region

ASIA
G-03-0001 1975 00574
NT East Asia
South Asia
Southeast Asia

ASSOCIATED STATES OF THE UNITED KINGDOM
1975-1979 00004
USE United Kingdom

ATLANTIC OCEAN REGION
G-04-0001 1979 00000
NT Ascension Island
Azores
Bermuda
Bouvet Island
Canary Islands
Cape Verde Islands
Gough Island
Iceland
Madeira
Saint Helena

AUSTRALASIA
1975-1979 00040
USE Australia
Oceania

AUSTRALIA
G-05-0001 1975 00037
UF Australasia

AUSTRIA
G-06-0016 1975 00017
BT Western Europe

AZORES
G-04-0003 1979 00000
BT Atlantic Ocean Region

BAHAMAS
G-02-0004 1975 00002
BT Caribbean Islands

BAHRAIN
G-08-0003 1979 00000
BT Middle East

BANGLADESH
G-03-0012 1975 00022
BT South Asia

BANKS ISLAND
G-09-0003 1979 00000
BT Melanesia

BARBADOS
G-02-0005 1979 00000
BT Caribbean Islands

BELGIAN CONGO
USE Zaire

BELGIUM
G-06-0017 1975 00016
BT Western Europe

BELIZE
G-02-0028 1979 00000
UF British Honduras
BT Central America

BENIN
G-01-0037 1979 00000
UF Dahomey
BT West Africa

BERMUDA
G-04-0004 1975 00000
BT Atlantic Ocean Region

BHUTAN
G-03-0013 1975 00000
BT South Asia

BOLIVIA
G-02-0043 1975 00011
BT South America

BOTSWANA
G-01-0026 1975 00006
BT South Africa

BOUVET ISLAND
G-04-0005 1979 00000
BT Atlantic Ocean Region

BRAZIL
G-02-0044 1975 00088
BT South America

BRITISH HONDURAS
1975-1979 00001
USE Belize

BRUNEI
1975-1979 00000
USE Malaysia

BULGARIA
G-06-0004 1975 00012
BT Eastern Europe

BURMA
G-03-0019 1975 00011
BT Southeast Asia

BURUNDI
G-01-0003 1975 00000
BT Central Africa

CAMBODIA
USE Democratic Kampuchea

CAMEROON
G-01-0038 1975 00007
UF Cameroun
BT West Africa

CAMEROUN
USE Cameroon

CANADA
G-02-0037 1975 00137
BT North America

CANARY ISLANDS
G-04-0006 1979 00000
BT Atlantic Ocean Region

CANTON AND ENDERBY ISLANDS
G-09-0014 1979 00000
BT Micronesia

CAPE VERDE ISLANDS
G-04-0007 1979 00000
BT Atlantic Ocean Region

CARIBBEAN ISLANDS
G-02-0002 1979 00000
UF West Indies
BT America
NT Antigua
Bahamas
Barbados
Cayman Islands

Cuba
Dominica
Dominican Republic
Grenada
Guadeloupe
Haiti
Jamaica
Martinique
Montserrat
Netherlands Antilles
Puerto Rico
Saint Barthelemy
Saint Kitt-Nevis-Anguilla
Saint Lucia
Saint Martin
Saint Vincent
Trinidad And Tobago
Turks And Caicos Islands
Virgin Islands (UK)
Virgin Islands (USA)

CAROLINE ISLANDS
G-09-0015 1979 00000
BT Micronesia

CAYMAN ISLANDS
G-02-0006 1979 00000
BT Caribbean Islands

CENTRAL AFRICA
G-01-0002 1975 00003
UF Africa South Of Sahara
BT Africa
NT Burundi
Central African Empire
Chad
Congo
Rwanda
Uganda
Zaire

CENTRAL AFRICA REPUBLIC
USE Central African Empire

CENTRAL AFRICAN EMPIRE
G-01-0004 1979 00000
UF Central Africa Republic
BT Central Africa

CENTRAL AFRICAN REPUBLIC
1975-1979 00002

CENTRAL AMERICA
G-02-0027 1975 00080
BT America
NT Belize
Costa Rica
El Salvador
Guatemala
Honduras
Nicaragua
Panama
Panama Canal Zone

CENTRAL PACIFIC OCEAN REGION
USE Polynesia

CEYLON
USE Sri Lanka

CHAD
G-01-0005 1975 00003
BT Central Africa

CHAGOS ARCHIPELAGO
G-07-0004 1979 00000
BT Indian Ocean Region

CHILE
G-02-0045 1975 00037
BT South America

CHINA
USE Peoples Republic Of China
Taiwan

CHRISTMAS ISLAND
G-07-0005 1979 00000
BT Indian Ocean Region

COCOS ISLANDS
G-07-0006 1979 00000
BT Indian Ocean Region

COLOMBIA
G-02-0046 1975 00038
BT South America

COMORO ISLAND
G-07-0007 1979 00000
BT Indian Ocean Region

CONGO
G-01-0006 1979 00000
UF Congo (Brazzaville)
Republic Of The Congo
BT Central Africa

CONGO (BRAZZAVILLE)
USE Congo

COOK ISLAND
G-09-0023 1979 00000
BT Polynesia

COSTA RICA
G-02-0029 1975 00014
BT Central America

CROZET ISLAND
G-07-0008 1979 00000
BT Indian Ocean Region

CUBA
G-02-0007 1975 00057
BT Caribbean Islands

CYPRUS
G-08-0004 1975 00011
BT Middle East

CZECHOSLOVAKIA
G-06-0005 1975 00036
BT Eastern Europe

DAHOMEY
1975-1979 00000
USE Benin

DEMOCRATIC KAMPUCHEA
G-03-0020 1979 00000
UF Cambodia
Khmer Republic
BT Southeast Asia

DEMOCRATIC REPUBLIC OF GERMANY
G-06-0006 1975 00022
UF East Germany
Germany
BT Eastern Europe

DEMOCRATIC REPUBLIC OF VIETNAM
1975-1979 00045
USE Vietnam

DENMARK
G-06-0018 1975 00015
BT Western Europe

DJIBOUTI
G-01-0011 1979 00000
BT East Africa

DOMINICA
G-02-0008 1975 00001
BT Caribbean Islands

DOMINICAN REPUBLIC
G-02-0009 1975 00003
BT Caribbean Islands

DUTCH GUIANA
USE Surinam

EAST AFRICA
G-01-0010 1975 00040
UF Africa South Of Sahara
BT Africa
NT Djibouti
Ethiopia
Kenya
Somalia
Sudan
Tanzania

EAST ASIA
G-03-0002 1975 00277
UF Far East
BT Asia
NT Hongkong
Japan
Macao
Mongolia
Peoples Democratic Republic Of Korea
Peoples Republic Of China
Republic Of Korea
Taiwan

EAST GERMANY
USE Democratic Republic Of Germany

EASTER ISLAND
G-09-0024 1979 00000
BT Polynesia

EASTERN EUROPE
G-06-0002 1975 00476
BT Europe
NT Albania
Bulgaria
Czechoslovakia
Democratic Republic Of Germany
Finland
Greece
Hungary
Poland
Romania
Union Of Soviet Socialist Republics
Yugoslavia

ECUADOR
G-02-0047 1975 00007
BT South America

EGYPT
G-01-0019 1975 00056
UF Arab Republic Of Egypt
United Arab Republic
BT North Africa

EIRE
USE Ireland

EL SALVADOR
G-02-0030 1975 00004
UF Salvador
BT Central America

ENGLAND
G-06-0036 1979 00000
BT United Kingdom

EQUATORIAL GUINEA
G-01-0039 1975 00000
BT West Africa

ETHIOPIA
G-01-0012 1975 00009
BT East Africa

EUROPE
G-06-0001 1975 00905
NT Eastern Europe
Western Europe

FAR EAST
USE East Asia

FEDERAL REPUBLIC OF GERMANY
G-06-0019 1975 00114
UF Germany
West Germany
BT Western Europe

FIJI
G-09-0004 1975 00004
BT Melanesia

FINLAND
G-06-0007 1975 00006
BT Eastern Europe

FORMOSA
USE Taiwan

FRANCE
G-06-0020 1975 00166
BT Western Europe

FRENCH GUIANA
G-02-0048 1975 00000
BT South America

FRENCH POLYNESIA
G-09-0025 1979 00000
BT Polynesia

GABON
G-01-0040 1975 00001
BT West Africa

GAMBIA
G-01-0041 1975 00001
BT West Africa

GERMANY
USE Democratic Republic Of Germany
Federal Republic Of Germany

GHANA
G-01-0042 1975 00017
BT West Africa

GIBRALTAR
G-06-0021 1975 00000
BT Western Europe

GILBERT AND ELLICE ISLANDS
G-09-0016 1979 00000
BT Micronesia

GOUGH ISLAND
G-04-0008 1979 00000
BT Atlantic Ocean Region

GREAT BRITAIN
USE United Kingdom

GREECE
G-06-0008 1975 00023
BT Eastern Europe

GREENLAND
G-02-0038 1975 00001
BT North America

GRENADA
G-02-0010 1975 00000
BT Caribbean Islands

GUADELOUPE
G-02-0011 1979 00000
BT Caribbean Islands

GUAM
G-09-0018 1979 00000
BT Mariana Islands

GUATEMALA
G-02-0031 1975 00011
BT Central America

GUINEA
G-01-0043 1975 00005
BT West Africa

GUINEA-BISSAU
G-01-0044 1979 00000
UF Portuguese Guinea
BT West Africa

GUYANA
G-02-0049 1975 00008
BT South America

HAITI
G-02-0012 1975 00006
BT Caribbean Islands

HEARD ISLAND
G-07-0009 1979 00000
BT Indian Ocean Region

HOLLAND
USE Netherlands

HONDURAS
G-02-0032 1975 00002
BT Central America

HONGKONG
G-03-0003 1975 00007
BT East Asia

HUNGARY
G-06-0009 1975 00037
BT Eastern Europe

ICELAND
G-04-0009 1975 00004
BT Atlantic Ocean Region

INDEPENDENT CONGO REPUBLIC
1975-1979 00004
USE Zaire

INDIA
G-03-0014 1975 00149
BT South Asia

INDIAN OCEAN REGION
G-07-0001 1979 00000
NT Amirante Island
Andaman Island
Chagos Archipelago
Christmas Island
Cocos Islands
Comoro Island
Crozet Island
Heard Island
Laccadive Islands
Maldives
Mauritius
Prince Edward Island
Reunion Island
Seychelles

INDONESIA
G-03-0021 1975 00034
UF Portuguese Timor
BT Southeast Asia

IRAN
G-08-0005 1975 00032
BT Middle East

IRAQ
G-08-0006 1975 00013
BT Middle East

IRELAND
G-06-0022 1975 00012
UF Eire
BT Western Europe

ISRAEL
G-08-0007 1975 00107
BT Middle East

ITALY
G-06-0023 1975 00089
BT Western Europe

IVORY COAST
G-01-0045 1975 00004
BT West Africa

JAMAICA
G-02-0013 1975 00006
BT Caribbean Islands

JAPAN
G-03-0004 1975 00177
BT East Asia

JOHNSTON ISLAND
G-09-0026 1979 00000
BT Polynesia

JORDAN
G-08-0008 1975 00014
BT Middle East

KENYA
G-01-0013 1975 00027
BT East Africa

KHMER REPUBLIC
1975-1979 00014
USE Democratic Kampuchea

KOREA
USE Peoples Democratic Republic Of Korea
Republic Of Korea

KUWAIT
G-08-0009 1975 00004
BT Middle East

LACCADIVE ISLANDS
G-07-0010 1979 00000
BT Indian Ocean Region

LAOS
G-03-0022 1975 00013
BT Southeast Asia

LEBANON
G-08-0010 1975 00019
BT Middle East

LESOTHO
G-01-0027 1975 00003
BT South Africa

LIBERIA
G-01-0046 1975 00005
BT West Africa

LIBYA
G-01-0020 1975 00006
BT North Africa

LIECHTENSTEIN
G-06-0024 1975 00000
BT Western Europe

LINE ISLANDS
G-09-0027 1979 00000
BT Polynesia

LUXEMBOURG
G-06-0025 1975 00004
BT Western Europe

MACAO
G-03-0005 1975 00000
BT East Asia

MADEIRA
G-04-0010 1979 00000
BT Atlantic Ocean Region

MAINLAND CHINA
USE Peoples Republic Of China

MALAGASY REPUBLIC
G-01-0028 1975 00000
BT South Africa

MALAWI
G-01-0029 1975 00001
BT South Africa

MALAYSIA
G-03-0023 1975 00027
UF Brunei
BT Southeast Asia

MALDIVES
G-07-0011 1979 00000
UF Republic Of Maldives
BT Indian Ocean Region

MALI
G-01-0047 1975 00004
BT West Africa

MALTA
G-06-0026 1975 00001
BT Western Europe

MANIHIKI ISLANDS
G-09-0028 1979 00000
BT Polynesia

MARIANA ISLANDS
G-09-0017 1979 00000
BT Micronesia
NT Guam

MARSHALL ISLANDS
G-09-0019 1979 00000
BT Micronesia

MARTINIQUE
G-02-0014 1979 00000
BT Caribbean Islands

MAURITANIA
G-01-0048 1975 00001
BT West Africa

MAURITIUS
G-07-0012 1975 00000
BT Indian Ocean Region

MELANESIA
G-09-0002 1979 00000
UF South Western Pacific Ocean Region
BT Oceania
NT Banks Island
Fiji
New Caledonia
New Guinea
New Hebrides
New Zealand
Papua New Guinea
Santa Cruz Islands
Solomon Islands
Tasmania

MEXICO
G-02-0039 1975 00117
BT North America

MICRONESIA
G-09-0013 1979 00000
UF West Pacific Ocean Region
BT Oceania
NT Canton And Enderby Islands
Caroline Islands
Gilbert And Ellice Islands
Mariana Islands
Marshall Islands
Nauru

MIDDLE EAST
G-08-0001 1975 00212
NT Afghanistan
Bahrain
Cyprus
Iran
Iraq
Israel
Jordan
Kuwait
Lebanon
Oman
Peoples Democratic Republic Of Yemen
Qatar
Saudi Arabia
Syria
Turkey
United Arab Emirates
Yemen Arab Republic

MIDWAY ISLANDS
G-09-0029 1979 00000
BT Polynesia

MONACO
G-06-0027 1975 00000
BT Western Europe

MONGOLIA
G-03-0006 1975 00003
BT East Asia

MONTSERRAT
G-02-0015 1979 00000
BT Caribbean Islands

MOROCCO
G-01-0021 1975 00015
BT North Africa

MOZAMBIQUE
G-01-0030 1975 00018
BT South Africa

MUSCAT AND OMAN
1975-1979 00002
USE Oman

NAMIBIA
G-01-0031 1975 00006
UF South-West Africa
BT South Africa

NAURU
G-09-0020 1975 00000
BT Micronesia

NEPAL
G-03-0015 1975 00008
BT South Asia

NETHERLANDS
G-06-0028 1975 00027
UF Holland
BT Western Europe

NETHERLANDS ANTILLES
G-02-0016 1975 00001
BT Caribbean Islands

NETHERLANDS GUIANA
USE Surinam

NEW CALEDONIA
G-09-0005 1975 00000
BT Melanesia

NEW GUINEA
G-09-0006 1975 00016
BT Melanesia

NEW HEBRIDES
G-09-0007 1979 00000
BT Melanesia

NEW ZEALAND
G-09-0008 1975 00011
BT Melanesia

NICARAGUA
G-02-0033 1975 00004
BT Central America

NIGER
G-01-0049 1975 00002
BT West Africa

NIGERIA
G-01-0050 1975 00045
BT West Africa

NIUE ISLAND
G-09-0030 1979 00000
BT Polynesia

NORTH AFRICA
G-01-0017 1975 00053
BT Africa
NT Algeria
Egypt
Libya
Morocco
Tunisia
Western Sahara

NORTH AMERICA
G-02-0036 1975 02736
BT America
NT Canada
Greenland
Mexico
United States Of America

NORTH KOREA
USE Peoples Democratic Republic Of Korea

NORTH VIETNAM
USE Vietnam

NORTHERN IRELAND
G-06-0037 1979 00000
BT United Kingdom

NORWAY
G-06-0029 1975 00025
BT Western Europe

OCEANIA
G-09-0001 1975 00050
UF Australasia
Pacific Ocean Region
NT Melanesia
Micronesia
Polynesia

OMAN
G-08-0011 1979 00000
UF Muscat And Oman
BT Middle East

ORKNEY ISLANDS
G-06-0041 1979 00000
BT Western Isles

PACIFIC OCEAN REGION
USE Oceania

PAKISTAN
G-03-0016 1975 00039
BT South Asia

PANAMA
G-02-0034 1975 00010
BT Central America

PANAMA CANAL ZONE
G-02-0035 1975 00009
BT Central America

PAPUA NEW GUINEA
G-09-0009 1979 00000
BT Melanesia

PARAGUAY
G-02-0050 1975 00004
BT South America

PEOPLE'S DEMOCRATIC REPUBLIC OF KOREA
1975-1979 00026
USE Peoples Democratic Republic Of Korea

PEOPLE'S REPUBLIC OF CHINA
1975-1979 00223
USE Peoples Republic Of China

PEOPLE'S REPUBLIC OF SOUTHERN YEMEN
1975-1979 00000
USE Peoples Republic Of Southern Yemen

PEOPLES DEMOCRATIC REPUBLIC OF KOREA
G-03-0007 1979 00000
UF Korea
North Korea
People's Democratic Republic Of Korea
BT East Asia

PEOPLES DEMOCRATIC REPUBLIC OF YEMEN
G-08-0012 1979 00000
UF Peoples Republic Of Southern Yemen
Southern Yemen
Yemen
BT Middle East

PEOPLES REPUBLIC OF CHINA
G-03-0008 1979 00000
UF China
Mainland China
People's Republic Of China
BT East Asia

PEOPLES REPUBLIC OF SOUTHERN YEMEN
UF People's Republic Of Southern Yemen
USE Peoples Democratic Republic Of Yemen

PERU
G-02-0051 1975 00032
BT South America

PHILIPPINES
G-03-0024 1975 00041
BT Southeast Asia

PITCAIRN ISLANDS
G-09-0031 1979 00000
BT Polynesia

POLAND
G-06-0010 1975 00077
BT Eastern Europe

POLAR REGIONS
G-10-0001 1979 00000
NT Antarctic Regions
Arctic Regions

POLYNESIA
G-09-0021 1979 00000
UF Central Pacific Ocean Region
BT Oceania
NT American Samoa
Cook Island
Easter Island
French Polynesia
Johnston Island
Line Islands
Manihiki Islands
Midway Islands
Niue Island
Pitcairn Islands
Tahiti
Tokelau Islands
Tonga
Wallis And Futuna Islands
Western Samoa

PORTUGAL
G-06-0030 1975 00027
BT Western Europe

PORTUGUESE GUINEA
1975-1979 00000
USE Guinea-Bissau

PORTUGUESE TIMOR
1975-1979 00001
USE Indonesia

PRINCE EDWARD ISLAND
G-07-0013 1979 00000
BT Indian Ocean Region

PUERTO RICO
G-02-0017 1975 00010
BT Caribbean Islands

QATAR
G-08-0013 1975 00000
BT Middle East

REPUBLIC OF CHINA
1975-1979 00037
USE Taiwan

REPUBLIC OF KOREA
G-03-0009 1975 00043
UF Korea
South Korea
BT East Asia

REPUBLIC OF MALDIVES
1975-1979 00001
USE Maldives

REPUBLIC OF SOUTH AFRICA
G-01-0032 1975 00061
UF South African Republic
BT South Africa

REPUBLIC OF THE CONGO
1975-1979 00001
USE Congo

REPUBLIC OF VIETNAM
1975-1979 00033
USE Vietnam

REPUBLIC OF YEMEN
1975-1979 00000
USE Yemen Arab Republic

REUNION ISLAND
G-07-0014 1979 00000
BT Indian Ocean Region

RHODESIA
1975-1979 00024
USE Zimbabwe-Rhodesia

ROMANIA
G-06-0011 1975 00033
BT Eastern Europe

RUSSIA
USE Union Of Soviet Socialist Republics

RWANDA
G-01-0007 1975 00000
BT Central Africa

SAINT BARTHELEMY
G-02-0018 1979 00000
BT Caribbean Islands

SAINT CHRISTOPHER-NEVIS-ANGUILLA
USE Saint Kitts-Nevis-Anguilla

SAINT HELENA
G-04-0011 1979 00000
BT Atlantic Ocean Region

SAINT KITTS-NEVIS-ANGUILLA
G-02-0019 1979 00000
UF Saint Christopher-Nevis-Anguilla
BT Caribbean Islands

SAINT LUCIA
G-02-0020 1979 00000
UF St. Lucia
BT Caribbean Islands

SAINT MARTIN
G-02-0021 1979 00000
UF St. Martin
BT Caribbean Islands

SAINT VINCENT
G-02-0022 1979 00000
UF St. Vincent
BT Caribbean Islands

SALVADOR
USE El Salvador

SAN MARINO
G-06-0031 1975 00000
BT Western Europe

SANTA CRUZ ISLANDS
G-09-0010 1979 00000
BT Melanesia

SAO TOME AND PRINCIPE
G-01-0051 1979 00000
BT West Africa

SAUDI ARABIA
G-08-0014 1975 00014
BT Middle East

SCOTLAND
G-06-0038 1979 00000
BT United Kingdom

SENEGAL
G-01-0052 1975 00005
BT West Africa

SEYCHELLES
G-07-0015 1979 00000
BT Indian Ocean Region

SHETLAND ISLANDS
G-06-0042 1979 00000
BT Western Isles

SIERRA LEONE
G-01-0053 1975 00004
BT West Africa

SINGAPORE
G-03-0025 1975 00012
BT Southeast Asia

SOLOMON ISLANDS
G-09-0011 1979 00000
BT Melanesia

SOMALIA
G-01-0014 1975 00003
BT East Africa

SOUTH AFRICA
G-01-0024 1979 00000
UF Africa South Of Sahara
BT Africa
NT Angola
Botswana
Lesotho
Malagasy Republic
Malawi
Mozambique
Namibia
Republic Of South Africa
Swaziland
Zambia
Zimbabwe-Rhodesia

SOUTH AFRICAN REPUBLIC
USE Republic Of South Africa

SOUTH AMERICA
G-02-0041 1975 00259
BT America
NT Argentina
Bolivia
Brazil
Chile
Colombia
Ecuador
French Guiana
Guyana
Paraguay
Peru
Surinam
Uruguay
Venezuela

SOUTH ASIA
G-03-0011 1975 00140
BT Asia
NT Bangladesh
Bhutan
India
Nepal
Pakistan
Sri Lanka

SOUTH KOREA
USE Republic Of Korea

SOUTH VIETNAM
USE Vietnam

SOUTH WESTERN PACIFIC OCEAN REGION
USE Melanesia

SOUTH-WEST AFRICA
USE Namibia

SOUTHEAST ASIA
G-03-0018 1975 00164
BT Asia
NT Burma
Democratic Kampuchea
Indonesia
Laos
Malaysia
Philippines
Singapore
Thailand
Vietnam

SOUTHERN AFRICA
1975-1979 00053

SOUTHERN YEMEN
USE Peoples Democratic Republic Of Yemen

SPAIN
G-06-0032 1975 00048
BT Western Europe

SPANISH SAHARA
USE Western Sahara

SRI LANKA
G-03-0017 1975 00017
UF Ceylon
BT South Asia

ST. KITTS-NEVIS-ANGUILLA
1975-1979 00000
USE Saint Kitts-Nevis-Anguilla

ST. LUCIA
1975-1979 00002
USE Saint Lucia

ST. MARTIN
USE Saint Martin

ST. VINCENT
1975-1979 00001
USE Saint Vincent

SUDAN
G-01-0015 1975 00006
BT East Africa

SURINAM
G-02-0052 1975 00001
UF Dutch Guiana
Netherlands Guiana
BT South America

SWAZILAND
G-01-0033 1975 00005
BT South Africa

SWEDEN
G-06-0033 1975 00038
BT Western Europe

SWITZERLAND
G-06-0034 1975 00014
BT Western Europe

SYRIA
G-08-0015 1975 00025
UF Syria Arab Republic
BT Middle East

SYRIA ARAB REPUBLIC
USE Syria

TAHITI
G-09-0032 1979 00000
BT Polynesia

TAIWAN
G-03-0010 1979 00000
UF China
Formosa
Republic Of China
BT East Asia

TANZANIA
G-01-0016 1975 00015
BT East Africa

TASMANIA
G-09-0012 1979 00000
BT Melanesia

THAILAND
G-03-0026 1975 00039
BT Southeast Asia

TOGO
G-01-0054 1975 00000
BT West Africa

TOKELAU ISLANDS
G-09-0033 1979 00000
BT Polynesia

TONGA
G-09-0034 1979 00000
BT Polynesia

TRINIDAD AND TOBAGO
G-02-0023 1975 00003
BT Caribbean Islands

TUNISIA
G-01-0022 1975 00008
BT North Africa

TURKEY
G-08-0016 1975 00039
BT Middle East

TURKS AND CAICOS ISLANDS
G-02-0024 1979 00000
BT Caribbean Islands

UGANDA
G-01-0008 1975 00015
BT Central Africa

UNION OF SOVIET SOCIALIST REPUBLICS
G-06-0012 1975 00553
UF Russia
USSR
BT Eastern Europe

UNITED ARAB EMIRATES
G-08-0017 1979 00000
BT Middle East

UNITED ARAB REPUBLIC
USE Egypt

UNITED KINGDOM
G-06-0035 1975 00269
UF Associated States Of The United Kingdom
Great Britain
BT Western Europe
NT England
Northern Ireland
Scotland
Wales
Western Isles

UNITED STATES OF AMERICA
G-02-0040 1975 04539
UF USA
BT North America

UPPER VOLTA
G-01-0055 1975 00002
BT West Africa

URUGUAY
G-02-0053 1975 00007
BT South America

USA
USE United States Of America

USSR
USE Union Of Soviet Socialist Republics

VATICAN
1975-1979 00000
USE Vatican City

VATICAN CITY
G-06-0043 1979 00000
UF Vatican
BT Western Europe

VENEZUELA
G-02-0054 1975 00021
BT South America

VIETNAM
G-03-0027 1979 00000
UF Democratic Republic Of Vietnam
North Vietnam
Republic Of Vietnam
South Vietnam
BT Southeast Asia

VIRGIN ISLANDS
1975-1979 00001

VIRGIN ISLANDS (UK)
G-02-0025 1979 00000
BT Caribbean Islands

VIRGIN ISLANDS (USA)
G-02-0026 1979 00000
BT Caribbean Islands

WALES
G-06-0039 1979 00000
BT United Kingdom

WALLIS AND FUTUNA ISLANDS
G-09-0035 1979 00000
BT Polynesia

WEST AFRICA
G-01-0036 1975 00063
UF Africa South Of Sahara
BT Africa
NT Benin
Cameroon
Equatorial Guinea
Gabon
Gambia
Ghana
Guinea
Guinea-Bissau
Ivory Coast
Liberia
Mali
Mauritania
Niger
Nigeria
Sao Tome And Principe
Senegal
Sierra Leone
Togo
Upper Volta

WEST GERMANY
USE Federal Republic Of Germany

WEST INDIES
1975-1979 00068
USE Caribbean Islands

WEST PACIFIC OCEAN REGION
USE Micronesia

WESTERN EUROPE
G-06-0014 1975 00546
BT Europe
NT Andorra
Austria
Belgium
Denmark
Federal Republic Of Germany
France
Gibraltar
Ireland
Italy
Liechtenstein
Luxembourg
Malta
Monaco
Netherlands
Norway
Portugal
San Marino
Spain
Sweden
Switzerland
United Kingdom
Vatican City

WESTERN ISLES
G-06-0040 1979 00000
BT United Kingdom
NT Orkney Islands
Shetland Islands

WESTERN SAHARA
G-01-0023 1979 00000
UF Spanish Sahara
BT North Africa

WESTERN SAMOA
G-09-0036 1975 00003
BT Polynesia

YEMEN
USE Peoples Democratic Republic Of Yemen
Yemen Arab Republic

YEMEN ARAB REPUBLIC
G-08-0018 1979 00000
UF Republic Of Yemen
Yemen
BT Middle East

YUGOSLAVIA
G-06-0013 1975 00054
BT Eastern Europe

ZAIRE

ROTATED DESCRIPTOR DISPLAY

ROTATED DESCRIPTOR DISPLAY

Code	Prefix	Descriptor
S-31-0461		Abdication
S-31-0147	Slavery	Abolition
S-10-0030	Criminal	Abortion
S-10-0033	Illegal	Abortion
S-21-0085		Abortion Law
S-26-0372		Abortion Policy
S-29-0157		Absentee Ballot
S-37-0051		Absentee Landlord System
S-32-0294		Absentee Voter
S-29-0122		Absentee Voting
S		Absenteeism
S-29-0112		Absolute Majority Electoral Outcome
S-36-0055		Absolute Monarch
S-16-0073		Absolute Monarchy
S-38-0177		Absolutism
S-38-0392	Hobbesian	Absolutism
S-16-0003		Absolutist Government
S-29-0118	Negative Voting	Abstention
S-29-0119	Positive Voting	Abstention
S-29-0117	Voting	Abstention
S-24-0154		Abstracting
S-18-0047		Abstracting Service
S	Drug	Abuse
S-29-0224	Power	Abuse
S-32-0002		Academic
S-01-0001		Academic Areas
S-07-0002		Academic Community
S		Academic Departments
S-14-0002		Academic Elite
S-15-0011		Academic Freedom
S-37-0067		Academic Imperialism
S		Academic Management
S-06-0362		Academic Specialization
S-26-0209		Academic Tenure Policy
S		Academician
S-19-0202		Academy Of Science
S-31-0301	Media	Access
S-26-0027	Broadcast	Access Policy
S-26-0039	Mass Media	Access Policy
S-26-0030	Prime Time	Access Policy
S-26-0284	Public Information	Access Policy
S	Prime Time	Access Rule
S	Direct	Access Storage
S	Random	Access Storage
S		Access To Culture
S		Access To Education
S		Access To University
S-26-0299		Accident Insurance
S-31-0221		Accommodation
S	Individual	Accommodation
S-05-0023		Accommodative Social Behavior
S-06-0432	Administrative	Accountability
S-06-0434	Chief Executive	Accountability
S-06-0433	Executive	Accountability
S-06-0370	Government	Accountability
S-06-0418	Legislative	Accountability
S-06-0435	Presidential	Accountability
S		Accountant
S-31-0692	Financial	Accounting
S-31-0696	Social	Accounting
S-09-0050	National	Accounts Analysis
S-19-0035	Education	Accreditation Agency
S-31-0002		Accreditation Process
S-31-0003	Education	Accreditation Process

Code	Qualifier	Term
S		Bolshevik Party
S-28-0012		Bolshevik Political Party
S-08-0073		Bolshevik Revolution
S-38-0315		Bolshevism
S-33-0021		Bomb
S-22-0002		Bonapartism
S-37-0090	Bail	Bond System
S		Book
S		Book Acquisition
S-31-0268		Book Censorship
S		Book Censorship Agency
S-17-0018		Book Industry
S-08-0099		Border Conflict
S-16-0160		Border State
S-08-0098		Border War
S-36-0018	Native	Born Citizen
S-24-0366		Borough
S-16-0100		Borough Government
S-31-0407	Government	Borrowing
S-32-0054	Local Political	Boss
S	Local Political Party	Boss
S-32-0156	Political	Boss
S-29-0217		Boss Politics
G-01-0026		Botswana
S-06-0480	National	Boundary
S-06-0574	System	Boundary
S-37-0014		Bourgeois Capitalism
S-16-0013		Bourgeois Democracy
S-16-0037		Bourgeois Dictatorship
S-08-0076		Bourgeois Revolution
S-35-0010		Bourgeois Society
S-06-0769		Bourgeoisie
S-06-0770	Black	Bourgeoisie
S-06-0771	Petite	Bourgeoisie
G-04-0005		Bouvet Island
S-29-0162	Ballot	Box
S-26-0121	International Economic	Boycott
S-08-0012	Labor	Boycott
S-06-0235		Braindrain
S-24-0012		Brainstorming
S-31-0304		Brainwashing
G-02-0044		Brazil
S-31-0352	Diplomatic Relations	Break
S-08-0036	Strike	Breaking
S-31-0219	Treaty	Breaking
S-10-0015	Economic	Bribery
S-10-0067	Political	Bribery
S	Legal	Brief
S-26-0252		Brinkmanship
G	Great	Britain
S-01-0040		British Commonwealth Area Studies
G		British Honduras
S-38-0442		Broad Constructionism
S-26-0027		Broadcast Access Policy
S-26-0031		Broadcast Censorship Policy
S-26-0032		Broadcast Jamming Policy
S-26-0033		Broadcast Regulation Policy
S-26-0034		Broadcast Subsidization Policy
S		Broadcaster Licensing Policy
S		Broadcaster Liscensing Policy
S-31-0180		Broadcasting
S-31-0181	Public	Broadcasting
S-19-0047		Broadcasting Agency
S-31-0277		Broadcasting Censorship
S-17-0007		Broadcasting Industry
S-17-0008	Commercial	Broadcasting Industry
S-17-0009	Public	Broadcasting Industry
S-26-0035		Broadcasting Licensing Policy
S-26-0026		Broadcasting Policy

Code		Term
S-16-0023	Participatory	Democracy
S	Party	Democracy
S-16-0028	Plebiscitary	Democracy
S-16-0029	Pluralist	Democracy
S-16-0024	Political Party	Democracy
S	Procedural	Democracy
S-16-0030	Representative	Democracy
S-16-0031	Social	Democracy
S-16-0032	Socialist	Democracy
S-16-0033	Stable	Democracy
S-16-0034	Tutelary	Democracy
S	Two Party	Democracy
S-16-0027	Two Political Party	Democracy
S-38-0088	Guided	Democracy Theory
S-32-0271		Democrat
S-32-0272	Christian	Democrat
S-32-0285		Democrat Socialist
S-38-0324		Democratic Centralism
S-02-0020		Democratic Coalition
S-21-0010		Democratic Constitution
S-31-0644		Democratic Economic Planning
S-38-0085		Democratic Elite Theory
S-16-0011		Democratic Government
G-03-0020		Democratic Kampuchea
S-22-0017		Democratic Leadership
S-27-0011	Christian	Democratic Movement
S-27-0022	Social	Democratic Movement
S		Democratic Party
S	Christian	Democratic Party
S	Liberal	Democratic Party
S	National	Democratic Party
S	Social	Democratic Party
S-28-0003		Democratic Political Party
S-28-0004	Christian	Democratic Political Party
S-28-0005	Liberal	Democratic Political Party
S-28-0006	National	Democratic Political Party
S-28-0007	Social	Democratic Political Party
S-08-0069		Democratic Political Revolution
S-37-0108		Democratic Political System
S-16-0137		Democratic Regime
G-06-0006		Democratic Republic Of Germany
G	People's	Democratic Republic Of Korea
G-03-0007	Peoples	Democratic Republic Of Korea
G		Democratic Republic Of Vietnam
G-08-0012	Peoples	Democratic Republic Of Yemen
S-38-0292		Democratic Socialism
S-08-0074		Democratic Socialist Revolution
S-16-0169	Peoples	Democratic State
S-38-0082		Democratic Theory
S-38-0083	Athenian	Democratic Theory
S-38-0087	General Will	Democratic Theory
S-38-0091	Jacksonian	Democratic Theory
S-38-0092	Jeffersonian	Democratic Theory
S-38-0094	Minority Rights	Democratic Theory
S-38-0095	Participatory	Democratic Theory
S	Polyarachic	Democratic Theory
S	Polyarchal	Democratic Theory
S-38-0096	Polyarchical	Democratic Theory
S-38-0097	Populist	Democratic Theory
S-38-0098	Procedural	Democratic Theory
S-38-0100	Socialist	Democratic Theory
S-31-0791		Democratization
S-24-0380		Demographic Analysis
S-06-0179		Demographic Characteristics
S-06-0187		Demographic Indicator
S-06-0188		Demographic Profile
S-06-0197		Demographic Projection
S-01-0056		Demographic Studies
S-31-0254		Demonstrating

Code		Term
S		Detention Camp
S-19-0295		Detention Center
S-06-0487	National Self	Determination
S-25-0011	Cultural	Determinism
S-38-0307	Marxist Economic	Determinism
S-25-0028	Scientific	Determinism
S-38-0009	Geographic	Determinism Theory
S-26-0063	Criminal	Deterrence
S-26-0062		Deterrence Policy
S-26-0064	Mutual	Deterrence Policy
S-26-0065	Nuclear	Deterrence Policy
S-33-0011	Mutual	Deterrence System
S-38-0342		Deterrence Theory
S-33-0025		Deterrent Weapon
S	Money	Devaluation
S-26-0112	Currency	Devaluation Policy
S-16-0016		Developed Democracy
S-12-0018		Developed Economy
S-16-0119		Developed Nation
S-12-0019		Developing Economy
S-16-0120		Developing Nation
S-37-0109		Developing Political System
S-31-0130	Agricultural	Development
S-31-0017	Coalition	Development
S-31-0083	Cognitive	Development
S-31-0154	Colonial	Development
S-31-0576	Constitutional	Development
S-31-0060	Economic	Development
S-31-0062	Education	Development
S-31-0151	Extraterritorial	Development
S-31-0024	Group	Development
S-06-0176	Human Resources	Development
S-31-0061	Industrial	Development
S-31-0073	Institutional	Development
S-06-0177	Legal	Development
S-31-0075	Local	Development
S-31-0038	Organization	Development
S-31-0082	Personality	Development
S-31-0687	Policy	Development
S-06-0178	Political	Development
S-34-0047	Political Orientation	Development
S-31-0101	Regional	Development
S-26-0349	Research And	Development
S-31-0102	Resource	Development
S-31-0129	Rural	Development
S-24-0152	Search Strategy	Development
S-31-0131	Urban	Development
S-31-0076	Village	Development
S-06-0141		Development Characteristics
S-06-0143	Economic	Development Characteristics
S-31-0406		Development Financing
S-06-0301		Development Fund
S-24-0229		Development Index
S-24-0230	Economic	Development Index
S-24-0231	Political	Development Index
S-24-0232	Social	Development Index
S-24-0259	Economic	Development Indicator
S-06-0144	Economic	Development Level
S-06-0149	International Economic	Development Level
S-06-0151	Local Economic	Development Level
S-06-0147	National Economic	Development Level
S-06-0148	Regional Economic	Development Level
S-06-0150	Subnational Economic	Development Level
S-23-0008		Development Management
S-24-0296		Development Model
S-24-0297	Economic	Development Model
S-31-0640		Development Planning
S-26-0079		Development Policy
S-26-0080	Cultural	Development Policy

Code	Modifier	Term
S-37-0026		Economic Sector
S-06-0643		Economic Security
S-06-0644		Economic Sovereignty
S-26-0090		Economic Stabilization Policy
S-38-0112		Economic Stabilization Theory
S-06-0160	Agricultural	Economic Stage
S-06-0161	Feudal	Economic Stage
S-06-0162	Industrial	Economic Stage
S-06-0163	Post Industrial	Economic Stage
S-18-0081		Economic Statistics
S-06-0645		Economic Stratification
S-26-0091		Economic Subsidization Policy
S-37-0010		Economic System
S-37-0011	Barter	Economic System
S-37-0022	Command	Economic System
S-37-0023	Communist	Economic System
S-37-0024	Diversified	Economic System
S-37-0033	Feudal	Economic System
S	Feudalist	Economic System
S-37-0042	International	Economic System
S-37-0045	Mercantile	Economic System
S-37-0046	Mixed	Economic System
S-37-0060	Socialist	Economic System
S-06-0620		Economic System Characteristics
S-38-0106		Economic Theory
S-38-0108	Classical	Economic Theory
S-38-0114	Keynesian	Economic Theory
S-38-0115	Marxist	Economic Theory
S-38-0116	Mercantile	Economic Theory
S-38-0117	Monetary	Economic Theory
S-38-0118	Neoclassical	Economic Theory
S-38-0086		Economic Theory Of Democracy
S-02-0078		Economic Treaty
S-24-0447		Economic Variable
S-01-0060	Business	Economics
S-01-0061	Consumer	Economics
S-01-0063	Evolutionary	Economics
S-01-0064	Industrial	Economics
S-01-0065	Institutional	Economics
S-01-0066	International	Economics
S-01-0069	Keynesian	Economics
S-01-0067	Labor	Economics
S-01-0070	Marxist	Economics
S-01-0072	Regional	Economics
S-01-0073	Social	Economics
S-01-0074	Transportation	Economics
S-01-0075	Urban	Economics
S-01-0076	Welfare	Economics
S-01-0059		Economics Discipline
S-32-0109		Economist
S		Economy
S-12-0002	Agrarian	Economy
S-12-0042	Autarchic	Economy
S-12-0010	Balanced	Economy
S-12-0011	Barter	Economy
S-12-0012	Capital Investment	Economy
S-12-0027	Capitalist	Economy
S-12-0035	Centrally Planned	Economy
S-12-0004	Collective Farm	Economy
S-12-0036	Command	Economy
S-12-0013	Consumer	Economy
S-12-0005	Cooperative Farm	Economy
S-12-0037	Corporate	Economy
S-31-0429	Corporate Farm	Economy
S-12-0014	Cottage Industry	Economy
S-12-0015	Craft	Economy
S-12-0016	Depressed	Economy
S-12-0018	Developed	Economy
S-12-0019	Developing	Economy

Code	Qualifier	Term
S-32-0209		Female Chauvinist
S-32-0312		Female Voter
S-06-0511		Femininity
S-38-0236		Feminism
S-29-0231		Feminist Politics
S-06-0190		Fertility Rate
S-06-0161		Feudal Economic Stage
S-37-0033		Feudal Economic System
S-16-0059		Feudal Government
S-36-0078		Feudal Lord
S-38-0169		Feudal Reaction Theory
S-35-0018		Feudal Society
S-16-0164		Feudal State
S-37-0114		Feudal System
S		Feudalist Economic System
S-18-0068	Political	Fiction
S-31-0169	Communication	Field
S-18-0083		Field Data
S-24-0077		Field Research
S-38-0583		Field Theory
S-38-0354	International	Field Theory
G-09-0004		Fiji
S-32-0177	Rank And	File Member
S-31-0608		Filibustering
S		Film
S-18-0075	Political	Film
S		Film Censorship Agency
S-31-0382	International	Finance
S	Political Party	Finance Committee
S	Campaign	Finance Disclosure
S-26-0136	Public	Finance Policy
S	Political Party	Finance Record
S-38-0119	Public	Finance Theory
S-31-0692		Financial Accounting
S-06-0309		Financial Aid
S-19-0318	Political Party	Financial Committee
S-29-0019	Election Campaign	Financial Disclosure
S-14-0008		Financial Elite
S-19-0188		Financial Market
S-18-0011		Financial Record
S-18-0015	Political Party	Financial Record
S-37-0034		Financial System
S-32-0075		Financier
S-31-0389		Financing
S	Campaign	Financing
S-31-0402	Debt	Financing
S-31-0405	Deficit	Financing
S-31-0406	Development	Financing
S-29-0016	Election Campaign	Financing
S-31-0408	Local	Financing
S-31-0403	National Debt	Financing
S-31-0400	Public	Financing
S-31-0404	War Debt	Financing
S-01-0124		Fine Arts
S-31-0502		Fining
G-06-0007		Finland
S-16-0092		Fire District
S-26-0303		Fire Insurance
S-26-0327	Cease	Fire Policy
S		First Nuclear Strike Weapon
S-36-0254	Local Political Party	First Secretary
S-36-0243	National Political Party	First Secretary
S-36-0255	Regional Political Party	First Secretary
S-36-0253	Subnational Political Party	First Secretary
S-06-0464		First Strike Capability
S-33-0036		First Strike Nuclear Weapon
S-26-0071		First Strike Policy
S-19-0021		Fiscal Agency
S-19-0178		Fiscal Institution

Code	Qualifier	Term
G-06-0008		Greece
S-11-0007		Greek Civilization
S-08-0067		Green Revolution
G-02-0038		Greenland
S-06-0512		Gregariousness
G-02-0010		Grenada
S-31-0540		Grievance Procedure
S-31-0441		Gross National Product
S-31-0442	Per Capita	Gross National Product
S-03-0014	Association Interest	Group
S-03-0015	Consumer Interest	Group
S-03-0012	Cultural	Group
S-03-0016	Cultural Interest	Group
S-03-0017	Economic Interest	Group
S-03-0025	Ethnic	Group
S-03-0026	Face To Face	Group
S-03-0013	Interest	Group
S-03-0028	Kinship	Group
S	Latent	Group
S-03-0019	Latent Interest	Group
S-06-0021	Minority	Group
S-03-0029	Nationality	Group
S-03-0020	Occupational Interest	Group
S-03-0035	Peer	Group
S-03-0022	Policy Interest	Group
S-03-0021	Political Interest	Group
S	Potential Elite	Group
S-03-0027	Primary	Group
S-03-0030	Racial	Group
S-03-0031	Reference	Group
S-03-0032	Religious	Group
S-03-0034	Secondary	Group
S-03-0024	Social	Group
S-09-0024		Group Analysis
S-09-0025	Small	Group Analysis
S-06-0010		Group Attitude
S-05-0029		Group Behavior
S	Large	Group Behavior
S-05-0030	Small	Group Behavior
S-32-0314		Group Benefits Voter
S-06-0011		Group Capability Characteristics
S-31-0023		Group Change
S-06-0009		Group Characteristics
S-06-0048		Group Cleavage Characteristics
S-02-0023	Interest	Group Coalition
S-06-0040		Group Cohesion
S-06-0041	Cultural	Group Cohesion
S-06-0043	Ethnic	Group Cohesion
S-06-0042	Minority	Group Cohesion
S		Group Cohesiveness
S-06-0014		Group Composition
S-08-0115		Group Conflict
S-08-0119	Ethnic	Group Conflict
S-08-0121	Language	Group Conflict
S-31-0028		Group Consolidation
S-06-0026		Group Constraint
S-31-0024		Group Development
S-06-0027		Group Discipline
S-31-0030		Group Disintegration
S-06-0024		Group Dynamics
S-06-0012		Group Effectiveness
S-06-0013		Group Efficiency
S-24-0106	Small	Group Experiment
S	Small	Group Experimentation
S-12-0008	Single	Group Farm Economy
S-06-0049		Group Flexibility
S-31-0025		Group Formation
S-06-0028		Group Goal
S-06-0050		Group Hierarchy

S-26-0292 . . . . Propaganda Policy
S-26-0036 . . . . Public Broadcasting Policy
S-26-0133 . . . . Public Debt Policy
S-26-0194 . . . . Public Education Policy
S-26-0320 . . . . Public Employee Union Policy
S-26-0136 . . . . Public Finance Policy
S-26-0272 . . . . Public Health Policy
S-26-0387 . . . . Public Housing Policy
S-26-0284 . . . . Public Information Access Policy
S-26-0216 . . . . Public Land Use Policy
S-26-0137 . . . . Public Utility Regulation Policy
S-26-0206 . . . . Public Works Policy
S-26-0236 . . . . Quota Policy
S-26-0207 . . . . Quota System Policy
S-26-0380 . . . . Racial Policy
S-26-0037 . . . . Radio Policy
S-26-0426 . . . . Railroad Policy
S-38-0346 . . . . Realist Foreign Policy
S-26-0075 . . . . Rearmament Policy
S-26-0353 . . . . Regional Planning Policy
S . . . . Regressive Taxation Policy
S-26-0195 . . . . Rehabilitation Education Policy
S-26-0397 . . . . Religious Policy
S-26-0388 . . . . Relocation Policy
S-26-0336 . . . . Reprisal Policy
S-26-0184 . . . . Restrictive Trade Policy
S-26-0138 . . . . Revenue Policy
S-26-0100 . . . . Revenue Sharing Policy
S-26-0321 . . . . Right To Work Policy
S-26-0400 . . . . Safety Policy
S-26-0228 . . . . Sanitation Policy
S-26-0384 . . . . School Desegregation Policy
S-26-0399 . . . . School Prayer Policy
S-26-0359 . . . . Science Policy
S-26-0289 . . . . Science Information Policy
S-26-0408 . . . . Scientific Manpower Policy
S-26-0358 . . . . Seabed Policy
S-26-0074 . . . . Second Strike Policy
S-26-0237 . . . . Segregation Policy
S-26-0360 . . . . Service Policy
S-26-0279 . . . . Service Industry Policy
S-26-0371 . . . . Social Policy
S-26-0084 . . . . Social Development Policy
S-26-0407 . . . . Social Resource Distribution Policy
S-26-0413 . . . . Social Security Policy
S-26-0409 . . . . Social Welfare Policy
S-26-0008 . . . . Soil Bank Policy
S-26-0230 . . . . Space Policy
S-26-0231 . . . . Space Exploration Policy
S-26-0232 . . . . Space Use Policy
S-26-0354 . . . . State Planning Policy
S-26-0076 . . . . Strategic Policy
S-26-0056 . . . . Strategic Arms Reduction Policy
S-26-0350 . . . . Subnational Planning Policy
S-26-0188 . . . . Tariff Policy
S-26-0139 . . . . Taxation Policy
S-26-0260 . . . . Technical Aid Policy
S-26-0416 . . . . Technology Policy
S-26-0417 . . . . Technology Constraint Policy
S-26-0418 . . . . Technology Development Policy
S-26-0419 . . . . Technology Transfer Policy
S-26-0021 . . . . Telephone Policy
S-26-0022 . . . . Telephone Allocation Policy
S-26-0038 . . . . Television Policy
S-26-0208 . . . . Tenure Policy
S-26-0343 . . . . Total War Policy
S-26-0180 . . . . Trade Policy
S-26-0322 . . . . Trade Union Policy
S-26-0403 . . . . Traffic Safety Policy

Code	Qualifier	Term
S-26-0420	Transportation	Policy
S-26-0210	Unemployment	Policy
S-26-0309	Unemployment Insurance	Policy
S-26-0261	Unilateral Aid	Policy
S-26-0415	Urban Renewal	Policy
S-26-0427	Urban Transit	Policy
S-26-0196	Vocation Training	Policy
S-26-0106	Wage	Policy
S-26-0109	Wage Freeze	Policy
S-26-0108	Wage Stabilization	Policy
S-26-0337	War	Policy
S-26-0078	War Declaration	Policy
S-26-0344	War Reparation	Policy
S-26-0293	Wartime Propaganda	Policy
S-26-0233	Waste Treatment	Policy
S-26-0229	Water Pollution	Policy
S-26-0223	Water Use	Policy
S-26-0414	Welfare	Policy
S-26-0023	Wiretapping	Policy
S-26-0132	Work Norm	Policy
S-26-0218	Zoning	Policy
S-19-0043	Foreign	Policy Advisory Board
S-09-0054		Policy Analysis
S-09-0056	Public	Policy Analysis
S-31-0684		Policy Articulation
S-31-0685		Policy Compliance
S-31-0686		Policy Conflict
S-31-0687		Policy Development
S-14-0025		Policy Elite
S-14-0026	Foreign	Policy Elite
S-31-0689		Policy Enforcement
S-31-0690		Policy Evaluation
S-24-0391		Policy Evaluation Research
S-26-0392		Policy For Disadvantaged
S-31-0698		Policy Format
S-31-0699		Policy Implementation
S-31-0700		Policy Incrementalism
S-03-0022		Policy Interest Group
S-31-0675	Administrative	Policy Making
S-31-0676	Collective	Policy Making
S-31-0677	Domestic	Policy Making
S-31-0678	Economic	Policy Making
S-31-0679	Education	Policy Making
S-31-0680	Foreign	Policy Making
S-31-0681	International	Policy Making
S-31-0682	Judicial	Policy Making
S-31-0702	Local	Policy Making
S-31-0683	National	Policy Making
S-31-0701	Subnational	Policy Making
S-31-0674		Policy Making Process
S-23-0038	Public	Policy Management
S	Presidential	Policy Message
S		Policy Output Index
S-24-0243		Policy Output Scale
S-32-0137	Foreign	Policy Planner
S-31-0665	City	Policy Planning
S-31-0662	International	Policy Planning
S-31-0666	Local	Policy Planning
S-31-0663	National	Policy Planning
S-31-0661	Public	Policy Planning
S-31-0667	Rural	Policy Planning
S-31-0668	State	Policy Planning
S-31-0664	Subnational	Policy Planning
S-31-0669	Urban	Policy Planning
S-31-0688		Policy Public Opinion Linkage
S-24-0390		Policy Research
S-01-0159		Policy Science Studies
S-32-0112		Policy Scientist
S	Executive	Policy Statement

S-11-0034 . . . . . Traditional	Political Culture
S-06-0079	Political Cynicism
S . . . . . Macro	Political Data
S-31-0058	Political Decay
S-32-0030	Political Decision Maker
S-06-0178	Political Development
S-24-0231	Political Development Index
S-26-0083	Political Development Policy
S-38-0025	Political Development Theory
S-06-0690	Political Dissensus
S-06-0081	Political Distrust
S-24-0358 . . . . . Local	Political Division
S-24-0355 . . . . . National	Political Division
S-24-0365 . . . . . State	Political Division
S-24-0357 . . . . . Subnational	Political Division
S-01-0161	Political Economy Studies
S-13-0029	Political Education
S-06-0099	Political Efficacy
S-14-0022	Political Elite
S-14-0023 . . . . . Local	Political Elite
S-14-0024 . . . . . Modernizing	Political Elite
S-14-0031 . . . . . Traditional	Political Elite
S-14-0032 . . . . . Transitional	Political Elite
S-06-0727	Political Equality
S-10-0070	Political Espionage
S-06-0083	Political Estrangement
S-31-0068	Political Evolution
S-31-0287	Political Exploitation
S-06-0101	Political Extremism
S-18-0068	Political Fiction
S-18-0075	Political Film
S-24-0016	Political Forecasting
S-31-0794	Political Fragmentation
S-10-0071	Political Fraud
S-38-0465	Political Freedom Theory
S-02-0052	Political Front
S-10-0074	Political Fund Misuse
S-32-0217	Political Gatekeeper
S-01-0093	Political Geography
S-10-0068	Political Graft
S-01-0115	Political History
S-06-0393	Political Identity
S-38-0285	Political Ideology
S-37-0071	Political Imperialism
S-24-0261	Political Indicator
S-31-0303	Political Indoctrination
S-06-0737	Political Inequality
S-31-0474	Political Influence
S-10-0075	Political Information Manipulation
S-32-0218	Political Informer
S-06-0686	Political Injustice
S-06-0691	Political Instability
S-24-0265	Political Instability Indicator
S-31-0819	Political Integration
S-31-0820 . . . . . International	Political Integration
S-31-0821 . . . . . International Regional	Political Integration
S-31-0826 . . . . . Local	Political Integration
S-31-0823 . . . . . National	Political Integration
S-31-0825 . . . . . Subnational	Political Integration
S-38-0159	Political Integration Theory
S-03-0021	Political Interest Group
S-26-0265	Political Interference Policy
S-26-0268	Political Intervention Policy
S-21-0066	Political Law
S-32-0052	Political Leader
S-22-0022	Political Leadership
S-38-0485	Political Legitimacy Theory
S-15-0026	Political Liberty
S-18-0065	Political Literature

Code		Term
S-29-0232	Gay	Politics
S-29-0206	Global	Politics
S-29-0202	Group	Politics
S-29-0203	Interest Group	Politics
S-29-0205	International	Politics
S-29-0211	Labor	Politics
S-29-0204	Language Group	Politics
S-29-0213	Linkage	Politics
S-29-0235	Local	Politics
S-29-0218	Machine	Politics
S-29-0237	Metropolitan	Politics
S-29-0219	Multiparty	Politics
S-29-0214	National	Politics
S	One Party	Politics
S-29-0220	One Political Party	Politics
S-29-0215	Parliamentary	Politics
S-29-0216	Partisan	Politics
S-29-0221	Patronage	Politics
S-29-0223	Power	Politics
S-29-0226	Progressive	Politics
S-29-0227	Protest	Politics
S-29-0228	Racial	Politics
S-29-0229	Religious	Politics
S-29-0230	Sexual	Politics
S-29-0233	Spoils	Politics
S-29-0241	State	Politics
S-29-0234	Subnational	Politics
S-29-0239	Suburban	Politics
S-29-0209	Superpower	Politics
S-29-0243	Symbolic	Politics
S-29-0244	Technocratic	Politics
S-29-0212	Trade Union	Politics
S-29-0245	Transitional	Politics
S-29-0210	Transnational	Politics
S-29-0242	Tribal	Politics
S	Two Party	Politics
S-29-0222	Two Political Party	Politics
S-29-0238	Urban	Politics
S-29-0240	Village	Politics
S-29-0207	World	Politics
S-29-0246	Youth	Politics
S-01-0167	Urban	Politics Studies
S		Polity
S		Poll
S-29-0176		Poll Tax
S-29-0197		Polling Place
S-31-0104	Air	Pollution
S-31-0103	Environmental	Pollution
S-31-0105	Noise	Pollution
S	Radioactive	Pollution
S-31-0106	Water	Pollution
S-26-0224		Pollution Policy
S-26-0225	Air	Pollution Policy
S-26-0226	Land	Pollution Policy
S-26-0227	Noise	Pollution Policy
S-26-0229	Water	Pollution Policy
S-20-0027		Polyandry
S		Polyarachic Democratic Theory
S		Polyarchal Democratic Theory
S-38-0096		Polyarchical Democratic Theory
S-16-0082		Polyarchy
S-37-0122		Polycentric International Political System
S-38-0330		Polycentrism
S-20-0026		Polygamy
S-20-0028		Polygyny
G-09-0021		Polynesia
G-09-0025	French	Polynesia
S-19-0211		Polytechnical Institute
S-13-0015		Polytechnical Institute Education

S-31-0345 ... Deregulation Process
S-31-0344 ... Destalinization Process
S-31-0054 ... Development Process
S-31-0362 ... Economic Process
S-31-0446 ... Education Process
S-31-0003 ... Education Accreditation Process
S-31-0619 ... Emigration Process
S-31-0285 ... Exploitation Process
S-31-0290 ... Expropriation Process
S-31-0420 ... Fiscal Process
S-31-0458 ... Government Process
S-31-0459 ... Government Dissolution Process
S-31-0465 ... Government Formation Process
S-31-0022 ... Group Process
S-31-0620 ... Immigration Process
S-31-0329 ... Implementation Process
S-31-0473 ... Influence Process
S-31-0330 ... International Decision Making Process
S-31-0475 ... Judicial Process
S ... Legislating Amendment Process
S-31-0573 ... Legislative Process
S ... Legislative Amending Process
S-31-0584 ... Legislative Amendment Process
S-31-0739 ... Legislative Nominating Process
S-31-0144 ... Liberation Process
S-31-0618 ... Migration Process
S-31-0626 ... Mobilization Process
S-31-0421 ... Monetary Process
S-31-0331 ... National Decision Making Process
S-31-0292 ... Nationalization Process
S-31-0738 ... Nominating Process
S ... Nomination Process
S-31-0036 ... Organization Process
S-31-0634 ... Planning Process
S-31-0674 ... Policy Making Process
S-31-0740 ... Presidential Nominating Process
S-31-0551 ... Procedural Due Process
S-31-0424 ... Production Process
S-31-0004 ... Professional Accreditation Process
S-31-0741 ... Recruitment Process
S-31-0310 ... Regulation Process
S-31-0312 ... Repression Process
S-15-0049 ... Right To Due Process
S-31-0728 ... Selection Process
S-31-0752 ... Social Process
S-31-0757 ... Social Role Process
S-31-0770 ... Social Stratification Process
S-31-0833 ... Specialization Process
S-31-0786 ... Structural Process
S-31-0332 ... Subnational Decision Making Process
S-31-0422 ... Subsidization Process
S-31-0552 ... Substantive Due Process
S-31-0165 ... Urbanization Process
S-24-0313 ... Process Model
S-24-0147 ... Computer Processing
S-24-0146 ... Data Processing
S-24-0144 ... Information Processing
S-24-0327 ... Data Processing Equipment
S-24-0324 ... Information Processing Equipment
S-18-0022 ... Proclamation
S-08-0028 ... Consumer Producer Conflict
S-03-0008 ... Producer Cooperative
S ... Producer Demonstration
S-31-0441 ... Gross National Product
S-31-0442 ... Per Capita Gross National Product
S-24-0035 ... Product Moment Correlation
S-31-0425 ... Agricultural Production
S-31-0433 ... Automated Production
S-31-0435 ... Commodity Production

Code	Qualifier	Term
S-31-0272		Religious Censorship
S-07-0044		Religious Community
S-06-0224		Religious Composition
S-08-0026		Religious Conflict
S-03-0033		Religious Cult
S-11-0041		Religious Culture
S-32-0341		Religious Dissenter
S-13-0044		Religious Education
S-14-0036		Religious Elite
S-06-0397		Religious Fanaticism
S-38-0573		Religious Fundamentalism
S-03-0032		Religious Group
S-01-0120		Religious History
S-06-0395		Religious Identity
S-21-0081		Religious Law
S-32-0340		Religious Leader
S-22-0011		Religious Leadership
S-32-0099		Religious Minister
S-27-0064		Religious Movement
S-10-0082		Religious Offense
S-03-0057		Religious Organization
S		Religious Party
S-31-0319		Religious Persecution
S-26-0397		Religious Policy
S-28-0051		Religious Political Party
S-29-0229		Religious Politics
S-32-0339		Religious Role
S-19-0224		Religious School
S-34-0035		Religious Socialization
S-35-0047		Religious Society
S-01-0181		Religious Studies
S-38-0552		Religious Thought
S-29-0135		Religious Voting
S-08-0106		Religious War
S-26-0388		Relocation Policy
S-29-0170	Largest	Remainder Voting Method
S-38-0482		Remedial Justice Theory
S-24-0330		Remote Terminal
S-06-0174		Renaissance
S-38-0516		Renaissance Political Thought
S-38-0525		Renaissance State Theory
S-31-0133	Urban	Renewal
S-26-0415	Urban	Renewal Policy
S-08-0011		Rent Strike
S	Personnel	Records
S-31-0091	Cabinet	Reorganization
S-31-0090	Executive	Reorganization
S-31-0099	Legislative	Reorganization
S-26-0332	Military	Reorganization Policy
S-26-0344	War	Reparation Policy
S-36-0026		Repatriate
S-24-0143		Replication
S-18-0031	Court	Report
S-31-0273		Report Censorship
S-31-0274	Government	Report Censorship
S-31-0275	Scientific	Report Censorship
S-31-0185	News	Reporting
S		Repository
S-31-0705		Representation
S-31-0716	At Large	Representation
S-31-0717	District	Representation
S-31-0718	Functional	Representation
S-31-0719	Geographic	Representation
S-31-0720	Indirect	Representation
S-31-0721	Interest Group	Representation
S-31-0722	Minority Group	Representation
S-31-0723	Multiple Member District	Representation
S-31-0724	One Man One Vote	Representation
S-31-0725	Proportional	Representation

HIERARCHICAL DISPLAYS

HIERARCHICAL DISPLAYS

S-01 ACADEMIC AREAS

S-01-0001	1975	00011	Academic Areas
S-01-0002	1975	00023	.Administrative Science
S-01-0003	1975	00016	.Agricultural Science
S-01-0004	1979	00000	..Agronomy
S-01-0005	1979	00000	..Animal Husbandry
S-01-0006	1979	00000	..Horticulture
S-01-0007	1975	00039	.Anthropology Discipline
S-01-0008	1979	00000	..Applied Anthropology
S-01-0009	1975	00040	..Cultural Anthropology
S-01-0010	1975	00026	...Ethnography
S-01-0011	1975	00017	...Ethnolinguistics
S-01-0012	1975	00026	...Ethnology
S-01-0013	1975	00005	....Mythology
S-01-0014	1975	00019	.....Ritual
S-01-0015	1975	00021	...Structural Linguistics
S-01-0016	1975	00006	....Morphology
S-01-0017	1979	00000	..Philosophical Anthropology
S-01-0018	1975	00005	..Physical Anthropology
S-01-0019	1975	00005	..Political Anthropology
S-01-0020	1975	00000	..Psychological Anthropology
S-01-0021	1975	00031	..Social Anthropology
S-01-0022	1975	00015	.Archaeology
S-01-0023	1979	00000	.Architectural Studies
S-01-0024	1975	00003	.Area Studies
S-01-0025	1975	00094	..African Area Studies
S-01-0026	1979	00000	...Central African Area Studies
S-01-0027	1979	00000	...East African Area Studies
S-01-0028	1975	00055	...North African Area Studies
S-01-0029	1979	00000	...South African Area Studies
S-01-0030	1979	00000	...West African Area Studies
S-01-0031	1975	00037	..American Area Studies
S-01-0032	1975	00090	...Caribbean Area Studies
S-01-0033	1975	00088	...Central American Area Studies
S-01-0034	1975	00395	...Latin American Area Studies
S-01-0035	1975	00172	...North American Area Studies
S-01-0036	1975	00113	..Asian Area Studies
S-01-0037	1975	00443	...East Asian Area Studies
S-01-0038	1975	00189	...South Asian Area Studies
S-01-0039	1975	00211	...Southeast Asian Area Studies
S-01-0040	1975	00010	..British Commonwealth Area Studies
S-01-0041	1975	00302	..Middle East Area Studies
S-01-0042	1975	00727	..Soviet And East European Area Studies
S-01-0043	1979	00000	...East European Area Studies
S-01-0044	1979	00000	...Russian Studies
S-01-0045	1979	00000	...Soviet Studies
S-01-0046	1975	00799	..West European Area Studies
S-01-0047	1975	00036	...Common Market Area Studies
S-01-0048	1975	00039	...Scandinavian Area Studies
S-01-0049	1975	00007	.Behavioral Science
S-01-0050	1979	00000	.Biological Sciences
S-01-0051	1979	00000	..Eugenics
S-01-0052	1979	00000	.Business Studies
S-01-0053	1979	00000	..Management Training Program
S-01-0054	1975	00074	.Communist Studies
S-01-0055	1975	00006	.Computer Science
S-01-0056	1975	00022	.Demographic Studies
S-01-0057	1975	00001	.Earth Sciences
S-01-0058	1975	00002	.Ecology Discipline
S-01-0059	1975	00023	.Economics Discipline
S-01-0060	1979	00000	..Business Economics
S-01-0061	1975	00014	..Consumer Economics
S-01-0062	1975	00003	..Econometrics
S-01-0063	1979	00000	..Evolutionary Economics
S-01-0064	1979	00000	..Industrial Economics
S-01-0065	1979	00000	..Institutional Economics
S-01-0066	1975	00033	..International Economics
S-01-0067	1979	00000	..Labor Economics
S-01-0068	1975	00010	..Macroeconomics
S-01-0069	1975	00011	...Keynesian Economics
S-01-0070	1975	00004	...Marxist Economics
S-01-0071	1975	00008	..Microeconomics
S-01-0072	1979	00000	..Regional Economics
S-01-0073	1979	00000	..Social Economics
S-01-0074	1979	00000	..Transportation Economics
S-01-0075	1979	00000	..Urban Economics
S-01-0076	1975	00018	..Welfare Economics
S-01-0077	1975	00013	.Education Discipline
S-01-0078	1975	00075	..Education Philosophy
S-01-0079	1979	00000	..Education Psychology
S-01-0080	1975	00003	.Engineering Discipline
S-01-0081	1979	00000	.Environmental Studies
S-01-0082	1975	00076	.Ethnic Studies
S-01-0083	1975	00142	..American Indian Studies
S-01-0084	1975	00247	..Black Studies
S-01-0085	1975	00053	..Chicano Studies
S-01-0086	1975	00005	..Puerto Rican Studies
S-01-0087	1975	00004	.Geography Discipline
S-01-0088	1975	00015	..Economic Geography
S-01-0089	1975	00012	..Human Geography
S-01-0090	1975	00003	..Physical Geography
S-01-0091	1979	00000	...Climatology
S-01-0092	1979	00000	...Topography
S-01-0093	1975	00014	..Political Geography
S-01-0094	1975	00003	...Electoral Geography
S-01-0095	1975	00028	..Urban Geography
S-01-0096	1979	00000	.Gerontology
S-01-0097	1975	00028	.History Discipline
S-01-0098	1979	00000	..Ancient History
S-01-0099	1979	00000	..Art History
S-01-0100	1975	00024	..Black History
S-01-0101	1975	00209	..Cultural History
S-01-0102	1979	00000	..Diplomatic History
S-01-0103	1975	00141	..Economic History
S-01-0104	1979	00000	...Agricultural History
S-01-0105	1975	00061	...Labor History
S-01-0106	1975	00129	..Historiography
S-01-0107	1975	00019	..History Of Philosophy
S-01-0108	1975	00019	..History Of Science
S-01-0109	1979	00000	...History Of Technology
S-01-0110	1979	00000	..Institutional History
S-01-0111	1979	00000	..Intellectual History
S-01-0112	1979	00000	..Legal History
S-01-0113	1975	00100	..Military History
S-01-0114	1975	00011	..Oral History
S-01-0115	1975	00511	..Political History
S-01-0116	1975	00042	...Electoral History
S-01-0117	1975	00021	...Legislative History
S-01-0118	1979	00000	..Psychohistory
S-01-0119	1979	00000	..Quantitative History
S-01-0120	1979	00000	..Religious History
S-01-0121	1975	00359	..Social History
S-01-0122	1979	00000	..Urban History
S-01-0123	1975	00019	.Humanities Discipline
S-01-0124	1979	00000	..Fine Arts

S-01-0125	1979	00000	...Graphic Arts
S-01-0126	1979	00000	...Plastic Arts
S-01-0127	1979	00000	...Visual Arts
S-01-0128	1975	00003	.Information Science
S-01-0129	1979	00000	.Interdisciplinary Studies
S-01-0130	1979	00000	.Language Studies
S-01-0131	1975	00066	.Legal Studies
S-01-0132	1979	00000	..Comparative Law
S-01-0133	1979	00000	.Library Science Studies
S-01-0134	1975	00011	.Linguistics
S-01-0135	1979	00000	..Applied Linguistics
S-01-0136	1979	00000	..Etymology
S-01-0137	1975	00013	..Psycholinguistics
S-01-0138	1975	00038	..Sociolinguistics
S-01-0139	1979	00000	.Literature Studies
S-01-0140	1979	00000	..Comparative Literature Studies
S-01-0141	1975	00001	.Mathematics Discipline
S-01-0142	1979	00000	.Medical Science
S-01-0143	1979	00000	..Psychiatry
S-01-0144	1979	00000	...Social Psychiatry
S-01-0145	1975	00019	.Military Science
S-01-0146	1975	00010	.Natural Science Discipline
S-01-0147	1975	00002	..Ideographic Science
S-01-0148	1975	00007	..Physical Science
S-01-0149	1975	00044	.Peace Studies
S-01-0150	1975	00010	.Philosophy Discipline
S-01-0151	1979	00000	..Logic
S-01-0152	1979	00000	..Philosophy Of Action
S-01-0153	1979	00000	..Philosophy Of Mind
S-01-0154	1975	00070	..Philosophy Of Science Studies
S-01-0155	1975	00021	..Social Philosophy
S-01-0156	1975	00028	.Political Science Discipline
S-01-0157	1975	00069	..Comparative Political Studies
S-01-0158	1975	00207	..International Relations Studies
S-01-0159	1975	00128	..Policy Science Studies
S-01-0160	1975	00040	..Political Behavior Studies
S-01-0161	1975	00042	..Political Economy Studies
S-01-0162	1975	00084	..Political Philosophy Studies
S-01-0163	1975	00052	..Political Science Methodology Studies
S-01-0164	1975	00022	..Political Theory Studies
S-01-0165	1975	00212	..Public Administration Studies
S-01-0166	1979	00000	..Public Policy Studies
S-01-0167	1975	00047	..Urban Politics Studies
S-01-0168	1975	00011	.Psychology Discipline
S-01-0169	1975	00036	..Behavioral Psychology
S-01-0170	1979	00000	..Child Psychology
S-01-0171	1979	00000	..Clinical Psychology
S-01-0172	1979	00000	..Developmental Psychology
S-01-0173	1975	00008	..Freudian Psychology
S-01-0174	1979	00000	..Gestalt Psychology
S-01-0175	1975	00056	..Learning Psychology
S-01-0176	1979	00000	..Parapsychology
S-01-0177	1975	00056	..Psychopathology
S-01-0178	1975	00131	..Social Psychology
S-01-0179	1975	00005	...Industrial Psychology
S-01-0180	1975	00013	...Political Psychology
S-01-0181	1979	00000	.Religious Studies
S-01-0182	1975	00042	.Sociology Discipline
S-01-0183	1979	00000	..Applied Sociology
S-01-0184	1975	00008	..Comparative Sociology
S-01-0185	1975	00018	..Criminology
S-01-0186	1975	00021	..Historical Sociology
S-01-0187	1975	00014	..Industrial Sociology
S-01-0188	1975	00010	..Macrosociology
S-01-0189	1975	00014	..Marxist Sociology
S-01-0190	1979	00000	..Parsonsian Sociology
S-01-0191	1975	00009	..Political Sociology
S-01-0192	1975	00012	..Rural Sociology
S-01-0193	1975	00011	..Social Pathology
S-01-0194	1979	00000	..Sociobiology
S-01-0195	1979	00000	..Sociology Of Art
S-01-0196	1975	00149	..Sociology Of Knowledge
S-01-0197	1975	00022	..Sociology Of Law
S-01-0198	1979	00000	..Sociology Of Religion
S-01-0199	1979	00000	..Sociology Of Science
S-01-0200	1979	00000	..Sociology Of The Professions
S-01-0201	1979	00000	..Sociology Of Work
S-01-0202	1975	00050	..Urban Sociology
S-01-0203	1979	00000	.Statistics Discipline
S-01-0204	1975	00109	.Strategic Studies
S-01-0205	1979	00000	.Urban Studies
S-01-0206	1975	00188	.Womens Studies

S-02 AGREEMENT TYPE

S-02-0001	1975	00003	Agreement Type
S-02-0002	1975	00023	.Alliance
S-02-0003	1975	00012	..Economic Alliance
S-02-0004	1975	00004	..Electoral Alliance
S-02-0005	1975	00031	..Military Alliance
S-02-0006	1975	00018	...Defense Alliance
S-02-0007	1975	00009	....Protective Alliance
S-02-0008	1975	00032	...Regional Military Alliance
S-02-0009	1975	00006	..Multilateral Alliance
S-02-0010	1975	00004	..Wartime Alliance
S-02-0011	1975	00003	..World Alliance
S-02-0012	1975	00003	...League Of Nations
S-02-0013	1975	00106	...United Nations
S-02-0014	1975	00004	.Coalition Type
S-02-0015	1975	00001	..Class Based Coalition
S-02-0016	1975	00000	..Economic Coalition
S-02-0017	1975	00000	..Multiethnic Coalition
S-02-0018	1975	00000	..Opinion Coalition
S-02-0019	1979	00000	..Political Coalition
S-02-0020	1975	00001	...Democratic Coalition
S-02-0021	1975	00011	...Electoral Coalition
S-02-0022	1975	00005	...Governing Coalition
S-02-0023	1975	00005	...Interest Group Coalition
S-02-0024	1975	00010	...Legislative Coalition
S-02-0025	1975	00004	....Parliamentary Coalition
S-02-0026	1975	00018	...Political Party Coalition
S-02-0027	1975	00000	....All Party Coalition
S-02-0028	1975	00001	.....Grand Coalition
S-02-0029	1979	00000	....Intraparty Coalition
S-02-0030	1975	00005	....Multiparty Coalition
S-02-0031	1975	00000	....Negative Coalition
S-02-0032	1975	00007	...Voting Coalition
S-02-0033	1975	00003	..Winning Coalition
S-02-0034	1975	00004	...Minimum Winning Coalition
S-02-0035	1975	00000	.Compact
S-02-0036	1975	00000	..Interstate Compact
S-02-0037	1979	00000	.Contract Type
S-02-0038	1979	00000	..Business Contract
S-02-0039	1979	00000	..Labor Management Contract
S-02-0040	1979	00000	..Marriage Contract
S-02-0041	1975	00001	.Extranational Bloc
S-02-0042	1975	00030	..Atlantic Community
S-02-0043	1975	00022	..Communist Bloc
S-02-0044	1975	00010	..Security Community
S-02-0045	1975	00066	..Third World Bloc
S-02-0046	1975	00001	...Afro Asian Bloc
S-02-0047	1975	00027	...Arab Bloc
S-02-0048	1975	00000	...Latin American Bloc
S-02-0049	1975	00002	...Neutral Bloc
S-02-0050	1975	00010	..Western Bloc
S-02-0051	1975	00007	.International Bloc

S-02-0052	1975	00001	.Political Front
S-02-0053	1975	00006	..Liberation Front
S-02-0054	1975	00001	..National Front
S-02-0055	1975	00002	..Popular Front
S-02-0056	1975	00006	..United Front
S-02-0057	1975	00003	.State Agreement Declaration
S-02-0058	1975	00000	..Mutual Support Declaration
S-02-0059	1975	00003	..Unilateral Declaration
S-02-0060	1975	00001	.State Agreement Form
S-02-0061	1975	00028	..Bilateral State Agreement
S-02-0062	1975	00011	..Bilateral Treaty
S-02-0063	1975	00003	..Executive Agreement
S-02-0064	1975	00016	..Multilateral State Agreement
S-02-0065	1975	00004	..Multilateral Treaty
S-02-0066	1975	00002	.State Agreement Type
S-02-0067	1975	00026	..Arms Control Agreement
S-02-0068	1975	00013	...Arms Control Treaty
S-02-0069	1979	00000	..Arms Sales
S-02-0070	1975	00006	..Commercial Agreement
S-02-0071	1975	00003	...Commercial Treaty
S-02-0072	1975	00003	..Cultural Agreement
S-02-0073	1975	00042	...Cultural Exchange Agreement
S-02-0074	1975	00001	....Cultural Exchange Treaty
S-02-0075	1975	00007	..Disarmament Agreement
S-02-0076	1975	00001	...Disarmament Treaty
S-02-0077	1975	00008	..Economic Agreement
S-02-0078	1975	00002	...Economic Treaty
S-02-0079	1975	00001	..Education Agreement
S-02-0080	1975	00039	...Education Exchange Agreement
S-02-0081	1975	00001	....Education Exchange Treaty
S-02-0082	1975	00000	..Friendship Agreement
S-02-0083	1975	00001	...Friendship Treaty
S-02-0084	1975	00006	..Military Agreement
S-02-0085	1975	00004	...Military Treaty
S-02-0086	1975	00001	..Monetary Agreement
S-02-0087	1975	00001	..Neutrality Agreement
S-02-0088	1975	00000	...Neutrality Treaty
S-02-0089	1975	00001	..Nonaggression Agreement
S-02-0090	1975	00001	...Nonaggression Treaty
S-02-0091	1975	00013	..Nuclear Nonproliferation Agreement
S-02-0092	1975	00019	...Nuclear Nonproliferation Treaty
S-02-0093	1975	00009	..Payment Agreement
S-02-0094	1975	00011	..Peace Proposal
S-02-0095	1975	00005	..Peace Treaty
S-02-0096	1975	00005	..Test Ban Agreement
S-02-0097	1975	00007	...Test Ban Treaty
S-02-0098	1975	00006	..Trade Agreement

S-03 ASSOCIATIONS

S-03-0001	1975	00001	Associations
S-03-0002	1975	00003	.Cooperatives
S-03-0003	1975	00007	..Agricultural Cooperative
S-03-0004	1975	00003	..Credit Cooperative
S-03-0005	1975	00002	..Housing Cooperative
S-03-0006	1975	00001	..Marketing Cooperative
S-03-0007	1975	00002	..Peasant Cooperative
S-03-0008	1975	00005	..Producer Cooperative
S-03-0009	1975	00001	..Village Cooperative
S-03-0010	1975	00002	..Worker Cooperative
S-03-0011	1975	00004	.Groups
S-03-0012	1979	00000	..Cultural Group
S-03-0013	1975	00020	..Interest Group
S-03-0014	1975	00005	...Association Interest Group
S-03-0015	1979	00000	...Consumer Interest Group
S-03-0016	1975	00003	...Cultural Interest Group
S-03-0017	1975	00024	...Economic Interest Group
S-03-0018	1979	00000	....Industrial Association
S-03-0019	1975	00001	...Latent Interest Group
S-03-0020	1975	00005	...Occupational Interest Group
S-03-0021	1975	00013	...Political Interest Group
S-03-0022	1975	00046	....Policy Interest Group
S-03-0023	1975	00000	....Political Club
S-03-0024	1975	00012	..Social Group
S-03-0025	1975	00156	...Ethnic Group
S-03-0026	1975	00003	...Face To Face Group
S-03-0027	1975	00005	....Primary Group
S-03-0028	1975	00016	...Kinship Group
S-03-0029	1975	00007	...Nationality Group
S-03-0030	1975	00049	...Racial Group
S-03-0031	1975	00011	...Reference Group
S-03-0032	1975	00041	...Religious Group
S-03-0033	1979	00000	....Religious Cult
S-03-0034	1975	00000	...Secondary Group
S-03-0035	1975	00008	....Peer Group
S-03-0036	1975	00009	.Organizations
S-03-0037	1975	00011	..Civic Organization
S-03-0038	1975	00007	..Cultural Organization
S-03-0039	1975	00008	..Economic Organization
S-03-0040	1975	00029	...International Economic Organization
S-03-0041	1975	00001	....Customs Union
S-03-0042	1975	00003	....Monetary Union
S-03-0043	1975	00000	..Employer Organization
S-03-0044	1975	00016	..Ethnic Organization
S-03-0045	1975	00002	..Fraternal Organization
S-03-0046	1979	00000	..International Organization
S-03-0047	1979	00000	...International Conference
S-03-0048	1979	00000	....Summit Meeting
S-03-0049	1975	00006	..Peasant Organization
S-03-0050	1979	00000	..Philanthropic Organization
S-03-0051	1979	00000	...Charitable Organization
S-03-0052	1975	00017	..Professional Organization
S-03-0053	1975	00002	...Bar Association
S-03-0054	1979	00000	...Education Association
S-03-0055	1975	00005	...Medical Association
S-03-0056	1975	00003	...Teacher Organization
S-03-0057	1975	00017	..Religious Organization
S-03-0058	1975	00001	..Trade Organization
S-03-0059	1975	00009	...International Trade Organization
S-03-0060	1975	00011	....Trade Bloc
S-03-0061	1975	00000	..Veterans Organization
S-03-0062	1975	00003	..Worker Organization
S-03-0063	1975	00005	...International Labor Organization
S-03-0064	1975	00004	...Public Employee Organization
S-03-0065	1975	00015	....Union
S-03-0066	1975	00003	.....Civil Service Union
S-03-0067	1975	00000	.....Craft Union
S-03-0068	1975	00000	.....Farmer Union
S-03-0069	1975	00004	.....Industrial Union
S-03-0070	1975	00036	.....Labor Union
S-03-0071	1975	00011	.....Trade Union
S-03-0072	1979	00000	.Youth Organization
S-03-0073	1975	00030	.Voluntary Association

S-04 AUTHORITY

S-04-0001	1975	00012	Authority
S-04-0002	1975	00002	.Authority Mode
S-04-0003	1975	00008	..Charismatic Authority
S-04-0004	1975	00003	..Derived Authority
S-04-0005	1979	00000	..Just Authority
S-04-0006	1975	00003	..Legal Rational Authority
S-04-0007	1975	00026	..Moral Authority
S-04-0008	1979	00000	..Scientific Authority
S-04-0009	1975	00009	..Traditional Authority
S-04-0010	1975	00014	.Authority Structure

S-04-0011	1975	00004	..Anarchy
S-04-0012	1975	00027	..Centralized Authority
S-04-0013	1975	00039	..Decentralized Authority
S-04-0014	1979	00000	..Delegated Authority
S-04-0015	1975	00000	..Diffuse Authority
S-04-0016	1975	00003	..Formal Authority
S-04-0017	1975	00006	..Hierarchical Authority
S-04-0018	1975	00004	..Independent Authority
S-04-0019	1975	00003	..Informal Authority
S-04-0020	1975	00001	..Integrated Authority
S-04-0021	1975	00008	.Authority Type
S-04-0022	1975	00023	..Parental Authority
S-04-0023	1975	00005	..Religious Authority
S-04-0024	1979	00000	...Civil Religion
S-04-0025	1975	00003	...Theocratic Authority
S-04-0026	1975	00001	..Secular Authority
S-04-0027	1975	00013	...Political Authority
S-04-0028	1975	00015	....Constitutional Authority
S-04-0029	1975	00009	....Government Authority
S-04-0030	1975	00001	.....Civil Authority
S-04-0031	1975	00002	......Education Compulsion Authority
S-04-0032	1975	00001	......Eminent Domain
S-04-0033	1975	00005	......Police Power
S-04-0034	1975	00006	......Tax Power
S-04-0035	1975	00000	......Testimony Compulsion Authority
S-04-0036	1975	00049	.....Civil Military Authority
S-04-0037	1975	00000	......Conscription Power
S-04-0038	1975	00007	......War Power

S-05 BEHAVIOR

S-05-0001	1975	00006	Behavior
S-05-0002	1975	00024	.Administrative Behavior
S-05-0003	1975	00043	..Bureaucratic Behavior
S-05-0004	1975	00013	..Executive Behavior
S-05-0005	1975	00062	..Organization Behavior
S-05-0006	1979	00000	.Animal Behavior
S-05-0007	1975	00042	.Economic Behavior
S-05-0008	1979	00000	..Consumer Behavior
S-05-0009	1975	00018	.Personal Behavior
S-05-0010	1979	00000	..Coping Behavior
S-05-0011	1979	00000	..Pathological Behavior
S-05-0012	1979	00000	..Sexual Behavior
S-05-0013	1975	00049	.Political Behavior
S-05-0014	1975	00015	..Elite Behavior
S-05-0015	1975	00030	..Judicial Behavior
S-05-0016	1975	00007	..Legal Behavior
S-05-0017	1975	00051	..Legislative Behavior
S-05-0018	1975	00041	...Legislative Voting Behavior
S-05-0019	1979	00000	..Obedience
S-05-0020	1975	00102	..Voting Behavior
S-05-0021	1979	00000	.Problem Solving Behavior
S-05-0022	1975	00066	.Social Behavior
S-05-0023	1975	00026	..Accommodative Social Behavior
S-05-0024	1975	00040	...Adaptive Behavior
S-05-0025	1975	00037	...Conformity Behavior
S-05-0026	1979	00000	...Cooperative Behavior
S-05-0027	1979	00000	..Avoidance Behavior
S-05-0028	1975	00039	..Deviant Behavior
S-05-0029	1975	00030	..Group Behavior
S-05-0030	1975	00026	...Small Group Behavior
S-05-0031	1979	00000	..Habitual Behavior
S-05-0032	1975	00022	..Mass Behavior
S-05-0033	1975	00008	...Crowd Behavior
S-05-0034	1979	00000	..Symbolic Action

S-06 CHARACTERISTICS

S-06-0001	1975	00000	Characteristics
S-06-0002	1975	00003	.Association Characteristics
S-06-0003	1975	00034	..Community Characteristics
S-06-0004	1975	00010	...Community Composition
S-06-0005	1975	00003	....Community Homogeneity
S-06-0006	1975	00013	...Community Structural Characteristics
S-06-0007	1975	00005	....Community Cleavage Characteristics
S-06-0008	1975	00027	....Community Size Characteristics
S-06-0009	1975	00015	..Group Characteristics
S-06-0010	1975	00039	...Group Attitude
S-06-0011	1975	00005	...Group Capability Characteristics
S-06-0012	1975	00003	....Group Effectiveness
S-06-0013	1975	00001	....Group Efficiency
S-06-0014	1975	00007	...Group Composition
S-06-0015	1975	00028	....Elite Composition
S-06-0016	1975	00007	.....Elite Heterogeneity
S-06-0017	1975	00008	.....Elite Homogeneity
S-06-0018	1975	00004	....Heterogeneous Group Membership
S-06-0019	1975	00004	....Homogeneous Group Membership
S-06-0020	1975	00006	....Interlocking Group Membership
S-06-0021	1979	00000	....Minority Group
S-06-0022	1975	00001	....Multiple Group Membership
S-06-0023	1975	00002	....Overlapping Membership
S-06-0024	1975	00015	...Group Dynamics
S-06-0025	1975	00015	...Group Normative Characteristics
S-06-0026	1975	00001	....Group Constraint
S-06-0027	1975	00001	....Group Discipline
S-06-0028	1975	00003	....Group Goal
S-06-0029	1975	00002	....Group Pluralism
S-06-0030	1979	00000	....Group Psychology
S-06-0031	1975	00003	....Group Rationality
S-06-0032	1975	00006	...Group Solidarity
S-06-0033	1975	00001	....Brotherhood
S-06-0034	1975	00001	....Caste Solidarity
S-06-0035	1975	00004	....Class Solidarity
S-06-0036	1975	00001	.....Proletarian Unity
S-06-0037	1975	00008	....Communal Solidarity
S-06-0038	1975	00001	....Gemeinschaft
S-06-0039	1975	00000	....Gesellschaft
S-06-0040	1979	00000	....Group Cohesion
S-06-0041	1975	00007	.....Cultural Group Cohesion
S-06-0042	1975	00009	.....Minority Group Cohesion
S-06-0043	1975	00038	......Ethnic Group Cohesion
S-06-0044	1975	00006	....Social Solidarity
S-06-0045	1975	00010	.....Social Unity
S-06-0046	1975	00010	...Group Status
S-06-0047	1975	00019	...Group Structural Characteristics
S-06-0048	1975	00009	....Group Cleavage Characteristics
S-06-0049	1975	00000	....Group Flexibility
S-06-0050	1975	00004	....Group Hierarchy
S-06-0051	1975	00000	....Group Inertia
S-06-0052	1975	00015	....Group Size
S-06-0053	1975	00004	....Group Stability
S-06-0054	1975	00051	..Organization Characteristics
S-06-0055	1975	00015	...Organization Capability Characteristics
S-06-0056	1975	00049	....Organization Effectiveness
S-06-0057	1975	00013	....Organization Efficiency
S-06-0058	1975	00007	...Organization Composition
S-06-0059	1975	00016	....Organization Membership
S-06-0060	1979	00000	...Organization Environment
S-06-0061	1975	00019	...Organization Normative Characteristics
S-06-0062	1975	00011	....Organization Constraint
S-06-0063	1975	00018	....Organization Goal
S-06-0064	1975	00007	....Organization Pluralism
S-06-0065	1975	00009	....Organization Rationality
S-06-0066	1975	00003	...Organization Status

Code	Year	Count	Term
S-06-0067	1975	00078	...Organization Structural Characteristics
S-06-0068	1975	00009	....Organization Cleavage Characteristics
S-06-0069	1979	00000	.....Organization Conflict
S-06-0070	1975	00007	....Organization Flexibility
S-06-0071	1975	00023	....Organization Hierarchy
S-06-0072	1975	00002	....Organization Inertia
S-06-0073	1975	00001	....Organization Level
S-06-0074	1975	00017	....Organization Size
S-06-0075	1975	00310	.Attitude Characteristics
S-06-0076	1975	00035	..Alienation
S-06-0077	1975	00008	...Cultural Alienation
S-06-0078	1975	00003	...Cynicism
S-06-0079	1975	00011	....Political Cynicism
S-06-0080	1975	00005	...Distrust
S-06-0081	1975	00024	....Political Distrust
S-06-0082	1975	00022	...Estrangement
S-06-0083	1975	00015	....Political Estrangement
S-06-0084	1975	00008	...Normlessness
S-06-0085	1975	00002	....Political Normlessness
S-06-0086	1975	00024	...Political Alienation
S-06-0087	1975	00012	...Powerlessness
S-06-0088	1975	00013	....Political Powerlessness
S-06-0089	1975	00016	..Anomie
S-06-0090	1975	00010	..Apathy
S-06-0091	1975	00016	...Political Apathy
S-06-0092	1975	00043	..Attitude Cluster
S-06-0093	1975	00046	...Perception
S-06-0094	1975	00094	....Decision Maker Perception
S-06-0095	1975	00005	..Authoritarian Attitude
S-06-0096	1979	00000	..Deference
S-06-0097	1975	00009	..Dogmatism
S-06-0098	1975	00024	..Efficacy
S-06-0099	1975	00046	...Political Efficacy
S-06-0100	1975	00001	..Extremism
S-06-0101	1975	00003	...Political Extremism
S-06-0102	1975	00013	..Hostility
S-06-0103	1975	00015	...Aggressiveness
S-06-0104	1975	00004	....Belligerence
S-06-0105	1975	00003	..Inner Directedness
S-06-0106	1975	00003	..Intolerance
S-06-0107	1975	00004	...Bigotry
S-06-0108	1975	00003	...Racial Intolerance
S-06-0109	1975	00011	..Militancy
S-06-0110	1975	00001	...Ethnic Militancy
S-06-0111	1975	00001	...Racial Militancy
S-06-0112	1975	00006	....Black Militancy
S-06-0113	1975	00000	....White Militancy
S-06-0114	1975	00004	...Student Militancy
S-06-0115	1975	00007	..Military Mind
S-06-0116	1975	00002	..Other Directedness
S-06-0117	1979	00000	..Political Attitude
S-06-0118	1975	00029	..Political Awareness
S-06-0119	1975	00017	..Prejudice
S-06-0120	1975	00028	...Bias
S-06-0121	1975	00046	..Racial Attitude
S-06-0122	1975	00026	...Racial Prejudice
S-06-0123	1975	00002	...Racial Pride
S-06-0124	1975	00002	...Racial Supremacy
S-06-0125	1975	00040	..Satisfaction
S-06-0126	1975	00008	...Deprivation
S-06-0127	1975	00012	....Relative Deprivation
S-06-0128	1979	00000	...Life Satisfaction
S-06-0129	1975	00015	...Political Satisfaction
S-06-0130	1975	00032	..Self Interest
S-06-0131	1975	00062	...Achievement Motivation
S-06-0132	1975	00020	...Ambition
S-06-0133	1975	00004	...Enlightened Self Interest
S-06-0134	1975	00001	..Submissiveness
S-06-0135	1975	00013	..Tolerance
S-06-0136	1975	00007	...Political Tolerance
S-06-0137	1975	00008	...Racial Tolerance
S-06-0138	1979	00000	..Trust
S-06-0139	1979	00000	...Political Trust
S-06-0140	1975	00050	.Change Characteristics
S-06-0141	1975	00046	..Development Characteristics
S-06-0142	1975	00021	...Development Potential
S-06-0143	1975	00063	...Economic Development Characteristics
S-06-0144	1975	00036	....Economic Development Level
S-06-0145	1975	00080	.....Industrialization Level
S-06-0146	1975	00002	.....Investment Ratio
S-06-0147	1975	00007	.....National Economic Development Level
S-06-0148	1975	00018	.....Regional Economic Development Level
S-06-0149	1975	00006	......International Economic Development Level
S-06-0150	1975	00005	......Subnational Economic Development Level
S-06-0151	1975	00006	.......Local Economic Development Level
S-06-0152	1975	00022	....Economic Development Rate
S-06-0153	1975	00060	.....Economic Growth Rate
S-06-0154	1975	00014	......Agricultural Growth Rate
S-06-0155	1975	00009	......Capital Growth Rate
S-06-0156	1975	00036	......Productivity Rate
S-06-0157	1975	00056	.......Cost Effectiveness
S-06-0158	1975	00044	.......Worker Productivity
S-06-0159	1975	00026	....Economic Development Stage
S-06-0160	1975	00007	.....Agricultural Economic Stage
S-06-0161	1975	00003	.....Feudal Economic Stage
S-06-0162	1975	00005	.....Industrial Economic Stage
S-06-0163	1975	00003	.....Post Industrial Economic Stage
S-06-0164	1975	00001	.....Pretakeoff Period
S-06-0165	1975	00000	.....Takeoff Stage
S-06-0166	1979	00000	....Entrepreneurship
S-06-0167	1979	00000	...Historical Periods
S-06-0168	1979	00000	....Ancient Times
S-06-0169	1979	00000	.....Antiquity
S-06-0170	1979	00000	....Classical Period
S-06-0171	1979	00000	....Dark Ages
S-06-0172	1979	00000	....Medieval Ages
S-06-0173	1979	00000	....Prehistorical Times
S-06-0174	1979	00000	....Renaissance
S-06-0175	1979	00000	....Modern Ages
S-06-0176	1979	00000	...Human Resources Development
S-06-0177	1979	00000	...Legal Development
S-06-0178	1979	00000	...Political Development
S-06-0179	1975	00057	.Demographic Characteristics
S-06-0180	1975	00061	..Age
S-06-0181	1975	00019	...Adolescence
S-06-0182	1975	00082	...Childhood
S-06-0183	1975	00010	...Infancy
S-06-0184	1975	00004	...Middle Age
S-06-0185	1975	00021	...Old Age
S-06-0186	1975	00038	...Youth
S-06-0187	1975	00006	..Demographic Indicator
S-06-0188	1975	00024	..Demographic Profile
S-06-0189	1975	00020	...Birth Rate
S-06-0190	1975	00051	...Fertility Rate
S-06-0191	1975	00019	...Household Size
S-06-0192	1975	00006	...Illiteracy Rate
S-06-0193	1975	00009	...Life Expectancy
S-06-0194	1975	00012	...Literacy Rate
S-06-0195	1975	00023	...Mortality Rate
S-06-0196	1975	00010	....Infant Mortality Rate
S-06-0197	1975	00014	..Demographic Projection
S-06-0198	1975	00002	..Origin
S-06-0199	1975	00002	...Ancestry
S-06-0200	1975	00000	....Black Ancestry

S-06-0201	1975	00012	...Class Origin
S-06-0202	1975	00026	....Social Class Origin
S-06-0203	1975	00013	...Ethnic Origin
S-06-0204	1975	00016	....Ethnic Background
S-06-0205	1975	00038	....Racial Background
S-06-0206	1975	00002	...Geographic Origin
S-06-0207	1975	00002	...National Origin
S-06-0208	1975	00119	...Socioeconomic Background
S-06-0209	1975	00024	....Economic Background
S-06-0210	1975	00088	....Education Background
S-06-0211	1975	00046	....Social Background
S-06-0212	1975	00037	..Population Attribute
S-06-0213	1975	00012	...Migrant Population
S-06-0214	1979	00000	...Population Growth
S-06-0215	1979	00000	....Zero Population Growth
S-06-0216	1975	00023	...Rural Population
S-06-0217	1975	00002	...Stable Population
S-06-0218	1975	00002	...Suburban Population
S-06-0219	1975	00041	...Urban Population
S-06-0220	1975	00036	..Population Composition
S-06-0221	1975	00028	...Ethnic Composition
S-06-0222	1975	00004	...Nationality Composition
S-06-0223	1975	00033	...Racial Composition
S-06-0224	1975	00006	...Religious Composition
S-06-0225	1975	00047	..Population Distribution
S-06-0226	1975	00024	...Metropolitan Growth Pattern
S-06-0227	1975	00056	...Population Concentration
S-06-0228	1975	00064	...Residential Pattern
S-06-0229	1975	00001	....Multiple Family Dwelling
S-06-0230	1975	00001	....Single Family Dwelling
S-06-0231	1975	00028	...Urbanization Pattern
S-06-0232	1979	00000	....Urban Sprawl
S-06-0233	1975	00013	..Population Movement
S-06-0234	1975	00026	...Migration Pattern
S-06-0235	1979	00000	....Braindrain
S-06-0236	1975	00007	....Emigration Pattern
S-06-0237	1975	00028	....Immigration Pattern
S-06-0238	1975	00015	.....Immigration Flow
S-06-0239	1975	00020	....Internal Migration Pattern
S-06-0240	1975	00004	.....Rural Migration Pattern
S-06-0241	1975	00009	.....Suburban Migration Pattern
S-06-0242	1975	00023	.....Urban Migration Pattern
S-06-0243	1975	00008	...Population Mobility
S-06-0244	1975	00023	....Geographic Mobility
S-06-0245	1979	00000	...Population Transition
S-06-0246	1975	00024	.Economic Characteristics
S-06-0247	1975	00015	..Budget
S-06-0248	1975	00001	...Balanced Budget
S-06-0249	1975	00001	...Budget Discrepancy
S-06-0250	1975	00003	....Budget Deficit
S-06-0251	1975	00001	....Budget Surplus
S-06-0252	1975	00000	...Capital Budget
S-06-0253	1975	00002	....Executive Budget
S-06-0254	1975	00005	....Incremental Budget
S-06-0255	1979	00000	....Military Budget
S-06-0256	1975	00008	....Performance Budget
S-06-0257	1975	00009	....Program Budget
S-06-0258	1979	00000	....Zero Based Budget
S-06-0259	1975	00015	..Capital
S-06-0260	1975	00017	...Accumulated Capital
S-06-0261	1979	00000	...Assets
S-06-0262	1979	00000	....Fixed Assets
S-06-0263	1975	00007	...Capital Surplus
S-06-0264	1975	00010	...Foreign Capital
S-06-0265	1975	00028	...Investment Capital
S-06-0266	1975	00004	...Private Capital
S-06-0267	1975	00005	...Public Capital
S-06-0268	1975	00008	..Consumption
S-06-0269	1975	00001	...Conspicuous Consumption
S-06-0270	1975	00053	...Consumption Pattern
S-06-0271	1975	00003	...Domestic Consumption
S-06-0272	1975	00068	...Energy Consumption
S-06-0273	1975	00003	...Mass Consumption
S-06-0274	1975	00001	...Private Consumption
S-06-0275	1975	00001	...Public Consumption
S-06-0276	1975	00020	..Division Of Labor
S-06-0277	1975	00003	...International Division Of Labor
S-06-0278	1975	00000	...National Division Of Labor
S-06-0279	1975	00000	...Socialist Division Of Labor
S-06-0280	1975	00020	..Economic Cycle
S-06-0281	1975	00019	...Economic Depression
S-06-0282	1975	00027	....Economic Recession
S-06-0283	1975	00075	...Economic Inflation
S-06-0284	1975	00013	...Economic Recovery
S-06-0285	1979	00000	..Economic Gain
S-06-0286	1975	00009	..Economic Index
S-06-0287	1975	00001	...Cost Of Living Index
S-06-0288	1975	00006	...Demand Curve
S-06-0289	1979	00000	....Demand Elasticity
S-06-0290	1975	00001	...Economic Competition Index
S-06-0291	1975	00006	...Economic Growth Index
S-06-0292	1975	00008	...Employment Index
S-06-0293	1975	00000	....Cyclical Employment
S-06-0294	1975	00000	....Seasonal Employment
S-06-0295	1979	00000	...Industrial Index
S-06-0296	1975	00010	...Supply Curve
S-06-0297	1979	00000	....Supply Elasticity
S-06-0298	1979	00000	..Economic Loss
S-06-0299	1979	00000	..Economic Scarcity
S-06-0300	1975	00057	..Government Expenditure
S-06-0301	1975	00017	...Development Fund
S-06-0302	1975	00019	...Education Subsidy
S-06-0303	1975	00000	....Parochial School Subsidy
S-06-0304	1975	00001	....Private School Subsidy
S-06-0305	1975	00001	....Vocational Subsidy
S-06-0306	1975	00000	...Farm Subsidy
S-06-0307	1975	00037	...Foreign Aid
S-06-0308	1975	00005	....Bilateral Aid
S-06-0309	1975	00014	....Financial Aid
S-06-0310	1975	00002	....Multilateral Aid
S-06-0311	1975	00027	...Foreign Assistance
S-06-0312	1975	00026	....Military Assistance
S-06-0313	1975	00024	....Technical Assistance
S-06-0314	1975	00016	....Training Assistance
S-06-0315	1975	00015	...Government Grant
S-06-0316	1975	00026	....Federal Grant In Aid
S-06-0317	1975	00006	...Government Loan
S-06-0318	1975	00024	...Government Research Support
S-06-0319	1975	00002	...Industrial Subsidy
S-06-0320	1975	00013	...Public Assistance
S-06-0321	1975	00017	....Welfare
S-06-0322	1975	00005	...Social Security
S-06-0323	1975	00005	...Unemployment Compensation
S-06-0324	1975	00037	..Income
S-06-0325	1975	00004	...Business Income
S-06-0326	1975	00007	....Corporate Income
S-06-0327	1975	00020	...Family Income
S-06-0328	1975	00004	...Farm Income
S-06-0329	1975	00000	...Foreign Income
S-06-0330	1975	00006	...Guaranteed Annual Income
S-06-0331	1975	00012	...Income Measure
S-06-0332	1975	00003	....Average Income
S-06-0333	1975	00000	....Disposable Income
S-06-0334	1975	00000	....Fixed Income
S-06-0335	1975	00002	....Median Income
S-06-0336	1975	00000	....Net Income

S-06-0337	1975	00004	....Real Income
S-06-0338	1975	00003	...National Income
S-06-0339	1975	00013	....Per Capita Income
S-06-0340	1975	00004	.....Per Capita Annual Income
S-06-0341	1975	00029	...Personal Income
S-06-0342	1979	00000	...Profit Income
S-06-0343	1975	00009	...Tax Exempt Income
S-06-0344	1979	00000	...Unearned Income
S-06-0345	1975	00062	..International Economic Characteristics
S-06-0346	1975	00014	...Balance Of Payments
S-06-0347	1975	00010	...Balance Of Trade
S-06-0348	1975	00004	...Export Quota
S-06-0349	1975	00033	...Foreign Trade Pattern
S-06-0350	1975	00011	...Import Export Ratio
S-06-0351	1975	00007	...Import Quota
S-06-0352	1975	00009	..Money
S-06-0353	1975	00004	...Money Creation
S-06-0354	1975	00002	....Bank Reserve
S-06-0355	1975	00004	....Discount Rate
S-06-0356	1975	00000	....Prime Loan Rate
S-06-0357	1975	00004	...Money Demand
S-06-0358	1975	00006	...Money Supply
S-06-0359	1975	00001	....Gold Reserve
S-06-0360	1975	00002	....National Currency
S-06-0361	1979	00000	.Education Characteristics
S-06-0362	1979	00000	..Academic Specialization
S-06-0363	1979	00000	.Environmental Characteristics
S-06-0364	1979	00000	..Population Density
S-06-0365	1979	00000	..Quality Of Life
S-06-0366	1979	00000	..Radiation Level
S-06-0367	1979	00000	.Expertise
S-06-0368	1975	00016	.Genetic Characteristics
S-06-0369	1979	00000	.Government Characteristics
S-06-0370	1979	00000	..Government Accountability
S-06-0371	1979	00000	..Government Responsiveness
S-06-0372	1979	00000	.Health Characteristics
S-06-0373	1979	00000	..Alcoholism
S-06-0374	1979	00000	..Disease
S-06-0375	1979	00000	..Drug Addiction
S-06-0376	1979	00000	..Epidemic
S-06-0377	1975	00031	.Identity Characteristics
S-06-0378	1975	00011	..Community Identity
S-06-0379	1975	00011	...Community Interest
S-06-0380	1975	00055	..Cultural Identity
S-06-0381	1975	00079	...Ethnicity
S-06-0382	1975	00016	....Ethnic Group Loyalty
S-06-0383	1975	00023	...Racial Identity
S-06-0384	1975	00014	....Black Identity
S-06-0385	1975	00020	..Folkways
S-06-0386	1975	00019	..Identity Change
S-06-0387	1975	00001	..Identity Crisis
S-06-0388	1975	00011	..Language Loyalty
S-06-0389	1975	00038	..National Identity
S-06-0390	1975	00009	...National Pride
S-06-0391	1975	00003	....National Prestige
S-06-0392	1975	00044	..Occupational Identity
S-06-0393	1975	00008	..Political Identity
S-06-0394	1975	00040	...Political Party Identification
S-06-0395	1975	00049	..Religious Identity
S-06-0396	1979	00000	...Religious Affiliation
S-06-0397	1975	00004	...Religious Fanaticism
S-06-0398	1975	00017	..Social Identity
S-06-0399	1975	00013	...Social Class Identification
S-06-0400	1975	00005	.Jurisdiction Characteristics
S-06-0401	1975	00013	..Administrative Jurisdiction
S-06-0402	1975	00000	..Executive Jurisdiction
S-06-0403	1975	00015	..Legal Jurisdiction
S-06-0404	1975	00012	...Court Jurisdiction

S-06-0405	1975	00003	....Appellate Jurisdiction
S-06-0406	1975	00008	....Constitutional Jurisdiction
S-06-0407	1975	00000	....Original Jurisdiction
S-06-0408	1975	00003	..Legislative Jurisdiction
S-06-0409	1975	00030	..Territory Jurisdiction
S-06-0410	1975	00000	..Union Jurisdiction
S-06-0411	1979	00000	.Language Characteristics
S-06-0412	1979	00000	..Grammar
S-06-0413	1979	00000	..Semantics
S-06-0414	1979	00000	..Speech
S-06-0415	1979	00000	..Stylistics
S-06-0416	1979	00000	..Vocabulary
S-06-0417	1975	00014	.Legislative Characteristics
S-06-0418	1979	00000	..Legislative Accountability
S-06-0419	1975	00005	..Legislative Norms
S-06-0420	1975	00000	...Legislative Courtesy
S-06-0421	1975	00000	...:Senatorial Courtesy
S-06-0422	1975	00000	...Legislative Patriotism
S-06-0423	1975	00004	...Log Rolling
S-06-0424	1975	00001	...Pork Barrel
S-06-0425	1975	00005	...Seniority
S-06-0426	1975	00032	.Management Characteristics
S-06-0427	1975	00021	..Administrative Characteristics
S-06-0428	1975	00009	...Administrative Capability Characteristics
S-06-0429	1975	00017	....Administrative Effectiveness
S-06-0430	1975	00015	....Administrative Efficiency
S-06-0431	1975	00009	...Administrative Normative Characteristics
S-06-0432	1975	00029	....Administrative Accountability
S-06-0433	1975	00007	.....Executive Accountability
S-06-0434	1975	00004	......Chief Executive Accountability
S-06-0435	1975	00013	.......Presidential Accountability
S-06-0436	1975	00000	.....Ministerial Responsibility
S-06-0437	1975	00003	....Administrative Discretion
S-06-0438	1975	00002	.....Executive Discretion
S-06-0439	1975	00001	......Chief Executive Discretion
S-06-0440	1975	00002	.......Presidential Discretion
S-06-0441	1975	00001	.....Executive Prerogative
S-06-0442	1975	00001	......Chief Executive Prerogative
S-06-0443	1975	00003	.....Executive Privilege
S-06-0444	1975	00031	...Bureaucratic Characteristics
S-06-0445	1975	00010	....Bureaucratic Capability Characteristics
S-06-0446	1975	00010	.....Bureaucratic Efficiency
S-06-0447	1975	00009	....Bureaucratic Normative Characteristics
S-06-0448	1975	00005	.....Bureaucratic Ethos
S-06-0449	1975	00003	.....Bureaucratic Rationality
S-06-0450	1975	00004	.....Bureaucratic Rule
S-06-0451	1975	00015	....Bureaucratic Structural Characteristics
S-06-0452	1975	00011	.....Bureaucratic Autonomy
S-06-0453	1975	00003	.....Bureaucratic Goal
S-06-0454	1975	00005	.....Bureaucratic Hierarchy
S-06-0455	1975	00002	......Line Staff
S-06-0456	1975	00007	.....Bureaucratic Inertia
S-06-0457	1975	00000	.....Bureaucratic Parallelism
S-06-0458	1975	00010	.....Bureaucratic Rigidity
S-06-0459	1975	00026	.Military Characteristics
S-06-0460	1975	00028	..Defensive Capability
S-06-0461	1975	00018	..Military Intelligence
S-06-0462	1975	00005	..Military Size
S-06-0463	1975	00036	..Nuclear Capability
S-06-0464	1975	00005	...First Strike Capability
S-06-0465	1975	00006	...Offensive Nuclear Capability
S-06-0466	1975	00004	...Second Strike Capability
S-06-0467	1975	00019	..Offensive Capability
S-06-0468	1975	00005	..Retaliatory Capability
S-06-0469	1975	00028	..Strategic Advantage
S-06-0470	1975	00004	.National Characteristics
S-06-0471	1975	00024	..Cultural Diversity

S-06-0472	1975	00015	...Cultural Cleavage
S-06-0473	1975	00004	...Linguistic Diversity
S-06-0474	1975	00006	...Racial Diversity
S-06-0475	1975	00013	....Racial Cleavage
S-06-0476	1975	00019	..Ethnic Diversity
S-06-0477	1975	00011	...Ethnic Cleavage
S-06-0478	1975	00013	...Ethnic Heterogeneity
S-06-0479	1975	00009	...Ethnic Homogeneity
S-06-0480	1975	00011	..National Boundary
S-06-0481	1975	00015	..National Character
S-06-0482	1975	00011	..National Image
S-06-0483	1975	00042	..National Interest
S-06-0484	1975	00033	...National Goal
S-06-0485	1975	00017	....National Priority
S-06-0486	1975	00118	....National Security
S-06-0487	1979	00000	..National Self Determination
S-06-0488	1975	00003	..Social Diversity
S-06-0489	1975	00014	...Social Cleavage
S-06-0490	1979	00000	.Occupation Characteristics
S-06-0491	1979	00000	..Job Discrimination
S-06-0492	1979	00000	..Job Dissatisfaction
S-06-0493	1979	00000	..Job Preference
S-06-0494	1979	00000	..Job Satisfaction
S-06-0495	1975	00022	.Opportunity Characteristics
S-06-0496	1975	00056	..Education Opportunity
S-06-0497	1975	00080	..Employment Opportunity
S-06-0498	1975	00041	..Equal Opportunity
S-06-0499	1975	00132	.Personality Characteristics
S-06-0500	1975	00023	..Altruism
S-06-0501	1975	00001	..Ambivalence
S-06-0502	1975	00013	...Role Ambivalence
S-06-0503	1979	00000	..Assertiveness
S-06-0504	1979	00000	..Charity
S-06-0505	1979	00000	..Courage
S-06-0506	1979	00000	..Creativity
S-06-0507	1979	00000	..Culture Shock
S-06-0508	1979	00000	..Curiosity
S-06-0509	1979	00000	..Egocentrism
S-06-0510	1975	00008	..Empathy
S-06-0511	1979	00000	..Femininity
S-06-0512	1979	00000	..Gregariousness
S-06-0513	1979	00000	..Happiness
S-06-0514	1979	00000	..Honesty
S-06-0515	1979	00000	..Imagination
S-06-0516	1979	00000	..Masculinity
S-06-0517	1979	00000	..Optimism
S-06-0518	1979	00000	..Virtue
S-06-0519	1979	00000	...Political Virtue
S-06-0520	1975	00015	..Personality Disorder
S-06-0521	1975	00001	...Hysteria
S-06-0522	1975	00005	...Neurosis
S-06-0523	1975	00013	...Psychosis
S-06-0524	1975	00006	....Paranoia
S-06-0525	1975	00034	....Schizophrenia
S-06-0526	1979	00000	..Persistence
S-06-0527	1975	00017	..Personality Type
S-06-0528	1975	00005	...Authoritarian Personality
S-06-0529	1975	00006	...Basic Personality
S-06-0530	1975	00007	...Deviant Personality
S-06-0531	1975	00003	...Inner Directed Personality
S-06-0532	1975	00002	...Modal Personality
S-06-0533	1975	00002	...Other Directed Personality
S-06-0534	1979	00000	..Pessimism
S-06-0535	1975	00024	.Political Party Characteristics
S-06-0536	1975	00017	..Political Party Capability Characteristics
S-06-0537	1975	00004	..Political Party Composition
S-06-0538	1975	00004	...Political Party Constituency
S-06-0539	1975	00038	....Political Party Electoral Strength
S-06-0540	1975	00009	...Political Party Membership
S-06-0541	1975	00020	....Political Party Affiliation
S-06-0542	1975	00012	....Political Party Recruitment Pattern
S-06-0543	1975	00015	..Political Party Normative Characteristics
S-06-0544	1975	00001	...Political Party Discipline
S-06-0545	1975	00044	...Political Party Ideology
S-06-0546	1975	00020	...Political Party Loyalty
S-06-0547	1975	00006	....Political Party Loyalty Intensity
S-06-0548	1975	00000	...Political Party Manifesto
S-06-0549	1975	00001	...Political Party Norms
S-06-0550	1975	00016	..Political Party Structural Characteristics
S-06-0551	1975	00008	...Intraparty Conflict
S-06-0552	1975	00026	....Political Party Factional Cleavage
S-06-0553	1975	00000	...Intraparty Democracy
S-06-0554	1979	00000	...Political Party Alignment
S-06-0555	1975	00002	...Political Party Centralization
S-06-0556	1975	00002	....Centralized Political Party
S-06-0557	1975	00016	...Political Party Cohesion
S-06-0558	1975	00002	...Political Party Decentralization
S-06-0559	1975	00001	....Decentralized Political Party
S-06-0560	1975	00014	...Political Party Faction
S-06-0561	1975	00003	...Political Party Hierarchy
S-06-0562	1975	00006	...Political Party Institutionalization
S-06-0563	1975	00017	...Political Party Organization
S-06-0564	1975	00003	....Political Party Bureaucracy
S-06-0565	1975	00007	....Political Party Congress
S-06-0566	1975	00000	....Political Party Machine
S-06-0567	1975	00000	....Political Party Nominating Committee
S-06-0568	1975	00020	...Political Party Realignment
S-06-0569	1975	00008	.System Characteristics
S-06-0570	1975	00002	..Analytic System Characteristics
S-06-0571	1979	00000	...Feedback Loop
S-06-0572	1979	00000	....Communication Feedback
S-06-0573	1979	00000	....Learning Feedback
S-06-0574	1975	00012	...System Boundary
S-06-0575	1975	00006	...System Capacity
S-06-0576	1975	00009	....System Adaptive Capacity
S-06-0577	1975	00007	....System Maintenance Capacity
S-06-0578	1975	00005	....System Persistence Capacity
S-06-0579	1975	00018	...System Change
S-06-0580	1975	00012	....System Adaptation
S-06-0581	1975	00008	.....Functional Adaptation
S-06-0582	1975	00013	.....Structural Adaptation
S-06-0583	1975	00009	....System Innovation
S-06-0584	1975	00004	...System Disequilibrium
S-06-0585	1975	00003	...System Function
S-06-0586	1975	00005	....Functional Specificity
S-06-0587	1975	00002	....Latent Function
S-06-0588	1975	00000	....Manifest Function
S-06-0589	1975	00002	...System Inputs
S-06-0590	1975	00011	....System Demands
S-06-0591	1975	00006	.....Endogenous System Demands
S-06-0592	1975	00003	.....Exogenous System Demands
S-06-0593	1975	00020	....System Supports
S-06-0594	1979	00000	.....Diffuse System Supports
S-06-0595	1979	00000	.....Specific System Supports
S-06-0596	1975	00004	...System Integration
S-06-0597	1975	00026	...System Interdependence
S-06-0598	1975	00002	....System Independence
S-06-0599	1975	00016	...System Maintenance
S-06-0600	1975	00001	....Pattern Maintenance
S-06-0601	1975	00008	...System Outputs
S-06-0602	1975	00001	....System Goal
S-06-0603	1975	00004	.....Goal Ambiguity
S-06-0604	1975	00006	.....Goal Satisfaction
S-06-0605	1975	00024	.....Goal Setting
S-06-0606	1975	00002	.....Goal Specificity
S-06-0607	1975	00007	.....Value Allocation

S-06-0608	1975	00002	......Authoritative Value Allocation
S-06-0609	1975	00026	....System Performance
S-06-0610	1979	00000	....System Requisite
S-06-0611	1979	00000	.....Functional Requisites
S-06-0612	1979	00000	.....Structural Requisites
S-06-0613	1975	00040	....System Stability
S-06-0614	1975	00006	.....System Equilibrium
S-06-0615	1975	00001	......Dynamic Equilibrium
S-06-0616	1975	00004	......Homeostatic Equilibrium
S-06-0617	1975	00005	....System Stress
S-06-0618	1975	00002	.....Endogenous System Stress
S-06-0619	1975	00004	.....Exogenous System Stress
S-06-0620	1975	00067	..Economic System Characteristics
S-06-0621	1975	00062	...Economic Dependency
S-06-0622	1975	00017	...Economic Deprivation
S-06-0623	1975	00005	...Economic Diversification
S-06-0624	1975	00008	....Production Distribution
S-06-0625	1975	00039	...Economic Power Distribution
S-06-0626	1975	00004	....Industrial Distribution
S-06-0627	1975	00021	....Land Distribution
S-06-0628	1975	00037	.....Land Ownership Pattern
S-06-0629	1975	00010	....Monopoly
S-06-0630	1975	00007	.....Oligopoly
S-06-0631	1975	00001	.....Perfect Monopoly
S-06-0632	1975	00001	.....Private Monopoly
S-06-0633	1975	00003	.....Public Monopoly
S-06-0634	1975	00048	....Wealth Distribution
S-06-0635	1975	00090	.....Income Distribution
S-06-0636	1979	00000	.....Income Elasticity
S-06-0637	1975	00043	.....Poverty
S-06-0638	1975	00005	.....Prosperity
S-06-0639	1975	00005	.....Subsistence Level
S-06-0640	1975	00048	.....Wage Level
S-06-0641	1975	00003	......Subsistence Wage Level
S-06-0642	1975	00026	.....Wealth Redistribution
S-06-0643	1975	00010	...Economic Security
S-06-0644	1975	00009	...Economic Sovereignty
S-06-0645	1975	00012	...Economic Stratification
S-06-0646	1975	00155	...Employment Characteristics
S-06-0647	1975	00020	....Full Employment
S-06-0648	1979	00000	....Labor Force
S-06-0649	1979	00000	....Labor Market
S-06-0650	1979	00000	....Labor Supply
S-06-0651	1979	00000	....Labor Surplus
S-06-0652	1975	00000	....Overemployment
S-06-0653	1979	00000	....Retirement
S-06-0654	1975	00015	....Underemployment
S-06-0655	1975	00063	....Unemployment
S-06-0656	1975	00006	.....Structural Unemployment
S-06-0657	1975	00002	.....Technological Unemployment
S-06-0658	1975	00054	..Political System Characteristics
S-06-0659	1975	00109	...International Political System Characteristics
S-06-0660	1975	00050	....Arms Race
S-06-0661	1975	00026	.....Nuclear Arms Race
S-06-0662	1975	00069	.....Nuclear Weapon Proliferation
S-06-0663	1975	00017	.....Strategic Arms Race
S-06-0664	1975	00057	....Balance Of Power
S-06-0665	1975	00008	.....Balance Of Terror
S-06-0666	1975	00009	......Nuclear Parity
S-06-0667	1975	00000	.....Balkanization
S-06-0668	1975	00012	....Collective Security
S-06-0669	1975	00033	.....Regional Security
S-06-0670	1975	00015	.....Supranational Security
S-06-0671	1975	00014	....Peace
S-06-0672	1975	00027	.....International Peace
S-06-0673	1975	00004	.....Limited Peace
S-06-0674	1975	00018	....Peaceful Coexistence
S-06-0675	1975	00031	.....Detente
S-06-0676	1975	00076	......East West Detente
S-06-0677	1975	00018	.....Disarmament
S-06-0678	1975	00049	.....Strategic Arms Limitation
S-06-0679	1979	00000	....Rapproachment
S-06-0680	1975	00010	....Sphere Of Influence
S-06-0681	1975	00011	...National Political System Characteristics
S-06-0682	1975	00017	...Political System Capability Characteristics
S-06-0683	1975	00011	....Political System Effectiveness
S-06-0684	1975	00002	....Political System Efficiency
S-06-0685	1975	00007	...Political System Normative Characteristics
S-06-0686	1979	00000	....Political Injustice
S-06-0687	1975	00015	....Political Style
S-06-0688	1975	00052	...Political System Structural Characteristics
S-06-0689	1975	00010	....Political Consensus
S-06-0690	1975	00008	....Political Dissensus
S-06-0691	1975	00051	....Political Instability
S-06-0692	1975	00019	.....Government Instability
S-06-0693	1975	00017	.....Regime Instability
S-06-0694	1975	00002	......Cabinet Instability
S-06-0695	1975	00000	.......Ministerial Instability
S-06-0696	1975	00009	....Political Opportunity Structure
S-06-0697	1975	00017	....Political Opposition
S-06-0698	1975	00005	.....Electoral Opposition
S-06-0699	1975	00002	.....Parliamentary Opposition
S-06-0700	1975	00060	..Social System Characteristics
S-06-0701	1975	00038	...Social System Environment Characteristics
S-06-0702	1979	00000	....Living Conditions
S-06-0703	1975	00020	....Rural Environment
S-06-0704	1975	00006	....Suburban Environment
S-06-0705	1975	00058	....Urban Environment
S-06-0706	1979	00000	....Working Conditions
S-06-0707	1975	00039	...Social System Normative Characteristics
S-06-0708	1975	00012	....Social Goal
S-06-0709	1979	00000	....Social Injustice
S-06-0710	1979	00000	.....Economic Injustice
S-06-0711	1979	00000	.....Education Injustice
S-06-0712	1975	00006	.....Racial Injustice
S-06-0713	1979	00000	.....Sexual Injustice
S-06-0714	1975	00023	....Social Mores
S-06-0715	1975	00024	.....Middle Class Values
S-06-0716	1975	00010	.....Socially Desirable Behavior
S-06-0717	1975	00050	....Social Norms
S-06-0718	1975	00005	.....Consensual Norms
S-06-0719	1975	00012	.....Constraining Norms
S-06-0720	1979	00000	.....Elite Norms
S-06-0721	1975	00015	....Social Utility
S-06-0722	1975	00022	.....Public Interest
S-06-0723	1975	00075	...Social System Structural Characteristics
S-06-0724	1979	00000	....Equality
S-06-0725	1979	00000	.....Economic Equality
S-06-0726	1979	00000	......Income Equality
S-06-0727	1979	00000	.....Political Equality
S-06-0728	1979	00000	.....Social Equality
S-06-0729	1979	00000	......Class Equality
S-06-0730	1979	00000	......Education Equality
S-06-0731	1979	00000	......Racial Equality
S-06-0732	1979	00000	......Sex Equality
S-06-0733	1979	00000	......Status Equality
S-06-0734	1979	00000	....Inequality
S-06-0735	1979	00000	.....Economic Inequality
S-06-0736	1979	00000	......Income Inequality
S-06-0737	1979	00000	.....Political Inequality
S-06-0738	1975	00051	.....Social Inequality

S-06-0739	1975	00024	......Class Inequality
S-06-0740	1975	00020	......Education Inequality
S-06-0741	1975	00044	......Racial Inequality
S-06-0742	1975	00044	......Sex Inequality
S-06-0743	1975	00033	......Status Inequality
S-06-0744	1979	00000	....Prestige Hierarchy
S-06-0745	1979	00000	.....Social Prestige
S-06-0746	1975	00089	....Social Mobility
S-06-0747	1975	00039	.....Status Mobility
S-06-0748	1975	00004	......Horizontal Mobility
S-06-0749	1975	00019	......Intergenerational Mobility
S-06-0750	1975	00008	......Intragenerational Mobility
S-06-0751	1975	00005	......Vertical Mobility
S-06-0752	1975	00008	.......Downward Mobility
S-06-0753	1975	00030	.......Upward Mobility
S-06-0754	1975	00019	....Social Stability
S-06-0755	1975	00014	....Social Stratification Division
S-06-0756	1975	00004	.....Caste Stratification Division
S-06-0757	1975	00001	......Lower Caste
S-06-0758	1975	00000	.......Untouchables
S-06-0759	1975	00000	......Middle Caste
S-06-0760	1975	00001	......Upper Caste
S-06-0761	1975	00021	.....Class Stratification Division
S-06-0762	1975	00009	......Aristocratic Class
S-06-0763	1975	00001	......Capitalist Class
S-06-0764	1975	00004	......Entrepreneur Class
S-06-0765	1975	00014	......Landowning Class
S-06-0766	1975	00012	......Lower Class
S-06-0767	1975	00001	......Lumpen Proletariat
S-06-0768	1975	00017	......Middle Class
S-06-0769	1975	00005	.......Bourgeoisie
S-06-0770	1975	00001	........Black Bourgeoisie
S-06-0771	1975	00004	........Petite Bourgeoisie
S-06-0772	1975	00002	.......New Middle Class
S-06-0773	1975	00001	.......Old Middle Class
S-06-0774	1975	00014	......Nobility
S-06-0775	1975	00025	......Peasant Class
S-06-0776	1975	00006	.......Landless Peasant Class
S-06-0777	1975	00003	......Propertied Class
S-06-0778	1975	00004	......Ruling Class
S-06-0779	1975	00004	......Upper Class
S-06-0780	1975	00034	......Working Class
S-06-0781	1975	00010	.......Agricultural Working Class
S-06-0782	1975	00010	.......Industrial Working Class
S-06-0783	1975	00003	.......Proletariat
S-06-0784	1975	00003	.......Unionized Working Class
S-06-0785	1975	00004	.....Horizontal Stratification Division
S-06-0786	1975	00037	.....Status Stratification Division
S-06-0787	1975	00030	......Achieved Status
S-06-0788	1975	00023	......Ascribed Status
S-06-0789	1979	00000	......Objectively Derived Status
S-06-0790	1979	00000	......Subjectively Derived Status
S-06-0791	1975	00005	.....Vertical Stratification Division
S-06-0792	1975	00030	....Social Stress
S-06-0793	1975	00044	.....Ethnic Conflict
S-06-0794	1975	00016	.....Racial Tension
S-06-0795	1975	00007	.....Social Criticism
S-06-0796	1975	00021	.....Social Deviance
S-06-0797	1975	00013	.....Social Disorder
S-06-0798	1975	00024	.....Social Instability
S-06-0799	1975	00053	.Technology
S-06-0800	1975	00043	..Advanced Technology
S-06-0801	1975	00012	..Middle Level Technology
S-06-0802	1975	00001	..Technological Obsolescence
S-06-0803	1975	00086	..Technology Transfer

S-07 COMMUNITY TYPE

S-07-0001	1975	00008	Community Type
S-07-0002	1979	00000	.Academic Community
S-07-0003	1975	00014	.City
S-07-0004	1979	00000	..Central City
S-07-0005	1975	00008	..Decentralized City
S-07-0006	1975	00002	..Federated City
S-07-0007	1975	00014	..Inner City
S-07-0008	1975	00035	..Metropolitan City
S-07-0009	1975	00004	...Megalopolis
S-07-0010	1975	00003	...Metropolis
S-07-0011	1975	00002	...Outer City
S-07-0012	1975	00012	..Municipality
S-07-0013	1975	00002	..Preindustrial City
S-07-0014	1975	00007	..Village
S-07-0015	1975	00000	...Hamlet
S-07-0016	1979	00000	.Compound
S-07-0017	1975	00003	.Cooperative Community
S-07-0018	1975	00003	..Collective Community
S-07-0019	1975	00010	..Communal Community
S-07-0020	1975	00004	...Red Commune
S-07-0021	1975	00007	..Kibbutz
S-07-0022	1975	00003	..Utopian Community
S-07-0023	1975	00007	.Economic Community
S-07-0024	1975	00062	.Ethnic Community
S-07-0025	1975	00005	.Ghetto Community
S-07-0026	1975	00008	..Ethnic Ghetto
S-07-0027	1975	00007	...Black Ghetto
S-07-0028	1975	00001	..Suburban Ghetto Community
S-07-0029	1975	00006	...Black Suburban Community
S-07-0030	1975	00014	..Urban Ghetto Community
S-07-0031	1975	00001	.Heterogeneous Community
S-07-0032	1975	00002	..Integrated Community
S-07-0033	1975	00002	..Multiethnic Community
S-07-0034	1975	00001	..Multilingual Community
S-07-0035	1975	00002	...Bilingual Community
S-07-0036	1975	00004	..Multiracial Community
S-07-0037	1975	00003	.Homogeneous Community
S-07-0038	1979	00000	..Language Community
S-07-0039	1975	00016	.Neighborhood
S-07-0040	1979	00000	.Planned Community
S-07-0041	1979	00000	..Model City
S-07-0042	1979	00000	..New Town
S-07-0043	1975	00008	.Political Community
S-07-0044	1975	00009	.Religious Community
S-07-0045	1979	00000	.Reservation
S-07-0046	1975	00049	.Rural Community
S-07-0047	1975	00017	.Segregated Community
S-07-0048	1975	00005	.Slum Community
S-07-0049	1979	00000	.Squatter Community
S-07-0050	1975	00010	.Suburb
S-07-0051	1979	00000	..Bedroom Community
S-07-0052	1975	00005	.Town
S-07-0053	1975	00018	.Village Community

S-08 CONFLICT TYPE

S-08-0001	1975	00012	Conflict Type
S-08-0002	1975	00024	.Aggression
S-08-0003	1975	00008	..Cultural Aggression
S-08-0004	1975	00009	..Military Aggression
S-08-0005	1975	00001	...Limited Military Aggression
S-08-0006	1975	00008	..Psychological Aggression
S-08-0007	1975	00000	.Agitation
S-08-0008	1975	00002	..Economic Agitation
S-08-0009	1975	00000	...Economic Demonstration
S-08-0010	1975	00001	....Consumer Demonstration

S-08-0011	1975	00000	....Rent Strike
S-08-0012	1975	00001	...Labor Boycott
S-08-0013	1975	00000	..Political Agitation
S-08-0014	1975	00001	...Agitation Propaganda
S-08-0015	1975	00005	...Demonstration
S-08-0016	1975	00003	....Civil Rights Demonstration
S-08-0017	1975	00000	.....Sit In
S-08-0018	1975	00002	....General Strike
S-08-0019	1975	00000	....Peace Demonstration
S-08-0020	1975	00004	....Student Demonstration
S-08-0021	1979	00000	.....Student Riot
S-08-0022	1975	00000	....Veterans Demonstration
S-08-0023	1975	00000	....Worker Demonstration
S-08-0024	1979	00000	.Conflict Of Interest
S-08-0025	1979	00000	.Cultural Conflict
S-08-0026	1975	00016	..Religious Conflict
S-08-0027	1975	00009	.Economic Conflict
S-08-0028	1975	00040	..Consumer Producer Conflict
S-08-0029	1975	00014	..Labor Conflict
S-08-0030	1975	00018	...Labor Strike
S-08-0031	1975	00000	....Jurisdiction Strike
S-08-0032	1975	00000	.....Sit Down Strike
S-08-0033	1975	00000	....Walkout
S-08-0034	1975	00000	....Wildcat Strike
S-08-0035	1975	00000	...Lockout
S-08-0036	1975	00002	...Strike Breaking
S-08-0037	1975	00011	.Government Overthrow
S-08-0038	1975	00019	..Coup D'Etat
S-08-0039	1975	00029	...Military Coup
S-08-0040	1975	00000	..Putsch
S-08-0041	1975	00032	.Ideological Conflict
S-08-0042	1975	00005	.Institutional Conflict
S-08-0043	1975	00002	..Routinized Conflict
S-08-0044	1975	00015	.Insurgency
S-08-0045	1975	00006	..Counterinsurgency
S-08-0046	1979	00000	.Internal Conflict
S-08-0047	1975	00017	..Internal War
S-08-0048	1975	00037	...Civil War
S-08-0049	1975	00018	...Guerrilla War
S-08-0050	1975	00016	....Guerrilla Activity
S-08-0051	1975	00020	...National Liberation War
S-08-0052	1975	00001	....Partisan War
S-08-0053	1975	00013	..Rebellion
S-08-0054	1975	00004	...Economic Rebellion
S-08-0055	1975	00015	...Political Rebellion
S-08-0056	1975	00009	...Social Rebellion
S-08-0057	1975	00003	....Class Rebellion
S-08-0058	1975	00029	....Peasant Rebellion
S-08-0059	1975	00002	....Slave Rebellion
S-08-0060	1975	00006	...Student Rebellion
S-08-0061	1975	00005	...Worker Rebellion
S-08-0062	1975	00028	..Revolution
S-08-0063	1975	00007	...Counterrevolution
S-08-0064	1975	00010	...Cultural Revolution
S-08-0065	1975	00014	....Chinese Cultural Revolution
S-08-0066	1975	00002	...Ecological Revolution
S-08-0067	1975	00013	....Green Revolution
S-08-0068	1975	00020	...Political Revolution
S-08-0069	1975	00001	....Democratic Political Revolution
S-08-0070	1975	00020	....National Political Revolution
S-08-0071	1975	00011	....Socialist Revolution
S-08-0072	1975	00026	.....Communist Revolution
S-08-0073	1975	00005	......Bolshevik Revolution
S-08-0074	1975	00000	.....Democratic Socialist Revolution
S-08-0075	1975	00013	...Social Revolution
S-08-0076	1975	00006	....Bourgeois Revolution
S-08-0077	1975	00007	....Industrial Revolution
S-08-0078	1975	00005	....Proletarian Revolution
S-08-0079	1975	00000	....Racial Revolution
S-08-0080	1975	00002	.....Black Revolution
S-08-0081	1975	00000	...Spontaneous Revolution
S-08-0082	1975	00008	...Technological Revolution
S-08-0083	1975	00001	...Thermidor
S-08-0084	1979	00000	.International Conflict
S-08-0085	1979	00000	..International Regional Conflict
S-08-0086	1979	00000	..North South Conflict
S-08-0087	1975	00075	..War
S-08-0088	1979	00000	...Biological War
S-08-0089	1979	00000	...Chemical War
S-08-0090	1975	00048	...Cold War
S-08-0091	1975	00021	...Conventional War
S-08-0092	1975	00000	...Declared War
S-08-0093	1975	00002	...Expansionist War
S-08-0094	1975	00005	....Imperialist War
S-08-0095	1975	00005	...Ideological War
S-08-0096	1975	00003	...Just War
S-08-0097	1975	00010	...Limited War
S-08-0098	1975	00003	....Border War
S-08-0099	1975	00007	.....Border Conflict
S-08-0100	1975	00000	....Brushfire War
S-08-0101	1979	00000	....Tactical War
S-08-0102	1975	00022	...Nuclear War
S-08-0103	1979	00000	...Proxy War
S-08-0104	1975	00008	...Psychological War
S-08-0105	1975	00001	....Propaganda War
S-08-0106	1979	00000	...Religious War
S-08-0107	1975	00001	....Holy War
S-08-0108	1975	00020	...Revolutionary War
S-08-0109	1975	00001	...Total War
S-08-0110	1975	00047	....World War
S-08-0111	1975	00002	...Undeclared War
S-08-0112	1979	00000	...War By Proxy
S-08-0113	1979	00000	.Interpersonal Conflict
S-08-0114	1975	00029	.Social Conflict
S-08-0115	1975	00015	..Group Conflict
S-08-0116	1975	00029	...Class Conflict
S-08-0117	1975	00003	....Class Antagonism
S-08-0118	1975	00005	...Class Polarization
S-08-0119	1979	00000	...Ethnic Group Conflict
S-08-0120	1979	00000	...Ghetto Conflict
S-08-0121	1975	00007	...Language Group Conflict
S-08-0122	1975	00021	..Racial Conflict
S-08-0123	1975	00002	...Black Insurrection
S-08-0124	1975	00004	...Race Riot
S-08-0125	1979	00000	....Urban Race Riot
S-08-0126	1975	00003	.Struggle
S-08-0127	1975	00005	..Class Struggle
S-08-0128	1975	00016	..Ideological Struggle
S-08-0129	1975	00037	..Succession Struggle
S-08-0130	1979	00000	.Violence
S-08-0131	1975	00010	..Mob Violence
S-08-0132	1975	00039	..Political Violence

S-09 CONTEMPORARY ANALYTIC MODES

S-09-0001	1975	00004	Contemporary Analytic Modes
S-09-0002	1975	00023	.Aggregate Data Analysis
S-09-0003	1979	00000	.Analysis Of Play
S-09-0004	1975	00057	.Behavior Analysis
S-09-0005	1975	00113	.Biographical Analysis
S-09-0006	1979	00000	..Career Analysis
S-09-0007	1979	00000	.Catastrophe Analysis
S-09-0008	1975	00058	.Class Analysis
S-09-0009	1975	00053	.Communication Analysis
S-09-0010	1975	00076	..Mass Media Analysis
S-09-0011	1979	00000	.Contextual Analysis

S-09-0012	1975	00082	.Cost Benefit Analysis
S-09-0013	1975	00019	.Critical Theory Analysis
S-09-0014	1975	00011	.Cybernetic Analysis
S-09-0015	1975	00032	.Demand Analysis
S-09-0016	1975	00005	.Eastonian Analysis
S-09-0017	1975	00022	.Ecological Analysis
S-09-0018	1975	00062	.Elite Analysis
S-09-0019	1975	00006	..Elite Identification
S-09-0020	1975	00002	...Institutional Elite Identification
S-09-0021	1975	00005	...Issue Elite Identification
S-09-0022	1975	00009	...Reputational Elite Identification
S-09-0023	1979	00000	.Graph Theory Analysis
S-09-0024	1975	00012	.Group Analysis
S-09-0025	1975	00015	..Small Group Analysis
S-09-0026	1975	00224	.Historical Analysis
S-09-0027	1975	00018	..Historical Sociology Analysis
S-09-0028	1975	00011	..Revisionist Historical Analysis
S-09-0029	1975	00006	.Ideal Type Analysis
S-09-0030	1975	00041	.Identity Analysis
S-09-0031	1975	00016	.Input Output Analysis
S-09-0032	1975	00144	.Interaction Analysis
S-09-0033	1975	00167	.Issue Analysis
S-09-0034	1979	00000	..Issue Intensity
S-09-0035	1979	00000	..Issue Salience
S-09-0036	1975	00089	.Leadership Analysis
S-09-0037	1975	00033	..Leadership Political Analysis
S-09-0038	1975	00025	..Leadership Psychological Analysis
S-09-0039	1975	00022	..Leadership Sociological Analysis
S-09-0040	1979	00000	.Leisure Time Analysis
S-09-0041	1975	00089	.Linguistic Analysis
S-09-0042	1979	00000	..Grammatical Analysis
S-09-0043	1979	00000	..Semantic Analysis
S-09-0044	1979	00000	..Verbal Analysis
S-09-0045	1979	00000	.Literature Analysis
S-09-0046	1975	00003	.Marginal Analysis
S-09-0047	1975	00014	..Marginal Utility Analysis
S-09-0048	1975	00026	.Marxist Analysis
S-09-0049	1979	00000	.Motivational Analysis
S-09-0050	1975	00000	.National Accounts Analysis
S-09-0051	1975	00008	.National Income Analysis
S-09-0052	1975	00022	.Network Analysis
S-09-0053	1975	00007	.Pluralist Analysis
S-09-0054	1975	00157	.Policy Analysis
S-09-0055	1979	00000	..PERT Analysis
S-09-0056	1975	00247	..Public Policy Analysis
S-09-0057	1975	00012	.Political Psychology Analysis
S-09-0058	1975	00001	..Lasswellian Analysis
S-09-0059	1979	00000	.Psychoanalysis
S-09-0060	1979	00000	..Psychotherapy
S-09-0061	1975	00010	.Rational Man Analysis
S-09-0062	1975	00000	.Reductionist Analysis
S-09-0063	1979	00000	.Situational Analysis
S-09-0064	1975	00001	.Social Area Analysis
S-09-0065	1975	00025	.Socialization Analysis
S-09-0066	1979	00000	.Sociological Analysis
S-09-0067	1979	00000	..Durkheimian Analysis
S-09-0068	1979	00000	..Marginal Man Analysis
S-09-0069	1979	00000	..Parsonsian Analysis
S-09-0070	1975	00020	..Weberian Analysis
S-09-0071	1975	00049	.Spatial Analysis
S-09-0072	1975	00030	.Structural Functional Analysis
S-09-0073	1975	00034	.Survey Analysis
S-09-0074	1975	00012	.Transactional Analysis
S-09-0075	1975	00118	.Value Analysis
S-09-0076	1975	00072	.Voting Behavior Analysis
S-09-0077	1975	00023	..Roll Call Analysis
S-09-0078	1975	00002	..Spatial Voting Analysis

S-10 CRIME

S-10-0001	1975	00059	Crime
S-10-0002	1975	00000	.Court Crime
S-10-0003	1975	00000	..Bail Skipping
S-10-0004	1975	00002	..Contempt Of Court
S-10-0005	1975	00000	..Jury Tampering
S-10-0006	1975	00001	..Perjury
S-10-0007	1975	00002	.Crime Against Humanity
S-10-0008	1979	00000	..Euthanasia
S-10-0009	1975	00009	..Genocide
S-10-0010	1975	00003	..War Crime
S-10-0011	1975	00001	...Massacre
S-10-0012	1975	00002	...War Atrocity
S-10-0013	1979	00000	.Crime Rate
S-10-0014	1975	00005	.Economic Crime
S-10-0015	1975	00005	..Economic Bribery
S-10-0016	1975	00000	..Economic Conspiracy
S-10-0017	1975	00000	..Economic Espionage
S-10-0018	1975	00001	...Industrial Espionage
S-10-0019	1975	00002	..Economic Sabotage
S-10-0020	1975	00003	..Fraud
S-10-0021	1975	00008	..Property Crime
S-10-0022	1975	00003	...Robbery
S-10-0023	1975	00001	...Vandalism
S-10-0024	1975	00001	..Tax Evasion
S-10-0025	1975	00002	..White Collar Crime
S-10-0026	1975	00001	.Individual Crime
S-10-0027	1975	00004	..Assault
S-10-0028	1975	00003	..Blackmail
S-10-0029	1979	00000	..Child Neglect
S-10-0030	1975	00002	..Criminal Abortion
S-10-0031	1975	00001	..Extortion
S-10-0032	1979	00000	..Highjacking
S-10-0033	1979	00000	..Illegal Abortion
S-10-0034	1975	00007	..Juvenile Crime
S-10-0035	1975	00013	...Juvenile Delinquency
S-10-0036	1979	00000	..Kidnapping
S-10-0037	1975	00001	..Libel
S-10-0038	1979	00000	..Malpractice
S-10-0039	1979	00000	...Legal Malpractice
S-10-0040	1979	00000	...Medical Malpractice
S-10-0041	1979	00000	..Marital Offense
S-10-0042	1975	00005	..Morals Offense
S-10-0043	1975	00008	..Murder
S-10-0044	1979	00000	..Police Brutality
S-10-0045	1975	00012	..Sex Crime
S-10-0046	1979	00000	...Child Molestation
S-10-0047	1979	00000	...Rape
S-10-0048	1975	00000	..Slander
S-10-0049	1979	00000	...Character Assassination
S-10-0050	1975	00001	..Street Crime
S-10-0051	1975	00002	.Organized Crime
S-10-0052	1975	00000	.Piracy
S-10-0053	1975	00001	..Air Piracy
S-10-0054	1975	00000	..Sea Piracy
S-10-0055	1975	00004	.Political Crime
S-10-0056	1975	00004	..Assassination
S-10-0057	1975	00000	...Tyrannicide
S-10-0058	1975	00000	..Defection
S-10-0059	1975	00003	...Desertion
S-10-0060	1979	00000	..Illegal Immigration
S-10-0061	1975	00000	..Malfeasance
S-10-0062	1975	00002	..Military Conspiracy
S-10-0063	1975	00001	..Military Espionage
S-10-0064	1975	00000	..Misfeasance
S-10-0065	1975	00002	..Political Conspiracy
S-10-0066	1975	00023	..Political Corruption

S-10-0067	1975	00002	...Political Bribery
S-10-0068	1975	00002	...Political Graft
S-10-0069	1975	00002	...Spoils System
S-10-0070	1975	00004	..Political Espionage
S-10-0071	1975	00002	..Political Fraud
S-10-0072	1975	00000	...Election Fraud
S-10-0073	1975	00000	....Vote Fraud
S-10-0074	1975	00001	...Political Fund Misuse
S-10-0075	1975	00002	...Political Information Manipulation
S-10-0076	1975	00000	...Political Record Falsification
S-10-0077	1975	00005	..Political Sabotage
S-10-0078	1975	00001	..Sedition
S-10-0079	1975	00002	..Treason
S-10-0080	1979	00000	.Pornographic Crime
S-10-0081	1979	00000	.Recidivism
S-10-0082	1979	00000	.Religious Offense
S-10-0083	1979	00000	.Violent Crime

S-11 CULTURE TYPE

S-11-0001	1975	00007	Culture Type
S-11-0002	1979	00000	.Civilization
S-11-0003	1979	00000	..African Civilization
S-11-0004	1979	00000	..Ancient Civilization
S-11-0005	1979	00000	..Byzantine Civilization
S-11-0006	1979	00000	..Eastern Civilization
S-11-0007	1979	00000	..Greek Civilization
S-11-0008	1979	00000	..Islamic Civilization
S-11-0009	1979	00000	..Roman Civilization
S-11-0010	1979	00000	..Western Civilization
S-11-0011	1975	00014	.Community Culture
S-11-0012	1975	00012	..Village Culture
S-11-0013	1975	00011	.Counter Culture
S-11-0014	1975	00010	.Drug Culture
S-11-0015	1975	00043	.Ethnic Culture
S-11-0016	1975	00014	..Black Culture
S-11-0017	1975	00007	.Heterogeneous Culture
S-11-0018	1975	00004	.Homogeneous Culture
S-11-0019	1979	00000	.Mass Culture
S-11-0020	1979	00000	..Popular Culture
S-11-0021	1975	00009	.Nonwestern Culture
S-11-0022	1975	00019	..Eastern Culture
S-11-0023	1975	00055	.Political Culture
S-11-0024	1975	00003	..Modern Political Culture
S-11-0025	1975	00002	...Political Professionalization
S-11-0026	1975	00001	...Political Secularization
S-11-0027	1975	00014	..National Political Culture
S-11-0028	1975	00007	...Civic Culture
S-11-0029	1975	00000	....Legalistic Political Culture
S-11-0030	1979	00000	....Parochial Political Culture
S-11-0031	1975	00003	....Pragmatic Political Culture
S-11-0032	1975	00002	....Secular Political Culture
S-11-0033	1975	00002	....Subject Participant Culture
S-11-0034	1975	00007	....Traditional Political Culture
S-11-0035	1975	00006	...Fragmented Political Culture
S-11-0036	1975	00013	...Generational Political Culture
S-11-0037	1975	00012	....Generation Gap
S-11-0038	1975	00012	...Ideological Political Culture
S-11-0039	1979	00000	...Political Subculture
S-11-0040	1975	00017	.Poverty Culture
S-11-0041	1975	00064	.Religious Culture
S-11-0042	1975	00008	.Secular Culture
S-11-0043	1979	00000	.Subculture
S-11-0044	1975	00014	.Technological Culture
S-11-0045	1975	00053	.Traditional Culture
S-11-0046	1975	00003	..Nomadic Culture
S-11-0047	1975	00028	..Peasant Culture
S-11-0048	1975	00029	.Urban Culture
S-11-0049	1975	00048	.Western Culture
S-11-0050	1979	00000	.Work Culture
S-11-0051	1979	00000	..Labor Discipline
S-11-0052	1979	00000	..Protestant Ethic
S-11-0053	1979	00000	..Work Ethic
S-11-0054	1975	00009	.Youth Culture

S-12 ECONOMY TYPE

S-12-0001	1979	00000	Economy Type
S-12-0002	1975	00025	.Agrarian Economy
S-12-0003	1975	00010	..Farm Economy
S-12-0004	1975	00006	...Collective Farm Economy
S-12-0005	1975	00002	...Cooperative Farm Economy
S-12-0006	1975	00003	...Family Farm Economy
S-12-0007	1975	00009	...Plantation Economy
S-12-0008	1975	00001	...Single Group Farm Economy
S-12-0009	1975	00002	...State Farm Economy
S-12-0010	1975	00001	.Balanced Economy
S-12-0011	1975	00001	.Barter Economy
S-12-0012	1979	00000	.Capital Investment Economy
S-12-0013	1979	00000	.Consumer Economy
S-12-0014	1979	00000	.Cottage Industry Economy
S-12-0015	1979	00000	..Craft Economy
S-12-0016	1975	00005	.Depressed Economy
S-12-0017	1975	00004	..Depressed Area
S-12-0018	1975	00011	.Developed Economy
S-12-0019	1975	00043	.Developing Economy
S-12-0020	1975	00004	.Dual Economy
S-12-0021	1975	00009	.Export Economy
S-12-0022	1979	00000	.Grants Economy
S-12-0023	1979	00000	.Hunting And Trapping Economy
S-12-0024	1975	00018	.Industrial Economy
S-12-0025	1979	00000	.Labor Intensive Economy
S-12-0026	1975	00031	.Market Economy
S-12-0027	1975	00030	..Capitalist Economy
S-12-0028	1975	00000	..Imperialist Economy
S-12-0029	1979	00000	..Socialist Market Economy
S-12-0030	1975	00004	.Mixed Economy
S-12-0031	1979	00000	.Modernizing Economy
S-12-0032	1975	00002	.Nomadic Economy
S-12-0033	1975	00026	.Peasant Economy
S-12-0034	1975	00004	.Planned Economy
S-12-0035	1979	00000	..Centrally Planned Economy
S-12-0036	1975	00003	...Command Economy
S-12-0037	1975	00004	..Corporate Economy
S-12-0038	1979	00000	...Fascist Economy
S-12-0039	1975	00001	..Nationalized Economy
S-12-0040	1975	00017	..Socialist Economy
S-12-0041	1975	00009	.Self Sufficient Economy
S-12-0042	1975	00004	..Autarchic Economy
S-12-0043	1975	00013	.Subsistence Economy
S-12-0044	1975	00030	.Underdeveloped Economy
S-12-0045	1975	00009	.War Economy
S-12-0046	1979	00000	.Welfare Economy
S-12-0047	1979	00000	.World Economy

S-13 EDUCATION TYPE

S-13-0001	1975	00014	Education Type
S-13-0002	1979	00000	.Adult Education
S-13-0003	1975	00004	.Alternative Education
S-13-0004	1975	00001	.Apprenticeship
S-13-0005	1975	00008	.Civic Education
S-13-0006	1975	00005	.Compulsory Education
S-13-0007	1975	00006	.Continuing Education
S-13-0008	1979	00000	.Foreign Language Education
S-13-0009	1979	00000	.Global Education

S-13-0010	1975	00087	.Higher Education
S-13-0011	1975	00025	..Graduate Education
S-13-0012	1975	00002	...Political Science Training
S-13-0013	1975	00002	..Pedagogical Institute Education
S-13-0014	1979	00000	...Teacher Education
S-13-0015	1975	00000	..Polytechnical Institute Education
S-13-0016	1975	00006	..Private Higher Education
S-13-0017	1975	00004	..State Supported Higher Education
S-13-0018	1975	00051	..University Education
S-13-0019	1979	00000	.Humanities Education
S-13-0020	1979	00000	..Classical Education
S-13-0021	1979	00000	..Liberal Arts Education
S-13-0022	1975	00003	...Humanistic Education
S-13-0023	1979	00000	.Informal Education
S-13-0024	1975	00012	.Mass Education
S-13-0025	1975	00015	.Military Education
S-13-0026	1975	00032	..Military Training
S-13-0027	1979	00000	.Natural Science Education
S-13-0028	1979	00000	.Outreach Education
S-13-0029	1975	00003	.Political Education
S-13-0030	1979	00000	..Communist Education
S-13-0031	1979	00000	..Fascist Education
S-13-0032	1975	00004	..Ideological Education
S-13-0033	1975	00007	..Socialist Education
S-13-0034	1975	00007	.Primary Education
S-13-0035	1975	00020	..Elementary Education
S-13-0036	1975	00002	.Private School Education
S-13-0037	1975	00041	.Professional Education
S-13-0038	1979	00000	..Business Administration Education
S-13-0039	1979	00000	..Health Education
S-13-0040	1975	00012	...Medical Education
S-13-0041	1979	00000	...Public Health Education
S-13-0042	1975	00006	..Legal Education
S-13-0043	1975	00007	.Progressive Education
S-13-0044	1979	00000	.Religious Education
S-13-0045	1975	00017	.Secondary Education
S-13-0046	1975	00001	.Self Taught Education
S-13-0047	1979	00000	.Sex Education
S-13-0048	1975	00011	.Technical Education
S-13-0049	1979	00000	..Agricultural Education
S-13-0050	1979	00000	..Manpower Training
S-13-0051	1975	00037	...Job Training
S-13-0052	1975	00012	...Vocational Education
S-13-0053	1975	00007	.Traditional Education
S-13-0054	1979	00000	..Urban Education

S-14 ELITE TYPE

S-14-0001	1975	00004	Elite Type
S-14-0002	1975	00012	.Academic Elite
S-14-0003	1975	00017	.Decision Making Elite
S-14-0004	1975	00007	.Economic Elite
S-14-0005	1975	00011	..Business Elite
S-14-0006	1975	00004	...Commercial Elite
S-14-0007	1979	00000	...Corporate Elite
S-14-0008	1979	00000	...Financial Elite
S-14-0009	1975	00023	.Governing Elite
S-14-0010	1975	00028	.Intellectual Elite
S-14-0011	1975	00008	..Cultural Elite
S-14-0012	1979	00000	...Artistic Elite
S-14-0013	1975	00044	...Literary Elite
S-14-0014	1975	00014	..Intelligentsia
S-14-0015	1975	00007	.Managerial Elite
S-14-0016	1975	00019	..Bureaucratic Elite
S-14-0017	1975	00023	.Military Elite
S-14-0018	1975	00005	.Modernizing Elite
S-14-0019	1975	00002	.Opinion Elite
S-14-0020	1975	00013	..Attentive Public
S-14-0021	1975	00005	.Pluralist Elite
S-14-0022	1975	00042	.Political Elite
S-14-0023	1975	00026	..Local Political Elite
S-14-0024	1975	00007	..Modernizing Political Elite
S-14-0025	1975	00032	..Policy Elite
S-14-0026	1975	00035	...Foreign Policy Elite
S-14-0027	1975	00002	..Potential Elite
S-14-0028	1975	00007	..Power Elite
S-14-0029	1975	00004	..Provincial Elite
S-14-0030	1975	00008	..Revolutionary Elite
S-14-0031	1975	00003	..Traditional Political Elite
S-14-0032	1975	00003	..Transitional Political Elite
S-14-0033	1975	00007	.Scientific Elite
S-14-0034	1975	00011	.Social Elite
S-14-0035	1975	00004	..Modernizing Social Elite
S-14-0036	1975	00008	..Religious Elite
S-14-0037	1975	00005	..Traditional Social Elite
S-14-0038	1975	00001	.Subnational Elite
S-14-0039	1975	00004	..Community Elite
S-14-0040	1975	00015	..Local Elite
S-14-0041	1975	00004	.Technological Elite

S-15 FREEDOM

S-15-0001	1975	00010	Freedom
S-15-0002	1975	00002	.Economic Freedom
S-15-0003	1975	00000	..Freedom Of Competition
S-15-0004	1975	00010	...Market Freedom
S-15-0005	1975	00002	..Freedom Of Contract
S-15-0006	1975	00000	...Right To Strike
S-15-0007	1975	00004	...Right To Work
S-15-0008	1975	00034	..Property Rights
S-15-0009	1979	00000	..Right To Job Security
S-15-0010	1975	00005	.Freedom Of Inquiry
S-15-0011	1975	00006	..Academic Freedom
S-15-0012	1975	00012	..Freedom Of Information
S-15-0013	1975	00007	..Scientific Freedom
S-15-0014	1979	00000	.Human Rights
S-15-0015	1975	00000	.Immunity
S-15-0016	1975	00000	..Citizenship Immunity
S-15-0017	1975	00003	...Citizenship Privilege
S-15-0018	1975	00001	..Diplomatic Immunity
S-15-0019	1975	00000	...Diplomatic Privilege
S-15-0020	1975	00000	..Executive Immunity
S-15-0021	1975	00005	..Legal Immunity
S-15-0022	1975	00000	..Legislative Immunity
S-15-0023	1975	00000	...Member Privilege
S-15-0024	1979	00000	..Political Asylum
S-15-0025	1975	00002	..Prosecution Immunity
S-15-0026	1975	00008	.Political Liberty
S-15-0027	1975	00079	..Civil Liberty
S-15-0028	1975	00002	...Freedom Of Association
S-15-0029	1975	00009	...Freedom Of Press
S-15-0030	1975	00007	...Freedom Of Religion
S-15-0031	1975	00017	...Freedom Of Speech
S-15-0032	1979	00000	...Freedom Of Thought
S-15-0033	1975	00000	...Freedom Of Travel
S-15-0034	1975	00002	...Right Of Assembly
S-15-0035	1975	00001	...Right Of Petition
S-15-0036	1975	00031	...Right Of Privacy
S-15-0037	1975	00002	...Right To Bear Arms
S-15-0038	1975	00077	..Civil Rights
S-15-0039	1975	00021	...Equal Rights
S-15-0040	1975	00016	....Minority Rights
S-15-0041	1975	00020	....Womens Rights
S-15-0042	1975	00009	..Procedural Rights
S-15-0043	1975	00011	...Defendants Rights
S-15-0044	1975	00000	....Bill Of Attainder

S-15-0045	1975	00001	....Double Jeopardy
S-15-0046	1975	00003	....Habeas Corpus
S-15-0047	1975	00002	....Right Against Cruel And Unusual Punishment
S-15-0048	1975	00000	....Right To Bail
S-15-0049	1975	00011	....Right To Due Process
S-15-0050	1975	00014	....Right To Equal Protection
S-15-0051	1975	00000	....Right To Trial
S-15-0052	1975	00000	.....Burden Of Proof
S-15-0053	1975	00000	.....Cross Examination
S-15-0054	1975	00003	.....Evidence Admissibility
S-15-0055	1979	00000	......Circumstantial Evidence
S-15-0056	1975	00000	.....Ex Post Facto Protection
S-15-0057	1975	00000	.....Grand Jury Indictment
S-15-0058	1975	00000	.....Right To Appeal
S-15-0059	1975	00003	.....Right To Counsel
S-15-0060	1975	00000	.....Right To Jury Trial
S-15-0061	1975	00000	.....Right To Speedy Trial
S-15-0062	1975	00002	.....Self Incrimination
S-15-0063	1975	00001	....Sanity Plea
S-15-0064	1975	00002	....Search And Seizure
S-15-0065	1975	00001	....Statute Of Limitations
S-15-0066	1975	00002	...Military Justice
S-15-0067	1975	00001	..Right Of Opposition
S-15-0068	1975	00014	...Civil Disobedience
S-15-0069	1975	00003	...Right Of Protest
S-15-0070	1975	00000	...Right Of Revolution
S-15-0071	1975	00001	...Right Of Secession
S-15-0072	1975	00032	..Social Rights
S-15-0073	1979	00000	...Childrens Rights
S-15-0074	1975	00030	...Health Care Rights
S-15-0075	1975	00007	...Housing Rights
S-15-0076	1975	00002	...Income Rights
S-15-0077	1979	00000	...Marriage Rights
S-15-0078	1979	00000	...Right To Die
S-15-0079	1979	00000	...Right To Education
S-15-0080	1979	00000	...Sexual Freedom
S-15-0081	1975	00005	..Voting Rights
S-15-0082	1975	00004	...Suffrage Equality
S-15-0083	1975	00000	...Voter Qualification
S-15-0084	1975	00000	....Property Voting Qualification
S-15-0085	1975	00000	....Registration Requirement
S-15-0086	1975	00003	....Residence Requirement
S-15-0087	1979	00000	....Voting Age Requirement

S-16 GOVERNMENT

S-16-0001	1975	00017	Government
S-16-0002	1975	00002	.Government Type
S-16-0003	1975	00003	..Absolutist Government
S-16-0004	1975	00002	..Autarchic Government
S-16-0005	1975	00003	..Autocratic Government
S-16-0006	1975	00001	..Cabinet Government
S-16-0007	1975	00027	..Centralized Government
S-16-0008	1975	00016	..Coalition Government
S-16-0009	1975	00149	..Communist Government
S-16-0010	1975	00027	..Decentralized Government
S-16-0011	1975	00024	..Democratic Government
S-16-0012	1975	00000	...Agrarian Democracy
S-16-0013	1975	00001	...Bourgeois Democracy
S-16-0014	1975	00003	...Consociational Democracy
S-16-0015	1975	00016	...Constitutional Democracy
S-16-0016	1975	00000	...Developed Democracy
S-16-0017	1975	00005	...Direct Democracy
S-16-0018	1975	00004	...Elitist Democracy
S-16-0019	1975	00000	...Guided Democracy
S-16-0020	1975	00007	...Majoritarian Democracy
S-16-0021	1975	00006	...Mass Democracy
S-16-0022	1975	00005	...Parliamentary Democracy
S-16-0023	1975	00011	...Participatory Democracy
S-16-0024	1979	00000	...Political Party Democracy
S-16-0025	1975	00002	....Multiparty Democracy
S-16-0026	1979	00000	....One Political Party Democracy
S-16-0027	1979	00000	....Two Political Party Democracy
S-16-0028	1975	00000	...Plebiscitary Democracy
S-16-0029	1975	00016	...Pluralist Democracy
S-16-0030	1975	00008	...Representative Democracy
S-16-0031	1975	00002	...Social Democracy
S-16-0032	1975	00008	...Socialist Democracy
S-16-0033	1975	00004	...Stable Democracy
S-16-0034	1975	00000	...Tutelary Democracy
S-16-0035	1975	00006	..Dictatorship
S-16-0036	1975	00002	...Benevolent Dictatorship
S-16-0037	1975	00000	...Bourgeois Dictatorship
S-16-0038	1975	00000	...Constitutional Dictatorship
S-16-0039	1975	00009	...Military Dictatorship
S-16-0040	1975	00002	...Modernizing Dictatorship
S-16-0041	1975	00000	...Progressive Dictatorship
S-16-0042	1975	00001	...Proletarian Dictatorship
S-16-0043	1975	00004	...Totalitarian Dictatorship
S-16-0044	1975	00003	..Extranational Government Structure
S-16-0045	1975	00016	...Colony
S-16-0046	1975	00017	....Former Colony
S-16-0047	1975	00000	....Proprietary Colony
S-16-0048	1975	00018	...Empire
S-16-0049	1975	00000	....Capitalist Empire
S-16-0050	1975	00015	....Colonial Empire
S-16-0051	1975	00002	....Communist Empire
S-16-0052	1975	00000	....World Empire
S-16-0053	1975	00000	...Extranational Commonwealth
S-16-0054	1975	00001	...International Trusteeship
S-16-0055	1975	00002	...Mandate Territory
S-16-0056	1975	00004	...Protectorate
S-16-0057	1975	00092	..Federal Government
S-16-0058	1975	00004	...Confederal Government
S-16-0059	1975	00002	..Feudal Government
S-16-0060	1975	00000	..Gerontocracy
S-16-0061	1979	00000	..Interim Government
S-16-0062	1979	00000	...Caretaker Government
S-16-0063	1975	00003	..International Government
S-16-0064	1975	00017	...Imperial Government
S-16-0065	1975	00006	...World Government
S-16-0066	1979	00000	..Limited Government
S-16-0067	1975	00000	..Matriarchic Government
S-16-0068	1975	00053	..Military Government
S-16-0069	1979	00000	...Military Occupation
S-16-0070	1975	00003	..Minority Government
S-16-0071	1975	00002	..Mixed Government
S-16-0072	1975	00013	..Monarchy
S-16-0073	1975	00001	...Absolute Monarchy
S-16-0074	1975	00002	...Constitutional Monarchy
S-16-0075	1975	00001	...Limited Monarchy
S-16-0076	1975	00001	...Republican Monarchy
S-16-0077	1975	00016	..National Government
S-16-0078	1975	00002	..Oligarchic Government
S-16-0079	1975	00007	..Parliamentary Government
S-16-0080	1979	00000	..Patriarchical Government
S-16-0081	1975	00000	..Plutocracy
S-16-0082	1975	00003	..Polyarchy
S-16-0083	1975	00008	..Presidential Government
S-16-0084	1975	00008	..Representative Government
S-16-0085	1975	00002	..Republic
S-16-0086	1975	00001	..Sheikdom
S-16-0087	1975	00018	..Socialist Government
S-16-0088	1975	00014	..Subnational Government
S-16-0089	1975	00014	...County Government

S-16-0090 1975 00000 ....County Manager Government
S-16-0091 1975 00001 ...District Government Type
S-16-0092 1975 00002 ....Fire District
S-16-0093 1975 00005 ....Recreation District
S-16-0094 1975 00019 ....School District
S-16-0095 1975 00000 ....Sewer District
S-16-0096 1975 00002 ....Transportation District
S-16-0097 1975 00000 ....Water District
S-16-0098 1975 00000 ....Zoning District
S-16-0099 1975 00097 ...Local Government
S-16-0100 1975 00000 ....Borough Government
S-16-0101 1975 00046 ....City Government
S-16-0102 1975 00001 .....City Council Government
S-16-0103 1975 00001 .....City Manager Government
S-16-0104 1975 00000 .....Commission Government
S-16-0105 1975 00002 .....Council Manager Government
S-16-0106 1975 00002 .....Strong Mayor Government
S-16-0107 1975 00001 .....Weak Mayor Government
S-16-0108 1975 00001 ....Township Government
S-16-0109 1975 00016 ...Metropolitan Government
S-16-0110 1975 00014 ....Provincial Government
S-16-0111 1975 00098 ...State Government
S-16-0112 1975 00059 ...Urban Government
S-16-0113 1975 00002 ..Unitary Government
S-16-0114 1975 00003 .Nation Type
S-16-0115 1975 00003 ..Aligned Nation
S-16-0116 1975 00001 ..Client Nation
S-16-0117 1975 00003 ..Debtor Nation
S-16-0118 1975 00068 ..Dependent Nation
S-16-0119 1975 00067 ..Developed Nation
S-16-0120 1975 00264 ..Developing Nation
S-16-0121 1979 00000 ..Divided Nation
S-16-0122 1979 00000 ..Fourth World Nation
S-16-0123 1975 00001 ..Hostile Nation
S-16-0124 1975 00009 ..Multiethnic Nation
S-16-0125 1975 00015 ..Nonaligned Nation
S-16-0126 1975 00031 ..Poor Nation
S-16-0127 1975 00012 ..Rich Nation
S-16-0128 1975 00003 ..Sovereign Nation
S-16-0129 1979 00000 ..Third World Nation
S-16-0130 1975 00073 ..Underdeveloped Nation
S-16-0131 1975 00010 .Regime Type
S-16-0132 1975 00006 ..Political Regime
S-16-0133 1975 00001 ...Ancient Regime
S-16-0134 1975 00035 ...Authoritarian Regime
S-16-0135 1975 00006 ....Modernizing Authoritarian Regime
S-16-0136 1975 00002 ...Conservative Regime
S-16-0137 1975 00005 ...Democratic Regime
S-16-0138 1975 00008 ...Dictatorial Regime
S-16-0139 1975 00000 ...Puppet Regime
S-16-0140 1975 00004 .Rule Type
S-16-0141 1975 00000 ..Despotism
S-16-0142 1975 00000 ...Benevolent Despotism
S-16-0143 1975 00002 ...Oriental Despotism
S-16-0144 1975 00000 ..Direct Rule
S-16-0145 1975 00003 ..Foreign Rule
S-16-0146 1975 00004 ..Home Rule
S-16-0147 1975 00001 ..Indirect Rule
S-16-0148 1975 00004 ..Military Directorate
S-16-0149 1975 00001 ..Revolutionary Directorate
S-16-0150 1975 00020 ..Technocracy
S-16-0151 1975 00003 ..Tyranny
S-16-0152 1975 00017 .Sovereignty
S-16-0153 1975 00003 ..Divided Sovereignty
S-16-0154 1975 00006 ..Limited Sovereignty
S-16-0155 1975 00001 ..Papal Sovereignty
S-16-0156 1975 00003 ..Popular Sovereignty
S-16-0157 1975 00024 ..Territory Sovereignty
S-16-0158 1975 00010 .State Type
S-16-0159 1975 00002 ..Aggressor State
S-16-0160 1975 00001 ..Border State
S-16-0161 1975 00000 ..City State
S-16-0162 1975 00002 ..Client State
S-16-0163 1975 00003 ..Corporate State
S-16-0164 1975 00003 ..Feudal State
S-16-0165 1975 00001 ..Garrison State
S-16-0166 1975 00004 ..Military State
S-16-0167 1975 00012 ..Multiethnic State
S-16-0168 1975 00011 ..Nation State
S-16-0169 1975 00000 ..Peoples Democratic State
S-16-0170 1975 00000 ..Police State
S-16-0171 1975 00000 ..Puppet State
S-16-0172 1975 00001 ..Warfare State
S-16-0173 1975 00012 ..Welfare State

S-17 INDUSTRY

S-17-0001 1975 00010 Industry
S-17-0002 1975 00005 .Chemical Industry
S-17-0003 1979 00000 ..Agrochemical Industry
S-17-0004 1979 00000 ..Rubber Industry
S-17-0005 1979 00000 ..Synthetics Industry
S-17-0006 1975 00008 .Communication Industry
S-17-0007 1975 00011 ..Broadcasting Industry
S-17-0008 1975 00012 ...Commercial Broadcasting Industry
S-17-0009 1975 00006 ...Public Broadcasting Industry
S-17-0010 1975 00009 ...Radio Industry
S-17-0011 1975 00095 ...Television Industry
S-17-0012 1979 00000 ....Cable Television
S-17-0013 1979 00000 ....Commercial Television
S-17-0014 1979 00000 ....Public Television
S-17-0015 1979 00000 ....State Controlled Television
S-17-0016 1975 00004 ..News Agency
S-17-0017 1975 00019 ..Publication Industry
S-17-0018 1975 00013 ...Book Industry
S-17-0019 1975 00008 ...Magazine Industry
S-17-0020 1975 00017 ...Newspaper Industry
S-17-0021 1975 00001 ....Black Press
S-17-0022 1975 00009 ....National Press
S-17-0023 1975 00001 ....Radical Press
S-17-0024 1975 00001 ....Underground Press
S-17-0025 1975 00015 ..Telecommunications Industry
S-17-0026 1975 00003 ..Telephone Industry
S-17-0027 1975 00005 .Construction Industry
S-17-0028 1979 00000 ..Building Supplies Industry
S-17-0029 1975 00019 ..Housing Industry
S-17-0030 1979 00000 ..Ship Building Industry
S-17-0031 1975 00010 .Consumer Industry
S-17-0032 1975 00000 ..Dairy Industry
S-17-0033 1975 00006 ..Farm Industry
S-17-0034 1975 00019 ..Fishing Industry
S-17-0035 1975 00004 .Defense Industry
S-17-0036 1975 00006 ..Aerospace Industry
S-17-0037 1979 00000 ..Arms Industry
S-17-0038 1979 00000 .Energy Industry
S-17-0039 1979 00000 ..Electrical Industry
S-17-0040 1979 00000 ..Nuclear Energy Industry
S-17-0041 1975 00013 .Extractive Industry
S-17-0042 1979 00000 ..Coal Industry
S-17-0043 1975 00004 ..Forestry Industry
S-17-0044 1979 00000 ...Lumber Industry
S-17-0045 1979 00000 ..Gas Industry
S-17-0046 1975 00131 ..Oil Industry
S-17-0047 1975 00006 ..Ore Industry
S-17-0048 1975 00071 .Food Industry
S-17-0049 1975 00001 .Infant Industry

S-17-0050	1975	00003	.Nationalized Industry
S-17-0051	1975	00012	.Private Industry
S-17-0052	1975	00003	.Production Industry
S-17-0053	1975	00001	..Heavy Industry
S-17-0054	1975	00005	...Steel Industry
S-17-0055	1975	00037	..Manufacturing Industry
S-17-0056	1975	00004	...Light Industry
S-17-0057	1979	00000	....Appliance Industry
S-17-0058	1975	00002	....Cottage Industry
S-17-0059	1979	00000	...Machinery Industry
S-17-0060	1979	00000	...Paper Industry
S-17-0061	1979	00000	...Textile Industry
S-17-0062	1979	00000	....Clothing Industry
S-17-0063	1979	00000	..Metallurgical Industry
S-17-0064	1975	00002	.Protected Industry
S-17-0065	1975	00006	.Public Utility Industry
S-17-0066	1979	00000	.Service Industry
S-17-0067	1979	00000	..Advertising Industry
S-17-0068	1975	00003	..Sanitation Industry
S-17-0069	1975	00011	..Tourist Industry
S-17-0070	1975	00016	.Transportation Industry
S-17-0071	1975	00012	..Air Transportation Industry
S-17-0072	1979	00000	...Aircraft Industry
S-17-0073	1975	00012	..Land Transportation Industry
S-17-0074	1975	00005	...Motor Vehicle Industry
S-17-0075	1979	00000	....Automobile Industry
S-17-0076	1979	00000	....Trucking Industry
S-17-0077	1975	00013	...Railway Industry
S-17-0078	1975	00006	..Mass Transportation Industry
S-17-0079	1975	00017	..Water Transportation Industry
S-17-0080	1979	00000	...Shipping Industry

S-18 INFORMATION SOURCES

S-18-0001	1975	00048	Information Sources
S-18-0002	1975	00004	.Archives
S-18-0003	1975	00014	..Data Bank
S-18-0004	1975	00013	...Data Archives
S-18-0005	1975	00001	..National Archives
S-18-0006	1975	00009	.Confidential Information
S-18-0007	1975	00003	.Documents
S-18-0008	1975	00001	..Commission Record
S-18-0009	1975	00002	..Committee Record
S-18-0010	1975	00019	..Employment Record
S-18-0011	1975	00007	..Financial Record
S-18-0012	1975	00007	...Budget Record
S-18-0013	1975	00016	...Expenditure Record
S-18-0014	1975	00009	...Income Record
S-18-0015	1979	00000	...Political Party Financial Record
S-18-0016	1975	00004	...Revenue Record
S-18-0017	1975	00000	....Tariff Record
S-18-0018	1975	00001	....Tax Record
S-18-0019	1975	00007	..Government Document
S-18-0020	1975	00001	...Administrative Record
S-18-0021	1975	00017	....Census Record
S-18-0022	1975	00001	....Proclamation
S-18-0023	1975	00004	....Regulatory Agency Record
S-18-0024	1975	00000	....Veto Message
S-18-0025	1975	00001	...Intergovernmental Document
S-18-0026	1975	00003	....Domestic Intergovernmental Document
S-18-0027	1975	00001	....Foreign Intergovernmental Document
S-18-0028	1975	00000	.....Trade Document
S-18-0029	1975	00001	.....Treaty Document
S-18-0030	1975	00012	...Judicial Record
S-18-0031	1975	00000	....Court Report
S-18-0032	1975	00002	....Court Transcript
S-18-0033	1975	00002	...Legislative Record
S-18-0034	1975	00005	....Legislative Voting Record
S-18-0035	1975	00006	.....Legislative Roll Call Record
S-18-0036	1975	00000	....Parliamentary Paper
S-18-0037	1975	00003	.....White Paper
S-18-0038	1975	00003	...Licensing Record
S-18-0039	1975	00041	..International Organization Record
S-18-0040	1975	00004	..Political Party Record
S-18-0041	1975	00000	..Pronouncement
S-18-0042	1975	00007	..Public Record
S-18-0043	1979	00000	.Essay
S-18-0044	1979	00000	.Encyclopedia
S-18-0045	1979	00000	.Folk Literature
S-18-0046	1975	00002	.Information Service
S-18-0047	1975	00000	..Abstracting Service
S-18-0048	1975	00009	..Bibliographic Service
S-18-0049	1979	00000	...Bibliographic Control
S-18-0050	1975	00002	..Documentation Service
S-18-0051	1979	00000	..Government Information Service
S-18-0052	1979	00000	...Legislative Information Service
S-18-0053	1979	00000	..Private Information Service
S-18-0054	1979	00000	..University Information Service
S-18-0055	1979	00000	.Journal
S-18-0056	1975	00008	.Library
S-18-0057	1979	00000	.Literature Review
S-18-0058	1975	00002	.Machine Readable Information
S-18-0059	1975	00007	..Machine Readable Data
S-18-0060	1975	00001	..Software
S-18-0061	1975	00002	...Information Retrieval Program
S-18-0062	1975	00001	.Monographs
S-18-0063	1979	00000	..Autobiography
S-18-0064	1979	00000	..Biography
S-18-0065	1975	00052	..Political Literature
S-18-0066	1975	00082	...Political Biography
S-18-0067	1975	00004	....Political Autobiography
S-18-0068	1975	00007	...Political Fiction
S-18-0069	1975	00004	...Political Memoir
S-18-0070	1975	00000	.Newsletters
S-18-0071	1975	00020	.Newspapers
S-18-0072	1979	00000	.Novel
S-18-0073	1975	00000	.Obituaries
S-18-0074	1979	00000	.Poetry
S-18-0075	1975	00001	.Political Film
S-18-0076	1975	00002	.Privileged Information
S-18-0077	1979	00000	.Short Story
S-18-0078	1975	00005	.Speeches
S-18-0079	1975	00010	.Statistical Data
S-18-0080	1975	00006	..Aggregate Data Statistics
S-18-0081	1975	00007	..Economic Statistics
S-18-0082	1975	00019	...Wage Statistics
S-18-0083	1979	00000	..Field Data
S-18-0084	1975	00000	..Political Statistics
S-18-0085	1975	00023	...Electoral Data
S-18-0086	1979	00000	...Macropolitical Data
S-18-0087	1975	00020	...Voting Data
S-18-0088	1975	00003	..Social Statistics
S-18-0089	1975	00036	...Ethnographic Data
S-18-0090	1975	00025	...Morbidity Data
S-18-0091	1975	00036	...Social Psychological Data
S-18-0092	1975	00035	...Socioeconomic Data
S-18-0093	1975	00006	...Vital Statistics Data
S-18-0094	1975	00003	..Statistical Table
S-18-0095	1975	00033	..Survey Data
S-18-0096	1979	00000	...Cross Cultural Data
S-18-0097	1975	00088	...Public Opinion Survey
S-18-0098	1979	00000	....Mass Public Opinion
S-18-0099	1979	00000	..Test Results
S-18-0100	1979	00000	.Surveillance
S-18-0101	1979	00000	..Spying
S-18-0102	1979	00000	.Textbook

Code	Year	Count	Term
S-18-0103	1979	00000	.Thesaurus
S-18-0104	1975	00000	.Thesis

S-19 INSTITUTIONS

Code	Year	Count	Term
S-19-0001	1975	00006	Institutions
S-19-0002	1975	00015	.Agencies
S-19-0003	1975	00004	..Agricultural Agency
S-19-0004	1975	00000	...Agricultural Advisory Board
S-19-0005	1975	00001	..Business Agency
S-19-0006	1975	00011	...Business Regulation Agency
S-19-0007	1975	00001	....Antitrust Agency
S-19-0008	1975	00000	..Censorship Agency
S-19-0009	1975	00003	...Government Censorship Agency
S-19-0010	1975	00000	..Consumer Agency
S-19-0011	1975	00001	...Consumer Advisory Board
S-19-0012	1975	00003	...Consumer Protection Agency
S-19-0013	1975	00006	..Cultural Agency
S-19-0014	1975	00001	...Cultural Advisory Board
S-19-0015	1975	00009	..Economic Agency
S-19-0016	1975	00000	...Economic Advisory Board
S-19-0017	1975	00006	...Economic Control Agency
S-19-0018	1975	00003	....Price Control Agency
S-19-0019	1975	00000	....Price Support Agency
S-19-0020	1975	00000	....Rationing Agency
S-19-0021	1975	00004	...Fiscal Agency
S-19-0022	1975	00003	....Appropriation Agency
S-19-0023	1975	00010	....Budget Agency
S-19-0024	1975	00002	....Monetary Agency
S-19-0025	1975	00013	.....Banking Agency
S-19-0026	1975	00002	....Public Treasury
S-19-0027	1975	00003	....Revenue Agency
S-19-0028	1975	00001	....Tax Agency
S-19-0029	1975	00003	...Labor Relations Agency
S-19-0030	1975	00003	...Production Agency
S-19-0031	1975	00001	....Trade Agency
S-19-0032	1975	00013	..Education Agency
S-19-0033	1975	00000	...Board Of Regents
S-19-0034	1975	00000	...Board Of Trustees
S-19-0035	1975	00001	...Education Accreditation Agency
S-19-0036	1975	00002	...Examination Agency
S-19-0037	1975	00008	...Scholarship Agency
S-19-0038	1975	00007	...School Board
S-19-0039	1975	00006	..Environmental Agency
S-19-0040	1975	00002	...Environmental Advisory Agency
S-19-0041	1975	00008	...Environmental Control Agency
S-19-0042	1975	00009	..Foreign Affairs Agency
S-19-0043	1975	00000	...Foreign Policy Advisory Board
S-19-0044	1979	00000	..Government Agency
S-19-0045	1975	00002	..Information Agency
S-19-0046	1975	00004	...Communication Agency
S-19-0047	1975	00001	....Broadcasting Agency
S-19-0048	1975	00001	....Publication Agency
S-19-0049	1975	00001	....Telephone Agency
S-19-0050	1975	00001	...Foreign Information Agency
S-19-0051	1975	00016	..Intelligence Agency
S-19-0052	1975	00000	...Military Intelligence Agency
S-19-0053	1975	00002	...Secret Service
S-19-0054	1975	00028	..International Agency
S-19-0055	1975	00000	..Judicial Administration Agency
S-19-0056	1975	00000	...Police Board
S-19-0057	1975	00004	..Justice Administration Agency
S-19-0058	1975	00005	..Military Agency
S-19-0059	1975	00010	...Defense Agency
S-19-0060	1975	00003	....Arms Control Agency
S-19-0061	1975	00010	..Planning Agency
S-19-0062	1979	00000	..Testing Agency
S-19-0063	1975	00007	..Transportation Agency
S-19-0064	1975	00015	..Welfare Agency
S-19-0065	1975	00013	...Health Care Agency
S-19-0066	1975	00000	.Authorities
S-19-0067	1979	00000	..Interstate Authorities
S-19-0068	1975	00008	..Municipal Authorities
S-19-0069	1975	00005	..Public Authorities
S-19-0070	1975	00033	.Bureaucracy
S-19-0071	1975	00000	..Economic Bureaucracy
S-19-0072	1975	00001	...Corporate Bureaucracy
S-19-0073	1979	00000	..Merit Bureaucracy
S-19-0074	1975	00031	..Public Bureaucracy
S-19-0075	1975	00034	...Government Bureaucracy
S-19-0076	1975	00001	....International Government Bureaucracy
S-19-0077	1975	00050	....National Government Bureaucracy
S-19-0078	1979	00000	....Patronage Bureaucracy
S-19-0079	1975	00007	....Subnational Government Bureaucracy
S-19-0080	1975	00010	.....Local Government Bureaucracy
S-19-0081	1975	00002	..Religious Bureaucracy
S-19-0082	1975	00001	.Commissions
S-19-0083	1975	00005	..Federal Commission
S-19-0084	1979	00000	...Interstate Commerce Commission
S-19-0085	1979	00000	..Investigation Commission
S-19-0086	1975	00001	...Commission Of Inquiry
S-19-0087	1975	00001	....Legislative Commission Of Inquiry
S-19-0088	1979	00000	.....Congressional Investigation Committee
S-19-0089	1975	00000	.....Parliamentary Commission Of Inquiry
S-19-0090	1975	00002	....Presidential Commission Of Inquiry
S-19-0091	1975	00002	....Royal Commission Of Inquiry
S-19-0092	1975	00001	...Crime Commission
S-19-0093	1975	00005	..Legislative Commission
S-19-0094	1975	00002	..Planning Commission
S-19-0095	1975	00010	...International Planning Commission
S-19-0096	1975	00001	...National Planning Commission
S-19-0097	1975	00002	...Subnational Planning Commission
S-19-0098	1975	00002	....Local Planning Commission
S-19-0099	1975	00001	.....City Planning Commission
S-19-0100	1975	00003	..Presidential Commission
S-19-0101	1975	00022	..Regulatory Commission
S-19-0102	1975	00007	...Independent Regulatory Commission
S-19-0103	1975	00003	.Constitutional Convention
S-19-0104	1975	00001	..International Constitutional Convention
S-19-0105	1975	00001	..National Constitutional Convention
S-19-0106	1975	00005	..State Constitutional Convention
S-19-0107	1975	00000	.Councils
S-19-0108	1975	00001	..Economic Council
S-19-0109	1975	00002	..International Government Council
S-19-0110	1975	00002	..National Government Council
S-19-0111	1975	00003	...Cabinet
S-19-0112	1975	00000	....Cabinet Committee
S-19-0113	1975	00001	....Ministerial Committee
S-19-0114	1975	00000	....Shadow Cabinet
S-19-0115	1975	00004	...Council Of Ministers
S-19-0116	1975	00006	...Presidential Advisory Council
S-19-0117	1975	00002	...Privy Council
S-19-0118	1975	00001	..Subnational Government Council
S-19-0119	1975	00004	...Local Government Council
S-19-0120	1975	00001	....City Council
S-19-0121	1975	00000	....Town Council
S-19-0122	1975	00000	.....Town Meeting
S-19-0123	1975	00000	....Village Council
S-19-0124	1975	00006	.Courts
S-19-0125	1975	00001	..Administrative Court
S-19-0126	1975	00000	...Administrative Tribunal
S-19-0127	1975	00000	...Tax Court
S-19-0128	1975	00005	..Civil Court
S-19-0129	1975	00000	...Common Law Court
S-19-0130	1975	00001	...Family Court
S-19-0131	1975	00000	...Housing Court

S-19-0132	1975	00003	...Juvenile Court
S-19-0133	1975	00001	...Probate Court
S-19-0134	1975	00001	..Colonial Court
S-19-0135	1975	00007	..Constitutional Court
S-19-0136	1975	00006	...Appellate Court
S-19-0137	1975	00009	...District Court
S-19-0138	1975	00061	...Supreme Court
S-19-0139	1975	00050	....National Supreme Court
S-19-0140	1975	00000	....Subnational Supreme Court
S-19-0141	1975	00007	.....State Supreme Court
S-19-0142	1975	00005	..Criminal Court
S-19-0143	1975	00003	...Trial Court
S-19-0144	1975	00009	..International Court
S-19-0145	1975	00001	...International Tribunal
S-19-0146	1975	00002	...World Court
S-19-0147	1975	00003	..Jury
S-19-0148	1975	00000	...Grand Jury
S-19-0149	1975	00000	...Trial Jury
S-19-0150	1975	00003	..Local Court
S-19-0151	1975	00000	...County Level Court
S-19-0152	1975	00000	...Municipal Court
S-19-0153	1975	00000	...Peoples Court
S-19-0154	1975	00000	..Maritime Court
S-19-0155	1975	00000	..Military Court
S-19-0156	1975	00001	...Military Tribunal
S-19-0157	1979	00000	.Day Care Center
S-19-0158	1975	00008	.Economic Institution
S-19-0159	1975	00015	..Business
S-19-0160	1975	00007	...Big Business
S-19-0161	1975	00003	...Ghetto Business
S-19-0162	1975	00011	...Small Business
S-19-0163	1975	00028	..Corporation
S-19-0164	1975	00025	...Cartel
S-19-0165	1975	00002	...Economic Conglomerate
S-19-0166	1975	00000	...Holding Company
S-19-0167	1975	00019	...International Corporation
S-19-0168	1975	00002	....Foreign Subsidiary
S-19-0169	1975	00065	....Multinational Corporation
S-19-0170	1975	00009	...Public Corporation
S-19-0171	1975	00007	...Quasipublic Corporation
S-19-0172	1975	00001	..Enterprise
S-19-0173	1975	00002	...Government Enterprise
S-19-0174	1975	00003	....Government Agricultural Enterprise
S-19-0175	1975	00000	....Government Production Enterprise
S-19-0176	1975	00000	...Mixed Enterprise
S-19-0177	1975	00005	..Factory
S-19-0178	1979	00000	..Fiscal Institution
S-19-0179	1975	00010	..Market
S-19-0180	1975	00003	...Black Market
S-19-0181	1975	00020	...Commodity Market
S-19-0182	1975	00029	....International Commodity Market
S-19-0183	1975	00020	...Common Market
S-19-0184	1975	00012	...Consumer Market
S-19-0185	1975	00001	...Differentiated Market
S-19-0186	1975	00013	...Domestic Market
S-19-0187	1975	00013	...Export Market
S-19-0188	1975	00017	...Financial Market
S-19-0189	1975	00002	....Foreign Capital Market
S-19-0190	1975	00005	...Free Market
S-19-0191	1979	00000	..International Market
S-19-0192	1975	00010	...Marketplace
S-19-0193	1975	00003	...Mass Market
S-19-0194	1975	00003	...National Market
S-19-0195	1975	00003	....Internal Market
S-19-0196	1975	00004	...Stock Market
S-19-0197	1975	00014	...World Market
S-19-0198	1979	00000	..Monetary Institution
S-19-0199	1979	00000	...World Bank
S-19-0200	1975	00045	.Education Institution
S-19-0201	1975	00050	..Higher Education Institution
S-19-0202	1975	00002	...Academy Of Science
S-19-0203	1975	00048	...College
S-19-0204	1975	00003	....Community College
S-19-0205	1975	00002	....Junior College
S-19-0206	1975	00003	....Private College
S-19-0207	1975	00001	....State Supported College
S-19-0208	1975	00000	...Higher Party School
S-19-0209	1975	00003	...Military Institute
S-19-0210	1975	00001	...Pedagogical Institute
S-19-0211	1975	00000	...Polytechnical Institute
S-19-0212	1975	00080	...University
S-19-0213	1975	00007	....Graduate School
S-19-0214	1979	00000	....Open University
S-19-0215	1975	00005	....Private University
S-19-0216	1979	00000	....Public University
S-19-0217	1975	00002	.....State Supported University
S-19-0218	1975	00015	...Professional School
S-19-0219	1975	00009	....Law School
S-19-0220	1975	00012	..Neighborhood School
S-19-0221	1975	00016	..Primary School
S-19-0222	1975	00003	..Private School
S-19-0223	1975	00032	..Public School
S-19-0224	1975	00001	..Religious School
S-19-0225	1975	00004	...Parochial School
S-19-0226	1975	00020	..Secondary School
S-19-0227	1975	00018	...High School
S-19-0228	1975	00002	...Middle School
S-19-0229	1975	00021	..Urban School
S-19-0230	1975	00009	...Inner City School
S-19-0231	1975	00000	..Vocational Training School
S-19-0232	1975	00002	.Executive Government Institution
S-19-0233	1975	00000	..Chancellery
S-19-0234	1975	00000	..Fascist Council
S-19-0235	1975	00000	..Governorship
S-19-0236	1975	00001	..Military Executive Council
S-19-0237	1975	00000	..Plural Executive
S-19-0238	1975	00000	..Premiership
S-19-0239	1975	00044	..Presidency
S-19-0240	1979	00000	...Imperial Presidency
S-19-0241	1975	00002	..Secretariat
S-19-0242	1975	00016	.Health Care Institution
S-19-0243	1979	00000	..Halfway House
S-19-0244	1975	00007	..Health Clinic
S-19-0245	1975	00000	...Neighborhood Clinic
S-19-0246	1975	00014	..Hospital
S-19-0247	1979	00000	...Private Hospital
S-19-0248	1975	00006	...Public Hospital
S-19-0249	1979	00000	..Mental Institution
S-19-0250	1979	00000	..Nursing Home
S-19-0251	1979	00000	..Public Health Institution
S-19-0252	1975	00015	.Legislatures
S-19-0253	1975	00002	..Legislature Type
S-19-0254	1975	00004	...Bicameral Legislature
S-19-0255	1975	00001	...Unicameral Legislature
S-19-0256	1975	00019	..National Legislature
S-19-0257	1975	00059	...Congress
S-19-0258	1975	00006	....Congressional System
S-19-0259	1975	00005	.....Congressional Agency
S-19-0260	1975	00002	.....Congressional Caucus
S-19-0261	1975	00014	.....Congressional Committee System
S-19-0262	1975	00014	......Congressional Committee
S-19-0263	1979	00000	.......Ad Hoc Congressional Committee
S-19-0264	1975	00003	.......Congressional Subcommittee
S-19-0265	1979	00000	.......Joint Congressional Committee
S-19-0266	1979	00000	.......Standing Congressional Committee
S-19-0267	1979	00000	........Joint Standing Congressional Committee

S-19-0268	1975	00002	......Senate House Conference Committee
S-19-0269	1975	00000	.....Congressional Delegation
S-19-0270	1975	00007	.....Congressional Seniority System
S-19-0271	1979	00000	....House Of Representatives
S-19-0272	1979	00000	....Senate
S-19-0273	1975	00003	...National Assembly
S-19-0274	1975	00001	....Diet
S-19-0275	1975	00000	....Peoples Assembly
S-19-0276	1975	00000	....Popular Assembly
S-19-0277	1975	00007	...Parliament
S-19-0278	1979	00000	...Parliamentary Committee System
S-19-0279	1975	00004	....Parliamentary Committee
S-19-0280	1975	00001	....Parliamentary Faction
S-19-0281	1975	00007	..Subnational Legislature
S-19-0282	1975	00001	...Local Legislature
S-19-0283	1975	00000	...Provincial Parliament
S-19-0284	1975	00041	...State Legislature
S-19-0285	1975	00003	....State Assembly
S-19-0286	1975	00006	....State House Of Representatives
S-19-0287	1975	00002	....State Senate
S-19-0288	1975	00004	.Military Industrial Complex
S-19-0289	1975	00009	.Multinational Organization
S-19-0290	1979	00000	.Nonprofit Institution
S-19-0291	1975	00011	.Penal Institution
S-19-0292	1975	00012	..Correctional Institution
S-19-0293	1979	00000	...Jail
S-19-0294	1979	00000	...Juvenile Center
S-19-0295	1979	00000	..Detention Center
S-19-0296	1975	00002	...Concentration Camp
S-19-0297	1975	00001	...Prisoner Of War Camp
S-19-0298	1975	00000	...Slave Labor Camp
S-19-0299	1975	00010	..Prison
S-19-0300	1975	00007	...Criminal Prison
S-19-0301	1975	00000	...Military Prison
S-19-0302	1975	00029	.Police
S-19-0303	1975	00000	..International Police
S-19-0304	1975	00000	..Military Police
S-19-0305	1975	00006	..National Police
S-19-0306	1975	00000	..Paramilitary Police
S-19-0307	1975	00000	..Private Police
S-19-0308	1975	00002	..Secret Police
S-19-0309	1975	00004	..Subnational Police
S-19-0310	1975	00030	...Local Police
S-19-0311	1975	00001	...State Police
S-19-0312	1975	00000	.Political Party Institution
S-19-0313	1979	00000	..Political Party Campaign
S-19-0314	1975	00001	..Political Party Caucus
S-19-0315	1975	00000	..Political Party Committee
S-19-0316	1975	00001	...Political Party Central Committee
S-19-0317	1975	00003	...Political Party Executive Committee
S-19-0318	1979	00000	...Political Party Financial Committee
S-19-0319	1979	00000	...Political Party National Committee
S-19-0320	1975	00005	...Political Party Politburo
S-19-0321	1975	00002	...Political Party Secretariat
S-19-0322	1975	00000	...Political Party State Committee
S-19-0323	1975	00013	..Political Party Convention
S-19-0324	1975	00017	.Research Institution
S-19-0325	1975	00004	..Research Council
S-19-0326	1975	00011	..Research Unit
S-19-0327	1975	00008	...Research Center
S-19-0328	1975	00002	...Research Laboratory
S-19-0329	1975	00001	.Task Force
S-19-0330	1975	00001	..Presidential Task Force

S-20 KINSHIP

S-20-0001	1975	00018	Kinship
S-20-0002	1975	00018	.Family Descent Pattern
S-20-0003	1975	00001	..Bilateral Family Descent Pattern
S-20-0004	1975	00003	..Matrilineal Family Descent Pattern
S-20-0005	1975	00006	..Patrilineal Family Descent Pattern
S-20-0006	1975	00063	.Family Type
S-20-0007	1975	00000	..Atomistic Family
S-20-0008	1975	00000	..Communal Family
S-20-0009	1975	00000	..Concubinage
S-20-0010	1975	00008	..Extended Family
S-20-0011	1975	00000	..Kindred Family
S-20-0012	1975	00004	..Matriarchal Family
S-20-0013	1975	00025	..Nuclear Family
S-20-0014	1975	00003	..Paternalistic Family
S-20-0015	1975	00001	..Patrilineal Family
S-20-0016	1975	00002	..Stem Family
S-20-0017	1975	00033	.Kinship System
S-20-0018	1975	00001	..Extended Kinship System
S-20-0019	1975	00001	...Clan Kinship System
S-20-0020	1975	00003	...Matriarchal Kinship System
S-20-0021	1975	00005	...Patriarchal Kinship System
S-20-0022	1975	00074	.Marriage Type
S-20-0023	1975	00007	..Intermarriage
S-20-0024	1975	00001	..Monogamy
S-20-0025	1975	00000	...Serial Monogamy
S-20-0026	1975	00001	..Polygamy
S-20-0027	1975	00000	...Polyandry
S-20-0028	1975	00001	...Polygyny

S-21 LAW TYPE

S-21-0001	1975	00006	Law Type
S-21-0002	1975	00006	.Administrative Law
S-21-0003	1975	00000	.Basic Law
S-21-0004	1975	00000	..City Charter
S-21-0005	1975	00000	...Colonial Charter
S-21-0006	1975	00009	..Constitution
S-21-0007	1975	00051	...Constitutional Law
S-21-0008	1975	00012	....Constitutional Amendment
S-21-0009	1975	00009	.....Bill Of Rights
S-21-0010	1975	00000	...Democratic Constitution
S-21-0011	1975	00009	...National Constitution
S-21-0012	1975	00013	....Federal Constitution
S-21-0013	1975	00001	....Unitary Constitution
S-21-0014	1975	00002	...State Constitution
S-21-0015	1975	00000	...Unwritten Constitution
S-21-0016	1975	00001	...Written Constitution
S-21-0017	1975	00011	.Civil Law
S-21-0018	1975	00003	..Civil Code
S-21-0019	1975	00010	.Commercial Law
S-21-0020	1975	00011	.Common Law
S-21-0021	1975	00000	..Case Law
S-21-0022	1975	00004	..Judge Made Law
S-21-0023	1975	00012	.Contract Law
S-21-0024	1979	00000	..Negligence Law
S-21-0025	1979	00000	..Tort
S-21-0026	1975	00025	.Criminal Law
S-21-0027	1979	00000	..Death Penalty Law
S-21-0028	1975	00003	..Penal Law
S-21-0029	1975	00006	.Customary Law
S-21-0030	1979	00000	.Decriminalization
S-21-0031	1975	00004	.Economic Law
S-21-0032	1975	00009	..Antitrust Law
S-21-0033	1975	00004	..Bankruptcy Law
S-21-0034	1979	00000	..Consumer Protection Law
S-21-0035	1979	00000	..Industrial Safety Law
S-21-0036	1979	00000	...Mine Safety Law
S-21-0037	1975	00011	..Labor Law
S-21-0038	1975	00005	...Fair Employment Law
S-21-0039	1975	00001	...Minimum Wage Law

S-21-0040	1975	00003	...Pension Law
S-21-0041	1975	00002	...Right To Work Law
S-21-0042	1975	00004	..Patent Law
S-21-0043	1975	00004	..Price Control Law
S-21-0044	1979	00000	..Property Law
S-21-0045	1975	00004	..Tax Code
S-21-0046	1975	00014	..Tax Law
S-21-0047	1975	00003	...National Tax Law
S-21-0048	1975	00002	..Trade Union Law
S-21-0049	1975	00003	..Welfare Law
S-21-0050	1975	00003	..Zoning Law
S-21-0051	1975	00002	...Building Code
S-21-0052	1975	00005	...Housing Code
S-21-0053	1979	00000	.Environmental Law
S-21-0054	1979	00000	..Conservation Law
S-21-0055	1979	00000	..Historical Preservation Law
S-21-0056	1975	00006	.Equity Law
S-21-0057	1975	00068	.International Law
S-21-0058	1979	00000	..Law Of The Sea
S-21-0059	1975	00002	..World Law
S-21-0060	1975	00032	.Maritime Law
S-21-0061	1975	00008	.Martial Law
S-21-0062	1975	00005	.Military Law
S-21-0063	1975	00000	..Uniform Code Of Military Justice
S-21-0064	1975	00011	.Natural Law
S-21-0065	1975	00005	.Outer Space Law
S-21-0066	1975	00001	.Political Law
S-21-0067	1975	00002	..Admiralty Law
S-21-0068	1975	00016	..Electoral Law
S-21-0069	1975	00002	...Suffrage Law
S-21-0070	1975	00000	...Voter Registration Law
S-21-0071	1975	00000	..Enabling Law
S-21-0072	1975	00000	..Home Rule Law
S-21-0073	1975	00000	..Sedition Law
S-21-0074	1979	00000	..Sunset Law
S-21-0075	1979	00000	..Sunshine Law
S-21-0076	1975	00002	.Procedural Law
S-21-0077	1975	00003	..Civil Procedure Law
S-21-0078	1975	00008	..Criminal Procedure Law
S-21-0079	1975	00000	..Parliamentary Procedure Law
S-21-0080	1975	00002	.Sacred Law
S-21-0081	1975	00003	..Religious Law
S-21-0082	1975	00000	...Canon Law
S-21-0083	1975	00001	...Church Law
S-21-0084	1975	00007	.Social Law
S-21-0085	1975	00024	..Abortion Law
S-21-0086	1979	00000	..Blue Law
S-21-0087	1975	00010	..Family Law
S-21-0088	1979	00000	..Gambling Law
S-21-0089	1975	00007	..Gun Control Law
S-21-0090	1975	00002	..Jim Crow Law
S-21-0091	1979	00000	..Marital Law
S-21-0092	1979	00000	...Divorce Law
S-21-0093	1975	00001	..Minority Law
S-21-0094	1975	00000	..Miscegenation Law
S-21-0095	1975	00002	..Nationalities Law
S-21-0096	1979	00000	..Pornography Law
S-21-0097	1975	00001	.Socialist Law
S-21-0098	1975	00000	..Socialist Legality
S-21-0099	1975	00019	.Statutory Law
S-21-0100	1975	00014	..Codified Law

S-22 LEADERSHIP TYPE

S-22-0001	1975	00013	Leadership Type
S-22-0002	1979	00000	.Bonapartism
S-22-0003	1979	00000	.Leadership Authority Base
S-22-0004	1975	00023	..Administrative Leadership
S-22-0005	1975	00012	...Bureaucratic Leadership
S-22-0006	1979	00000	..Moral Leadership
S-22-0007	1975	00017	..Personalized Leadership
S-22-0008	1975	00008	...Charismatic Leadership
S-22-0009	1975	00000	..Rational Legal Leadership
S-22-0010	1975	00003	..Traditional Leadership
S-22-0011	1979	00000	...Religious Leadership
S-22-0012	1975	00002	....Ecclesiastical Leadership
S-22-0013	1979	00000	.Leadership Structure Type
S-22-0014	1975	00001	..Closed Leadership
S-22-0015	1975	00003	..Collective Leadership
S-22-0016	1975	00000	..Collegial Leadership
S-22-0017	1975	00002	..Democratic Leadership
S-22-0018	1975	00000	..Open Leadership
S-22-0019	1975	00004	..Small Group Leadership
S-22-0020	1975	00005	..Totalitarian Leadership
S-22-0021	1975	00001	.National Leadership
S-22-0022	1975	00056	.Political Leadership
S-22-0023	1979	00000	..Congressional Leadership
S-22-0024	1979	00000	..Executive Leadership
S-22-0025	1979	00000	...Presidential Leadership
S-22-0026	1979	00000	..Political Movement Leadership
S-22-0027	1975	00031	..Political Party Leadership

S-23 MANAGEMENT

S-23-0001	1975	00032	Management
S-23-0002	1975	00066	.Administrative Management
S-23-0003	1975	00034	..Personnel Management
S-23-0004	1975	00044	.Conflict Management
S-23-0005	1975	00021	..Conflict Control Management
S-23-0006	1979	00000	..Crisis Management
S-23-0007	1975	00009	.Defense Management
S-23-0008	1975	00036	.Development Management
S-23-0009	1975	00019	.Economic Management
S-23-0010	1975	00030	..Business Management
S-23-0011	1975	00018	...Corporate Management
S-23-0012	1975	00007	..Central Economic Management
S-23-0013	1975	00042	...Government Economic Management
S-23-0014	1975	00019	..Fiscal Management
S-23-0015	1975	00016	..Industrial Management
S-23-0016	1975	00021	..International Economic Management
S-23-0017	1975	00005	..Monetary Management
S-23-0018	1975	00033	..National Economic Management
S-23-0019	1975	00003	..Subnational Economic Management
S-23-0020	1975	00048	.Education Administration
S-23-0021	1975	00022	..Higher Education Administration
S-23-0022	1975	00033	.Environmental Management
S-23-0023	1975	00067	..Natural Resource Management
S-23-0024	1979	00000	...Energy Management
S-23-0025	1975	00010	.Health Administration
S-23-0026	1975	00013	.Information Management
S-23-0027	1975	00014	..Data Management
S-23-0028	1975	00006	.Law Administration
S-23-0029	1975	00004	..Judicial Administration
S-23-0030	1975	00013	..Justice Administration
S-23-0031	1975	00033	...Criminal Justice Administration
S-23-0032	1975	00009	...Police Administration
S-23-0033	1975	00030	.Military Management
S-23-0034	1975	00024	.Participatory Management
S-23-0035	1975	00040	..Worker Management Participation
S-23-0036	1975	00018	...Worker Self Management
S-23-0037	1975	00015	.Population Management
S-23-0038	1975	00070	.Public Policy Management
S-23-0039	1979	00000	.Research Management
S-23-0040	1975	00013	.Welfare Administration

S-24 METHODOLOGY

S-24-0001	1975	00104	Methodology
S-24-0002	1975	00143	.Analysis Methodology
S-24-0003	1979	00000	..Causal Analysis
S-24-0004	1979	00000	..Deductive Method
S-24-0005	1979	00000	..Education Testing
S-24-0006	1979	00000	...Degree Requirement
S-24-0007	1975	00002	...Literacy Test
S-24-0008	1979	00000	...Physiological Test
S-24-0009	1979	00000	...Psychological Test
S-24-0010	1979	00000	..Forecasting Methodology
S-24-0011	1979	00000	...Authority Forecasting
S-24-0012	1979	00000	...Brainstorming
S-24-0013	1979	00000	...Delphi Technique
S-24-0014	1979	00000	...Divergence Mapping
S-24-0015	1979	00000	...Economic Forecasting
S-24-0016	1979	00000	...Political Forecasting
S-24-0017	1979	00000	...Scenario Construction
S-24-0018	1979	00000	...Social Forecasting
S-24-0019	1979	00000	...Trend Analysis
S-24-0020	1979	00000	..Hermeneutical Analysis
S-24-0021	1979	00000	..Inductive Method
S-24-0022	1975	00007	..Logical Analysis
S-24-0023	1975	00012	..Mathematical Analysis
S-24-0024	1975	00001	...Calculus
S-24-0025	1975	00001	...Geometry
S-24-0026	1979	00000	...Graph Analysis
S-24-0027	1975	00016	...Linear Programming
S-24-0028	1975	00096	...Model Building
S-24-0029	1975	00000	...Trigonometry
S-24-0030	1975	00039	..Normative Analysis
S-24-0031	1975	00008	..Qualitative Analysis
S-24-0032	1975	00054	..Statistical Analysis
S-24-0033	1975	00014	...Bivariate Analysis
S-24-0034	1975	00084	....Correlation Analysis
S-24-0035	1975	00008	.....Product Moment Correlation
S-24-0036	1975	00005	.....Rank Order Correlation
S-24-0037	1975	00053	.....Regression Analysis
S-24-0038	1975	00046	...Multivariate Analysis
S-24-0039	1975	00021	....Analysis Of Variance
S-24-0040	1975	00000	....Automatic Interaction Detection
S-24-0041	1975	00002	....Canonical Correlation Analysis
S-24-0042	1975	00007	....Cluster Analysis
S-24-0043	1975	00006	....Covariance Analysis
S-24-0044	1975	00004	....Dimensional Analysis
S-24-0045	1975	00006	....Discriminant Analysis
S-24-0046	1975	00021	....Factor Analysis
S-24-0047	1975	00006	....Multiple Correlation Analysis
S-24-0048	1975	00017	....Multiple Regression Analysis
S-24-0049	1975	00011	....Partial Correlation Analysis
S-24-0050	1975	00024	....Path Analysis
S-24-0051	1975	00027	...Probability Estimation
S-24-0052	1975	00005	....Bayesian Analysis
S-24-0053	1975	00004	....Subjective Probability Estimation
S-24-0054	1975	00007	...Statistical Significance Test
S-24-0055	1975	00001	....Binomial Test
S-24-0056	1975	00004	....Chi Square Test
S-24-0057	1975	00000	....F Ratio
S-24-0058	1975	00000	....Interval Significance Test
S-24-0059	1979	00000	....Mann Whitney U Test
S-24-0060	1975	00002	....Nominal Significance Test
S-24-0061	1975	00000	....Ordinal Significance Test
S-24-0062	1975	00000	....Wald Wolfowitz Runs Test
S-24-0063	1979	00000	....Wilcoxian T Test
S-24-0064	1975	00002	...Statistics Type
S-24-0065	1975	00004	....Descriptive Statistics
S-24-0066	1975	00003	....Inferential Statistics
S-24-0067	1975	00001	....Nonparametric Statistics
S-24-0068	1975	00003	....Parametric Statistics
S-24-0069	1975	00002	...Univariate Analysis
S-24-0070	1975	00002	....Central Tendency Measure
S-24-0071	1975	00000	....Dispersion Measure
S-24-0072	1975	00016	....Population Estimation
S-24-0073	1975	00006	.....Parameter Estimation
S-24-0074	1975	00013	.....Statistical Inference
S-24-0075	1975	00007	.....Unbiased Estimation
S-24-0076	1975	00076	.Data Collection Methodology
S-24-0077	1975	00027	..Field Research
S-24-0078	1975	00000	..Nonreactive Observation
S-24-0079	1975	00031	...Documentary Research
S-24-0080	1975	00002	....Citation Analysis
S-24-0081	1975	00002	...Library Research
S-24-0082	1975	00002	...Nonparticipant Observation
S-24-0083	1975	00000	..Observation Time
S-24-0084	1975	00020	...Cross Sectional Analysis
S-24-0085	1975	00063	...Longitudinal Analysis
S-24-0086	1975	00027	....Cohort Analysis
S-24-0087	1975	00002	....Panel Technique
S-24-0088	1975	00012	....Time Series Analysis
S-24-0089	1975	00000	.....Cross Lagged Panel Analysis
S-24-0090	1975	00025	..Questionnaire
S-24-0091	1975	00002	...Closed Questionnaire
S-24-0092	1975	00012	...Mail Questionnaire
S-24-0093	1975	00002	...Open Ended Questionnaire
S-24-0094	1975	00004	...Self Administered Questionnaire
S-24-0095	1975	00001	...Telephone Questionnaire
S-24-0096	1975	00002	..Reactive Observation
S-24-0097	1975	00016	...Experimental Observation
S-24-0098	1975	00051	....Gaming
S-24-0099	1975	00000	.....Fixed Sum Gaming
S-24-0100	1975	00010	.....N Person Gaming
S-24-0101	1975	00001	.....Nonzero Sum Gaming
S-24-0102	1975	00013	.....Prisoner Dilemma Gaming
S-24-0103	1975	00013	.....Two Person Gaming
S-24-0104	1975	00000	.....Variable Sum Gaming
S-24-0105	1975	00004	.....Zero Sum Gaming
S-24-0106	1979	00000	....Small Group Experiment
S-24-0107	1975	00012	...Interview
S-24-0108	1975	00000	....Depth Interview
S-24-0109	1975	00000	....Group Interview
S-24-0110	1975	00010	....Personal Interview
S-24-0111	1975	00000	....Structured Interview
S-24-0112	1975	00004	....Telephone Interview
S-24-0113	1975	00000	....Unstructured Interview
S-24-0114	1975	00009	...Participant Observation
S-24-0115	1975	00104	...Survey Research
S-24-0116	1975	00018	..Sampling Procedure
S-24-0117	1975	00001	...Area Sampling
S-24-0118	1975	00000	...Nonprobability Sampling
S-24-0119	1975	00000	....Haphazard Sampling
S-24-0120	1975	00001	....Purposive Sampling
S-24-0121	1975	00000	....Quota Sampling
S-24-0122	1975	00001	...Probability Sampling
S-24-0123	1975	00002	....Cluster Sampling
S-24-0124	1975	00005	....Simple Random Sampling
S-24-0125	1975	00001	....Stratified Sampling
S-24-0126	1975	00000	....Systematic Sampling
S-24-0127	1975	00048	..Simulation
S-24-0128	1975	00021	...Computer Simulation
S-24-0129	1975	00002	...Man Machine Simulation
S-24-0130	1975	00017	.Data Presentation Methodology
S-24-0131	1975	00000	..Chart
S-24-0132	1975	00001	...Curve
S-24-0133	1975	00001	..Diagram
S-24-0134	1975	00000	...Venn Diagram

S-24-0135	1975	00002	..Graph
S-24-0136	1975	00000	..Plot
S-24-0137	1975	00000	...Scatter Plot
S-24-0138	1975	00000	..Table
S-24-0139	1975	00002	...Frequency Table
S-24-0140	1975	00077	.Hypothesis Testing
S-24-0141	1975	00003	..Confirmation
S-24-0142	1975	00002	..Falsification
S-24-0143	1975	00014	..Replication
S-24-0144	1975	00022	.Information Processing
S-24-0145	1979	00000	..Data Format
S-24-0146	1975	00007	..Data Processing
S-24-0147	1975	00016	...Computer Processing
S-24-0148	1975	00008	...Computer Programming
S-24-0149	1975	00002	..Information Retrieval
S-24-0150	1975	00006	...Data Retrieval
S-24-0151	1975	00001	...Question Formulation
S-24-0152	1975	00004	...Search Strategy Development
S-24-0153	1975	00004	..Information Storage
S-24-0154	1975	00000	...Abstracting
S-24-0155	1975	00004	...Data Storage
S-24-0156	1975	00009	...Indexing
S-24-0157	1975	00023	.Measurement
S-24-0158	1975	00105	..Measurement Evaluation
S-24-0159	1975	00020	...Reliability Measurement
S-24-0160	1975	00005	....Intercoder Reliability
S-24-0161	1975	00010	....Internal Consistency Reliability
S-24-0162	1975	00021	....Interviewer Effect
S-24-0163	1975	00002	....Test Retest Reliability
S-24-0164	1975	00024	...Validity Measurement
S-24-0165	1975	00020	....Construct Validity
S-24-0166	1975	00013	....Criterion Validity
S-24-0167	1975	00004	....Discriminant Validity
S-24-0168	1975	00002	....Face Validity
S-24-0169	1975	00003	..Measurement Level
S-24-0170	1975	00002	...Interval Measurement
S-24-0171	1975	00002	...Nominal Measurement
S-24-0172	1975	00006	....Classification
S-24-0173	1975	00022	.....Typology
S-24-0174	1975	00005	...Ordinal Measurement
S-24-0175	1975	00002	...Ratio Scale Measurement
S-24-0176	1975	00001	..Measurement Object
S-24-0177	1979	00000	...Aptitude Measurement
S-24-0178	1979	00000	....Intelligence Quotient
S-24-0179	1975	00094	...Attitude Measurement
S-24-0180	1975	00080	....Affective Measurement
S-24-0181	1975	00029	....Belief Measurement
S-24-0182	1975	00058	....Cognitive Measurement
S-24-0183	1975	00016	....Motivation Measurement
S-24-0184	1975	00027	...Behavioral Measurement
S-24-0185	1975	00013	...Change Measurement
S-24-0186	1975	00001	...Event Measurement
S-24-0187	1975	00001	...Group Measurement
S-24-0188	1975	00006	...Individual Measurement
S-24-0189	1975	00108	...Perception Measurement
S-24-0190	1979	00000	...Power Measurement
S-24-0191	1975	00053	..Measurement Problem
S-24-0192	1975	00002	...Autocorrelation
S-24-0193	1975	00045	...Measurement Bias
S-24-0194	1975	00030	....Response Bias
S-24-0195	1975	00031	...Measurement Error
S-24-0196	1975	00007	...Missing Data
S-24-0197	1975	00001	...Random Error
S-24-0198	1975	00007	...Sampling Error
S-24-0199	1975	00005	....Sampling Bias
S-24-0200	1975	00004	...Systematic Error
S-24-0201	1975	00084	..Measurement Procedure
S-24-0202	1975	00018	..Measurement Scale
S-24-0203	1975	00026	...Scale Construction Methodology
S-24-0204	1975	00000	....Composite Scale
S-24-0205	1975	00010	....Cross Cultural Index
S-24-0206	1975	00002	....Cumulative Scale
S-24-0207	1975	00005	....Factor Structure
S-24-0208	1975	00004	....Guttman Scale
S-24-0209	1975	00001	....Interval Scale
S-24-0210	1975	00006	....Likert Scale
S-24-0211	1975	00001	....Measurement Level Scale
S-24-0212	1975	00021	....Multidimensional Scale
S-24-0213	1975	00004	.....Nonmetric Multidimensional Scale
S-24-0214	1975	00001	....Nominal Scale
S-24-0215	1975	00004	....Ordinal Scale
S-24-0216	1975	00000	....Ratio Scale
S-24-0217	1975	00003	....Scalability Index
S-24-0218	1975	00011	....Semantic Differential
S-24-0219	1975	00001	....Thurstone Scale
S-24-0220	1975	00005	....Unidimensional Scale
S-24-0221	1975	00007	...Scale Type
S-24-0222	1975	00002	....Aggression Scale
S-24-0223	1975	00001	....Alienation Scale
S-24-0224	1975	00003	.....Political Alienation Scale
S-24-0225	1975	00004	....Anomie Scale
S-24-0226	1975	00008	....Authoritarianism Scale
S-24-0227	1975	00004	....Civic Competence Scale
S-24-0228	1975	00000	....Cynicism Scale
S-24-0229	1975	00007	....Development Index
S-24-0230	1975	00009	.....Economic Development Index
S-24-0231	1975	00010	.....Political Development Index
S-24-0232	1975	00008	.....Social Development Index
S-24-0233	1975	00001	....Dogmatism Scale
S-24-0234	1975	00011	....Efficacy Scale
S-24-0235	1975	00003	....Frustration Scale
S-24-0236	1975	00017	....Internal External Reinforcement Scale
S-24-0237	1975	00001	....Left Right Scale
S-24-0238	1975	00001	....Legitimacy Scale
S-24-0239	1975	00014	....Liberalism Conservatism Scale
S-24-0240	1975	00010	....Modernity Scale
S-24-0241	1979	00000	....Modernization Scale
S-24-0242	1975	00003	....Optimism Pessimism Scale
S-24-0243	1979	00000	....Policy Output Scale
S-24-0244	1975	00017	....Satisfaction Scale
S-24-0245	1975	00007	....Social Change Index
S-24-0246	1975	00025	....Social Distance Scale
S-24-0247	1975	00000	....Social Frustration Scale
S-24-0248	1975	00003	....Stability Index
S-24-0249	1975	00003	....Support Opposition Scale
S-24-0250	1975	00015	....Urbanization Index
S-24-0251	1975	00000	....Voting Duty Scale
S-24-0252	1975	00025	..Operationalization
S-24-0253	1975	00019	...Coding
S-24-0254	1975	00007	...Conceptual Equivalence
S-24-0255	1975	00005	....Functional Equivalent
S-24-0256	1975	00012	...Indicator
S-24-0257	1975	00010	....Change Indicator
S-24-0258	1975	00007	....Economic Indicator
S-24-0259	1975	00008	.....Economic Development Indicator
S-24-0260	1975	00000	....Multiple Indicator
S-24-0261	1975	00003	....Political Indicator
S-24-0262	1975	00013	.....Conflict Indicator
S-24-0263	1975	00010	......Threat Indicator
S-24-0264	1975	00046	.....Influence Indicator
S-24-0265	1975	00004	.....Political Instability Indicator
S-24-0266	1975	00003	.....Political Resource Indicator
S-24-0267	1975	00040	.....Public Opinion Indicator
S-24-0268	1975	00014	.....Voting Indicator
S-24-0269	1975	00005	......Legislative Voting Indicator
S-24-0270	1975	00017	......Political Party Voting Indicator

S-24-0271	1979	00000	......Two Political Party Voting Indicator
S-24-0272	1975	00010	......Voting Turnout Indicator
S-24-0273	1975	00010	....Social Indicator
S-24-0274	1975	00005	.....Social Cleavage Indicator
S-24-0275	1975	00024	.....Sociometric Indicator
S-24-0276	1975	00005	.....Stress Indicator
S-24-0277	1975	00003	...Measures
S-24-0278	1975	00001	...Multiple Operationalization
S-24-0279	1975	00095	.Models
S-24-0280	1975	00106	..Mathematical Model
S-24-0281	1975	00008	...Differential Equation Model
S-24-0282	1979	00000	...Economic Mathematical Model
S-24-0283	1975	00007	...Simultaneous Equation Model
S-24-0284	1975	00029	...Stochastic Model
S-24-0285	1975	00019	..Natural Science Model
S-24-0286	1975	00105	...Biological Model
S-24-0287	1975	00025	...Ecological Model
S-24-0288	1975	00047	..Social Science Model
S-24-0289	1975	00000	...Atomistic Model
S-24-0290	1975	00029	...Cognitive Model
S-24-0291	1975	00024	...Communication Model
S-24-0292	1975	00019	...Computer Simulation Model
S-24-0293	1975	00033	...Conflict Model
S-24-0294	1975	00013	...Consensus Model
S-24-0295	1975	00014	...Cybernetic Model
S-24-0296	1979	00000	...Development Model
S-24-0297	1979	00000	....Economic Development Model
S-24-0298	1975	00029	...Diffusion Model
S-24-0299	1975	00020	...Econometric Model
S-24-0300	1975	00009	...Equilibrium Model
S-24-0301	1975	00038	...Growth Model
S-24-0302	1979	00000	....Economic Growth Model
S-24-0303	1975	00007	...Hierarchical Model
S-24-0304	1975	00004	...Ideal Type Model
S-24-0305	1979	00000	...Individualism Model
S-24-0306	1975	00018	...Input Output Model
S-24-0307	1975	00064	...Interaction Model
S-24-0308	1975	00040	...Market Model
S-24-0309	1975	00053	...Optimizing Model
S-24-0310	1975	00029	...Organization Model
S-24-0311	1975	00012	...Pluralist Model
S-24-0312	1979	00000	...Probability Model
S-24-0313	1975	00022	...Process Model
S-24-0314	1975	00005	...Psychometric Model
S-24-0315	1975	00039	...Rational Choice Model
S-24-0316	1975	00017	...Social Power Model
S-24-0317	1975	00016	...Social System Model
S-24-0318	1975	00039	...Spatial Model
S-24-0319	1975	00005	...Static Model
S-24-0320	1975	00023	...Structural Model
S-24-0321	1975	00005	...Teleological Model
S-24-0322	1975	00003	...Voluntarism Model
S-24-0323	1975	00007	.Research Apparatus
S-24-0324	1975	00001	..Information Processing Equipment
S-24-0325	1975	00002	...Computer Software
S-24-0326	1975	00025	....Computer Program
S-24-0327	1975	00002	...Data Processing Equipment
S-24-0328	1975	00007	....Computer Equipment
S-24-0329	1975	00000	.....Input Output Device
S-24-0330	1975	00000	......Remote Terminal
S-24-0331	1975	00000	....Unit Record Equipment
S-24-0332	1975	00000	...Information Recording Equipment
S-24-0333	1975	00003	....Interviewing Material
S-24-0334	1975	00001	.....Response Recording Equipment
S-24-0335	1975	00001	....Microfilm Equipment
S-24-0336	1975	00000	...Laboratory
S-24-0337	1975	00000	....Laboratory Equipment
S-24-0338	1975	00010	....Small Group Laboratory
S-24-0339	1975	00007	...Simulation Material
S-24-0340	1975	00105	.Research Design
S-24-0341	1975	00108	..Analysis Framework
S-24-0342	1975	00002	...Analysis Unit
S-24-0343	1975	00000	....Event
S-24-0344	1975	00000	....Individual
S-24-0345	1975	00004	....Social Classification
S-24-0346	1975	00002	.....Population Identification
S-24-0347	1975	00025	......Rural Population Area
S-24-0348	1975	00005	......Suburban Population Area
S-24-0349	1975	00044	......Urban Population Area
S-24-0350	1975	00001	....Territory Classification
S-24-0351	1975	00093	.....Global System
S-24-0352	1975	00017	......World Region
S-24-0353	1979	00000	.......International Region
S-24-0354	1975	00054	.......National Region
S-24-0355	1975	00000	........National Political Division
S-24-0356	1975	00001	.........Nation
S-24-0357	1975	00001	........Subnational Political Division
S-24-0358	1975	00001	.........Local Political Division
S-24-0359	1975	00005	..........City Unit
S-24-0360	1975	00007	...........Census Tract
S-24-0361	1975	00000	...........Street Block
S-24-0362	1975	00007	..........Commune
S-24-0363	1975	00002	.........Province
S-24-0364	1975	00000	.........State
S-24-0365	1975	00000	.........State Political Division
S-24-0366	1979	00000	..........Borough
S-24-0367	1975	00004	..........County
S-24-0368	1975	00007	..........Legislative District
S-24-0369	1975	00001	..........Township
S-24-0370	1975	00001	..Most Different System Design
S-24-0371	1975	00001	..Most Similar System Design
S-24-0372	1975	00041	..Paradigm
S-24-0373	1975	00171	.Research Orientation
S-24-0374	1979	00000	..Advocacy Research
S-24-0375	1975	00092	..Applied Research
S-24-0376	1975	00029	..Basic Research
S-24-0377	1975	00009	..Data Selection Orientation
S-24-0378	1975	00004	...Aggregate Data Selection
S-24-0379	1975	00106	...Content Analysis
S-24-0380	1975	00046	...Demographic Analysis
S-24-0381	1975	00043	...Event Analysis
S-24-0382	1975	00090	..Descriptive Research
S-24-0383	1975	00002	...Ideographic Research
S-24-0384	1975	00122	..Experimental Research
S-24-0385	1975	00097	..Explanatory Research
S-24-0386	1975	00017	...Quasiexperimental Research
S-24-0387	1975	00010	..Humanistic Research
S-24-0388	1975	00029	..Interdisciplinary Research
S-24-0389	1979	00000	..Market Research
S-24-0390	1975	00321	..Policy Research
S-24-0391	1975	00093	...Policy Evaluation Research
S-24-0392	1975	00065	..Predictive Research
S-24-0393	1975	00004	..Qualitative Research
S-24-0394	1975	00029	..Quantitative Research
S-24-0395	1975	00084	..Scientific Research
S-24-0396	1975	00026	...Behavioral Science Research
S-24-0397	1975	00130	..Theoretical Research
S-24-0398	1979	00000	...Concept Explication Research
S-24-0399	1975	00004	.Study Scope
S-24-0400	1975	00100	..Case Study
S-24-0401	1975	00001	...Deviant Case Analysis
S-24-0402	1975	00000	...Ideal Case Analysis
S-24-0403	1975	00264	..Comparative Analysis
S-24-0404	1975	00253	...Cross Cultural Analysis
S-24-0405	1975	00014	...Cross Level Analysis
S-24-0406	1975	00198	...Cross National Analysis

S-24-0407 1975 00068 ...International Analysis
S-24-0408 1975 00004 ...Intracultural Analysis
S-24-0409 1975 00002 ..Configurative Analysis
S-24-0410 1975 00010 ..Panel Analysis
S-24-0411 1979 00000 ..Propositional Inventory
S-24-0412 1975 00095 .Theoretical Framework
S-24-0413 1979 00000 ..Macrolevel Analysis
S-24-0414 1975 00037 ...System Analysis
S-24-0415 1979 00000 ..Microlevel Analysis
S-24-0416 1975 00084 ...Decision Making Analysis
S-24-0417 1975 00022 ...Public Choice Analysis
S-24-0418 1975 00108 ...Role Analysis
S-24-0419 1975 00016 ..Variable
S-24-0420 1975 00007 ...Variable Control
S-24-0421 1975 00013 ....Experiment
S-24-0422 1975 00000 ....Nonexperiment
S-24-0423 1975 00009 ....Quasiexperiment
S-24-0424 1975 00000 .....Matching Case
S-24-0425 1975 00000 .....Natural Experiment
S-24-0426 1975 00020 ...Variable Logical Status
S-24-0427 1975 00011 ....Dependent Variable
S-24-0428 1975 00003 ....Endogenous Variable
S-24-0429 1975 00005 ....Exogenous Variable
S-24-0430 1975 00015 ....Independent Variable
S-24-0431 1975 00010 .....Explanatory Variable
S-24-0432 1975 00005 ....Interdependent Variable
S-24-0433 1975 00008 ....Intervening Variable
S-24-0434 1975 00003 .....Control Variable
S-24-0435 1975 00001 ...Variable Phenomenological Status
S-24-0436 1975 00001 ....Group Phenomena
S-24-0437 1975 00032 .....Group Perception
S-24-0438 1979 00000 ......Elite Perception
S-24-0439 1975 00000 ....Individual Phenomena
S-24-0440 1975 00036 .....Individual Attitude
S-24-0441 1975 00075 .....Individual Behavior
S-24-0442 1975 00165 .....Individual Perception
S-24-0443 1979 00000 ......Reality Construction
S-24-0444 1979 00000 ......Reality Testing
S-24-0445 1975 00004 ...Variable Substantive Content
S-24-0446 1975 00038 ....Cultural Variable
S-24-0447 1975 00025 ....Economic Variable
S-24-0448 1975 00000 ....Historical Variable
S-24-0449 1975 00015 ....Institutional Variable
S-24-0450 1975 00010 ....Political Variable
S-24-0451 1975 00019 ....Psychological Variable
S-24-0452 1975 00007 ....Social Variable
S-24-0453 1975 00008 .....Organization Variable
S-24-0454 1975 00050 ....Time Variable

S-25 PHILOSOPHICAL CONCEPT

S-25-0001 1975 00008 Philosophical Concept
S-25-0002 1975 00166 .Aesthetics
S-25-0003 1975 00004 .Cosmology
S-25-0004 1975 00002 .Eschatology
S-25-0005 1975 00004 ..Fatalism
S-25-0006 1975 00001 ..Prophetic Tradition
S-25-0007 1975 00026 .Jurisprudence
S-25-0008 1975 00002 ..Legal Positivism
S-25-0009 1975 00016 .Metaphysics
S-25-0010 1975 00041 ..Epistemology
S-25-0011 1975 00010 ...Cultural Determinism
S-25-0012 1975 00009 ...Cultural Relativism
S-25-0013 1979 00000 ...Cultural Universalism
S-25-0014 1975 00010 ...Dialectic
S-25-0015 1975 00006 ...Empiricism
S-25-0016 1975 00004 ....Holism
S-25-0017 1975 00001 ....Methodological Individualism
S-25-0018 1975 00003 ....Reductionism
S-25-0019 1975 00001 ...Essentialism
S-25-0020 1975 00010 ...Historicism
S-25-0021 1975 00009 ...Logical Positivism
S-25-0022 1975 00006 ...Materialism
S-25-0023 1975 00004 ....Philosophical Materialism
S-25-0024 1975 00000 ...Neopositivism
S-25-0025 1975 00003 ...Objectivism
S-25-0026 1975 00010 ...Philosophical Idealism
S-25-0027 1975 00003 ...Philosophical Realism
S-25-0028 1975 00004 ...Scientific Determinism
S-25-0029 1975 00012 ...Scientism
S-25-0030 1975 00005 ...Subjectivism
S-25-0031 1975 00003 ...Teleology
S-25-0032 1975 00006 ...Verstehen Theory
S-25-0033 1975 00164 ..Ethical Theory
S-25-0034 1975 00001 ...Axiology
S-25-0035 1979 00000 ...Bioethics
S-25-0036 1975 00001 ...Emotive Ethical Theory
S-25-0037 1975 00006 ...Ethical Naturalism
S-25-0038 1975 00008 ...Ethical Relativism
S-25-0039 1975 00001 ...Hedonism
S-25-0040 1975 00005 ...Instrumentalism
S-25-0041 1975 00002 ...Intuitionism
S-25-0042 1975 00005 ...Linguistic Ethical Theory
S-25-0043 1979 00000 ...Professional Ethics
S-25-0044 1979 00000 ...Research Ethics
S-25-0045 1979 00000 ....Use Of Human Subjects
S-25-0046 1979 00000 .....Human Subject Rights
S-25-0047 1975 00025 ...Situational Ethics
S-25-0048 1975 00002 ..Metaethical Theory
S-25-0049 1979 00000 ...Moral Theory
S-25-0050 1979 00000 ....Moral Reasoning
S-25-0051 1979 00000 ..Ontology
S-25-0052 1975 00010 ..Voluntarism

S-26 POLICY

S-26-0001 1975 00017 Policy
S-26-0002 1979 00000 .Admission Policy
S-26-0003 1975 00035 .Agricultural Policy
S-26-0004 1975 00014 ..Agrarian Reform Policy
S-26-0005 1975 00025 ...Land Reform Policy
S-26-0006 1975 00009 ..Agricultural Collectivization Policy
S-26-0007 1975 00004 ..Agricultural Subsidization Policy
S-26-0008 1975 00000 ...Soil Bank Policy
S-26-0009 1979 00000 ..Food Policy
S-26-0010 1979 00000 ..Forced Requisitioning
S-26-0011 1975 00017 .Business Policy
S-26-0012 1979 00000 ..Business Credit Policy
S-26-0013 1975 00052 ..Business Regulation Policy
S-26-0014 1975 00005 ...Antitrust Policy
S-26-0015 1975 00006 ..Business Subsidization Policy
S-26-0016 1975 00011 .Communication Policy
S-26-0017 1975 00007 ..Individual Communication Policy
S-26-0018 1975 00002 ...Postal Communication Policy
S-26-0019 1975 00000 ...Postal Telephone Telegraph Policy
S-26-0020 1975 00000 ....Postal Rate Policy
S-26-0021 1975 00001 ...Telephone Policy
S-26-0022 1975 00000 ....Telephone Allocation Policy
S-26-0023 1975 00005 ....Wiretapping Policy
S-26-0024 1975 00000 .....Wiretap Evidence Admissibility
S-26-0025 1975 00017 ..Mass Media Policy
S-26-0026 1975 00007 ...Broadcasting Policy
S-26-0027 1975 00004 ....Broadcast Access Policy
S-26-0028 1975 00003 .....Equal Time Provision Policy
S-26-0029 1975 00001 .....Fairness Doctrine
S-26-0030 1979 00000 .....Prime Time Access Policy

S-26-0031	1975	00000	....Broadcast Censorship Policy
S-26-0032	1975	00000	.....Broadcast Jamming Policy
S-26-0033	1975	00012	....Broadcast Regulation Policy
S-26-0034	1975	00002	....Broadcast Subsidization Policy
S-26-0035	1979	00000	....Broadcasting Licensing Policy
S-26-0036	1975	00003	....Public Broadcasting Policy
S-26-0037	1975	00004	....Radio Policy
S-26-0038	1975	00030	....Television Policy
S-26-0039	1975	00009	...Mass Media Access Policy
S-26-0040	1975	00003	...Mass Media Censorship Policy
S-26-0041	1975	00000	...Mass Media Licensing Policy
S-26-0042	1975	00005	...Mass Media Regulation Policy
S-26-0043	1975	00002	...Mass Media Subsidization Policy
S-26-0044	1975	00009	.Consumer Policy
S-26-0045	1979	00000	..Consumer Credit Policy
S-26-0046	1975	00013	..Consumer Protection Policy
S-26-0047	1975	00010	.Cultural Policy
S-26-0048	1975	00046	..Arts Policy
S-26-0049	1975	00016	..Language Policy
S-26-0050	1975	00115	.Defense Policy
S-26-0051	1975	00003	..Armistice Policy
S-26-0052	1975	00063	..Arms Control Policy
S-26-0053	1975	00003	...Arms Inspection Policy
S-26-0054	1975	00020	...Arms Reduction Policy
S-26-0055	1975	00006	....Balanced Force Reduction Policy
S-26-0056	1975	00022	....Strategic Arms Reduction Policy
S-26-0057	1979	00000	...Arms Verification Policy
S-26-0058	1975	00001	...Disarmament Policy
S-26-0059	1975	00018	....Nuclear Disarmament Policy
S-26-0060	1975	00027	...Nuclear Weapon Nonproliferation Policy
S-26-0061	1975	00005	..Civil Defense Policy
S-26-0062	1975	00031	..Deterrence Policy
S-26-0063	1979	00000	...Criminal Deterrence
S-26-0064	1975	00010	...Mutual Deterrence Policy
S-26-0065	1975	00024	...Nuclear Deterrence Policy
S-26-0066	1975	00038	..Nuclear Strategy
S-26-0067	1979	00000	...Assured Destruction Policy
S-26-0068	1975	00003	...Damage Limiting Strategy
S-26-0069	1979	00000	...Massive Retaliation Policy
S-26-0070	1975	00014	...Nuclear Strike Policy
S-26-0071	1975	00001	....First Strike Policy
S-26-0072	1975	00008	....Preemptive Attack Policy
S-26-0073	1975	00000	....Preventive Attack Policy
S-26-0074	1975	00001	....Second Strike Policy
S-26-0075	1975	00000	..Rearmament Policy
S-26-0076	1979	00000	..Strategic Policy
S-26-0077	1975	00000	..Truce
S-26-0078	1975	00002	..War Declaration Policy
S-26-0079	1979	00000	.Development Policy
S-26-0080	1979	00000	..Cultural Development Policy
S-26-0081	1979	00000	...Ethnic Heritage Policy
S-26-0082	1979	00000	..Economic Development Policy
S-26-0083	1979	00000	..Political Development Policy
S-26-0084	1979	00000	..Social Development Policy
S-26-0085	1975	00103	.Economic Policy
S-26-0086	1975	00040	..Economic Growth Policy
S-26-0087	1975	00008	...Economic Program
S-26-0088	1975	00009	....Economic Plan
S-26-0089	1975	00004	.....Multiple Year Economic Plan
S-26-0090	1975	00011	..Economic Stabilization Policy
S-26-0091	1975	00012	..Economic Subsidization Policy
S-26-0092	1975	00045	..Fiscal Policy
S-26-0093	1979	00000	...Antiinflation Policy
S-26-0094	1975	00021	...Budget Policy
S-26-0095	1979	00000	...Capital Formation Policy
S-26-0096	1979	00000	...Capital Investment Policy
S-26-0097	1975	00004	...Deflation Policy
S-26-0098	1979	00000	....Currency Revaluation Policy
S-26-0099	1975	00047	...Expenditure Policy
S-26-0100	1975	00034	....Revenue Sharing Policy
S-26-0101	1975	00021	...Income Policy
S-26-0102	1979	00000	....Income Maintenance Policy
S-26-0103	1975	00030	....Income Redistribution Policy
S-26-0104	1975	00011	....Income Subsidy Policy
S-26-0105	1975	00006	.....Guaranteed Annual Income Policy
S-26-0106	1975	00037	....Wage Policy
S-26-0107	1975	00003	.....Minimum Wage Policy
S-26-0108	1975	00004	.....Wage Stabilization Policy
S-26-0109	1975	00001	.....Wage Freeze Policy
S-26-0110	1975	00021	....Inflation Policy
S-26-0111	1975	00027	....Inflation Control Policy
S-26-0112	1975	00007	.....Currency Devaluation Policy
S-26-0113	1975	00052	....Price Policy
S-26-0114	1975	00022	....Price Control Policy
S-26-0115	1975	00015	....Price Fixing Policy
S-26-0116	1979	00000	....Price Freeze Policy
S-26-0117	1979	00000	..Grants
S-26-0118	1979	00000	...Education Grant
S-26-0119	1979	00000	...Grant In Aid
S-26-0120	1979	00000	...Research Grant
S-26-0121	1979	00000	..International Economic Boycott
S-26-0122	1975	00034	..Investment Policy
S-26-0123	1975	00027	..Monetary Policy
S-26-0124	1975	00015	...Banking Policy
S-26-0125	1975	00015	...Credit Policy
S-26-0126	1975	00004	...Money Supply Policy
S-26-0127	1975	00001	..Price Support Policy
S-26-0128	1975	00001	...Agricultural Price Support Policy
S-26-0129	1975	00000	...Business Price Support Policy
S-26-0130	1975	00018	..Productivity Policy
S-26-0131	1975	00002	...Production Quota
S-26-0132	1975	00009	...Work Norm Policy
S-26-0133	1975	00003	..Public Debt Policy
S-26-0134	1975	00000	...Debt Ceiling Policy
S-26-0135	1975	00001	...National Debt Policy
S-26-0136	1979	00000	..Public Finance Policy
S-26-0137	1975	00005	..Public Utility Regulation Policy
S-26-0138	1975	00020	..Revenue Policy
S-26-0139	1975	00080	...Taxation Policy
S-26-0140	1975	00001	....Confiscatory Taxation
S-26-0141	1975	00001	....Direct Taxation
S-26-0142	1975	00001	....Excise Taxation Policy
S-26-0143	1975	00003	....Gift Taxation
S-26-0144	1975	00001	....Import Duty
S-26-0145	1975	00011	....Incentive Taxation Policy
S-26-0146	1975	00025	....Income Taxation
S-26-0147	1975	00008	.....National Income Taxation
S-26-0148	1975	00000	.....Subnational Income Taxation
S-26-0149	1975	00001	......Local Income Taxation
S-26-0150	1975	00000	.......City Income Taxation
S-26-0151	1975	00000	......State Income Taxation
S-26-0152	1975	00007	....Incentive Taxation
S-26-0153	1975	00002	....Indirect Taxation
S-26-0154	1975	00003	....Inheritance Taxation
S-26-0155	1975	00001	....Luxury Taxation
S-26-0156	1975	00001	....National Taxation
S-26-0157	1975	00003	.....Federal Taxation
S-26-0158	1975	00000	....Nuisance Taxation
S-26-0159	1975	00005	....Progressive Taxation
S-26-0160	1975	00001	.....Graduated Taxation
S-26-0161	1975	00028	....Property Taxation
S-26-0162	1975	00003	....Regressive Taxation
S-26-0163	1975	00004	....Sales Taxation
S-26-0164	1975	00003	....School Taxation
S-26-0165	1975	00004	....Social Security Taxation
S-26-0166	1975	00001	....Subnational Taxation

S-26-0167	1975	00009	.....Local Taxation
S-26-0168	1975	00003	......Municipal Taxation
S-26-0169	1975	00004	.....State Taxation
S-26-0170	1975	00001	....Tariff
S-26-0171	1975	00006	.....Protective Tariff
S-26-0172	1979	00000	....Tax Assessment
S-26-0173	1979	00000	....Tax Credit
S-26-0174	1979	00000	....Tax Cut
S-26-0175	1979	00000	....Tax Base
S-26-0176	1979	00000	....Tax Rebate
S-26-0177	1979	00000	....Tax Shelter
S-26-0178	1975	00001	....Value Added Taxation
S-26-0179	1975	00003	....Wage Taxation
S-26-0180	1975	00047	..Trade Policy
S-26-0181	1975	00002	...Export Subsidization Policy
S-26-0182	1975	00004	...Free Trade Policy
S-26-0183	1975	00007	...Most Favored Nation Policy
S-26-0184	1975	00026	...Restrictive Trade Policy
S-26-0185	1975	00005	....Blockade Policy
S-26-0186	1975	00055	....Export Policy
S-26-0187	1975	00041	....Import Policy
S-26-0188	1975	00012	....Tariff Policy
S-26-0189	1975	00194	.Education Policy
S-26-0190	1979	00000	..Education Curriculum
S-26-0191	1975	00078	..Higher Education Policy
S-26-0192	1975	00006	..Literacy Policy
S-26-0193	1975	00003	..Private Education Policy
S-26-0194	1975	00040	..Public Education Policy
S-26-0195	1975	00031	..Rehabilitation Education Policy
S-26-0196	1975	00005	..Vocation Training Policy
S-26-0197	1975	00063	.Employment Policy
S-26-0198	1975	00023	..Affirmative Action Employment Policy
S-26-0199	1975	00010	..Civil Service System
S-26-0200	1975	00023	..Equal Employment Policy
S-26-0201	1975	00004	..Fair Employment Policy
S-26-0202	1975	00020	..Full Employment Policy
S-26-0203	1975	00049	..Manpower Policy
S-26-0204	1975	00004	..Merit Policy
S-26-0205	1975	00001	..Patronage Policy
S-26-0206	1975	00011	..Public Works Policy
S-26-0207	1975	00003	..Quota System Policy
S-26-0208	1975	00003	..Tenure Policy
S-26-0209	1975	00003	...Academic Tenure Policy
S-26-0210	1975	00024	..Unemployment Policy
S-26-0211	1979	00000	.Energy Policy
S-26-0212	1975	00112	..Energy Use Policy
S-26-0213	1979	00000	.Environment Policy
S-26-0214	1975	00027	..Land Policy
S-26-0215	1975	00068	...Land Use Policy
S-26-0216	1975	00013	....Public Land Use Policy
S-26-0217	1975	00001	.....Eminent Domain Policy
S-26-0218	1975	00012	....Zoning Policy
S-26-0219	1975	00058	..Natural Resource Policy
S-26-0220	1975	00003	...Fish And Wildlife Policy
S-26-0221	1975	00004	...Forest Land Policy
S-26-0222	1975	00001	...Grazing Land Policy
S-26-0223	1975	00064	...Water Use Policy
S-26-0224	1975	00015	..Pollution Policy
S-26-0225	1975	00015	...Air Pollution Policy
S-26-0226	1975	00001	...Land Pollution Policy
S-26-0227	1975	00003	...Noise Pollution Policy
S-26-0228	1975	00001	...Sanitation Policy
S-26-0229	1975	00017	...Water Pollution Policy
S-26-0230	1975	00005	..Space Policy
S-26-0231	1975	00006	...Space Exploration Policy
S-26-0232	1975	00011	...Space Use Policy
S-26-0233	1979	00000	...Waste Treatment Policy
S-26-0234	1975	00007	.Exclusionary Policy
S-26-0235	1975	00000	..Blacklisting Policy
S-26-0236	1975	00004	..Quota Policy
S-26-0237	1975	00018	..Segregation Policy
S-26-0238	1979	00000	...Residential Segregation
S-26-0239	1975	00007	.Executive Policy
S-26-0240	1975	00001	..Executive Budget Proposal
S-26-0241	1975	00003	..Executive Communique
S-26-0242	1975	00000	..Executive Judicial Policy
S-26-0243	1975	00003	..Executive Legislative Policy
S-26-0244	1975	00007	...Presidential Legislative Program
S-26-0245	1975	00003	..Executive Pardon
S-26-0246	1975	00000	..Executive Pronouncement
S-26-0247	1975	00000	..Executive Trial Balloon Policy
S-26-0248	1979	00000	..Presidential Policy
S-26-0249	1975	00000	...Inaugural Address
S-26-0250	1979	00000	....State Of The Union
S-26-0251	1975	00532	.Foreign Policy
S-26-0252	1975	00000	..Brinkmanship
S-26-0253	1975	00018	..Containment Policy
S-26-0254	1975	00013	..Expansionist Policy
S-26-0255	1975	00033	..Foreign Aid Policy
S-26-0256	1975	00005	...Bilateral Aid Policy
S-26-0257	1975	00025	...Economic Aid Policy
S-26-0258	1975	00023	...Military Aid Policy
S-26-0259	1975	00005	...Multilateral Aid Policy
S-26-0260	1975	00012	...Technical Aid Policy
S-26-0261	1975	00000	...Unilateral Aid Policy
S-26-0262	1975	00058	..Intervention Policy
S-26-0263	1975	00015	...Interference Policy
S-26-0264	1975	00009	....Economic Interference Policy
S-26-0265	1979	00000	....Political Interference Policy
S-26-0266	1975	00051	...Military Intervention Policy
S-26-0267	1979	00000	....Military Invasion
S-26-0268	1979	00000	...Political Intervention Policy
S-26-0269	1975	00000	..Open Door Policy
S-26-0270	1979	00000	.Health Care Policy
S-26-0271	1975	00082	..Medical Care Policy
S-26-0272	1975	00056	..Public Health Policy
S-26-0273	1979	00000	.Gambling Policy
S-26-0274	1979	00000	.Human Rights Policy
S-26-0275	1975	00012	.Industrial Policy
S-26-0276	1975	00002	..Consumer Industrial Policy
S-26-0277	1975	00000	..Heavy Industrial Policy
S-26-0278	1975	00000	..Light Industrial Policy
S-26-0279	1979	00000	..Service Industry Policy
S-26-0280	1975	00014	.Information Policy
S-26-0281	1975	00003	..Domestic Information Policy
S-26-0282	1975	00002	...Government Document Classification Policy
S-26-0283	1975	00010	....Government Secrecy Policy
S-26-0284	1975	00009	.....Public Information Access Policy
S-26-0285	1975	00012	...Government Information Diffusion Policy
S-26-0286	1975	00002	....Clientele Information Policy
S-26-0287	1975	00011	....Consumer Information Policy
S-26-0288	1975	00003	....Copyright Policy
S-26-0289	1975	00008	....Science Information Policy
S-26-0290	1975	00002	...Government Media Regulation Policy
S-26-0291	1975	00007	..Foreign Information Policy
S-26-0292	1975	00001	..Propaganda Policy
S-26-0293	1975	00002	...Wartime Propaganda Policy
S-26-0294	1975	00082	.International Policy
S-26-0295	1979	00000	..International Exchange Program
S-26-0296	1975	00115	..International Organization Policy
S-26-0297	1975	00012	..International Sanction
S-26-0298	1979	00000	.Insurance
S-26-0299	1979	00000	..Accident Insurance
S-26-0300	1979	00000	..Catastrophe Insurance

Code	Year	Count	Term
S-26-0301	1979	00000	..Compulsory Insurance
S-26-0302	1979	00000	..Disability Insurance
S-26-0303	1979	00000	..Fire Insurance
S-26-0304	1979	00000	..Life Insurance
S-26-0305	1979	00000	..Malpractice Insurance
S-26-0306	1979	00000	..Motor Vehicle Insurance
S-26-0307	1975	00021	..National Health Insurance
S-26-0308	1979	00000	..No Fault Insurance
S-26-0309	1975	00004	..Unemployment Insurance Policy
S-26-0310	1975	00010	.Justice Administration Policy
S-26-0311	1975	00003	..Judicial Appointment Policy
S-26-0312	1975	00036	..Law Enforcement Policy
S-26-0313	1975	00000	..Police Board Policy
S-26-0314	1975	00026	.Labor Policy
S-26-0315	1975	00024	..Labor Management Relations Policy
S-26-0316	1975	00018	...Collective Bargaining Policy
S-26-0317	1975	00001	....Labor Mediation Policy
S-26-0318	1975	00002	...Labor Arbitration Policy
S-26-0319	1975	00000	....Compulsory Arbitration Policy
S-26-0320	1975	00011	...Public Employee Union Policy
S-26-0321	1975	00003	...Right To Work Policy
S-26-0322	1975	00013	...Trade Union Policy
S-26-0323	1975	00007	..Labor Regulation Policy
S-26-0324	1975	00001	..Labor Subsidization Policy
S-26-0325	1975	00167	.Military Policy
S-26-0326	1975	00012	..Armed Intervention Policy
S-26-0327	1975	00001	..Cease Fire Policy
S-26-0328	1975	00001	..Deescalation Policy
S-26-0329	1975	00005	..Demilitarization Policy
S-26-0330	1975	00000	..Demobilization Policy
S-26-0331	1975	00001	..Escalation Policy
S-26-0332	1975	00012	..Military Reorganization Policy
S-26-0333	1975	00002	...Military Integration Policy
S-26-0334	1975	00015	...Military Reform Policy
S-26-0335	1975	00002	..Mobilization Policy
S-26-0336	1975	00001	..Reprisal Policy
S-26-0337	1975	00056	..War Policy
S-26-0338	1975	00008	...Global War Policy
S-26-0339	1975	00013	...Limited War Policy
S-26-0340	1975	00002	...Local War Policy
S-26-0341	1975	00001	...Pacification Policy
S-26-0342	1975	00003	...Peoples War Policy
S-26-0343	1975	00001	...Total War Policy
S-26-0344	1979	00000	...War Reparation Policy
S-26-0345	1975	00009	.Planning Policy
S-26-0346	1975	00007	..National Planning Policy
S-26-0347	1979	00000	..Needs Assessment
S-26-0348	1979	00000	...Education Needs
S-26-0349	1979	00000	..Research And Development
S-26-0350	1975	00003	..Subnational Planning Policy
S-26-0351	1975	00016	...Local Planning Policy
S-26-0352	1979	00000	....City Planning Policy
S-26-0353	1975	00017	...Regional Planning Policy
S-26-0354	1975	00003	...State Planning Policy
S-26-0355	1975	00031	.Political Party Policy
S-26-0356	1975	00004	..Political Party Platform
S-26-0357	1975	00011	..Political Party Program
S-26-0358	1979	00000	.Seabed Policy
S-26-0359	1975	00041	.Science Policy
S-26-0360	1979	00000	.Service Policy
S-26-0361	1979	00000	..Education Service
S-26-0362	1979	00000	..Employment Service
S-26-0363	1979	00000	..Health Service
S-26-0364	1979	00000	...Medical Care Service
S-26-0365	1979	00000	..Legal Service
S-26-0366	1979	00000	..Social Service
S-26-0367	1979	00000	...Child Care Service
S-26-0368	1979	00000	...Community Service
S-26-0369	1979	00000	...Family Service
S-26-0370	1979	00000	..Psychological Service
S-26-0371	1975	00052	.Social Policy
S-26-0372	1979	00000	..Abortion Policy
S-26-0373	1975	00077	..Discrimination Policy
S-26-0374	1979	00000	...Racial Discrimination
S-26-0375	1979	00000	...Reverse Discrimination
S-26-0376	1979	00000	...Sex Discrimination
S-26-0377	1975	00032	..Drug Control Policy
S-26-0378	1975	00021	..Ethnic Policy
S-26-0379	1975	00015	...Nationality Policy
S-26-0380	1975	00020	...Racial Policy
S-26-0381	1975	00028	....Apartheid
S-26-0382	1975	00020	....Desegregation Policy
S-26-0383	1975	00004	.....Community Desegregation Policy
S-26-0384	1975	00048	.....School Desegregation Policy
S-26-0385	1975	00061	..Housing Policy
S-26-0386	1975	00004	...Open Housing Policy
S-26-0387	1979	00000	...Public Housing Policy
S-26-0388	1975	00003	...Relocation Policy
S-26-0389	1975	00008	..Migration Policy
S-26-0390	1975	00003	...Emigration Policy
S-26-0391	1975	00016	...Immigration Policy
S-26-0392	1979	00000	..Policy For Disadvantaged
S-26-0393	1975	00046	..Population Policy
S-26-0394	1975	00034	...Birth Control Policy
S-26-0395	1975	00017	...Family Policy
S-26-0396	1975	00004	....Family Subsidization Policy
S-26-0397	1975	00011	..Religious Policy
S-26-0398	1975	00005	...Church State Policy
S-26-0399	1975	00001	...School Prayer Policy
S-26-0400	1975	00011	..Safety Policy
S-26-0401	1975	00007	...Industrial Safety Policy
S-26-0402	1975	00000	...Mine Safety Policy
S-26-0403	1975	00008	...Traffic Safety Policy
S-26-0404	1975	00002	....Air Safety Policy
S-26-0405	1975	00002	....Highway Safety Policy
S-26-0406	1975	00000	.....Driver Licensing Policy
S-26-0407	1975	00018	..Social Resource Distribution Policy
S-26-0408	1975	00002	...Scientific Manpower Policy
S-26-0409	1975	00062	..Social Welfare Policy
S-26-0410	1975	00046	...Mental Health Policy
S-26-0411	1975	00010	...Old Age Assistance Policy
S-26-0412	1975	00037	...Poverty Policy
S-26-0413	1975	00016	...Social Security Policy
S-26-0414	1975	00024	...Welfare Policy
S-26-0415	1975	00011	..Urban Renewal Policy
S-26-0416	1979	00000	.Technology Policy
S-26-0417	1979	00000	..Technology Constraint Policy
S-26-0418	1979	00000	..Technology Development Policy
S-26-0419	1979	00000	..Technology Transfer Policy
S-26-0420	1975	00024	.Transportation Policy
S-26-0421	1975	00007	..Highway Policy
S-26-0422	1975	00013	..Mass Transit Policy
S-26-0423	1975	00010	...Air Transportation Policy
S-26-0424	1979	00000	....Airline Regulation Policy
S-26-0425	1979	00000	.....Air Fare Regulation Policy
S-26-0426	1975	00008	...Railroad Policy
S-26-0427	1975	00021	...Urban Transit Policy

S-27 POLITICAL MOVEMENT

Code	Year	Count	Term
S-27-0001	1975	00012	Political Movement
S-27-0002	1975	00001	.Chiliastic Movement
S-27-0003	1975	00004	.Confederation Movement
S-27-0004	1975	00009	.Ecology Movement
S-27-0005	1979	00000	.Economic Movement
S-27-0006	1979	00000	..Consumer Rights Movement

S-27-0007	1975	00017	..Trade Union Movement
S-27-0008	1975	00001	..Welfare Rights Movement
S-27-0009	1975	00002	.Federation Movement
S-27-0010	1979	00000	.Ideological Spectrum Political Movement
S-27-0011	1979	00000	..Christian Democratic Movement
S-27-0012	1979	00000	..Communist Movement
S-27-0013	1979	00000	...International Communist Movement
S-27-0014	1975	00002	..Extremist Movement
S-27-0015	1979	00000	...Terrorist Movement
S-27-0016	1975	00003	..Fascist Movement
S-27-0017	1975	00004	..Maoist Movement
S-27-0018	1975	00012	..Radical Movement
S-27-0019	1975	00006	...Radical Student Movement
S-27-0020	1975	00040	..Revolutionary Movement
S-27-0021	1975	00004	...Mass Revolutionary Movement
S-27-0022	1975	00002	..Social Democratic Movement
S-27-0023	1975	00032	.Independence Movement
S-27-0024	1975	00014	..Liberation Movement
S-27-0025	1975	00004	...Black Liberation Movement
S-27-0026	1975	00021	...National Liberation Movement
S-27-0027	1975	00001	...Peoples Liberation Movement
S-27-0028	1975	00019	...Womens Liberation Movement
S-27-0029	1979	00000	..Separatist Movement
S-27-0030	1975	00002	...Black Separatist Movement
S-27-0031	1975	00011	...Ethnic Separatist Movement
S-27-0032	1975	00000	.Luddite Movement
S-27-0033	1975	00001	.Messianic Movement
S-27-0034	1975	00017	.Nationalist Movement
S-27-0035	1975	00004	..Black Nationalist Movement
S-27-0036	1975	00004	..Pan African Movement
S-27-0037	1975	00002	..Pan Arab Movement
S-27-0038	1975	00000	..Pan Slav Movement
S-27-0039	1975	00015	..Zionist Movement
S-27-0040	1975	00002	.Peace Movement
S-27-0041	1975	00006	..Antiwar Movement
S-27-0042	1975	00030	.Reform Movement
S-27-0043	1975	00016	..Municipal Reform Movement
S-27-0044	1979	00000	..Tax Reform Movement
S-27-0045	1975	00010	.Resistance Movement
S-27-0046	1979	00000	.Sector Based Political Movement
S-27-0047	1975	00007	..Agrarian Movement
S-27-0048	1975	00003	...Agrarian Reform Movement
S-27-0049	1979	00000	..Class Based Movement
S-27-0050	1979	00000	...Middle Class Movement
S-27-0051	1975	00001	...Proletarian Movement
S-27-0052	1975	00006	....Proletarian Cultural Revolution Movement
S-27-0053	1975	00003	....Proletarian Socialist Movement
S-27-0054	1975	00010	...Working Class Movement
S-27-0055	1975	00004	..Grass Roots Movement
S-27-0056	1975	00004	..Populist Movement
S-27-0057	1975	00001	..Transnational Political Movement
S-27-0058	1975	00032	.Social Movement
S-27-0059	1975	00000	..Civic Action Movement
S-27-0060	1975	00016	..Civil Rights Movement
S-27-0061	1975	00002	..Communal Movement
S-27-0062	1975	00010	..Ethnic Movement
S-27-0063	1975	00004	..Language Movement
S-27-0064	1975	00027	..Religious Movement
S-27-0065	1975	00000	...Ecumenical Movement
S-27-0066	1975	00002	..Sectarian Movement
S-27-0067	1979	00000	..Senior Citizen Movement
S-27-0068	1975	00007	..Youth Movement
S-27-0069	1975	00000	...Hippie Movement
S-27-0070	1975	00001	.Totalitarian Movement

S-28 POLITICAL PARTY TYPE

S-28-0001	1975	00005	Political Party Type
S-28-0002	1979	00000	.Authoritarian Political Party
S-28-0003	1979	00000	.Democratic Political Party
S-28-0004	1979	00000	..Christian Democratic Political Party
S-28-0005	1979	00000	..Liberal Democratic Political Party
S-28-0006	1979	00000	..National Democratic Political Party
S-28-0007	1979	00000	..Social Democratic Political Party
S-28-0008	1979	00000	.Ideological Political Party
S-28-0009	1979	00000	.Ideological Spectrum Political Party Type
S-28-0010	1979	00000	..Center Political Party
S-28-0011	1979	00000	..Communist Political Party
S-28-0012	1979	00000	...Bolshevik Political Party
S-28-0013	1979	00000	...Maoist Political Party
S-28-0014	1979	00000	...Trotskyite Political Party
S-28-0015	1979	00000	..Conservative Political Party
S-28-0016	1979	00000	..Fascist Political Party
S-28-0017	1979	00000	...Flangist Political Party
S-28-0018	1979	00000	...National Socialist Political Party
S-28-0019	1979	00000	..Leftist Political Party
S-28-0020	1979	00000	..Liberal Political Party
S-28-0021	1979	00000	..Radical Political Party
S-28-0022	1979	00000	..Rightist Political Party
S-28-0023	1979	00000	..Socialist Political Party
S-28-0024	1979	00000	.International Political Party
S-28-0025	1979	00000	.Major Political Party
S-28-0026	1979	00000	.Majority Political Party
S-28-0027	1979	00000	.Minor Political Party
S-28-0028	1979	00000	.Monarchist Political Party
S-28-0029	1979	00000	.Nationalist Political Party
S-28-0030	1979	00000	.Opposition Political Party
S-28-0031	1979	00000	.Republican Political Party
S-28-0032	1979	00000	.Revolutionary Political Party
S-28-0033	1979	00000	.Ruling Political Party
S-28-0034	1979	00000	.Sector Based Political Party Type
S-28-0035	1979	00000	..Agrarian Political Party
S-28-0036	1979	00000	..Class Based Political Party
S-28-0037	1979	00000	...Aristocracy Political Party
S-28-0038	1979	00000	...Middle Class Political Party
S-28-0039	1979	00000	...Peasant Political Party
S-28-0040	1979	00000	...Proletarian Political Party
S-28-0041	1979	00000	...Labor Political Party
S-28-0042	1979	00000	....Working Class Political Party
S-28-0043	1979	00000	..Government Political Party
S-28-0044	1979	00000	..Legislative Political Party
S-28-0045	1979	00000	...National Legislative Political Party
S-28-0046	1979	00000	....Congressional Political Party
S-28-0047	1979	00000	....Parliamentary Political Party
S-28-0048	1979	00000	..Military Political Party
S-28-0049	1979	00000	..Minority Political Party
S-28-0050	1979	00000	..Traditional Political Party
S-28-0051	1979	00000	...Religious Political Party
S-28-0052	1979	00000	.National Political Party
S-28-0053	1979	00000	..Subnational Political Party
S-28-0054	1979	00000	...Local Political Party
S-28-0055	1979	00000	...Provincial Political Party
S-28-0056	1979	00000	...State Political Party
S-28-0057	1979	00000	.Separatist Political Party
S-28-0058	1979	00000	.Structure Specific Political Party Type
S-28-0059	1979	00000	..Cadre Political Party
S-28-0060	1979	00000	..Elite Political Party
S-28-0061	1979	00000	..Mass Political Party
S-28-0062	1979	00000	..Splinter Political Party
S-28-0063	1979	00000	..Third Political Party
S-28-0064	1979	00000	..Totalitarian Political Party
S-28-0065	1979	00000	.Underground Political Party

S-29 POLITICS

Code	Year	Count	Term
S-29-0001	1975	00009	Politics
S-29-0002	1975	00019	.Administrative Politics
S-29-0003	1975	00057	..Bureaucratic Politics
S-29-0004	1975	00003	..Interagency Rivalry
S-29-0005	1975	00000	.Biopolitics
S-29-0006	1975	00013	.Class Politics
S-29-0007	1975	00019	.Coalition Politics
S-29-0008	1975	00009	.Confrontation Politics
S-29-0009	1975	00007	.Consensual Politics
S-29-0010	1979	00000	.Constituency Politics
S-29-0011	1979	00000	.Cultural Politics
S-29-0012	1975	00025	.Education Politics
S-29-0013	1975	00046	.Electoral Politics
S-29-0014	1975	00017	..Election Campaign
S-29-0015	1979	00000	...Election Campaign Advertising
S-29-0016	1979	00000	...Election Campaign Financing
S-29-0017	1979	00000	....Election Campaign Contribution
S-29-0018	1979	00000	....Election Campaign Expenditure
S-29-0019	1979	00000	....Election Campaign Financial Disclosure
S-29-0020	1979	00000	...Election Campaign Organization
S-29-0021	1979	00000	...Election Campaign Strategy
S-29-0022	1979	00000	....Election Campaign Tactics
S-29-0023	1975	00001	...Canvassing
S-29-0024	1975	00006	...National Election Campaign
S-29-0025	1975	00003	....National Chief Executive Election Campaign
S-29-0026	1979	00000	.....Chancellor Election Campaign
S-29-0027	1979	00000	.....Presidential Election Campaign
S-29-0028	1979	00000	.....Prime Minister Election Campaign
S-29-0029	1975	00000	....National Judicial Election Campaign
S-29-0030	1975	00002	....National Legislative Election Campaign
S-29-0031	1979	00000	.....Congressional Election Campaign
S-29-0032	1979	00000	.....Parliamentary Election Campaign
S-29-0033	1975	00001	...Subnational Election Campaign
S-29-0034	1975	00001	....Local Election Campaign
S-29-0035	1975	00000	....Subnational Chief Executive Election Campaign
S-29-0036	1975	00000	.....Local Chief Executive Election Campaign
S-29-0037	1979	00000	......Mayoralty Election Campaign
S-29-0038	1975	00000	....Subnational Judicial Election Campaign
S-29-0039	1975	00000	.....Local Judicial Election Campaign
S-29-0040	1975	00000	....Subnational Legislative Election Campaign
S-29-0041	1975	00001	.....Local Legislative Election Campaign
S-29-0042	1975	00008	..Election Type
S-29-0043	1975	00001	...Contested Election
S-29-0044	1975	00005	...Critical Election
S-29-0045	1975	00002	...Deviating Election
S-29-0046	1975	00003	...Direct Election
S-29-0047	1975	00004	...General Election
S-29-0048	1975	00000	...Indirect Election
S-29-0049	1979	00000	...Initiative Election
S-29-0050	1975	00001	...Maintaining Election
S-29-0051	1975	00018	...National Election
S-29-0052	1975	00010	....National Chief Executive Election
S-29-0053	1975	00000	.....Chancellor Election
S-29-0054	1975	00056	.....Presidential Election
S-29-0055	1975	00000	.....Prime Minister Election
S-29-0056	1975	00000	....National Judicial Election
S-29-0057	1975	00009	....National Legislative Election
S-29-0058	1975	00031	.....Congressional Election
S-29-0059	1975	00017	.....Parliamentary Election
S-29-0060	1975	00005	...Nonpartisan Election
S-29-0061	1975	00004	...Partisan Election
S-29-0062	1979	00000	...Plebiscite Election
S-29-0063	1975	00009	...Primary Election
S-29-0064	1975	00000	....Blanket Primary
S-29-0065	1975	00000	....Closed Primary
S-29-0066	1975	00000	.....Partisan Primary
S-29-0067	1975	00003	......Political Party Primary
S-29-0068	1975	00000	....National Primary
S-29-0069	1975	00001	.....National Chief Executive Primary
S-29-0070	1975	00008	......Presidential Primary
S-29-0071	1975	00000	.....National Judicial Primary
S-29-0072	1975	00000	.....National Legislative Primary
S-29-0073	1975	00000	......Congressional Primary
S-29-0074	1975	00001	...Open Primary
S-29-0075	1975	00000	....Nonpartisan Primary
S-29-0076	1975	00002	...Preference Primary
S-29-0077	1975	00001	...Subnational Primary
S-29-0078	1975	00000	....Local Primary
S-29-0079	1975	00001	....Subnational Chief Executive Primary
S-29-0080	1975	00000	.....Local Chief Executive Primary
S-29-0081	1975	00000	....Subnational Judicial Primary
S-29-0082	1975	00000	.....Local Judicial Primary
S-29-0083	1975	00000	....Subnational Legislative Primary
S-29-0084	1975	00000	.....Local Legislative Primary
S-29-0085	1975	00010	...Realigning Election
S-29-0086	1975	00002	...Reinstating Election
S-29-0087	1975	00002	...Runoff Election
S-29-0088	1975	00001	...Special Election
S-29-0089	1975	00002	....By Election
S-29-0090	1975	00003	...Subnational Election
S-29-0091	1975	00003	....Local Election
S-29-0092	1975	00005	.....Municipal Election
S-29-0093	1975	00001	....Provincial Election
S-29-0094	1975	00000	....Subnational Chief Executive Election
S-29-0095	1975	00008	.....Gubernatorial Election
S-29-0096	1975	00000	.....Local Chief Executive Election
S-29-0097	1975	00004	......Mayoralty Election
S-29-0098	1975	00001	....Subnational Judicial Election
S-29-0099	1975	00000	.....Local Judicial Election
S-29-0100	1975	00003	....Subnational Legislative Election
S-29-0101	1975	00002	.....Local Legislative Election
S-29-0102	1975	00006	......City Council Election
S-29-0103	1975	00003	.....State Legislative Election
S-29-0104	1975	00019	..Electoral Competition
S-29-0105	1975	00018	...Political Party Electoral Competition
S-29-0106	1975	00040	..Electoral Outcome
S-29-0107	1975	00006	...Bandwagon Effect
S-29-0108	1975	00000	...Coattail Effect
S-29-0109	1975	00004	....Presidential Coattail Effect
S-29-0110	1975	00000	...Landslide Electoral Outcome
S-29-0111	1975	00012	...Majority Electoral Outcome
S-29-0112	1975	00002	....Absolute Majority Electoral Outcome
S-29-0113	1975	00000	...Vote Distribution
S-29-0114	1975	00055	..Electoral Participation
S-29-0115	1975	00001	...Nonvoting
S-29-0116	1975	00000	....Disenfranchisement
S-29-0117	1975	00000	....Voting Abstention
S-29-0118	1975	00000	.....Negative Voting Abstention
S-29-0119	1975	00000	.....Positive Voting Abstention
S-29-0120	1975	00001	...Suffrage Extension
S-29-0121	1975	00013	...Voting
S-29-0122	1975	00000	....Absentee Voting
S-29-0123	1975	00000	....Compulsory Voting
S-29-0124	1975	00001	....Confidence Voting
S-29-0125	1975	00005	....Floating Voting
S-29-0126	1979	00000	....Geographic Voting
S-29-0127	1979	00000	.....Regional Voting
S-29-0128	1979	00000	....Group Voting
S-29-0129	1975	00009	.....Age Group Voting
S-29-0130	1975	00008	.....Bloc Voting

S-29-0131	1975	00019	.....Class Voting
S-29-0132	1975	00009	.....Ethnic Group Voting
S-29-0133	1975	00007	.....Racial Voting
S-29-0134	1975	00008	......Black Voting
S-29-0135	1975	00008	.....Religious Voting
S-29-0136	1975	00008	.....Rural Voting
S-29-0137	1975	00003	.....Sex Group Voting
S-29-0138	1975	00000	.....Student Voting
S-29-0139	1975	00001	.....Suburban Voting
S-29-0140	1975	00002	....Independent Voting
S-29-0141	1975	00002	....Plural Voting
S-29-0142	1975	00010	....Political Party Ticket Voting
S-29-0143	1975	00002	....Protest Voting
S-29-0144	1979	00000	.....Backlash Voting
S-29-0145	1975	00000	....Proxy Voting
S-29-0146	1975	00004	....Split Ticket Voting
S-29-0147	1975	00006	....Straight Ticket Voting
S-29-0148	1975	00009	....Urban Voting
S-29-0149	1975	00002	....Voting Device
S-29-0150	1975	00003	.....Ballot
S-29-0151	1975	00000	......Australian Ballot
S-29-0152	1975	00001	......Long Ballot
S-29-0153	1975	00000	......Machine Ballot
S-29-0154	1975	00000	......Nonpartisan Ballot
S-29-0155	1975	00000	......Office Block Ballot
S-29-0156	1975	00000	......Paper Ballot
S-29-0157	1975	00000	.......Absentee Ballot
S-29-0158	1975	00000	......Political Party Column Ballot
S-29-0159	1975	00000	......Political Party List Ballot
S-29-0160	1975	00000	......Secret Ballot
S-29-0161	1975	00000	......Short Ballot
S-29-0162	1975	00000	.....Ballot Box
S-29-0163	1975	00000	.....Electronic Roll Call Device
S-29-0164	1975	00000	.....Voting Machine
S-29-0165	1975	00000	....Write In Voting
S-29-0166	1975	00004	...Voting Formulae
S-29-0167	1975	00000	....Cumulative Voting
S-29-0168	1979	00000	....D'Hont Voting Method
S-29-0169	1975	00000	....Largest Average Voting Method
S-29-0170	1975	00000	....Largest Remainder Voting Method
S-29-0171	1975	00001	....List Voting
S-29-0172	1975	00001	....Single Transferable Vote
S-29-0173	1975	00034	...Voting Pattern
S-29-0174	1975	00007	...Voting Procedure
S-29-0175	1979	00000	....Literacy Voting Test
S-29-0176	1975	00000	....Poll Tax
S-29-0177	1975	00004	....Voter Registration
S-29-0178	1975	00056	...Voting Result Interpretation
S-29-0179	1975	00004	....Election Turnout
S-29-0180	1975	00025	.....Voter Turnout
S-29-0181	1975	00001	......Average Voter Turnout Election
S-29-0182	1975	00001	......High Turnout Election
S-29-0183	1975	00000	......Low Turnout Election
S-29-0184	1975	00016	..Electoral Procedure
S-29-0185	1975	00000	...Electoral Board
S-29-0186	1975	00002	...Electoral College
S-29-0187	1975	00008	..Electoral Strategy
S-29-0188	1975	00001	...Electoral Tactics
S-29-0189	1975	00001	.....Voting Tactics
S-29-0190	1975	00002	..Electoral Unit
S-29-0191	1975	00004	...Constituency Size
S-29-0192	1975	00005	...Electoral District
S-29-0193	1975	00001	....Multimember District
S-29-0194	1975	00002	....Single Member District
S-29-0195	1975	00002	...Local Election District
S-29-0196	1975	00002	....Precinct
S-29-0197	1975	00000	.....Polling Place
S-29-0198	1975	00000	....Ward
S-29-0199	1975	00036	.Ethnic Politics
S-29-0200	1975	00000	.Extraparliamentary Politics
S-29-0201	1975	00016	.Geopolitics
S-29-0202	1975	00005	.Group Politics
S-29-0203	1975	00079	..Interest Group Politics
S-29-0204	1979	00000	..Language Group Politics
S-29-0205	1975	00141	.International Politics
S-29-0206	1975	00023	..Global Politics
S-29-0207	1975	00028	..World Politics
S-29-0208	1975	00003	...Communal Politics
S-29-0209	1975	00189	...Superpower Politics
S-29-0210	1975	00004	...Transnational Politics
S-29-0211	1975	00014	.Labor Politics
S-29-0212	1975	00010	..Trade Union Politics
S-29-0213	1979	00000	.Linkage Politics
S-29-0214	1975	00015	.National Politics
S-29-0215	1975	00015	.Parliamentary Politics
S-29-0216	1975	00017	.Partisan Politics
S-29-0217	1975	00002	..Boss Politics
S-29-0218	1975	00001	..Machine Politics
S-29-0219	1975	00005	..Multiparty Politics
S-29-0220	1979	00000	..One Political Party Politics
S-29-0221	1975	00010	..Patronage Politics
S-29-0222	1979	00000	..Two Political Party Politics
S-29-0223	1975	00020	.Power Politics
S-29-0224	1979	00000	..Power Abuse
S-29-0225	1975	00002	..Realpolitik
S-29-0226	1975	00001	.Progressive Politics
S-29-0227	1975	00024	.Protest Politics
S-29-0228	1975	00020	.Racial Politics
S-29-0229	1975	00018	.Religious Politics
S-29-0230	1979	00000	.Sexual Politics
S-29-0231	1979	00000	..Feminist Politics
S-29-0232	1979	00000	..Gay Politics
S-29-0233	1975	00000	.Spoils Politics
S-29-0234	1975	00007	.Subnational Politics
S-29-0235	1975	00033	..Local Politics
S-29-0236	1975	00022	...City Politics
S-29-0237	1975	00012	...Metropolitan Politics
S-29-0238	1975	00060	...Urban Politics
S-29-0239	1975	00005	....Suburban Politics
S-29-0240	1975	00010	...Village Politics
S-29-0241	1975	00021	..State Politics
S-29-0242	1975	00010	..Tribal Politics
S-29-0243	1975	00032	.Symbolic Politics
S-29-0244	1975	00008	.Technocratic Politics
S-29-0245	1975	00012	.Transitional Politics
S-29-0246	1975	00011	.Youth Politics

S-30 POWER TYPE

S-30-0001	1975	00007	Power Type
S-30-0002	1975	00008	.Concentrated Power
S-30-0003	1975	00004	.Dispersed Power
S-30-0004	1975	00032	.Economic Power
S-30-0005	1975	00009	..Corporate Power
S-30-0006	1975	00003	..Countervailing Power
S-30-0007	1975	00000	..Power Of The Purse
S-30-0008	1975	00001	.Formal Power
S-30-0009	1979	00000	..Institutional Power
S-30-0010	1975	00005	.Informal Power
S-30-0011	1975	00026	.Political Power
S-30-0012	1975	00012	..Emergency Power
S-30-0013	1975	00014	..Executive Power
S-30-0014	1975	00073	...Presidential Power
S-30-0015	1975	00018	..Judicial Power
S-30-0016	1975	00025	..Legislative Power
S-30-0017	1975	00026	..Separation Of Power

S-30-0018	1975	00015	...Federal State Separation
S-30-0019	1975	00004	...Legislative Executive Separation
S-30-0020	1975	00009	.State Power
S-30-0021	1975	00001	.Wartime Power

S-31 PROCESS

S-31-0001	1975	00002	Process
S-31-0002	1979	00000	.Accreditation Process
S-31-0003	1979	00000	..Education Accreditation Process
S-31-0004	1979	00000	..Professional Accreditation Process
S-31-0005	1975	00009	.Analytic Process
S-31-0006	1975	00021	..Classification Process
S-31-0007	1979	00000	..Evaluating
S-31-0008	1975	00000	..Formalization
S-31-0009	1979	00000	..Judging
S-31-0010	1979	00000	...Value Judgment
S-31-0011	1979	00000	..Testing
S-31-0012	1975	00011	..Typologizing
S-31-0013	1975	00003	.Associational Process
S-31-0014	1975	00025	..Alliance Process
S-31-0015	1975	00019	..Coalition Process
S-31-0016	1975	00003	...Coalition Change
S-31-0017	1975	00014	....Coalition Development
S-31-0018	1975	00034	.....Coalition Formation
S-31-0019	1975	00004	....Coalition Structural Change
S-31-0020	1975	00008	.....Coalition Disintegration
S-31-0021	1975	00003	.....Coalition Dissolution
S-31-0022	1975	00006	..Group Process
S-31-0023	1975	00003	...Group Change
S-31-0024	1975	00005	....Group Development
S-31-0025	1975	00008	.....Group Formation
S-31-0026	1975	00005	......Elite Formation
S-31-0027	1975	00004	....Group Structural Change
S-31-0028	1975	00000	.....Group Consolidation
S-31-0029	1975	00009	......Elite Consolidation
S-31-0030	1975	00000	.....Group Disintegration
S-31-0031	1975	00001	......Elite Disintegration
S-31-0032	1975	00001	...Group Innovation
S-31-0033	1975	00003	...Group Maintenance
S-31-0034	1975	00005	...Interest Aggregation
S-31-0035	1975	00013	...Interest Articulation
S-31-0036	1975	00018	..Organization Process
S-31-0037	1975	00051	...Organization Change
S-31-0038	1975	00048	....Organization Development
S-31-0039	1975	00012	.....Organization Formation
S-31-0040	1975	00022	....Organization Structural Change
S-31-0041	1975	00005	.....Organization Consolidation
S-31-0042	1975	00009	.....Organization Disintegration
S-31-0043	1975	00029	...Organization Innovation
S-31-0044	1975	00008	...Organization Maintenance
S-31-0045	1975	00086	.Change Process
S-31-0046	1975	00003	..Building Process
S-31-0047	1975	00013	...Community Building
S-31-0048	1975	00013	...Institution Building
S-31-0049	1975	00033	...Nation Building
S-31-0050	1975	00054	..Cultural Change Process
S-31-0051	1975	00029	...Cultural Adaptation
S-31-0052	1975	00010	...Cultural Differentiation
S-31-0053	1975	00002	...Cultural Lag
S-31-0054	1975	00111	..Development Process
S-31-0055	1979	00000	...Aging
S-31-0056	1975	00006	...Decay
S-31-0057	1975	00008	....Institutional Decay
S-31-0058	1975	00014	....Political Decay
S-31-0059	1979	00000	....Urban Decay
S-31-0060	1975	00163	...Economic Development
S-31-0061	1979	00000	....Industrial Development
S-31-0062	1975	00092	...Education Development
S-31-0063	1975	00000	...Evolution
S-31-0064	1975	00014	....Cultural Evolution
S-31-0065	1975	00007	....Genetic Evolution
S-31-0066	1975	00001	.....Natural Selection
S-31-0067	1975	00013	....Human Evolution
S-31-0068	1975	00005	....Political Evolution
S-31-0069	1975	00008	....Social Evolution
S-31-0070	1975	00060	...Innovation
S-31-0071	1975	00023	....Institutional Innovation
S-31-0072	1979	00000	....Political Party Innovation
S-31-0073	1975	00044	...Institutional Development
S-31-0074	1975	00029	....Institutionalization
S-31-0075	1975	00018	...Local Development
S-31-0076	1975	00007	....Village Development
S-31-0077	1975	00090	...Modernization
S-31-0078	1975	00022	....Cultural Modernization
S-31-0079	1975	00035	....Economic Modernization
S-31-0080	1975	00024	....Political Modernization
S-31-0081	1975	00040	....Social Modernization
S-31-0082	1975	00026	...Personality Development
S-31-0083	1975	00066	....Cognitive Development
S-31-0084	1975	00002	...Progress
S-31-0085	1975	00051	....Technological Progress
S-31-0086	1975	00129	...Reform
S-31-0087	1979	00000	....Administrative Reform
S-31-0088	1979	00000	....Education Reform
S-31-0089	1975	00008	....Executive Reform
S-31-0090	1975	00011	.....Executive Reorganization
S-31-0091	1975	00003	......Cabinet Reorganization
S-31-0092	1975	00011	....Judicial Reform
S-31-0093	1975	00005	.....Court Reform
S-31-0094	1975	00020	.....Penal Reform
S-31-0095	1975	00006	......Prison Reform
S-31-0096	1975	00018	....Legislative Reform
S-31-0097	1975	00002	.....Apportionment Reform
S-31-0098	1975	00022	.....Congressional Reform
S-31-0099	1975	00011	.....Legislative Reorganization
S-31-0100	1975	00001	.....Parliamentary Reform
S-31-0101	1975	00046	...Regional Development
S-31-0102	1975	00041	...Resource Development
S-31-0103	1975	00022	....Environmental Pollution
S-31-0104	1975	00009	.....Air Pollution
S-31-0105	1975	00004	.....Noise Pollution
S-31-0106	1975	00011	.....Water Pollution
S-31-0107	1975	00061	....Resource Allocation
S-31-0108	1975	00069	....Resource Distribution
S-31-0109	1975	00059	....Resource Utilization
S-31-0110	1979	00000	.....Scarcity
S-31-0111	1979	00000	......Energy Scarcity
S-31-0112	1979	00000	......Food Scarcity
S-31-0113	1979	00000	.......Hunger
S-31-0114	1979	00000	.......Malnutrition
S-31-0115	1979	00000	.......Starvation
S-31-0116	1979	00000	......Housing Scarcity
S-31-0117	1979	00000	......Labor Scarcity
S-31-0118	1979	00000	......Water Scarcity
S-31-0119	1975	00048	.....Natural Resource Exploitation
S-31-0120	1979	00000	......Coal Energy
S-31-0121	1979	00000	......Gas Energy
S-31-0122	1979	00000	......Geothermal Energy
S-31-0123	1979	00000	......Hydroelectric Energy
S-31-0124	1979	00000	......Nuclear Energy
S-31-0125	1979	00000	......Oil Energy
S-31-0126	1979	00000	......Solar Energy
S-31-0127	1979	00000	......Tidal Energy
S-31-0128	1979	00000	......Wind Energy
S-31-0129	1975	00061	...Rural Development

S-31-0130	1975	00070	....Agricultural Development
S-31-0131	1975	00099	...Urban Development
S-31-0132	1975	00012	....Urban Redevelopment
S-31-0133	1975	00010	.....Urban Renewal
S-31-0134	1975	00003	......Slum Rehabilitation
S-31-0135	1975	00046	..Economic Change
S-31-0136	1975	00003	...Deflation
S-31-0137	1975	00013	...Depression
S-31-0138	1975	00051	...Inflation
S-31-0139	1975	00021	..Elite Change
S-31-0140	1975	00011	...Elite Circulation
S-31-0141	1975	00009	..Evolutionary Change
S-31-0142	1975	00001	...Homeostatic Change
S-31-0143	1975	00040	..Institutional Change
S-31-0144	1975	00008	..Liberation Process
S-31-0145	1975	00001	...Emancipation
S-31-0146	1975	00003	....Black Emancipation
S-31-0147	1975	00009	.....Slavery Abolition
S-31-0148	1975	00012	....Womens Emancipation
S-31-0149	1975	00000	....Working Class Emancipation
S-31-0150	1975	00076	..Political Change
S-31-0151	1975	00003	...Extraterritorial Development
S-31-0152	1975	00006	....Annexation
S-31-0153	1975	00015	....Colonization
S-31-0154	1975	00024	.....Colonial Development
S-31-0155	1975	00024	....Decolonization
S-31-0156	1979	00000	....Political Succession
S-31-0157	1975	00007	....Secession
S-31-0158	1975	00023	...Politicization
S-31-0159	1975	00016	....Issue Politicization
S-31-0160	1979	00000	....System Politicization
S-31-0161	1975	00031	...Revolutionary Change
S-31-0162	1975	00121	...Social Change
S-31-0163	1975	00015	....Planned Social Change
S-31-0164	1975	00050	...Technological Change
S-31-0165	1975	00056	...Urbanization Process
S-31-0166	1975	00067	.Communication Process
S-31-0167	1975	00024	..Communication Flow
S-31-0168	1975	00019	...Communication Channel
S-31-0169	1975	00001	...Communication Field
S-31-0170	1975	00001	...Two Step Communication Flow
S-31-0171	1975	00017	..Informal Communication
S-31-0172	1979	00000	..Information Acquisition
S-31-0173	1979	00000	...Knowledge Acquisition
S-31-0174	1975	00040	..Information Dissemination
S-31-0175	1975	00005	..Information Explosion
S-31-0176	1979	00000	..Information Utilization
S-31-0177	1975	00055	..International Communication
S-31-0178	1975	00136	..Interpersonal Communication
S-31-0179	1975	00017	..Mass Communication
S-31-0180	1975	00002	...Broadcasting
S-31-0181	1975	00003	....Public Broadcasting
S-31-0182	1975	00010	...Media Editorializing
S-31-0183	1975	00002	...News Conference
S-31-0184	1975	00006	...News Flow
S-31-0185	1975	00030	...News Reporting
S-31-0186	1975	00030	....News Coverage
S-31-0187	1975	00001	...Newspaper Circulation
S-31-0188	1975	00048	..Nonverbal Communication
S-31-0189	1975	00006	...Political Propaganda
S-31-0190	1979	00000	....Election Campaign Propaganda
S-31-0191	1975	00004	....Government Propaganda
S-31-0192	1975	00002	....Political Party Propaganda
S-31-0193	1975	00002	....War Propaganda
S-31-0194	1975	00019	...Political Communication
S-31-0195	1975	00000	....Political Advertising
S-31-0196	1975	00000	..Political Party Advertising
S-31-0197	1979	00000	.Child Rearing Practices
S-31-0198	1975	00046	.Conflict Process
S-31-0199	1975	00029	..Competition
S-31-0200	1975	00000	...Direct Competition
S-31-0201	1975	00035	...Economic Competition
S-31-0202	1975	00018	...Elite Competition
S-31-0203	1975	00001	...External Competition
S-31-0204	1975	00006	...Foreign Competition
S-31-0205	1975	00000	...Formal Competition
S-31-0206	1975	00001	...Imperfect Competition
S-31-0207	1975	00000	...Indirect Competition
S-31-0208	1975	00003	...Internal Competition
S-31-0209	1975	00025	...International Competition
S-31-0210	1975	00001	...Perfect Competition
S-31-0211	1975	00014	...Political Competition
S-31-0212	1975	00029	...Political Party Competition
S-31-0213	1975	00010	....Interparty Competition
S-31-0214	1975	00007	....Intraparty Competition
S-31-0215	1975	00000	...Unfair Competition
S-31-0216	1975	00010	..Conflict Intensification
S-31-0217	1975	00000	...Escalation
S-31-0218	1975	00000	...Treaty Dissolution
S-31-0219	1975	00003	....Treaty Breaking
S-31-0220	1975	00051	..Conflict Resolution
S-31-0221	1975	00008	...Accommodation
S-31-0222	1975	00013	...Adjudication
S-31-0223	1975	00005	....International Adjudication
S-31-0224	1975	00030	....International Conciliation
S-31-0225	1975	00005	...Agreement
S-31-0226	1975	00015	....Treaty Making
S-31-0227	1975	00003	...Appeasement
S-31-0228	1975	00022	...Bargaining
S-31-0229	1975	00035	....Bargaining Strategy Process
S-31-0230	1975	00013	....Economic Bargaining
S-31-0231	1975	00007	....Political Bargaining
S-31-0232	1975	00036	.....International Political Bargaining
S-31-0233	1975	00017	...Coercion
S-31-0234	1975	00004	...Conciliation
S-31-0235	1975	00000	...Deescalation
S-31-0236	1975	00011	...Mediation
S-31-0237	1975	00001	....Arbitration
S-31-0238	1975	00007	.....International Arbitration
S-31-0239	1975	00003	.....Labor Arbitration
S-31-0240	1975	00021	....International Mediation
S-31-0241	1975	00003	....Labor Mediation
S-31-0242	1975	00020	...Negotiation
S-31-0243	1975	00088	....International Negotiation
S-31-0244	1975	00020	.....International Peace Negotiation
S-31-0245	1975	00007	....Labor Negotiation
S-31-0246	1979	00000	..Crisis
S-31-0247	1979	00000	...Economic Crisis
S-31-0248	1979	00000	...Natural Catastrophe
S-31-0249	1979	00000	...Personality Crisis
S-31-0250	1979	00000	...Political Crisis
S-31-0251	1979	00000	....International Crisis
S-31-0252	1979	00000	...Social Crisis
S-31-0253	1975	00034	..Dissent
S-31-0254	1975	00000	...Demonstrating
S-31-0255	1975	00001	...Mutiny
S-31-0256	1975	00019	...Protest
S-31-0257	1975	00004	....Peaceful Protest
S-31-0258	1975	00016	....Social Protest
S-31-0259	1975	00007	....Student Protest
S-31-0260	1975	00006	...Resistance
S-31-0261	1975	00002	....Draft Resistance
S-31-0262	1975	00000	....Passive Resistance
S-31-0263	1975	00085	.Control Process
S-31-0264	1975	00005	..Censorship Process
S-31-0265	1975	00001	...Graphic Arts Censorship

S-31-0266 1975 00004 ...Political Censorship
S-31-0267 1975 00003 ...Published Media Censorship
S-31-0268 1975 00002 ....Book Censorship
S-31-0269 1975 00000 ....Periodical Publication Censorship
S-31-0270 1975 00000 .....Journal Censorship
S-31-0271 1975 00002 .....Newspaper Censorship
S-31-0272 1975 00000 ...Religious Censorship
S-31-0273 1975 00000 ...Report Censorship
S-31-0274 1975 00000 ....Government Report Censorship
S-31-0275 1975 00000 ....Scientific Report Censorship
S-31-0276 1975 00000 ...Unpublished Media Censorship
S-31-0277 1975 00001 ....Broadcasting Censorship
S-31-0278 1975 00001 .....Radio Censorship
S-31-0279 1975 00004 .....Television Censorship
S-31-0280 1975 00001 ....Intelligence Censorship
S-31-0281 1975 00000 ....Performing Arts Censorship
S-31-0282 1975 00001 .....Cinema Censorship
S-31-0283 1975 00000 .....Music Censorship
S-31-0284 1979 00000 .....Theater Censorship
S-31-0285 1975 00015 ..Exploitation Process
S-31-0286 1975 00013 ...Economic Exploitation
S-31-0287 1975 00000 ...Political Exploitation
S-31-0288 1975 00005 ...Racial Exploitation
S-31-0289 1979 00000 ...Sex Exploitation
S-31-0290 1975 00003 ..Expropriation Process
S-31-0291 1975 00004 ...Government Expropriation
S-31-0292 1975 00010 ....Nationalization Process
S-31-0293 1975 00001 .....Bank Nationalization
S-31-0294 1975 00005 .....Industry Nationalization
S-31-0295 1975 00003 ......Basic Industry Nationalization
S-31-0296 1975 00000 .....Land Nationalization
S-31-0297 1975 00000 .....Utility Nationalization
S-31-0298 1975 00008 ..Information Manipulation
S-31-0299 1975 00006 ...Editorial Control
S-31-0300 1975 00003 ...Information Leaking
S-31-0301 1975 00013 ...Media Access
S-31-0302 1975 00028 ..Political Control
S-31-0303 1975 00003 ...Political Indoctrination
S-31-0304 1975 00003 ....Brainwashing
S-31-0305 1975 00005 ....Ideological Indoctrination
S-31-0306 1975 00000 ...Political Self Criticism
S-31-0307 1979 00000 ..Purge
S-31-0308 1979 00000 ...Catharsis
S-31-0309 1979 00000 ...Political Purge
S-31-0310 1979 00000 ..Regulation Process
S-31-0311 1979 00000 ...Government Regulation
S-31-0312 1975 00033 ..Repression Process
S-31-0313 1975 00001 ...Persecution
S-31-0314 1975 00017 ....Ethnic Persecution
S-31-0315 1975 00008 ....Minority Persecution
S-31-0316 1975 00001 ....Nationality Persecution
S-31-0317 1975 00002 ....Political Persecution
S-31-0318 1975 00006 ....Racial Persecution
S-31-0319 1975 00010 ....Religious Persecution
S-31-0320 1975 00006 ....Sex Persecution
S-31-0321 1979 00000 ...Political Repression
S-31-0322 1975 00135 .Decision Making Process
S-31-0323 1975 00043 ..Allocation Process
S-31-0324 1975 00000 ..Approval Process
S-31-0325 1975 00000 ..Authorization Process
S-31-0326 1975 00006 ..Collegial Decision Making
S-31-0327 1975 00008 ..Committee Decision Making
S-31-0328 1975 00001 ..Confirmation Process
S-31-0329 1975 00017 ..Implementation Process
S-31-0330 1975 00028 ..International Decision Making Process
S-31-0331 1975 00009 ..National Decision Making Process
S-31-0332 1975 00004 ..Subnational Decision Making Process
S-31-0333 1975 00024 ...Community Decision Making
S-31-0334 1975 00018 ...Local Decision Making
S-31-0335 1975 00002 ..Veto
S-31-0336 1975 00001 ...Executive Veto
S-31-0337 1975 00000 ....Gubernatorial Veto
S-31-0338 1975 00004 ....Presidential Veto
S-31-0339 1975 00000 ...Item Veto
S-31-0340 1975 00000 ...Pocket Veto
S-31-0341 1975 00000 ...Security Council Veto
S-31-0342 1979 00000 .Decontrol Process
S-31-0343 1979 00000 ..Denationalization Process
S-31-0344 1979 00000 ..Destalinization Process
S-31-0345 1979 00000 ..Deregulation Process
S-31-0346 1979 00000 ...Government Deregulation
S-31-0347 1975 00071 .Diplomacy
S-31-0348 1975 00016 ..Diplomatic Recognition
S-31-0349 1979 00000 ...DeFacto Recognition
S-31-0350 1979 00000 ...DeJure Recognition
S-31-0351 1975 00072 ..Diplomatic Relations
S-31-0352 1975 00005 ..Diplomatic Relations Break
S-31-0353 1979 00000 ..Diplomatic Relations Normalization
S-31-0354 1975 00001 ..Dollar Diplomacy
S-31-0355 1975 00003 ..Executive Diplomacy
S-31-0356 1975 00006 ...Presidential Diplomacy
S-31-0357 1975 00001 ..Gunboat Diplomacy
S-31-0358 1975 00007 ..Person To Person Diplomacy
S-31-0359 1975 00004 ...Citizen To Citizen Diplomacy
S-31-0360 1975 00002 ..Secret Diplomacy
S-31-0361 1975 00003 ..Summit Diplomacy
S-31-0362 1975 00007 .Economic Process
S-31-0363 1979 00000 ..Budget Process
S-31-0364 1975 00008 ...Budget Cutting
S-31-0365 1975 00014 ...Budget Formulation
S-31-0366 1975 00010 ....Budget Estimation
S-31-0367 1975 00002 ....Budget Proposing
S-31-0368 1975 00009 ...Budget Reviewing
S-31-0369 1975 00003 ....Budget Auditing
S-31-0370 1975 00011 ..Consumption Process
S-31-0371 1975 00018 ..Economic Relations
S-31-0372 1975 00005 ...Commerce
S-31-0373 1975 00027 ....International Commerce
S-31-0374 1975 00007 ....Interstate Commerce
S-31-0375 1975 00000 ....Intrastate Commerce
S-31-0376 1975 00003 ....World Commerce
S-31-0377 1975 00015 ...Industrial Relations
S-31-0378 1975 00184 ...International Economic Relations
S-31-0379 1975 00006 ....Economic Retaliation
S-31-0380 1975 00012 ....International Capital Movement
S-31-0381 1975 00069 ....International Economic Interdependence
S-31-0382 1975 00012 ....International Finance
S-31-0383 1975 00014 ....International Investment
S-31-0384 1975 00029 ...Trade
S-31-0385 1975 00026 ....Foreign Trade
S-31-0386 1975 00071 ....International Trade
S-31-0387 1975 00015 .....East West Trade
S-31-0388 1975 00061 ..Economic Resource Allocation
S-31-0389 1975 00027 ...Financing
S-31-0390 1975 00026 ....Investment
S-31-0391 1979 00000 .....Capital Flow
S-31-0392 1979 00000 .....Capital Formation
S-31-0393 1975 00013 .....Private Investment
S-31-0394 1975 00027 ......Private Foreign Investment
S-31-0395 1975 00004 ....Private Overseas Investment
S-31-0396 1975 00008 ......Private Industrial Investment
S-31-0397 1975 00000 ......Private Rural Investment
S-31-0398 1979 00000 .....Public Investment
S-31-0399 1979 00000 ......Public Foreign Investment
S-31-0400 1975 00041 .....Public Financing
S-31-0401 1975 00005 ......Cost Sharing

Code	Year	Count	Term
S-31-0402	1975	00005	......Debt Financing
S-31-0403	1975	00000	.......National Debt Financing
S-31-0404	1975	00002	.......War Debt Financing
S-31-0405	1975	00001	......Deficit Financing
S-31-0406	1975	00029	......Development Financing
S-31-0407	1975	00001	......Government Borrowing
S-31-0408	1975	00018	......Local Financing
S-31-0409	1979	00000	...Saving
S-31-0410	1979	00000	....Private Saving
S-31-0411	1979	00000	....Public Saving
S-31-0412	1975	00011	...Spending
S-31-0413	1975	00000	....Private Spending
S-31-0414	1975	00013	....Public Spending
S-31-0415	1975	00059	.....Defense Spending
S-31-0416	1975	00000	.....Deficit Spending
S-31-0417	1975	00001	.....Economy Pump Priming
S-31-0418	1975	00015	.....Poverty Program Spending
S-31-0419	1975	00013	.....Welfare Spending
S-31-0420	1975	00019	..Fiscal Process
S-31-0421	1975	00006	...Monetary Process
S-31-0422	1975	00008	...Subsidization Process
S-31-0423	1979	00000	..Marketing
S-31-0424	1975	00044	..Production Process
S-31-0425	1975	00079	...Agricultural Production
S-31-0426	1975	00012	....Farm Production
S-31-0427	1975	00007	.....Farming
S-31-0428	1979	00000	......Collective Farming
S-31-0429	1975	00000	......Corporate Farm Economy
S-31-0430	1975	00001	......Migrant Farming
S-31-0431	1975	00010	......Subsistence Farming
S-31-0432	1975	00003	......Tenant Farming
S-31-0433	1975	00001	...Automated Production
S-31-0434	1975	00017	...Industrial Production
S-31-0435	1975	00013	....Commodity Production
S-31-0436	1975	00002	....Mass Production
S-31-0437	1975	00019	....Raw Material Production
S-31-0438	1979	00000	...Knowledge Production
S-31-0439	1979	00000	....Discovery
S-31-0440	1975	00002	...National Production
S-31-0441	1975	00013	....Gross National Product
S-31-0442	1975	00002	.....Per Capita Gross National Product
S-31-0443	1975	00011	....Standard Of Living
S-31-0444	1975	00004	...Subsistence Production
S-31-0445	1975	00003	...War Production
S-31-0446	1975	00093	.Education Process
S-31-0447	1975	00005	..Computer Assisted Instruction
S-31-0448	1979	00000	..Instruction Methodology
S-31-0449	1979	00000	...Instructional Material
S-31-0450	1979	00000	....Learning Package
S-31-0451	1975	00011	..Programmed Instruction
S-31-0452	1979	00000	..Teaching
S-31-0453	1975	00011	...Political Science Teaching
S-31-0454	1979	00000	.Elite Mass Relations
S-31-0455	1979	00000	..Cult Of Personality
S-31-0456	1979	00000	.Exploration
S-31-0457	1979	00000	..Geographic Exploration
S-31-0458	1975	00021	.Government Process
S-31-0459	1975	00002	..Government Dissolution Process
S-31-0460	1975	00000	...Executive Dissolution
S-31-0461	1975	00000	....Abdication
S-31-0462	1975	00002	....Impeachment
S-31-0463	1975	00001	....Resignation
S-31-0464	1975	00000	...Legislative Dissolution
S-31-0465	1975	00001	..Government Formation Process
S-31-0466	1979	00000	..Intergovernmental Relations
S-31-0467	1979	00000	...Center Periphery Government Relations
S-31-0468	1979	00000	...City State Relations
S-31-0469	1979	00000	...Civil Military Relations
S-31-0470	1979	00000	...Federal City Relations
S-31-0471	1979	00000	...Federal State Relations
S-31-0472	1979	00000	...Police Community Relations
S-31-0473	1975	00107	.Influence Process
S-31-0474	1975	00046	..Political Influence
S-31-0475	1975	00018	.Judicial Process
S-31-0476	1975	00003	..Adversary Process
S-31-0477	1975	00030	..Court Action
S-31-0478	1975	00000	...Acquittal
S-31-0479	1975	00000	...Cease Desist Order
S-31-0480	1975	00000	...Certiorari
S-31-0481	1975	00000	...Consent Judgment
S-31-0482	1975	00003	...Conviction
S-31-0483	1975	00003	...Injunction
S-31-0484	1975	00001	...Life Sentence
S-31-0485	1975	00000	...Obiter Dicta
S-31-0486	1975	00000	...Subpoena
S-31-0487	1975	00000	...Verdict
S-31-0488	1975	00000	...Warrant
S-31-0489	1975	00000	...Writ Of Mandamus
S-31-0490	1975	00008	..Court Procedure
S-31-0491	1975	00000	...Post Trial Procedure
S-31-0492	1975	00003	....Imprisonment
S-31-0493	1975	00000	.....Arbitrary Imprisonment
S-31-0494	1975	00000	....Internment
S-31-0495	1975	00009	....Legal Settlement
S-31-0496	1975	00000	.....Imposed Legal Settlement
S-31-0497	1975	00003	.....Negotiated Legal Settlement
S-31-0498	1975	00005	......Plea Bargaining
S-31-0499	1975	00005	....Parole
S-31-0500	1975	00000	....Presentence Investigation
S-31-0501	1975	00015	....Sentencing
S-31-0502	1975	00000	.....Fining
S-31-0503	1975	00001	.....Jailing
S-31-0504	1975	00000	.....Probation
S-31-0505	1975	00003	...Pretrial Procedure
S-31-0506	1975	00000	....Arraignment
S-31-0507	1975	00004	....Arrest
S-31-0508	1975	00001	.....Arbitrary Arrest
S-31-0509	1975	00000	.....On View Arrest
S-31-0510	1975	00000	.....Political Arrest
S-31-0511	1975	00000	.....Warrant Arrest
S-31-0512	1975	00001	....Bail
S-31-0513	1975	00001	....Detention
S-31-0514	1975	00001	.....Preventive Detention
S-31-0515	1975	00000	....Indictment
S-31-0516	1975	00000	....Pretrial Release
S-31-0517	1975	00001	...Trial
S-31-0518	1975	00003	....Fair Trial
S-31-0519	1975	00000	....Military Trial
S-31-0520	1975	00002	.....Court Martial
S-31-0521	1975	00001	.....War Crime Trial
S-31-0522	1975	00001	....Political Trial
S-31-0523	1975	00001	....Public Trial
S-31-0524	1975	00000	.....Bench Trial
S-31-0525	1975	00000	.....Jury Trial
S-31-0526	1975	00000	....Secret Trial
S-31-0527	1975	00000	.....Star Chamber Proceeding
S-31-0528	1975	00003	...Trial Procedure
S-31-0529	1975	00003	....Jury Selection
S-31-0530	1975	00000	....Trial Oral Argument
S-31-0531	1975	00000	....Trial Strategy
S-31-0532	1975	00003	.....Self Defense
S-31-0533	1975	00003	.....Testimony
S-31-0534	1975	00039	..Judicial Decision Making
S-31-0535	1975	00016	..Judicial Procedure
S-31-0536	1975	00003	...Amnesty
S-31-0537	1975	00001	...Appeal Procedure

S-31-0538	1975	00002	...Clemency
S-31-0539	1975	00000	...Common Law Procedure
S-31-0540	1975	00004	...Grievance Procedure
S-31-0541	1975	00000	...Jeopardy
S-31-0542	1975	00010	...Judicial Discretion
S-31-0543	1975	00025	...Judicial Review
S-31-0544	1975	00007	....Appellate Court Review
S-31-0545	1975	00007	....Supreme Court Review
S-31-0546	1975	00002	...Justiciable Question
S-31-0547	1975	00012	...Legal Discrimination
S-31-0548	1975	00005	...Legal Precedent
S-31-0549	1975	00002	....Stare Decisis
S-31-0550	1975	00000	...Preemptory Challenge
S-31-0551	1975	00006	...Procedural Due Process
S-31-0552	1975	00007	...Substantive Due Process
S-31-0553	1975	00002	..Judicial Selection
S-31-0554	1975	00001	...Judicial Appointment
S-31-0555	1975	00000	...Judicial Retention
S-31-0556	1975	00029	..Litigation
S-31-0557	1975	00017	...Civil Rights Litigation
S-31-0558	1975	00005	...Class Action Litigation
S-31-0559	1975	00012	...Constitutional Litigation
S-31-0560	1975	00007	...Consumer Protection Litigation
S-31-0561	1975	00007	...Damage Suit
S-31-0562	1975	00006	..Public Order Maintenance
S-31-0563	1975	00035	...Law Enforcement
S-31-0564	1975	00005	....Code Enforcement
S-31-0565	1975	00001	.....Equal Law Enforcement
S-31-0566	1975	00011	....International Law Enforcement
S-31-0567	1975	00001	....National Law Enforcement
S-31-0568	1975	00022	....Punishment
S-31-0569	1975	00033	.....Criminal Punishment
S-31-0570	1975	00006	......Capital Punishment
S-31-0571	1975	00001	....Subnational Law Enforcement
S-31-0572	1975	00002	.....Local Law Enforcement
S-31-0573	1975	00033	.Legislative Process
S-31-0574	1975	00045	..Constituency Relations
S-31-0575	1975	00042	..Law Formulation
S-31-0576	1975	00019	...Constitutional Development
S-31-0577	1975	00006	....Constitution Making
S-31-0578	1979	00000	....Constitution Amendment Process
S-31-0579	1975	00012	....Constitutional Reform
S-31-0580	1975	00007	....Constitutional Revision
S-31-0581	1979	00000	...Legislative Action
S-31-0582	1975	00000	....Adjournment Debate
S-31-0583	1975	00002	....Bill Drafting
S-31-0584	1979	00000	....Legislative Amendment Process
S-31-0585	1975	00012	....Legislative Appropriation
S-31-0586	1975	00004	....Legislative Authorization
S-31-0587	1979	00000	....Legislative Bill Rejection
S-31-0588	1975	00045	....Legislative Decision Making
S-31-0589	1975	00003	....Legislative Resolution
S-31-0590	1975	00007	....Legislative Voting
S-31-0591	1975	00002	.....Bipartisan Voting
S-31-0592	1975	00000	.....Censure Motion
S-31-0593	1975	00000	......No Confidence Motion
S-31-0594	1975	00000	.....Cloture
S-31-0595	1975	00000	.....Discharge Petition
S-31-0596	1975	00000	....Question Time Debate
S-31-0597	1975	00004	...Treaty Ratification
S-31-0598	1975	00026	..Legislative Executive Relations
S-31-0599	1975	00057	...Congressional Executive Relations
S-31-0600	1975	00001	...Parliament Cabinet Relations
S-31-0601	1975	00000	....Interpellation
S-31-0602	1975	00000	.....Question Period
S-31-0603	1975	00005	..Legislative Procedure
S-31-0604	1975	00000	...Committee Rules
S-31-0605	1975	00000	...Committee Staffing
S-31-0606	1975	00006	...Congressional Procedure
S-31-0607	1975	00001	....Contempt Of Congress
S-31-0608	1975	00000	....Filibustering
S-31-0609	1975	00000	...Legislative Calendar
S-31-0610	1975	00000	...Legislative Hearing
S-31-0611	1975	00003	....Congressional Hearing
S-31-0612	1975	00030	.....Congressional Oversight
S-31-0613	1975	00000	...Parliamentary Procedure
S-31-0614	1975	00000	....Committee Of The Whole
S-31-0615	1975	00000	....Executive Session
S-31-0616	1975	00015	..Lobbying
S-31-0617	1979	00000	...Lobbying Tactic
S-31-0618	1975	00028	.Migration Process
S-31-0619	1975	00007	..Emigration Process
S-31-0620	1975	00010	..Immigration Process
S-31-0621	1975	00020	..Internal Migration
S-31-0622	1975	00019	...Rural Migration
S-31-0623	1975	00007	...Suburban Migration
S-31-0624	1975	00034	...Urban Migration
S-31-0625	1975	00005	..Refugee Migration
S-31-0626	1975	00029	.Mobilization Process
S-31-0627	1975	00008	..Economic Mobilization
S-31-0628	1975	00018	..Mass Mobilization
S-31-0629	1975	00014	..Military Mobilization
S-31-0630	1979	00000	..Peasant Mobilization
S-31-0631	1979	00000	..Political Mobilization
S-31-0632	1975	00026	..Social Mobilization
S-31-0633	1975	00006	..Worker Mobilization
S-31-0634	1975	00040	.Planning Process
S-31-0635	1975	00009	..Administrative Planning
S-31-0636	1975	00001	...Planification
S-31-0637	1975	00014	..Defense Planning
S-31-0638	1975	00004	...Defense Appropriation
S-31-0639	1975	00001	...Defense Authorization
S-31-0640	1975	00068	..Development Planning
S-31-0641	1975	00031	..Economic Planning
S-31-0642	1975	00007	...Central Economic Planning
S-31-0643	1975	00028	....Government Economic Planning
S-31-0644	1975	00000	.....Democratic Economic Planning
S-31-0645	1975	00009	.....Five Year Economic Planning
S-31-0646	1975	00008	.....Socialist Economic Planning
S-31-0647	1975	00010	...Fiscal Planning
S-31-0648	1975	00001	...Industrial Economic Planning
S-31-0649	1975	00017	...International Economic Planning
S-31-0650	1975	00033	...National Economic Planning
S-31-0651	1975	00000	...Subnational Economic Planning
S-31-0652	1975	00005	....Local Economic Planning
S-31-0653	1975	00006	....State Economic Planning
S-31-0654	1975	00056	..Education Planning
S-31-0655	1975	00027	...Higher Education Planning
S-31-0656	1975	00027	..Environmental Planning
S-31-0657	1979	00000	..Long Range Planning
S-31-0658	1975	00030	..Military Planning
S-31-0659	1975	00020	..Population Planning
S-31-0660	1975	00022	...Family Planning
S-31-0661	1975	00072	..Public Policy Planning
S-31-0662	1975	00019	...International Policy Planning
S-31-0663	1975	00025	...National Policy Planning
S-31-0664	1975	00005	...Subnational Policy Planning
S-31-0665	1975	00017	....City Policy Planning
S-31-0666	1975	00029	....Local Policy Planning
S-31-0667	1975	00008	....Rural Policy Planning
S-31-0668	1975	00019	....State Policy Planning
S-31-0669	1975	00065	....Urban Policy Planning
S-31-0670	1979	00000	.....Urban Design
S-31-0671	1979	00000	..Short Range Planning
S-31-0672	1975	00010	..Social Planning
S-31-0673	1975	00005	...Social Engineering

S-31-0674 1975 00215 .Policy Making Process
S-31-0675 1975 00013 ..Administrative Policy Making
S-31-0676 1975 00028 ..Collective Policy Making
S-31-0677 1975 00034 ..Domestic Policy Making
S-31-0678 1975 00026 ..Economic Policy Making
S-31-0679 1975 00059 ..Education Policy Making
S-31-0680 1975 00116 ..Foreign Policy Making
S-31-0681 1975 00040 ..International Policy Making
S-31-0682 1975 00076 ..Judicial Policy Making
S-31-0683 1975 00020 ..National Policy Making
S-31-0684 1975 00027 ..Policy Articulation
S-31-0685 1979 00000 ..Policy Compliance
S-31-0686 1975 00033 ..Policy Conflict
S-31-0687 1975 00145 ..Policy Development
S-31-0688 1979 00000 ...Policy Public Opinion Linkage
S-31-0689 1979 00000 ..Policy Enforcement
S-31-0690 1975 00687 ..Policy Evaluation
S-31-0691 1979 00000 ...Education Evaluation
S-31-0692 1979 00000 ...Financial Accounting
S-31-0693 1975 00010 ...Formative Evaluation
S-31-0694 1975 00034 ...Normative Evaluation
S-31-0695 1975 00775 ...Research Evaluation
S-31-0696 1975 00003 ...Social Accounting
S-31-0697 1975 00012 ...Summative Evaluation
S-31-0698 1975 00103 ..Policy Format
S-31-0699 1975 00112 ..Policy Implementation
S-31-0700 1975 00012 ..Policy Incrementalism
S-31-0701 1975 00009 ..Subnational Policy Making
S-31-0702 1975 00016 ...Local Policy Making
S-31-0703 1979 00000 .Political Participation
S-31-0704 1975 00125 ..Citizen Participation
S-31-0705 1975 00019 .Representation
S-31-0706 1975 00001 ..Apportionment
S-31-0707 1975 00000 ...Districting
S-31-0708 1975 00001 ....Gerrymandering
S-31-0709 1975 00000 ....Legislative Districting
S-31-0710 1975 00001 ....Legislative Redistricting
S-31-0711 1975 00000 ....Multiple Member Districting
S-31-0712 1975 00000 ....Single Member Districting
S-31-0713 1975 00001 ...Malapportionment
S-31-0714 1975 00002 ...Reapportionment
S-31-0715 1975 00008 ..Representation Type
S-31-0716 1975 00001 ...At Large Representation
S-31-0717 1975 00006 ...District Representation
S-31-0718 1975 00001 ...Functional Representation
S-31-0719 1975 00004 ...Geographic Representation
S-31-0720 1975 00000 ...Indirect Representation
S-31-0721 1975 00016 ...Interest Group Representation
S-31-0722 1975 00030 ...Minority Group Representation
S-31-0723 1975 00000 ...Multiple Member District Representation
S-31-0724 1975 00002 ...One Man One Vote Representation
S-31-0725 1975 00004 ...Proportional Representation
S-31-0726 1975 00001 ...Single Member District Representation
S-31-0727 1979 00000 ...Token Representation
S-31-0728 1975 00024 .Selection Process
S-31-0729 1975 00003 ..Appointment Process
S-31-0730 1975 00005 ...Presidential Appointment
S-31-0731 1975 00000 ...Reappointment
S-31-0732 1975 00006 ..Candidate Selection
S-31-0733 1975 00001 ..Delegate Selection
S-31-0734 1975 00001 ...Convention Delegate Selection
S-31-0735 1975 00001 ....Constitutional Convention Delegate Selection
S-31-0736 1975 00004 ....Political Party Convention Delegate Selection
S-31-0737 1975 00001 ..Endorsement
S-31-0738 1979 00000 ..Nominating Process
S-31-0739 1979 00000 ...Legislative Nominating Process
S-31-0740 1975 00010 ...Presidential Nominating Process
S-31-0741 1975 00028 ..Recruitment Process
S-31-0742 1975 00001 ...Cooptation
S-31-0743 1975 00019 ...Elite Recruitment
S-31-0744 1975 00025 ...Military Recruitment
S-31-0745 1975 00001 ...Nepotism
S-31-0746 1975 00009 ...Political Recruitment
S-31-0747 1975 00004 ....Judicial Recruitment
S-31-0748 1975 00008 ....Leadership Recruitment
S-31-0749 1975 00008 ....Legislative Recruitment
S-31-0750 1975 00008 ....Political Party Recruitment
S-31-0751 1975 00000 ..Slate Making
S-31-0752 1979 00000 .Social Process
S-31-0753 1979 00000 ..Ostracism
S-31-0754 1979 00000 ..Social Interaction
S-31-0755 1979 00000 ...Interpersonal Cooperation
S-31-0756 1979 00000 ...Friendship
S-31-0757 1975 00028 ..Social Role Process
S-31-0758 1979 00000 ...Role Acquisition
S-31-0759 1975 00031 ...Role Allocation
S-31-0760 1975 00012 ...Role Conflict
S-31-0761 1975 00026 ...Role Differentiation
S-31-0762 1975 00019 ....Role Specialization
S-31-0763 1975 00041 ...Role Expectation
S-31-0764 1975 00044 ...Role Orientation
S-31-0765 1975 00007 ....Executive Role Orientation
S-31-0766 1975 00014 ....Judicial Role Orientation
S-31-0767 1975 00026 ....Legislative Role Orientation
S-31-0768 1975 00012 ....Political Role Orientation
S-31-0769 1975 00087 ...Role Performance
S-31-0770 1975 00029 .Social Stratification Process
S-31-0771 1975 00003 ..Social Stratification Dissolution
S-31-0772 1975 00000 ...Caste Dissolution
S-31-0773 1975 00000 ...Class Dissolution
S-31-0774 1975 00004 ...Status Dissolution
S-31-0775 1975 00008 ..Social Stratification Formation
S-31-0776 1975 00000 ...Caste Formation
S-31-0777 1975 00011 ...Class Formation
S-31-0778 1975 00012 ...Status Formation
S-31-0779 1975 00012 ..Social Stratification Maintenance
S-31-0780 1975 00002 ...Caste Maintenance
S-31-0781 1975 00008 ...Class Maintenance
S-31-0782 1975 00014 ...Status Maintenance
S-31-0783 1979 00000 .Sports
S-31-0784 1979 00000 ..Amateur Sports
S-31-0785 1979 00000 ..Professional Sports
S-31-0786 1975 00001 .Structural Process
S-31-0787 1975 00015 ..Alienation Process
S-31-0788 1975 00017 ..Cleavage Process
S-31-0789 1975 00000 ...Horizontal Cleavage
S-31-0790 1975 00001 ...Vertical Cleavage
S-31-0791 1975 00019 ..Democratization
S-31-0792 1975 00016 ..Fragmentation
S-31-0793 1975 00006 ...Anomic Process
S-31-0794 1979 00000 ...Political Fragmentation
S-31-0795 1975 00013 ...Social Fragmentation
S-31-0796 1975 00029 ..Integration
S-31-0797 1975 00015 ...Assimilation
S-31-0798 1975 00034 ....Cultural Assimilation
S-31-0799 1975 00047 ....Ethnic Assimilation
S-31-0800 1975 00005 ....Linguistic Assimilation
S-31-0801 1975 00010 ....Racial Assimilation
S-31-0802 1975 00019 ...Cultural Integration
S-31-0803 1975 00007 ...Economic Integration
S-31-0804 1979 00000 ....Horizontal Economic Integration
S-31-0805 1975 00016 ....International Economic Integration
S-31-0806 1975 00034 .....International Regional Economic Integration

S-31-0807	1975	00002	....National Economic Integration
S-31-0808	1975	00000	....Subnational Economic Integration
S-31-0809	1975	00003	.....Local Economic Integration
S-31-0810	1979	00000	....Vertical Economic Integration
S-31-0811	1975	00025	...Ethnic Integration
S-31-0812	1975	00004	...Functional Integration
S-31-0813	1979	00000	...Horizontal Integration
S-31-0814	1975	00002	...Linguistic Integration
S-31-0815	1975	00015	....Bilingualism
S-31-0816	1975	00011	...Polarization
S-31-0817	1975	00014	....Ideological Polarization
S-31-0818	1979	00000	....International System Polarization
S-31-0819	1975	00029	...Political Integration
S-31-0820	1975	00008	....International Political Integration
S-31-0821	1975	00026	.....International Regional Political Integration
S-31-0822	1975	00007	.....Supranational Integration
S-31-0823	1975	00011	....National Political Integration
S-31-0824	1975	00025	....Political Unification
S-31-0825	1975	00002	....Subnational Political Integration
S-31-0826	1975	00002	.....Local Political Integration
S-31-0827	1975	00032	...Racial Integration
S-31-0828	1975	00007	....Housing Integration
S-31-0829	1975	00026	....School Integration
S-31-0830	1975	00030	...Social Integration
S-31-0831	1975	00000	...Vertical Integration
S-31-0832	1975	00000	....Hierarchical Integration
S-31-0833	1979	00000	..Specialization Process
S-31-0834	1979	00000	...Over Specialization

S-32 ROLES

S-32-0001	1975	00006	Roles
S-32-0002	1979	00000	.Academic
S-32-0003	1975	00000	.Adjudicator
S-32-0004	1975	00000	..Arbitrator
S-32-0005	1975	00001	..Bargainer
S-32-0006	1975	00002	..Broker
S-32-0007	1975	00001	..Mediator
S-32-0008	1975	00000	..Moderator
S-32-0009	1975	00006	..Negotiator
S-32-0010	1975	00004	..Ombudsman
S-32-0011	1975	00002	.Advisor
S-32-0012	1975	00005	..Administrative Advisor
S-32-0013	1975	00002	...Chief Executive Advisor
S-32-0014	1975	00004	....Presidential Advisor
S-32-0015	1975	00003	..Economic Advisor
S-32-0016	1975	00004	..Education Advisor
S-32-0017	1975	00003	..Legal Advisor
S-32-0018	1975	00002	..Military Advisor
S-32-0019	1975	00002	..Political Advisor
S-32-0020	1979	00000	...Election Campaign Advisor
S-32-0021	1975	00017	..Science Advisor
S-32-0022	1975	00006	..Technical Advisor
S-32-0023	1979	00000	.Athlete
S-32-0024	1979	00000	..Amateur Athlete
S-32-0025	1979	00000	..Professional Athlete
S-32-0026	1975	00013	.Decision Maker
S-32-0027	1975	00003	..Cultural Decision Maker
S-32-0028	1975	00005	..Economic Decision Maker
S-32-0029	1975	00014	..Organization Decision Maker
S-32-0030	1975	00010	..Political Decision Maker
S-32-0031	1975	00004	..Social Decision Maker
S-32-0032	1979	00000	.Explorer
S-32-0033	1975	00012	.Kinship Role
S-32-0034	1975	00003	..Clan Role
S-32-0035	1975	00065	..Family Role
S-32-0036	1979	00000	...Child
S-32-0037	1979	00000	....Exceptional Child
S-32-0038	1979	00000	....Handicapped Child
S-32-0039	1975	00014	...Household Head
S-32-0040	1975	00004	...Housewife
S-32-0041	1975	00016	...Husband
S-32-0042	1975	00010	...Maternal Role
S-32-0043	1975	00015	....Mother
S-32-0044	1979	00000	...Parent
S-32-0045	1975	00004	...Paternal Role
S-32-0046	1975	00003	....Father
S-32-0047	1975	00000	...Sibling
S-32-0048	1975	00020	...Wife
S-32-0049	1975	00002	.Leader
S-32-0050	1975	00000	..Economic Leader
S-32-0051	1975	00003	...Business Leader
S-32-0052	1975	00021	..Political Leader
S-32-0053	1975	00002	...Civil Rights Leader
S-32-0054	1975	00000	...Local Political Boss
S-32-0055	1975	00000	...Titular Leader
S-32-0056	1975	00003	..Social Leader
S-32-0057	1975	00006	...Charismatic Leader
S-32-0058	1975	00006	...Community Leader
S-32-0059	1975	00006	...Opinion Leader
S-32-0060	1975	00008	....Public Opinion Leader
S-32-0061	1975	00141	.Occupational Role
S-32-0062	1975	00005	..Agricultural Occupation
S-32-0063	1975	00013	...Agricultural Worker
S-32-0064	1975	00016	....Migrant Worker
S-32-0065	1975	00010	...Farmer
S-32-0066	1975	00001	....Collective Farmer
S-32-0067	1975	00000	....Private Farmer
S-32-0068	1975	00003	....Sharecropper
S-32-0069	1975	00004	....Tenant Farmer
S-32-0070	1979	00000	..Artisan
S-32-0071	1975	00002	..Commercial Occupation
S-32-0072	1975	00010	...Businessman
S-32-0073	1975	00010	....Entrepreneur
S-32-0074	1975	00003	....Small Businessman
S-32-0075	1975	00003	...Financier
S-32-0076	1975	00001	....Investor
S-32-0077	1975	00006	.....Foreign Investor
S-32-0078	1975	00002	...Speculator
S-32-0079	1975	00003	..Foreign Worker
S-32-0080	1975	00009	..Government Employee
S-32-0081	1975	00016	...Civil Service Employee
S-32-0082	1975	00001	...Patronage Worker
S-32-0083	1975	00006	..Industrial Occupation
S-32-0084	1975	00004	...Industrial Supervisor
S-32-0085	1975	00000	....Foreman
S-32-0086	1975	00022	...Industrial Worker
S-32-0087	1975	00014	....Blue Collar Worker
S-32-0088	1975	00003	.....Semiskilled Worker
S-32-0089	1975	00010	.....Skilled Worker
S-32-0090	1975	00007	.....Unskilled Worker
S-32-0091	1975	00000	......Day Laborer
S-32-0092	1975	00158	..Professional Occupational Role
S-32-0093	1975	00020	...Lawyer
S-32-0094	1975	00004	....Civil Lawyer
S-32-0095	1975	00006	....Corporation Lawyer
S-32-0096	1975	00004	....Criminal Lawyer
S-32-0097	1975	00010	...Manager
S-32-0098	1975	00006	....White Collar Worker
S-32-0099	1979	00000	...Religious Minister
S-32-0100	1979	00000	....Ayatallah
S-32-0101	1979	00000	....Lama
S-32-0102	1979	00000	....Missionary
S-32-0103	1979	00000	....Monk
S-32-0104	1979	00000	....Priest

S-32-0105	1979	00000	....Rabbi
S-32-0106	1975	00036	...Physician
S-32-0107	1975	00049	...Social Scientist
S-32-0108	1979	00000	....Anthropologist
S-32-0109	1979	00000	....Economist
S-32-0110	1979	00000	....Geographer
S-32-0111	1979	00000	....Historian
S-32-0112	1975	00011	....Policy Scientist
S-32-0113	1975	00005	....Political Scientist
S-32-0114	1979	00000	....Psychologist
S-32-0115	1979	00000	.....Clinical Psychologist
S-32-0116	1979	00000	.....Learning Psychologist
S-32-0117	1979	00000	.....Social Psychologist
S-32-0118	1979	00000	...Social Worker
S-32-0119	1979	00000	...Sociologist
S-32-0120	1975	00033	...Teacher
S-32-0121	1975	00025	....Professor
S-32-0122	1975	00025	....School Teacher
S-32-0123	1975	00001	...Technical Occupation
S-32-0124	1975	00004	....Engineer
S-32-0125	1975	00024	....Scientist
S-32-0126	1975	00001	....Technician
S-32-0127	1975	00009	..Unemployed Person
S-32-0128	1979	00000	..Union Worker
S-32-0129	1975	00007	.Planner
S-32-0130	1975	00003	..Economic Planner
S-32-0131	1975	00001	...Fiscal Planner
S-32-0132	1975	00005	....Budget Planner
S-32-0133	1975	00001	..International Planner
S-32-0134	1975	00000	..National Planner
S-32-0135	1975	00000	..Political Planner
S-32-0136	1975	00004	...Government Planner
S-32-0137	1975	00007	....Foreign Policy Planner
S-32-0138	1975	00000	..Social Planner
S-32-0139	1975	00006	...Education Planner
S-32-0140	1975	00004	..Subnational Planner
S-32-0141	1975	00008	...Local Planner
S-32-0142	1975	00005	....City Planner
S-32-0143	1975	00008	....Urban Planner
S-32-0144	1975	00007	...Regional Planner
S-32-0145	1975	00002	...State Planner
S-32-0146	1975	00028	.Political Party Role
S-32-0147	1975	00007	..Political Party Leader
S-32-0148	1975	00003	...Backbencher
S-32-0149	1975	00001	...Bloc Leader
S-32-0150	1975	00001	...Campaign Manager
S-32-0151	1975	00000	...Cell Leader
S-32-0152	1975	00000	...Formal Political Party Leader
S-32-0153	1975	00000	...Frontbencher
S-32-0154	1975	00002	...Opposition Political Party Leader
S-32-0155	1975	00001	...Politburo Member
S-32-0156	1975	00000	...Political Boss
S-32-0157	1975	00002	....National Political Party Leader
S-32-0158	1975	00007	...Political Party Cadre
S-32-0159	1975	00000	...Political Party Chief
S-32-0160	1975	00004	...Political Party Professional
S-32-0161	1975	00000	...Political Party Whip
S-32-0162	1975	00000	...Precinct Captain
S-32-0163	1975	00001	...Ward Chairperson
S-32-0164	1975	00005	..Political Party Member
S-32-0165	1975	00002	...Delegation Member
S-32-0166	1975	00002	....Delegate
S-32-0167	1975	00010	.....Convention Delegate
S-32-0168	1975	00000	.....Delegate At Large
S-32-0169	1975	00022	...Political Party Supporter
S-32-0170	1975	00006	....Campaign Contributor
S-32-0171	1975	00011	....Political Party Loyalist
S-32-0172	1975	00003	....Strong Political Party Identifier
S-32-0173	1975	00002	....Weak Political Party Identifier
S-32-0174	1975	00002	...Political Party Worker
S-32-0175	1975	00004	....Campaign Worker
S-32-0176	1975	00000	....Precinct Worker
S-32-0177	1975	00000	...Rank And File Member
S-32-0178	1975	00028	.Political Role
S-32-0179	1975	00010	..Activist
S-32-0180	1975	00001	...Demonstrator
S-32-0181	1975	00000	...Economic Activist
S-32-0182	1975	00004	....Consumer Activist
S-32-0183	1975	00025	...Political Activist
S-32-0184	1975	00002	....Militant
S-32-0185	1975	00001	.....Black Militant
S-32-0186	1975	00001	......Black Muslim
S-32-0187	1975	00002	......Black Panther
S-32-0188	1975	00001	.....New Left Militant
S-32-0189	1975	00002	.....Student Militant
S-32-0190	1975	00001	....Peace Activist
S-32-0191	1975	00000	....Political Agitator
S-32-0192	1975	00001	....Political Conspirator
S-32-0193	1975	00009	....Political Party Activist
S-32-0194	1975	00003	....Political Party Dissident
S-32-0195	1975	00005	....Political Party Follower
S-32-0196	1975	00010	....Revolutionary
S-32-0197	1975	00003	.....Guerrilla
S-32-0198	1975	00002	......Urban Guerrilla
S-32-0199	1975	00002	.....Insurrectionist
S-32-0200	1975	00004	.....Maoist Revolutionary
S-32-0201	1975	00001	....Right Wing Activist
S-32-0202	1975	00001	....Suffragette
S-32-0203	1975	00032	....Terrorist
S-32-0204	1975	00001	...Rioter
S-32-0205	1975	00000	....Ghetto Rioter
S-32-0206	1975	00004	...Student Activist
S-32-0207	1975	00001	...War Protestor
S-32-0208	1975	00001	..Chauvinist
S-32-0209	1975	00000	...Female Chauvinist
S-32-0210	1975	00000	...Jingoist
S-32-0211	1975	00001	...Male Chauvinist
S-32-0212	1975	00002	...National Chauvinist
S-32-0213	1975	00001	...Sexist
S-32-0214	1975	00000	...Xenophobe
S-32-0215	1975	00002	..Conscientious Objector
S-32-0216	1975	00008	..Lobbyist
S-32-0217	1975	00001	..Political Gatekeeper
S-32-0218	1975	00001	..Political Informer
S-32-0219	1975	00003	..Politician
S-32-0220	1975	00001	...Autocrat
S-32-0221	1975	00000	...Despot
S-32-0222	1975	00000	....Benevolent Despot
S-32-0223	1975	00000	....Oriental Despot
S-32-0224	1975	00005	...Political Broker
S-32-0225	1975	00009	...Political Candidate
S-32-0226	1975	00000	....Dark Horse Candidate
S-32-0227	1975	00000	....Machine Candidate
S-32-0228	1975	00002	....National Candidate
S-32-0229	1975	00001	.....National Chief Executive Candidate
S-32-0230	1975	00000	......Chancellor Candidate
S-32-0231	1975	00019	......Presidential Candidate
S-32-0232	1975	00000	.......Favorite Son Candidate
S-32-0233	1975	00001	......Prime Minister Candidate
S-32-0234	1975	00000	.....National Judicial Candidate
S-32-0235	1979	00000	.....National Legislative Candidate
S-32-0236	1975	00010	......Congressional Candidate
S-32-0237	1975	00001	......Parliamentary Candidate
S-32-0238	1975	00000	...Subnational Candidate
S-32-0239	1975	00000	.....Subnational Chief Executive Candidate
S-32-0240	1975	00000	......Local Chief Executive Candidate

S-32-0241	1975	00002	.......Mayoralty Candidate
S-32-0242	1975	00000	......State Chief Executive Candidate
S-32-0243	1975	00001	.......Gubernatorial Candidate
S-32-0244	1975	00000	.....Subnational Judicial Candidate
S-32-0245	1975	00000	......Local Judicial Candidate
S-32-0246	1975	00001	......State Judicial Candidate
S-32-0247	1979	00000	.....Subnational Legislative Candidate
S-32-0248	1979	00000	......Local Legislative Candidate
S-32-0249	1979	00000	......State Legislative Candidate
S-32-0250	1975	00002	...Political Official
S-32-0251	1975	00001	....Political Appointee
S-32-0252	1975	00002	...Political Patron
S-32-0253	1975	00005	...Professional Politician
S-32-0254	1975	00001	..Politicist
S-32-0255	1975	00000	...Spectrum Politicist
S-32-0256	1975	00001	....Centrist
S-32-0257	1975	00003	....Conservative
S-32-0258	1975	00001	....Extremist
S-32-0259	1975	00007	....Ideologue
S-32-0260	1975	00006	....Leftist
S-32-0261	1975	00005	....Liberal
S-32-0262	1975	00000	....Political Neutralist
S-32-0263	1975	00009	....Political Radical
S-32-0264	1975	00001	....Reactionary
S-32-0265	1975	00003	....Rightist
S-32-0266	1975	00000	...System Politicist
S-32-0267	1975	00001	....Anarchist
S-32-0268	1975	00000	....Anticleric
S-32-0269	1975	00002	....Colonialist
S-32-0270	1975	00001	....Communalist
S-32-0271	1975	00000	....Democrat
S-32-0272	1975	00000	.....Christian Democrat
S-32-0273	1975	00001	....Fascist
S-32-0274	1975	00000	.....Falangist
S-32-0275	1975	00001	.....National Socialist
S-32-0276	1975	00000	....Imperialist
S-32-0277	1975	00004	....Nationalist
S-32-0278	1975	00002	....Republican
S-32-0279	1975	00000	....Royalist
S-32-0280	1975	00001	....Sectarian
S-32-0281	1975	00015	....Socialist
S-32-0282	1975	00003	.....Communist
S-32-0283	1975	00001	......Maoist
S-32-0284	1975	00000	......Stalinist
S-32-0285	1975	00000	.....Democrat Socialist
S-32-0286	1975	00002	..Separatist
S-32-0287	1975	00007	...Factionalist
S-32-0288	1975	00003	...Isolationist
S-32-0289	1975	00004	...Secessionist
S-32-0290	1975	00000	...Sectionalist
S-32-0291	1975	00001	...Segregationist
S-32-0292	1975	00002	....Racist
S-32-0293	1975	00008	..Voter
S-32-0294	1975	00000	...Absentee Voter
S-32-0295	1975	00004	...Alienated Voter
S-32-0296	1975	00003	...Apathetic Voter
S-32-0297	1975	00003	...Black Voter
S-32-0298	1975	00009	...Candidate Voter
S-32-0299	1975	00013	....Candidate Image Voter
S-32-0300	1975	00022	....Candidate Preference Voter
S-32-0301	1975	00006	...Class Voter
S-32-0302	1975	00000	....Middle Class Voter
S-32-0303	1975	00001	....Upper Class Voter
S-32-0304	1975	00008	....Working Class Voter
S-32-0305	1975	00002	...Deferential Voter
S-32-0306	1975	00002	...Efficacious Voter
S-32-0307	1975	00000	...Eligible Voter
S-32-0308	1975	00000	....Potential Voter
S-32-0309	1975	00000	.....Registered Voter
S-32-0310	1975	00003	...Ethnic Voter
S-32-0311	1975	00002	...Farm Voter
S-32-0312	1975	00001	...Female Voter
S-32-0313	1975	00008	...Floating Voter
S-32-0314	1975	00003	...Group Benefits Voter
S-32-0315	1975	00015	...Ideological Voter
S-32-0316	1975	00004	...Independent Voter
S-32-0317	1975	00008	...Informed Voter
S-32-0318	1975	00025	...Issue Voter
S-32-0319	1975	00002	....Single Issue Voter
S-32-0320	1975	00001	...Marginal Voter
S-32-0321	1975	00002	...Minority Voter
S-32-0322	1975	00001	...New Voter
S-32-0323	1975	00000	...Nonvoter
S-32-0324	1975	00031	...Political Party Voter
S-32-0325	1975	00017	....Partisan Image Voter
S-32-0326	1975	00004	....Straight Party Voter
S-32-0327	1975	00003	...Protest Voter
S-32-0328	1975	00004	...Rural Voter
S-32-0329	1975	00002	...Situation Of The Times Voter
S-32-0330	1975	00002	...Student Voter
S-32-0331	1975	00001	...Suburban Voter
S-32-0332	1975	00000	...Ticket Splitter
S-32-0333	1975	00005	...Urban Voter
S-32-0334	1975	00052	...Voter Orientation
S-32-0335	1975	00010	....Candidate Orientation
S-32-0336	1975	00037	....Issue Orientation
S-32-0337	1975	00021	....Political Party Orientation
S-32-0338	1979	00000	...Youth Voter
S-32-0339	1975	00008	.Religious Role
S-32-0340	1975	00013	..Religious Leader
S-32-0341	1975	00002	..Religious Dissenter
S-32-0342	1975	00228	.Sex Role
S-32-0343	1975	00124	.Student
S-32-0344	1979	00000	..Foreign Student

S-33 SECURITY FORCES

S-33-0001	1975	00005	Security Forces
S-33-0002	1975	00005	.Multinational Security Forces
S-33-0003	1975	00001	..Multilateral Security Forces
S-33-0004	1975	00004	..Peacekeeping Forces
S-33-0005	1975	00010	...International Peacekeeping Forces
S-33-0006	1975	00006	.National Security Forces
S-33-0007	1975	00024	..Defense System
S-33-0008	1975	00004	...Balanced Force
S-33-0009	1975	00019	...Tactical Force
S-33-0010	1975	00037	...War Technology
S-33-0011	1975	00003	....Mutual Deterrence System
S-33-0012	1975	00079	....Nuclear Power
S-33-0013	1975	00007	....Offensive Weapon System
S-33-0014	1975	00018	.....Weapon Delivery System
S-33-0015	1975	00001	......Weapon Delivery Subsystem
S-33-0016	1975	00007	....Weapon
S-33-0017	1975	00004	.....Civilian Weapon
S-33-0018	1975	00003	......Handgun
S-33-0019	1975	00021	.....Military Weapon
S-33-0020	1975	00005	......Biological Weapon
S-33-0021	1979	00000	......Bomb
S-33-0022	1975	00004	......Chemical Weapon
S-33-0023	1975	00016	......Conventional Weapon
S-33-0024	1975	00004	......Defensive Weapon
S-33-0025	1975	00003	......Deterrent Weapon
S-33-0026	1975	00015	.....Missile
S-33-0027	1975	00011	......Ballistic Missile
S-33-0028	1975	00006	.......Antiballistic Missile
S-33-0029	1975	00002	......Multiple Warhead Missile

S-33-0030	1979	00000	.......MARV
S-33-0031	1979	00000	.......MIRV
S-33-0032	1975	00000	.....Munitions
S-33-0033	1975	00032	......Military Aircraft
S-33-0034	1975	00020	......Warship
S-33-0035	1975	00039	.....Nuclear Weapon
S-33-0036	1979	00000	......First Strike Nuclear Weapon
S-33-0037	1979	00000	......Nuclear Stockpiling
S-33-0038	1979	00000	......Second Strike Nuclear Weapon
S-33-0039	1975	00023	.....Strategic Weapon
S-33-0040	1975	00016	.....Tactical Weapon
S-33-0041	1975	00001	.....Unconventional Weapon
S-33-0042	1975	00000	..Irregular Forces
S-33-0043	1975	00000	...Irregular Military Forces
S-33-0044	1975	00005	....Paramilitary Forces
S-33-0045	1975	00001	.....Paramilitary Organization
S-33-0046	1975	00000	....Private Army
S-33-0047	1975	00073	..Military Forces
S-33-0048	1975	00022	...Military Establishment
S-33-0049	1975	00037	....Armed Forces
S-33-0050	1975	00001	.....Admiralty
S-33-0051	1979	00000	.....Air Force
S-33-0052	1975	00052	.....Army
S-33-0053	1975	00007	......Army Organization
S-33-0054	1975	00004	.......Mass Militia Army
S-33-0055	1975	00002	.......National Guard
S-33-0056	1975	00003	.......Regular Army
S-33-0057	1975	00023	........Officer Corps
S-33-0058	1975	00001	.......Standing Army
S-33-0059	1975	00004	.....Coast Guard
S-33-0060	1975	00010	.....Conscripted Armed Forces
S-33-0061	1975	00013	.....Marines
S-33-0062	1975	00001	.....Mercenary Armed Forces
S-33-0063	1979	00000	.....Merchant Marine
S-33-0064	1975	00077	.....Navy
S-33-0065	1975	00069	......Naval Forces
S-33-0066	1975	00022	.......Naval Power
S-33-0067	1975	00017	........Sea Power
S-33-0068	1975	00010	.....Peoples Army
S-33-0069	1975	00030	.....Voluntary Armed Forces
S-33-0070	1975	00027	...Professional Military Forces
S-33-0071	1975	00010	...Reserve Military Forces

S-34 SOCIALIZATION

S-34-0001	1975	00036	Socialization
S-34-0002	1975	00024	.Acculturation
S-34-0003	1975	00004	.Enculturation
S-34-0004	1975	00008	..Americanization
S-34-0005	1979	00000	.Learning
S-34-0006	1979	00000	..Behavior Modification
S-34-0007	1979	00000	..Language Acquisition
S-34-0008	1979	00000	...Language Learning
S-34-0009	1979	00000	..Moral Learning
S-34-0010	1979	00000	..Nonverbal Learning
S-34-0011	1979	00000	..Rote Learning
S-34-0012	1979	00000	..Serial Learning
S-34-0013	1979	00000	..Skill Acquisition
S-34-0014	1979	00000	..Symbol Learning
S-34-0015	1979	00000	..Verbal Learning
S-34-0016	1975	00019	.Socialization Context
S-34-0017	1975	00016	..Group Socialization
S-34-0018	1975	00018	...Adolescent Socialization
S-34-0019	1975	00015	....Adolescent Political Socialization
S-34-0020	1975	00007	...Adult Socialization
S-34-0021	1975	00006	....Adult Political Socialization
S-34-0022	1975	00084	...Childhood Socialization
S-34-0023	1975	00028	....Childhood Political Socialization
S-34-0024	1975	00008	...Cohort Group Socialization
S-34-0025	1975	00015	...Elite Socialization
S-34-0026	1975	00030	...Family Socialization
S-34-0027	1975	00012	....Family Political Socialization
S-34-0028	1975	00000	...Interest Group Socialization
S-34-0029	1979	00000	...Job Socialization
S-34-0030	1975	00016	...Peer Group Socialization
S-34-0031	1975	00009	...Primary Group Socialization
S-34-0032	1975	00010	..Institutional Socialization
S-34-0033	1975	00004	...Bureaucratic Socialization
S-34-0034	1975	00002	...Legislative Socialization
S-34-0035	1979	00000	...Religious Socialization
S-34-0036	1975	00023	..Professional Socialization
S-34-0037	1975	00045	...Education Socialization
S-34-0038	1975	00001	...Legal Socialization
S-34-0039	1975	00001	.Socialization Type
S-34-0040	1979	00000	..Ethical Socialization
S-34-0041	1975	00009	..Opinion Socialization
S-34-0042	1975	00032	...Opinion Change
S-34-0043	1975	00040	...Opinion Formation
S-34-0044	1975	00013	...Opinion Stability
S-34-0045	1975	00024	..Perception Socialization
S-34-0046	1975	00051	..Political Socialization
S-34-0047	1975	00029	...Political Orientation Development
S-34-0048	1975	00020	...Political Value Acquisition
S-34-0049	1975	00028	..Role Socialization
S-34-0050	1975	00002	..Social Conditioning
S-34-0051	1975	00000	...Political Conditioning
S-34-0052	1979	00000	...Social Adjustment
S-34-0053	1975	00054	...Stereotyping

S-35 SOCIETY TYPE

S-35-0001	1975	00010	Society Type
S-35-0002	1975	00009	.Achieving Society
S-35-0003	1975	00009	.Affluent Society
S-35-0004	1975	00005	.Meritocracy
S-35-0005	1975	00019	.Modernizing Society
S-35-0006	1975	00006	.Nonwestern Society
S-35-0007	1975	00015	.Primitive Society
S-35-0008	1975	00006	.Secular Society
S-35-0009	1979	00000	.Society Type Base
S-35-0010	1975	00004	..Bourgeois Society
S-35-0011	1975	00008	..Bureaucratic Society
S-35-0012	1975	00025	..Capitalist Society
S-35-0013	1975	00007	..Caste Society
S-35-0014	1975	00003	..Clan Society
S-35-0015	1975	00008	..Class Society
S-35-0016	1975	00001	..Classless Society
S-35-0017	1979	00000	...Communist Society
S-35-0018	1975	00010	..Feudal Society
S-35-0019	1979	00000	..Hunting And Fishing Society
S-35-0020	1975	00039	..Industrial Society
S-35-0021	1975	00047	...Advanced Industrial Society
S-35-0022	1975	00015	...Post Industrial Society
S-35-0023	1975	00011	..Mass Society
S-35-0024	1975	00002	...Atomistic Society
S-35-0025	1975	00003	..Nomadic Society
S-35-0026	1975	00048	..Peasant Society
S-35-0027	1975	00008	..Slave Society
S-35-0028	1979	00000	..Squatter Society
S-35-0029	1975	00044	..Tribal Society
S-35-0030	1975	00052	..Urban Society
S-35-0031	1979	00000	.Society Type Structure
S-35-0032	1975	00004	..Closed Society
S-35-0033	1975	00002	...Secret Society
S-35-0034	1979	00000	....Freemasonry
S-35-0035	1975	00007	..Heterogeneous Society

S-35-0036	1979	00000	...Multicultural Society
S-35-0037	1975	00002	....Bicultural Society
S-35-0038	1975	00012	...Multiethnic Society
S-35-0039	1975	00002	...Multilingual Society
S-35-0040	1975	00002	...Multiracial Society
S-35-0041	1975	00004	...Plural Society
S-35-0042	1975	00005	..Homogeneous Society
S-35-0043	1975	00004	..Open Society
S-35-0044	1979	00000	..Pluralistic Society
S-35-0045	1975	00048	.Traditional Society
S-35-0046	1975	00010	..Preindustrial Society
S-35-0047	1979	00000	..Religious Society
S-35-0048	1979	00000	...Islamic Society
S-35-0049	1975	00019	.Transitional Society
S-35-0050	1975	00016	.Western Society

S-36 STATUS

S-36-0001	1975	00028	Status
S-36-0002	1975	00009	.Administrative Personnel
S-36-0003	1975	00006	..Administrative Officer
S-36-0004	1975	00000	...Bureau Chief
S-36-0005	1975	00000	...Dean
S-36-0006	1975	00000	...Department Head
S-36-0007	1975	00001	...Executive Director
S-36-0008	1975	00001	....Executive Assistant
S-36-0009	1975	00003	..Administrative Staff Personnel
S-36-0010	1975	00003	...Executive Staff Personnel
S-36-0011	1975	00002	....Chief Executive Staff Personnel
S-36-0012	1975	00013	.....Presidential Staff Personnel
S-36-0013	1975	00000	...Judicial Staff Personnel
S-36-0014	1975	00005	...Legislative Staff Personnel
S-36-0015	1975	00006	.Citizenship Status
S-36-0016	1975	00007	..Alien
S-36-0017	1975	00001	...Dual Citizen
S-36-0018	1975	00001	...Native Born Citizen
S-36-0019	1975	00003	...Naturalized Citizen
S-36-0020	1979	00000	..Exile
S-36-0021	1975	00049	..Immigrant
S-36-0022	1975	00005	...Emigre
S-36-0023	1975	00002	...Expatriate
S-36-0024	1975	00008	...Refugee
S-36-0025	1975	00004	....Political Refugee
S-36-0026	1975	00000	..Repatriate
S-36-0027	1975	00000	..Stateless Person
S-36-0028	1975	00026	.Criminal
S-36-0029	1975	00002	..Economic Criminal
S-36-0030	1975	00004	..Personal Crime Criminal
S-36-0031	1975	00000	...Blackmailer
S-36-0032	1975	00000	...Extortionist
S-36-0033	1975	00000	...Murderer
S-36-0034	1975	00000	...Slanderer
S-36-0035	1975	00000	..Political Criminal
S-36-0036	1975	00000	...Political Assassin
S-36-0037	1975	00000	...Traitor
S-36-0038	1975	00004	..War Criminal
S-36-0039	1979	00000	.Expert
S-36-0040	1975	00010	.Government Official
S-36-0041	1975	00004	..Cabinet Member
S-36-0042	1975	00004	...International Commission Member
S-36-0043	1975	00001	...International Council Member
S-36-0044	1975	00002	...Minister
S-36-0045	1975	00004	....Cabinet Secretary
S-36-0046	1975	00000	.....Cabinet Undersecretary
S-36-0047	1975	00001	...Privy Councilor
S-36-0048	1975	00001	..Chief Government Executive
S-36-0049	1975	00003	...Dictator
S-36-0050	1975	00000	....Benevolent Dictator
S-36-0051	1975	00001	...International Government Executive
S-36-0052	1975	00000	...Military Governor
S-36-0053	1975	00003	....Warlord
S-36-0054	1975	00003	...Monarch
S-36-0055	1975	00000	....Absolute Monarch
S-36-0056	1975	00002	....Constitutional Monarch
S-36-0057	1975	00006	....Emperor
S-36-0058	1975	00000	.....Kaiser
S-36-0059	1975	00000	.....Khan
S-36-0060	1975	00002	.....Shah
S-36-0061	1975	00001	.....Sheik
S-36-0062	1975	00004	.....Tsar
S-36-0063	1975	00002	....Hereditary Ruler
S-36-0064	1975	00007	....King
S-36-0065	1975	00004	....Prince
S-36-0066	1975	00000	....Queen
S-36-0067	1975	00000	....Regent
S-36-0068	1975	00001	....Sultan
S-36-0069	1975	00007	...National Chief Government Executive
S-36-0070	1975	00001	....Chancellor
S-36-0071	1975	00005	....Colonial Ruler
S-36-0072	1975	00000	.....Governor General
S-36-0073	1975	00001	....Premier
S-36-0074	1975	00036	....President
S-36-0075	1975	00004	.....Vice President
S-36-0076	1975	00010	....Prime Minister
S-36-0077	1975	00002	...Subnational Chief Government Executive
S-36-0078	1975	00002	....Feudal Lord
S-36-0079	1975	00002	....Governor
S-36-0080	1975	00006	.....State Governor
S-36-0081	1975	00000	......Lieutenant Governor
S-36-0082	1975	00002	...Local Chief Government Executive
S-36-0083	1975	00013	....City Manager
S-36-0084	1975	00000	....Council Manager
S-36-0085	1975	00005	....Mayor
S-36-0086	1975	00002	....Village Chief
S-36-0087	1975	00001	...Prefect
S-36-0088	1975	00012	..Civil Servant
S-36-0089	1975	00001	...International Civil Servant
S-36-0090	1975	00006	...National Civil Servant
S-36-0091	1975	00001	...Subnational Civil Servant
S-36-0092	1975	00000	....Local Civil Servant
S-36-0093	1975	00002	..Court Official
S-36-0094	1975	00000	...Amicus Curiae
S-36-0095	1975	00001	...Bailiff
S-36-0096	1975	00000	...Coroner
S-36-0097	1975	00000	...Court Attorney
S-36-0098	1975	00000	....Barrister
S-36-0099	1975	00005	....Defense Attorney
S-36-0100	1975	00001	.....Defender
S-36-0101	1975	00001	......Public Defender
S-36-0102	1975	00004	....Prosecuting Attorney
S-36-0103	1975	00000	.....Attorney General
S-36-0104	1975	00001	......District Attorney
S-36-0105	1975	00000	......Military Prosecutor
S-36-0106	1975	00000	....Solicitor
S-36-0107	1975	00004	...Judge
S-36-0108	1975	00001	....International Judge
S-36-0109	1975	00002	....National Judge
S-36-0110	1975	00001	....Subnational Judge
S-36-0111	1975	00003	.....Local Judge
S-36-0112	1975	00000	......Justice Of The Peace
S-36-0113	1975	00000	.....Magistrate
S-36-0114	1975	00000	......Chief Magistrate
S-36-0115	1975	00002	......Local Magistrate
S-36-0116	1975	00013	....Supreme Court Justice
S-36-0117	1975	00003	.....Chief Justice

Code	Year	Count	Term
S-36-0118	1975	00001	...Juror
S-36-0119	1975	00013	..Diplomat
S-36-0120	1975	00002	...Embassy Official
S-36-0121	1975	00003	....Ambassador
S-36-0122	1975	00000	....Charge D'Affaires
S-36-0123	1975	00000	....Consul General
S-36-0124	1975	00000	....Embassy Attache
S-36-0125	1979	00000	.....Commercial Attache
S-36-0126	1975	00000	.....Cultural Attache
S-36-0127	1975	00000	.....Economic Attache
S-36-0128	1975	00000	.....Information Attache
S-36-0129	1975	00001	.....Military Attache
S-36-0130	1975	00000	.....Political Attache
S-36-0131	1979	00000	.....Scientific Attache
S-36-0132	1975	00003	...Foreign Minister
S-36-0133	1975	00003	...Foreign Service Officer
S-36-0134	1979	00000	..Incumbent
S-36-0135	1975	00009	..Law Enforcement Official
S-36-0136	1975	00000	...International Police Official
S-36-0137	1975	00000	...National Police Official
S-36-0138	1975	00000	....National Police Commissioner
S-36-0139	1975	00000	...Secret Police Official
S-36-0140	1975	00001	...Subnational Police Official
S-36-0141	1975	00002	....Local Police Official
S-36-0142	1975	00000	.....Constable
S-36-0143	1975	00001	.....Local Police Chief
S-36-0144	1975	00001	.....Sheriff
S-36-0145	1975	00000	....State Police Official
S-36-0146	1975	00000	..Legislative Official
S-36-0147	1975	00001	...Legislative Committee Chairperson
S-36-0148	1975	00000	....National Legislative Committee Chairperson
S-36-0149	1975	00002	.....Congressional Committee Chairperson
S-36-0150	1975	00000	.....Parliamentary Committee Chairperson
S-36-0151	1975	00000	....Subnational Legislative Committee Chairperson
S-36-0152	1975	00000	.....Local Legislative Committee Chairperson
S-36-0153	1975	00000	.....State Legislative Committee Chairperson
S-36-0154	1975	00005	...Legislative Committee Member
S-36-0155	1975	00000	....Ranking Minority Member
S-36-0156	1975	00002	...Legislative Leader
S-36-0157	1975	00001	....Floor Leader
S-36-0158	1975	00000	....Leader Of Opposition
S-36-0159	1975	00001	....Legislative Speaker
S-36-0160	1975	00000	.....National Legislative Speaker
S-36-0161	1975	00000	......Congressional Speaker
S-36-0162	1975	00000	.......House Of Representatives Speaker
S-36-0163	1975	00000	.......Senate Speaker
S-36-0164	1975	00000	......Parliamentary Speaker
S-36-0165	1975	00000	.......Lower House Speaker
S-36-0166	1975	00000	.......Upper House Speaker
S-36-0167	1975	00001	.....Subnational Legislative Speaker
S-36-0168	1975	00000	......Local Legislative Speaker
S-36-0169	1975	00001	......State Legislative Speaker
S-36-0170	1975	00001	....Legislative Whip
S-36-0171	1975	00000	.....National Legislative Whip
S-36-0172	1975	00000	......Congressional Whip
S-36-0173	1975	00000	......Parliamentary Whip
S-36-0174	1975	00000	.....Subnational Legislative Whip
S-36-0175	1975	00000	......Local Legislative Whip
S-36-0176	1975	00000	......State Legislative Whip
S-36-0177	1975	00001	....Majority Leader
S-36-0178	1975	00001	....Minority Leader
S-36-0179	1975	00001	....National Legislative Leader
S-36-0180	1975	00001	.....Congressional Leader
S-36-0181	1975	00003	......House Of Representatives Leader
S-36-0182	1975	00003	......Senate Leader
S-36-0183	1975	00004	.....Parliamentary Leader
S-36-0184	1975	00001	....Subnational Legislative Leader
S-36-0185	1975	00000	.....Local Legislative Leader
S-36-0186	1975	00001	.....State Legislative Leader
S-36-0187	1975	00008	...Legislative Member
S-36-0188	1975	00004	....National Legislative Member
S-36-0189	1975	00026	.....Congressional Member
S-36-0190	1975	00004	......Representative
S-36-0191	1975	00012	......Senator
S-36-0192	1975	00006	.....Parliamentary Member
S-36-0193	1975	00002	......Lower House Member
S-36-0194	1975	00000	......Upper House Member
S-36-0195	1975	00002	....Subnational Legislative Member
S-36-0196	1975	00001	.....Local Legislative Member
S-36-0197	1975	00002	......Alderman
S-36-0198	1975	00003	......City Councilman
S-36-0199	1975	00014	.....State Legislative Member
S-36-0200	1975	00001	......State Senator
S-36-0201	1975	00001	...Legislative Ombudsman
S-36-0202	1975	00006	...Legislative Staff
S-36-0203	1975	00001	....Legislative Committee Staff
S-36-0204	1975	00000	....National Legislative Staff
S-36-0205	1975	00003	.....Congressional Legislative Staff
S-36-0206	1975	00002	......Congressional Aide
S-36-0207	1975	00000	......Congressional Intern
S-36-0208	1975	00000	.....Parliamentary Legislative Staff
S-36-0209	1975	00002	....Subnational Legislative Staff
S-36-0210	1975	00000	.....Local Legislative Staff
S-36-0211	1975	00004	.....State Legislative Staff
S-36-0212	1975	00025	..Military Personnel
S-36-0213	1975	00034	...Military Officer
S-36-0214	1975	00001	....Commander In Chief
S-36-0215	1975	00014	....Commanding Officer
S-36-0216	1975	00000	....Joint Chiefs Of Staff
S-36-0217	1975	00000	...Military Recruit
S-36-0218	1975	00000	....Draftee
S-36-0219	1975	00001	....Mercenary
S-36-0220	1975	00003	....Volunteer
S-36-0221	1975	00020	...Military Service Personnel
S-36-0222	1975	00000	....Marine
S-36-0223	1975	00003	....Pilot
S-36-0224	1975	00004	....Sailor
S-36-0225	1975	00012	....Soldier
S-36-0226	1975	00015	....Veteran
S-36-0227	1979	00000	.Marital Status
S-36-0228	1979	00000	..Divorced
S-36-0229	1979	00000	..Married
S-36-0230	1979	00000	..Single
S-36-0231	1979	00000	..Widow
S-36-0232	1979	00000	..Widower
S-36-0233	1975	00002	.Political Party Official
S-36-0234	1975	00000	..International Political Party Executive Member
S-36-0235	1975	00000	...International Political Party Chairperson
S-36-0236	1975	00000	...International Political Party Committee Member
S-36-0237	1975	00001	..National Political Party Executive Member
S-36-0238	1975	00000	...National Political Party Chairperson
S-36-0239	1975	00000	...National Political Party Committee Member
S-36-0240	1975	00004	....National Political Party Central Committee Member
S-36-0241	1975	00000	...National Political Party Politburo Member
S-36-0242	1975	00000	...National Political Party Secretary
S-36-0243	1975	00002	....National Political Party First Secretary

S-36-0244	1975	00000	..Subnational Political Party Executive Member
S-36-0245	1975	00000	...Subnational Political Party Chairperson
S-36-0246	1975	00002	....Local Political Party Chairperson
S-36-0247	1975	00000	...Subnational Political Party Committee Member
S-36-0248	1975	00000	....Subnational Political Party Central Committee Member
S-36-0249	1975	00000	.....Local Political Party Central Committee Member
S-36-0250	1975	00000	...Subnational Political Party Politburo Member
S-36-0251	1975	00000	....Local Political Party Politburo Member
S-36-0252	1975	00001	...Subnational Political Party Secretary
S-36-0253	1975	00001	....Subnational Political Party First Secretary
S-36-0254	1975	00001	.....Local Political Party First Secretary
S-36-0255	1975	00002	.....Regional Political Party First Secretary
S-36-0256	1975	00012	.Prisoner
S-36-0257	1975	00000	..Detainee
S-36-0258	1975	00001	..Hostage
S-36-0259	1975	00000	..Political Prisoner
S-36-0260	1975	00006	..Prisoner Of War
S-36-0261	1975	00000	.Suborganization Official
S-36-0262	1975	00000	..Caucus Member
S-36-0263	1975	00000	...Caucus Staff Personnel
S-36-0264	1975	00000	..Chairperson
S-36-0265	1975	00000	...Caucus Chairperson
S-36-0266	1975	00000	...Committee Chairperson
S-36-0267	1975	00004	..Committee Member
S-36-0268	1975	00001	...Committee Staff Personnel

S-37 SYSTEM TYPE

S-37-0001	1975	00002	System Type
S-37-0002	1975	00074	.Belief System
S-37-0003	1979	00000	..Mass Belief System
S-37-0004	1975	00015	.Cognitive System
S-37-0005	1975	00048	.Cultural System
S-37-0006	1975	00009	.Cybernetic System
S-37-0007	1975	00003	.Differentiated System
S-37-0008	1975	00007	..Functional Differentiated System
S-37-0009	1975	00007	..Structural Differentiated System
S-37-0010	1975	00039	.Economic System
S-37-0011	1975	00000	..Barter Economic System
S-37-0012	1975	00029	..Capitalism
S-37-0013	1975	00005	...Black Capitalism
S-37-0014	1975	00002	...Bourgeois Capitalism
S-37-0015	1975	00006	...Industrial Capitalism
S-37-0016	1975	00004	...Mature Capitalism
S-37-0017	1975	00003	...Mercantile Capitalism
S-37-0018	1975	00002	...Monopoly Capitalism
S-37-0019	1975	00003	...State Capitalism
S-37-0020	1975	00001	...Warfare Capitalism
S-37-0021	1975	00004	...Welfare Capitalism
S-37-0022	1975	00001	..Command Economic System
S-37-0023	1975	00037	..Communist Economic System
S-37-0024	1975	00001	..Diversified Economic System
S-37-0025	1975	00051	..Economic Incentive System
S-37-0026	1975	00007	..Economic Sector
S-37-0027	1975	00014	...Agricultural Sector
S-37-0028	1975	00014	...Commercial Sector
S-37-0029	1975	00002	....Free Trade Sector
S-37-0030	1975	00010	...Industrial Sector
S-37-0031	1975	00046	...Private Sector
S-37-0032	1975	00036	...Public Sector
S-37-0033	1979	00000	..Feudal Economic System
S-37-0034	1975	00013	..Financial System
S-37-0035	1975	00003	...Central Banking System
S-37-0036	1975	00005	...Federal Reserve System
S-37-0037	1975	00013	...International Banking System
S-37-0038	1975	00005	...National Banking System
S-37-0039	1975	00000	...Subnational Banking System
S-37-0040	1979	00000	..Free Enterprise System
S-37-0041	1979	00000	..Inheritance System
S-37-0042	1979	00000	..International Economic System
S-37-0043	1979	00000	...New International Economic Order
S-37-0044	1979	00000	..Market System
S-37-0045	1975	00006	..Mercantile Economic System
S-37-0046	1975	00002	..Mixed Economic System
S-37-0047	1975	00026	..Monetary System
S-37-0048	1975	00012	...Monetary Exchange System
S-37-0049	1979	00000	..Patron System
S-37-0050	1975	00025	..Property Ownership System
S-37-0051	1975	00000	...Absentee Landlord System
S-37-0052	1975	00005	...Collective Ownership
S-37-0053	1975	00008	...Foreign Ownership
S-37-0054	1975	00002	...Government Ownership
S-37-0055	1975	00010	...Land Estate System
S-37-0056	1975	00021	...Land Tenure System
S-37-0057	1975	00000	...Primogeniture
S-37-0058	1975	00017	...Private Ownership
S-37-0059	1975	00033	...Slavery
S-37-0060	1975	00012	..Socialist Economic System
S-37-0061	1975	00011	.Ecosystem
S-37-0062	1975	00102	.Education System
S-37-0063	1975	00104	.Health Care System
S-37-0064	1975	00056	..Medical Care System
S-37-0065	1975	00003	...Socialized Medicine System
S-37-0066	1975	00011	.Imperialism System
S-37-0067	1975	00005	..Academic Imperialism
S-37-0068	1975	00026	..Cultural Imperialism
S-37-0069	1975	00018	..Economic Imperialism
S-37-0070	1975	00015	...Capitalist Imperialism
S-37-0071	1975	00005	..Political Imperialism
S-37-0072	1975	00007	...Communist Imperialism
S-37-0073	1975	00019	...Western Imperialism
S-37-0074	1975	00007	...Yankee Imperialism
S-37-0075	1975	00027	.Information System
S-37-0076	1979	00000	..Computer Network
S-37-0077	1975	00017	..Information Network
S-37-0078	1975	00006	..Information Retrieval System
S-37-0079	1975	00005	..Management Information System
S-37-0080	1975	00034	.Legal System
S-37-0081	1975	00015	..Judicial System
S-37-0082	1975	00006	...International Judicial System
S-37-0083	1975	00001	...National Judicial System
S-37-0084	1975	00012	....Federal Judicial System
S-37-0085	1975	00000	...Subnational Judicial System
S-37-0086	1975	00000	....Local Judicial System
S-37-0087	1975	00009	....State Judicial System
S-37-0088	1975	00014	..Justice System
S-37-0089	1975	00003	...Adversary System
S-37-0090	1975	00000	...Bail Bond System
S-37-0091	1975	00000	...Grand Jury System
S-37-0092	1975	00029	...Law Enforcement System
S-37-0093	1975	00012	....Prison System
S-37-0094	1975	00002	...Trial System
S-37-0095	1975	00002	....Jury System
S-37-0096	1975	00020	..Law System
S-37-0097	1975	00000	...Administrative Law System
S-37-0098	1975	00007	...Civil Law System
S-37-0099	1975	00006	...Common Law System
S-37-0100	1975	00011	...Constitutional Law System
S-37-0101	1975	00014	...Criminal Law System
S-37-0102	1975	00010	...International Law System

S-37-0103	1975	00004	...Military Law System
S-37-0104	1975	00000	...Natural Law System
S-37-0105	1975	00002	...Socialist Law System
S-37-0106	1979	00000	.Political System Type
S-37-0107	1975	00001	..City State Political System
S-37-0108	1975	00036	..Democratic Political System
S-37-0109	1975	00019	..Developing Political System
S-37-0110	1979	00000	..Federalism
S-37-0111	1975	00002	...Conflict Federalism
S-37-0112	1975	00004	...Cooperative Federalism
S-37-0113	1975	00015	...New Federalism
S-37-0114	1975	00014	..Feudal System
S-37-0115	1975	00042	..International Political System
S-37-0116	1975	00009	...Bipolar International System
S-37-0117	1975	00001	....Loose Bipolar International Political System
S-37-0118	1975	00001	....Tight Bipolar International Political System
S-37-0119	1975	00003	...Commonwealth International System
S-37-0120	1975	00008	...Hegemonic System
S-37-0121	1975	00016	...Multipolar International Political System
S-37-0122	1975	00002	....Polycentric International Political System
S-37-0123	1975	00059	...Regional International Political System
S-37-0124	1979	00000	..Modernizing Political System
S-37-0125	1979	00000	..Political Party System
S-37-0126	1975	00009	...Multiparty System
S-37-0127	1979	00000	...One Political Party System
S-37-0128	1975	00000	....Hegemonic One Party System
S-37-0129	1975	00000	....Modified One Party System
S-37-0130	1979	00000	...Two Political Party System
S-37-0131	1975	00000	....Disciplined Two Party System
S-37-0132	1975	00006	....Responsible Two Party System
S-37-0133	1975	00018	..Totalitarian Political System
S-37-0134	1975	00004	..Traditional Political System
S-37-0135	1975	00013	..Transitional Political System
S-37-0136	1975	00013	..Tribal Political System
S-37-0137	1979	00000	.Service Delivery System
S-37-0138	1979	00000	..Agricultural Extension Service
S-37-0139	1975	00019	.Social System
S-37-0140	1975	00042	..Social Stratification System
S-37-0141	1975	00008	...Caste Social System
S-37-0142	1975	00014	...Class Social System
S-37-0143	1975	00002	....Closed Class Social System
S-37-0144	1975	00004	....Open Class Social System
S-37-0145	1975	00029	...Status Social System
S-37-0146	1975	00014	....Achieved Status System
S-37-0147	1975	00011	....Ascribed Status System
S-37-0148	1979	00000	.Transportation System
S-37-0149	1975	00131	.Value System
S-37-0150	1979	00000	..Value Of Life
S-37-0151	1975	00025	.Welfare System

S-38 THEORY

S-38-0001	1975	00017	Theory
S-38-0002	1975	00036	.Anthropological Theory
S-38-0003	1975	00006	..Acculturation Theory
S-38-0004	1975	00002	..Anthropological Functionalism
S-38-0005	1975	00007	..Anthropological Linguistic Theory
S-38-0006	1975	00000	..Antievolutionist Anthropological Theory
S-38-0007	1975	00002	..Cultural Evolutionism
S-38-0008	1975	00008	..Ethnographic Theory
S-38-0009	1975	00006	..Geographic Determinism Theory
S-38-0010	1975	00002	..Hydraulic Theory
S-38-0011	1975	00009	..Kinship Systematics Theory
S-38-0012	1975	00024	..Myth Analysis
S-38-0013	1975	00008	...Magic
S-38-0014	1975	00002	...Shamanism
S-38-0015	1975	00003	...Superstition
S-38-0016	1975	00003	...Taboo
S-38-0017	1975	00002	...Witchcraft
S-38-0018	1975	00009	..Structuralism
S-38-0019	1975	00019	.Behavioral Theory
S-38-0020	1975	00010	.Data Theory
S-38-0021	1975	00122	.Development Theory
S-38-0022	1975	00012	..Administrative Development Theory
S-38-0023	1975	00117	..Economic Development Theory
S-38-0024	1975	00041	...Economic Growth Theory
S-38-0025	1975	00064	..Political Development Theory
S-38-0026	1975	00054	..Social Development Theory
S-38-0027	1975	00034	..Technological Development Theory
S-38-0028	1975	00060	..Urban Development Theory
S-38-0029	1975	00014	.General System Theory
S-38-0030	1975	00039	..Communication Theory
S-38-0031	1975	00008	..Cybernetic Theory
S-38-0032	1975	00009	..Equilibrium Theory
S-38-0033	1979	00000	.Information Theory
S-38-0034	1979	00000	.Linguistic Theory
S-38-0035	1975	00060	.Modernization Theory
S-38-0036	1975	00010	..Convergence Theory
S-38-0037	1975	00004	..Divergence Theory
S-38-0038	1975	00096	.Organization Theory
S-38-0039	1975	00043	..Administrative Theory
S-38-0040	1975	00021	..Bureaucratic Theory
S-38-0041	1975	00004	...Iron Law Of Oligarchy
S-38-0042	1975	00009	..Multinational Organization Theory
S-38-0043	1975	00042	..Social Organization Theory
S-38-0044	1975	00040	.Planning Theory
S-38-0045	1979	00000	..Contingency Theory
S-38-0046	1975	00027	.Political Theory
S-38-0047	1975	00008	..Classical Political Thought
S-38-0048	1975	00011	...Aristotelian Thought
S-38-0049	1979	00000	...Cynic Thought
S-38-0050	1979	00000	...Epicurean Thought
S-38-0051	1975	00000	...Neoplatonic Political Thought
S-38-0052	1975	00015	...Platonic Political Thought
S-38-0053	1975	00001	...Presocratic Political Thought
S-38-0054	1979	00000	...Pythagorean Thought
S-38-0055	1975	00004	...Roman Legal Thought
S-38-0056	1979	00000	...Skeptic Thought
S-38-0057	1979	00000	...Socratic Political Thought
S-38-0058	1979	00000	...Stoic Thought
S-38-0059	1975	00001	...Thucydidean Political Thought
S-38-0060	1975	00002	..Contemporary Political Thought
S-38-0061	1975	00005	...Black Political Thought
S-38-0062	1975	00004	...Existentialism
S-38-0063	1975	00001	....Christian Existentialism
S-38-0064	1975	00002	....Existential Psychologism
S-38-0065	1975	00001	....Marxist Existentialism
S-38-0066	1975	00003	....Ontological Existentialism
S-38-0067	1975	00001	...Neohegelianism
S-38-0068	1975	00005	...Neomarxism
S-38-0069	1975	00007	...Ordinary Language Philosophy
S-38-0070	1975	00000	....Wittgensteinian Thought
S-38-0071	1975	00014	...Phenomenological Thought
S-38-0072	1975	00005	....Phenomenological Existentialism
S-38-0073	1975	00002	....Phenomenological Marxism
S-38-0074	1975	00002	....Phenomenological Psychologism
S-38-0075	1975	00010	...Pragmatism
S-38-0076	1975	00006	...Progressivism
S-38-0077	1975	00024	...Radicalism
S-38-0078	1979	00000	...Straussian Thought
S-38-0079	1975	00002	...Structural Marxism
S-38-0080	1975	00000	...Teilhardean Thought
S-38-0081	1975	00007	...Utopianism

Code	Year	Count	Term
S-38-0082	1975	00056	..Democratic Theory
S-38-0083	1975	00001	...Athenian Democratic Theory
S-38-0084	1975	00000	...Concurrent Majority Theory
S-38-0085	1975	00005	...Democratic Elite Theory
S-38-0086	1975	00008	...Economic Theory Of Democracy
S-38-0087	1975	00001	...General Will Democratic Theory
S-38-0088	1975	00001	...Guided Democracy Theory
S-38-0089	1979	00000	...Industrial Democracy
S-38-0090	1975	00010	...Interest Group Pluralism
S-38-0091	1975	00002	...Jacksonian Democratic Theory
S-38-0092	1975	00002	...Jeffersonian Democratic Theory
S-38-0093	1975	00008	...Majoritarianism
S-38-0094	1975	00001	...Minority Rights Democratic Theory
S-38-0095	1975	00008	...Participatory Democratic Theory
S-38-0096	1979	00000	...Polyarchical Democratic Theory
S-38-0097	1975	00001	...Populist Democratic Theory
S-38-0098	1979	00000	...Procedural Democratic Theory
S-38-0099	1975	00004	...Republic Theory
S-38-0100	1975	00003	...Socialist Democratic Theory
S-38-0101	1975	00004	..Eastern Political Thought
S-38-0102	1975	00003	...Confucian Political Theory
S-38-0103	1975	00000	....Mandate Of Heaven Theory
S-38-0104	1975	00002	...Eastern Legalist Theory
S-38-0105	1975	00000	...Neoconfucian Political Theory
S-38-0106	1979	00000	..Economic Theory
S-38-0107	1975	00022	...Capitalism Theory
S-38-0108	1975	00021	...Classical Economic Theory
S-38-0109	1975	00006	....Laissez Faire Theory
S-38-0110	1975	00002	....Malthusian Theory
S-38-0111	1975	00003	....Ricardian Theory
S-38-0112	1979	00000	...Economic Stabilization Theory
S-38-0113	1979	00000	...Fiscal Theory
S-38-0114	1975	00009	...Keynesian Economic Theory
S-38-0115	1975	00009	...Marxist Economic Theory
S-38-0116	1975	00002	...Mercantile Economic Theory
S-38-0117	1979	00000	...Monetary Economic Theory
S-38-0118	1979	00000	...Neoclassical Economic Theory
S-38-0119	1979	00000	...Public Finance Theory
S-38-0120	1975	00013	..Explanatory Political Theory
S-38-0121	1975	00070	...Conflict Theory
S-38-0122	1975	00020	....Aggression Theory
S-38-0123	1975	00033	....Conflict Resolution Theory
S-38-0124	1975	00069	...Decision Making Theory
S-38-0125	1975	00012	...Elite Theory
S-38-0126	1975	00005	...Formal Political Theory
S-38-0127	1975	00023	....Bargaining Theory
S-38-0128	1975	00022	....Coalition Theory
S-38-0129	1975	00017	.....Alliance Theory
S-38-0130	1975	00103	....Economic Model
S-38-0131	1975	00033	....Exchange Theory
S-38-0132	1975	00030	....Game Theory
S-38-0133	1975	00001	.....Constant Sum Game Theory
S-38-0134	1975	00007	.....N Person Game Theory
S-38-0135	1975	00013	.....Prisoner Dilemma Theory
S-38-0136	1975	00006	.....Two Person Game Theory
S-38-0137	1975	00005	.....Zero Sum Game Theory
S-38-0138	1975	00005	....Mathematical Political Theory
S-38-0139	1975	00023	....Rational Model
S-38-0140	1975	00037	.....Rational Choice Theory
S-38-0141	1975	00003	....Set Theory
S-38-0142	1975	00043	...Futurology
S-38-0143	1975	00009	...Group Theory
S-38-0144	1975	00009	....Interest Group Theory
S-38-0145	1975	00002	....Pluralist Group Theory
S-38-0146	1975	00012	....Reference Group Theory
S-38-0147	1975	00023	...Ideology Explanatory Theory
S-38-0148	1975	00001	....End Of Ideology Analysis
S-38-0149	1975	00002	....Mannheim Ideology Explanation
S-38-0150	1975	00010	....Marxist Ideology Explanation
S-38-0151	1975	00009	...Mass Society Theory
S-38-0152	1979	00000	...Micropolitical Theory
S-38-0153	1975	00007	...Nation State Explanatory Theory
S-38-0154	1975	00016	....Nation Building Theory
S-38-0155	1975	00010	....National Identity Theory
S-38-0156	1975	00008	....National Sovereignty Theory
S-38-0157	1975	00001	....Statecraft Theory
S-38-0158	1979	00000	...Political Behaviorism
S-38-0159	1975	00017	...Political Integration Theory
S-38-0160	1975	00050	...Political System Theory
S-38-0161	1975	00013	...Post Industrial Society Theory
S-38-0162	1975	00048	...Power Theory
S-38-0163	1975	00017	....Community Power Theory
S-38-0164	1975	00019	....Control Theory
S-38-0165	1975	00110	....International Power Theory
S-38-0166	1975	00037	...Public Choice Theory
S-38-0167	1979	00000	...Public Good Theory
S-38-0168	1975	00048	...Revolution Theory
S-38-0169	1975	00000	....Feudal Reaction Theory
S-38-0170	1975	00002	....Permanent Revolution Theory
S-38-0171	1975	00008	....Rising Expectation Theory
S-38-0172	1979	00000	...Social Choice Theory
S-38-0173	1975	00000	...Structural Functional Political Theory
S-38-0174	1975	00001	...Transactional Theory
S-38-0175	1975	00037	...Voting Theory
S-38-0176	1975	00013	..Ideologies
S-38-0177	1975	00004	...Absolutism
S-38-0178	1975	00005	...Agrarianism
S-38-0179	1975	00011	...Anarchism
S-38-0180	1975	00000	...Anarchosyndicalism
S-38-0181	1975	00000	...Anticlericalism
S-38-0182	1975	00010	...Anticolonialism
S-38-0183	1975	00018	...Anticommunism
S-38-0184	1975	00003	....McCarthyism
S-38-0185	1975	00000	...Antifascism
S-38-0186	1975	00008	...Antiimperialism
S-38-0187	1975	00002	...Antimilitarism
S-38-0188	1975	00015	...Authoritarianism
S-38-0189	1975	00000	...Caudillism
S-38-0190	1975	00000	...Chartism
S-38-0191	1975	00018	...Clientelism
S-38-0192	1975	00005	...Communalism
S-38-0193	1975	00024	...Conservatism
S-38-0194	1975	00000	....American Conservatism
S-38-0195	1979	00000	....Bureaucratic Conservatism
S-38-0196	1975	00001	....Burkean Conservatism
S-38-0197	1975	00002	....Christian Conservatism
S-38-0198	1975	00001	....Neoconservatism
S-38-0199	1975	00000	....Objectivist Political Thought
S-38-0200	1975	00000	....Reactionary Conservatism
S-38-0201	1979	00000	....Status Quo Conservatism
S-38-0202	1975	00013	...Corporatism
S-38-0203	1975	00011	...Economic Ideology
S-38-0204	1975	00014	....Consumerism
S-38-0205	1975	00004	....Cooperativism
S-38-0206	1975	00006	....Economic Egalitarianism
S-38-0207	1979	00000	....Trickle Down Theory
S-38-0208	1975	00033	...Egalitarianism
S-38-0209	1975	00005	...Elitism
S-38-0210	1975	00008	...Ethnic Ideology
S-38-0211	1975	00015	....Ethnic Assimilation Theory
S-38-0212	1975	00019	.....Racial Integration Theory
S-38-0213	1975	00035	....Ethnic Nationalism
S-38-0214	1975	00004	....Ethnic Particularism
S-38-0215	1975	00012	....Ethnic Separatism
S-38-0216	1975	00014	....Ethnocentrism
S-38-0217	1975	00039	....Racism

S-38-0218	1975	00034	.....Antisemitism
S-38-0219	1975	00002	.....Apartheid Theory
S-38-0220	1975	00001	.....Black Racism
S-38-0221	1979	00000	.....Institutional Racism
S-38-0222	1975	00017	.....White Racism
S-38-0223	1979	00000	...Eurocommunism
S-38-0224	1975	00003	...Fascist Theory
S-38-0225	1975	00000	....Corporate Fascism
S-38-0226	1975	00000	....Falangism
S-38-0227	1975	00001	....Francoism
S-38-0228	1975	00006	....Italian Fascism
S-38-0229	1975	00013	....National Socialism
S-38-0230	1975	00000	....Neofascism
S-38-0231	1975	00007	....Peronism
S-38-0232	1975	00000	...Free Masonry
S-38-0233	1975	00004	...Gender Ideology
S-38-0234	1975	00003	....Gay Liberation
S-38-0235	1975	00033	....Sexism
S-38-0236	1975	00016	.....Feminism
S-38-0237	1975	00000	......Female Chauvinism
S-38-0238	1975	00012	......Womens Liberation
S-38-0239	1975	00002	.....Male Chauvinism
S-38-0240	1975	00019	...Humanism
S-38-0241	1975	00001	....Christian Humanism
S-38-0242	1975	00020	....Humanitarianism
S-38-0243	1975	00001	....Scientific Humanism
S-38-0244	1975	00002	....Socialist Humanism
S-38-0245	1975	00022	...Imperialism
S-38-0246	1975	00046	....Colonialism
S-38-0247	1975	00012	....Neocolonialism
S-38-0248	1975	00002	....Neoimperialism
S-38-0249	1975	00033	...Liberalism
S-38-0250	1975	00003	....Civil Liberty Liberalism
S-38-0251	1975	00000	....Civil Rights Liberalism
S-38-0252	1975	00004	....Classical Liberalism
S-38-0253	1975	00009	....Economic Liberalism
S-38-0254	1975	00009	....Laissez Faire Liberalism
S-38-0255	1975	00001	....Nineteenth Century Liberalism
S-38-0256	1975	00002	....Welfare Liberalism
S-38-0257	1975	00011	...Libertarianism
S-38-0258	1975	00009	...Militarism
S-38-0259	1975	00005	...Millenarianism
S-38-0260	1975	00019	...Modernizing Ideology
S-38-0261	1975	00077	...Nationalism
S-38-0262	1975	00003	....Americanism
S-38-0263	1975	00024	....Cultural Nationalism
S-38-0264	1975	00007	.....Black Nationalism
S-38-0265	1975	00002	.....Irredentism
S-38-0266	1975	00007	.....Pan Africanism
S-38-0267	1975	00003	.....Pan Arabism
S-38-0268	1975	00001	.....Pan Islamism
S-38-0269	1975	00002	.....Pan Slavism
S-38-0270	1975	00005	.....Tribalism
S-38-0271	1975	00011	.....Zionism
S-38-0272	1975	00016	....Isolationism
S-38-0273	1975	00007	....Neutralism
S-38-0274	1975	00007	....Patriotism
S-38-0275	1975	00009	....Separatism
S-38-0276	1979	00000	...New Left
S-38-0277	1975	00006	....Counter Culture Ideology
S-38-0278	1975	00014	....Student Activism
S-38-0279	1975	00005	....Student Radicalism
S-38-0280	1975	00004	...Nihilism
S-38-0281	1975	00003	...Pacifism
S-38-0282	1975	00000	....International Pacifism
S-38-0283	1975	00004	....Nonviolent Resistance Theory
S-38-0284	1975	00001	.....Gandhiism
S-38-0285	1979	00000	...Political Ideology

S-38-0286	1975	00013	...Populism
S-38-0287	1975	00005	...Social Darwinism
S-38-0288	1975	00027	...Socialist Theory
S-38-0289	1975	00001	....Agrarian Socialism
S-38-0290	1975	00000	....Aprista Socialism
S-38-0291	1975	00001	....Christian Socialism
S-38-0292	1975	00002	....Democratic Socialism
S-38-0293	1975	00002	....Evolutionary Socialism
S-38-0294	1975	00001	.....Bernsteinian Socialism
S-38-0295	1975	00002	.....Fabian Socialism
S-38-0296	1975	00004	.....Saint Simonianism
S-38-0297	1975	00000	....Guild Socialism
S-38-0298	1975	00050	....Marxist Theory
S-38-0299	1979	00000	.....Dictatorship Of The Proletariat
S-38-0300	1975	00004	.....Marxist Alienation Theory
S-38-0301	1975	00017	.....Marxist Capitalism Theory
S-38-0302	1975	00008	.....Marxist Class Theory
S-38-0303	1975	00018	......Marxist Class Consciousness Theory
S-38-0304	1979	00000	.......Proletarian Internationalism
S-38-0305	1975	00001	......Marxist Immiseration Theory
S-38-0306	1975	00007	.....Marxist Communism Theory
S-38-0307	1975	00008	.....Marxist Economic Determinism
S-38-0308	1975	00004	.....Marxist Labor Value Theory
S-38-0309	1975	00003	.....Marxist Materialism
S-38-0310	1975	00004	......Dialectical Materialism
S-38-0311	1975	00004	......Historical Materialism
S-38-0312	1979	00000	.....Marxist Revolution Theory
S-38-0313	1979	00000	.....Praxis
S-38-0314	1975	00028	....Marxism
S-38-0315	1975	00006	.....Bolshevism
S-38-0316	1975	00006	.....Castroism
S-38-0317	1975	00027	.....Communism
S-38-0318	1975	00014	......International Communism
S-38-0319	1975	00018	......National Communism
S-38-0320	1975	00006	......Socialist Realism
S-38-0321	1975	00002	.....Evolutionary Marxism
S-38-0322	1975	00002	.....Hegelian Marxism
S-38-0323	1975	00011	.....Leninism
S-38-0324	1975	00002	......Democratic Centralism
S-38-0325	1975	00002	......Leninist Imperialism Theory
S-38-0326	1975	00045	.....Maoism
S-38-0327	1975	00009	.....Marxist Revisionism
S-38-0328	1975	00009	......Communist Deviationism
S-38-0329	1975	00021	.....Marxism Leninism
S-38-0330	1975	00005	.....Polycentrism
S-38-0331	1975	00019	.....Stalinism
S-38-0332	1975	00001	.....Titoism
S-38-0333	1975	00016	.....Trotskyism
S-38-0334	1975	00003	....Scientific Socialism
S-38-0335	1975	00003	....Utopian Socialism
S-38-0336	1975	00003	...Syndicalism
S-38-0337	1975	00001	....Agrarian Syndicalism
S-38-0338	1979	00000	...Terrorism
S-38-0339	1975	00011	...Trade Unionism
S-38-0340	1975	00035	..International Political Theory
S-38-0341	1975	00017	...Balance Of Power Theory
S-38-0342	1975	00027	...Deterrence Theory
S-38-0343	1975	00005	...Domino Theory
S-38-0344	1975	00123	...Foreign Policy Theory
S-38-0345	1979	00000	....Idealist Foreign Policy
S-38-0346	1979	00000	....Realist Foreign Policy
S-38-0347	1975	00007	...Geopolitical Theory
S-38-0348	1975	00001	....Buffer Zone Theory
S-38-0349	1975	00006	....Frontier Theory
S-38-0350	1975	00000	....Heartland Theory
S-38-0351	1975	00041	...International Alliance Theory
S-38-0352	1975	00085	...International Conflict Resolution Theory
S-38-0353	1975	00022	...International Decision Making Theory

S-38-0354	1975	00002	...International Field Theory
S-38-0355	1975	00123	...International Influence Theory
S-38-0356	1975	00019	...International Integration Theory
S-38-0357	1975	00016	....European Integration Theory
S-38-0358	1975	00000	....International Commonwealth Theory
S-38-0359	1975	00010	....International Economic Organization Theory
S-38-0360	1975	00005	....Security Community Theory
S-38-0361	1975	00004	...International Law Theory
S-38-0362	1975	00041	...International Organization Theory
S-38-0363	1979	00000	..Macropolitical Theory
S-38-0364	1975	00000	..Medieval Political Thought
S-38-0365	1975	00001	...Augustinian Analysis
S-38-0366	1975	00000	...Erastianism
S-38-0367	1975	00002	...Medieval Corporatism
S-38-0368	1975	00000	...Medieval International Theory
S-38-0369	1975	00003	...Medieval Islamic Thought
S-38-0370	1975	00002	...Medieval State Theory
S-38-0371	1975	00001	...Monasticism
S-38-0372	1975	00001	...Nominalism
S-38-0373	1975	00000	...Quietistic Thought
S-38-0374	1975	00000	....Anabaptism
S-38-0375	1975	00000	....Antitrinitarianism
S-38-0376	1975	00002	...Scholasticism
S-38-0377	1975	00001	....Hagiology
S-38-0378	1975	00001	....Scholastic Method
S-38-0379	1975	00002	...Thomism
S-38-0380	1975	00000	...Trentine Doctrine
S-38-0381	1975	00000	...Two Swords Theory
S-38-0382	1975	00000	....Conciliar Movement Doctrine
S-38-0383	1975	00000	....Gelasian Doctrine
S-38-0384	1975	00000	....Investiture Controversy
S-38-0385	1979	00000	..Micropolitical Thought
S-38-0386	1975	00003	..Modern Political Thought
S-38-0387	1979	00000	..American Political Thought
S-38-0388	1975	00002	...Burkean Analysis
S-38-0389	1975	00004	...Comtean Positivism
S-38-0390	1975	00001	...Early Modern Theory Of The State
S-38-0391	1975	00002	....Divine Right Theory
S-38-0392	1975	00001	....Hobbesian Absolutism
S-38-0393	1975	00001	....Instrumental State Theory
S-38-0394	1975	00003	....Lockean Contractualism
S-38-0395	1975	00000	....Newtonian Mechanistic State Theory
S-38-0396	1975	00009	....Republican Constitutionalism
S-38-0397	1975	00019	...Enlightenment Thought
S-38-0398	1975	00003	....American Enlightenment Thought
S-38-0399	1975	00002	.....Jeffersonian Thought
S-38-0400	1975	00002	.....Madisonian Thought
S-38-0401	1979	00000	....Encyclopedist Thought
S-38-0402	1975	00004	....French Revolutionary Thought
S-38-0403	1975	00001	.....Jacobinism
S-38-0404	1975	00013	....Kantian Analysis
S-38-0405	1975	00000	....Philosophe Thought
S-38-0406	1975	00012	....Rousseauian Analysis
S-38-0407	1975	00000	....Voltairean Analysis
S-38-0408	1975	00008	...Hegelian Analysis
S-38-0409	1975	00000	....Left Hegelianism
S-38-0410	1975	00000	....Right Hegelianism
S-38-0411	1975	00014	...Hobbesian Analysis
S-38-0412	1975	00002	...Humean Analysis
S-38-0413	1975	00017	...Liberal Political Thought
S-38-0414	1975	00001	....Enlightenment Liberalism
S-38-0415	1975	00009	....Lockean Liberalism
S-38-0416	1975	00009	...Marxist Political Thought
S-38-0417	1975	00000	...Modern Idealism
S-38-0418	1975	00002	....German Idealism
S-38-0419	1975	00000	....Oxford Idealism
S-38-0420	1975	00001	....Transcendentalism
S-38-0421	1975	00005	...Nietzschean Analysis
S-38-0422	1975	00014	...Progress Theory
S-38-0423	1979	00000	...Romanticism
S-38-0424	1975	00002	....German Romanticism
S-38-0425	1975	00002	...Tocquevillian Analysis
S-38-0426	1975	00016	...Utilitarianism
S-38-0427	1975	00001	....Benthamism
S-38-0428	1975	00056	..Political Philosophy Concept
S-38-0429	1975	00016	...Authority Theory
S-38-0430	1975	00018	...Common Good Theory
S-38-0431	1975	00000	....Common Wealth Theory
S-38-0432	1975	00006	....General Interest Theory
S-38-0433	1975	00003	....General Will Theory
S-38-0434	1975	00015	....Public Interest Theory
S-38-0435	1979	00000	...Community Philosophical Concept
S-38-0436	1975	00000	....Commonwealth Community Theory
S-38-0437	1975	00002	....Fraternity Theory
S-38-0438	1975	00006	....Organic State Theory
S-38-0439	1975	00006	...Consensus Theory
S-38-0440	1975	00011	...Consent Theory
S-38-0441	1975	00032	...Constitutional Interpretation Theory
S-38-0442	1975	00001	....Broad Constructionism
S-38-0443	1975	00000	....Constitutional Realism
S-38-0444	1975	00005	....Judicial Restraint Theory
S-38-0445	1975	00009	....Legalism
S-38-0446	1975	00003	....Strict Constructionism
S-38-0447	1975	00003	...Constitutional Structural Theory
S-38-0448	1975	00011	....Check And Balance Theory
S-38-0449	1975	00004	....Church State Separation Doctrine
S-38-0450	1975	00003	....Extended Republic Theory
S-38-0451	1975	00000	....Interposition Doctrine
S-38-0452	1975	00000	....Nullification Doctrine
S-38-0453	1975	00011	....Separation Of Power Theory
S-38-0454	1975	00004	....State Rights Doctrine
S-38-0455	1975	00042	...Equality Theory
S-38-0456	1975	00016	...Freedom Theory
S-38-0457	1975	00000	....Classical Corporate Freedom Theory
S-38-0458	1975	00002	....Economic Freedom Theory
S-38-0459	1975	00001	....Freedom And Necessity Doctrine
S-38-0460	1975	00021	....Individual Freedom Theory
S-38-0461	1975	00014	....Moral Freedom Theory
S-38-0462	1979	00000	.....Moral Choice
S-38-0463	1979	00000	.....Moral Responsibility
S-38-0464	1975	00004	....Negative Freedom Theory
S-38-0465	1975	00009	....Political Freedom Theory
S-38-0466	1975	00002	....Positive Freedom Theory
S-38-0467	1975	00001	....Psychological Freedom Theory
S-38-0468	1975	00017	...Human Condition Theory
S-38-0469	1975	00029	...Human Dignity Theory
S-38-0470	1975	00042	...Human Nature Theory
S-38-0471	1975	00023	...Individualism Theory
S-38-0472	1975	00007	....Possessive Individualism
S-38-0473	1975	00060	...Justice Theory
S-38-0474	1979	00000	....Compensatory Justice
S-38-0475	1975	00034	....Distributive Justice Theory
S-38-0476	1975	00000	....Divine Justice Theory
S-38-0477	1975	00004	....Egalitarian Justice Theory
S-38-0478	1979	00000	....Equity
S-38-0479	1975	00007	....Justice As Fairness Doctrine
S-38-0480	1975	00001	....Natural Justice Theory
S-38-0481	1975	00001	....Relative Justice Theory
S-38-0482	1975	00002	....Remedial Justice Theory
S-38-0483	1975	00003	....Utilitarian Justice Theory
S-38-0484	1975	00021	...Legitimacy Theory
S-38-0485	1975	00038	....Political Legitimacy Theory
S-38-0486	1975	00016	...Liberty Theory
S-38-0487	1975	00001	...Natural Law Conventionalism Theory
S-38-0488	1975	00010	....Classical Natural Right Doctrine

S-38-0489	1975	00000	....Great Chain Of Being Doctrine
S-38-0490	1975	00002	....Medieval Natural Law Theory
S-38-0491	1975	00000	....Right Reason Doctrine
S-38-0492	1975	00019	....Rights Of Man Doctrine
S-38-0493	1975	00001	....Roman Natural Law Theory
S-38-0494	1975	00001	....Scientific Natural Law Theory
S-38-0495	1975	00000	....Stoic Natural Law Theory
S-38-0496	1975	00034	...Obligation Theory
S-38-0497	1975	00003	...Open Society Theory
S-38-0498	1975	00014	...Order Theory
S-38-0499	1975	00008	...Political Alienation Theory
S-38-0500	1975	00001	...Political Man Theory
S-38-0501	1975	00026	...Rationality Theory
S-38-0502	1975	00016	...Representation Theory
S-38-0503	1975	00001	....Delegate Representation Theory
S-38-0504	1975	00000	....Functional Representation Theory
S-38-0505	1975	00004	....Group Representation Theory
S-38-0506	1975	00007	....Linkage Representation Theory
S-38-0507	1975	00000	....Territory Representation Theory
S-38-0508	1975	00001	....Trustee Representation Theory
S-38-0509	1975	00001	....Virtual Representation Theory
S-38-0510	1975	00010	...Responsibility Doctrine
S-38-0511	1975	00009	...Social Contract Theory
S-38-0512	1975	00001	....Government Contract Theory
S-38-0513	1975	00002	....Societal Contract Theory
S-38-0514	1975	00004	....State Of Nature Theory
S-38-0515	1975	00017	...Sovereignty Theory
S-38-0516	1975	00003	..Renaissance Political Thought
S-38-0517	1975	00000	...Baconian Analysis
S-38-0518	1975	00003	...Cartesian Analysis
S-38-0519	1975	00000	...Early Radical Thought
S-38-0520	1975	00000	....Diggers Political Thought
S-38-0521	1975	00006	....Early Republicanism
S-38-0522	1975	00000	....Levellers Political Thought
S-38-0523	1975	00005	...Machiavellian Thought
S-38-0524	1975	00001	...Reformation Theory
S-38-0525	1975	00001	...Renaissance State Theory
S-38-0526	1975	00000	...Royalist State Theory
S-38-0527	1975	00088	..Strategic Theory
S-38-0528	1979	00000	...Counterforce Theory
S-38-0529	1975	00063	.Psychological Theory
S-38-0530	1975	00034	..Achievement Theory
S-38-0531	1975	00005	..Alienation Psychological Theory
S-38-0532	1975	00122	..Attitude Change Theory
S-38-0533	1975	00023	...Cognitive Dissonance Theory
S-38-0534	1979	00000	..Attribution Theory
S-38-0535	1975	00035	..Cognitive Theory
S-38-0536	1975	00006	..Cross Pressure Theory
S-38-0537	1975	00008	..Freudian Theory
S-38-0538	1975	00006	..Frustration Aggression Theory
S-38-0539	1975	00002	..Gestalt Theory
S-38-0540	1979	00000	..Human Needs Theory
S-38-0541	1975	00031	..Identity Theory
S-38-0542	1979	00000	..Jungian Theory
S-38-0543	1975	00073	..Learning Theory
S-38-0544	1975	00067	..Motivation Theory
S-38-0545	1975	00057	..Personality Theory
S-38-0546	1975	00008	..Psychological Behavioralism
S-38-0547	1975	00001	..Psychological Behaviorism
S-38-0548	1979	00000	...Psychological Programming
S-38-0549	1979	00000	....Psychological Deprogramming
S-38-0550	1975	00007	..Psychopolitical Theory
S-38-0551	1975	00007	..Relative Deprivation Theory
S-38-0552	1975	00037	.Religious Thought
S-38-0553	1979	00000	..Atheism
S-38-0554	1975	00015	..Buddhism
S-38-0555	1975	00001	...Lamaism
S-38-0556	1975	00013	..Confucianism
S-38-0557	1975	00002	...Neoconfucianism
S-38-0558	1975	00011	..Hinduism
S-38-0559	1975	00019	..Islamic Thought
S-38-0560	1975	00003	..Judeo Christian Thought
S-38-0561	1975	00020	...Christian Thought
S-38-0562	1975	00013	....Catholicism
S-38-0563	1975	00004	.....Eastern Orthodox Thought
S-38-0564	1975	00027	.....Roman Catholicism
S-38-0565	1975	00013	....Protestantism
S-38-0566	1975	00000	.....Anglicanism
S-38-0567	1975	00005	.....Calvinism
S-38-0568	1975	00000	.....Hussite Thought
S-38-0569	1975	00000	.....Lutheranism
S-38-0570	1975	00005	.....Protestant Sectarianism
S-38-0571	1975	00000	.....Unitarianism
S-38-0572	1975	00010	...Judaic Thought
S-38-0573	1979	00000	..Religious Fundamentalism
S-38-0574	1975	00000	..Shintoism
S-38-0575	1975	00001	..Taoism
S-38-0576	1975	00001	..Zoroastrianism
S-38-0577	1975	00019	.Scientific Theory
S-38-0578	1975	00014	..Empirical Theory
S-38-0579	1979	00000	..Theory Of Causality
S-38-0580	1975	00023	..Value Free Science Theory
S-38-0581	1975	00062	.Social Theory
S-38-0582	1975	00014	..Assimilation Theory
S-38-0583	1975	00001	..Field Theory
S-38-0584	1979	00000	..Riot Theory
S-38-0585	1975	00033	..Role Theory
S-38-0586	1975	00032	..Social Action Theory
S-38-0587	1975	00029	...Collective Action Theory
S-38-0588	1975	00231	...Social Interaction Theory
S-38-0589	1979	00000	..Social Distance Theory
S-38-0590	1975	00022	..Social Integration Theory
S-38-0591	1975	00034	..Social Learning Theory
S-38-0592	1975	00029	..Socialization Theory
S-38-0593	1975	00023	..Weberian Theory
S-38-0594	1975	00004	.Theoretical Range
S-38-0595	1975	00003	..General Theory
S-38-0596	1975	00004	..Middle Range Theory
S-38-0597	1975	00066	.Theory Construction

.END

G-01 AFRICA

G-01-0001	1975	00253	Africa
G-01-0002	1975	00003	.Central Africa
G-01-0003	1975	00000	..Burundi
G-01-0004	1979	00000	..Central African Empire
G-01-0005	1975	00003	..Chad
G-01-0006	1979	00000	..Congo
G-01-0007	1975	00000	..Rwanda
G-01-0008	1975	00015	..Uganda
G-01-0009	1979	00000	..Zaire
G-01-0010	1975	00040	.East Africa
G-01-0011	1979	00000	..Djibouti
G-01-0012	1975	00009	..Ethiopia
G-01-0013	1975	00027	..Kenya
G-01-0014	1975	00003	..Somalia
G-01-0015	1975	00006	..Sudan
G-01-0016	1975	00015	..Tanzania
G-01-0017	1975	00053	.North Africa
G-01-0018	1975	00011	..Algeria
G-01-0019	1975	00056	..Egypt
G-01-0020	1975	00006	..Libya
G-01-0021	1975	00015	..Morocco
G-01-0022	1975	00008	..Tunisia
G-01-0023	1979	00000	..Western Sahara

G-01-0024	1979	00000	.South Africa
G-01-0025	1975	00025	..Angola
G-01-0026	1975	00006	..Botswana
G-01-0027	1975	00003	..Lesotho
G-01-0028	1975	00000	..Malagasy Republic
G-01-0029	1975	00001	..Malawi
G-01-0030	1975	00018	..Mozambique
G-01-0031	1975	00006	..Namibia
G-01-0032	1975	00061	..Republic Of South Africa
G-01-0033	1975	00005	..Swaziland
G-01-0034	1975	00006	..Zambia
G-01-0035	1979	00000	..Zimbabwe-Rhodesia
G-01-0036	1975	00063	.West Africa
G-01-0037	1979	00000	..Benin
G-01-0038	1975	00007	..Cameroon
G-01-0039	1975	00000	..Equatorial Guinea
G-01-0040	1975	00001	..Gabon
G-01-0041	1975	00001	..Gambia
G-01-0042	1975	00017	..Ghana
G-01-0043	1975	00005	..Guinea
G-01-0044	1979	00000	..Guinea-Bissau
G-01-0045	1975	00004	..Ivory Coast
G-01-0046	1975	00005	..Liberia
G-01-0047	1975	00004	..Mali
G-01-0048	1975	00001	..Mauritania
G-01-0049	1975	00002	..Niger
G-01-0050	1975	00045	..Nigeria
G-01-0051	1979	00000	..Sao Tome And Principe
G-01-0052	1975	00005	..Senegal
G-01-0053	1975	00004	..Sierra Leone
G-01-0054	1975	00000	..Togo
G-01-0055	1975	00002	..Upper Volta

G-02 AMERICA

G-02-0001	1975	02955	America
G-02-0002	1979	00000	.Caribbean Islands
G-02-0003	1975	00000	..Antigua
G-02-0004	1975	00002	..Bahamas
G-02-0005	1979	00000	..Barbados
G-02-0006	1979	00000	..Cayman Islands
G-02-0007	1975	00057	..Cuba
G-02-0008	1975	00001	..Dominica
G-02-0009	1975	00003	..Dominican Republic
G-02-0010	1975	00000	..Grenada
G-02-0011	1979	00000	..Guadeloupe
G-02-0012	1975	00006	..Haiti
G-02-0013	1975	00006	..Jamaica
G-02-0014	1979	00000	..Martinique
G-02-0015	1979	00000	..Montserrat
G-02-0016	1975	00001	..Netherlands Antilles
G-02-0017	1975	00010	..Puerto Rico
G-02-0018	1979	00000	..Saint Barthelemy
G-02-0019	1979	00000	..Saint Kitt-Nevis-Anguilla
G-02-0020	1979	00000	..Saint Lucia
G-02-0021	1979	00000	..Saint Martin
G-02-0022	1979	00000	..Saint Vincent
G-02-0023	1975	00003	..Trinidad And Tobago
G-02-0024	1979	00000	..Turks And Caicos Islands
G-02-0025	1979	00000	..Virgin Islands (UK)
G-02-0026	1979	00000	..Virgin Islands (USA)
G-02-0027	1975	00080	.Central America
G-02-0028	1979	00000	..Belize
G-02-0029	1975	00014	..Costa Rica
G-02-0030	1975	00004	..El Salvador
G-02-0031	1975	00011	..Guatemala
G-02-0032	1975	00002	..Honduras
G-02-0033	1975	00004	..Nicaragua
G-02-0034	1975	00010	..Panama
G-02-0035	1975	00009	..Panama Canal Zone
G-02-0036	1975	02736	.North America
G-02-0037	1975	00137	..Canada
G-02-0038	1975	00001	..Greenland
G-02-0039	1975	00117	..Mexico
G-02-0040	1975	04539	..United States Of America
G-02-0041	1975	00259	.South America
G-02-0042	1975	00031	..Argentina
G-02-0043	1975	00011	..Bolivia
G-02-0044	1975	00088	..Brazil
G-02-0045	1975	00037	..Chile
G-02-0046	1975	00038	..Colombia
G-02-0047	1975	00007	..Ecuador
G-02-0048	1975	00000	..French Guiana
G-02-0049	1975	00008	..Guyana
G-02-0050	1975	00004	..Paraguay
G-02-0051	1975	00032	..Peru
G-02-0052	1975	00001	..Surinam
G-02-0053	1975	00007	..Uruguay
G-02-0054	1975	00021	..Venezuela

G-03 ASIA

G-03-0001	1975	00574	Asia
G-03-0002	1975	00277	.East Asia
G-03-0003	1975	00007	..Hongkong
G-03-0004	1975	00177	..Japan
G-03-0005	1975	00000	..Macao
G-03-0006	1975	00003	..Mongolia
G-03-0007	1979	00000	..Peoples Democratic Republic Of Korea
G-03-0008	1979	00000	..Peoples Republic Of China
G-03-0009	1975	00043	..Republic Of Korea
G-03-0010	1979	00000	..Taiwan
G-03-0011	1975	00140	.South Asia
G-03-0012	1975	00022	..Bangladesh
G-03-0013	1975	00000	..Bhutan
G-03-0014	1975	00149	..India
G-03-0015	1975	00008	..Nepal
G-03-0016	1975	00039	..Pakistan
G-03-0017	1975	00017	..Sri Lanka
G-03-0018	1975	00164	.Southeast Asia
G-03-0019	1975	00011	..Burma
G-03-0020	1979	00000	..Democratic Kampuchea
G-03-0021	1975	00034	..Indonesia
G-03-0022	1975	00013	..Laos
G-03-0023	1975	00027	..Malaysia
G-03-0024	1975	00041	..Philippines
G-03-0025	1975	00012	..Singapore
G-03-0026	1975	00039	..Thailand
G-03-0027	1979	00000	..Vietnam

G-04 ATLANTIC OCEAN REGION

G-04-0001	1979	00000	Atlantic Ocean Region
G-04-0002	1979	00000	.Ascension Island
G-04-0003	1979	00000	.Azores
G-04-0004	1975	00000	.Bermuda
G-04-0005	1979	00000	.Bouvet Island
G-04-0006	1979	00000	.Canary Islands
G-04-0007	1979	00000	.Cape Verde Islands
G-04-0008	1979	00000	.Gough Island
G-04-0009	1975	00004	.Iceland
G-04-0010	1979	00000	.Madeira
G-04-0011	1979	00000	.Saint Helena

G-05 AUSTRALIA

G-05-0001	1975	00037	Australia

G-06 EUROPE

G-06-0001	1975	00905	Europe
G-06-0002	1975	00476	.Eastern Europe
G-06-0003	1975	00007	..Albania
G-06-0004	1975	00012	..Bulgaria
G-06-0005	1975	00036	..Czechoslovakia
G-06-0006	1975	00022	..Democratic Republic Of Germany
G-06-0007	1975	00006	..Finland
G-06-0008	1975	00023	..Greece
G-06-0009	1975	00037	..Hungary
G-06-0010	1975	00077	..Poland
G-06-0011	1975	00033	..Romania
G-06-0012	1975	00553	..Union Of Soviet Socialist Republics
G-06-0013	1975	00054	..Yugoslavia
G-06-0014	1975	00546	.Western Europe
G-06-0015	1975	00000	..Andorra
G-06-0016	1975	00017	..Austria
G-06-0017	1975	00016	..Belgium
G-06-0018	1975	00015	..Denmark
G-06-0019	1975	00114	..Federal Republic Of Germany
G-06-0020	1975	00166	..France
G-06-0021	1975	00000	..Gibraltar
G-06-0022	1975	00012	..Ireland
G-06-0023	1975	00089	..Italy
G-06-0024	1975	00000	..Liechtenstein
G-06-0025	1975	00004	..Luxembourg
G-06-0026	1975	00001	..Malta
G-06-0027	1975	00000	..Monaco
G-06-0028	1975	00027	..Netherlands
G-06-0029	1975	00025	..Norway
G-06-0030	1975	00027	..Portugal
G-06-0031	1975	00000	..San Marino
G-06-0032	1975	00048	..Spain
G-06-0033	1975	00038	..Sweden
G-06-0034	1975	00014	..Switzerland
G-06-0035	1975	00269	..United Kingdom
G-06-0036	1979	00000	...England
G-06-0037	1979	00000	...Northern Ireland
G-06-0038	1979	00000	...Scotland
G-06-0039	1979	00000	...Wales
G-06-0040	1979	00000	...Western Isles
G-06-0041	1979	00000	....Orkney Islands
G-06-0042	1979	00000	....Shetland Islands
G-06-0043	1979	00000	..Vatican City

G-07 INDIAN OCEAN REGION

G-07-0001	1979	00000	Indian Ocean Region
G-07-0002	1979	00000	.Amirante Island
G-07-0003	1979	00000	.Andaman Island
G-07-0004	1979	00000	.Chagos Archipelago
G-07-0005	1979	00000	.Christmas Island
G-07-0006	1979	00000	.Cocos Islands
G-07-0007	1979	00000	.Comoro Island
G-07-0008	1979	00000	.Crozet Island
G-07-0009	1979	00000	.Heard Island
G-07-0010	1979	00000	.Laccadive Islands
G-07-0011	1979	00000	.Maldives
G-07-0012	1975	00000	.Mauritius
G-07-0013	1979	00000	.Prince Edward Island
G-07-0014	1979	00000	.Reunion Island
G-07-0015	1979	00000	.Seychelles

G-08 MIDDLE EAST

G-08-0001	1975	00212	Middle East
G-08-0002	1975	00006	.Afghanistan
G-08-0003	1979	00000	.Bahrain
G-08-0004	1975	00011	.Cyprus
G-08-0005	1975	00032	.Iran
G-08-0006	1975	00013	.Iraq
G-08-0007	1975	00107	.Israel
G-08-0008	1975	00014	.Jordan
G-08-0009	1975	00004	.Kuwait
G-08-0010	1975	00019	.Lebanon
G-08-0011	1979	00000	.Oman
G-08-0012	1979	00000	.Peoples Democratic Republic Of Yemen
G-08-0013	1975	00000	.Qatar
G-08-0014	1975	00014	.Saudi Arabia
G-08-0015	1975	00025	.Syria
G-08-0016	1975	00039	.Turkey
G-08-0017	1979	00000	.United Arab Emirates
G-08-0018	1979	00000	.Yemen Arab Republic

G-09 OCEANIA

G-09-0001	1975	00050	Oceania
G-09-0002	1979	00000	.Melanesia
G-09-0003	1979	00000	..Banks Island
G-09-0004	1975	00004	..Fiji
G-09-0005	1975	00000	..New Caledonia
G-09-0006	1975	00016	..New Guinea
G-09-0007	1979	00000	..New Hebrides
G-09-0008	1975	00011	..New Zealand
G-09-0009	1979	00000	..Papua New Guinea
G-09-0010	1979	00000	..Santa Cruz Islands
G-09-0011	1979	00000	..Solomon Islands
G-09-0012	1979	00000	..Tasmania
G-09-0013	1979	00000	.Micronesia
G-09-0014	1979	00000	..Canton And Enderby Islands
G-09-0015	1979	00000	..Caroline Islands
G-09-0016	1979	00000	..Gilbert And Ellice Islands
G-09-0017	1979	00000	..Mariana Islands
G-09-0018	1979	00000	...Guam
G-09-0019	1979	00000	..Marshall Islands
G-09-0020	1975	00000	..Nauru
G-09-0021	1979	00000	.Polynesia
G-09-0022	1979	00000	..American Samoa
G-09-0023	1979	00000	..Cook Island
G-09-0024	1979	00000	..Easter Island
G-09-0025	1979	00000	..French Polynesia
G-09-0026	1979	00000	..Johnston Island
G-09-0027	1979	00000	..Line Islands
G-09-0028	1979	00000	..Manihiki Islands
G-09-0029	1979	00000	..Midway Islands
G-09-0030	1979	00000	..Niue Island
G-09-0031	1979	00000	..Pitcairn Islands
G-09-0032	1979	00000	..Tahiti
G-09-0033	1979	00000	..Tokelau Islands
G-09-0034	1979	00000	..Tonga
G-09-0035	1979	00000	..Wallis And Futuna Islands
G-09-0036	1975	00003	..Western Samoa

G-10 POLAR REGIONS

G-10-0001	1979	00000	Polar Regions
G-10-0002	1979	00000	.Antarctic Regions
G-10-0003	1979	00000	.Arctic Regions

APPENDICES

APPENDIX I
RULES AND CONVENTIONS

I. Testing and Evaluations

Prior to general distribution of the Political Science Thesaurus, a period of testing, employing a sampling of documents from the various areas of political science, will be performed. The results of this testing and the Thesaurus itself will be critically evaluated by a representative number of political scientists, information scientists, indexers and/or abstractors, and potential users.

II. Introduction to the Thesaurus

An introduction will be provided for the Thesaurus stating:

1. its purpose and structure;
2. the subject areas covered;
3. the rules for establishment, including-
   a. methods and sources employed in term identification,
   b. technique employed in term analysis (e.g., "roadmap," *see* Section V),
   c. process and criteria employed in relating terms within analytical groups,
   d. standards employed in alphabetizing and punctuating, and
   e. procedures developed for updating terms and relationships;
4. the rules for usage and the limits of applicability;
5. the desire for comments and suggestions from users for improving the Thesaurus; and
6. the total number of main entries, non-postable entries (e.g., USE references, *see* Section VI,A), hierarchical chains, and related concepts contained in the Thesaurus.

III. Indexes to the Thesaurus

The Thesuarus will contain an index that lists alphabetically each individual term that has been included in the hierarchical, related section, and an index that provides a categorized listing of the terms as analyzed by the "roadmap" (*see* Section V).

IV. Identification of Candidate Terms

Terms identified for inclusion in the Thesaurus may be single or multi-word descriptors related to discrete concepts encountered in political science and relevant, associated subject fields (e.g., sociology).

A. *Collection:* Numerous sources will be employed in identifying candidate terms to insure that the current and historical language of political science is identified as well as that terminology employed in analyzing (e.g., indexing and abstracting) the literature of the field.

B. *Editing and verification*: Due to the variety of sources employed in term identification, the list of candidate terms will be reviewed to eliminate duplicates, variant forms, prepositional phrases (unless standard in the vocabulary; e.g., "balance of power"), and standardize word form.

1. SPELLING—Discrepancies in spelling will be verified, and the standard form determined (e.g., color preferred to colour).

2. NOUN FORM—The noun form of a term will be used whenever possible. Exceptions to this will be certain terms requiring adjectives or equivalent expressions. Verbs will not be used.

3. NUMBER—The singular form will be used for specific material or property terms, process terms, and disciplinary areas. The plural form will be used for generic terms. When the singular and plural forms of a term denote different concepts, both will be used.

4. ABBREVIATIONS AND ACRONYMS—Abbreviated word forms and acronyms will not be used as primary terms unless the abbreviation or acronym has, through usage, become an accepted word; e.g., radar.

---

*The suggestions provided in the UNESCO *Guidelines for the Establishment and Development of Monolingual Scientific and Technical Thesauri for Information Retrieval* have served as a basis for these "Rules and Conventions." United Nations Education, Scientific and Cultural Organization. *Guidelines for the Establishment and Development of Monolingual Scientific and Technical Thesauri for Information Retrieval* (SC/MD/20). UNESCO, Paris, July 6, 1970 (distributed by U.S. Department of Health, Education and Welfare: EDO42464)

5. TERM ORDER—The natural word order of a multi-word term will be used rather than the inverted word order; e.g., "behavioral theory" rather than "theory, behavioral."

6. PUNCTUATION MARKS AND SPECIAL CHARACTERS—In general, the use of punctuation and special diacritics will be confined to right and left parentheses for scope notes following terms.

V. Analysis of Candidate Terms

To insure that the Thesaurus contains current terminology of import to the field of political science, it will be necessary to analyze each candidate term and establish its meaning for the field of political science. since many of the candidate terms may be employed in other disciplines and/or fields; e.g., sociology, economics, education, law; term analysis will be performed by individuals with adequate technical knowledge of political science, and they will subject each term to a unique analysis technique.

A. *Analysts:* The team of term analysts will represent the various academic and pragmatic divisions of political science as well as the variety of positions within these divisions. Members of the Advisory Committee, Project Staff (with subject knowledge), and the American Political Science Association will constitute the analytical team.

B. *Analysis technique:* This technique can best be described as that of a "roadmap"* by which the areas of political science will be divided into major (or generic) headings (or categories) and, then, subdivided into more and more specific categories. Once an analyst has decided that a candidate term should be processed by way of the "roadmap" (initial decision being "process" or "omit"), subsequent analytical decisions will be made by following the arrows (direction indicators) to locate all terms into common and homogeneous categories.

1. DEVELOPMENT OF "ROADMAP"—The taxonomy of the vocabulary of political science will be represented by the analytical "roadmap." The roadmap will be developed by identifying the most generic categories for political science terminology and then more speicfic categories as required.

2. APPLICATION OF "ROADMAP"—Each candidate term will be analyzed *via* the roadmap by a subject expert. If a term has more than one accepted meaning in the field of political science, a roadmap will be completed to represent each meaning. By this multi-analysis, ambiguities among terms will be resolved. The roadmap will also provide for the indication of preferred terms and common usage terms.

VI. Interrelationships Between Descriptors

Candidate terms analyzed *via* the roadmap will be grouped by the determined categories, and preferential, hierarchical, and affinitive relationships established between terms in a group. The symbols employed for these relationships will be:

Use	USE
Used For	UF
Broader Term	BT
Narrower Term	NT
Related Term	RT

A. *Preferential:* This relationship determines preferred terms among synonyms and quasi-synonyms, alternate spellings, and abbreviations and acronyms; and is cross referenced by the USE and UF symbols.

1. SYNONYMS—If two descriptors are true synonyms (a one for one relationship; e.g., mercury and quicksilver) one is selected as the main entry:

Mercury
  UF Quicksilver
Quicksilver
  USE Mercury

2. QUASI-SYNONYMS—Descriptors that overlap significantly in meaning or represent different aspects of the same property will be treated as synonyms:

Armed Forces
  UF Army
Army
  USE Armed Forces

---

*Dym, Eleanor D. "A New Approach to the Development of a Technical Thesaurus." *Proceedings of the American Documentation Institute*, vol. 4, New York, October 22-27, 1967. pp. 126-31.

3. ALTERNATE SPELLING—Based upon the preferred spelling established in Section IV, B, 1, the alternate spelling will be cross referenced:

Color
  UF Colour
Colour
  USE Color

4. ABBREVIATIONS AND ACRONYMS—Based upon the preferred word form established in Section IV, B, 4, the abbreviated form or acronym will be cross referenced:

North Atlantic Treaty Organization
  UF NATO
NATO
  USE North Atlantic Treaty Organization

B. *Hierarchical:* The broader and narrower relationships are used to display the position of a descriptor within a given class of concepts; e.g., generic or specific:

Government
  NT Local Government
Local Government
  BT Government

C. *Affinitive:* The affinitive relationship will be used to indicate those terms that are related in concept, but do not possess a hierarchical or preferential relationship:

Military
  RT War
War
  RT Military

VII. Format of Thesaurus

The main section of the Thesaurus will be an alphabetic display of the descriptors with established relationships listed under each term. In addition, two indexes (*see* Section III) will be included. Following each descriptor, will be a category code indicating the location of the term in the "categorized index." For those terms that have more than one meaning in political science (*see* Section V, B, 2), and, therefore, are related in more than one category group, a multi-listing with appropriate category codes will be made.

The alphabetizing for all sections of the Thesaurus will be word-by-word, according to the following rules:

1. a space indicates the end of a word;

2. ignore all characters other than letters, numerals and left parenthesis; and

3. file in sequence as follows:
   a. left parenthesis,
   b. letters in order by word,
   c. numerals preceded by letters in numeric order, and
   d. numerals at beginning of descriptor by word.

VIII. Updating

Once the Thesaurus is subjected to practical application, the ability to include additional terms and eliminate terms will be needed.

A. *New Descriptors:* When through user or indexer recommendations, the desirability of adding a new term is indicated, the candidate term will be analyzed *via* the roadmap (Section V) and its relationship to other terms in the determined concept group established (Section VI).

B. *Elimination of Descriptors:* Since the Thesaurus is to serve as the terminology guide for political science in general, as well as a vocabulary base for an information storage and retrieval system, prudent judgement will be required in eliminating descriptors. Low frequency of usage in indexing would, therefore, be an insufficient reason for elimination. Rather, the elimination of a term would require that its concept or meaning in political science had been eliminated.

APPENDIX II
SOURCES OF TERMS USED IN THE FIRST EDITION

ABC political science. Santa Barbara, California: American Bibliographical Center, Clio Press.

Administrative science quarterly. Ithaca, New York: Graduate School of Business and Public Administration, Cornell University

American Academy of Political and Social Science. *Annals.* Philadelphia, Pennsylvania: The American Academy of Political and Social Science.

American anthropologist. Washington, D.C.: American Anthropological Association.

American behavioral scientist. Beverly Hills, California: Sage Publications, Inc.

American journal of economics and sociology. Lancaster, Pennsylvania: Journal of Economics and Sociology, Inc.

American journal of international law. Washington, D.C.: American Society of International Law.

American political science review. Washington, D.C.: American Political Science Association.

American sociological review. Washington, D.C.: American Sociological Association.

Australian journal of politics and history. Brisbane, Australia: University of Queensland Press.

Behavioral science. Ann Arbor, Michigan: Mental Health Research Institute, University of Michigan.

Black lines. Pittsburgh, Pennsylvania: Department of Black Studies, University of Pittsburgh.

Canadian journal of political science (Revue Canadienne de sciences politiques). (Canadian Political Science Association) Toronto, Canada: University of Toronto Press.

Canadian public administration (Administration publique du Canada). Toronto, Canada: Institute of Public Administration of Canada.

Columbia law review. New York, New York: Columbia Law Students.

Commentary. New York, New York: American Jewish Committee.

Comparative political studies. Beverly Hills, California: Sage Publications, Inc.

Contemporary sociology. Albany, New York: American Sociological Association.

Control or fate in economic affairs: selections from the proceedings of the Academy of Political Science. (Academy of Political Science) New York, New York: Columbia University.

Daedalus. Boston, Massachusetts: American Academy of Arts and Sciences. .o DeCrespigny, Anthony, and Wertheimer, Alan. *Contemporary political theory.* New York, New York: Aldine, 1970.

Deutsch, Karl. *Politics and government: how people decide their fate.* New York, New York: Houghton-Mifflin, 1970.

Dissent. New York, New York: Dissent Publishing Corporation.

Dunner, Joseph, ed. *Dictionary of political science.* New York, New York: Philosophical Library, 1964.

Economic development and cultural change. (Research Center in Economic Development and Cultural Change, University of Chicago) Chicago, Illinois: University of Chicago Press.

Ehenstein, William. *Modern political thought.* New York, New York: Holt, 1960.

Ethics: an international journal of social and political philosophy. Chicago, Illinois: University of Chicago Press.

Foreign affairs: an American quartely review. New York, New York: Council on Foreign Relations, Inc.

Foreign affairs (concordance). vol. 46, no. 3/vol. 49, no. 1 (April 1968 through October 1970).

Foreign policy. New York, New York: National Affairs, Inc.

Fundamentals of Marxism-Leninism: manual. Moscow, U.S.S.R.: Foreign Languages Publishing House, 1961.

Harvard law review. Cambridge, Massachusetts: Harvard Law Review Association.

Ibele, Oscar, *Political science: an introduction.* London, England: Chandler Pub., 1971.

The Indian journal of public administration. New Delhi, India: Indian Institute of Public Administration.

Industrial and labor relations review. Ithaca, New York: New York State School of Industrial and Labor Relations.

International bibliography of political science—1969. vol. 18.

International conciliation. New York, New York: Carnegie Endowment for International Peace.

International encyclopedia of the social sciences. vol. 17, index. New York, New York: McMillan, 1968.

International information notes (concordance). July 1969/November 1970.

International journal. (Canadian Institute of International Affairs) Toronto, Canada: International Journal.

International organization. Boston, Massachusetts: World Peace Foundation.

International political science abstracts. (International Political Science Association) Oxford, England: Basil Blackwell & Mott, Ltd.

International political science abstracts (concordance). vol. 19, no. 1/vol. 20, no. 1 (June 1969 through June 1970).

International studies quarterly. (International Studies Association) Beverly Hills, California: Sage Publications, Inc.

Iris, Mark, compiler. *Cumulative index to the proceedings of the American Political Science Association: 1904-1910, 1912, 1956-1969.* Ann Arbor, Michigan: Xerox-University Microfilms, 1970.

Janda, Kenneth, ed. *Cumulative index to the American political science review, 1906-1968.* vol. 1-620. Ann Arbor, Michigan: Xerox-University Microfilms, 1969.

Journal of administration overseas. (Foreign and Commonwealth Office, Overseas Development Administration) London, England: Her Majesty's Stationery Office.

Journal of comparative administration. (Comparative Administration Group) Beverly Hills, California: Sage Publications, Inc.
Journal of conflict resolution: a quarterly for research related to war and peace. Ann Arbor, Michigan: Center for Research on Conflict Resolution, University of Michigan.
Journal of contemporary history. London, England: Weidenfeld and Nicolson.
Journal of developing areas. Macomb, Illinois: Western Illinois University.
Journal of development studies. London, England: Frank Cass and Co., Ltd.
Journal of law and economics. Chicago, Illinois: University of Chicago Law School.
Journal of peach research. Oslo, Norway: Universitatsforlaget.
Journal of personality and social psychology. Washington, D.C.: American Psychological Association.
Journal of social psychology. Provincetown, Massachusetts: Journal Press.
Journalism quarterly. (Association for Education in Journalism) Minneapolis, Minnesota: School of Journalism, University of Minnesota.
Latin American research review. (Latin American Studies Association) Washington, D.C.: Hispanic Foundation, Library of Congress.
Law and society review. (Law and Society Association) Beverly Hills, California, Sage Publications, Inc.
MacIves, Robert M. *Politics and society.* New York, New York: Atherton, 1969.
The Middle East journal. Washington, D.C.: Middle East Institute.
Middle Eastern studies. London, England: Frank Cass and Co., Ltd.
Midwest journal of political science. (Midwest Political Science Association) Detroit, Michigan: Wayne State University Press.
New York University law review. New York, New York: New York University.
New Zealand journal of public administration. Wellington, New Zealand.
Northwestern Data I (concordance).
Northwestern Data II (concordance).
Orbis: a quarterly journal of world affairs. Philadelphia, Pennsylvania: Foreign Policy Research Institute, University of Pennsylvania, in association with The Fletcher School of Law and Diplomacy, Tufts University.
Pacific affairs. (Institute of Pacific Relations) Vancouver, British Columbia: University of British Columbia.
Philippine journal of public administration. Manila, Philippines: College of Public Administration, University of the Philippines.
Political quarterly. London, England: Political Quarterly Publishing Co., Ltd.
Political science quarterly. (Academy of Political Science) New York, New York: Columbia University.
Politics and society. Los Altos, California: Geron-X Publishers, Inc.
Polity. (Northeastern Political Science Association) Amherst, Massachusetts: University of Massachusetts Press.
PS. (U.S.) Washington, D.C.: American Political Science Review.
Psychiatry. Washington, D.C.: William Alanson White Psychiatric Foundation, Inc.
Public administration review. (U.S.) Washington, D.C.: American Society for Public Administration.
The public interest. (Freedom House, New York) New York, New York: Basic Books, Inc.
Public opinion quarterly. (Opinion Research Corporation, Princeton) New York, New York: Columbia University.
Public policy. (John F. Kennedy School of Government, Harvard University) Cambridge, Massachusetts: Harvard University Press.
The review of politics. Notre Dame, Indiana: University of Notre Dame.
Science and society. New York, New York: Science and Society, Inc.
Simulation and games: an international journal of theory, design, and research. Beverly Hills, California: Sage Publications, Inc.
Slavic review. Seattle, Washington: American Association for the Advancement of Slavic Studies, University of Washington.
Sloan, Harold S., and Zurcher, Arnold J. *A dictionary of economics.* 4th ed., New York, New York: Barnes and Noble, Inc.
Social forces. Chapel Hill, North Carolina: University of North Carolina Press.
Social research: an international quarterly of the social sciences. New York, New York: Graduate Faculty of Political and Social Science of the New School for Social Research.
Social science information. The Hague, Netherlands: Mouton & Co.
Sociological inquiry. Toronto, Canada: Alpha Kappa Delta-National Honor Society.
Soviet studies. Glasgow, Scotland: Institute of Soviet and East European Studies. University of Glasgow.
Studies in comparative communism. Los Angeles, California: University of Southern California Press.
Studies in comparative international development. Beverly Hills, California: Sage Publications, Inc.
Theodorson, George A., and Theodorson, Achilles G. *A modern dictionary of sociology.* New York, New York: Thomas V. Crowell Co., 1971.
Trans-action: social science and modern society. New Brunswick, New Jersey: Rutgers University.
Urban affairs quarterly. Beverly Hills, California: Sage Publications, Inc.
Western political quarterly. (Western Political Science Association, Pacific Northwest Political Science Association, Southern California Political Science Association) Salt Lake City, Utah: Institute of Government, University of Utah.
World politics: a quarterly journal of international relations. (Center of International Studies, Princeton) Princeton, New Jersey: Princeton University Press.
Yale review: a national quarterly. New Haven, Connecticut: Yale University.

APPENDIX III
SOURCES OF TERMS USED IN THE SECOND EDITION

Administration and Society
Administrative Science Quarterly
Air University Review
American Anthropologist
American Behavioral Scientist
American Historical Review
American Jewish Historical Quarterly
American Journal of Comparative Law
American Journal of Economics and Sociology
American Journal of International Law
American Journal of Political Science
American Journal of Sociology
American Political Science Review
American Politics Quarterly
American Review of Canadian Studies
American Sociological Review
Annals of the American Academy of Political & Social Science
Armed Forces & Society
Asian Survey

Behavior Science Research
Behavioral Science
Bulletin of the Atomic Scientists
Bureaucrat

Canadian-American Slavic Studies
Civil Liberties Review
Columbia Journal of Law & Social Problems
Comparative Political Studies
Comparative Politics
Comparative Strategy
Comparative Studies in Society & History
Comparative Urban Research
Common Ground
Cuban Studies
Current History

Daedalus

East European Quarterly
Economic Development & Cultural Change
Economic Working Papers Bibliography
Education & Urban Society
Emory Law Journal
Ethics
Ethnicity
Ethnology

Foreign Affairs
Foreign Polity

Growth and Change

Harvard Educational Review
Harvard Law Review
Hastings Center Report
Hispanic American Historical Review
Historical Abstracts
Historical Methods Newsletter
History and Theory

Human Organization
Human Relations
Human Relations Area Files

Indian Historian
Industrial and Labor Relations Review
Inter-American Economic Affairs
International and Comparative Public Policy
International Development Review
International Educational & Cultural Exchange
International Interactions
International Journal of Intercultural Relations
International Journal of Middle East Studies
International Migration Review
International Organization
International Security
International Studies Notes
International Studies Quarterly

Jewish Social Studies
Journal of African Studies
Journal of American History
Journal of Applied Behavioral Science
Journal of Asian Affairs
Journal of Asian Studies
Journal of Black Studies
Journal of Communication
Journal of Conflict Resolution
Journal of Cross-Cultural Psychology
Journal of Developing Areas
Journal of Economic History
Journal of Economic Issues
Journal of Economic Literature
Journal of Ethnic Studies
Journal of Interamerican Studies & World Affairs
Journal of Interdisciplinary History
Journal of International Affairs
Journal of International Business Studies
Journal of Japanese Studies
Journal of Modern History
Journal of Peace Science
Journal of Political Economy
Journal of Politics
Journal of Social and Political Studies
Journal of Social History
Journal of Social Issues
Journal of Social Psychology
Journal of Southern African Affairs
Journal of the American Institute of Planners
Journal of the History of Ideas
Journal of Urban History

Korean Studies Forum

Latin American Research Review
Law & Contemporary Problems
Law & Society Review
Legislative Studies Quarterly

Middle East Review
Midwest Review of Public Administration
Military Review
Modern China

Natural Resources Journal
New York Times Data Bank

Orbis

Pacific Sociological Review
Papers of the Peace Science Society
Parameters
Peasant Studies
Philosophical Forum
Philosophy & Public Affairs
Policy Analysis
Policy Review
Policy Studies Journal
Polish American Studies
Polish Review
Political Science Quarterly
Political Theory
Politics & Society
Polity
Presidential Studies Quarterly
Problems of Communism
Proceedings of the Academy of Political Science
Public Administration Review
Public Choice
Public Finance Quarterly
Public Interest
Public Opinion Quarterly
Public Policy
Publius

Review of Black Political Economy
Review of Politics
Russian Review

Simulation and Games
Slavic Review
Slavonic & East European Review
Social Forces
Social Research
Social Science History
Social Science Quarterly
Social Science Research
Social Sciences Information Utilization Laboratory (retrieval service)
Sociological Abstracts
Sociological Methods and Research
Sociological Quarterly
Sociometry
State and Local Government Review
Strategic Review
Studies in Comparative Communism
Studies in Comparative International Development

Thesaurus of ERIC Descriptors
(Educational Resources Information Center)
Thesaurus of the Modern Language Association (in draft)
Thesaurus of Psychological Index Terms
(American Psychological Association)
Topics in Culture Learning

UNESCO Thesaurus
United States Naval Institute Proceedings
Urban Affairs Quarterly
Urban Studies
Urbanism Past & Present

Western Political Quarterly
Wilson Quarterly
World Affairs
World Politics

Youth & Society

APPENDIX IV
PARTICIPANTS—FIRST EDITION

Beck, Carl
Professor, Department of Political Science
Director, University Center for International Studies
University of Pittsburgh

Bonn, Frank
Professor, Department of Political Science
University of Indiana—South Bend

Brenner, Marjorie
Administrative Specialist, University Center for International Studies
University of Pittsburgh

Brewer, Gary
The RAND Corporation
Santa Monica, California

Brock, Clifton
Professor, University Library
University of North Carolina

Budge, Ian
Professor, Department of Government
University of Essex
Essex, United Kingdom

Burgess, Phillip
Director, Behavioral Science Laboratory
Ohio State University

Carroll, James
Professor, Department of Political Science
Maxwell School—Syracuse University

Corrado, Raymond R.
Instructor, Department of Political Science
University of Pittsburgh

Daniels, William
Professor, Department of Political Science
Union College

Dennis, Jack
Professor, Department of Political Science
University of Wisconsin

Diamond, Martin
Professor, Department of Political Science
Northern Illinois University

Dowdell Arnetta
Keypuncher, Knowledge Availability Systems Center
University of Pittsburgh

Dym, Eleanor
Assistant Director, Knowledge Availability Systems Center
University of Pittsburgh

Dym, Victoria
Student Assistant
University of Pittsburgh

Easton, David
Professor, Andrew MacLeish Distinguished Service,
Department of Political Science
University of Chicago
Chairman, Scientific Information Exchange Committee,
American Political Science Association

Farber, Karen
Assistant to Director of Personnel
University of Pittsburgh

Foster, Lynn
Assistant Instructor, Department of Political Science
University of Pittsburgh

Flurry, William H.
Research Associate, University Center for International Studies
University of Pittsburgh

Gattuso, Karin
Research Assistant, Knowledge Availability Systems Center
University of Pittsburgh

Graham, George
Professor, Department of Political Science
Vanderbilt University

Golden Carolyn
Research Assistant, University Center for International Studies
University of Pittsburgh

Hofstetter, Richard
Professor, Department of Political Science
Ohio State University

Humphrey, Lorraine
Senior Secretary, University Center for International Studies
University of Pittsburgh

Hurtig, Serge
Editor, International Political Science Abstracts
Paris, France

Janda, Kenneth
Professor, Department of Political Science
Northwestern University

Kent, Allen
Director, Office of Communications Program
University

King, Erika
Instructor, Department of Political Science
Chatham Colllge

Koller, Mary
Secretary, Knowldege Availability Systems Center
University of Pittsburgh

Kowalski, Jean
Library Systems Specialist, Information Utilization Laboratory,
University Center for International Studies
University of Pittsburgh

Lane, Robert, E.
Professor, Department of Political Science
Yale University

Lijphart, Arend
Professor, Department of Political Science
Rijks—Universiteit de Leiden
Leiden, The Netherlands

Livingston, William
Professor, Department of Government
University of Texas—Austin

Luce, Diane
Teaching Assistant, Department of Political Science
University of Pittsburgh

Mann, Thomas
Staff Associate, American Political Science Association

McAtee, Ellen
Research Assistant, Knowledge Availability Systems Center
University of Pittsburgh

McKechnie, John T.
Instructor, Department of Political Science
Chatham College

Meyriat, Jean
Secretary General, International Committee for Social Sciences
Paris, France

Mouly, Ruth
Lecturer, Department of Political Science
University of Pittsburgh

Nesvold, Betty
Professor, Department of Political Science
University of California—San Diego

Ogul, Morris
Professor, Department of Political Science
University of Pittsburgh

Ostrom, Lynn
Professor, Department of Political Science
Indiana University

Patterson, Samuel
Professor, Department of Political Science
University of Iowa

Peters, Paul
Information Systems Analyst, Information Utilization Laboratory,
University Center for International Studies
University of Pittsburgh

Pool, Jonathan
Professor, Department of Political Science
State University of New York—Stony Brook

Rawling Karen E.
Associate Director, International Studies Association
Lecturer, Department of Political Science
University of Pittsburgh

Reiding, Read R.
Assistant Professor, Department of Political Science
University of Pittsburgh

Rogers, Rosemarie
Professor, Fletcher School of Law and Diplomacy
Tufts University

Rokkan, Stein
Chairman, Michelsen Institute
Bergen, Norway

Shanks, Merrill
Professor, Department of Political Science
University of California—Berkeley

Tilton, Timothy
Professor, Department of Political Science
Indiana University

Viet, Jean
Directeur, Service d'Echange d'Information Scientifiques,
Maison des Sciences de l'Homme
Paris, France

Wall, Eugene
President, Lex Inc.
Rockville, Maryland

Whitman, Gertrude
Executive Secretary, University Center for International Studies
University of Pittsburgh

Woodring, Ruth
Administrative Secretary, Knowledge Availability Systems Center
University of Pittsburgh

Wyner, Alan
Professor, Department of Political Science
University of California—Santa Barbara

Wildemann, Rudolf
Professor, Lehrstuhl Fur Politische Wissenschaft,
der Universitat Mannheim (W.H.)
Mannheim, West German

Zisk, Betty
Professor, Department of Political Science
Ohio State University

APPENDIX V

FOREWARD TO THE FIRST EDITION

The publication of this *Thesaurus* clears away the first major hurdle to the development of an indexing and abstracting service for political science in the United States. Simultaneously it lays the groundwork for a broad automated information service capable of meeting the growing research and teaching needs of our discipline. The *Thesaurus* has been organized in such a way as to ensure that the information acquired through its use will cover all major areas of interest to the discipline, and that inquiries made with its terms will obtain responses of maximum relevance. In addition, the design of the *Thesaurus* permits continuous revision so as to keep pace with the changing emphasis in the discipline. The information system of which, hopefully, it will become an integral part should help to democratize the access to published knowledge in political science. Some day, whether through direct on-line computer connections or through rapid response to mail or phone inquiries, teachers and students of political science at the smallest and most remote college could have a capacity identical with those at larger institutions for quickly and comprehensively searching the literature for relevant publications.

Two personal experiences are indirectly associated with the appearance of this *Thesaurus*. They impressed on me the need to mount a concerted effort toward improving the quality of our methods in political science for storing, recovering, and disseminating the kinds of information that we characteristically need and use for research and teaching, regardless of whether we are concerned with surveys or with philosophical inquiry.

In 1965 I chaired a newly formed Committee on Information in the Behavioral Sciences of the National Academy of Sciences—National Research Council. This committee addressed itself to the information needs of the social sciences as a whole, the state of automated technology in the information field, and knowledge about the possible consequences of machine-usable data for the improvement of research and teaching. In 1967 the Committee offered some far-reaching recommendations for reorganizing and strengthening the information systems for the social sciences in the United States.[1]

As a member of the International Committee on Social Science Information and Documentation, a UNESCO-supported group, and later, from 1969 to 1971, as its Chairman, I was confronted with the even less well developed state of scientific information exchange in the international social science community. It became clear, however, that without the prior improvement of national methods for managing scientific information, the necessary and desirable infrastructure for an international system would never become available, even if the obvious technical and political barriers could be surmounted.

As President Elect of the American Political Science Association during 1967-68, and in the next year as President, I took advantage of the opportunity to urge upon the Association the need to initiate a program for increasing our knowledge about the information practices of political scientists in the United States and for considering ways to improve our information services and capabilities. During those years social changes were occurring that were clearly critical for the future character of our discipline and its professional organizations. The APSA Council did share with me the conviction, however, that the information needs of all political scientists would continue regardless of other significant changes in the discipline. The steps taken during those years led to the sequence of events of which this *Thesaurus* is the first operational product.

The organizational history of the Association's efforts in this area needs to be briefly described. It is a short tale of aroused expectations, financial disappointments, and frustrated hopes. But it is also a story of a small but growing community of concerned scholars from all branches and outlooks in the discipline, of deep commitment by a few and, toward the end, of steady progress even on a virtually non-existent budget.

Early in 1968 the Executive Committee of the Association authorized the establishment of a Committee on Communications;[2] its name was shortly changed to its present form, the Committee on Scientific Information Exchange. On the well-grounded assumption that as a discipline we had little reliable understanding of how in fact our knowledge, findings, and data get disseminated, the objective of the Committee was to consider the need for a full-scale study of the information practices among political scientists in the United States.

Like any good group of independent scholars, the members of this committee immediately went about redefining the issue. They concluded that the Harvey and Griffith reports for the American Psychological Association on scientific information exchange within that discipline could probably be extended without excessive error to political science.[3] In place of a replicating study for political science, the Committee proposed substituting research in an area about which to this day we have little reliable understanding: the impact of changes in the dissemination of information upon both teaching and research. Unfortunately this suggestion was never funded. It served, however, to keep the issue of scientific information alive until the Presidency of Robert Lane, who was also concerned with the relatively undeveloped state of our information resources. Under his guidance the Council authorized the reorganization of the Committee and charged it with the following considerably enlarged responsibilities: "(1) to advise and recommend to the Council policies on matters relating to scientific information exchange; (2) to supervise and evaluate the proposed United States Abstracts Center (including the development of a thesaurus, if funded); and (3) to advise on publication programs and services."[4] In effect the jurisdiction of the Committee was broadened to include the charges of two earlier committees whose terms had expired: a Committee on Journals and an Ad Hoc Committee on Abstracts. It is this new Committee that has had the responsibility for supervising the planning, production, and publication of this *Thesaurus*.

These various committees have labored hard and long in exploring the various dimensions of the current information practices found in the discipline and in formulating alternative programs for improvement. The minutes of the Committee include detailed proposals for a fully developed system for the selective dissemination of information in the United States and for coordinating our activities with the *International Political Science Abstracts*. Unfortunately the scope and intensity of our efforts have been blocked at almost every turn by lack of funds. In the end this forced the Committee to restrict its interests to only one aspect of its general responsibilities, the construction of an indexing and abstracting center. The fulfillment of its other charges will continue to be contingent upon the availability of financial resources.

A word of explanation about this circumscription of its activities is in order. When the Committee was first founded, in 1967, the climate was such in the information field that there was reasonable hope of funds, from public or private sources, for the establishment and improvement of automated information systems in the social and natural sciences alike. But following the social unrest of the 1960's, the reordering of national priorities quickly reduced information services, which had never ranked high at best, to the bottom rung of the ladder. The accident of timing alone enabled the Committee to obtain funding from the National Science Foundation for the construction of the present *Thesaurus* before financial sources dried up completely.

Fortunately the Committee found greater success with its human resources. It has consistently been able to attract members of the discipline who have been enthusiastic about efforts to improve our antiquated and unwittingly costly information practices. In Carl Beck, Director of the University Center for International Studies at the University of Pittsburgh, the Committee was rewarded with a contractor for its work to whom, it would seem the creation of a mechanized information system for the discipline represented a major challenge to be met with unrelenting energy and perseverance. Our staff associate at the American Political Science Association, Thomas Mann, displayed a sense of dedication that went far beyond the call of duty. Without a high level of commitment from many other colleagues in the discipline, as well as staff persons identified elsewhere in this publication, the monumental undertaking that this *Thesaurus* alone represents could never have been brought to completion.

This *Thesaurus* is, however, only a first even if vital step, in several senses. It represents a first step for, even with the enormous labor that has gone into it, we are all only too painfully aware that important omissions, redundancies, and errors could not help but occur. these are not to be viewed as irreparable disasters however. The design of the *Thesaurus* takes into account its own inevitable initial deficiencies. It is to be conceived as a living system, open and expansible. Built into it are rules for periodic and regular updating based upon the experience of its users. Its self-correcting capacity should help allay any anxieties or dissatisfactions at the discovery of its inevitable shortcomings.

This *Thesaurus* is a first step in another sense. A thesaurus is only a means to an end. The end is the improvement of the capabilities for research and teaching in all areas of political science as far apart as statistical analysis and moral inquiry. Between a thesaurus and this broader goal stands the need for a structure that will permit the rapid and efficient dissemination of information and knowledge directly relevant to teaching and research needs. It is appropriate, therefore, that the publication of this *Thesaurus* should coincide with the introduction of a Demonstration Year. Through the Association, the Committee has entered into an arrangement with the University Center for International Studies to conduct "a twelve month developmental project to try out a selective dissemination of information system for political science. The principal objectives of this demonstration project are the creation of a meaningful but limited data base, the development of staff capabilities and procedures for tagging documents with thesaurus terms, and the evaluation and improvement of the Selective Dissemination of Information system. "[5]

The *Thesaurus* stands as a beginning in another sense as well. In the hard-headed world of information science we find more visionaries perhaps than in what is often thought to be the softer world of fiction. Behind this *Thesaurus*, in the minds of some, lies the image of an information network for political science in the United States in which research workers, teachers, and students will be able, at low cost, to command materials (bibliographies, abstracts, and citations from journals, books, fugitive conference papers and the like) most relevant to their changing interests. At its best they should be able to obtain this information at low cost in minimal time from specialized storage centers dispersed throughout the country but linked in an automated network through a central clearing house.[6] Such a decentralized information system would not only be able to put pertinent information at the fingertips of all political scientists, but it would continuously and automatically keep current profiles of the academic interests of all its users. In this way searches of the files could be effectively and comprehensively conducted.

The vision extends beyond the United States. For the distant future it includes an international network of academic informalities in each major research area in the world. Very practical organizations such as UNISIST[7] have already taken steps in this direction for the natural sciences and discussion regarding the social sciences has also begun. Through this international network scholars in each country would be able to dip directly and selectively into the publicly available information and documents stored in automated information centers in any other cooperating country.

Political, economic, linguistic and not a few technical barriers leave the realization of this image somewhere off in the distant future, if ever at all. But whether fantasies such as these will come to pass is of no immediate moment. For some they do serve to provide the psychic stimulus for the painstaking labors demanded by the very limited and specific objectives of the here and now. But for all information scientists the day of easy access to essential information in our discipline will never be even a remote possibility without an infrastructure of national information systems in the social sciences. Such a national system, in turn, whether as a goal in itself or as part of a broader world-wide network, is inconceivable without the prior construction of thesauri encompassing the objectives of the one presented here.

David Easton
Chairman, Committee on Scientific Information Exchange
American Political Science Association

Footnotes

1. *Communication Systems and Resources in the Behavioral Sciences*, a report by the Committee on Information in the Behavioral Sciences (Chairman: David Easton), Division of the Behavioral Sciences of the National Research Council—National Academy of Sciences, Publication 1575, Washington, D.C., 1967.

2. Carl Beck (Chairman), Kenneth Janda, Kenneth Prewitt, Albert Somit. This Committee was expanded by 1970 in include Michael Hudson, Warren Miller, and Ray Tanter.

3. W.D. Garvey and B.C. Griffith, *Reports of the American Psychological Association's Project on Scientific Information Exchange in Psychology*, American Psychological Association, Washington, D.C., 1963-65.

4. See Minutes of the Council, American Political Science Association, June, 1971. The changing membership of the Committee from 1971 to the present day has included the following: Carl Beck, Gary Brewer*, David Easton* (Chairman, 1972 ff.), George Graham*, Richard Hofstetter*, Kenneth Janda*, Robert Lane* (Chairman, 1970-72), William Livingston, Betty Nesvold, Samuel Patterson, Nelson Polsby, rosemarie rogers*, Stein Rokkan, Merrill Shanks*, Albert Somit*. [*current members]

5. Letter of Agreement, December 14, 1973, files of American Political Science Association.

6. See *communication Systems and Resources in the Behavioral Sciences.*

7. A United Nations program for voluntary cooperation among existing and future information systems in the areas of science and technology.

APPENDIX VI
PREFACE TO THE FIRST EDITION

Political scientists, as users and generators of information, have been hampered by the complications created by the broad interdisciplinary nature of the field's literature. The scope of the literature and the lack of a comprehensive information system have a number of negative consequences on teaching, research, and program development within political science. They lead (1) to a premature reification of concepts, (2) to a failure to identify and use new conceptual framework and methodologies, (3) to the perpetuation of artificial class and category disciplines which affect both institutions and individuals, and (4) to the perpetuation of outworn and outdated myths. The present information milieu in political science, also, results in a drain on time, money, and talent.

In the spring of 1968, the American Political Science Association (APSA) established the Committee on Scientific Information Exchange. This Committee was charged with developing mechanisms that would enable political scientists to come to grips with the discipline's information problems. During the first three years of its existence, the Committee drafted statements and proposals aimed at conceptualizing the information problems and designing an approach to changing the present information structures and behaviors in political science. The major study of the Committee, *Classification of Knowledge and Information Retrieval in Political Science*, assessed services available to political scientists and presented the design of a computer dependent information system. The design included approaches to handling three of the major problems associated with the effective operation and utilization of an information system: (1) the development of a terminology control mechanism, (2) the development of a user oriented document format for information storage, and (3) the development of a user oriented information retrieval system.

After many long discussions with Federal agencies, private foundations, and publishers, one component of the proposed system was funded. The Office of Scientific Information Services of the National Science Foundation, under the leadership of Dr. Melvin S. Day, subsidized the creation of a Thesaurus of political science. The Thesaurus was to be created from English language sources and it was to be machine oriented. The Thesaurus project was a combined effort of the American Political Science Association (APSA) through its Committee on Scientific Information Exchange and the University of Pittsburgh through the University Center for International Studies (UCIS) and the Knowledge Availability Systems Center (KASC). Since one goal of the Thesaurus project was to assemble a community of interested scholars who would be involved in the development and evaluation of the final *Thesaurus*, over a hundred political scientists were invited to participate in the project. Originally, three evaluations, one through machine access and manipulation, were planned for the *Thesaurus*. In reality, it was necessary to perform a more extensive evaluation process than was originally perceived. This had the consequence of extending the time frame of the project. Fortunately, funding was provided by UCIS for a year beyond the original project date.

It is felt that a seminal *Thesaurus* for political science which represents an adequate taxonomy of the terminology used by political scientists has been developed. It is acknowledged that the *Thesaurus* will have to be revised on the basis of usage, and a demonstration system for updating and revising the *Thesaurus* has already been designed. The major mechanism for any revision, therefore, will be actual usage.

The *Political Science* (PS) *Thesaurus* was to be one of the underpinings of an information system for political science. Following extensive discussions with Federal agencies, private foundations, and publishers in an attempt to obtain support for an information system, APSA and UCIS decided to underwrite a demonstration year of a political science information system which will serve as a pilot and evaluation project for all parts of the information system including the *Thesaurus*. For the pilot information system, articles contained in approximately 70 journals published in the United States which are of interest to political scientists will be analyzed and stored in machine readable form. Of the eleven levels of information recorded for each document, one level will be *Thesaurus* normalized index entries. Techniques for evaluating each component of the information system have also been developed, and throughout the demonstration year the opportunity to field test the *PS Thesaurus* from the perspective of both the analyst and the user will be exploited. This intensive evaluation is a critical phase in the process of amending the information milieu of contemporary political science.

The test of an operating information system lies in its ability to provide users with the information that they seek. Most users fall into two broad categories: the user who evaluates the system in terms of recall and the user who evaluates the system in terms of precision. Recall is a measure of the systems ability to assure the user that he or she has received a high percentage of all relevant documents from the system which match the interest profile. The recall oriented user is interested in a positive answer to the question: ". . . am I getting all the material that is in the file which is relevant to my query?" Precision is a measure of the exactness of the match between a user's profile and the documents retrieved. The precision oriented user is interested in a positive answer to the question: ". . . do all the documents that I am getting match precisely my interests?" A thesaurus is the only effective interface by which both groups of users can be satisfied.

This *Thesaurus* is designed to be but one building block in an operating information system for political science. We hope to have in operation a system whose data bases include books, convention papers and articles, drawn not only from the United States but from other countries as well. We hope to have in operation a system which will provide continuous service to clients on a regularized current awareness basis and with the capability for retrospective searching as well. The *Thesaurus* is the first step toward this goal. The demonstration year is the second. The third, an operating system, will depend upon our ability to attract users, to create networking arrangements with other systems, and to design a fiscal and management system which will make the information system feasible.

In the "Description and Use of the Thesaurus" section, the methodology employed in creating the *Thesaurus* is described. It is an important statement on thesaurus construction, editing and evaluation. What is not described are the traumas of the project. The first traumatic period occurred when it was-found that the number of candidate terms had been underestimated. It had been expected that from the current literature approximately 100,000 terms would be identified which would have to be sorted and edited to obtain a list of approximately 30,000 candidate terms that would be intensively analyzed for possible inclusion in the *Thesaurus*. Instead, 300,000 terms were initially identified and the sorting and editing procedures resulted in a listing of approximately 25,000 candidate terms for the analysis process.

The second traumatic period occurred during the candidate term analysis stage. In order to group (or categorize) the 40,000 candidate terms into linguistically similar classes, so that hierarchical relationships could be established, each term was analyzed *via* the political science "roadmap."* Approximately 100 political scientists, representing the various fields of the discipline, participated in the "roadmap" analysis effort. Comprehension of the principle of the analysis technique varied among the participating political scientists. Rather than accepting a term as recorded and determining its linguistic structure from the graphic representation, many of the participants tended to provide context for the term. The result was that many of the term groupings obtained from the "roadmap" contained terms that were not linguistically similar. For example, the term *governing*, which linguistically represents a process, was associated with government and analyzed as an institution. The term *husband*, which linguistically represents a role or status, was associated with the family and analyzed as an institution. Of particular value in identifying linguistic violations was an evaluation by Mr. Eugene Wall, President of Lex, Inc., who served as a consultant to the project.

As a result, it was necessary for project staff members from UCIS and KASC to review and reconstruct each of the 43 hierarchies. This task was greatly aided by professor Jonathan Pool, State University of New York at Stony Brook, who painstakingly went completely through each of the partially reconstructed hierarchies.

The third traumatic period occurred when a group of participants were asked to identify related terms between the hierarchies. Related terms within the hierarchies had already been identified by UCIS project staff. An aggregate number of over 700,000 interhierarchical relationships were noted by this group. Even more interestingly, with this apparent over-kill of related terms, a number of seminal relationships were missed. Again, it was necessary to prune the identified related terms to compensate for misinterpretation. During the demonstration and evaluation year, the character of the existing related terms will be carefully documented.

In the original proposal to the National Science Foundation, the creation of the *Thesaurus* was described as both an act of science and an act of intuition. As Project Director, I have concluded that the important variables are neither science nor intuition but the commitment and energy of some key individuals who have to be willing to devote time and energy to the project.

I would like to particularly thank a few of the key individuals of this *Thesaurus* project. The first two are, of course, the co-authors: Eleanor D. Dym, Associate Director of KASC, and J. Thomas McKechnie, Instructor, Chatham College. Both devoted hundreds of hours to this project and shared with me all of the problems that arose. Caroline Golden, Research Assistant of UCIS, stayed with the project from the beginning as a key research assistant. William H. Flurry and Paul H. Ernandez, Research Assistants in the Center, contributed many hours in supervising the relating of terms and preparing the final document for production. Paul Peters, Manager of the Information Utilization Laboratory of UCIS, provided programming assistance and, more importantly, significant insights into users' needs. The IUL serves, per month, over 500 users of mechanized data bases, and the insights into pragmatic behavior coupled with experimental data were invaluable. Georgia S. McClellan, Manager of the Publications Program of UCIS, was responsible for the generation of camera-ready copy for the *Thesaurus*. Thomas Mann, Staff Associate of the American Political Science Association, served as an effective diplomatic liaison between the project staff, the Association, the Committee, and the National Science Foundation. Mrs. Gertrude Whitman, my secretary, coordinated all of the activities and meetings connected with the project. Mrs. Whitman possesses the marvelous facility of keeping track of various activities and making people feel comfortable and attended to at the same time. I would also like to express my gratitude to Rhoten A. Smith, Provost of the University of Pittsburgh, who supported the unique financial arrangements that made the demonstration year possible.

I can only acknowledge the assistance of my family in the breech. There is an euphemism that describes conflict in terms of "we had words." Never did that euphemism have such a massive reality.

Carl Beck

---

*Dym, Eleanor D. "A New Approach to the Development of a Technical Thesaurus," *Proceedings of the American Documentation Institute,* annual meeting, vol. 4. New York, American Documentation Institute, October 22-27, 1967. pp. 126-131.

APPENDIX VII
UNITED STATES POLITICAL SCIENCE DOCUMENTS DESIGN PHILOSOPHY

Publications like UNITED STATES POLITICAL SCIENCE DOCUMENTS (USPSD) are responses to the so-called "information explosion." They are designed to offer their readers information about the growing literature record so that useful materials can be identified quickly and accurately. Although all "secondary publications" share this objective they all don't go about accomplishing it in the same way. USPSD is a case in point because it is devoted to an intensive coverage of a well-constrained set of information sources rather than to an extensive coverage of an ill-defined set of information sources. The remarks which follow are offered to develop this design philosophy and to illustrate its application.

It is important to recognize that the information explosion which has become so prevalent an aspect of modern life is in fact the result of the combination of two realities. First, there is more information available today than ever before and it becomes available at an ever increasing rate. This situation, which is what most people think of when they think of the "information explosion", is most aptly characterized as a "publication explosion" because its measurement and impact assessment is always stated in terms of journal titles, journal articles, technical reports, and the like. The other situation, much less discussed and studied, can be called a "utilization explosion". Here the concern is that there are more people looking for information than ever before and new problems on which information is to be brought to bear are being introduced at an ever increasing rate. To understand the information explosion requires attention to both the publication and utilization explosions because they express the essential supply versus demand dynamics of an important social reality.

This distinction, moreover, is useful as a means for distinguishing between types of secondary publications. It is possible, for instance, to think of existing secondary publications as being primarily motivated by the publication rather than utilization explosion.They are concerned with surveying as large a number of journal titles producing as large a number of entries as quickly as possible. Characteristically, they do not furnish very much detail of a subject analytic nature and many provide none at all. Although disappointing, the fact that this is the case is not surprising. It is merely a question of priorities and cost. If the goal of a secondary publication is primarily one of covering as much information in as short a period of time as possible then subject analytic features such as in-depth indexing using a thesaurus and abstracts may have to be omitted to control costs and to reduce delays. This is very understandable and publication-minded secondary materials are very helpful for keeping up with new information. This design, though, is not the only one possible and USPSD can be cited as an example of a different approach.

The basic principle upon which the design of USPSD rests is that not all sources of information are of equal stature. There are some sources of information in any field which are more highly regarded than others and the degree of this regard can be fairly reliably sensed by examining such measures as subscription and citation data. What's more, this "informational nucleus" of a field is often rather modest in size. This view is *not* a speculation. Studies of information flows within communities of researchers have been unanimous in their conclusion that a very small number of information sources account for a very large number of *used* materials. That this is the case has been known and discussed since the late 1940s when S.C. Bradford's ground-breaking work *Documentation* originally appeared. The effect has been so regular in its occurrence that it's been accorded the status of a bibliometric law, "Bradford's Law". What has not been commonly recognized, though, is that this empirical generalization has implications for the design of secondary and other informational/reference publications. p. To illustrate how this is the case consider the following. Carl Jung is a psychologist whose stature is such that his works have been collected and carefully indexed so that students and scholars can have easy and ready access to his thinking on a wide-range of topics. The works of other psychologists who are not as highly regarded as Jung are not handled in as intensive a manner because the demand is not acute enough to warrant.the time and expense involved. Of course, Jung provides simply a case in point. In any field there are those leaders, always very small in number, whose publications and findings are repeatedly studied and debated by a very much larger number of practitioners and so time is taken to organize the literature record of the leaders in a manner appropriate to the interest in it. USPSD organizes the information from leading journals with an analagous intent. The journals covered by USPSD are regarded as those with the highest standing among observers with an interest in political science in the United States. As such, they merit intensive, in-depth examination and organization not appropriate for *all* journals. Whereas a publication-explosion motivated secondary publications cover all sources of information as though they were of equal stature, USPSD is devoted to providing a higher level of analysis than is usually the case for that core of journals with the highest standing. In this context, then, USPSD is complementary to other secondary publications in that it improves upon the bibliographic control of materials which other secondary publications treat too lightly in their efforts to keep up with the publication explosion.

USPSD accomplishes its intensive coverage in a number of ways. First, it is important to note that USPSD acquisition decisions are made at the level of the journal *title* and not the *article,* as is usually the case. A user of USPSD is assured that if a journal is said to be covered then *every* article published therein appears in USPSD. Secondly, as many as eleven distinct categories of information are furnished for each article. These include the familiar categories of author, title, journal citation, and abstract together with the unique "titled special features" (recording figures, tables, charts, maps, etc.) and "cited people" (recording the names of people cited in text, footnotes, and references). Entries in USPSD are indexed as to their subject and geographic area themes, using a thesaurus developed especially for this purpose, and a list of proper names is supplied to call attention to notable events, articles of legislation, organizations, ethnic groups, etc. (The indexing process itself entails work by two separate analysts followed by a discussion to resolve differences; this is in the interest of inter-indexer consistency. USPSD is printed using a type-face and a lay-out design which facilitates scanning (browsing) and reduces fatigue. It is also bound in two parts so that its users can go from indexes to document descriptions and back again with a minimum of page turning and, consequently, place losing. As well, five separate indexes (authors, subject, geographic area, proper name, and journal) are provided to maximize the number of avenues by which its users can approach finding information. USPSD analysts, moreover, are not limited to a number of words per abstract or a number of index terms per entry so they are free to describe USPSD entries as completely as they deem warranted.

These, then, are the features of USPSD which derive directly from its design philosophy. USPSD has other features and there are aspects to the process by which USPSD is produced which are also of interest. These matters are best discussed elsewhere. The essential message that these brief notes have tried to convey is that USPSD is based upon a novel, innovative design philosophy. The pivotal tenet of this philosophy is that there are some sources of information whose stature invites more careful analysis than heretofore offered by conventional secondary publications and that if these sources of information were to be more intensively organized than has been the case then users of information would greatly benefit. Almost all of what USPSD can be said to represent proceeds from this starting point.